Rereading America

Cultural Contexts for
Critical Thinking and Writing

Rereading America

Cultural Contexts for
Critical Thinking and Writing

Fourth Edition

Edited by

Gary Colombo
LOS ANGELES CITY COLLEGE

Robert Cullen
SAN JOSE STATE UNIVERSITY

Bonnie Lisle
UNIVERSITY OF CALIFORNIA, LOS ANGELES

Bedford/St. Martin's
Boston ◆ New York

For Bedford/St. Martin's

President and Publisher: Charles H. Christensen
General Manager and Associate Publisher: Joan E. Feinberg
Managing Editor: Elizabeth M. Schaff
Developmental Editor: John Sullivan
Production Editor: Tony Periello
Production Assistants: Deborah Baker and Melissa Cook
Copyeditor: Lisa Wehrle
Cover Design: Hannus Design Associates
Cover Art: Untitled (American Flag), c. 1987, photography collage on cut
  paper, by Conrad Jorgensen.
Composition: Pine Tree Composition
Printing and Binding: Bloomsburg Graftsmen

Library of Congress Catalog Card Number: 97–74958

Manufactured in the United States of America

3   2   1   0
f   e

For information, write: Bedford/St. Martin's, 75 Arlington Street, Boston,
  MA 02116 (617–426–7440)

ISBN: 0–312–14837–2

Preface for Instructors

About *Rereading America*

Designed for first-year writing and critical thinking courses, *Rereading America* anthologizes a diverse set of readings focused on the myths that dominate U.S. culture. This central theme brings together thought-provoking selections on a broad range of topics — family, education, success, gender roles, race, and freedom — topics that raise controversial issues meaningful to college students of all backgrounds. We've drawn these readings from many sources, both within the academy and outside of it; the selections are both multicultural and cross-curricular, and thus represent an unusual variety of voices, styles, and subjects.

The readings in this anthology speak directly to students' experiences and concerns. Every college student has had some brush with prejudice, and most have something to say about education, the family, or the gender stereotypes they see on film and television. The issues raised here help students to link their personal experiences with broader cultural perspectives and lead them to analyze, or "read," the cultural forces that have shaped and continue to shape their lives. By linking the personal and the cultural, students begin to recognize that they are not academic outsiders — that they do have knowledge, assumptions, and intellectual frameworks that give them authority in academic culture. Connecting personal knowledge and academic discourse helps students see that they are able to think, speak, and write academically and that they don't have to absorb passively what the "experts" say.

Features of the Fourth Edition

A Cultural Approach to Critical Thinking *Rereading America* is committed to the premise that learning to think critically means learning to identify and see beyond dominant cultural myths — collective and often unconsciously held beliefs that influence our thinking, reading, and writing. Instead of treating cultural diversity as just another topic to be studied or "appreciated," *Rereading America* encourages students to grapple with the real differences in perspective that arise in a pluralistic society like ours. This method helps students to break through conventional assumptions and patterns of thought that hinder fresh critical responses and inhibit dialogue. It helps them recognize that even the most apparently "natural" fact or obvious idea results from a process of social construction. And it helps them to develop the intellectual independence essential to critical thinking, reading, and writing.

New Classic and Conservative Perspectives   To provide students with the historical context they often need, each chapter in this edition of *Rereading America* begins with a "classic" expression of the myth under examination. Approaching the myth of success, for example, by way of Horatio Alger's "Ragged Dick"—or the myth of racial superiority by way of Thomas Jefferson's infamous diatribe against "race mixing"—gives students a better sense of the myth's origin and impact. We've also included, in response to popular demand, at least one recent conservative revision of the myth in each chapter, so you'll find more readings by cultural critics who stand to the right of center, writers like Charles Murray, Lynne Cheney, and Ken Hamblin, and even some radical Libertarian views by authors like David Boaz and John Taylor Gatto.

Timely New Readings   Over the past few years there's been an explosion of important writing on topics like race, gender, freedom, and success, and we've worked hard in this edition to bring you the best new voices speaking on these issues. We've kept old favorites like Gloria Anzaldúa, Malcolm X, Shelby Steele, Jamaica Kincaid, bell hooks, Maxine Hong Kingston, Ronald Takaki, Bebe Moore Campbell, June Jordan, Judith Ortiz Cofer, Gloria Naylor, and Mike Rose. But you'll also find a host of new selections by such authors as Ellis Cose, Dagoberto Gilb, Jimmy Santiago Baca, Nancy Mairs, Patricia J. Williams, Stephanie Coontz, John R. Gillis, and Leslie Marmon Silko. And like earlier versions, this edition of *Rereading America* includes a healthy mix of personal and academic writing, representing a wide variety of genres, styles, and rhetorical strategies.

New Chapter Sequence   To make *Rereading America* as accessible as possible for first-year students, we've adopted a new ordering for our exploration of American cultural myths:

Harmony at Home: The Myth of the Model Family
Learning Power: The Myth of Educational Empowerment
Money and Success: The Myth of Individual Opportunity
True Women and Real Men: Myths of Gender
Created Equal: The Myth of the Melting Pot
Liberty and Justice for All: The Myth of Freedom

We've structured the first half of the book around myths associated with family, education, and success because students generally have little trouble making productive personal connections with these themes. Most first-year college students don't need much encouragement to engage and analyze the cultural myths that inform our thinking about families, schooling, or the American Dream. The second half of the book addresses topics that may prove more intellectually and emotionally challenging. Here students will have the chance to explore issues like the social construction of gender roles and racial categories — issues that are closely involved with personal identity and that have powerful social and personal implications. By making greater demands on students, the readings in these concluding chapters help them develop the kind of analytic and interpretive skills they'll use throughout their college careers.

Media Essays and Visual Images   As in the last edition, we've included one or more selections focusing on media in each chapter of *Rereading America*. This distribution of media pieces throughout the book allows you to discuss media representations in the context of the specific myths your class addresses. And recognizing the growing importance of computers in American life, we've included authors like Theodore Roszak on the limits of computers in college and Stephanie Brail on freedom and the Internet. We've also updated and expanded the visual images and cartoons that were featured in the last edition. The first chapter, for example, presents a selection of Norman Rockwell paintings as its "classic" expression of the mythic American family. The photos that open each chapter are integrated into the pre-reading assignments found in the chapter introductions. The cartoons, offered as a bit of comic relief and an opportunity for some visual thinking, are paired with appropriate readings throughout the text.

Focus on Struggle and Resistance   Most multicultural readers approach diversity in one of two ways: either they adopt a pluralist approach and conceive of American society as a kind of salad bowl of cultures, or, in response to recent worries about the lack of "objectivity" in the new multicultural curriculum, they take what might be called the "talk show" approach and present American culture as a series of pro-and-con debates on a number of social issues. The fourth edition of *Rereading America*, like its predecessors, follows neither of these approaches. Pluralist readers, we feel, make a promise that's impossible to keep: no single text, and no single course, can do justice to the many complex cultures that inhabit the United States. Thus, the materials selected for *Rereading America* aren't meant to offer a taste of what "family" means for Native Americans, or the flavor of gender relations among recent immigrants. Instead, we've included selections like Melvin Dixon's "Aunt Ida Pieces a Quilt" or Harlon Dalton's "Horatio Alger," because they offer us fresh critical perspectives on the common myths that shape our ideas, values, and beliefs. Rather than seeing this anthology as a mosaic or kaleidoscope of cultural fragments that combine to form a beautiful picture, it's more accurate to think of *Rereading America* as a handbook that helps students explore the ways that the dominant culture shapes their ideas, values, and beliefs.

This notion of cultural dominance is studiously avoided in most recent multicultural anthologies. Salad bowl readers generally sidestep the issue of cultural dynamics: intent on celebrating America's cultural diversity, they offer a relatively static picture of a nation fragmented into a kind of cultural archipelago. Talk show readers admit the idea of conflict, but they distort the reality of cultural dynamics by presenting cultural conflict as a matter of rational — and equally balanced — pro and con debate. All of the materials anthologized in *Rereading America* address the cultural struggles that animate American society — the tensions that result from the expectations established by our dominant cultural myths and the diverse realities that these myths often contradict.

Ultimately, *Rereading America* is about resistance. In this new edition we continue to include readings that offer positive alternatives to the dilemmas of cultural conflict — from the students in Deborah Meier's and Paul Schwarz's "The Hard Part is Making it Happen," who take an active role in the development of their school's curriculum, to the teens who are rewriting the myth of the melting pot in Lynell George's "Gray Boys, Funky Aztecs, and Honorary Homegirls." To make this commitment to resistance as visible as possible, we've tried to conclude every chapter of this new edition with a suite of readings offering creative, and we hope empowering, examples of Americans who work together to redefine our national myths.

Extensive Apparatus   *Rereading America* offers a wealth of features to help students hone their analytic abilities and to aid instructors as they plan class discussions, critical thinking activities, and writing assignments. These include:

- *A Comprehensive Introductory Essay* The book begins with a comprehensive essay, "Thinking Critically, Challenging Cultural Myths," that introduces students to the relationships between thinking, cultural diversity, and the notion of dominant cultural myths, and shows how such myths can influence their academic performance. We've also included a section devoted to active reading, which offers suggestions for prereading, prewriting, note taking, text marking, and keeping a reading journal.

- *Detailed Chapter Introductions* An introductory essay at the beginning of each chapter offers students a thorough overview of each cultural myth, placing it in historical context, raising some of the chapter's central questions, and orienting students to the chapter's internal structure.

- *Prereading Activities* Following each chapter introduction you'll find prereading activities designed to encourage students to reflect on what they already know about the cultural myth in question. Often connected to the photographs that open every chapter, these prereading activities help students to engage the topic even before they begin to read.

- *Questions to Stimulate Critical Thinking* Three groups of questions following each selection encourage students to consider the reading carefully in several contexts: "Engaging the Text" focuses on close reading of the selection itself; "Exploring Connections" puts the selection into dialogue with other selections throughout the book; "Extending the Critical Context" invites students to connect the ideas they read about here with sources of knowledge outside the anthology, including library research, personal experience, interviews, ethnographic-style observations, and so forth. As in past editions we've included a number of questions linking readings with contemporary television shows and feature films for instructors who want to address the interplay of cultural myths and the mass media.

- *Extensive Instructor's Manual, Resources for Teaching Rereading America: Cultural Contexts for Critical Thinking and Writing*, provides detailed advice about ways to make the most of both the readings and the questions; it also offers further ideas for discussion, class activities, and writing assignments, as well as practical hints and suggestions that we've garnered from our own classroom experiences.

- *Online Resources* A Web site for *Rereading America* contains annotated links, and an electronic mailing list allows you to correspond easily and share ideas with other instructors about using *Rereading America* in the classroom. Whether you are teaching for the first time, or you've been using *Rereading America* since the first edition, you'll find topics of interest. You can ask questions, offer suggestions, discuss your current teaching strategies and explore new ones, discover new ways of teaching familiar material, or find other classes with which your students can develop collaborative writing projects. For more information, visit the Bedford Books Web site at www.bedfordbooks.com, or speak to your Scientific American/St. Martin's Press sales representative.

Acknowledgments

The fourth edition of *Rereading America*, like its predecessors, emerges from a nation-wide collaboration of teachers who remind us, again and again, that critical thinking always renews itself and that there's always a new reading or a new classroom activity worth exploring. Among the many instructors who shared their insights with us as we reworked this edition, we'd particularly like to thank the following: Dan Armstrong, Lane Community College; H. Inness Asher, University of Southwestern Louisiana, Lafayette; Margot Gayle Backis, St. John Fisher College; Marlow Belschner, Southern Illinois University; Nancy Botkin, University of Indiana, South Bend; Carol Brown, South Puget Sound Community College; William Carroll, Norfolk State University; Dolores Crim, Purdue University, Hammond; Linda L. Danielson, Lane Community College; Emily Detiner, Miami University; Kathy Doherty, Bentley College; Melinda M.

Fiala, University of Missouri, Kansas City; Sara Gogol, Portland Community College; Joyce Huff, George Washington University; Kim Lang, Shippensburg University; Uvieja Leighton, The Union Institute; Elizabeth L. Lewis, Vermilion Community College; Jennifer Lowood, Vista Community College; Brij Lurine, University of New Mexico; Eunice M. Madison, Purdue University, Calumet; Kenneth K. Martin, Community College of Philadelphia; James McWard, University of Kansas; Kevin A. Moberg, University of North Dakota; John G. Morris, Cameron University; Craig J. Nauman, University of Wisconsin, Madison; Bruce Ouderkirk, University of Nebraska, Lincoln; E. Suzanne Owens, Lorain County Community College; Elizabeth Paulson, California State University; Amy Sapowith, University of California, Los Angeles; Jurgen Schlunk, West Virginia University; Tony Slagle, The Ohio State University; Penny L. Smith, Gannon University; Sharon Snyder, Purdue University, Calumet; Deborah Tenneg, Yale University; Ruthe Thompson, University of Arizona; Lorraine Threadgill, Community College of Philadelphia; Steve Turnwall, Los Medanos College; Riley Vann, West Virginia University; Nancy Wallace, Temple University; Ellen Weinauer, University of Southern Mississippi; Claudia L. Whitling, South Puget Sound Community College; Judy Wilkinson, Skyline College; Mark Wollarges, Vanderbilt University; Phyllis Zrzuay, Franklin Pierce College.

We are also grateful to the following people for responding to a questionnaire for previous editions: Katya Amato, Portland State University; Jeanne Anderson, University of Louisville; Julie Drew Anderson, University of South Florida; Sharon K. Anthony, Portland Community College; Rodney Ash, Western State College of Colorado; David Axelson, Western State College of Colorado; Valerie Babb, Georgetown University; Flavia Bacarella, Herbert H. Lehman College; Michael A. Balas, Nassau Community College; Gwen Barday, East Carolina University; Jim Baril, Western State College of Colorado; Richard Barney, University of Oklahoma; Jeannette Batz, Saint Louis University; Les Belikian, Los Angeles City College; Patricia Ann Bender, Rutgers University, Newark; Jon Bentley, Albuquerque Technical Vocational Institute; Sara Blake, El Camino College; Jean L. Blanning, Michigan Technological University; Maurice Blauf, Hutchins School of Liberal Studies; Joseph Bodziock, Clarion University; Will Bohnaker, Portland State University; Susan R. Bowers, Susquehanna University; Laura Brady, George Mason University; Eugenia M. Bragen, Baruch College; Byron Caminero-Santangelo, Saddleback College; Julianna de Magalhaes Castro, Highline Community College; Cheryl Christiansen, California State University, Stanislaus; Ann Christie, Goucher College; Stuart Christie, University of California, Santa Cruz; Renny Christopher, Cabrillo College; Gloria Collins, San Jose State University; Richard Conway, Lamar Community College; Harry James Cook, Dundalk Community College; Richard Courage, Westchester Community College; Cynthia Cox, Belmont University; Dulce M. Cruz, Indiana University; Wendy J. Cutler, Hocking Technical College; Patricia A. Daskivich, Los Angeles Harbor College; Anthony Dawahare, Loyola University, Chicago; Thomas Dean, Cardinal Stritch College; Elise Donovan, Union County College; Miriam Dow, George Washington University; Douglass T. Doyle, University of South Florida; Diana Dreyer, Slippery Rock University; Michele Driscoll, San Francisco State University; Cynthia Dubielak, Hocking Technical College; M. H. Dunlop, Iowa State University; Steve Dunn, Western State College of Colorado; Mary DuPree, University of Idaho; Harriet Dwinell, American University; K. C. Eapen, Clark Atlanta University; Iain J. W. Ellis, Bowling Green State University; Sharon Emmons, University of Portland; G. Euridge, Ohio State University; Rand Floren, Santa Rosa Junior College; Marie Foley, Santa Barbara City College; Barry Fruchter, Nassau Community College; Sandy Fugate, Western Michigan University; Arra M. Garab, Northern Illinois University; Peter Gardner, Berklee College of Music; Mary R. Georges, University of California, Los Angeles; Paul Gery, Western State College of Colorado; Michele Glazer, Portland Community College–Sylvania; William Gleason, University of California, Los Angeles; Sara Gogal, Portland Community College; Krystyna Golkowska, Ithaca College; Jim Gorman; Andrea Greenbaum, University of South Florida; Ervene Gulley, Bloomsburg University; James C. Hall, University of Iowa; Craig Hancock, State University of New York, Albany; Jan Hayhurst, Community College of Pittsburgh; G. Held, Queens College; Jay W. Helman, Western State College of Colorado; Penny L. Hirsch, Northwestern University; Roseanne L. Hoefel, Iowa State University; Carol Hovanec, Ramapo College; Allison A. Hutira, Youngstown State University; John M. Jakaitis, Indiana State University; Jeannette J. Jeneault, Syracuse University; Robert T. Kelley, Urstnus College; Kathleen Kelly, Northeastern University; Kathleen Kiehl, Cabrillo College; Frances E. Kino, Iona College, Yonkers Campus; Blanche Jamson, Southeastern Oklahoma State University; Ron Johnson, Skyline College; Elizabeth Mary Kirchen, University of Michigan, Dearborn; Judith Kirscht, University of California, Santa Barbara; Jeffrey A. Kisner, Waynesburg College; Phil Klingsmith, Western State College of Colorado; Philip A. Korth, Michigan State University; S. J. Kotz, Virginia Polytechnic Institute and State University; Joann Kricg, Hofstra University; Catherine W. Kroll, Sonoma State American Language Institute; Jim Krusoe, Santa Monica College; Frank La Ferriere, Los Angeles City College; Susan Latta, Purdue University; Sheila A. Lebo, University of California, Los Angeles; D. Lebofsky, Temple University; Mitzi Lewellen, Normandale Community College; Lis Leyson, Fullerton College; Joseph Like, Beloit College; Don Lipman, Los Angeles City College; Solange Lira, Boston University; L. Loeffel, Syracuse University; Paul Loukides, Albion College; Bernadette Flynn Low, Dundalk Community College; Paul Lowdenslager, Western State College of Colorado; Susan G. Luck, Lorain County Community College; Janet Madden-Simpson, El Camino College; Annette March, Cabrillo College; Kathleen Marley, Fairleigh Dickinson University; Lorraine Mercer, Portland State University; Clifford Marks, University of

Wyoming; Peggy Marron, University of Wyoming; David Martinez, University of California, Los Angeles; Laura McCall, Western State College of Colorado; K. Ann McCarthy, Shoreline Community College; Richard McGowan, St. Joseph's College; Grace McLaughlin, Portland Community College; Ann A. Merrill, Emory University; Dale Metcalfe, University of California, Davis; Charles Miller, Western State College of Colorado; Carol Porterfield Milowski, Bemidji State University; Ann Mine, Oregon State University; Kathy Molloy, Santa Barbara City College; Candace Montoya, University of Oregon; Amy Mooney, South Puget Sound Community College; Fred Moss, University of Wisconsin–Waukesha; Merlyn E. Mowrey, Central Michigan University; Denise Muller, San Jose State University; William Murphy, University of Maine, Machias; Susan Nance, Bowling Green State University; Patricia M. Naulty, Canisius College; Scott R. Nelson, Louisiana State University; Robert Newman, State University of New York at Buffalo; Thu Nguyen, Irvine Valley College; Todd T. Nilson, University of Kentucky; Fran O'Connor, Nassau Community College; Sarah-Hope Parmeter, University of California, Santa Cruz; Sandra Patterson, Western State College of Colorado; Marsha Penti, Michigan Technological University; Erik Peterson, University of Minnesota; Linda Peterson, Salt Lake Community College; Michele Peterson, Santa Barbara City College; Madeleine Picciotto, Oglethorpe University; Kirsten Pierce, Villanova University; Dan Pinti, Ohio State University; Fritz H. Pointer, Contra Costa College; Paige S. Price, University of Oregon; Teresa M. Redd, Howard University; Thomas C. Renzi, State University College at Buffalo; Geri Rhodes, Albuquerque Technical Vocational Institute; Walter G. Rice, Dundalk Community College; Bruce Richardson, University of Wyoming; Randall Rightmire, Los Angeles Southwest College; Jeffrey Ritchie, Northern Kentucky University; Patricia Roberts, Allentown College of St. Francis de Sales; Marjorie Roemer, University of Cincinnati; Bonnie Ross, Los Angeles Valley College; Renee Ruderman, Metropolitan State College, Denver; Lillian Ruiz-Powell, Miracosta College; Geoffrey J. Sadock, Bergen Community College; Mollie Sandock, Valparaiso University; Bryan Scanlon, Western Michigan University; Wayne Scheer, Atlanta Metro College; Linda Scholer, College of San Mateo; Jurgen E. Schlunk, West Virginia University; Esther L. Schwartz, Allegheny County Community College; David Seitz, University of Illinois, Chicago; Jennifer A. Senft, University of California, Los Angeles; Ann Shapiro, State University of New York, Farmingdale; Nancy Shaw, Ursinus College; Eric Shibuya, University of Oklahoma; Jeanette Shumaker, San Diego State University; Michele Moragne e Silva, St. Edward's University; Rashna B. Singh, Holyoke Community College; Craig Sirles, De Paul University; Bill Siverly, Portland Community College; Antony Sloan, Bowling Green State University; Susan Belasco Smith, Allegheny College; Cynthia Solem, Cabrillo College; Andrew M. Stauffer, University of Virginia; Joseph Steinbach, Purdue University; Skai Stelzer, University of Toledo; Susan Sterr, Santa Monica College; Mark Stiger,

Western State College of Colorado; Ann Marie Stock, Hamline University; John B. Stoker, Kent State University; Ann Stolls, University of Illinois, Chicago; Brendan D. Strasser, Bowling Green State University; David Strong, Indiana University; Miriam Stuarts, Loyola University; Bonnie Surfus, University of South Florida; Karen Thomas, University of California, Los Angeles; Alice L. Trupe, Community College of Allegheny County; Eileen Turaff, Cleveland State University; Ruth Ann Thompson, Fordham University; Mark Todd, Western State College of Colorado; Michael Uebel, University of Virginia; James Varn, Morris College; Keith Walters, Ohio State University; Robert R. Watson, Grand Valley State University; Nola J. Wegman, Valparaiso University; Edwin Weihe, Seattle University; R. L. Welker, University of Virginia; Douglas Wixson, University of Missouri; Janice M. Wolff, Saginaw Valley State University; Brent Yaciw, University of South Florida; Nancy Young, Bentley, Curry, and Regis Colleges; and Naomi F. Zucker, University of Rhode Island.

We'd also like to thank our wonderful collaborators at Bedford Books for their guidance and support. Charles Christensen and Joan Feinberg, our publishers extraordinaire, deserve special recognition for the kindness and trust they bring to the business of bookmaking. During the many months he spent nurturing this edition, John Sullivan was a model editor: indefatigably helpful, wonderfully wise, and infinitely patient. At Bedford we also want to thank Tony Perriello, who served as production manager on this edition, Susan Pace, who designed our new cover, Amanda Bristow, who gathered biographical information, Michelle Clark and Susan Doheny, for clearing permissions under a tight deadline with unfailing good grace, and Lisa Wehrle for careful copyediting. And as always, we owe a heavy debt of gratitude to Elena Barcia, Liz Silver, and Roy Weitz, who have learned by now to meet a new season of midnight faxes and last-minute dashes to the post office with unfailing grace.

Contents

1

Harmony at Home:
The Myth of the Model Family   17

2

Learning Power:
The Myth of Education
and Empowerment

5

Created Equal: *The Myth of the Melting Pot* 528

6

Liberty and Justice for All:
The Myth of Freedom **678**

Rereading America

Cultural Contexts for
Critical Thinking and Writing

Thinking Critically,
Challenging Cultural Myths

Becoming a College Student

Beginning college can be a disconcerting experience. It may be the first time you've lived away from home and had to deal with the stresses and pleasures of independence. There's increased academic competition, increased temptation, and a whole new set of peer pressures. In the dorms you may find yourself among people whose backgrounds make them seem foreign and unapproachable. If you commute, you may be struggling against a feeling of isolation that you've never faced before. And then there are increased expectations. For an introductory history class you may read as many books as you covered in a year of high school coursework. In anthropology, you might be asked to conduct ethnographic research — when you've barely heard of an ethnography before, much less written one. In English you may tackle more formal analytic writing in a single semester than you've ever done in your life.

College typically imposes fewer rules than high school, but also gives you less guidance and makes greater demands — demands that affect the quality as well as the quantity of your work. By your first midterm exam, you may suspect that your previous academic experience is irrelevant, that nothing you've done in school has prepared you to think, read, or write in the ways your professors expect. Your sociology instructor says she doesn't care whether you can remember all the examples in the textbook as long as you can apply the theoretical concepts to real situations. In your composition class, the perfect five-paragraph essay you turn in for your first assignment is dismissed as "superficial, mechanical, and dull." Meanwhile, the lecturer in your political science or psychology course is rejecting ideas about country, religion, family, and self that have always been a part of your deepest beliefs. How can you cope with these new expectations and challenges?

There is no simple solution, no infallible five-step method that works for everyone. As you meet the personal challenges of college, you'll grow as a human being. You'll begin to look critically at your old habits, beliefs, and values, to see them in relation to the new world you're entering. You may have to re-examine your relationships to family, friends, neighborhood, and heritage. You'll have to sort out your strengths from your weaknesses and make tough choices about who you are and who you want to become. Your academic work demands the same process of serious self-examination. To excel in college work you need to grow intellectually — to become a critical thinker.

What Is Critical Thinking?

What do instructors mean when they tell you to think critically? Most would say that it involves asking questions rather than memorizing information. Instead of simply collecting the "facts," a critical thinker probes them, looking for underlying assumptions and ideas. Instead of focusing on dates and events in history or symptoms in psychology, she probes for motives, causes — an explanation of how these things came to be. A critical thinker cultivates the ability to imagine and value points of view different from her own — then strengthens, refines, enlarges, or reshapes her ideas in light of those other perspectives. She is at once open and skeptical: receptive to new ideas yet careful to test them against previous experience and knowledge. In short, a critical thinker is an active learner, someone with the ability to shape, not merely absorb, knowledge.

All this is difficult to put into practice, because it requires getting outside your own skin and seeing the world from multiple perspectives. To see why critical thinking doesn't come naturally, take another look at the cover of this book. Many would scan the title, *Rereading America,* take in the surface meaning — to reconsider America — and go on to page one. There isn't much to question here; it just "makes sense." But what happens with the student who brings a different perspective? For example, a student from El Salvador might justly complain that the title reflects an ethnocentric view of what it means to be an American. After all, since America encompasses all the countries of North, South, and Central America, he lived in "America" long before arriving in the United States. When this student reads the title, then, he actually does *reread* it; he reads it once in the "commonsense" way but also from the perspective of someone who has lived in a country dominated by U.S. intervention and interests. This double vision or double perspective frees him to look beyond the "obvious" meaning of the book and to question its assumptions.

Of course, you don't have to be bicultural to become a proficient critical thinker. You can develop a genuine sensitivity to alternative perspectives even if you've never lived outside your hometown. But to do so you need to recognize that there are no "obvious meanings." The automatic equation that the native-born student makes between "America" and the United States seems to make sense only because our culture has traditionally endorsed the idea that the United States *is* America and, by implication, that other countries in this hemisphere are somehow inferior — not the genuine article. We tend to accept this equation and its unfortunate implications because we are products of our culture.

The Power of Cultural Myths

Culture shapes the way we think; it tells us what "makes sense." It holds people together by providing us with a shared set of customs, values, ideas, and beliefs, as well as a common language. We live enmeshed in this cultural web: it influences the way we relate to others, the way we look, our tastes, our habits; it enters our dreams and desires. But as culture binds us together it also selectively blinds us. As we grow up, we accept ways of looking at the world, ways of thinking and being that might best be characterized as cultural frames of reference or cultural myths. These myths help us understand our place in the world — our place as prescribed by our culture. They define our relationships to friends and lovers, to the past and future, to nature, to power, and to nation. Becoming a critical thinker means learning how to look beyond these cultural myths and the assumptions embedded in them.

You may associate the word "myth" primarily with the myths of the ancient Greeks. The legends of gods and heroes like Athena, Zeus, and Oedipus embodied the central ideals and values of Greek civilization — notions like civic responsibility, the primacy of male authority, and humility before the gods. The stories were "true" not in a literal sense but as reflections of important cultural beliefs. These myths assured the Greeks of the nobility of their origins; they provided models for the roles that Greeks would play in their public and private lives; they justified inequities in Greek society; they helped the Greeks understand human life and destiny in terms that "made sense" within the framework of that culture.

Our cultural myths do much the same. Take, for example, the myth of freedom. A strong belief in freedom unites us; we have only to reflect on the number of lives lost in wars fought "for freedom" to grasp its power as a cultural myth. However, look beneath the surface of our collective belief in freedom, and you'll find that we understand it in very different ways. Some see freedom as the right to participate in the electoral process by casting a ballot and electing representatives and leaders. Others say it's freedom of choice, or speech, or unlimited economic opportunity. One person will argue passionately that all government exists solely to guarantee the freedoms enjoyed by individual citizens. The next one will argue just as passionately that our obsession with freedom has become the single biggest problem in modern society. The list of possible definitions is endless, and so is the debate about whether each of us is genuinely free. But the power of myth lies in its ability to override these differences. Politicians and advertisers rely on our automatic emotional response to treasured cultural ideas: when they invoke the ideal of freedom, they expect us to feel a surge of patriotism and count on us not to ask whether the candidate or product really embodies the specific values we associate with freedom.

Cultural myths gain such enormous power over us by insinuating themselves into our thinking before we're aware of them. Most are learned at a deep, even unconscious level. Gender roles are a good example. As children we get gender role models from our families, our schools, our churches, and other important institutions. We see them acted out in the relationships between family members or portrayed on television, in the movies, or in song lyrics. Before long, the culturally determined roles we see for women and men appear to us as "self-evident": it seems "natural" for a man to be strong, responsible, competitive, and heterosexual, just as it may seem "unnatural" for a man to shun competitive activity or to take a romantic interest in other men. Our most dominant cultural myths shape the way we perceive the world and blind us to alternative ways of seeing and being. When something violates the expectations that such myths create, it may even be called unnatural, immoral, or perverse.

Cultural Myths as Obstacles to Critical Thinking

Cultural myths can have more subtle effects as well. In academic work they can reduce the complexity of our reading and thinking. A few years ago, for example, a professor at Los Angeles City College noted that he and his students couldn't agree in their interpretations of the following poem by Theodore Roethke:

My Papa's Waltz

The whiskey on your breath
Could make a small boy dizzy;
But I hung on like death:
Such waltzing was not easy.

We romped until the pans
Slid from the kitchen shelf;
My mother's countenance
Could not unfrown itself.

The hand that held my wrist
Was battered on one knuckle;
At every step you missed
My right ear scraped a buckle.

You beat time on my head
With a palm caked hard by dirt,
Then waltzed me off to bed
Still clinging to your shirt.

The instructor read this poem as a clear expression of a child's love for his blue-collar father, a rough-and-tumble man who had worked hard all his life ("a palm caked hard by dirt"), who was not above taking a drink of whiskey to ease his mind, but who also found the time to "waltz" his son off to bed. The students didn't see this at all. They saw the poem as a story about an abusive father and heavy drinker. They seemed unwilling to look beyond the father's roughness and the whiskey on his breath, equating these with drunken violence. Although the poem does suggest an element of fear mingled with the boy's excitement ("I hung on like death"), the class ignored its complexity — the mixture of fear, love, and boisterous fun that colors the son's memory of his father. It's possible that some students might overlook the positive traits in the father in this poem because they have suffered child abuse themselves. But this couldn't be true for all the students in the class. The difference between these interpretations lies, instead, in the influence of cultural myths. After all, in a culture now dominated by images of the family that emphasize "positive" parenting, middle-class values, and sensitive fathers, it's no wonder that students refused to see this father sympathetically. Our culture simply doesn't associate good, loving families with drinking or with even the suggestion of physical roughness.

Years of acculturation — the process of internalizing cultural values — leave us with a set of rigid categories for "good" and "bad" parents, narrow conceptions of how parents should look, talk, and behave toward their children. These cultural categories work like mental pigeonholes: they help us sort out and evaluate our experiences rapidly, almost before we're consciously aware of them. They give us a helpful shorthand for interpreting the world; after all, we can't stop to ponder every new situation we meet as if it were a puzzle or a philosophical problem. But while cultural categories help us make practical decisions in everyday life, they also impose their inherent rigidity on our thinking and thus limit our ability to understand the complexity of our experience. They reduce the world to dichotomies — simplified either/or choices: either women or men, either heterosexuals or homosexuals, either nature or culture, either animal or human, either "alien" or American, either them or us.

Rigid cultural beliefs can present serious obstacles to success for first-year college students. In a psychology class, for example, a student's cultural myths may so color her thinking that she finds it nearly impossible to comprehend Freud's ideas about infant sexuality. Her ingrained assumptions about childhood innocence and sexual guilt may make it impossible for her to see children as sexual beings — a concept absolutely basic to an understanding of the history of psychoanalytic theory. Yet college-level critical inquiry thrives on exactly this kind of revision of common sense: academics prize the unusual, the subtle, the ambiguous, the complex — and expect students to appreciate them as well. Good critical thinkers in all academic disciplines welcome the opportunity to challenge conventional ways of seeing the world; they seem to take delight in questioning everything that appears clear and self-evident.

Questioning: The Basis of Critical Thinking

By questioning the myths that dominate our culture, we can begin to resist the limits they impose on our vision. In fact, they invite such questioning. Often our personal experience fails to fit the images the myths project: a young woman's ambition to be a test pilot may clash with the ideal of femininity our culture promotes; a Cambodian immigrant who has suffered from racism in the United States may question our professed commitment to equality; a student in the vocational track may not see education as the road to success that we assume it is; and few of our families these days fit the mythic model of husband, wife, two kids, a dog, and a house in the suburbs.

Moreover, because cultural myths serve such large and varied needs, they're not always coherent or consistent. Powerful contradictory myths coexist in our society and our own minds. For example, while the myth of freedom celebrates equality, the myth of individual success pushes us to strive for inequality — to "get ahead" of everyone else. Likewise, our attitudes toward education are deeply paradoxical: on one level Americans tend to see schooling as a valuable experience that unites us in a common culture and helps us bring out the best in ourselves; yet at the same time we suspect that formal classroom instruction stifles creativity and chokes off natural intelligence and enthusiasm. These contradictions infuse our history, literature, and popular culture; they're so much a part of our thinking that we tend to take them for granted, unaware of their inconsistencies.

Learning to recognize contradictions lies at the very heart of critical thinking, for intellectual conflict inevitably generates questions. Can both (or all) perspectives be true? What evidence do I have for the validity of each? Is there some way to reconcile them? Are there still other alternatives? Questions like these represent the beginning of serious academic analysis. They stimulate the reflection, discussion, and research that are the essence of good scholarship. Thus, whether we find contradictions between myth and lived experience, or between opposing myths, the wealth of powerful, conflicting material generated by our cultural mythology offers a particularly rich context for critical inquiry.

The Structure of *Rereading America*

We've designed this book to help you develop the habits of mind you'll need to become a critical thinker — someone who recognizes the way that cultural myths shape thinking and can move beyond them to evaluate issues from multiple perspectives. Each of the book's six chapters addresses one of the dominant myths of American culture. We begin with the myth that's literally closest to home — the myth of the model family. In "Harmony at Home" we look at the impact that the idea of the nuclear family has had on generations of Americans, including those who don't fit comfortably within its limitations. We also present some serious challenges to this time-honored definition of American family life. Next we turn to a topic that every student should have a lot to say about — the myth of educational empowerment. "Learning Power" gives you the chance to reflect on how the "hidden curriculum" of schooling has shaped your own attitudes towards learning. We begin our exploration of American cultural myths by focusing on home and education because most students find it easy to make personal connections with these topics and because they both involve institutions — families and schools — that are surrounded by a rich legacy of cultural stories and myths. These two introductory chapters are followed by consideration of what is perhaps the most famous of all American myths, the American Dream. Chapter Three, "Money and Success," addresses the idea of unlimited personal opportunity that brought millions of immigrants to our shores and set the story of America in motion. It invites you to weigh some of the human costs of the dream and to reconsider your own definition of a successful life.

The second half of the book focuses on three cultural myths that offer greater intellectual and emotional challenges, in part because they are so intertwined with every American's personal identity and because they touch on highly charged social issues. "True Women and Real Men" considers the socially constructed categories of gender — the traditional roles that enforce differences between women and men. This chapter also explores the perspectives of Americans who defy conventional gender boundaries. The book's fifth chapter, "Created Equal," examines two myths that have powerfully shaped racial and ethnic relations in the United States: the myth of the melting pot, which celebrates cultural homogenization, and the myth of racial and ethnic superiority, which promotes separateness and inequality. This chapter probes the nature of prejudice, explores the ways that prejudicial attitudes are created, and examines several alternatives to a race-divided society. Each of these two chapters questions how our culture divides and defines our world, how it artificially channels our experience into oppositions like black and white, male and female, straight and gay. The book concludes by addressing what is perhaps the most central, and also the most elusive, of all American cultural myths — the myth of freedom. In "Liberty and Justice for All" we pause to reflect on what the idea of freedom means in contemporary America, and we explore some of the dilemmas that arise in a society committed to the pursuit of liberty. Ultimately, this final chapter challenges you to reconsider the role that freedom plays in your own life as an American.

The Selections

Our identities — who we are and how we relate to others — are deeply entangled with the cultural values we have internalized since infancy. Cultural myths become so closely identified with our personal beliefs that rereading them actually means rereading ourselves, rethinking the way we see the world. Questioning long-held assumptions can be an exhilarating experience, but it can be distressing too. Thus, you may find certain selections in *Rereading America* difficult, controversial, or even downright offensive. They are meant to challenge you and to provoke classroom debate. But as you discuss the ideas you encounter in this book, remind yourself that your classmates may bring with them very different, and equally profound, beliefs. Keep an open mind, listen carefully, and treat other perspectives with the same respect you'd expect other people to show for your own. It's by encountering new ideas and engaging with others in open dialogue that we learn to grow.

Because *Rereading America* explores cultural myths that shape our thinking, it doesn't focus on the kind of well-defined public issues you might expect to find in a traditional composition anthology. You won't be reading any arguments for and against affirmative action, bilingual education, or the death penalty here. Although we do include conservative as well as liberal — and even radical — perspectives, we've deliberately avoided the traditional pro-and-con approach because we want you to aim deeper than that; we want you to focus on the subtle cultural beliefs that underlie, and frequently determine, the debates that are waged on public issues. We've also steered clear of the "issues approach" because we feel it reinforces simplistic either/or thinking. Polarizing American culture into a series of debates doesn't encourage you to examine your own beliefs or explore how they've been shaped by the cultures you're part of. To begin to appreciate the influence of your own cultural myths, you need new perspectives: you need to stand outside the ideological machinery that makes American culture run to begin to appreciate its power. That's why we've included many strongly dissenting views: there are works by disabled activists, gay rights activists, socialists, libertarians, and more. You may find that their views confirm your own experience of what it means to be an American, or you may find that you bitterly disagree with them. We only hope that you will use the materials here to gain some insight into the values and beliefs that shape our thinking and our national identity. This book is meant to complicate the mental categories that our cultural myths have established for us. Our intention is not to present a new "truth" to replace the old but to expand the range of ideas you bring to all your reading and writing in college. We believe that learning to see and value other perspectives will enable you to think more critically — to question, for yourself, the truth of any statement.

You may also note that several selections in *Rereading America* challenge the way you think writing is supposed to look or sound. You won't find many "classic" essays in this book, the finely crafted reflective essays on general topics that are often held up as models of "good writing." It's not that we reject this type of essay in principle. It's just that most writers who stand outside mainstream culture seem to have little use for it. The kind of writing that challenges dominant cultural values often comes out of scholarly research, so you can expect to cut your teeth on some serious academic analysis in this book. We also believe that unusual styles and uses of language, like unconventional ideas, offer points of entry into critical thinking. You will come across some selections — like Gloria Anzaldúa's "La conciencia de la mestiza" — that seem to violate all the conventions of writing and even include passages in another language or dialect. Although such readings may seem disorienting at first, we'll do our best to get you over the tough spots by offering help in chapter introductions, headnotes, and footnotes. We think these selections will reward the extra trouble it may take you to read them, because encountering new styles, besides being intellectually stimulating, can help you become a more flexible reader and writer.

Our selections come from a wide variety of sources: professional books and journals from many disciplines, popular magazines, college textbooks, autobiographies, oral histories, and literary works. We've included this variety partly for the very practical reason that you're likely to encounter texts like these in your college coursework. But we also see textual diversity, like ethnic and political diversity, as a way to multiply perspectives and stimulate critical analysis. For example, an academic article like Jean Anyon's study of social class and school curriculum might give you a new way of understanding Mike Rose's personal narrative about his classroom experiences. On the other hand, you may find that some of the teachers Rose encounters don't neatly fit Anyon's theoretical model. Do such discrepancies mean that Anyon's argument is invalid? That her analysis needs to be modified to account for these teachers? That the teachers are simply exceptions to the rule? You'll probably want to consider your own classroom experience as you wrestle with such questions. Throughout the book, we've chosen readings that "talk to each other" in this way and that draw on the cultural knowledge you bring with you. These readings invite you to join the conversation; we hope they raise difficult questions, prompt lively discussion, and stimulate critical inquiry.

The Power of Dialogue

Good thinking, like good writing and good reading, is an intensely social activity. Thinking, reading, and writing are all forms of relationship — when you read, you enter into dialogue with an author about the subject at hand; when you write, you address an imaginary reader, testing your ideas against probable responses, reservations, and arguments. Thus, you can't become an accomplished writer simply by declaring your right to speak or by criticizing as an act of principle: real authority comes when you enter into the discipline of an active exchange of opinions and interpretations.

Critical thinking, then, is always a matter of dialogue and debate — discovering relationships between apparently unrelated ideas, finding parallels between your own experiences and the ideas you read about, exploring points of agreement and conflict between yourself and other people.

We've designed the readings and questions in this text to encourage you to make just these kinds of connections. You'll notice, for example, that we often ask you to divide into small groups to discuss readings, and we frequently suggest that you take part in projects that require you to collaborate with your classmates. We're convinced that the only way you can learn critical reading, thinking, and writing is by actively engaging others in an intellectual exchange. So we've built into the text many opportunities for listening, discussion, and debate.

The questions that follow each selection should guide you in critical thinking. Like the readings, they're intended to get you started, not to set limits; we strongly recommend that you also devise your own questions and pursue them either individually or in study groups. We've divided our questions into three categories. Here's what to expect from each:

- Those labeled "Engaging the Text" focus on the individual selection they follow. They're designed to highlight important issues in the reading, to help you begin questioning and evaluating what you've read, and sometimes to remind you to consider the author's choices of language, evidence, structure, and style.

- The questions labeled "Exploring Connections" will lead you from the selection you've just finished to one or more other readings in this book. It's hard to make sparks fly from just one stone; if you think hard about these connecting questions, though, you'll see some real collisions of ideas and perspectives, not just polite and predictable "differences of opinion."

- The final questions for each reading, "Extending the Critical Context," invite you to extend your thinking beyond the book — to your family, your community, your college, the media, or the more traditional research environment of the library. The emphasis here is on creating new knowledge by applying ideas from this book to the world around you and by testing these ideas in your world.

Active Reading

You've undoubtedly read many textbooks, but it's unlikely that you've had to deal with the kind of analytic, argumentative, and scholarly writing you'll find in college and in *Rereading America*. These different writing styles require a different approach to reading as well. In high school you probably read to "take in" information, often for the sole purpose of reproducing it later on a test. In college you'll also be expected to recognize larger issues, such as the author's theoretical slant, her goals and methods, her assumptions, and her relationship to other writers and researchers.

These expectations can be especially difficult in the first two years of college, when you take introductory courses that survey large, complex fields of knowledge. With all these demands on your attention, you'll need to read actively to keep your bearings. Think of active reading as a conversation between you and the text: instead of listening passively as the writer talks, respond to what she says with questions and comments of your own. Here are some specific techniques you can practice to become a more active reader.

Prereading and Prewriting

It's best with most college reading to "preread" the text. In prereading, you briefly look over whatever information you have on the author and the selection itself. Reading chapter introductions and headnotes like those provided in this book can save you time and effort by giving you information about the author's background and concerns, the subject or thesis of the selection, and its place in the chapter as a whole. Also take a look at the title and at any headings or subheadings in the piece. These will give you further clues about an article's general scope and organization. Next, quickly skim the entire selection, paying a bit more attention to the first few paragraphs and the conclusion. Now you should have a pretty good sense of the author's position — what she's trying to say in this piece of writing.

At this point you may do one of several things before you settle down to in-depth reading. You may want to jot down in a few lines what you think the author is doing. Or you may want to make a list of questions you can ask about this topic based on your prereading. Or you may want to freewrite a page or so on the subject. Informally writing out your own ideas will prepare you for more in-depth reading by recalling what you already know about the topic.

We emphasize writing about what you've read because reading and writing are complementary activities: being an avid reader will help you as a writer by familiarizing you with a wide range of ideas and styles to draw on; likewise, writing about what you've read will give you a deeper understanding of your reading. In fact, the more actively you "process" or reshape what you've read, the better you'll comprehend and remember it. So you'll learn more effectively by marking a text as you read than by simply reading; taking notes as you read is even more effective than marking, and writing about the material for your own purposes (putting it in your own words and connecting it with what you already know) is better still.

Marking the Text
and Taking Notes

After prereading and prewriting, you're ready to begin critical reading in earnest. As you read, be sure to highlight ideas and phrases that strike you as especially significant — those that seem to capture the gist of a particular paragraph or section, or those that relate directly to the author's purpose or argument. While prereading can help you identify central ideas, you may find that you need to reread difficult sections or flip back and skim an earlier passage if you feel yourself getting lost. Many students think of themselves as poor readers if they can't whip through an article at high speed without pausing. However, the best readers read recursively — that is, they shuttle back and forth, browsing, skimming, and rereading as necessary, depending on their interest, their familiarity with the subject, and the difficulty of the material. This shuttling actually parallels what goes on in your mind when you read actively, as you alternately recall prior knowledge or experience and predict or look for clues about where the writer is going next.

Keep a record of your mental shuttling by writing comments in the margins as you read. It's often useful to gloss the contents of each paragraph or section, to summarize it in a word or two written alongside the text. This note will serve as a reminder or key to the section when you return to it for further thinking, discussion, or writing. You may also want to note passages that puzzled you. Or you may want to write down personal reactions or questions stimulated by the reading. Take time to ponder why you felt confused or annoyed or affirmed by a particular passage. Let yourself wonder "out loud" in the margins as you read.

Presented below are one student's notes on a few stanzas of Inés Hernández-Ávila's "Para Teresa" (p. 216). In this example, you can see that the reader puts glosses or summary comments to the left of the poem and questions or personal responses to the right. You should experiment and create your own system of note taking, one that works best for the way you read. Just remember that your main goals in taking notes are to help you understand the author's overall position, to deepen and refine your responses to the selection, and to create a permanent record of those responses.

Para Teresa[1]

INÉS HERNÁNDEZ-ÁVILA

This poem explores and attempts to resolve an old conflict between its speaker and her schoolmate, two Chicanas at "Alamo which-had-to-be-its-name" Elementary School who have radically different ideas about what education means and does. Inés Hernández-Ávila (b. 1947) is a professor of Native American studies at the University of California, Davis. This poem appeared in her collection Con Razón, Corazón *(1987).*

[1]For Teresa. [Author's note]

Writes to Teresa

A tí-Teresa Compean — *Why in Spanish?*
Te dedico las palabras estás
que (explotan) de mi corazón[2] — *Why do her words explode?*
That day during lunch hour
at Alamo which-had-to-be-its-name   *!Why?*

The day of their con- fron- tation

Elementary — *Feels close to T. (?)*
my dear raza
That day in the bathroom
Door guarded
Myself cornered
I was accused by you, Teresa
Tú y las demás de tus amigas
Pachucas todas
Eran Uds. cinco.[3]

T.'s accusa- tion

Me gritaban que porque me creía tan grande[4]
What was I trying to do, you growled
Show you up? — *Teachers must be white / Anglo.*
Make the teachers like me, pet me,
Tell me what a credit (to my people) I was?
I was playing right into their hands, you challenged
And you would have none of it. — *Speaker is a "good student."*
I was to stop.

[2]To you, Teresa Compean, I dedicate these words that explode from my heart. [Author's note]

[3]You and the rest of your friends, all Pachucas, there were five of you. [Author's note]

[4]You were screaming at me, asking me why I thought I was so hot. [Author's note]

Keeping a Reading Journal

You may also want (or be required) to keep a reading journal in response to the selections you cover in *Rereading America*. In such a journal you'd keep all the freewriting that you do either before or after reading. Some students find it helpful to keep a double-entry journal, writing initial responses on the left side of the page and adding later reflections and reconsiderations on the right. You may want to use your journal as a place to explore personal reactions to your reading. You can do this by writing out imaginary dialogues — between two writers who address the same subject, between yourself and the writer of the selection, or between two parts of yourself. You can use the journal as a place to rewrite passages from a poem or essay in your own voice and from your own point of view. You can write letters to an author you particularly like or dislike or to a character in a story or poem. You might even draw a cartoon that comments on one of the reading selections.

Many students don't write as well as they could because they're afraid to take risks. They may have been repeatedly penalized for breaking "rules" of grammar or essay form; their main concern in writing becomes avoiding trouble rather than exploring ideas or experimenting with style. But without risk and experimentation, there's little possibility of growth. One of the benefits of journal writing is that it gives you a place to experiment with ideas, free from worries about "correctness." Here are two examples of student journal entries, in response to "Para Teresa" (we reprint the entries as they were written):

Entry 1: Internal Dialogue

ME 1:   I agree with Inés Hernández-Ávila's speaker. Her actions were justifiable in a way that if you can't fight 'em, join 'em. After all, Teresa Compean is just making the situation worse for her because not only is she sabotaging the teacher-student relationship, she's also destroying her chance for a good education.

ME 2:   Hey, Teresa's action was justifiable. Why else would the speaker admit at the end of the poem that what Teresa did was fine thus she respects Teresa more?

ME 1:   The reason the speaker respected Teresa was because she (Teresa) was still keeping her culture alive, although through different means. It wasn't her action that the speaker respected, it was the representation of it.

ME 2:   The reason I think Teresa acted the way she did was because she felt she had something to prove to society. She wanted to show that no one could push her people around; that her people were tough.

Entry 2: Personal Response

"Con cố gắng học gioi, cho Bá Má,
Rồi sau nây đời sống cua con sẽ thõai mái lắm.[5]
What if I don't want to?
What if I can't?
Sometimes I feel my parents don't understand what
I'm going through.
To them, education is money.
And money is success.
They don't see beyond that.
Sometimes I want to fail my classes purposely to
See their reaction, but that is too cruel.
They have taught me to value education.
Education makes you a person, makes you somebody, they say.
I agree.
They are proud I am going to UCLA.
They brag to their friends, our Vietnamese community, people
I don't even know.
            . . .
They believe in me, but I doubt myself. . . .

[5]"Daughter, study hard (for us, your Mom and Dad), so your future will be bright and easy."

You'll notice that neither of these students talks directly about "Para Teresa" as a poem. Instead, each uses it as a point of departure for her own reflections on ethnicity, identity, and education. Although we've included a number of literary works in *Rereading America,* we don't expect you to do literary analysis. We want you to use these pieces to stimulate your own thinking about the cultural myths they address. So don't feel you have to discuss imagery in Inés Hernández-Ávila's "Para Teresa" or characterization in Toni Cade Bambara's "The Lesson" in order to understand and appreciate them.

Finally, remember that the readings are just a starting point for discussion: you have access to a wealth of other perspectives and ideas among your family, friends, classmates; in your college library; in your personal experience; and in your own imagination. We urge you to consult them all as you grapple with the perspectives you encounter in this text.

1

Harmony at Home
The Myth of the Model Family

What would an American political campaign be without wholesome photographs of the candidates kissing babies and posing with their loving families? Politicians understand the cultural power of these symbols; they appreciate the family as one of our most sacred American institutions. The vision of the ideal nuclear family — Dad, Mom, a couple of kids, maybe a dog, and a spacious suburban home — is a cliché but also a potent myth, a dream that millions of Americans work to fulfill. The image is so compelling that it's easy to forget what a short time it's been around, especially compared with the long history of the family itself.

In fact, what we call the "traditional" family, headed by a breadwinner-father and a housewife-mother, has existed for little more than two hundred years, and the suburbs only came into being in the 1950s. But the family as a social institution was legally recognized in Western culture at least as far back as the Code of Hammurabi, published in ancient Mesopotamia some four thousand years ago. To appreciate how profoundly concepts of family life have changed, consider the absolute power of the Mesopotamian father, the patriarch: the law allowed him to use any of his dependents, including his wife, as collateral for loans or even to sell family members outright to pay his debts.

Although patriarchal authority was less absolute in Puritan America, fathers remained the undisputed heads of families. Seventeenth-century Connecticut, Massachusetts, and New Hampshire enacted laws condemning rebellious children to severe punishment and, in extreme cases, to death. In the early years of the American colonies, as in Western culture stretching back to Hammurabi's time, unquestioned authority within the family served as both the model for and the basis of state authority. Just as family members owed complete obedience to the father, so all citizens owed unquestioned loyalty to the king and his legal representatives. In his influential volume *Democracy in America* (1835), French aristocrat Alexis de Tocqueville describes the relationship between the traditional European family and the old political order:

> ... Among aristocratic nations, social institutions recognize, in truth, no one in the family but the father; children are received by society at his hands; society governs him, he governs them. Thus, the parent not only has a natural right, but acquires a political right to command them; he is the author and the support of his family; but he is also its constituted ruler.

By the mid-eighteenth century, however, new ideas about individual freedom and democracy were stirring the colonies. And by the time Tocqueville visited the United States in 1831, they had evidently worked a revolution in the family as well as in the nation's political structure: he observes, "When the condition of society becomes democratic, and men adopt as their general principle that it is good and lawful to judge of all things for one's self, . . . the power which the opinions of a father exercise over those of his sons diminishes, as well as his legal power." To Tocqueville, this shift away from strict patriarchal rule signaled a change in the emotional climate of families: "in proportion as manners and laws become more democratic, the relation of father and son becomes more intimate and more affectionate; rules and authority are less talked of, confidence and tenderness are oftentimes increased, and it would seem that the natural bond is drawn closer. . . ." In his view, the American family heralded a new era in human relations. Freed from the rigid hierarchy of the past, parents and children could meet as near equals, joined by "filial love and fraternal affection."

This vision of the democratic family — a harmonious association of parents and children united by love and trust — has mesmerized popular culture in the United States. From the nineteenth century to the present, popular novels, magazines, music, and advertising images have glorified the comforts of loving domesticity. In recent years, we've probably absorbed our strongest impressions of the ideal family from television situation comedies. In the 1950s we had the Andersons on *Father Knows Best*, the Stones on *The Donna Reed Show*, and the real-life Nelson family on *The Adventures of Ozzie & Harriet*. Over the next three decades, the model stretched to include single parents, second marriages, and interracial adoptions on *My Three Sons, The Brady Bunch,* and *Diff'rent Strokes*, but the underlying ideal of wise, loving parents and harmonious, happy families remained unchanged. But today, America has begun to worry about the health of its families: even the families on TV no longer reflect the domestic tranquility of the Anderson clan. America is becoming increasingly ambivalent about the future of family life, and perhaps with good reason. The myth of the family scarcely reflects the complexities of modern American life. High divorce rates, the rise of the single-parent household, the impact of remarriage, and a growing frankness about domestic violence are transforming the way we see family life; many families must also contend with the stresses of urban life and economic hardship. Such pressures on and within the family can be particularly devastating to young people: the suicide rate among fifteen- to nineteen-year-olds has more than tripled in the last thirty years. In our world it's no longer clear whether the family is a blessing to be cherished or an ordeal to be survived.

This chapter examines the myth of the model family and explores alternative visions of family life. It opens with three paintings by Norman Rockwell that capture some of the power of "family values" circa 1950, an era some consider the heyday of American family life. The next four readings challenge the ideal of the harmonious nuclear family. Historian John R. Gillis dismantles numerous "myths of families past" and shows that many of our most cherished images of family life are relatively recent inventions. In "Looking for Work," Gary Soto recalls his boyhood desire to live the myth and recounts his humorously futile attempts to transform his working-class Chicano family into a facsimile of the Cleavers on *Leave It to Beaver*. Anndee Hochman's painful memoir about her parents' response to her coming out as a lesbian invites you to consider the chilling idea that behind family unity lurks the demand for utter conformity. Stephanie Coontz then takes a hard look at the 1950s family, explaining its appeal to some Americans but also documenting its dark side. In the chapter's media selection, Elizabeth Dodson Gray argues that television has exposed domestic violence against women and children that has been present but rarely seen.

The next trio of readings addresses the issue of unwed mothers, a group that has come to symbolize, for many Americans, the dissolution of traditional family values. Conservative writer Charles Murray warns that an epidemic of illegitimacy threatens to create a white underclass in the United States and thus jeopardizes the American way of life. Benjamin Franklin's "The Speech of Miss Polly Baker" adds not only a historical but also a women's perspective. Next, Kristin Luker explores the realities behind everyday (mis)conceptions about teenage pregnancy and makes some recommendations radically different from Murray's call to eliminate welfare assistance to unwed mothers and spend "lavishly" on orphanages instead.

The chapter concludes with four readings that explore alternative family structures and show families functioning well under trying circumstances. In "An Indian Story," Roger Jack paints a warm, magical portrait of the bond between a Native American boy and his caretaker aunt. Bebe Moore Campbell's "Envy" is a fascinating personal account of growing up father-hungry in a female-dominated African American family. In "Black Women and Motherhood," Patricia Hill Collins presents another perspective on the many roles played by black mothers and offers a model of the extended family that defies the narrow definitions of the Eurocentric family myth. Finally, Melvin Dixon's poem "Aunt Ida Pieces a Quilt" celebrates a woman who rises above prejudice to commemorate a nephew lost to AIDS. These closing selections affirm the continuing power of families as sources of acceptance, love, and support.

Sources

Gerda Lerner, *The Creation of Patriarchy*. New York: Oxford University Press, 1986.

Steven Mintz and Susan Kellogg, *Domestic Revolutions: A Social History of American Family Life*. New York: Free Press, 1988.

Alexis de Tocqueville, *Democracy in America*. 1835; New York: Vintage Books, 1990.

BEFORE READING

- Spend ten minutes or so jotting down every word, phrase, or image you associate with the idea of "family." Write as freely as possible, without censoring your thoughts or worrying about grammatical correctness.

Working in small groups, compare lists and try to categorize your responses. What assumptions about families do they reveal?

- Draw a visual representation of your family. This could take the form of a graph, chart, diagram, map, cartoon, symbolic picture, or literal portrait. Don't worry if you're not a skillful artist: the main point is to convey an idea, and even stick figures can speak eloquently. When you're finished, write a journal entry about your drawing. Was it easier to depict some feelings or ideas visually than it would have been to describe them in words? Did you find some things about your family difficult or impossible to convey visually? Does your drawing "say" anything that surprises you?

- Do a brief freewrite about the mother and son pictured on the title page of this chapter (p. 17). What can you tell about their relationship? What does this image suggest to you about the ideals and realities of American family life?

A Family Tree, Freedom from Want, and Freedom from Fear

NORMAN ROCKWELL

The first "reading" for this book consists of three paintings by Norman Rockwell (1894–1978), one of America's most prolific and popular artists. Together they capture what the idea of family meant to the nation half a century ago, a time some consider the golden age of American family life. A Family Tree *(1959) is an oil painting that, like hundreds of Rockwell's images, became cover art for* The Saturday Evening Post. Freedom from Want *and* Freedom from Fear *are part of Rockwell's Four Freedoms series (1943). Their appearance in the* Post, *along with* Freedom of Speech *and* Freedom of Worship, *generated millions of requests for reprints.*

A Family Tree, by Norman Rockwell.

Freedom from Want, by Norman Rockwell.

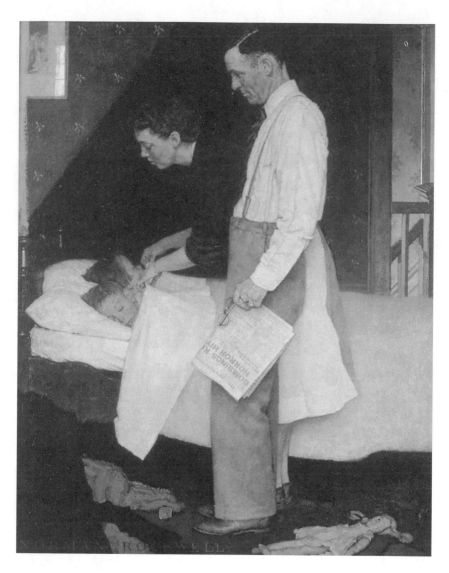

Freedom from Fear, by Norman Rockwell.

ENGAGING THE TEXT

1. What is the usual purpose of family trees? Why do you think they are important to many Americans? How significant is a family tree to you or others in your family?
2. Discuss the details of *A Family Tree* and their significance. For example, identify each figure and explain what it contributes to Rockwell's composite picture of America.
3. How does Rockwell's painting differ from your image of a typical family tree? What is its basic message? How accurate do you consider its portrayal of the American family?
4. What is the appeal of *Freedom from Want?* What ideas about family does it assume or promote? What's your own reaction to Rockwell's image? Support your answers with reference to details of the painting.
5. In *Freedom from Fear,* why did Rockwell choose this moment to paint? What can you guess about the relationships within the family? What about its relationship to the rest of the world?

EXPLORING CONNECTIONS

6. Compare Rockwell's paintings to the frontispiece photo for this chapter (p. 17). How does Rockwell's vision of family life differ from that depicted by the photo?

EXTENDING THE CRITICAL CONTEXT

7. Research your family tree and make your own drawing of it. How does it compare to the family tree Rockwell has created? Write a journal entry or short essay about your family tree.
8. Rockwell's family tree appeared in 1959. Draw an updated version for the 1990s.
9. What might pictures entitled *Freedom from Want* and *Freedom from Fear* look like if they were painted today? Describe in detail a scene or image to fit each of these titles; if possible, draw, paint, or photograph your image.

Myths of Family Past
JOHN R. GILLIS

Listening to politicians talk about the sanctity of "family values," you might think that the nuclear family had a long pedigree in American society. But as John R. Gillis demonstrates in this selection, you'd be dead wrong. The 1950s television image of family life is only a few decades old and bears little resemblance to the real living arrangements of the past. Whatever aspect of family life you can think of — marriage, childbearing, even family trees — Gillis is likely to tell you something surprising about the disparity between myth and reality. John R. Gillis (b. 1939) is a professor of history at Rutgers University; this selection comes from his book A World of Their Own Making: Myth, Ritual, and the Quest for Family Values *(1996).*

> This acute awareness of tradition is a modern phenomenon that reflects a desire for custom and routine in a world characterized by constant change and innovation. Reverence for the past has become so strong that when traditions do not exist, they are frequently invented.
> — WITOLD RYBCZYNSKI, *Home*[1]

Much about modern family life is changing, but one thing that never seems to change is the notion that family is not what it used to be. Families past are presented to us not only as more stable but as more authentic than families present. We imagine their times to have been the days when fathers were really fathers, mothers true mothers, and children still children. Families past are invariably portrayed as simpler, less problematic. We imagine them not only as large but as better integrated, untroubled by generational divisions, close to kin, respectful of the old, honoring the dead. Families past are imagined as rooted and centered, identified with particular places and loyal to their own pasts. We think of them as "traditional," not only because they belong to the past but because they were supposedly more attached to it. And because we imagine previous generations to have been such dedicated keepers of custom, we regard all our own family occasions in the same light in which we regard the old furniture passed down from generation to generation — as having seen better days.

But like antiques, family traditions have actually acquired their value by the passage of time and are far more treasured today than when they were new. It comes as a considerable surprise to most people that our cherished family traditions are of relatively recent origins, few older than the mid-nineteenth century. It was the European and American Protestant middle classes, the Victorians, who were the first to value the old as such. They invented the modern notion of antiques and were also the first to assign the past that quality of authenticity we so readily accept.[2] The more things change, the more we desire to keep them the same. Never has the old silver shown brighter or custom been kept in such mint condition. No period in

---

[1]Witold Rybczynski, *Home: A Short History of an Idea* (New York: Penguin, 1987), p. 9. [Author's note]

[2]David Lowenthal, *The Past Is a Foreign Country* (Cambridge: Cambridge University Press, 1985), p. 122. [Author's note]

human history has been so devoted to preservation, restoration, and reen-actment as our own. In earlier times, the past belonged only to elites, who kept heritage just as they kept offices and land — for themselves. Today the past has been democratized and we all must have our own history. What was once a luxury has become a necessity. What was once a privilege is now a right.

It is the present that endows antiques with their current value, and it is the present that has given family past its huge significance. The unity, conti-nuity, rootedness, and traditionalism ascribed to families past, first by the Victorians and then by each succeeding modern generation, parallels the way in which community is seen as being in a perpetual state of disintegra-tion. On both sides of the Atlantic there has been a tendency to pick a par-ticular time and place as the epitome of community — for Americans the New England town, for Swedes the villages of the Dalarna region, for Ger-mans the small walled city, for the English the villages of the so-called Home Counties — and to designate it the epitome of the traditional com-munity, causing everything that followed to be seen in terms of destruction and loss.[3]

When we talk about family in terms of tradition, the result is the same. In projecting a static image of family onto a particular past time and place, we immediately begin to describe change in terms of "decline" or "loss." Ironically, we are also in the habit of updating the traditional community and family periodically so that the location of the golden age is constantly changing. For the Victorians, the traditional family, imagined to be rooted and extended, was located sometime before industrialization and urbaniza-tion, but for those who came of age during the First World War, tradition was associated with the Victorians themselves; today we think of the 1950s and early 1960s as the location of the family and community life we imagine we have lost.

Summoning images from the past is one of the ways we generate the hope and energy necessary to strive for better communities and families in the future. But when the remembered past becomes an end in itself, be-coming "mere nostalgia, it degenerates into a terminal bubble of the past that closes one off from the living spontaneity of the present and denies the

5

[3]On American notions of community, see Thomas Bender, *Community and Social Change in America* (New Brunswick, N.J.: Rutgers University Press, 1978), chaps. 1 and 2; on Sweden, see Orvar Löfgren and Jonas Frykman, *Culture Builders: A Historical Anthropology of Middle-Class Life* (New Brunswick, N.J.: Rutgers University Press, 1987), pp. 59–60; on Germany, see Mack Walker, *German Home Towns, Community, State, and General Estates, 1640–1871* (Ithaca, N.Y.: Cornell University Press, 1971), and Alon Confino, *Nation as a Local Metaphor: Wuertemburg, the German Empire, and National Empire, 1871–1918* (Chapel Hill: University of North Carolina Press, forthcoming); on England, see Robert Colls and Philip Dodd, eds., *Englishness: Politics and Culture, 1880–1920* (London: Croom Helm, 1986), and Anthony P. Cohen, *The Symbolic Construction of Community* (London: Routledge, 1985). [Author's note]

possibility of a future."[4] Either way, the notion of the traditional family is a myth many families live by.

Looking back from the 1990s, and preoccupied with rising divorce and illegitimacy rates, we perceive the 1950s as a rock of stability. But that was a decade gripped by anxiety about family life, and especially about the threat posed by the new youth cultures. The 1950s version of the traditional family was an idealized image of the Depression family, which was imagined as holding on by holding tight to one another.[5] But those who lived through the 1920s and 1930s would not have recognized themselves in the myths that later generations made of them, for these were the same people who saw themselves to be in the midst of a sexual revolution.[6] The so-called Lost Generation felt wholly cut off from a past they imagined to have been as stable as their present was chaotic. For them, the Victorian family was tradition. But as we have seen, the Victorians were by no means sure of themselves when it came to family matters. They were deeply anxious about the loss of community resulting from rapid urbanization and no more secure in their family life than we are. In 1851 the American Horace Bushnell looked back with regret on the passing of the days when families were "harnessed, all together, into the producing process, young and old, male and female, from the boy who rode the plough-horse to the grandmother knitting under her spectacles."[7]. . .

Middle-class Victorians were not necessarily the first to invent a usable family past. For centuries, those pretending to aristocratic or patrician[8] status had been creating pedigrees for themselves. But prior to the nineteenth century, genealogy had been a very exclusive enterprise; very few families were conscious of their own origins, much less interested in the history of family generally.[9] The working classes were anything but nostalgic about their pasts. Until very recently, their family stories were about hard times, and their memories of childhood often bitter.[10] Middle-class Victorians

---

[4]Eugene Rochberg-Halton, *Meaning and Modernity: Social Theory in the Pragmatic Attitude* (Chicago: University of Chicago Press, 1986), p. 188; Stephanie Coontz, *The Way We Never Were: American Families and the Nostalgia Trap* (New York: Basic Books, 1992), chap. 1. [Author's note]

[5]Arlene Skolnick, *Embattled Paradise: The American Family in an Age of Uncertainty* (New York: Basic Books, 1991), pp. 47, 50–51, 77–78. [Author's note]

[6]Paula Fass, *The Damned and the Beautiful: American Youth in the 1920s* (New York: Oxford University Press, 1977). [Author's note]

[7]Quoted in Coontz, *The Way We Never Were*, p. 12. [Author's note]

[8]*patrician:* Of high social rank.

[9]Alex Shoumatoff, *The Mountain of Names: A History of the Human Family* (New York: Simon & Schuster, 1985), pp. 213–24; see also Anthony Richard Wagner, *English Genealogy* (Oxford: Clarendon Press, 1972), pp. 3–4, 397–407. [Author's note]

[10]Mary Jo Maynes, "The Contours of Childhood: Demography, Strategy, and Mythology of Childhood in French and German Lower-Class Adults," *The European Experience of Declining Fertility, 1850–1970: The Quiet Revolution,* ed. John Gillis, David Levine, and Louise Tilly (Oxford: Basil Blackwell, 1992), pp. 101–24. [Author's note]

started by inventing traditions for their own families, but they quickly became advocates of tradition in general. By 1900 they had founded hundreds of genealogical and historical societies in Europe and North America. Enthusiasm for family traditions was slower to arrive at other social levels, but by the 1970s the search for roots had become a mass preoccupation, and today everyone is a family historian. Children learn to value family history in school, magazines tell us how to refurbish our family traditions, and software programs make it ever easier to construct the family tree. Today every family wants its own history and its own traditions. Arising alongside the new familism is a new ethnicity, which stresses the uniqueness of every group's identity based on the uniqueness of its particular history.

Yet despite all the diversity, there is a certain uniformity: the "traditional family" imagined by WASPS is strikingly like that conjured up by Jews, Germans, and Mexican Americans. All these visions of family past emphasize stability and unity, rootedness and continuity. When they remember earlier generations as more cooperative and caring, African Americans are no different than Asian or Irish Americans. Cross-national comparisons show a similar uniformity. The images of the old homestead held by Swedes and Poles are not all that different from those held by Californians and Australians. It turns out that we are all seeking essentially the same thing, namely, a reassuring myth of family past that can serve our present needs and future aspirations.

We must be careful not to confuse the family past we live by with the families that previous generations actually lived with. Until quite recently, historians also failed to make this distinction, but in the last two decades demographic and social history research has revealed a very different picture of families past, one that suggests much more continuity between families past and present in actual behavior than anyone would have imagined. It seems that the fragmentation, instability, and discontinuity that we feel so keenly today has been part of the European experience of family life since at least the late Middle Ages. Europeans who came to the Americas carried a dream of caring and cooperation with them but were unable to realize it in the new land. Throughout the seventeenth and eighteenth centuries, family unity and continuity remained elusive on both sides of the Atlantic, and, in the great industrial and political upheavals of the nineteenth century, it became even more so.

Human reproduction has never been straightforward, and no society has   10
found a way to eliminate its contradictions. Different peoples have found a bewildering variety of ways of coping; over time it is not the problems that have changed but the answers. The questions that Western civilization has had to face over the centuries are to some degree the same as those that every preindustrial society has to confront, namely, how to manage the fragmenting effects of high levels of mortality and fertility along with low levels of very unevenly distributed resources. Until our own century, no part of the

world was able to control death or birth rates or produce the levels of affluence that would have given hope that all families might share in roughly the
same resources.

We know that Europe, and particularly northwestern Europe, departed
from the preexisting domestic practices of both the classical Mediterranean
world and Germanic peoples beginning in the Middle Ages, setting in on a
course of development different from most parts of the world.[11] At the core
of the unique European family system, and distinguishing it from the family
systems of Africa, Asia, and the pre-Columbian Americas, was the single-
family household established by monogamous marriage. The first "rule" was
that marriage should not take place without the couple first having established a basis of economic independence. "When thou art married, if it may
be, live of thyself with thy wife, in a family of thine own," was the advice offered to English young people by William Whateley in 1624.[12] Colonial settlers also heeded his maxim that "the mixing of governours in a household,
or subordinating or uniting of two Masters, or two Dames under one roof,
doth fall out most times, to be a matter of unquietness to all parties."[13]

Multiple-family households continued to predominate in southern and
eastern Europe, but in northwestern Europe and those parts of the world
its peoples settled, the single-family household contributed to a second
unique characteristic: a relatively high age of marriage. From at least the
fourteenth century onward, the marriage age of men averaged about
twenty-six years, and women generally married at twenty-three. In contrast
to other world regions, these ages were both remarkably high and relatively
evenly matched. European marriage age did not fall significantly until the
late eighteenth century, but even then it remained high by world standards.
And today it seems to be returning to its old levels once again, confirming a
pattern that has lasted for almost six centuries.

The linkage between late age of marriage and household formation led
to two more unique features of the Western family system. The late age of
marriage gave rise to a very large pool of unmarried young people. Most of
them hoped to gain a household and marry eventually, but given the strait-
ened circumstances of the medieval and early modern economies, not all
would have this opportunity. Rates of lifetime celibacy therefore never fell

[11]John Hajnal, "European Marriage Patterns in Perspective," in *Population in History:
Essays in Historical Demography*, ed. D. V. Glass and D. E. C. Eversley (London: Edward
Arnold, 1965); and Hajnal, "Two Kinds of Pre-Industrial Household Systems," *Population and
Development Review* 8, no. 3 (1982): pp. 449–94; Wally Seccombe, *A Millennium of Family
Change: Feudalism to Capitalism in Northwestern Europe* (London: Verso, 1992), chap. 3;
David Herlihy, *Medieval Households* (Cambridge: Cambridge University Press, 1985), chaps.
1–3. [Author's note]

[12]Quoted in Alan Macfarlane, *The Origins of English Individualism* (Oxford: Basil Blackwell, 1978), p. 75. [Author's note]

[13]Quoted in Laurel Thatcher Ulrich, *A Midwife's Tale: The Life of Martha Ballard, Based
on Her Diary, 1785–1812* (New York: Vintage, 1991), p. 281. [Author's note]

below 10 percent and sometimes went as high as 20 percent, in sharp contrast to other world regions where some form of marriage was virtually universal. Wedlock did not become universal in the West until the twentieth century; now, as we approach a new millennium, the old pattern of late marriage and low marriage rates seems to be reasserting itself.[14]

Only the wealthy and powerful were ever guaranteed access to marriage, but even they could not escape the effects of the high mortality rates that prevailed right up to the present century.[15] Mortality before the twentieth century was catastrophic by any standard. The average life expectancy was the midforties for both sexes, mortality was distributed across the age spectrum, and rates of infant mortality ranged from 15 to 30 percent for the first year of life. By the age of twenty, a half or more of the birth cohort was deceased, and life remained very uncertain throughout middle age as well. It was not until the twentieth century that mortality declined significantly: two-thirds of the longevity gains in the entire history of the human race have been attained in the last one hundred years.[16]

High rates of mortality have always been associated with high rates of fertility. Simply to replace the children who died, women in the past had to devote their entire married life to childbearing. From the fourteenth through the nineteenth centuries, married women had an average of four to six children. They might have had more had not the age of marriage been so high and so many women either died or reached the limits of their physical capacity to have children. In any case, population growth in Europe and North America remained moderate by the standards of today's Third World, where early marriage combines with lengthening life expectancies to produce very high birth rates.

Despite the relatively moderate nature of European population growth, families in the past had difficulty rearing all their children, partly owing to parental mortality: in England prior to the mid-nineteenth century, 17 percent of children were fatherless by age ten, and 27 percent by age fifteen. Peter Laslett has estimated that one-half to two-thirds of all young women had lost their fathers by the time they married in their midtwenties.[17] Given this very high level of orphanage, it is not surprising that children lived elsewhere than in their natal homes. What is astonishing is that even children with two parents moved out of the natal house at a very young age in large

15

---

[14]Hajnal, "Two Kinds of Pre-Industrial Household Systems," pp. 449–94. [Author's note]

[15]David Herlihy rightly argues that the Western family system enhanced the "poor man's chances of gaining a wife and producing progeny," but relative only to the ancient and Germanic worlds. *Medieval Households,* p. 158. [Author's note]

[16]Lawrence Stone, *The Family, Sex, and Marriage in England, 1500–1800* (New York: Harper & Row, 1977), pp. 58–64. [Author's note]

[17]Peter Laslett, *Family Life and Illicit Love in Earlier Generations* (Cambridge: Cambridge University Press, 1977), p. 169; see also Illana Krausman Ben-Amos, *Adolescence and Youth in Early Modern England* (New Haven, Conn.: Yale University Press, 1994), p. 48. [Author's note]

numbers. Some did so as mere children, but the greatest exodus happened in the midteens, when virtually all young people lived and worked in another dwelling for shorter or longer periods of time. David Herlihy has estimated that in late medieval and early modern Europe, two-thirds to three-quarters of the entire population spent some part of their childhood and youth living away from their families of birth.[18] In England, one-fifth of all rural people in the early modern period were living in households other than their own.[19]

Extrafamilial residents included not only orphaned children but large numbers of unmarried servants and apprentices, plus a fair number of married adults who were forced by poverty or other circumstances to work away from home. On the death of a marriage partner, it was common for the surviving spouse to remarry immediately so as to maintain the household, but when he or she was unable to remarry, the household was likely to disperse, with widows and widowers constituting a large part of the adults living apart from their families of birth and marriage.

Thus, contrary to myth, the three-generation household was relatively rare. Throughout the late medieval and early modern periods, the two groups least likely to be living with their own kin were children in their teens and old persons. The young were accommodated by the institutions of apprenticeship and servanthood, which had been fixtures in the West since at least the fourteenth century. The elderly were taken care of by a combination of poor relief and arrangements worked out when they were no longer able to sustain their own households. While some old folks made out "retirement" contracts with their own families, a surprising number lived in the households of nonrelatives. Most, especially those whose children had predeceased them, had little choice, but others chose such a living arrangement because it sustained some small part of their independence.

Today we are so used to thinking of the poor as having the greatest numbers of children that it comes as a shock to learn that, before the nineteenth century, the largest households were those of the wealthy. Not only were the wealthy better able to afford to keep more of their own children, but they actively recruited the largest numbers of servants and live-in workers. In the household economy that prevailed from the fourteenth to the nineteenth centuries, the "big houses" benefited from the surplus labor of their less fortunate neighbors, whose own residences were not ordinarily dignified with the word *house,* much less the word *home.* The upward circulation of young people in their teens and twenties also benefited poorer families by relieving them of feeding and housing costs, and thus there functioned a unique system of exchange of children that sustained the economic, social, and political order of Europe and North America until the nineteenth century.

---

[18]Herlihy, *Medieval Households,* p. 159. [Author's note]
[19]Ben-Amos, *Adolescence and Youth in Early Modern England,* p. 69. [Author's note]

Even moderately well off families regularly ceded their rights over their   20
children through apprenticeship contracts that ensured good treatment of
youngsters in return for their loyalty to their masters and mistresses.[20]
Parental rights were socially and legally rather than naturally defined. The
social order was understood to depend on a hierarchy of households, with
each head of house, starting with the monarchy, exercising parental (usually
patriarchal but sometimes matriarchal) authority over all the inhabitants, related or not. In this multitiered system, only a minority of families could rely
solely on their own reproduction to form and sustain a household. All families, rich and poor, were dependent on one another to some degree. And
this central fact of economic, social, and political life was contingent on the
ability of everyone to imagine family as something other than that constituted by birth or marriage. For most of its history, therefore, the Western
family system has functioned with an imaginary [web] that has enabled individuals to form familial relations with strangers and to feel at home away
from home.

Our myths of family past tell us that people used to be more monogamous and that sex was always contained within marriage, but here again the
historical reality proves to be quite different. It took a very long time for the
church to assert its control over marriage and divorce, and, even as late as
the nineteenth century, common-law nuptials and folk customs of divorce
were common in both Europe and North America. Until then, the line between married and unmarried persons was often somewhat indistinct.
While illegitimacy rates remained moderate in most places throughout the
centuries, premarital pregnancy rates were somewhat higher, never falling
below 10 percent and sometimes rising to 30 percent.[21]
    In the agrarian and rural manufacturing economies that prevailed until
the nineteenth century, there were never enough resources to afford everyone access to a farm or a trade and thus to marry and have a family of their
own. But this fact did not prevent people from establishing intimate relationships outside the single-family household system. The distinction between the big house and the little house had its parallel in the distinction
between big weddings, solemnized by the church and recognized in law,
and the little marriages that people conducted to sustain ties that did not receive the same official or even social recognition. Prior to the church's regulation of marriage in the twelfth century, Europeans had legitimated their
sexual unions and the resulting children in all kinds of rituals of their own

[20]John Gillis, *Youth and History: Tradition and Change in European Age Relations, 1750 to the Present* (New York: Academic Press, 1975), pp. 5–12, 21–26. [Author's note]

[21]Laslett, *A Fresh Map of Life: The Emergence of the Third Age* (Cambridge, Mass.: Harvard University Press, 1991), chap. 3; E. A. Wrigley and Roger Schofield, *The Population History of England, 1541–1871: A Reconstruction* (Cambridge, Mass.: Harvard University Press, 1981), chap. 8; on American rates, see Stone, *The Family, Sex, and Marriage in England*, p. 609; Seccombe, *A Millennium of Family Change*, pp. 225–26. [Author's note]

making. Wells, bridges, and prominent natural features served as altars where vows were exchanged. Rings and other love tokens predated church marriage, which ultimately, but somewhat reluctantly, incorporated these pagan symbols into its ceremonies.[22] For a very long time the church itself accepted the consent of the parties as sufficient validation of a marriage. Its own rites did not triumph completely until the nineteenth century.

We may like to think of the big church wedding as traditional, but it too is of very recent origins. Before the nineteenth century, no great fuss was made about premarital pregnancy or even illegitimate birth as long as the community was assured that it would not be unduly burdened by the child.[23] Merely having a child did not change a person's social status. In eighteenth-century Maine, Martha Ballard's son Jonathan continued living with his mother as her son even though he was the father of Sally Pierce's child. And Sally remained with her own family until, some four months after the birth, she married the reluctant Jonathan. Yet the couple lived with both the Ballards and the Pierces for another month before they "went to housekeeping." Only when they had their own household did Jonathan take his place among the town fathers of Hallowell. His rite of passage was quite public and formal. He became a man of the town when, along with six other recently married men, he was initiated into the mock office of "hog reeve."[24]

The rites of female passage were typically less public, but we can be fairly sure that having her own house changed Sally's status from girl to woman. It surprises us that giving birth to a child was not the transformative event then that it is today, but prior to the nineteenth century, motherhood, fatherhood, and childhood were all socially rather than biologically defined statuses. Mothers were those women, including many who had not given birth, who were engaged in the tasks of mothering; fathers were those men, including bachelors, who headed households. The various tasks of mothering were shareable and separable from childbearing. Wet-nursing was common on both sides of the Atlantic, and infants were often removed from the birth family for long periods. In households where mothers were either busy or absent, older daughters frequently acted as "little mothers" to their younger siblings.

Indeed, child-rearing was by no means exclusively the domain of   25
women: prior to the midnineteenth century, fathers were expected to be at least as involved as mothers with the raising of children. Fatherhood, like motherhood, was defined socially rather than biologically. Fathering meant much more than inseminating: it was understood as a well-defined set of domestic skills — provisioning, hospitality, and child-rearing — that male heads of households were expected to acquire and share with other men.

---

[22]John Gillis, *For Better, For Worse: British Marriages, 1600 to the Present* (New York: Oxford University Press, 1985), chaps. 1–2. [Author's note]

[23]Ulrich, *A Midwife's Tale*, pp. 138, 152–67; Gillis, *For Better, For Worse*, chap. 4. [Author's note]

[24]Ulrich, *A Midwife's Tale*, pp. 138, 147, 155, 160. [Author's note]

Many a bachelor head of house had "his own family" in the eighteenth century, and over a lifetime the German *Hausvater* would be father to many children not his own, while his children were being fathered elsewhere.[25]

Today we think of motherhood, fatherhood, and childhood as natural conditions inherent in the biological relationship itself, a conception quite the opposite of these earlier understandings of mothering and fathering as skills to be acquired, used, and then set aside. Even children were expected to learn to be children, for until the midnineteenth century, domestic advice manuals were directed as much to them as to their parents. Treated as a social role rather than as a biologically defined age category, both childhood and youth were something to adjust to. In fact, all family relationships were achieved rather than natural. Social definitions of family invariably prevailed over biological definitions. The social father, the *pater,* took precedence over the natural father, the *genitor,* just as natural mothers gave pride of place to social mothers in a world where a child's survival often depended on having a variety of nurturers, male as well as female.

The economic necessity that compelled young people to postpone and even forgo marriage and forced parents to give up their children was made palatable by a contemporary understanding of family flexible and capacious enough to provide everyone with surrogate family relations of one kind or another. Origins did not matter much to the very large part of the population who, because of mortality or mobility, were cut off from their pasts.

Prior to the nineteenth century, families on both sides of the Atlantic had little of the stability and continuity we now want to attribute to them. In the Old Country as well as in the New World, families rarely dwelled in one place (much less the same house) for even two generations. Farms and townhouses had an identity of their own independent of the succession of families who inhabited them. Places gave their names to people, not vice versa. Elite families were sometimes referred to as "houses" only because the house defined the family. The term "family" still meant all the members of the house — servants, boarders, live-in employees, as well as resident blood relations. In those days, even visitors were regarded as part of the family.[26]

[25]Naomi Tadmore, "'Family' and 'Friend' in *Pamela:* A Case Study in the History of the Family in Eighteenth-Century England," *Social History* 14. no. 3 (October 1989): 289–306. [Author's note]

[26]On the language of family, see Raymond Williams, *Key Words,* rev. ed. (New York: Oxford University Press, 1983); Petrus Spierenberg, *The Broken Spell: A Cultural and Anthropological History of Preindustrial Europe* (New Brunswick, N.J.: Rutgers University Press, 1991), p. 283; and Jean-Louis Flandrin, *Families in Former Times: Kinship, Household, and Sexuality* (New York: Cambridge University Press, 1979), pp. 4–10. On the languages of household and home, see Orvar Löfgren, "Family and Household: Images and Realities: Cultural Change in Swedish Society," in *Households: Comparative and Historical Structure of the Domestic Group,* ed. R. Netting, R. Wilk, and E. Arnould (Berkeley: University of California Press, 1984), pp. 457–58; and Lawrence Stone and Jeanne C. Stone, *An Open Elite? England, 1540–1880,* abr. ed. (New York: Oxford University Press, 1986), p. 212. [Author's note]

This constant changeover was built into a hierarchical social order in which everyone knew his or her place, even if they knew little of their pasts. The rich could claim not only the productive and reproductive capacity of the poor but their very identities. This prerogative was most evident in slave-holding regions, where the big house claimed rights superior to those of the natural families under its purview by forbidding slave marriages and refusing to legitimate slave offspring. Such patriarchy was not confined to plantations, however, for all masters claimed the right to the loyalty of those who lived under their roofs, including the right to forbid the marriages of servants and apprentices. What millions of African Americans were forced to do by enslavement, the European poor were compelled to do by the terms of their bonded labor.[27]. . .

Until the mid-nineteenth century, most Americans and Europeans still located themselves spatially in the Great Chain of Being rather than temporally in the Great Line of Progress. It was through place rather than history that they made themselves at home in the world. We who have lost that sense of place depend much more on time for our bearings, and specifically on origins, which we believe give meaning and value to both things and people.[28] A person, a family, a nation — nothing without a past can have meaning or substance.[29] But apart from the genealogies of the aristocratic elites, premodern knowledge of ancestors did not extend back more than two generations. Most would neither have known nor cared where their forefathers were buried. Except for the elites, nobody tended family graves or organized formal anniversaries. Ralph Josselin, a seventeenth-century English clergyman, showed little interest in his forebears; he thought of himself and his wife as the trunk of a tree and his children as its branches. What is striking is that Josselin's family tree had no roots.[30]

Such an attitude does not fit with our cherished myths of family past, through which we project our obsession with ancestors onto earlier generations. Partly because of communication difficulties and partly because of employment conditions, family reunions were rare before the nineteenth century, though family members were usually dispersed over only a ten- or twenty-mile distance. But there is also little evidence that anyone cared to

30

[27]Mechal Sobel, *The World They Made Together: Black and White Values in Eighteenth-Century Virginia* (Princeton, N.J.: Princeton University Press, 1987); Herbert G. Gutman, *The Black Family in Slavery and Freedom, 1750–1925* (New York: Random House, 1977). [Author's note]

[28]As articulated by Mircea Eliade, *Myth and Reality* (New York: Harper & Row, 1974), p. 34. [Author's note]

[29]For a general discussion of the modern cult of origins, see Barry Schwartz, "The Social Context of Commemoration: A Study in Collective Memory," *Social Forces* 61, no. 2 (December 1982): 374–402. [Author's note]

[30]Alan Macfarlane, *The Family Life of Ralph Josselin* (New York: W. W. Norton, 1970), p. 83. [Author's note]

come together in a regular, ritualized way.[31] Baptisms, weddings, and funerals, which we imagine to have been bigger family events in the past than they are now, were rarely attended by kin and often not even by the immediate family. Baptisms were often hurried affairs that took place while mothers were still confined to the house by the prescribed lying-in period. Betrothal largely ended the family role in marriage, and the bride was escorted to the church by a raucous crowd, not by her father. Parents played a very minor role in premodern weddings. Gifts came from the community rather than from family and kin, and it was also the community that gave the dead their final send-off. Only in the nineteenth century did funerals become family occasions.

In the language of preindustrial Europe and colonial America, the distinctions between kin, and between kin and nonkin, were much more ambiguous than they are today. Before the nineteenth century, no one made a sharp distinction between friendship, by implication a matter of choice, and kinship, with its sense of obligation. Families past were not especially familiar with their relatives, especially those who lived at a distance, and they did not distinguish clearly between their various in-laws. The terms "mother-in-law" and "stepmother" were often used interchangeably, and grandmothers and grandfathers could be any older female or male relative, or sometimes a familiar older person. The more intimate language of "grandma" and "grandpa" did not emerge until the middle of the eighteenth century and was not popularly adopted until much later.[32] The term "friend" was used for relatives, neighbors, and members of the same religious faith. In turn, the familial idiom was extended to guilds, confraternities, monasteries, and the military — groups that today we would not call families.[33]

The language of family was kept open and fluid for good reason. Parents taught their children not to be too reliant on blood ties alone, and New England Puritans reminded themselves constantly not to love their spouses and children too much, for doing so might detract from their love of God. "Look not for Perfection in your relations. God reserves that for another state where marriage is not needed," they told themselves.[34] Parenthood, childhood, and marriage were all terminated at death. Thomas

[31]Keith Wrightson, *English Society, 1580–1680* (New Brunswick, N.J.: Rutgers University Press, 1982), pp. 44–51; Ben-Amos, *Adolescence and Youth in Early Modern England*, pp. 54–69. [Author's note]

[32]According to Wrightson *(English Society)*, the terms "friend" and "kin" were interchangeable (55); Macfarlane, *The Family Life of Ralph Josselin*, chap. 10; Ralph Houlbrooke, *English Family Life, 1576–1716: An Anthology from Diaries* (Oxford: Basil Blackwell, 1989), pp. 219–20. [Author's note]

[33]On the language of friendship, see Ellen Rothman, *Hearts and Hands: A History of Courtship in America* (Cambridge, Mass.: Harvard University Press, 1987), p. 36; Macfarlane, *The Family Life of Ralph Josselin*, p. 150. [Author's note]

[34]Quoted in Edmund Morgan, *The Puritan Family: Essays on Religion and Domestic Relations in Seventeenth-Century New England* (New York: Harper & Row, 1966), p. 52. [Author's note]

Hooker wrote that there would be "no marrying in heaven," for, as he and his contemporaries imagined Paradise, everyone would be "as dear to another, as if all relations of husbands, and wives, of parents, and children, and friends, were in every one of them."[35] Until well into the nineteenth century, heaven was represented not as a community of families but as one large community of friends.[36]

Prior to the nineteenth century, when it was place, not past, that gave people their sense of identity, almost everyone lived in a household. In parts of New England, it was illegal to live on one's own, while in Europe lone-standing household and hostel systems kept the number of those living alone to a minimum. Home was the place that sheltered you at the moment, not the one special place associated with childhood or family of origin.[37]. . .

Our ancestors were anything but homebodies. They had a stronger   35 sense of place and felt more at home in the world at large than we do. They moved easily in and out of one another's households, for the ancient traditions of hospitality were by no means dead; the presence of strangers in the household was still perceived as an enhancement to status.[38] In the eighteenth century, comfort had not yet triumphed over generosity; for instance, William Byrd II, the head of one of Virginia's great families, was either visited or visited others on more than three-quarters of the days of the year. At a humbler level, it seems that visiting enhanced vital bonds of community, creating interdependencies that were invaluable in times of illness or hardship. Some visits were brief, but others, especially those of young people, could be quite extended. In big as well as little houses, the constant traffic of people precluded the cozy home life we imagine to have existed in the past.[39]

In eighteenth-century North America, women may well have done more moving about than men. They referred to this as "gadding"; it had little of the formal, ritualistic character that the Victorians associated with female visiting.[40] People entered without knocking, even without acknowledgment, and seated themselves at the hearth or the table with an air of familiarity that we would find quite astonishing and disturbing. Even the middle classes moved between households so frequently that it was often

[35]Quoted in ibid., p. 49. [Author's note]

[36]Irene Quenzler Brown, "Death, Friendship, and Female Identity during New England's Second Great Awakening," *Journal of Family History* 12, no. 4 (1987): 367–87. [Author's note]

[37]See Leslie Moch, *Moving Europeans: Migration in Western Europe since 1650* (Bloomington: Indiana University Press, 1992), p. 58. [Author's note]

[38]Felicity Heal, *Hospitality in Early Modern England* (Oxford: Clarendon Press, 1990). [Author's note]

[39]Stone and Stone, *An Open Elite?* p. 212. [Author's note]

[40]Ulrich, *A Midwife's Tale,* pp. 91–94. [Author's note]

difficult to tell which family belonged where.[41] The house had yet to become a strictly private space associated exclusively with the nuclear family. It was still the primary place of work and the meeting place of different classes, genders, and ages. Little about it conforms to the myth of the old homestead as a peaceful refuge, the original home sweet home.

We must also dispense with the notion that families past were more concerned with maintaining custom and tradition, and that they maintained the "quality time" we see as so threatened in our own day and age. By and large, premodern Europeans and Americans were less concerned with the economy of time than with the economy of space. Households took their time together pretty much for granted, allowing it to be governed by the rhythms of work and leisure and not setting apart any strictly family times. As we shall see, they lived by an entirely different culture of time than we do. The past had not yet taken on that quality of irrecoverable pastness that causes us so much anguish. Even the dead were within reach in the village graveyard, and people were more likely to be haunted by them, troubled by their presence.[42] It is we, rather than they, who are ancestor worshipers.

The eighteenth century did not think of generations as we do. The term itself simply meant the offspring of a common parent and implied sameness rather than difference.[43] By this definition, all generations occupied the same capacious present. The young were not necessarily identified with the future, nor the old with the past. In the premodern economy of time all ages were conceived of as equidistant from death, and the age differences we make so much of today mattered much less.

People then may have been less obsessed with temporal differences than we are now, and less aware of age than we are, but when it came to sharing space, trouble could erupt. This was precisely what happened when Martha Ballard was forced to share her house with her son Jonathan and his wife Sally. It was common under such circumstances for the parties to draw up an agreement about the rationing of space and resources so as to avoid strife. The Ballards made such an agreement, but it was not sufficient to prevent tensions between Martha and her daughter-in-law.[44]

Contrary to another of our favorite images of families past, the desire for   40
closeness for closeness' sake was notably absent. Families usually gathered to work or to pursue communally organized leisure, not to have family occasions as such. Most such gatherings were returns to community rather than to family

---

[41]E. M. Forster, *Marianne Thornton: A Domestic Biography 1797–1887* (New York: Harcourt, Brace, and Co., 1956), p. 32; see also Robert Fishman, *Bourgeois Utopia: The Rise and Fall of Suburbia* (New York: Basic Books, 1987), pp. 51–62. [Author's note]

[42]Natalie Zemon Davis, "Ghosts, Kin, and Progeny: Some Features of Family Life in Early Modern France," in *The Family,* ed. Alice Rossi, Jerome Kagan, and Tamara Hareven (New York: W. W. Norton, 1978), p. 92. [Author's note]

[43]Williams, *Key Words,* pp. 140–42. [Author's note]

[44]Ulrich, *A Midwife's Tale,* pp. 281–82. [Author's note]

as such, and the nostalgia we associate with family occasions was entirely missing. No graves were visited or ancestors remembered. In the premodern economy of time, no rupture between past and present was visible, and there was no compelling need to connect with other generations or to memorialize the dead.

Given the separation and loss that resulted from the demographic and economic realities of the preindustrial era, it is no wonder that our ancestors regarded forgetfulness as a kind of blessing. We like to think of our ancestors as having better memories, but like so many of our ideas about the past, this belief is more a projection of our fears of forgetting than a true reflection of what was important to them. Montaigne was convinced that "an excellent memory is often conjoined with the weakest intellects."[45] In premodern Europe and North America, people were under no religious obligation to remember earthly things, not even their own families. "The things and relationships of this life are like prints in the Sand, there is not the least appearance of remembrance of them," declared Thomas Hooker. "The King remembers not his Crown, the Husband the Wife, the Father the child."[46] It was God, not man, who remembered.

We want to believe that families past were less fragmented, discontinuous, and divided than families now, but historical reality is anything but reassuring on this point. Lawrence Stone has calculated that the proportion of marriages broken up by death in earlier centuries is just about the same as the proportion broken up by divorce today.[47] Of course, one kind of separation is involuntary and the other is a choice, but it is hard to argue that fragmentation and loss of family ties are anything new, or that we are facing today a situation unprecedented in the history of Western civilization.[48] What has changed are the cultural resources that different periods have had at their disposal to cope with the perpetual challenge of creating a sense of continuity and permanence. Propagating the myth of families past as more stable and united than families present is contemporary culture's way of achieving this result.

It is imperative that we disabuse ourselves of our misconceptions of family past, but we must not stop there. Those who would simply debunk the myths of family past seem to think that we can transcend myth entirely. Marina Warner is right to warn us that "pleas for a return to reason, for simply stripping away illusion, ignore the necessity and the vitality of mythical material in the consciousness as well as unconsciousness."[49] We are no

---

[45]Quoted in James Fentress and Chris Wickham, *Social Memory* (Oxford: Basil Blackwell, 1992), p. 14. [Author's note]

[46]Quoted in Morgan, *The Puritan Family,* p. 20. [Author's note]

[47]Stone, *The Family, Sex, and Marriage in England,* p. 56. [Author's note]

[48]For a contrary point of view, see David Popenoe, "American Family Decline, 1960–1990," *Journal of Marriage and the Family* 55, no. 3 (August 1993): 527–42. [Author's note]

[49]Marina Warner, *Six Myths of Our Time: Little Angels, Little Monsters, Beautiful Beasts, and More* (New York: Vintage, 1994), p. 20. [Author's note]

more able to live without our imagined families than were our ancestors. The only difference lies in the fact that their myths, rituals, and icons were provided by religion and community, while ours are self-generated. We will not understand our own engagement with myth and ritual until we understand how earlier generations engaged with theirs. In this way, we can use the past to throw light on the present.

ENGAGING THE TEXT

1. In his opening paragraph, Gillis makes a number of generalizations about how Americans imagine families of the past. Do you think most Americans see families of the past the way Gillis describes?

2. Working in groups, chart the key myths Gillis defines, plus the "reality" he describes. Here's a start:

Myth	Reality
Families in the past were stable, unified, and firmly rooted.	For centuries, families have been fragmented and unstable.

   When your chart is complete, discuss why it's important to understand the reality and not simply accept the myth.

3. Gillis observes that the mythical "golden age" of the family keeps shifting, but pinpoints the 1950s as the decade contemporary Americans look back on most nostalgically. To what extent do you (or did you) share this view of the 1950s? To what extent has Gillis modified your image of the 1950s family?

4. What activities usually associated with families were performed in the past by the community or by people outside the immediate family? Why is this significant?

5. Gillis writes that motherhood, fatherhood, and childhood, now biologically defined in our society, were once socially defined (para. 24). What does he mean, and why is the distinction important?

EXPLORING CONNECTIONS

6. How do the three paintings by Norman Rockwell (p. 21) reflect the myths of family past that Gillis discusses?

EXTENDING THE CRITICAL CONTEXT

7. Gillis believes that many Americans are nostalgic about family life in the past. Look for evidence of this nostalgia in your reading, on television, in advertisements, in conversations, and so on. After a few days of observation, compare notes with classmates and write a journal entry or short essay based on what you've seen and heard.

8. Gillis writes that "the past has been democratized" (para. 2). What does he mean by this phrase? What evidence do you see in American society or in your own family life that the past has been democratized?

Looking for Work

GARY SOTO

"Looking for Work" is the narrative of a nine-year-old Mexican American boy who wants his family to imitate the "perfect families" he sees on TV. Much of the humor in this essay comes from the author's perspective as an adult looking back at his childhood self, but Soto also respects the child's point of view. In the marvelous details of this midsummer day, Soto captures the interplay of seductive myth and complex reality. Gary Soto (b. 1952) grew up "on the industrial side of Fresno, right smack against a junkyard and the junkyard's cross-eyed German shepherd." Having discovered poetry almost by chance in a city college library, he has now published several volumes of his own, including The Elements of San Joaquin *(1977),* Father Is a Pillow Tied to a Broom *(1980), and* Home Course in Religion *(1991). He has also published essays, prose memoirs, and novels for young readers. "Looking for Work" appeared in* Living Up the Street: Narrative Recollections *(1985).*

One July, while killing ants on the kitchen sink with a rolled newspaper, I had a nine-year-old's vision of wealth that would save us from ourselves. For weeks I had drunk Kool-Aid and watched morning reruns of *Father Knows Best*, whose family was so uncomplicated in its routine that I very much wanted to imitate it. The first step was to get my brother and sister to wear shoes at dinner.

"Come on, Rick — come on, Deb," I whined. But Rick mimicked me and the same day that I asked him to wear shoes he came to the dinner table in only his swim trunks. My mother didn't notice, nor did my sister, as we sat to eat our beans and tortillas in the stifling heat of our kitchen. We all gleamed like cellophane, wiping the sweat from our brows with the backs of our hands as we talked about the day: Frankie our neighbor was beat up by Faustino; the swimming pool at the playground would be closed for a day because the pump was broken.

Such was our life. So that morning, while doing-in the train of ants which arrived each day, I decided to become wealthy, and right away! After downing a bowl of cereal, I took a rake from the garage and started up the block to look for work.

We lived on an ordinary block of mostly working class people: warehousemen, egg candlers,[1] welders, mechanics, and a union plumber. And there were many retired people who kept their lawns green and the gut-

---

[1]*egg candler:* One who inspects eggs by holding them up to a light.

ters uncluttered of the chewing gum wrappers we dropped as we rode by on our bikes. They bent down to gather our litter, muttering at our evilness.

At the corner house I rapped the screen door and a very large woman   5
in a muu-muu answered. She sized me up and then asked what I could do.

"Rake leaves," I answered smiling.

"It's summer, and there ain't no leaves," she countered. Her face was pinched with lines; fat jiggled under her chin. She pointed to the lawn, then the flower bed, and said: "You see any leaves there — or there?" I followed her pointing arm, stupidly. But she had a job for me and that was to get her a Coke at the liquor store. She gave me twenty cents, and after ditching my rake in a bush, off I ran. I returned with an unbagged Pepsi, for which she thanked me and gave me a nickel from her apron.

I skipped off her porch, fetched my rake, and crossed the street to the next block where Mrs. Moore, mother of Earl the retarded man, let me weed a flower bed. She handed me a trowel and for a good part of the morning my fingers dipped into the moist dirt, ripping up runners of Bermuda grass. Worms surfaced in my search for deep roots, and I cut them in halves, tossing them to Mrs. Moore's cat who pawed them playfully as they dried in the sun. I made out Earl whose face was pressed to the back window of the house, and although he was calling to me I couldn't understand what he was trying to say. Embarrassed, I worked without looking up, but I imagined his contorted mouth and the ring of keys attached to his belt — keys that jingled with each palsied step. He scared me and I worked quickly to finish the flower bed. When I did finish Mrs. Moore gave me a quarter and two peaches from her tree, which I washed there but ate in the alley behind my house.

I was sucking on the second one, a bit of juice staining the front of my T-shirt, when Little John, my best friend, came walking down the alley with a baseball bat over his shoulder, knocking over trash cans as he made his way toward me.

Little John and I went to St. John's Catholic School, where we sat among   10
the "stupids." Miss Marino, our teacher, alternated the rows of good students with the bad, hoping that by sitting side-by-side with the bright students the stupids might become more intelligent, as though intelligence were contagious. But we didn't progress as she had hoped. She grew frustrated when one day, while dismissing class for recess, Little John couldn't get up because his arms were stuck in the slats of the chair's backrest. She scolded us with a shaking finger when we knocked over the globe, denting the already troubled Africa. She muttered curses when Leroy White, a real stupid but a great softball player with the gift to hit to all fields, openly chewed his host[2] when he made his First Communion; his hands swung at his sides as he returned to the pew looking around with a big smile.

[2]*his host:* The wafer that represents, in the Catholic sacrament of Communion, the bread of the Last Supper and the body of Christ.

Little John asked what I was doing, and I told him that I was taking a break from work, as I sat comfortably among high weeds. He wanted to join me, but I reminded him that the last time he'd gone door-to-door asking for work his mother had whipped him. I was with him when his mother, a New Jersey Italian who could rise up in anger one moment and love the next, told me in a polite but matter-of-fact voice that I had to leave because she was going to beat her son. She gave me a homemade popsicle, ushered me to the door, and said that I could see Little John the next day. But it was sooner than that. I went around to his bedroom window to suck my popsicle and watch Little John dodge his mother's blows, a few hitting their mark but many whirring air.

It was midday when Little John and I converged in the alley, the sun blazing in the high nineties, and he suggested that we go to Roosevelt High School to swim. He needed five cents to make fifteen, the cost of admission, and I lent him a nickel. We ran home for my bike and when my sister found out that we were going swimming, she started to cry because she didn't have the fifteen cents but only an empty Coke bottle. I waved for her to come and three of us mounted the bike — Debra on the cross bar, Little John on the handle bars and holding the Coke bottle which we would cash for a nickel and make up the difference that would allow all of us to get in, and me pumping up the crooked streets, dodging cars and pot holes. We spent the day swimming under the afternoon sun, so that when we got home our mom asked us what was darker, the floor or us? She feigned a stern posture, her hands on her hips and her mouth puckered. We played along. Looking down, Debbie and I said in unison, "Us."

That evening at dinner we all sat down in our bathing suits to eat our beans, laughing and chewing loudly. Our mom was in a good mood, so I took a risk and asked her if sometime we could have turtle soup. A few days before I had watched a television program in which a Polynesian tribe killed a large turtle, gutted it, and then stewed it over an open fire. The turtle, basted in a sugary sauce, looked delicious as I ate an afternoon bowl of cereal, but my sister, who was watching the program with a glass of Kool-Aid between her knees, said, "Caca."

My mother looked at me in bewilderment. "Boy, are you a crazy Mexican. Where did you get the idea that people eat turtles?"

"On television," I said, explaining the program. Then I took it a step 15 further. "Mom, do you think we could get dressed up for dinner one of these days? David King does."

"*Ay, Dios,*" my mother laughed. She started collecting the dinner plates, but my brother wouldn't let go of his. He was still drawing a picture in the bean sauce. Giggling, he said it was me, but I didn't want to listen because I wanted an answer from Mom. This was the summer when I spent the mornings in front of the television that showed the comfortable lives of white kids. There were no beatings, no rifts in the family. They wore bright clothes; toys tumbled from their closets. They hopped into bed with kisses and woke to glasses of fresh orange juice, and to a father sitting before his morning coffee while the mother buttered his toast. They hurried through the day making friends and gobs of money, returning home to a warmly lit living room, and then dinner. *Leave It to Beaver* was the program I re-played in my mind:

"May I have the mashed potatoes?" asks Beaver with a smile.

"Sure, Beav," replies Wally as he taps the corners of his mouth with a starched napkin.

The father looks on in his suit. The mother, decked out in earrings and a pearl necklace, cuts into her steak and blushes. Their conversation is po-litely clipped.

"Swell," says Beaver, his cheeks puffed with food.   20

Our own talk at dinner was loud with belly laughs and marked by our pointing forks at one another. The subjects were commonplace.

"Gary, let's go to the ditch tomorrow," my brother suggests. He ex-plains that he has made a life preserver out of four empty detergent bottles strung together with twine and that he will make me one if I can find more bottles. "No way are we going to drown."

"Yeah, then we could have a dirt clod fight," I reply, so happy to be alive.

Whereas the Beaver's family enjoyed dessert in dishes at the table, our mom sent us outside, and more often than not I went into the alley to peek over the neighbor's fences and spy out fruit, apricot or peaches.

I had asked my mom and again she laughed that I was a crazy *chavalo*[3]   25 as she stood in front of the sink, her arms rising and falling with suds, face glistening from the heat. She sent me outside where my brother and sister were sitting in the shade that the fence threw out like a blanket. They were talking about me when I plopped down next to them. They looked at one another and then Debbie, my eight-year-old sister, started in.

"What's this crap about getting dressed up?"

She had entered her *profanity* stage. A year later she would give up such words and slip into her Catholic uniform, and into squealing on my brother and me when we "cussed this" and "cussed that."

I tried to convince them that if we improved the way we looked we might get along better in life. White people would like us more. They might invite us to places, like their homes or front yards. They might not hate us so much.

My sister called me a "craphead," and got up to leave with a stalk of grass dangling from her mouth. "They'll never like us."

My brother's mood lightened as he talked about the ditch — the white   30 water, the broken pieces of glass, and the rusted car fenders that awaited our knees. There would be toads, and rocks to smash them.

[3]*chavalo:* Kid.

David King, the only person we knew who resembled the middle class, called from over the fence. David was Catholic, of Armenian and French descent, and his closet was filled with toys. A bear-shaped cookie jar, like the ones on television, sat on the kitchen counter. His mother was remarkably kind while she put up with the racket we made on the street. Evenings, she often watered the front yard and it must have upset her to see us — my brother and I and others — jump from trees laughing, the unkillable kids of the very poor, who got up unshaken, brushed off, and climbed into another one to try again.

David called again. Rick got up and slapped grass from his pants. When I asked if I could come along he said no. David said no. They were two years older so their affairs were different from mine. They greeted one another with foul names and took off down the alley to look for trouble.

I went inside the house, turned on the television, and was about to sit down with a glass of Kool-Aid when Mom shooed me outside.

"It's still light," she said. "Later you'll bug me to let you stay out longer. So go on."

I downed my Kool-Aid and went outside to the front yard. No one was around. The day had cooled and a breeze rustled the trees. Mr. Jackson, the plumber, was watering his lawn and when he saw me he turned away to wash off his front steps. There was more than an hour of light left, so I took advantage of it and decided to look for work. I felt suddenly alive as I skipped down the block in search of an overgrown flower bed and the dime that would end the day right.   35

ENGAGING THE TEXT

1. Why is the narrator attracted to the kind of family life depicted on TV? What, if anything, does he think is wrong with his life? Why do his desires apparently have so little impact on his family?

2. Why does the narrator first go looking for work? How has the meaning of work changed by the end of the story, when he goes out again "in search of an overgrown flower bed and the dime that would end the day right"? Explain.

3. As Soto looks back on his nine-year-old self, he has a different perspective on things than he had as a child. How would you characterize the mature Soto's thoughts about his childhood family life? (Was it "a good family"? What was wrong with Soto's thinking as a nine-year-old?) Back up your remarks with specific references to the narrative.

4. Review the story to find each mention of food or drink. Explain the role these references play.

5. Review the cast of "supporting characters" in this narrative — the mother, sister, brother, friends, and neighbors. What does each contribute to the story and in particular to the meaning of family within the story?

EXPLORING CONNECTIONS

6. Read Bebe Moore Campbell's "Envy" (p. 118) or Roger Jack's "An Indian Story" (p. 109) and compare Soto's family to one of the families portrayed in these selections. In particular, consider gender roles, the household atmosphere, and the expectations placed on children and parents.

7. Compare and contrast the relationship of school and family in this narrative to that described by Mike Rose (p. 174), Richard Rodriguez (p. 202), Inés Hernández-Ávila (p. 216), or Maxine Hong Kingston (p. 251).

8. Like Soto's story, the cartoon on page 49 attests to the power of the media to shape our ideas about family. Write a journal entry describing the media family that most accurately reflects your image of family life. Discuss these entries, and the impact of media on your image of the family, with your classmates.

EXTENDING THE CRITICAL CONTEXT

9. Write a journal entry about a time when you wished your family were somehow different. What caused your dissatisfaction? What did you want your family to be like? Was your dissatisfaction ever resolved?

10. "Looking for Work" is essentially the story of a single day. Write a narrative of one day when you were eight or nine or ten; use details as Soto does to give the events of the day broader significance.

Growing Pains: Beyond "One Big Happy Family"

ANNDEE HOCHMAN

This narrative shows how life in what looks like "one big happy family" can be a lot more complicated when viewed from the inside. Hochman writes evocatively about her childhood and about how her emerging lesbian identity tested the boundaries of family love. Hochman (b. 1962) has worked as a reporter for the Washington Post, *a VISTA volunteer, a counselor for homeless teenagers, and a creative writing teacher. She is now a freelance writer; "Growing Pains" comes from her book* Everyday Acts and Small Subversions: Women Reinventing Family, Community, and Home *(1994).*

I remember waking up to the smell of salt.

Each August when I was little, my parents loaded the car with Bermuda shorts and groceries, beach towels and Scrabble board, and drove to the New Jersey shore. My great-uncle Bernie Ochman had bought a $16,000 bay-front house there in the mid-1950s; he imagined it as a sort of free-wheeling compound, where all the aunts, grandparents, and cousins of my mother's large extended family could gather each summer.

Bernie died before my parents were married, but my mother carried out his vision with her usual zest. She made sure the taxes on the house were paid quarterly, the water valve was turned on each May, and there were enough hamburgers for everyone on Memorial Day and the Fourth of July.

In August, my parents worked feverishly for two weeks, then packed up and headed to the shore for what my father used to call, with some sarcasm, "a little peace and quiet." We left at night to avoid traffic on the Atlantic City Expressway. I always fell asleep in the car and always woke up as we came over the bay bridge, where the smell of salt, moist and thick, would touch me like a mitten dipped in the ocean.

"Are we there yet?" I'd mumble from the back seat.   5

"Almost," my mom would say, and my dad would turn left, then left again, and park the car as close as he could to the big white house.

I loved the shore house because it was so different from home. The front steps tilted a little. Gray paint flaked off the window frames. Two daybeds in the living room were draped with pea green spreads, and the loveseats wore crunchy plastic slipcovers. The picket fence was red.

Even the architecture broke rules. The front room had been added as an afterthought, a low-budget job. The carpenters never removed what had once been the house's front window, now ridiculous in the wall between the front room and the kitchen. I used to sit on the stairs, tapping on the kitchen window and making faces until my mother or my grandmother or Aunt Sadie looked up from the dishes and waved at me. Then I would collapse in giggles.

Upstairs, there was no hall, no doors on the bedrooms. In fact, the bedrooms were not really separate rooms at all, just thin-walled divisions of the upper floor. The front stairs climbed right into the middle of Aunt Charlotte and Uncle Freddie's room; you could stand on the top step and almost tickle Uncle Freddie's feet.

Walk through that bedroom, and the next one, and the next, and you   10
arrived at the bathroom, which had its own quirks — a white claw-foot tub, a hasty shower rigged up with red rubber tubing, and two doors. When I was older, I would check the sliding locks on both doors several times before I dared to unpeel my damp, sandy bathing suit.

Aunt Sadie and Uncle Izzy slept in the larger of the two rear bedrooms, in twin beds pushed together to make one. The very back room was long and narrow, like a single-lane swimming pool, with windows that let in wet salty air off the bay. My grandparents — Bubie and Pop-pop — slept here.

My mother loves to tell the story of my father's first visit to this family compound, during their courtship. He recoiled at the upstairs setup; a pri-

ROGER REALIZES A CHERISHED CHILDHOOD MEMORY IS ACTUALLY A SCENE FROM AN OLD MOVIE.

vate motel room, with a door that locked, was more what he had in mind. My mother informed him firmly that she was a package deal; if he loved her, he would learn to love her family — the father who smoked terrible cigars, the sister who rolled her hair in Kotex sanitary pads, the mother who stewed bruised peaches in the hot, tiny kitchen. And he could start loving them here, in their peculiar summer habitat.

I thought the house was wonderful. The connecting rooms reminded me of a maze, the sort of place where surprises could hunch in old dressers, under beds. Later I realized how the physical space shaped our time there, dissolving the barriers that, in most houses, separate adults from children, private from communal space, eating from work. At the shore, my friends and I played jacks in the middle of the living room, hide and seek in the freestanding metal closets. When people got hungry, they helped themselves from one of the three refrigerators. If I wanted to be alone, I opened a book.

There was one last room upstairs, an odd sixth bedroom lodged in the center of the house. It was the only bedroom with a door, and it belonged to my parents. When I was younger, I assumed they took that room out of generosity. It was small and dark and hot, and you had to grope for the light switch behind a high wooden headboard. It was also the only room in the house in which two people could have a private talk, or take a nap, without somebody else clomping through on her way to the bathroom.

Much later, the summer I was twenty-two, I finally grasped the full significance of that room and made love with Jon Feldstein in it one June weekend when the family wasn't there. "Do you want to have sex?" he had asked, without expectation in his voice, as if it were a foregone conclusion. Later he said, "Well, you know, it gets better with practice."

I did not practice with Jon Feldstein again. In fact, I didn't practice with anyone until more than two years later. By then, I had fallen into a deep and surprising infatuation with one of my closest friends, driven my Datsun cross-country alone, and settled in Portland.

Early in the summer of 1987, I flew back east to tell my parents I was in love with a woman and believed I was destined to be in love with women throughout the foreseeable future. It was Memorial Day weekend, the time we traditionally turned on the water valve and began to inhabit the house at the shore. My mother and I drove there in her blue Honda.

"I think that's how it's going to be for me. With women, I mean," I told her.

"Well, your father thought so," she said finally. "He thought so back in November. I told him that was ridiculous, that you'd always had boyfriends."

She said a lot of other things after that, about not having grandchildren and what a hard path I'd chosen and how she and my father weren't going to be around forever and had hoped to see me taken care of. I concentrated on driving and on the way blood was beating in my ankles, my thumbs, my neck, my ears. I wanted to go to sleep and not wake up until I smelled salt. When we came close to the bay, my mother asked me to pull into a parking lot so she could cry for a while. "I'm sorry," I said, but it didn't seem to help.

At the house, I walked around, touching things, while my mother told my father that he was right, I *was* having an affair with a woman. I wanted to eat something, anything, off the familiar mismatched dishes, play Scrabble until the stars came out, stand on the back porch and watch boats slip under the bridge, tap on the kitchen window until someone waved at me. Instead I went into the bathroom and locked both doors.

About midnight, while I lay sleepless in Aunt Sadie and Uncle Izzy's room, my mother came in and crawled into the other twin bed. "I feel so empty," she said. "I feel empty inside. . . . I don't feel any joy anymore. I feel like the family is breaking apart. I remember how the family was when Uncle Bernie was alive, how this house was. . . ." And her voice, already thin, cracked like a bowl dropped on a tile floor — a splintering and then silence where something used to be.

2 A.M. 3 A.M. Everyone had trooped off to bed in pairs — cousins Joni and Gerry, cousins Debbie and Ralph. Except for my grandfather, who had always stayed up late to watch television and stayed up even later since my grandmother died three years before. Finally he switched off the set, and the house went dark and quiet.

"Don't you feel it's unnatural?" my mother asked. "Don't you feel it's just wrong, that it's weird?"

How can you ask me about being weird in this house, I wanted to   25
shout. This house, with its bedrooms barging into each other and its mismatched dishes, its double-doored bathroom and its red picket fence. When I used to complain that our family wasn't like other families, you laughed and said, "Well, we may not be normal, but we have a lot of fun."

I didn't say these things. I only thought them. And it wasn't until much later, until very recently, that I began to understand why my mother could tolerate the quirks in that house. The madcap shell at the shore housed a solid, predictable center. Relatives came and went in pairs. Someday, presumably, I would join the procession; one of my children would tap on the kitchen window and giggle when I waved. The house might be a little cracked, but the family was predictable, enduring.

I understand why you are so upset, I could tell my mother now. The world has gone crazy and all the walls are too thin and your mother is dead and your sister divorced and your daughter loves women and everything is coming unglued and nothing turns out the way we plan.

4 A.M. 5 A.M. My mother stayed in my room all night, talking and weeping. Toward morning, as boats began to slosh in the bay, I fell into an exhausted, tear-stained sleep. When I woke up at noon, we ate tuna subs and drove back to Philadelphia.

The New Jersey beach house was never just a summertime shelter. It housed my family's favorite image of itself at our expansive best — gathered around the huge dining room table, traipsing through the bedrooms, one big happy family. Just like all the television shows I watched and worshipped.

It is no accident that this particular image clung. The picture of such   30
charmed and cheerful families took hold in the decade preceding my birth,

a bit of postwar propaganda that paid homage to the supposedly idyllic families of Victorian times. Mass-marketed by television, the Cleaver clan and others were burned into our minds by millions of cathode-ray tubes.

The feminist movement challenged that postwar myth as women began to examine the contents inside the "happy family" cliché. Feminists of the late 1960s and 1970s urged their sisters to live authentic lives and to begin them at home. They insisted that personal choices had political import — that is, the daily, minute interactions of our lives *mattered,* not just for each of us alone, but potentially for everyone, for the world. "When a woman tells the truth," Adrienne Rich wrote, "she is creating the possibility for more truth around her."

Women pointed out that families maintained the illusion of happiness only by denying important facts — about adoptions, abortions, illness and illegitimate births, divorces and deaths. Some families devoted their lives to maintaining the secret of a son's homosexuality, a grandmother's alcoholism, a father's violent rage. Melancholy and despair split family members not only from outsiders but from each other; certain topics, one understood, were simply not discussed.

In consciousness-raising groups, women discovered the exhilaration of telling each other unvarnished stories of their bodies, relationships, and families. Back at home, in their kitchens and living rooms, they began to apply these feminist ideals: that *how* people talked meant as much as the conclusions they reached; that the only way to solve problems was to actively engage them; that keeping secrets cost too much.

It was feminism, in part, that prompted me to tell my own family a difficult truth, one I was sure would cause misunderstanding and pain. I was frightened to disturb the jovial peace that was a source of such family pride; at the same time, I could not visit that unpretentious house and pretend I was someone else. I wanted to be known, and seen, in the ways I had come to know and see myself.

I did it because I chose truth over tranquility. Because I had come to   35 believe that real families fight and resist, sob and explode, apologize and forgive. Beneath the fiction of happiness lies the raw, important tissue of human relationships.

And I did it because I had watched other women live without lying. For some, that meant no longer passing as heterosexual. For others, it meant acknowledging they did not want partners or children. Some urged their biological relatives and chosen kin to talk about subjects long considered taboo. Their example made my own convictions more fierce. Their bravery buoyed me.

"It's hard. We argue and struggle," Selma Miriam of the Bloodroot restaurant collective told me, with a glance around the room at her "cronies."

"You know each other's weaknesses," said Betsey Beaven, another Bloodroot member. "Love requires a lot of cultivation. It can be tenuous.

You have to work on it all the time. It's very difficult at times, but so reward-ing when you get through to the other side."

I remember my friend Susan's assessment, at the end of a long discus-sion about what separates family from friends. "Family," she said, "are the people I've struggled through things with."

Again, always, the personal becomes political. Women striving daily to   40
make plain the good and the bad of their lives also contribute to a larger change, the breakdown of fictions that divide us from each other — white from black, lesbian from straight, old from young. Women who refuse to act out lies at home can turn the same honest scrutiny outside, demanding truth in their work, their education, their politics.

Maybe happiness, I have come to think, is a limiting proposition, a flat summary of human emotion in the same way a sitcom is a flat summary of real life. "Happy families" don't account for the ways people are knit by sor-row, the way bonds grow stronger through anger and grief.

This is it, I tell myself now; this mess is as real as it gets. I try to cherish flux — the mercurial moods, the feelings that flood and recede, the infinite chaos in which families become families.

Two days after I came out to my parents at the beach house, I returned to Portland, with my bicycle packed in a United Airlines baggage carrier and my grandmother's cameo ring on the pinky finger of my left hand. I'd found the ring in a jewelry box in my bedroom. It was delicate, a filigree set-ting with a small oblong cameo, the ivory-faced women profiled on a peach background.

The thin silver band barely eased over the knuckle on my pinky — les-bians' traditional ring-bearing finger. Wearing it, I felt marked, as though I were bringing contraband across the border in broad daylight, all my con-flicting allegiances exposed.

My head ached. Would my relatives still love me if I failed to do my   45
part by marrying and enlarging the family with children? Could I ever bring a woman lover to the shore? Where would we sleep?

How would I reconcile my relatives with the various families I devel-oped as a writer, a Jew, a lesbian, a social worker, an East Coast expatriate in the Northwest? How far could everyone stretch without snapping, refus-ing wholeness, flying apart like shrapnel?

I stumbled off the plane at midnight into a solid hug from Marian, a coworker at the social service agency where I counseled street youth. At work that week, I walked numbly through my routine. On Friday, while cleaning up the drop-in center after the last round of kids, I looked at my left hand. Where the cameo of my grandmother's ring had been, a little rec-tangle of skin showed through the filigree window. In the agency's dim basement, I leaned against a paneled wall and sobbed.

All the rest of that summer my parents and I exchanged letters, en-velopes full of anger and accusation, concern and caution, guilt and grief. I had been such a good child, cheerful, diligent, and brainy — good citizen awards in ninth grade, acceptance to Yale, an internship, then a job, at *The Washington Post.* It was bad enough that I had left the *Post* after two years, moved 3,000 miles away and begun to work with homeless teenagers. Now this! Where had I gotten such subversive ideas?

Perhaps in a certain south Jersey beach house, in a maze of doorless rooms.

From the West Coast, I glanced anxiously over my shoulder: Were my   50
relatives still there, with their shopping and their sweaters, their softening faces and their stiff resistance to change? If I returned, would I be swallowed up? If I stayed, would I be left adrift? Is that the brittle choice that, ultimately, forms the boundary line of every family: Be like us, or be alone?

I took off the empty ring and put it in a drawer. I spent that summer prowling my past, looking for signposts to help navigate the present. I heard voices, comforting and cautionary, joyous and pained, voices that chased in endless loops through my head.

"You can do anything you set your mind to."

"Don't leave."

"The world is full of interesting people and places."

"This family is the only safe spot on earth."   55

"Follow your dreams."

"Stay put."

I listened, and remembered, and wrote things down.

ENGAGING THE TEXT

1. How do you explain the title of this piece? What tone does it set, and what message does it convey?

2. Throughout this essay, Hochman uses the shore house as a symbol of her family. Review her descriptions of the house and discuss in some detail what made the house special to her. To what extent is it an apt symbol for her family life?

3. Why does the revelation that Hochman is in love with a woman so disturb her family? How — and how well — do the author and her family deal with this situation?

4. What is Hochman's notion of "family"? Aside from the issue of homosexuality, does it differ from "mainstream" or "traditional" views, and if so, how?

5. Why did Hochman include the description of her brief "affair" with Jon Feldstein? How do you interpret this incident?

EXPLORING CONNECTIONS

6. In the previous selection (p. 42), Gary Soto is frustrated because his parents won't or can't meet his expectations of what ideal parents should be. Brainstorm a list of qualities that both Soto and Hochman seem to expect

in their ideal parents. Are these qualities what any child might desire in a parent? What other qualities would you add to this list?

7. Write a conversation among Richard Rodriguez, Kathleen Boatwright, and Anndee Hochman on the costs of conformity to and rebellion against family traditions and values.

EXTENDING THE CRITICAL CONTEXT

8. At the end of Hochman's essay she offers a brief sample of past family voices that continue to haunt her (para. 51). Make your own list of voices from your family's past. What do these voices tell you? What do they say about your family's beliefs, values, and attitudes?

9. Hochman's essay challenges us to consider the chilling idea that families demand that sons and daughters "be like us, or be alone" (para. 50). To what extent do you agree that families are held together by conformity?

10. Think back to a particular time or place in your childhood that seemed as special or meaningful to you as her summer house seemed to Hochman. Try to describe this time or place in as much detail as possible, and then explain how it shaped your own view of family life.

11. Watch *The Wedding Banquet,* and compare the actions and reactions of the parents and children in this film with those of Hochman and her parents. What underlying values and assumptions about family unity do these responses suggest?

What We Really Miss About the 1950s

STEPHANIE COONTZ

Popular myth has it that the 1950s were the ideal decade for the American family. In this example of academic writing at its best, Stephanie Coontz provides a clear, well-documented, and insightful analysis of what was really going on and suggests that our nostalgia for the 1950s could mislead us today. Stephanie Coontz teaches history and family studies at The Evergreen State College in Olympia, Washington. An award-winning writer and nationally recognized expert on the family, she has published her work in numerous popular magazines and academic journals, testified before a House Select Committee on families, and appeared in several television documentaries. This selection is from her latest book, The Way We Really Are: Coming to Terms with America's Changing Families *(1997).*

In a 1996 poll by the Knight-Ridder news agency, more Americans chose the 1950s than any other single decade as the best time for children to grow up.[1] And despite the research I've done on the underside of 1950s families, I don't think it's crazy for people to feel nostalgic about the period. For one thing, it's easy to see why people might look back fondly to a decade when real wages grew more in any single year than in the entire ten years of the 1980s combined, a time when the average 30-year-old man could buy a median-priced home on only 15–18 percent of his salary.[2]

But it's more than just a financial issue. When I talk with modern parents, even ones who grew up in unhappy families, they associate the 1950s with a yearning they feel for a time when there were fewer complicated choices for kids or parents to grapple with, when there was more predictability in how people formed and maintained families, and when there was a coherent "moral order" in their community to serve as a reference point for family norms. Even people who found that moral order grossly unfair or repressive often say that its presence provided them with something concrete to push against.

I can sympathize entirely. One of my most empowering moments occurred the summer I turned 12, when my mother marched down to the library with me to confront a librarian who'd curtly refused to let me check out a book that was "not appropriate" for my age. "Don't you *ever* tell my daughter what she can and can't read," fumed my mom. "She's a mature young lady and she can make her own choices." In recent years I've often thought back to the gratitude I felt toward my mother for that act of trust in me. I wish I had some way of earning similar points from my own son. But much as I've always respected his values, I certainly wouldn't have walked into my local video store when he was 12 and demanded that he be allowed to check out absolutely anything he wanted!

Still, I have no illusions that I'd actually like to go back to the 1950s, and neither do most people who express such occasional nostalgia. For example, although the 1950s got more votes than any other decade in the Knight-Ridder poll, it did not win an outright majority: 38 percent of respondents picked the 1950s; 27 percent picked the 1960s or the 1970s. Voters between the ages of 50 and 64 were most likely to choose the 1950s, the decade in which they themselves came of age, as the best time for kids; voters under 30 were more likely to choose the 1970s. African Americans dif-

---

[1]Steven Thomma, "Nostalgia for '50s Surfaces," *Philadelphia Inquirer,* Feb. 4, 1996. [All notes are the author's.]

[2]Frank Levy, *Dollars and Dreams: The Changing American Income Distribution* (New York: Russell Sage, 1987), p. 6; Frank Levy, "Incomes and Income Inequality," in Reynolds Farley, ed., *State of the Union: America in the 1990s,* vol. 1 (New York: Russell Sage, 1995), pp. 1–57; Richard May and Kathryn Porter, "Poverty and Income Trends, 1994," Washington, D.C.: Center on Budget and Policy Priorities, March 1996; Rob Nelson and Jon Cowan, "Buster Power," *USA Weekend,* October 14–16, 1994, p. 10.

fered over whether the 1960s, 1970s, or 1980s were best, but all age groups of blacks agreed that later decades were definitely preferable to the 1950s.

Nostalgia for the 1950s is real and deserves to be taken seriously, but it usually shouldn't be taken literally. Even people who *do* pick the 1950s as the best decade generally end up saying, once they start discussing their feelings in depth, that it's not the family arrangements in and of themselves that they want to revive. They don't miss the way women used to be treated, they sure wouldn't want to live with most of the fathers they knew in their neighborhoods, and "come to think of it" — I don't know how many times I've recorded these exact words — "I communicate with my kids *much* better than my parents or grandparents did." When Judith Wallerstein recently interviewed 100 spouses in "happy" marriages, she found that only five "wanted a marriage like their parents'." The husbands "consciously rejected the role models provided by their fathers. The women said they could never be happy living as their mothers did."[3]

People today understandably feel that their lives are out of balance, but they yearn for something totally *new* — a more equal distribution of work, family, and community time for both men and women, children and adults. If the 1990s are lopsided in one direction, the 1950s were equally lopsided in the opposite direction.

What most people really feel nostalgic about has little to do with the internal structure of 1950s families. It is the belief that the 1950s provided a more family-friendly economic and social environment, an easier climate in which to keep kids on the straight and narrow, and above all, a greater feeling of hope for a family's long-term future, especially for its young. The contrast between the perceived hopefulness of the fifties and our own misgivings about the future is key to contemporary nostalgia for the period. Greater optimism *did* exist then, even among many individuals and groups who were in terrible circumstances. But if we are to take people's sense of loss seriously, rather than merely to capitalize on it for a hidden political agenda, we need to develop a historical perspective on where that hope came from.

Part of it came from families comparing their prospects in the 1950s to their unstable, often grindingly uncomfortable pasts, especially the two horrible decades just before. In the 1920s, after two centuries of child labor and income insecurity, and for the first time in American history, a bare majority of children had come to live in a family with a male breadwinner, a female homemaker, and a chance at a high school education. Yet no sooner did the ideals associated with such a family begin to blossom than they were buried by the stock market crash of 1929 and the Great Depression of the 1930s. During the 1930s domestic violence soared; divorce rates fell, but

[3]Judith Wallerstein and Sandra Blakeslee, *The Good Marriage: How and Why Love Lasts* (Boston: Houghton Mifflin, 1995), p. 15.

informal separations jumped; fertility plummeted. Murder rates were higher in 1933 than they were in the 1980s. Families were uprooted or torn apart. Thousands of young people left home to seek work, often riding the rails across the country.[4]

World War II brought the beginning of economic recovery, and people's renewed interest in forming families resulted in a marriage and childbearing boom, but stability was still beyond most people's grasp. Postwar communities were rocked by racial tensions, labor strife, and a right-wing backlash against the radical union movement of the 1930s. Many women resented being fired from wartime jobs they had grown to enjoy. Veterans often came home to find that they had to elbow their way back into their families, with wives and children resisting their attempts to reassert domestic authority. In one recent study of fathers who returned from the war, four times as many reported painful, even traumatic, reunions as remembered happy ones.[5]

By 1946 one in every three marriages was ending in divorce. Even 10 couples who stayed together went through rough times, as an acute housing shortage forced families to double up with relatives or friends. Tempers frayed and generational relations grew strained. "No home is big enough to house two families, particularly two of different generations, with opposite theories on child training," warned a 1948 film on the problems of modern marriage.[6]

So after the widespread domestic strife, family disruptions, and violence of the 1930s and the instability of the World War II period, people were ready to try something new. The postwar economic boom gave them the chance. The 1950s was the first time that a majority of Americans could even *dream* of creating a secure oasis in their immediate nuclear families. There they could focus their emotional and financial investments, reduce obligations to others that might keep them from seizing their own chance at a new start, and escape the interference of an older generation of neighbors or relatives who tried to tell them how to run their lives and raise their kids. Oral histories of the postwar period resound with the theme of escaping from in-laws, maiden aunts, older parents, even needy siblings.

The private family also provided a refuge from the anxieties of the new nuclear age and the cold war, as well as a place to get away from the political witch-hunts led by Senator Joe McCarthy and his allies. When having the wrong friends at the wrong time or belonging to any "suspicious" orga-

[4]Donald Hernandez, *America's Children: Resources from Family, Government and the Economy* (New York: Russell Sage, 1993), pp. 99, 102; James Morone, "The Corrosive Politics of Virtue," *American Prospect* 26 (May–June 1996), p. 37; "Study Finds U.S. No. 1 in Violence," *Olympian*, November 13, 1992. See also Stephen Mintz and Susan Kellogg, *Domestic Revolutions: A Social History of American Family Life* (New York: The Free Press, 1988).

[5]William Tuttle, Jr., *"Daddy's Gone to War": The Second World War in the Lives of America's Children* (New York: Oxford University Press, 1993).

[6]"Marriage and Divorce," *March of Time*, film series 14 (1948).

nization could ruin your career and reputation, it was safer to pull out of groups you might have joined earlier and to focus on your family. On a more positive note, the nuclear family was where people could try to satisfy their long-pent-up desires for a more stable marriage, a decent home, and the chance to really enjoy their children.

The 1950s Family Experiment

The key to understanding the successes, failures, and comparatively short life of 1950s family forms and values is to understand the period as one of *experimentation* with the possibilities of a new kind of family, not as the expression of some longstanding tradition. At the end of the 1940s, the divorce rate, which had been rising steadily since the 1890s, dropped sharply; the age of marriage fell to a 100-year low; and the birth rate soared. Women who had worked during the Depression or World War II quit their jobs as soon as they became pregnant, which meant quite a few women were specializing in child raising; fewer women remained childless during the 1950s than in any decade since the late nineteenth century. The timing and spacing of childbearing became far more compressed, so that young mothers were likely to have two or more children in diapers at once, with no older sibling to help in their care. At the same time, again for the first time in 100 years, the educational gap between young middle-class women and men increased, while job segregation for working men and women seems to have peaked. These demographic changes increased the dependence of women on marriage, in contrast to gradual trends in the opposite direction since the early twentieth century.[7]

The result was that family life and gender roles became much more predictable, orderly, and settled in the 1950s than they were either twenty years earlier or would be twenty years later. Only slightly more than one in four marriages ended in divorce during the 1950s. Very few young people spent any extended period of time in a nonfamily setting: They moved from their parents' family into their own family, after just a brief experience with independent living, and they started having children soon after marriage. Whereas two-thirds of women aged 20 to 24 were not yet married in 1990, only 28 percent of women this age were still single in 1960.[8]

---

[7]Arlene Skolnick and Stacey Rosencrantz, "The New Crusade for the Old Family," *American Prospect,* Summer 1994, p. 65; Hernandez, *America's Children,* pp. 128–32; Andrew Cherlin, "Changing Family and Household: Contemporary Lessons from Historical Research," *Annual Review of Sociology* 9 (1983), pp. 54–58; Sam Roberts, *Who We Are: A Portrait of America Based on the Latest Census* (New York: Times Books, 1995), p. 45.

[8]Levy, "Incomes and Income Inequality," p. 20; Arthur Norton and Louisa Miller, *Marriage, Divorce, and Remarriage in the 1990s,* Current Population Reports Series P23–180 (Washington, D.C.: Bureau of the Census, October 1992); Roberts, *Who We Are* (1995 ed.), pp. 50–53.

Ninety percent of all the households in the country were families in the   15
1950s, in comparison with only 71 percent by 1990. Eighty-six percent of all
children lived in two-parent homes in 1950, as opposed to just 72 percent in
1990. And the percentage living with both biological parents — rather than,
say, a parent and stepparent — was dramatically higher than it had been at
the turn of the century or is today: seventy percent in 1950, compared with
only 50 percent in 1990. Nearly 60 percent of kids — an all-time high —
were born into male breadwinner–female homemaker families; only a minority of the rest had mothers who worked in the paid labor force.[9]

If the organization and uniformity of family life in the 1950s were new,
so were the values, especially the emphasis on putting all one's emotional
and financial eggs in the small basket of the immediate nuclear family.
Right up through the 1940s, ties of work, friendship, neighborhood, ethnicity, extended kin, and voluntary organizations were as important a source of
identity for most Americans, and sometimes a *more* important source of
obligation, than marriage and the nuclear family. All this changed in the
postwar era. The spread of suburbs and automobiles, combined with the
destruction of older ethnic neighborhoods in many cities, led to the decline
of the neighborhood social club. Young couples moved away from parents
and kin, cutting ties with traditional extrafamilial networks that might compete for their attention. A critical factor in this trend was the emergence of
a group of family sociologists and marriage counselors who followed Talcott
Parsons in claiming that the nuclear family, built on a sharp division of labor
between husband and wife, was the cornerstone of modern society.

The new family experts tended to advocate views such as those first
raised in a 1946 book, *Their Mothers' Sons,* by psychiatrist Edward
Strecker. Strecker and his followers argued that American boys were infan-
tilized and emasculated by women who were old-fashioned "moms" instead
of modern "mothers." One sign that you might be that dreaded "mom,"
Strecker warned women, was if you felt you should take your aging parents
into your own home, rather than putting them in "a good institution . . .
where they will receive adequate care and comfort." Modern "mothers"
placed their parents in nursing homes and poured all their energies into
their nuclear family. They were discouraged from diluting their wifely and
maternal commitments by maintaining "competing" interests in friends,
jobs, or extended family networks, yet they were also supposed to cheerfully
grant early independence to their (male) children — an emotional double

[9]Dennis Hogan and Daniel Lichter, "Children and Youth: Living Arrangements and Welfare," in Farley, ed., *State of the Union,* vol. 2, p. 99; Richard Gelles, *Contemporary Families: A
Sociological View* (Thousand Oaks, Calif.: Sage, 1995), p. 115; Hernandez, *America's Children,*
p. 102. The fact that only a small percentage of children had mothers in the paid labor force,
though a full 40 percent did not live in male breadwinner–female homemaker families, was because some children had mothers who worked, unpaid, in farms or family businesses, or fathers
who were unemployed, or the children were not living with both parents.

bind that may explain why so many women who took this advice to heart ended up abusing alcohol or tranquilizers over the course of the decade.[10]

The call for young couples to break from their parents and youthful friends was a consistent theme in 1950s popular culture. In *Marty,* one of the most highly praised TV plays and movies of the 1950s, the hero almost loses his chance at love by listening to the carping of his mother and aunt and letting himself be influenced by old friends who resent the time he spends with his new girlfriend. In the end, he turns his back on mother, aunt, and friends to get his new marriage and a little business of his own off to a good start. Other movies, novels, and popular psychology tracts portrayed the dreadful things that happened when women became more interested in careers than marriage or men resisted domestic conformity.

Yet many people felt guilty about moving away from older parents and relatives; "modern mothers" worried that fostering independence in their kids could lead to defiance or even juvenile delinquency (the recurring nightmare of the age); there was considerable confusion about how men and women could maintain clear breadwinner-homemaker distinctions in a period of expanding education, job openings, and consumer aspirations. People clamored for advice. They got it from the new family education specialists and marriage counselors, from columns in women's magazines, from government pamphlets, and above all from television. While 1950s TV melodramas warned against letting anything dilute the commitment to getting married and having kids, the new family sitcoms gave people nightly lessons on how to make their marriage or rapidly expanding family work — or, in the case of *I Love Lucy,* probably the most popular show of the era, how *not* to make their marriage and family work. Lucy and Ricky gave weekly comic reminders of how much trouble a woman could get into by wanting a career or hatching some hare-brained scheme behind her husband's back.

At the time, everyone knew that shows such as *Donna Reed, Ozzie and Harriet, Leave It to Beaver,* and *Father Knows Best* were not the way families really were. People didn't watch those shows to see their own lives reflected back at them. They watched them to see how families were *supposed* to live — and also to get a little reassurance that they were headed in the right direction. The sitcoms were simultaneously advertisements, etiquette manuals, and how-to lessons for a new way of organizing marriage and child raising. I have studied the scripts of these shows for years, since I often use them in my classes on family history, but it wasn't until I became a parent that I felt their extraordinary pull. The secret of their appeal, I suddenly realized, was that they offered 1950s viewers, wracked with the same feelings of parental inadequacy as was I, the promise that there were easy answers and surefire techniques for raising kids.

20

[10]Edward Strecker, *Their Mothers' Sons: The Psychiatrist Examines an American Problem* (Philadelphia: J. B. Lippincott, 1946), p. 209.

Ever since, I have found it useful to think of the sitcoms as the 1950s equivalent of today's beer ads. As most people know, beer ads are consciously aimed at men who *aren't* as strong and sexy as the models in the commercials, guys who are uneasily aware of the gap between the ideal masculine pursuits and their own achievements. The promise is that if the viewers on the couch will just drink brand X, they too will be able to run 10 miles without gasping for breath. Their bodies will firm up, their complexions will clear up, and maybe the Swedish bikini team will come over and hang out at their place.

Similarly, the 1950s sitcoms were aimed at young couples who had married in haste, women who had tasted new freedoms during World War II and given up their jobs with regret, veterans whose children resented their attempts to reassert paternal authority, and individuals disturbed by the changing racial and ethnic mix of postwar America. The message was clear: Buy these ranch houses, Hotpoint appliances, and child-raising ideals; relate to your spouse like this; get a new car to wash with your kids on Sunday afternoons; organize your dinners like that — and you too can escape from the conflicts of race, class, and political witch-hunts into harmonious families where father knows best, mothers are never bored or irritated, and teenagers rush to the dinner table each night, eager to get their latest dose of parental wisdom.

Many families found it possible to put together a good imitation of this way of living during the 1950s and 1960s. Couples were often able to construct marriages that were much more harmonious than those in which they had grown up, and to devote far more time to their children. Even when marriages were deeply unhappy, as many were, the new stability, economic security, and educational advantages parents were able to offer their kids counted for a lot in people's assessment of their life satisfaction. And in some matters, ignorance could be bliss: The lack of media coverage of problems such as abuse or incest was terribly hard on the casualties, but it protected more fortunate families from knowledge and fear of many social ills.[11]

There was tremendous hostility to people who could be defined as "others": Jews, African Americans, Puerto Ricans, the poor, gays or lesbians, and "the red menace." Yet on a day-to-day basis, the civility that prevailed in homogeneous neighborhoods allowed people to ignore larger patterns of racial and political repression. Racial clashes were ever-present in the 1950s, sometimes escalating into full-scale antiblack riots, but individual homicide rates fell to almost half the levels of the 1930s. As nuclear families

---

[11]For discussion of the discontents, and often searing misery, that were considered normal in a "good-enough" marriage in the 1950s and 1960s, see Lillian Rubin, *Worlds of Pain: Life in the Working-Class Family* (New York: Basic Books, 1976); Mirra Komarovsky, *Blue Collar Marriage* (New Haven, Conn.: Vintage, 1962); Elaine Tyler May, *Homeward Bound: American Families in the Cold War Era* (New York: Basic Books, 1988).

moved into the suburbs, they retreated from social activism but entered voluntary relationships with people who had children the same age; they became involved in PTAs together, joined bridge clubs, went bowling. There does seem to have been a stronger sense of neighborly commonalities than many of us feel today. Even though this local community was often the product of exclusion or repression, it sometimes looks attractive to modern Americans whose commutes are getting longer and whose family or work patterns give them little in common with their neighbors.[12]

The optimism that allowed many families to rise above their internal   25
difficulties and to put limits on their individualistic values during the 1950s came from the sense that America was on a dramatically different trajectory than it had been in the past, an upward and expansionary path that had already taken people to better places than they had ever seen before and would certainly take their children even further. This confidence that almost everyone could look forward to a better future stands in sharp contrast to how most contemporary Americans feel, and it explains why a period in which many people were much worse off than today sometimes still looks like a better period for families than our own.

Throughout the 1950s, poverty was higher than it is today, but it was less concentrated in pockets of blight existing side-by-side with extremes of wealth, and, unlike today, it was falling rather than rising. At the end of the 1930s, almost two-thirds of the population had incomes below the poverty standards of the day, while only one in eight had a middle-class income (defined as two to five times the poverty line). By 1960, a majority of the population had climbed into the middle-income range.[13]

Unmarried people were hardly sexually abstinent in the 1950s, but the age of first intercourse was somewhat higher than it is now, and despite a tripling of nonmarital birth rates between 1940 and 1958, more than 70

[12]See Robert Putnam, "The Strange Disappearance of Civic America," *American Prospect*, Winter 1996. For a glowing if somewhat lopsided picture of 1950s community solidarities, see Alan Ehrenhalt, *The Lost City: Discovering the Forgotten Virtues of Community in the Chicago of the 1950s* (New York: Basic Books, 1995). For a chilling account of communities uniting against perceived outsiders, in the same city, see Arnold Hirsch, *Making the Second Ghetto: Race and Housing in Chicago, 1940–1960* (Cambridge, Mass.: Harvard University Press, 1983). On homicide rates, see "Study Finds United States No. 1 in Violence," *Olympian*, November 13, 1992; *New York Times*, November 13, 1992, p. A9; and Douglas Lee Eckberg, "Estimates of Early Twentieth-Century U.S. Homicide Rates: A Econometric Forecasting Approach," *Demography* 32 (1995), p. 14. On lengthening commutes, see "It's Taking Longer to Get to Work," *Olympian*, December 6, 1995.

[13]The figures in this and the following paragraph come from Levy, "Incomes and Income Inequality," pp. 1–57; May and Porter, "Poverty and Income Trends, 1994"; Reynolds Farley, *The New American Reality: Who We Are, How We Got Here, Where We Are Going* (New York: Russell Sage, 1996), pp. 83–85; Gelles, *Contemporary Families*, p. 115; David Grissmer, Sheila Nataraj Kirby, Mark Bender, and Stephanie Williamson, *Student Achievement and the Changing American Family*, Rand Institute on Education and Training (Santa Monica, Calif: Rand, 1994), p. 106.

percent of nonmarital pregnancies led to weddings before the child was born. Teenage birth rates were almost twice as high in 1957 as in the 1990s, but most teen births were to married couples, and the effect of teen pregnancy in reducing further schooling for young people did not hurt their life prospects the way it does today. High school graduation rates were lower in the 1950s than they are today, and minority students had far worse test scores, but there were jobs for people who dropped out of high school or graduated without good reading skills — jobs that actually had a future. People entering the job market in the 1950s had no way of knowing that they would be the last generation to have a good shot at reaching middle-class status without the benefit of postsecondary schooling.

Millions of men from impoverished, rural, unemployed, or poorly educated family backgrounds found steady jobs in the steel, auto, appliance, construction, and shipping industries. Lower middle-class men went further on in college during the 1950s than they would have been able to expect in earlier decades, enabling them to make the transition to secure white-collar work. The experience of shared sacrifices in the Depression and war, reinforced by a New Deal–inspired belief in the ability of government to make life better, gave people a sense of hope for the future. Confidence in government, business, education, and other institutions was on the rise. This general optimism affected people's experience and assessment of family life. It is no wonder modern Americans yearn for a similar sense of hope.

But before we sign on to any attempts to turn the family clock back to the 1950s we should note that the family successes and community solidarities of the 1950s rested on a totally different set of political and economic conditions than we have today. Contrary to widespread belief, the 1950s was not an age of laissez-faire government and free market competition. A major cause of the social mobility of young families in the 1950s was that federal assistance programs were much more generous and widespread than they are today.

In the most ambitious and successful affirmative action program ever 30 adopted in America, 40 percent of young men were eligible for veterans' benefits, and these benefits were far more extensive than those available to Vietnam-era vets. Financed in part by a federal income tax on the rich that went up to 87 percent and a corporate tax rate of 52 percent, such benefits provided quite a jump start for a generation of young families. The GI bill paid most tuition costs for vets who attended college, doubling the percentage of college students from prewar levels. At the other end of the life span, Social Security began to build up a significant safety net for the elderly, formerly the poorest segment of the population. Starting in 1950, the federal government regularly mandated raises in the minimum wage to keep pace with inflation. The minimum wage may have been only $1.40 as late as 1968, but a person who worked for that amount full-time, year-round, earned 118 percent of the poverty figure for a family of three. By 1995, a full-time minimum-wage worker could earn only 72 percent of the poverty level.[14]

An important source of the economic expansion of the 1950s was that public works spending at all levels of government comprised nearly 20 percent of total expenditures in 1950, as compared to less than 7 percent in 1984. Between 1950 and 1960, nonmilitary, nonresidential public construction rose by 58 percent. Construction expenditures for new schools (in dollar amounts adjusted for inflation) rose by 72 percent; funding on sewers and waterworks rose by 46 percent. Government paid 90 percent of the costs of building the new Interstate Highway System. These programs opened up suburbia to growing numbers of middle-class Americans and created secure, well-paying jobs for blue-collar workers.[15]

Government also reorganized home financing, underwriting low down payments and long-term mortgages that had been rejected as bad business by private industry. To do this, government put public assets behind housing lending programs, created two new national financial institutions to facilitate home loans, allowed veterans to put down payments as low as a dollar on a house, and offered tax breaks to people who bought homes. The National Education Defense Act funded the socioeconomic mobility of thousands of young men who trained themselves for well-paying jobs in such fields as engineering.[16]

Unlike contemporary welfare programs, government investment in 1950s families was not just for immediate subsistence but encouraged long-term asset development, rewarding people for increasing their investment in homes and education. Thus it was far less likely that such families or individuals would ever fall back to where they started, even after a string of bad luck. Subsidies for higher education were greater the longer people stayed in school and the more expensive the school they selected. Mortgage deductions got bigger as people traded up to better houses.[17]

---

[14]William Chafe, *The Unfinished Journey: America Since World War II* (New York: Oxford University Press, 1986), pp. 113, 143; Marc Linder, "Eisenhower-Era Marxist-Confiscatory Taxation: Requiem for the Rhetoric of Rate Reduction for the Rich," *Tulane Law Review* 70 (1996), p. 917; Barry Bluestone and Teresa Ghilarducci, "Rewarding Work: Feasible Antipoverty Policy," *American Prospect* 28 (1996), p. 42; Theda Skocpol, "Delivering for Young Families," *American Prospect* 28 (1996), p. 67.

[15]Joel Tarr, "The Evolution of the Urban Infrastructure in the Nineteenth and Twentieth Centuries," ed. Royce Hanson, ed., *Perspectives on Urban Infrastructure* (Washington, D.C.: National Academy Press, 1984); Mark Aldrich, *A History of Public Works Investment in the United States,* report prepared by the CPNSAD Research Corporation for the U.S. Department of Commerce, April 1980.

[16]For more information on this government financing, see Kenneth Jackson, *Crabgrass Frontier: The Suburbanization of the United States* (New York: Oxford University Press, 1985); and *The Way We Never Were,* chapter 4.

[17]John Cook and Laura Sherman, "Economic Security Among America's Poor: The Impact of State Welfare Waivers on Asset Accumulation," Center on Hunger, Poverty, and Nutrition Policy, Tufts University, May 1996.

These social and political support systems magnified the impact of the postwar economic boom. "In the years between 1947 and 1973," reports economist Robert Kuttner, "the median paycheck more than doubled, and the bottom 20 percent enjoyed the greatest gains." High rates of unionization meant that blue-collar workers were making much more financial progress than most of their counterparts today. In 1952, when eager home buyers flocked to the opening of Levittown, Pennsylvania, the largest planned community yet constructed, "it took a factory worker one day to earn enough money to pay the closing costs on a new Levittown house, then selling for $10,000." By 1991, such a home was selling for $100,000 or more, and it took a factory worker *eighteen weeks* to earn enough money for just the closing costs.[18]

The legacy of the union struggle of the 1930s and 1940s, combined   35 with government support for raising people's living standards, set limits on corporations that have disappeared in recent decades. Corporations paid 23 percent of federal income taxes in the 1950s, as compared to just 9.2 percent in 1991. Big companies earned higher profit margins than smaller firms, partly due to their dominance of the market, partly to America's postwar economic advantage. They chose (or were forced) to share these extra earnings, which economists call "rents," with employees. Economists at the Brookings Institution and Harvard University estimate that 70 percent of such corporate rents were passed on to workers at all levels of the firm, benefiting secretaries and janitors as well as CEOs. Corporations routinely retained workers even in slack periods, as a way of ensuring workplace stability. Although they often received more generous tax breaks from communities than they gave back in investment, at least they kept their plants and employment offices in the same place. AT&T, for example, received much of the technology it used to finance its postwar expansion from publicly funded communications research conducted as part of the war effort, and, as current AT&T Chairman Robert Allen puts it, there "used to be a lifelong commitment on the employee's part and on our part." Today, however, he admits, "the contract doesn't exist anymore."[19]

Television trivia experts still argue over exactly what the fathers in many 1950s sitcoms did for a living. Whatever it was, though, they obviously didn't have to worry about downsizing. If most married people stayed in

[18]Robert Kuttner, "The Incredible Shrinking American Paycheck," *Washington Post National Weekly Edition,* November 6–12, 1995, p. 23; Donald Bartlett and James Steele, *America: What Went Wrong?* (Kansas City: Andrews McMeel, 1992), p. 20.

[19]Richard Barnet, "Lords of the Global Economy," *Nation,* December 19, 1994, p. 756; Clay Chandler, "U.S. Corporations: Good Citizens or Bad?" *Washington Post National Weekly Edition,* May 20–26, 1996, p. 16; Steven Pearlstein, "No More Mr. Nice Guy: Corporate America Has Done an About-Face in How It Pays and Treats Employees," *Washington Post National Weekly Edition,* December 18–24, 1995, p. 10; Robert Kuttner, "Ducking Class Warfare," *Washington Post National Weekly Edition,* March 11–17, 1996, p. 5; Henry Allen, "Ha! So Much for Loyalty," *Washington Post National Weekly Edition,* March 4–10, 1996, p. 11.

long-term relationships during the 1950s, so did most corporations, sticking with the communities they grew up in and the employees they originally hired. Corporations were not constantly relocating in search of cheap labor during the 1950s; unlike today, increases in worker productivity usually led to increases in wages. The number of workers covered by corporate pension plans and health benefits increased steadily. So did limits on the work week. There is good reason that people look back to the 1950s as a less hurried age: The average American was working a shorter workday in the 1950s than his or her counterpart today, when a quarter of the workforce puts in 49 or more hours a week.[20]

So politicians are practicing quite a double standard when they tell us to return to the family forms of the 1950s while they do nothing to restore the job programs and family subsidies of that era, the limits on corporate relocation and financial wheeling-dealing, the much higher share of taxes paid by corporations then, the availability of union jobs for noncollege youth, and the subsidies for higher education such as the National Defense Education Act loans. Furthermore, they're not telling the whole story when they claim that the 1950s was the most prosperous time for families and the most secure decade for children. Instead, playing to our understandable nostalgia for a time when things seemed to be getting better, not worse, they engage in a tricky chronological shell game with their figures, diverting our attention from two important points. First, many individuals, families, and groups were excluded from the economic prosperity, family optimism, and social civility of the 1950s. Second, the all-time high point of child well-being and family economic security came not during the 1950s but *at the end of the 1960s.*

We now know that 1950s family culture was not only nontraditional; it was also not idyllic. In important ways, the stability of family and community life during the 1950s rested on pervasive discrimination against women, gays, political dissidents, non-Christians, and racial or ethnic minorities, as well as on a systematic cover-up of the underside of many families. Families that were harmonious and fair of their own free will may have been able to function more easily in the fifties, but few alternatives existed for members of discordant or oppressive families. Victims of child abuse, incest, alcoholism, spousal rape, and wife battering had no recourse, no place to go, until well into the 1960s.[21]

At the end of the 1950s, despite ten years of economic growth, 27.3 percent of the nation's children were poor, including those in white "underclass"

---

[20]Ehrenhalt, *The Lost City,* pp. 11–12; Jeremy Rifken, *The End of Work: The Decline of the Global Labor Force and the Dawn of the Post-Market Era* (New York: G. P. Putnam's Sons, 1995), pp. 169, 170, 231; Juliet Schorr, *The Overworked American: The Unexpected Decline of Leisure* (New York: Basic Books, 1991).

[21]For documentation that these problems existed, see chapter 2 of *The Way We Never Were.*

communities such as Appalachia. Almost 50 percent of married-couple African-American families were impoverished — a figure far higher than today. It's no wonder African Americans are not likely to pick the 1950s as a golden age, even in comparison with the setbacks they experienced in the 1980s. When blacks moved north to find jobs in the postwar urban manufacturing boom they met vicious harassment and violence, first to prevent them from moving out of the central cities, then to exclude them from public space such as parks or beaches.

In Philadelphia, for example, the City of Brotherly Love, there were more than 200 racial incidents over housing in the first six months of 1955 alone. The Federal Housing Authority, such a boon to white working-class families, refused to insure homes in all-black or in racially mixed neighborhoods. Two-thirds of the city dwellers evicted by the urban renewal projects of the decade were African Americans and Latinos; government did almost nothing to help such displaced families find substitute housing.[22]   40

Women were unable to take out loans or even credit cards in their own names. They were excluded from juries in many states. A lack of options outside marriage led some women to remain in desperately unhappy unions that were often not in the best interests of their children or themselves. Even women in happy marriages often felt humiliated by the constant messages they received that their whole lives had to revolve around a man. "You are not ready when he calls — miss one turn," was a rule in the Barbie game marketed to 1950s girls; "he criticizes your hairdo — go to the beauty shop." Episodes of *Father Knows Best* advised young women: "The worst thing you can do is to try to beat a man at his own game. You just beat the women at theirs." One character on the show told women to always ask themselves, "Are you after a job or a man? You can't have both."[23]

The Fifties Experiment Comes to an End

The social stability of the 1950s, then, was a response to the stick of racism, sexism, and repression as well as to the carrot of economic opportunity and government aid. Because social protest mounted in the 1960s and unsettling challenges were posed to the gender roles and sexual mores of the previous decade, many people forget that families continued to make gains throughout the 1960s and into the first few years of the 1970s. By 1969, child poverty was down to 14 percent, its lowest level ever; it hovered just above that marker until 1975, when it began its steady climb up to con-

[22]The poverty figures come from census data collected in *The State of America's Children Yearbook, 1996* (Washington, D.C.: Children's Defense Fund, 1996), p. 77. See also Hirsch, *Making the Second Ghetto;* Raymond Mohl, "Making the Second Ghetto in Metropolitan Miami, 1940–1960," *Journal of Urban History* 25 (1995), p. 396; Micaela di Leonardo, "Boys on the Hood," *Nation,* August 17–24, 1992, p. 180; Jackson, *Crabgrass Frontier,* pp. 226–227.

[23]Susan Douglas, *Where the Girls Are: Growing Up Female with the Mass Media* (New York: Times Books, 1994), pp. 25, 37.

temporary figures (22 percent in 1993; 21.2 percent in 1994). The high point of health and nutrition for poor children was reached in the early 1970s.[24]

So commentators are being misleading when they claim that the 1950s was the golden age of American families. They are disregarding the number of people who were excluded during that decade and ignoring the socioeconomic gains that continued to be made through the 1960s. But they are quite right to note that the improvements of the 1950s and 1960s came to an end at some point in the 1970s (though not for the elderly, who continued to make progress).

Ironically, it was the children of those stable, enduring, supposedly idyllic 1950s families, the recipients of so much maternal time and attention, that pioneered the sharp break with their parents' family forms and gender roles in the 1970s. This was not because they were led astray by some youthful Murphy Brown in her student rebel days or inadvertently spoiled by parents who read too many of Dr. Spock's child-raising manuals.

Partly, the departure from 1950s family arrangements was a logical extension of trends and beliefs pioneered in the 1950s, or of inherent contradictions in those patterns. For example, early and close-spaced childbearing freed more wives up to join the labor force, and married women began to flock to work. By 1960, more than 40 percent of women over the age of 16 held a job, and working mothers were the fastest growing component of the labor force. The educational aspirations and opportunities that opened up for kids of the baby boom could not be confined to males, and many tight-knit, male-breadwinner, nuclear families in the 1950s instilled in their daughters the ambition to be something other than a homemaker.[25]   45

Another part of the transformation was a shift in values. Most people would probably agree that some changes in values were urgently needed: the extension of civil rights to racial minorities and to women; a rejection of property rights in children by parents and in women by husbands; a reaction against the political intolerance and the wasteful materialism of 1950s culture. Other changes in values remain more controversial: opposition to American intervention abroad; repudiation of the traditional sexual double standard; rebellion against what many young people saw as the hypocrisy of parents who preached sexual morality but ignored social immorality such as racism and militarism.

Still other developments, such as the growth of me-first individualism, are widely regarded as problematic by people on all points along the political

[24]*The State of America's Children Yearbook, 1966,* p. 77; May and Porter, "Poverty and Income Trends: 1994," p. 23; Sara McLanahan et al., *Losing Ground: A Critique,* University of Wisconsin Institute for Research on Poverty, Special Report No. 38, 1985.

[25]For studies of how both middle-class and working-class women in the 1950s quickly departed from, or never quite accepted, the predominant image of women, see Joanne Meyerowitz, ed., *Not June Cleaver: Women and Gender in Postwar America, 1945–1960* (Philadelphia: Temple University Press, 1994).

spectrum. It's worth noting, though, that the origins of antisocial individual- ism and self-indulgent consumerism lay at least as much in the family values of the 1950s as in the youth rebellion of the 1960s. The marketing experts who never allowed the kids in *Ozzie and Harriet* sitcoms to be shown drinking milk, for fear of offending soft-drink companies that might sponsor the show in syndication, were ultimately the same people who slightly later invested billions of dollars to channel sexual rebelliousness and a depoliticized individ- ualism into mainstream culture.

There were big cultural changes brewing by the beginning of the 1970s, and tremendous upheavals in social, sexual, and family values. And yes, there were sometimes reckless or simply laughable excesses in some of the early ex- periments with new gender roles, family forms, and personal expression. But the excesses of 1950s gender roles and family forms were every bit as repel- lent and stupid as the excesses of the sixties: Just watch a dating etiquette film of the time period, or recall that therapists of the day often told victims of in- cest that they were merely having unconscious oedipal fantasies.

Ultimately, though, changes in values were not what brought the 1950s family experiment to an end. The postwar family compacts between hus- bands and wives, parents and children, young and old, were based on the postwar social compact between government, corporations, and workers. While there was some discontent with those family bargains among women and youth, the old relations did not really start to unravel until people began to face the erosion of the corporate wage bargain and government broke its tacit societal bargain that it would continue to invest in jobs and education for the younger generation.

In the 1970s, new economic trends began to clash with all the social ex-   50 pectations that 1950s families had instilled in their children. That clash, not the willful abandonment of responsibility and commitment, has been the primary cause of both family rearrangements and the growing social prob- lems that are usually attributed to such family changes, but in fact have *sep- arate* origins.

ENGAGING THE TEXT

1. According to Coontz, what do we really miss about the 1950s? In addition, what *don't* we miss?
2. In Coontz's view, what was the role of the government in making the 1950s in America what they were? What part did broader historical forces or other circumstances play?
3. Although she concentrates on the 1950s, Coontz also describes the other decades from the 1920s to the present. Use her information to create a brief chart naming the key characteristics of each decade. Then consider your own family history and see how well it fits the pattern Coontz outlines. Discuss the results with classmates or write a journal entry reflecting on what you learn.

EXPLORING CONNECTIONS

4. Review "Looking for Work," by Gary Soto (p. 42) and "Growing Pains" by Anndee Hochman (p. 47). How do these narratives evoke nostalgia for a simpler, better era for families? Do they reveal any of the problems with the 1950s that Coontz describes?

EXTENDING THE CRITICAL CONTEXT

5. Coontz suggests that an uninformed nostalgia for the 1950s could promote harmful political agendas today. (See, for example, paras. 7 and 37.) What evidence, if any, do you see in contemporary media that nostalgia for the 1950s is on the rise? Do you agree with Coontz that such nostalgia can be dangerous? Why or why not?

6. Watch an episode of a 1950s sitcom (if possible, videotape it) such as *Father Knows Best, The Donna Reed Show, Leave It to Beaver,* or *I Love Lucy.* Analyze the extent to which it reveals both positive and negative aspects of the 1950s that Coontz discusses (for example, an authoritarian father figure, limited roles for wives, economic prosperity, or a sense of a secure community).

Television's Transformative Role in Courtroom Justice for Women and Children

ELIZABETH DODSON GRAY

*Ever since Newton Minow declared TV a vast wasteland back in the early 1960s, television has been a favorite target of America's cultural critics. Television programming has been blamed for causing almost every social ill during the past forty years, from decreasing reading scores for American students to increasing violence in the streets. And in the post–*Married with Children *era cultural critics have reserved special condemnation for what they see as television's corrosive effect on the American family. Perhaps that's what makes Elizabeth Dodson Gray's perspective on TV so refreshing: according to Gray, television has been a progressive force in American life, educating us about important social issues — particularly issues that have special relevance for women, like domestic violence and child abuse. Coordinator of the Theological Opportunities Program at Harvard University since 1978, Gray has published several books spanning her interests in feminism, religion, and the environment. This selection is from*

Women Transforming Communications: Global Intersections *(1996), edited by Donna Allen, Ramona R. Rush, and Susan J. Kaufman.*

First, there was great consternation at a woman "daring" to cut off her husband's penis after he had raped her. Were you then surprised (as I was) that Lorena Bobbitt was tried — and acquitted? She was acquitted by a mixed jury of both males and females, with a nice-looking early-thirties male as foreman of the jury.

What a surprise that acquittal was! And how was it possible, when her husband's body provided indisputable evidence of her deed?

Then there were the Menendez brothers, Erik and Lyle. Once again, there was no doubt they had murdered their parents. As with Lorena Bobbitt, their guilt was not contested. What was at issue was the interpretation to be given to that guilt, and what was to be a suitable punishment.

The outcome, once again, was a surprise. The first trials of each of the brothers resulted in "hung" juries. Again, how could that be possible in a popular culture in which Hillary Clinton's work with the Children's Defense fund on behalf of the legal rights of children has been widely viewed with apprehension, one media pundit speculating that "soon your children will sue you if you ask them to take out the garbage"! So how could two separate juries not return verdicts of guilty against the Menendez brothers?

The larger question is this: What has recently intervened in our culture   5
to make such verdicts possible now?

It seems to me the likely answer is a decade of TV talk shows and news shows about, among other topics, domestic violence against women and children. Ten years ago, I think such jury verdicts would have been impossible.

But by the early 1970s, increasing numbers of women were being employed in the industry, and many of them were working internally to get greater visibility in news and programming for events and issues affecting women. Even that would not have been enough, had there not also been the focus on these issues by the emerging organizations and media of the women's movement itself also beginning in the early 1970s. What the issue-oriented women's activist organizations provided was something for the TV women to find and then lobby to get on the air.[1]

So finally television gave voice to enough human experience of domestic abuse, including marital rape and the sexual abuse of children by their

---

[1] For a more detailed account of the history of how this happened, see Donna Allen (1989). Also see Allen's Chapter 34 in this volume [Donna Allen, Ramona R. Rush, and Susan J. Kaufman, eds., *Women Transforming Communications: Global Intersections* (Newbury Park, Cal.: Sage Publications, 1996)].

parents, to make a defense based upon those realities credible to jurors. Let us look now at selected examples of how television coverage contributed to this change.

Night After Night, Day After Day

First, there has been the ordinary nightly news. The local evening news not only convinces viewers of the reality of crime in our society, but in these last years it has served also as witness to the increasing numbers of brutal murders coming out of so-called domestic violence.

Watching either the early or the late local news regularly, you hear not   10
only of drive-by shootings on urban streets but also again and again of a husband (or boyfriend) who kills his wife, his children, himself, his girlfriend, her sister's family when he cannot find her, or he kills those with whom she has taken refuge. One recent spring in Boston over a period of a few weeks, we learned of three teenage girls killed by their boyfriends when the girls tried to break off the dating relationship, in one case after three weeks since its inception. One girl was shot to death, another knifed to death, a third beaten to death with a baseball bat!

The night-after-night repetitions of variations on this same theme finally convince you as a viewer that this is not fantasy or nightmare. This is the reality of everyday life for some people in this culture of ours.

You-the-Viewer Meet "Experts" and Participants

If you come from these nightly accounts at all confused and asking, "What is going on in our culture, that such things can be happening?" — other aspects of TV media step in to interpret for you. We now have a growing genre of hour-long TV newsmagazines: *60 Minutes, 20/20, Prime Time Live, Dateline NBC, 48 Hours*. Most of these programs have done segments on domestic violence and domestic abuse, exploring both events and the issues with commentary by anchor people, in-depth psychological interpretation by visiting "experts" with psychological training, and sometimes even interviews with couples themselves.

Exposure to even a few of these newsmagazine segments lets you begin to perceive an emerging picture that has been hidden in that euphemistic cover-up phrase *domestic violence* (as though the walls were turning in and beating up women and children). It is a nasty picture of male violence to women and children, violence repeated in home after home, city after city, town after town, in all social classes.

Then there are the TV talk shows. Watch Phil Donahue, Oprah Winfrey, Geraldo Rivera, Sally Jessy Raphaël, Montel Williams, Jerry Springer, Vicki, Rolonda, Maury Povich, or their more recent colleagues in this competitive genre — and you will see again and again the real-life stories of battered women. The women talk of being beaten, kicked, knifed, threatened with being killed. They tell 10 or 20 million television viewers of their experience of marital rape with a brutally invasive penis or with a Coke bottle or a curling iron or whatever.

"You don't have to be a rocket scientist to understand" that sex with a   15
violent man would never be erotic; it would be simply brutal. And you hear these women's sobbing voices and see their faces, and you begin to believe what would have seemed to many of us unbelievable 10 years ago.

Then you watch two-hour made-for-television movies, often fact-based (or so *TV Guide* tells you) and you see all these same stories again. This is a typical *TV Guide* listing: *Shattered Dreams* (1990), a fact-based movie recounting the 17-year ordeal of the battered wife (Lindsay Wagner) of a prominent Washington, D.C., lawyer (Michael Nouri).

You see Farrah Fawcett star in *The Burning Bed,* and you watch with sickening horror as her abuse continues and increases and crescendos until she finally does burn the bed. And you hear about the Framingham Eight, who are some of the women in prison in Massachusetts who finally did kill their abusive, stalking, threatening, restraining-order-ignoring former husbands and boyfriends. Now you can see that battered women are white and black, Hispanic and Asian, rich and poor, society matron and blue collar.

Without Reading the Book

Whether you have ever read Lenore Walker's classic *The Battered Woman* (1979) — whether you have ever heard her on a TV talk show or TV newsmagazine focused on battered women — whether or not you have ever heard the phrase *battered woman syndrome* — you as a viewer of present-day television, you understand. You are ready, whether male or female, to be on Lorena Bobbitt's jury. Television has opened up to you, in living color, the reality of battered women in today's culture.

Television has given battered women faces you have seen. And it has given them voices, so they speak to you of this awesomely terrible life experience that for hundreds of years in patriarchy has been silenced, suppressed, covered up. Oh, the valiant and determined Victorian women of the Women's Christian Temperance Union (WCTU) knew of these realities. But given the conventions of their day, they could not speak them. They could only inveigh against the evils of what they called "drink," knowing (as their audiences also knew) that drunken angry men often came home to beat and abuse their children and wives. But the women of the WCTU could only speak against alcohol, not against these unspeakable abuses themselves.

A lot of that covering up has been ripped away. Now all of us who have   20
not experienced such abuse personally can see the reality of those who have, and we can tremble for what we have missed.

Beholding the Crucifixion
of Children

Not only battered wives but abused children have become visible through the miracle of television. I think we all naively assumed for "all" families a "normative" decent pattern of child rearing. This included some degree of disciplinary "spanking." But it certainly did not extend to behavior such as burning a child's skin with a hot cigarette, or breaking a child's arm or leg or ribs, or throwing the child down a flight of stairs, chaining a child to a water pipe or radiator, or locking a child up in a basement, starving a child, and so on.

Yet recently we have seen all this on the evening news, happening sometimes in unknown families, sometimes in much heralded ones, as in the Lisa Steinberg case in New York City. Can anyone doubt such abuse happens, when you see it not only on the evening news but read about it over breakfast on the front page of the *New York Times* (which promises you "all the news that is fit to print")?

There have also been talk shows where we have seen with our own eyes many women (and some men) recall, and recount to us, their experiences of being sexually abused many years earlier. We search their faces: Are they really telling us the truth? Could any parent in this culture (usually a male) do this to his child (usually a female)? It boggles our minds, but we realize eventually that when we have difficulty imagining something, it does not mean that it is not true.

We watch their eyes, we see their tears, we begin to feel their pain. We begin to believe. We also see their diversity — again, white and black and Hispanic and Asian — again, rich and middle class and poor.

We watch that terribly attractive former Miss America, Marilyn Van-   25
Debur, look directly into the camera's eye as she tells us how her father, the Denver socialite, a pillar of society, a seemingly upright man, "pried her legs open at night" to molest her. She tells us how she repressed those "night memories" but became too terrified to sleep in her too-tightly clamped muscles of resistance — until years into her marriage, she "fell apart" in midlife and regained those memories. We sense as we hear her speak her deep commitment to making everyone understand that it happens, and what it means to those children to whom it happens.

Other Prominent Voices Speak Out

Even if we have never read Harvard psychiatrist Judith Herman's classic *Father-Daughter Incest* (1981), with its profile of the incestuous father as "good provider, pillar of the church, pillar of the community," we begin to believe that sexual abuse and incest can happen. We begin to understand that it does happen. We have taken into our minds and hearts the sickening reality of child sexual abuse — the reality of incest.

Then media celebrities such as Roseanne Arnold and Oprah Winfrey add their voices to the chorus, and we marvel at their courage to join poet Maya Angelou in letting us see into the violence they have experienced earlier in their lives in such a private way.

Word gradually leaks out about scandals in churches and sexual abuse by priests, first in the *National Catholic Reporter* and the specialized religious press. Then suddenly it is on the nightly television news and we are watching arrests and allegations and court trials. Then we see survivors speaking out on talk shows and television newsmagazines — especially the men, lots of men, confessing their shame and lifelong trauma from being sexually abused — sodomized — as young schoolboys by their priest, their "Father in God." And we exclaim, like Marie Fortune, "Is nothing sacred?"[2]

In a follow-up story on a TV newsmagazine, we see the journalist who first broke into print with accounts of pedophilia by priests. He has been following this diocese by diocese, and he tells how many million dollars Roman Catholic dioceses in the United States have spent paying off survivors and "settling" out of court in return for survivors' silence. Then he and Roman Catholic priest-sociologist Andrew Greeley are on the *Phil Donahue Show*.

The film *The Prince of Tides* was in movie houses across the country a 30 year or more before. Even though the novel does not culminate in the sodomy-rape of the son, the movie does. It helps us begin to believe that child sexual abuse happens to little boys as well as little girls, and that when it happens, it is as life-distorting, as traumatic, and perhaps even more deeply repressed with men than with women.

Now we are ready to sit through the Menendez brothers' trial as jurors, and at least consider seriously the possibility that their father's sexual abuse through the years could indeed have made the brothers fear for their own lives and have driven them to murder in self-defense.

TV as Ally in Feminist Consciousness Change

How does all this make me feel as a feminist who is interested in consciousness change? It makes me feel we should "thank our lucky (feminist) stars!" that we live in a TV age.

Television has taken parts of the reality of women's lives and it has made them "seen and heard" as a part of the visible and taken-seriously reality of our culture. It has taken women's experience, aptly named by sociologist Elise Boulding "the underside of history" (1976/1992), and made it noteworthy, even with patriarchy's determination to focus only on male experience as normative and visible. It has allowed the voices of women and children, long silenced as victims of abuse, to resonate loud and clear until we can hear them as survivors and not just as victims. It has done this with male talk show hosts

---

[2]Marie Fortune is a United Church of Christ minister and a consultant on preventing clergy sexual abuse and on procedures for dealing with it when it does occur. See Fortune (1989).

(Donahue, Geraldo, Montel, Jerry, Maury), with male commentators on newsmagazines (Sam Donaldson, Hugh Downs, Stone Phillips), and with a male news anchor as host of a TV special on rape (Peter Jennings).

I do not think I will ever forget the incredible feeling I had when Peter Jennings in the ABC rape special (March 1992) looked directly into the camera and said that rape is a man's problem because we men are always doing it to women! Men like Peter Jennings bring a huge reservoir of credibility to a women's issue because when important men declare an issue to be important and urgent, it *becomes* important and urgent in the male world that dominates our public life.

What to Make of O. J. Simpson?

For millions of sports fans, the struggle originally was whether they   35
could imagine that their beloved O. J., the sports hero and superior athlete of almost mythic dimensions, actually could have committed such a violent and awful crime — the double murder of Nicole Brown Simpson and Ronald Goldman. But television — because it cares about ratings and money, and not because it cares particularly about women's issues — was to cover every moment of the trial it was allowed to, bringing out every gory detail a million times on every TV station and every newsmagazine. That O. J. might have done it became thinkable. At the start, it appeared that the hyper-coverage might accomplish what the women's movement by itself could never have accomplished. It appeared that this trial might finally make it commonplace in our culture to perceive the relationship between the macho sports male mystique and violence itself, not just in our sports but in our personal relationships.

At about that time, I saw at my supermarket checkout the latest issue of the *National Enquirer*, with a full-page article by two men, Reginald Fitz and John Blosser (1994), on what they are now calling the "Super Jock Syndrome." The title of the article promises to tell its readers "why O. J. and other sports stars turn violent toward women." "Many sports figures have shown signs of the syndrome," the article continues, "including Sugar Ray Leonard who confessed to punching his wife; Mike Tyson, convicted of rape, and San Francisco Giants slugger Darryl Strawberry who admitted beating his spouse" (p. 41). The more recent book, *Sex, Violence and Power in Sports: Rethinking Masculinity*, by Michael Messner and Donald Sabo (1994), is also concerned to investigate this connection between athletes and violence to the women in their lives.

Finally Racist Violence Overwhelmed Sexist Violence

The yearlong O. J. trial developed a complexity all its own, in which the focus shifted away many times from the dead victims. The lawyers defending O. J. attacked the forensic procedures and conclusions of the Los Angeles Police Department. With a screenwriter's disclosure that LAPD detective Mark

Fuhrman had been talking to her on tape for a decade, it almost became the Mark Fuhrman trial, for on the tapes Fuhrman described how officers fabricated evidence to convict defendants, beat up blacks, and administered street justice in a racially biased and hostile way.

At the end of the trial, the acquittal of O. J. Simpson still seemed unthinkable and unjust to a substantial majority of white America. But for a jury of mostly black women, this was a trial about the long history of violence and injustice of whites toward blacks, rather than of men toward women. There was, in their judgment, "reasonable doubt," and the media focus shifted to explore another dark and dangerous tradition of violence, that of whites against blacks. Violence has moved along racial as well as sexual divisions, and both are important, both need to be understood and acknowledged — and both need to cease.

"Go, Tell It on the Mountain"

In ancient times, people would seek the height of mountaintops to help them amplify their voices and help in getting their message out: "Go, tell it on the mountain, / Over the hills, and everywhere. / Go tell it on the mountain." Television has provided contemporary feminism, and now American blacks, with a modern equivalent of such a mountaintop, providing just such an amplifying voice for at least certain of our messages about women's (and blacks') experience in this culture.

I do not say that television does this for love of women or affection for the women's movement. Rather, the driving forces are more likely television news managers' and network managers' insatiable needs for news that is highly visual and also emotionally powerful and very involving for their viewers — a large number of whom are women. Networks and stations are also driven by concerns about advertising revenues and market share, and so they are constantly creating and showing whatever is the hottest and latest issue or newest trend. This means that, in the midst of television's coverage of issues which concern and affect women, it also continues to show and maintain the old stereotypes of women and it has all the other flaws of a well-invested patriarchal institution.

But despite itself, television as the great amplifying voice of our time has made possible some unexpected and truly incredible cultural leaps in consciousness symbolized by Clarence Thomas, the priestly pedophile Father Porter, Lorena Bobbitt, and O. J. Simpson. These leaps of consciousness on the issues of wife battering, incest and sexual abuse of children, violence to women, and sexual harassment could not have been produced by the women's movement alone, or by the courts alone. A crucial role is played by the harsh glare of publicity and celebrity, the amplifying "voice" of television.

The extent of these changes in consciousness, and in general awareness of these issues, is suggested by the jury verdicts in the Lorena Bobbitt and first of the Menendez brothers trials, and perhaps by white America's will-

40

ingness to consider an exemplary black sports hero a batterer and then the murderer of his wife.

The Continuing Struggle to "Name" What Is Happening

Where such a cultural shift takes place, providing a gain in cultural power for some group, the shift often provokes a backlash. I take *The Abuse Excuse: Cop-Outs, Sob Stories and Other Evasions of Responsibility,* by Harvard law professor Alan M. Dershowitz (1994), to be an expression of just such a patriarchal backlash against these very real recent gains for women and children in a still violent patriarchal culture. I think the publication of *The Abuse Excuse* indicates that my quick sketch of women's and children's recent search for safety and justice is not the end of the story. On the contrary, we all know such violence will continue. But there is, for me, clear evidence in the publication of this book, by such an eminent defense lawyer, that a lot of progress has indeed already been made, perhaps more than we noticed. We need to appreciate that progress, and honor the women in the women's movement and in the communications industry whose efforts made it possible.

References

Allen, D. (1989). From opportunity to strategy: Women contribute to the communications future. In R. Rush & D. Allen (Eds.), *Communications at the crossroads: The gender gap connection* (pp. 59–79). Norwood, NJ: Ablex.

Boulding, E. (1992). *The underside of history: A view of women through time* (rev. ed.). Thousand Oaks, CA: Sage. (Original work published 1976, Boulder, CO: Westview)

Dershowitz, A. (1994). *The abuse excuse: Cop-outs, sob stories and other evasions of responsibility.* Boston: Little, Brown.

Fitz, R., & Blosser, J. (1994, August 2). Why O. J. and other sports stars turn violent toward women. *National Enquirer,* 41.

Fortune, M. (1989). *Is nothing sacred? When sex invades the pastoral relationship.* San Francisco: Harper SanFrancisco.

Herman, J. L. (M.D.). (1981). *Father-daughter incest.* Cambridge, MA: Harvard University Press.

Messner, M. A., & Sabo, D. F. (1994). *Sex, violence and power in sports: Rethinking masculinity.* Freedom, CA: Crossing Press.

Walker, L. E. (1979). *The battered woman.* New York: Harper & Row, Colophon.

ENGAGING THE TEXT

1. In what ways, according to Gray, does television "give voice" to women's experience? How do different types of programming serve to amplify the voice of advocates for women and children?

2. What motivates television producers to highlight issues like domestic violence and child abuse, according to Gray? Overall, how accurately do you think shows like those she mentions portray American society?

3. Gray offers two contrasting interpretations of the O. J. Simpson trial in this article — one from the perspective of "white America," another from that of the African American women who were part of the jury. How accurate and how fair is this analysis of how the trial was viewed? What other meanings may the Simpson trial have conveyed to the American public?

4. Toward the end of her essay Gray says that "in the midst of television's coverage of issues which concern and affect women, it also continues to show and maintain the old stereotypes of women" (para. 40). How accurate is Gray's assessment of TV's portrayal of women? Does television portray women as being more than victims of abuse or old-fashioned stereotypes?

EXPLORING CONNECTIONS

5. Compare Norman Rockwell's enormously popular portrayals of family life (p. 21) with the television portrayals mentioned by Gray. Could paintings like Rockwell's be interpreted as part of a cultural conspiracy to deny violence against women and children?

6. Consider the gulf separating the ideas about family the young Gary Soto got from television (p. 42) and ideas and attitudes about family and relationships projected by programs like those described by Gray. What effect would such shows be likely to have on an impressionable child's ideas about family? What evidence of such influence, if any, do you see in younger acquaintances and family members?

7. Compare Gray's view of television's influence with that of Bill McKibben (p. 718) and Patricia J. Williams (p. 604). Which of these contrasting interpretations of TV's cultural impact seems most plausible to you and why?

EXTENDING THE CRITICAL CONTEXT

8. Organize a group to split up the work of surveying a week's worth of TV coverage of domestic violence. One individual, for example, might be responsible for scanning talk shows, another for sampling soap operas, another for watching local news programs, and so on. Pool your findings to assess the quantity and quality of coverage of domestic abuse. Do your findings support Gray's claim that television is having a positive impact on the way we view violence against women and children?

9. Gray notes that television, whatever its intent, has led to leaps of cultural consciousness that have benefited women. Brainstorm about the next decade of television coverage of women's issues. What topics would you like to see television raise for public discussion?

10. Look up one or two detailed news stories about the trial of Lorena Bobbitt or the Menendez brothers. Does the case seem to support Alan Dershowitz's charge that "the abuse excuse" is evoked by guilty defendants to avoid responsibility for their actions? Which view of the case, Gray's or Dershowitz's, do you find more compelling? Why?

The Coming White Underclass
CHARLES MURRAY

*Over the past three decades, conservative critics have deplored the ero-
sion of traditional values in American life. One of the statistics they commonly cite to support their claims about America's decline is the rising number of "illegitimate" births. In this provocative essay, Murray argues that
the nation is at risk now that an "epidemic" of illegitimacy is threatening
white as well as black Americans. Charles Murray (b. 1943) is a fellow at the
American Enterprise Institute and one of the nation's most influential conservative writers. He is author of three books on social policy, including* The
Bell Curve *(1994, with Richard Herrnstein).*

Every once in a while the sky really is falling, and this seems to be the
case with the latest national figures on illegitimacy. The unadorned statistic
is that, in 1991, 1.2 million children were born to unmarried mothers,
within a hair of 30 percent of all live births. How high is 30 percent? About
four percent points higher than the black illegitimacy rate in the early 1960s
that motivated Daniel Patrick Moynihan[1] to write his famous memorandum
on the breakdown of the black family.

The 1991 story for blacks is that illegitimacy has now reached 68 percent of births to black women. In inner cities, the figure is typically in excess
of 80 percent. Many of us have heard these numbers so often that we are in-
ured. It is time to think about them as if we were back in the mid-1960s
with the young Moynihan and asked to predict what would happen if the
black illegitimacy rate were 68 percent.

Impossible, we would have said. But if the proportion of fatherless boys
in a given community were to reach such levels, surely the culture must be
Lord of the Flies[2] writ large, the values of unsocialized male adolescents
made norms — physical violence, immediate gratification, and predatory
sex. That is the culture now taking over the black inner city.

But the black story, however dismaying, is old news. The new trend
that threatens the United States is white illegitimacy. Matters have not yet
quite gotten out of hand, but they are on the brink. If we want to act, now is
the time.

In 1991 707,502 babies were born to single white women, representing   5
22 percent of white births. The elite wisdom holds that this phenomenon

---

[1]*Daniel Patrick Moynihan:* Four-term Democratic senator from New York.
[2]*Lord of the Flies:* 1954 William Golding novel in which English schoolboys stranded on
an island degenerate into savagery.

cuts across social classes, as if the increase in Murphy Browns[3] were pushing the trend line. Thus, a few months ago, a Census Bureau study of fertility among all American women got headlines for a few days because it
showed that births to single women with college degrees doubled in the last
decade to 6 percent from 3 percent. This is an interesting trend, but of
minor social importance. The real news of that study is that the proportion
of single mothers with less than a high-school education jumped to 48 percent from 35 percent in a single decade.

These numbers are dominated by whites. Breaking down the numbers
by race (using data not available in the published version), women with college degrees contribute only 4 percent of white illegitimate babies, while
women with a high-school education or less contribute 82 percent. Women
with family incomes of $75,000 or more contribute 1 percent of white ille-
gitimate babies, while women with family incomes under $20,000 con-
tribute 69 percent.

The National Longitudinal Study of Youth, a Labor Department study
that has tracked more than ten thousand youths since 1979, shows an even
more dramatic picture. For white women below the poverty line in the year
prior to giving birth, 44 percent of births have been illegitimate, compared
with only 6 percent for women above the poverty line. White illegitimacy is
overwhelmingly a lower-class phenomenon.

This brings us to the emergence of a white underclass. In raw numbers,
European-American whites are the ethnic group with the most people in
poverty, most illegitimate children, most women on welfare, most unemployed men, and most arrests for serious crimes. And yet whites have not
had an "underclass" as such, because the whites who might qualify have
been scattered among the working class. Instead, whites have had "white
trash" concentrated in a few streets on the outskirts of town, sometimes a
skid row of unattached white men in the large cities. But these scatterings
have seldom been large enough to make up a neighborhood. An underclass
needs a critical mass, and white America has not had one.

But now the overall white illegitimacy rate is 22 percent. The figure in
low-income, working-class communities may be twice that. How much illegitimacy can a community tolerate? Nobody knows, but the historical fact is
that the trend lines on black crime, dropout from the labor force, and illegitimacy all shifted sharply upward as the overall black illegitimacy rate
passed 25 percent.

The causal connection is murky — I blame the revolution in social policy   10
during that period, while others blame the sexual revolution, broad shifts in
cultural norms, or structural changes in the economy. But the white illegitimacy rate is approaching that same problematic 25 percent region at a time

---

[3]*Murphy Browns:* The popular TV comedy *Murphy Brown* stirred controversy in 1992
when the title character, a successful journalist, chose to have a baby without marrying.

when social policy is more comprehensively wrongheaded than it was in the mid-1960s, and the cultural and sexual norms are still more degraded.

The white underclass will begin to show its face in isolated ways. Look for certain schools in white neighborhoods to get a reputation as being unteachable, with large numbers of disruptive students and indifferent parents. Talk to the police; listen for stories about white neighborhoods where the incidence of domestic disputes and casual violence has been shooting up. Look for white neighborhoods with high concentrations of drug activity and large numbers of men who have dropped out of the labor force. Some readers will recall reading the occasional news story about such places already.

As the spatial concentration of illegitimacy reaches critical mass, we should expect the deterioration to be as fast among low-income whites in the 1990s as it was among low-income blacks in the 1960s. My proposition is that illegitimacy is the single most important social problem of our time — more important than crime, drugs, poverty, illiteracy, welfare, or homelessness because it drives everything else. Doing something about it is not just one more item on the American policy agenda, but should be at the top. Here is what to do:

In the calculus of illegitimacy, the constants are that boys like to sleep with girls and that girls think babies are endearing. Human societies have historically channeled these elemental forces of human behavior via thick walls of rewards and penalties that constrained the overwhelming majority of births to take place within marriage. The past thirty years have seen those walls cave in. It is time to rebuild them.

The ethical underpinning for the policies I am about to describe is this: Bringing a child into the world is the most important thing that most human beings ever do. Bringing a child into the world when one is not emotionally or financially prepared to be a parent is wrong. The child deserves society's support. The parent does not.

The social justification is this· A society with broad legal freedoms de-   15
pends crucially on strong nongovernmental institutions to temper and restrain behavior. Of these, marriage is paramount. Either we reverse the current trends in illegitimacy — especially white illegitimacy — or America must, willy-nilly, become an unrecognizably authoritarian, socially segregated, centralized state.

To restore the rewards and penalties of marriage does not require social engineering. Rather, it requires that the state stop interfering with the natural forces that have done the job quite effectively for millennia. Some of the changes I will describe can occur at the federal level; others would involve state laws. For now, the important thing is to agree on what should be done.

I begin with the penalties, of which the most obvious are economic. Throughout human history, a single woman with a small child has not been a viable economic unit. Not being a viable economic unit, neither have the single woman and child been a legitimate social unit. In small numbers, they must be a net drain on the community's resources. In large numbers, they must destroy the community's capacity to sustain itself. Mirabile dictu,[4] communities everywhere have augmented the economic penalties of single parenthood with severe social stigma.

Restoring economic penalties translates into the first and central policy prescription: to end all economic support for single mothers. The AFDC (Aid to Families with Dependent Children) payment goes to zero. Single mothers are not eligible for subsidized housing or for food stamps. An assortment of other subsidies and in-kind benefits disappear. Since universal medical coverage appears to be an idea whose time has come, I will stipulate that all children have medical coverage. But with that exception, the signal is loud and unmistakable: From society's perspective, to have a baby that you cannot care for yourself is profoundly irresponsible, and the government will no longer subsidize it.

How does a poor young mother survive without government support? The same way she has since time immemorial. If she wants to keep a child, she must enlist support from her parents, boyfriend, siblings, neighbors, church, or philanthropies. She must get support from somewhere, anywhere, other than the government. The objectives are threefold.

First, enlisting the support of others raises the probability that other mature adults are going to be involved with the upbringing of the child, and this is a great good in itself.

Second, the need to find support forces a self-selection process. One of the most shortsighted excuses made for current behavior is that an adolescent who is utterly unprepared to be a mother "needs someone to love." Childish yearning isn't a good enough selection device. We need to raise the probability that a young single woman who keeps her child is doing so volitionally and thoughtfully. Forcing her to find a way of supporting the child does this. It will lead many young women who shouldn't be mothers to place their babies for adoption. This is good. It will lead others, watching what happens to their sisters, to take steps not to get pregnant. This is also good. Many others will get abortions. Whether this is good depends on what one thinks of abortion.

Third, stigma will regenerate. The pressure on relatives and communities to pay for the folly of their children will make an illegitimate birth the socially horrific act it used to be, and getting a girl pregnant something boys do at the risk of facing a shotgun. Stigma and shotgun marriages may or may not be good for those on the receiving end, but their deterrent effect on others is wonderful — and indispensable.

What about women who can find no support but keep the baby anyway? There are laws already on the books about the right of the state to take a child from a neglectful parent. We have some 360,000 children in foster care because of them. Those laws would still apply. Society's main response, however, should be to make it as easy as possible for those mothers to place

20

---

[4]*Mirabile dictu:* "Strange to say/marvelous to relate" (often used ironically, as it is here).

their children for adoption at infancy. To that end, state governments must strip adoption of the nonsense that has encumbered it in recent decades.

The first step is to make adoption easy for any married couple who can show reasonable evidence of having the resources and stability to raise a child. Lift all restrictions on interracial adoption. Ease age limitations for adoptive parents.

The second step is to restore the traditional legal principle that placing a child for adoption means irrevocably relinquishing all legal rights to the child. The adoptive parents are parents without qualification. Records are sealed until the child reaches adulthood, at which time they may be unsealed only with the consent of biological child and parent.

Given these straightforward changes — going back to the old way, which worked — there is reason to believe that some extremely large proportion of infants given up by their mothers will be adopted into good homes. This is true not just for flawless blue-eyed blond infants but for babies of all colors and conditions. The demand for infants to adopt is huge.

Some small proportion of infants and larger proportion of older children will not be adopted. For them, the government should spend lavishly on orphanages. I am not recommending Dickensian barracks. In 1993, we know a lot about how to provide a warm, nurturing environment for children, and getting rid of the welfare system frees up lots of money to do it. Those who find the word "orphanages" objectionable may think of them as twenty-four-hour-a-day preschools. Those who prattle about the importance of keeping children with their biological mothers may wish to spend some time in a patrol car or with a social worker seeing what the reality of life with welfare-dependent biological mothers can be like.

Finally, there is the matter of restoring the rewards of marriage. Here, I am pessimistic about how much government can do and optimistic about how little it needs to do. The rewards of raising children within marriage are real and deep. The main task is to shepherd children through adolescence so that they can reach adulthood — when they are likely to recognize the value of those rewards — free to take on marriage and family. The main purpose of the penalties for single parenthood is to make that task easier.

One of the few concrete things that the government can do to increase the rewards of marriage is make the tax code favor marriage and children. Those of us who are nervous about using the tax code for social purposes can advocate making the tax code at least neutral.

A more abstract but ultimately crucial step in raising the rewards of marriage is to make marriage once again the sole legal institution through which parental rights and responsibilities are defined and exercised.

Little boys should grow up knowing from their earliest memories that if they want to have any rights whatsoever regarding a child that they sire — more vividly, if they want to grow up to be a daddy — they must marry. Little girls should grow up knowing from their earliest memories that if they want to have any legal claims whatsoever on the father of their children, they must marry. A marriage certificate should establish that a man and a woman have entered into a unique legal relationship. The changes in recent years that have blurred the distinctiveness of marriage are subtly but importantly destructive.

Together, these measures add up to a set of signals, some with immediate and tangible consequences, others with long-term consequences, still others symbolic. They should be supplemented by others based on a reexamination of divorce laws, and their consequences.

That these policy changes seem drastic and unrealistic is a peculiarity of our age, not of the policies themselves. With embellishments, I have endorsed the policies that were the uncontroversial law of the land as recently as John Kennedy's presidency. Then, America's elites accepted as a matter of course that a free society such as America's can sustain itself only through virtue and temperance in the people, that virtue and temperance depend centrally on the

socialization of each new generation, and that the socialization of each generation depends on the matrix of care and resources fostered by marriage.

Three decades after that consensus disappeared, we face an emerging crisis. The long, steep climb in black illegitimacy has been calamitous for black communities and painful for the nation. The reforms I have described will work for blacks as for whites, and have been needed for years. But the brutal truth is that American society as a whole could survive when illegitimacy became epidemic within a comparatively small ethnic minority. It cannot survive the same epidemic among whites.

ENGAGING THE TEXT

1. Why does Murray believe that a high illegitimacy rate for whites will produce a white underclass? Explain why you agree or disagree.

2. Summarize the penalties Murray would endorse for having a baby outside of marriage. Debate the impact these would have on rates of "illegitimacy." What drawbacks, if any, do you see to imposing such penalties? Do you see any other ways of reducing the number of children born out of wedlock?

3. Murray states that one should be "financially prepared" (para. 14) to bring a child into the world. Do you agree that childbearing should be restricted to financially adequate parents? If so, how much income would you consider adequate for a mother or a couple to have one child?

4. Analyze the roles of race and gender in Murray's essay. For example, in what ways does he equate or distinguish between white and black Americans, and how do *fathers* of "illegitimate" children fit into Murray's proposals?

5. Debate Murray's statement that "throughout human history, a single woman with a small child has not been a viable economic unit" (para. 17). Do you think it's true today that a single mother is not a viable economic unit?

6. Murray writes that today's "social policy is more comprehensively wrong-headed than it was in the mid-1960s, and the cultural and sexual norms are still more degraded" (para. 10). What do you think he means by these statements? What is your own view?

EXPLORING CONNECTIONS

7. How might John Gillis (p. 25) respond to Murray's bleak assessment of the decline of the American family?

8. Read the excerpt from *Dubious Conceptions* by Kristin Luker (p. 91). Work in small groups to identify two or three fundamental disagreements between Luker and Murray. Debate these, being careful to examine the evidence and logic of each writer.

9. Read "The Speech of Miss Polly Baker" (p. 88) and write a letter from Baker to Murray responding to his views of unwed mothers.

10. Look at the cartoon by Lloyd Dangle on page 86. Is your point of view on teen pregnancy and unwed mothers closer to Murray's or Dangle's? Explain why.

EXTENDING THE CRITICAL CONTEXT

11. Murray says that Aid to Families with Dependent Children is essentially an undeserved subsidy awarded to single mothers. Brainstorm with classmates to think of other government subsidies and debate whether their recipients are more deserving than single mothers.

The Speech of Miss Polly Baker

BENJAMIN FRANKLIN

Unwed mothers are scarcely a new phenomenon. This selection concerns an instance dating back to colonial New England. Franklin, writing for the Maryland Gazette *in 1747, described the piece as "the Speech of Miss Polly Baker, before a Court of Judicature, at Connecticut in New England, where she was prosecuted the fifth Time for having a Bastard Child; which influenced the Court to dispense with her Punishment, and induced one of her Judges to marry her the next Day." Benjamin Franklin (1706–1790), in addition to being a "founding father" of the United States, was a printer, publisher, statesman, scientist, journalist, cartoonist, inventor, military strategist, mathematician, vegetarian, postmaster, Freemason, slaveholder and (later) abolitionist.*

May it please the Honourable Bench to indulge me a few Words: I am a poor unhappy Woman; who have no Money to Fee Lawyers to plead for me, being hard put to it to get a tolerable Living. I shall not trouble your Honours with long Speeches; for I have not the presumption to expect, that you may, by any Means, be prevailed on to deviate in your Sentence from the Law, in my Favour. All I humbly hope is, that your Honours would charitably move the Governor's Goodness on my Behalf, that my Fine may be remitted. This is the Fifth Time, Gentlemen, that I have been dragg'd before your Courts on the same Account; twice I have paid heavy Fines, and twice have been brought to public Punishment, for want of Money to pay those Fines. This may have been agreeable to the Laws; I do not dispute it: But since Laws are sometimes unreasonable in themselves, and therefore repealed; and others bear too hard on the Subject in particular Circumstances; and therefore there is left a Power somewhere to dispense with the Execution of them; I take the Liberty to say, that I think this Law, by which I am punished, is both unreasonable in itself, and particularly severe with regard to me, who have always lived an inoffensive Life in the Neighbourhood where I was born, and defy my Enemies (if I have any) to say I ever wrong'd Man, Woman, or Child. Abstracted from the law, I cannot conceive (may it please your Honours) what the Nature of my Offence is. I have brought Five fine Children into the World, at the Risque of my Life: I have maintained them well by my own Industry, without burthening the Township, and could have done it better, if it had not been for the heavy Charges and Fines I have paid. Can it be a Crime (in the Nature of Things I mean) to add to the Number of the King's Subjects, in a new Country that really wants People? I own I should think it rather a Praise worthy, than a Punishable Action. I have debauch'd no other Woman's Husband, nor inticed any innocent Youth: These Things I never was charged with; nor has any one the least cause of Complaint against me, unless, perhaps the Minister, or the Justice, because I have had Children without being Married, by which they have miss'd a Wedding Fee. But, can even this be a Fault of mine? I appeal to your Honours. You are pleased to allow I don't want Sense; but I must be stupid to the last Degree, not to prefer the Honourable State of Wedlock, to the Condition I have lived in. I always was, and still am, willing to enter into it; I doubt not my Behaving well in it, having all the Industry, Frugality, Fertility, and Skill in Oeconomy, appertaining to a good Wife's Character. I defy any Person to say I ever Refused an Offer of that Sort: On the contrary, I readily Consented to the only Proposal of Marriage that ever was made me, which was when I was a Virgin; but too easily confiding in the Person's Sincerity that made it, I unhappily lost my own Honour, by trusting to his; for he got me with Child, and then forsook me: That very Person you all know; he is now become a Magistrate of this County; and I had hopes he would have appeared this Day on the Bench, and have endeavoured to moderate the Court in my Favour; then I should have scorn'd to have mention'd it; but I must Complain of it as unjust and unequal, that my Betrayer and Undoer, the first Cause of all my Faults and Miscarriages (if they must be deemed such) should be advanced to Honour and Power, in the same Government that punishes my Misfortunes with Stripes and Infamy. I shall be told, 'tis like, that were there no Act of Assembly in the Case, the Precepts of Religion are violated by my Transgressions. If mine, then, is a religious Offence, leave it, Gentlemen, to religious Punishments. You have already excluded me from all the Comforts of your Church Communion: Is not that sufficient? You believe I have offended Heaven, and must suffer eternal Fire: Will not that be sufficient? What need is there, then, of your additional Fines and Whippings? I own, I do not think as you do; for, if I thought, what you call a Sin, was really such, I would not presumptuously commit it. But how can it be believed, that Heaven is angry at my having Children, when, to the little done by me towards it, God has been pleased to add his divine Skill and admirable Workmanship in the Formation of their Bodies, and crown'd it by furnishing them with rational and immortal Souls? Forgive me gentlemen, if I talk a little extravagantly on these Matters; I am no Divine: But if you, great Men,[1] must be making Laws, do not turn natural and useful Actions into Crimes, by your Prohibitions. Reflect a little on the horrid Consequences of this Law in particular: What Numbers of procur'd Abortions! and how many distress'd Mothers have been driven, by the Terror of Punishment and public Shame, to imbrue,[2] contrary to nature, their own trembling hands in the Blood of their helpless Offspring! Nature would have induc'd them to nurse it up with a Parent's Fondness. 'Tis the Law therefore, 'tis the Law itself that is guilty of all these Barbarities and Murders. Repeal it then, Gentlemen; let it be expung'd for ever from your Books: And on the other hand, take into your wise Consideration, the great and growing Number of Batchelors in the Country, many of whom, from the mean Fear of the Expence of a Family, have never sincerely and honourably Courted a Woman in their Lives; and by their Manner of Living, leave unproduced (which I think is little better than Murder) Hundreds of their Posterity to the Thousandth Generation. Is not theirs a greater Offence against the Public Good, than mine? Compel them then, by a Law, either to Marry, or pay double the Fine of Fornication every Year. What must poor young Women do, whom Custom has forbid to sollicit the Men, and who cannot force themselves upon Husbands, when the Laws take no Care to provide them any, and yet severely punish if they do their Duty without them? Yes, Gentlemen, I venture to call it a Duty; 'tis the Duty of the first and great Command of Nature, and of Nature's God, *Increase and multiply*: A Duty, from the steady Performance of which nothing has ever been able to deter me; but for its Sake, I have hazarded the Loss of the public Esteem, and frequently incurr'd public Disgrace and Punishment; and therefore ought, in my humble Opinion, instead of a Whipping, to have a Statue erected to my Memory.

---

[1]Turning to some Gentlemen of the Assembly, then in Court.
[2]*imbrue:* Drench or soak, especially in blood.

ENGAGING THE TEXT

1. Outline Polly Baker's argument in skeleton form. How well does it hold up to close scrutiny? What parts, if any, do you consider relevant to current attitudes and policies concerning unwed mothers?
2. What charges does Polly Baker make against men? Do you think these remain important issues today? Why or why not?
3. Identify the rhetorical strategies employed by Baker to sway her judges; try to explain what made them so effective that she was not punished.

EXPLORING CONNECTIONS

4. Using "Calculators, not Condoms" (p. 86) for inspiration, draw a cartoon for the 1747 *Maryland Gazette* to accompany "The Speech of Miss Polly Baker."

5. Imagine if Charles Murray (p. 81) tried to convince Polly Baker to give up her children for adoption. What would he say to her? How might she respond?

EXTENDING THE CRITICAL CONTEXT

6. Look up some recent newspaper or magazine articles and editorials about unwed mothers. How are such women generally portrayed? How do these images compare to Franklin's portrait of Polly Baker?

From *Dubious Conceptions:*
The Politics of Teenage Pregnancy
KRISTIN LUKER

Since the end of the 1950s, the number of U.S. households headed by single mothers has steadily increased for all ethnicities and economic groups, and continues to grow despite the efforts of America's political and religious leaders. In this selection, Kristin Luker examines the complex reasons behind this trend. Instead of rushing to condemn unwed mothers, Luker explores the social, economic, and political sides of the issue, separating fact from fiction. Kristin Luker (b. 1946) is a sociologist with special expertise in family issues, including contraception and abortion. This selection is from Dubious Conceptions: The Politics of Teenage Pregnancy *(1996).*

At the Eileen Sullivan Daycare Center, in the sunny playroom for toddlers, young David Winters sits entranced in front of a colorful bead-and-wire toy.[1] His chubby fingers tease the beads up and across the bright red,

[1]David and his mother are real people, but their names and personal characteristics have been changed to protect their privacy. The Eileen Sullivan Daycare Center, likewise referred to here under a pseudonym, is funded by the school district and by the state. Located in a medium-sized community in the western United States, it is a reasonably typical program designed to help teenagers with problems relating to pregnancy and parenting. [Author's note]

blue, and green wires, his solemnity lightened by rare and dazzling smiles as he conquers a particularly tricky corner in the game.

Born a month prematurely, David has gone on to flourish at the Sullivan Center after a rocky start. Across the street, in the high school to which the daycare center belongs, David's mother, Michelle Brown, is taking her algebra exam. If all goes well and Michelle gets the B she hopes for, she may well succeed at being the first member of her family to graduate from high school. And if she does, she has every intention of crossing that auditorium stage three months from now, dressed in her graduation robes and holding baby David in her arms.

Meanwhile, beyond the walls of the school and the daycare center, Michelle and her baby are at the heart of important and troubling questions that are being asked by people from all walks of life. In the United States, although teenagers give birth to only 12 percent of all babies, they represent about a third of all unmarried mothers. These young mothers are somewhat less likely than older mothers to start prenatal care on time, and are slightly more likely to have low-birthweight babies and complications during pregnancy and childbirth — all of which are factors associated with medical and sometimes developmental problems in their children.[2]

Michelle is not sure she's old enough to get married, though she never considered herself too young to have or to raise David, despite the fact that she was only seventeen when he was born. She did think briefly about having an abortion, but both her mother and grandmother were adamantly opposed; and truth to tell, Michelle was secretly happy they were. Their support, combined with her own experiences and those of many of her friends, makes her sure that she can successfully handle being both a young mother and a student. Being a wife is another story, though.

Michelle's reluctance to marry is strengthened by some harsh economic realities. The father of her baby works full time at McDonald's, but his minimum-wage salary of $684 a month just won't support the three of them. He's a diligent and even desperate worker (he competed against more than a hundred other applicants for his job), and he's been promised a promotion to manager. Even managers don't get medical benefits at McDonald's, however, and David's health still calls for frequent and expensive visits to the pediatrician. Although Michelle squirms under what she sees as the shame attached to welfare, she can't afford to give up the money (and especially the medical services that come with it) in order to marry.   5

Michelle and David's situation illustrates a host of important questions about age, sex, and marriage. To many people over forty, the idea of pregnant teenagers walking openly down school corridors, not to mention the existence of high school daycare centers, is something that outstrips the

---

[2]National Center for Health Statistics, *Advance Report of Final Natality Statistics* 43, no. 5 (1992), Supplement October 25, 1994. . . . [Author's note]

imagination. Until the mid-1970s visibly pregnant *married* women, whether students or teachers, were formally banned from school grounds, lest their swelling bellies cross that invisible boundary separating the real world (where sex and pregnancy existed) from the schools (where they did not). The idea that a pregnant *unmarried* woman would show herself not only in public but in schools, where the minds of innocent children could be corrupted, was more unthinkable still.

And what role does David's father play in all this? Like many of the fathers in discussions of early pregnancy, he is largely invisible to the public eye. We do know that most fathers are relatively young themselves (about 80 percent of teenage mothers have a partner who is within five years of their own age).[3] And we also have reason to suspect that this young man's faithful visits to the neonatal intensive care unit during David's lengthy stay there and his eager willingness to be a good father mark him as more typical than the stereotype would have it. Still, some twenty-five years after the most recent round of feminist activism, most people focus on teenage mothers instead of on young parents, so our knowledge about such men is surprisingly limited. This book will try to focus on both men and women as much as possible, but the available data force us to speak more often and with more authority about young women. The focus on young women in a book about early pregnancy should not, however, be taken as "natural."

For similar reasons, this book focuses largely on blacks and whites. Despite the fact that the U.S. Census gathers data on a number of races, and despite the fact that pregnancy among teenagers has been a national concern for the past two decades, reasonably comparable data exist only for whites and African Americans. More problematically, "race" is a social rather than a biological category and as such is defined differently in different historical eras.[4] Furthermore, the National Center for Health Statistics and the Bureau of the Census, which provide the data that underlie studies

---

[3]Alan Guttmacher Institute, *Sex and America's Teenagers* (New York: Alan Guttmacher Institute, 1994), p. 53. Mike Males, "School Age Pregnancy: Why Hasn't Prevention Worked?" *Journal of School Health* 63, no. 10 (1993): 429–432. [Author's note]

[4]The notions of "race" and "ethnicity" also vary within groups, and may even vary from situation to situation within a person's lifetime. See William Peterson, "Politics and the Measurement of Ethnicity," in William Alonso and Paul Starr, eds., *The Politics of Numbers* (New York: Russell Sage, 1987), esp. p. 189. The first census of 1790 counted free white males and females, "all other free persons" (indentured servants and a few free blacks), and "slaves." From 1790 to 1840 there were no specific directives, and classification was presumably left up to the census taker. Between 1840 and 1910 there were various efforts to subdivide the category of black Americans (into mulattos, quadroons, octoroons, and so on). But until the mid-1960s, government survey and research documents typically examined only two categories of people: whites and "nonwhites." In 1990 the U.S. Census reported a total population of approximately 250 million people, of which 85 percent were white, 12 percent black, and 3 percent "other races" (including Native Americans, Asian Americans, and Pacific Islanders). But research data on these other races are still scarce. [Author's note]

such as this, use different systems of racial classification.[5] Thus, for the sake of accuracy, the discussion that follows will center on blacks and whites (providing data on other groups where possible), but readers should keep in mind that this dichotomy only partly reflects the rich tapestry of modern America.

The changes that have occurred over the last twenty years are more far-reaching than most people, even those most intimately involved, can appreciate. For example, Michelle and David raise questions not only about sex, age, and marriage but about other issues that Americans are currently struggling with — issues such as poverty, dependency, and the difficulties of getting ahead in the increasingly competitive global economy. More subtly, they raise questions about "family values," about the relationship of individuals to the community, and about the competing claims of rights and obligations in this new economy. For example, have doors already been closed to David because his mother is a teenager and has not married his father? Has an inevitable sequence of life events — premature birth, impaired health, failure in school, poverty, perhaps even a tendency to violent behavior — been set in motion for David by his mother's behavior? In the opinion of many people, David's future is already blighted and his right to participate as an equal in the pursuit of the American dream has already begun to diminish, all by virtue of decisions in which he has had no say. The little boy whose imagination is fired by a colorful bead-game is, in the eyes of many, already well on the way to a life of trouble and failure.

A great number of Americans think that children like young David   10 are being lost in a particularly painful and troubling fashion which has important implications for the larger society. One way of reading the story

[5]Virtually all of the statistics reported in this book have been compiled from these two sources. The National Center for Health Statistics gathered the data on "vital statistics" used for the numerator, and the Bureau of the Census collected the population data used for the denominator. Yet their systems of racial coding differ. For example, whereas the Bureau of the Census allows people to classify themselves and their children, the Center for Health Statistics defines "race" as synonymous with "national origin" and follows a complex set of rules governing the assignment of race of newborn based on race of parent. When only one parent is "white," the child is assigned the other parent's race or national origin. When neither parent is "white," the child is assigned the father's race or national origin — unless one of the parents is Hawaiian, in which case the child is "always assigned to Hawaiian." When information concerning race or national origin is lacking, the child is "allocated electronically" on the basis of previous records. But this system has changed over time: prior to 1964 all births for which race or national origin was unstated were classified as white. Births reported as white or "Hispanic" (an ethnic category) are coded as white, despite the fact that the extent to which Hispanic Americans identify themselves as white varies greatly. When it comes to marriage registration (and the Center for Health Statistics records only licenses to marry, not actual marriages), a different system is used: optional categories are listed (black, white, American Indian, etc.), and the code is often entered by a clerk. In short, the concept of race is extremely unstable and imprecise — a fact that readers should keep in mind throughout this book. [Author's note]

of Michelle and her baby is to say that David's future is being compromised by the selfishness of his mother, by her inability to put the long-term needs of a vulnerable baby before her own longings and desires. According to the most generous interpretation, Michelle is doing this out of youth and ignorance. The liberal view of Michelle's actions — from having sex in the first place, to not using contraception when she does have sex, to not getting an abortion despite the fact that she is young and poor, to trying to raise David without bothering to marry his father — is that she is simply too immature to appreciate the consequences of her actions. The harm is being done unwittingly, and Michelle is as much a victim as David.[6]

This view has the virtue of protecting Michelle from moral censure for her actions (when advocates speak of "babies having babies," they imply that Michelle cannot be held to the standards expected of adults any more than David can). At the same time, however, it denies her the status of full personhood, exempting her from the obligations of being a moral actor held accountable for the choices she makes. In turn, people deemed incapable of making meaningful moral choices often find themselves the targets of those who would make choices for them. The problem is that Americans have a rather mixed history of doing bad things to young or otherwise vulnerable people "for their own good," of confusing an unwillingness to make the "right" choice with an incapacity to do so.

A darker reading of Michelle's actions and motives exists alongside the narrative of the young mother as innocent victim who unwittingly harms her baby. According to this reading, Michelle is the calculating, knowing, "rational actor" of neoclassical economics: she coolly assesses the costs of having a baby, analyzes the benefits of welfare, and "invests" in a course of action that will get her what she wants. This view at least has the virtue of granting her the status of a real decisionmaker whose choices must be taken seriously. But when looked at closely, the dilemma of early pregnancy highlights the limitations of rational-actor theory as a useful way of looking at human behavior. Part of what makes economic theories of human interaction so elegant and parsimonious is that all motives are reduced to the easily observed ones of the marketplace. Passion, conviction, altruism, and morality become, in this view of the social

---

[6]This "discourse," which refers to young women in trouble as ignorant but not bad, is very old. In 1910 reformer Annie Allen compared such young women to a baby who "may wreck a railroad train and not even be naughty." She emphasized that "choice — volition — must enter into a wrong deed before the doer can be called wicked. A person must intend not only his act, but the consequences of his act before he can be held accountable." She admitted frankly that "these girls are generally silly and ignorant; if they were not they would not get into trouble." But she maintained that this was the worst that could be said of them. "Very few of them are malicious or even defiant; they seldom have any desire to be mischievous or to do harm of any serious sort to any one." Annie W. Allen, "How to Save Girls Who Have Fallen," *The Survey* 24, no. 1 (1910): 692. [Author's note]

world, either "externalities" or "revealed preferences" and are reduced to the status of "utilities."[7]

Yet careful scrutiny makes it clear that the rational actor of neoclassical economics is not an *individual* in the generic sense of the word, but rather a *male individual:* the concepts of "work" and "family" have assumptions about gender deeply embedded within them. In the nineteenth century, American society came to rely on a cultural division of labor whereby men went out into the marketplace and engaged in the kind of selfish, disconnected, amoral, and autonomous behavior lauded in economic theory. Bruised and tattered by the harshness of this dog-eat-dog world, they then came home to the pious, altruistic, caring, connected, and profoundly moral world of women where the values of the marketplace were held at bay and older, more humane values were honored.[8]

Part of the cultural schizophrenia of our own time is that this old division of moral labor is breaking down. We have come to expect women to emulate competitive, "selfish" male behavior in the workplace but to carry on their traditional roles of altruistic nurturers everywhere else.[9] Michelle and the problem of early pregnancy highlight these dilemmas in particularly compelling ways. At some level we intuit that teenage mothers are doing things that in another time and place would be acceptable and often praiseworthy, because they are just doing the same things that earlier generations of women did from time immemorial. Teenage mothers often get pregnant because they *aren't* being rational actors who put self first — they may have sex to please a man, and they may fail to use contraception because the man

[7]For explorations of this point, see Paula England, "The Separative Self: Androcentric Bias in Neoclassical Economics," in Marianne A. Ferber and Julie A. Nelson, eds., *Beyond Economic Man: Feminist Theory and Economics* (Chicago: University of Chicago Press, 1993), pp. 37–53. See also Nancy Folbre, *Who Pays for the Kids? Gender and the Structure of Constraint* (London: Routledge, 1994). [Author's note]

[8]The classic exposition of this cultural shift is Barbara Welter, "The Cult of True Womanhood, 1820–1860," *American Quarterly* 18, no. 2, part I (1966): 151–174. For further variations on the theme, see Ann Douglas, *The Feminization of American Culture* (New York: Knopf, 1977); and Christopher Lasch, *Haven in a Heartless World: The Family Besieged* (New York: Basic Books, 1972). In this context, the literary theorist Jane Tompkins makes a most interesting point — namely, that the vitality of the Western as a literary genre comes from the fact that it represents for the male reader a resounding rejection of the "feminized" culture of the late nineteenth century. See Jane Tompkins, *West of Everything: The Inner Life of Westerns* (New York: Oxford University Press, 1992). [Author's note]

[9]Following Arlie Hochschild, who argues that women these days must work a "second shift" at home after a long day at work, one could argue that women are required to work a second *moral* shift as well, doing all the emotional caretaking of home, family, and society after they have expended much energy in the competitive world of the marketplace. See Arlie Hochschild with Anne Machung, *The Second Shift: Working Parents and the Revolution at Home* (New York: Viking, 1989). For a particularly insightful view of how women "care" in ways that are invisible both to themselves and others, see Marjorie Devault, *Feeding the Family: The Organization of Caring as Gendered Work* (Chicago: University of Chicago Press, 1991). [Author's note]

either actively objects or makes it difficult by complaining that a condom reduces his pleasure. And filled with images from movies and magazines, young women may read a man's unwillingness to use contraception as a tacit commitment to the consequences, namely a baby. Teenage mothers, like other mothers, have also been known to get pregnant hoping that the pregnancy will solidify a partnership, making a couple out of two individuals. Many of them choose to forego an abortion because they have moral objections, and because they feel a commitment to this new person in the making. Most poignantly, in the vast majority of cases, giving birth while still a teenager is a pledge of hope, an acted-out wish that the lives of the next generation will be better than those of the current generation, that this young mother can give her child something she never had.[10]

It is teenagers' unwillingness (or inability) to be rational actors that   15
frustrates concerned adults: these young mothers seemingly refuse to think ahead and see how young they are, and how poor, and how dubious a prospect for marriage and fatherhood most of their young men are. Yet the thought of women being self-centered rational actors in the intimate realms of sex, childbearing, family, and home is a rather chilling one.[11] And one that few people really accept, no matter how militant their views in other areas of life. If some Americans are uneasy at the thought of eliminating all welfare for unwed teenage mothers, and if Republican congressmen suggest creating orphanages on a vast scale as a backup remedy, it is because they suspect that even the most draconian[12] changes will have very little effect on what really happens in bedrooms and in abortion clinics, except, as economists say, "at the margin."[13] Even the most militant conservatives would be hard pressed to imagine a scenario in which a passionate

---

[10] ... These are hopes — not expectations — of a better life. To put this in the starkest terms: for most teenage mothers, having a child represents very little in the way of losses and brings at least the potential that things might change for the better. Early motherhood occurs mostly among the discouraged and disadvantaged, and rarely forces a successful young woman off the path to a rewarding life. [Author's note]

[11] A cartoon in the *New Yorker* (September 3, 1979, p. 83) highlights this contradiction. It shows an affluent executive standing next to a desk, shaking the hand of his young child. The boy says, "Forget I'm your son, Dad. Give it to me straight." Father: "You're fired. Sorry, son. We're downsizing this family and we're going to have to let you go." [Author's note]

[12] *draconian:* Unusually severe or cruel.

[13] The phrase "at the margin" comes from the mathematical notion that changes in the value of a variable within a function ($f[x]$) can make a difference. The size of the difference, however, depends on the mathematical function — if it's even possible to model something as complex as joint and contingent decisions related to engaging in sex, using contraception, and having an abortion, all in the light of welfare policies. The difficulty of modeling this relationship, and of predicting the complex way in which welfare-policy changes may affect sexual and reproductive behavior, is suggested by the fact that the real value of welfare has declined considerably since 1973. (Some analysts put the decline, in real terms, on the order of 25 percent.) During this period the overall birthrate among teenagers did not change greatly, but the proportion of out-of-wedlock births did, and in exactly the opposite direction from what we would expect if rational economic calculations had been at play. [Author's note]

midnight embrace is interrupted at the last moment when the young woman insists that her partner don a condom because, after all, their state has just eliminated welfare benefits for mothers under twenty-one.[14] These competing views of family and marketplace, of men and women, of rationality and morality, of rights and obligations are very much front and center in nearly every aspect of American life these days. Teenage mothers and their babies reflect and illuminate these cultural and social wars because they pose so pointedly the contradictions inherent in our ways of thinking about them. To the extent that we view young mothers as young *women,* we want them to be sensitive to the needs of others, altruistic, committed to relationships and to nurturing the next generation. Yet to the extent that we see them as *poor* women, we want them to be careful, forward-thinking, attuned to the market, and prepared to invest in themselves, not in others. We want them to be both more and less selfish, in a society that is constantly redefining what "selfish" means. And because they are women, their lapses from "good" behavior are seen, as enormously threatening. Just as women who have abortions call into question the boundaries of self and other, of motherhood and marketplace, so, in a more subtle way, do teenage mothers.[15]

These tensions between self-supporting work in the marketplace and the needs of the family, between self and other, fuel a growing uneasiness over welfare. In a country with a long (though ambiguous) history of attention to vulnerable children, many citizens have come to accept unquestioningly the notion that some amorphous "we" — be it the community, society, voluntary agencies, or the government — have a moral obligation to make sure that children born in less-than-ideal circumstances are not condemned to failure before they can walk. But many of these same citizens are rightly concerned about how difficult and costly it is to help children like David. And some people worry that helping mothers like Michelle will merely produce a great many more babies like David.[16]

The public's apprehensions about poverty and dependency are in turn almost always intertwined with questions of race, given America's complex history on the matter. Many readers, in their mind's eye, will immediately see Michelle and her baby as African American, and this is understandable: the public quite commonly thinks of African Americans as prone to

[14]This image leaves it up to the young woman to interrupt the sexual embrace in order to "be responsible." Yet for the reasons hinted at here and examined in later chapters, young women are subject to a cultural handicap that assigns them virtually all of the responsibility for preventing pregnancy but relatively little power to do so. [Author's note]

[15]For the argument that abortion is a highly controversial issue precisely because it encapsulates in essential form a range of cultural and social conflicts, see Kristin Luker, *Abortion and the Politics of Motherhood* (Berkeley: University of California Press, 1984). [Author's note]

[16]Charles Murray, *Losing Ground: American Social Policy, 1950–1980* (New York: Basic Books, 1984). [Author's note]

bear children at early ages and out of wedlock. The image is not false — but it's not entirely true, either. African Americans, who make up only about 15 percent of the population of teenage girls, account for more than a third of all teenage mothers. And whereas six out of every ten white teenagers who give birth are unmarried, among black teenagers the ratio is nine out of ten.[17]

But although African Americans do account for a disproportionate share of births to teenagers and unmarried women, unmarried African American teenage mothers are not, statistically speaking, typical unwed teenage mothers. In 1990, for example, 57 percent of all babies born to unmarried teenage mothers were born to whites.[18] And since 1985, birthrates among unmarried white teenagers have been increasing rapidly, while those among unmarried black teens have been largely stable. (Women of all ages — both African Americans and whites, married as well as unmarried — have been having more babies since 1988).

Some commentators, among them Charles Murray, who has long been a critic of welfare policies and their putative effects on illegitimacy, say that the rising birthrates among white unmarried teenagers presage the growth of a white underclass, which will take its place alongside historically disadvantaged African Americans. In essence, Murray argues that as racial differences become less important in the life of the country, Americans will separate into two new nations — no longer black and white, but married and affluent on the one hand and unmarried and poor on the other.[19]

So Michelle at her algebra exam and David at his bead-game have come to represent a tangle of difficult issues — pertaining to sex, marriage, teenagers, race, dependency (as the condition of those who accept means-tested support from the government is conventionally labeled) — that confront the United States on the eve of a new century. If we queried a stranger on the street and a neighbor over coffee, we would not be surprised to find that they, like much of the American public, find early pregnancy a very serious problem. Or that they have concluded that doing

20

---

[17]U.S. Bureau of the Census, *General Population Characteristics, United States, 1990* (Washington, D.C.: Government Printing Office, 1992), p. 34; National Center for Health Statistics, *Advance Report of Final Natality Statistics* 43, no. 5 (1992), Supplement October 25, 1994, p. 48, Table 14, "Number, Rate, and Ratio of Births to Unmarried Women by Age and Race of Mother, United States, 1992." [Author's note]

[18]In 1990 there were 349,970 births to women aged fifteen to nineteen (360,615 if births to those younger than fifteen are considered). Of these, 199,896 (204,053 including those under fifteen) were to whites, 139,442 (145,682) to blacks, and 10,910 to women of other races. See National Center for Health Statistics, *Advance Report of Final Natality Statistics* 41, no. 9 (1990), Supplement February 25, 1993, Table 16. [Author's note]

[19]Charles Murray, "The Coming White Underclass," *Wall Street Journal,* October 29, 1993. It was William Julius Wilson who formulated the notion of the "declining significance of race"; see Wilson, *The Truly Disadvantaged: The Inner City, the Underclass, and Public Policy* (Chicago: University of Chicago Press, 1987). [Author's note]

something about "babies having babies" is one way of confronting these troubling issues.[20]

As with many issues that arouse a great deal of public worry and passion, that of "teenage pregnancy" is complex in nature and a challenge to conventional wisdom. Not only are Michelle and David more likely to be white than black, but as a high school student Michelle is younger than the statistically typical teenage mother. The majority of teenage mothers — almost six out of ten — are eighteen or nineteen when their babies are born, and they are legal adults in most states.[21] Furthermore, although many people worry that pregnancy among teenagers has attained "epidemic" proportions, teenage women right now are having babies at about the same rate as they have for most of the century. The "epidemic" years were the 1950s, when teenagers were having twice as many babies as they had had in previous decades but few people worried about them.[22] Even the teenage mothers who arouse the most concern — those who are under fifteen, the "babies having babies" — are simply doing what such "babies" did in the 1940s and 1950s, although they are more visible now than their counterparts were then.[23]

Of course, it is true that in the 1950s almost all teenage mothers (in fact, almost all mothers) were married, at least by the time their babies arrived. But within the broader context — the number of babies being born

[20]Roper Poll, 1986, in *Public Opinion Online,* LEXIS, Market Library, R-Poll File, Accession no. 0126650 (eight out of ten Americans surveyed thought teen pregnancy was a major problem); Riter Research Poll for the National Association of Private Psychiatric Hospitals, 1988, in *Public Opinion Online,* LEXIS, Market Library, R-Poll File, Accession no. 0109142 (a survey of people who knew a child or teen coping with unwanted pregnancy); Harris, 1985, in *Public Opinion Online,* LEXIS, Market Library, R-Poll File, Accession no. 0071940 (84 percent of the respondents said teenage pregnancy was a serious problem); Gordon Black for *USA Today,* 1987, LEXIS, Market Library, R-Poll File, Accession no. 0183794 (72 percent of those polled said teenage pregnancy was a very important problem); Riter Poll, 1988, LEXIS, Market Library, R-Poll File, Accession 0109089 (71 percent said teenage pregnancy was an extremely serious or very serious problem); Hart, 1987, LEXIS, Market Library, R-Poll File, Accession no. 0075049 (44 percent said that they would like to see a great deal more attention paid to the issue in election campaigns); Harris, 1986, LEXIS, Market Library, R-Poll File, Accession no. 0072806 (47 percent said they were very interested in the issue). [Author's note]

[21]In 1992, among women of all races, 505,415 babies were born to women aged fifteen to nineteen; 287,866 (56.9 percent) were born to women aged eighteen to nineteen. See National Center for Health Statistics, *Advance Report of Final Natality Statistics* 43, no. 5 (1992), Supplement October 25, 1994, p. 33. [Author's note]

[22]Prior to the baby boom years (1946–1964), the birthrate among teenagers was roughly 50–60 per thousand. At the peak of the boom, it rose to 97 per thousand. See Robert L. Heuser, *Fertility Tables for Birth Cohort by Color: United States, 1917–1973,* DHEW Publication (HRA)76–1152 (Rockville, Md.: National Center for Health Statistics, 1976); National Center for Health Statistics, *Advance Report of Final Natality Statistics* 38, no. 3 (1987), Supplement June 29, 1989, pp. 1–5. [Author's note]

[23]Heuser, *Fertility Tables for Birth Cohort by Color: United States, 1917–1973;* National Center for Health Statistics, *Advance Report of Final Natality Statistics* 38, no. 3 (1987), Supplement June 29, 1989, pp. 1–5. [Author's note]

to unmarried women — teenagers account for only a small subset of the problem. Two-thirds of unwed mothers are not teenagers, and in fact about one-fourth of America's unwed mothers are actually "no longer wed" mothers — that is, women who once were married but are not at the time their baby is born.[24]

Out-of-wedlock births are becoming more common around the globe. In Europe, the proportion of babies born out of wedlock has doubled and tripled in the past twenty years. Many people assume that this is because European welfare states support single mothers (and the poor overall) more generously than the U.S. government does. And this belief is prevalent in a more extreme form: some people believe that unwed mothers (especially teens) get pregnant and have a baby just to get a welfare check, and that consequently it's not surprising that European countries have increasing rates. But all industrialized countries, including the United States, are cutting back on welfare provision as a result of the tightening global economy, and out-of-wedlock births have responded by *increasing*. In the United States, the real value of a welfare check has been declining since 1973, even as women of all ages were choosing more often to become single mothers.[25] In fact, the nation with the sharpest increase in the proportion of babies born out of wedlock has been England, which has instituted conservative, antiwelfare policies: in the early 1970s England had a lower proportion of out-of-wedlock births than did the United States, but after twenty years of Thatcherism[26] the figure has quadrupled.[27]

Yet unmarried parents in England have not for the most part been teenagers. Throughout modern Europe, parenthood has historically been limited to older individuals, and teenage mothers have been found only in those countries on the periphery, such as Greece and Portugal. But the United States has always had an anomalous birth pattern. Compared to Europeans, Americans start their families at a younger age, and have done so for a very long time. In the 1950s, for example, there were more married teenagers in the United States, as a proportion of the age group, than in any other first-world country.[28]

[24]Larry Bumpass and James A. Sweet, "Children's Experience in Single-Parent Families: Implications of Cohabitation and Marital Transition," *Family Planning Perspectives* 21, no. 6 (November–December, 1989): 256–260. [Author's note]

[25]U.S. Congress, House Committee on Ways and Means, "Overview of Entitlement Programs, 1994" (Green Book), 103rd Congress, 2nd sess., July 15, 1994, p. 325. [Author's note]

[26]*Thatcherism:* The politics of Margaret Thatcher, England's prime minister from 1979 to 1990.

[27]U.K. Office of Population Censuses and Surveys, *Birth Statistics: Review of the Registrar General on Births and Patterns of Family Building in England and Wales, 1992* (London: HMSO, 1994), p. 49, Table 9.6, "Live Births: Country of Birth of Mother, Occurrence Inside/Outside Marriages and Previous Liveborn Children, 1982–1992." [Author's note]

[28]United Nations Department of International Economic and Social Affairs, "Adolescent Reproductive Behavior: Evidence from Developed Countries," *Population Studies* 1, no. 109 (1988). [Author's note]

Similarly, the rates of abortion among women of all ages are much   25
lower in most European countries than they are in the United States, despite the fact that (according to the limited data available) teenagers in
Great Britain, France, Germany, and Scandinavia are about as likely to be
sexually active as those in the United States. Although European teenagers
have sex — and, like their American counterparts, are increasingly doing so
outside marriage — they are much less likely to seek abortions, or to get
pregnant in the first place.[29]

Finally, despite what we all think we know about motherhood among
teenagers and its effects on later life, having a baby as a teenager does not
inevitably lead to abbreviated schooling and economic hardship, either for
the mother or for the child. According to some older sources of data, pregnant teenagers *were* very likely to "truncate" their education, as the experts
put it — but this curtailment resulted not so much from pregnancy per se as
from the strictures that banned pregnant teachers and students from school
grounds. Prior to 1975, when such policies were outlawed nationally, pregnant schoolgirls were "throwouts" more often than "dropouts."[30] Now that
secondary schools often have daycare facilities like the Sullivan Center, students who become pregnant in high school are increasingly likely to graduate and are beginning to do so at rates approaching those of nonpregnant
teens. This is all the more surprising since the kinds of young people who
get pregnant (and, in these days of legal abortion, *stay* pregnant) are usually
the kinds of young people who are floundering in school long before a pregnancy occurs.

So if the easy assumptions about early pregnancy (that there's an epidemic of early births, that unwed mothers and teenage mothers are one and
the same, that being a teenage mother is a short, quick route to poverty)
aren't quite tenable, what do we know about pregnancy among teenagers?
How did we come to think about it as a social problem? And what can we —
should we — do about it?

In most of the public discussion of early pregnancy and motherhood
that has taken place to date, the question about what we *should* do has pre-
dominated. Since pregnant teenagers in general and teenage mothers in
particular raise such troubling questions about sex and gender, poverty and
welfare, selfishness and altruism, self-indulgence and self-discipline, there
is something approaching a consensus about what they and we should do.
For their part, teenagers shouldn't have sex; if they have sex they should use
contraception; if they get pregnant despite using contraception, they should
have an abortion or give up the child for adoption; and failing all of that,

[29]Ibid., p. 23; Elise F. Jones, Jacqueline Forrest, Noreen Goldman, Stanley Henshaw,
Richard Lincoln, Jeannie Rosoff, Charles F. Westoff, and Deirdre Wulf, *Teenage Pregnancy in
Industrialized Countries* (New Haven: Yale University Press, 1986). [Author's note]
[30]*Ordway v. Hargraves*, 323 F. Supp. 1155 (1971). Title IX of the Educational Amend-
ments of 1972 also outlawed such policies. . . . [Author's note]

they should marry the fathers of their babies. In terms of that amorphous "we" of the public, our obligation is to use moral suasion, economic incentives, and the whole repertoire of public policy to enable and sometimes coerce teenagers to do the right thing.

The only problem with such a consensus about what teenagers should do is that it seems to be falling on remarkably deaf ears. The picture here is a mixed one: teens are having more sex at the same time that they are using more contraception and using it more effectively. Compared with teenagers of twenty years ago, today's teens are getting pregnant less often but are also more likely, once pregnant, to go ahead and have their babies. Moreover, these days very few teens give up their children for adoption, and relatively few get married in order to make their babies "legal" — the two really notable revolutions in this area of American life.

On the national level it seems that society has recreated a situation familiar to all families with teenagers: adults are expressing strong, even violent opinions about what teenagers should be doing, and teenagers are just not listening. Not surprisingly, U.S. public policy concerning early pregnancy reflects the rather limited set of options that frustrated adults have at their disposal in the face of recalcitrant teenagers. Easygoing, liberal people conclude that the problem is merely lack of information: if adults just tell teenagers more clearly what they should do and why it's good for them, they will do it. More old-fashioned and authority-conscious people conclude that the problem is one of incentives and controls: if adults just cut off teens' allowance and limit their access to those privileges that society has under its control, teenagers will straighten up and do the right thing.

Neither of these strategies is working very well at present, and it is probably a waste of time to expend much more energy in this book or elsewhere debating whether "soft" or "tough" love is more effective in combating early pregnancy. The real question here is why teenagers do what they do, and how the world looks from their vantage point. Clearly, teenagers are not ignorant victims, but neither are they rational actors. The declining value of a welfare check over the last twenty years, and the increasingly tight eligibility requirements for receiving one in the first place, should make it immediately clear that if teenagers are simply "investors" they are exceedingly foolish ones.

Luckily, more than two decades of research on early pregnancy have given us a rich and complex body of information about teenagers and why they do what they do. The short answer to why teenagers get pregnant and especially to why they continue those pregnancies is that a fairly substantial number of them just don't believe what adults tell them, be it about sex, contraception, marriage, or babies. They don't believe in adult conventional wisdom — not because they are defiant or because they are developmentally too immature to process the information (although many are one or the other and some are both), but because the conventional wisdom does not accord with the world they see around them. When adults talk to teenagers,

30

they draw on a lived reality that is now ten, twenty, thirty, forty or more years out of date. But today's teenagers live in a world whose demographic, social, economic, and sexual circumstances are almost unimaginable to older generations. Unless we can begin to understand that world, complete with its radically new circumstances, most of what adults tell teenagers will be just blather. . . .

How can society's concern about teenagers and their babies be mobilized to good effect? How can such anxiety be made less confused and inchoate — be made to reflect real problems? Most centrally, how can society ensure that this anxiety — which relates to sexuality, race, poverty, gender, and a changing world economy — not simply exacerbate the existing problems of young women and their babies? Both the Clinton administration and the Republican-dominated Congress, despite their many differences, agree that efforts to reduce the rates of pregnancy among teenagers should be the cornerstone of any welfare reform plan. But the ambitious schemes that have been proposed will almost surely fail, as their predecessors did, because they are based on a fundamental misunderstanding of the problem; and there is a very real risk that yet another failed program will lead to even more draconian and punitive measures aimed at young women.

Michelle and David represent a challenge to American social attitudes and policies, one whose contours are only now becoming clear. As we consider the young woman at her algebra exam, her baby at play at the Sullivan Center, and the young man who cannot earn enough money to support that woman and child, we owe them our clearest thinking. In trying to find a way to better their lives and the lives of others like them, American society will have to confront some hard choices — choices that it would be easier to avoid facing. But to give these young people anything less than the nation's best effort would be a tragedy. For better or for worse, they are America's future. . . .

In view of all the evidence that public policies have done a reasonably   35
good job of containing early pregnancy despite a vast increase in sexual activity among teens, the current conservative initiatives seem paradoxical at best and self-defeating at worst. There are powerful pressures to cut public funding for contraceptive programs, even as these programs are becoming recognized for the success story they are. Similarly, people who oppose abortions, much like people in the nineteenth century who opposed contraception, have been stymied in their attempts to make abortion either illegal or unpopular for the affluent. They have instead contented themselves with policies that make abortion more difficult for young people and poor people to obtain. Finally, just as we have begun to sort out which sex education techniques work and which ones don't, the very notion of sex education is more contested than it has ever been. In the face of accumulating evidence which suggests that more students than ever are receiving sex education and that well-designed programs can indeed modify adolescents' risk-taking

behavior, politically mobilized activists all over the United States are pushing for hasty adoption of abstinence-based programs before rigorous evaluation has been able to show whether they are capable of doing anything
other than making adults feel better.

To put this in the bluntest terms, society seems to have become committed to *increasing* the rates of pregnancy among teens, especially among
those who are poor and those who are most at risk. Affluent and successful
young women see real costs to early pregnancy and thus have strong incentives to avoid it;[31] but poor young women face greater obstacles, both internal and external. Cutting funding for public contraceptive clinics, imposing
parental-consent requirements, and limiting access to abortion all increase
the likelihood that a young woman will get pregnant and have a baby. Conversely, providing widespread contraceptive services (perhaps even making
the Pill available over the counter), extending clinic hours, and affording
greater access to abortion will give at least some poor young women an alternative to early childbearing.

The news is even grimmer when it comes to preventing or postponing
childbearing among teenagers who are not highly motivated in the first
place. Even as we amass evidence showing that early childbearing is not a
root cause of poverty in the United States, we are also realizing more clearly
that the high rate of early childbearing is a measure of how bleak life is for
young people who are living in poor communities and who have no obvious
arenas for success. Here, too, just as we are developing a better sense of
what it would take to offer these young women and men more choice in life,
the political temper of the times makes even modest investments in young
people seem like utopian dreams. Far from making lives easier for actual
and potential teenage parents, society seems committed to making things
harder.

A quarter-century of research on poverty and early childbearing has
yielded some solid leads on ways to reduce early pregnancy and childbearing. But because the young people involved have multiple problems, the solutions aren't cheap. In order to reduce the number of teenagers who want
babies, society would have to be restructured so that poor people in the
United States would no longer be the poorest poor people in the developed
world. Early childbearing would decrease if poor teenagers had better
schools and safer neighborhoods, and if their mothers and fathers had decent jobs so that teens could afford the luxury of being children for a while
longer. If in 1994 the United States had finally succeeded in creating a national health care system (becoming the last industrialized country to do so),
this change alone would have had a dramatic impact on poor people generally and poor women specifically. Providing wider access to health care, for

---

[31]Even in affluent communities boys and young men seem much less interested in preventing pregnancy, and this is a real problem. [Author's note]

example, would have eliminated some obstacles to contraception and possibly even to abortion. More fundamentally, it would have meant that young women and men, even if they did have babies and even if they did have them out of wedlock, could have afforded to raise them without going on welfare.

This is no time to be advocating expensive social programs, however. These days, policymakers seem inclined to shred what remains of the safety net, so the best that teenage mothers and potential teenage mothers can hope for is that programs which make life easier will not be totally eliminated in the drive to reduce the federal deficit. If the few employment programs that exist in the United States survive the budget cutting and if they can increase their outreach to young women, greater employment opportunities may reduce pregnancy rates. A 1978 evaluation of the federally funded Job Corps, for example, revealed that young men and women who were enrolled in the program tended to postpone childbearing and had fewer out-of-wedlock babies.[32] And women who found jobs through other federally funded programs seemed to have lower birthrates than women living in similar communities that had no such programs.[33] Some evidence also shows that macroeconomic forces can affect the rates of early childbearing: communities whose job markets are open to young women tend to have fewer teenage mothers.[34]

A widespread misconception is that many poor women live on welfare   40
instead of finding a job. In fact, most women on welfare use their grants to supplement the low wages they earn in the work force and to see them through periods of unemployment or poor health.[35] The kinds of jobs they have usually pay very little and provide no benefits; even if they worked full time and year round, their incomes would still be below the poverty level. Recent expansions in the Earned Income Tax Credit[36] made life a little easier for those at the bottom. Now, the cessation of AFDC[37] as an entitlement program and inevitable cutbacks in the Earned Income Tax Credit will make life on the bottom much harder. Their effects on early childbearing are unknown, but they are unlikely to reduce it. Although it is a cherished

---

[32]C. Mallar et al., *Evaluation of the Economic Impact of the Job Corps Program* (Princeton, N.J.: Mathematica, 1978). [Author's note]

[33]R. J. Olsen and G. Farkas, *The Effects of Economic Opportunity and Family Background on Adolescent Fertility among Low Income Blacks* (Rockville, Md.: U.S. Department of Health and Human Services, 1987). [Author's note]

[34]Elaine McCrate, "Employment Opportunities and Teenage Childbearing," paper delivered at first annual meeting of the Women's Policy Institute, Washington, D.C., May 1989. [Author's note]

[35]Katherine Edin and Christopher Jencks, "The Real Welfare Problem," *American Prospect* (1990): 31–50. [Author's note]

[36]*Earned Income Tax Credit:* A special tax break for low-income workers with children living at home.

[37]*AFDC:* Aid to Families with Dependent Children.

belief among conservatives that the level of available welfare affects child-bearing among teenagers, and among unmarried teens in particular, if this were true the rate of such childbearing would have declined dramatically over the past twenty years as the real value of welfare plummeted.

Society could also do a number of other things that, although they would not reduce early childbearing, would make the children of teenage parents better off, thereby reducing the ranks of disadvantaged and discouraged people at risk of being the next generation's teenage parents. These measures, too, have come to seem hopelessly utopian in the current political climate. For example, most other industrialized nations provide high-quality, publicly subsidized daycare for poor children; in the best of all possible worlds, the United States would, too. A national childcare and preschool system would ideally be part of the public schools, as is the case in France. Daycare workers would be trained like teachers and paid at similar levels. In this way, children born to young or poor parents would be challenged and educated from their earliest years. As things stand now, most poor mothers rely on a relative to provide daycare for their children. But this family-oriented system might actually motivate teens to have babies at an early age, since a young mother's claim on her female kin — usually her own mother — seems much more reasonable if she is sixteen than if she is twenty-four. If she knows that someone other than her mother will be able to help care for her children, she may wait a few years before having her first baby. . . .

The more one knows about early pregnancy and childbearing, the more skeptical one becomes that they correlate with poverty in any simple way. Poverty is not exclusively or even primarily limited to single mothers; most single mothers are not teenagers; many teenage mothers have husbands or partners; and many pregnant teenagers do not become mothers. The rates of pregnancy and childbearing among teenagers *are* a serious problem. But early childbearing doesn't make young women poor; rather, poverty makes women bear children at an early age. Society should worry not about some epidemic of "teenage pregnancy" but about the hopeless, discouraged, and empty lives that early childbearing denotes. Teenagers and their children desperately need a better future, one with brighter opportunities and greater rewards. Making the United States the kind of country in which — as in most European countries — early childbearing is rare would entail profound changes in public policy and perhaps even in American society as a whole. Such measures would be costly, and some of them would fail.

Any observer of the current scene would have to conclude that these days the chances of implementing costly social programs are extremely small. Americans seem bent on making the lives of teenage parents and their children even harder than they already are. Society has failed teenage parents all along the line — they are people for whom the schools, the health care system, and the labor market have been painful and unrewarding places. Now, it seems, young parents are being assigned responsibility for society's failures. Michelle and her baby have never needed help more, yet never have Americans been less willing to help and more willing to blame.

ENGAGING THE TEXT

1. Why does Luker begin with the story of Michelle and David? Is it important to you that they are real people? Why or why not?

2. In paragraphs 10–12 Luker sketches some faulty interpretations or "readings" of Michelle's actions. Review these and Luker's objections to them. Why does she bother to include such misinterpretations?

3. Throughout this selection, Luker challenges myths and "easy assumptions" about early pregnancy. Working in groups, identify each of the "misconceptions" and Luker's objection to it. To what extent do you agree with her analysis?

4. Luker points to a generation gap between teens and adults, claiming that teens are "just not listening" to adults (para. 30) and that they "just don't believe what adults tell them" (para. 32). How accurate do you think Luker's assessment is? Whom, if anyone, does Luker blame? Whom, if anyone, do you blame?

5. Working in small groups, list the "solutions" or partial solutions Luker would like to see. Debate whether or not they are likely to alleviate the problems often associated with teen pregnancy. Why is Luker skeptical about our society making rapid progress on this issue?

EXPLORING CONNECTIONS

6. How do Michelle and David think about their situation? How do you think someone in the 1950s, according to Stephanie Coontz (p. 55), might view Michelle's and David's situation? How might someone in America's past, according to John Gillis (p. 25), think about what Michelle and David do? How do you account for the differences?

7. Read "The Coming White Underclass" by Charles Murray (p. 81). To what extent does Murray treat unwed mothers as "rational actors" (para. 12)? How applicable to Murray's argument is Luker's criticism of the "rational actor" approach?

8. Charles Murray (p. 81) writes that illegitimacy among whites is reaching "epidemic" levels. Luker (paras. 21–22) points out that the real "epidemic" of teenage mothering was the 1950s (though almost all the 1950s mothers were married). Whose interpretation of the data do you find more sensible or insightful, and why?

9. The Troubletown cartoon on page 86 points out that one reason teens conceive is that they are "hella-mega-horny." What other motivations does Luker mention? Does she persuade you that these other motives are also important?

EXTENDING THE CRITICAL CONTEXT

10. Imagine, if you can, an adult or a parent whose voice would not be "just blather" (para. 32). What would such a person tell a teenager about "dubious conceptions"?

11. Review Luker's claim that society may be inadvertently increasing rates of teen pregnancy (paras. 35–36). Then assess the resources available in your city or town such as contraceptive clinics, sex education in the schools, and access to abortion. Do your findings match the trend Luker describes?

An Indian Story

ROGER JACK

This narrative concerns growing up away from one's father in one of the Indian cultures of the Pacific Northwest. It's also an intimate view of a nonnuclear family; the author is interested in the family not as a static set of defined relationships but as a social network that adapts to the ever-changing circumstances and needs of its members. Roger Jack's work has been published in several journals and anthologies, including Spawning the Medicine River, Earth Power Coming, *and* The Clouds Threw This Light. *"An Indian Story" appeared in* Dancing on the Rim of the World: An Anthology of Contemporary Northwest Native American Writing *(1990), edited by Andrea Lerner.*

Aunt Greta was always a slow person. Grandpa used to say she was like an old lady out of the old days who never hurried herself for anything, no matter what. She was only forty-five, heavyset, dark-complexioned, and very knowledgeable of the old ways, which made her seem even older. Most of the time she wore her hair straight up or in a ponytail that hung below her beltline. At home she wore pants and big, baggy shirts, but at ritual gatherings she wore her light blue calico dress, beaded moccasins, hair braided and clasped with beaded barrettes. Sometimes she wore a scarf on her head like ladies older than she. She said we emulate those we love and care for. I liked seeing her dressed for ceremonials. Even more, I liked seeing her stand before crowds of tribal members and guests translating the old language to the new for our elders, or speaking on behalf of the younger people who had no understanding of the Indian language. It made me proud to be her nephew and her son.

My mom died when I was little. Dad took care of me as best he could after that. He worked hard and earned good money as an accountant at the agency. But about a year after Mom died he married a half-breed Indian and this made me feel very uncomfortable. Besides, she had a child of her own who was white. We fought a lot — me and Jeffrey Pine — and then I'd get into trouble because I was older and was supposed to know better than to misbehave.

I ran away from home one day when everyone was gone — actually, I walked to Aunt Greta's and asked if I could move in with her since I had already spent so much time with her anyway. Then after I had gone to bed that night, Dad came looking for me and Aunt Greta told him what I had told her about my wanting to move in with her. He said it would be all right for a while, then we would decide what to do about it later. That was a long time ago. Now I am out of high school and going to college. Meanwhile, Jeffrey Pine is a high-school dropout and living with the folks.

Aunt Greta was married a long time ago. She married a guy named Mathew who made her very happy. They never had children, but when persistent people asked either of them what was wrong, they would simply reply they were working on it. Then Mathew died during their fifth year of marriage. No children. No legacy. After that Aunt Greta took care of Grandpa, who had moved in with them earlier when Grandma died. Grandpa wasn't too old, but sometimes he acted like it. I guess it came from that long, drawn-out transition from horse riding and breeding out in the wild country to reservation life in buggies, dirt roads, and cars. He walked slowly everywhere he went; he and Aunt Greta complemented each other that way.

Eventually, Aunt Greta became interested in tribal politics and threatened to run for tribal council, so Grandpa changed her Indian name from Little Girl Heart to Old Woman Walking, which he had called Grandma when she was alive. Aunt Greta didn't mind. In fact, she was proud of her new name. Little Girl Heart was her baby name, she said. When Grandpa died a couple of years later she was all alone. She decided tribal politics wasn't for her but began teaching Indian culture and language classes. That's when I walked into her life like a newborn Mathew or Grandpa or the baby she never had. She had so much love and knowledge to share, which she passed on to me naturally and freely; she received wages for teaching others. But that was gesticulation, she said.

My home and academic life improved a lot after I had moved in with Aunt Greta. Dad and his wife had a baby boy, and then a girl, but I didn't see too much of them. It was like we were strangers living a quarter mile from one another. Aunt Greta and I went on vacations together from the time I graduated from the eighth grade. We were trailblazers, she said, because our ancestors never traveled very far from the homeland.

The first year we went to Maryhill, Washington, which is about a tenhour drive from our reservation home in Park City, and saw the imitation

5

Stonehenge Monument. We arrived there late in the evening because we had to stop off in every other town along the road to eat, whether or not we were hungry, because that was Aunt Greta's way and Grandma's and all the other old ladies of the tribe. You have to eat to survive, they would say. It was almost dark when we arrived at the park. We saw the huge outlines of the massive hewn stones placed in a circular position and towering well over our heads. We stood small and in awe of their magnificence, especially seeing darkness fall upon us. Stars grew brighter and we saw them more keenly as time passed. Then they started falling, dropping out of the sky to meet us where we stood. I could see the power of Aunt Greta protruding through her eyes; if I had power I wouldn't have to explore, physically, the sensation I imagined her feeling. She said nothing for a long time. Then, barely audible, she murmured something like, "I have no teepee. I need no cover. This moment has been waiting for me here all this time." She paused. Then, "I wasn't sure what I would find here, but I'm glad we came. I was going to say something goofy like 'we should have brought the teepee and we could call upon Coyote to come and knock over these poles so we could drape our canvas over the skeleton and camp!' But I won't. I'm just glad we came here."

"Oh no, you aren't flipping out on me, are you?" I ribbed her. She always said good Indians remember two things: their humor and their history. These are the elements that dictate our culture and our survival in this crazy world. If these are somehow destroyed or forgotten, we would be doomed to extinction. Our power gone. And she had the biggest, silliest grin on her face. She said, "I want to camp right here!" and I knew she was serious.

We camped in the car, in the parking lot, that night. But neither of us slept until nearly daybreak. She told me Coyote stories and Indian stories and asked me what I planned to do with my life. "I want to be like you," I told her. Then she reminded me that I had a Dad to think about, too, and that maybe I should think about taking up his trade. I thought about a lot of stories I had heard about boys following in their father's footsteps — good or bad — and I told Aunt Greta that I wasn't too sure about living on the reservation and working at the agency all my life. Then I tried to sleep, keeping in mind everything we had talked about. I was young, but my Indian memory was good and strong.

On our way home from Maryhill we stopped off at Coyote's Sweat-   10
house down by Soap Lake. I crawled inside the small cavernous stone structure and Aunt Greta said to make a wish for something good. She tossed a coin inside before we left the site. Then we drove through miles of desert country and basalt cliffs and canyons, but we knew we were getting closer to home when the pine trees starting weeding out the sagebrush, and the mountains overrode the flatland.

Our annual treks after that brought us to the Olympic Peninsula on the coast and the Redwood Forest in northern California; Yellowstone National Park in Wyoming and Glacier Park in Montana; and the Crazy Horse / Mount Rushmore Monuments in South Dakota. We were careful in coordinating our trips with pow-wows too. Then we talked about going all the way to Washington, D.C., and New York City to see the sights and how the other half lived, but we never did.

After high-school graduation we went to Calgary for a pow-wow and I got into trouble for drinking and fighting with some local Indians I had met. They talked me into it. The fight occurred when a girlfriend of one of the guys started acting very friendly toward me. Her boyfriend got jealous and started pushing me around and calling me names; only after I defended myself did the others join in the fight. Three of us were thrown into the tribe's makeshift jail. Aunt Greta was not happy when she came to pay my bail. As a matter of fact, I had never seen her angry before. Our neighbors at the campground thought it was funny that I had been arrested and thrown into jail and treated the incident as an everyday occurrence. I sat in the car imagining my own untimely death. I was so sick.

After dropping the ear poles, I watched Aunt Greta take down the rest of the teepee with the same meticulousness with which we had set it up. She went around the radius of the teepee removing wooden stakes from the ground that held fast the teepee's body to the earth. Then she stood on a folding chair to reach the pins that held the face of the teepee together. She folded the teepee into halves as it hung, still, on the center pole. She folded it again and again until it grew clumsy and uneven, then she motioned for me to come and drop the pole so she could untie the fastener that made the teepee our home. Meanwhile, I had to drop all skeletal poles from the sky and all that remained were a few holes in the ground and flattened patches of grass that said we had been there. I stood looking over the crowd. Lots of people had come from throughout Canada and the northern states for the pow-wow. Hundreds of people sat watching the war dance. Other people watched the stick-games and card games. But what caught my attention were the obvious drunks in the crowd. I was "one of them" now.

Aunt Greta didn't talk much while we drove home. It was a long, lonely drive. We stopped only twice to eat cold, tasteless meals. Once in Canada and once stateside. When we finally got home, Aunt Greta said, "Good night," and went to bed. It was only eight o'clock in the evening. I felt a heavy calling to go talk to Dad about what had happened. So I did.

He was alone when I arrived at his house. As usual I walked through   15
the front door without knocking, but immediately heard him call out, "Son?"

"Yeah," I said as I went to sit on a couch facing him. "How did you know it was me?"

He smiled, said hello, and told me a father is always tuned in to his son. Then he sensed my hesitation to speak and asked, "What's wrong?"

"I got drunk in Calgary." My voice cracked. "I got into a fight and thrown in jail too. Aunt Greta had to bail me out. Now she's mad at me. She hasn't said much since we packed to come home."

"Did you tell her you were sorry for screwing up?" Dad asked.

"Yeah. I tried to tell her. But she clammed up on me."   20

"I wouldn't worry about it," Dad said. "This was bound to happen sooner or later. You really feel guilty when you take that first drink and get caught doing it. Hell, when I got drunk the first time, my Mom and Dad took turns preaching to me about the evils of drinking, fornication, and loose living. It didn't stop me though. I was one of those smart asses who had to have his own way. What you have to do is come up with some sort of reparation. Something that will get you back on Greta's good side."

"I guess that's what got to me. She didn't holler or preach to me. All the while I was driving I could feel her staring at me." My voice strengthened, "But she wouldn't say anything."

"Well, Son. You have to try to imagine what's going through her mind too. As much as I love you, you have been Greta's boy since you were knee-high to a grasshopper. She has done nothing but try to provide all the love and proper caring that she can for you. Maybe she thinks she has done something wrong in your upbringing. She probably feels more guilty about what happened than you. Maybe she hasn't said anything because she isn't handling this very well either." Dad became a little less serious before adding. "Of course, Greta's been around the block a time or two herself."

Stunned, I asked, "What do you mean?"

"Son, as much as Greta's life has changed, there are some of us who re-   25 member her younger days. She liked drinking, partying, and loud music along with war dancing, stick-games, and pow-wows. She got along wherever she went looking for a good time. She was one of the few who could do that. The rest of us either took to drinking all the time, or we hit the pow-wow circuit all straight-faced and sober, never mixing up the two. Another good thing about Greta was that when she found her mate and decided to settle down, she did it right. After she married Mathew she quit running around." Dad smiled, "Of course, Mathew may have had some influence on her behavior, since he worked for the alcohol program."

"I wonder why she never remarried?" I asked.

"Some women just don't," Dad said authoritatively. "But she never had a shortage of men to take care of. She had your Grandpa — and YOU!" We laughed. Then he continued, "Greta could have had her pick of any man on the reservation. A lot of men chased after her before she married, and a lot of them chased after her after Mathew died. But she never had time for them."

"I wonder if she would have gotten married again if I hadn't moved in on her?"

"That's a question only Greta can answer. You know, she may work in tribal programs and college programs, but if she had to give it all up for one reason in the world, it would be you." Dad became intent, "You are her bloodline. You know that? Otherwise I wouldn't have let you stay with her all these years. The way her family believes is that two sisters coming from the same mother and father are the same. Especially blood. After your Mother died and you asked to go and live with your Aunt, that was all right.

As a matter of fact, according to her way, we were supposed to have gotten married after our period of mourning was over."

"You — married to Aunt Greta!" I half-bellowed and again we laughed.   30

"Yeah. We could have made a hell of a family, don't you think?" Dad tried steadying his mood. "But, you know, maybe Greta's afraid of losing you too. Maybe she's afraid that you're entering manhood and that you'll be leaving her. Like when you go away to college. You are still going to college, aren't you?"

"Yeah. But I never thought of it as leaving her. I thought it more like going out and doing what's expected of me. Ain't I supposed to strike out on my own one day?"

"Yeah. Your leaving your family and friends behind may be expected, but like I said, 'you are everything to Greta,' and maybe she has other plans for you." Dad looked down to the floor and I caught a glimpse of graying streaks of hair on top of his head. Then he asked me which college I planned on attending.

"One in Spokane," I answered. "I ain't decided which one yet."

Then we talked about other things and before we knew it his missus   35 and the kids were home. Junior was nine, Anna Lee eight; they had gone to the last day of the tribe's celebration and carnival in Nespelem, which was what Aunt Greta and I had gone to Calgary to get away from for once. I sat quietly and wondered what Aunt Greta must have felt for my wrongdoing. The kids got louder as they told Dad about their carnival rides and games and prizes they had won. They shared their goodies with him and he looked to be having a good time eating popcorn and cotton candy.

I remembered a time when Mom and Dad brought me to the carnival. Grandpa and Grandma were with us. Mom and Dad stuck me on a big, black merry-go-round horse with flaming red nostrils and fiery eyes. Its long, dangling tongue hung out of its mouth. I didn't really want to ride that horse, but I felt I had to because Grandpa kept telling Mom and Dad that I belonged on a real horse and not some wooden thing. I didn't like the horse, when it hit certain angles it jolted and scared me even more. Mom and Dad offered me another ride on it, but I refused.

"Want some cotton candy?" Junior brought me back to reality. "We had fun going on the rides and trying to win some prizes. Here, you can have this one." He handed me one of his prizes. And, "Are you gonna stay with us tonight?"

I didn't realize it was after eleven o'clock.

"You can sleep in my bed," Junior offered.

"Yeah. Maybe I will, Little Brother." Junior smiled. I bade everyone   40 good night and went to his room and pulled back his top blanket revealing his Star Wars sheets. I chuckled at the sight of them before lying down and trying to sleep on them. This would be my first time sleeping away from Aunt Greta in a long time. I still felt tired from my drinking and the long drive home, but I was glad to have talked to Dad. I smiled in thinking that he said he loved me, because Indian men hardly ever verbalize their emotions. I went to sleep thinking how alone Aunt Greta must have felt after I had left home and promised myself to return there as early as I could.

I ate breakfast with the family before leaving. Dad told me one last thing that he and Aunt Greta had talked about sometime before. "You know, she talked about giving you an Indian name. She asked me if you had one and I said 'no.' She talked about it and I thought maybe she would go ahead and do it too, but her way of doing this is: boys are named for their father's side and girls are named for their mother's. Maybe she's still waiting for me to give you a name. I don't know."

"I remember when Grandpa named her, but I never thought of having a name myself. What was the name?" I asked.

"I don't remember. Something about stars."

Aunt Greta was sitting at the kitchen table drinking coffee and listening to an Elvis album when I got home. Elvis always made her lonesome for the old days or it cheered her up when she felt down. I didn't know what to say, but showed her the toy totem pole Junior had given me.

"That's cute," she said. "So you spent the night at the carnival?" 45

"No. Junior gave it to me," I explained. "I camped at Dad's."

"Are you hungry?" she was about to get up from the table.

"No. I've eaten." I saw a stack of pancakes on the stove. I hesitated another moment before asking, "What's with Elvis?"

"He's dead!" she said and smiled, because that's what I usually said to her. "Oh well, I just needed a little cheering up, I guess."

I remember hearing a story about Aunt Greta that happened a long 50 time ago. She was a teenager when the Elvis craze hit the reservation. Back then hardly any families had television sets, so they couldn't see Elvis. But when his songs hit the airwaves on the radio the girls went crazy. The guys went kind of crazy too — but they were pissed off crazy. A guy can't be that good looking and talented too, they claimed. They were jealous of Elvis. Elvis had a concert in Seattle and my Mom and Aunt Greta and a couple other girls went to it. Legend said that Elvis kissed Aunt Greta on the cheek during his performance and she took to heart the old "ain't never going to wash that cheek again" promissory and never washed her cheek for a long time and it got chapped and cracked until Grandpa and Grandma finally had to order her to go to the clinic to get some medicine to clean up her face. She hated them for a while, still swearing Elvis would be her number one man forever.

"How's your Dad?"

"He's all right. The kids were at the carnival when I got to his house, so we had a nice, long visit." I paused momentarily before adding, "And he told me some stories about you too."

"Oh?" she acted concerned even though her crow's feet showed.

"Yeah. He said you were quite a fox when you were young. And he said you probably could have had any man you wanted before you married

Uncle Mathew, and you could have had any man after Uncle Mathew died. So, how come you never snagged yourself another husband?"

Aunt Greta sat quietly for a moment. I could see her slumping into the   55 old way of doing things which said you thought things through before saying them. "I suppose I could have had my pick of the litter. It's just that after my old man died I didn't want anyone else. He was so good to me that I didn't think I could find any better. Besides, I had you and Grandpa to care for, didn't I? Have I ever complained about that?"

"Yeah," I persisted, "but haven't you ever thought about what might have happened if you had gotten married again? You might have done like Dad and started a whole new family. Babies, even!"

Aunt Greta was truly embarrassed. "Will you get away from here with talk like that. I don't need babies. Probably won't be long now and you'll be bringing them home for me to take care of anyhow."

Now I was embarrassed. We got along great after that initial conversation. It was like we had never gone to Calgary and I had never gotten on to her wrong side at all. We were like kids rediscovering what it was worth to have a real good friend go away for a while and then come back. To be appreciative of each other, I imagined Aunt Greta might have said.

Our trip to Calgary happened in July. August and September found me dumbfounded as to what to do with myself college-wise. I felt grateful that Indian parents don't throw out their offspring when they reach a certain age. Aunt Greta said it was too late for fall term and that I should rest my brain for a while and think about going to college after Christmas. So I explored different schools in the area and talked to people who had gone to them. Meanwhile, some of my friends were going to Haskell Indian Junior College in Kansas. Aunt Greta frowned upon my going there. She said it was too far away from home, people die of malaria there, and if you're not drunk, you're just crazy. So I stuck with the Spokane plan.

That fall Aunt Greta was invited to attend a language seminar in Port-   60 land. She taught Indian language classes when asked to. So we decided to take a side trip to our old campsite at Stonehenge. This time we arrived early in the morning and it was foggy and drizzling rain. The sight of the stones didn't provide the feeling we had experienced earlier. To us, the sight seemed to be just a bunch of rocks standing, overlooking the Columbia River, a lot of sagebrush, and two state highways. It didn't offer us feelings of mysticism and power anymore. Unhappy with the mood, Aunt Greta said we might as well leave; her words hung heavy on the air.

We stayed in Portland for a week and then made it a special point to leave late in the afternoon so we could stop by Stonehenge again at dusk. So with careful planning we arrived with just enough light to take a couple pictures and then darkness began settling in. We sat in the car eating baloney sandwiches and potato chips and drinking pop because we were tired of restaurant food and we didn't want people staring at us when we ate. That's where we were when an early evening star fell. Aunt Greta's mouth fell open, potato chip crumbs clung to the sides of her mouth. "This is it!" she squealed in English, Indian, and English again. "Get out of the car, Son," and she half pushed me out the door. "Go and stand in the middle of the circle and pray for something good to happen to you." I ran out and stood waiting and wondering what was supposed to happen. I knew better than to doubt Aunt Greta's wishes or superstitions. Then the moment came to pass.

"Did you feel it?" she asked as she led me back to the car.

"I don't know," I told her because I didn't think anything had happened.

"I guess it just takes some people a little longer to realize," she said.

I never quite understood what was supposed to have happened that day. A couple months later I was packing up to move to Spokane. I decided to go into the accounting business, like Dad. Aunt Greta quizzed me hourly before I was to leave whether I was all right and if I would be all right in the city. "Yeah, yeah," I heard myself repeating. So by the time I really was to leave she clued me in on her new philosophy: it wasn't that I was leaving her, it was just that she wouldn't be around to take care of me much anymore. She told me, "Good Indians stick together," and that I should search out our people who were already there, but not forget those who were still at home.

After I arrived in Spokane and settled down I went home all too frequently to actually experience what Aunt Greta and everyone told me. Then my studies got so intense that I didn't think I could travel home as much anymore. So I stayed in Spokane a lot more than before. Finally it got so I didn't worry as much about the folks at home. I would be out walking in the evening and know someone's presence was with me. I never bothered telephoning Dad at his office at the agency; and I never knew where or when Aunt Greta worked. She might have been at the agency or school. Then one day Dad telephoned me at school. After asking how I was doing, he told me why he was calling. "Your Aunt Greta is sick. The doctors don't know what's wrong with her yet. They just told me to advise her family of the possibility that it could be serious." I only half heard what he was saying, "Son, are you there?"

"Yeah."

"Did you hear me? Did you hear what I said?"

"Yeah. I don't think you have to worry about Aunt Greta though. She'll be all right. Like the old timers used to say, 'she might go away for a while, but she'll be back,'" and I hung up the telephone unalarmed.

ENGAGING THE TEXT

1. Give specific examples of how the narrator's extended family or kinship structure works to solve family problems. What problems does it seem to create or make worse?

65

2. What key choices does the narrator make in this story? How are these choices influenced by family members or family considerations?

3. Is the family portrayed here matriarchal, patriarchal, egalitarian, or something else? Explain. To what extent is parenting influenced by gender roles?

4. What events narrated in this story might threaten the survival of a nuclear family? How well does the extended family manage these crises?

5. How strong an influence does the narrator's father have on him? How can you explain the father's influence given how rarely the two see each other?

6. How do you interpret the narrator's reaction when he hears about Aunt Greta's failing health? What is implied in the story's closing lines?

Exploring Connections

7. In what ways is Roger Jack's family life similar to the lives of families of the past that John Gillis (p. 25) talks about?

8. Review Patricia Hill Collins's "Black Women and Motherhood" (p. 131). To what extent does Aunt Greta fulfill the roles of "othermother" and "community othermother" as defined by Collins? In what ways does her parenting depart from the African American models Collins describes?

Extending the Critical Context

9. This story celebrates the power of stories to connect people and to shape or affirm one's identity. Throughout, the narrator relates family stories about his father and his aunt that give him a clearer sense of himself and his relationship to those he loves. In a journal entry or essay, relate one or two family stories that are important to you and explain how they help you define who you are.

Envy

Bebe Moore Campbell

What would make a schoolgirl who is afraid to chew gum in class threaten to stab her teacher? In this narrative, at least, it's not grammar drills or sentence diagrams — it's anger, frustration, and envy caused by an absentee father. Like Gary Soto's "Looking for Work" (p. 42), this personal recollection of childhood combines the authenticity of actual experience with the artistry of expert storytelling. Bebe Moore Campbell (b. 1950) has published articles in many national newspapers and magazines, including The New York Times Magazine, Ebony, Working Mother, Ms., *and the* Los Angeles Times. *A frequent contributor to National Public Radio, she lives in Los Angeles, where she recently received the NAACP Image Award for outstanding literary work. Her books include* Your Blues Ain't Like Mine *(1992);* Brothers and Sisters *(1995); and* Sweet Summer: Growing Up With and Without My Dad *(1989), from which this selection is taken. Her latest is called* Singing in the Comeback Choir *(1998).*

The red bricks of 2239 North 16th Street melded into the uniformity of look-alike doors, windows, and brownstone-steps. From the outside our rowhouse looked the same as any other. When I was a toddler, the similarity was unsettling. The family story was that my mother and I were out walking on the street one day when panic rumbled through me. "Where's our house? Where's our house?" I cried, grabbing my mother's hand.

My mother walked me to our house, pointed to the numbers painted next to the door. "Twenty-two thirty-nine," she said, slapping the wall. "This is our house."

Much later I learned that the real difference was inside.

In my house there was no morning stubble, no long johns or Fruit of the Loom on the clothesline, no baritone hollering for keys that were sitting on the table. There was no beer in the refrigerator, no ball game on TV, no loud cussing. After dark the snores that emanated from the bedrooms were subtle, ladylike, little moans really.

Growing up, I could have died from overexposure to femininity.   5
Women ruled at 2239. A grandmother, a mother, occasionally an aunt, grown-up girlfriends from at least two generations, all the time rubbing up against me, fixing my food, running my bathwater, telling me to sit still and be good in those grown-up, girly-girl voices. Chanel and Prince Matchabelli wafting through the bedrooms. Bubble bath and Jergens came from the bathroom, scents unbroken by aftershave, macho beer breath, a good he-man funk. I remember a house full of 'do rags and rollers, the soft, sweet allure of Dixie peach and bergamot;[1] brown-skinned queens wearing pastel housecoats and worn-out size six-and-a-half flip-flops that slapped softly against the wood as the royal women climbed the stairs at night carrying their paperbacks to bed.

The outside world offered no retreat. School was taught by stern, old-maid white women with age spots and merciless gray eyes; ballet lessons, piano lessons, Sunday school, and choir were all led by colored sisters with a hands-on-their-hips attitude who cajoled and screeched in distaff[2] tongues.

And what did they want from me, these Bosoms? Achievement! This desire had nothing to do with the pittance they collected from the Philadelphia

[1]*bergamot:* A citrus tree with a fragrant fruit.
[2]*distaff:* Female, maternal.

Board of Education or the few dollars my mother paid them. Pushing little colored girls forward was in their blood. They made it clear: a life of white picket fences and teas was for other girls to aspire to. I was to *do* something. And if I didn't climb willingly up their ladder, they'd drag me to the top. Rap my knuckles hard for not practicing. Make me lift my leg until I wanted to die. Stay after school and write "I will listen to the teacher" five hundred times. They were not playing. "Obey them," my mother commanded.

When I entered 2B — the Philadelphia school system divided grades into A and B — in September 1957, I sensed immediately that Miss Bradley was not a woman to be challenged. She looked like one of those evil old spinsters Shirley Temple[3] was always getting shipped off to live with; she was kind of hefty, but so tightly corseted that if she happened to grab you or if you fell against her during recess, it felt as if you were bouncing into a steel wall. In reality she was a sweet lady who was probably a good five years past her retirement age when I wound up in her class. Miss Bradley remained at Logan for one reason and one reason only: she was dedicated. She wanted her students to learn! learn! learn! Miss Bradley was halfway sick, hacking and coughing her lungs out through every lesson, spitting the phlegm into fluffy white tissues from the box on her desk, but she was *never* absent. Each day at three o'clock she kissed each one of her "little pupils" on the cheek, sending a faint scent of Emeraude home with us. Her rules for teaching children seemed to be: love them; discipline them; reward them; and make sure they are clean.

Every morning she ran a hygiene check on the entire class. She marched down the aisle like a stormtrooper, rummaging through the ears of hapless students, checking for embedded wax. She looked under our fingernails for dirt. Too bad on you if she found any. Once she made David, a stringy-haired white boy who thought Elvis Presley was a living deity and who was the most notorious booger-eater in the entire school, go to the nurse's office to have the dirt cleaned from under his fingernails. Everybody knew that what was under David's fingernails was most likely dried-up boogies and not dirt, but nobody said anything.

If she was death on dirt and earwax, Miss Bradley's specialty was head-lice patrol. Down the aisles she stomped in her black Enna Jettick shoes,[4] stopping at each student to part strands of blond, brown, or dark hair, looking for cooties. Miss Bradley would flip through plaits, curls, kinks — the woman was relentless. I always passed inspection. Nana put enough Nu Nile in my hair to suffocate any living creature that had the nerve to come tipping up on my scalp. Nu Nile was the official cootie killer. I was clean, wax-free, bug-free, and smart. The folder inside my desk contained a stack of spelling and arithmetic papers with A's emblazoned across the top, gold

10

---

[3]*Shirley Temple:* Famous child actor (b. 1928); later, Shirley Temple Black, U.S. ambassador.

[4]*Enna Jettick shoes:* Brand name of "sensible" women's shoes.

stars in the corner. Miss Bradley always called on me. She sent me to run errands for her too. I was her pet.

When Mrs. Clark, my piano teacher and my mother's good friend, told my mother that Logan Elementary School was accepting children who didn't live in the neighborhood, my mother immediately enrolled Michael and later me. "It's not crowded and it's mixed," she told a nodding, smiling Nana. The fact that Logan was integrated was the main reason Michael and I were sent there. Nana and Mommy, like most upwardly mobile colored women, believed that to have the same education as a white child was the first step up the rocky road to success. This viewpoint was buttressed by the fact that George Washington Carver, my neighborhood school, was severely overcrowded. Logan was just barely integrated, with only a handful of black kids thrown in with hordes of square-jawed, pale-eyed second-generation Ukrainians whose immigrant parents and grandparents populated the neighborhood near the school. There were a few dark-haired Jews and aristocratic-looking WASPs too. My first day in kindergarten it was Nana who enthusiastically grabbed Michael's and my hands, pulling us away from North Philly's stacked-up row-houses, from the hucksters whose wagons bounced down the streets with trucks full of ripe fruits and vegetables, from the street-corner singers and jitterbugs who filled my block with all-day doo-wahs. It was Nana who resolutely walked me past the early-morning hordes of colored kids heading two blocks away to Carver Elementary School, Nana who pulled me by the hand and led me in another direction.

We went underground at the Susquehanna and Dauphin subway station, leaving behind the unremitting asphalt and bricks and the bits of paper strewn in the streets above us. We emerged at Logan station, where sunlight, brilliant red and pink roses and yellow chrysanthemums, and neatly clipped lawns and clean streets startled me. There were robins and blue jays flying overhead. The only birds in my neighborhood were sparrows and pigeons. Delivering me at the schoolyard, Nana firmly cupped my chin with her hand as she bent down to instruct me. "Your mother's sending you up here to learn, so you do everything your teacher tells you to, okay?" To Michael she turned and said, "You're not up here to be a monkey on a stick." Then to both of us: "Don't talk. Listen. Act like you've got some home training. You've got as much brains as anybody up here. Do you know that? All right now. Make Nana proud of you."

A month after I returned from Pasquotank County,[5] I sat in Miss Bradley's classroom on a rainy Monday watching her write spelling words on the blackboard. The harsh scurr, scurr of Miss Bradley's chalk and the tinny sound the rain made against the window took my mind to faraway places. I couldn't get as far away as I wanted. Wallace, the bane of the whole class, had only moments earlier laid the most gigunda fart in history,

---

[5]*Pasquotank County:* County in North Carolina where Campbell's father lived; she visited him there every summer.

one in a never-ending series, and the air was just clearing. His farts were silent wonders. Not a hint, not the slightest sound. You could be in the middle of a sentence and then wham! bam! Mystery Funk would knock you down.

Two seats ahead of me was Leonard, a lean colored boy from West Philly who always wore suits and ties to school, waving his hand like a crazy man. A showoff if ever there was one.

I was bored that day. I looked around at the walls. Miss Bradley had dec-   15
orated the room with pictures of the ABCs in cursive. Portraits of the presidents were hanging in a row on one wall above the blackboard. On the bulletin board there was a display of the Russian satellite, *Sputnik I,* and the American satellite, *Explorer I.* Miss Bradley was satellite-crazy. She thought it was just wonderful that America was in the "space race" and she constantly filled our heads with space fantasies. "Boys and girls," she told us, "one day man will walk on the moon." In the far corner on another bulletin board there was a Thanksgiving scene of turkeys and pilgrims. And stuck in the corner was a picture of Sacajawea.[6] Sacajawea, Indian Woman Guide. I preferred looking at Sacajawea over satellites any day.

Thinking about the bubble gum that lay in my pocket, I decided to sneak a piece, even though gum chewing was strictly forbidden. I rarely broke the rules. Could anyone hear the loud drumming of my heart, I wondered, as I slid my hand into my skirt pocket and felt for the Double Bubble? I peeked cautiously to either side of me. Then I managed to unwrap it without even rustling the paper; I drew my hands to my lips, coughed, and popped the gum in my mouth. Ahhh! Miss Bradley's back was to the class. I chomped down hard on the Double Bubble. Miss Bradley turned around. I quickly packed the gum under my tongue. My hands were folded on top of my desk. "Who can give me a sentence for 'birthday'?" Leonard just about went nuts. Miss Bradley ignored him, which she did a lot. "Sandra," Miss Bradley called.

A petite white girl rose obediently. I liked Sandra. She had shared her crayons with me once when I left mine at home. I remember her drawing: a white house with smoke coming out of the chimney, a little girl with yellow hair like hers, a mommy, a daddy, a little boy, and a dog standing in front of the house in a yard full of flowers. Her voice was crystal clear when she spoke. There were smiles in that voice. She said, "My father made me a beautiful dollhouse for my birthday."

The lump under my tongue was suddenly a stone and when I swallowed, the taste was bitter. I coughed into a piece of tablet paper, spit out the bubble gum, and crumpled up the wad and pushed it inside my desk. The center of my chest was burning. I breathed deeply and slowly. Sandra sat down as demurely as a princess. She crossed her ankles. Her words

[6]*Sacajawea:* A Shoshone Indian woman (1786–1812), captured and sold to a white man; she became the famous guide of the 1804 Lewis and Clark expedition.

came back to me in a rush. "Muuuy fatha made me a bee-yoo-tee-ful doll-house." Miss Bradley said, "Very good," and moved on to the next word. Around me hands were waving, waving. Pick me! Pick me! Behind me I could hear David softly crooning, "You ain't nothin' but a hound dog, cryin' all the time." Sometimes he would stick his head inside his desk, sing Elvis songs, and pick his boogies at the same time. Somebody was jabbing pins in my chest. Ping! Ping! Ping! I wanted to holler, "Yowee! Stop!" as loud as I could, but I pressed my lips together hard.

"Now who can give me a sentence?" Miss Bradley asked. I put my head down on my desk and when Miss Bradley asked me what was wrong I told her that I didn't feel well and that I didn't want to be chosen. When Leonard collected the homework, I shoved mine at him so hard all the papers he was carrying fell on the floor.

Bile was still clogging my throat when Miss Bradley sent me into the cloakroom to get my lunchbox. The rule was, only one student in the cloakroom at a time. When the second one came in, the first one had to leave. I was still rummaging around in my bookbag when I saw Sandra.   20

"Miss Bradley said for you to come out," she said. She was smiling. That dollhouse girl was always smiling. I glared at her.

"Leave when I get ready to," I said, my words full of venom.

Sandra's eyes darted around in confusion. "Miss Bradley said . . ." she began again, still trying to smile as if she expected somebody to crown her Miss America or something and come take her picture any minute.

In my head a dam broke. Terrible waters rushed out. "I don't care about any Miss Bradley. If she messes with me I'll, I'll . . . I'll take my butcher knife and stab her until she bleeds." What I lacked in props I made up for in drama. My balled-up hand swung menacingly in the air. I aimed the invisible dagger toward Sandra. Her Miss America smile faded instantly. Her eyes grew round and frightened as she blinked rapidly. "Think I won't, huh? Huh?" I whispered, enjoying my meanness, liking the scared look on Sandra's face. Scaredy cat! Scaredy cat! Muuuy fatha made me a bee-yoo-tee-full dollhouse. "What do you think about that?" I added viciously, look-ing into her eyes to see the total effect of my daring words.

But Sandra wasn't looking at me. Upon closer inspection, I realized that   25 she was looking *over* me with sudden relief in her face. I turned to see what was so interesting, and my chin jammed smack into the Emeraude-scented iron bosom of Miss Bradley. Even as my mind scrambled for an excuse, I knew I was lost.

Miss Bradley had a look of horror on her face. For a minute she didn't say anything, just stood there looking as though someone had slapped her across the face. Sandra didn't say anything. I didn't move. Finally, "Would you mind repeating what you just said, Bebe."

"I didn't say anything, Miss Bradley." I could feel my dress sticking to my body.

"Sandra, what did Bebe say?"

Sandra was crying softly, little delicate tears streaming down her face. For just a second she paused, giving a tiny shudder. I rubbed my ear vigorously, thinking, "Oh, please . . ."

"She said, she said, if you bothered with her she would cut you with her knife."   30

"Unh unh, Miss Bradley, I didn't say that. I didn't. I didn't say anything like that."

Miss Bradley's gray eyes penetrated mine. She locked me into her gaze until I looked down at the floor. Then she looked at Sandra.

"Bebe, you and I had better go see the principal."

The floor blurred. The principal!! Jennie G., the students called her with awe and fear. As Miss Bradley wrapped her thick knuckles around my forearm and dutifully steered me from the cloakroom and out the classroom door, I completely lost what little cool I had left. I began to cry, a jerky, hiccuping, snot-filled cry for mercy. "I didn't say it. I didn't say it," I moaned.

Miss Bradley was nonplussed. Dedication and duty overruled compassion. Always. "Too late for that now," she said grimly.   35

Jennie G.'s office was small, neat, and dim. The principal was dwarfed by the large brown desk she sat behind, and when she stood up she wasn't much bigger than I. But she was big enough to make me tremble as I stood in front of her, listening to Miss Bradley recount the sordid details of my downfall. Jennie G. was one of those pale, pale vein-showing white women. She had a vocabulary of about six horrible phrases, designed to send chills of despair down the spine of any young transgressor. Phrases like "We'll just see about that" or "come with me, young lady," spoken ominously. Her face was impassive as she listened to Miss Bradley. I'd been told that she had a six-foot paddle in her office used solely to beat young transgressors. Suppose she tried to beat me? My heart gave a lurch. I tugged rapidly at my ears. I longed to suck my thumb.

"Well, Bebe, I think we'll have to call your mother."

My mother! I wanted the floor to swallow me up and take me whole. My mother! As Jennie G. dialed the number, I envisioned my mother's face, clouded with disappointment and shame. I started crying again as I listened to the principal telling my mother what had happened. They talked for a pretty long time. When she hung up, ole Jennie G. flipped through some paper on her desk before looking at me sternly.

"You go back to class and watch your mouth, young lady."

As I was closing the door to her office I heard her say to Miss Bradley, "What can you expect?"   40

"Ooooh, you're gonna get it girl," is how Michael greeted me after school. Logan's colored world was small, and news of my demise had blazed its way through hallways and classrooms, via the brown-skinned grapevine. Everyone from North Philly, West Philly, and Germantown knew about my crime. The subway ride home was depressing. My fellow commuters kept coming up to me and asking, "Are you gonna get in trouble?" Did they think my mother would give me a reward or something? I stared at the floor for most of the ride, looking up only when the train came to a stop and the doors hissed open. Logan. Wyoming. Hunting Park. Each station drew me closer to my doom, whatever that was going to be. "What can you expect?" I mulled over those words. What did she mean? My mother rarely spanked, although Nana would give Michael or me, usually Michael, a whack across the butt from time to time. My mother's social-worker instincts were too strong for such undignified displays; Doris believed in talking things out, which was sometimes worse than a thousand beatings. As the train drew closer to Susquehanna and Dauphin I thought of how much I hated for my mother to be disappointed in me. And now she would be. "What can you expect?"

Of me? Didn't Jennie G. know that I was riding a subway halfway across town as opposed to walking around the corner to Carver Elementary School, for a reason: the same reason I was dragged away from Saturday cartoons and pulled from museum to museum, to Judimar School of Dance for ballet (art class for Michael), to Mrs. Clark for piano. The Bosoms wanted me to Be Somebody, to be the second generation to live out my life as far away from a mop and scrub brush and Miss Ann's floors as possible.

My mother had won a full scholarship to the University of Pennsylvania. The story of that miracle was a treasured family heirloom. Sometimes Nana told the tale and sometimes my mother described how the old Jewish counselor at William Penn High School approached her and asked why a girl with straight E's (for "excellent") was taking the commercial course. My mother replied that Nana couldn't afford to send her to college, that she planned to become a secretary. "Sweetheart, you switch to academic," the woman told her. "You'll get to college." When her graduation day approached, the counselor pulled her aside. "I have two scholarships for you. One to Cheyney State Teacher's College and the other to the University of Pennsylvania." Cheyney was a small black school outside of Philadelphia. My mother chose Penn. I had been born to a family of hopeful women. One miracle had already taken place. They expected more. And now I'd thrown away my chance. Michael, who was seated next to me on the subway and whose generosity of spirit had lasted a record five subway stops, poked me in my arm. "Bebe," he told me gleefully, "your ass is grass."

Nana took one look at my guilty face, scowled at me, and sucked her teeth until they whistled. My mother had called her and told her what happened and now she was possessed by a legion of demons. I had barely entered the room when she exploded. "Don't. Come. In. Here. Crying," Nana said, her voice booming, her lips quivering and puffy with anger. When Nana talked in staccato language she was beyond pissed off. Waaaay beyond. "What. Could. Possess. You. To. Say. Such. A. Thing? Embarrassingyourmotherlikethatinfrontof *those people!*" Before I could answer she started singing some Dinah Washington[7] song, real loud. Volume all the way up. With every word she sang I sank deeper and deeper into gloom.

Later that evening, when my mother got home and Aunt Ruth,   45
Michael's mother, came to visit, the three women lectured me in unison. The room was full of flying feathers. Three hens clucking away at me, their breasts heaving with emotion. Cluck! Cluck! Cluck! How could I have said such a thing? What on earth was I thinking about? Cluck! Cluck! Cluck! A knife, such a *colored* weapon.

"But I didn't do anything," I wailed, the tears that had been trickling all day now falling in full force.

"Umph, umph, umph," Nana said, and started singing. Billie Holiday[8] this time.

"You call threatening somebody with a knife nothing?" Aunt Ruth asked. Ruth was Nana's middle girl. She was the family beauty, as pretty as Dorothy Dandridge[9] or Lena Horne.[10] Now her coral lips were curled up in disdain and her Maybelline eyebrows were raised in judgment against me. "They expect us to act like animals and you have to go and say that. My God."

Animals. Oh. Oh. Oh.

My mother glared at her sister, but I looked at Aunt Ruth in momen-   50
tary wonder and appreciation. Now I understood. The unspoken rule that I had sensed all my life was that a colored child had to be on her best behavior whenever she visited the white world. Otherwise, whatever opportunity was being presented would be snatched away. I had broken the rule. I had committed the unpardonable sin of embarrassing my family in front of *them.* Sensing my remorse and shame, Mommy led me out of the kitchen. We sat down on the living room sofa; my mother took my hand, "Bebe, I want you to go to your room and think about what you've done. I don't understand your behavior. It was very hard for me to get you in Logan." She drew a breath. I drew a breath and looked into the eyes of a social worker. "I'm extremely disappointed in you."

I didn't go straight to my room. Instead I sneaked into Michael's room, which overlooked Mole Street, the tiny, one-sided alley of narrow rowhouses that faced the backyards of 16th Street. Michael and I usually played on the "back street." Alone in Michael's room with the window open, I could hear Mr. Watson, our neighbor, hollering at one of his kids. Why had I said what I said? What had possessed me? Then I remembered. "Muuuy fatha made me a bee-yoo-tee-ful dollhouse for muuuuy birthday." Some-

---

[7]*Dinah Washington:* Blues singer, born Ruth Jones (1924–1963).

[8]*Billie Holiday:* Celebrated jazz singer (1915–1959).

[9]*Dorothy Dandridge:* Glamorous film star (1923–1965).

[10]*Lena Horne:* Singer, actor (b. 1917); first black woman vocalist to be featured with a white band.

thing pinched me inside my chest when I heard those words. Pain oozed from my heart like a tube of toothpaste bursting open, going every whichaway. Blue-eyes kept yapping away with her golden hair and her goofy little smile. Who cared what her fatha did? Who cared? I couldn't help it. When she came into the cloakroom I got mad all over again. When I said I had a knife, she looked just like Grandma Mary's chickens. Scared. And my chest stopped hurting. Just stopped.

Mr. Watson's baritone voice was a seismic rumble echoing with the threat of upheaval, violence. His words floated over Mole Street and into the bedroom window. Whoever was in trouble over there was really gonna get it. None of this "go to your room" stuff. None of this corny "I'm disappointed in you" stuff. Mr. Watson was getting ready to beat somebody's ass.

Adam's. He was the youngest and one of my playmates. I could tell by his pleading voice. "Please, Daddy. I won't do it anymore, Daddy. I'm sorry, Daddy."

Michael came into the room. "What are you doing?" he whispered.

"Shhh. Adam's getting a whipping." 55

"You better go to your room before Aunt Doris comes upstairs."

"Shhhh."

My playmate's misery took my mind off my own. His father's exotic yelling hypnotized me. From downstairs I could hear the hens, still clucking away. Michael and I sat quietly, not making a sound. Mr. Watson's voice sounded so foreign coming into our house. For a moment I pretended that his anger was emanating from Michael's bedroom, and I remembered how only last year he got mad and ran after all of us kids — Jackie, Jane, and Adam, his own three, and me. His face was covered with shaving cream and he held a razor in one hand and a thick leather belt in the other. I don't recall what we had done, but I remember him chasing us and yelling ferociously, "This belt's got your name on it too, Miss Bebe!" And I recall that I was thrilled when the leather grazed my hincy with the vengeance of a father's wrath.

My mind drifted back a few years. The memory was vague and fuzzy. When I was four or five I was playing on Mole Street when my ten-year-old neighbor, a boy named Buddy, asked me to come inside his yard. He was sitting on an old soda crate. "Come closer," he told me. "Wanna play doctor?"

"Uh huh." 60

"You can examine me."

I told my mother, prattling on about the "game" I had played. She sat me down on her bed. "Did he touch your private parts?"

"Nope." Why was Mommy's face so serious?

"Did you touch his?"

"I touched his zipper." Had I done something wrong? 65

Nana went into hysterics, singing and screeching like a wild woman. "Mother, just calm down," Mommy told her.

Mommy was cool, every inch the social worker; she took my hand and we walked down the street to Buddy's house. He was in his yard making a scooter out of the crate. "Buddy," my mother said softly. When he saw the two of us, he dropped his hammer. "Buddy, I want to talk with you."

My mother questioned him. Calmly put the fear of God in him. Warned him of penalties for a repeat performance. And that was that. Not quite. Weeks, maybe months later, my father came to visit me, one of his pop-in, no-real-occasion visits. My mother, my father, and I were sitting in his car and she told him about my playing doctor. His leg shot out in wild, uncontrollable spasms. His face became contorted and he started yelling. Nana's screeching paled in contrast. This was rage that my mother and Nana could not even begin to muster. And it was in my honor. This energy was for my avengement, my protection. Or should have been. But the sound of his fury frightened me. I remember angling away from my father, this man who was yelling like an animal in pain. I leaned toward my mother, and she put one arm around me and with her other hand tried to pat my father's shoulder, only he snatched [it] away. He leaned forward and started reaching for his chair.[11] "I may not be able to walk, goddammit, but I can tear that little son of a bitch's ass up."

My mother kept talking very softly, saying, "No, no, no. It's all right. He's just a kid. I took care of it. It's okay." I leaned away from my father's anger, his determination. He frightened me. But the rage was fascinating too. And after a while, when my father was shouting only a little, I moved closer to him. I wanted to see the natural progression of his hot words. If he snatched his wheelchair out of the backseat and rolled up to Buddy's house, what would he do? What should he do in my honor? My mother calmed my father. His shouting subsided. I was relieved. I was disappointed.

"Hey" — I suddenly heard Michael's persistent voice — "ain't you glad   70 Mr. Watson ain't your father?" I felt Michael's hands, shaking my shoulder. "Ain't you?"

I didn't answer. I was thinking about Miss Bradley, Jennie G., Aunt Ruth, Nana, and Mommy. All these women with power over me. I could hear Mrs. Watson telling her husband that enough was enough and then the baritone telling her he knew when to stop and Adam letting out another feeble little yelp. "Muuuy fatha made me a bee-yoo-tee-ful dollhouse." Maybe my mother would write my daddy and tell him how bad I had been. Maybe he would get so mad he would get into his car and drive all the way to Philly just to whip my behind. Or tell me he was disappointed in me. Either one.

The Bosoms decided to forgive me. My mother woke me up with a kiss and a snuggle and then a crisp, "All right, Bebe. It's a brand-new day. Forget about yesterday." When I went to get a bowl of cereal that morning, my

---

[11]*his chair:* Campbell's father had lost the use of his legs in an automobile accident.

Aunt Ruth was sitting in the kitchen drinking coffee and reading the newspaper. She had spent the night. "Did you comb your hair?" she asked me.

I nodded.

"That's not what I call combed. Go get me the comb and brush."

She combed out my hair and braided it all over again. This time there   75
were no wispy little ends sticking out. "Now you look nice," she said. "Now you look like a pretty girl, and when you go to school today, act like a pretty girl. All right?"

I nodded.

Last night Nana had hissed at me between her teeth. "If you want to behave like a little *heathen,* if you want go up there acting like a, a . . . *monkey on a stick* . . . well, thenyoucangotoschoolrightaroundthecornerand I'llwalkyoubackhomeandI'llcomeandgetyouforlunchnowyou*behave*yourself!" But today she was sanguine, even jovial, as she fixed my lunch. She kissed me when I left for school.

On my way out the door my mother handed me two elegant letters, one to Miss Bradley and the other to Jennie G., assuring them that I had an overactive imagination, that I had no access to butcher knives or weapons of any kind, that she had spoken to me at length about my unfortunate outburst, and that henceforth my behavior would be exemplary. These letters were written on her very best personalized stationery. The paper was light pink and had "D.C.M." in embossed letters across the top. Doris C. knew lots of big words and she had used every single one of them in those letters. I knew that all of her *i*'s were dotted and all of her *t*'s were crossed. I knew the letters were extremely dignified. My mother was very big on personal dignity. Anyone who messed with her dignity was in serious trouble.

I was only five when an unfortunate teller at her bank called her by her first name loud enough for the other customers to hear. My mother's body stiffened when she heard, "Doris, oh Doris," coming from a girl almost young enough to be her child.

"Are you talking to *me,* dear?" Her English was so clipped, her words so   80 razor sharp she could have taken one, stabbed the teller, and drawn blood. The girl nodded, her speckled green eyes wide and gaping, aware that something was going on, not quite sure what, and speechless because she was no match at all for this imperious little brown-skinned woman. "The people in *my* office all call me *Mrs. Moore.*"

And she grabbed me by the hand and we swept out of the bank. Me and Bette Davis.[12] Me and Claudia McNeil.[13] People stepped aside to let us pass.

---

[12]*Bette Davis:* Actor (1908–1989) known for her portrayals of strong, beautiful, intelligent women.

[13]*Claudia McNeil:* Emmy-winning actor (b. 1917).

So I knew my mother's letters not only would impress Miss Bradley and Jennie G. but also would go a long way toward redeeming me. After Miss Bradley read the note she told me I have a very nice mother and let me know that if I was willing to be exemplary she would let bygones be bygones and I could get back into her good graces. She was, after all, a dedicated teacher. And I had learned my lesson.

My mother wrote my father about the knife incident. I waited anxiously to hear from him. Would he suddenly appear? I searched the street in front of the school every afternoon. At home I jumped up nervously whenever I heard a horn beep. Finally, a letter from my dad arrived — one page of southpaw scribble.

Dear Bebe,
Your mother told me what happened in school about the knife. That wasn't a good thing to say. I think maybe you were joking. Remember, a lot of times white people don't understand how colored people joke, so you have to be careful what you say around them. Be a good girl.
                                                            Lots of love,
                                                            Daddy.

The crumpled letter hit the edge of the wastepaper basket in my mother's room and landed in front of her bureau. I picked it up and slammed it into the basket, hitting my hand in the process. I flung myself across the bed, buried my face into my pillow, and howled with pain, rage, and sadness. "It's not fair," I wailed. Ole Blondie had her dollhouse-making daddy whenever she wanted him. "Muuuy fatha . . ." Jackie, Jane, and Adam had their wild, ass-whipping daddy. All they had to do was walk outside their house, look under a car, and there he was, tinkering away. Ole ugly grease-monkey man. Why couldn't I have my daddy all the time too? I didn't want a letter signed "Lots of love," I wanted my father to come and yell at me for acting like a monkey on a stick. I wanted him to come and beat my butt or shake his finger in my face, or tell me that what I did wasn't so bad after all. Anything, I just wanted him to come.

ENGAGING THE TEXT

1. Why does Sandra's sentence in Miss Bradley's class so upset Bebe?
2. The family in "Envy" is clearly matriarchal: "Women ruled at 2239" (para. 5). What positive and negative effects did this matriarchal family have on the author when she was a child?
3. How did the matriarchs groom young Bebe for success? What lessons were taught in this family? Do you think the women's methods of raising the child were the best possible?
4. What does the young Bebe think she is missing with her father's absence? What might he provide that the women do not? Do you think the mature author sees the situation much differently than she did as a child?

5. What traditionally male roles do the women in Bebe's family play? How well do you think they perform these roles?

EXPLORING CONNECTIONS

6. Compare and contrast Campbell's family life with Roger Jack's in "An Indian Story (p. 109). In what ways and for what reasons does each depart from the structure of the Western European nuclear family?

7. Compare and contrast the mother-daughter relationships portrayed in this story, in Anndee Hochman's "Growing Pains" (p. 47), and in Maxine Hong Kingston's "Silence" (p. 251). Which relationship is closest to your ideal, and why?

EXTENDING THE CRITICAL CONTEXT

8. If you have ever felt the lack of a father, mother, sister, brother, or grandparent in your family, write a journal entry or narrative memoir exploring your memories and emotions.

9. At the end of *Sweet Summer*, Campbell decides that, while she saw her father only during the summer, her extended family, including uncles, boarders, and family friends, had provided her with plenty of healthy male influences. Read the rest of the book and report to the class on Campbell's portrayal of her relationship with her immediate and extended family.

Black Women and Motherhood

PATRICIA HILL COLLINS

For decades many American sociologists failed to understand African American families because their assumption that Western European families were "normal" made any different families seem flawed or deficient. Even today, politicians and religious leaders sometimes criticize family relationships and parenting styles that fall outside the norm of the nuclear family. This essay by Patricia Hill Collins, focusing on women within the black family, offers a close look at the positive roles that black women have played in American family and community life. Collins (b. 1948) is a professor of sociology and African American studies at the University of Cincinnati. This selection is taken from her award-winning book Black Feminist Thought: Knowledge, Consciousness, and the Politics of Empowerment *(1991).*

The institution of Black motherhood consists of a series of constantly renegotiated relationships that African-American women experience with one another, with Black children, with the larger African-American community, and with self. These relationships occur in specific locations such as the individual households that make up African-American extended family networks, as well as in Black community institutions (Martin and Martin 1978; Sudarkasa 1981b). Moreover, just as Black women's work and family experiences varied during the transition from slavery to the post–World War II political economy, how Black women define, value, and shape Black motherhood as an institution shows comparable diversity.

Black motherhood as an institution is both dynamic and dialectical.[1] An ongoing tension exists between efforts to mold the institution of Black motherhood to benefit systems of race, gender, and class oppression and efforts by African-American women to define and value our own experiences with motherhood. The controlling images of the mammy, the matriarch, and the welfare mother and the practices they justify are designed to oppress. In contrast, motherhood can serve as a site where Black women express and learn the power of self-definition, the importance of valuing and respecting ourselves, the necessity of self-reliance and independence, and a belief in Black women's empowerment. This tension leads to a continuum of responses. Some women view motherhood as a truly burdensome condition that stifles their creativity, exploits their labor, and makes them partners in their own oppression. Others see motherhood as providing a base for self-actualization, status in the Black community, and a catalyst for social activism. These alleged contradictions can exist side by side in African-American communities and families and even within individual women.

Embedded in these changing relationships are [a number of] enduring themes that characterize a Black woman's standpoint on Black motherhood. For any given historical moment, the particular form that Black women's relationships with one another, children, community, and self actually take depends on how this dialectical relationship between the severity of oppression facing African-American women and our actions in resisting that oppression is expressed.

Bloodmothers, Othermothers, and Women-Centered Networks

In African-American communities, fluid and changing boundaries often distinguish biological mothers from other women who care for children. Biological mothers, or bloodmothers, are expected to care for their children.

---

[1]*dialectical:* Based on opposition or tension between competing "truths" or viewpoints. An example follows in Collins's text: the stereotype of the black "mammy" versus the image of a self-reliant, independent mother.

But African and African-American communities have also recognized that vesting one person with full responsibility for mothering a child may not be wise or possible. As a result, othermothers — women who assist bloodmothers by sharing mothering responsibilities — traditionally have been central to the institution of Black motherhood (Troester 1984).

The centrality of women in African-American extended families reflects both a continuation of West African cultural values and functional adaptations to race and gender oppression (Tanner 1974; Stack 1974; Aschenbrenner 1975; Martin and Martin 1978; Sudarkasa 1981b; Reagon 1987). This centrality is not characterized by the absence of husbands and fathers. Men may be physically present and/or have well-defined and culturally significant roles in the extended family and the kin unit may be woman-centered. Bebe Moore Campbell's (1989) parents separated when she was small. Even though she spent the school year in the North Philadelphia household maintained by her grandmother and mother, Campbell's father assumed an important role in her life. "My father took care of me," Campbell remembers. "Our separation didn't stunt me or condemn me to a lesser humanity. His absence never made me a fatherless child. I'm not fatherless now" (p. 271). In woman-centered kin units such as Campbell's — whether a mother-child household unit, a married couple household, or a larger unit extending over several households — the centrality of mothers is not predicated on male powerlessness (Tanner 1974, 133).

Organized, resilient, women-centered networks of bloodmothers and othermothers are key in understanding this centrality. Grandmothers, sisters, aunts, or cousins act as othermothers by taking on child-care responsibilities for one another's children. When needed, temporary child-care arrangements can turn into long-term care or informal adoption (Stack 1974; Gutman 1976). Despite strong cultural norms encouraging women to become biological mothers, women who choose not to do so often receive recognition and status from othermother relationships that they establish with Black children.

In African-American communities these women-centered networks of community-based child care often extend beyond the boundaries of biologically related individuals and include "fictive kin" (Stack 1974). Civil rights activist Ella Baker describes how informal adoption by othermothers functioned in the rural southern community of her childhood:

> My aunt who had thirteen children of her own raised three more. She had become a midwife, and a child was born who was covered with sores. Nobody was particularly wanting the child, so she took the child and raised him . . . and another mother decided she didn't want to be bothered with two children. So my aunt took one and raised him . . . they were part of the family. (Cantarow 1980, 59)

Even when relationships are not between kin or fictive kin, African-American community norms traditionally were such that neighbors cared

5

for one another's children. Sara Brooks, a southern domestic worker, describes the importance that the community-based child care a neighbor offered her daughter had for her: "She kept Vivian and she didn't charge me nothin' either. You see, people used to look after each other, but now it's not that way. I reckon it's because we all was poor, and I guess they put theirself in the place of the person that they was helpin'" (Simonsen 1986, 181). Brooks's experiences demonstrate how the African-American cultural value placed on cooperative child care traditionally found institutional support in the adverse conditions under which so many Black women mothered.

Othermothers are key not only in supporting children but also in helping bloodmothers who, for whatever reason, lack the preparation or desire for motherhood. In confronting racial oppression, maintaining community-based child care and respecting othermothers who assume child-care responsibilities serve a critical function in African-American communities. Children orphaned by sale or death of their parents under slavery, children conceived through rape, children of young mothers, children born into extreme poverty or to alcoholic or drug-addicted mothers, or children who for other reasons cannot remain with their bloodmothers have all been supported by othermothers, who, like Ella Baker's aunt, take in additional children even when they have enough of their own.

Young women are often carefully groomed at an early age to become   10
othermothers. As a ten-year-old, civil rights activist Ella Baker learned to be an othermother by caring for the children of a widowed neighbor: "Mama would say, 'You must take the clothes to Mr. Powell's house, and give so-and-so a bath.' The children were running wild. . . . The kids . . . would take off across the field. We'd chase them down, and bring them back, and put 'em in the tub, and wash 'em off, and change clothes, and carry the dirty ones home, and wash them. Those kind of things were routine" (Cantarow 1980, 59).

Many Black men also value community-based child care but exercise these values to a lesser extent. Young Black men are taught how to care for children (Young 1970; Lewis 1975). During slavery, for example, Black children under age ten experienced little division of labor. They were dressed alike and performed similar tasks. If the activities of work and play are any indication of the degree of gender role differentiation that existed among slave children, "then young girls probably grew up minimizing the difference between the sexes while learning far more about the differences between the races" (D. White 1985, 94). Differences among Black men and women in attitudes toward children may have more to do with male labor force patterns. As Ella Baker observes, "my father took care of people too, but . . . my father had to work" (Cantarow 1980, 60).

Historically, community-based child care and the relationships among bloodmothers and othermothers in women-centered networks have taken diverse institutional forms. In some polygynous West African societies, the children of the same father but different mothers referred to one another as brothers and sisters. While a strong bond existed between the biological mother and her child — one so strong that, among the Ashanti for example, "to show disrespect towards one's mother is tantamount to sacrilege" (Fortes 1950, 263) — children could be disciplined by any of their other "mothers." Cross-culturally, the high status given to othermothers and the cooperative nature of child-care arrangements among bloodmothers and othermothers in Caribbean and other Black societies gives credence to the importance that people of African descent place on mothering (Clarke 1966; Shimkin et al. 1978; Sudarkasa 1981a, 1981b).

Although the political economy of slavery brought profound changes to enslaved Africans, cultural values concerning the importance of motherhood and the value of cooperative approaches to child care continued. While older women served as nurses and midwives, their most common occupation was caring for the children of parents who worked (D. White 1985). Informal adoption of orphaned children reinforced the importance of social motherhood in African-American communities (Gutman 1976).

The relationship between bloodmothers and othermothers survived the transition from a slave economy to postemancipation southern rural agriculture. Children in southern rural communities were not solely the responsibility of their biological mothers. Aunts, grandmothers, and others who had time to supervise children served as othermothers (Young 1970; Dougherty 1978). The significant status women enjoyed in family networks and in African-American communities continued to be linked to their bloodmother and othermother activities.

The entire community structure of bloodmothers and othermothers is under assault in many inner-city neighborhoods, where the very fabric of African-American community life is being eroded by illegal drugs. But even in the most troubled communities, remnants of the othermother tradition endure. Bebe Moore Campbell's 1950s North Philadelphia neighborhood underwent some startling changes when crack cocaine flooded the streets in the 1980s. Increases in birth defects, child abuse, and parental neglect left many children without care. But some residents, such as Miss Nee, continue the othermother tradition. After raising her younger brothers and sisters and five children of her own, Miss Nee cares for three additional children whose families fell apart. Moreover, on any given night Miss Nee's house may be filled by up to a dozen children because she has a reputation for never turning away a needy child ("Children of the Underclass" 1989).

Traditionally, community-based child care certainly has been functional for African-American communities and for Black women. Black feminist theorist bell hooks suggests that the relationships among bloodmothers and othermothers may have greater theoretical importance than currently recognized:

This form of parenting is revolutionary in this society because it takes place in opposition to the ideas that parents, especially mothers, should be the only childrearers. . . . This kind of shared responsibility for child care can happen in small community settings where people know and trust one another. It cannot happen in those settings if parents regard children as their "property," their possession. (1984, 144)

The resiliency of women-centered family networks illustrates how traditional cultural values — namely, the African origins of community-based child care — can help people cope with and resist oppression. By continuing community-based child care, African-American women challenge one fundamental assumption underlying the capitalist system itself: that children are "private property" and can be disposed of as such. Notions of property, child care, and gender differences in parenting styles are embedded in the institutional arrangements of any given political economy. Under the property model stemming from capitalist patriarchal families, parents may not literally assert that their children are pieces of property, but their parenting may reflect assumptions analogous to those they make in connection with property (J. Smith 1983). For example, the exclusive parental "right" to discipline children as parents see fit, even if discipline borders on abuse, parallels the widespread assumption that property owners may dispose of their property without consulting members of the larger community. By seeing the larger community as responsible for children and by giving othermothers and other nonparents "rights" in child rearing, African-Americans challenge prevailing property relations. It is in this sense that traditional bloodmother/othermother relationships in women-centered networks are "revolutionary."

Mothers, Daughters, and Socialization for Survival

Black mothers of daughters face a troubling dilemma. On one hand, to ensure their daughters' physical survival, mothers must teach them to fit into systems of oppression. For example, as a young girl Black activist Ann Moody questioned why she was paid so little for the domestic work she began at age nine, why Black women domestics were sexually harassed by their white male employers, why no one would explain the activities of the National Association for the Advancement of Colored People to her, and why whites had so much more than Blacks. But her mother refused to answer her questions and actually chastised her for questioning the system and stepping out of her "place" (Moody 1968). Like Ann Moody, Black daughters learn to expect to work, to strive for an education so they can support themselves, and to anticipate carrying heavy responsibilities in their families and communities because these skills are essential to their own survival and those for whom they will eventually be responsible (Ladner 1972; Joseph 1981). New Yorker Michele Wallace recounts: "I can't remember when I first learned that my family expected me to work, to be able to take care of myself when I grew up. . . . It had been drilled into me that the best and only sure support was self-support" (1978, 89–90). Mothers also know that if their daughters uncritically accept the limited opportunities offered Black women, they become willing participants in their own subordination. Mothers may have ensured their daughters' physical survival, but at the high cost of their emotional destruction.

On the other hand, Black daughters with strong self-definitions and self-valuations who offer serious challenges to oppressive situations may not physically survive. When Ann Moody became active in the early 1960s in sit-ins and voter registration activities, her mother first begged her not to participate and then told her not to come home because she feared the whites in Moody's hometown would kill her. Despite the dangers, mothers routinely encourage Black daughters to develop skills to confront oppressive conditions. Learning that they will work and that education is a vehicle for advancement can also be seen as ways of enhancing positive self-definitions and self-valuations in Black girls. Emotional strength is essential, but not at the cost of physical survival.

Historian Elsa Barkley Brown captures this delicate balance Black mothers negotiate by pointing out that her mother's behavior demonstrated the "need to teach me to live my life one way and, at the same time, to provide all the tools I would need to live it quite differently" (1989, 929). Black daughters must learn how to survive in interlocking structures of race, class, and gender oppression while rejecting and transcending those same structures. In order to develop these skills in their daughters, mothers demonstrate varying combinations of behaviors devoted to ensuring their daughters' survival — such as providing them with basic necessities and protecting them in dangerous environments — to helping their daughters go further than mothers themselves were allowed to go.

This special vision of Black mothers may grow from the nature of work 20 women have done to ensure Black children's survival. These work experiences have provided Black women with a unique angle of vision, a particular perspective on the world to be passed on to Black daughters. African and African-American women have long integrated economic self-reliance with mothering. In contrast to the cult of true womanhood,[2] in which work is defined as being in opposition to and incompatible with motherhood, work for Black women has been an important and valued dimension of Afrocentric definitions of Black motherhood. Sara Brooks describes the powerful connections that economic self-reliance and mothering had in her childhood: "When I was about nine I was nursin' my sister Sally — I'm about seven or eight years older than Sally. And when I would put her to sleep, instead of

---

[2]*cult of true womanhood:* The nineteenth-century ideal of women as saintly, even angelic, beings — passive and innocent creatures who should be sheltered from the rough world of men.

me goin' somewhere and sit down and play, I'd get my little old hoe and get out there and work right in the field around the house" (in Simonsen 1986, 86).

Mothers who are domestic workers or who work in proximity to whites may experience a unique relationship with the dominant group. For example, African-American women domestics are exposed to all the intimate details of the lives of their white employers. Working for whites offers domestic workers a view from the inside and exposes them to ideas and resources that might aid in their children's upward mobility. In some cases domestic workers form close, long-lasting relationships with their employers. But domestic workers also encounter some of the harshest exploitation confronting women of color. The work is low paid, has few benefits, and exposes women to the threat and reality of sexual harassment. Black domestics could see the dangers awaiting their daughters.

Willi Coleman's mother used a Saturday-night hair-combing ritual to impart a Black women's standpoint on domestic work to her daughters:

> Except for special occasions mama came home from work early on Saturdays. She spent six days a week mopping, waxing, and dusting other women's houses and keeping out of reach of other women's husbands. Saturday nights were reserved for "taking care of them girls" hair and the telling of stories. Some of which included a recitation of what she had endured and how she had triumphed over "folks that were lower than dirt" and "no-good snakes in the grass." She combed, patted, twisted, and talked, saying things which would have embarrassed or shamed her at other times. (Coleman 1987, 34)

Bonnie Thornton Dill's (1980) study of the child-rearing goals of domestic workers illustrates how African-American women see their work as both contributing to their children's survival and instilling values that will encourage their children to reject their proscribed "place" as Blacks and strive for more. Providing a better chance for their children was a dominant theme among Black women. Domestic workers described themselves as "struggling to give their children the skills and training they did not have; and as praying that opportunities which had not been open to them would be open to their children" (p. 110). But the women also realized that while they wanted to communicate the value of their work as part of the ethics of caring and personal accountability, the work itself was undesirable. Bebe Moore Campbell's (1989) grandmother and college-educated mother stressed the importance of education. Campbell remembers, "[they] wanted me to Be Somebody, to be the second generation to live out my life as far away from a mop and scrub brush and Miss Ann's floors as possible" (p. 83).

Understanding this goal of balancing the need for the physical survival of their daughters with the vision of encouraging them to transcend the boundaries confronting them explains many apparent contradictions in Black mother-daughter relationships. Black mothers are often described as strong disciplinarians and overly protective; yet these same women manage to raise daughters who are self-reliant and assertive. To explain this apparent contradiction, Gloria Wade-Gayles suggests that Black mothers:

> do not socialize their daughters to be "passive" or "irrational." Quite the contrary, they socialize their daughters to be independent, strong, and self-confident. Black mothers are suffocatingly protective and domineering precisely because they are determined to mold their daughters into whole and self-actualizing persons in a society that devalues Black women. (1984, 12)

African-American mothers place a strong emphasis on protection, either by trying to shield their daughters as long as possible from the penalties attached to their race, class, and gender status or by teaching them skills of independence and self-reliance so that they will be able to protect themselves. Consider the following verse from a traditional blues song:

> I ain't good lookin' and ain't got waist-long hair
> I say I ain't good lookin' and I ain't got waist-long hair
> But my mama gave me something that'll take me anywhere.
> (Washington 184, 144)

Unlike white women, symbolized by "good looks" and "waist-long hair," Black women have been denied male protection. Under such conditions it becomes essential that Black mothers teach their daughters skills that will "take them anywhere."

Black women's autobiographies and fiction can be read as texts revealing the multiple ways that African-American mothers aim to shield their daughters from the demands of being Black women in oppressive conditions. Michele Wallace describes her growing understanding of how her mother viewed raising Black daughters in Harlem: "My mother has since explained to me that since it was obvious her attempt to protect me was going to prove a failure, she was determined to make me realize that as a black girl in white America I was going to find it an uphill climb to keep myself together" (1978, 98). In discussing the mother-daughter relationship in Paule Marshall's *Brown Girl, Brownstones,* Rosalie Troester catalogues the ways mothers have aimed to protect their daughters and the impact this may have on relationships themselves:

> Black mothers, particularly those with strong ties to their community, sometimes build high banks around their young daughters, isolating them from the dangers of the larger world until they are old and strong enough to function as autonomous women. Often these dikes are religious, but sometimes they are built with education, family, or the restrictions of a close-knit and homogeneous community. . . . This isolation causes the currents between Black mothers and daughters to run deep and the relationship to be fraught with an emotional intensity often missing from the lives of women with more freedom. (1984, 13)

Michele Wallace's mother built banks around her headstrong adolescent daughter by institutionalizing her in a Catholic home for troubled girls. Wallace went willingly, believing "I thought at the time that I would rather live in hell than be with my mother" (1978, 98). But years later Wallace's evaluation of her mother's decision changed: "Now that I know my mother better, I know that her sense of powerlessness made it all the more essential to her that she take radical action" (p. 98).

African-American mothers try to protect their daughters from the dangers that lie ahead by offering them a sense of their own unique self-worth. Many contemporary Black women writers report the experience of being singled out, of being given a sense of specialness at an early age which encouraged them to develop their talents. My own mother marched me to the public library at age five, helped me get my first library card, and told me that I could do anything if I learned how to read. In discussing the works of Paule Marshall, Dorothy West, and Alice Walker, Mary Helen Washington observes that all three writers make special claims about the roles their mothers played in the development of their creativity: "The bond with their mothers is such a fundamental and powerful source that the term 'mothering the mind' might have been coined specifically to define their experiences as writers" (1984, 144).

Black women's efforts to provide a physical and psychic base for their children can affect mothering styles and the emotional intensity of Black mother-daughter relationships. As Gloria Wade-Gayles points out, "mothers in Black Women's fiction are strong and devoted . . . they are rarely affectionate" (1984, 10). For example, in Toni Morrison's *Sula* (1974), Eva Peace's husband ran off, leaving her with three small children and no money. Despite her feelings, "the demands of feeding her three children were so acute she had to postpone her anger for two years until she had both the time and energy for it" (p. 32). Later in the novel Eva's daughter Hannah asks, "Mamma, did you ever love us?" (p. 67). Eva angrily replies, "What you talkin' bout did I love you girl I stayed alive for you" (p. 69). For far too many Black mothers, the demands of providing for children in interlocking systems of oppression are sometimes so demanding that they have neither the time nor the patience for affection. And yet most Black daughters love and admire their mothers and are convinced that their mothers truly love them (Joseph 1981).

Black daughters raised by mothers grappling with hostile environments have to come to terms with their feelings about the difference between the idealized versions of maternal love extant in popular culture and the strict and often troubled mothers in their lives. For a daughter, growing up means developing a better understanding that even though she may desire more affection and greater freedom, her mother's physical care and protection are acts of maternal love. Ann Moody describes her growing awareness of the cost her mother paid as a domestic worker who was a single mother of three. Watching her mother sleep after the birth of another child, Moody remembers:

> For a long time I stood there looking at her. I didn't want to wake her up. I wanted to enjoy and preserve that calm, peaceful look on her face, I wanted to think she would always be that happy. . . . Adline and Junior were too young to feel the things I felt and know the things I knew about Mama. They couldn't remember when she and Daddy separated. They had never heard her cry at night as I had or worked and helped as I had done when we were starving. (1968, 57)

Moody initially sees her mother as a strict disciplinarian, a woman who tries to protect her daughter by withholding information. But as Moody matures and better understands the oppression in her community, her ideas change. On one occasion Moody left school early the day after a Black family had been brutally murdered by local whites. Moody's description of her mother's reaction reflects her deepening understanding: "When I walked in the house Mama didn't even ask me why I came home. She just looked at me. And for the first time I realized she understood what was going on within me or was trying to anyway" (1968, 136).

Another example of a daughter's efforts to understand her mother is offered in Renita Weems's account of coming to grips with maternal desertion. In the following passage Weems struggles with the difference between the stereotypical image of the superstrong Black mother and her own alcoholic mother's decision to leave her children: "My mother loved us. I must believe that. She worked all day in a department store bakery to buy shoes and school tablets, came home to curse out neighbors who wrongly accused her children of any impropriety (which in an apartment complex usually meant stealing), and kept her house cleaner than most sober women" (1984, 26). Weems concludes that her mother loved her because she provided for her to the best of her ability.

Othermothers often help to defuse the emotional intensity of relation-   30
ships between bloodmothers and their daughters. In recounting how she dealt with the intensity of her relationship with her mother, Weems describes the women teachers, neighbors, friends, and othermothers she turned to — women who, she observes, "did not have the onus of providing for me, and so had the luxury of talking to me" (1984, 27). Cheryl West's household included her brother, her lesbian mother, and Jan, her mother's lover. Jan became an othermother to West: "Yellow-colored, rotund and short in stature, Jan was like a second mother. . . . Jan braided my hair in the morning, mother worked two jobs and tucked me in at night. Loving, gentle, and fastidious in the domestic arena, Jan could be a rigid disciplinarian. . . . To the outside world . . . she was my 'aunt' who happened to live with us. But she was much more involved and nurturing than any of my 'real' aunts" (1987, 43).

June Jordan offers an eloquent analysis of one daughter's realization of the high personal cost African-American women can pay in providing an economic and emotional foundation for their children. In the following passage Jordan offers a powerful testament of how she came to see that her mother's work was an act of love:

> As a child I noticed the sadness of my mother as she sat alone in the kitchen at night. . . . Her woman's work never won permanent victories of any kind. It never enlarged the universe of her imagination or her power to influence what happened beyond the front door of our house. Her woman's work never tickled her to laugh or shout or dance. But she did raise me to respect her way of offering love and to believe that hard work is often the irreducible factor for survival, not something to avoid. Her woman's work produced a reliable home base where I could pursue the privileges of books and music. Her woman's work invented the potential for a completely different kind of work for us, the next generation of Black women: huge, rewarding hard work demanded by the huge, new ambitions that her perfect confidence in us engendered. (1985, 105)

Community Othermothers and Political Activism

Black women's experiences as othermothers provide a foundation for Black women's political activism. Nurturing children in Black extended family networks stimulates a more generalized ethic of caring and personal accountability among African-American women who often feel accountable to all the Black community's children.

This notion of Black women as community othermothers for all Black children traditionally allowed African-American women to treat biologically unrelated children as if they were members of their own families. For example, sociologist Karen Fields describes how her grandmother, Mamie Garvin Fields, draws on her power as a community othermother when dealing with unfamiliar children: "She will say to a child on the street who looks up to no good, picking out a name at random, 'Aren't you Miz Pinckney's boy?' in that same reproving tone. If the reply is, 'No, *ma'am,* my mother is Miz Gadsden,' whatever threat there was dissipates" (Fields and Fields 1983, xvii).

The use of family language in referring to members of the African-American community also illustrates this dimension of Black motherhood. In the following passage, Mamie Garvin Fields describes how she became active in surveying substandard housing conditions among African-Americans in Charleston. Note her explanation of why she uses family language:

> I was one of the volunteers they got to make a survey of the places where we were paying extortious rents for indescribable property. I said "we," although it wasn't Bob and me. We had our own home, and so did many of the Federated Women. Yet we still felt like it really was "we" living in those terrible places, and it was up to us to do something about them. (Fields and Fields 1983, 195)

Black women frequently describe Black children using family language. In recounting her increasingly successful efforts to teach a boy who had given other teachers problems, my daughter's kindergarten teacher stated, "You know how it can be — the majority of children in the learning disabled classes are *our children*. I know he didn't belong there, so I volunteered to take him." In their statements both women use family language to describe the ties that bind them as Black women to their responsibilities as members of an African-American community/family.

In explaining why the South Carolina Federation of Colored Women's 35 Clubs founded a home for girls, Ms. Fields observes, "We all could see that we had a responsibility for those girls: they were the daughters of our community coming up" (Fields and Fields 1983, 197). Ms. Fields's activities as a community othermother on behalf of the "daughters" of her community represent an established tradition among educated Black women. Serving as othermothers to women in the Black community has a long history. A study of 108 of the first generation of Black club women found that three-quarters were married, three-quarters worked outside the home, but only one-fourth had children (Giddings 1984). These women emphasized self-report for Black women, whether married or not, and realized that self-sufficient community othermothers were important. "Not all women are intended for mothers," declares an 1894 edition of the *Woman's Era*. "Some of us have not the temperament for family life. . . . Clubs will make women think seriously of their future lives, and not make girls think their only alternative is to marry" (Giddings 1984, 108).

Black women writers also explore this theme of the African-American community othermother who nurtures the Black community. One of the earliest examples is found in Frances Ellen Watkins Harper's 1892 novel *Iola Leroy*. By rejecting an opportunity to marry a prestigious physician and dissociate herself from the Black community, nearly white Iola, the main character, chooses instead to serve the African-American community. Similarly, in Alice Walker's *Meridian* (1976), the main character rejects the controlling image of the "happy slave," the self-sacrificing Black mother, and chooses to become a community othermother. Giving up her biological child to the care of an othermother, Meridian gets an education, works in the civil rights movement, and eventually takes on responsibility for the children of a small southern town. She engages in a "quest that will take her beyond the society's narrow meaning of the word *mother* as a physical state and expand its meaning to those who create, nurture, and save life in social and psychological as well as physical terms" (Christian 1985, 242).

Sociologist Cheryl Gilkes (1980, 1982, 1983b) suggests that community othermother relationships can be key in stimulating Black women's decisions to become community activists. Gilkes asserts that many of the Black women community activists in her study became involved in community organizing in response to the needs of their own children and of those in their communities. The following comment is typical of how many of the Black women in Gilkes's study relate to Black children: "There were a lot of summer programs springing up for kids, but they were exclusive . . . and I found that most of *our kids* were excluded" (1980, 219). For many women what began as the daily expression of their obligations as community othermothers, as was the case for the kindergarten teacher, developed into full-fledged actions as community leaders.

This community othermother tradition also explains the "mothering the mind" relationships that can develop between Black women teachers and their Black women students. Unlike the traditional mentoring so widely reported in educational literature, this relationship goes far beyond that of providing students with either technical skills or a network of academic and professional contacts. Bell hooks shares the special vision that teachers who see our work in community othermother terms can pass on to our students: "I understood from the teachers in those segregated schools that the work of any teacher committed to the full self-realization of students was necessarily and fundamentally radical, that ideas were not neutral, that to teach in a way that liberates, that expands consciousness, that awakens, is to challenge domination at its very core" (1989, 50). Like the mother-daughter relationship, this "mothering the mind" among Black women seeks to move toward the mutuality of a shared sisterhood that binds African-American women as community othermothers.

Community othermothers have made important contributions in building a different type of community in often hostile political and economic surroundings (Reagon 1987). Community othermothers' actions demonstrate a clear rejection of separateness and individual interest as the basis of either community organization or individual self-actualization. Instead, the connectedness with others and common interest expressed by community othermothers models a very different value system, one whereby Afrocentric feminist ethics of caring and personal accountability move communities forward.

Motherhood as a Symbol of Power

Motherhood — whether bloodmother, othermother, or community othermother — can be invoked by African-American communities as a symbol of power. Much of Black women's status in African-American communities stems not only from actions as mothers in Black family networks but from contributions as community othermothers.

Black women's involvement in fostering African-American community development forms the basis for community-based power. This is the type of power many African-Americans have in mind when they describe the "strong Black women" they see around them in traditional African-American communities. Community othermothers work on behalf of the Black community by expressing ethics of caring and personal accountability which embrace conceptions of transformative power and mutuality (Kuykendall 1983). Such power is transformative in that Black women's relationships

Drawing by R. Chast © 1992, The New Yorker Magazine, Inc.

with children and other vulnerable community members is not intended to dominate or control. Rather, its purpose is to bring people along, to — in the words of late-nineteenth-century Black feminists — "uplift the race" so that vulnerable members of the community will be able to attain the self-reliance and independence essential for resistance.

When older African-American women invoke their power as community othermothers, the results can be quite striking. Karen Fields recounts a telling incident:

> One night . . . as Grandmother sat crocheting alone at about two in the morning, a young man walked into the living room carrying the portable TV from upstairs. She said, "Who are you looking for *this* time of night?" As Grandmother [described] the incident to me over the phone, I could hear a tone of voice that I know well. It said, "Nice boys don't do that." So I imagine the burglar heard his own mother or grandmother at that moment. He joined in the familial game just created: "Well, he told me that I could borrow it." "*Who* told you?" "John." "Um um, no *John* lives here. You got the wrong house." (Fields and Fields, 1983, xvi)

After this dialogue, the teenager turned around, went back upstairs, and returned the television.

In local African-American communities, community othermothers become identified as powerful figures through furthering the community's well-being. Sociologist Charles Johnson (1934/1979) describes the behavior of an elderly Black woman at a church service in rural 1930s Alabama. Even though she was not on the program, the woman stood up to speak. The master of ceremonies rang for her to sit down, but she refused to do so claiming, "I am the mother of this church, and I will say what I please" (p. 172). The master of ceremonies offered the following explanation to the congregation as to why he let the woman continue: "Brothers, I know you all honor Sister Moore. Course our time is short but she has acted as a mother to me. . . . Any time old folks get up I give way to them" (p. 173).

References

Aschenbrenner, Joyce. 1975. *Lifelines, Black Families in Chicago.* Prospect Heights, IL: Waveland Press.

Brown, Elsa Barkley. 1989. "African-American Women's Quilting: A Framework for Conceptualizing and Teaching African-American Women's History." *Signs* 14 (4): 921–29.

Campbell, Bebe Moore. 1989. *Sweet Summer: Growing Up with and Without My Dad.* New York: Putnam.

Cantarow, Ellen. 1980. *Moving the Mountain: Women Working for Social Change.* Old Westbury, NY: Feminist Press.

Christian, Barbara. 1985. *Black Feminist Criticism, Perspectives on Black Women Writers.* New York: Pergamon.

Clarke, Edith. 1966. *My Mother Who Fathered Me.* 2d ed. London: Allen and Unwin.

Coleman, Willi. 1987. "Closets and Keepsakes." *Sage: A Scholarly Journal on Black Women* 4 (2): 34–35.

Dill, Bonnie Thornton. 1980. "'The Means to Put My Children Through': Child-Rearing Goals and Strategies among Black Female Domestic Servants." In *The Black Woman,* edited by La Frances Rodgers-Rose, 107–23. Beverly Hills, CA: Sage.

Dougherty, Molly C. 1978. *Becoming a Woman in Rural Black Culture.* New York: Holt, Rinehart and Winston.

Fields, Mamie Garvin, and Karen Fields. 1983. *Lemon Swamp and Other Places: A Carolina Memoir.* New York: Free Press.

Fortes, Meyer. 1950. "Kinship and Marriage among the Ashanti." In *African Systems of Kinship and Marriage,* edited by A. R. Radcliffe-Brown and Daryll Forde, 252–84. New York: Oxford University Press.

Giddings, Paula. 1984. *When and Where I Enter . . . The Impact of Black Women on Race and Sex in America.* New York: William Morrow.

Gilkes, Cheryl Townsend. 1980. "'Holding Back the Ocean with a Broom': Black Women and Community Work." In *The Black Woman,* edited by La Frances Rodgers-Rose, 217–32. Beverly Hills, CA: Sage.

———. 1982. "Successful Rebellious Professionals: The Black Woman's Professional Identity and Community Commitment." *Psychology of Women Quarterly* 6 (3): 289–311.

———. 1983b. "Going Up for the Oppressed: The Career Mobility of Black Women Community Workers." *Journal of Social Issues* 39 (3): 1115–39.

Gutman, Herbert. 1976. *The Black Family in Slavery and Freedom, 1750–1925.* New York: Random House.

hooks, bell. 1984. *From Margin to Center.* Boston: South End Press.

———. 1989. *Talking Back: Thinking Feminist, Thinking Black.* Boston: South End Press.

Johnson, Charles S. [1934] 1979. *Shadow of the Plantation.* Chicago: University of Chicago Press.

Jordan, June. 1985. *On Call.* Boston: South End Press.

Joseph, Gloria. 1981. "Black Mothers and Daughters: Their Roles and Functions in American Society." In *Common Differences,* edited by Gloria Joseph and Jill Lewis, 75–126. Garden City, NY: Anchor.

Kuykendall, Eleanor H. 1983. "Toward an Ethic of Nurturance: Luce Irigaray on Mothering and Power." In *Motherhood: Essays in Feminist Theory,* edited by Joyce Treblicot, 263–74. Totowa, NJ: Rowman & Allanheld.

Ladner, Joyce. 1972. *Tomorrow's Tomorrow.* Garden City, NJ: Doubleday.

Lewis, Diane K. 1975. "The Black Family: Socialization and Sex Roles." *Phylon* 36 (3): 221–37.

Martin, Elmer, and Joanne Mitchell Martin. 1978. *The Black Extended Family.* Chicago: University of Chicago Press.

Moody, Ann. 1968. *Coming of Age in Mississippi.* New York: Dell.

Morrison, Toni. 1974. *Sula.* New York: Random House.

Reagon, Bernice Johnson. 1987. "African Diaspora Women: The Making of Cultural Workers." In *Women in Africa and the African Diaspora,* edited by Rosalyn Terborg-Penn, Sharon Harley, and Andrea Benton Rushing, 167–80. Washington, DC: Howard University Press.

Shimkin, Demitri B., Edith M. Shimkin, and Dennis A. Frate, eds. 1978. *The Extended Family in Black Societies.* Chicago: Aldine.

Simonsen, Thordis, ed. 1986. *You May Plow Here: The Narrative of Sara Brooks.* New York: Touchstone.

Smith, Janet Farrell. 1983. "Parenting as Property." In *Mothering: Essays in Feminist Theory,* edited by Joyce Treblicot, 199–212. Totowa, NJ: Rowman & Allanheld.

Stack, Carol D. 1974. *All Our Kin: Strategies for Survival in a Black Community.* New York: Harper & Row.

Sudarkasa, Niara. 1981a. "Female Employment and Family Organization in West Africa." In *The Black Woman Cross-Culturally,* edited by Filomina Chioma Steady. 49–64. Cambridge, MA: Schenkman.

———. 1981b. "Interpreting the African Heritage in Afro-American Family Organization." In *Black Families,* edited by Harriette Pipes McAdoo, 37–53. Beverly Hills, CA: Sage.

Tanner, Nancy. 1974. "Matrifocality in Indonesia and Africa and among Black Americans." In *Woman, Culture, and Society,* edited by Michelle Z. Rosaldo and Louise Lamphere, 129–56. Stanford: Stanford University Press.

Troester, Rosalie Riegle. 1984. "Turbulence and Tenderness: Mothers, Daughters, and 'Othermothers' in Paule Marshall's *Brown Girl, Brownstones.*" *Sage: A Scholarly Journal on Black Women* 1 (2): 13–16.

Wade-Gayles, Gloria. 1984. "The Truths of Our Mothers' Lives: Mother-Daughter Relationships in Black Women's Fiction." *Sage: A Scholarly Journal on Black Women* 1 (2): 8–12.

Walker, Alice. 1976. *Meridian.* New York: Pocket Books.

Wallace, Michele. 1978. *Black Macho and the Myth of the Superwoman.* New York: Dial Press.

Washington, Mary Helen. 1984. "I Sign My Mother's Name: Alice Walker, Dorothy West and Paule Marshall." In *Mothering the Mind: Twelve Studies of Writers and Their Silent Partners,* edited by Ruth Perry and Martine Watson Broronley, 143–63. New York: Holmes & Meier.

Weems, Renita. 1984. "'Hush. Mama's Gotta Go Bye Bye': A Personal Narrative." *Sage: A Scholarly Journal on Black Women* 1 (2): 25–28.

West, Cheryl. 1987. "Lesbian Daughter." *Sage: A Scholarly Journal on Black Women* 4 (2): 42–44.

White, Deborah Gray. 1985. *Ar'n't I a Woman? Female Slaves in the Plantation South.* New York: W. W. Norton.

Young, Virginia Heyer. 1970. "Family and Childhood in a Southern Negro Community." *American Anthropologist* 72 (32): 269–88.

ENGAGING THE TEXT

1. In what ways do the African American families described by Collins differ from traditional Eurocentric views of family structure?

2. Define "othermother" and "fictive kin." Why are these roles important to the African American family? Can you think of similar roles in families that are not African American?

3. What explanations does Collins give for the centrality of women in extended African American families?

4. Explain what Collins means by "socialization for survival" (para. 17) and define the dilemma it presents to black mothers. Do you think this dilemma still exists?

5. Explain the connections Collins sees between African American family life and political struggle.

EXPLORING CONNECTIONS

6. Apply Collins's terms and ideas to Bebe Moore Campbell's "Envy" (p. 118). To what extent does Collins's analysis help explain Campbell's narrative? Does it change your understanding of "Envy"?

7. Read Toni Cade Bambara's "The Lesson" (p. 348) and discuss how Collins's description of community othermothers might illuminate Miss Moore's attitude toward Sylvia and her friends.

8. What interests and values does Roz Chast suggest lie at the heart of the "nontraditional family units" that she depicts in the cartoon on page 145? How do these differ from the interests and values that unite the alternative families described by Collins?

EXTENDING THE CRITICAL CONTEXT

9. Survey several depictions of African American family life on recent TV shows. To what extent do the mothers on these shows display the attitudes, values, and behaviors that Collins describes? What images of black motherhood does TV create?

10. As a class, watch Spike Lee's *Crooklyn* and explore the roles that African American women are given in this film. To what extent do their portrayals confirm or complicate Collins's analysis of the roles typically played by African American women?

11. Write a paper exploring the dynamics of a particular family relationship (for example, father-son, sisters) within some group in American society *other than* African American. Following Collins's example, you may wish to include anecdotal support as well as published research. In any case, try to identify the definitive characteristics or patterns of the chosen relationship. How does this relationship connect to the family, the community, or one's sense of self?

Aunt Ida Pieces a Quilt

MELVIN DIXON

This is an extraordinary poem about AIDS, love, and family life. Its author, Melvin Dixon (b. 1950), received his Ph.D. from Brown University; in addition to teaching English at Queens College in New York, he published poetry, literary criticism, translations, and two novels. "Aunt Ida" appeared in Brother to Brother: New Writings by Black Gay Men *(1991). Dixon died of complications from AIDS in 1992.*

> You are right, but your patch isn't big enough.
> — JESSE JACKSON

> *When a cure is found and the last panel is*
> *sewn into place, the Quilt will be displayed*
> *in a permanent home as a national monument*
> *to the individual, irreplaceable people lost to AIDS —*
> *and the people who knew and loved them most.*
> — CLEVE JONES, *founder, The NAMES Project*

They brought me some of his clothes. The hospital gown,
those too-tight dungarees, his blue choir robe
with the gold sash. How that boy could sing!
His favorite color in a necktie. A Sunday shirt.
What I'm gonna do with all this stuff?   5
I can remember Junie without this business.
My niece Francine say they quilting all over the country.
So many good boys like her boy, gone.

At my age I ain't studying no needle and thread.
My eyes ain't so good now and my fingers lock in a fist,   10
they so eaten up with arthritis. This old back
don't take kindly to bending over a frame no more.
Francine say ain't I a mess carrying on like this.
I could make two quilts the time I spend running my mouth.

Just cut his name out the cloths, stitch something nice   15
about him. Something to bring him back. You can do it,
Francine say. Best sewing our family ever had.
Quilting ain't that easy, I say. Never was easy.
Y'all got to help me remember him good.

Most of my quilts was made down South. My mama   20
And my mama's mama taught me. Popped me on the tail
if I missed a stitch or threw the pattern out of line.
I did "Bright Star" and "Lonesome Square" and "Rally Round,"
what many folks don't bother with nowadays. Then Elmo and me
married and came North where the cold in Connecticut   25
cuts you like a knife. We was warm, though.
We had sackcloth and calico and cotton, 100% pure.
What they got now but polyester rayon. Factory made.

Let me tell you something. In all my quilts there's a secret
nobody knows. Every last one of them got my name Ida   30
stitched on the back side in red thread.
That's where Junie got his flair. Don't let nobody fool you.
When he got the Youth Choir standing up and singing
the whole church would rock. He'd throw up his hands

from them wide blue sleeves and the church would hush   35
right down to the funeral parlor fans whisking the air.
He'd toss his head back and holler and we'd all cry holy.

And nevermind his too-tight dungarees.
I caught him switching down the street one Saturday night,
and I seen him more than once. I said, Junie,   40
you ain't got to let the world know all your business.
Who cared where he went when he wanted to have fun.
He'd be singing his heart out come Sunday morning.

When Francine say she gonna hang this quilt in the church
I like to fall out. A quilt ain't no showpiece,   45
it's to keep you warm. Francine say it can do both.
Now I ain't so old-fashioned I can't change,
but I made Francine come over and bring her daughter
Belinda. We cut and tacked his name, *JUNIE*.
Just plain and simple, *"JUNIE, our boy."*   50
Cut the *J* in blue, the *U* in gold. *N* in dungarees
just as tight as you please. The *I* from the hospital gown
and the white shirt he wore First Sunday. Belinda
put the necktie in *E* in the cross stitch I showed her.

Wouldn't you know we got to talking about Junie.   55
We could smell him in the cloth.
Underarm. Afro Sheen pomade.[1] Gravy stains.
I forgot all about my arthritis.
When Francine left me to finish up, I swear
I heard Junie giggling right along with me   60
as I stitched Ida on the back side in red thread.

Francine say she gonna send this quilt to Washington
like folks doing from all 'cross the country,
so many good people gone. Babies, mothers, fathers
and boys like our Junie. Francine say   65
they gonna piece this quilt to another one,
another name and another patch
all in a larger quilt getting larger and larger.

Maybe we all like that, patches waiting to be pieced.
Well, I don't know about Washington.   70
We need Junie here with us. And Maxine,
she cousin May's husband's sister's people,
she having a baby and here comes winter already.
The cold cutting like knives. Now where did I put that needle?

[1]*Afro Sheen pomade:* Hair-care product for African Americans.

ENGAGING THE TEXT

1. Identify all of the characters and their relationships in the poem. Then retell the story of the poem in your own words.

2. Discuss the movement of Aunt Ida's mind and her emotions as we move from stanza to stanza. What happens to Aunt Ida in the poem? What is the dominant feeling at the end of the poem?

3. Junie's clothes take on symbolic weight in the quilt and, of course, in the poem as well. What do the hospital gown, the dungarees, the choir robe, and the white shirt and necktie represent?

4. What is Aunt Ida about to make at the end of the poem, and what is its significance?

EXPLORING CONNECTIONS

5. Discuss the actions of the women in this poem in light of Patricia Hill Collins's discussion of African American families (p. 131). To what extent do the authors share similar beliefs about black families?

6. How might Melvin Dixon (p. 149) and Roger Jack (p. 109) respond to Anndee Hochman's suggestion (p. 47) that belonging to a family requires complete conformity? Which vision of family membership seems the most realistic to you?

EXTENDING THE CRITICAL CONTEXT

7. Write a screenplay or dramatic script to "translate" the story of "Aunt Ida Pieces a Quilt" into dramatic form. Time permitting, organize a group to read or perform the piece for the class.

8. Through this chapter, families have been portrayed through a variety of metaphors: they have appeared as a nuclear unit, a house with many connecting rooms, a network of relationships, and a quilt with many parts. What are the implications of each of these metaphors? How do they affect our view of family? What other metaphors might capture your vision of American family life?

9. Watch the documentary *Common Threads: Stories from the Quilt* and write a poem based on the life of one of the people profiled in this film.

2

Learning Power

The Myth of Education and Empowerment

> Broke out of Chester gaol,[1] last night, one James Rockett, a very short
> well set fellow, pretends to be a schoolmaster, of a fair complexion,
> and smooth fac'd; Had on when he went away, a light colored camblet
> coat, a blue cloth jacket, without sleeves, a check shirt, a pair of old
> dy'd leather breaches, gray worsted stockings, a pair of half worn
> pumps, and an almost new beaver hat; his hair is cut off, and wears a
> cap; he is a great taker of snuff, and very apt to get drunk; he has with
> him two certificates, one from some inhabitants in Burlington county,
> Jersey, which he will no doubt produce as a pass. Who ever takes up
> and secures said Rockett in any gaol, shall have two Pistoles reward,
> paid by October 27, 1756. — SAMUEL SMITH, Gaoler
>
> — Advertisement for a "runaway schoolmaster"
> Pennsylvania Gazette, November 25, 1756

Americans have always had mixed feelings about schooling. Today,
most Americans tend to see education as something intrinsically valuable or
important. After all, education is the engine that drives the American
Dream. The chance to learn, better oneself, and gain the skills that pay off
in upward mobility has sustained the hope of millions of Americans. As a
nation we look up to figures like Abraham Lincoln and Frederick Douglass,
who learned to see beyond poverty and slavery by learning to read. Education tells us that the American Dream can work for everyone. It reassures us
that we are, in fact, "created equal" and that the path to achievement lies
through individual effort and hard work, not blind luck or birth.

But as the advertisement quoted above suggests, American attitudes toward teachers and teaching haven't always been overwhelmingly positive.
The Puritans who established the Massachusetts Bay Colony viewed education with respectful skepticism. Schooling in Puritan society was a force for
spiritual rather than worldly advancement. Lessons were designed to reinforce moral and religious training and to teach children to read the Bible for
themselves. Education was important to the Puritan "Divines" because it was
a source of order, control, and discipline. But when education aimed at more
worldly goals or was undertaken for self-improvement, it was seen as a menacing, sinful luxury. Little wonder, then, that the Puritans often viewed teaching as something less than an ennobling profession. In fact, teachers in the
early colonies were commonly treated as menial employees by the families and
communities they served. The following list of the "Duties of a Schoolmaster"
gives you some idea of the status of American educators in the year 1661:

1. Act as court-messenger
2. Serve summonses
3. Conduct certain ceremonial church services
4. Lead Sunday choir
5. Ring bell for public worship

[1]*gaol:* Jail.

6. Dig graves
7. Take charge of school
8. Perform other occasional duties

Colonial American teachers were frequently indentured servants who had sold themselves for five to ten years, often for the price of passage to the New World. Once here, they drilled their masters' children in spiritual exercises until they earned their freedom — or escaped.

The reputation of education in America began to improve with the onset of the Revolutionary War. Following the overthrow of British rule, leaders sought to create a spirit of nationalism that would unify the former colonies. Differences were to be set aside, for, as George Washington pointed out, "the more homogeneous our citizens can be made ... the greater will be our prospect of permanent union." The goal of schooling became the creation of uniformly loyal, patriotic Americans. In the words of Benjamin Rush, one of the signers of the Declaration of Independence, "Our schools of learning, by producing one general and uniform system of education, will render the mass of people more homogeneous and thereby fit them more easily for uniform and peaceable government."

Thomas Jefferson saw school as a training ground for citizenship and democratic leadership. Recognizing that an illiterate and ill-informed population would be unable to assume the responsibilities of self-government, Jefferson laid out a comprehensive plan in 1781 for public education in the state of Virginia. According to Jefferson's blueprint, all children would be eligible for three years of free public instruction. Of those who could not afford further schooling, one promising "genius" from each school was to be "raked from the rubbish" and given six more years of free education. At the end of that time, ten boys would be selected to attend college at public expense. Jeffersonian Virginia may have been the first place in the United States where education so clearly offered the penniless boy a path to self-improvement. However, this path was open to very few, and Jefferson, like Washington and Rush, was more concerned with benefiting the state than serving the individual student: "We hope to avail the state of those talents which nature has sown as liberally among the poor as the rich, but which perish without use, if not sought for and cultivated." For leaders of the American Revolution, education was seen as a tool for nation-building, not personal development.

Perhaps that's why Native American leaders remained lukewarm to the idea of formal education despite its growing popularity with their colonial neighbors. When, according to Ben Franklin's report, the government of Virginia offered to provide six American Indian youths with the best college education it could afford in 1744, the tribal leaders of the Six Nations politely declined, pointing out that

> our ideas of this kind of education happen not to be the same with yours. We have had some experience of it; several of our young people were formerly brought up at the colleges of the northern provinces; they were instructed in all your sciences; but when they came back to

us, they were bad runners; ignorant of every means of living in the woods; unable to bear either cold or hunger; knew neither how to build a cabin, take a deer, or kill an enemy; spoke our language imperfectly; were therefore neither fit for hunters, warriors, or counselors: they were totally good for nothing.

It's not surprising that these tribal leaders saw American education as useless. Education works to socialize young people — to teach them the values, beliefs, and skills central to their society; the same schooling that prepared students for life in Anglo-American culture made them singularly unfit for tribal life. As people who stood outside the dominant society, Native Americans were quick to realize education's potential as a tool for enforcing cultural conformity. But despite their resistance, by the 1880s the U.S. government had established special "Indian schools" dedicated to assimilating Indian children into Anglo-American culture and destroying tribal knowledge and tribal ways.

In the nineteenth century two great historical forces — industrialization and immigration — combined to exert even greater pressure for the "homogenization" of young Americans. Massive immigration from Ireland and Eastern and Central Europe led to fears that "non-native" peoples would undermine the cultural identity of the United States. Many saw school as the first line of defense against this perceived threat, a place where the children of "foreigners" could become Americanized. In a meeting of educators in 1836, one college professor stated the problem as bluntly as possible:

> Let us now be reminded, that unless we educate our immigrants, they will be our ruin. It is no longer a mere question of benevolence, of duty, or of enlightened self-interest, but the intellectual and religious training of our foreign population has become essential to our own safety; we are prompted to it by the instinct of self-preservation.

Industrialization gave rise to another kind of uniformity in nineteenth-century public education. Factory work didn't require the kind of educational preparation needed to transform a child into a craftsman or merchant. So, for the first time in American history, school systems began to categorize students into different educational "tracks" that offered qualitatively different kinds of education to different groups. Some — typically students from well-to-do homes — were prepared for professional and managerial positions. But most were consigned to education for life "on the line." Increasing demand for factory workers put a premium on young people who were obedient and able to work in large groups according to fixed schedules. As a result, leading educators in 1874 proposed a system of schooling that would meet the needs of the "modern industrial community" by stressing "punctuality, regularity, attention, and silence, as habits necessary through life." History complicates the myth of education as a source of personal empowerment. School can bind as effectively as it can liberate; it can enforce conformity and limit life chances as well as foster individual talent.

But history also supplies examples of education serving the idealistic goals of democracy, equality, and self-improvement. Nineteenth-century educator and reformer Horace Mann worked to expand educational opportunity to all Americans. Mann believed that genuine democratic self-government would become a reality only if every citizen were sufficiently educated to make reasoned judgments about even the thorniest public issues. "Education," according to Mann, "must prepare our citizens to become municipal officers, intelligent jurors, honest witnesses, legislators, or competent judges of legislation — in fine, to fill all the manifold relations of life." In Mann's conception, the "common school," offering educational opportunity to anyone with the will to learn, would make good on the central promise of American democracy; it would become "the great equalizer of the conditions of men."

At the turn of the century, philosopher and educational theorist John Dewey made even greater claims for educational empowerment. A fierce opponent of the kind of "tracking" associated with industrial education, Dewey proposed that schools should strive to produce thinking citizens rather than obedient workers. As members of a democracy, all men and women, according to Dewey, are entitled to an education that helps them make the best of their natural talents and enables them to participate as fully as possible in the life of their community: "only by being true to the full growth of the individuals who make it up, can society by any chance be true to itself." Most of our current myths of education echo the optimism of Mann and Dewey. Guided by these two men's ideas, most Americans still believe that education leads to self-improvement and can help us empower ourselves — and perhaps even transform our society.

Does education empower us? Or does it stifle personal growth by squeezing us into prefabricated cultural molds? This chapter takes a critical look at American education: what it can do and how it shapes or enhances our identities. The first three readings provide a starting point for exploring the myth of educational empowerment. We begin with an excerpt from a nineteenth-century French study of American schools that offers an overview of some of our most enduring myths of education. Next we turn to a veteran teacher, John Taylor Gatto, and his searing analysis of schooling's implicit agenda. In "I Just Wanna Be Average," Mike Rose offers a moving personal account of the power that teachers can exert, for good or ill, over the students' lives.

The next section takes a closer look at how education works to define us — how it molds our perceptions, values, and destinies. In the excerpt from *Social Class and the Hidden Curriculum of Work,* Jean Anyon suggests that schools virtually program students for success or failure according to their socioeconomic status. The autobiographical selection by Richard Rodriguez raises questions about the ambivalent role education plays in the lives of many Americans who come from families new to the world of higher education. In her dramatic narrative poem "Para Teresa," Inés Hernández-Ávila asks whether academic achievement demands cultural conformity or whether it can become a form of protest against oppression and racism. "Learning to Read" closes this section with the moving story of Malcolm X's spiritual and political rebirth through his self-made education in prison.

The trio of selections that follows focuses more specifically on the experiences of women in the classroom. Myra and David Sadker's "Higher Education: Colder by Degrees" describes a variety of inequalities and abuses suffered by women in higher education. "Connected Education for Women," by psychologist Blythe McVicker Clinchy and her three colleagues, offers an alternative to the traditional model of teaching and learning for women — a model that emphasizes cooperation and personal engagement. Maxine Hong Kingston's "Silence" shows how a cultural mismatch between student and school leads a Chinese American girl to doubt the power of her own voice.

The next pair of readings present dissenting opinions on recent trends in American education. In "Politics in the Schoolroom" former Reagan appointee Lynne V. Cheney offers a conservative critique of two cultural forces — multiculturalism and feminism — that she sees as distorting the true purpose of education in America. Next, cultural critic Theodore Roszak takes on the idea of electronic empowerment in "The Computerized Campus." The chapter closes with a detailed description of one of the most successful contemporary experiments in democratic education — Central Park East Secondary School. In "The Hard Part Is Making It Happen," Deborah Meier and Paul Schwarz offer a model of schooling that suggests that education can be empowering if students are encouraged to take responsibility for their own intellectual development.

Sources

John Hardin Best and Robert T. Sidwell, eds. *The American Legacy of Learning: Readings in the History of Education*. Philadelphia: J. B. Lippincott Co., 1966.

Sol Cohen, ed., *Education in the United States: A Documentary History*, 5 vols. New York: Random House, 1974.

John Dewey, "The School and Society" (1899) and "My Pedagogic Creed" (1897). In *John Dewey on Education*. New York: Modern Library, 1964.

Benjamin Franklin, "Remarks Concerning the Savages of North America." In *The Works of Dr. Benjamin Franklin*. Hartford: S. Andrus and Son, 1849.

Thomas Jefferson, *Notes on the State of Virginia*. Chapel Hill: University of North Carolina Press, 1955.

Lorraine Smith Pangle and Thomas L. Pangle, *The Learning of Liberty: The Educational Ideas of the American Founders*. Lawrence: University Press of Kansas, 1993.

Leonard Pitt, *We Americans,* vol. 2, 3rd ed. Dubuque: Kendall/Hunt, 1987.

Edward Stevens and George H. Wood, *Justice, Ideology, and Education: An Introduction to the Social Foundations of Education.* New York: Random House, 1987.

Elizabeth Vallance, "Hiding the Hidden Curriculum: An Interpretation of the Language of Justification in Nineteenth-Century Educational Reform." *Curriculum Theory Network,* vol. 4. no. 1 (1973–74), pp. 5–21.

Robert B. Westbrook, "Public Schooling and American Democracy." In *Democracy, Education, and the Schools,* Roger Soder, ed. San Francisco: Jossey-Bass Publishers, 1996.

BEFORE READING

- Freewrite for fifteen or twenty minutes about your best and worst educational experiences. Then, working in groups, compare notes to see if you can find recurring themes or ideas in what you've written. What aspects of school seem to stand out most clearly in your memories? Do the best experiences have anything in common? How about the worst? What aspects of your school experience didn't show up in the freewriting?

- Work in small groups to draw a collective picture that expresses your experience of high school or college. Don't worry about your drawing skill — just load the page with imagery, feelings, and ideas. Then show your work to other class members and let them try to interpret it.

- Write a journal entry from the point of view of the girl pictured on the title page of this chapter (p. 153). Try to capture the thoughts that are going through her head. What has her day in school been like? What is she looking forward to? What is she dreading? Share your entries with your classmates and discuss your responses.

From *Report of the French Commission on American Education, 1879*

After winning political independence from Europe, American leaders were anxious to declare their intellectual independence as well. The first generation of U.S. citizens wanted to fashion a new society — one that would fight free of the old ideas, prejudices, and animosities associated with the Old World. The tool they chose to bring about this cultural revolution was the school. Thinkers like Benjamin Franklin and Daniel Webster wanted to create a distinctly American approach to education, an approach that would be practical, worldly, and free — the exact opposite of the rigid, aristocratic value system that dominated instruction in European schools. Yet, oddly enough, it was often Europeans who most admired early American efforts to rethink schooling. The following selection, excerpted from a report delivered to the French government by a delegation sent to document American educational innovations, reflects Europe's fascination with schooling in the United States. It also offers a snapshot of what American schools were meant to do in the last quarter of the nineteenth century, just when industrialization and immigration were shaping modern American attitudes toward education. This selection appears in Education in the United States: A Documentary History *(1974). Sol Cohen, the editor of this five-volume series, is professor of social sciences and comparative education at the University of California, Los Angeles.*

"A republican government needs the whole power of education." These words of Montesquieu have, perhaps, never found a more striking application than in the subject which we are now about to consider. If there be a nation which has expected everything from this power of education, which has intimately united its national destinies with the development of its schools, which has made public instruction the supreme guarantee of its liberties, the condition of its prosperity, and the safeguard of its institutions, that nation certainly is the people of the United States.

The peculiar position assigned to the school in American social life has always been one of the first points to attract the attention of foreigners.

The great zeal for the education of the young which grows as the population increases, penetrates into the public mind more and more, and manifests itself in more and more decided ways. What may have seemed at first a transient glow of enthusiasm, a generous impulse, has in time assumed all the force of a logical conviction or rather of a positive certainty. It is no longer a movement of a few philanthropists or of a few religious societies, but it is an essential part of the public administration for which the States, the cities, and townships appropriate every year more money than any other country in the world has hitherto devoted to the education of the people. Far from limiting this generosity as much as possible to primary instruction, it goes so far as to declare free for all not only primary but even secondary schools.

The laws and customs of the country are in perfect harmony in regard to this practice; public opinion approves and even insists upon these sacrifices, so evident has it become to every one that the future of the American people will be whatever its schools make it.

Among the many influences which gave the American school this unique importance, the influence of Protestant ideas was one of the first. 5

The early settlers of New England did not recognize a more important duty or a greater privilege than that of reading the Bible. The first charter of every settlement compelled it to establish schools and compelled every family to educate its children.

As soon as democratic institutions were more fully developed, the former religious duty became gradually a political necessity. The form of the United States Government established a hundred years ago, making everything depend upon the will of the people, assumes that will to be enlightened as the only safeguard against the worst calamities.

The United States have been peopled by continuous immigration. But what does this immigration bring to the country? People of different origins, classes, and religions. The many thousands that arrive have frequently nothing in common except the desire which animates nearly all immigrants, viz, to improve their condition. No previous education has prepared them for this new political and social government which was not intended for them; for what could less resemble the Puritan colonists of New England than the heterogeneous, unstable, and ignorant mass which constitutes the greater part of the immigration? These are the elements of which a nation has to be made; without roughly assailing, too, the veneration immigrants feel for any former national or religious customs, all must be "Americanized" as fast as possible. It is necessary that within one or two generations the Irish, Germans, French, Scandinavians, Spaniards, shall not have the slightest inclination to constitute nations within the nation, but that they shall all have become Americans themselves, and be proud of being so.

What is the cause of this wonderful transformation? What instrumentality infuses American blood into the veins of these thousands of people who have hardly had time to forget Europe? Every statesman will tell you, "It is the public school"; and this single service which the school renders to the nation is considered by many Americans sufficient to justify all the expense it involves. Suppose the immigrants were left to their own inspirations, and instead of public schools should find only private institutions; everything would be different: each person would keep up his own customs or preferences; each group would constitute itself separately, preserve its own language, traditions, religious customs, its old national spirit, and its prejudices. In denominational schools the distinction between rich and poor, paying and non-paying pupils, would necessarily be perpetuated and emphasized. And without fusion of races, without a uniform language, without equality of social classes, without reciprocal toleration among the different denominations, and, above all, without an ardent love for the new country and its institutions, would the United States still be united? . . .

If the political future of the United States depends on the efficiency of her schools, her commercial future is no less directly interested. The conditions of labor in the New World are such that success depends, as it were, on a certain degree of education. In industrial, commercial, agricultural, financial, or other occupations, the success of each will be almost in proportion to his intelligence. No one finds his career definitely marked out. If it is becoming rare in the Old World to see sons follow the profession of their fathers during several generations, in the United States it is still more exceptional. The spirit of initiative, of enterprise, of adventure, even, is the result of this entirely new civilization; there is no America without the "go ahead." Work without any other aim than a moderate salary, the humble prospect of a life of toil, is not the ideal of the American. No people works more, but, also, no other people attaches a higher value to its labor than the American people. What Europeans call Yankee greed or speculation is nothing but the effect of this intelligence which accompanies their work and of the high price which they demand for their labor. "To be content with little," advice of ancient philosophy, finds no credit in the New World. Under these circumstances education has a double value: it has besides its real value a kind of surplus value, resulting from its practical and commercial usefulness. The whole political economy of the United States takes this for granted; without it, neither the farmer nor the business man would be able to calculate his chances of success; the artisan and the laborer would not endeavor to improve their work, to lessen their hardships, or to increase their profits. The wealth of the United States is incalculable precisely because intellectual wealth counts for an enormous proportion. We sometimes think that the eagerness of the Americans to support and improve schools is a kind of national pride, vanity, or show. Not at all. It is a calculation, and a sound one; enormous advances are made, but it is known that they will be returned a hundredfold.

In 1870 the United States Bureau of Education sent several thousand   10
circulars to workmen, employers, and observers who were supposed to know the condition of the working classes. These circulars solicited information in regard to difference of skill, aptitude, or amount of work executed by persons employed which arose from a difference in their education and independent of their natural abilities; whether those who could read and write showed any greater skill, and how such skill tends to increase their wages; whether they are more economical; whether, finally, educated laborers were preferred. The answers sent to the Bureau of Education are most interesting. With one exception, all the correspondents recommend, for economical reasons, the education of the people, because, they say, intelligence increases the value of manual labor. The only exception was in the planters of the Southern States, who were almost all opposed to the education of the negroes. Some asserted that the colored people are not fit for education or civilization; others, that the negroes do not need education, and that the more they resemble beasts of burden the more easily they can be made to work.

Besides political and economical motives, there is still another, the moral motive, which must encourage the United States in their zeal for public education. If the Americans expect their public schools to prepare citizens who shall be permeated with the national spirit, it is not less nec-

essary that the young generation be imbued with sufficient moral principles; and to accomplish this the school is the principal, often the surest,
instrumentality.

From a variety of causes, family ties are far less strong in the United
States than in Europe. The frequent separation of the parents which results
from commercial and agricultural occupations in an immense territory; the
feverish zeal of many fathers in business; the general spirit of independence; the custom of self government which the young American draws, as
it were, from the air he inhales; the custom which excuses even young
women from asking the permission of their parents for most of their actions,
and from giving an account thereof; the laws, finally, which sanction the existing customs, frequently shorten the duration of childhood and weaken
parental authority. These are some of the causes which have greatly reduced the moral influence of the family. Does the school supply this want of
moral and domestic education? It is difficult to believe that it supplies it entirely, but it certainly does partially. The children of the lower classes will
learn at school how to behave and will lose some of the rudeness of their
manners. In school they hear the duties of respectable people authoritatively explained and receive moral directions of an elementary character for
practical life; here they are trained to be members of a civilized country.

ENGAGING THE TEXT

1. What basic functions does education perform in U.S. society according to
   the authors of the *Report of the French Commission*? Which of these do
   you feel is the most important? Why? Which, if any, seems inappropriate?
   In your opinion, what other important purposes or functions of education
   do the authors fail to mention?

2. What assumptions do the authors of this report make about American culture, the average American's chances for self-improvement, and the American family? Do these assumptions hold true today?

EXPLORING CONNECTIONS

3. Contrast the view of education presented in the *Report of the French Commission* to that suggested by the Matt Groening cartoons that follow this
   selection (pp. 164–65). Which of these visions of education seems more accurate to you? Why?

EXTENDING THE CRITICAL CONTEXT

4. Conduct a mini-poll of three to five people to find out what they think the
   primary goals of education in American society should be. Share your results in small groups and compare them with the statements made in the
   Report of the French Commission. In general, how have attitudes toward
   education changed over the past hundred years?

5. Working in small groups, make a report card for American education, grading how effectively U.S. schools fulfill the functions spelled out in the *Report of the French Commission.* You may also want to give grades for other goals or functions that your group feels are important. When you're finished, compare and discuss your results with the rest of the class.

From School is Hell © 1987 Matt Groening. All Rights Reserved. Reprinted by permission of Pantheon, a division of Random House Publishers, Inc., New York.

The Seven-Lesson Schoolteacher
JOHN TAYLOR GATTO

There's no doubt that America's schools are meant to benefit the students they serve; they're intended to transmit a body of knowledge — a curriculum — that equips students with all the ideas, skills, and attitudes necessary to help them lead happy and productive lives. But even the best intentions can go awry; as John Taylor Gatto argues in this selection, education in the United States may harbor a "hidden curriculum" — an unwritten, unacknowledged set of lessons about self and society that schooling inflicts on every student from kindergarten to graduate school. An award-winning educator and ardent Libertarian, Gatto suggests that what school does best is to inculcate seven such unconscious and debilitating lessons. Gatto has taught in New York City public schools for more than two decades. In 1990 he was named New York City Teacher of the Year. This selection comes from Dumbing Us Down: The Hidden Curriculum of Compulsory Schooling *(1992).*

I

Call me Mr. Gatto, please. Twenty-six years ago, having nothing better to do with myself at the time, I tried my hand at schoolteaching. The license I have certifies that I am an instructor of English language and English literature, but that isn't what I do at all. I don't teach English, I teach school — and I win awards doing it.

Teaching means different things in different places, but seven lessons are universally taught from Harlem to Hollywood Hills. They constitute a national curriculum you pay for in more ways than you can imagine, so you might as well know what it is. You are at liberty, of course, to regard these lessons any way you like, but believe me when I say I intend no irony in this presentation. These are the things I teach, these are the things you pay me to teach. Make of them what you will.

1. Confusion

A lady named Kathy wrote this to me from Dubois, Indiana the other day:

> What big ideas are important to little kids? Well, the biggest idea I think they need is that what they are learning isn't idiosyncratic — that there is some system to it all and it's not just raining down on them as they helplessly absorb. That's the task, to understand, to make coherent.

Kathy has it wrong. *The first lesson I teach is confusion. Everything* I teach is out of context. I teach the un-relating of everything. I teach disconnections. I teach too much: the orbiting of planets, the law of large numbers, slavery, adjectives, architectural drawing, dance, gymnasium, choral singing, assemblies, surprise guests, fire drills, computer languages, parents' nights, staff-development days, pull-out programs, guidance with strangers my students may never see again, standardized tests, age-segregation unlike anything seen in the outside world. . . . What do any of these things have to do with each other?

Even in the best schools a close examination of curriculum and its sequences turns up a lack of coherence, full of internal contradictions. Fortunately the children have no words to define the panic and anger they feel *at constant violations of natural order and sequence* fobbed off on them as quality in education. The logic of the school-mind is that it is better to leave school with a tool kit of superficial jargon derived from economics, sociology, natural science, and so on, than with one genuine enthusiasm. But quality in education entails learning about something in depth. Confusion is thrust upon kids by too many strange adults, each working alone with only the thinnest relationship with each other, pretending, for the most part, to an expertise they do not possess.

Meaning, not disconnected facts, is what sane human beings seek, and education is a set of codes for processing raw data into meaning. Behind the patchwork quilt of school sequences and the school obsession with facts and theories, the age-old human search for meaning lies well concealed. This is harder to see in elementary school where the hierarchy of school experience seems to make better sense because the good-natured simple relationship between "let's do this" and "let's do that" is just assumed to mean something and the clientele has not yet consciously discerned how little substance is behind the play and pretense.

Think of the great natural sequences — like learning to walk and learning to talk; the progression of light from sunrise to sunset; the ancient procedures of a farmer, a smithy, or a shoemaker; or the preparation of a Thanksgiving feast — all of the parts are in perfect harmony with each other, each action justifies itself and illuminates the past and the future. School sequences aren't like that, not inside a single class and not among the total menu of daily classes. School sequences are crazy. There is no particular reason for any of them, nothing that bears close scrutiny. Few teachers would dare to teach the tools whereby dogmas of a school or a teacher could be criticized, since everything must be accepted. School subjects are learned, if they *can* be learned, like children learn the catechism or memorize the Thirty-nine Articles of Anglicanism.

I teach the un-relating of everything, an infinite fragmentation the opposite of cohesion; what I do is more related to television programming than to making a scheme of order. In a world where home is only a ghost, because both parents work, or because of too many moves or too many job changes or too much ambition, or because something else has left every-body too confused to maintain a family relation, I teach you how to accept confusion as your destiny. That's the first lesson I teach.

2. Class Position

The second lesson I teach is class position. I teach that students must stay in the class where they belong. I don't know who decides my kids belong there but that's not my business. The children are numbered so that if any get away they can be returned to the right class. Over the years the variety of ways children are numbered by schools has increased dramatically, until it is hard to see the human beings plainly under the weight of numbers they carry. Numbering children is a big and very profitable undertaking, though what the strategy is designed to accomplish is elusive. I don't even know why parents would, without a fight, allow it to be done to their kids.

In any case, that's not my business. My job is to make them like being   10
locked together with children who bear numbers like their own. Or at the least to endure it like good sports. If I do my job well, the kids can't even *imagine* themselves somewhere else, because I've shown them how to envy and fear the better classes and how to have contempt for the dumb classes. Under this efficient discipline the class mostly polices itself into good marching order. That's the real lesson of any rigged competition like school. You come to know your place.

In spite of the overall class blueprint, which assumes that ninety-nine percent of the kids are in their class to stay, I nevertheless make a public effort to exhort children to higher levels of test success, hinting at eventual transfer from the lower class as a reward. I frequently insinuate the day will come when an employer will hire them on the basis of test scores and grades, even though my own experience is that employers are rightly indifferent to such things. I never lie outright, but I've come to see that truth and schoolteaching are, at bottom, incompatible, just as Socrates said thousands of years ago. The lesson of numbered classes is that everyone has a proper place in the pyramid and there is no way out of your class except by number magic. Failing that, you must stay where you are put.

3. Indifference

The third lesson I teach is indifference. I teach children not to care too much about anything, even though they want to make it appear that they do. How I do this is very subtle. I do it by demanding that they become totally involved in my lessons, jumping up and down in their seats with anticipation, competing vigorously with each other for my favor. It's heartwarming when they do that; it impresses everyone, even me. When I'm at my best I plan lessons very carefully in order to produce this show of enthusiasm. But when the bell rings I insist they drop whatever it is we have been doing and proceed quickly to the next work station. They must turn on and off like a light switch. Nothing important is ever finished in my class nor in any class I know of. Students never have a complete experience except on the installment plan.

Indeed, the lesson of bells is that no work is worth finishing, so why care too deeply about anything? Years of bells will condition all but the strongest to a world that can no longer offer important work to do. Bells are the secret logic of schooltime; their logic is inexorable. Bells destroy the past and future, rendering every interval the same as any other, as the abstraction of a map renders every living mountain and river the same, even though they are not. Bells inoculate each undertaking with indifference.

4. Emotional Dependency

The fourth lesson I teach is emotional dependency. By stars and red checks, smiles and frowns, prizes, honors, and disgraces, I teach kids to surrender their will to the predestinated chain of command. Rights may be granted or withheld by any authority without appeal, because rights do not exist inside a school — not even the right of free speech, as the Supreme Court has ruled — unless school authorities say they do. As a schoolteacher, I intervene in many personal decisions, issuing a pass for those I deem legitimate, or initiating a disciplinary confrontation for behavior that threatens my control. Individuality is constantly trying to assert itself among children and teenagers, so my judgments come thick and fast. Individuality is a contradiction of class theory, a curse to all systems of classification.

Here are some common ways it shows up: children sneak away for a   15
private moment in the toilet on the pretext of moving their bowels, or they steal a private instant in the hallway on the grounds they need water. I know they don't, but I allow them to "deceive" me because this conditions them to depend on my favors. Sometimes free will appears right in front of me in pockets of children angry, depressed, or unhappy about things outside my ken; rights in such matters cannot be recognized by schoolteachers, only privileges that can be withdrawn, hostages to good behavior.

5. Intellectual Dependency

The fifth lesson I teach is intellectual dependency. Good students wait for a teacher to tell them what to do. It is the most important lesson, that we must wait for other people, better trained than ourselves, to make the meanings of our lives. The expert makes all the important choices; only I, the teacher, can determine what my kids must study, or rather, only the people who pay me can make those decisions, which I then enforce. If I'm told that evolution is a fact instead of a theory, I transmit that as ordered, punishing deviants who resist what I have been told to tell them to think. This power to control what children will think lets me separate successful students from failures very easily.

Successful children do the thinking I assign them with a minimum of resistance and a decent show of enthusiasm. Of the millions of things of value to study, I decide what few we have time for, or actually it is decided by my faceless employers. The choices are theirs, why should I argue? Curiosity has no important place in my work, only conformity.

Bad kids fight this, of course, even though they lack the concepts to know what they are fighting, struggling to make decisions for themselves about what they will learn and when they will learn it. How can we allow that and survive as schoolteachers? Fortunately there are tested procedures to break the will of those who resist; it is more difficult, naturally, if the kids have respectable parents who come to their aid, but that happens less and less in spite of the bad reputation of schools. No middle-class parents I have ever met actually believe that *their* kid's school is one of the bad ones. Not one single parent in twenty-six years of teaching. That's amazing, and probably the best testimony to what happens to families when mother and father have been well-schooled themselves, learning the seven lessons.

Good people wait for an expert to tell them what to do. It is hardly an exaggeration to say that our entire economy depends upon this lesson being learned. Think of what might fall apart if children weren't trained to be dependent: the social services could hardly survive; they would vanish, I think, into the recent historical limbo out of which they arose. Counselors and therapists would look on in horror as the supply of psychic invalids vanished. Commercial entertainment of all sorts, including television, would wither as people learned again how to make their own fun. Restaurants, the prepared-food industry, and a whole host of other assorted food services would be drastically down-sized if people returned to making their own meals rather than depending on strangers to plant, pick, chop, and cook for them. Much of modern law, medicine, and engineering would go too, the clothing business and schoolteaching as well, unless a guaranteed supply of helpless people continued to pour out of our schools each year.

Don't be too quick to vote for radical school reform if you want to continue getting a paycheck. We've built a way of life that depends on people doing what they are told because they don't know how to tell *themselves* what to do. It's one of the biggest lessons I teach.   20

6. *Provisional Self-Esteem*

The sixth lesson I teach is provisional self-esteem. If you've ever tried to wrestle into line kids whose parents have convinced them to believe they'll be loved in spite of anything, you know how impossible it is to make self-confident spirits conform. Our world wouldn't survive a flood of confident people very long, so I teach that a kid's self-respect should depend on expert opinion. My kids are constantly evaluated and judged.

A monthly report, impressive in its provision, is sent into a student's home to elicit approval or mark exactly, down to a single percentage point, how dissatisfied with the child a parent should be. The ecology of "good" schooling depends on perpetuating dissatisfaction, just as the commercial economy depends on the same fertilizer. Although some people might be surprised how little time or reflection goes into making up these mathematical records, the cumulative weight of these objective-seeming documents establishes a profile that compels children to arrive at certain decisions about themselves and their futures based on the casual judgment of strangers. Self-evaluation, the staple of every major philosophical system that ever appeared on the planet, is never considered a factor. The lesson of report cards, grades, and tests is that children should not trust themselves or their parents but should instead rely on the evaluation of certified officials. People need to be told what they are worth.

7. One Can't Hide

The seventh lesson I teach is that one can't hide. I teach students they are always watched, that each is under constant surveillance by myself and my colleagues. There are no private spaces for children, there is no private time. Class change lasts exactly three hundred seconds to keep promiscuous fraternization at low levels. Students are encouraged to tattle on each other or even to tattle on their own parents. Of course, I encourage parents to file reports about their own child's waywardness too. A family trained to snitch on itself isn't likely to conceal any dangerous secrets.

I assign a type of extended schooling called "homework," so that the effect of surveillance, if not that surveillance itself, travels into private households, where students might otherwise use free time to learn something unauthorized from a father or mother, by exploration, or by apprenticing to some wise person in the neighborhood. Disloyalty to the idea of schooling is a devil always ready to find work for idle hands.

The meaning of constant surveillance and denial of privacy is that no one can be trusted, that privacy is not legitimate. Surveillance is an ancient imperative, espoused by certain influential thinkers, a central prescription set down in *The Republic*, in *The City of God*, in the *Institutes of the Christian Religion*, in *New Atlantis*, in *Leviathan*,[1] and in a host of other places. All these childless men who wrote these books discovered the same thing: children must be closely watched if you want to keep a society under tight central control. Children will follow a private drummer if you can't get them into a uniformed marching band.

25

II

It is the great triumph of compulsory government monopoly mass-schooling that among even the best of my fellow teachers, and among even the best of my students' parents, only a small number can imagine a different way to do things. "The kids have to know how to read and write, don't they?" "They have to know how to add and subtract, don't they?" "They have to learn to follow orders if they ever expect to keep a job."

---

[1]*The Republic,* in *The City of God . . . Leviathan:* Famous political and philosophical writings by authors like Plato, St. Augustine, and Thomas Hobbes.

Only a few lifetimes ago things were very different in the United States. Originality and variety were common currency; our freedom from regimentation made us the miracle of the world; social-class boundaries were relatively easy to cross; our citizenry was marvelously confident, inventive, and able to do much for themselves independently, and to think for themselves. We were something special, we Americans, all by ourselves, without government sticking its nose into and measuring every aspect of our lives, without institutions and social agencies telling us how to think and feel. We were something special, as individuals, as Americans.

But we've had a society essentially under central control in the United States since just before the Civil War, and such a society requires compulsory schooling, government monopoly schooling, to maintain itself. Before this development schooling wasn't very important anywhere. We had it, but not too much of it, and only as much as an individual *wanted*. People learned to read, write, and do arithmetic just fine anyway; there are some studies that suggest literacy at the time of the American Revolution, at least for non-slaves on the Eastern seaboard, was close to total. Thomas Paine's *Common Sense*[2] sold 600,000 copies to a population of 3,000,000, twenty percent of whom were slaves, and fifty percent indentured servants.

Were the colonists geniuses? No, the truth is that reading, writing, and arithmetic only take about one hundred hours to transmit as long as the audience is eager and willing to learn. The trick is to wait until someone asks and then move fast while the mood is on. Millions of people teach themselves these things, it really isn't very hard. Pick up a fifth-grade math or rhetoric textbook from 1850 and you'll see that the texts were pitched then on what would today be considered college level. The continuing cry for "basic skills" practice is a smoke screen behind which schools preempt the time of children for twelve years and teach them the seven lessons I've just described to you.

The society that has come increasingly under central control since just before the Civil War shows itself in the lives we lead, the clothes we wear, the food we eat, and the green highway signs we drive by from coast to coast, all of which are the products of this control. So too, I think, are the epidemics of drugs, suicide, divorce, violence, cruelty, and hardening of class into caste in the United States products of the dehumanization of our lives, the lessening of individual, family, and community importance, a diminishment that proceeds from central control. The character of large compulsory institutions is inevitable; they want more and more until there isn't any more to give. School takes our children away from any possibility of an active role in community life — in fact it destroys communities by relegating the training of children to the hands of certified experts — and by doing so it ensures our children cannot grow up fully human. Aristotle taught that without a fully active role in   30

[2]*Common Sense:* Paine's fifty-page pamphlet, published January 10, 1776, was recognized as the war-cry of the American revolutionary movement.

community life one could not hope to become a healthy human being. Surely he was right. Look around you the next time you are near a school or an old people's reservation if you wish a demonstration.

School as it was built is an essential support system for a model of social engineering that condemns most people to be subordinate stones in a pyramid that narrows as it ascends to a terminal of control. School is an artifice that makes such a pyramidical social order seem inevitable, although such a premise is a fundamental betrayal of the American Revolution. From Colonial days through the period of the Republic we had no schools to speak of — read Benjamin Franklin's *Autobiography* for an example of a man who had no time to waste in school — and yet the promise of democracy was beginning to be realized. We turned our backs on this promise by bringing to life the ancient pharaonic dream of Egypt: compulsory subordination for all. That was the secret Plato reluctantly transmitted in *The Republic* when Glaucon and Adeimantus extort from Socrates the plan for total state control of human life, a plan necessary to maintain a society where some people take more than their share. "'I will show you,'" says Socrates, "'how to bring about such a feverish city, but you will not like what I am going to say.'" And so the blueprint of the seven-lesson school was first sketched.

The current debate about whether we should have a national curriculum is phony. We already have a national curriculum locked up in the seven lessons I have just outlined. Such a curriculum produces physical, moral, and intellectual paralysis, and no curriculum of content will be sufficient to reverse its hideous effects. What is currently under discussion in our national hysteria about failing academic performance misses the point. Schools teach exactly what they are intended to teach and they do it well: how to be a good Egyptian and remain in your place in the pyramid.

ENGAGING THE TEXT

1. Working in groups, try to summarize each of the seven lessons that Gatto claims are taught as part of the hidden curriculum in all American schools. To what extent does the collective experience of your group support or challenge Gatto's claims?

2. Working together in small groups, construct an imaginary profile of the kind of student that Gatto's seven-lesson teacher would be likely to produce. How accurately does this portrait describe most high school graduates intellectually, socially, and emotionally?

3. Freewrite for a page or two about a particular teacher you had who didn't fit Gatto's description of the seven-lesson teacher. What set this teacher apart or made her stand out for you? To what extent did she teach any or all of the lessons outlined by Gatto?

4. What does Gatto mean when he says that "truth and schoolteaching are, at bottom, incompatible" (para. 11)? Given his concerns about the impact of public education, why do you think Gatto continues to teach?

EXPLORING CONNECTIONS

5. How might Gatto assess the vision of education presented in excerpt from the *Report of the French Commission* (p. 159)? How can you explain the gulf between Gatto's analysis of the function of education and that presented in the *Report*? Try to generate several possible explanations; which strikes you as the most interesting or plausible?

6. Compare the "lessons" taught in the Matt Groening cartoons that preceded this selection (pp. 164–65) with those described by Gatto. To what extent is Gatto's indictment of education simply a matter of perspective?

7. Look ahead to Jean Anyon's excerpt from *Social Class and the Hidden Curriculum of Work* (p. 186) and compare Anyon's analysis of the hidden agenda of American education with that described by Gatto. Which of Gatto's seven lessons might be explained by differences of social class? Which, if any, seem unrelated to issues of status or class position?

EXTENDING THE CRITICAL CONTEXT

8. Evaluate the hidden curriculum of the college courses you've taken or are currently enrolled in. To what extent do they reinforce or counter the lessons that Gatto describes?

9. Working in groups, brainstorm a design for a school that would make it *impossible* to teach the hidden curriculum that Gatto describes. How would classes be structured in such a school? What roles would teachers and students play? What would students study? How would they be graded?

"I Just Wanna Be Average"

MIKE ROSE

Mike Rose is anything but average: he has published poetry, scholarly research, a textbook, and two widely praised books on education in America. A professor in the School of Education at UCLA, Rose has won awards from the National Academy of Education, the National Council of Teachers of English, and the John Simon Guggenheim Memorial Foundation. Below you'll read the story of how this highly successful teacher and writer started high school in the "vocational education" track, learning dead-end skills from teachers who were often underprepared or incompetent. Rose shows that students whom the system has written off can have tremendous unrealized potential, and his critique of the school system specifies several reasons for the "failure" of students who go through high school belligerent, fearful, stoned, frustrated, or just plain bored. This selection comes from Lives on

the Boundary *(1989), Rose's exploration of America's educationally under-*
privileged. His most recent book, Possible Lives *(1996), offers a nationwide*
tour of creative classrooms and innovative educational programs.

It took two buses to get to Our Lady of Mercy. The first started deep in
South Los Angeles and caught me at midpoint. The second drifted through
neighborhoods with trees, parks, big lawns, and lots of flowers. The rides
were long but were livened up by a group of South L.A. veterans whose parents also thought that Hope had set up shop in the west end of the county.
There was Christy Biggars, who, at sixteen, was dealing and was, according
to rumor, a pimp as well. There were Bill Cobb and Johnny Gonzales,
grease-pencil artists extraordinaire, who left Nembutal-enhanced[1] swirls of
"Cobb" and "Johnny" on the corrugated walls of the bus. And then there
was Tyrrell Wilson. Tyrrell was the coolest kid I knew. He ran the dozens[2]
like a metric halfback, laid down a rap that outrhymed and outpointed
Cobb, whose rap was good but not great — the curse of a moderately soul-
ful kid trapped in white skin. But it was Cobb who would sneak a radio onto
the bus, and thus underwrote his patter with Little Richard, Fats Domino,
Chuck Berry, the Coasters,[3] and Ernie K. Doe's mother-in-law, an awful
woman who was "sent from down below." And so it was that Christy and
Cobb and Johnny G. and Tyrrell and I and assorted others picked up along
the way passed our days in the back of the bus, a funny mix brought together by geography and parental desire.

Entrance to school brings with it forms and releases and assessments.
Mercy relied on a series of tests, mostly the Stanford-Binet,[4] for placement,
and somehow the results of my tests got confused with those of another student named Rose. The other Rose apparently didn't do very well, for I was
placed in the vocational track, a euphemism for the bottom level. Neither I
nor my parents realized what this meant. We had no sense that Business
Math, Typing, and English–Level D were dead ends. The current spate of
reports on the schools criticizes parents for not involving themselves in the
education of their children. But how would someone like Tommy Rose,
with his two years of Italian schooling, know what to ask? And what sort of
pressure could an exhausted waitress apply? The error went undetected,
and I remained in the vocational track for two years. What a place.

[1]*Nembutal:* Trade name for pentobarbital, a sedative drug.

[2]*the dozens:* A verbal game of African origin in which competitors try to top each other's
insults.

[3]*Little Richard, Fats Domino, Chuck Berry, the Coasters:* Popular black musicians of the
1950s.

[4]*Stanford-Binet:* An IQ test.

My homeroom was supervised by Brother Dill, a troubled and unstable man who also taught freshman English. When his class drifted away from him, which was often, his voice would rise in paranoid accusations, and occasionally he would lose control and shake or smack us. I hadn't been there two months when one of his brisk, face-turning slaps had my glasses sliding down the aisle. Physical education was also pretty harsh. Our teacher was a stubby ex-lineman who had played old-time pro ball in the Midwest. He routinely had us grabbing our ankles to receive his stinging paddle across our butts. He did that, he said, to make men of us. "Rose," he bellowed on our first encounter; me standing geeky in line in my baggy shorts. "'Rose'? What the hell kind of name is that?"

"Italian, sir," I squeaked.

"Italian! Ho. Rose, do you know the sound a bag of shit makes when it   5
hits the wall?"

"No, sir."

"Wop!"[5]

Sophomore English was taught by Mr. Mitropetros. He was a large, bejeweled man who managed the parking lot at the Shrine Auditorium. He would crow and preen and list for us the stars he'd brushed against. We'd ask questions and glance knowingly and snicker, and all that fueled the poor guy to brag some more. Parking cars was his night job. He had little training in English, so his lesson plan for his day work had us reading the district's required text, *Julius Caesar,* aloud for the semester. We'd finished the play way before the twenty weeks was up, so he'd have us switch parts again and again and start again: Dave Snyder, the fastest guy at Mercy, muscling through Caesar to the breathless squeals of Calpurnia, as interpreted by Steve Fusco, a surfer who owned the school's most envied paneled wagon. Week ten and Dave and Steve would take on new roles, as would we all, and render a water-logged Cassius and a Brutus that are beyond my powers of description.

Spanish I — taken in the second year — fell into the hands of a new recruit. Mr. Montez was a tiny man, slight, five foot six at the most, soft-spoken and delicate. Spanish was a particularly rowdy class, and Mr. Montez was as prepared for it as a doily maker at a hammer throw. He would tap his pencil to a room in which Steve Fusco was propelling spitballs from his heavy lips, in which Mike Dweetz was taunting Billy Hawk, a half-Indian, half-Spanish, reed-thin, quietly explosive boy. The vocational track at Our Lady of Mercy mixed kids traveling in from South L.A. with South Bay surfers and a few Slavs and Chicanos from the harbors of San Pedro. This was a dangerous miscellany: surfers and hodads[6] and South-Central blacks all ablaze to the metronomic tapping of Hector Montez's pencil.

---

[5]*Wop:* Derogatory term for Italian.
[6]*hodads:* Nonsurfers.

One day Billy lost it. Out of the corner of my eye I saw him strike out   10
with his right arm and catch Dweetz across the neck. Quick as a spasm,
Dweetz was out of his seat, scattering desks, cracking Billy on the side of
the head, right behind the eye. Snyder and Fusco and others broke it up,
but the room felt hot and close and naked. Mr. Montez's tenuous authority
was finally ripped to shreds, and I think everyone felt a little strange about
that. The charade was over, and when it came down to it, I don't think any
of the kids really wanted it to end this way. They had pushed and pushed
and bullied their way into a freedom that both scared and embarrassed
them.

Students will float to the mark you set. I and the others in the vocational classes were bobbing in pretty shallow water. Vocational education
has aimed at increasing the economic opportunities of students who do not
do well in our schools. Some serious programs succeed in doing that, and
through exceptional teachers — like Mr. Gross in *Horace's Compromise*[7] —
students learn to develop hypotheses and troubleshoot, reason through a
problem, and communicate effectively — the true job skills. The vocational
track, however, is most often a place for those who are just not making it, a
dumping ground for the disaffected. There were a few teachers who worked
hard at education; young Brother Slattery, for example, combined a stern
voice with weekly quizzes to try to pass along to us a skeletal outline of
world history. But mostly the teachers had no idea of how to engage the
imaginations of us kids who were scuttling along at the bottom of the pond.

And the teachers would have needed some inventiveness, for none of
us was groomed for the classroom. It wasn't just that I didn't know things —
didn't know how to simplify algebraic fractions, couldn't identify different
kinds of clauses, bungled Spanish translations — but that I had developed
various faulty and inadequate ways of doing algebra and making sense of
Spanish. Worse yet, the years of defensive tuning out in elementary school
had given me a way to escape quickly while seeming at least half alert. During my time in Voc. Ed., I developed further into a mediocre student and a
somnambulant problem solver, and that affected the subjects I did have the
wherewithal to handle: I detested Shakespeare; I got bored with history. My
attention flitted here and there. I fooled around in class and read my books
indifferently — the intellectual equivalent of playing with your food. I did
what I had to do to get by, and I did it with half a mind.

But I did learn things about people and eventually came into my own
socially. I liked the guys in Voc. Ed. Growing up where I did, I understood
and admired physical prowess, and there was an abundance of muscle here.
There was Dave Snyder, a sprinter and halfback of true quality. Dave's ability and his quick wit gave him a natural appeal, and he was welcome in any

---

[7]*Horace's Compromise:* A book on American education by Theodore Sizer.

clique, though he always kept a little independent. He enjoyed acting the fool and could care less about studies, but he possessed a certain maturity and never caused the faculty much trouble. It was a testament to his independence that he included me among his friends — I eventually went out for track, but I was no jock. Owing to the Latin alphabet and a dearth of *R*s and *S*s, Snyder sat behind Rose, and we started exchanging one-liners and became friends.

There was Ted Richard, a much-touted Little League pitcher. He was chunky and had a baby face and came to Our Lady of Mercy as a seasoned street fighter. Ted was quick to laugh and he had a loud, jolly laugh, but when he got angry he'd smile a little smile, the kind that simply raises the corner of the mouth a quarter of an inch. For those who knew, it was an eerie signal. Those who didn't found themselves in big trouble, for Ted was very quick. He loved to carry on what we would come to call philosophical discussions: What is courage? Does God exist? He also loved words, enjoyed picking up big ones like *salubrious* and *equivocal* and using them in our conversations — laughing at himself as the word hit a chuckhole rolling off his tongue. Ted didn't do all that well in school — baseball and parties and testing the courage he'd speculated about took up his time. His textbooks were *Argosy* and *Field and Stream,* whatever newspapers he'd find on the bus stop — from the *Daily Worker* to pornography — conversations with uncles or hobos or businessmen he'd meet in a coffee shop, *The Old Man and the Sea.* With hindsight, I can see that Ted was developing into one of those rough-hewn intellectuals whose sources are a mix of the learned and the apocryphal, whose discussions are both assured and sad.

And then there was Ken Harvey. Ken was good-looking in a puffy way and had a full and oily ducktail and was a car enthusiast . . . a hodad. One day in religion class, he said the sentence that turned out to be one of the most memorable of the hundreds of thousands I heard in those Voc. Ed. years. We were talking about the parable of the talents, about achievement, working hard, doing the best you can do, blah-blah-blah, when the teacher called on the restive Ken Harvey for an opinion. Ken thought about it, but just for a second, and said (with studied, minimal affect), "I just wanna be average." That woke me up. Average? Who wants to be average? Then the athletes chimed in with the clichés that make you want to laryngectomize them, and the exchange became a platitudinous melee. At the time, I thought Ken's assertion was stupid, and I wrote him off. But his sentence has stayed with me all these years, and I think I am finally coming to understand it.

Ken Harvey was gasping for air. School can be a tremendously disorienting place. No matter how bad the school, you're going to encounter notions that don't fit with the assumptions and beliefs that you grew up with — maybe you'll hear these dissonant notions from teachers, maybe from the other students, and maybe you'll read them. You'll also be thrown in with all kinds of kids from all kinds of backgrounds, and that can be unsettling — this

15

is especially true in places of rich ethnic and linguistic mix, like the L.A. basin. You'll see a handful of students far excel you in courses that sound exotic and that are only in the curriculum of the elite: French, physics, trigonometry. And all this is happening while you're trying to shape an identity, your body is changing, and your emotions are running wild. If you're a working-class kid in the vocational track, the options you'll have to deal with this will be constrained in certain ways: you're defined by your school as "slow"; you're placed in a curriculum that isn't designed to liberate you but to occupy you, or, if you're lucky, train you, though the training is for work the society does not esteem; other students are picking up the cues from your school and your curriculum and interacting with you in particular ways. If you're a kid like Ted Richard, you turn your back on all this and let your mind roam where it may. But youngsters like Ted are rare. What Ken and so many others do is protect themselves from such suffocating madness by taking on with a vengeance the identity implied in the vocational track. Reject the confusion and frustration by openly defining yourself as the Common Joe. Champion the average. Rely on your own good sense. Fuck this bullshit. Bullshit, of course, is everything you — and the others — fear is beyond you: books, essays, tests, academic scrambling, complexity, scientific reasoning, philosophical inquiry.

The tragedy is that you have to twist the knife in your own gray matter to make this defense work. You'll have to shut down, have to reject intellectual stimuli or diffuse them with sarcasm, have to cultivate stupidity, have to convert boredom from a malady into a way of confronting the world. Keep your vocabulary simple, act stoned when you're not or act more stoned than you are, flaunt ignorance, materialize your dreams. It is a powerful and effective defense — it neutralizes the insult and the frustration of being a vocational kid and, when perfected, it drives teachers up the wall, a delightful secondary effect. But like all strong magic, it exacts a price.

My own deliverance from the Voc. Ed. world began with sophomore biology. Every student, college prep to vocational, had to take biology, and unlike the other courses, the same person taught all sections. When teaching the vocational group, Brother Clint probably slowed down a bit or omitted a little of the fundamental biochemistry, but he used the same book and more or less the same syllabus across the board. If one class got tough, he could get tougher. He was young and powerful and very handsome, and looks and physical strength were high currency. No one gave him any trouble.

I was pretty bad at the dissecting table, but the lectures and the textbook were interesting: plastic overlays that, with each turned page, peeled away skin, then veins and muscle, then organs, down to the very bones that Brother Clint, pointer in hand, would tap out on our hanging skeleton. Dave Snyder was in big trouble, for the study of life — versus the living of it — was sticking in his craw. We worked out a code for our multiple-choice exams. He'd poke me in the back: once for the answer under *A*, twice for *B*, and so on; and when he'd hit the right one, I'd look up to the ceiling as though I were lost in thought. Poke: cytoplasm. Poke, poke: methane. Poke, poke, poke: William Harvey. Poke, poke, poke, poke: islets of Langerhans. This didn't work out perfectly, but Dave passed the course, and I mastered the dreamy look of a guy on a record jacket. And something else happened. Brother Clint puzzled over this Voc. Ed. kid who was racking up 98s and 99s on his tests. He checked the school's records and discovered the error. He recommended that I begin my junior year in the College Prep program. According to all I've read since, such a shift, as one report put it, is virtually impossible. Kids at that level rarely cross tracks. The telling thing is how chancy both my placement into and exit from Voc. Ed. was; neither I nor my parents had anything to do with it. I lived in one world during spring semester, and when I came back to school in the fall, I was living in another.

Switching to College Prep was a mixed blessing. I was an erratic student. I was undisciplined. And I hadn't caught onto the rules of the game: why work hard in a class that didn't grab my fancy? I was also hopelessly behind in math. Chemistry was hard; toying with my chemistry set years before hadn't prepared me for the chemist's equations. Fortunately, the priest who taught both chemistry and second-year algebra was also the school's athletic director. Membership on the track team covered me; I knew I wouldn't get lower than a C. U.S. history was taught pretty well, and I did okay. But civics was taken over by a football coach who had trouble reading the textbook aloud — and reading aloud was the centerpiece of his pedagogy. College Prep at Mercy was certainly an improvement over the vocational program — at least it carried some status — but the social science curriculum was weak, and the mathematics and physical sciences were simply beyond me. I had a miserable quantitative background and ended up copying some assignments and finessing the rest as best I could. Let me try to explain how it feels to see again and again material you should once have learned but didn't.

You are given a problem. It requires you to simplify algebraic fractions or to multiply expressions containing square roots. You know this is pretty basic material because you've seen it for years. Once a teacher took some time with you, and you learned how to carry out these operations. Simple versions, anyway. But that was a year or two or more in the past, and these are more complex versions, and now you're not sure. And this, you keep telling yourself, is ninth- or even eighth-grade stuff.

Next it's a word problem. This is also old hat. The basic elements are as familiar as story characters: trains speeding so many miles per hour or shadows of buildings angling so many degrees. Maybe you know enough, have sat through enough explanations, to be able to begin setting up the problem: "If one train is going this fast . . ." or "This shadow is really one line of a triangle . . ." Then: "Let's see . . ." "How did Jones do this?" "Hmmmm." "No." "No, that won't work." Your attention wavers. You wonder about other things: a football game, a dance, that cute new checker at the market. You try to focus on the problem again. You scribble on paper for a while,

20

but the tension wins out and your attention flits elsewhere. You crumple the paper and begin daydreaming to ease the frustration.

The particulars will vary, but in essence this is what a number of students go through, especially those in so-called remedial classes. They open their textbooks and see once again the familiar and impenetrable formulas and diagrams and terms that have stumped them for years. There is no excitement here. *No* excitement. Regardless of what the teacher says, this is not a new challenge. There is, rather, embarrassment and frustration and, not surprisingly, some anger in being reminded once again of long-standing inadequacies. No wonder so many students finally attribute their difficulties to something inborn, organic: "That part of my brain just doesn't work." Given the troubling histories many of these students have, it's miraculous that any of them can lift the shroud of hopelessness sufficiently to make deliverance from these classes possible.

Through this entire period, my father's health was deteriorating with cruel momentum. His arteriosclerosis progressed to the point where a simple nick on his shin wouldn't heal. Eventually it ulcerated and widened. Lou Minton would come by daily to change the dressing. We tried renting an oscillating bed — which we placed in the front room — to force blood through the constricted arteries in my father's legs. The bed hummed through the night, moving in place to ward off the inevitable. The ulcer continued to spread, and the doctors finally had to amputate. My grandfather had lost his leg in a stockyard accident. Now my father too was crippled. His convalescence was slow but steady, and the doctors placed him in the Santa Monica Rehabilitation Center, a sun-bleached building that opened out onto the warm spray of the Pacific. The place gave him some strength and some color and some training in walking with an artificial leg. He did pretty well for a year or so until he slipped and broke his hip. He was confined to a wheelchair after that, and the confinement contributed to the diminishing of his body and spirit.

I am holding a picture of him. He is sitting in his wheelchair and smiling   25 at the camera. The smile appears forced, unsteady, seems to quaver, though it is frozen in silver nitrate. He is in his mid-sixties and looks eighty. Late in my junior year, he had a stroke and never came out of the resulting coma. After that, I would see him only in dreams, and to this day that is how I join him. Sometimes the dreams are sad and grisly and primal: my father lying in a bed soaked with his suppuration,[8] holding me, rocking me. But sometimes the dreams bring him back to me healthy: him talking to me on an empty street, or buying some pictures to decorate our old house, or transformed somehow into someone strong and adept with tools and the physical.

Jack MacFarland couldn't have come into my life at a better time. My father was dead, and I had logged up too many years of scholastic indifference. Mr. MacFarland had a master's degree from Columbia and decided,

---

[8]*suppuration:* Discharge from wounds.

at twenty-six, to find a little school and teach his heart out. He never took any credentialing courses, couldn't bear to, he said, so he had to find employment in a private system. He ended up at Our Lady of Mercy teaching five sections of senior English. He was a beatnik who was born too late. His teeth were stained, he tucked his sorry tie in between the third and fourth buttons of his shirt, and his pants were chronically wrinkled. At first, we couldn't believe this guy, thought he slept in his car. But within no time, he had us so startled with work that we didn't much worry about where he slept or if he slept at all. We wrote three or four essays a month. We read a book every two to three weeks, starting with the *Iliad* and ending up with Hemingway. He gave us a quiz on the reading every other day. He brought a prep school curriculum to Mercy High.

MacFarland's lectures were crafted, and as he delivered them he would pace the room jiggling a piece of chalk in his cupped hand, using it to scribble on the board the names of all the writers and philosophers and plays and novels he was weaving into his discussion. He asked questions often, raised everything from Zeno's paradox to the repeated last line of Frost's "Stopping by Woods on a Snowy Evening." He slowly and carefully built up our knowledge of Western intellectual history — with facts, with connections, with speculations. We learned about Greek philosophy, about Dante, the Elizabethan world view, the Age of Reason, existentialism. He analyzed poems with us, had us reading sections from John Ciardi's *How Does a Poem Mean?*, making a potentially difficult book accessible with his own explanations. We gave oral reports on poems Ciardi didn't cover. We imitated the styles of Conrad, Hemingway, and *Time* magazine. We wrote and talked, wrote and talked. The man immersed us in language.

Even MacFarland's barbs were literary. If Jim Fitzsimmons, hung over and irritable, tried to smart-ass him, he'd rejoin with a flourish that would spark the indomitable Skip Madison — who'd lost his front teeth in a hapless tackle — to flick his tongue through the gap and opine, "good chop," drawing out the single "o" in stinging indictment. Jack MacFarland, this tobacco-stained intellectual, brandished linguistic weapons of a kind I hadn't encountered before. Here was this *egghead,* for God's sake, keeping some pretty difficult people in line. And from what I heard, Mike Dweetz and Steve Fusco and all the notorious Voc. Ed. crowd settled down as well when MacFarland took the podium. Though a lot of guys groused in the schoolyard, it just seemed that giving trouble to this particular teacher was a silly thing to do. Tomfoolery, not to mention assault, had no place in the world he was trying to create for us, and instinctively everyone knew that. If nothing else, we all recognized MacFarland's considerable intelligence and respected the hours he put into his work. It came to this: the troublemaker would look foolish rather than daring. Even Jim Fitzsimmons was reading *On the Road* and turning his incipient alcoholism to literary ends.

There were some lives that were already beyond Jack MacFarland's ministrations, but mine was not. I started reading again as I hadn't since elementary school. I would go into our gloomy little bedroom or sit at the dinner table while, on the television, Danny McShane was paralyzing Mr. Moto with the atomic drop, and work slowly back through *Heart of Darkness,* trying to catch the words in Conrad's sentences. I certainly was not Mac-Farland's best student; most of the other guys in College Prep, even my fellow slackers, had better backgrounds than I did. But I worked very hard, for MacFarland had hooked me. He tapped my old interest in reading and creating stories. He gave me a way to feel special by using my mind. And he provided a role model that wasn't shaped on physical prowess alone, and something inside me that I wasn't quite aware of responded to that. Jack MacFarland established a literacy club, to borrow a phrase of Frank Smith's, and invited me — invited all of us — to join.

There's been a good deal of research and speculation suggesting that 30 the acknowledgment of school performance with extrinsic rewards — smiling faces, stars, numbers, grades — diminishes the intrinsic satisfaction children experience by engaging in reading or writing or problem solving. While it's certainly true that we've created an educational system that encourages our best and brightest to become cynical grade collectors and, in general, have developed an obsession with evaluation and assessment, I must tell you that venal though it may have been, I loved getting good grades from MacFarland. I now know how subjective grades can be, but then they came tucked in the back of essays like bits of scientific data, some sort of spectroscopic readout that said, objectively and publicly, that I had made something of value. I suppose I'd been mediocre for too long and enjoyed a public redefinition. And I suppose the workings of my mind, such as they were, had been private for too long. My linguistic play moved into the world; ... these papers with their circled, red B-pluses and A-minuses linked my mind to something outside it. I carried them around like a club emblem.

One day in the December of my senior year, Mr. MacFarland asked me where I was going to go to college. I hadn't thought much about it. Many of the students I teach today spent their last year in high school with a physics text in one hand and the Stanford catalog in the other, but I wasn't even aware of what "entrance requirements" were. My folks would say that they wanted me to go to college and be a doctor, but I don't know how seriously I ever took that; it seemed a sweet thing to say, a bit of supportive family chatter, like telling a gangly daughter she's graceful. The reality of higher education wasn't in my scheme of things: no one in the family had gone to college; only two of my uncles had completed high school. I figured I'd get a night job and go to the local junior college because I knew that Snyder and Company were going there to play ball. But I hadn't even prepared for that. When I finally said, "I don't know," MacFarland looked down at me — I was seated in his office — and said, "Listen, you can write."

My grades stank. I had A's in biology and a handful of B's in a few English and social science classes. All the rest were C's — or worse. MacFarland said I would do well in his class and laid down the law about doing well in the others. Still, the record for my first three years wouldn't have been acceptable to any four-year school. To nobody's surprise, I was turned down flat by USC and UCLA. But Jack MacFarland was on the case. He had received his bachelor's degree from Loyola University, so he made calls to old professors and talked to somebody in admissions and wrote me a strong letter. Loyola finally accepted me as a probationary student. I would be on trial for the first year, and if I did okay, I would be granted regular status. MacFarland also intervened to get me a loan, for I could never have afforded a private college without it. Four more years of religion classes and four more years of boys at one school, girls at another. But at least I was going to college. Amazing.

In my last semester of high school, I elected a special English course fashioned by Mr. MacFarland, and it was through this elective that there arose at Mercy a fledgling literati. Art Mitz, the editor of the school newspaper and a very smart guy, was the kingpin. He was joined by me and by Mark Dever, a quiet boy who wrote beautifully and who would die before he was forty. MacFarland occasionally invited us to his apartment, and those visits became the high point of our apprenticeship: we'd clamp on our training wheels and drive to his salon.

He lived in a cramped and cluttered place near the airport, tucked away in the kind of building that architectural critic Reyner Banham calls a *dingbat.* Books were all over: stacked, piled, tossed, and crated, underlined and dog eared, well worn and new. Cigarette ashes crusted with coffee in saucers or spilling over the sides of motel ashtrays. The little bedroom had, along two of its walls, bricks and boards loaded with notes, magazines, and oversized books. The kitchen joined the living room, and there was a stack of German newspapers under the sink. I had never seen anything like it: a great flophouse of language furnished by City Lights and Café le Metro. I read every title. I flipped through paperbacks and scanned jackets and memorized names: Gogol, *Finnegans Wake,* Djuna Barnes, Jackson Pollock, *A Coney Island of the Mind,* F. O. Matthiessen's *American Renaissance,* all sorts of Freud, *Troubled Sleep,* Man Ray, *The Education of Henry Adams,* Richard Wright, *Film as Art,* William Butler Yeats, Marguerite Duras, *Redburn, A Season in Hell, Kapital.* On the cover of Alain-Fournier's *The Wanderer* was an Edward Gorey drawing of a young man on a road winding into dark trees. By the hotplate sat a strange Kafka novel called *Amerika,* in which an adolescent hero crosses the Atlantic to find the Nature Theater of Oklahoma. Art and Mark would be talking about a movie or the school newspaper, and I would be consuming my English teacher's library. It was heady stuff. I felt like a Pop Warner[9] athlete on steroids.

Art, Mark, and I would buy stogies and triangulate from MacFarland's apartment to the Cinema, which now shows X-rated films but was then L.A.'s premier art theater, and then to the musty Cherokee Bookstore in

35

[9]*Pop Warner:* A nationwide youth athletics organization.

Hollywood to hobnob with beatnik homosexuals — smoking, drinking bourbon and coffee, and trying out awkward phrases we'd gleaned from our mentor's bookshelves. I was happy and precocious and a little scared as well, for Hollywood Boulevard was thick with a kind of decadence that was foreign to the South Side. After the Cherokee, we would head back to the security of MacFarland's apartment, slaphappy with hipness.

Let me be the first to admit that there was a good deal of adolescent passion in this embrace of the avant-garde: self-absorption, sexually charged pedantry, an elevation of the odd and abandoned. Still it was a time during which I absorbed an awful lot of information: long lists of titles, images from expressionist paintings, new wave shibboleths,[10] snippets of philosophy, and names that read like Steve Fusco's misspellings — Goethe, Nietzsche, Kierkegaard. Now this is hardly the stuff of deep understanding. But it was an introduction, a phrase book, a Baedeker[11] to a vocabulary of ideas, and it felt good at the time to know all these words. With hindsight I realize how layered and important that knowledge was.

It enabled me to do things in the world. I could browse bohemian bookstores in far-off, mysterious Hollywood; I could go to the Cinema and see events through the lenses of European directors; and, most of all, I could share an evening, talk that talk, with Jack MacFarland, the man I most admired at the time. Knowledge was becoming a bonding agent. Within a year or two, the persona of the disaffected hipster would prove too cynical, too alienated to last. But for a time it was new and exciting: it provided a critical perspective on society, and it allowed me to act as though I were living beyond the limiting boundaries of South Vermont.[12]

---

[10]*new wave shibboleths:* Trendy phrases or jargon.
[11]*Baedeker:* Travel guide.
[12]*South Vermont:* A street in an economically depressed area of Los Angeles.

ENGAGING THE TEXT

1. Describe Rose's life in Voc. Ed. What were his teachers like? Have you ever had experience with teachers like these?
2. What did Voc. Ed. do to Rose and his fellow students? How did it affect them intellectually, emotionally, and socially? Why was it subsequently so hard for Rose to catch up in math?
3. Why is high school so disorienting to students like Ken Harvey? How does he cope with it? What other strategies do students use to cope with the pressures and judgments they encounter in school?
4. What does Jack MacFarland offer Rose that finally helps him learn? Do you think it was inevitable that someone with Rose's intelligence would eventually succeed?

EXPLORING CONNECTIONS

5. To what extent do Rose's experiences challenge or confirm John Taylor Gatto's critique of public education in "The Seven-Lesson Schoolteacher" (p. 166)?

6. Draw a Groening-style cartoon (see pp. 164–65) or comic strip of Rose in the vocational track, or of Rose before and after his liberation from Voc. Ed.

7. Read Gregory Mantsios's "Rewards and Opportunities: The Politics and Economics of Class in the U.S." (p. 331) and write an imaginary dialogue between Rose and Mantsios about why some students, like Rose, seem to be able to break through social class barriers and others, like Dave Snyder, Ted Richard, and Ken Harvey, do not.

EXTENDING THE CRITICAL CONTEXT

8. Rose explains that high school can be a "tremendously disorienting place" (para. 16). What, if anything, do you find disorienting about college? What steps can students at your school take to lessen feelings of disorientation? What could the college do to help them?

9. Review one or more of Rose's descriptions of his high school classmates; then write a description of one of your own high school classmates, trying to capture in a nutshell how that person coped or failed to cope with the educational system.

10. Watch on videotape any one of the many films that have been made in the last ten years about charismatic teachers (for example, *Dangerous Minds, Renaissance Man, Stand and Deliver*, or *Dead Poets Society*) and compare Hollywood's depiction of a dynamic teacher to Rose's portrayal of Jack MacFarland. What do such charismatic teachers offer their students personally and intellectually? Do you see any disadvantages to classes taught by teachers like these?

From *Social Class and the Hidden Curriculum of Work*

JEAN ANYON

It's no surprise that schools in wealthy communities are better than those in poor communities, or that they better prepare their students for desirable jobs. It may be shocking, however, to learn how vast the differences in schools are — not so much in resources as in teaching methods and philosophies of education. Jean Anyon observed five elementary schools over the course of a full school year and concluded that fifth-graders of different economic backgrounds are already being prepared to occupy particular rungs on the social ladder. In a sense, some whole schools are on the vocational education track, while others are geared to produce future doctors, lawyers, and business leaders. Anyon's main audience is professional educators, so you may find her style and vocabulary challenging, but, once you've read her descriptions of specific classroom activities, the more analytic parts of the essay should prove easier to understand. Anyon is chairperson of the Department of Education at Rutgers University, Newark; this essay first appeared in the Journal of Education *in 1980.*

Scholars in political economy and the sociology of knowledge have recently argued that public schools in complex industrial societies like our own make available different types of educational experience and curriculum knowledge to students in different social classes. Bowles and Gintis[1] for example, have argued that students in different social-class backgrounds are rewarded for classroom behaviors that correspond to personality traits allegedly rewarded in the different occupational strata — the working classes for docility and obedience, the managerial classes for initiative and personal assertiveness. Basil Bernstein, Pierre Bourdieu, and Michael W. Apple,[2] focusing on school knowledge, have argued that knowledge and skills leading to social power and regard (medical, legal, managerial) are made available to the advantaged social groups but are withheld from the working classes, to whom a more "practical" curriculum is offered (manual skills, clerical knowledge). While there has been considerable argumentation of these points regarding education in England, France, and North America, there has been little or no attempt to investigate these ideas empirically in elementary or secondary schools and classrooms in this country.[3]

This article offers tentative empirical support (and qualification) of the above arguments by providing illustrative examples of differences in student *work* in classrooms in contrasting social class communities. The examples were gathered as part of an ethnographical[4] study of curricular, pedagogical,

[1]S. Bowles and H. Gintis, *Schooling in Capitalist America: Educational Reform and the Contradictions of Economic Life* (New York: Basic Books, 1976). [Author's note]

[2]B. Bernstein, *Class, Codes and Control, Vol. 3. Towards a Theory of Educational Transmission,* 2d ed. (London: Routledge & Kegan Paul, 1977); P. Bourdieu and J. Passeron, *Reproduction in Education, Society and Culture* (Beverly Hills, Calif.: Sage, 1977): M. W. Apple, *Ideology and Curriculum* (Boston: Routledge & Kegan Paul, 1979). [Author's note]

[3]But see, in a related vein, M. W. Apple and N. King, "What Do Schools Teach?" *Curriculum Inquiry* 6 (1977): 341–58; R. C. Rist, *The Urban School: A Factory for Failure* (Cambridge, Mass.: MIT Press, 1973). [Author's note]

[4]*ethnographical:* Based on an anthropological study of cultures or subcultures — the "cultures" in this case being the five schools observed.

and pupil evaluation practices in five elementary schools. The article attempts a theoretical contribution as well and assesses student work in the light of a theoretical approach to social-class analysis. . . . It will be suggested that there is a "hidden curriculum" in schoolwork that has profound implications for the theory — and consequence — of everyday activity in education. . . .

The Sample of Schools

. . . The social-class designation of each of the five schools will be identified, and the income, occupation, and other relevant available social characteristics of the students and their parents will be described. The first three schools are in a medium-sized city district in northern New Jersey, and the other two are in a nearby New Jersey suburb.

The first two schools I will call *working-class schools.* Most of the parents have blue-collar jobs. Less than a third of the fathers are skilled, while the majority are in unskilled or semiskilled jobs. During the period of the study (1978–1979), approximately 15 percent of the fathers were unemployed. The large majority (85 percent) of the families are white. The following occupations are typical: platform, storeroom, and stockroom workers; foundrymen, pipe welders, and boilermakers; semiskilled and unskilled assemblyline operatives; gas station attendants, auto mechanics, maintenance workers, and security guards. Less than 30 percent of the women work, some part-time and some full-time, on assembly lines, in storerooms and stockrooms, as waitresses, barmaids, or sales clerks. Of the fifth-grade parents, none of the wives of the skilled workers had jobs. Approximately 15 percent of the families in each school are at or below the federal "poverty" level;[5] most of the rest of the family incomes are at or below $12,000, except some of the skilled workers whose incomes are higher. The incomes of the majority of the families in these two schools (at or below $12,000) are typical of 38.6 percent of the families in the United States.[6]

The third school is called the *middle-class school,* although because of   5
neighborhood residence patterns, the population is a mixture of several social classes. The parents' occupations can be divided into three groups: a small group of blue-collar "rich," who are skilled, well-paid workers such as printers, carpenters, plumbers, and construction workers. The second group is composed of parents in working-class and middle-class white-collar jobs: women in office jobs, technicians, supervisors in industry, and parents employed by the city (such as firemen, policemen, and several of the

---

[5]The U.S. Bureau of the Census defines *poverty* for a nonfarm family of four as a yearly income of $6,191 a year or less. U.S. Bureau of the Census, *Statistical Abstract of the United States: 1978* (Washington, D.C.: U.S. Government Printing Office, 1978), 465, table 754. [Author's note]

[6]U.S. Bureau of the Census, "Money Income in 1977 of Families and Persons in the United States," *Current Population Reports* Series P-60, no. 118 (Washington, D.C.: U.S. Government Printing Office, 1979), p. 2, table A. [Author's note]

school's teachers). The third group is composed of occupations such as personnel directors in local firms, accountants, "middle management," and a few small capitalists (owners of shops in the area). The children of several local doctors attend this school. Most family incomes are between $13,000 and $25,000, with a few higher. This income range is typical of 38.9 percent of the families in the United States.[7]

The fourth school has a parent population that is at the upper income level of the upper middle class and is predominantly professional. This school will be called the *affluent professional school.* Typical jobs are: cardiologist, interior designer, corporate lawyer or engineer, executive in advertising or television. There are some families who are not as affluent as the majority (the family of the superintendent of the district's schools, and the one or two families in which the fathers are skilled workers). In addition, a few of the families are more affluent than the majority and can be classified in the capitalist class (a partner in a prestigious Wall Street stock brokerage firm). Approximately 90 percent of the children in this school are white. Most family incomes are between $40,000 and $80,000. This income span represents approximately 7 percent of the families in the United States.[8]

In the fifth school the majority of the families belong to the capitalist class. This school will be called the *executive elite school* because most of the fathers are top executives (for example, presidents and vice-presidents) in major United States–based multinational corporations — for example, AT&T, RCA, Citibank, American Express, U.S. Steel. A sizable group of fathers are top executives in financial firms on Wall Street. There are also a number of fathers who list their occupations as "general counsel" to a particular corporation, and these corporations are also among the large multinationals. Many of the mothers do volunteer work in the Junior League, Junior Fortnightly, or other service groups; some are intricately involved in town politics; and some are themselves in well-paid occupations. There are no minority children in the school. Almost all the family incomes are over $100,000, with some in the $500,000 range. The incomes in this school represent less than 1 percent of the families in the United States.[9]

Since each of the five schools is only one instance of elementary education in a particular social class context, I will not generalize beyond the sample. However, the examples of schoolwork which follow will suggest characteristics of education in each social setting that appear to have theoretical and social significance and to be worth investigation in a larger number of schools. . . .

[7]Ibid. [Author's note]

[8]This figure is an estimate. According to the Bureau of the Census, only 2.6 percent of families in the United States have money income of $50,000 or over. U.S. Bureau of the Census, *Current Population Reports* Series P-60. For figures on income at these higher levels, see J. D. Smith and S. Franklin, "The Concentration of Personal Wealth, 1922–1969," *American Economic Review* 64 (1974): 162–67. [Author's note]

[9]Smith and Franklin, "The Concentration of Personal Wealth." [Author's note]

The Working-Class Schools

In the two working-class schools, work is following the steps of a procedure. The procedure is usually mechanical, involving rote behavior and very
little decision making or choice. The teachers rarely explain why the work is
being assigned, how it might connect to other assignments, or what the idea
is that lies behind the procedure or gives it coherence and perhaps meaning
or significance. Available textbooks are not always used, and the teachers
often prepare their own dittos or put work examples on the board. Most of
the rules regarding work are designations of what the children are to do; the
rules are steps to follow. These steps are told to the children by the teachers
and are often written on the board. The children are usually told to copy the
steps as notes. These notes are to be studied. Work is often evaluated not
according to whether it is right or wrong but according to whether the children followed the right steps.

The following examples illustrate these points. In math, when two-digit   10
division was introduced, the teacher in one school gave a four-minute lecture on what the terms are called (which number is the divisor, dividend,
quotient, and remainder). The children were told to copy these names in
their notebooks. Then the teacher told them the steps to follow to do the
problems, saying, "This is how you do them." The teacher listed the steps
on the board, and they appeared several days later as a chart hung in the
middle of the front wall: "Divide, Multiply, Subtract, Bring Down." The
children often did examples of two-digit division. When the teacher went
over the examples with them, he told them what the procedure was for each
problem, rarely asking them to conceptualize or explain it themselves:
"Three into twenty-two is seven; do your subtraction and one is left over."
During the week that two-digit division was introduced (or at any other
time), the investigator did not observe any discussion of the idea of grouping involved in division, any use of manipulables, or any attempt to relate
two-digit division to any other mathematical process. Nor was there any attempt to relate the steps to an actual or possible thought process of the children. The observer did not hear the terms *dividend, quotient,* and so on,
used again. The math teacher in the other working-class school followed
similar procedures regarding two-digit division and at one point her class
seemed confused. She said, "You're confusing yourselves. You're tensing
up. Remember, when you do this, it's the same steps over and over again —
and that's the way division always is." Several weeks later, after a test, a
group of her children "still didn't get it," and she made no attempt to explain the concept of dividing things into groups or to give them manipulables for their own investigation. Rather, she went over the steps with them
again and told them that they "needed more practice."

In other areas of math, work is also carrying out often unexplained fragmented procedures. For example, one of the teachers led the children
through a series of steps to make a 1-inch grid on their paper *without* telling
them that they were making a 1-inch grid or that it would be used to study

scale. She said, "Take your ruler. Put it across the top. Make a mark at every number. Then move your ruler down to the bottom. No, put it across the bottom. Now make a mark on top of every number. Now draw a line from . . ." At this point a girl said that she had a faster way to do it and the teacher said, "No, you don't; you don't even know what I'm making yet. Do it this way or it's wrong." After they had made the lines up and down and across, the teacher told them she wanted them to make a figure by connecting some dots and to measure that, using the scale of 1 inch equals 1 mile. Then they were to cut it out. She said, "Don't cut it until I check it."

In both working-class schools, work in language arts is mechanics of punctuation (commas, periods, question marks, exclamation points), capitalization, and the four kinds of sentences. One teacher explained to me, "Simple punctuation is all they'll ever use." Regarding punctuation, either a teacher or a ditto stated the rules for where, for example, to put commas. The investigator heard no classroom discussion of the aural context of punctuation (which, of course, is what gives each mark its meaning). Nor did the investigator hear any statement or inference that placing a punctuation mark could be a decision-making process, depending, for example, on one's intended meaning. Rather, the children were told to follow the rules. Language arts did not involve creative writing. There were several writing assignments throughout the year, but in each instance the children were given a ditto, and they wrote answers to questions on the sheet. For example, they wrote their "autobiography" by answering such questions as "Where were you born?" "What is your favorite animal?" on a sheet entitled "All About Me."

In one of the working-class schools, the class had a science period several times a week. On the three occasions observed, the children were not called upon to set up experiments or to give explanations for facts or concepts. Rather, on each occasion the teacher told them in his own words what the book said. The children copied the teacher's sentences from the board. Each day that preceded the day they were to do a science experiment, the teacher told them to copy the directions from the book for the procedure they would carry out the next day and to study the list at home that night. The day after each experiment, the teacher went over what they had "found" (they did the experiments as a class, and each was actually a class demonstration led by the teacher). Then the teacher wrote what they "found" on the board, and the children copied that in their notebooks. Once or twice a year there are science projects. The project is chosen and assigned by the teacher from a box of 3-by-5-inch cards. On the card the teacher has written the question to be answered, the books to use, and how much to write. Explaining the cards to the observer, the teacher said, "It tells them exactly what to do, or they couldn't do it."

Social studies in the working-class schools is also largely mechanical, rote work that was given little explanation or connection to larger contexts. In one school, for example, although there was a book available, social studies work was to copy the teacher's notes from the board. Several times a week for a period of several months the children copied these notes. The fifth grades in the district were to study United States history. The teacher used a booklet she had purchased called "The Fabulous Fifty States." Each day she put information from the booklet in outline form on the board and the children copied it. The type of information did not vary: the name of the state, its abbreviation, state capital, nickname of the state, its main products, main business, and a "Fabulous Fact" ("Idaho grew twenty-seven billion potatoes in one year. That's enough potatoes for each man, woman, and . . ."). As the children finished copying the sentences, the teacher erased them and wrote more. Children would occasionally go to the front to pull down the wall map in order to locate the states they were copying, and the teacher did not dissuade them. But the observer never saw her refer to the map; nor did the observer ever hear her make other than perfunctory remarks concerning the information the children were copying. Occasionally the children colored in a ditto and cut it out to make a stand-up figure (representing, for example, a man roping a cow in the Southwest). These were referred to by the teacher as their social studies "projects."

Rote behavior was often called for in classroom work. When going over   15
math and language arts skills sheets, for example, as the teacher asked for the answer to each problem, he fired the questions rapidly, staccato, and the scene reminded the observer of a sergeant drilling recruits: above all, the questions demanded that you stay at attention: "The next one? What do I put here? . . . Here? Give us the next." Or "How many commas in this sentence? Where do I put them . . . The next one?"

The four fifth-grade teachers observed in the working-class schools attempted to control classroom time and space by making decisions without consulting the children and without explaining the basis for their decisions. The teacher's control thus often seemed capricious. Teachers, for instance, very often ignored the bells to switch classes — deciding among themselves to keep the children after the period was officially over to continue with the work or for disciplinary reasons or so they (the teachers) could stand in the hall and talk. There were no clocks in the rooms in either school, and the children often asked, "What period is this?" "When do we go to gym?" The children had no access to materials. These were handed out by teachers and closely guarded. Things in the room "belonged" to the teacher: "Bob, bring me my garbage can." The teachers continually gave the children orders. Only three times did the investigator hear a teacher in either working-class school preface a directive with an unsarcastic "please," or "let's" or "would you." Instead, the teachers said, "Shut up," "Shut your mouth," "Open your books," "Throw your gum away — if you want to rot your teeth, do it on your own time." Teachers made every effort to control the movement of the children, and often shouted, "Why are you out of your seat??!!" If the children got permission to leave the room, they had to take a written pass with the date and time. . . .

Middle-Class School

In the middle-class school, work is getting the right answer. If one accumulates enough right answers, one gets a good grade. One must follow the directions in order to get the right answers, but the directions often call for some figuring, some choice, some decision making. For example, the children must often figure out by themselves what the directions ask them to do and how to get the answer: what do you do first, second, and perhaps third? Answers are usually found in books or by listening to the teacher. Answers are usually words, sentences, numbers, or facts and dates; one writes them on paper, and one should be neat. Answers must be given in the right order, and one cannot make them up.

The following activities are illustrative. Math involves some choice: one may do two-digit division the long way or the short way, and there are some math problems that can be done "in your head." When the teacher explains how to do two-digit division, there is recognition that a cognitive process is involved; she gives you several ways and says, "I want to make sure you understand what you're doing — so you get it right"; and, when they go over the homework, she asks the *children* to tell how they did the problem and what answer they got.

In social studies the daily work is to read the assigned pages in the textbook and to answer the teacher's questions. The questions are almost always designed to check on whether the students have read the assignment and understood it: who did so-and-so; what happened after that; when did it happen, where, and sometimes, why did it happen? The answers are in the book and in one's understanding of the book; the teacher's hints when one doesn't know the answers are to "read it again" or to look at the picture or at the rest of the paragraph. One is to search for the answer in the "context," in what is given.

Language arts is "simple grammar, what they need for everyday life." 20
The language arts teacher says, "They should learn to speak properly, to write business letters and thank-you letters, and to understand what nouns and verbs and simple subjects are." Here, as well, actual work is to choose the right answers, to understand what is given. The teacher often says, "Please read the next sentence and then I'll question you about it." One teacher said in some exasperation to a boy who was fooling around in class, "If you don't know the answers to the questions I ask, then you can't stay in this *class!* [pause] You *never* know the answers to the questions I ask, and it's not fair to me — and certainly not to you!"

Most lessons are based on the textbook. This does not involve a critical perspective on what is given there. For example, a critical perspective in social studies is perceived as dangerous by these teachers because it may lead to controversial topics; the parents might complain. The children, however, are often curious, especially in social studies. Their questions are tolerated and usually answered perfunctorily. But after a few minutes the teacher will say, "All right, we're not going any farther. Please open your social studies workbook." While the teachers spend a lot of time explaining and expanding on what the textbooks say, there is little attempt to analyze how or why things happen, or to give thought to how pieces of a culture, or, say, a system of numbers or elements of a language fit together or can be analyzed. What has happened in the past and what exists now may not be equitable or fair, but (shrug) that is the way things are and one does not confront such matters in school. For example, in social studies after a child is called on to read a passage about the pilgrims, the teacher summarizes the paragraph and then says, "So you can see how strict they were about everything." A child asks, "Why?" "Well, because they felt that if you weren't busy you'd get into trouble." Another child asks, "Is it true that they burned women at the stake?" The teacher says, "Yes, if a woman did anything strange, they hanged them. [*sic*] What would a woman do, do you think, to make them burn them? [*sic*] See if you can come up with better answers than my other [social studies] class." Several children offer suggestions, to which the teacher nods but does not comment. Then she says, "Okay, good," and calls on the next child to read.

Work tasks do not usually request creativity. Serious attention is rarely given in school work on *how* the children develop or express their own feelings and ideas, either linguistically or in graphic form. On the occasions when creativity or self-expression is requested, it is peripheral to the main activity or it is "enrichment" or "for fun." During a lesson on what similes are, for example, the teacher explains what they are, puts several on the board, gives some other examples herself, and then asks the children if they can "make some up." She calls on three children who give similes, two of which are actually in the book they have open before them. The teacher does not comment on this and then asks several others to choose similes from the list of phrases in the book. Several do so correctly, and she says, "Oh good! You're picking them out! See how good we are?" Their homework is to pick out the rest of the similes from the list.

Creativity is not often requested in social studies and science projects, either. Social studies projects, for example, are given with directions to "find information on your topic" and write it up. The children are not supposed to copy but to "put it in your own words." Although a number of the projects subsequently went beyond the teacher's direction to find information and had quite expressive covers and inside illustrations, the teacher's evaluative comments had to do with the amount of information, whether they had "copied," and if their work was neat.

The style of control of the three fifth-grade teachers observed in this school varied from somewhat easygoing to strict, but in contrast to the working-class schools, the teachers' decisions were usually based on external rules and regulations — for example, on criteria that were known or available to the children. Thus, the teachers always honor the bells for changing classes, and they usually evaluate children's work by what is in the textbooks and answer booklets.

There is little excitement in schoolwork for the children, and the assignments are perceived as having little to do with their interests and feelings. As one child said, what you do is "store facts up in your head like cold storage — until you need it later for a test or your job." Thus, doing well is important because there are thought to be *other*, likely rewards: a good job or college.[10]

Affluent Professional School

In the affluent professional school, work is creative activity carried out independently. The students are continually asked to express and apply ideas and concepts. Work involves individual thought and expressiveness, expansion and illustration of ideas, and choice of appropriate method and material. (The class is not considered an open classroom, and the principal explained that because of the large number of discipline problems in the fifth grade this year they did not departmentalize. The teacher who agreed to take part in the study said she is "more structured" this year than she usually is.) The products of work in this class are often written stories, editorials and essays, or representations of ideas in mural, graph, or craft form. The products of work should not be like everybody else's and should show individuality. They should exhibit good design, and (this is important) they must also fit empirical reality. Moreover, one's work should attempt to interpret or "make sense" of reality. The relatively few rules to be followed regarding work are usually criteria for, or limits on, individual activity. One's product is usually evaluated for the quality of its expression and for the appropriateness of its conception to the task. In many cases, one's own satisfaction with the product is an important criterion for its evaluation. When right answers are called for, as in commercial materials like SRA (Science Research Associates) and math, it is important that the children decide on an answer as a result of thinking about the idea involved in what they're being asked to do. Teacher's hints are to "think about it some more."

The following activities are illustrative. The class takes home a sheet requesting each child's parents to fill in the number of cars they have, the number of television sets, refrigerators, games, or rooms in the house, and so on. Each child is to figure the average number of a type of possession owned by the fifth grade. Each child must compile the "data" from all the sheets. A calculator is available in the classroom to do the mechanics of finding the average. Some children decide to send sheets to the fourth-grade families for comparison. Their work should be "verified" by a classmate before it is handed in.

---

[10]A dominant feeling, expressed directly and indirectly by teachers in this school, was boredom with their work. They did, however, in contrast to the working-class schools, almost always carry out lessons during class times. [Author's note]

Each child and his or her family has made a geoboard. The teacher asks the class to get their geoboards from the side cabinet, to take a handful of rubber bands, and then to listen to what she would like them to do. She says, "I would like you to design a figure and then find the perimeter and area. When you have it, check with your neighbor. After you've done that, please transfer it to graph paper and tomorrow I'll ask you to make up a question about it for someone. When you hand it in, please let me know whose it is and who verified it. Then I have something else for you to do that's really fun. [pause] Find the average number of chocolate chips in three cookies. I'll give you three cookies, and you'll have to *eat* your way through, I'm afraid!" Then she goes around the room and gives help, suggestions, praise, and admonitions that they are getting noisy. They work sitting, or standing up at their desks, at benches in the back, or on the floor. A child hands the teacher his paper and she comments, "I'm not accepting this paper. Do a better design." To another child she says, "That's fantastic! But you'll never find the area. Why don't you draw a figure inside [the big one] and subtract to get the area?"

The school district requires the fifth grade to study ancient civilization (in particular, Egypt, Athens, and Sumer). In this classroom, the emphasis is on illustrating and re-creating the culture of the people of ancient times. The following are typical activities: the children made an 8mm film on Egypt, which one of the parents edited. A girl in the class wrote the script, and the class acted it out. They put the sound on themselves. They read stories of those days. They wrote essays and stories depicting the lives of the people and the societal and occupational divisions. They chose from a list of projects, all of which involved graphic representations of ideas: for example, "Make a mural depicting the division of labor in Egyptian society."

Each child wrote and exchanged a letter in hieroglyphics with a fifth   30
grader in another class, and they also exchanged stories they wrote in cuneiform. They made a scroll and singed the edges so it looked authentic. They each chose an occupation and made an Egyptian plaque representing that occupation, simulating the appropriate Egyptian design. They carved their design on a cylinder of wax, pressed the wax into clay, and then baked the clay. Although one girl did not choose an occupation but carved instead a series of gods and slaves, the teacher said, "That's all right, Amber, it's beautiful." As they were working the teacher said, "Don't cut into your clay until you're satisfied with your design."

Social studies also involves almost daily presentation by the children of some event from the news. The teacher's questions ask the children to expand what they say, to give more details, and to be more specific. Occasionally she adds some remarks to help them see connections between events.

The emphasis on expressing and illustrating ideas in social studies is accompanied in language arts by an emphasis on creative writing. Each child wrote a rebus story for a first grader whom they had interviewed to see what kind of story the child liked best. They wrote editorials on pending decisions by the school board and radio plays, some of which were read over the school intercom from the office and one of which was performed in the auditorium. There is no language arts textbook because, the teacher said, "The principal wants us to be creative." There is not much grammar, but there is punctuation. One morning when the observer arrived, the class was doing a punctuation ditto. The teacher later apologized for using the ditto. "It's just for review," she said. "I don't teach punctuation that way. We use their language." The ditto had three unambiguous rules for where to put commas in a sentence. As the teacher was going around to help the children with the ditto, she repeated several times, "Where you put commas depends on how you say the sentence; it depends on the situation and what you want to say." Several weeks later the observer saw another punctuation activity. The teacher had printed a five-paragraph story on an oak tag and then cut it into phrases. She read the whole story to the class from the book, then passed out the phrases. The group had to decide how the phrases could best be put together again. (They arranged the phrases on the floor.) The point was not to replicate the story, although that was not irrelevant, but to "decide what you think the best way is." Punctuation marks on cardboard pieces were then handed out, and the children discussed and then decided what mark was best at each place they thought one was needed. At the end of each paragraph the teacher asked, "Are you satisfied with the way the paragraphs are now? Read it to yourself and see how it sounds." Then she read the original story again, and they compared the two.

Describing her goals in science to the investigator, the teacher said, "We use ESS (Elementary Science Study). It's very good because it gives a hands-on experience — so they can make *sense* out of it. It doesn't matter whether it [what they find] is right or wrong. I bring them together and there's value in discussing their ideas."

The products of work in this class are often highly valued by the children and the teacher. In fact, this was the only school in which the investigator was not allowed to take original pieces of the children's work for her files. If the work was small enough, however, and was on paper, the investigator could duplicate it on the copying machine in the office.

The teacher's attempt to control the class involves constant negotiation. 35 She does not give direct orders unless she is angry because the children have been too noisy. Normally, she tries to get them to foresee the consequences of their actions and to decide accordingly. For example, lining them up to go see a play written by the sixth graders, she says, "I presume you're lined up by someone with whom you want to sit. I hope you're lined up by someone you won't get in trouble with." . . .

One of the few rules governing the children's movement is that no more than three children may be out of the room at once. There is a school rule that anyone can go to the library at any time to get a book. In the fifth grade I observed, they sign their name on the chalkboard and leave. There are no passes. Finally, the children have a fair amount of officially sanctioned say over what happens in the class. For example, they often negotiate what work is to be done. If the teacher wants to move on to the next subject, but the children say they are not ready, they want to work on their present projects some more, she very often lets them do it.

Executive Elite School

In the executive elite school, work is developing one's analytical intellectual powers. Children are continually asked to reason through a problem, to produce intellectual products that are both logically sound and of top academic quality. A primary goal of thought is to conceptualize rules by which elements may fit together in systems and then to apply these rules in solving a problem. Schoolwork helps one to achieve, to excel, to prepare for life.

The following are illustrative. The math teacher teaches area and perimeter by having the children derive formulas for each. First she helps them, through discussion at the board, to arrive at $A = W \times L$ as a formula (not *the* formula) for area. After discussing several, she says, "Can anyone make up a formula for perimeter? Can you figure that out yourselves? [pause] Knowing what we know, can we think of a formula?" She works out three children's suggestions at the board, saying to two, "Yes, that's a good one," and then asks the class if they can think of any more. No one volunteers. To prod them, she says, "If you use rules and good reasoning, you get many ways. Chris, can you think up a formula?"

She discusses two-digit division with the children as a decision-making process. Presenting a new type of problem to them, she asks, "What's the *first* decision you'd make if presented with this kind of example? What is the first thing you'd *think?* Craig?" Craig says, "To find my first partial quotient." She responds, "Yes, that would be your first decision. How would you do that?" Craig explains, and then the teacher says, "OK, we'll see how that works for you." The class tries his way. Subsequently, she comments on the merits and shortcomings of several other children's decisions. Later, she tells the investigator that her goals in math are to develop their reasoning and mathematical thinking and that, unfortunately, "there's no *time* for manipulables."

While right answers are important in math, they are not "given" by the book or by the teacher but may be challenged by the children. Going over some problems in late September the teacher says, "Raise your hand if you do not agree." A child says, "I don't agree with sixty-four." The teacher responds, "OK, there's a question about sixty-four. [to class] Please check it. Owen, they're disagreeing with you. Kristen, they're checking yours." The teacher emphasized this repeatedly during September and October with statements like "Don't be afraid to say you disagree. In the last [math] class, somebody disagreed, and they were right. Before you disagree, check yours, and if you still think we're wrong, then we'll check it out." By Thanksgiving, 40 the children did not often speak in terms of right and wrong math problems but of whether they agreed with the answer that had been given.

There are complicated math mimeos with many word problems. Whenever they go over the examples, they discuss how each child has set up the problem. The children must explain it precisely. On one occasion the teacher said, "I'm more — just as interested in *how* you set up the problem as in what answer you find. If you set up a problem in a good way, the answer is *easy* to find."

Social studies work is most often reading and discussion of concepts and independent research. There are only occasional artistic, expressive, or illustrative projects. Ancient Athens and Sumer are, rather, societies to analyze. The following questions are typical of those that guide the children's independent research. "What mistakes did Pericles make after the war?" "What mistakes did the citizens of Athens make?" "What are the elements of a civilization?" "How did Greece build an economic empire?" "Compare the way Athens chose its leaders with the way we choose ours." Occasionally the children are asked to make up sample questions for their social studies tests. On an occasion when the investigator was present, the social studies teacher rejected a child's question by saying, "That's just fact. If I asked you that question on a test, you'd complain it was just memory! Good questions ask for concepts."

In social studies — but also in reading, science, and health — the teachers initiate classroom discussions of current social issues and problems. These discussions occurred on every one of the investigator's visits, and a teacher told me, "These children's opinions are important — it's important that they learn to reason things through." The classroom discussions always struck the observer as quite realistic and analytical, dealing with concrete social issues like the following: "Why do workers strike?" "Is that right or wrong?" "Why do we have inflation, and what can be done to stop it?" "Why do companies put chemicals in food when the natural ingredients are available?" and so on. Usually the children did not have to be prodded to give their opinions. In fact, their statements and the interchanges between them struck the observer as quite sophisticated conceptually and verbally, and well-informed. Occasionally the teachers would prod with statements such as, "Even if you don't know [the answers], if you think logically about it, you can figure it out." And "I'm asking you [these] questions to help you think this through."

Language arts emphasizes language as a complex system, one that should be mastered. The children are asked to diagram sentences of complex grammatical construction, to memorize irregular verb conjugations (he lay, he has lain, and so on . . .), and to use the proper participles, conjunctions, and interjections in their speech. The teacher (the same one who teaches social studies) told them, "It is not enough to get these right on tests; you must use what you learn [in grammar classes] in your written and oral work. I will grade you on that."

Most writing assignments are either research reports and essays for social   45
studies or experiment analyses and write-ups for science. There is only an occasional story or other "creative writing" assignment. On the occasion observed by
the investigator (the writing of a Halloween story), the points the teacher
stressed in preparing the children to write involved the structural aspects of a
story rather than the expression of feelings or other ideas. The teacher showed
them a filmstrip, "The Seven Parts of a Story," and lectured them on plot development, mood setting, character development, consistency, and the use of a
logical or appropriate ending. The stories they subsequently wrote were, in fact,
well-structured, but many were also personal and expressive. The teacher's
evaluative comments, however, did not refer to the expressiveness or artistry
but were all directed toward whether they had "developed" the story well.

Language arts work also involved a large amount of practice in presentation of the self and in managing situations where the child was expected to
be in charge. For example, there was a series of assignments in which each
child had to be a "student teacher." The child had to plan a lesson in grammar, outlining, punctuation, or other language arts topic and explain the
concept to the class. Each child was to prepare a worksheet or game and a
homework assignment as well. After each presentation, the teacher and
other children gave a critical appraisal of the "student teacher's" performance. Their criteria were: whether the student spoke clearly, whether the
lesson was interesting, whether the student made any mistakes, and
whether he or she kept control of the class. On an occasion when a child did
not maintain control, the teacher said, "When you're up there, you have authority and you have to use it. I'll back you up." . . .

The executive elite school is the only school where bells do not demar-
cate the periods of time. The two fifth-grade teachers were very strict about
changing classes on schedule, however, as specific plans for each session
had been made. The teachers attempted to keep tight control over the children during lessons, and the children were sometimes flippant, boisterous,
and occasionally rude. However, the children may be brought into line by
reminding them that "It is up to you." "You must control yourself," "you are
responsible for your work," you must "set your own priorities." One teacher
told a child, "You are the only driver of your car — and only you can regulate your speed." A new teacher complained to the observer that she had
thought "these children" would have more control.

While strict attention to the lesson at hand is required, the teachers
make relatively little attempt to regulate the movement of the children at
other times. For example, except for the kindergartners the children in this
school do not have to wait for the bell to ring in the morning; they may go to
their classroom when they arrive at school. Fifth graders often came early to
read, to finish work, or to catch up. After the first two months of school, the
fifth-grade teachers did not line the children up to change classes or to go to
gym, and so on, but, when the children were ready and quiet, they were
told they could go — sometimes without the teachers.

In the classroom, the children could get materials when they needed them and took what they needed from closets and from the teacher's desk. They were in charge of the office at lunchtime. During class they did not have to sign out or ask permission to leave the room; they just got up and left. Because of the pressure to get work done, however, they did not leave the room very often. The teachers were very polite to the children, and the investigator heard no sarcasm, no nasty remarks, and few direct orders. The teachers never called the children "honey" or "dear" but always called them by name. The teachers were expected to be available before school, after school, and for part of their lunchtime to provide extra help if needed. . . .

The foregoing analysis of differences in schoolwork in contrasting social   50
class contexts suggests the following conclusion: the "hidden curriculum" of schoolwork is tacit preparation for relating to the process of production in a particular way. Differing curricular, pedagogical, and pupil evaluation practices emphasize different cognitive and behavioral skills in each social setting and thus contribute to the development in the children of certain potential relationships to physical and symbolic capital,[11] to authority, and to the process of work. School experience, in the sample of schools discussed here, differed qualitatively by social class. These differences may not only contribute to the development in the children in each social class of certain types of economically significant relationships and not others but would thereby help to *reproduce* this system of relations in society. In the contribution to the reproduction of unequal social relations lies a theoretical meaning and social consequence of classroom practice.

The identification of different emphases in classrooms in a sample of contrasting social class contexts implies that further research should be conducted in a large number of schools to investigate the types of work tasks and interactions in each to see if they differ in the ways discussed here and to see if similar potential relationships are uncovered. Such research could have as a product the further elucidation of complex but not readily apparent connections between everyday activity in schools and classrooms and the unequal structure of economic relationships in which we work and live.

---

[11]*physical and symbolic capital:* Elsewhere Anyon defines *capital* as "property that is used to produce profit, interest, or rent"; she defines *symbolic capital* as the knowledge and skills that "may yield social and cultural power."

ENGAGING THE TEXT

1. Examine the ways any single subject is taught in the four types of schools Anyon describes. What differences in teaching methods and in the student-teacher relationship do they reflect? What other differences do you note in the schools? What schools in your geographic region would

closely approximate the working-class, middle-class, affluent professional, and executive elite schools of her article?

2. What attitudes toward knowledge and work are the four types of schools teaching their students? What kinds of jobs are students being prepared to do? Do you see any evidence that the schools in your community are producing particular kinds of workers?

3. What is the "hidden curriculum" of Anyon's title? How is this curriculum taught, and what social, cultural, or political purposes does it serve?

EXPLORING CONNECTIONS

4. Contrast Anyon's depiction of the "hidden curriculum" of American education with that proposed by John Taylor Gatto (p. 166). How common would you expect the "Seven-Lesson Schoolteacher" to be in each of the four types of school Anyon mentions?

5. Draw a Groening-like (see pp. 164–65) cartoon or comic strip about a classroom situation in a working-class, middle-class, professional, or elite school (but do not identify the type of school explicitly). Pool all the cartoons from the class. In small groups, sort the comics according to the type of school they represent.

6. Analyze the teaching styles that Mike Rose encounters at Our Lady of Mercy (p. 174). Which of Anyon's categories would they fit best? Do Rose's experiences at his high school tend to confirm or complicate Anyon's analysis?

EXTENDING THE CRITICAL CONTEXT

7. Should all schools be run like professional or elite schools? What would be the advantages of making these schools models for all social classes? Do you see any possible disadvantages?

8. Choose a common elementary school task or skill that Anyon does not mention. Outline four ways it might be taught in the four types of schools.

The Achievement of Desire

RICHARD RODRIGUEZ

Hunger of Memory, *the autobiography of Richard Rodriguez and the source of the following selection, set off a storm of controversy in the Chicano community when it appeared in 1981. Some hailed it as an uncompromising portrayal of the difficulties of growing up between two cultures; others condemned it because it seemed to blame Mexican Americans for the difficulties they encountered assimilating into mainstream American society. Rodriguez was born in 1944 into an immigrant family outside San Francisco. Though he was unable to speak English when he entered school, his educational career can only be described as brilliant: undergraduate work at Stanford University, graduate study at Berkeley and Columbia, a Fulbright fellowship to study English literature in London, a subsequent grant from the National Endowment for the Humanities. In this selection, Rodriguez analyzes the motives that led him to abandon his study of Renaissance literature and return to live with his parents. He is currently an associate editor with the Pacific News Service in San Francisco, an essayist for* the Newshour with Jim Lehrer, *and a contributing editor for* Harper's *magazine and for the Opinion section of the* Los Angeles Times. *Recent books include* Mexico's Children *(1991) and* Days of Obligation: An Argument with My Mexican Father *(1993), which was nominated for the Pulitzer Prize in nonfiction.*

I stand in the ghetto classroom — "the guest speaker" — attempting to lecture on the mystery of the sounds of our words to rows of diffident students. "Don't you hear it? Listen! The music of our words. '*Sumer is i-cumen in.*[1] . . .' And songs on the car radio. We need Aretha Franklin's voice to fill plain words with music — her life." In the face of their empty stares, I try to create an enthusiasm. But the girls in the back row turn to watch some boy passing outside. There are flutters of smiles, waves. And someone's mouth elongates heavy, silent words through the barrier of glass. Silent words — the lips straining to shape each voiceless syllable: *"Meet meee late errr."* By the door, the instructor smiles at me, apparently hoping that I will be able to spark some enthusiasm in the class. But only one student seems to be listening. A girl, maybe fourteen. In this gray room her eyes shine with ambition. She keeps nodding and nodding at all that I say; she even takes notes. And each time I ask a question, she jerks up and down in her desk like a marionette, while her hand waves over the bowed heads of her classmates. It is myself (as a boy) I see as she faces me now (a man in my thirties).

The boy who first entered a classroom barely able to speak English, twenty years later concluded his studies in the stately quiet of the reading room in the British Museum. Thus with one sentence I can summarize my academic career. It will be harder to summarize what sort of life connects the boy to the man.

With every award, each graduation from one level of education to the next, people I'd meet would congratulate me. Their refrain always the

---

[1]*Sumer is i-cumen in:* Opening line of a Middle English poem ("Summer has come").

same: "Your parents must be very proud." Sometimes then they'd ask me how I managed it — my "success." (How?) After a while, I had several quick answers to give in reply. I'd admit, for one thing, that I went to an excellent grammar school. (My earliest teachers, the nuns, made my success their ambition.) And my brother and both my sisters were very good students. (They often brought home the shiny school trophies I came to want.) And my mother and father always encouraged me. (At every graduation they were behind the stunning flash of the camera when I turned to look at the crowd.)

As important as these factors were, however, they account inadequately for my academic advance. Nor do they suggest what an odd success I managed. For although I was a very good student, I was also a very bad student. I was a "scholarship boy," a certain kind of scholarship boy. Always successful, I was always unconfident. Exhilarated by my progress. Sad. I became the prized student — anxious and eager to learn. Too eager, too anxious — an imitative and unoriginal pupil. My brother and two sisters enjoyed the advantages I did, and they grew to be as successful as I, but none of them ever seemed so anxious about their schooling. A second-grade student, I was the one who came home and corrected the "simple" grammatical mistakes of our parents. ("Two negatives make a positive.") Proudly I announced — to my family's startled silence — that a teacher had said I was losing all trace of a Spanish accent. I was oddly annoyed when I was unable to get parental help with a homework assignment. The night my father tried to help me with an arithmetic exercise, he kept reading the instructions, each time more deliberately, until I pried the textbook out of his hands, saying, "I'll try to figure it out some more by myself."

When I reached the third grade, I outgrew such behavior. I became   5
more tactful, careful to keep separate the two very different worlds of my day. But then, with ever-increasing intensity, I devoted myself to my studies. I became bookish, puzzling to all my family. Ambition set me apart. When my brother saw me struggling home with stacks of library books, he would laugh, shouting: "Hey, Four Eyes!" My father opened a closet one day and was startled to find me inside, reading a novel. My mother would find me reading when I was supposed to be asleep or helping around the house or playing outside. In a voice angry or worried or just curious, she'd ask: "What do you see in your books?" It became the family's joke. When I was called and wouldn't reply, someone would say I must be hiding under my bed with a book.

(How did I manage my success?)

What I am about to say to you has taken me more than twenty years to admit: *A primary reason for my success in the classroom was that I couldn't forget that schooling was changing me and separating me from the life I enjoyed before becoming a student.* That simple realization! For years I never spoke to anyone about it. Never mentioned a thing to my family or my teachers or classmates. From a very early age, I understood enough, just enough about my classroom experiences to keep what I knew repressed, hidden beneath layers of embarrassment. Not until my last months as a graduate student, nearly thirty years old, was it possible for me to think much about the reasons for my academic success. Only then. At the end of my schooling, I needed to determine how far I had moved from my past. The adult finally confronted, and now must publicly say, what the child shuddered from knowing and could never admit to himself or to those many faces that smiled at his every success. ("Your parents must be very proud. . . .")

At the end, in the British Museum (too distracted to finish my dissertation) for weeks I read, speed-read, books by modern educational theorists, only to find infrequent and slight mention of students like me. (Much more is written about the more typical case, the lower-class student who barely is helped by his schooling.) Then one day, leafing through Richard Hoggart's *The Uses of Literacy*, I found, in his description of the scholarship boy, myself. For the first time I realized that there were other students like me, and so I was able to frame the meaning of my academic success, its consequent price — the loss.

Hoggart's description is distinguished, at least initially, by deep understanding. What he grasps very well is that the scholarship boy must move between environments, his home and the classroom, which are at cultural extremes, opposed. With his family, the boy has the intense pleasure of intimacy, the family's consolation in feeling public alienation. Lavish emotions texture home life. *Then,* at school, the instruction bids him to trust lonely reason primarily. Immediate needs set the pace of his parents' lives. From his mother and father the boy learns to trust spontaneity and nonrational ways of knowing. *Then,* at school, there is mental calm. Teachers emphasize the value of a reflectiveness that opens a space between thinking and immediate action.

Years of schooling must pass before the boy will be able to sketch the   10
cultural differences in his day as abstractly as this. But he senses those differences early. Perhaps as early as the night he brings home an assignment from school and finds the house too noisy for study.

> He has to be more and more alone, if he is going to "get on." He will have, probably unconsciously, to oppose the ethos[2] of the hearth, the intense gregariousness of the working-class family group. Since everything centres upon the living-room, there is unlikely to be a room of his own; the bedrooms are cold and inhospitable, and to warm them or the front room, if there is one, would not only be expensive, but would require an imaginative leap — out of the tradition — which most families are not capable of making. There is a corner of the living-room

---

[2]*ethos:* The fundamental spirit or character of a thing.

table. On the other side Mother is ironing, the wireless is on, someone is singing a snatch of song or Father says intermittently whatever comes into his head. The boy has to cut himself off mentally, so as to do his homework, as well as he can.[3]

The next day, the lesson is as apparent at school. There are even rows of desks. Discussion is ordered. The boy must rehearse his thoughts and raise his hand before speaking out in a loud voice to an audience of class-mates. And there is time enough, and silence, to think about ideas (big ideas) never considered at home by his parents.

Not for the working-class child alone is adjustment to the classroom difficult. Good schooling requires that any student alter early childhood habits. But the working-class child is usually least prepared for the change. And, unlike many middle-class children, he goes home and sees in his par-ents a way of life not only different but starkly opposed to that of the class-room. (He enters the house and hears his parents talking in ways his teach-ers discourage.)

Without extraordinary determination and the great assistance of oth-ers — at home and at school — there is little chance for success. Typically most working-class children are barely changed by the classroom. The ex-ception succeeds. The relative few become scholarship students. Of these, Richard Hoggart estimates, most manage a fairly graceful transition. Some-how they learn to live in the two very different worlds of their day. There are some others, however, those Hoggart pejoratively terms "scholarship boys," for whom success comes with special anxiety. Scholarship boy: good student, troubled son. The child is "moderately endowed," intellectually mediocre, Hoggart supposes — though it may be more pertinent to note the special qualities of temperament in the child. High-strung child. Brood-ing. Sensitive. Haunted by the knowledge that one *chooses* to become a stu-dent. (Education is not an inevitable or natural step in growing up.) Here is a child who cannot forget that his academic success distances him from a life he loved, even from his own memory of himself.

Initially, he wavers, balances allegiance. ("The boy is himself [until he reaches, say, the upper forms[4]] very much of *both* the worlds of home and school. He is enormously obedient to the dictates of the world of school, but emotionally still strongly wants to continue as part of the family circle.") Gradually, necessarily, the balance is lost. The boy needs to spend more and more time studying, each night enclosing himself in the silence permitted and required by intense concentration. He takes his first step toward aca-demic success, away from his family.

---

[3]All quotations are from Richard Hoggart, *The Uses of Literacy* (London: Chatto and Windus, 1957), chapter 10. [Author's note]

[4]*upper forms:* Upper grades or classes in British secondary schools.

From the very first days, through the years following, it will be with his   15
parents — the figures of lost authority, the persons toward whom he feels
deepest love — that the change will be most powerfully measured. A separation will unravel between them. Advancing in his studies, the boy notices
that his mother and father have not changed as much as he. Rather, when
he sees them, they often remind him of the person he once was and the life
he earlier shared with them. He realizes what some Romantics[5] also know
when they praise the working class for the capacity for human closeness,
qualities of passion and spontaneity, that the rest of us experience in like
measure only in the earliest part of our youth. For the Romantic, this
doesn't make working-class life childish. Working-class life challenges precisely because it is an *adult* way of life.

The scholarship boy reaches a different conclusion. He cannot afford to
admire his parents. (How could he and still pursue such a contrary life?) He
permits himself embarrassment at their lack of education. And to evade
nostalgia for the life he has lost, he concentrates on the benefits education
will bestow upon him. He becomes especially ambitious. Without the support of old certainties and consolations, almost mechanically, he assumes
the procedures and doctrines of the classroom. The kind of allegiance the
young student might have given his mother and father only days earlier, he
transfers to the teacher, the new figure of authority. "[The scholarship boy]
tends to make a father-figure of his form-master,"[6] Hoggart observes.

But Hoggart's calm prose only makes me recall the urgency with which I
came to idolize my grammar school teachers. I began by imitating their accents, using their diction, trusting their every direction. The very first facts
they dispensed, I grasped with awe. Any book they told me to read, I read —
then waited for them to tell me which books I enjoyed. Their every casual
opinion I came to adopt and to trumpet when I returned home. I stayed after
school "to help" — to get my teacher's undivided attention. It was the nun's
encouragement that mattered most to me. (She understood exactly what —
my parents never seemed to appraise so well — all my achievements entailed.)
Memory gently caressed each word of praise bestowed in the classroom so that
compliments teachers paid me years ago come quickly to mind even today.

The enthusiasm I felt in second-grade classes I flaunted before both my
parents. The docile, obedient student came home a shrill and precocious
son who insisted on correcting and teaching his parents with the remark:
"My teacher told us. . . ."

I intended to hurt my mother and father. I was still angry at them for
having encouraged me toward classroom English. But gradually this anger

---

[5]*Romantics:* Adherents of the principles of romanticism — a literary and philosophical
movement that emphasized the imagination, freedom, nature, the return to a simple life, and
the ordinary individual.

[6]*form-master:* A teacher in a British secondary school.

was exhausted, replaced by guilt as school grew more and more attractive to me. I grew increasingly successful, a talkative student. My hand was raised in the classroom; I yearned to answer any question. At home, life was less noisy than it had been. (I spoke to classmates and teachers more often each day than to family members.) Quiet at home, I sat with my papers for hours each night. I never forgot that schooling had irretrievably changed my family's life. That knowledge, however, did not weaken ambition. Instead, it strengthened resolve. Those times I remembered the loss of my past with regret, I quickly reminded myself of all the things my teachers could give me. (They could make me an educated man.) I tightened my grip on pencil and books. I evaded nostalgia. Tried hard to forget. But one does not forget by trying to forget. One only remembers. I remembered too well that education had changed my family's life. I would not have become a scholarship boy had I not so often remembered.

Once she was sure that her children knew English, my mother would   20
tell us, "You should keep up your Spanish." Voices playfully groaned in response. "¡Pochos!"[7] my mother would tease. I listened silently.

After a while, I grew more calm at home. I developed tact. A fourth-grade student, I was no longer the show-off in front of my parents. I became a conventionally dutiful son, politely affectionate, cheerful enough, even — for reasons beyond choosing — my father's favorite. And much about my family life was easy then, comfortable, happy in the rhythm of our living together: hearing my father getting ready for work; eating the breakfast my mother had made me; looking up from a novel to hear my brother or one of my sisters playing with friends in the backyard; in winter, coming upon the house all lighted up after dark.

But withheld from my mother and father was any mention of what most mattered to me: the extraordinary experience of first-learning. Late afternoon: in the midst of preparing dinner, my mother would come up behind me while I was trying to read. Her head just over mine, her breath warmly scented with food. "What are you reading?" Or, "Tell me about your new courses." I would barely respond, "Just the usual things, nothing special." (A half smile, then silence. Her head moving back in the silence. Silence! Instead of the flood of intimate sounds that had once flowed smoothly between us, there was this silence.) After dinner, I would rush to a bedroom with papers and books. As often as possible, I resisted parental pleas to "save lights" by coming to the kitchen to work. I kept so much, so often, to myself. Sad. Enthusiastic. Troubled by the excitement of coming upon new ideas. Eager. Fascinated by the promising texture of a brand-new book. I hoarded the pleasures of learning. Alone for hours. Enthralled. Nervous. I rarely looked away from my books — or back on my memories. Nights when relatives visited and

[7]*Pocho:* A derogatory Spanish word for a Mexican American who has adopted the attitudes, values, and lifestyle of Anglo culture.

the front rooms were warmed by Spanish sounds, I slipped quietly out of the house.

It mattered that education was changing me. It never ceased to matter. My brother and sisters would giggle at our mother's mispronounced words. They'd correct her gently. My mother laughed girlishly one night, trying not to pronounce *sheep* as *ship*. From a distance I listened sullenly. From that distance, pretending not to notice on another occasion, I saw my father looking at the title pages of my library books. That was the scene on my mind when I walked home with a fourth-grade companion and heard him say that his parents read to him every night. (A strange-sounding book — *Winnie the Pooh*.) Immediately, I wanted to know, "What is it like?" My companion, however, thought I wanted to know about the plot of the book. Another day, my mother surprised me by asking for a "nice" book to read. "Something not too hard you think I might like." Carefully I chose one, Willa Cather's[8] *My Antonia*. But when, several weeks later, I happened to see it next to her bed unread except for the first few pages, I was furious and suddenly wanted to cry. I grabbed up the book and took it back to my room and placed it in its place, alphabetically on my shelf.

"Your parents must be very proud of you." People began to say that to me about the time I was in sixth grade. To answer affirmatively, I'd smile. Shyly I'd smile, never betraying my sense of the irony: I was not proud of my mother and father. I was embarrassed by their lack of education. It was not that I ever thought they were stupid, though stupidly I took for granted their enormous native intelligence. Simply, what mattered to me was that they were not like my teachers.

But, "Why didn't you tell us about the award?" my mother demanded,   25 her frown weakened by pride. At the grammar school ceremony several weeks after, her eyes were brighter than the trophy I'd won. Pushing back the hair from my forehead, she whispered that I had "shown" the *gringos*.[9] A few minutes later, I heard my father speak to my teacher and felt ashamed of his labored, accented words. Then guilty for the shame. I felt such contrary feelings. (There is no simple roadmap through the heart of the scholarship boy.) My teacher was so soft-spoken and her words were edged sharp and clean. I admired her until it seemed to me that she spoke too carefully. Sensing that she was condescending to them, I became nervous. Resentful. Protective. I tried to move my parents away. "You both must be very proud of Richard," the nun said. They responded quickly. (They were proud.) "We are proud of all our children." Then this afterthought: "They sure didn't get their brains from us." They all laughed. I smiled.

[8]*Willa Cather:* American novelist (1876–1947).
[9]*gringos:* Anglos.

In fourth grade I embarked upon a grandiose reading program. "Give me the names of important books," I would say to startled teachers. They soon found out that I had in mind "adult books." I ignored their suggestion of anything I suspected was written for children. (Not until I was in college, as a result, did I read *Huckleberry Finn* or *Alice's Adventures in Wonderland*.) Instead, I read *The Scarlet Letter* and Franklin's *Autobiography*. And whatever I read I read for extra credit. Each time I finished a book, I reported the achievement to a teacher and basked in the praise my effort earned. Despite my best efforts, however, there seemed to be more and more books I needed to read. At the library I would literally tremble as I came upon whole shelves of books I hadn't read. So I read and I read and I read: *Great Expectations;* all the short stories of Kipling; *The Babe Ruth Story;* the entire first volume of the *Encyclopaedia Britannica* (A–ANSTEY); the *Iliad; Moby Dick; Gone with the Wind; The Good Earth; Ramona; Forever Amber; The Lives of the Saints; Crime and Punishment; The Pearl. . . .* Librarians who initially frowned when I checked out the maximum ten books at a time started saving books they thought I might like. Teachers would say to the rest of the class, "I only wish the rest of you took reading as seriously as Richard obviously does."

But at home I would hear my mother wondering, "What do you see in your books?" (Was reading a hobby like her knitting? Was so much reading even healthy for a boy? Was it the sign of "brains"? Or was it just a convenient excuse for not helping around the house on Saturday mornings?) Always, "What do you see. . . ?"

What *did* I see in my books? I had the idea that they were crucial for my academic success, though I couldn't have said exactly how or why. In the sixth grade I simply concluded that what gave a book its value was some major idea or theme it contained. If that core essence could be mined and memorized, I would become learned like my teachers. I decided to record in a notebook the themes of the books that I read. After reading *Robinson Crusoe,* I wrote that its theme was "the value of learning to live by oneself." When I completed *Wuthering Heights,* I noted the danger of "letting emotions get out of control." Rereading these brief moralistic appraisals usually left me disheartened. I couldn't believe that they were really the source of reading's value. But for many more years, they constituted the only means I had of describing to myself the educational value of books.

I entered high school having read hundreds of books. My habit of reading made me a confident speaker and writer of English. Reading also enabled me to sense something of the shape, the major concerns, of Western thought. (I was able to say something about Dante[10] and Descartes[11] and

---

[10]*Dante:* Dante Alighieri, Italian poet (1265–1321); author of the *Divine Comedy.*
[11]*Descartes:* René Descartes, French philosopher and mathematician (1596–1650).

Engels[12] and James Baldwin[13] in my high school term papers.) In these various ways, books brought me academic success as I hoped that they would. But I was not a good reader. Merely bookish, I lacked a point of view when I read. Rather, I read in order to acquire a point of view. I vacuumed books for epigrams, scraps of information, ideas, themes — anything to fill the hollow within me and make me feel educated. When one of my teachers suggested to his drowsy tenth-grade English class that a person could not have a "complicated idea" until he had read at least two thousand books, I heard the remark without detecting either its irony or its very complicated truth. I merely determined to compile a list of all the books I had ever read. Harsh with myself, I included only once a title I might have read several times. (How, after all, could one read a book more than once?) And I included only those books over a hundred pages in length. (Could anything shorter be a book?)

There was yet another high school list I compiled. One day I came   30 across a newspaper article about the retirement of an English professor at a nearby state college. The article was accompanied by a list of the "hundred most important books of Western Civilization." "More than anything else in my life," the professor told the reporter with finality, "these books have made me all that I am." That was the kind of remark I couldn't ignore. I clipped out the list and kept it for the several months it took me to read all of the titles. Most books, of course, I barely understood. While reading Plato's *Republic,* for instance, I needed to keep looking at the book jacket comments to remind myself what the text was about. Nevertheless, with the special patience and superstition of a scholarship boy, I looked at every word of the text. And by the time I reached the last word, relieved, I convinced myself that I had read *The Republic.* In a ceremony of great pride, I solemnly crossed Plato off my list.

. . . The scholarship boy does not straddle, cannot reconcile, the two great opposing cultures of his life. His success is unromantic and plain. He sits in the classroom and offers those sitting beside him no calming reassurance about their own lives. He sits in the seminar room — a man with brown skin, the son of working-class Mexican immigrant parents. (Addressing the professor at the head of the table, his voice catches with nervousness.) There is no trace of his parents' accent in his speech. Instead he approximates the accents of teachers and classmates. Coming from *him* those sounds seem suddenly odd. Odd too is the effect produced when *he* uses academic jargon — bubbles at the tip of his tongue: "*Topos* . . . negative capability . . . vegetation imagery in Shakespearean comedy."[14] He lifts an

---

[12]*Engels:* Friedrich Engels, German socialist (1820–1895); coauthor with Karl Marx of the *Communist Manifesto* in 1848.

[13]*James Baldwin:* American novelist and essayist (1924–1987).

[14]*topos . . . negative capability . . . :* Technical terms associated with the study of literary criticism.

opinion from Coleridge, takes something else from Frye or Empson or Leavis.[15] He even repeats exactly his professor's earlier comment. All his ideas are clearly borrowed. He seems to have no thought of his own. He chatters while his listeners smile — their look one of disdain.

When he is older and thus when so little of the person he was survives, the scholarship boy makes only too apparent his profound lack of *self*-confidence. This is the conventional assessment that even Richard Hoggart repeats:

> [The scholarship boy] tends to over-stress the importance of examinations, of the piling-up of knowledge and of received opinions. He discovers a technique of apparent learning, of the acquiring of facts rather than of the handling and use of facts. He learns how to receive a purely literate education, one using only a small part of the personality and challenging only a limited area of his being. He begins to see life as a ladder, as a permanent examination with some praise and some further exhortation at each stage. He becomes an expert imbiber and dolerout; his competence will vary, but will rarely be accompanied by genuine enthusiasms. He rarely feels the reality of knowledge, of other men's thoughts and imaginings, on his own pulses. . . . He has something of the blinkered pony about him. . . .

But this is criticism more accurate than fair. The scholarship boy is a very bad student. He is the great mimic; a collector of thoughts, not a thinker; the very last person in class who ever feels obliged to have an opinion of his own. In large part, however, the reason he is such a bad student is because he realizes more often and more acutely than most other students — than Hoggart himself — that education requires radical self-reformation. As a very young boy, regarding his parents, as he struggles with an early homework assignment, he knows this too well. That is why he lacks self-assurance. He does not forget that the classroom is responsible for remaking him. He relies on his teacher, depends on all that he hears in the classroom and reads in his books. He becomes in every obvious way the worst student, a dummy mouthing the opinions of others. But he would not be so bad — nor would he become so successful, a *scholarship* boy — if he did not accurately perceive that the best synonym for primary "education" is "imitation."

Like me, Hoggart's imagined scholarship boy spends most of his years in the classroom afraid to long for his past. Only at the very end of his schooling does the boy-man become nostalgic. In this sudden change of heart, Richard Hoggart notes:

> He longs for the membership he lost, "he pines for some Nameless Eden where he never was." The nostalgia is the stronger and the more

---

[15]*Coleridge . . . Frye . . . Empson . . . Leavis:* Important literary critics.

ambiguous because he is really "in quest of his own absconded self yet scared to find it." He both wants to go back and yet thinks he has gone beyond his class, feels himself weighted with knowledge of his own and their situation, which hereafter forbids him the simpler pleasures of his father and mother. . . .

According to Hoggart, the scholarship boy grows nostalgic because he   35 remains the uncertain scholar, bright enough to have moved from his past, yet unable to feel easy, a part of a community of academics.

This analysis, however, only partially suggests what happened to me in my last years as a graduate student. When I traveled to London to write a dissertation on English Renaissance literature, I was finally confident of membership in a "community of scholars." But the pleasure that confidence gave me faded rapidly. After only two or three months in the reading room of the British Museum, it became clear that I had joined a lonely community. Around me each day were dour faces eclipsed by large piles of books. There were the regulars, like the old couple who arrived every morning, each holding a loop of the shopping bag which contained all their notes. And there was the historian who chattered madly to herself. ("Oh dear! Oh! Now, what's this? What? Oh, my!") There were also the faces of young men and women worn by long study. And everywhere eyes turned away the moment our glance accidentally met. Some persons I sat beside day after day, yet we passed silently at the end of the day, strangers. Still, we were united by a common respect for the written word and for scholarship. We did form a union, though one in which we remained distant from one another.

More profound and unsettling was the bond I recognized with those writers whose books I consulted. Whenever I opened a text that hadn't been used for years, I realized that my special interests and skills united me to a mere handful of academics. We formed an exclusive — eccentric! — society, separated from others who would never care or be able to share our concerns. (The pages I turned were stiff like layers of dead skin.) I began to wonder: Who, beside my dissertation director and a few faculty members, would ever read what I wrote? and: Was my dissertation much more than an act of social withdrawal? These questions went unanswered in the silence of the Museum reading room. They remained to trouble me after I'd leave the library each afternoon and feel myself shy — unsteady, speaking simple sentences at the grocer's or the butcher's on my way back to my bed-sitter.[16]

Meanwhile my file cards accumulated. A professional, I knew exactly how to search a book for pertinent information. I could quickly assess and summarize the usability of the many books I consulted. But whenever I started to write, I knew too much (and not enough) to be able to write anything but sentences that were overly cautious, timid, strained brittle under

---

[16]*bed-sitter:* A one-room apartment.

the heavy weight of footnotes and qualifications. I seemed unable to dare a passionate statement. I felt drawn by professionalism to the edge of sterility, capable of no more than pedantic, lifeless, unassailable prose.

Then nostalgia began.

After years spent unwilling to admit its attractions, I gestured nostalgi-   40
cally toward the past. I yearned for that time when I had not been so alone. I became impatient with books. I wanted experience more immediate. I feared the library's silence. I silently scorned the gray, timid faces around me. I grew to hate the growing pages of my dissertation on genre[17] and Renaissance literature. (In my mind I heard relatives laughing as they tried to make sense of its title.) I wanted something — I couldn't say exactly what. I told myself that I wanted a more passionate life. And a life less thoughtful. And above all, I wanted to be less alone. One day I heard some Spanish academics whispering back and forth to each other, and their sounds seemed ghostly voices recalling my life. Yearning became preoccupation then. Boyhood memories beckoned, flooded my mind. (Laughing intimate voices. Bounding up the front steps of the porch. A sudden embrace inside the door.)

For weeks after, I turned to books by educational experts. I needed to learn how far I had moved from my past — to determine how fast I would be able to recover something of it once again. But I found little. Only a chapter in a book by Richard Hoggart. . . I left the reading room and the circle of faces.

I came home. After the year in England, I spent three summer months living with my mother and father, relieved by how easy it was to be home. It no longer seemed very important to me that we had little to say. I felt easy sitting and eating and walking with them. I watched them, nevertheless, looking for evidence of those elastic, sturdy strands that bind generations in a web of inheritance. I thought as I watched my mother one night: of course a friend had been right when she told me that I gestured and laughed just like my mother. Another time I saw for myself: my father's eyes were much like my own, constantly watchful.

But after the early relief, this return, came suspicion, nagging until I realized that I had not neatly sidestepped the impact of schooling. My desire to do so was precisely the measure of how much I remained an academic. *Negatively* (for that is how this idea first occurred to me): my need to think so much and so abstractly about my parents and our relationship was in itself an indication of my long education. My father and mother did not pass their time thinking about the cultural meanings of their experience. It was I who described their daily lives with airy ideas. And yet, *positively:* the ability to consider experience so abstractly allowed me to shape into desire what would otherwise have remained indefinite, meaningless longing in the

---

[17]*genre:* A class or category of artistic work; e.g., the genre of poetry.

British Museum. If, because of my schooling, I had grown culturally separated from my parents, my education finally had given me ways of speaking and caring about that fact.

My best teachers in college and graduate school, years before, had tried to prepare me for this conclusion, I think, when they discussed texts of aristocratic pastoral literature. Faithfully, I wrote down all that they said. I memorized it: "The praise of the unlettered by the highly educated is one of the primary themes of 'elitist' literature." But, "the importance of the praise given the unsolitary, richly passionate and spontaneous life is that it simultaneously reflects the value of a reflective life." I heard it all. But there was no way for any of it to mean very much to me. I was a scholarship boy at the time, busily laddering my way up the rungs of education. To pass an examination, I copied down exactly what my teachers told me. It would require many more years of schooling (an inevitable miseducation) in which I came to trust the silence of reading and the habit of abstracting from immediate experience — moving away from a life of closeness and immediacy I remembered with my parents, growing older — before I turned unafraid to desire the past, and thereby achieved what had eluded me for so long — the end of education.

ENGAGING THE TEXT

1. How does education affect Rodriguez's relationship to his family, his past, and his culture? Do you agree with him that education requires "radical self-reformation" (para. 33)?

2. What is a "scholarship boy"? Why does Rodriguez consider himself a bad student despite his academic success?

3. What happens to Rodriguez in London? Why does he ultimately abandon his studies there?

4. What drives Rodriguez to succeed? What does education represent to him? To his father and mother?

5. What is Rodriguez's final assessment of what he has gained and lost through his education? Do you agree with his analysis?

EXPLORING CONNECTIONS

6. Compare Rodriguez's attitude toward education and success with that of Mike Rose (p. 174) in "I Just Wanna Be Average."

7. To what extent do Rodriguez's experiences as a "scholarship boy" confirm or complicate Jean Anyon's analysis (p. 186) of the relationship between social class, education, and success?

8. Read "Stephen Cruz" (p. 326) and compare his attitudes toward education and success with those of Rodriguez.

EXTENDING THE CRITICAL CONTEXT

9. What are your personal motives for academic success? How do they compare with those of Rodriguez?

10. Today many college students find that they're following in the footsteps of family members — not breaking ground as Rodriguez did. What special difficulties do such second- or third-generation college students face?

Para Teresa[1]

INÉS HERNÁNDEZ-ÁVILA

This poem explores and attempts to resolve an old conflict between its speaker and her schoolmate, two Chicanas at "Alamo which-had-to-be-its-name" Elementary School who have radically different ideas about what education means and does. Inés Hernández-Ávila (b. 1947) is a professor of Native American studies at the University of California, Davis. This poem appeared in her collection Con Razón, Corazón *(1987).*

A tí-Teresa Compean
Te dedico las palabras estás
que explotan de mi corazón[2]

That day during lunch hour
at Alamo which-had-to-be-its-name   5
Elementary
my dear raza
That day in the bathroom
Door guarded
Myself cornered   10
I was accused by you, Teresa
Tú y las demás de tus amigas
Pachucas todas
Eran Uds. cinco.[3]

---

[1]For Teresa. [Author's note]
[2]To you, Teresa Compean, I dedicate these words that explode from my heart. [Author's note]
[3]You and the rest of your friends, all Pachucas, there were five of you. [Author's note]

Me gritaban que porque me creía tan grande[4]   15
What was I trying to do, you growled
Show you up?
Make the teachers like me, pet me,
Tell me what a credit to my people I was?
I was playing right into their hands, you challenged   20
And you would have none of it.
I was to stop.

I was to be like you
I was to play your game of deadly defiance
Arrogance, refusal to submit.   25
The game in which the winner takes nothing
Asks for nothing
Never lets his weaknesses show.

But I didn't understand.
My fear salted with confusion   30
Charged me to explain to you
I did nothing *for the teachers.*
I studied for my parents and for my grandparents
Who cut out honor roll lists
Whenever their nietos'[5] names appeared   35
For my shy mother who mastered her terror
to demand her place in mother's clubs
For my carpenter-father who helped me patiently with my math.
For my abuelos que me regalaron lápices en la Navidad[6]
And for myself.   40

Porque reconocí en aquel entonces
una verdad tremenda
que me hizo a mi un rebelde
Aunque tú no te habías dadocuenta[7]
We were not inferior   45
You and I, y las demás de tus amigas
Y los demás de nuestra gente[8]
I knew it the way I knew I was alive
We were good, honorable, brave
Genuine, loyal, strong   50
And smart.

[4]You were screaming at me, asking me why I thought I was so hot. [Author's note]
[5]Grandchildren's. [Author's note]
[6]Grandparents who gave me gifts of pencils at Christmas. [Author's note]
[7]Because I recognized a great truth then that made me a rebel, even though you didn't realize it. [Author's note]
[8]And the rest of your friends / And the rest of our people. [Author's note]

Mine was a deadly game of defiance, also.
My contest was to prove
beyond any doubt
that we were not only equal but superior to them.   55
That was why I studied.
If I could do it, we all could.

You let me go then.
Your friends unblocked the way
I who-did-not-know-how-to-fight   60
was not made to engage with you-who-grew-up-fighting
Tu y yo, Teresa[9]
We went in different directions
Pero fuimos juntas.[10]
                                                                     65
In sixth grade we did not understand
Uds. with the teased, dyed-black-but-reddening hair,
Full petticoats, red lipsticks
and sweaters with the sleeves
pushed up
Y yo conformándome con lo que deseaba mi mamá[11]   70
Certainly never allowed to dye, to tease, to paint myself
I did not accept your way of anger,
Your judgements
You did not accept mine.
                                                                     75
But now in 1975, when I am twenty-eight
Teresa Compean
I remember you.
Y sabes —
Te comprendo,
Es más, te respeto.   80
Y si me permites,
Te nombro — "hermana."[12]

[9]You and I. [Author's note]
[10]But we were together. [Author's note]
[11]And I conforming to my mother's wishes. [Author's note]
[12]And do you know what, I understand you. Even more, I respect you. And, if you permit me, I name you my sister. [Author's note]

ENGAGING THE TEXT

1. The speaker says that she didn't understand Teresa at the time of the incident she describes. What didn't she understand, and why? How have her views of Teresa and of herself changed since then? What seems to have brought about this change?

2. What attitudes toward school and the majority culture do Teresa and the speaker represent? What about the speaker's family? In what way are both girls playing a game of "deadly defiance"? What arguments can you make for each form of rebellion?

3. Why do you think Hernández-Ávila wrote this poem in both Spanish and English? What does doing so say about the speaker's life? About her change of attitude toward Teresa?

EXPLORING CONNECTIONS

4. Compare and contrast the speaker's attitude toward school and family with those of Richard Rodriguez (p. 202). What motivates each of them? What tensions do they feel?

5. Write a dialogue between the speaker of this poem, who wants to excel, and Ken Harvey, the boy whom Mike Rose said just wanted to be average (p. 174). Explore the uncertainties, pressures, and desires that these students felt. In what ways are these two apparently contrasting students actually similar?

EXTENDING THE CRITICAL CONTEXT

6. Was there a person or group you disliked, feared, or fought with in elementary school? Has your understanding of your adversary or of your own motives changed since then? If so, what brought about this change?

Learning to Read

MALCOLM X

Born Malcolm Little on May 19, 1925, Malcolm X was one of the most articulate and powerful leaders of black America during the 1960s. A street hustler convicted of robbery in 1946, he spent seven years in prison, where he educated himself and became a disciple of Elijah Muhammad, founder of the Nation of Islam. In the days of the civil rights movement, Malcolm X emerged as the leading spokesman for black separatism, a philosophy that urged black Americans to cut political, social, and economic ties with the white community. After a pilgrimage to Mecca, the capital of the Muslim world, in 1964, he became an orthodox Muslim, adopted the Muslim name El Hajj Malik El-Shabazz, and distanced himself from the teachings of the black Muslims. He was assassinated in 1965. In the following excerpt from his autobiography (1965), coauthored with Alex Haley and published the year of his death, Malcolm X describes his self-education.

It was because of my letters that I happened to stumble upon starting to acquire some kind of a homemade education.

I became increasingly frustrated at not being able to express what I wanted to convey in letters that I wrote, especially those to Mr. Elijah Muhammad.[1] In the street, I had been the most articulate hustler out there — I had commanded attention when I said something. But now, trying to write simple English, I not only wasn't articulate, I wasn't even functional. How would I sound writing in slang, the way I would *say* it, something such as, "Look, daddy, let me pull your coat about a cat, Elijah Muhammad — "

Many who today hear me somewhere in person, or on television, or those who read something I've said, will think I went to school far beyond the eighth grade. This impression is due entirely to my prison studies.

It had really begun back in the Charlestown Prison, when Bimbi[2] first made me feel envy of his stock of knowledge. Bimbi had always taken charge of any conversations he was in, and I had tried to emulate him. But every book I picked up had few sentences which didn't contain anywhere from one to nearly all of the words that might as well have been in Chinese. When I just skipped those words, of course, I really ended up with little idea of what the book said. So I had come to the Norfolk Prison Colony still going through only book-reading motions. Pretty soon, I would have quit even these motions, unless I had received the motivation that I did.

I saw that the best thing I could do was get hold of a dictionary — to study, to learn some words. I was lucky enough to reason also that I should try to improve my penmanship. It was sad. I couldn't even write in a straight line. It was both ideas together that moved me to request a dictionary along with some tablets and pencils from the Norfolk Prison Colony school.

I spent two days just riffling uncertainly through the dictionary's pages. I'd never realized so many words existed! I didn't know *which* words I needed to learn. Finally, just to start some kind of action, I began copying.

In my slow, painstaking, ragged handwriting, I copied into my tablet everything printed on that first page, down to the punctuation marks.

I believe it took me a day. Then, aloud, I read back, to myself, everything I'd written on the tablet. Over and over, aloud, to myself, I read my own handwriting.

I woke up the next morning, thinking about those words — immensely proud to realize that not only had I written so much at one time, but I'd written words that I never knew were in the world. Moreover, with a little effort, I also could remember what many of these words meant. I reviewed the words whose meanings I didn't remember. Funny thing, from the dic-

5

---

[1]*Elijah Muhammad:* American clergyman (1897–1975); leader of the Nation of Islam, 1935–1975.

[2]*Bimbi:* A fellow inmate whose encyclopedic learning and verbal facility greatly impressed Malcolm X.

tionary first page right now, that "aardvark" springs to my mind. The dictionary had a picture of it, a long-tailed, long-eared, burrowing African mammal, which lives off termites caught by sticking out its tongue as an anteater does for ants.

I was so fascinated that I went on — I copied the dictionary's next   10
page. And the same experience came when I studied that. With every succeeding page, I also learned of people and places and events from history. Actually the dictionary is like a miniature encyclopedia. Finally the dictionary's A section had filled a whole tablet — and I went on into the B's. That was the way I started copying what eventually became the entire dictionary. It went a lot faster after so much practice helped me to pick up handwriting speed. Between what I wrote in my tablet, and writing letters, during the rest of my time in prison I would guess I wrote a million words.

I suppose it was inevitable that as my word-base broadened, I could for the first time pick up a book and read and now begin to understand what the book was saying. Anyone who has read a great deal can imagine the new world that opened. Let me tell you something: from then until I left that prison, in every free moment I had, if I was not reading in the library, I was reading on my bunk. You couldn't have gotten me out of books with a wedge. Between Mr. Muhammad's teachings, my correspondence, my visitors, . . . and my reading of books, months passed without my even thinking about being imprisoned. In fact, up to then, I never had been so truly free in my life.

The Norfolk Prison Colony's library was in the school building. A variety of classes was taught there by instructors who came from such places as Harvard and Boston universities. The weekly debates between inmate teams were also held in the school building. You would be astonished to know how worked up convict debaters and audiences would get over subjects like "Should Babies Be Fed Milk?"

Available on the prison library's shelves were books on just about every general subject. Much of the big private collection that Parkhurst[3] had willed to the prison was still in crates and boxes in the back of the library — thousands of old books. Some of them looked ancient: covers faded, old-time parchment-looking binding. Parkhurst . . . seemed to have been principally interested in history and religion. He had the money and the special interest to have a lot of books that you wouldn't have in a general circulation. Any college library would have been lucky to get that collection.

As you can imagine, especially in a prison where there was heavy emphasis on rehabilitation, an inmate was smiled upon if he demonstrated an

---

[3]*Parkhurst:* Charles Henry Parkhurst (1842–1933); American clergyman, reformer, and president of the Society for the Prevention of Crime.

unusually intense interest in books. There was a sizable number of well-read inmates, especially the popular debaters. Some were said by many to be practically walking encyclopedias. They were almost celebrities. No university would ask any student to devour literature as I did when this new world opened to me, of being able to read and *understand*.

I read more in my room than in the library itself. An inmate who was   15
known to read a lot could check out more than the permitted maximum number of books. I preferred reading in the total isolation of my own room.

When I had progressed to really serious reading, every night at about ten P.M. I would be outraged with the "lights out." It always seemed to catch me right in the middle of something engrossing.

Fortunately, right outside my door was a corridor light that cast a glow into my room. The glow was enough to read by, once my eyes adjusted to it. So when "lights out" came, I would sit on the floor where I could continue reading in that glow.

At one-hour intervals at night guards paced past every room. Each time I heard the approaching footsteps, I jumped into bed and feigned sleep. And as soon as the guard passed, I got back out of bed onto the floor area of that light-glow, where I would read for another fifty-eight minutes until the guard approached again. That went on until three or four every morning. Three or four hours of sleep a night was enough for me. Often in the years in the streets I had slept less than that.

The teachings of Mr. Muhammad stressed how history had been "whitened" — when white men had written history books, the black man simply had been left out. Mr. Muhammad couldn't have said anything that would have struck me much harder. I had never forgotten how when my class, me and all of those whites, had studied seventh-grade United States history back in Mason, the history of the Negro had been covered in one paragraph, and the teacher had gotten a big laugh with his joke, "Negroes' feet are so big that when they walk, they leave a hole in the ground."

This is one reason why Mr. Muhammad's teachings spread so swiftly all   20
over the United States, among *all* Negroes, whether or not they became followers of Mr. Muhammad. The teachings ring true — to every Negro. You can hardly show me a black adult in America — or a white one, for that matter — who knows from the history books anything like the truth about the black man's role. In my own case, once I heard of the "glorious history of the black man," I took special pains to hunt in the library for books that would inform me on details about black history.

I can remember accurately the very first set of books that really impressed me. I have since bought that set of books and I have it at home for my children to read as they grow up. It's called *Wonders of the World*. It's full of pictures of archeological finds, statues that depict, usually, non-European people.

I found books like Will Durant's[4] *Story of Civilization.* I read H. G. Wells'[5] *Outline of History. Souls of Black Folk* by W. E. B. Du Bois[6] gave me a glimpse into the black people's history before they came to this country. Carter G. Woodson's[7] *Negro History* opened my eyes about black empires before the black slave was brought to the United States, and the early Negro struggles for freedom.

J. A. Rogers'[8] three volumes of *Sex and Race* told about race-mixing before Christ's time; and Aesop being a black man who told fables; about Egypt's Pharaohs; about the great Coptic Christian Empires;[9] about Ethiopia, the earth's oldest continuous black civilization, as China is the oldest continuous civilization.

Mr. Muhammad's teaching about how the white man had been created led me to *Findings In Genetics,* by Gregor Mendel.[10] (The dictionary's G section was where I had learned what "genetics" meant.) I really studied this book by the Austrian monk. Reading it over and over, especially certain sections, helped me to understand that if you started with a black man, a white man could be produced; but starting with a white man, you never could produce a black man — because the white chromosome is recessive. And since no one disputes that there was but one Original Man, the conclusion is clear.

During the last year or so, in the *New York Times,* Arnold Toynbee[11] 25 used the word "bleached" in describing the white man. His words were: "White (i.e., bleached) human beings of North European origin. . . ." Toynbee also referred to the European geographic area as only a peninsula of Asia. He said there was no such thing as Europe. And if you look at the globe, you will see for yourself that America is only an extension of Asia. (But at the same time Toynbee is among those who have helped to bleach history. He has written that Africa was the only continent that produced no history. He won't write that again. Every day now, the truth is coming to light.)

I never will forget how shocked I was when I began reading about slavery's total horror. It made such an impact upon me that it later became one of my favorite subjects when I became a minister of Mr. Muhammad's. The

---

[4]*Will Durant:* American author and historian (1885–1981).

[5]*H. G. Wells:* English novelist and historian (1866–1946).

[6]*W. E. B. Du Bois:* William Edward Burghardt Du Bois, distinguished black scholar, author, and activist (1868–1963). Du Bois was the first director of the NAACP and was an important figure in the Harlem Renaissance; his best-known book is *Souls of Black Folk.*

[7]*Carter G. Woodson:* Distinguished African American historian (1875–1950); considered the father of black history.

[8]*J. A. Rogers:* African American historian and journalist (1883–1965).

[9]*Coptic Christian Empire:* The domain of the Coptic Church, a native Egyptian Christian church that retains elements of its African origins.

[10]*Gregor Mendel:* Austrian monk, botanist, and pioneer in genetic research (1822–1884).

[11]*Arnold Toynbee:* English historian (1889–1975).

world's most monstrous crime, the sin and the blood on the white man's hands, are almost impossible to believe. Books like the one by Frederick Olmsted[12] opened my eyes to the horrors suffered when the slave was landed in the United States. The European woman, Fanny Kemble,[13] who had married a Southern white slaveowner, described how human beings were degraded. Of course I read *Uncle Tom's Cabin*.[14] In fact, I believe that's the only novel I have ever read since I started serious reading.

Parkhurst's collection also contained some bound pamphlets of the Abolitionist[15] Anti-Slavery Society of New England. I read descriptions of atrocities, saw those illustrations of black slave women tied up and flogged with whips; of black mothers watching their babies being dragged off, never to be seen by their mothers again; of dogs after slaves, and of the fugitive slave catchers, evil white men with whips and clubs and chains and guns. I read about the slave preacher Nat Turner, who put the fear of God into the white slavemaster. Nat Turner wasn't going around preaching pie-in-the-sky and "non-violent" freedom for the black man. There in Virginia one night in 1831, Nat and seven other slaves started out at his master's home and through the night they went from one plantation "big house" to the next, killing, until by the next morning 57 white people were dead and Nat had about 70 slaves following him. White people, terrified for their lives, fled from their homes, locked themselves up in public buildings, hid in the woods, and some even left the state. A small army of soldiers took two months to catch and hang Nat Turner. Somewhere I have read where Nat Turner's example is said to have inspired John Brown[16] to invade Virginia and attack Harpers Ferry nearly thirty years later, with thirteen white men and five Negroes.

I read Herodotus,[17] "the father of History," or, rather, I read about him. And I read the histories of various nations, which opened my eyes gradually, then wider and wider, to how the whole world's white men had indeed acted like devils, pillaging and raping and bleeding and draining the whole world's non-white people. I remember, for instance, books such as Will Durant's *The Story of Oriental Civilization*, and Mahatma Gandhi's[18] accounts of the struggle to drive the British out of India.

---

[12]*Frederick Olmsted:* Frederick Law Olmsted (1822–1903), American landscape architect, city planner, and opponent of slavery.

[13]*Fanny Kemble:* Frances Anne Kemble, English actress and author (1809–1893); best known for her autobiographical *Journal of a Residence on a Georgia Plantation,* published in 1863 to win support in Britain for the abolitionist cause.

[14]*Uncle Tom's Cabin:* Harriet Beecher Stowe's 1852 antislavery novel.

[15]*Abolitionist:* Advocating the prohibition of slavery.

[16]*John Brown:* American abolitionist (1800–1859); leader of an attack on Harpers Ferry, West Virginia, in 1859.

[17]*Herodotus:* Early Greek historian (484?–425? B.C.).

[18]*Mahatma Gandhi:* Hindu religious leader, social reformer, and advocate of nonviolence (1869–1948).

Book after book showed me how the white man had brought upon the world's black, brown, red, and yellow peoples every variety of the suffering of exploitation. I saw how since the sixteenth century, the so-called "Christian trader" white man began to ply the seas in his lust for Asian and African empires, and plunder, and power. I read, I saw, how the white man never has gone among the non-white peoples bearing the Cross in the true manner and spirit of Christ's teachings — meek, humble, and Christlike.

I perceived, as I read, how the collective white man had been actually   30 nothing but a piratical opportunist who used Faustian machinations[19] to make his own Christianity his initial wedge in criminal conquests. First, always "religiously," he branded "heathen" and "pagan" labels upon ancient non-white cultures and civilizations. The stage thus set, he then turned upon his non-white victims his weapons of war.

I read how, entering India — half a *billion* deeply religious brown people — the British white man, by 1759, through promises, trickery, and manipulations, controlled much of India through Great Britain's East India Company. The parasitical British administration kept tentacling out to half of the sub-continent. In 1857, some of the desperate people of India finally mutinied — and, excepting the African slave trade, nowhere has history recorded any more unnecessary bestial and ruthless human carnage than the British suppression of the non-white Indian people.

Over 115 million African blacks — close to the 1930's population of the United States — were murdered or enslaved during the slave trade. And I read how when the slave market was glutted, the cannibalistic white powers of Europe next carved up, as their colonies, the richest areas of the black continent. And Europe's chancelleries for the next century played a chess game of naked exploitation and power from Cape Horn to Cairo.

Ten guards and the warden couldn't have torn me out of those books. Not even Elijah Muhammad could have been more eloquent than those books were in providing indisputable proof that the collective white man had acted like a devil in virtually every contact he had with the world's collective non-white man. I listen today to the radio, and watch television, and read the headlines about the collective white man's fear and tension concerning China. When the white man professes ignorance about why the Chinese hate him so, my mind can't help flashing back to what I read, there in prison, about how the blood forebears of this same white man raped China at a time when China was trusting and helpless. Those original white "Christian traders" sent into China millions of pounds of opium. By 1839, so many of the Chinese were addicts that China's desperate government destroyed twenty thousand chests of opium. The first Opium War[20] was

---

[19]*Faustian machinations:* Evil plots or schemes. Faust was a legendary character who sold his soul to the devil for knowledge and power.

[20]*Opium War:* 1839–1842 war between Britain and China that ended with China's cession of Hong Kong to British rule.

promptly declared by the white man. Imagine! Declaring *war* upon someone who objects to being narcotized! The Chinese were severely beaten,
with Chinese-invented gunpowder.

The Treaty of Nanking made China pay the British white man for the
destroyed opium; forced open China's major ports to British trade; forced
China to abandon Hong Kong; fixed China's import tariffs so low that cheap
British articles soon flooded in, maiming China's industrial development.

After a second Opium War, the Tientsin Treaties legalized the ravaging   35
opium trade, legalized a British-French-American control of China's customs.
China tried delaying that Treaty's ratification; Peking was looted and burned.

"Kill the foreign white devils!" was the 1901 Chinese war cry in the
Boxer Rebellion.[21] Losing again, this time the Chinese were driven from
Peking's choicest areas. The vicious, arrogant white man put up the famous
signs, "Chinese and dogs not allowed."

Red China after World War II closed its doors to the Western white
world. Massive Chinese agricultural, scientific, and industrial efforts are described in a book that *Life* magazine recently published. Some observers inside Red China have reported that the world never has known such a hate-
white campaign as is now going on in this non-white country where, present
birth-rates continuing, in fifty more years Chinese will be half the earth's
population. And it seems that some Chinese chickens will soon come home
to roost, with China's recent successful nuclear tests.

Let us face reality. We can see in the United Nations a new world order
being shaped, along color lines — an alliance among the non-white nations.
America's U.N. Ambassador Adlai Stevenson[22] complained not long ago that
in the United Nations "a skin game"[23] was being played. He was right. He was
facing reality. A "skin game" *is* being played. But Ambassador Stevenson
sounded like Jesse James accusing the marshal of carrying a gun. Because who
in the world's history ever has played a worse "skin game" than the white man?

Mr. Muhammad, to whom I was writing daily, had no idea of what a
new world had opened up to me through my efforts to document his teachings in books.

When I discovered philosophy, I tried to touch all the landmarks of   40
philosophical development. Gradually, I read most of the old philosophers,
Occidental and Oriental. The Oriental philosophers were the ones I came
to prefer; finally, my impression was that most Occidental philosophy had
largely been borrowed from the Oriental thinkers. Socrates, for instance,
traveled in Egypt. Some sources even say that Socrates was initiated into

---

[21]*Boxer Rebellion:* The 1898–1900 uprising by members of a secret Chinese society who
opposed foreign influence in Chinese affairs.
[22]*Adlai Stevenson:* American politician (1900–1965); Democratic candidate for the presidency in 1952 and 1956.
[23]*skin game:* A dishonest or fraudulent scheme, business operation, or trick, with the
added reference in this instance to skin color.

some of the Egyptian mysteries. Obviously Socrates got some of his wisdom among the East's wise men.

I have often reflected upon the new vistas that reading opened to me. I knew right there in prison that reading had changed forever the course of my life. As I see it today, the ability to read awoke inside me some long dormant craving to be mentally alive. I certainly wasn't seeking any degree, the way a college confers a status symbol upon its students. My homemade education gave me, with every additional book that I read, a little bit more sensitivity to the deafness, dumbness, and blindness that was afflicting the black race in America. Not long ago, an English writer telephoned me from London, asking questions. One was, "What's your alma mater?" I told him, "Books." You will never catch me with a free fifteen minutes in which I'm not studying something I feel might be able to help the black man.

Yesterday I spoke in London, and both ways on the plane across the Atlantic I was studying a document about how the United Nations proposes to insure the human rights of the oppressed minorities of the world. The American black man is the world's most shameful case of minority oppression. What makes the black man think of himself as only an internal United States issue is just a catch-phrase, two words, "civil rights." How is the black man going to get "civil rights" before first he wins his *human* rights? If the American black man will start thinking about his *human* rights, and then start thinking of himself as part of one of the world's great peoples, he will see he has a case for the United Nations.

I can't think of a better case! Four hundred years of black blood and sweat invested here in America, and the white man still has the black man begging for what every immigrant fresh off the ship can take for granted the minute he walks down the gangplank.

But I'm digressing. I told the Englishman that my alma mater was books, a good library. Every time I catch a plane, I have with me a book that I want to read — and that's a lot of books these days. If I weren't out here every day battling the white man, I could spend the rest of my life reading, just satisfying my curiosity — because you can hardly mention anything I'm not curious about. I don't think anybody ever got more out of going to prison than I did. In fact, prison enabled me to study far more intensively than I would have if my life had gone differently and I had attended some college. I imagine that one of the biggest troubles with colleges is there are too many distractions, too much panty-raiding, fraternities, and boola-boola and all of that. Where else but in a prison could I have attacked my ignorance by being able to study intensely sometimes as much as fifteen hours a day?

ENGAGING THE TEXT

1. What motivated Malcolm X to educate himself?
2. What kind of knowledge did Malcolm X gain by learning to read? How did this knowledge free or empower him?

3. Would it be possible for public schools to empower students in the way that Malcolm X's self-education empowered him? If so, how? If not, why not?

4. Some readers are offended by the strength of Malcolm X's accusations and by his grouping of all members of a given race into "collectives." Given the history of racial injustice he recounts here, do you feel he is justified in taking such a position?

EXPLORING CONNECTIONS

5. Compare and contrast Malcolm X's views on the meaning and purpose of education — or on the value and nature of reading — with those of Richard Rodriguez (p. 202). How can you account for the differences in their attitudes?

6. Imagine that John Taylor Gatto (p. 166), Mike Rose (p. 174), Richard Rodriguez (p. 202), and Malcolm X have been appointed to redesign American education. Working in groups, role-play a meeting in which the committee attempts to reach consensus on its recommendations. Report to the class the results of the committee's deliberations and discuss them.

EXTENDING THE CRITICAL CONTEXT

7. Survey some typical elementary or secondary school textbooks to test the currency of Malcolm X's charge that the educational establishment presents a "whitened" view of America. What view of America is presently being projected in public school history and social science texts?

8. Go to the library and read one page of the dictionary chosen at random. Study the meanings of any unfamiliar words and follow up on the information on your page by consulting encyclopedias, books, or articles. Let yourself be guided by chance and by your interests. After you've tried this experiment, discuss in class the benefits and drawbacks of an unsystematic self-education like Malcolm X's.

Higher Education: Colder by Degrees

MYRA SADKER AND DAVID SADKER

Following the civil rights movement, race- and gender-segregated colleges and universities across the country began to integrate their student populations. After decades of "separate-but-equal" schooling, women and ethnic minority groups were eager to compete as equals in college classrooms. But recently, critics have questioned the effectiveness and equity of

*institutions that claim to offer color- and gender-blind education. In this se-
lection from* Failing at Fairness: How America's Schools Cheat Girls *(1994),
the Sadkers document pervasive sexism in American colleges, from gender
bias in the lecture hall to acquaintance rape on fraternity row. A professor
of education at The American University in Washington, D.C., David Sadker (b. 1942) has published a number of books and articles on sexism in education, several of them with Myra Sadker (1943–1995).*

The Divided Campus

Graduation day is a family milestone, official recognition of full and active partnership in the American Dream. Parents crowd the bookstore to
buy sweatshirts and baseball caps emblazoned with school insignia. Even
the car shows its colors with a college decal affixed to the window, proclaiming to all the world previous accomplishments and future promise. Amid all
this celebration it is easy to forget that little more than a century ago higher
education was mainly a man's world.

In the late 1800s college was the place to be for rich young men; it was
a source of social polish and a rollicking good time. Informal sporting events
and athletic competitions were harbingers of today's lucrative college football and basketball seasons. Fraternities created a world without adult rules,
a haven for males in their late teens and early twenties who drank, gambled,
and talked about loose women. While a few focused on academics, most
worked at fitting in and getting along, the marks of a successful student. In
the vernacular of the 1800s, working to win the approval of the professor by
class participation was ridiculed as "sticking your neck out" or "fishing."
Cheaters were shielded by fraternities and secret societies, and peer loyalty
was the measure of integrity.[1]

The first women to enter this male-ordered campus were venturing
into unmapped terrain. True pioneers who defied conventions to settle in
hostile territory, they were not greeted with open arms or the hospitality accorded welcome guests. At the University of Michigan after the Civil War,
women could not join the campus newspaper or college yearbook staffs.
Michigaum, the prestigious honor society, closed its doors to females and
kept the portals shut throughout the century. Cornell's response to the newcomers was undisguised disgust, and the school excluded them from clubs
and social activities. Even speaking to women on campus was an infraction
of fraternity rules. At Wesleyan, male students beat other men who talked
to women.

---

[1]An interesting and lively discussion of this period is provided in Helen Lefkowitz
Horowitz, *Campus Life: Undergraduate Cultures from the End of the Eighteenth Century to
the Present* (New York: Alfred A. Knopf, 1987). [Authors' note]

When they graduated, these pioneering women cultivated new careers. Many worked in elementary schools or the recently created high schools. By 1918, 84 percent of the nation's teaching force were women, and in this profession they could earn more than unskilled men and could support themselves. Like Jane Addams[2] and her Hull House colleagues, some women became settlement workers in the new profession of social work, while others studied to become doctors. As this wave of college women surged into emerging careers, they often abandoned the traditional life-style of marriage and motherhood.

Many college administrators were not ecstatic about these new students. At Stanford, 102 men and 98 women graduated in 1901, but the women received more honors and awards. In 1904, Stanford corrected the problem by setting a quota for future enrollments of three males for every female admitted, a policy maintained until 1933.[3] But the rate of women flooding the nation's colleges could not be halted. In 1870, two out of three postsecondary institutions turned women away; only thirty years later, more than two out of three admitted them; and by 1900, 19 percent of college graduates were female. But as their numbers increased, they became more conventional and less courageous. . . .

The trickle of female pioneers fighting for admission to male universities in the 1870s eventually became a tidal wave. A century later most remaining holdouts, including many Ivy League schools, finally capitulated and opened their doors. Today, women are the majority, 53 percent of the nation's postsecondary students, and the barriers once separating the sexes seem to have been demolished. But appearances deceive. The brick walls have been replaced with those of glass; the partitions are so transparent that they are all but invisible. The campus remains a divided one; it channels women and men into different educations that lead to separate and unequal futures.

The "hard" sciences are still housed on the male side of the glass wall. Almost 70 percent of today's students who major in physics, chemistry, and computer science are male. Engineering tops all of these, however, with 85 percent of bachelor degrees going to men. The overwhelmingly male majority extends beyond the hard sciences and engineering to theology (75 percent male), philosophy (64 percent), agriculture (69 percent), and architecture (61 percent).[4]

[2]*Jane Addams:* American reformer (1860–1935), author, suffragist, and recipient of the 1931 Nobel Peace Prize. In 1889, with Ellen Gates Starr, Addams founded Hull House, a community center for Chicago's poor which became an internationally recognized symbol of social reform.

[3]Miriam K. Chamberlain (ed.), *Women in Academe: Progress and Prospects* (New York: Russell Sage Foundation, 1988), p. 4. [Authors' note]

[4]Thomas Snyder and Charlene Hoffman, *Digest of Education Statistics 1992* (Washington, DC: U.S. Department of Education, 1992), pp. 275, 277, 295, 296. Michael R. Ransom, "Gender Segregation by Field in Higher Education," *Researcher in Higher Education* 31:5 (October 5, 1990): pp. 477–94. Judith G. Touchton and Lynne Davis with the assistance of Vivian Parker Makosky, *Fact Book on Women in Higher Education* (New York: Macmillan, 1991). [Authors' note]

But it would be a mistake to view the male campus only in terms of academic courses because the heart of extracurricular life beats there, too. Male athletes enjoy an impressive array of "perks," including special meal allowances, exclusive living arrangements, lucrative scholarships, and at all too many institutions, academic dispensation when studies and game schedules conflict. This side of the campus also has valuable real estate, precious land that was turned over to fraternity row. In fact, this is the part of the campus where the lion's share of financial and educational resources are invested.

On the other side of the glass wall, the "soft" sciences and humanities are taught to classes populated mostly by women. On this second campus, females receive 90 percent of the bachelor degrees in home economics, 84 percent in health sciences, and 67 percent in general liberal arts. Here women are awarded three out of every four degrees in education and foreign language, and two out of three in psychology, communications, and the performing arts. On the women's side of the glass wall, class schedules are less likely to include advanced courses in mathematics, science, and technology. If graduation requirements insist on science courses, women typically opt for biology rather than physics or chemistry. Science, after all, is what many worked hard to avoid in high school. Although they pay the same tuition, study in the same libraries, reside in the same dorms, and receive diplomas with the name of the same college, the female students are less likely to take the courses that lead to lucrative and prestigious careers.

Women who move on to graduate and professional schools, where they   10
earn half as many doctorates as men, also discover the divided campus:[5] men receive 75 percent of the doctoral degrees in business and 91 percent of those in engineering, but women acquire more doctorates than men in education. Despite this, three out of every four professors are male, and nine out of ten are white and non-Hispanic. Even prestigious Ivy League schools, the ones with their pick of the most talented women, seem unable to find them. Only 10 percent to 13 percent of Ivy League faculties are female, and they earn on average almost $14,000 less annually than their male colleagues.[6] Nationally, 68 percent of male faculty members have tenure, while only 45 percent of the women enjoy this lifetime job security. It is no secret among faculty members who is valued, vested, and rewarded. Through comments, attitudes, and behavior, the message is clear that female faculty members have second-class citizenship on campus; and this message filters down to the students.

If students somehow miss the salary and tenure subtleties, the power of numbers overwhelms. Ninety-eight percent of the engineering faculty is

[5]Even in the social sciences and humanities, women earn only 46 percent of the doctoral degrees. In the life sciences, as in biology, women earn 37 percent of all doctorates. Although women acquire close to half of the bachelor's degrees in mathematics, their share drops to 40 percent at the master's level and less than 18 percent at the doctoral level. [Authors' note]

[6]Anthony DePalma, "Rare in Ivy League: Women Who Work as Full Professors." *New York Times* (January 24, 1993), pp. 1, 23. [Authors' note]

male. While this is the most extreme imbalance, in every field students see mainly male professors: more than 60 percent in the humanities, 75 percent in business, fine arts, and the social sciences, and 83 percent in the natural sciences. Again, women are best represented in education, but even here, where they claim almost 58 percent of the doctorates, they are only 45 percent of the faculty.[7] Female students who are looking for role models, counselors, and mentors must search long and hard. With Hispanic and African-American women comprising only 1 percent of the faculty, students who are both minority and female receive an even stronger signal of their place on campus. Lacking role models and missing the mentoring connection, college women are less likely to pursue graduate work. The process becomes a continuing cycle: mainly male professors prepare men to become the faculty of the future, and the campus remains divided and unequal.

Every now and then the glass wall separating the two campuses is almost visible. For example, when we visited the school of education at one university, we entered a building and turned right. If we had turned left, we would have arrived at the physics department and met a faculty that was 100 percent male. As we observed students entering the building, it was like watching gender-segregated lines in elementary school: those who turned left for physics were male, those who turned right for the school of education were female.

Sometimes the difference between the two campuses is as simple as turning right or left in a building, but other differences can be observed in a different school: the community college. These two-year institutions offer a less expensive education, but they are also less prestigious. As the prestige factor dips, the proportion of women rises: women hold 47 percent of community college faculty positions and comprise 57 percent of the students.[8]

While females are more likely to attend community colleges, they are less likely to find themselves at the most highly selective schools. Harvard may not be able to list by name the students who will be admitted next year, but it does know that only 40 percent of them will be women. Since females face occupational and income barriers, they will probably earn less than men and therefore will have less to donate to the university. From this perspective, admitting more men who will earn more money may be seen as good business practice. So economic discrimination becomes grounds for admissions discrimination, which in turn leads to further economic discrimination.

Although there are now more female applicants to college, most Ivy   15 League schools also seem hard-pressed to locate acceptable female candidates.[9] Only Columbia University accepts approximately equal numbers of

[7]Snyder and Hoffman, *Digest of Education Statistics, 1992,* p. 296. [Authors' note]

[8]Susan Klein and Karen Bogart, "Achieving Sex Equity in Education: A Comparison of Pre- and Post-Secondary Levels." *Equity and Excellence* 23:1–2 (Spring 1987), pp. 114–22. [Authors' note]

[9]*The Insider's Guide to Colleges,* compiled and edited by the staff of the *Yale Daily News* (New York: St. Martin's Press, 1993). [Authors' note]

female and male students. The frightening possibility of women comprising the majority of the student body can be reason enough to tinker with the admissions machinery.[10] In 1987, officials at the University of North Carolina noted that more than half of their new students were women. They recommended placing more weight on SAT tests and less on high school grades in order to achieve the "desirable" balance.

Although sex segregation on campus has become a way of life, there are times when students attend classes in equal numbers. The glass walls come down in general subjects required of everybody, courses such as English and political science. In these classrooms, parallel campuses converge, and all students sit in the same rooms, read the same texts, and are taught by the same professors. But even as men and women share the same space, they receive substantially different teaching.

In a Silent Voice

At the highest educational level, where the instructors are the most credentialed and the students the most capable, teaching is the most biased. We discovered this during a two-year grant in which we and a staff of trained raters observed and coded postsecondary classrooms. When we analyzed the data, we discovered how hidden lessons, rooted in elementary school and exacerbated in high school, emerged full-blown in the college classroom. Drawn from our research files, the following classroom scene offers more than a discussion of the Constitution; it shows how earlier subtle sexism has evolved and intensified.

> The course on the U.S. Constitution is required for graduation, and more than fifty students, approximately half male and half female, file in. The professor begins by asking if there are questions on next week's midterm. Several hands go up.
>
> BERNIE: Do we have to memorize names and dates in the book? Or will the test be more general?
> PROFESSOR: You do have to know those critical dates and people. Not every one but the important ones. If I were you, Bernie, I would spend time learning them. Ellen?
> ELLEN: What kind of short-answer questions will there be?
> PROFESSOR: All multiple choice.
> ELLEN: Will we have the whole class time?
> PROFESSOR: Yes, we'll have the whole class time. Anyone else?
> BEN (calling out):   Will there be an extra-credit question?
> PROFESSOR: I hadn't planned on it. What do you think?

[10]Caroline Hodges Persell, Sophia Catsambis, and Peter W. Cookson, Jr., "Differential Asset Conversion: Class and Gendered Pathways to Selective Colleges," *Sociology of Education* 65:3 (July 1992), pp. 208–25. [Authors' note]

BEN: I really like them. They take some of the pressure off. You can also see who is doing extra work.

PROFESSOR: I'll take it under advisement. Charles?

CHARLES: How much of our final grade is this?

PROFESSOR: The midterm is 25 percent. But remember, class participation counts as well. Why don't we begin?

The professor lectures on the Constitution for twenty minutes before he asks a question about the electoral college. The electoral college is not as hot a topic as the midterm, so only four hands are raised. The professor calls on Ben.

BEN: The electoral college was created because there was a lack of faith in the people. Rather than have them vote for the president, they voted for the electors.

PROFESSOR: I like the way you think. (He smiles at Ben, and Ben smiles back.) Who could vote? (Five hands go up, five out of fifty.) Angie?

ANGIE: I don't know if this is right, but I thought only men could vote.

BEN (calling out):   That was a great idea. We began going downhill when we let women vote. (Angie looks surprised but says nothing. Some of the students laugh, and so does the professor. He calls on Barbara.)

BARBARA: I think you had to be pretty wealthy, own property —

JOSH (not waiting for Barbara to finish, calls out):   That's right. There was a distrust of the poor, who could upset the democracy. But if you had property, if you had something at stake, you could be trusted not to do something wild. Only property owners could be trusted.

PROFESSOR: Nice job, Josh. But why do we still have electors today? Mike?

MIKE: Tradition, I guess.

PROFESSOR: Do you think it's tradition? If you walked down the street and asked people their views of the electoral college, what would they say?

MIKE: Probably they'd be clueless. Maybe they would think that it elects the Pope. People don't know how it works.

PROFESSOR: Good, Mike. Judy, do you want to say something? (Judy's hand is at "half-mast," raised but just barely. When the professor calls her name, she looks a bit startled.)

JUDY (speaking very softly):   Maybe we would need a whole new constitutional convention to change it. And once they get together to change that, they could change anything. That frightens people, doesn't it? (As Judy speaks, a number of students fidget, pass notes, and leaf through their books; a few even begin to whisper.)

A visit to the typical college class, which is a stop on the campus tour that most parents never make, shows that students behave as if they, too, are visitors. While 80 percent of pupils in elementary and secondary classes contribute at least one comment in each of their classes, approximately half of the college class says nothing at all. One in two sits through an entire class without ever answering a question, asking one, or making a comment. Women's silence is loudest at college, with twice as many females voiceless. Considering the rising cost of college tuition, the female rule of speech seems to be: the more you pay, the less you say.

At the other end of the college speech spectrum are the salient students who monopolize the discussion. Their hands shoot up for attention even before the professor finishes the question. Others don't bother to wave for recognition; they blurt out answers, sometimes way off the mark, before other students formulate their ideas. As in the class we described, these aggressive, Jeopardy-like players are usually male. In our research we have found that men are twice as likely to monopolize class discussions, and women are twice as likely to be silent. The college classroom is the finale of a twelve-year rehearsal, the culminating showcase for a manly display of verbal dominance.

Studying classrooms at Harvard, Catherine Krupnick also discovered this gender divide, one where males perform and females watch. Here were the most academically talented women in the nation, and even they were silenced. When they did speak, they were more likely to be interrupted. Males talked more often, and they talked longer. When the professor as well as most of the students were male, the stage was set for women to be minor players, a virtual Harvard underclass.[11]

Bernice Sandler and Roberta Hall found that professors give males   20 more nonverbal attention as well. They make more eye contact with men, wait longer for them to answer, and are more likely to remember their names. The result, Sandler and Hall concluded, is a "chilly classroom climate," one that silently robs women of knowledge and self-esteem.[12]

When females do volunteer comments, the impact of years of silence and self-devaluation becomes evident. In our class scenario above, Angie showed this loss. Like many women, she has learned to preface her speech with phrases like "I'm not sure if this is what you want" or "This probably isn't right but. . . ." These female preambles of self-deprecation are a predictable part of the college classroom. In our coding system we called them "self-put-downs." In class after class we were disheartened at how many

[11]Catherine Krupnick, "Unlearning Gender Roles," in Kenneth Winston and Mary Jo Bane (eds.), *Gender and Public Policy: Cases and Comments* (Boulder, CO: Westview Press, 1992). Catherine Krupnick, "Women and Men in the Classroom: Inequality and Its Remedies," *Teaching and Learning: Journal of the Harvard Danforth Center* 1:1 (May 1985):18–25. [Authors' note]

[12]Roberta Hall and Bernice Sandler, *The Classroom Climate: A Chilly One for Women?* (Washington, DC: Project on the Status and Education of Women, Association of American Colleges, 1982). For a summary of differences in women's and men's views of Harvard, see Richard Light, *The Harvard Assessment Seminars, First Report* (Cambridge, MA: Harvard University Press, 1990). [Authors' note]

times women compromised superb comments: "I'm not really sure," "This is just a guess," "I don't know, but could the answer be. . . ." Or like Judy they spoke in such a soft and tentative manner that their classmates don't even bother to listen.

When we asked college women why they neutralized the power of their own speech, they offered revealing explanations:

> I do it to lower expectations. If my answer is wrong, so what? I don't lose anything. I already said it might be wrong.

> I don't want to seem like I'm taking over the class or anything. If I disguise that I know the answers, then the other students won't resent me.

> I say I'm not sure because I'm really not sure. I'm not certain that I'm following the professor, and I'm just being honest about it.

> I didn't know I was talking like that.

The last one is the reaction we hear most frequently. Self-doubt has become part of women's public voice, and most are unaware it has happened.[13] This pattern of uncertain speech is reminiscent of the standardized science test taken in elementary and middle school, the exam where many girls selected the "I don't know" option rather than take a guess at the correct response. By the time these schoolgirls become college women, the "I don't know" option, the only one guaranteed not to garner any points, has insinuated itself into speech, a tacit acknowledgment of diminished status.

We also found that one-third of the college classrooms that contain both males and females are characterized by informally sex-segregated seating, patterns formed by the students themselves. The salient students, usually male, are well versed in the concept of strategic seating; they choose places where they can be spotted quickly by the professor. Those who want to hide, the silent students, who are more likely to be female, prize the corners, the unobtrusive areas, and the anonymity that grows with distance. It is as if a transparent gender divide was erected within the classroom.

While not as stark, the parallel with the sex segregation of elementary school is obvious. And teachers continue their patterns, too. The subtle bias in teacher reactions that we detected in lower grades resurfaces in college. Professors usually respond to student answers with neutral silence or a vague "Okay." But when praise is awarded, when criticism is leveled, or when help is given, the male student is more likely to be on the receiving end. In the class scene we described, Mike was challenged to improve his answer and then rewarded for the correction. In fact, the professor praised

---

[13]For a discussion of how classroom communication is more compatible with male communication training, see Deborah Tannen, "Teachers' Classroom Strategies Should Recognize That Men and Women Use Language Differently," *Chronicle of Higher Education* 37 (June 19, 1991), pp. B1–B3. [Authors' note]

three male students: Ben, Josh, and Mike. Women's comments never received the professor's stamp of approval. At best they were merely acknowledged, at worst interrupted or ridiculed. So, like boys in elementary school, men in college receive not only more attention from the professor but better attention as well.

The professor in the previous example did not intervene when Ben   25
poked fun at women and at Angie's comment, but he did not say anything sexist or sexual himself. But many professors do. At Iowa State, 65 percent of female students said they had been the target of sexist comments, and 43 percent said professors flirted with them. At Harvard University, almost half the women graduate students reported sexual harassment. This is how women described the incidents:

> He came into class, looked directly at me, and announced to everyone, "Your sweater is too tight." I felt terrible. The next week he whispered to me, "You look like you had a tough night." I just dropped his course and had to go to summer school.

> One day this professor requested that I come to his office to discuss a paper. When I arrived, he escorted me to a chair and closed the office door. He walked over to me, put his hands on either side of my face, and told me I was a very beautiful woman. Then he kissed my forehead. We never discussed any of my academic work. . . . I disregarded his constant requests to visit his office and hurriedly left his class. I received my lowest grade in his course.

Joseph Thorpe, a professor at the University of Missouri, knows just how bad it can get. He sent questionnaires to over one thousand women who were recent recipients of psychology doctorates and were members of the American Psychological Association. Thorpe found that many students had been propositioned by their professors. Most of these overtures were turned down, but almost half said they suffered academic penalties for refusing. The survey also revealed that one in every four or five women studying for their psychology doctorates was having sex with the teacher, adviser, or mentor responsible for her academic career.[14]

"These figures seem terribly high," we said in an interview with Thorpe. "Do you think they're inflated?"

"I think they underpredict what's going on," he said. "The study did not interview any of the women who dropped out, the ones who became so emotionally devastated that they never finished their programs. If we knew

[14]Robert D. Glaser and Joseph S. Thorpe, "Unethical Intimacy: A Survey of Sexual Contact and Advances Between Psychology Educators and Female Graduate Students," *American Psychologist* 40 (January 1986), pp. 43–51. Billie Wright Dziech and Linda Weiner, *The Lecherous Professor: Sexual Harassment on Campus* (Boston: Beacon Press, 1984), pp. 13, 115–16. Claudia Dreifus, "Sex with Professors," *Glamour* (August 1986), pp. 264–65, 308–09, 311. [Authors' note]

those numbers, the figures would be higher. In fact, for subgroups in our sample, the numbers were higher. When we looked at the responses from single, separated, or divorced female students, the sex-with-adviser rate climbed to 33 percent."

Senior professors are overwhelmingly male and critically important. These professors distribute funds in the form of assistantships and fellowships. They can offer coauthorships on publications crucial to a fledgling career. With the right phone calls, they can land prestigious jobs for their students. Male students are more likely to be part of this mentoring relationship, but when women are mentored, the dynamics sometimes become sexual.

With grades and professional careers at stake, female students may feel vulnerable and powerless to object.[15] If a professor is a senior faculty member and distinguished in his field, it becomes even more difficult. When one of our students at The American University told us of harassment she was experiencing in a course, we urged her to bring charges. "It's useless," she told us. "This professor is a nationally known scholar. When I said I was going to report him, he laughed. 'No one would believe you,' he said. 'Do you know how many awards I have won? I'm like a god on this campus.'" This young woman did not report the professor; she dropped the course instead.

The alienation of female students on the male campus emerges even in the quiet alcoves of the university library. Surrounded by books with few if any females, women continue to learn they are worth less.   30

Out of Sight, Out of Mind

The first grant we ever received was to investigate sex bias in college books. In the late 1970s, we spent more than a year examining the twenty-four best-selling teacher education textbooks. We read each line, evaluated every photo, and assessed the books from cover to cover — from the table of contents to the index. Twenty-three of the twenty-four texts gave the issue of gender equity less than 1 percent of book space. One-third never mentioned the topic. Those least likely to include girls and women were the books about how to teach mathematics and science courses. Not one of the

---

[15]Patricia L. Bask, Joanne L. Jensen, and Jami Price, "Women's Graduate School Experiences, Professional Career Expectations and Their Relationship," paper presented at the American Educational Research Association, Chicago, Illinois, April 1991. S. Y. Jenkins, *Gender Differences in Graduate Student Relationships with Their Major Faculty Advisor,* unpublished doctoral dissertation, University of Oregon, 1985. Kenneth S. Pope, Hanna Levinson, and L. R. Schover, "Sexual Relationships in Psychology Training: Results and Implications of a National Survey," *American Psychologist* 34 (1979), pp. 682–89. Corinna A. Ethington and Rita Bode, "Differences in the Graduate Experience for Males and Females," paper presented at the American Educational Research Association, San Francisco, California, April 1991. [Authors' note]

twenty-four texts provided teachers with strategies or resources to eliminate sexism from the classroom.

Using these college texts, tomorrow's teachers would actually learn to be more sexist. One book offered a lengthy rationale for paying female teachers less than male teachers. Another author advised prospective teachers to stock their classroom libraries with twice as many books about males as females. The author explained that "boys will not read 'girl books' but girls will read 'boy books.'" An educational psychology text offered this helpful tidbit to increase teacher efficiency: "If all the boys in a high school class routinely get distracted when a curvaceous and provocative coed undulates into the room to pick up attendance slips, tape the attendance slips to the outside of the door."[16]

A science textbook explained that girls "know less, do less, explore less, and are prone to be more superstitious than boys." Another education text emphasized the impact of technology with a fascinating analogy: if it were not for recent technological breakthroughs, "all women over twenty years of age in the United States would have to be telephone operators to handle all the phone calls." A reading textbook offered recommendations for bringing parent power into the classroom: "Some fathers could help the third-grade boys make birdhouses easier than the teacher could; some mothers could teach sixth-grade girls how to knit; many mothers would be glad to drive a carload of children to the airport, to the museum, or to the public library."[17]

Adding to the stereotyped narrative was the male world presented by the books. From the photographs to the index listings, education was pictured as populated and experienced by boys and men. One text highlighted seventy-three famous educators, seventy-two of whom were male. Another text featured the work of thirty renowned educators, all men. The message to tomorrow's teachers, most of whom are women, was clear: even in this female profession, it is the men who deserve to be remembered.

To turn this picture around, we developed a set of nonsexist guidelines,   35
suggestions for publishers interested in creating fairer college texts. Several publishers distributed our guidelines to their authors. A few publishers actually sent our research findings to the authors of the textbooks we had critiqued and requested that they "repair" their work in future editions.

Considering the job done, we turned our attention to classroom interaction, but in 1991 we were jolted back into the world of college books. The second edition of our own teacher education textbook had just been published, and we were sent an advance copy. We had taken special care to integrate women and minorities throughout the narrative of the book, but the outside of the book was something else. Without our knowledge the publisher had chosen a vibrant multicultural photograph, but it included

---

[16]Myra Sadker and David Sadker, *Beyond Pictures and Pronouns: Sexism in Teacher Education Textbooks* (Washington, DC: Office of Education, 1980), pp. 8, 38. [Authors' note]

[17]Sadker and Sadker, *Beyond Pictures and Pronouns,* pp. 38, 39. [Authors' note]

four times more boys than girls. A call to the publisher cleared up the matter. It was all a "terrible mistake"; the photograph had been chosen to reflect cultural diversity, but the publisher, sensitive to racial representation, had not noticed that girls were left out. We began calling other publishers about their guidelines. Here is a typical exchange:

"Guidelines? What guidelines?"

"The nonsexist guidelines you agreed to follow over a decade ago."

"Over a decade ago. That's way before I arrived here. I don't remember seeing any nonsexist guidelines."

Many college textbooks have withstood the winds of change. From philosophy to psychology, from history to the sciences, students may still learn about a world of male accomplishment and female invisibility. Centuries of recorded history parade before today's college students, but women continue to make only a rare appearance. For example, a classic text in English literature survey courses is the two-volume *Norton Anthology*. Here the culture's great works are collected, and the literary canon is offered to the next generation. Norton has introduced students to centuries of literature: Chaucer, Shakespeare, Milton, Byron, Shelley, Keats, Matthew Arnold, T. S. Eliot; the showcase of male literary accomplishment is extensive. The 3,450 pages of the initial 1962 edition were expanded to 5,000 pages in the 1986 (fifth) edition, where the preface discusses efforts to reflect "contemporary culture." Less than 15 percent of these new pages included women writers. In fact, the percentage of women in the *Norton Anthology* was greater in 1962 than in 1986.[18]

Women in higher education are frequently aware that their lives are left out of books, and they feel excluded from a recorded culture that is not their own. As one student said: "In history we never talked about what women did; in geography it was always what was important to men; it was the same in our English class — we hardly ever studied women authors. I won't even talk about math and science. . . . I always felt as though I didn't belong. . . . Now I just deaden myself against it so I don't hear it anymore. But I really feel alienated."[19]

Centuries of bias cannot be undone in a single chapter or insert, but authors and publishers try nonetheless. The results of their efforts to rectify imbalance can be seen in chapters or boxes called "Women and Art," "Female Authors," "Famous Women Scientists," or "American Diversity: Founding Mothers." This last title came from a popular 1991 political science textbook

---

[18]William Sullivan, "The *Norton Anthology* and the Canon of English Literature," paper presented at the Annual Meeting of the College English Association, San Antonio, Texas, 1991. Jordan J. Titus, "Gender Messages in Education Foundations Textbooks," *Journal of Teacher Education* 44:1 (January–February 1993), pp. 38–44. [Authors' note]

[19]Magda Lewis, "Interrupting Patriarchy: Politics, Resistance, and Transformation in the Feminist Classroom," *Harvard Educational Review* 60:4 (November 1990), pp. 467–88. [Authors' note]

that offers information about women's contributions during the revolution.[20] The authors tell how the "daughters of the revolution" boycotted British goods, wrote political pamphlets, were leaders in the fight for independence, and fought in the Revolutionary War disguised as men. In fact, the only Revolutionary War veteran buried at West Point is a woman who took full advantage of the absence of pre-induction physicals and joined the Continental army. The "Founding Mothers" represents a step forward, but it is only one page long, which is the problem with boxes and chapters. The student is left with a fragmented world view: males are the main story and women are a sideshow, confined to a brief insert, anecdote, or biographical summary.

Sometimes women do not even make sideshow status. The controversy over generic male pronouns and nouns is a case in point. Some professors and students say that words such as "he" and "mankind" exclude women, while others charge that all the fuss is a tempest in a teapot, a case of semantic hypersensitivity. But studies show that words are powerful indeed. When a career or job is described using male pronouns, females find the job less appealing than when neutral terms are used. When a job applicant is referred to as a "girl" instead of a "woman," she is seen as less tough, less dignified, and of course less well paid.[21]

Despite studies showing that when "man" is said, in the mind's eye man is seen, many college texts persist in using these deceptive generics. Some authors even resort to creative strategies such as asking readers to imagine that inclusive language has been used, as if saying makes it so.

> Note that we have not made a distinction between the sexes. The theory is intended to apply to adolescent boys as well as adolescent girls. We have used the masculine gender in this report for convenience; it should be considered a neutral, general usage.[22]

When textbooks exclude them, some women develop their own defense. We were discussing generic words with our class when one of our students, Paul, showed us a copy of *Everyone Wins! A Citizen's Guide to Development,* a book about protecting the environment.[23] "This book belongs to my

---

[20]Susan Welch et al., *Understanding American Government* (St. Paul, MN: West Publishing Co., 1991), p. 24. [Authors' note]

[21]Barbara Westbrook Eakins and R. Gene Eakins, *Sex Differences in Human Communication* (Boston: Houghton Mifflin, 1978). Joseph Schneider and Sally Hacker, "Sex Role Imagery and the Use of Generic 'Man' in Introductory Texts: A Case in the Sociology of Sociology," *American Sociologist* 8 (February 1973), pp. 12–18. Cheris Kramer, Barrie Thorne, and Nancy Henley, "Perspectives on Language and Communication," *Signs: Journal of Women in Culture and Society* 3:3 (1978), pp. 638–51. Robert Brannon, "The Consequences of Sexist Language," paper presented at the American Psychological Association, August 1978. [Authors' note]

[22]Martin Gold and David Mann, *Expelled to a Friendlier Place: A Study of Effective Alternative Schools* (Ann Arbor, MI: University of Michigan Press, 1984), p. 6. [Authors' note]

[23]Richard Klein, *Everyone Wins! A Citizen's Guide to Development* (Chicago: Planners Press, 1990). [Authors' note]

friend Connie at Portland State," he told us. "I want you to see what she did." As we leafed through the text, we saw how Connie had laboriously crossed out all the *he* and *him* pronouns and replaced them with *she* and *her*. "Connie felt as though the book was talking to someone else," Paul said, "So as she read through it, she included herself."

We asked our students to analyze the content of their textbooks to see   45
how widespread sex bias was in the books read at our own university. They found psychology, economics, and sociology textbooks that rarely even mentioned a woman's name. One art book included 245 photographs, but only 18 depicted women. Other studies have also noted the slow pace of textbook change, but not all textbooks are frozen in time; several contain nonsexist language and include males and females in relatively equal numbers. Why such extremes? Unlike elementary and high schools, postsecondary schools do not have committees to evaluate and select books. At the college level, professors choose their own texts and call it academic freedom. For students, it's *caveat emptor.*[24]

The Girls Next Door

When I entered college in North Carolina in the 1960s, I was given my official women's rule book, a thirty-four-page tome filled with guidelines and expectations for all coeds. (Female students were "coeds"; male students were "gentlemen.") The following are some of the rules:

- No beer in the dorm, even to use as a hair rinse, as was the custom of the day. Men, of course, could have as much beer in their rooms as they wished.
- No smoking while walking on campus since this was considered "unladylike" conduct.
- No visiting a boy's apartment unless there was another couple present.
- No dates outside the town line unless you were "signed out" to do so. Male students could go wherever they pleased.

The rules went on and on. I don't believe male students had a rule book. To be fair, I should note that by the time I graduated in 1970, the rule book had been shortened to pamphlet length. In the 1970s, when students reinvented dorm life, they abridged and then discarded the rule book completely. Almost overnight single-sex dorms seemed out of date and coeducational living became the arrangement of choice. Researchers found both positive and negative sides to these new coed dorms. Men told fewer off-

---

[24]*caveat emptor*: Latin for "let the buyer beware," this legal principle relieves sellers of responsibility for the quality of a product. Students are advised, then, to scrutinize their colleges as carefully as they would a used car.

color jokes, drank less, and talked with women more; women became more outgoing and were more likely to attend university events. Cross-sex friendships flourished as residents went to classes, meals, and university activities together. But there were problems as well as benefits. While men studied more, women in coed dorms took their academic work less seriously, held lower career aspirations, and dropped out of school more often. And stories of unwanted teasing and touching became increasingly frequent.[25]

Stories that surfaced in the 1970s have become commonplace on today's campus. A survey of Cornell students found that four out of five women experienced sexist comments and 68 percent received unwanted attention from men. At the Massachusetts Institute of Technology, 92 percent of the women reported receiving unwanted sexual attention. At the University of Rhode Island, seven out of ten women said they were sexually insulted by men. Sexual harassment can occur anywhere on campus, but students are especially vulnerable when it happens where they live.[26]

> My dorm at Stanford is composed of fifty men and women who reside on two coed hallways. We are all freshmen. Last week several of the girls, including me, discovered that the men on the second floor had posted in the men's room a "rating and ranking" sheet of the second-floor women. The ranking was obviously based on the relative physical attractiveness of the girls in the dorm and was accompanied by various and sundry disgusting comments. Naturally, many of the second-floor women were upset by this list. . . . I decided that this was something so fundamentally wrong, I couldn't ignore it.
>
> As the week progressed, I began to discuss "the list" with some of the second-floor men, explaining my objections. I felt that the list was dehumanizing and humiliating . . . immature and childish, a remnant of middle school days. How could these guys whom we'd been living with for eight months think of their closest friends in such superficial terms? How could they degrade us in that way? And most of all, how could they be sitting in front of me and defending themselves instead of apologizing for their actions?
>
> Eventually a male resident adviser decided to hold a house meeting to discuss the problem in a more formal setting. This meeting became a battle between me and the ten to twelve men on the second

---

[25]Judith Corbett and Robert Sommer, "Anatomy of a Coed Residence Hall," *Journal of College Student Personnel* 13:3 (May 1972), pp. 215–17, Rudolf H. Moos and Jean Otto, "The Impact of Coed Living on Males and Females," *Journal of College Student Personnel* 16:6 (November 1975), pp. 459–67. Robert Brown, John Winkworth, and Larry Brakskamp, "Student Development in a Good Residence Hall: Promiscuity, Prophylactic, or Panacea?" *Journal of College Student Personnel* 14:2 (March 1973), pp. 98–104. Charles C. Schroeder and Morris LeMay, "The Impact of Coed Residence Halls on Self-Actualization," *Journal of College Student Personnel* 14:2 (March 1973), pp. 105–10. [Authors' note]

[26]"Harassing Women Becomes a Sick College Sport," *Utne Reader* (May–June 1990), - pp. 70–71. Linda J. Rubin and Sherry B. Borgers, "Sexual Harassment in Universities During the 1980s," *Sex Roles* 23:7–8 (1990), pp. 397–411. [Authors' note]

floor who could find nothing wrong with their "list." Amazingly enough, throughout the entire argument not one of the other second-floor women who had initially been so angered . . . had the strength to help validate my arguments with her support. In fact, several were so afraid to become embroiled in an argument that they pretended they knew nothing about the list. The men who were not part of the ranking and who I knew were opposed to it . . . didn't attack my position, but they certainly were not willing to put themselves on the line to defend it. After this confrontation and for the next few days, however, many of the women in the dorm . . . came to me separately and thanked me for standing up for them and myself, and for trying to explain how disturbing and upsetting the situation was.

In this case, words created a psychological betrayal, shattering the veneer of honest communication. When the betrayal is physical instead of verbal, it is far more threatening.

> I was driving home from a bar with five guys who lived in my dorm. Most of them were drunk (I wasn't). I was sitting on the lap of one of my friends. He kept trying to touch me on my inner thighs or my buttocks. I was squirming and telling him to stop, but he ignored me. The other guys kept laughing. One kept grabbing my breasts while another whispered in my ear that I should go to his room tonight. I felt like Jodie Foster in *The Accused*. I was trapped in a car with no way to escape.

The young woman from The American University who described this incident to us said that the "guys were just messing around," and nothing else happened; but she felt "frightened, helpless, and violated." She said, "When I tell people the story, they say that being with five drunk guys is just asking for trouble. But they don't understand. These guys were my *friends*." Another college student also described the frightening transformation of someone else considered a friend, the man who lived next door.

> John and I were friends in the same dorm. Just friends. He knew I had a boyfriend and that I saw him as a friend. One day I was in his room talking with him. We were always hanging out in each other's rooms, listening to music and watching TV. When I got up to leave, he blocked the door, grabbed my arms, and forcefully kissed me. I was shocked. I didn't know what to do. I mean, this was a pretty good friend of mine acting like this. He picked me up and threw me down on his bed. . . . He started kissing me and saying how much he wanted to make love to me. I said no. I was completely pinned down. I have never felt so lacking in control in my own life. I realized that something I didn't want to happen could — and I didn't have any say in the situation. He didn't care about my feelings. I must have said no about a thousand times. I kept struggling, and I finally convinced him to stop. . . .

To this day (and I know this for sure because he lives next door to me) he doesn't feel as if he did anything wrong. I still haven't been able to make him understand how he affected me that day. Almost being raped. . . . I can only begin to imagine what I would have felt like if a rape had really happened.

Baffled by the way her trusted friend treated her, this young woman keeps playing the incident over and over in her mind, trying to understand why it happened. But these terrifying experiences are not even distant possibilities in the minds of new students as they unload their cars and move into their dorms. And most parents, as they wave good-bye, have no inkling of the alarming extracurricular activities their tuition dollars may be buying.

The Years of Living Dangerously

During the 1980s fraternity and sorority membership grew, and by the 1990s over a million students were part of the resurgence of Greek associations on campus. Fraternities often set the social rhythm of undergraduate life because they have more and bigger houses for parties; sometimes they have the only location on campus.

Walk through the typical campus and you are far more likely to see a fraternity house than a sorority house. When we asked college students why fraternities were more likely to claim campus real estate, we often heard a rendition of the bordello story, which goes something like this: "It's an ancient law here in [the District of Columbia, St. Louis, Boston, or the city of your choice]. When three or four women rent or buy a house together, it's considered a brothel. Back then it was called a bordello. That's why sorority houses are illegal. It has nothing to do with campus inequality, it's just these stupid, outdated bordello laws."

The longer history of fraternities and their greater wealth and influ- 50 ence, not bordello laws, have created the real estate gender gap. But we have heard this explanation at so many different colleges and universities, it qualifies as campus mythology.

Nationally there are more than twice as many fraternities as sororities. And on the typical campus, sorority row is a weak reflection of its male counterpart. On some campuses the sorority house is big enough only for meetings and parties; no one lives there. On others, there are no sorority houses, just dorm areas where sorority sisters live together. In many cases there is not even dorm space; all that is available is a meeting room in a university building.

This less well-appointed sorority life still produces enthusiastic supporters. As one woman said, "Living like sisters creates a lifelong bond. The sorority gave me friendship and support." Both fraternity and sorority members are quick to point out that they raise money for charitable causes and do good work for children, the poor, and the homeless. But it is the social activities — and scandals — that gain public attention, and these usually take place on the male side of the campus.

Fraternity row is home to an all-male society, one separate from the rest of the world where secret rituals bond new brothers into a surrogate family. Here the stage is set for life's last fling before the onset of work and family responsibilities. Alcohol, parties, good times, and close friendships characterize fraternity life. But along with horseplay and harmless fun, there exists a menacing, darker side:

> The theme for Dartmouth's winter carnival was *Camelot,* so a group of fraternity brothers built a snow sculpture for the event — a woman's breast pierced by a sword and captioned GUINEVERE — THANKS FOR THE MAMMARIES, ARTHUR.[27]
>
> At Middlebury, the 1988 toga party was hosted by one of the biggest fraternities on campus. As part of the decor, the torso of a female mannequin was hung from the balcony and splattered with red paint to look like blood. A sign underneath suggested the female body was available for sex.[28]
>
> One fraternity sponsored a campus scavenger hunt. Points were awarded to those who could produce photocopies of female genitalia.
>
> A fraternity on a New England college campus hosted "pig parties." Females from a nearby state teacher's college were imported, and the date of the one voted ugliest was the winner.
>
> At UCLA a fraternity manual, forgotten in an apartment, found its way into a campus magazine. The fraternity's history, traditions, and bylaws were included, as well as a series of songs the pledges were supposed to memorize. Many of the lyrics described sexual scenes that were shockingly graphic, unbelievably bizarre, and revoltingly sadistic. For example, one song recounted the life of a Mexican girl named Lupe who performed any sexual act imaginable. She first had intercourse when she was eight years old, and even in death, "while maggots crawl[ed] out of her decomposed womb," the smile on her face signaled that she still wanted more sex.[29]

When fraternity members are involved in these pranks and songs, they create a mind-set that turns women into objects, animals, prey. Then the college campus becomes a setting of very real danger.

---

[27]Andrew Merton, "Return to Brotherhood," *Ms.* September 1985, pp. 60–62. [Authors' note]

[28]Beth Ann Krier, "Frat Row," *Los Angeles Times* (February 9, 1990), pp. E1, E7–9. [Authors' note]

[29]For additional examples and analyses of these activities, see Jean O'Gorman Hughes and Bernice Sandler, *Peer Harassment: Hassles for Women on Campus* (Washington, DC: Project on the Status and Education of Women, Association of American Colleges, 1988). [Authors' note]

The young woman, newly arrived on campus, was seeking acceptance from her classmates. She looked forward to attending the fraternity party, a beginning event in her college social life. At the party she was encouraged to drink, and eventually she passed out. The brothers had a name for this practice: "working a Yes out." She was carried upstairs, stripped, and raped by a number of men. They lined up outside the door and took turns, an approach called "pulling train." Several times she regained consciousness and pleaded for them to stop. The university learned of the incident and punished those involved. Several were required to do community service projects. Some additional reading and writing projects were also assigned for the fraternity members involved. The woman who was gang-raped left without graduating.[30]

The police had a difficult time piecing together the sordid details. A gang rape was reported at the Pi Kappa Alpha house at Florida State University, and a witness alleged that a visiting brother from Auburn University helped dump the body of the unconscious woman at a neighboring fraternity house. Even though they were charged with obstructing justice, all the brothers kept their pledge of secrecy. Although two were on trial facing life sentences, no one would cooperate with the police.[31]

Campus rape is more common than college officials care to admit, and they are far less well equipped to deal with it than most parents realize. According to national studies, approximately one in four college women says she has been forced into having sex, and one in six reports having been raped.[32] While most people think of rape as an assault by a violent stranger, in nine out of ten college incidents, the sex is forced by a friend or acquaintance. Victims experience a maelstrom of emotions: shock, disbelief, fear, and depression. They also agonize over every nuance of their own behavior and are likely to find themselves at fault: "How could I have been so wrong about him?" "What did I do to lead him on?" When the perpetrator is a "friend,"[33] college women are not even sure they have a right to call the ordeal "rape."

While the victim is at a loss to figure out how it happened, the perpetrator fits a predictable profile. Socialized into the aggressive male role, he

[30]Lis McMillen, "An Anthropologist's Disturbing Picture of Gang Rape on Campus," *Chronicle of Higher Education* 37 (September 19, 1990), p. A3. Peggy Reeves Sanday, *Fraternity Gang Rape: Sex, Brotherhood, and Privilege on Campus* (New York: New York University Press, 1990). [Authors' note]

[31]Michael Hirschorn, "Two Colleges Drop Recognition of Fraternities, Sororities Amid Continuing Concern Over Groups' Behavior," *Chronicle of Higher Education* (May 11, 1988), pp. A27–28. [Authors' note]

[32]Mary P. Koss, Christine A. Gidycz, and Nadine Wisniewski, "The Scope of Rape: Incidence and Prevalence of Sexual Aggression and Victimization in a National Sample of Higher Education Students," *Journal of Consulting and Clinical Psychology* 55:2 (1987), pp. 162–70. [Authors' note]

[33]Aileen Adams and Gail Abarbanel, *Sexual Assault on Campus: What Colleges Can Do* (Santa Monica, CA: Rape Treatment Center, 1988). Diana E. H. Russell, *Sexual Exploitation: Rape, Child Sexual Assault, and Workplace Harassment* (Beverly Hills, CA: Sage, 1984). [Authors' note]

believes that women tease and lead him on, that they provoke and enjoy sexual encounters and later cry rape falsely. To these men it is not rape at all but part of a game men and women play. More than one in every three college men believes that a woman who says "no" to sex really means "yes," or at least "maybe." According to one study, a shocking 30 percent of men admitted they would rape a woman if they thought they could get away with it.[34]

Drugs and alcohol trigger sexual violence. Intoxicated men are more   55
likely to be violent, and intoxicated women are less able to resist. This dangerous situation is viewed very differently by females and males. When asked, "If a woman is heavily intoxicated, is it okay to have sex with her?" only one in fifty women agreed. But one in four college men said that an intoxicated female was an appropriate target for sex. In addition to alcohol or drugs, location and date can be danger factors. Women who find themselves in a man's living quarters, at his party, or even in his car are more vulnerable.[35] So are women who go out with athletes.

Basking in status and popularity, male athletes are like campus nobility. In athletic events and on television, their physical exploits garner glory, network dollars, and alumni contributions. But off the field, physical exploits of a different nature can bring disgrace. The National Institute of Mental Health found athletes involved in one out of every three sexual assaults nationally. At Maryland's Towson State, athletes are five times more likely than others to be involved in gang rapes. A major southern university found that 27 percent of its athletes had threatened women into having sex against their will. In just one year, from 1989 to 1990, at least fifteen gang rapes were reported, involving fifty athletes. No one knows how many gang rapes went unreported.[36]

Meg Davis called them her friends; she "buddied" with them. In the spring semester her "friends," all on the university's football team, sexually assaulted her. For three hours, seven to nine men took turns. She blacked out as she was being sodomized. Back at the dorm, she showered until the hot water ran out. "I felt so dirty. Even so, I didn't call what hap-

[34]Alan Berkowitz, "College Men as Perpetrators of Acquaintance Rape and Sexual Assault: A Review of Recent Research," *College Health* 40 (January 1992), pp. 175–81. Mary Koss, Thomas E. Dinero, Cynthia Seibel, and Susan Cox, "Stranger and Acquaintance Rape: Are There Differences in the Victim's Experience?," *Psychology of Women Quarterly* 12 (March 1988), pp. 1–24. [Authors' note]

[35]Charlene Muehlenhard and Melaney Linton, "Date Rape and Sexual Aggression in Dating Situations: Incidence and Risk Factors," *Journal of Counseling Psychology* 34:2 (1987), pp. 186–96. Kelly Elizabeth Naylor, *Gender Role Strain: A Contributing Factor to Acquaintance Rape in a College Population at Risk,* unpublished doctoral dissertation, DePaul University, 1991. [Authors' note]

[36]Thomas Jackson, "A University Athletic Department's Rape and Assault Experiences," *Journal of College Student Development* 32 (January 1991), pp. 77–78. Merrill Melnick, "Male Athletes and Sexual Assault," *Journal of Physical Education, Recreation and Dance* 63 (May–June 1992), pp. 32–35. [Authors' note]

pened to me rape. These were guys I knew. It wasn't until I went to a women's center in town that someone explained I'd been gang-raped."[37]

After fraternities, athletic teams are most likely to be involved in gang rapes. Whether called "brotherhood," as in fraternity houses, or "teamwork," as in sports, the mind-set generated by male bonding can suppress independent thought and morality. A director of a rape treatment center described the impact of this bonding: "There has never been a single case in all the gang rapes we've seen where one man tried to stop it. . . . It's more important to be part of the group than to be the person who does what's right."[38]

At Carleton College in Northfield, Minnesota, women took matters into their own hands. As one woman said, "I had been on the campus for five weeks when I was raped. The college knew this man was a rapist, and they could have prevented this from happening."[39] After hearing the evidence, Carleton suspended the male offender for less than a year. When he returned to campus, he harassed the woman who had reported the rape. She and others sued the college, and then they did something else. On the wall of the women's bathroom at the university's library, as a warning to other women on campus, they posted an unofficial list of the names of Carleton men who had raped.

Colleges are not always slow to respond. Many institute special programs to sensitize the campus community, but when these programs are evaluated, the results are surprising. Female participants become more sensitive to the problem even before the training begins. Just responding to questions about rape on a survey changes their attitudes, heightens their level of concern, and causes them to become more sympathetic toward rape victims. Once in the program, they place even more importance on stopping college rape. But males respond differently. Traditional educational programs have little impact on their attitudes, and evaluation results show that many who continue to believe pro-rape myths blame the victim. These starkly different reactions to rape prevention reveal not only a profound gender gap in perception but also a fundamental difference in campus entitlement and power.[40]

[37]Jill Neimark, "Out of Bounds: The Truth About Athletes and Rape," *Mademoiselle* (May 1991), pp. 198, 244. [Authors' note]

[38]Gail Abarbanel quoted in Neimark, "The Truth About Athletes and Rape," p. 198. [Authors' note]

[39]Michelle Collison, "Increase in Reports of Sexual Assaults Strains Campus Disciplinary Systems," *Chronicle of Higher Education* (May 15, 1991), pp. A29–A30. [Authors' note]

[40]Genie O. Lenihan et al., "Gender Differences in Rape Supportive Attitudes Before and After Date Rape Education Intervention." *Journal of College Student Development* 33:4 (July 1992), pp. 331–38. Patricia Yancey Martin and Robert A. Hummer, "Fraternities and Rape on Campus," *Gender and Society* 3:4 (December 1989), pp. 457–73. David Ellis, "Setting New Goals for the Greek System," *Educational Record* 70:3–4 (Summer–Fall 1989), pp. 48–53. *Status of the College Fraternity and Sorority, 1990* (Bloomington, IN: Center for the Study of the College Fraternity, 1990). Patrick J. Harrison, Jeanette Downes, and Michael D. Williams, "Date and Acquaintance Rape: Perceptions and Attitude Change Strategies," *Journal of College Student Development* 32 (March 1991), pp. 131–39. [Authors' note]

ENGAGING THE TEXT

1. Working in groups, write up study notes for this selection, charting Sadker and Sadker's key claims and evidence in the following areas:
   - the history of women at the university
   - current structural/numerical biases
   - bias in the classroom
   - books
   - "campus life," including housing and extracurricular activities
   - sexual harassment/rape

2. Write a journal entry evaluating your own college experiences in light of Sadker and Sadker's revelations about campus life. To what extent do your experiences and observations confirm or challenge their analysis of sexism in higher education?

3. Test the Sadkers' claims by closely observing one class on your campus. Take notes on all the things they analyzed: female vs. male seating, frequency and nature of speech, amount of attention received from the professor, and so on. Compare notes with students who observed other classes. What patterns, if any, do you see?

EXPLORING CONNECTIONS

4. In examining social class and educational opportunities, Jean Anyon (p. 186) describes a "hidden curriculum." Compare and contrast Anyon's hidden curriculum with the one revealed in this selection.

5. Explain each panel of the "Doonesbury" cartoon that follows (p. 251), in light of Sadker and Sadker's observations about "a girl's education."

EXTENDING THE CRITICAL CONTEXT

6. Ask your school's administration for data on the percentage of female and male faculty, tenured and untenured, by department. Also find out the number of male and female majors in various departments. (You may have to divide the work and approach department chairs directly.) Do your data support Sadker and Sadker's claims?

7. Read Leora Tanenbaum's review of *Failing at Fairness* in the February 28, 1994, edition of *The Nation*—a review that is in some respects severely critical of the book. Report to the class on the issues Tanembaum raises. When experts disagree, how does the college student know whom to believe?

8. In recent years, there has been growing interest in returning to same-sex schooling at all educational levels. Working in groups, brainstorm the advantages and disadvantages of gender-segregated education.

9. Sadker and Sadker note that efforts at sensitivity education to stop rape appear to have little impact on male students. Research what your college does to address sexual harassment and rape. Beyond sensitivity training,

what can institutions of higher education do to reduce the threat of violence to women on campus?

Doonesbury   BY GARRY TRUDEAU

Doonesbury © G. B. Trudeau. Reprinted with permission of Universal Press Syndicate. All rights reserved.

Silence

MAXINE HONG KINGSTON

To the Chinese immigrant, white Americans are "ghosts" — threatening and occasionally comical specters who speak an incomprehensible tongue. For many immigrants, becoming American means living among "ghosts," finding a new voice, adopting new values, defining a new self. This selection, from Maxine Hong Kingston's enormously popular autobiography, The Woman Warrior, *describes the conflicts experienced by a young Chinese girl as she struggles to adapt to new ways in her American school. Maxine Hong Kingston (b. 1940) teaches at the University of California, Berkeley.* The Woman Warrior *won the National Book Critics Circle Award for nonfiction in 1976 and was named by* Time *magazine as one of the top ten nonfiction works of the 1970s. Kingston has since published* China Men *(1980) and* Tripmaster Monkey *(1989), in addition to numerous poems, short stories, and articles in national magazines. The stage play* The Woman Warrior *debuted in Berkeley in 1994.*

Long ago in China, knot-makers tied string into buttons and frogs, and rope into bell pulls. There was one knot so complicated that it blinded the knot-maker. Finally an emperor outlawed this cruel knot, and the nobles could not order it anymore. If I had lived in China, I would have been an outlaw knot-maker.

Maybe that's why my mother cut my tongue. She pushed my tongue up and sliced the frenum. Or maybe she snipped it with a pair of nail scissors. I don't remember her doing it, only her telling me about it, but all during childhood I felt sorry for the baby whose mother waited with scissors or knife in hand for it to cry — and then, when its mouth was wide open like a baby bird's, cut. The Chinese say "a ready tongue is an evil."

I used to curl up my tongue in front of the mirror and tauten my frenum into a white line, itself as thin as a razor blade. I saw no scars in my mouth. I thought perhaps I had had two frena, and she had cut one. I made other children open their mouths so I could compare theirs to mine. I saw perfect pink membranes stretching into precise edges that looked easy enough to cut. Sometimes I felt very proud that my mother committed such a powerful act upon me. At other times I was terrified — the first thing my mother did when she saw me was to cut my tongue.

"Why did you do that to me, Mother?"

"I told you."   5

"Tell me again."

"I cut it so that you would not be tongue-tied. Your tongue would be able to move in any language. You'll be able to speak languages that are completely different from one another. You'll be able to pronounce anything. Your frenum looked too tight to do those things, so I cut it."

"But isn't 'a ready tongue an evil'?"

"Things are different in this ghost country."

"Did it hurt me? Did I cry and bleed?"   10

"I don't remember. Probably."

She didn't cut the other children's. When I asked cousins and other Chinese children whether their mothers had cut their tongues loose, they said, "What?"

"Why didn't you cut my brothers' and sisters' tongues?"

"They didn't need it."

"Why not? Were theirs longer than mine?"   15

"Why don't you quit blabbering and get to work?"

If my mother was not lying she should have cut more, scraped away the rest of the frenum skin, because I have a terrible time talking. Or she should not have cut at all, tampering with my speech. When I went to kindergarten and had to speak English for the first time, I became silent. A dumbness — a shame — still cracks my voice in two, even when I want to say "hello" casually, or ask any easy question in front of the check-out counter, or ask directions of a bus driver. I stand frozen, or I hold up the line with the complete, grammatical sentence that comes squeaking out at impossible length. "What did you say?" says the cab driver, or "Speak up," so I have to perform again, only weaker the second time. A telephone call makes my throat bleed and takes up that day's courage. It spoils my day with self-disgust when I hear my broken voice come skittering out into the open. It makes people wince to hear it. I'm getting better, though. Recently I asked the postman for special-issue stamps; I've waited since childhood for postmen to give me some of their own accord. I am making progress, a little every day.

My silence was thickest — total — during the three years that I covered my school paintings with black paint. I painted layers of black over houses and flowers and suns, and when I drew on the blackboard, I put a layer of chalk on top. I was making a stage curtain, and it was the moment before the curtain parted or rose. The teachers called my parents to school, and I saw they had been saving my pictures, curling and cracking, all alike and black. The teachers pointed to the pictures and looked serious, talked seriously too, but my parents did not understand English. ("The parents and teachers of criminals were executed," said my father.) My parents took the pictures home. I spread them out (so black and full of possibilities) and pretended the curtains were swinging open, flying up, one after another, sunlight underneath, mighty operas.

During the first silent year I spoke to no one at school, did not ask before going to the lavatory, and flunked kindergarten. My sister also said nothing for three years, silent in the playground and silent at lunch. There were other quiet Chinese girls not of our family, but most of them got over it sooner than we did. I enjoyed the silence. At first it did not occur to me I was supposed to talk or to pass kindergarten. I talked at home and to one or two of the Chinese kids in the class. I made motions and even made some jokes. I drank out of a toy saucer when the water spilled out of the cup, and everybody laughed, pointing at me, so I did it some more. I didn't know that Americans don't drink out of saucers.

I liked the Negro students (Black Ghosts) best because they laughed the loudest and talked to me as if I were a daring talker too. One of the Negro girls had her mother coil braids over her ears Shanghai-style like mine; we were Shanghai twins except that she was covered with black like my paintings. Two Negro kids enrolled in Chinese school, and the teachers gave them Chinese names. Some Negro kids walked me to school and home, protecting me from the Japanese kids, who hit me and chased me and stuck gum in my ears. The Japanese kids were noisy and tough. They appeared one day in kindergarten, released from concentration camp,[1] which was a tic-tac-toe mark, like barbed wire, on the map.

It was when I found out I had to talk that school became a misery, that the silence became a misery. I did not speak and felt bad each time that I did not speak. I read aloud in first grade, though, and heard the barest whisper with little squeaks come out of my throat. "Louder," said the teacher,

20

---

[1]*concentration camp:* Refers to one of the U.S. camps where Japanese Americans were imprisoned during World War II.

who scared the voice away again. The other Chinese girls did not talk either, so I knew the silence had to do with being a Chinese girl.

Reading out loud was easier than speaking because we did not have to make up what to say, but I stopped often, and the teacher would think I'd gone quiet again. I could not understand "I." The Chinese "I" has seven strokes, intricacies. How could the American "I," assuredly wearing a hat like the Chinese, have only three strokes, the middle so straight? Was it out of politeness that this writer left off strokes the way a Chinese has to write her own name small and crooked? No, it was not politeness; "I" is a capital and "you" is a lower-case. I stared at that middle line and waited so long for its black center to resolve into tight strokes and dots that I forgot to pronounce it. The other troublesome word was "here," no strong consonant to hang on to, and so flat, when "here" is two mountainous ideographs.[2] The teacher, who had already told me every day how to read "I" and "here," put me in the low corner under the stairs again, where the noisy boys usually sat.

When my second grade class did a play, the whole class went to the auditorium except the Chinese girls. The teacher, lovely and Hawaiian, should have understood about us, but instead left us behind in the classroom. Our voices were too soft or nonexistent, and our parents never signed the permission slips anyway. They never signed anything unnecessary. We opened the door a crack and peeked out, but closed it again quickly. One of us (not me) won every spelling bee, though.

I remember telling the Hawaiian teacher, "We Chinese can't sing 'land where our fathers died.' " She argued with me about politics, while I meant because of curses. But how can I have that memory when I couldn't talk? My mother says that we, like the ghosts, have no memories.

After American school, we picked up our cigar boxes in which we had   25
arranged books, brushes, and an inkbox neatly, and went to Chinese school, from 5:00 to 7:30 P.M. There we chanted together, voices rising and falling, loud and soft, some boys shouting, everybody reading together, reciting together and not alone with one voice. When we had a memorization test, the teacher let each of us come to his desk and say the lesson to him privately, while the rest of the class practiced copying or tracing. Most of the teachers were men. The boys who were so well behaved in the American school played tricks on them and talked back to them. The girls were not mute. They screamed and yelled during recess, when there were no rules; they had fistfights. Nobody was afraid of children hurting themselves or of children hurting school property. The glass doors to the red and green balconies with the gold joy symbols were left wide open so that we could run out and climb the fire escapes. We played capture-the-flag in the audito-

[2]*ideographs:* Composite characters in Chinese writing made by combining two or more other characters.

rium, where Sun Yat-sen[3] and Chiang Kai-shek's[4] pictures hung at the back of the stage, the Chinese flag on their left and the American flag on their right. We climbed the teak ceremonial chairs and made flying leaps off the stage. One flag headquarters was behind the glass door and the other on stage right. Our feet drummed on the hollow stage. During recess the teachers locked themselves up in their office with the shelves of books, copybooks, inks from China. They drank tea and warmed their hands at a stove. There was no play supervision. At recess we had the school to ourselves, and also we could roam as far as we could go — downtown, Chinatown stores, home — as long as we returned before the bell rang.

At exactly 7:30 the teacher again picked up the brass bell that sat on his desk and swung it over our heads, while we charged down the stairs, our cheering magnified in the stairwell. Nobody had to line up.

Not all of the children who were silent at American school found voice at Chinese school. One new teacher said each of us had to get up and recite in front of the class, who was to listen. My sister and I had memorized the lesson perfectly. We said it to each other at home, one chanting, one listening. The teacher called on my sister to recite first. It was the first time a teacher had called on the second-born to go first. My sister was scared. She glanced at me and looked away; I looked down at my desk. I hoped that she could do it because if she could, then I would have to. She opened her mouth and a voice came out that wasn't a whisper, but it wasn't a proper voice either. I hoped that she would not cry, fear breaking up her voice like twigs underfoot. She sounded as if she were trying to sing through weeping and strangling. She did not pause or stop to end the embarrassment. She kept going until she said the last word, and then she sat down. When it was my turn, the same voice came out, a crippled animal running on broken legs. You could hear splinters in my voice, bones rubbing jagged against one another. I was loud, though. I was glad I didn't whisper. There was one little girl who whispered.

[3]*Sun Yat-sen:* Chinese politician, intellectual, and revolutionary (1866–1925).

[4]*Chiang Kai-shek:* Military leader of the Chinese Revolution (1887–1975), later leader of the Nationalist government driven to Taiwan by their former allies, the Chinese Communists.

ENGAGING THE TEXT

1. Explain the significance of the first paragraph and Kingston's assertion that she "would have been an outlaw knot-maker."

2. Did Kingston's mother literally cut her tongue? If so, why, and what was the result? If not, why does Kingston create this elaborate and graphic story?

3. Why is the young Kingston silent in American school? What's the connection for her between being silent and being Chinese? Between being silent and being female?

4. Kingston writes that school became "a misery" (para. 21). Was this misery avoidable? What, if anything, could Kingston, her American school, her parents, or her Chinese school have done better?

5. Compare and contrast the two schools Kingston attended. Consider their activities, their rules, the behavior of the students and teachers, their probable goals. Why are the schools so different?

EXPLORING CONNECTIONS

6. Compare and contrast Kingston's experience with that of the speaker in Inés Hernández-Ávila's "Para Teresa" (p. 216). Consider each girl's relationship to her family, her attitude toward school, and her strategy for coping with or fitting into Anglo society.

7. Richard Rodriguez (p. 202) also reports a period of silence and discomfort in school. How does his situation compare with Kingston's? Are the differences you see a matter of degree, or were the two students silent for different reasons?

8. How might the Sadkers (p. 228) explain Kingston's silence in school?

9. Write a scenario in which the silent young Kingston encounters a "connected teacher" (see "Connected Education for Women," p. 256). What would the teacher do, and how might the young Kingston respond? Read your scenario aloud in class.

EXTENDING THE CRITICAL CONTEXT

10. Write a journal entry or essay about a time you felt silenced in school. Describe the situation in detail. How did you perceive yourself? How do you think others perceived you? What factors, both in and outside the classroom, led to the situation?

Connected Education for Women

BLYTHE MCVICKER CLINCHY,
MARY FIELD BELENKY,
NANCY GOLDBERGER,
AND JILL MATTUCK TARULE

Like Myra Sadker and David Sadker (p. 228), the authors of this excerpt believe that higher education in the United States unnecessarily intimidates and alienates women students, and that schools usually fail to teach in the productive and humane ways they should. They based their conclusions on extensive interviews with more than a hundred women in widely diverse colleges and adult education programs. In this brief selection, they explain how "connected education" might solve some of the problems women experience in school. The authors are all psychologists — Blythe Clinchy at Wellesley College, Mary Belenky at the University of Vermont, Nancy Goldberger at the Fielding Institute in Santa Barbara, and Jill Tarule at the University of Vermont, where she is dean of education. The article from which this reading is excerpted appeared in the Journal of Education *in 1985. In 1988 the same authors published* Women's Ways of Knowing: The Development of Self, Voice, and Mind, *which won the Distinguished Publication Award from the Association of Women in Psychology. The authors have recently revisited their award-winning project in* Knowledge, Difference, and Power: Essays Inspired by Women's Ways of Knowing *(1997).*

Most of the institutions of higher education in this country were designed by men, and most continue to be run by men. In recent years feminist teachers and scholars have begun to question the structure, the curriculum, and the pedagogical practices of these institutions, and they have put forth useful proposals for change (e.g., Bowles & Duelli Klein, 1983; Martin, 1984; Nicholson, 1980; Rich, 1979; Spanier, Bloom, & Borovik, 1984). But in order to design an education appropriate for women we must learn about the academic experiences of ordinary women, women who are, in most cases, neither teachers nor scholars nor even feminists, but simply students.

In a project on "Education for Women's Development," supported by the Fund for the Improvement of Post-secondary Education, we asked 135 ordinary women to share their educational experiences with us. The women were drawn from three private liberal arts colleges (a women's college, an "early college" which admits younger students, and a progressive coeducational college), an inner-city community college, an urban public high school, two adult education programs, and three rural human service agencies which we call "invisible colleges." The women ranged in age from 16 to 65 and came from a variety of ethnic, class, and religious backgrounds. Some were single, some divorced, some married. Many had borne and raised children.

Connected Teaching

Not one of the women we interviewed advocated the traditional form of education characterized by Paulo Freire[1] as a "banking model," in which

---

[1]*Paulo Freire:* Noted Brazilian educator, philosopher, and political activist (b. 1921).

the teacher's role is "to 'fill' the students by making deposits of information which he considers to constitute true knowledge," and the student's job is merely to "store the deposits" (Freire, 1971, p. 60). Even a woman who, heavily dependent upon knowledge received from authorities, said, "I just want to listen to the instructor" said, in almost the next breath, "I don't really think that anybody can put something into someone that isn't there. It has to be there."

Many women expressed — some firmly, some shakily — this belief that they possessed latent knowledge. The kind of teacher they praised and the kind they yearned for was a teacher who would help them articulate and expand their latent knowledge: a midwife-teacher. The midwife-teacher is the opposite of the banker-teacher. While the bank clerk deposits knowledge in the learner's head, the midwife draws it out. She assists the students in giving birth to their own ideas, in making their own tacit knowledge explicit and elaborating it.

Here are some examples of women talking about their midwife-   5
teachers: "She helped me to be able to say what I wanted to say." "He said to me, 'What you're thinking is fine, but think more.' " "She let me do what I wanted to do [with my poetry] and helped me do it and pushed it further." "She told me, 'Go home and write what you feel, because then you can look at it and see how you felt.' " "I told her that I'd had this dream that inspired my painting, and she said, 'Keep drawing from that dream until you can't draw from it any more.' "

In Freire's banking model the teacher constructs knowledge in private and talks about it in public, so that the students may store it. In the connected education model, as in Freire's "problem-posing" model, teacher and students construct knowledge together. Several women cherished memories of classes like this. One woman told us about a connected class that had occurred by accident. Usually, she said, her English teacher "just hands you his thoughts," but on one memorable occasion he allowed a discussion to erupt.

> We were all raising our hands and talking about I forget what book, and some of the students brought up things that he hadn't thought about that made him see it in a whole different way, and he was really excited, and we all came to a conclusion that none of us had started out with. We came up with an answer to a question we thought was unanswerable in the beginning, and it just made you all feel really good when you walked out of class. You felt you had accomplished something and that you understood the book. And he was pleased, too.

At the next class meeting, however, the teacher had reverted to the banking mode. "I guess he doesn't like that method," the student said.

The connected class provides a culture in which ideas can grow. It is, in the writer Peter Elbow's[2] (1973) words, a "yoghurt" class, as opposed to a "movie" class. Members of the connected class are not mere spectators; they actively nurture each other's ideas. A senior at the women's college tries to explain what goes on in her art history seminar: "Somebody will say, 'Well, do you mean . . . ?' and then somebody else says, 'No, I mean . . .' It's clarifying." The teacher has fostered a special atmosphere in the class.

> It's allowing everyone to voice things that they think are uncertain. It's allowing people to realize that they're not stupid for questioning things. It's okay to say, "Why" or "How" or "What." I think it's important to let everybody voice their uncertainties.

In a connected class no one apologizes for uncertainty. It is assumed that evolving thought must be tentative.

Connected classes seem to work best when members of the group meet over a long period of time and get to know each other well. The early college, a small college in which most classes are conducted as seminars, came closest to fulfilling these conditions. One of the women we interviewed attended the early college for two years and then transferred to a larger school. There she enrolled in a seminar on modern British poetry, one of her favorite topics. "It was awful," she says. "The people didn't know how to talk about anything. They didn't know how to share ideas. It was always an argument. It wasn't an idea to be developed, to be explored." At the early college, students came to know their classmates' styles of thinking. "It was like a family group trying to work out a family problem, except it was an idea." In most colleges there is no chance to form family groups. Each course starts with a new cast of characters, runs for 13 weeks or so, and then disperses.

In a community, unlike a hierarchy, people get to know each other. They do not act as representatives of positions to be attacked or defended or as occupants of roles but as individuals with particular modes of thinking. A first-year student remarked that her editing group composed of three classmates in a writing course was not working: "We just talk about commas and junk like that."

> I had a peer editing group in high school, and it was terrific. But we all knew each other inside out, so you knew what each person was trying to do in her writing, and you knew what kinds of criticisms helped her and what kind hurt her feelings. You can't really help if you don't know people.

Unless she knows the critic personally and the critic knows her personally, she says, she finds criticism of her work "hurtful, but not helpful."

---

[2]*Peter Elbow:* American educator (b. 1935) specializing in writing instruction.

Connected teaching is personal. Connected teachers present them- 10
selves as genuine, flawed human beings. They allow students to observe the
imperfect processes of their thinking. Connected teachers take a personal
interest in their students. They want to know how each individual student is
thinking. But connected teaching is not "soft." It is rigorous. And it is objective, although not coldly impersonal.

Connected teachers practice a sophisticated form of what we call "connected knowing," a "technique of *disciplined* subjectivity" (Erikson, 1964)
requiring them to "systematically empathize" with their students (Wilson,
1977, p. 259). They try to practice what Peter Elbow (1973, p. 171) calls
"projection in the good sense," using their own reactions to the material the
class is studying to formulate hypotheses about the students' reactions.

Cynthia, an alumna quoted earlier, told us about an English teacher
who could serve as an ideal prototype.

> This woman and her method of teaching and her attitude towards life
> moved me very much. She was so rigorous. She wanted things always
> to add up. You had to have a system and you had to make everything
> work. You had to assume that there was a purpose to everything the
> artist did. And if something seemed odd, you couldn't overlook it or ig-
> nore it or throw it out.

This teacher was thoroughly "objective" in treating the students' responses as real and independent of her own.

> She was intensely, genuinely interested in everybody's feelings about
> things. She asked a question and wanted to know what your response
> was. She wanted to know because she wanted to see what sort of effect
> this writing was having. She wasn't using us as a sounding board for
> her own feelings about things. She really wanted to know. . . .

Cynthia's English teacher does not treat her own experience of the material under study as primary, and she does not assume that her students experience the material as she does; this would be undisciplined subjectivity
or, as Elbow (1973, p. 171) puts it, "projection in the bad sense." She "really
wants to know" how the students are experiencing the material. . . .

Belief, Doubt, and Development

Midwives are believers. They trust their students' thinking and encour- 15
age them to expand it. But in the psychological literature concerning the factors promoting cognitive development, doubt has played a more prominent
role than belief and the adversarial model has dominated institutions of
higher education (Rich, 1979). In order to stimulate cognitive growth, according to this model, the teacher should point out flaws in the students'
thinking, put forth opposing notions, encourage debate, and challenge students to defend their ideas. One should attempt to induce cognitive conflict

in students' minds. We do not deny that cognitive conflict can act as an impetus to growth, but in all our interviews only a handful of women described a powerful and positive learning experience in which a teacher challenged their ideas in this fashion. The women did mention such incidents, but they did not describe them as occasions for cognitive growth. On the whole, women found the experience of being doubted debilitating, rather than energizing.

Because so many women are already filled with self-doubt, doubts imposed from outside seem at best redundant ("I'm always reprimanding myself ":), and at worst destructive, confirming their own sense of themselves as inadequate knowers. The doubting model, then, may be peculiarly inappropriate for women (although we are not convinced that it is appropriate for men, either).

We believe that most women want and need an education in which connection is emphasized over separation, understanding and acceptance over judgment and assessment, and collaboration over debate. They need a curriculum which accords respect to and allows time for the knowledge that emerges from firsthand experience. They need a system which, instead of imposing its own expectations and arbitrary requirements, helps them to define their own questions and evolve their own patterns of work for pursuing these questions. These are the lessons we think we have learned in listening to ordinary women.

References

Bowles, G., & Duelli Klein, R. (1983). *Theories of women's studies*. London: Routledge & Kegan Paul.

Elbow, P. (1973). *Writing without teachers*. London: Oxford University Press.

Erikson, E. (1964). On the nature of clinical evidence. In E. Erikson, *Insight and responsibility* (pp. 49–80). New York: Norton.

Freire, P. (1971). *Pedagogy of the oppressed*. New York: Seaview.

Martin, J. (1984). Bringing women into educational thought. *Educational Theory, 34*, 341–353.

Nicholson, L. (1980). Women and schooling. *Educational Theory 30*, 225–233.

Rich, A. (1979). *On Lies, Secrets, and Silence: Selected prose: 1966–78*. New York: Norton.

Spanier, B., Bloom, A., & Borovik, D. (1984). *Toward a balanced curriculum: A source book for initiating gender integration projects*. Cambridge, MA: Schenkman.

Wilson, S. (1977). The use of ethnographic techniques in educational research. *Review of Educational Research, 47*, 245–265.

ENGAGING THE TEXT

1. Explain in your own words what is meant by the "banking model" (para. 3), by "midwife-teachers" (para. 4), by a "yoghurt class" (para. 7), and by "connected education".

2. Write an extended journal entry about a class you've taken, either in college or in the past, that illustrates the "banking model" of education. How would you evaluate the experience? Do you agree with the suggestion that a traditional "banking" approach affects women more than men?

3. Write another journal entry, this time about your educational experience that most closely resembled "connected education." Was this experience as positive as Clinchy et al. portray it to be? Why do you think connected education is so rare?

EXPLORING CONNECTIONS

4. To what extent does the model of connected education presented by Clinchy et al. address the gender inequities described by Myra and David Sadker (p. 228)? What more might be necessary to ensure equity for women?

5. In the excerpt from *Social Class and the Hidden Curriculum of Work* (p. 186), Jean Anyon links specific classroom practices with the social status and jobs different schools expect their students to hold later in life. Write your own analysis of how traditional practices in higher education relate to the expected social status and jobs of women.

6. Drawing on the analysis of traditional and connected teaching in this article, discuss which model best describes Jack MacFarland in Mike Rose's "'I Just Wanna Be Average'" (p. 174).

7. Clinchy et al. recognize that many women students, like the students in Matt Groening's cartoons (pp. 164–65), find themselves in a hostile environment. Draw a cartoon or comic strip that captures some of the feelings and ideas of the dissatisfied women discussed above.

EXTENDING THE CRITICAL CONTEXT

8. Analyze your current classes for evidence of connected and traditional teaching techniques. Write a journal entry on your reactions to the teaching styles you observe, and compare notes with classmates.

9. When teachers attempt to practice connected teaching (peer editing groups, collaborative learning groups, small group discussions, and so on), they find that some students resist these efforts. Why do you think some students reject them?

10. Many contemporary writers — including scholars, poets, novelists, and political activists — suggest that women experience and respond to the world differently than men. Write a short narrative about a world in which "women's values" dominate. Share your story in class and discuss.

Politics in the Schoolroom

LYNNE V. CHENEY

The last few decades have witnessed a sea change in American educa-
tion. Forty years ago the typical American college classroom was filled with
mostly white male students listening to a white male instructor lecturing
about the achievements of — you guessed it — their white male predeces-
sors. But after the civil rights movement, American education began to open
its doors, not only to a new, more ethnically and racially diverse group of
students, but to the ideas, experiences, and perspectives they brought with
them. The presence of growing numbers of minority, low-income, and fe-
male students at all instructional levels has challenged America's educators
to rethink and revise their pedagogy and the content of their classrooms.
Not all cultural commentators, however, are invigorated by the direction of
these changes. Some, like former Reagan appointee Lynne V. Cheney, see
classroom innovations that feature multicultural or feminist perspectives as
an unnecessary diversion from more important academic concerns. The fol-
lowing selection, excerpted from Cheney's Telling the Truth: Why Our Culture and Our Country Have Stopped Making Sense — and What We Can
Do About It *(1996), presents a conservative critique of what Cheney sees as*
the recent politicization of our nation's classrooms. Cheney served as Chair-
man of the National Endowment for the Humanities from 1986 to 1992. She
is currently a Senior Fellow at the American Enterprise Institute.

> Ignorance is strength.
> — One of the mottoes of the Party in GEORGE ORWELL, *1984*

- A Massachusetts educator warns teachers about using *The Story of
  Babar* because it "extols the virtues of a European, middle-class
  lifestyle and disparages the animals and people who have remained
  in the jungle."[1]
- A teacher of "radical math literacy" warns against bombarding students with "oppressive procapitalist ideology." Among the practical
  applications of mathematics that she says should be avoided is totaling a grocery bill since such an exercise "carries the nonneutral message that paying for food is natural."[2]

[1]Patricia G. Ramsey, *Teaching and Learning in a Diverse World: Multicultural Education
for Young Children* (New York: Teachers College Press, 1987), 73. [Author's note]

[2]Marilyn Frankenstein, "A Different Third R: Radical Math," *Politics of Education: Essays from* Radical Teacher, Susan Gushee O'Malley, Robert C. Rosen, and Leonard Vogt, eds.
(Albany: State University of New York Press, 1990), 220. [Author's note]

· The author of a textbook for future teachers urges skepticism for the
idea that the people now known as American Indians came to this
hemisphere across the Bering land bridge. Indian myths do not tell
this story, she writes. Moreover, she observes, the scientific account
has nothing "except logic" to recommend it. A committee of parents
and teachers in Berkeley, California, subsequently offers this argument as reason for rejecting a fourth-grade history text.[3]

Disparate as these examples seem, the people in them have a common
goal. They want to be sure that American schools show no favor to — and,
indeed, positively downgrade — ideas and practices associated with the
United States and its Western heritage, including, in the last instance, the
Enlightenment legacy of scientific thought. While such efforts can seem
foolish and extreme (someone really wants to ban *Babar*?), it would be a
mistake to overlook the trend they represent: the growing tendency for politics to drive the education of the young in this country, very often at the expense of truth.

A teacher in New Jersey describes at length her way of teaching fourth-
graders that Columbus wasn't a hero who "discovered" America, but a
"greedy" man and a "murderer" who "stole" it. In order to help them understand why they have been taught lies about 1492, she has the children in her
class imagine that every year the principal of their school speaks of Columbus as a man to be respected. Meanwhile, the fourth-graders are further to
imagine, the principal regularly leads an army of the school's strongest students on raids of neighboring schools where they confiscate valuable materials and round up prisoners to be the principal's servants. By asking the
fourth-graders "to explain the connection between the principal's spirited
promotion of the Columbus myth and the invasions of neighboring
schools," the teacher claims to help her students understand how the positive Columbus myth is used by their government "to forestall any critical
questioning of U.S. imperialistic foreign policy today." As the teacher explains it:

Widespread belief in the myth makes it easy for U.S. officials to get
away with invading Vietnam, Grenada, Panama, and so on. Those
books (containing the myth) teach children that any nation with sufficient military power has the right to invade other lands. In particular,
they reinforce blind patriotism and the belief that the United States
has a moral imperative to control the "New World Order."[4]

[3]Christine I. Bennett, *Comprehensive Multicultural Education: Theory and Practice*
(Boston: Allyn and Bacon, 1990), 287; Eugenie C. Scott, "The Social Context of Pseudo-
science," *The Natural History of Paradigms*, J. H. Langdon and M. E. McGann, eds. (Indianapolis: University of Indianapolis Press, 1993), 350. [Author's note]

[4]Maria Sweeney, "Columbus, A Hero? Rethinking Columbus in an Elementary Classroom," *Radical Teacher* (Fall 1993), 25–29. [Author's note]

Although this teacher is particularly expansive about the views she presents in the classroom, she is hardly unique in conveying to those she teaches that the events leading up to their country's founding should be regarded with loathing. At a multicultural conference in California, a teacher offers her colleagues an example of how to deal with students who want to be positive instead of negative about Columbus and study him as an exemplar of the Age of Exploration. When faced with this in her own classroom, says the teacher, she simply told the student, "That would be like a Jew celebrating Hitler because he had a dream."[5]

Fourth-graders in Chapel Hill, North Carolina, have had to use the following words in a fill-in-the-blank test about Columbus: *conquer, genocide, holocaust, subjugate, annihilate,* and *propaganda.*[6] A seventh-grader in Minnesota recounted for me her difficulties with a writing assignment about Columbus:

> The history teacher wanted us to write a story for first-graders, wanted us to tell the story over the way it was supposed to be. We were supposed to write a negative story on the bad things Columbus did.

The seventh-grader went on to explain that she didn't follow instructions: "I didn't think we should go out and tell first-graders he was so awful." As a result, she got what she called "a really bad grade." She wrote the story again, "half and half" this time, and thus managed to get by.[7]

We should not, of course, retreat into the old myths, should not hide   5
from students that Columbus and other European explorers were often brutal. But there was also brutality in indigenous cultures — as well as much to be admired. And much to praise about Europeans as well, who did, after all, bring with them the foundations for our legal, educational, and political institutions. But instead of being encouraged to search for a complicated truth, students are increasingly presented with oversimple versions of the American past that focus on the negative.

Sandra Stotsky, a researcher at Harvard University, reviewed teaching materials being used in the Brookline, Massachusetts, high school and concluded in 1991 that there was "one major theme" running through the course outlines and examinations for social studies: "the systematic denigration of America's Western heritage." A ninth-grade exam on ancient history, for example, asked students to identify the "Hellenic epic which established egotistical individualism as heroic." Almost all the questions on Greece and Rome, according to Stotsky, emphasized negative aspects, while "all items about ancient China . . . were worded positively or drew attention only to China's positive features, such

---

[5]Quoted in Robert Holland, "Re-education, the Multicultural Way," *Richmond Times-Dispatch* (21 February 1993), F7. [Author's note]

[6]"Spelling Test 3" given in October 1992 to a fourth-grade gifted and talented class in the Chapel Hill–Carrboro, North Carolina, school district. [Author's note]

[7]Conversation with author, 27 May 1993. [Author's note]

as 'Chinese belief in pacifism and relativism.' Not a word, for example, about the existence of slavery in ancient China and the thousands of slaves who built, and died building, the Great Wall." Similarly, Stotsky observed:

> Students . . . learn about racism as an American and European phe-
> nomenon only. Even though Islamic and African history are exten-
> sively covered in the curriculum . . . students learn only about the
> trans-Atlantic slave trade and nothing about the slave trade conducted
> by African kings or Arab traders for centuries preceding and following
> the trans-Atlantic slave trade.[8]

The National History Standards[9] developed at the University of California at Los Angeles and released in the fall of 1994 are the most egregious example to date of encouraging students to take a benign view of — or totally
overlook — the failings of other cultures while being hypercritical of the one
in which they live. Published in two volumes — one for U.S. history and one
for world history — and intended for schools across the nation, the standards
suggest that students consider the architecture, labor systems, and agriculture of the Aztecs — but not their practice of human sacrifice. The gathering
of wealth, presented as an admirable activity when an African king, Mansa
Musa, undertakes it, is presented as cause for outrage when it occurs in the
American context. One suggested student activity is to "conduct a trial of
John D. Rockefeller on the following charge: 'The plaintiff [sic] had knowingly and willfully participated in unethical and amoral business practices designed to undermine traditions of fair and open competition for personal and
private aggrandizement in direct violation of the common welfare.' "[10]

Although the standards for U.S. history neglect to mention that George
Washington was our first president or that James Madison was the father of
the Constitution, they do manage to include a great deal about the Ku Klux
Klan (which appears seventeen times in the document), Senator Joe Mc-
Carthy and McCarthyism (cited nineteen times), and the Great Depression
(cited twenty-five times). The U.S. standards also pay little attention to scientific and technological achievement. Among the figures *not* discussed are
Alexander Graham Bell, the Wright Brothers, Thomas Edison, Albert Einstein, Jonas Salk, and Neil Armstrong (or any astronaut). The exquisite consciousness of race and gender that characterizes the standards may have
contributed to the omission of this group (its members are all white males),
but it is also the case that science and technology are now held in extremely

---

[8]Sandra Stotsky, "Multicultural Education in the Brookline Public Schools: The Deconstruction of an Academic Curriculum," *Network News & Views* (October 1991), 30, 32. [Au-
thor's note]

[9]*The National History Standards:* After heated public debate, the curriculum standards
discussed here were not adopted by the state of California.

[10]Charlotte Crabtree and Gary B. Nash, *National Standards for United States History:
Exploring the American Experience, Grades 5–12* (Los Angeles: National Center for History in
the Schools, University of California at Los Angeles, 1994), 48, 44, 139. [Author's note]

low regard in certain parts of the academy. Feminists argue that science represents destructive male thinking. Why not call Newton's *Principia* Newton's "rape manual"? asks one.[11] Both feminists and environmentalists argue that because of the high value that science places on objectivity and rationality, it is now in deep and deserved crisis — information that tends to come as a surprise to practicing scientists.[12] Did the authors of the U.S. standards decide that in the case of a field so disdained by so many of their colleagues, the less said the better? Whatever the motive, to overlook American accomplishment in science and technology is to omit some of our most dazzling achievements.

The World History Standards do mention Edison and Einstein; and while there is heavy emphasis on the role that technological advancement has had in increasing the brutality of war, there is also some recognition that science has played a role in improving quality of life — though it is usually coupled with a reminder that not everyone has benefited equally. Students are asked, for example, to assess "why scientific, technological, and medical advances have improved living standards for many but have failed to eradicate hunger, poverty, and epidemic disease."[13]

In the World History Standards, the fact that women generally had different roles from men in the ancient world is seen simply as a matter of gender "differentiation" — until it happens in Athens, the birthplace of Western civilization. Then it becomes a matter of "restrictions on the rights and freedoms of women." Just as sexism is first introduced in the context of Greek civilization, so, too, is ethnocentrism — as though in previous cultures in Asia and Africa, people had never considered their ethnic group superior.[14] Nowhere is it mentioned that it was, in fact, in Western civilization that the unjust treatment of women and minorities was first condemned and curiosity about other cultures first encouraged. 10

In one of the sillier sections of the World History Standards — and one of the most quintessentially politically correct — students are asked to read a book about Michelangelo, not in order to discuss art, but so that they can "discuss social oppression and conflict in Europe during the Renaissance." In what may be the most irresponsible section of the World History Standards, fifth- and sixth-graders are asked to read a book about a Japanese girl of their age who died a painful death as a result of radiation from the atomic

---

[11]Sandra Harding, *The Science Question in Feminism* (Ithaca: Cornell University Press, 1986), 113. [Author's note]

[12]Andrew Ross, *Strange Weather: Culture, Science, and Technology in the Age of Limits* (London: Verso, 1991), 11; Paul R. Gross and Norman Levitt, *Higher Superstition: The Academic Left and Its Quarrels with Science* (Baltimore: Johns Hopkins University Press, 1994), 235. [Author's note]

[13]Charlotte Crabtree and Gary B. Nash, *National Standards for World History: Exploring Paths to the Present, Grades 5–12* (Los Angeles: National Center for History in the Schools, University of California at Los Angeles, 1994), 274. [Author's note]

[14]Ibid., 52, 79. [Author's note]

weapon dropped on Hiroshima in 1945.[15] No mention is made of why American leaders decided to use atomic weapons, about the casualties they believed an invasion of Japan would have entailed, for example. No mention is made of death and suffering caused by the Japanese. The rape of Nanking is not discussed, nor is Pearl Harbor, nor the Bataan death march. What fifth- and sixth-graders would be likely to conclude is that their country was guilty of a horrible — and completely unjustified — act of cruelty against innocents.

In the World History Standards, as in those for the United States, the Cold War is presented as a deadly competition between two equally culpable superpowers, each bent on world domination. Ignored is the most salient fact: that the struggle was between the communist totalitarianism of the Soviet Union, on the one hand, and the freedom offered by the United States, on the other. One might almost conclude from reading the standards that it would have made very little difference in terms of human freedom how the Cold War ended.[16]

It is sometimes said that the negative slant to what we are teaching now is overreaction to a too positive slant in the past, and it is true that in the past we sometimes presented celebratory history in our schools. But this explanation is of no help to students who were not around when prideful, positive stories were told, and who, day after day, are presented a drearily distorted picture of the society in which they live. Nor is this explanation complete. For those intent on political and social transformation, a bleak version of history is better than a balanced one. The grimmer the picture, the more heavily underscored is the need for the reforms they have in mind. . . .

One of the ways in which schools have changed — and for the better — is in recognizing the contributions that women have made and will continue to make to our society. But a 1992 study sponsored by the American Association of University Women (AAUW) claimed that education reformers have ignored girls, left them on the sidelines. Entitled *How Schools Shortchange Girls,* the report concluded that schools were biased in favor of boys, though, in fact, research in this area — including research cited in the AAUW report itself — is hardly clear on this point.[17] As education historian Diane Ravitch has pointed out, when one compares the educational record of females to males, it is very hard to find evidence that girls are victims of gender bias:

[15]Ibid., 177, 268. [Author's note]

[16]Ibid., 270–71; Crabtree and Nash, *National Standards for United States History,* 214–15. [Author's note]

[17]*How Schools Shortchange Girls* (Washington, D.C.: American Association of University Women, 1992). [Author's note]

While boys get higher scores in mathematics and science, girls get higher scores in reading and writing. Boys in eighth grade are 50 percent likelier than girls to be held back a grade, and boys in high school constitute 68 percent of the "special education" population.[18]

Research done shortly after the release of the AAUW report was especially devastating to its conclusions. A 1993 survey showed that female college freshmen — recent products, most of them, of American elementary and secondary schools — have higher aspirations than male college freshmen: 27.3 percent of the women declared their intention to pursue medical, law, or doctoral degrees; 25.8 percent of male freshmen had the same ambitions. Numbers for 1994 showed an even higher percentage for women — 28.1 — and a slightly lower one for men — 25.6. These numbers represent an enormous turnaround from a quarter century ago when three times as many male as female freshmen said they intended to pursue advanced degrees.[19]

The AAUW report found textbooks to be discriminatory, a claim that   15
was repeated uncritically in many news stories about the report. But as anyone who has looked at textbooks recently is aware, they have undergone enormous change. In order to make this point, I frequently cite for audiences a study showing that 83.8 percent of seventeen-year-olds know who Harriet Tubman is — more than know that George Washington was the commander of the American army during the Revolutionary War.[20] When I use this example, the over-thirty-five-year-olds in the audience almost always look disconcerted because they haven't the least idea of who Tubman — so familiar to seventeen-year-olds — was. Their puzzlement is testimony to how much textbooks — and, as a result, school curricula — have changed.

A group of researchers at Smith College in Massachusetts analyzed three leading high school American history textbooks and found that they not only include women, but show a pro-female bias. Wrote Robert Lerner, Althea K. Nagai, and Stanley Rothman:

> Of [the figures] they do evaluate, textbooks portray 99 percent of the women positively. Only one female character is portrayed both positively and negatively; no woman is depicted in a negative light. When textbooks rate men, they also portray them positively, but only 71 percent of the time. By contrast 14 percent of the men rated mixed portrayals, while 14 percent are portrayed negatively.

[18]Diane Ravitch, "What Gender Bias?" *Washington Post* (21 November 1993), C7. [Author's note]

[19]Alexander W. Astin, William S. Korn, and Ellyne R. Riggs, *The American Freshman: National Norms for Fall 1993* (Los Angeles: Higher Education Research Institute, December 1993), 2; Alexander W. Astin et al., *The American Freshman: National Norms for Fall 1994* (Los Angeles: Higher Education Research Institute, December 1994), 48, 32. [Author's note]

[20]See Diane Ravitch and Chester E. Finn, Jr., *What Do Our 17-Year-Olds Know?* (New York: Harper & Row, 1987), 263. [Author's note]

The researchers also noted a pro-feminist bias. The National Organization for Woman (NOW) and the Equal Rights Amendment (ERA), for example, both received uncritical, favorable coverage. Opposition to groups like NOW and legal measures like ERA was uniformly ignored.[21]

A study of elementary school textbooks published in 1986 found:

> Not one of the many families described in these books features a homemaker — that is, referred to a woman principally dedicated to acting as a wife and mother — as a model. . . . There are countless references to mothers and other women working outside of the home in occupations such as medicine, transportation, and politics. There is not one citation indicating that the occupation of a mother or housewife represents an important job, one with integrity, one that provides real satisfactions.[22]

In light of the results of this research — indeed, in light of what any parent who opens up a recently published textbook will see for him- or herself — it is astonishing that the president of the AAUW, Jackie DeFazio, in defending her organization's report, would write, "Textbooks rarely include references to the achievements of women, and when women are included, they are generally in sex-stereotyped roles."[23] Not even the report she was defending made that claim. Its primary concern, in fact, was almost the opposite: that the women in textbooks tended to be famous; that is, they had succeeded by supposedly male standards, rather than being representative of "women's perspectives and cultures."[24]

In 1993, the AAUW issued a second report, this one on sexual harassment. According to *Hostile Hallways,* 81 percent of students had experienced sexual harassment in school. Some of the instances of harassment cited were quite serious: 11 percent said they had been "forced to do something sexual at school other than kissing." But others were much less so. Two-thirds said they had been harassed by "sexual comments, jokes, ges-

---

[21]Robert Lerner, Althea K. Nagai, and Stanley Rothman, "Filler Feminism in High School History," *Academic Questions* (Winter 1991–1992), 31, 36–37. [Author's note]

[22]Paul C. Vitz, *Censorship: Evidence of Bias in Our Children's Textbooks* (Ann Arbor, Mich.: Servant Books, 1986), 38. An indignant mother in the Wallingford-Swarthmore school district of Philadelphia pointed out to me the way this theme carried over into exercises sixth-graders were asked to do in the school district in which she lived. A handout given to her son declared "the traditional nuclear family" to be a relic of the past and deservedly so since it "depended on the wife subordinating many of her individual interests to those of her husband and children." The handout further asked sixth-graders to assess who in their families was responsible for such tasks as grocery shopping, preparing meals, making major expenditures, and disciplining children. On the basis of the answers, each sixth-grader was to decide whether his or her family was "egalitarian or traditional" — and report the results to the school. [Author's note]

[23]Jackie DeFazio, letter to the editor, *Washington Post* (25 December 1993), A21. [Author's note]

[24]*How Schools Shortchange Girls,* 62. [Author's note]

tures, or looks."[25] One of the commentators to point out how expansive is the AAUW definition of sexual harassment was Albert Shanker, president of the American Federation of Teachers, who wrote:

> *Hostile Hallways* defines sexual harassment so broadly that it can be anything from being raped on the stairs to "unwelcome" words or gestures from someone you don't find attractive. . . . And the glance/gesture/remark kind of harassment is by far the most frequently reported.

Observing that an all-inclusive definition of sexual harassment trivializes the harm done to students who suffer serious abuse, Shanker asked, "What possible benefit is it to anyone to define sexual harassment so broadly that it includes most of the kids in a school — a girl who doesn't like the way a guy looked at her as well as one who suffered several broken bones when she was attacked?"[26]

The political point of the AAUW's research became clear when a "gender equity" bill was introduced in the Congress in 1993. In 1994, many provisions of this bill were enacted into law as part of the Elementary and Secondary Education Act. Millions of dollars of federal funds were thus dedicated to the purpose of making schools more congenial places for girls — despite statistics showing that males, in fact, have at least as much if not more difficulty than females at succeeding in school.

The research efforts of the AAUW illustrate well a point made by Cynthia Crossen in her book *Tainted Truth* about how postmodern thinking has affected the research enterprise. "Researchers have almost given up on the quaint notion that there is any such thing as 'fact' or 'objectivity,'" Crossen writes.[27] Instead, the point has become to amass data in order to support an agenda, in the case of the AAUW, an agenda that is moving sharply left, aligning it with organizations like the National Women's Studies Association. Vivien Ng, who as president of the NWSA expounded at that group's 1993 convention on her love for "political work, both inside the classroom and outside it,"[28] is a member of the AAUW foundation that funded *Hostile Hallways.* The other AAUW study, *How Schools Shortchange Girls,* was written in part by Peggy McIntosh, associate director of Wellesley College's Center for Research on Women, who has gained a certain measure of fame lecturing to parents and teachers across the country about how schools must

20

---

[25]*Hostile Hallways: The AAUW Survey on Sexual Harassment in America's Schools* (Washington, D.C.: American Association of University Women, 1993), 7, 10, 8. [Author's note]

[26]Albert Shanker, "Lewd or Rude?" *New Republic* (23–30 August 1993), Advertisement. [Author's note]

[27]Cynthia Crossen, *Tainted Truth: The Manipulation of Fact in America* (New York: Simon & Schuster, 1994), 17. [Author's note]

[28]Vivien Ng (Washington, D.C.: Presentation to National Women's Studies Association Annual Conference, 20 June 1993). [Author's note]

stress the "lateral" thinking typical of women and minorities and deempha-size the "vertical" thinking that white males exhibit. Lateral thinking, as McIntosh defines it, aims "not to win, but to be in a decent relationship with the universe." Vertical thinking, on the other hand, is what makes "our young white males dangerous to themselves and the rest of us — especially in a nuclear age."[29]

One of the worst ideas that vertical thinking produces, according to McIntosh, is the notion of excellence. It holds "in thrall," she explains, those who think of life in terms of advancement upward.[30] Many feminists — and other political activists as well — maintain that we should do away with the idea of excellence not only on the grounds that it is oppressive but because it is an illusion. Although they usually assert this point rather than explain it, their view seems to be that since complete objectivity is impossible, any judgment about excellence is completely subjective and meaningless. That this line of thought sets up a false dichotomy (complete objectivity and complete subjectivity are not the only choices; varying degrees of each are possible) and makes all valuations thoroughly arbitrary (including those that feminists would substitute) does nothing to slow down the attack. In her book *Ed School Follies*, educator Rita Kramer tells about listening to one of the most popular professors at Columbia University's Teacher College, one of the most prestigious institutions of teacher education in the country, condemn "norms of success, effectiveness, [and] efficiency"; assert that "we have to do something about our preoccupation with rewards and competition in this country"; and declare "relativism"[31] to be "a *good* thing." "There are no 'objective standards,'" the professor tells her students, "there is no such thing as 'objective norms.'"[32]

Inspired particularly by Harvard psychologist Carol Gilligan's *In a Different Voice*, as well as by *Women's Ways of Knowing*, a collaboratively written book, many feminists have declared excellence and objectivity to be male constructs, part of a male sphere where abstract principles, intellect, rationality, and logical thinking are valued.[33] The research on which these books depend is idiosyncratic and limited. *In a Different Voice* is based on three small studies, including one of twenty-nine women considering having

[29]McIntosh quoted in Robert Costrell, "The Mother of All Curriculums," *Brookline Citizen* (15 March 1991), 7. [Author's note]

[30]Ibid. [Author's note]

[31]*relativism:* The notion, frequently associated with feminist or multicultural approaches to education, that all values, beliefs, ideas, and so forth are culturally constructed and thus "true" only within a specific social, historical, or cultural context, the opposite of "absolutism" or "fundamentalism."

[32]Rita Kramer, *Ed School Follies: The Miseducation of America's Teachers* (New York: Free Press, 1991), 28–29. [Author's note]

[33]Carol Gilligan, *In a Different Voice: Psychological Theory and Women's Development* (Cambridge: Harvard University Press, 1982); Mary Field Belenky et al., *Women's Ways of Knowing: The Development of Self, Voice, and Mind* (New York: Basic Books, 1986). [Author's note]

an abortion; *Women's Ways of Knowing* reaches its conclusions on the basis of 135 open-ended interviews. The authors of these books do not claim to offer conclusive evidence (indeed, attempting to amass the data needed to do so would, by their lights, be a decidedly masculine undertaking). But despite this and despite the fact that the theories they offer portray women in stereotypical ways that previous generations of feminists would have found highly offensive, *In a Different Voice* and *Women's Ways of Knowing* have become widely influential. Among many professional educators, the conventional wisdom is that for female students, caring, sharing, and connectedness are what matter; that for them, feelings, emotions, and intuition provide natural ways of proceeding. Schools, which have traditionally undervalued these ways of knowing, must — so the thinking goes — now bring them to the fore.

One of the first steps in achieving this transformation is to do away with situations that create hierarchies, thus elevating some at the expense of others. Grades do this, of course, and one of the trends of our time at all levels of education has been to do away with meaningful grading:

- According to research reported by Randy Moore, editor of the *American Biology Teacher,* high school teachers gave twice as many C's as A's in 1966. By 1978, the ratio had changed dramatically, with the number of A's given exceeding the number of C's. By 1990, 20 percent of entering college students reported an A average for their entire high school career.[34]
- According to a survey conducted by the Higher Education Research Institute at the University of California at Los Angeles, in the fall of 1994, 28.1 percent of college freshmen reported average high school grades of A- or higher.[35]

The same phenomenon has occurred in higher education. At Stanford, over 70 percent of undergraduates get A's and B's; at Princeton, the number is 80 percent.[36] According to Harvard instructor William Cole, the "gentleman's C" has been replaced at his school by the " 'gentleperson's B,' and A- is gaining ground fast, especially in the humanities."[37]

Grade inflation is certainly not the accomplishment of feminists alone, but they have contributed mightily to the notion that the world in general

---

[34]Randy Moore, "Grades and Self-Esteem," *American Biology Teacher* (October 1993), 388. [Author's note]

[35]Astin et al., *The American Freshman* (1994), 13. [Author's note]

[36]Suzanne Alexander, "Trophy Transcript Hunters Are Finding Professors Have Become an Easy Mark," *Wall Street Journal* (27 April 1993), B1; Committee on Academic Appraisal and Achievement, "A Study of Grading Practices at Stanford University: Faculty Attitudes, Student Concerns, and Proposed Changes to Grading Policy" (Stanford, Calif.: Stanford University, April 1994), figure 3. [Author's note]

[37]William Cole, "By Rewarding Mediocrity We Discourage Excellence," *Chronicle of Higher Education* (6 January 1993), B1. [Author's note]

and schools in particular have for too long been run according to standards that have no justification except to advance the interests of white males. "Relativism is the key word today," explains Harvard's Cole. "There's a general conception in the literary-academic world that holding things to high standards — like logic, argument, having an interesting thesis — is patriarchal, Eurocentric and conservative."[38] So out of fashion has meaningful grading become that the *New York Times* declared Stanford University's 1994 decision to reinstitute the grade of F "an event of seismic proportions."[39]

One also senses the radical egalitarianism espoused by many feminists   25
in the movement to do away with other kinds of competition in the schools. In a section of *How Schools Shortchange Girls* that Peggy McIntosh helped write, current events and civics curricula are condemned for their tendency to focus on "controversy and conflict." Debate clubs are said to be harmful since they take for granted an "adversarial, win/lose orientation."[40] Other examples of this kind of thinking abound:

- According to an article in the *New York Times*, physical education is no longer what it used to be: "[In] the new P.E. . . . competition is out and cooperation is in." In every part of the country, schoolchildren are dancing and jumping rope, activities that do not involve competition, instead of playing games like dodgeball, from which a winner emerges.[41]

- A mother in Michigan reports to Ann Landers that her child's school no longer has spelling bees because they are regarded as unfair to children who are not good spellers.[42]

- The president of the Independent Schools Association of the Central States reports that the Illinois Junior Academy of Science prohibited a small independent school in Downers Grove, Illinois, from competing in the 1995 State Science Fair. The Downers Grove school, which makes a point of encouraging excellence, puts other schools at too much of a disadvantage, an Academy of Science official said: "We want to spread the wealth around."[43]

- Meanwhile, the executive director of the Maryland Coalition for Inclusive Education argues that honor rolls should be abolished. They

[38]Quoted in John Leo, "A for Effort. Or for Showing Up," *U.S. News & World Report* (18 October 1993), 22. [Author's note]

[39]"Making the Grades," *New York Times* (5 June 1994), Sec. 4, p. 16. [Author's note]

[40]*How Schools Shortchange Girls,* 66. [Author's note]

[41]Melinda Henneberger, "New Gym Class: No More Choosing Up Sides," *New York Times* (16 May 1993), A1. [Author's note]

[42]Ann Landers, "Part of Me Will Always Be Missing," *Chicago Tribune* (17 January 1994), Tempo section, 3. [Author's note]

[43]Quoted in Patrick F. Bassett, "The Academy of (Lesser) Science," *Education Week* (3 August 1994), 51. [Author's note]

rely on "objective" cutoff points, he complains, and reinforce "some of the least attractive aspects of our culture."[44]

Meritocracy in general has come under assault in the schools. A few years ago in the *Harvard Educational Review,* there appeared an article that has become something of a classic in the annals of educational egalitarianism. Entitled *"Tootle:* A Parable of Schooling and Destiny," the article warned about the lesson implicit in the Little Golden Book story *Tootle.* The story is about a talented young train who, after going through a period in which he breaks the first rule of trainhood and repeatedly jumps the tracks in order to wander through the meadows, learns that success, in the words of the *Harvard Educational Review* article, comes from "deferred gratification, hard work, and an achievement orientation." While one might think these good lessons to teach children, they are, according to the *Harvard Educational Review* article, part of the repressive "masculine world of technology [and] competition" to which Tootle's "sensitive, emotional, and relational qualities . . . must give way."[45]

Although this heavyhanded analysis of a simple story reads like a parody, it has been taken quite seriously. In her book *Ed School Follies,* Rita Kramer reports on a class for future teachers at Eastern Michigan University in which the professor assigns the *Harvard Educational Review* article. An older woman in the class is skeptical about the analysis it offers. "What would a six-year-old get out of [the story of Tootle]?" she asks. "I read it to my kid. 'Work hard in school' — isn't that what we all want?"

The teacher pounces on her question. "What does that sound like? Anyone?"

A young woman named Amy — the star of the class, according to Kramer — knows exactly what mistaken notion the older student is advancing: "Meritocracy! And if it doesn't work, if you don't succeed, you think, What's wrong with me?"[46]

[44]Mark A. Mlawer, " 'My Kid Beat Up Your Honor Student,' " *Education Week* (13 July 1994), 39. [Author's note]

[45]Nicholas C. Burbules, *"Tootle:* A Parable of Schooling and Destiny," *Harvard Educational Review* (August 1986), 253, 250. [Author's note]

[46]Quoted in Kramer, *Ed School Follies,* 95. [Author's note]

ENGAGING THE TEXT

1. Working in small groups, discuss the threat that Cheney sees in multicultural approaches to education. To what extent does your own experience in American classrooms support or complicate Cheney's claim that multiculturalism presents "a drearily distorted picture of [American] society"

(para. 13)? Do you agree that non-Western cultures are typically glorified in American classrooms today at the expense of American and European achievements?

2. Write a journal entry on your own experience in science classes. How accurate are Cheney's claims that American education "overlooks" the achievements of U.S. scientists and that students are taught to view science as an example of "destructive male thinking" (para. 8)?

3. Drawing on your own experiences, debate whether American schools and textbooks are overly influenced by a pro-female or feminist bias. To what extent has concern for promoting "female" behavioral and thinking styles been responsible for undermining the idea of excellence or the desire to compete and achieve in America's schools?

Exploring Connections

4. Contrast Cheney's interpretation of the position of women in education with that presented by Myra and David Sadker in "Higher Education: Colder by Degrees" (p. 228) or in "Connected Education for Women" (p. 256). Which of these analyses strikes you as more accurate? What specific aspects of each argument seem particularly persuasive or particularly weak?

5. Write an imaginary letter of response to Cheney from Mike Rose (p. 174), Richard Rodriguez (p. 202), Inés Hernández-Ávila (p. 216), or Malcolm X (p. 219). How might they react to her assessment of multicultural education and its impact on American students?

6. How might John Taylor Gatto (p. 166) or Jean Anyon (p. 186) respond to the idea that "politics" has only recently entered American classrooms through the inclusion of multicultural and feminist perspectives?

7. Look ahead to Ronald Takaki's "A Different Mirror" (p. 538). To what extent does his approach to American history support or challenge Cheney's claim that multiculturalism is unnecessarily politicizing and distorting education?

Extending the Critical Context

8. Working in small groups, research the way women and women's achievements are portrayed in a number of recent secondary school textbooks. Based on your findings, what conclusions can you reach about gender bias in textbooks?

9. Design a brief survey to test several of Cheney's claims (for example, her assertion that Americans know more about Harriet Tubman than George Washington or that Christopher Columbus is portrayed in American schoolrooms as a greedy murderer). Then administer your survey to a number of people who come from different age groups. To what extent do their responses sustain Cheney's depiction of what's happening in America's classrooms?

The Computerized Campus

THEODORE ROSZAK

Ever since the Clinton/Gore campaign of 1992 promised to take Amer-
ica for a spin on the "Information Superhighway," it seems you can't find a
visionary or pundit who doesn't see the whole country networked and
modemed by century's end. Indeed, America's rosy techno-future is the one
topic that everyone seems to agree on — from politicians on the right and
left, to cultural revolutionaries, to Fortune 500 mega-billionaires. America's
colleges and universities occupy a special place in this march toward a to-
tally wired tomorrow. The Internet was born on college campuses, and
higher education is probably the American institution that's closest to be-
coming a "virtual community." But the high-tech campus does have its skep-
tics, like Theodore Roszak, a self-proclaimed technophobe and the author of
this selection. In "The Computerized Campus," the media selection for this
chapter, Roszak offers a word of warning about mixing computers and col-
lege education and presents us with yet another version of the hidden cur-
riculum. Roszak teaches history and is director of the Ecopsychology Insti-
tute at California State University, Hayward. Twice nominated for the
National Book Award, he writes on issues of culture and the environment.
His works include The Voice of the Earth *(1993),* The Making of a Counter-
culture *(1969), and, the source of this selection,* The Cult of Information: A
Neo-Luddite Treatise on High Tech, Artificial Intelligence, and the True
Art of Thinking *(2nd ed. 1994).*

The computer has entered the world of higher education a great deal
more smoothly and decisively than it has made its way into the elementary
and secondary schools. Universities, after all, have more internal control
over their choices than do bureaucratically congested school systems. This
is also the province of learned men and women, scholars and experts who
are supposedly prepared to make discriminating judgments that rise above
the whims of the marketplace. Yet the campuses have also been targeted for
a massive merchandising campaign by the computer makers, and the effort
seems to be sweeping all before it.

Many leading universities purchased their first computer in the mid- to
late 1960s, one of the IBM hulking giants. It became *the* campus computer,
a proud and expensive possession that was frequently displayed as a sign of
status. It was usually parked in an air-conditioned computer center and
used mainly for administrative data processing. In short order, school

records became computer printouts; grades and scheduling were done with punchcards. The better endowed schools, especially those with strong science departments, quickly moved to acquire a few more of these big mainframes for their technicians; these were used as widely as possible on time-sharing arrangements that were often the arena of intense competition and bickering on the part of the faculty.

By the early 1970s, the universities began to set up multiterminal computer labs, where students as well as faculty might be permitted to lay their hands on the technology. Once again, prestigious departments would push to have their own, autonomous labs for their majors as a sign of status. About this time, optional courses in computer programming began to appear, mainly for students in the sciences, engineering, and business. The society was by then becoming highly computerized in all its major sectors; but there were few educators who thought computer literacy, in any interpretation of the term, had an urgent place in higher education. Significantly, things changed in the universities when the market changed. In the 1980s, with the advent of the microcomputer, a readily salable item, the computer industry went after academia with one of the most intense mass marketing efforts in business history. The goal has been nothing less than to place computers in the hands of every teacher and student. With the help of grants, donations, and stupendous discounts ranging up to 80 percent, the companies have succeeded in striking a number of what they hope will be bellwether deals with schools large and small. The campuses have not displayed much sales resistance to these blandishments.

Though there are only 3,400 degree-granting institutions in the United States, higher education is one of the richest markets in the information economy. It includes schools like the University of Texas, which owns more computers (18,500 Apple Macintoshes) than any other non-government operation in the world. Through the decade of the 1980s American universities are estimated to have spent some $8 billion dollars on computers. A big school like the three-campus University of Michigan (45,000 students) can budget as much as $50 million a year; but even a small school that sets out to achieve the goal of being fully wired can be a prodigious consumer of computer technology. For example, Carnegie-Mellon University with only 5,500 students has spent as much as $15 million in a single year on the new technology.[1]

Nor is it only the immediate demand they generate that makes the universities so attractive to the data merchants. The schools are the gateway to a student market populated by prospectively high-earning professionals and white collar workers, the ideal computer buyers of the future. When it comes to campaigning for computer literacy, the universities are a far richer prize than the high schools. Even schools as influential as Harvard, Yale,

[1]Linda Watkins, "On Many Campuses, Computers Now Are Vital and Ubiquitous," *Wall Street Journal,* November 30, 1984, p. 1.

and the University of California at Berkeley have seriously considered imposing such a requirement. Still more welcome than a literacy requirement would be a *property* requirement: namely, that owning a computer should be a condition of admission. This is happening, mainly at engineering schools but also at the three United States service academies. Though the machines may be well-discounted, this is surely a remarkable innovation. Has there ever been another instance of the universities making ownership of a piece of equipment mandatory for the pursuit of learning? One school, Dallas Baptist, which is among those that require every entering student to buy a computer, has gone so far as to reshape its curriculum to emphasize the computer; it insists that at least three assignments per term in each freshman course should require the use of a computer.[2]

The prospect of the fully networked university has made computer makers eager to strike ever more advantageous deals with the schools. Companies have resorted to all sorts of inducements, including generous giveaway programs. IBM has been part of $50–$70 million programs at both MIT and Brown. Since the mid-1980s, AT&T, the largest donor, has donated over $285 million in computer labs and equipment to some 60 universities.[3] In addition to offering faculty members discounted or even free computers, some companies have negotiated joint research and development projects that purchase and merchandise courseware developed by professors. The universities are a rich source for instructional innovation and the rewards can be handsome; the most widely marketed educational program, now used in hundreds of schools, is a chemistry course developed at the University of Illinois.

There is no question but that information technology will expand steadily at the universities, most obviously in technical and scientific fields. If only as word processors (the use that predominates among students) the computer has staked out a permanent place in every university department. But even the arts and humanities have a greater stake in the computer. Some of the most ambitious projects for full-text computer access, like the Center for Electronic Texts in the Humanities at Princeton and Rutgers, the E-Text Center at the University of Virginia, or the Center for Scholarly Technology at the University of Southern California, are campus-based. Since the initial euphoria that greeted the computer on campus in the early 1980s, however, some educators have grown cautious about the more extravagant pedagogical claims made for the new technology. In a major national forum in 1989, many teachers cited the troubling issues that arise from unlimited, often unmanageable information access; teaching in a "blizzard of information" raises as many problems as it solves. Some urgently

[2]For a survey of computers in the universities, see Donna Osgood, "A Computer on Every Desk," *Byte,* June 1984. Also see Judith A. Turner, "A Personal Computer for Every Freshman," *Chronicle of Higher Education,* February 20, 1985, p. 1.

[3]"AT&T Donates $7 Million in Computer Labs to 61 Schools," *Business Wire,* June 23, 1993.

called for a greater emphasis upon the distinction between raw data and knowledge, judgment, and intellectual integration.[4]

Despite these reservations, EDUCOM, the consortium of some 600 universities and 110 corporations that has become the principal lobbying agent on the campuses for new technology, continues to make ambitious predictions about the electronic campus of tomorrow. With each new computer development, EDUCOM spells out a scenario of dazzling possibilities. For example, EDUCOM tells us that when interactive multimedia finally reach the campus in full force, students will be able to find everything they need for a customized, self-paced education in one neat software package. Lecture courses will vanish; modem-to-modem tutorials with the instructor will take the place of class attendance. Instead of being "the sage on the stage," professors will become "the guide at the side" of the magic box.[5]

As if these predictions were not attractive enough, EUIT, EDUCOM's Educational Uses of Information Technology unit, has found a new enticement: cost cutting. Techniques like distance video instruction and interactive programs promise to reach more students with fewer teachers. Computerized instruction may become for the campus what automation has become for the assembly line: the royal road to down-sizing. This is a strong card to play in an era of budgetary restraint; it may even overcome the reservations some might have about the initial cost of the more expensive technology now on the market. The hardware necessary to run "Columbus," IBM's multimedia extravaganza on the life of the great explorer, is priced at $10,000 per system. Costly, but not if one considers how many teaching assistants and lecturers it will cut from the payroll.[6]

Cost cutting is the preferred managerial style of the 1990s. In that respect EDUCOM is in brisk step with the times. But as sophisticated as methods of down-sizing may be, the overall process is a bleak symptom of the nation's economic decline. And quite as much so on the campuses as in manufacturing and the white collar workplace. What EDUCOM's bright prospectus leaves out of account are the ambitions that bring many students to school in the first place. If the computer is used to slash salaries and eliminate teaching positions, what is a college degree going to be worth to those whose goal it is to become educators? There comes a point in the computer enthusiast's image of our cultural destiny that leaves creativity and imagination only one outlet: programming software, designing hardware. The fact that lecturing is an intellectual talent with its own distinct virtues, that the

10

[4]*Teaching and Technology: The Impact of Unlimited Information Access on Classroom Teaching,* Proceedings of a National Forum at Earlham College (Ann Arbor, MI.: The Pierian Press, 1991).

[5]"How Multimedia Computer Technology is Reshaping the Way Students Learn and Professors Teach," *U.S. News & World Report,* September 28, 1992.

[6]Thomas DeLoughry, "EDUCOM Hopes to Demonstrate How Computers Can Improve Instruction and Save Money," *The Chronicle of Higher Education,* July 14, 1993.

classroom encounter between teacher and student can be a rewarding experience in its own right, even the possibility that there are indispensably valuable things that can be done with the blackboard and the pencil elude the technician's worldview. A great deal that programmers see fit to eliminate in favor of their own narrow skills may be precisely that "human use of human beings" that was supposedly the greatest promise the computer had to offer.

If all works out as the computer makers would have it, there may one day be fully networked campuses where all the students and all the teachers do indeed have micros, and then perhaps they will rarely have to meet at all. They will simply exchange assignments and grades electronically. Networks may even outgrow the campuses that created them — as at the University of Houston, where teachers and students can link up from their own homes. Then, professors can not only grade their students electronically, but network with them at all hours of the day and night, and perhaps watch on line while assignments are processed across the video screen, making helpful suggestions along the way. (Of course, this sort of round-the-clock, unpredictably intrusive fraternization would be possible now by way of telephone. Which is why, in my experience, professors go to great lengths to keep their phone numbers private. I am not certain why the computer terminal, always on and demanding attention, is supposed to make unrestricted teacher-student interaction more enticing.) The ultimate goal of networking on the grandest scale is to become a "wired city" that expands into the surrounding community. Together with Bell Telephone and Warner Communications, which holds the local cable television franchise, Carnegie-Mellon University is planning to do just that in the Pittsburgh area.

One would be hard-pressed to find another time when a single industry was able to intrude its interests so aggressively upon the schools of the nation — and to find such enthusiastic receptivity (or timid surrender) on the part of educators. This is all the more remarkable when one considers that probably no two teachers or computer scientists could come up with the same definition of "computer literacy" — the goal that launched the campaign. As for the general intellectual benefits of that skill, of these there is no evidence to be found beyond the claims of the computer industry's self-promotional literature, filled with vague futuristic allusions to life in the Information Age. Yet if the computer makers succeed in their hard sell, we may soon be graduating students who believe (with their teachers' encouragement) that thinking is indeed a matter of information processing, and therefore without a computer no thinking can be done at all.

"The great university of the future will be that with a great computer system," Richard Cyert, president of Carnegie-Mellon, has announced.[7] A dramatic statement of conviction. Doubtless many educators wish their schools had the resources his university has been able to muster in laying claim to such greatness, even though it remains obscure how quantities of

[7]Cyert, quoted in *Wall Street Journal*, November 30, 1984, p. 18.

computational power translate into quality of learning. There is no question but that computers have a valuable role to play as computing devices in the technical fields, as electronic record keeping systems, or as word processors. Taken together, this is a sizable contribution for any single invention to make in the daily lives of students and teachers. But the computer enthusiasts have promised that the new technology will do more than merely replace the slide rule, the typewriter, and the filing cabinet. Its benefits supposedly reach to intellectual values at the highest level, nothing less than the radical transformation of educational methods and goals. The computer, after all, is the bountiful bringer of information, which is widely understood by educators themselves to be the substance of thought. Even Dr. Ernest Boyer, president of the Carnegie Foundation for the Advancement of Teaching, who has raised many keen criticisms on the waste and misuse of computers in the schools, agrees that "in the long run, electronic teachers may provide exchanges of information, ideas, and experiences more effectively (certainly differently) than the traditional classroom or the teacher. The promise of the new technology is to enrich the study of literature, science, mathematics, and the arts through words, pictures, and auditory messages."[8]

How disappointing it is, then, to see so much of this glowing promise come down to mere promotional gimmickry. There is, for example, the image of the fully networked campus which currently stands as the ultimate goal of computerization in the universities. Without leaving their dorms, students will be able to access the library card catalog; they will be able to log on to a student bulletin board to exchange advice, gossip, make dates, find a ride, buy used books. They will be able to submit assignments electronically to their instructors.

Yes, these things and a dozen more *can* be computerized. But why 15 *should* they be? They all get done now by the most obvious and economical means: students walk to the library, the student union, the bookstore, to a nearby coffeehouse or cafe, where they meet other human beings. They talk, they listen, they make arrangements. Outside of disabled students (for whom computers can be a boon), who ever found these ordinary perambulatory activities so burdensome as to be worth the cost of an expensive technology to eliminate them? Indeed, it has always been my thought that an intellectually vital campus is one designed in its architecture, grounds, and general spirit to make such daily human intercourse graceful and attractively frequent — rather than one that spends millions to spare its students the exercise of leaving their dorms.

When enthusiasts come up with artificial uses like these for the computer, they are really doing nothing more than teaching another lesson in technological dependence, a vice already ingrained in our culture. For obvi-

---

[8]Ernest L. Boyer, "Education's New Challenge," *Personal Computing,* September 1984, pp. 81–85.

ous commercial reasons, they are intruding a machine into places where it was never needed. Similarly, the prospect of having students submit assignments by some form of electronic mail is simply endorsing the sort of pseudo problem (like "static cling" or "wax buildup") that exists only because the hucksters invented it in the first place to sell a product. I have come across computer advertising that seems determined to make me forget that the red pencil — underscoring, circling, working along the margins and between the lines of the page (things no computer can do) — is one of the most practical teaching tools ever invented. Every experienced teacher knows this; but the ads are out to embarrass me into agreeing that, as a full-fledged member of the Information Age, I should be dealing exclusively with floppy disks, light pens, and video screens.

I will admit that, to a degree, one's criteria of educational greatness may involve matters of personal taste. Some people relish the image of schools where ranks of solitary students in private cubicles sit in motionless attendance upon computer terminals, their repertory of activities scaled down to a fixed stare and the repetitive stroking of a keyboard. I find this picture barely acceptable even where it may be justified episodically for a computer-specific exercise: some drill, computation, or graphics work. The image becomes no more appealing when I am told that working with computers is a marvelous occasion for socializing: the students cluster around the machines, taking their cues from its directives, debating the fine points of this or that response to its queries. As an educational ethos, both these situations strike me as simply another form of technological desiccation in our lives, appearing in the one place we might most want to save from its blight.

My own taste runs to another image: that of teachers and students in one another's face-to-face company, perhaps pondering a book, a work of art, even a crude scrawl on the blackboard. At the very least, that image reminds us of how marvelously simple, even primitive, education is. It is the unmediated encounter of two minds, one needing to learn, the other wanting to teach. The biological spontaneity of that encounter is a given fact of life; ideally, it should be kept close to the flesh and blood, as uncluttered and supple as possible. Too much apparatus, like too much bureaucracy, only inhibits the natural flow. Free human dialogue, wandering wherever the agility of the mind allows, lies at the heart of education. If teachers do not have the time, the incentive, or the wit to provide that, if students are too demoralized, bored, or distracted to muster the attention their teachers need of them, then *that* is the educational problem which has to be solved — and solved from inside the experience of the teachers and the students. Defaulting to the computer is not a solution; it is surrender.

But there are other issues that transcend taste, questions of educational theory, social policy, and professional ethics. It is simply wrong for any priorities about our schools to be set by those with commercial interests at stake. That vice has plagued public schools in the past; it may be more advanced now than ever, as the schools invest in glamorous machines without any clear idea of their use. They are doing so because they have absorbed mindless clichés about "information," its intellectual value and vocational urgency, that are little better than advertising copy. This has led them to overlook the degree to which educational problems are political and philosophical issues that will not yield to a technological fix.

To mention only the most obvious of the issues on which the ethics of   20 the teaching profession require candor:

- Disruptive or alienated students in the schools may reflect an anxiety, even a desperation that stems from their disadvantaged social condition or from the compulsory nature of the school system itself; no matter how equitably the computers are spread through the classrooms, these students are not apt to find the will to learn.
- Students who are being sold on computer literacy as an easy response to their job hunger are simply being deceived; what they are learning in a few computer lab experiences will not make them one iota more employable.
- Teachers who are falling back on flashy software as a convenient classroom entertainment are wasting their students' time and demeaning their own profession.

One senses how distorted the discussion of education has become in the Information Age when educators begin to draw not only upon the products but upon the language and imagery of the industrial marketplace. "Productivity" is the word Dr. Arthur S. Melmed of the Department of Education uses to define "the central problem of education. The key to productivity improvement in every other economic sector has been through technological innovation. Applications of modern information and communication technologies that are properly developed and appropriately used may soon offer education policy makers . . . a unique opportunity for productivity management."

Along the same lines, Richard Cyert of Carnegie-Mellon predicts that his school's computer network "will have the same role in student learning that the development of the assembly line in the 1920s had for the production of automobiles. The assembly line enabled large-scale manufacturing to develop. Likewise, the network personal computer system will enable students to increase significantly the amount of learning they do in the university."[9]

Computers, as the experts continually remind us, are nothing more than their programs make them. But as the sentiments above should make clear, the programs may have a program hidden within them, an agenda of values that counts for more than all the interactive virtues and graphic tricks of the technology. The essence of the machine is its software, but the essence of the software is its philosophy.

---

[9]The quotes from Melmed and Cyert come from Stephen L. Chorover, "Cautions on Computers in Education," *Byte,* June 1984, pp. 22–24.

Power and Dependency

Anyone who has watched children almost hypnotically absorbed by the dazzling display of a video game cannot help but recognize the computer's peculiar power to spellbind its users. Fortunately, the most excessive form of this electronic enchantment seems to have lost its hold on the adolescent imagination; the video arcades are fast declining in popularity. But what we have seen there at its extreme is a capacity to fascinate that has been connected with the computer since the earliest stored-program machines arrived in the universities. It reaches back to the first generation of young hackers at a few select computer labs, like that at MIT. Hackers have always been a freakish minority, highly gifted minds for whom the intricacies of the computer can become an obsession, if not an addiction; yet they play a crucial role in the history of the technology. They were the first to give themselves fully to the strange interplay between the human mind and its clever mechanical counterfeit. That interplay deserves the careful attention of educators because it carries within it a hidden curriculum that arrives in the classroom with the computer.

Among the hackers, one of the main attractions of the machine was the enthralling sense of power it gave its user, or rather its master. For one did not simply use a computer, one had to take intellectual control of it. This was a complex machine, an "embodiment of mind," as Warren McCulloch once described it, and it could easily elude effective application. Yet, even when it did so, its misbehavior arose from some rigorously consistent extension of its programming that demanded understanding. It was not like an automobile, which would malfunction simply because a part wore out; its problems were not merely physical. They could only be corrected by tracking the bug through the dense logic of the machine's program. But if the hacker mastered that logic, he could bend the computer to his will. ("His" is historically correct here; notably, nearly all the early hackers, like most hackers since, were male, many of them living in "bachelor mode.") As one computer genius reported to Steven Levy, who has written the best history of the early hackers, there was a day when he came to the "sudden realization" that "the computer wasn't so smart at all. It was just some dumb beast, following orders, doing what you told it to in exactly the order you determined. You could control it. You could be God."[10]

But the satisfaction of becoming the machine's God, of lowering it to the status of a "dumb beast," is not available to everyone; only to those who can outsmart the smart machine. First it has to be respected as an uncanny sort of mind, one that can perform many mental tricks better than its user. The relationship of the human being to the machine is, thus, an ambivalent one, a complex mixture of sensed inferiority and the need to dominate, of

25

[10]The quote is from Steven Levy, *Hackers: Heroes of the Computer Revolution* (New York: Anchor Doubleday, 1984) 284. In this section, I am following Levy's excellent and entertaining history of the early hackers.

dependence and mastery. "Like Aladdin's lamp, you could get it to do your bidding." That is how Levy describes a certain exhilarating moment of truth in the early hackers' encounter with the computer. But like Aladdin's lamp, the machine holds a genie more powerful than the human being who temporarily commands its obedience.

The word *power* is freely sprinkled through the literature of computers. The computer is a "powerful tool"; it is fueled by "powerful theories" and "powerful ideas." "Computers are not good or bad," Sherry Turkle concludes in her study of the psychology of young computer users. "They are powerful."[11] As we have seen, computer scientists have been willing to exaggerate that power to superhuman, even godlike dimensions. Perhaps it will soon be "an intelligence beyond man's." These heady speculations on the part of respected authorities are not simply whimsical diversions; they are images and aspirations that weave themselves into the folklore of the computer and become embedded in the priorities that guide its development. They are intimately involved in the sense of power that surrounds the machine, even as it is playfully presented to children at the basic level of computer literacy.

This can be a deeply illuminating educational moment for children — if it comes to them in the right way. It is their introduction to the form of power that most distinguishes their species: the power of the mind. At some point, they must learn that the phantom cunning and resourcefulness of the mind provides a greater biological advantage than size and strength, that intelligence counts for more than the brute force of muscle or of engines that replace muscle. In ancient Greece, children learned the value of cunning from the exploits of Odysseus, the man "of many devices." American Indian children learned cleverness from the mythic figure of Coyote the Trickster. All folklore features these masters of guile, who teach that a good trick may outdo the strongest sinews in the risky adventures of life.

In the modern West, the survival power of the mind has come to be concentrated in the "many devices" of our technology, and now most importantly in a smart machine which is the culmination of that technology. Whatever simple, gamelike computer exercises children may learn, they are also learning that the computer possesses what adults regard as the highest kind of power, a power that is similar to what human beings do when they lay plans, store up information, solve problems: something mindlike.

Because of this mindlikeness, the little box with the video screen on top, which doesn't look anything like a person, has come to be surrounded by all sorts of personifications. One "talks" to the computer. It "understands" — or doesn't understand. It "asks" and "answers" questions. It "remembers" things. It says "please" and "thank you." Above all, it "teaches"   30

---

[11]Sherry Turkle, *The Second Self: Computers and the Human Spirit* (New York: Simon and Schuster, 1984), p. 218.

and "corrects" because it "knows" things and knows them better. If computer literacy takes hold in our schools, students may not be learning these mindlike qualities from another human being, but most often from a machine. Even if they are also learning from a teacher, the teacher will not be a "powerful" device. No one — certainly no computer scientist — has ever described a teacher's mind as "a powerful tool." Why not? Because teachers cannot know as much as the box. The box can hold lots more information. Even if the little computer in the classroom is limited in its capacity, the children know there are other, bigger computers that are running the world they live in. They can be seen in the bank, the store, the doctor's office. And when all the computers are put together, they have a power no teacher can have. They never make mistakes. That is the power which adults respect and would have children aspire to: the power of always being right, quickly and absolutely. But this is a power that can only come through the machine. As one children's book puts it: "Computers never make mistakes. If there is a mistake, it is made by the people who are using the computer or because the computer is broken."[12] The mixture of loose, anthropomorphic metaphors, interactive software, and commercial imagery that accompany the computer into the classroom brings with it a clear, if subliminal, lesson. It is the lesson the computer's inventors and dominant users have ingrained in the technology: a conception of thinking, of order, of intellectual priorities. It goes something like this:

Here is a form of power. It is a power of the mind. It is the greatest power of the mind — the power to process limitless information with absolute correctness. We live in an Information Age that needs that power. Getting a job, being successful, means acquiring that power. The machine has it; you don't. As time goes on, the machine will have more and more of it. It will deserve that power because it fits better with the world than human brains. The only human brains that can be trusted are those that use the machine to help them think.

This lesson can be transmitted in an unthreatening, even inviting way. That is the style of all computer instruction. Start simple. Make it fun. Build confidence. Ideally, the machine should be "user friendly" — a curiously condescending phrase which suggests that the machine is being kind enough to simplify and slow down for less talented users who need to be babied along. Most encouraging of all, the machine will share its power with its users. It can be domesticated and brought into one's home as a mental servant. All one needs to do is adjust to the machine's way of thinking. Becoming computer literate, comments Paul Kalaghan, dean of computer science at Northeastern University, "is a chance to spend your life working with devices smarter than you are, and yet have control over them. It's like carrying a six-gun on the old frontier."[13]

---

[12]Melvin Berger, *Computers* (New York: Coward, McCann & Geohegan, 1972).

[13]Kalaghan, quoted in *New York Times,* January 13, 1985, p. A1.

ENGAGING THE TEXT

1. According to Roszak, what arguments or claims are commonly made for including computers in the classroom? Can you think of any other reasons
that are commonly put forward to support the use of information processing technology in educational settings?

2. Why does Roszak reject the idea of the electronic campus as a goal? What
is his vision of the ideal campus? To what extent are these visions mutually
exclusive? Which one do you prefer? Why?

3. Working in small groups, discuss how important computers have been in
your own education. What evidence does your group see to support the
claim that computers are changing the way we learn? Do you think that instructors should be required to involve computers in all college classes?

4. What, according to Roszak, is the hidden curriculum that comes along with
computerized instruction? Why does he feel that the unconscious "lessons"
that accompany computer-assisted instruction are so dangerous? To what
extent do you agree or disagree with his concerns? Why?

EXPLORING CONNECTIONS

5. How might computerized instruction change the educational "lessons"
taught by John Taylor Gatto's "Seven-Lesson Schoolteacher" (p. 166)?
Would the electronic campus be likely to intensify or diminish the negative effects Gatto associates with the hidden curriculum of American
education?

6. How might Myra and David Sadker (p. 228) explain the rapid spread
of computer technology throughout higher education? Do you think that
computers promote educational approaches and attitudes that are more
congenial to men than to women?

EXTENDING THE CRITICAL CONTEXT

7. Working in small groups, sketch a rough map of your campus, highlighting
places that encourage the kind of lively communal interaction that Roszak
describes. Then sketch a model of what a fully computerized campus
would look like. Which would you prefer? Why?

8. Poll ten or more students on your campus to find out if they would choose
to take classes from a computerized "instructor" if they had the option. As
part of your poll, ask them to explain the reasons that underlie their preferences. Share the results in small groups and try to reach some conclusions
about what your findings tell you about students, instructors, electronic
technology, and campus life.

The Hard Part Is Making It Happen
DEBORAH MEIER AND PAUL SCHWARZ

Throughout this chapter you've had the chance to ponder how "hidden curriculums" shape the thinking and values of American students. You've also met a few individuals — like Mike Rose, Richard Rodriguez, and Malcolm X — who learned to learn despite the obstacles they encountered in formal educational settings. Now you'll read about an entire school whose innovative methods have produced lots of successful students, exactly where you might least expect to find them. Central Park East Secondary School, founded by Deborah Meier and Paul Schwarz, represents a remarkable achievement. In one of the most ethnically diverse and economically depressed urban areas in the nation, a group of dedicated teachers threw away the rule book and the standard curriculum — hidden or otherwise — and learned how to make education work for their students. Deborah Meier began teaching as a kindergarten instructor in Chicago. Since then she has received honorary degrees from Harvard, Yale, Brown, and Columbia Universities for her work as an educational innovator. She is president of the Center for Collaborative Education in New York and serves as a part-time fellow at the Annenberg National Institute for School Reform at Brown University. Paul Schwarz is co-director of Central Park East Secondary School and is a Thompson Fellow at the Coalition of Essential Schools at Brown University. This selection originally appeared in Democratic Schools *(1995), edited by Michael W. Apple and James A. Beane.*

Central Park East Secondary School (CPESS), an alternative high school, expands on the successful learning environment created at the Central Park East Elementary Schools over the last 20 years. The secondary school is a cooperative project of Community School Board #4, the New York City Board of Education Alternative High School Division, and the Coalition of Essential Schools, a national high school network.

CPESS was started in the fall of 1985 with 80 7th graders. The school currently enrolls 450 students in grades 7–12 and although CPESS will not grow larger, we have begun the creation of 11 new Coalition high schools in New York City. The students who attend CPESS are mostly neighborhood (East Harlem) residents. Eighty-five percent of the students are African American or Latino, and more than 20 percent are eligible for service provided by special education. From careful tracking of our students, even when they move and attend other schools, we know that 97.3 percent of the students who have attended CPESS graduated from high school. And 90 percent of those graduates attended college.

The fundamental aim of CPESS is to teach students to use their minds well, to prepare them for a well-lived life that is productive, socially useful, and personally satisfying. The school's academic program stresses intellectual achievement and emphasizes the mastery of a limited number of centrally important subjects. This program goes hand in hand with an approach that emphasizes learning how to learn, how to reason, and how to investigate complex issues that require collaboration and personal responsibility.

The final high school diploma is not based on time spent in class or Carnegie units, but on each student's clear demonstration of achievement through the presentation of 14 portfolios to a graduation committee. The school's values include high expectations, trust, a sense of personal decency, and respect for diversity. The school is open to all students and expects a lot from each student.

The school is guided by the principles of the Coalition of Essential Schools, a national organization of high schools directed by Ted Sizer. The Coalition's principles include:

1. *Less is more.* It is more important to know some things well than to know many things superficially.

2. *Personalization.* Although the course of study is unified and universal, teaching and learning are personalized. No teacher is responsible for teaching more than 80 students (40 at CPESS) or advising more than 15.

3. *Goal setting.* High standards are set for all students. Students must clearly exhibit mastery of their school work.

4. *Student as worker.* CPESS teachers "coach" students, encouraging them to find answers and, in effect, to teach themselves. Thus, students discover answers and solutions and learn by doing rather than by simply repeating what textbooks (or teachers) say.

Habits of Mind, Work, and Heart

It was Friday, May 2, 1992. Our students had spent the week talking, organizing, and dealing with powerful feelings in the wake of the Rodney King verdict and the riots in Los Angeles. As luck would have it, an all-white choir from a small Michigan town was scheduled to sing for us that day. While L.A. was burning, and probably scared to death, the choir faced an audience of mostly African American and Latino teenagers, many still brimming with eagerness to protest. There was tension in the air as one of our seniors stepped up to ask if he could a say a few words that he thought might help.

"I took it on myself to come up here and talk to all you students about what we've been going through. I know from the Senior Institute that a lot of students have been talking about what's been going on in L.A., and it bothers them a lot.

"I just wanted to tell you that no one here is our enemy . . . and that we have to stick together.

" . . . and that there's lots of people from . . . Michigan, right?" The students laugh. "Michigan, not California, right?" There is more laughter from students.

"What they are doing here, they are doing for us. They are not here to 10
make us feel better. They are here because they like to sing, and they're here to show us what they've got.

"They are not our enemies either. There is no one in this room that is our enemy. If we can stick together and stay with each other, we can show these people that we are not falling apart like some other people are." Cheers and whoops fill the room.

"You got to do what you got to do, but showing your anger at these people here isn't going to do anything for any of us."

If the primary public responsibility and justification for tax-supported schooling is raising a generation of fellow citizens, then the school — of necessity — must be a place where students learn the habits of mind, work, and heart that lie at the core of such a democracy.

Since you can't learn to be good at something you've never experienced — even vicariously — then it stands to reason that schools are a good place to experience what such democratic habits might be. It's as simple as that, and as complex. You can't learn to play a game you've never seen played. No one would think of raising up musicians without being sure to place them in the company of musicians, including some at the top of their art.

Our task at CPESS was to take this idea seriously once again, and re- 15
turn the business of rearing our young to such basic principles. Instead of placing students in cohorts of equal ignorance and creating settings in which no expert ever performed his or her craft in the presence of novices and in which no one, novice or expert, ever showed what they could do, but only talked about it, we tried to turn the tables on it all.

We'd keep the idea of kindergarten, where we both began our careers, going all the way through high school — and long after, we hoped. We wanted a schoolhouse that was naturally organized to be interesting, just like a good kindergarten room. We wanted a place where young people and their teachers could work in shared ways around topics and materials they were inclined to enjoy, for long stretches of time, and without too many preconceived strictures. We wanted opportunities for the least expert to watch and observe the more expert, and then to practice out at their own pace. We wanted settings in which people knew each other through each other's works, through the close observation of actual practice — by our teacher colleagues and our student colleagues. A truly collegial setting.

So, we knew we had to be small, multi-aged, intimate, and interesting. Family and school would need to be allies, as the two institutions responsible for shared child-rearing tasks. Between us, we had to find ways to make the idea of growing up seem wonderful and enticing, and noticeably varied enough to include everyone. We had to make the idea of being a powerful citizen on an ever broadening platform, with the capacity to play effective roles both in public and private, seem feasible and imaginable and appealing.

That's what good schooling could do. But it took taking apart all this large and wordy rhetoric and finding the details that counted, just as we had both done when we daily set about putting together our kindergarten classrooms, from the block corner to the sand table, the selection of particular books, the organizing of pencils and paints, the placement of works of art, always with particular children in mind, always with particular purposes in mind.

So we put together CPESS, over time, collectively, modifying as we went, mindful of all the details of a place filled with many stories as well as common purposes. We created a structure in which people — students and students, students and teachers, and teachers and teachers, and their families — could think aloud together and jointly make decisions. We had to define what "using your mind well," the Coalition of Essential Schools' overarching mission, meant. What were the habits of mind that defined a democratic citizen? We thought of friends who were "good citizens" and tried to imagine what it was that they had in common. Surely it wasn't the ability to recall some body of facts or information, although they were curious about such mundane details. The two qualities that seemed to define our ideal citizen were *empathy* and *skepticism:* the ability to see a situation from the eyes of another and the tendency to wonder about the validity of what we encountered.

Our operational definition of a thoughtful person, a person whom we   20
would be proud to claim as a graduate of our school, was one who could demonstrate to us, in a variety of ways and in numerous disciplines, that he or she was in the habit of tackling the following five questions:

- How do you know what you know? (Evidence)
- From whose viewpoint is this being presented? (Perspective)
- How is this event or work connected to others? (Connections)
- What if things were different? (Supposition)
- Why is this important? (Relevance)

We have organized our curriculum and our assessment around the idea that a person in the habit of looking for answers to these five questions when presented with a novel situation is using his or her mind well. The nuances, the vocabulary, the tools change from physics to literature to geometry and so on. If these questions are the right ones, however, they ought also to apply to the playground and the workplace. Of course, such habits are neither learned nor used in a vacuum. They are embedded in appropriate subject matter; they depend on the ability of the learner to use skills of reading, writing, logic, computation, research, and scientific inquiry to give them substance. But we hold to the concept of their universality across subject matter and age. A person in the habit of asking these five questions is a thoughtful person.

In fact, the biggest step we took was deciding that a student would graduate CPESS almost entirely on the basis of evidence of such thoughtfulness, over and over again in 14 designated fields of work. We called this Graduation by Portfolio, although our portfolios are compilations not merely of written work, but of everything and anything students believe speaks to their meeting the graduation standards we have spelled out.

We invented graduation committees, which are a little like doctoral committees. Each committee includes at least two faculty members, an adult of the student's choice, and another student member. Their job is to read, review, observe, listen to the evidence, and make appropriate recommendations for revision or approval. When we started, it was hard for us to imagine such a process. But today stories like the one . . . [below] reinforce our commitment to this time-consuming process.

A Meeting of the Graduation Committee

It is a warm Friday afternoon in September and Monique's graduation committee has convened for the first time. As we wait for Monique's mother to arrive (each student is allowed to choose one adult, and Monique has chosen her mother — according to local wisdom, always a risky choice). Monique is so nervous she can't sit still. "I've got to go to the bathroom," she says, and makes her third trip in the last 15 minutes.

Finally, we all settle in around a table in my office and Monique begins   25
her presentation. She has chosen to present a paper on AIDS discrimination in health care. She refers to her paper, but only occasionally. At the start, she is somewhat ashen-faced. She sits bolt upright, as opposed to her usual adolescent slump, and begins nearly every sentence with "I put . . ." — as in "I put in an interview with a nurse who works in the emergency room to describe the feelings of a professional whose primary responsibility is not AIDS-related."

Monique finishes her presentation and asks if there are any questions. She knows there will be. This is the part of the meeting where committee members probe to see if she has acquired our five habits of mind, the hallmark of a CPESS graduate. We begin gently asking her for the source of some of her information. She handles these questions easily. Students always discuss committee experiences with their friends, and Monique expected questions about sources.

But the questions quickly become less predictable. "Monique," I ask, "you spoke of doctors who screened patients for the HIV virus without their

text continues on page 296

The 14 Portfolio Areas:
An Overview for Students and Parents

The primary responsibility of the Senior Institute student is to complete the 14 portfolio requirements listed below.

These portfolios reflect cumulative knowledge and skill in each area as well as the specific CPESS habits of mind and work. Students will present the work in all 14 portfolio areas to their Graduation Committee for review and acceptance. They will meet for a full review of their seven chosen "majors" to present, discuss, and defend their work. There are, therefore, two stages to keep in mind: (1) preparation of the portfolio materials in collaboration with the advisor and others, and (2) presentation and defense of the materials. In some cases, portfolio work will need to be expanded, modified, and represented for final approval. Students may also choose to present work a second time to earn a higher assessment.

It is important to remember that a majority of the work done in connection with a portfolio can and should be the outcome of the courses, seminars, internships, and independent study that a student has engaged in during the normal course of his or her Senior Institute years. In addition, some of the material may be an outgrowth of work initiated in Divisions I or II or, where appropriate (e.g., the Language Other Than English portfolio), work completed prior to entering the Senior Institute.

Portfolios include work in 14 areas: seven "majors" and seven "minors." There is no one way to complete these requirements, nor one way to present them. People are different, and the individual portfolio will reflect these differences. The term "portfolio" covers all the ways in which a student exhibits his or her knowledge, understanding, and skill. CPESS recommends interdisciplinary studies wherever possible, so work completed to meet one requirement may be used to fulfill other requirements as well.

While the final review is based on individual accomplishment, almost all portfolio requirements can be based on work done in collaboration with others, including group presentations. Such collaborative work is encouraged, since it often enables a student to engage in a much more complex and interesting project.

Quality and depth of understanding, good use of CPESS's five habits of mind, and the capacity to present competent and convincing evidence of mastery as relevant to each particular field are the major criteria used by the Graduation Committee; however, portfolio work must reflect a concern for both substance and style. For example, written work must be submitted in clear, grammatical English that reflects the expected proficiency level of a high school graduate in spelling, grammar, and legibility. Errors should be eliminated before the portfolio is presented to the committee. Written work must generally be submitted in typewritten form. The same care in preparation and presentation applies to all other forms of work. Portfolio work should represent a student's best effort. The same holds true for the manner of presentation.

Different characteristics are more or less relevant to each portfolio area. Each academic discipline, for example, has developed its own "scoring grid" to help students and Graduation Committee members focus objectively on the appropriate criteria. Over time, the criteria for acceptable performance will be more fully developed through both the creation of new scoring grids and the compilation of past student work that demonstrates accepted levels of skill. Students are expected to become familiar with the criteria by which they are measured (both the scoring grids and former student work).

At Graduation Committee meetings, students should be prepared to discuss not only the content of the portfolio, but their computer knowledge and growth in particular fields of work.

The following are the 14 Portfolio areas:

1. Postgraduate Plan
2. Science/Technology°
3. Mathematics°
4. History and Social Studies°
5. Literature°
6. Autobiography
7. School and Community Service and Internship
8. Ethics and Social Issues
9. Fine Arts/Aesthetics
10. Practical Skills
11. Media
12. Geography
13. Language Other Than English/Dual Language Proficiency
14. Physical Challenge

Senior Project

One of the above portfolio topics or items will be separately assessed as a final Senior project. Each student is required to make a major presentation in 7 of the 14 areas described above. These include the four starred Portfolios, and at least three others chosen in cooperation with the advisor. Grades of Distinguished, SatPlus, Sat, or Min-Sat will be used to grade work as a whole. In the seven "minor" portfolios, a student will be graded pass/fail. Passing will be upon recommendation of the advisor and approval of the full Graduation Committee.

The student may, however, request a grade from the advisor (Distinguished, SatPlus, etc.). In this case, the student must provide the committee with sufficient time to review all relevant materials and to discuss the recommended grade at a meeting of the committee. Such a grade would be subject to approval by the entire committee.

knowledge or permission. You see this as a bad thing, an invasion of their privacy. Just last Sunday I saw a TV program about Cuba and their response to the AIDS epidemic. In Cuba they test everyone. They don't ask permission. When they find an HIV-positive person, they quarantine them. They are put in a comfortable place with good food and excellent health care, but they must stay there. Period. One result is that they have greatly lessened the spread of the disease. What if they were to do that here?"

Monique is on her own here. She certainly did not anticipate this question, and she can't begin her answer with "I put." But something happens to her at that moment; a physical change takes place, one that I've often seen at a graduation committee meeting. Monique doesn't hesitate. She straightens up, leans forward, looks me right in the eye, and says, "My father died of AIDS and that's why I decided to present this portfolio first. It is real important to me."

She continues, "I would be in favor of anything that prevents AIDS or even slows it down a little bit, but I don't know about not telling people that you are testing them. I can see both sides of the question and I don't want to decide. I think we should take a vote."

"Who should vote?" I ask.   30

"Everyone," she answers immediately. "Even little kids. This is so important that everyone should be able to vote."

The committee meeting ends after an hour of presentation and questions. Committee members fill out grids that we have created here at CPESS: one to assess the major project in the portfolio (our portfolios are compilations of work) and a tabulation form that gives a grade for this portfolio, her first of seven major portfolios.

As I announce the grade to Monique — a better than satisfactory grade — and give her our feedback on what we thought was strong in her work and what we thought might have improved the portfolio, she grins from ear to ear. She is back to her younger self. She can hardly listen to us and immediately excuses herself to go and talk to Yuiza and Frances, her best friends, who are waiting in the lobby for her.

I put papers and forms and tabulation sheets away and prepare for my next graduation committee. Carlos is presenting his literature portfolio — or rather, he is presenting himself as a person in the habit of using his mind well, of using our habits of mind, and he is going to demonstrate these qualities through his work in the field of literature.

After school, I meet some school friends and they ask me why I am   35 so "high." It is because occasionally, during committee meetings like Monique's, I witness the fruits of our work together. I see the hidden hours of struggle that so many teachers and parents and students have invested in learning. The committee meetings are not only our final assessment, they are often "payoff time," a concrete reward for having studied and read and written and argued and thought so long and so hard.

And once in a while I see magic. Not sleight-of-hand magic, but the magic of a child's first step or her first word. Magic that has been earned. The magic of students growing up as thinkers, gaining confidence, showing off their minds — of a young person changing, in front of my eyes, into a woman who is confident, thoughtful, and competent.

The Choices We Have Made

How did we create graduation committees as rigorous and as personal as the one described above? How did we create a school organization that allows teachers to attend to details, the way early childhood teachers do? The changes we have made are not simple. They have forced us to make weighty choices, and there have been sacrifices involved in each of them.

Half-Day, Theme-Centered Classes

CPESS offers a common core curriculum for all students in grades 7 through 10, organized around two major fields: math/science for half the school day and humanities (art, history, social studies, and literature) for the other half.

Each class is centered around a theme. Here, for example, are two themes of study, one in humanities and one in math/science, both taken from the curriculum of our Division II, 9th and 10th grades:

Justice: Systems of Laws and Government. At least two very different   40 concepts of justice are explored in this year-long theme: one consensual and the other adversarial. Ideas of fairness, conflict resolution, and equity are examined in these two societies. The American justice system and critical legal landmarks are examined in detail. Students develop firsthand experience with the preparation and defense of a legal brief. They explore the jury system and the nature of evidence. The essential questions in the study are: How is authority justified? How are conflicts resolved? Are justice, morality, and fairness synonymous?

Motion and Forces of Energy is a two-year theme driven by the following essential questions: How do things move? How does energy behave in its different forms? Is energy ever made or lost? In the investigation of these questions, students work on projects such as designing and analyzing an original amusement park ride or doing a scientific analysis of a projectile (e.g., a basketball or a javelin in flight). They used a variety of commercially produced computer software to model and analyze projectile motion and collisions of two or more bodies. The theme includes an emphasis on the scientific method and the techniques of statistics and probability. Students also investigate the mathematical themes of counting, measuring, locating, and describing, which lead them to a more intense study of algebra, geometry, trigonometry, mathematical transformations, vectors, and matrices.

In grades 7 through 10, each class period is two hours long, and each teacher teaches two classes a day rather than the five classes that are common in many other schools. This change has meant a reconceptualization of instructional practice. Two-hour classes push teachers to use a variety of strategies, such as whole-group instruction, small-group collaborative work, library research, and hands-on problem solving. The teacher can't bore kids by lecturing them for two hours at a time.

Instruction in the Senior Institute — our name for grades 11 and 12 — works a little differently. Students in this transitional stage spend more time taking courses out of our building: at colleges and museums, at internships, and in independent study. A substantial portion of their day is also spent with their advisors, preparing for graduation and the steps beyond.

Small Classes

A second priority is to reduce not only the number of classes taught, but also class size. To accomplish this goal, we have chosen to concentrate the great bulk of the resources allotted to us in core classroom instruction. As we have grown from a single 7th grade class in 1985 to our full complement today, we have made the ratio of students to teachers our priority. We have no guidance counselors, no gym teacher (although we do have an extensive intramural program and a substantial afterschool athletic program), no music teacher, and a single art teacher for the whole school. We have no department chairs, no deans, and one social worker; in return for class sizes of under 20, other teachers have assumed many of the functions traditionally carried out by these personnel. All professional staff are advisors to a group of under 15 students for two years. This group meets for several hours each week, and it is the advisor who has long-range, in-depth relationships with each student's family.

Critical Friends

Powerful as this educational process is, it puts us at odds with ideas of curriculum and assessment that stress memorization and coverage. This kind of learning is personal; it requires internalizing, not just saying, difficult ideas. It assumes an active role by the learner and, like other creative acts, it is unpredictable and full of surprises. No textbooks or standardized tests exist for teaching this way. Adults must work together to constantly re-create curriculum, invent new forms for exhibiting knowledge, and decide when the school is ready to say, "She's done it. It's time to hand her a diploma." Such chutzpa requires that standards be constantly discussed and agreed on.

External colleagues, what we call "critical friends," are essential to help us look critically at the school's work. "Autonomy" can't be synonymous with privacy. Quite the opposite. CPESS, and its work, are always public. We bring in experts of various sorts several times a year to help us set standards and examine our curriculum. For instance, professors from local colleges and universities have come to our school and reviewed the writing quality of portfolio items, in almost all cases confirming our staff's own evaluations of the items. And we've even had critical friends join us for a full day of graduation portfolio review. These teachers from traditional public schools in New York City, state education department employees, principals of comprehensive high schools, principals and teachers from our sister schools, foundation representatives, and outside experts looked at portfolios of differing quality, talked to students about their studies, and watched videotapes of student presentations. They also met with us and with teachers, offering thought-provoking comments, criticisms, and advice on a range of topics, from the structure of our school to academic requirements. By opening our program to this kind of outside scrutiny, we hold ourselves accountable to the public while also providing rich collaborative experiences for the staff.

Time for Planning, Collaboration, and Assessment

To make such collaboration possible we had to address another priority: teacher time. We had to build into the professional life of teachers time for adults to do this new kind of planning, collaboration, and assessment. Every Monday, staff meet from 3:00 to 4:30. On Friday, we have classes from 8:00 to 1:00, and the staff meet again from 1:30 until 3:00. This is three hours a week that staff work together on whole-school issues. Some of that time is used by vertical teams (all the humanities teachers and all the math/science teachers) to meet and discuss scope and sequence and standards of work from 7th grade through graduation. At least once a month, our whole staff gathers to discuss issues of race, class, and gender. And once a month, we gather to consider school matters such as family conferences, report writing or reports, and recommendations from various working subgroups. Several times a year, we meet over weekends for public review of students' work and developing curriculum. We've even raised some funds to pay teachers a stipend for working during July on collaborative projects.

In addition, each week we have carved out a three-hour block of time for teams of teachers who work with the same students to meet. We have done this by requiring that each student in grades 7 through 10 have a community service placement. We have one teacher who is responsible for these placements. We organize the placements so that students who go into the community to work do so in constellations of 80 students per day. This arrangement frees teams of teachers to work together for that half day. The students check in with their advisor at 9:00 A.M. and then go to their placement. They return at noon and go to lunch and midday options (gym, library, etc.). Their teachers have until 1:00 to plan collaboratively, and the students have rich opportunities for using their minds in a wide variety of institutions, from day-care classrooms to museums, hospitals, and homes for the aged.

These formal and informal gatherings that take place all day long are where "staff development" occurs. They are where the newest teacher learns his or her trade, and senior staff reexamine and revisit old issues. While everyone complains occasionally of being exhausted — and so we skip a meeting here and there — we don't complain of burnout. We're never treated like appliances, but are in control of our own profession.

Through these varied forms of face-to-face meetings, the governance of   50
the school is enacted. Decisions are made, wherever possible, by those who must implement them. But decisions also belong to the wider community of staff, parents, and students, and they have always the right to ask that a decision be reconsidered, defended, and explained. In these open and accessible ways, staff and students learn about the complexities of democracy. They learn of its limitations and of the realities of institutional trade-offs. And they imagine how they might even do it better. We ourselves are forever tinkering with ways to govern better (and less), using the same habits of mind we ask of our students.

Altered Perceptions

We come back to the personal (as former kindergarten teachers, we couldn't do otherwise), which includes looking at children as members of their family and reflecting on how schooling has altered both children's and family's perceptions of themselves. One mother described to an audience of teachers how this kind of schooling has changed her family; her words convey what it is we hope for from our schooling:

> As we (our family) became familiar with the process of presenting work for criticism to a supportive group of peers, we all became involved with it.
>
> I remember when Zawadi (my middle daughter) was doing a portfolio item on Philip Parnell, a case of a teenager who was shot down and killed by a police officer in New Jersey. I went to the library with her and we did extensive research. She told me what to look for.
>
> She interviewed my brother, who is a NYC police officer, so she could get a feeling for what a police officer feels like when something like that happens. She didn't want her exhibition to be biased . . .
>
> I watched her formulate her questions. I watched her interview people. I watched her over a period of several years pull all that information into a play that she decided to use as a vehicle for her presentation.
>
> And then I watched her have her friends from school come to my living room. I watched her become the director. And I watched her listen to them — to take into account how they felt — how they would have responded in that case.

My son chose to focus on his experience as a child living in three different states and how they impacted on who he has become.

This having to define himself was insightful to us all. His accounts of specific instances of racism were validated by his sisters and led to family discussions about those instances and how they could be empowering if you change the anger to strength.

My youngest daughter has taken to documenting the family history, which has brought into the picture the total United States history and the history of the Caribbean. She has had to do extensive research around those oral histories, which are important to me because I grew up with them but never thought to document them. This process allowed her to do that and to give her the time so that she wasn't doing the rote kind of work our children used to do, but she was placing her time in something that was meaningful and important to her, and she was excited about that.

The history of progressive education has largely been written in schools for young children — in kindergartens and early childhood centers and Head Start centers. Its spokespeople have been professionals who have studied and practiced their craft with the young. Maria Montessori, Jean Piaget, John Dewey, Lillian Weber and Barbara Biber, and so many other teachers who have gone before. They created schools where what students studied was intimately connected to their lives, and where people had a chance to work and learn side by side. Our success at CPESS is to re-create those structures and to implement goals in settings where older students learn. It is also our challenge.

We have created a structure where it is possible to learn to know students well so they can learn to use their minds well; we have created a structure where teachers can be in responsible control of their professional lives and where there is a strong professional community supporting them; we have created an assessment system that can hold students to high standards without standardization; we have created a curriculum structure based on habits of mind that focus on tools for thinking, not just bits and pieces of information. That's the easy part; the hard part is making it happen.

ENGAGING THE TEXT

1. Skim Meier and Schwarz's description of Central Park East Secondary School (CPESS) and jot down, in your own words, a list of the main concepts that make this school work and that distinguish it from more traditional schools. Compare notes with other students and discuss which of these concepts are most important. Has your own schooling been built on a similar or different philosophy of education?

2. How, according to the authors, does CPESS work to promote democratic values? How does this approach compare with your own experience of the

way "citizenship" is typically taught? Do you agree with Meier and Schwarz
that school "must be a place where students learn the habits of mind, work,
and heart that lie at the core of . . . a democracy" (para. 13)?

3. Do you see any potential problems with the CPESS approach to education? If this model of education is so effective, why hasn't it become more
   widespread?

EXPLORING CONNECTIONS

4. How do the goals of CPESS compare with those described in *Report of the
   French Commission* (p. 159)? Working in groups, draw up your own priori-
   tized list of what you feel should be the top three or four purposes of public
   education.

5. To what extent do the innovations that underlie the CPESS approach to
   education challenge the seven lessons that John Taylor Gatto (p. 166) identifies with the hidden curriculum of public schooling? How do you think
   Gatto would respond to the model of education presented by Meier and
   Schwarz?

6. Jean Anyon describes four types of schools in her excerpt from *Social Class
   and the Hidden Curriculum of Work* (p. 186). Which of these four does
   CPESS most closely resemble, and why?

7. Contrast the differing notions of citizenship preparation that underlie
   CPESS and Lynne V. Cheney's approach to education (p. 263). What kinds
   of citizens would each be likely to produce?

EXTENDING THE CRITICAL CONTEXT

8. The approach to education at CPESS focuses on five "essential questions"
   and "Habits of Mind" (paras. 19–20). Organize a group to draft and post
   key questions or principles that you feel would be appropriate for guiding
   your own intellectual development as a writer.

9. Drawing on the CPESS model and ideas you've encountered in other readings in this chapter, work in groups to draft a proposal for an ideal school.
   Make your proposal as detailed as possible, addressing the structure of the
   school day, the kinds of materials taught, teaching and learning methods,
   student and teacher roles and responsibilities, class sizes, length of class periods, even the design and setting of campus buildings.

3

Money and Success

*The Myth of
Individual Opportunity*

Ask most people how they define the American Dream and chances are they'll say, "Success." The dream of individual opportunity has been at home in America since Europeans discovered a "new world" in the Western Hemisphere. Early immigrants like Hector St. Jean de Crèvecoeur extolled the freedom and opportunity to be found in this new land. His glowing descriptions of a classless society where anyone could attain success through honesty and hard work fired the imaginations of many European readers: in *Letters from an American Farmer* (1782) he wrote, "We are all animated with the spirit of an industry which is unfettered and unrestrained, because each person works for himself. . . . We have no princes, for whom we toil, starve, and bleed: we are the most perfect society now existing in the world." The promise of a land where "the rewards of [a man's] industry follow with equal steps the progress of his labor" drew poor immigrants from Europe and fueled national expansion into the western territories.

Our national mythology abounds with illustrations of the American success story. There's Benjamin Franklin, the very model of the self-educated, self-made man, who rose from modest origins to become a renowned scientist, philosopher, and statesman. In the nineteenth century, Horatio Alger, a writer of pulp fiction for young boys — fiction that you will get to sample below — became America's best-selling author with rags-to-riches tales like *Struggling Upward* (1886) and *Bound to Rise* (1873). The notion of success haunts us: we spend millions every year reading about the rich and famous, learning how to "make a fortune in real estate with no money down," and "dressing for success." The myth of success has even invaded our personal relationships: today it's as important to be "successful" in marriage or parenthood as it is to come out on top in business.

But dreams easily turn into nightmares. Every American who hopes to "make it" also knows the fear of failure, because the myth of success inevitably implies comparison between the haves and the have-nots, the achievers and the drones, the stars and the anonymous crowd. Under pressure of the myth, we become engrossed in status symbols: we try to live in the "right" neighborhoods, wear the "right" clothes, eat the "right" foods. These emblems of distinction assure us and others that we are different, that we stand out from the crowd. It is one of the great paradoxes of our culture that we believe passionately in the fundamental equality of all, yet strive as hard as we can to separate ourselves from our fellow citizens.

Steeped in a Puritan theology that vigorously preached the individual's responsibility to the larger community, colonial America balanced the drive for individual gain with concern for the common good. To Franklin, the way to wealth lay in practicing the virtues of honesty, hard work, and thrift: "Without industry and frugality nothing will do, and with them every thing. He that gets all he can honestly, and saves all he gets . . . will certainly become RICH" ("Advice to a Young Tradesman," 1748). And Alger's heroes were as concerned with moral rectitude as they were with financial gain: a benefactor advises Ragged Dick, "If you'll try to be somebody, and grow up into a respectable member of society, you will. You may not become rich, — it isn't everybody that becomes rich, you know, — but you can obtain a good position and be respected." But in the twentieth century the mood of the myth has changed. Contemporary guides to success, like Robert Ringer's enormously popular *Looking Out for Number One* (1977), urge readers to "forget foundationless traditions, forget the 'moral' standards others may have tried to cram down your throat . . . and, most important, think of yourself — Number One. . . . You and you alone will be responsible for your success or failure." The myth of success may have been responsible for making the United States what it is today, but it also seems to be pulling us apart. Can we exist as a living community if our greatest value can be summed up by the slogan "Me first"?

The chapter begins with two readings that define the myth of success. First, a selection from Alger's *Ragged Dick* serves as a classic expression of the American Dream. The myth is updated — and extended to African Americans — with the selection from Rose Blue and Corrine Naden's *Colin Powell: Straight to the Top*, a biography of the black military leader written for young readers. The rosy picture painted in these opening pieces is complicated by subsequent readings. Harlon Dalton's "Horatio Alger," for example, examines the myth that made Alger popular and finds it "socially destructive." The oral history of Stephen Cruz, a successful Mexican American engineer, reveals a man pursuing the Dream but gradually becoming disillusioned with it.

The myth of individual opportunity implies that social class is not very important: anyone can become President; anyone can get rich quick. As our next group of readings suggests, however, class can matter, even in America. In "Rewards and Opportunities," Gregory Mantsios explores the forces that maintain vast inequities of wealth, power, and opportunity. "The Lesson," by Toni Cade Bambara, dramatizes these inequities by presenting them through the eyes of a group of kids from Harlem who venture uptown to see how the rich live and spend. "Have-Mores and Have-Lesses," by Donald L. Barlett and James B. Steele, presents the discomforting thesis that rich and poor in the United States are getting farther and farther apart as the middle class disappears; if this is true, the American Dream can become a reality only for a tiny percentage of elite citizens.

Just as social class can matter, so can race. Curtis Chang's "Streets of Gold" complicates the myth of the American Dream by challenging the media-created stereotype of the successful Asian American. In contrast, "The Black Avenger" by conservative talk show host Ken Hamblin downplays the importance of race and celebrates the vitality of the American Dream, specifically its openness to black Americans willing to seize their opportunities. In "Number One!" African American journalist Jill Nelson offers a thought-provoking sketch of her father and the ambivalence he felt about making it in America.

The chapter closes with two positive rereadings of the meaning of success. In "Good Noise: Cora Tucker," Anne Witte Garland presents the story of an African American activist who measures success in terms of lives saved instead of dollars spent. Finally, Sucheng Chan's "You're Short, Besides!" profiles a woman who has resisted the definitions of race, gender, and physical ability imposed on her by a society obsessed with mythic images of success.

Sources

Peter Baida, *Poor Richard's Legacy: American Business Values from Benjamin Franklin to Donald Trump.* New York: William Morrow, 1990.

J. Hector St. Jean de Crèvecoeur, *Letters from an American Farmer.* New York: Dolphin Books, 1961. First published in London, 1782.

BEFORE READING

- Working alone or in groups, make a list of people who best represent your idea of success. (You may want to consider public and political figures, leaders in government, entertainment, sports, education, or other fields.) List the specific qualities or accomplishments that make these people successful. Compare notes with your classmates, then freewrite about the meaning of success: What does it mean to you? To the class as a whole?

- Keep your list and your definition. As you work through this chapter, reread and reflect on what you've written, comparing your ideas with those of the authors included here.

- Write a journal entry that captures the thoughts of the man pictured in the photo at the beginning of this chapter (p. 303). What feelings or attitudes can you read in his expression, his dress, and his body language? How do you think he got where he is today?

From *Ragged Dick*
HORATIO ALGER

The choice of Horatio Alger to exemplify the myth of individual opportunity is almost automatic. Alger's rags-to-riches stories have become synonymous with the notion that anyone can succeed — even to generations of Americans who have never read one of the books that were best-sellers a

*century ago. The excerpt below is typical of Alger's work in that it focuses on
a young man's progress from a poor background toward "fame and fortune." Alger (1832–1899) published over a hundred such stories; most observers agree that their popularity depended less on their literary accomplishments than on the promises they made about opportunity in America
and the rewards of hard work.*

Dick now began to look about for a position in a store or counting-
room. Until he should obtain one he determined to devote half the day to
blacking boots, not being willing to break in upon his small capital. He
found that he could earn enough in half a day to pay all his necessary ex-
penses, including the entire rent of the room. Fosdick desired to pay his
half; but Dick steadily refused, insisting upon paying so much as compensation for his friend's services as instructor.

It should be added that Dick's peculiar way of speaking and use of
slang terms had been somewhat modified by his education and his intimacy
with Henry Fosdick. Still he continued to indulge in them to some extent,
especially when he felt like joking, and it was natural to Dick to joke, as my
readers have probably found out by this time. Still his manners were considerably improved, so that he was more likely to obtain a situation than when
first introduced to our notice.

Just now, however, business was very dull, and merchants, instead of
hiring new assistants, were disposed to part with those already in their employ. After making several ineffectual applications, Dick began to think he
should be obliged to stick to his profession until the next season. But about
this time something occurred which considerably improved his chances of
preferment.

This is the way it happened.

As Dick, with a balance of more than a hundred dollars in the savings   5
bank, might fairly consider himself a young man of property, he thought
himself justified in occasionally taking a half holiday from business, and
going on an excursion. On Wednesday afternoon Henry Fosdick was sent by
his employer on an errand to that part of Brooklyn near Greenwood Cemetery. Dick hastily dressed himself in his best, and determined to accompany
him.

The two boys walked down to the South Ferry, and, paying their two
cents each, entered the ferry-boat. They remained at the stern, and stood by
the railing, watching the great city, with its crowded wharves, receding from
view. Beside them was a gentleman with two children, — a girl of eight and
a little boy of six. The children were talking gayly to their father. While he
was pointing out some object of interest to the little girl, the boy managed
to creep, unobserved, beneath the chain that extends across the boat, for

the protection of passengers, and, stepping incautiously to the edge of the boat, fell over into the foaming water.

At the child's scream, the father looked up, and, with a cry of horror, sprang to the edge of the boat. He would have plunged in, but, being unable to swim, would only have endangered his own life, without being able to save his child.

"My child!" he exclaimed in anguish, — "who will save my child? A thousand — ten thousand dollars to any one who will save him!"

There chanced to be but few passengers on board at the time, and nearly all these were either in the cabins or standing forward. Among the few who saw the child fall was our hero.

Now Dick was an expert swimmer. It was an accomplishment which he   10
had possessed for years, and he no sooner saw the boy fall than he resolved to rescue him. His determination was formed before he heard the liberal offer made by the boy's father. Indeed, I must do Dick the justice to say that, in the excitement of the moment, he did not hear it at all, nor would it have stimulated the alacrity with which he sprang to the rescue of the little boy.

Little Johnny had already risen once, and gone under for the second time, when our hero plunged in. He was obliged to strike out for the boy, and this took time. He reached him none too soon. Just as he was sinking for the third and last time, he caught him by the jacket. Dick was stout and strong, but Johnny clung to him so tightly, that it was with great difficulty he was able to sustain himself.

"Put your arms round my neck," said Dick.

The little boy mechanically obeyed, and clung with a grasp strengthened by his terror. In this position Dick could bear his weight better. But the ferry-boat was receding fast. It was quite impossible to reach it. The father, his face pale with terror and anguish, and his hands clasped in suspense, saw the brave boy's struggles, and prayed with agonizing fervor that he might be successful. But it is probable, for they were now midway of the river, that both Dick and the little boy whom he had bravely undertaken to rescue would have been drowned, had not a row-boat been fortunately near. The two men who were in it witnessed the accident, and hastened to the rescue of our hero.

"Keep up a little longer," they shouted, bending to their oars, "and we will save you."

Dick heard the shout, and it put fresh strength into him. He battled   15
manfully with the treacherous sea, his eyes fixed longingly upon the approaching boat.

"Hold on tight, little boy," he said. "There's a boat coming."

The little boy did not see the boat. His eyes were closed to shut out the fearful water, but he clung the closer to his young preserver. Six long, steady strokes, and the boat dashed along side. Strong hands seized Dick and his youthful burden, and drew them into the boat, both dripping with water.

"God be thanked!" exclaimed the father, as from the steamer he saw the child's rescue. "That brave boy shall be rewarded, if I sacrifice my whole fortune to compass it."

"You've had a pretty narrow escape, young chap," said one of the boatmen to Dick. "It was a pretty tough job you undertook."

"Yes," said Dick. "That's what I thought when I was in the water. If it hadn't been for you, I don't know what would have 'come of us."   20

"Anyhow you're a plucky boy, or you wouldn't have dared to jump into the water after this little chap. It was a risky thing to do."

"I'm used to the water," said Dick, modestly. "I didn't stop to think of the danger, but I wasn't going to see that little fellow drown without tryin' to save him."

The boat at once headed for the ferry wharf on the Brooklyn side. The captain of the ferry-boat, seeing the rescue, did not think it necessary to stop his boat, but kept on his way. The whole occurrence took place in less time than I have occupied in telling it.

The father was waiting on the wharf to receive his little boy, with what feeling of gratitude and joy can be easily understood. With a burst of happy tears he clasped him to his arms. Dick was about to withdraw modestly, but the gentleman perceived the movement, and, putting down the child, came forward, and, clasping his hand, said with emotion, "My brave boy, I owe you a debt I can never repay. But for your timely service I should now be plunged into an anguish which I cannot think of without a shudder."

Our hero was ready enough to speak on most occasions, but always felt   25
awkward when he was praised.

"It wasn't any trouble," he said, modestly. "I can swim like a top."

"But not many boys would have risked their lives for a stranger," said the gentleman. "But," he added with a sudden thought, as his glance rested on Dick's dripping garments, "both you and my little boy will take cold in wet clothes. Fortunately I have a friend living close at hand, at whose house you will have an opportunity of taking off your clothes, and having them dried."

Dick protested that he never took cold; but Fosdick, who had now joined them, and who, it is needless to say, had been greatly alarmed at Dick's danger, joined in urging compliance with the gentleman's proposal, and in the end our hero had to yield. His new friend secured a hack, the driver of which agreed for extra recompense to receive the dripping boys into his carriage, and they were whirled rapidly to a pleasant house in a side street, where matters were quickly explained, and both boys were put to bed.

"I aint used to goin' to bed quite so early," thought Dick. "This is the queerest excursion I ever took."

Like most active boys Dick did not enjoy the prospect of spending half   30
a day in bed; but his confinement did not last as long as he anticipated.

In about an hour the door of his chamber was opened, and a servant
appeared, bringing a new and handsome suit of clothes throughout.

"You are to put on these," said the servant to Dick; "but you needn't get
up till you feel like it."

"Whose clothes are they?" asked Dick.

"They are yours."

"Mine! Where did they come from?"   35

"Mr. Rockwell sent out and bought them for you. They are the same
size as your wet ones."

"Is he here now?"

"No. He bought another suit for the little boy, and has gone back to
New York. Here's a note he asked me to give you."

Dick opened the paper, and read as follows, —

"Please accept this outfit of clothes as the first instalment of a debt   40
which I can never repay. I have asked to have your wet suit dried, when you
can reclaim it. Will you oblige me by calling to-morrow at my counting
room, No. — , Pearl Street.

> "Your friend,
> "JAMES ROCKWELL."

When Dick was dressed in his new suit, he surveyed his figure with par-
donable complacency. It was the best he had ever worn, and fitted him as
well as if it had been made expressly for him.

"He's done the handsome thing," said Dick to himself; "but there
wasn't no 'casion for his givin' me these clothes. My lucky stars are shinin'
pretty bright now. Jumpin' into the water pays better than shinin' boots; but
I don't think I'd like to try it more'n once a week."

About eleven o'clock the next morning Dick repaired to Mr. Rockwell's
counting-room on Pearl Street. He found himself in front of a large and
handsome warehouse. The counting-room was on the lower floor. Our hero
entered, and found Mr. Rockwell sitting at a desk. No sooner did that
gentleman see him than he arose, and, advancing, shook Dick by the hand
in the most friendly manner.

"My young friend," he said, "you have done me so great a service that I
wish to be of some service to you in return. Tell me about yourself, and
what plans or wishes you have formed for the future."

Dick frankly related his past history, and told Mr. Rockwell of his de-   45
sire to get into a store or counting-room, and of the failure of all his applications thus far. The merchant listened attentively to Dick's statement, and,
when he had finished, placed a sheet of paper before him, and, handing him
a pen, said, "Will you write your name on this piece of paper?"

Dick wrote, in a free, bold hand, the name Richard Hunter. He had very much improved his penmanship, as has already been mentioned, and now had no cause to be ashamed of it.

Mr. Rockwell surveyed it approvingly.

"How would you like to enter my counting-room as clerk, Richard?" he asked.

Dick was about to say "Bully," when he recollected himself, and answered, "Very much."

"I suppose you know something of arithmetic, do you not?"   50

"Yes, sir."

"Then you may consider yourself engaged at a salary of ten dollars a week. You may come next Monday morning."

"Ten dollars!" repeated Dick, thinking he must have misunderstood.

"Yes; will that be sufficient?"

"It's more than I can earn," said Dick, honestly.   55

"Perhaps it is at first," said Mr. Rockwell, smiling; "but I am willing to pay you that. I will besides advance you as fast as your progress will justify it."

Dick was so elated that he hardly restrained himself from some demonstration which would have astonished the merchant; but he exercised self-control, and only said, "I'll try to serve you so faithfully, sir, that you won't repent having taken me into your service."

"And I think you will succeed," said Mr. Rockwell, encouragingly. "I will not detain you any longer, for I have some important business to attend to. I shall expect to see you on Monday morning."

Dick left the counting-room, hardly knowing whether he stood on his head or his heels, so overjoyed was he at the sudden change in his fortunes. Ten dollars a week was to him a fortune, and three times as much as he had expected to obtain at first. Indeed he would have been glad, only the day before, to get a place at three dollars a week. He reflected that with the stock of clothes which he had now on hand, he could save up at least half of it, and even then live better than he had been accustomed to do; so that his little fund in the savings bank, instead of being diminished, would be steadily increasing. Then he was to be advanced if he deserved it. It was indeed a bright prospect for a boy who, only a year before, could neither read nor write, and depended for a night's lodging upon the chance hospitality of an alley-way or old wagon. Dick's great ambition to "grow up 'spectable" seemed likely to be accomplished after all.

"I wish Fosdick was as well off as I am," he thought generously. But he   60
determined to help his less fortunate friend, and assist him up the ladder as he advanced himself.

When Dick entered his room on Mott Street, he discovered that some one else had been there before him, and two articles of wearing apparel had disappeared.

"By gracious!" he exclaimed; "somebody's stole my Washington coat and Napoleon pants. Maybe it's an agent of Barnum's, who expects to make a fortun' by exhibitin' the valooable wardrobe of a gentleman of fashion."

Dick did not shed many tears over his loss, as, in his present circumstances, he never expected to have any further use for the well-worn garments. It may be stated that he afterwards saw them adorning the figure of Micky Maguire; but whether that estimable young man stole them himself, he never ascertained. As to the loss, Dick was rather pleased that it had occurred. It seemed to cut him off from the old vagabond life which he hoped never to resume. Henceforward he meant to press onward, and rise as high as possible.

Although it was yet only noon, Dick did not go out again with his brush. He felt that it was time to retire from business. He would leave his share of the public patronage to other boys less fortunate than himself. That evening Dick and Fosdick had a long conversation. Fosdick rejoiced heartily in his friend's success, and on his side had the pleasant news to communicate that his pay had been advanced to six dollars a week.

"I think we can afford to leave Mott Street now," he continued. "This   65
house isn't as neat as it might be, and I should like to live in a nicer quarter of the city."

"All right," said Dick. "We'll hunt up a new room tomorrow. I shall have plenty of time, having retired from business. I'll try to get my reg'lar customers to take Johnny Nolan in my place. That boy hasn't any enterprise. He needs somebody to look out for him."

"You might give him your box and brush, too, Dick."

"No," said Dick; "I'll give him some new ones, but mine I want to keep, to remind me of the hard times I've had, when I was an ignorant boot-black, and never expected to be anything better."

"When, in short, you were 'Ragged Dick.' You must drop that name, and think of yourself now as" —

"Richard Hunter, Esq.," said our hero, smiling.   70

"A young gentleman on the way to fame and fortune," added Fosdick.

ENGAGING THE TEXT

1. List the values, characteristics, and actions that help Ragged Dick succeed. How valuable do you consider these today? How important is virtue compared to good luck — in the story and in your own experience?

2. Skim the Alger selection to find as many mentions of money as you can. How frequent are they? What seem to be Alger's ideas about money, wealth, salaries, and other financial issues?

3. Quite a few things have changed since Dick "was an ignorant boot-black, and never expected to be anything better" (para. 68). What are the changes? What seems to be Alger's attitude toward them?

4. Why is Alger careful to note that Dick does not hear Mr. Rockwell's offer of $10,000 to whomever would save Little Johnny? Is Dick being shortchanged by getting a job and clothes but not a $10,000 reward?

EXPLORING CONNECTIONS

5. Look ahead to "Horatio Alger" by Harlon Dalton (p. 320). Does Dalton's analysis of the Alger myth change your understanding of this excerpt? Explain. What elements in this story might Dalton cite to support his claims?

6. Read "Looking for Work" by Gary Soto (p. 42). Compare and contrast Alger's ideas about work, money, and aspiration to those found in Soto's narrative.

EXTENDING THE CRITICAL CONTEXT

7. Dick considers himself a "young man of property" when he has $100 in the bank. Talk to classmates and see if you can reach any consensus about what it would take today to be a "young man or woman of property." Similarly, see if you can agree on what a good starting salary would be for a recent college graduate, or on what levels of wealth and income define the poor, the middle class, and the upper class in the United States today.

8. If you did the first "Before Reading" assignment on page 306, compare and contrast the qualities that made the people on your list successful with the qualities Alger gives to Ragged Dick.

From *Colin Powell:*
Straight to the Top

ROSE BLUE AND CORINNE J. NADEN

Nowadays America's appetite for mythic heroes is fed by fact more than fiction. News shows and magazines profile "stars" who have achieved remarkable success in almost every field. But the stars that burn brightest are those, like General Colin Powell, who embody the rags-to-riches story of success. This selection comes from a book for young readers that reduces the full-length biographies of Powell to their mythic essence. Powell, who rose from humble roots to become the top-ranking U.S. military officer, has often been called the modern embodiment of the American Dream, a kind of real-life Horatio Alger hero. Most important, Powell's success is often cited as a validation of the Dream for African Americans. Working both independently and as collaborators, Rose Blue (b. 1931) and Corinne J. Naden (b. 1930) have published many books for children and young adults; this excerpt comes from one of their several co-authored biographies of famous Americans.

On August 2, 1990, Iraq invaded and conquered Kuwait. The news shocked the world. Kuwait is on the Persian Gulf, sandwiched between Iraq to the north and west and Saudi Arabia to the south. This is part of the troubled area called the Middle East.

Oil-rich Kuwait is a tiny desert land that is only a little larger than the state of Connecticut. Overpowered by Iraq, Kuwait asked the United Nations (U.N.) for help. Saudi Arabia, afraid of being invaded next, also turned to the world organization. The United Nations said Iraq was wrong. To protect Saudi Arabia, President George Bush sent U.S. troops there. This was the start of Operation Desert Shield. The U.S. forces were soon joined by troops from Britain, France, Egypt, and other U.N. members.

During the next few months, many countries urged Iraq to leave Kuwait. Iraq's leader, Saddam Hussein, refused. Finally, the United Nations ordered Iraq to get out of Kuwait by January 15, 1991. War was threatened.

January 15 came and went. Iraq did not budge. One day later, on January 16, Operation Desert Shield turned into Operation Desert Storm. The United States and its allies went to war against Iraq. U.S. Secretary of Defense Richard Cheney told the nation, "The liberation of Kuwait has begun."

The war became known as the Persian Gulf War. The allied forces   5
numbered more than half a million. Most were U.S. troops. They faced an
even larger Iraqi army. The Americans were fighting a war in a desert thousands of miles from home.

Even before the first shot was fired, President Bush counted on the
help of his top military adviser, the chairman of the Joint Chiefs of Staff
(JCS). The JCS includes the top people in all the branches of the U.S. military. The chairman that President Bush counted on was a four-star general
in the U.S. Army. His name is Colin Luther Powell.

As chairman of the JCS, Colin Powell was the highest-ranking military
officer in the United States and the world's most powerful soldier. He was
fifty-two years old when he took over as chairman on October 1, 1989. That
made him the youngest chairman ever. He was also the first black American
to have this job.

Colin Luther Powell is an impressive person. He stands six feet, one
inch tall and weighs two hundred pounds. His dark, close-cropped hair is
graying. It is said (although probably not to his face) that he has "teddy
bear" good looks. His husky frame is held straight. He *looks* like a general.

Powell is every inch the military professional. He is quiet, serious, and
businesslike. His manner is polished and even-tempered. He also has a
sense of humor, and he can talk to civilians and military people with the
same ease.

Powell was born into a poor black immigrant family. How did he rise to   10
become the country's top military man? There was no magic shortcut. Powell once said, "People keep asking the secret of my success. There isn't any
secret. I work hard and spend long hours. It's as simple as that." He advised
young people, "There is no substitute for hard work and study. Nothing
comes easy."

Things were not easy for young Colin Powell. He was born in Harlem
in New York City on April 5, 1937. Many blacks and other minorities live
in Harlem. It is part of the borough of Manhattan. New York City, the nation's largest city, has four other boroughs — Brooklyn, Queens, Staten Island, and the Bronx. When Colin was still a young child, his family moved
to the South Bronx. He grew up in a four-bedroom apartment on Kelly
Street.

The South Bronx was, and still is, a poor neighborhood. Colin's mother
and father came to America in the 1920s from the island of Jamaica in the
Caribbean. Both parents worked in the garment district of New York City.
Maud, Colin's mother, was a seamstress. Luther, his father, was a shipping
clerk.

Colin Powell grew up to be a serious, strong military leader. But tears
can still cloud his eyes when he speaks of his mother and father. They both
died in the 1980s. "As I grow older," he has said, "I have greater and greater
affection for my parents."

Maud and Luther Powell were serious people with a dream. They wanted a better life for Colin and his sister, Marilyn, who is five and a half years older than Colin. For the Powells, education was the key to a better life. Colin's mother graduated from high school; his father did not. If Maud Powell got annoyed at her husband, she would remind him just *who* had the high school diploma.

The Powells taught their children that success comes with hard work. 15 "You must set a goal and do your job well," they said.

A reporter once suggested that Colin Powell got to the top because his parents taught him values. The general had this reply: "Kids don't pick up training because parents sit around and talk to them about values. Children watch their parents *live* values. Youngsters don't care what you say, but they watch what you do."

The future general grew up in a warm, loving, hardworking family. His sister, Marilyn, remembers that when the family first moved to the South Bronx, there were few children his age in the neighborhood. So Colin went everywhere with her. "He was a tagalong brother," she says. She recalls that he was "really a pretty average boy," but he always "had a sense of direction." She was not surprised by his later success, only by the "greatness of it." Today Marilyn Powell Berns is married and is a teacher in Santa Ana, California.

The neighborhood around Kelly Street included people of many kinds. There were blacks and Puerto Ricans, and there was a large Jewish population. As Colin grew older, he played stickball on the streets with friends. He served as an altar boy at St. Margaret's Episcopal Church. And, of course, he went to school — first to the neighborhood elementary school, and then to Morris High School nearby. After school, he worked at a furniture store in his neighborhood. He learned a little of the Yiddish language from the store's Jewish owners. "I had a great childhood," he later recalled.

Colin was not an honor student. He admits that at school he sometimes "horsed around." His sister laughingly says that he was a "late bloomer." A late bloomer is someone who succeeds in school or at a career at an older age than most other people do. Colin Powell gives hope to all late bloomers who are C students. That was his grade average during high school and college.

Powell went to City College of New York (CCNY) in 1954. The school 20 is now part of City University of New York (CUNY). He had no career in mind, but City College was free to New York students. He worked part-time after classes.

In his second semester of college, Powell joined the Reserve Officers Training Corps (ROTC). This program trains college students to become officers in the army. Powell's group was known as the Pershing Rifles. He later said that he joined because he liked the uniform. Actually, the military had always impressed him. He was a young boy during World War II and a teenager during the Korean War.

According to an old saying, some people "find a home in the army." In other words, sometimes a person is just right for military life. Colin Powell and the army seemed just right together. This C student got straight A's in his ROTC classes in all four years of college. When his group took summer training at Fort Bragg, North Carolina, he was named "outstanding cadet."

Powell earned a degree in geology (the study of the history of the earth, especially through rocks) from CCNY in 1958. He graduated at the top of his ROTC group. He was a Pershing Rifles company commander, a cadet colonel (ROTC's highest rank), and a "distinguished military graduate." The late bloomer was blooming.

One of Powell's ROTC classmates at CCNY was Mitchell Strear, who later became a school principal in New York City. Strear recalls: "Even back then Colin drew attention when he entered a room. At the age of eighteen, his bearing, manner, and presence were special. You just knew he would become a leader. The infantry has a motto: 'Follow me.' Colin's manner of acceptance of responsibility and leadership all said 'Follow me.'"

Powell decided to follow the army. On June 9, 1958, he became a second lieutenant. He earned sixty dollars a week. His parents encouraged him. They felt that, like most young men at the time, he would have been drafted into the military anyway. The Powells thought that their son would serve a tour of duty, then come home and get a "real job." Instead, he went into the army to stay. He had "found a home." To him, a career in the military was "an honorable profession and a contribution to society."

But success in the military was not certain for Powell. In his profession, the most successful people have usually come from "the Point" — the U.S. Military Academy at West Point, New York. Many famous American generals were West Pointers. They include President Dwight D. Eisenhower and General Douglas MacArthur, who fought in World War II, and Robert E. Lee and Ulysses S. Grant, both generals in the Civil War.

General Colin Powell did not go to West Point. Yet he did make it to the top in the army. He once said: "Although I had to compete in my military schooling with West Pointers . . . my CCNY foundation was so solid, I never regretted going anywhere but to City."

Lieutenant Powell was sent to training school at Fort Benning, Georgia. At that time, blacks and whites were segregated — kept apart by law — in many places. In the South, blacks were required to attend separate schools, which were generally not as good as the schools for whites. Blacks ate at segregated restaurants, sat in separate seats on buses and in movie theaters, and drank from separate water fountains.

Late in the 1950s, that was beginning to change. Blacks all over the country were beginning to demand, and win, civil rights — the basic rights of all citizens. But many whites still wanted the races to be kept separate. Thus, when Colin Powell went to Fort Benning at the age of twenty-one, he felt the shock of racism for the first time.

25

"On Kelly Street in the South Bronx, everybody was a minority," Powell   30
later said. "I didn't know what a 'majority' was." But he realized his status
soon enough. When he stopped at a restaurant in Columbus, Georgia, the
waitress refused to serve him a hamburger unless he went around to the
back door.

Even after he became the army's top man, Powell never forgot how
much blacks had suffered. He became a student of black history and an ad-
mirer of Martin Luther King, Jr., who led the civil rights struggle in the
1950s and 1960s. Powell has advised young black Americans: "Don't let
your blackness, your minority status, be a problem to you. Let it be a problem to somebody else. . . . Beat them at it. Prove they're wrong. If you work
hard, do the best you can, take advantage of every opportunity that's put in
front of you, success will come your way."

In his own career, Powell has done just that. "In the army," he once
said, "I never felt I was looked down on by my white colleagues. I've been
given the opportunity to compete fair and square with them." It helped, he
added, that he "came along at a time of change, a time of growth in civil
rights."

Today, blacks make up about twelve percent of the U.S. population but
about thirty percent of the U.S. Army. Why? The main reason is opportunity. Segregation is against the law, but blacks still face many barriers to
success. The military offers a chance for education and advancement. It also
offers less racism than probably any other career.

Black Americans have fought with honor in all of America's wars. But
the military has not always treated them so honorably. Blacks fought in the
American Revolution, but many were slaves. During the War of 1812
against the British, blacks fought in the Battle of New Orleans. But General
Andrew Jackson had to argue with the government before they were paid.

Black troops fought in the Civil War, in World War I, and in World   35
War II. They served bravely and well. But they were segregated — in separate fighting units, separate officers' clubs, and separate jobs. Men who
cooked or served food to officers, for instance, were nearly always black.

In 1948, after World War II, President Harry S Truman signed Executive Order 9981. It *officially* ended segregation in the armed forces. The
problem didn't go away overnight. There was still racism. But today there is
no segregation in any of the U.S. armed services.

Besides Colin Powell, a number of blacks have had outstanding military
careers. During World War II, Benjamin O. Davis, Sr., became the first
black general in the U.S. Army. Benjamin O. Davis, Jr., his son, became a
lieutenant general in the U.S. Air Force and the highest-ranking black in
the military in 1965. At West Point in 1932, his classmates had refused to
talk to him because of his race.

Black women have also succeeded in the military. Such people have
made Colin Powell's path easier. "We should be grateful," he once said,

"for what all these men and women have done before. We cannot let the torch drop."

ENGAGING THE TEXT

1. Why do people point to Powell as the embodiment of the American Dream?

2. Asked about the secret of his success, Powell said, "There isn't any secret. I work hard and spend long hours. It's as simple as that" (para. 10). Is it that simple? Explain.

3. Aside from the biographical facts about Powell, what are the primary messages about success, hard work, and race embedded in this text? To what extent do you agree or disagree with them?

4. What features of this text mark it as having been written specifically for young readers?

EXPLORING CONNECTIONS

5. Compare and contrast Powell to Ragged Dick (p. 306). How can these two rather different figures both embody the same myth? Has the myth changed in any way between Dick's time and ours?

6. Look at the cartoon by Kristen Smith on page 312. How do the ideas about success in the cartoon contrast with the myth of success as embodied by Colin Powell and Ragged Dick? To what extent do you think Americans today equate success with an easy job and high pay?

EXTENDING THE CRITICAL CONTEXT

7. The brief account of the Persian Gulf War given above cannot, of course, explore the full complexity of that historical event. What are some of the Persian Gulf War issues that don't show up in this account for young readers? Also discuss other issues or events the authors simplify for their audience.

8. Find one or more of the full-length biographies of Powell in your college or community library. Read the "adult" version of some of the events mentioned above, such as Powell's schooling, his role in the Persian Gulf War, his experience with segregation, and so forth. Report to the class what you find, making special note of how accurately the biography for young readers reflects the fuller accounts you read.

Horatio Alger

Harlon Dalton

The two preceding selections dramatize the American Dream coming true: the success stories of the fictional Ragged Dick and the real-life Colin Powell exemplify the myth of individual success in America, as both men rise above poverty to reach their goals. This piece by Harlon Dalton questions that myth, calling it not only false, but worse — "socially destructive." Using Alger as his prime example, Dalton systematically explains how the rags-to-riches myth can conceal important social realities like race and class. Dalton is a professor at Yale Law School and author of Racial Healing: Confronting the Fear Between Blacks and Whites *(1995), from which this selection is taken.*

Ah, Horatio Alger, whose name more than any other is associated with the classic American hero. A writer of mediocre fiction, Alger had a formula for commercial success that was simple and straightforward: his lead characters, young boys born into poverty, invariably managed to transcend their station in life by dint of hard work, persistence, initiative, and daring.[1] Nice story line. There is just one problem — it is a myth. Not just in the sense that it is fictional, but more fundamentally because the lesson Alger conveys is a false one. To be sure, many myths are perfectly benign, and more than a few are salutary, but on balance Alger's myth is socially destructive.

The Horatio Alger myth conveys three basic messages: (1) each of us is judged solely on her or his own merits; (2) we each have a fair opportunity to develop those merits; and (3) ultimately, merit will out. Each of them is, to be charitable, problematic. The first message is a variant on the rugged individualism ethos. . . . In this form, it suggests that success in life has nothing to do with pedigree, race, class background, gender, national origin, sexual orientation — in short, with anything beyond our individual control. Those variables may exist, but they play no appreciable role in how our actions are appraised.

This simply flies in the face of reality. There are doubtless circumstances — the hiring of a letter carrier in a large metropolitan post office, for example — where none of this may matter, but that is the exception rather than the rule. Black folk certainly know what it is like to be favored, disfavored, scrutinized, and ignored all on the basis of our race. Sometimes

---

[1]Edwin P. Hoyt, *Horatio's Boys: The Life and Works of Horatio Alger, Jr.* (Radnor, Penn.: Chilton Book Company, 1974).

we are judged on a different scale altogether. Stephen Carter has written movingly about what he calls "the best black syndrome," the tendency of White folk to judge successful Black people only in relation to each other rather than against all comers. Thus, when Carter earned the second-highest score in his high school on the National Merit Scholarship qualifying test, he was readily recognized as "the best Black" around, but somehow not seen as one of the best students, period.[2]

Although I would like to think that things are much different now, I know better. Not long ago a student sought my advice regarding how to deal with the fact that a liberal colleague of mine (and of Stephen Carter's) had written a judicial clerkship recommendation for her in which he described her as the best Black student to have ever taken his class. Apparently the letter caused a mild stir among current law clerks in several courthouses, one of whom saw fit to inform the student. "What was the professor [whom she declined to name] thinking of?" she wondered aloud. "What does his comment mean? What is a judge supposed to make of it? 'If for some reason you think you have to hire one of them, then she's the way to go'? I could understand if he said I was one of the top ten students or even the top thousand, but what does the 'best Black' mean?"

Black folk also know what it is like to be underestimated because of the 5 color of their skin. For example, those of us who communicate in standard English are often praised unduly for how well we speak. This is, I might add, an experience all too familiar to Asian-Americans, including those born and bred in the U.S.A. And we know what it is like to be feared, pitied, admired, and scorned on account of our race, before we even have a chance to say boo! We, in turn, view White people through the prism of our own race-based expectations. I honestly am surprised every time I see a White man who can play basketball above the rim, just as Puerto Ricans and Cubans tend to be surprised to discover "Americans" who salsa truly well. All of which is to say that the notion that every individual is judged solely on personal merit, without regard for sociological wrapping, is mythical at best.

The second message conveyed by Horatio Alger is that we all have a shot at reaching our true potential. To be fair, neither Alger nor the myth he underwrote suggests that we start out equal. Nor does the myth necessarily require that we be given an equal opportunity to succeed. Rather, Alger's point is that each of us has the power to create our own opportunities. That turns out to be a difficult proposition to completely disprove, for no matter what evidence is offered up to show that a particular group of people have not fared well, it can always be argued that they did not try hard enough, or that they spent too much time wallowing in their predicament and not enough figuring out how to rise above it. Besides, there are always up-by-the-bootstraps examples to point to, like Colin Powell, whose

[2]Stephen L. Carter, *Reflections of an Affirmative Action Baby* (New York: Basic Books, 1991), 47–49.

name has so frequently been linked with that of Horatio Alger's that he must think they are related.[3] Nevertheless, it is by now generally agreed that there is a large category of Americans — some have called it the under-class — for whom upward mobility is practically impossible without massive changes in the structure of the economy and in the location of public resources.

As for the notion that merit will out, it assumes not only a commitment to merit-based decision making but also the existence of standards for mea-suring merit that do not unfairly favor one individual over another. Such standards, of course, must come from somewhere. They must be decided upon by somebody. And that somebody is rarely without a point of view. Ask a devotee of West Coast basketball what skills you should look for in re-cruiting talent and near the top of his list will be the ability to "get out on the break," to "be creative in the open court," and "to finish the play." On the other hand, ask someone who prefers East Coast basketball and her list will rank highly the ability "to d-up [play defense]," "to board [rebound]," and "to maintain focus and intensity."

Or, to take another example, what makes a great Supreme Court jus-tice? Brains to spare? Common sense? Proper judicial temperament? Politi-cal savvy? Extensive lawyering experience? A well-developed ability to ab-stract? Vision? Well-honed rhetorical skills? A reverence for our rich legal heritage? The capacity to adapt to changing times? Even if one is tempted to say "all of the above," how should these (or any other set of characteris-tics) be ranked? Measured? Evaluated?

The answers depend in part on whom you ask. Practicing lawyers, for example, are probably likely to rank extensive lawyering experience more highly than, say, brains. They are also likely to pay close attention to judicial temperament, which for them means whether the prospective justice would be inclined to treat them with respect during a court appearance. Sitting judges are also likely to rank judicial temperament highly, meaning whether the prospective justice would be a good colleague. In choosing among the other characteristics, they might each favor the ones that they happen to possess in abundance. Politicians might well see more merit in political savvy than would, say, academics, who could be expected to favor brains, the ability to abstract, and perhaps rhetorical skills.

---

[3]Sandy Grady, "Will He or Won't He?: Win or Lose, Presidential Pursuit by Colin Powell Would Do America a Necessary Service," *Kansas City Star,* 24 April 1995; Thomas B. Edsall, "For Powell, Timing Could be Crucial: As Gulf War Hero Hints at 1996 Bid, Associates Look into Details," *Washington Post,* 6 April 1995; J. F. O. McAllister, "The Candidate of Dreams," *Time,* 13 March 1995; Deroy Murdock, "Colin Powell: Many Things to Many People," *Wash-ington Times,* 16 January 1995; Doug Fischer, "U.S. Politics: War Hero Well-Placed to Be-come First Black President," *Ottawa Citizen,* 8 October 1994; "General Nice Guy: Profile Colin Powell," *Sunday Telegraph,* 25 September 1994; Otto Kreisher, "As a Civilian, Powell's Options are Enviable," *San Diego Union-Tribune,* 26 September 1993.

All of these relevant actors might be honestly trying to come up with   10
appropriate standards for measuring merit, but they would arrive at
markedly different results. And any given result would screen out people
who would succeed under another, equally plausible set of standards. Thus,
if there is a genuine commitment to merit-based decision making it is possible that merit will out, but only for those who have the right kind of merit.

Which brings us to the prior question: is merit all we care about in deciding who gets what share of life's goodies? Clearly not. Does anyone, for
example, honestly believe that any Supreme Court justice in recent memory
was nominated solely on the basis of merit (however defined)? Any President? Any member of Congress? Does anyone believe that America's
health-care resources are distributed solely on merit? That tax breaks are
distributed solely on merit? That baseball club owners are selected solely on
merit?

As I suggested earlier, the mere fact that a myth is based on false
premises or conveys a false image of the world does not necessarily make it
undesirable. Indeed, I place great stock in the idea that some illusions are,
or at least can be, positive. As social psychologist Shelley Taylor has observed, "[normal] people who are confronted with the normal rebuffs of
everyday life seem to construe their experience [so] as to develop and maintain an exaggeratedly positive view of their own attributes, an unrealistic optimism about the future, and a distorted faith in their ability to control what
goes on around them."[4] Taylor's research suggests that, up to a point, such
self-aggrandizement actually improves one's chances of worldly success.[5]

This may well explain the deep appeal of the Horatio Alger myth. True
or not, it can help to pull people in the direction they want to go. After all,
in order to succeed in life, especially when the odds are stacked against you,
it is often necessary to first convince yourself that there is a reason to get up
in the morning. So what is my beef? Where is the harm?

In a nutshell, my objection to the Alger myth is that it serves to maintain the racial pecking order. It does so by mentally bypassing the role of
race in American society. And it does so by fostering beliefs that themselves
serve to trivialize, if not erase, the social meaning of race. The Alger myth
encourages people to blink at the many barriers to racial equality (historical,
structural, and institutional) that litter the social landscape. Yes, slavery was
built on the notion that Africans were property and not persons; yes, even
after that "peculiar institution" collapsed, it continued to shape the life
prospects of those who previously were enslaved; yes, the enforced illiteracy
and cultural disruption of slavery, together with the collapse of Reconstruction, virtually assured that the vast majority of "freedmen" and "freed-
women" would not be successfully integrated into society; yes, Jim Crow

---

[4]Shelley E. Taylor, *Positive Illusions: Creative Self-Deception and the Healthy Mind*
(New York: Basic Books, 1989), xi.
[5]Ibid., xi, 7, 228–46.

laws, segregation, and a separate and unequal social reality severely undermined the prospects for Black achievement; yes, these and other features of our national life created a racial caste system that persists to this day; yes, the short-lived civil rights era of the 1950s and 1960s was undone by a broad and sustained White backlash; yes, the majority of Black people in America are mired in poverty; yes, economic mobility is not what it used to be, given the decline in our manufacturing and industrial base; yes, the siting of the illicit drug industry in our inner cities has had pernicious effects on Black and Latino neighborhoods; yes, yes, yes, BUT (drumroll) "all it takes to make it in America is initiative, hard work, persistence, and pluck." After all, just look at Colin Powell!

There is a fundamental tension between the promise of opportunity   15 enshrined in the Alger myth and the realities of a racial caste system. The main point of such a system is to promote and maintain inequality. The main point of the Alger myth is to proclaim that everyone can rise above her station in life. Despite this tension, it is possible for the myth to coexist with social reality. To quote Shelley Taylor once again:

> [T]he normal human mind is oriented toward mental health and . . . at every turn it construes events in a manner that promotes benign fictions about the self, the world, and the future. The mind is, with some significant exceptions, intrinsically adaptive, oriented toward overcoming rather than succumbing to the adverse events of life. . . . At one level, it constructs beneficent interpretations of threatening events that raise self-esteem and promote motivation; yet at another level, it recognizes the threat or challenge that is posed by these events.[6]

Not surprisingly, then, there are lots of Black folk who subscribe to the Alger myth and at the same time understand it to be deeply false. They live with the dissonance between myth and reality because both are helpful and healthful in dealing with "the adverse events of life." Many Whites, however, have a strong interest in resolving the dissonance in favor of the myth. Far from needing to be on guard against racial "threat[s] or challenge[s]," they would just as soon put the ugliness of racism out of mind. For them, the Horatio Alger myth provides them the opportunity to do just that.[7]

Quite apart from the general way in which the myth works to submerge the social realities of race, each of the messages it projects is also incompatible with the idea of race-based advantage or disadvantage. If, as the myth suggests, we are judged solely on our individual merits, then caste has little practical meaning. If we all can acquire the tools needed to reach our full potential, then how important can the disadvantage of race be? If merit will eventually carry the day, then shouldn't we be directing our energies to-

---

[6]Ibid., xi.

[7]Robert T. Carter, et al., "White Racial Identity Development and Work Values," *Journal of Vocational Behavior, Special Issue: Racial Identity and Vocational Behavior* 44, no. 2 (April 1994): 185–97.

ward encouraging Black initiative and follow-through rather than worrying about questions of power and privilege?

By interring the myth of Horatio Alger, or at least forcing it to coexist with social reality, we can accomplish two important goals. First, we can give the lie to the idea that Black people can simply lift themselves up by their own bootstraps. With that pesky idea out of the way, it is easier to see why White folk need to take joint ownership of the nation's race problem. Second, the realization that hard work and individual merit, while certainly critical, are not guarantors of success should lead at least some White people to reflect on whether their own achievements have been helped along by their preferred social position.

Finally, quite apart from race, it is in our national interest to give the Horatio Alger myth a rest, for it broadcasts a fourth message no less false than the first three — that we live in a land of unlimited potential. Although that belief may have served us well in the past, we live today in an era of diminished possibilities. We need to make a series of hard choices, followed by yet more hard choices regarding how to live with the promise of less. Confronting that reality is made that much harder by a mythology that assures us we can have it all.

ENGAGING THE TEXT

1. The first message communicated by the Alger myth, according to Dalton, is that "each of us is judged solely on her or his own merits" (para. 2). What does this message mean to Dalton, and why does he object to it? How does he make his case against it, and what kind of evidence does he provide? Explain why you agree or disagree with his claim that this first message "simply flies in the face of reality" (para. 3).

2. Dalton says it is "generally agreed," but do *you* agree that "there is a large category of Americans . . . for whom upward mobility is practically impossible" (para. 6)? Why or why not?

3. How persuasive do you find Dalton's claims that American society is far from operating as a strictly merit-based system?

4. Why does Dalton believe that the Alger myth is destructive? Do you think the power of the American Dream to inspire or motivate people is outweighed by the negative effects Dalton cites, or vice versa? Write a journal entry explaining your position.

EXPLORING CONNECTIONS

5. Test Dalton's claims against the actual excerpt from Horatio Alger's *Ragged Dick* (p. 306). For example, does the novel seem to match the formula Dalton summarizes in his first paragraph? Similarly, can you find in the novel any examples of the three messages Dalton identifies in his second paragraph? On balance, does the excerpt from Alger seem to promote ideas that you consider socially destructive? Why or why not?

6. How well does Colin Powell's story (p. 314) fit the Alger formula as defined in Dalton's first paragraph?

EXTENDING THE CRITICAL CONTEXT

7. Pick a few contemporary cultural heroes like Powell, Tiger Woods, and Oprah Winfrey. Conduct a mini-poll about what their success means to race relations in the United States. Do the responses you get support Dalton's contention that such heroes encourage people "to blink at the many barriers to racial equality" (para. 14)?

8. Dalton argues that the Alger myth should be buried, or, to use his word, "interred." Supposing for the moment that you agree, how could that be accomplished? How is a cultural myth challenged, revised, or robbed of its mythic power?

Stephen Cruz

STUDS TERKEL

The speaker of the following oral history is Stephen Cruz, a man who at first glance seems to be living the American Dream of success and upward mobility. He is never content, however, and he comes to question his own values and the meaning of success in the world of corporate America. Studs Terkel (b. 1912) is probably the best-known practitioner of oral history in the United States. He has compiled several books by interviewing dozens of widely varying people — ordinary people for the most part — about important subjects like work, social class, race, and the Great Depression. The edited versions of these interviews are often surprisingly powerful crystallizations of American social history: Terkel's subjects give voice to the frustrations and hopes of whole generations of Americans. Terkel won a Pulitzer Prize in 1985 for "The Good War": An Oral History of World War II. This selection first appeared in his American Dreams: Lost and Found *(1980).*

He is thirty-nine.
"The family came in stages from Mexico. Your grandparents usually came first, did a little work, found little roots, put together a few bucks, and brought the family in, one at a time. Those were the days when controls at the border didn't exist as they do now."

You just tried very hard to be whatever it is the system wanted of you. I was a good student and, as small as I was, a pretty good athlete. I was well liked, I thought. We were fairly affluent, but we lived down where all the trashy whites were. It was the only housing we could get. As kids, we never understood why. We did everything right. We didn't have those Mexican accents, we were never on welfare. Dad wouldn't be on welfare to save his soul. He woulda died first. He worked during the depression. He carries that pride with him, even today.

Of the five children, I'm the only one who really got into the business world. We learned quickly that you have to look for opportunities and add things up very quickly. I was in liberal arts, but as soon as Sputnik[1] went up, well, golly, hell, we knew where the bucks were. I went right over to the registrar's office and signed up for engineering. I got my degree in '62. If you had a master's in business as well, they were just paying all kinds of bucks. So that's what I did. Sure enough, the market was super. I had fourteen job offers. I could have had a hundred if I wanted to look around.

I never once associated these offers with my being a minority. I was aware   5
of the Civil Rights Act of 1964, but I was still self-confident enough to feel they wanted me because of my abilities. Looking back, the reason I got more offers than the other guys was because of the government edict. And I thought it was because I was so goddamned brilliant. (Laughs.) In 1962, I didn't get as many offers as those who were less qualified. You have a tendency to blame the job market. You just don't want to face the issue of discrimination.

I went to work with Procter & Gamble. After about two years, they told me I was one of the best supervisors they ever had and they were gonna promote me. Okay, I went into personnel. Again, I thought it was because I was such a brilliant guy. Now I started getting wise to the ways of the American Dream. My office was glass-enclosed, while all the other offices were enclosed so you couldn't see into them. I was the visible man.

They made sure I interviewed most of the people that came in. I just didn't really think there was anything wrong until we got a new plant manager, a southerner. I received instructions from him on how I should interview blacks. Just check and see if they smell, okay? That was the beginning of my training program. I started asking: Why weren't we hiring more minorities? I realized I was the only one in a management position.

I guess as a Mexican I was more acceptable because I wasn't really black. I was a good compromise. I was visibly good. I hired a black secretary, which was *verboten*. When I came back from my vacation, she was gone. My boss fired her while I was away. I asked why and never got a good reason.

Until then, I never questioned the American Dream. I was convinced if you worked hard, you could make it. I never considered myself different. That was the trouble. We had been discriminated against a lot, but I never

---

[1]*Sputnik:* Satellite launched by the Soviet Union in 1957; this launch signaled the beginning of the "space race" between the United States and the USSR.

associated it with society. I considered it an individual matter. Bad people, my mother used to say. In '68 I began to question.

I was doing fine. My very first year out of college, I was making twelve   10
thousand dollars. I left Procter & Gamble because I really saw no opportunity. They were content to leave me visible, but my thoughts were not really solicited. I may have overreacted a bit, with the plant manager's attitude, but I felt there's no way a Mexican could get ahead here.

I went to work for Blue Cross. It's 1969. The Great Society[2] is in full swing. Those who never thought of being minorities before are being turned on. Consciousness raising is going on. Black programs are popping up in universities. Cultural identity and all that. But what about the one issue in this country: economics? There were very few management jobs for minorities, especially blacks.

The stereotypes popped up again. If you're Oriental, you're real good in mathematics. If you're Mexican, you're a happy guy to have around, pleasant but emotional. Mexicans are either sleeping or laughing all the time. Life is just one big happy kind of event. *Mañana*. Good to have as part of the management team, as long as you weren't allowed to make decisions.

I was thinking there were two possibilities why minorities were not making it in business. One was deep, ingrained racism. But there was still the possibility that they were simply a bunch of bad managers who just couldn't cut it. You see, until now I believed everything I was taught about the dream: the American businessman is omnipotent and fair. If we could show these turkeys there's money to be made in hiring minorities, these businessmen — good managers, good decision makers — would respond. I naively thought American businessmen gave a damn about society, that given a choice they would do the right thing. I had that faith.

I was hungry for learning about decision-making criteria. I was still too far away from top management to see exactly how they were working. I needed to learn more. Hey, just learn more and you'll make it. That part of the dream hadn't left me yet. I was still clinging to the notion of work your ass off, learn more than anybody else, and you'll get in that sphere.

During my fifth year at Blue Cross, I discovered another flaw in the   15
American Dream. Minorities are as bad to other minorities as whites are to minorities. The strongest weapon the white manager had is the old divide and conquer routine. My mistake was thinking we were all at the same level of consciousness.

I had attempted to bring together some blacks with the other minorities. There weren't too many of them anyway. The Orientals never really got involved. The blacks misunderstood what I was presenting, perhaps I said it badly. They were on the cultural kick: a manager should be crucified for saying "Negro" instead of "black." I said as long as the Negro or the black gets the job, it doesn't mean a damn what he's called. We got into a huge

---

[2]*The Great Society:* President Lyndon B. Johnson's term for the American society he hoped to establish through social reforms, including an antipoverty program.

hassle. Management, of course, merely smiled. The whole struggle fell flat on its face. It crumpled from divisiveness. So I learned another lesson. People have their own agenda. It doesn't matter what group you're with, there is a tendency to put the other guy down regardless.

The American Dream began to look so damn complicated, I began to think: Hell, if I wanted, I could just back away and reap the harvest myself. By this time, I'm up to twenty-five thousand dollars a year. It's beginning to look good, and a lot of people are beginning to look good. And they're saying: "Hey, the American Dream, you got it. Why don't you lay off?" I wasn't falling in line.

My bosses were telling me I had all the "ingredients" for top management. All that was required was to "get to know our business." This term comes up all the time. If I could just warn all minorities and women whenever you hear "get to know our business," they're really saying "fall in line." Stay within that fence, and glory can be yours. I left Blue Cross disillusioned. They offered me a director's job at thirty thousand dollars before I quit.

All I had to do was behave myself. I had the "ingredients" of being a good Chicano, the equivalent of the good nigger. I was smart. I could articulate well. People didn't know by my speech patterns that I was of Mexican heritage. Some tell me I don't look Mexican, that I have a certain amount of Italian, Lebanese, or who knows. (Laughs.)

One could easily say: "Hey, what's your bitch? The American Dream has treated you beautifully. So just knock it off and quit this crap you're spreading around." It was a real problem. Every time I turned around, America seemed to be treating me very well.   20

Hell, I even thought of dropping out, the hell with it. Maybe get a job in a factory. But what happened? Offers kept coming in. I just said to myself: God, isn't this silly? You might as well take the bucks and continue looking for the answer. So I did that. But each time I took the money, the conflict in me got more intense, not less.

Wow, I'm up to thirty-five thousand a year. This is a savings and loan business. I have faith in the executive director. He was the kind of guy I was looking for in top management: understanding, humane, also looking for the formula. Until he was up for consideration as executive v.p. of the entire organization. All of a sudden everything changed. It wasn't until I saw this guy flip-flop that I realized how powerful vested interests are. Suddenly he's saying: "Don't rock the boat. Keep a low profile. Get in line." Another disappointment.

Subsequently, I went to work for a consulting firm. I said to myself: Okay, I've got to get close to the executive mind. I need to know how they work. Wow, a consulting firm.

Consulting firms are saving a lot of American businessmen. They're doing it in ways that defy the whole notion of capitalism. They're not allowing these businesses to fail. Lockheed was successful in getting U.S. funding guarantees because of the efforts of consulting firms working on their behalf, helping them look better. In this kind of work, you don't find minorities. You've got to be a proven success in business before you get there.

The American Dream, I see now, is governed not by education, opportunity, and hard work, but by power and fear. The higher up in the organization you go, the more you have to lose. The dream is *not losing*. This is the notion pervading America today: don't lose.

When I left the consulting business, I was making fifty thousand dollars a year. My last performance appraisal was: you can go a long way in this business, you can be a partner, but you gotta know our business. It came up again. At this point, I was incapable of being disillusioned any more. How easy it is to be swallowed up by the same set of values that governs the top guy. I was becoming that way. I was becoming concerned about losing that fifty grand or so a year. So I asked other minorities who had it made. I'd go up and ask 'em: "look, do you owe anything to others?" The answer was: "we owe nothing to anybody." They drew from the civil rights movement but felt no debt. They've quickly forgotten how it happened. It's like I was when I first got out of college. Hey, it's really me, I'm great. I'm great. I'm as angry with these guys as I am with the top guys.

Right now, it's confused. I've had fifteen years in the business world as "a success." Many Anglos would be envious of my progress. Fifty thousand dollars a year puts you in the one or two top percent of all Americans. Plus my wife making another thirty thousand. We had lots of money. When I gave it up, my cohorts looked at me not just as strange, but as something of a traitor. "You're screwing it up for all of us. You're part of our union, we're the elite, we should govern. What the hell are you doing?" So now I'm looked at suspiciously by my peer group as well.

I'm teaching at the University of Wisconsin at Platteville. It's nice. My colleagues tell me what's on their minds. I got a farm next-door to Platteville. With farm prices being what they are (laughs), it's a losing proposition. But with university work and what money we've saved, we're gonna be all right.

The American Dream is getting more elusive. The dream is being governed by a few people's notion of what the dream is. Sometimes I feel it's a small group of financiers that gets together once a year and decides all the world's issues.

It's getting so big. The small-business venture is not there any more. Business has become too big to influence. It can't be changed internally. A counterpower is needed.

ENGAGING THE TEXT

1. As Cruz moves up the economic ladder, he experiences growing conflict that keeps him from being content and proud of his accomplishments. To what do you attribute his discontent? Is his "solution" one that you would recommend?

2. Cruz says that the real force in America is the dream of "not losing" (para. 25). What does he mean by this? Do you agree?

3. What, according to Stephen Cruz, is wrong with the American Dream? Write an essay in which you first define and then either defend or critique his position.

4. Imagine the remainder of Stephen Cruz's life. Write a few paragraphs continuing his story. Read these aloud and discuss.

EXPLORING CONNECTIONS

5. Compare Stephen Cruz to Ragged Dick (p. 306) and Colin Powell (p. 314) in terms of the American Dream and individual success. How similar are Cruz's circumstances, goals, beliefs, and values to those examples of the Dream come true? What distinguishes him from those figures?

6. Compare Stephen Cruz to Richard Rodriguez (p. 202), Gary Soto (p. 42), and Mike Rose (p. 174) in terms of their attitudes toward education and success.

EXTENDING THE CRITICAL CONTEXT

7. According to Cruz, in 1969 few management positions were open to members of minority groups. Working in small groups, go to the library and look up current statistics on minorities in business (for example, the number of large minority-owned companies; the number of minority chief executives among major corporations; the distribution of minorities among top management, middle management, supervisory, and clerical positions). Compare notes with classmates and discuss.

Rewards and Opportunities: The Politics and Economics of Class in the U.S.[1]

GREGORY MANTSIOS

Which of these gifts might a high school graduate in your family receive — a corsage, a savings bond, or a BMW? The answer indicates your social class, a key factor in American lives that many of us conspire to deny or ignore. The selection below makes it hard to deny class distinctions and

[1]The author wishes to thank Bill Clark for his assistance in preparing this selection. [Author's note]

their nearly universal influence on our lives. The statistics linking social class to everything from educational opportunities to health care are staggering, as are the gaps between rich and poor. For example, the richest Americans may accumulate more wealth in one day than you are likely to earn in ten years; meanwhile, there are two million poor people in New York City alone. Mantsios is the director of Worker Education at Queens College of the City University of New York. His essay appeared in Race, Class and Gender in the United States, *2nd ed. (1992).*

> [Class is] for European democracies or something else — it isn't for the United States of America. We are not going to be divided by class.
> — GEORGE BUSH, 1988[2]

Strange words from a man presiding over a nation with more than 32 million people living in poverty and one of the largest income gaps between rich and poor in the industrialized world.[3] Politicians long before and long after George Bush have made and will continue to make statements proclaiming our egalitarian values and denying the existence of class in America. But they are not alone: most Americans dislike talking about class. We minimize the extent of inequality, pretend that class differences do not really matter, and erase the word "class" from our vocabulary and from our mind. In one survey, designed to solicit respondents' class identification, 35 percent of all those questioned told interviewers they had never thought about their class identification before that very moment.[4]

"We are all middle-class" or so it would seem. Our national consciousness, as shaped in large part by the media and our political leadership, provides us with a picture of ourselves as a nation of prosperity and opportunity with an ever expanding middle-class life-style. As a result, our class differences are muted and our collective character is homogenized.

Yet class divisions are real and arguably the most significant factor in determining both our very being in the world and the nature of the society we live in.

---

[2]Quoted in George Will, "A Case for Dukakis," in *The Washington Post,* November 13, 1988, p. A27. [Author's note]

[3]The income gap in the United States, measured as a percentage of total income held by the wealthiest 20 percent of the population vs. the poorest 20 percent is approximately 11 to 1. The ratio in Great Britain is 7 to 1; in Japan, it is 4 to 1. (See "U.N. National Accounts Statistics." Statistical Papers, Series M no. 79. N.Y. U.N. 1985, pp. 1–11.) [Author's note]

[4]Marian Irish and James Prothro, *The Politics of American Democracy,* Englewood Cliffs, N.J., Prentice-Hall, 1965, pp. 2, 38. [Author's note]

The Extent of Poverty in the U.S.

The official poverty line in 1990 was $12,675 for an urban family of four and $9,736 for a family of three. For years, critics have argued that the measurements used by the government woefully underestimate the extent of poverty in America.[5] Yet even by the government's conservative estimate, nearly one in eight Americans currently lives in poverty.

As deplorable as this is, the overall poverty rate for the nation effec-   5
tively masks both the level of deprivation and the extent of the problem within geographic areas and within specific populations. Three short years prior to George Bush's speech, the Physicians Task Force on Hunger in America declared that "Hunger is a problem of epidemic proportion across the nation." Upon completing their national field investigation of hunger and malnutrition, the team of twenty-two prominent physicians estimated that there were up to 20 million citizens hungry at least some period of time each month.

Touring rural Mississippi the Task Force filed this report from one of the many such homes they visited:

Inside the remnants of a house, alongside a dirt road in Green-wood, lived a family of thirteen people. Graciously welcomed by the mother and father, the doctors entered another world — a dwelling with no heat, no electricity, no windows, home for two parents, their children, and several nieces and nephews. Clothes were piled in the corner, the substitute location for closets which were missing; the two beds in the three-room house had no sheets, the torn mattresses covered by the bodies of three children who lay side by side. In the kitchen a small gas stove was the only appliance.

No food was in the house. The babies had no milk; two were crying as several of the older children tried to console them. "These people are starving," the local guide told the doctors. Twice a week she collected food from churches to bring to the family. . . . Only the flies which crawled on the face of the smallest child seemed to be well fed. The parents were not; they had not eaten for two days. The children had eaten some dried beans the previous evening.

— from *Hunger in America: The Growing Epidemic,*
the PHYSICIANS TASK FORCE[6]

---

[5]See, for example, Patricia Ruggles, "The Poverty Line — Too Low for the 90's, in the *New York Times,* April 26, 1990, p. A31. [Author's note]

[6]Physicians Task Force on Hunger in America, *Hunger in America: The Growing Epidemic* (Middletown, CT: Wesleyan University Press, 1985, p. 27. [Author's note]

Nearly a quarter of the population of the state of Mississippi lives below the federal poverty level. Over a third of the population of Mississippi is so poor it qualifies for food stamps, although only 15 percent actually receive them.[7]

The face of poverty in Greenwood, Mississippi, is not much different than that in other parts of the deep south and beyond. Appalling conditions of poverty are facts of life in the foothills of Appalachia, the reservations of Native America, the barrios of the Southwest, the abandoned towns of the industrial belt, and the ghettoes of the nation's urban centers. There are more than 2 million poor people in New York City alone, a figure that exceeds the entire population of some nations.

Today, the poor include the very young and the elderly, the rural poor and the urban homeless: increasingly, the poor also include men and women who work full time. When we examine the incidence of poverty within particular segments of the population, the figures can be both shameful and sobering:

- more than one out of every five children in the U.S. (all races) lives below the poverty line[8]
- 39 percent of Hispanic children and 45 percent of Black children in the U.S. live below the poverty line[9]
- one in every four rural children is poor[10]
- if you are Black and 65 years of age or older, your chances of being poor are one in three[11]
- roughly 60 percent of all poor work at least part-time or in seasonal work[12]
- 2 million Americans worked full-time throughout the year and were still poor[13]

Poverty statistics have either remained relatively constant over the years or have shown a marked increase in the incidence of poverty. The number of full-time workers below the poverty line, for example, increased by more than 50 percent from 1978 to 1986.[14]

The Level of Wealth

Business Week recently reported that the average salary for the CEO of   10
the nation's top 1,000 companies was $841,000.[15] As high as this figure is, however, it fails to capture the level of compensation at the top of the corporate

[7]Ibid. [Author's note]

[8]Bureau of Census, "Statistical Abstract of the U.S. 1990," Department of Commerce, Washington, D.C., 1990, p. 460. [Author's note]

[9]Ibid. [Author's note]

[10]Ibid. [Author's note]

[11]Ibid. [Author's note]

[12]*U.S. News and World Report,* January 1, 1988, pp. 18–24. [Author's note]

[13]Ibid. [Author's note]

[14]Ibid. [Author's note]

[15]*Business Week,* October 19, 1990, p. 11. [Author's note}

world. Short-term and long-term bonuses, stock options and stock awards can add significantly to annual compensation. Take the following examples:

- annual compensation in 1989, including short-term bonuses, for the Chief Executive Officer of UAL, came to $18.3 million; for the head of Reebok, compensation came to $14.6 million (in what was not a particularly hot year in the sneaker business).[16]
- annual compensation, including short-term and long-term bonuses and stock awards, for the head of Time Warner Inc. totaled $78.2 million; for the CEO of LIN Broadcasting, it came to a whopping $186 million.[17]

The distribution of income in the United States is outlined in Table 1.

Table 1   Income Inequality in the U.S.[18]

INCOME GROUP (FAMILIES)	PERCENT OF INCOME RECEIVED
Lowest fifth	4.6
Second fifth	10.8
Middle fifth	16.8
Fourth fifth	24.0
Highest fifth	43.7
(Highest 5 percent)	(17.0)

By 1990, according to economist Robert Reich, the top fifth of the population took home more money than the other four-fifths put together.[19]

Wealth, rather than income, is a more accurate indicator of economic inequality. Accumulated wealth by individuals and families runs into the billions, with the U.S. now boasting at least 58 billionaires, many of them multibillionaires. The distribution of wealth is far more skewed than the distribution of income. In 1986, the Joint Economic Committee of the U.S. Congress released a special report entitled "The Concentration of Wealth in the United States." Table 2 summarizes some of the findings.

Table 2   Distribution of Wealth in the U.S.[20]

FAMILIES	PERCENT OF WEALTH OWNED
The richest 10 percent	71.7
(The top 1/2 percent)	(35.1)
Everyone else, or 90 percent of all families	28.2

[16]Ibid., p. 12. [Author's note]

[17]*Business Week,* May 6, 1991, p. 90. [Author's note]

[18]U.S. Department of Commerce, "Statistical Abstract of the U.S. 1988," Washington, D.C., 1988, p. 428. [Author's note]

[19]Robert Reich, "Secession of the Successful," *New York Times,* January 20, 1991, p. M42. [Author's note]

[20]Joint Economic Committee of the U.S. Congress, "The Concentration of Wealth in the United States," Washington, D.C., 1986, p. 24. [Author's note]

It should be noted that because of the way the statistics were collected by the Congressional Committee, the figure for 90 percent of all other families includes half of the families who fall into the wealthiest quintile of the population. The "super rich," that is, the top one-half of one percent of the population, includes approximately 420,000 households with the average value of the wealth for each one of these households amounting to $8.9 million.[21]

Most people never see the opulence of the wealthy, except in the fantasy world of television and the movies. Society pages in local newspapers, however, often provide a glimpse into the real life-style of the wealthy. A recent article in the *New York Times* described the life-style of John and Patricia Kluge.

Mr. Kluge, chairman of the Metromedia Company, has an estimated worth of $5.2 billion. . . . The Kluges (pronounced Kloog-ee) have an apartment in Manhattan, an estate in the Virginia hunt country, and a horse farm in Scotland. . . .

They are known in Washington and New York social circles for opulent parties. Mr. Kluge had the ballroom of the Waldorf done up like the interior of a Viennese belle epoque palace for Mrs. Kluge's forty-ninth birthday.

Her birthday parties for him have been more intimate, friends say. Typically these involve only one or two other couples (once it was Frank and Barbara Sinatra) who take over L'Orangerie, a private dining room at Le Cirque that seats one hundred. The room was turned into an English garden for Mr. Kluge's seventieth birthday, with dirt covering the carpet, flowering plants, and trees. Hidden among the trees were nine violinists. The wine was a Chateau Lafite from 1914, the year of his birth. The birthday cake was in the shape of a $1 billion bill.[22]

The Plight of the Middle Class

The percentage of households with earnings at a middle-income level has been falling steadily.[23] The latest census figures show that the percentage of families with an annual income between $15,000 and $50,000 (approximately 50 percent and 200 percent of the median income) has fallen by nearly 10 percentage points since 1970.[24] While some of the households have moved upward and others have moved downward, what is clear is that

[21]Richard Roper, *Persistent Poverty: The American Dream Turned Nightmare* (New York: Plenum Press, 1991), p. 60. [Author's note]

[22]*New York Times*, April 29, 1990, p. 48. [Author's note]

[23]Chris Tilly, "U-Turn on Equality," *Dollars and Sense,* May 1986, p. 84. [Author's note]

[24]Bureau of Census, "Statistical Abstract of the U.S. 1990," p. 450. [Author's note]

the United States is experiencing a significant polarization in the distribution of income. The gap between rich and poor is wider and the share of income earned by middle-income Americans has fallen to the lowest level since the census bureau began keeping statistics in 1946. More and more individuals and families are finding themselves at one or the other end of the economic spectrum as the middle class steadily declines.

Furthermore, being in the middle class is no longer what it used to be. Once, middle-class status carried the promise that one's standard of living would steadily improve over time. Yet 60 percent of Americans will have experienced virtually no income gain between 1980 and 1990. (Compare this to the income gains experienced by the wealthiest fifth of the population — up by 33 percent, and the wealthiest one percent of the population — up by 87 percent).[25] One study showed that only one in five (males) will surpass the status, income, and prestige of their fathers.[26]

Nor does a middle-class income any longer guarantee the comforts it   15 once did. Home ownership, for example, has increasingly become out of reach for a growing number of citizens. During the last decade home ownership rates dropped from 44 percent to 36 percent among people in the 25–29 year old age-group and from 61 percent to 53 percent among those in their thirties.[27]

The Rewards of Money

The distribution of income and wealth in the U.S. is grossly unequal and becomes increasingly more so with time. The rewards of money, however, go well beyond those of consumption patterns and life-style. It is not simply that the wealthy live such opulent life-styles, it is that class position determines one's life chances. Life chances include such far-reaching factors as life expectancy, level of education, occupational status, exposure to industrial hazards, incidence of crime victimization, rate of incarceration, etc. In short, class position can play a critically important role in determining how long you live, whether you have a healthy life, if you fail in school, or if you succeed at work.

The link between economic status and health is perhaps the most revealing and most disheartening. Health professionals and social scientists have shown that income is closely correlated to such factors as infant mortality, cancer, chronic disease, and death due to surgical and medical complications and "misadventures."[28]

[25]"And the Rich Get Richer," *Dollars and Sense*, October 1990, p. 5. [Author's note]

[26]Richard DeLone, *Small Futures* (New York: Harcourt Brace Jovanovich, 1978), pp. 14–19. [Author's note]

[27]Roper, *Persistent Poverty*, p. 32. [Author's note]

[28]Melvin Krasner, *Poverty and Health in New York City*, United Hospital Fund of New York, 1989. See also U.S. Dept. of Health and Human Services, *Health Status of Minorities and Low Income Groups*, 1985; and Dana Hughes, Kay Johnson, Sara Rosenbaum, Elizabeth Butler, Janet Simons, *The Health of America's Children*, The Children's Defense Fund, 1988. [Author's note]

The infant mortality rate is an example that invites international as well as racial and economic comparisons. At 10.6 infant deaths per 1,000 live births, the U.S. places nineteenth in the world — behind such countries as Spain, Singapore, and Hong Kong; a statistic that is in and of itself shameful for the wealthiest nation in the world. When infant mortality only among Blacks in the U.S. is considered, the rate rises to 18.2 and places the U.S. twenty-eighth in rank — behind Bulgaria and equal to Costa Rica. The infant mortality rate in poverty stricken areas, such as Hale County, Alabama, is three times the national rate and nearly twice that of the nation of Malaysia (whose GNP per capita is one-tenth that of the U.S.).[29] [See Table 3.]

Table 3   Infant Mortality Rate Per 1,000 Births[30]

Total (national, all racial and ethnic groups)	10.6
Among Blacks only	18.2
In Hale County, Alabama	31.0

Analyses of the relationship between health and income are not always easy to come by. A recent study conducted in New York City, however, provided some important information. The study examined the difference in health status and delivery of health services among residents from different neighborhoods. The data provided allows for comparing incidents of health problems in neighborhoods where 40 percent or more of the population lives below the poverty line with those in other neighborhoods where less than 10 percent of the population lives below the poverty line. The study found that the incidence of health problems, in many categories, was several times as great in poorer neighborhoods. For example, death associated with vascular complications (from the heart or brain) occurred nearly twice as often in poor areas than in non-poor. Similarly, the chance of being afflicted with bronchitis is 5 times as great in poor areas than in non-poor areas.[31] The study concluded, "The findings clearly indicate that certain segments of the population — poor, minority, and other disadvantaged groups — are especially vulnerable and bear a disproportionate share of preventable, and therefore unnecessary deaths and diseases."[32]

The reasons for such a high correlation are many and varied: inadequate nutrition, exposure to occupational and environmental hazards, ac-

20

[29]Physicians Task Force, *Hunger in America;* Hughes et al., ibid.; and "World Development Report 1990," World Bank (New York: Oxford University Press, 1990, pp. 232–233. [Author's note]

[30]Ibid. [Author's note]

[31]Krasner, *Poverty and Health,* p. 134. [Author's note]

[32]Ibid., p. 166. It should be noted that the study was conducted in a major metropolitan area where hospitals and health-care facilities are in close proximity to the population, rich and poor. One might expect the discrepancies to be even greater in poor, rural areas where access to health care and medical attention is more problematic. [Author's note]

cess to health-care facilities, quality of health services provided, ability to pay and therefore receive medical services, etc. Inadequate nutrition, for example, is associated with low birth weights and growth failure among low-income children and with chronic disease among the elderly poor. It has also been shown that the uninsured and those covered by Medicaid are far less likely to be given common hospital procedures than are patients with private medical coverage.

The relationship between income and health is similar to that of income and rate of incarceration. One in four young Black men, age 20 to 29, are either in jail or court supervised (i.e., on parole or probation). This figure surpasses the number of Black men enrolled in higher education. The figure also compares negatively to that for white men where 1 in 16 are incarcerated in the same age-group.[33]

While it is often assumed that differences in rates of arrest and incarceration reflect differences in the incidence of crime, a recent study conducted in Pinellas County, Florida, found that most women prosecuted for using illegal drugs while pregnant have been poor members of racial minorities, even though drug use in pregnancy is equally prevalent in white middle-class women. Researchers found that about 15 percent of both the white and the Black women used drugs, but that the Black women were 10 times as likely as whites to be reported to the authorities and poor women were more likely to be reported than middle-class women. Sixty percent of the 133 women reported had incomes of less than $12,000 a year. Only 8 percent had incomes of more than $25,000 a year.

Differences in Opportunity

The opportunity for social and economic success are the hallmarks of the American Dream. The dream is rooted in two factors: education and jobs.

Our nation prides itself on its ability to provide unprecedented educational opportunities to its citizens. As well it should. It sends more of its young people to college than any other nation in the world. There are nearly 13 million Americans currently enrolled in colleges and universities around the country, a result of the tremendous expansion of higher education since World War II. The establishment of financial assistance for veterans and for the needy, and the growth of affordable public colleges all have had an important and positive effect on college enrollment. Most importantly from the point of view of a national consciousness, the swelling of college enrollments has affirmed our egalitarian values and convinced us that our educational system is just and democratic.

---

[33]*Washington Post,* February 27, 1990, p. A3, citing Marc Mauer, "Young Black Men and the Criminal Justice System: A Growing National Problem," The Sentencing Project, January 1990. [Author's note]

Our pride, however, is a false pride. For while we have made great   25
strides in opening the doors of academe, the system of education in the
United States leaves much to be desired and is anything but egalitarian.

More than a quarter of our adult population has not graduated from
high school, nearly three quarters do not hold a college degree.[34] This is a
record that does not bode well for the most industrialized and technologi-
cally advanced nation in the world. Perhaps more importantly, the level of
educational achievement is largely class determined.

At least equal in importance to the amount of education received, is the
quality of education. The quality of primary and secondary schools is largely
dependent on geography and proximity to schools with adequate resources.
Educational funding, and the tax base for it, are determined by residency
and who can afford to live where. Schools in poorer districts are just not as
likely to provide a high-quality education.

Student achievement in the classroom and on standardized tests is also
class determined. Studies from the late 1970s showed a direct relation between SAT scores and family income. Grouping SAT scores into twelve categories from highest to lowest, researchers found that the mean family income decreased consistently from one group to the next as test scores
declined. The study was done by examining the test results and family income of over 600,000 students![35] In other words, the higher the family income, the higher the test scores and vice versa.

Furthermore, for that segment of the population that does enter and
complete a college education (approximately 18 percent of the population,
including Associate degrees), the system is highly stratified. Precious few
from poor and working-class families have gained access to the elite colleges. For the most part, these have remained the bastion of the wealthy,
leaving the less prestigious two-year colleges almost exclusively the domain
of the poor and the disadvantaged. The result is that colleges today are performing the same sorting function previously performed by high schools,
where students are divided into vocational and academic tracks. The rate of
participation in vocational programs at the college level is closely related to
socioeconomic class, so that students from poorer backgrounds who do enroll in college are still being channeled into educational programs and institutions that are vocational in nature and that lead to less desirable occupations and futures.[36]

---

[34]The Chronicle of Higher Education, *The Almanac of Higher Education, 1989–1990*
(Chicago: The University of Chicago Press, 1989. [Author's note]

[35]DeLone, *Small Futures,* p. 102. [Author's note]

[36]David Karen, "The Politics of Class, Race, and Gender," paper presented at Conference
on "Class Bias in Higher Education," Queens College, Flushing, N.Y., November 1990. This
does not deny the intrinsic value of vocational education, but points to the fact that poor and
working class students are found in the sector of education that yields the smallest socioeconomic return. [Author's note]

The "junior" colleges, whose growth once promised to serve as a step-   30
ping stone for the disadvantaged and the underprepared to gain access to
four-year liberal arts colleges have been transformed into "community" colleges which provide vocational programs and terminal degrees in fields that
narrow occupational options. The effect is to limit opportunity and to provide what some critics have referred to as a "cooling out function" — the
managing of ambitions of the poor and working class who might otherwise
take the American dream seriously.[37]

Some might argue that intelligence and drive are more significant than
education in determining a young person's future. A *New York Times*
article, however, entitled "Status Not Brains Makes a Child's Future,"
neatly summed up the findings of a Carnegie Foundation study that examined the relationship between IQ scores and occupational success. Researchers compared economic success rates of individuals who had the
same IQ. Their findings: even when IQ test scores were the same, a young
person's ability to obtain a job that will pay in the top 10 percent of the income structure is 27 times as great if he or she comes from a wealthy background.[38]

Culture, the Media, and Ideology

If the U.S. is so highly stratified and if economic class makes such a difference, why is it, then, that we retain such illusions about an egalitarian[39]
society? In part, it is because for many of us it is simply more comfortable to
deny the class nature of our society and the rigid boundaries such a society
suggests: we would rather consider our economic predicament, whatever
our class standing, to be temporary and anticipate a brighter future in what
we prefer to believe is a fluid and open opportunity structure. In part, it is
also because we are constantly bombarded with cultural messages from the
media and other sources that tell us that class in America, if it exists at all,
does not really matter.

Both in entertainment and in relating the news of the day, the media
convey important, albeit contradictory messages: classes do not exist, the
poor and the working class are morally inferior, America is a land of great
social and economic mobility, class is irrelevant.

TV sitcoms and feature films have traditionally ignored class issues.
There have been relatively few serious portrayals of the poor or the working
class in the history of film and television. Television, in particular, presents a
view of America where everyone is a professional and middle class: daddy, it

---

[37]Steven Brint and Jerome Karabel, *Diverted Dream: Community Colleges and the Promise of Educational Opportunity in America, 1890 to 1985* (New York: Oxford University Press, 1989). [Author's note]

[38]DeLone, *Small Futures.* [Author's note]

[39]*egalitarian:* Based on equal social, political, and economic rights and privileges.

seems, always goes to the office, not to the factory.[40] There are notable exceptions and these are of particular interest in that they usually present story lines that distort class realities even further.

Story lines about class do one of three things. First, they present and re-   35
inforce negative class stereotypes. The poor are presented as hapless or dangerous and the working class as dumb, reactionary, and bigoted. Those not members of the professional middle class are to be laughed at, despised, or feared.[41] Second, they portray instances of upward mobility and class fluidity. These include rags-to-riches stories, Pygmalion tales,[42] and comic instances of downward mobility. Third, they stress that the people who think firm class lines exist come to discover that they are mistaken: everybody is really the same.[43] These are often rich girl/poor boy romances or their opposite.

Story lines about class make for good comedy, good romance, and in the last example, even good lessons in human relations. They also perform, however, a great disservice: "treating class differences as totally inconsequential strengthens the national delusion that class power and position are insignificant."[44]

A Structural Perspective

Vast differences in wealth have serious consequences and are neither justifiable nor a result of individual and personal deficiencies. People are poor because they have no money and no power to acquire money. The wealthy are rich because they have both.

The distribution of income and wealth occurs because a society is structured and policies are implemented in such a way to either produce or alleviate inequalities. A society can choose to minimize the gaps in wealth and power between its most privileged and its most disenfranchised. Government can serve as the equalizer by providing mechanisms to redistribute wealth from the top to the bottom. The promise of government as the great equalizer has clearly failed in the U.S. and rather than redoubling the efforts to redistribute wealth, traditional redistributive mechanisms, such as the progressive income tax, have declined in use in recent years. The tax rate for the wealthiest segment of the population, for example, steadily declined in spite of, or

---

[40]Barbara Ehrenreich, *Fear of Falling: The Inner Life of the Middle Class* (New York: Pantheon, 1989), p. 140. [Author's note]

[41]See Ehrenreich, ibid. [Author's note]

[42]*Pygmalion tales:* Tales in which a lower-class citizen is transformed into someone elegant and refined. In George Bernard Shaw's *Pygmalion* (1913), a British speech professor transforms a working girl; the musical version *My Fair Lady* (1956) is based on Shaw's play. In the original Greek myth, Pygmalion was an artist-king who fell in love with a beautiful statue, which the goddess Aphrodite then brought to life.

[43]Benjamin DeMott, *The Imperial Middle: Why Americans Can't Think Straight About Class* (New York: William Morrow, 1990). [Author's note]

[44]DeMott, ibid. [Author's note]

perhaps because of, the increasing concentration of wealth and power at the top. In 1944 the top tax rate was 94 percent, after World War II it was reduced to 91 percent, in 1964 to 72 percent, in 1981 to 50 percent, in 1990 to 28 percent (for those with an annual income over $155,000).[45]

Nor is it the case that conditions of wealth simply coexist side-by-side with conditions of poverty. The point is not that there are rich and poor, but that some are rich precisely because others are poor, and that one's privilege is predicated on the other's disenfranchisement. If it were not for the element of exploitation, we might celebrate inequality as reflective of our nation's great diversity.

The great antipoverty crusader, Michael Harrington, tells of the debate   40 in Congress over Richard Nixon's Family Assistance Plan during the 1970s. If the government provided a minimum income to everyone, "Who," asked a southern legislator, "will iron my shirts and rake the yard?"[46]

The legislator bluntly stated the more complex truth: the privileged in our society require a class-structured social order in order to maintain and enhance their economic and political well-being. Industrial profits depend on cheap labor and on a pool of unemployed to keep workers in check. Real estate speculators and developers create and depend on slums for tax-evading investments. These are the injustices and irrationalities of our economic system.

What is worse is that inequalities perpetuate themselves. People with wealth are the ones who have the opportunity to accumulate more wealth.

The fortune of Warren Buffett is estimated to be approximately $4 billion dollars. He is one of 71 billionaires in the United States (their average holding is about $3 billion each).[47] Calculated below is the interest generated by Buffett's wealth at an 8 percent return.
Interest generated by $4 billion, at 8 percent return

$10 each second
$600 each minute
$36,000 each hour
$864,000 each day
$6,048,000 each week
$320,000,000 each year ($320 million)

In other words, Mr. Buffett makes more money in two days of non-work than most people earn in a lifetime of work.

---

[45]Ironically those with an annual income between $75,000 and $150,000 pay a higher rate of 33 percent. [Author's note]

[46]Michael Harrington, *The New American Poverty* (New York: Penguin, 1985), p. 3. [Author's note]

[47]*Fortune Magazine,* September 10, 1990, p. 98; *Forbes,* October 21, 1991, pp. 145–160. [Author's note]

It is this ability to generate additional resources that most distinguishes the nation's upper class from the rest of society. It is not simply bank interest that generates more money, but income producing property: buildings, factories, natural resources; those assets Karl Marx referred to as the means of production. Today, unlike the early days of capitalism, these are owned either directly or indirectly through stocks. Economists estimate that for the super rich, the rate of return on such investments is approximately 30 percent.[48] Economists have also designed a device, called Net Financial Assets (NFA), to measure the level and concentration of income-producing property. While Net Worth (NW), a figure that considers all assets and debts, provides a picture of what kind of life-style is being supported, the NFA figure specifically excludes in its calculation ownership of homes and motor vehicles. By doing so, the NFA figure provides a more reliable measure of an individual's life chances and ability to accumulate future resources. A home or a car are not ordinarily converted to purchase other resources, such as a prep school or college education for one's children. Neither are these assets likely to be used to buy medical care, support political candidates, pursue justice in the courts, pay lobbyists to protect special interests, or finance a business or make other investments. Net financial assets include only those financial assets normally available for and used to generate income and wealth.[49] Stock ownership, for example, is a financial asset and is highly concentrated at the top, with the wealthiest 10 percent of the population owning over 89 percent of the corporate stocks.[50] Since home ownership is the major source of wealth for those who own a house, removing home equity as well as car ownership from the calculations has a significant impact on how we view the question of equity.

- The median net household income in the U.S. is $21,744, net worth in the U.S. is $32,609, and the median Net Financial Assets is $2,599.
- While the top 20 percent of American households earn over 43 percent of all income, that same 20 percent holds 67 percent of Net Worth, and nearly 90 percent of Net Financial Assets.
- The median income of the top one percent of the population is 22 times greater than that of the remaining 99 percent. The median Net Financial Assets of the top one percent is 237 times greater than the median of the other 99 percent of the population.[51]

[48]E. K. Hunt and Howard Sherman, *Economics* (New York: Harper and Row, 1990), pp. 254–257. [Author's note]

[49]Melvin Oliver and Thomas Shapiro, "Wealth of a Nation." *American Journal of Economics and Sociology,* April 1990, p. 129. [Author's note]

[50]Joint Economic Committee, "The Concentration of Wealth in the United States." [Author's note]

[51]Oliver and Shapiro, "Wealth of a Nation," p. 129. [Author's note]

The ability to generate wealth on the part of this class of owners is truly staggering. It contrasts sharply with the ability of those who rely on selling their labor power. For those with income under $25,000, wage and salary income from labor comprised 90 percent of their total income.

There is also an entrepreneurial middle class in America that includes   45
farmers, shopkeepers, and others. The small entrepreneurs, however, are becoming increasingly marginal in America and their income-producing property hardly exempts them from laboring.

The wealthy usually work too: their property income, however, is substantial enough to enable them to live without working if they chose to do so.

People with wealth and financial assets have disproportionate power in society. First, they have control of the workplace in enterprises they own. They determine what is produced and how it is produced. Second, they have enormous control over the media and other institutions that influence ideology and how we think about things, including class. Third, they have far greater influence over the nations' political institutions than their numbers warrant. They have the ability to influence not only decisions affecting their particular business ventures, but the general political climate of the nation.

Spheres of Power and Oppression

When we look at society and try to determine what it is that keeps most people down — what holds them back from realizing their potential as healthy, creative, productive individuals — we find institutionally oppressive forces that are largely beyond their individual control. Class domination is one of these forces. People do not choose to be poor or working class; instead they are limited and confined by the opportunities afforded or denied them by a social system. The class structure in the United States is a function of its economic system — capitalism, a system that is based on private rather then public ownership and control of commercial enterprises and on the class division between those who own and control and those who do not. Under capitalism, these enterprises are governed by the need to produce a profit for the owners, rather than to fulfill collective needs.

Racial and gender domination are other such forces that hold people down. Although there are significant differences in the way capitalism, racism and sexism affect our lives, there are also a multitude of parallels. And although race, class, and gender act independently of each other, they are at the same time very much interrelated.

On the one hand, issues of race and gender oppression cut across class   50
lines. Women experience the effects of sexism whether they are well-paid professionals or poorly paid clerks. As women, they face discrimination and male domination, as well as catcalls and stereotyping. Similarly, a Black man faces racial oppression whether he is an executive, an auto worker, or a

tenant farmer. As a Black, he will be subjected to racial slurs and be denied opportunities because of his color. Regardless of their class standing, women and members of minority races are confronted with oppressive forces precisely because of their gender, color, or both.

On the other hand, class oppression permeates other spheres of power and oppression, so that the oppression experienced by women and minorities is also differentiated along class lines. Although women and minorities find themselves in subordinate positions vis-à-vis white men, the particular issues they confront may be quite different depending on their position in the class structure. Inequalities in the class structure distinguish social functions and individual power, and these distinctions carry over to race and gender categories.

Power is incremental and class privileges can accrue to individual women and to individual members of a racial minority. At the same time, class-oppressed men, whether they are white or Black, have privileges afforded them as men in a sexist society. Similarly, class-oppressed whites, whether they are men or women, have privileges afforded them as whites in a racist society. Spheres of power and oppression divide us deeply in our society, and the schisms between us are often difficult to bridge.

Whereas power is incremental, oppression is cumulative, and those who are poor, Black, and female have all the forces of classism, racism, and sexism bearing down on them. This cumulative oppression is what is meant by the double and triple jeopardy of women and minorities.

Furthermore, oppression in one sphere is related to the likelihood of oppression in another. If you are Black and female, for example, you are much more likely to be poor and working class than you would be as a white male. Census figures show that the incidence of poverty and near-poverty (calculated as 125 percent of the poverty line) varies greatly by race and gender. [See Table 4.]

Table 4   Chances of Being Poor in America[52]

	WHITE MALE & FEMALE	WHITE FEMALE HEAD	BLACK MALE & FEMALE	BLACK FEMALE HEAD
Poverty	1 in 9	1 in 4	1 in 3	1 in 2
Near Poverty	1 in 6	1 in 3	1 in 2	2 in 3

In other words, being female and being nonwhite are attributes in our society that increase the chances of poverty and of lower-class standing. Racism and sexism compound the effects of classism in society.   55

---

[52]"Characteristics of the Population Below the Poverty Line: 1984," from Current Population Reports, Consumer Income Series P-60, No. 152, Washington, D.C., U.S. Department of Commerce, Bureau of the Census, June 1986, pp. 5–9. [Author's note]

ENGAGING THE TEXT

1. Explain the difference between wealth and income. Why is this such an important distinction to make?

2. Work out a rough budget for a family of four with an annual income of $12,675. Be sure to include costs for food, housing, health care, transportation, and other unavoidable expenses. Do you think this would be a reasonable poverty line, or is it too low or too high?

3. Look past all the evidence Mantsios provides and make a list of his key claims about class in the United States. Discuss these briefly in class to identify areas of consensus and disagreement; in any controversial areas, consult Mantsios's evidence and weigh its adequacy and the author's logic.

4. Are the wealthy in the United States exploiting or oppressing those less fortunate? Are the disparities in wealth a necessary by-product of a free society?

5. Mantsios says that government could redistribute wealth to reduce inequalities (para. 38). Clearly many wealthy Americans would oppose such steps. What do you believe most middle-class Americans would think, and why?

EXPLORING CONNECTIONS

6. Working in small groups, discuss which class each of the following would belong to and how this class affiliation would shape the life chances of each:

Gary Soto in "Looking for Work" (p. 42)	Stephen Cruz (p. 326)
	Miss Moore in "The Lesson"
Anndee Hochman in "Growing	(p. 348)
Pains" (p. 47)	Cora Tucker (p. 390)
the narrator in "An Indian	Nora Quealey (p. 430)
Story" (p. 109)	C. P. Ellis (p. 575)

7. Look ahead and compare the data provided by Mantsios with the information in "Have-Mores and Have-Lesses" (p. 356). Are the two pieces largely consistent in the pictures they draw of wealth in the United States? Do you see any discrepancies or inconsistencies?

8. Write an imaginary dialogue between Mantsios and Mike Rose (p. 174) about why some students, like Rose, seem to be able to break through social class barriers and others, like Ken Harvey, Dave Snyder, and Ted Richard, do not.

EXTENDING THE CRITICAL CONTEXT

9. Skim through several recent issues of a financial magazine like *Forbes* or *Money*. Who is the audience for these publications? What kind of advice is offered, and what levels of income and investment are discussed?

10. Study the employment pages of a major newspaper in your area. Roughly what percentage of the openings would you consider upper class, middle class, and lower class? On what do you base your distinctions?

11. Mantsios claims that while TV reinforces negative class stereotypes, it generally depicts a world where class scarcely exists. Work together in small groups to survey a week's worth of TV programming. In general, how are upper-, middle-, and working-class Americans portrayed? To what extent does TV deny the power of class differences?

The Lesson

TONI CADE BAMBARA

"The Lesson" looks at wealth through the eyes of a poor black girl whose education includes a field trip to one of the world's premier toy stores. The story speaks to serious social issues with a comic, energetic, and utterly engaging voice. Toni Cade Bambara (1939–1995) grew up in the

Harlem and Bedford-Stuyvesant areas of New York City. Trained at Queens College and City College of New York in dance, drama, and literature, she is best known for her collections of stories, Gorilla, My Love *(1972) and* The Seabirds Are Still Alive and Other Stories *(1977), and for her novels,* If Blessing Comes *(1987) and* The Salt Eaters *(1980), winner of the American Book Award. Late in her career Bambara collaborated on several TV documentaries and taught script writing at Scribe Video Center in Philadelphia. This story is taken from* Gorilla, My Love.

Back in the days when everyone was old and stupid or young and foolish and me and Sugar were the only ones just right, this lady moved on our block with nappy hair and proper speech and no makeup. And quite naturally we laughed at her, laughed the way we did at the junk man who went about his business like he was some big-time president and his sorry-ass horse his secretary. And we kinda hated her too, hated the way we did the winos who cluttered up our parks and pissed on our handball walls and stank up our hallways and stairs so you couldn't halfway play hide-and-seek without a goddamn gas mask. Miss Moore was her name. The only woman on the block with no first name. And she was black as hell, cept for her feet, which were fish-white and spooky. And she was always planning these boring-ass things for us to do, us being my cousin, mostly, who lived on the block cause we all moved North the same time and to the same apartment then spread out gradual to breathe. And our parents would yank our heads into some kinda shape and crisp up our clothes so we'd be presentable for travel with Miss Moore, who always looked like she was going to church, though she never did. Which is just one of the things the grownups talked about when they talked behind her back like a dog. But when she came calling with some sachet[1] she'd sewed up or some gingerbread she'd made or some book, why then they'd all be too embarrassed to turn her down and we'd get handed out all spruced up. She'd been to college and said it only right that she should take responsibility for the young ones' education, and she not even related by marriage or blood. So they'd go for it. Specially Aunt Gretchen. She was the main gofer in the family. You got some ole dumb shit foolishness you want somebody to go for, you send for Aunt Gretchen. She been screwed into the go-along for so long, it's a blood-deep natural thing with her. Which is how she got saddled with me and Sugar and Junior in the first place while our mothers were in a la-de-da apartment up the block having a good ole time.

---

[1]*sachet:* A small bag filled with a sweet-smelling substance. Sachets are often placed in drawers to scent clothes.

So this one day Miss Moore rounds us all up at the mailbox and it's puredee hot and she's knockin herself out about arithmetic. And school suppose to let up in summer I heard, but she don't never let up. And the starch in my pinafore scratching the shit outta me and I'm really hating this nappy-head bitch and her goddamn college degree. I'd much rather go to the pool or to the show where it's cool. So me and Sugar leaning on the mailbox being surly, which is a Miss Moore word. And Flyboy checking out what everybody brought for lunch. And Fat Butt already wasting his peanut-butter-and-jelly sandwich like the pig he is. And Junebug punchin on Q.T.'s arm for potato chips. And Rosie Giraffe shifting from one hip to the other waiting for somebody to step on her foot or ask her if she from Georgia so she can kick ass, preferably Mercedes'. And Miss Moore asking us do we know what money is, like we a bunch of retards. I mean real money, she say, like it's only poker chips or monopoly papers we lay on the grocer. So right away I'm tired of this and say so. And would much rather snatch Sugar and go to the Sunset and terrorize the West Indian kids and take their hair ribbons and their money too. And Miss Moore files that re-mark away for next week's lesson on brotherhood, I can tell. And finally I say we oughta get to the subway cause it's cooler and besides we might meet some cute boys. Sugar done swiped her mama's lipstick, so we ready.

So we heading down the street and she's boring us silly about what things cost and what our parents make and how much goes for rent and how money ain't divided up right in this country. And then she gets to the part about we all poor and live in the slums, which I don't feature. And I'm ready to speak on that, but she steps out in the street and hails two cabs just like that. Then she hustles half the crew in with her and hands me a five-dollar bill and tells me to calculate 10 percent tip for the driver. And we're off. Me and Sugar and Junebug and Flyboy hangin out the window and hollering to everybody, putting lipstick on each other cause Flyboy a faggot anyway, and making farts with our sweaty armpits. But I'm mostly trying to figure how to spend this money. But they all fascinated with the meter ticking and Junebug starts laying bets as to how much it'll read when Flyboy can't hold his breath no more. Then Sugar lays bets as to how much it'll be when we get there. So I'm stuck. Don't nobody want to go for my plan, which is to jump out at the next light and run off to the first bar-b-que we can find. Then the driver tells us to get the hell out cause we are there already. And the meter reads eighty-five cents. And I'm stalling to figure out the tip and Sugar say give him a dime. And I decide he don't need it bad as I do, so later for him. But then he tries to take off with Junebug foot still in the door so we talk about his mama something ferocious. Then we check out that we on Fifth Avenue[2] and everybody dressed up in stockings. One lady in a fur coat, hot as it is. White folks crazy.

---

[2]*Fifth Avenue:* The street in New York most famous for its expensive stores.

"This is the place," Miss Moore say, presenting it to us in the voice she uses at the museum. "Let's look in the windows before we go in."

"Can we steal?" Sugar asks very serious like she's getting the ground   5
rules square away before she plays. "I beg your pardon," say Miss Moore, and we fall out. So she leads us around the windows of the toy store and me and Sugar screamin, "This is mine, that's mine, I gotta have that, that was made for me, I was born for that," till Big Butt drowns us out.

"Hey, I'm goin to buy that there."

"That there? You don't even know what it is, stupid."

"I do so," he say punchin on Rosie Giraffe. "It's a microscope."

"Whatcha gonna do with a microscope, fool?"

"Look at things."   10

"Like what, Ronald?" ask Miss Moore. And Big Butt ain't got the first notion. So here go Miss Moore gabbing about the thousands of bacteria in a drop of water and the somethinorother in a speck of blood and the million and one living things in the air around us is invisible to the naked eye. And what she say that for? Junebug go to town on that "naked" and we rolling. Then Miss Moore ask what it cost. So we all jam into the window smudgin it up and the price tag say $300. So then she ask how long'd take for Big Butt and Junebug to save up their allowances. "Too long," I say. "Yeh," adds Sugar, "outgrown it by that time." And Miss Moore say no, you never out-grow learning instruments. "Why, even medical students and interns and," blah, blah, blah. And we ready to choke Big Butt for bringing it up in the first damn place.

"This here costs four hundred eighty dollars," say Rosie Giraffe. So we pile up all over her to see what she pointin out. My eyes tell me it's a chunk of glass cracked with something heavy, and different-color inks dripped into the splits, then the whole thing put into a oven or something. But for $480 it don't make sense.

"That's a paperweight made of semi precious stones fused together under tremendous pressure," she explains slowly, with her hands doing the mining and all the factory work.

"So what's paperweight?" asks Rosie Giraffe.

"To weight paper with, dumbbell," say Flyboy, the wise man from the   15
East.

"Not exactly," say Miss Moore, which is what she say when you warm or way off too. "It's to weigh paper down so it won't scatter and make your desk untidy." So right away me and Sugar curtsy to each other and then to Mercedes who is more the tidy type.

"We don't keep paper on top of the desk in my class," say Junebug, fig-uring Miss Moore crazy or lyin one.

"At home, then," she say. "Don't you have a calendar and a pencil case and a blotter and a letter-opener on your desk at home where you do your homework?" And she know damn well what our homes look like cause she nosys around in them every chance she gets.

"I don't even have a desk," say Junebug. "Do we?"

"No. And I don't get no homework neither," say Big Butt.   20

"And I don't even have a home," say Flyboy like he do at school to keep
the white folks off his back and sorry for him. Send this poor kid to camp
posters, is his speciality.

"I do," say Mercedes. "I have a box of stationery on my desk and a picture of my cat. My godmother bought the stationery and the desk. There's a
big rose on each sheet and the envelopes smell like roses."

"Who want to know about your smelly-ass stationery," say Rosie Giraffe
fore I can get my two cents in.

"It's important to have a work area all your own so that . . ."

"Will you look at this sailboat, please," say Flyboy, cuttin her off and   25
pointin to the thing like it was his. So once again we tumble all over each other
to gaze at this magnificent thing in the toy store which is just big enough to
maybe sail two kittens across the pond if you strap them to the posts tight. We
all start reciting the price tag like we in assembly. "Handcrafted sailboat of
fiberglass at one thousand one hundred ninety-five dollars."

"Unbelievable," I hear myself say and am really stunned. I read it again
for myself just in case the group recitation put me in a trance. Same thing.
For some reason this pisses me off. We look at Miss Moore and she lookin
at us, waiting for I dunno what.

"Who'd pay all that when you can buy a sailboat set for a quarter at
Pop's, a tube of glue for a dime, and a ball of string for eight cents? It must
have a motor and a whole lot else besides." I say. "My sailboat cost me
about fifty cents."

"But will it take water?" say Mercedes with her smart ass.

"Took mine to Alley Pond Park once," say Flyboy. "String broke. Lost
it. Pity."

"Sailed mine in Central Park and it keeled over and sank. Had to ask   30
my father for another dollar."

"And you got the strap," laugh Big Butt. "The jerk didn't even have a
string on it. My old man wailed on his behind."

Little Q.T. was staring hard at the sailboat and you could see he wanted
it bad. But he too little and somebody'd just take it from him. So what the
hell. "This boat for kids, Miss Moore?"

"Parents silly to buy something like that just to get all broke up," say
Rosie Giraffe.

"That much money it should last forever," I figure.

"My father'd buy it for me if I wanted it."   35

"Your father, my ass," say Rosie Giraffe getting a chance to finally push
Mercedes.

"Must be rich people shop here," say Q.T.

"You are a very bright boy," say Flyboy. "What was your first clue?" And
he rap him on the head with the back of his knuckles, since Q.T. the only

one he could get away with. Though Q.T. liable to come up behind you years later and get his licks in when you half expect it.

"What I want to know is," I says to Miss Moore though I never talk to her, I wouldn't give the bitch that satisfaction, "is how much a real boat costs? I figure a thousand'd get you a yacht any day."

"Why don't you check that out," she says, "and report back to the group?" Which really pains my ass. If you gonna mess up a perfectly good swim day least you could do is have some answers. "Let's go in," she say like she got something up her sleeve. Only she don't lead the way. So me and Sugar turn the corner to where the entrance is, but when we get there I kinda hang back. Not that I'm scared, what's there to be afraid of, just a toy store. But I feel funny, shame. But what I got to be shamed about? Got as much right to go in as anybody. But somehow I can't seem to get hold on the door, so I step away for Sugar to lead. But she hangs back too. And I look at her and she looks at me and this is ridiculous. I mean, damn, I have never ever been shy about doing nothing or going nowhere. But then Mercedes steps up and then Rosie Giraffe and Big Butt crowd in behind and shove, and next thing we all stuffed into the doorway with only Mercedes squeezing past us, smoothing out her jumper and walking right down the aisle. Then the rest of us tumble in like a glued-together jigsaw done all wrong. And people lookin at us. And it's like the time me and Sugar crashed into the Catholic church on a dare. But once we got in there and everything so hushed and holy and the candles and the bowin and the handkerchiefs on all the drooping heads, I just couldn't go through with the plan. Which was for me to run up to the altar and do a tap dance while Sugar played the nose flute and messed around in the holy water. And Sugar kept givin me the elbow. Then later teased me so bad I tied her up in the shower and turned it on and locked her in. And she'd be there till this day if Aunt Gretchen hadn't finally figured I was lying about the boarder takin a shower.

Same thing in the store. We all walkin on tiptoe and hardly touchin the games and puzzles and things. And I watched Miss Moore who is steady watchin us like she waitin for a sign. Like Mama Drewery watches the sky and sniffs the air and takes note of just how much slant is in the bird formation. Then me and Sugar bump smack into each other, so busy gazing at the toys, 'specially the sailboat. But we don't laugh and go into our fat-lady bump-stomach routine. We just stare at that price tag. Then Sugar run a finger over the whole boat. And I'm jealous and want to hit her. Maybe not her, but I sure want to punch somebody in the mouth.

"Watcha bring us here for, Miss Moore?"

"You sound angry, Sylvia. Are you mad about something?" Give me one of them grins like she tellin a grown-up joke that never turns out to be funny. And she's lookin very closely at me like maybe she plannin to do my portrait from memory. I'm mad, but I won't give her that satisfaction. So I slouch around the store bein very bored and say, "Let's go."

Me and Sugar at the back of the train watchin' the tracks whizzin by large then small then gettin gobbled up in the dark. I'm thinkin about this tricky toy I saw in the store. A clown that somersaults on a bar then does chin-ups just cause you yank lightly at his leg. Cost $35. I could see me askin my mother for a $35 birthday clown. "You wanna who that costs what?" she'd say, cockin her head to the side to get a better view of the hole in my head. Thirty-five dollars could buy new bunk beds for Junior and Gretchen's boy. Thirty-five dollars and the whole household could go visit Granddaddy Nelson in the country. Thirty-five dollars would pay for the rent and the piano bill too. Who are these people that spend that much for performing clowns and $1,000 for toy sailboats? What kinda work they do and how they live and how come we ain't in on it? Where we are is who we are, Miss Moore always pointin out. But it don't necessarily have to be that way, she always adds then waits for somebody to say that poor people have to wake up and demand their share of the pie and don't none of us know what kind of pie she talkin about in the first damn place. But she ain't so smart cause I still got her four dollars from the taxi and she sure ain't gettin it. Messin up my day with this shit. Sugar nudges me in my pocket and winks.

Miss Moore lines us up in front of the mailbox where we started from,   45
seem like years ago, and I got a headache for thinkin so hard. And we lean all over each other so we can hold up under the draggy-ass lecture she always finishes us off with at the end before we thank her for borin us to tears. But she just looks at us like she readin tea leaves. Finally she say, "Well, what did you think of F. A. O. Schwarz?"[3]

Rosie Giraffe mumbles, "White folks crazy."

"I'd like to go in there again when I get my birthday money," says Mercedes, and we shove her out the pack so she has to lean on the mailbox by herself.

"I'd like a shower. Tiring day," say Flyboy.

Then Sugar surprises me by saying. "You know, Miss Moore, I don't think all of us here put together eat in a year what that sailboat costs." And Miss Moore lights up like somebody goosed her. "And?" she say, urging Sugar on. Only I'm standin on her foot so she don't continue.

"Imagine for a minute what kind of society it is in which some people   50
can spend on a toy what it would cost to feed a family of six or seven. What do you think?"

"I think," say Sugar pushing me off her feet like she never done before, cause I whip her ass in a minute, "that this is not much of a democracy if you ask me. Equal chance to pursue happiness means an equal crack at the dough, don't it?" Miss Moore is besides herself and I am disgusted with

---

[3]*F. A. O. Schwarz:* The name and the toy store are real. The store, in fact, has become a tourist attraction.

Sugar's treachery. So I stand on her foot one more time to see if she'll shove me. She shuts up, and Miss Moore looks at me, sorrowfully I'm thinkin. And somethin weird is going on, I can feel it in my chest.

"Anybody else learn anything today?" lookin dead at me. I walk away and Sugar has to run to catch up and don't even seem to notice when I shrug her arm off my shoulder.

"Well, we got four dollars anyway," she says.

"Uh hunh."

"We could go to Hascombs and get half a chocolate layer and then go   55
to the Sunset and still have plenty money for potato chips and ice-cream sodas."

"Uh hunh."

"Race you to Hascombs," she say.

We start down the block and she gets ahead which is O.K. by me cause I'm goin to the West End and then over to the Drive to think this day through. She can run if she want to and even run faster. But ain't nobody gonna beat me at nuthin.

Engaging the Text

1. What is the lesson Miss Moore is trying to teach in this story? How well is it received by Mercedes, Sugar, and the narrator, Sylvia? Why does the narrator react differently from Sugar, and what is the meaning of her last line in the story, "But ain't nobody gonna beat me at nuthin"?

2. Why did Bambara write the story from Sylvia's point of view? How would the story change if told from Miss Moore's perspective? From Sugar's? How would it change if the story were set today as opposed to twenty years ago?

3. The story mentions several expensive items: a fur coat, a microscope, a paperweight, a sailboat, and a toy clown. Why do you think the author chose each of these details?

4. In paragraph 44 Sylvia says, "Where we are is who we are, Miss Moore always pointin out. But it don't necessarily have to be that way." What does Miss Moore mean by this? Do you agree? What does Miss Moore expect the children to do to change the situation?

Exploring Connections

5. Write a dialogue between Miss Moore and Gregory Mantsios, author of "Rewards and Opportunities" (p. 331), in which they discuss Sylvia's future and her chances for success.

6. Compare Miss Moore with the matriarchs in "Envy" by Bebe Moore Campbell (p. 118). In particular, examine the goals they set, the behavior they expect, and their means of influencing the young women in their charge.

7. Compare Miss Moore with the "Seven-Lesson Schoolteacher" described by John Taylor Gatto (p. 166). To what extent does Miss Moore's approach to education avoid the pitfalls Gatto identifies with formal schooling? Does Miss Moore's "lesson" have a hidden curriculum?

8. Compare Sylvia and Sugar's relationship here with that of Teresa and the speaker of the poem in "Para Teresa" (p. 216). Which girls stand the better chance of achieving success? Why?

EXTENDING THE CRITICAL CONTEXT

9. For the next class meeting, find the most overpriced, unnecessary item you can in a store, catalog, TV ad or newspaper. Spend a few minutes swapping examples, then discuss the information you've gathered: are there any lessons to be learned here about wealth, success, and status?

10. The opening lines of "The Lesson" suggest that Sylvia is now a mature woman looking back on her youth. Working in groups, write a brief biography explaining what has happened to Sylvia since the day of "The Lesson." What has she done? Who has she become? Read your profiles aloud to the class and explain your vision of Sylvia's development.

Have-Mores and Have-Lesses

DONALD L. BARLETT AND JAMES B. STEELE

Given the value Americans place on equality, freedom, and opportunity, it's not surprising that many tend to think of the United States as a classless society; part of the great experiment in democracy, after all, was to throw out the European system of aristocracy and strict social hierarchy. Generally, though, Americans have recognized that a three-class society does exist in the United States; we have prided ourselves on the prosperity of our huge middle class, whose standard of living led the world. Barlett and Steele argue that we are moving now toward a two-class society, with a small number of elite Americans enjoying a fabulous lifestyle while the majority work more and harder for fewer rewards. Business and government decisions have put the American Dream out of reach, they say, for ordinary Americans. Donald L. Barlett (b. 1936) and James B. Steele (b. 1943) are Pulitzer Prize–winning investigative reporters for the Philadelphia Inquirer. *In addition to writing* America: Who Stole the Dream? *(1996), from which this selection is excerpted, they authored the best-seller* America: What Went Wrong? *(1992).*

Who Revoked the Dream?

Let's suppose, for a moment, there was a country where the people in charge charted a course that eliminated millions of good-paying jobs. Suppose they gave away several million more jobs to other nations. Finally, imagine that the people running this country implemented economic policies that enabled those at the very top to grow ever richer while most others grew poorer.

You wouldn't want to live in such a place, would you?

Too bad.

You already do.

These are some of the consequences of failed U.S. government policies   5
that have been building over the last three decades — the same policies that people in Washington today are intent on keeping or expanding. Under them, 100 million Americans, mostly working families and individuals — blue-collar, white-collar, and professional — are being treated as though they were expendable.

Most significant of all, the American dream of the last half-century has been revoked for millions of people — a dream rooted in a secure job, a home in the suburbs, the option for families to live on one income rather than two, a better life than your parents had, and a still-better life for your children.

U.S. government policies consistently have failed to preserve that dream in the face of growing international competition. Instead they've favored the very forces that shift jobs, money, and influence abroad. As a result, the United States is about to enter the 21st century much the same way it left the 19th century: with a two-class society.

Both government and big business are encouraging the shift — dividing America into have-mores and have-lesses. While the nation's richest 1 percent is accumulating wealth not seen since the robber-baron era of the last century, the middle class is shrinking.

There are, to be sure, some notable differences from a century ago. In the 1890s, most Americans were struggling to reach a middle-class lifestyle. By the 1990s, an overwhelming majority, having achieved it, were either losing it or struggling to hold on to it. In the 1890s, government responded to the prodding of reform-minded citizens and began to slowly create a framework of rules to guide the economy, control the excesses of giant business trusts and their allies, and generally to protect the interests of the average citizen. By the 1990s, that framework was being dismantled.

Who is responsible?   10

In a word: Washington.

Or, more specifically, members of Congress and presidents of the last three decades, Democrats and Republicans alike. Of course, they've had a lot of help — from lobbyists, special-interest groups, executives of multinational corporations, bankers, economists, think-tank strategists and the wheelers and dealers of Wall Street. These are some of the emerging winners in this changing America.

The losers? Working Americans who have been forced to live in fear — fear of losing their jobs and benefits, fear of the inability to pay for their children's education, fear of what will happen to their aging parents, fear of losing everything they've struggled to achieve.

The winners say if you're not a part of this new America, you have no one to blame but yourself. They say the country is undergoing a massive structural change comparable to the Industrial Revolution of the 1800s, when Americans moved off the farms and into factories. They say you have failed to retrain yourselves for the new emerging economy. That you don't have enough education. That you're not working smarter. That you failed to grasp the fact that companies aren't in the business of providing lifetime employment. And, they say, it's all inevitable anyway.

It is inevitable that factories and offices will close, that jobs will move   15
overseas or be taken by newly arriving immigrants, that people's living standards will fall, that you may have to work two or three part-time jobs instead of one full-time job. These things are inevitable, they say, because they are the product of a market economy, and thus beyond the control of ordinary human beings and, most especially, beyond the control of government.

Don't believe it.

They are, in fact, the product of the interaction between market forces and government policies — laws and regulations enacted or not enacted, of people finding ways to turn government to their advantage. The policies that are driving these changes range across the breadth of government — from international trade to immigration, from antitrust enforcement to deregulation, from lobbying laws to tax laws.

Because of these changes, American society is being recast, as the bottom-line mentality of the global business world is transferred to the country at large. Along the way, workers, entire communities, and a way of life once the envy of people around the world have become dispensable.

Michael Rothbaum and Darlene Speer are at opposite ends of this new two-class society.

Rothbaum, a corporate executive, lives in an exclusive gated commu-   20
nity called St. Andrews Country Club in Boca Raton, Fla. Set amid 718 acres of lakes, fairways, and landscaped grounds, St. Andrews is typical of the luxury communities that many wealthy Americans now inhabit — self-contained enclaves sealed off from everyone else.

St. Andrews has its own 24-hour security patrol, shopping complex, sports pavilion, restaurants and two championship 18-hole golf courses where residents can play after paying a $75,000 membership fee. Rothbaum lives in a 5,000-square-foot home, with pool and spa, built in 1991. According to the Palm Beach county assessors's office, the property is valued at $636,000.

Darlene Speer, on the other hand, works two jobs. She is a full-time office worker for a furniture manufacturer and a part-time clerk at a video store in Marion, Va. She lives in a one-bedroom unit in an apartment complex in Marion, a community of 8,500 in the mountains of southwestern Virginia.

Until 1992, Speer worked in the sewing department of Harwood Industries, a clothing manufacturer that was one of Marion's largest private employers. But in August 1992, Harwood Industries, whose principal owner was Michael Rothbaum, announced it would close the department. After that, all apparel production was in Honduras and Costa Rica, where labor costs are much cheaper. The company said it was under pressure from retailers to cut costs.

Not that Darlene Speer and her coworkers drove Harwood Industries to Central America with their bloated salaries. After 13 years, Speer was earning less than nine dollars an hour. But women in Honduras work for a lot less — about 48 cents an hour.

Before leaving town, Rothbaum's company agreed to pay severance of 25 about $1,200 to each employee. The total for 120 women, who had collectively worked more than 1,500 years in the sewing department, amounted to less than one-quarter of the value of Rothbaum's home . . . .

Marion is in the heart of what Virginians call the Mountain Empire, a region of lovely rolling hills, pleasant valleys and gentle streams. It is a place where jobs have never been plentiful. But small manufacturing facilities, especially clothing plants, have dotted stretches of the countryside along Interstate 81, providing jobs for area women.

For more than half a century Harwood Industries, a maker of men's pajamas, robes, and casual clothing, was one of the fixtures of the Marion economy. At its plant on the outskirts of town, Harwood employed several hundred seamstresses, cutters, warehousemen, packers, mechanics, and office workers. By national standards, the pay was never good. In 1992, the average wage for women in the sewing department was $6.75 an hour, or roughly $14,000 a year. But Harwood did have a health plan, the women were close to family and friends, and at least it provided steady work.

Until August 31, 1992. On that day, Harwood announced it was closing the sewing operation, eliminating 120 jobs. In a statement all too familiar to American workers, Harwood officials said they regretted the decision but that it was "necessary because we were not competitive on most of the products we were producing." The company said it planned to keep open a distribution center and office "to maintain a substantial presence in Marion." But they, too, were phased out over the next 18 months.

For years, Harwood had been shuttering plants in the United States and, under pressure from retailers to cut costs, shifting production offshore — first to Puerto Rico, then Nicaragua, and finally to Honduras and Costa Rica. The employees at Marion had watched as the company closed other plants, and had seen other manufacturers in their area shut down. They knew the signs did not look good. Yet the layoff still came as a shock.

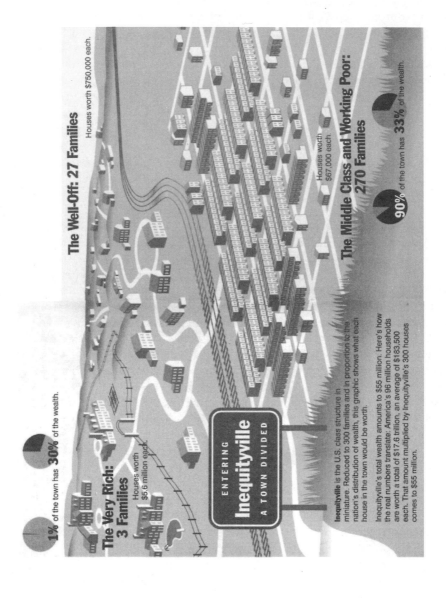

The Very Rich: 3 Families
Houses worth $6.6 million each.

1% of the town has **30%** of the wealth.

ENTERING
Inequityville
A TOWN DIVIDED

Inequityville is the U.S. class structure in miniature. Reduced to 300 families and in proportion to the nation's distribution of wealth, this graphic shows what each house in the town would be worth.

Inequityville's total wealth amounts to $55 million. Here's how the real numbers translate: America's 96 million households are worth a total of $17.6 trillion, an average of $183,500 each. That amount multiplied by Inequityville's 300 houses comes to $55 million.

The Well-Off: 27 Families
Houses worth $750,000 each.

The Middle Class and Working Poor: 270 Families
Houses worth $67,000 each.

90% of the town has **33%** of the wealth.

America: Who Stole the Dream? © by Donald Barlett and James B. Steele. Reprinted with permission of Andrews and McMeel. All rights reserved.

"It does something to your self-esteem," said Ann Williams, who closed   30
out her 20 years at Harwood working in the office. "You don't get over it. I
don't know anyone who has really gotten over it. Even those of us who have
gone on and been fortunate enough to find work feel that way. We all knew
we hadn't been singled out. Everybody had been let go. But you still take it
personally. I don't think there is any one of us who didn't take it personally."

For Darlene Speer, the shutdown hurt, both personally and financially.
"I loved my job, but after the way they treated us at the end, I was almost
glad to get out of there," she said. "We all worked so hard. They didn't close
it because of our work. I don't think there's any one of us now who is not
glad to be away from there, even though we might not be making the same
money."

Speer, who is divorced and the mother of two grown children, ultimately wound up with two jobs, with the furniture maker and the video
store, and together, she said, the two equal roughly what she earned annually at Harwood. "But you can't look back," she said. "I've gone ahead with
my life. And, for the most part, I'm happy. But I'll tell you it's hard to start
over."

One of her coworkers, Nancy Anders, who worked in the sewing department for 25 years, recalled how she'd felt such a sense of responsibility
toward the job. She went to work regardless — "when I was sick, when my
family was sick," she said. At the company's request, she even went to
Nicaragua in the late 1970s to help train new employees at a plant Harwood
had built there. Anders spent six weeks showing Nicaraguan women how to
operate sewing machines. At the time, she didn't think much about it. She
felt sorry for the people, who were so poor. It was only years later, reflecting
on the trip, that she realized she'd been "training them to take our jobs but
didn't know it."

She did everything she was asked because that was her nature. "When I
worked there, I thought this company can't get by without me," Anders
said. "And when I found out they could, it hurt. I was bitter at first. It
seemed like they shouldn't have closed it. But the more I thought about it, I
thought, 'If they don't want me, then I can find a job somewhere.' "

Eventually, Anders did find one, for less money. "I have a good job   35
now," she said. "It's a part-time job. I'm Wal-Mart's people-greeter, and I
love it. And I think I'm the best people-greeter Wal-Mart's got."

Smiling and upbeat, Nancy Anders has gone on with her life, even
though she earns less and must pay for her health coverage. Yet for her, the
greatest loss can't be measured in dollars and cents. Harwood's closing
cheated her out of a chapter of her life.

For 25 years, she had gone to festive dinners sponsored by the employees when fellow workers retired. On these occasions, employees chipped in
to buy the retiree a finely crafted oak rocking chair made at a nearby furniture factory. It was a lasting gesture of affection from those who stayed to
those who were departing, and the rocking chair came to symbolize not only

a life of leisure but also a kind of closure to a life of working at the Harwood plant. "I went to the retirement dinners for 25 years and I couldn't wait to retire so I could get one of those great big rocking chairs," she said. "I just dreamed about that day. That was my goal, getting that rocking chair."

When Harwood announced the shutdown in 1992, Nancy Anders knew there would be no retirement dinner, no rocking chair. "I went home that night and I cried," she said. "My husband thought I was crazy being so upset over a rocking chair. He said, 'Go get one.' I could have bought the rocking chair. But it wouldn't have meant the same after all those years. I missed getting that rocking chair almost as much as I hated to lose my job."

Wendell Watkins, a Harwood vice-president and the last manager of the Marion plant, said the company regretted the closing but had no choice if it wanted to remain "competitive." "We have always manufactured private-label goods for big firms [department stores] who can shop the world and get the best price they can," Watkins said. "Now, that's great for the U.S. consumer, and they are the real beneficiaries. Our major customers always insist on having the lowest price. They tell us, 'We'll bring it in from the Orient if you can't do something to match the cost.' I think we did a great job of keeping it open as long as we did and we would have loved to have continued to operate it, but we just could not compete with the competition we had to meet and pay U.S. labor prices."

Watkins said he knew the closing was hard on many employees, but he felt   40
it was the right decision — not just for Harwood but for the nation as a whole. "As much as this has hurt my industry, it is my belief and feeling that our government is going about this in the correct manner," Watkins said. "I think that they have to write the industry off and go for high-tech and let the less-expensive labor countries produce the apparel and other things. I have lived in the industry all my life and it has been good to me, and as much as I hate to admit it, I think we are taking the proper approach. I know it has hurt a lot of people, but it is also helping a lot of people in the long run, the consumers."

When Harwood shut Marion, the company ceased to manufacture in the United States. The gradual move of its plants offshore was complete to three new facilities — two in Honduras and one in Costa Rica. For many American apparel makers, Honduras has become the country of choice in recent years. The Central American nation of 5.3 million people has been highly successful in attracting U.S. plants because of cheap labor, no taxes and a solicitous government. American companies that manufacture products in specially created export zones are exempt from all import and export duties, from currency charges when they ship profits back to the United States, and from all Honduran taxes — a "Permanent Tax Holiday," as the Honduran government describes it.

Best of all, they are exempt from U.S.-style wages. The minimum wage of the Honduran factory worker, according to that government's statistics, is 48 cents an hour, including benefits — or less than $20 a week in take-home pay. Even by Latin American standards, that's low. Mexicans who work in American plants in the north of Mexico now earn, on average, $60 a week — three times the average pay of Hondurans. And Mexican wages, of course, are only a fraction of the $7 to $8 an hour that a U.S. worker would be paid. In short, for all the talk about the need to be "competitive," there is no way a plant in the United States paying minimum wages and no benefits could compete with a Honduran plant that pays 48 cents an hour and where profits are exempt from taxes.

Not surprisingly, many American companies have moved some operations to Honduras in recent years. The list includes such familiar names as Sara Lee, Bestform, U.S. Shoe, Fruit of the Loom, and Wrangler. One of those companies, Sara Lee, in turn announced plans in the summer of 1996 to acquire Harwood. "Harwood's manufacturing expertise complements Sara Lee's knowledge of the underwear [industry]," said Donald J. Franceschini, executive vice-president of Sara Lee.

Harwood was one of the first to capitalize on Honduran incentives; its first plant was built there in 1980. When Harwood's Watkins was asked if labor was the main reason for going to Central America, he answered: "It's the only benefit. And you do it only so you can compete, not because you want to."

Having successfully transferred all of Harwood's operations abroad, the company's chief executive officer and principal owner, Michael Rothbaum, subsequently offered some words of advice to American manufacturers who might be considering a Caribbean operation. After first warning that the process was not easy — think of it "as if you were starting a plant on the moon," he wrote in a trade journal — he then assured them it was worth it. If "approached correctly, the savings in labor costs can be significant." 45

Rothbaum went on to paint a picture of the average worker: "Caribbean employees work longer hours, from 44 to 48 per week, and they travel further to work, sometimes two hours by bus each way. Some also attend school at night. For many, the only decent meal they get each day is the one served in your cafeteria. Also remember that Caribbean employees are younger than your domestic workforce. The average age in a Caribbean plant may be 19 to 20.

"Medical care as we know it is not available, and people come to work when they're sick — because that is where they may find a doctor or nurse. To a great extent, you, the employer, must compensate for these differences in conditions through the social contract you make with your employees in order to achieve acceptable performance."

If Rothbaum believes U.S. employers must enter into a social contract with their Caribbean employees, it is just such a contract that their abandoned employees in the United States believe has been broken — by cutting off jobs, wiping out benefits, lowering their standard of living.

And the outlook for a long-term social contract in countries such as Honduras is not good, either, if history is any guide. Harwood's first offshore plant was in Puerto Rico. When wage rates rose there, the company moved its

apparel production to a lower-wage country, Nicaragua. But after political upheaval there in the late 1970s, Harwood relocated to Honduras and Costa Rica.

One longtime Harwood employee at Marion, Garney Powers, after   50
noticing how the company kept moving its operations from one developing
country to the next to cut costs, said he once asked a Harwood manager if
there was any chance, as wages rose in developing countries, that Harwood
might shift some of its manufacturing back to the States. No way, he said
the manager told him:

"There's too many countries out there."

ENGAGING THE TEXT

1. Spend some time in class telling stories from your family's and friends' experience that illustrate or challenge some of the themes Barlett and Steele
   raise (for example, downward mobility, jobs going overseas, two-job workers). How common are these problems in the community or communities
   you and your classmates come from?

Toles © 1994 The Buffalo News. Reprinted with permission of Universal Press Syndicate. All rights reserved.

2. Do the authors persuade you that there is indeed a serious threat to the American Dream — that it has perhaps been stolen? Do you expect to live in a two-class society after you graduate from college? Why or why not? What class do you expect to belong to, and why?

3. Analyze the illustration of "Inequityville" (p. 360): What is its overall message? How do the various details of the drawing support that message?

4. Review the point of view espoused by Wendell Watkins in paragraphs 39–40. Do you agree that the decisions by Harwood Industries ultimately benefit American consumers? Explain.

5. Paragraphs 46–49 describe the "social contract" between employers and employees. What is meant by this term? What kind of social contract, if any, do you expect to govern your own employment?

EXPLORING CONNECTIONS

6. In paragraph 6, the authors give a brief definition of the American Dream. Compare and contrast their understanding of the Dream to those you encountered in the excerpt from *Ragged Dick* (p. 306) and from "Horatio Alger" (p. 320). Do you see evidence that the meaning of the American Dream has shifted over time? Whose definition, if any, is most meaningful to you today?

7. Look ahead to the story of blue-collar worker Nora Quealey on page 430. Assume that she told her story in 1982. In small groups, brainstorm what Barlett and Steele might expect her to have experienced since then. Be as specific as possible. Then compare your imagined scenarios to those of other groups.

8. Look at the cartoons by Tom Tomorrow (p. 346) and Tom Toles (p. 364). What ideas about have-mores and have-lesses does each cartoon suggest? To what extent does the selection by Barlett and Steele support the perspectives of the cartoons?

EXTENDING THE CRITICAL CONTEXT

9. The "Inequityville" illustration (p. 360) uses the metaphor of a city to show the disparity in wealth between American have-mores and have-lesses. Draw your own illustration of the same idea but use a different metaphor of your choice (for example, food).

10. Draw a map of your city or town that shows how you think the wealth is distributed. Are there, for instance, prestigious gated communities featuring amenities like golf courses?

Streets of Gold:
The Myth of the Model Minority
CURTIS CHANG

According to conventional wisdom, Asian Americans offer the best evidence that the American Dream is alive and well. Publications like Time *and* Newsweek *have celebrated Asian Americans as a "super minority" that has adopted the Puritan work ethic and outshone even the Anglo majority in terms of education and financial success. In this essay, Curtis Chang probes the data used in such media reports and questions this new embodiment of the success myth. Since the educational achievement of Asians is an important component of the myth, the essay may prompt you to take a fresh look at the status of Asian American students on your campus. Chang was born in Taiwan and immigrated to the United States in 1971. This essay was written in 1987, when he was a freshman at Harvard; since graduating in 1990 Chang has taught in Harvard's government department and traveled to Soweto, South Africa, on a Michael C. Rockefeller Fellowship for Travel Abroad.*

Over 100 years ago, an American myth misled many of my ancestors. Seeking cheap labor, railroad companies convinced numerous Chinese that American streets were paved with gold. Today, the media portrays Asian-Americans as finally mining those golden streets. Major publications like *Time, Newsweek, U.S. News and World Report, Fortune, The New Republic,* the *Wall Street Journal,* and the *New York Times* have all recently published congratulatory "Model Minority" headline stories with such titles:

America's Super Minority
An American Success Story
A Model Minority
Why They Succeed
The Ultimate Assimilation
The Triumph of the Asian Americans

But the Model Minority is another "Streets of Gold" tale. It distorts Asian-Americans' true status and ignores our racial handicaps. And the Model Minority's ideology is even worse than its mythology. It attempts to justify the existing system of racial inequality by blaming the victims rather than the system itself.

The Model Minority myth introduces us as an ethnic minority that is finally "making it in America" (*Time,* July 8, 1985). The media consistently defines "making it" as achieving material wealth, wealth that flows from our successes in the workplace and the schoolroom. This economic achievement allegedly proves a minority can "lay claim to the American dream" (*Fortune,* Nov. 24, 1986).

Trying to show how "Asian-Americans present a picture of affluence and economic success" (*N.Y. Times Magazine,* Nov. 30, 1986), 9 out of 10 of the major Model Minority stories of the last four years relied heavily on one statistic: the family median income. The median Asian-American family income, according to the U.S. Census Survey of Income and Education data, is $22,713 compared to $20,800 for white Americans. Armed with that figure, national magazines have trumpeted our "remarkable, ever-mounting achievements" (*Newsweek,* Dec. 6, 1982).

Such assertions demonstrate the truth of the aphorism "Statistics are   5
like a bikini. What they reveal is suggestive, but what they conceal is vital." The family median income statistic conceals the fact that Asian-American families generally (1) have more children and live-in relatives and thus have more mouths to feed; (2) are often forced by necessity to have everyone in the family work, averaging more than two family income earners (whites only have 1.6) (Cabezas, 1979, p. 402); and (3) live disproportionately in high cost of living areas (i.e., New York, Chicago, Los Angeles, and Honolulu) which artificially inflate income figures. Dr. Robert S. Mariano, professor of economics at the University of Pennsylvania, has calculated that

> when such appropriate adjustments and comparisons are made, a different and rather disturbing picture emerges, showing indeed a clearly disadvantaged group. . . . Filipino and Chinese men *are no better off than black men with regard to median incomes.* (Mariano, 1979, p. 55)[1]

Along with other racial minorities, Asian-Americans are still scraping for the crumbs of the economic pie.

Throughout its distortion of our status, the media propagates two crucial assumptions. First, it lumps all Asian-Americans into one monolithic, homogeneous, yellow skinned mass. Such a view ignores the existence of an incredibly disadvantaged Asian-American underclass. Asians work in low income and low status jobs 2 to 3 times more than whites (Cabezas, 1979, p. 438). Recent Vietnamese refugees in California are living like the Appalachian poor. While going to his Manhattan office, multimillionaire architect I. M. Pei's car passes Chinese restaurants and laundries where

---

[1]The picture becomes even more disturbing when one realizes that higher income figures do not necessarily equal higher quality of life. For instance, in New York Chinatown, more than 1 out of 5 residents work more than 57 hours per week, almost 1 out of 10 elderly must labor more than 55 hours per week (Nishi, 1979, p. 503). [Author's note]

72 percent of all New York Chinese men still work (U.S. Bureau of the Census, 1977, Table 7).

But the media makes an even more dangerous assumption. It suggests that (alleged) material success is the same thing as basic racial equality. Citing that venerable family median income figure, magazines claim Asian-Americans are "obviously nondisadvantaged folks" (*Fortune,* May 17, 1982). Yet a 1979 United States Equal Employment Opportunity Commission study on Asian-Americans discovered widespread anti-Asian hiring and promotion practices. Asian-Americans "in the professional, technical, and managerial occupations" often face "modern racism — the subtle, sophisticated, systemic patterns and practices which function to effect and to obscure the discriminatory outcomes" (Nishi, 1979, p. 398). One myth simply does not prove another: neither our "astonishing economic prosperity" (*Fortune,* Nov. 24, 1986) nor a racially equal America exist.

An emphasis on material success also pervades the media's stress on Asian-Americans' educational status at "the top of the class" (*Newsweek on Campus,* April 2, 1984). Our "march into the ranks of the educational elite" (*U.S. News,* April 2, 1984) is significant because "all that education is paying off spectacularly" (*Fortune,* Nov. 24, 1986). Once again, the same fallacious assumptions plague this "whiz kids" image of Asian-Americans.

The media again ignores the fact that class division accounts for much of the publicized success. Until 1976, the U.S. Immigration Department only admitted Asian immigrants that were termed "skilled" workers. "Skilled" generally meant college educated, usually in the sciences since poor English would not be a handicap. The result was that the vast majority of pre-1976 Asian immigrants came from already well-educated, upper-class backgrounds — the classic "brain drain" syndrome (Hirschman and Wong, 1981, pp. 507–510).

The post-1976 immigrants, however, come generally from the lower, less educated classes (Kim, 1986, p. 24). A study by Professor Elizabeth Ahn Toupin of Tufts University matched similar Asian and non-Asian students *along class lines* and found that Asian-Americans "did not perform at a superior academic level to non-Asian students. Asian-Americans were more likely to be placed on academic probation than their white counterparts . . . twice as many Asian American students withdrew from the university" (Toupin, 1986, p. 12). 10

Thus, it is doubtful whether the perceived widespread educational success will continue as the Asian-American population eventually balances out along class lines. When 16.2 percent of all Chinese have less than 4 years of schooling (*four times* that of whites) (Azores, 1979, p. 73), it seems many future Asian-Americans will worry more about being able to read a newspaper rather than a Harvard acceptance letter.

Most important, the media assumes once again that achieving a certain level of material or educational success means achieving real equality. People easily forget that to begin with, Asians invest heavily in education since other means of upward mobility are barred to them by race. Until recently, for instance, Asian-Americans were barred from unions and traditional lines of credit (Yun, 1986, pp. 23–24).[2] Other "white" avenues to success, such as the "old boy network," are still closed to Asian-Americans.

When *Time* (July 8, 1985) claims "as a result of their academic achievement Asians are climbing the economic ladder with remarkable speed," it glosses over an inescapable fact: there is a white ladder and then there is a yellow one. Almost all of the academic studies on the *actual returns Asians receive* from their education point to prevalent discrimination. A striking example of this was found in a City University of New York research project which constructed resumes with equivalent educational backgrounds. Applications were then sent to employers, one group under an Asian name and a similar group under a Caucasian name. Whites received interviews 5 times more than Asians (Nishi, 1979, p. 399). The media never headlines even more shocking data that can be easily found in the U.S. Census. For instance, Chinese and Filipino males only earned respectively 74 and 52 percent as much as their *equally educated* white counterparts. Asian females fared even worse. Their salaries were only 44 to 54 percent as large as equivalent white males' paychecks (Cabezas, 1979, p. 391). Blacks suffer from this same statistical disparity. We Asian-Americans are indeed a Model Minority — a perfect model of racial discrimination in America.

Yet this media myth encourages neglect of our pressing needs. "Clearly, many Asian-Americans and Pacific peoples are invisible to the governmental agencies," one state agency reported. "Discrimination against Asian-Americans and Pacific peoples is as much the result of omission as commission" (California State Advisory Committee, 1975, p. 75). In 1979, while the president praised Asian-Americans' "successful integration into American society," his administration revoked Asian-Americans' eligibility for minority small business loans, devastating thousands of struggling, newly arrived small businessmen. Hosts of other minority issues, ranging from reparations for the Japanese-American internment[3] to the ominous rise of anti-Asian violence, are widely ignored by the general public.

The media, in fact, insist to the general populace that we are not a true   15
racial minority. In its attack on affirmative action, the *Boston Globe* (Jan. 14, 1985) pointed out that universities, like many people, "obviously feel that Asian-Americans, especially those of Chinese and Japanese descent, are brilliant, privileged, and wrongly classified as minorities." Harvard Dean Henry Rosovsky remarked in the same article that "it does not seem to me

---

[2]For further analysis on the role racism plays in Asian-Americans' stress on education and certain technical and scientific fields, see Suzuki, 1977, p. 44. [Author's note]

[3]*reparations . . . internment:* During World War II, over one hundred twenty thousand Japanese Americans on the West Coast were sent to prison camps by order of the U.S. government; many lost their homes, businesses, and possessions because of this forced relocation. After decades of work by Asian American activists, Congress in 1988 ordered the government to pay $20,000 to each internee as partial recompense for these losses.

that as a group, they are disadvantaged. . . . Asian-Americans appear to be in an odd category among other protected minorities."

The image that we Asians aren't like "other minorities" is fundamental to the Model Minority ideology. Any elementary school student knows that the teacher designates one student the model, the "teacher's pet," in order to set an example for others to follow. One only sets up a "model minority" in order to communicate to the other "students," the blacks and Hispanics, "Why can't you be like that?" The media, in fact, almost admit to "grading" minorities as they headline Model Minority stories, "Asian-Americans: Are They Making the Grade?" (*U.S. News,* April 2, 1984). And Asians have earned the highest grade by fulfilling one important assignment: identifying with the white majority, with its values and wishes.

Unlike blacks, for instance, we Asian-Americans have not vigorously asserted our ethnic identity (a.k.a. Black Power). And the American public has historically demanded assimilation over racial pluralism.[4] Over the years, *Newsweek* has published titles from "Success Story: Outwhiting the Whites" (*Newsweek,* June 21, 1971) to "Ultimate Assimilation" (*Newsweek,* Nov. 24, 1986), which lauded the increasing number of Asian-White marriages as evidence of Asian-Americans' "acceptance into American society."

Even more significant is the public's approval of how we have succeeded in the "American tradition" (*Fortune,* Nov. 24, 1986). Unlike the Blacks and Hispanics, we "Puritan-like" Asians (*N.Y. Times Magazine,* Nov. 30, 1986) disdain governmental assistance. A *New Republic* piece, "America's Greatest Success Story" (July 15, 1985), similarly applauded how "Asian-Americans pose no problems at all." The media consistently compares the crime-ridden image of other minorities with the picture of law abiding Asian parents whose "well-behaved kids" (*Newsweek on Campus,* April 1984) hit books and not the streets.

Some insist there is nothing terrible about whites conjuring up our "tremendous" success, divining from it model American traits, then preaching, "Why can't you blacks and Hispanics be like that?" After all, one might argue, aren't those traits desirable?

Such a view, as mentioned, neglects Asian-Americans' true and pressing needs. Moreover, this view completely misses the Model Minority image's fundamental ideology, an ideology meant to falsely grant America absolution from its racial barriers. 20

David O. Sears and Donald R. Kinder, two social scientists, have recently published significant empirical studies on the underpinnings of American racial attitudes. They consistently discovered that Americans'

---

[4]A full discussion of racial pluralism vs. assimilation is impossible here. But suffice it to say that pluralism accepts ethnic cultures as equally different; assimilation asks for a "melting" into the majority. An example of the assimilation philosophy is the massive "Americanization" programs of the late 1800s which successfully erased Eastern European immigrants' customs in favor of Anglo-Saxon ones. [Author's note]

stress on "values, such as 'individualism and self-reliance, the work ethic, obedience, and discipline' . . . can be invoked, however perversely, to feed racist appetites" (Kennedy, 1987, p. 88). In other words, the Model Minority image lets Americans' consciences rest easy. They can think: "It's not our fault those blacks and Hispanics can't make it. They're just too lazy. After all, look at the Asians."[5] Consequently, American society never confronts the systemic racial and economic factors underlying such inequality. The victims instead bear the blame.

This ideology behind the Model Minority image is best seen when we examine one of the first Model Minority stories, which suddenly appeared in the mid 1960s. It is important to note that the period was marked by newfound, strident black demands for equality and power.

> At a time when it is being proposed that hundreds of billions be spent to uplift Negroes and other minorities, the nation's 300,000 Chinese Americans are moving ahead on their own — with no help from anyone else . . . few Chinese-Americans are getting welfare handouts — or even want them . . . they don't sit around moaning. (*U.S. News,* Dec. 26, 1966)

The same article then concludes that the Chinese-American history and accomplishment "would shock those now complaining about the hardships endured by today's Negroes" (*U.S. News,* Dec. 26, 1966).

Not surprisingly, the dunce-capped blacks and Hispanics resent us apple polishing, "well-behaved" teacher's pets. Black comedian Richard Pryor performs a revealing routine in which new Asian immigrants learn from whites their first English word: "Nigger." And Asian-Americans themselves succumb to the Model Minority's deceptive mythology and racist ideology.[6] "I made it without help," one often hears among Asian circles, "why can't they?" In a 1986 nationwide poll, only 27 percent of Asian-American students rated "racial understanding" as "essential." The figure plunged 9 percent in the last year alone (a year marked by a torrent of Model Minority stories) (Hune, 1987). We "white-washed" Asians have simply lost our identity as a fellow, disadvantaged minority.

---

[5]This phenomenon of blaming the victim for racial inequality is as old as America itself. For instance, Southerners once eased their consciences over slavery by labeling blacks as animals lacking humanity. Today, America does it by labeling them as inferior people lacking "desirable" traits. For an excellent further analysis of this ideology, actually widespread among American intellectuals, see *Iron Cages: Race and Culture in 19th-Century America* by Ronald T. Takaki. [Author's note]

[6]America has a long history of playing off one minority against the other. During the early 1900s, for instance, mining companies in the west often hired Asians solely as scabs against striking black miners. Black versus Asian hostility and violence usually followed. This pattern was repeated in numerous industries. In a larger historical sense, almost every immigrant group has assimilated, to some degree, the culture of anti-black racism. [Author's note]

But we don't even need to look beyond the Model Minority stories themselves to realize that whites see us as "whiter" than blacks — but not quite white enough. For instance, citing that familiar median family income figure, *Fortune* magazine of May 17, 1982, complained that Asian-Americans are in fact "getting *more* than [their] share of the pie." For decades, when white Americans were leading the nation in every single economic measure, editorials arguing that whites were getting more than *their* share of the pie were rather rare.

No matter how "well behaved" we are, Asian-Americans are still excluded from the real pie, the "positions of institutional power and political power" (Kuo, 1979, p. 289). Professor Harry Kitano of UCLA has written extensively on the plight of Asian-Americans as the "middle-man minority," a minority supposedly satisfied materially but forever racially barred from a true, *significant* role in society. Empirical studies indicate that Asian-Americans "have been channeled into lower-echelon white-collar jobs having little or no decision making authority" (Suzuki, 1977, p. 38). For example, in *Fortune*'s 1,000 largest companies, Asian-American nameplates rest on a mere half of one percent of all officers' and directors' desks (a statistical disparity worsened by the fact that most of the Asians founded their companies) (*Fortune,* Nov. 24, 1986). While the education of the upper-class Asians may save them from the bread lines, their race still keeps them from the boardroom.

Our docile acceptance of such exclusion is actually one of our "model" traits. When Asian-Americans in San Francisco showed their first hint of political activism and protested Asian exclusion from city boards, *The Washington Monthly* (May 1986) warned in a long Asian-American article, "Watch out, here comes another group to pander to." *The New Republic* (July 15, 1985) praised Asian-American political movements because

> unlike blacks or Hispanics, Asian-American politicians have the luxury of not having to devote the bulk of their time to an "Asian-American agenda," and thus escape becoming prisoners of such an agenda. . . . The most important thing for Asian-Americans . . . is simply being part of the process.

This is strikingly reminiscent of another of the first Model Minority stories:

> As the Black and Brown communities push for changes in the present system, the Oriental is set forth as an example to be followed — a minority group that has achieved success through adaptation rather than confrontation. (*Gidra,* 1969)

But it is precisely this "present system," this system of subtle, persistent racism that we all must confront, not adapt to. For example, we Asians gained our right to vote from the 1964 Civil Rights Act that blacks marched, bled, died, and in the words of that original Model Minority story, "sat

CHANG • STREETS OF GOLD **373**

around moaning for." Unless we assert our true identity as a minority and challenge racial misconceptions and inequalities, we will be nothing more than techno-coolies[7] — collecting our wages but silently enduring basic political and economic inequality.

This country perpetuated a myth once. Today, no one can afford to dreamily chase after that gold in the streets, oblivious to the genuine treasure of racial equality. When racism persists, can one really call any minority a "model"?

List of Sources

Azores, Fortunata M., "Census Methodology and the Development of Social Indicators for Asian and Pacific Americans," *U.S. Commission on Civil Rights: Testimony on Civil Rights Issues of Asian and Pacific Americans* (1979), pp. 70–79.

Boston Globe, "Affirmative Non-actions," Jan. 14, 1985, p. 10.

Cabezas, Dr. Armado, "Employment Issues of Asian Americans," *U.S. Commission on Civil Rights: Testimony on Civil Rights Issues of Asian and Pacific Americans* (1979), pp. 389–399, 402, 434–444.

California State Advisory Committee to the U.S. Commission on Civil Rights, *Asian American and Pacific Peoples: A Case of Mistaken Identity* (1975) (quoted in Chun, 1980, p. 7).

Chun, Ki-Taek, "The Myth of Asian American Success and Its Educational Ramifications," *IRCD Bulletin* (Winter/Spring 1980).

Dutta, Manoranjan, "Asian/Pacific American Employment Profile: Myth and Reality — Issues and Answers," *U.S. Commission on Civil Rights: Testimony on Civil Rights Issues of Asian and Pacific Americans* (1979), pp. 445–489.

Fortune: "America's Super Minority," Nov. 24, 1986, pp. 148–149; "Working Smarter," May 17, 1982, p. 64.

Gidra (1969), pp. 6–7 (quoted in Chun, p. 7).

Hirschman, Charles, and Wong, Morrison, "Trends in Socioeconomic Achievement Among Immigrant and Native-Born Asian-Americans, 1960–1976," *The Sociological Quarterly* (Autumn 1981), pp. 495–513.

Hune, Shirley, keynote address, East Coast Asian Student Union Conference, Boston University, Feb. 14, 1987.

Kahng, Dr. Anthony, "Employment Issues," *U.S. Commission on Civil Rights: Testimony on Civil Rights Issues of Asian and Pacific Americans* (1979), pp. 411–413.

Kennedy, David M., "The Making of a Classic, Gunnar Myrdal and Black-White Relations: The Use and Abuse of *An American Dilemma,*" *The Atlantic* (May 1987), pp. 86–89.

Kiang, Peter, professor of sociology, University of Massachusetts, Boston, personal interview, May 1, 1987.

[7]*techno-coolies:* The original coolies were unskilled laborers from the Far East who were often paid subsistence wages in the United States.

Kim, Illsoo, "Class Division Among Asian Immigrants: Its Implications for Social Welfare Policy," *Asian American Studies: Contemporary Issues, Proceedings from East Coast Asian American Scholars Conference* (1986), pp. 24–25.

Kuo, Wen H. "On the Study of Asian-Americans: Its Current State and Agenda," *Sociological Quarterly* (1979), pp. 279–290.

Mariano, Dr. Robert S., "Census Issues," *U.S. Commission on Civil Rights: Testimony on Civil Rights Issues of Asian and Pacific Americans* (1979), pp. 54–59.

New Republic, "The Triumph of Asian Americans" (July 15–22, 1985), pp. 24–31.

The New York Times Magazine, "Why They Succeed" (Nov. 30, 1986), pp. 72 + .

Newsweek: "The Ultimate Assimilation" (Nov. 24, 1986), p. 80; "Asian-Americans: A 'Model Minority'" (Dec. 6, 1982), pp. 39–51: "Success Story: Outwhiting the Whites" (June 21, 1971), pp. 24–25.

Newsweek on Campus: "Asian Americans, the Drive to Excel" (April 1984), pp. 4–13.

Nishi, Dr. Setsuko Matsunaga, "Asian American Employment Issues: Myths and Realities," *U.S. Commission on Civil Rights: Testimony on Civil Rights Issues of Asian and Pacific Americans*(1979), pp. 397–399, 495–507.

Sung, Betty Lee, *Chinese American Manpower and Employment* (1975).

Suzuki, Bob H., "Education and the Socialization of Asian Americans: A Revisionist Analysis of the 'Model Minority' Thesis," *Amerasia Journal,* vol. 4, issue 2 (1977), pp. 23–51.

Time, "To America with Skills" (July 8, 1985), p. 42.

Toupin, Dr. Elizabeth Ahn, "A Model University for A 'Model Minority,'" *Asian American Studies: Contemporary Issues, Proceedings from East Coast Asian American Scholars Conference* (1986), pp. 10–12.

U.S. Bureau of the Census, *Survey of Minority-Owned Business Enterprises* (1977) (as quoted in Cabezas, p. 443).

U.S. News & World Report: "Asian-Americans, Are They Making the Grade?" (April 2, 1984), pp. 41–42; "Success Story of One Minority Group in U.S." (Dec. 26, 1966), pp. 6–9.

Washington Monthly, "The Wrong Way to Court Ethnics" (May 1986), pp. 21–26.

Yun, Grace, "Notes from Discussions on Asian American Education," *Asian American Studies: Contemporary Issues, Proceedings from East Coast Asian American Scholars Conference* (1986), pp. 20–24.

Engaging the Text

1. In Chang's view, what are the key elements of the stereotype of Asian Americans as a model minority? Have you encountered these yourself? How pervasive do you believe they are in your school or community?

2. What is wrong with this positive image of Asian Americans, according to Chang? What assumptions does it make, and how do they mislead us about the situation of many Asian Americans?

3. Why has the myth of the model minority been so widely embraced, according to Chang? What does it do for the United States as a country? What is the effect of the model minority myth on other ethnic minorities?

4. Many scholars who question the image of the model minority are themselves Asian Americans. Does this fact make their claims more or less persuasive? Explain.

5. Chang's essay analyzes news stories, interprets census data, and reports on work by other scholars, but it does not present any original research. What purpose do essays like this serve when all of the data they contain is already available elsewhere?

EXPLORING CONNECTIONS

6. When Stephen Cruz (p. 326) became successful, he was seen not as a member of a model minority group but rather as a model member of a minority group. To what extent was his situation as a successful young Chicano engineer comparable to that of Asian Americans today?

7. Compare and contrast the idea of the "model minority" with the idea of the "scholarship boy" as defined by Richard Rodriguez (p. 202). On what assumptions does each concept rest? What expectations does each create? Why is each of these labels dangerous?

EXTENDING THE CRITICAL CONTEXT

8. Discuss in small groups how you learned of the myth of the model minority. Was it through TV, family, reading? Be as specific as possible. Then try to draw some conclusions about how this type of cultural "knowledge" is taught.

9. Although the news media have been quick to extol the virtues of Asian Americans as models of achievement, representations of Asians and Asian Americans are scarce in most forms of mass entertainment. Survey movies, TV shows, music videos, song lyrics, and other forms of popular culture. How are Asian Americans represented, and how do these images compare with those implied by the myth of the model minority?

10. Chang's essay is now more than a decade old. Do you see any evidence that stereotypes of the "model minority" have changed significantly since 1987?

The Black Avenger

KEN HAMBLIN

If radio talk show hosts are paid to be controversial, Ken Hamblin earns his money. He refers to young black women who bear children out of wedlock as "brood mares"; most of their children were sired, he writes, by "black thugs." Hamblin's main theme is the vitality of the American Dream and, in particular, his belief that black Americans should embrace that dream, quit whining about white racism, forget affirmative action, and make successes of themselves in the best country on earth. "The Black Avenger" touches on many of Hamblin's most provocative ideas. It is excerpted from his book Pick a Better Country: An Unassuming Colored Guy Speaks His Mind about America *(1996). Hamblin has himself lived a version of the American Dream. Raised in a poor area of Brooklyn by West Indian immigrant parents, his work in varied media fields (photojournalism, cinematography, TV production, newspapers, talk radio) has led to national recognition and an audience of over two million for* The Ken Hamblin Show.

Broad brushstrokes have been used over the last couple of years to paint a simplistic picture of the serious grievances emanating from middle America.

This picture painted and broadcast by the mainstream media is far different from the complex white backlash that I see and fear, however. The mainstream media have reduced nearly every political and social phenomenon I have written about in this book to a simple sound bite and a three-word headline: "Angry White Men."

The premise is that the black race and the white race are moving farther and farther apart because these angry white men are coming together in a collective backlash against the benefits afforded blacks through civil rights over the last three decades.

The evidence frequently cited is that these men, who for years held an unfair advantage in the workplace and in society in general, now are attacking programs such as affirmative action, which were designed to give minorities the edge to compensate for the years they were not treated as equals.

The predominantly liberal media report that these white men make up   5
the core of the growing conservative audience of talk radio. As a nationally syndicated talk radio host who is on the air for three hours five days a week, I guess this means that I should be among the first to hear from these guys.

But in actuality, that misconception is shattered regularly on *The Ken Hamblin Show*. The most interesting evidence against the stereotype comes in call after call, day after day, from white men, white southern men in particular, whom I hear crying uncle in this tired debate about race.

They are not crying uncle in the sense that they are rolling over.

What they are saying is: "Look, I personally didn't do it. I've gone through the family Bible. I haven't found one instance where we owned slaves. But I'll admit that at one time in America an injustice was committed against people of color — against black people, African Americans, Negroes. And as a white person, I am willing to atone for that."

In January of 1994 my local Denver radio program was broadcast live on C-Span and then repeated several times over the following week. On that show I addressed this guilt factor among white Americans and, as a spoof, offered to send my listeners and my viewers a copy of my very own "Certificate of Absolution."

Some months earlier, a man had called me on the air, identified himself   10
as white, and told me with candor and some degree of desperation that he was tired of feeling guilty about "my people."

That prompted me to come up with an official pardon in the form of a certificate, which only a clear-thinking black American would be authorized to issue. Soon after that, a Denver printer named Rex Kniss, who listened to my show, called and said he would be willing to print the certificate.

Rex added some "certificate" language to my thoughts and we ended up with the following:

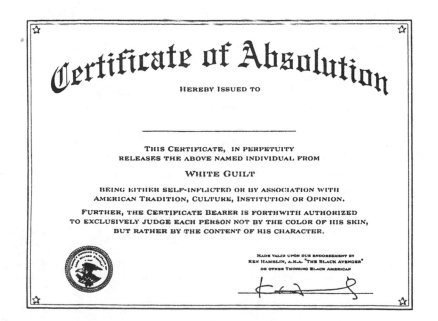

☆   ☆

𝕮ertificate of Absolution

HEREBY ISSUED TO

_____

THIS CERTIFICATE, IN PERPETUITY
RELEASES THE ABOVE NAMED INDIVIDUAL FROM

WHITE GUILT

BEING EITHER SELF-INFLICTED OR BY ASSOCIATION WITH
AMERICAN TRADITION, CULTURE, INSTITUTION OR OPINION.

FURTHER, THE CERTIFICATE BEARER IS FORTHWITH AUTHORIZED
TO EXCLUSIVELY JUDGE EACH PERSON NOT BY THE COLOR OF HIS SKIN,
BUT RATHER BY THE CONTENT OF HIS CHARACTER.

MADE VALID UPON DUE ENDORSEMENT BY
KEN HAMBLIN, A.K.A. "THE BLACK AVENGER"
OR OTHER THINKING BLACK AMERICAN

☆   ☆

I signed the Certificate "The Black Avenger," a moniker that I use particularly with my radio listeners. The idea behind the name was that I wanted to avenge the lies and the disinformation that more than thirty years of liberalism have brought about in this country. More to the point, I wanted to present myself as living proof that America works for black people too. As the Black Avenger, I was a living, breathing challenge to the well-honed Myth of the Hobbled Black.[1]

"The Black Avenger" caught on among my fans in 1993 while I was on a local Denver radio station that also carried Rush Limbaugh. Limbaugh was hyping his newsletter by promoting an appearance in Colorado after one of his callers from Fort Collins, a man named Dan, said his wife wouldn't let him spend the money to buy a subscription. Limbaugh said he'd personally come out to Fort Collins if Dan would organize a bake sale to raise money for the subscription. The result was "Dan's Bake Sale," which drew Limbaugh fans from all over the country and raised money not only for Dan's newsletter but also for charity.

My local station got behind the event by lining up buses to take our   15
Limbaugh fans fifty miles north to Fort Collins.

Meanwhile, I had just gotten back into motorcycles — a couple of years late, I might add. As I tell my wife and all of my male friends circa fifty years of age, it's a male rite of passage to buy a motorcycle when you turn fifty. I was fifty-two, pushing fifty-three, and hadn't ridden one since I had a Honda 150 in the late 1960s.

A fellow motorcyclist called my show and said he didn't want to go to Dan's Bake Sale by bus, but that he and I should go on our scoots. That prompted a lot of on-air bravado, and I ended up leading a cavalcade of some forty bikes in front of that many more buses to Fort Collins. On the ride, I was dressed in black leather from head to toe and wearing a black helmet with a tinted face guard — exhibiting some resemblance to Darth Vader or — you got it — the Black Avenger. After that trip, the Black Avenger moniker stuck.

Over time, when asked why I called myself the Black Avenger, I must admit I started answering a bit flippantly, mocking the comic book characters of my youth: "Truth, justice, and the American way . . . honey."[2]

I added "honey" after a black caller, in all seriousness, challenged me, claiming that "truth, justice, and the American way" were not "black" values because these American principles weren't afforded to black people. He further insinuated that I was trying to "act white." Of course, I stood my ground.

---

[1]*Myth of the Hobbled Black:* Hamblin's name for the notions that African Americans are helplessly victimized by past and present racial discrimination, that few blacks are successful in America, that blacks can't make it without special assistance.

[2]*Truth, justice, and the American way:* The values that Superman stands for.

I am an American first, I replied. Don't ask me to choose between this   20
Republic and the color of my skin. If you're a Pan-Africanist or a black nationalist, you won't like that answer.

After thinking about the absurdity of this man trying to discount blacks
as beneficiaries of the American Way, I decided to add "honey" with an ethnic ghetto drawl for the sole purpose of messing with self-righteous African
Americans like him who still feed off the Myth of the Hobbled Black.

As a result of my appearance on C-Span, I received nearly 8,000 pieces
of mail, more than 5,000 of them requesting the Certificate of Absolution.
To this day I hear from people from all over America who remember the
program, and my staff continues to fill orders for the certificate every week.

Needless to say, it warms my heart to know that so many white people
are sleeping better at night, no longer writhing in pain brought about by
their white guilt.

All joking aside, the extent of white guilt in this country is immense. It
directly correlates with the endless depiction by the mass media of the profound pain that black people purportedly still suffer as a result of the years
they were excluded from America's mainstream.

The constant reports of this pain and suffering that are broadcast   25
through the media, combined with the "blame whitey" syndrome that em-
anates from the black-trash[3] welfare culture, have caused some white Americans to suffer such a high degree of guilt that they have an almost fanatic
desire to undo the injustices of slavery, perhaps beginning with guilt about
not having delivered the forty acres and a mule promised to every Negro
after the Civil War.

The greater majority of white Americans have passed on a nagging
sense of social obligation from one generation to the next. After four or five
generations, however, mass amnesia has set in. The people who are haunted
by this guilt — the white majority, mainstream Americans obsessed with
undoing this injustice — have forgotten exactly what their crime was. In
fact, they have no idea what their particular crime was.

As is the case with my southern callers, most Americans can't trace
their family tree back to the equivalent of Tara, the fictitious plantation in
Gone With the Wind, or to the ownership of slaves. So the guilt no longer
arises from having once personally owned slaves, be they black people or indentured Irishmen. The guilt now is imposed just because of a lack of
melanin in their skin, just because they are white. Simply by virtue of the
birth of a white child, another guilty American is created. It's as if we were
talking about the burden of the national debt. That baby inherits the guilt of
slavery, the guilt of an injustice of long, long ago.

---

[3]*black-trash:* Hamblin's counterpart to "white trash," these are black Americans who, in
his words, are "unskilled and unemployed" and who "tend to be socially inept, possess limited
education and few salable job skills."

Because of this guilt and the ongoing stories of black oppression, white people have been conditioned to accept just about any level of black rage and the illogical demands resulting from it.

All of which brings us back around to modern-day African-American revolutionaries like welfare queen Dorothy King.

Despite her crassness, in some ways King is very sophisticated. She 30 knowingly touches a little secret in white people who have been conditioned by years of hearing about black hardships — the little secret that they are glad, they are relieved, to have been born white rather than a disenfranchised minority. These white middle-class citizens — especially the thirty- and forty-something crowd — have been inundated from the cradle with news reports about the dreadful burden of being black in America — reports of suffering the hardships of poverty, racism, and second-class citizenship.

While going through college, these white folks saw liberal administrators and professors excuse low test scores from black students because of these inherent hardships. They felt sorry for affirmative action students who obviously must have been scared, because they refused to compete. And though clearly this discrimination was self-imposed by the blacks themselves, they watched black students segregate themselves at all levels of campus life — from African-American studies to African-American student unions to African-American graduations — in essence implementing a post–civil rights version of "white only" and "colored" sections.

These white people graduated, got married, and began family life in comfortable suburbs . . . and bingo! They see Dorothy King on the nightly TV news, cataloging all the black hardships they have been conditioned to believe exist.

So when King makes absurd demands, like "give me" a house, these guilt-ridden white people shy away from standing up to her with what should be the logical American response: "Heavens no, we won't give you a house. Go out and work for it."

Nope. They stay out of it. Because they fear that X-ray vision might discern their little secret — the secret that they are eternally thankful they are white, and just having that thought makes them racists.

I have heard white Americans express so much racial guilt that, being 35 the old Catholic that I am, on some days I feel as though my radio show has become a confessional.

Because of the earnestness with which these people come to my show, it has dawned on me that if we as minority people, as black Americans, can't cut a deal with these average white Americans who are sitting at the table apologizing for the past, then we are a flawed and a lost people.

Or we are a disingenuous people who demand to prolong the negotiation with no intention of ever ending the strife and the separation, with no intention of ever doing our part to fill up the moat between the races or of getting on with the business of continuing to build a strong America that will benefit all of us.

I have a bigger, more selfish reason for wanting to avenge white guilt, however, a reason that goes beyond relieving the strain on white America. Guilt almost certainly inspires pity for the injured party — in this case black Americans. I contend that we can never stand tall as a people and expect to be treated as equals so long as we allow ourselves to be patronized in this fashion.

I also hear from white people across the country who call my radio show and say essentially, "Get over it."

They respond to the poverty pimps' demands for more and more repa-   40
rations for black people by asking what credit they get for all the taxes they have paid to support decades of Great Society programs that benefited black recipients. They want consideration for the years of affirmative action that gave black Americans a pass to automatically step to the front of the employment line.

Those kinds of queries undoubtedly contribute to the notion that there are angry white men. And I am certain there are, in fact, some white men who are angry, perhaps even racist. But the truth is that, as a black man, I ask some of the same questions, albeit from a different perspective.

When will black people recognize that we are able and willing to stand on our own? When will we acknowledge that we are able and willing to stand side by side with other Americans to compete for jobs and our piece of the American Dream? When will we get over that ugly and unjust period in our American history and evolve into healthy citizens of this great country?

I don't perceive that the majority of white Americans I talk to are saying "Get over it" sarcastically in order to dismiss the subject or to lobby for a return to the days of yore.

Rather, I think they are saying to black Americans: "Get over it, because even if we haven't paid the bill in full, we certainly have made enough of an effort to make amends that you should acknowledge some sincerity on our part."

Personally, I heartily second the call to get over it.   45
I am absolutely convinced that if we black Americans unequivocally throw in our lot with mainstream America today, we have much more to gain in the future than we have lost in the past. We have more to gain by putting our energies into the pursuit of the American Dream than we have to gain by continuing to whine about being compensated for having been kept out of the game in the past. We have an opportunity to realize all the benefits of being an American in the name of all of those who came before us, those Negroes who were kept unfairly from the full potential of this great country.

I would go so far as to say that we *owe* it to our forefathers to seize the opportunity that they helped to make available to us by their own stalwart faith in the American Dream. I know that all of my life I have felt I owed it to my mother and her sisters to make something of myself, to achieve the level of success that they only dreamed would be possible in their new homeland.

Today mainstream America has opened its full society and culture to us. The white majority has supported legislation that makes the American Dream truly accessible to all black citizens.

Oh, sure, there's still the old-guard club or the snooty neighborhood where the members or residents may look down their noses at black newcomers. But I would wager that those scenarios are few and far between.

And I am also willing to bet that in most cases the feelings of discrimi- 50 nation and exclusion are self-imposed by xenophobic quota blacks.

In fact, some of today's cries of racism have become downright ludicrous.

I wrote a column in the *Denver Post* in the summer of 1994 about a group of Denver area black women who claimed that a white shopkeeper in a Western Slope mountain town "stripped away our dignity, making us feel frustrated and powerless" by making an offhand remark when they walked into his store.

It seems one of the women was complaining about the heat, and the shopkeeper responded, "Hey! Watermelon's not served until one o'clock."

When he realized the ladies were seriously offended, he reportedly tried to make light of the situation, but alas, the oppressed travelers bustled out the door and followed up by writing a critical letter to the editor of the local newspaper.

I wrote that had I been presented with the watermelon-serving sched- 55 ule, I promptly would have inquired about the cantaloupe.

I don't doubt there are some angry white men. I'm still unconvinced that this shopkeeper was one of them, however.

More important is the fact that I am one black man who refuses to be shamed or made to feel powerless anymore by white bigots and racists. White folks can no longer intimidate me. I know better.

What I am constantly amazed at is how thin-skinned, how delicate, and how utterly afraid the beneficiaries of Dr. Martin Luther King's proud march for liberation have become.

Furthermore, as a black American, I am shamed by the Myth of the Hobbled Black. I am shamed that so many of my people have allowed themselves in one way or another to become part of the sham.

Someone must have the courage to kill this myth. Someone has to be 60 embarrassed that, with the opportunities available to us today, so many black Americans remain in a declining state of existence in Dark Town. Someone has to be embarrassed for the great number of middle-class black Americans who live in seclusion, apparently afraid to celebrate their success as educated and sophisticated Americans.

Someone must speak out to avenge the mythical disability of the Hobbled Black, and I think it's only logical that successful middle-class black Americans take the lead to meet this challenge.

White liberals won't do it because they continue to feed off the myth in order to further their own political and social agenda. White conservatives who speak out about ending the welfare culture have no credibility. They are summarily labeled racists.

And so I have lobbed a loud salvo by declaring myself the Black Avenger, standing tall to dispel the Myth of the Hobbled Black. I am standing up to put an end to the decades of liberal propaganda which deny that today opportunity exists for any American man or woman willing to pursue it.

I fully understand that it's not easy to be black and publicly refute the Myth of the Hobbled Black, because the quota blacks, the poverty pimps, the African Americans, will do all in their collective power to try to de-black you: "You ain't black no more. You don't understand the pain and suffering. You forgot your roots, boy."

But their admonishments have nothing to do with pain and suffering.   65
The real reason they are trying to de-black me and people like me is that we are telling the truth. And the truth is that being poor and black does not give you an excuse to gang-bang, to ruin a city, to make parks unsafe, to terrorize senior citizens, and to denounce the American Dream.

I am not a mean person. But I have run the gauntlet of ghetto life, and I have survived. I understand the value of life. And I understand that being poor is never an excuse to become a mugger or a killer.

Like a lot of black babies, I started out on the lowest social rung. I was raised by women. I grew up on welfare. I lived on the toughest streets of New York.

But I was not raised to be black trash or to be a victim. I never went through a drug rehab center. I have never been a guest of the government beyond my enlistment in the service. I have never believed — because I was never told — that because of the color of my skin I could never get the fullest measure of opportunity in America.

When you are poor, you may be so busy trying to survive that you miss the opportunity to smell the roses. You may miss the pure joy of watching your children grow up. But none of that gives you a valid reason to disregard what's right and what's wrong.

I am one American who is saying no to the myth that all people of color   70
are weak, illiterate, potentially violent, and substandard in their expectations for themselves and their children as contributors to the community.

Despite the attempted intimidation emanating from the black-trash welfare culture, every day I hear from more and more healthy black Americans — and guilt-free white Americans — who are joining the crusade to tell the truth about black people and their good fortune to be Americans.

My personal adventure in America is at its pinnacle today because I am able to talk every day on my radio show with so many people from coast to coast and from all walks of life. I hear personally from hundreds more Americans off the air every day through the Internet and via letters to the editors of newspapers that carry my column.

And every day I am reassured that the heartbeat of America remains strong. I am reassured that the great majority of Americans maintain the true American spirit, the spirit that ultimately will make it possible for us to prevail.

I draw my strength from that heartbeat of America; it gives me the power to be the Black Avenger.

ENGAGING THE TEXT

1. Working in groups, summarize the central claims Hamblin makes about the United States and the American Dream. To what extent do you agree or disagree with these assertions, and why?

2. Assess Hamblin's assertion that some white Americans "suffer such a high degree of guilt that they have an almost fanatic desire to undo the injustices of slavery" (para. 25). Have you seen evidence of such a compulsion in the media, in your education or reading, in your community? Discuss.

3. Hamblin often uses language that is rhetorically daring, to say the least — language that is pointedly *not* politically correct. What do you think he means by the terms listed below? What effect does such language have on you as a reader?

   welfare queen (para. 29)
   poverty pimp (para. 40)
   quota blacks (para. 50)
   Dark Town (para. 60)

4. Review Hamblin's account of how he assumed his alias, "The Black Avenger" (paras. 13–18); note the various components of this persona, including the motorcycle and motorcycle outfit, the Darth Vader connection, the Superman/comic books connection, and his ghetto pronunciation of "honey." What impression do you think Hamblin is trying to create? How well do you think he succeeds?

EXPLORING CONNECTIONS

5. Look ahead to Anne Witte Garland's "Good Noise: Cora Tucker" (p. 390). Compare and contrast her ideas about success with Hamblin's. Be sure to touch on Tucker's and Hamblin's views of poverty, welfare, and obstacles to success for African Americans.

6. Hamblin believes there are few barriers in the United States today for African Americans who are motivated to succeed. Read "From Individual to Structural Discrimination" by Fred L. Pincus (p. 586). Do you think the kinds of discrimination Pincus defines present formidable barriers to success for black Americans? Explain why or why not.

7. Read "Town Hall Television" by Patricia J. Williams (p. 604). What might she say about the incident involving the Denver shopkeeper (paras. 52–57) and Hamblin's assertion that the women overreacted to an "offhand remark"?

8. What parts of Hamblin's piece do you think are meant to be humorous? In each case, explain how Patricia J. Williams (p. 604) might respond to the intended humor. How do you respond?

EXTENDING THE CRITICAL CONTEXT

9. In paragraph 31, Hamblin offers a brief description of black students segregating themselves on college campuses. How well would his description fit your campus today: to what extent are ethnic groups segregated or self-segregated?

10. Listen to one or more broadcasts of *The Ken Hamblin Show* and analyze what you hear. What issues are being discussed? What sort of persona does Hamblin project? How would you characterize his audience? To what extent does Hamblin echo themes found in the reading selection above?

Number One!

JILL NELSON

In this brief excerpt from Volunteer Slavery: My Authentic Negro Experience *(1993), Jill Nelson paints an unforgettable portrait of her father. Successful professional, head of an affluent black family, and member of a privileged class, Nelson's father made very sure his children didn't grow complacent about their social and economic position. Nelson (b. 1952) studied at the City University of New York and at Columbia and became a radical journalist; in 1986, "sick of committing class suicide in the name of righteousness," she accepted a position at the prestigious* Washington Post's *Sunday magazine, becoming the newsmagazine's first black and first female writer. After a brief period with the* Post, *she quit her job because of the bias of the paper's managerial and editorial policies. Her work has appeared in numerous publications, including* Essence, Ms., USA Weekend, *and the* Village Voice.

That night I dream about my father, but it is really more a memory than a dream.

"Number one! Not two! Number one!" my father intones from the head of the breakfast table. The four of us sit at attention, two on each side of the ten-foot teak expanse, our brown faces rigid. At the foot, my mother looks up at my father, the expression on her face a mixture of pride, anxiety, and, could it be, boredom? I am twelve. It is 1965.

"You kids have got to be, not number two," he roars, his dark face turning darker from the effort to communicate. He holds up his index and middle fingers. "But number —" here, he pauses dramatically, a preacher going for revelation, his four children a rapt congregation, my mother a smitten church sister. "Number one!"

These last words he shouts while lowering his index finger. My father has great, big black hands, long, perfectly shaped fingers with oval nails so vast they seem landscapes all their own. The half moons leading to the cuticle take up most of the nail and seem ever encroaching, threatening to swallow up first his fingertips, then his whole hand. I always wondered if he became a dentist just to mess with people by putting those enormous fingers in their mouths, each day surprising his patients and himself by the delicacy of the work he did.

Years later my father told me that when a woman came to him with an   5
infant she asserted was his, he simply looked at the baby's hands. If they lacked the size, enormous nails, and half-moon cuticles like an ocean eroding the shore of the fingers, he dismissed them.

Early on, what I remember of my father were Sunday morning breakfasts and those hands, index finger coyly lowering, leaving the middle finger standing alone.

When he shouted "Number one!" that finger seemed to grow, thicken and harden, thrust up and at us, a phallic symbol to spur us, my sister Lynn, fifteen, brothers Stanley and Ralph, thirteen and nine, on to greatness, to number oneness. My father's rich, heavy voice rolled down the length of the table, breaking and washing over our four trembling bodies.

When I wake up I am trembling again, but it's because the air conditioner, a luxury in New York but a necessity in D.C., is set too high. I turn it down, check on Misu,[1] light a cigarette, and think about the dream.

It wasn't until my parents had separated and Sunday breakfasts were no more that I faced the fact that my father's symbol for number one was the world's sign language for "fuck you." I know my father knew this, but I still haven't figured out what he meant by it. Were we to become number one and go out and fuck the world? If we didn't, would life fuck us? Was he intentionally sending his children a mixed message? If so, what was he trying to say?

I never went to church with my family. While other black middle-class   10
families journeyed to Baptist church on Sundays, both to thank the Lord for their prosperity and donate a few dollars to the less fortunate brethren

---

[1]*Misu:* Nelson's daughter.

they'd left behind, we had what was reverentially known as "Sunday break-fast." That was our church.

In the dining room of the eleven-room apartment we lived in, the only black family in a building my father had threatened to file a discrimination suit to get into, my father delivered the gospel according to him. The recurring theme was the necessity that each of us be "number one," but my father preached about whatever was on his mind: current events, great black heroes, lousy black sell-outs, our responsibility as privileged children, his personal family history.

His requirements were the same as those at church: that we be on time, not fidget, hear and heed the gospel, and give generously. But Daddy's church boasted no collection plate; dropping a few nickels into a bowl would have been too easy. Instead, my father asked that we absorb his lessons and become what he wanted us to be, number one. He never told us what that meant or how to get there. It was years before I was able to forgive my father for not being more specific. It was even longer before I understood and accepted that he couldn't be.

Like most preachers, my father was stronger on imagery, oratory, and instilling fear than he was on process. I came away from fifteen years of Sunday breakfasts knowing that to be number two was not enough, and having no idea what number one was or how to become it, only that it was better.

When I was a kid, I just listened, kept a sober face, and tried to understand what was going on. Thanks to my father, my older sister Lynn and I, usually at odds, found spiritual communion. The family dishwashers, our spirits met wordlessly as my father talked. We shared each other's anguish as we watched egg yolk harden on plates, sausage fat congeal, chicken livers separate silently from gravy.

We all had our favorite sermons. Mine was the "Rockefeller wouldn't let his dog shit in our dining room" sermon. 15

"You think we're doing well?" my father would begin, looking into each of our four faces. We know better than to venture a response. For my father, even now, conversations are lectures. Please save your applause — and questions — until the end.

"And we are," he'd answer his own query. "We live on West End Avenue, I'm a professional, your mother doesn't *have* to work, you all go to private school, we go to Martha's Vineyard in the summer. But what we have, we have because 100,000 other black people haven't made it. Have nothing! Live like dogs!"

My father has a wonderfully expressive voice. When he said dogs, you could almost hear them whimpering. In my head, I saw an uncountable mass of black faces attached to the bodies of mutts, scrambling to elevate themselves to a better life. For some reason, they were always on 125th Street, under the Apollo Theatre marquee. Years later, when I got political and decided to be the number-one black nationalist, I was thrilled by the notion that my father might have been inspired by Claude McKay's[2] poem that begins, "If we must die, let it not be like dogs."

"There is a quota system in this country for black folks, and your mother and me were allowed to make it," my father went on. It was hard to imagine anyone allowing my six-foot-three, suave, smart, take-no-shit father to do anything. Maybe his use of the word was a rhetorical device.

"Look around you," he continued. With the long arm that supported his   20 heavy hand he indicated the dining room. I looked around. At the eight-foot china cabinet gleaming from the weekly oiling administered by Margie, our housekeeper, filled to bursting with my maternal grandmother's china and silver. At the lush green carpeting, the sideboard that on holidays sagged from the weight of cakes, pies, and cookies, at the paintings on the walls. We were living kind of good, I thought. That notion lasted only an instant.

My father's arm slashed left. It was as though he had stripped the room bare. I could almost hear the china crashing to the floor, all that teak splintering, silver clanging.

"Nelson Rockefeller wouldn't let his dog shit in here!" my father roared. "What we have, compared to what Rockefeller and the people who rule the world have, is nothing. Nothing! Not even good enough for his dog. You four have to remember that and do better than I have. Not just for yourselves, but for our people, black people. You have to be number one."

My father went on, but right about there was where my mind usually started drifting. I was entranced by the image of Rockefeller's dog — which I imagined to be a Corgi or Afghan or Scottish Terrier — bladder and rectum full to bursting, sniffing around the green carpet of our dining room, refusing to relieve himself.

The possible reasons for this fascinated me. Didn't he like green carpets? Was he used to defecating on rare Persian rugs and our 100 percent wool carpeting wasn't good enough? Was it because we were black? But weren't dogs colorblind?

I've spent a good part of my life trying to figure out what my father   25 meant by number one. Born poor and dark in Washington, I think he was trying, in his own way, to protect us from the crushing assumptions of failure that he and his generation grew up with. I like to think he was simply saying, like the army, "Be all that you can be," but I'm still not sure. For years, I was haunted by the specter of number two gaining on me, of never having a house nice enough for Rockefeller dog shit, of my father's middle finger admonishing me. It's hard to move forward when you're looking over your shoulder.

When I was younger, I didn't ask my father what he meant. By the time I was confident enough to ask, my father had been through so many trans-

---

[2]*Claude McKay:* African American poet (1890–1948).

formations — from dentist to hippie to lay guru — that he'd managed to forget, or convince himself he'd forgotten, those Sunday morning sermons. When I brought them up he'd look blank, his eyes would glaze over, and he'd say something like, "Jill, what are you talking about? With your dramatic imagination you should have been an actress."

But I'm not an actress. I'm a journalist, my father's daughter. I've spent a good portion of my life trying to be a good race woman and number one at the same time. Tomorrow, I go to work at the *Washington Post* magazine, a first. Falling asleep, I wonder if that's the same as being number one.

ENGAGING THE TEXT

1. What lessons do you think Nelson's father meant to teach his children? Were these good lessons to teach? What do you think he meant by holding up his middle finger when he shouted, "Number one"?

2. Debate the father's assertion that "there is a quota system in this country for black folks" (para. 19). What does he mean by this? Do you think this is still true, was once true, or was never true?

3. What admirable traits and what flaws does Nelson reveal about her father? How has her attitude toward him changed over the years? Do you think he was a good father?

4. How do you interpret this line in Nelson's account: "It's hard to move forward when you're looking over your shoulder" (para. 25)?

EXPLORING CONNECTIONS

5. Compare the attitude toward success expressed by Nelson's father with the family attitudes seen in "Looking for Work" (p. 42), "The Achievement of Desire" (p. 202), or "Para Teresa" (p. 216). How energetically do you think families should encourage children to excel?

6. Review Bebe Moore Campbell's "Envy" (p. 118) and compare what she learned about success from the women in her family with the lessons taught by Nelson's father. Which seem the more important or useful to you?

EXTENDING THE CRITICAL CONTEXT

7. In this brief story, Nelson captures a single moment in her childhood that expresses her own eventual feelings about success. In an extended journal entry or as a short paper, write a story from your own life that captures the most important lesson you ever learned about the meaning of success.

8. Write an interview of Jill Nelson hosted by Ken Hamblin for his radio show, or write an interview of Ken Hamblin carried out by Jill Nelson as a freelance journalist. Whichever approach you take, be sure to take into account their differing views of what success means for African Americans. How might the style and format of the two interviews differ?

Good Noise: Cora Tucker

ANNE WITTE GARLAND

When most people think about the American Dream, they don't visual-
ize a factory job and a cluttered house right next to the railroad tracks. As
you read this selection about community activist Cora Tucker, however,
think about the connection of her life to core American values like democ-
racy, progress, and individual rights. Author Anne Witte Garland is a free-
lance writer covering environmental, public health, consumer, and women's
issues. This selection comes from her 1988 book Women Activists: Challenging the Abuse of Power.

Cora Tucker's house is so close to the railroad tracks that at night when
trains thunder by, the beds shake. The house and furniture are modest, and
in the kitchen there's a lingering smell of the lard Cora cooks with. There
are traces of Virginia red clay on the kitchen floor, and piled up on the bedroom floor are cardboard boxes overflowing with newspaper clippings and
other papers.

Cora admits she doesn't like housekeeping anymore. The plaques and
photographs hanging in the kitchen and living room attest to what she does
enjoy; alongside religious pictures and photos of her children and grandchildren, there are several citizenship awards, certificates acknowledging her
work in civil rights, and photos of her — a pretty, smiling black woman —
with various politicians. One framed picture in the kitchen was handmade
for Cora by some of the inmates in a nearby prison, whom Cora has visited
and helped. In it, Old English letters made of foil spell out, "God grant me
the serenity to accept the things I cannot change, the courage to change the
things I can, and wisdom to know the difference." Cora has plenty of all
three virtues, although "serene" probably isn't the first adjective a stranger
would pin on her. But then, there isn't much that Cora would say she can't
change, either.

Cora Tucker is something of an institution in Halifax County, Virginia,
a rural county bordering North Carolina. In more than a dozen years, she
has missed only a handful of the county board of supervisors' monthly meetings. Her name appears in the letters columns of the two daily newspapers
several times a week — either signed onto her own letter or, almost as
often, vilified in someone else's. She seems to know and be known by every
black person on the street, in the post offices, and in stores and restaurants.
And she is known by white and black people alike as having taken on many

of the local, white-controlled institutions. Her main concern is simply fighting for the underdog, which she does in many ways — from social work–like visits to the elderly and invalids, to legal fights against racial discrimination, registering people to vote, and lobbying on issues like health care and the environment.

Cora was born in 1941 ten miles from where she lives now, near the Halifax county seat, in the small town of South Boston. Her father was a school teacher and later a railway porter. He died when Cora was three, and her mother and the nine children became sharecroppers on white men's farms. It was as a sharecropper, Cora says, that she learned how to do community organizing. She started by trying to help other sharecroppers to get things like better heating and food stamps. "I didn't call it 'organizing,' then," she says. "I just called it 'being concerned.' When you do sharecropping, you move around a lot. So I got to know everybody in the county, and to know what people's problems were.

"Sharecropping is the worst form of drudgery; it's slavery really. You   5
work on a man's farm, supposedly for half the profit on the crops you grow. That's what the contract says. But you pay for all the stuff that goes into the crop — seeds, fertilizer, and all. You get free housing, but most sharecroppers' housing is dilapidated and cold. It isn't insulated — it's just shacks, really. Sharecroppers are poor. I know of a family of twelve who grew fifteen acres of tobacco, and at the end of the year, they had earned just fifty dollars. And I know sharecroppers who needed food and applied for food stamps, but couldn't get them because they supposedly made too much money; the boss went to the food stamp office, and said they made such and such, so they couldn't qualify."

Cora went to work very young, planting and plowing with the others in the family. Her mother taught her to cook when she was six; Cora remembers having to stand on a crate to reach the kitchen counter. She was a curious and intelligent child who loved school and was unhappy when she had to stay out of school to clean house for the white woman on the farm where they lived.

Cora always adored her mother. Bertha Plenty Moesley was a "chief stringer" — a step in tobacco processing that involves picking the green tobacco leaves from the plants one at a time, and stringing them together three leaves to a stick, so that they can be hung to dry and cure. "My mama worked hard," Cora says. "She would plow and do all the things the men did. She was independent; she raised her children alone for eighteen years. When I was little, I felt so bad that she had to work that hard just so we could survive. There was welfare out there — all kinds of help, if only somebody had told her how to go about getting it. She had very little education, and didn't know to go down to the welfare office for help. As I got older, I was upset by that and made up my mind, when I was about eight or nine years old, that if I ever got grown, I'd make sure that everybody knew how to get everything there was to get. And I really meant it. I learned early how to get things done, and I learned it would take initiative to get what I wanted."

By the time Cora learned about welfare, her mother wouldn't take advantage of it. She was proud, and she told the children to have self-respect. "We didn't have anything else," Cora's mother says. "The kids had only themselves to be proud of." Cora took the advice to heart. There's a story she tells about growing up that has found a permanent place in community-organizing lore. In her high school, which was segregated at the time (Halifax County schools didn't integrate until 1969, under court order), Cora entered an essay contest on the topic of "what America means to me." She was taken by surprise when her bitter essay about growing up black in the South won a statewide award. But on awards night she was in for another surprise. The winners were to have their essays read, and then shake hands with the Virginia governor. Cora's mother was in the audience beaming, along with Cora's friends and teachers. But when her essay was read, Cora didn't recognize it — it had been rewritten, and the less critical sentiments weren't hers at all. She refused to greet the governor. "I disappointed everyone — my mother even cried."

The only person who supported her that night, she says, was a high school literature teacher, whom she credits as an important influence on her. "He spent a lot of time with me, encouraging me. Every time an issue came up that I felt strongly about, he'd have me write about it — letters to the editor that never got printed. He told me, 'Nobody can make you a second-class citizen but you. You should be involved in what's going on around you.'"

Instead, at seventeen she dropped out of high school to get married. As she describes it, the next several years were consumed with housekeeping and having children — six of them in rapid succession. She and her husband adopted a seventh. At first, Cora says, she threw herself enthusiastically into her new role. "I just wanted to be married. My father-in-law used to tease me about making myself so busy just being married. He'd say, 'You ain't going to keep this up for long.' But I'd say yes I would. Every morning, I put clean sheets on our beds — washed and ironed them. I ironed every diaper. I read all the housekeeping magazines; my house was immaculate. But I was beginning to find myself so bored, even then. My husband was farming then, sharecropping, and he'd get up early; I'd get up too, and feed him and the kids, and then do the cleaning. But when you clean every day, there just isn't that much to do, so I'd be finished by ten in the morning! I joined a book club, so that I would get a book every month — but I would get bored in between. I would read the book in two days — I tried to savor it, but I couldn't make it last any longer. Then, when the kids started growing up and going to school, that would occupy me a little more. I'd feed them, then take them to school, and come back and clean and then start making lunch. But just as soon as my baby started school, I went out and got a job."

Halifax County has several textile and garment factories, and Cora went to work as a seamstress for one of the largest, a knit sportswear manufacturer. It was a fairly new operation, and the mostly women employees were expected to do everything, from lifting fabric bolts weighing forty or fifty pounds each, to sitting at sewing machines for eight hour stretches. There was no union; the county boasts in promotional material that less than 5 percent of the county's workforce is unionized. "Every time I used to talk to the girls there, my boss thought I was trying to get a union started. And I sure thought there *should* be a union; there were lots of health hazards, and people were always getting hurt. People got back injuries, two people even had heart attacks in the factory, because of the working conditions. I once got a woman to come down from Baltimore to talk about forming a union, but people got frightened because the bosses warned us that if there was any union activity, we'd lose our jobs."

Cora worked at the factory for seven years. The first thing she did with the money she was earning was to buy land for a house. "We had lived in places where we were so cold," she says. "We'd have no windows, and no wood. My dream was always to grow up and build me a house — my own house, out of brick. My husband never really wanted one; he was just as happy moving around. But after I had the babies and went to work at the factory, I told him I was going to build me a house. So the first year I worked, I saved a thousand dollars. The next year I saved another thousand, and then borrowed some from the company, to buy some land. Then I started saving again, for the house. But when I went to the FHA, they said I couldn't get a house without my husband's permission. At first, he said he wasn't going to have anything to do with it, so I said I'd buy a trailer instead. When he found out, he figured I might just as well put the money into a house, so he signed the papers. We built the house; it was the first time any of us had been inside a new house. I was crazy about it; we could sit down and say exactly where we wanted things. And while I was working, I bought every stick of furniture in it."

In 1976 Cora hurt her back and had to leave her job. Over the next few years she underwent surgery several times — first for her back, and then for cancer (for which she has had to have periodic treatments ever since). In the meantime, she had become active in the community. In the 1960s, she had participated in organizations like the National Association for the Advancement of Colored People, and another group called the Assemblies, but they moved too slowly for her tastes. ("They weren't really interested in taking on the power structure," she complains.) She had also organized her own letter-writing campaign in support of the federal Voting Rights Act to make it easier for blacks to vote. She had gone around to local churches, speaking to people and encouraging them to write to their representatives in Washington. She also took advantage of knowing women who ran beauty parlors — she provided the paper and pens, so that women could write letters while they sat under the hair dryers. "People would say to me, 'What good will it do?' But I think politicians have to be responsive if enough pressure can be brought to bear on them. You can complain, I can complain, but that's just two people. A politician needs to get piles of letters saying vote for this bill, because if you don't, you won't be in office much longer!" Cora was responsible for generating about five hundred letters supporting the voting law.

She takes voting very seriously. In 1977, she campaigned for a populist candidate for Virginia governor. She was undergoing cancer treatments at the time, but they made her tired, so she stopped the treatments in order to register people to vote. She had taught herself to drive, and personally rode around the county from house to house, filling her car with everyone there who was of voting age, driving them to the court house to register, and then home again. She's credited with having registered over one thousand people this way, and on election day, she personally drove many of them to the polling place.

While Cora was growing up, her mother's house was always filled with people — besides her own family, several cousins lived with them, and aunts and uncles who had moved up north and came back to visit would stay with Cora's mother. Cora's own house was the same way — always filled with neighborhood teenagers, white and black. Cora became a confidante for the young people, and she encouraged them to read about black history, and to be concerned about the community. One of the things that upset the teenagers was the fate of a county recreation center. Halifax had no recreation facilities, and the county had applied for money from the federal Department of Housing and Urban Development (HUD) to build a center. When HUD awarded the county $500,000, however, the county turned it down because, as Cora puts it, there were "too many strings attached" — meaning it would have to be integrated. At home because of her back trouble and cancer, Cora took it on herself to help steer the teenagers' anger toward research into community problems. "When I heard about the recreation center, I went to the county board meeting and raised hell," she says. "But they went ahead and did what they wanted anyway. What I realized then was that if I had had all those kids come with me to the meeting, there would have been some changes. You need warm bodies — persons present and accounted for — if you want to get things done."

In 1975, Cora founded her own organization, Citizens for a Better America. CBA's first project was a study of black spending and employment patterns in the county. The study was based on a survey of three hundred people; it took two years to complete, with Cora's teenage friends doing much of the legwork. The findings painted a clear picture of inequality. Blacks made up nearly half the county population, and according to the survey, spent a disproportionate share of their salaries on food, cars, and furniture. But, as the study pointed out, there were very few black employees at the grocery stores where the money was spent, not a single black salesperson in the furniture stores, and no black salesperson at the auto dealerships. Blacks weren't represented at all on newspaper or radio station staffs.

Cora saw to it that the survey results were published in the local newspaper. The next step was to act on the results. The survey had uncovered problems with hiring practices and promotions of blacks in the school system, so Cora complained to the school board. After waiting in vain for the board to respond, CBA filed a complaint with what was then the federal Department of Health, Education, and Welfare. An HEW investigation confirmed the problems, and the agency threatened to cut off federal education funds to the county if the discrimination wasn't corrected. The county promised that the next principals it hired would be black.

CBA then took on other aspects of the county government. The survey had found that of all the county employees, only 7 percent were black — chiefly custodial workers or workers hired with federal Comprehensive Employment Training Administration (CETA) funds. Only one black person in the county government made over $20,000 a year. When the county refused to negotiate with Cora's organization about their hiring practices, CBA filed a complaint with the federal revenue sharing program. A Virginia state senator was successful in getting a federal investigation into the complaint stalled, but Cora went over his head, to the congressional Black Caucus and Maryland's black congressman, Parren Mitchell. Mitchell contacted Senator Edward Kennedy's office, which pressed to have the investigation completed. The findings confirmed CBA's, and the county was told to improve its hiring practices or stand to lose federal revenues.

CBA also initiated a boycott of local businesses that didn't hire minorities — Cora avoided the term "boycott," and instead called the action the "Spend Your Money Wisely Campaign." Leaflets were distributed listing the stores that hired black employees, and urging people, "Where Blacks are not HIRED, Blacks should not buy!"

Cora was developing a reputation. She started having frequent contact   20
with the congressional Black Caucus, and would be called occasionally to testify in Washington on welfare issues. "They don't usually get people like me to testify; they get all these 'experts' instead. But every once in a while, it's good for them to hear from someone who isn't a professional, whose English isn't good, and who talks from a grassroots level."

It wasn't just in Washington that her reputation was growing, but back home, too. "I have a lot of enemies," she says. "There are derogatory things in the papers about me all the time. And the county government doesn't like me, because I keep going to all those board meetings and raising hell about what they do. When I go sometimes, they say, 'Yes, what do you want now, Ms. Tucker?' But I don't care what they think — I just tell them what I want. So a lot of the white power structure don't really like me. They think

I'm a troublemaker, but I'm not really. I just believe what I believe in. Then there are black people too, who think that I want too much too soon. But when you think about it, black people have been in America 360-some years, so when is the time ever going to be right? The time doesn't *get* right; you make it right. So I'm not offended by what anybody says about me."

Sometimes the problem isn't just what people say; it's what they do. Cora has had many experiences with harassment. At first it was phone calls, from people threatening to burn her house down or telling her to "go back to Africa." Once she wrote a letter to the editor saying, "This is an open letter to all the people who call me and ask, what do you niggers want now? and hang up before I can tell them. . . .

"Blacks and poor people want to share in the economic progress of Hal-ifax County, and when we get our children educated and motivated we would like them to come back to Halifax County and do something other than push mops and brooms. And a few of us would like our grandchildren to grow up near us, and if our children decide to make their home elsewhere it will be due to choice and not an economic necessity."

The harassment has taken other forms as well. Cora was followed and run off the highway one night, and had all four tires slashed one day when her car was parked in town. Once she was in the post office and a man recognized her, walked over, and spit on her; another time a car with out-of-state license plates pulled up next to her car as if to ask directions, and the man spat into her face. She came home from a meeting one night to find that someone had broken into her home and drenched her bed with gasoline. But Cora views the abuses with amazing equanimity: "If you stop doing things because somebody says something bad about you or does something to you," she says, "then you'll never get *anything* done."

And she wasn't making only enemies; she was also gaining a following.   25
One woman, who now works in the local legal aid office where Cora stops in frequently to get answers to legal questions, tells how she first met Cora. The woman had been born in Halifax, but had moved to New Jersey when she was a young girl. The civil rights movement progressed, and when the woman was finished with school, she moved back to Virginia, thinking that things there would be much better than they *had* been for blacks. But she found that any progress had been superficial only. When she started looking for work, she discovered that there were no blacks in responsible positions. She wore her hair in an Afro, and in hindsight thinks that it cost her jobs: at one point, it seemed she would be offered a position with the county, but when the man who was to be her boss saw her, he didn't give her the job. Another prospective employer turned her down with the flat statement that he didn't want any union people around.

She became disillusioned, and was shocked at the complacency around her. About that time, she saw Cora Tucker's name in the paper. She was impressed, and started asking around about Cora. Not too long afterwards, she went to a community action program meeting, and noticed that Cora was scheduled to speak. "I was excited. I thought, finally, I'm going to meet a black person who's alive!" But she was initially disappointed. "I had pictured her as a towering woman — a fiery, eloquent speaker, like Barbara Jordan. Instead, there she was, short, and not that articulate."

But she quickly got drawn to Cora's strengths. "Cora wouldn't be happy at home, doing housekeeping," she says. "She's just not cut out for that. She's cut out for doing exactly what she's doing — getting out and raising hell about issues that affect people. She keeps pushing. When I get burned, I back off. But when Cora gets burned, she just blows out the fire and goes on."

Even people who don't like Cora give her credit: "I'm not a Cora Tucker fan," says one South Boston resident. "But I admit that she might just be the most informed person on political issues in this county." People credit Cora with having stamina and with inspiring others. An old friend of hers who runs a corner grocery says, "She keeps people fired up; she won't let us get lazy. It's because of her that I even watch the news!" One woman who was in school with Cora and now works for the county government says, "She was always making noise at school. We knew she'd grow up noisy. But it's *good* noise. When Cora talks, she knows what she's talking about."

And although Cora thinks she'll never be much of a public speaker, others disagree. One man who has worked with Cora for several years described a dinner ceremony sponsored by a human rights coalition in Richmond. "They had asked Cora to come and be a featured speaker. The woman who spoke before her gave this very polished speech. And then Cora got up, and gave her very unpolished speech. But it was moving to everyone in the room, because it was so much from the heart. It was the contrast of day and night between her and the previous speaker. What she had to say was so honest and down to earth, that people were very touched by it. And that's just the way she is."

Cora is very religious. "I believe in God, and in the providence of   30 prayer. I go to church regularly." The churches in her area are still segregated; she attends the Crystal Hill Baptist Church, which, she points out with a chuckle, is brick-colored, while the white congregation down the road painted their brick church white. In an essay called "Halifax County and Blacks," under a subtitle "Things Blacks Must Do To Succeed," Cora once wrote, "First, blacks must go to church. The church is the backbone of black progress." Every summer for several years Cora has organized a "Citizenship Day of Prayer" on the lawn of the county courthouse in South Boston, which attracts hundreds of people who probably wouldn't gather if the event were called a rally. At the event a list of grievances is always read off — including complaints about such things as how people are treated by the welfare system, unfair employment practices, or disproportionate suspensions of black pupils in the schools.

Problems like that — and what to do about them — are raised regularly at Citizens for a Better America meetings, held the fourth Friday of each month at a local funeral home. CBA has several hundred members, and with help from friends, Cora publishes a monthly one-page newsletter, which she decorates with American flag stickers and short religious sayings. The newsletter is a hodgepodge of useful information, including notices of food stamp law changes, regular updates on what the Virginia General Assembly is considering, board of supervisors' actions, community news, and news about other subjects that Cora is currently concerned with. One issue might have an essay on education, something on federal budget cutbacks and poor people, and a paragraph on the dangers of uranium mining. In 1986, when the federal government was considering southern Virginia, including part of Halifax County, as a possible site for a high-level nuclear waste dump, Cora and CBA fought back, using a section of the federal law requiring that the siting consideration take Indians and other minorities into account. Among other things, CBA found that blacks owned more farmland in Halifax County than in any other county in the country, and that historically, the first black-owned businesses and land in the country were on the site that would be affected by the nuclear waste dump.

Cora learns facts quickly; she can attend a meeting on the problems of family farmers one day, and the next, go to another meeting and be able to reel off facts and figures about farm foreclosures, the cost of fertilizers, trends in agribusiness, and the harmful effect of various pesticides. She reads constantly — newspapers, books, anything on an issue that interests her. "I save newspaper clippings — especially statements from politicians. That way, five years from now when they say, 'I'm definitely against that,' I can go back and say, 'But on such and such a date, you said *this*.'"

Cora stays extremely busy. Several years ago, she went back and got her graduate equivalency diploma, and took some courses at the community college. She thought she might want her degree: "I used to think I wanted to be a social worker. But I changed my mind, because you can't do as much inside the system as you can on the outside. There are so many people who become social workers, and then sit there with their hands tied. What people really need is somebody on the outside who's going to go and raise hell for them about laws and regulations."

Besides CBA gatherings, meetings of the county board of supervisors, and her usual rounds to the legal aid office and the county office building, Cora still visits elderly people, helps women without cars to do their shopping, reads and explains people's mail about food stamps and social security to them, and answers frequent letters. She takes every letter seriously. One, for instance, addressed simply to "Cora Tucker, Halifax, Virginia," read, "Dear Mrs. Tucker, Please don't let the county send us to be experimented on. We heard that they are going to take people on welfare to be experimented on." Cora remembered that there had been separate articles in the newspaper recently, on the "workfare" program to employ welfare recipients, and on a county decision to allow dogs from the animal pound to be used for medical experiments. Cora concluded that the person who wrote the letter had gotten the two issues confused — but she wasn't satisfied until she had called the county administrator and had gotten him to pledge to do a better job of explaining the issues publicly.

Cora's work goes far beyond Halifax. CBA itself has chapters in several   35
other places, including one started in Baltimore by one of Cora's sisters. In addition, when a new coalition group, Virginia Action, was started in the state in 1980, Cora was on the founding committee and was elected its first president. She also became active on the board of its national affiliate, Citizen Action. And in 1981, on top of everything else she was doing, this woman who as a girl had refused to shake the governor's hand was talked into running as a write-in protest candidate for governor by several black groups. She didn't get many votes, but her campaign was covered in the press, and she thinks that she raised issues about black people's concerns that otherwise would have been ignored.

Cora hasn't received much support in her work from her family, except from her mother. She and her husband are estranged, and her children haven't taken an active interest in Cora's work. Cora visits her mother often, in an old house several miles away that has woodburning stoves for heat, religious pictures in the downstairs room, and, hanging in the stairway, a plastic placemat depicting Martin Luther King's tomb. Cora's mother is clearly proud of her; she emphasizes what a smart girl Cora was, and is, and how courageous.

Others agree. As a man who works with Cora at Virginia Action puts it, "All of the issues Cora has taken on — like voting rights and employment discrimination — had been problems in Halifax County for decades. But nobody was willing to fight. And the reason was that it's very, very hard to be somebody going against the mainstream in a small rural community. It's a hell of a lot easier to play the role of the gadfly when you live in an urban environment, where you have your own community of friends, and you don't have to worry about the world. In a small rural community, your community *is* your world. And it's hard to fight the people you have to face every single day. Cora's able to do it because she's got guts. There's just nothing else to it but courage. In a small community those people writing nasty letters to the editor about you are people you're going to run into at the grocery, or whose kids go to school with yours. In addition, being black in a southern rural community, and being a woman, make it that much harder. She hasn't even had the active support of a large part of the black community — they feel threatened by her; she's stolen a lot of their fire. And she's always fighting back as opposed to the blacks who always cooperate with the white power structure. She just reached a point where she decided that slow-moving efforts weren't enough for the things that needed doing — things that were clear in her mind. She recognized the dangers that would be involved, but went ahead because she knew she was right."

ENGAGING THE TEXT

1. How might Cora Tucker define success? To what extent has she achieved it?

2. What motivates Cora Tucker? How do you explain her courage and commitment? Can you think of any ways to encourage more people to emulate some of her virtues?

3. What has her experience taught Cora Tucker about "organizing"? What are her strategies for getting things done?

4. Do you think people in small towns or rural communities are better able than urban dwellers to influence political decisions that affect them? Why or why not?

EXPLORING CONNECTIONS

5. Review the stories of *Ragged Dick* (p. 306) and Colin Powell (p. 314) to refresh in your mind those definitive, archetypal versions of the American Dream. What, if anything, does Cora Tucker have in common with Dick and Powell? How does she differ? What, if anything, will keep Cora Tucker from becoming a mythic figure in our culture?

6. In "Rewards and Opportunities" (p. 331), Gregory Mantsios writes that "people do not choose to be poor or working class; instead they are limited and confined by the opportunities afforded or denied them by a social system" (para. 48). How well does this description fit Cora Tucker? To what extent does her story make your rethink this claim or others by Mantsios?

EXTENDING THE CRITICAL CONTEXT

7. Research grass-roots organizations like Citizens for a Better America in your community. Choose one and attend a meeting and interview members of the organization. Report to the class on its goals, strategies, accomplishments, and current objectives and challenges.

8. This chapter of *Rereading America* has been criticized by conservatives for undermining the work ethic of American college students. Rush Limbaugh, for example, claims that the chapter "presents America as a stacked deck," thus "robbing people of the ability to see the enormous opportunities directly in front of them." Do you agree? Write a journal entry in which you explain whether or how these readings have influenced your attitudes toward work and success.

You're Short, Besides!

SUCHENG CHAN

In this essay, Sucheng Chan analyzes her experiences as a "physically handicapped Asian American woman," showing how cultural myths about "disabilities" kept people from seeing her capacity for real achievement. Chan is a professor of Asian American studies at the University of California, Santa Barbara. The distinguished teaching award mentioned in the essay is just one of several prizes she has won for her excellence in teaching and scholarship. She is author of the award-winning The Asian Americans: An Interpretive History *(1991) and has written or edited another dozen books, most dealing with Asian American history. This essay first appeared in* Making Waves: An Anthology of Writing By and About Asian American Women *(1989).*

When asked to write about being a physically handicapped Asian American woman, I considered it an insult. After all, my accomplishments are many, yet I was not asked to write about any of them. Is being handicapped the most salient feature about me? The fact that it might be in the eyes of others made me decide to write the essay as requested. I realized that the way I think about myself may differ considerably from the way others perceive me. And maybe that's what being physically handicapped is all about.

I was stricken simultaneously with pneumonia and polio at the age of four. Uncertain whether I had polio of the lungs, seven of the eight doctors who attended me — all practitioners of Western medicine — told my parents they should not feel optimistic about my survival. A Chinese fortune teller my mother consulted also gave a grim prognosis, but for an entirely different reason: I had been stricken because my name was offensive to the gods. My grandmother had named me "grandchild of wisdom," a name that the fortune teller said was too presumptuous for a girl. So he advised my parents to change my name to "chaste virgin." All these pessimistic predictions notwithstanding, I hung onto life, if only by a thread. For three years, my body was periodically pierced with electric shocks as the muscles of my legs atrophied. Before my illness, I had been an active, rambunctious, precocious, and very curious child. Being confined to bed was thus a mental agony as great as my physical pain. Living in war-torn China, I received little medical attention; physical therapy was unheard of. But I was determined to walk. So one day, when I was six or seven, I instructed my mother to set up two rows of chairs to face each other so that I could use them as I would parallel bars. I attempted to walk by holding my body up and moving it forward with my arms while dragging my legs along behind. Each time I fell, my mother gasped, but I badgered her until she let me try again. After four nonambulatory years, I finally walked once more by pressing my hands against my thighs so my knees wouldn't buckle.

My father had been away from home during most of those years because of the war. When he returned. I had to confront the guilt he felt about my condition. In many East Asian cultures, there is a strong folk belief that a person's physical state in this life is a reflection of how morally or sinfully he or she lived in previous lives. Furthermore, because of the tendency to view the family as a single unit, it is believed that the fate of one member can be caused by the behavior of another. Some of my father's relatives told him that my illness had doubtless been caused by the wild carousing he did in his youth. A well-meaning but somewhat simple man, my father believed them.

Throughout my childhood, he sometimes apologized to me for having to suffer retribution for his former bad behavior. This upset me; it was bad enough that I had to deal with the anguish of not being able to walk, but to have to assuage his guilt as well was a real burden! In other ways, my father was very good to me. He took me out often, carrying me on his shoulders or back, to give me fresh air and sunshine. He did this until I was too large and heavy for him to carry. And ever since I can remember, he has told me that I am pretty.

After getting over her anxieties about my constant falls, my mother decided to send me to school. I had already learned to read some words of Chinese at the age of three by asking my parents to teach me the sounds and meaning of various characters in the daily newspaper. But between the ages of four and eight, I received no education since just staying alive was a full-time job. Much to her chagrin, my mother found no school in Shanghai, where we lived at the time, which would accept me as a student. Finally, as a last resort, she approached the American School which agreed to enroll me only if my family kept an *amah* (a servant who takes care of children) by my side at all times. The tuition at the school was twenty U.S. dollars per month — a huge sum of money during those years of runaway inflation in China — and payable only in U.S. dollars. My family afforded the high cost of tuition and the expense of employing a full-time *amah* for less than a year.

We left China as the Communist forces swept across the country in victory. We found an apartment in Hong Kong across the street from a school run by Seventh-Day Adventists.[1] By that time I could walk a little, so the principal was persuaded to accept me. An *amah* now had to take care of me

₅

---

[1]*Seventh-Day Adventists:* A Protestant sect noted for their evangelical missionary work and their belief in the imminent and visible return of Christ, which would herald the coming of the Christian millennium.

only during recess when my classmates might easily knock me over as they ran about the playground.

After a year and a half in Hong Kong, we moved to Malaysia, where my father's family had lived for four generations. There I learned to swim in the lovely warm waters of the tropics and fell in love with the sea. On land I was a cripple; in the ocean I could move with the grace of a fish. I liked the freedom of being in the water so much that many years later, when I was a graduate student in Hawaii, I became greatly enamored with a man just because he called me a "Polynesian water nymph."

As my overall health improved, my mother became less anxious about all aspects of my life. She did everything possible to enable me to lead as normal a life as possible. I remember how once some of her colleagues in the high school where she taught criticized her for letting me wear short skirts. They felt my legs should not be exposed to public view. My mother's response was, "All girls her age wear short skirts, so why shouldn't she?"

The years in Malaysia were the happiest of my childhood, even though I was constantly fending off children who ran after me calling, "*Baikah! Baikah!*" ("Cripple! Cripple!" in the Hokkien dialect commonly spoken in Malaysia). The taunts of children mattered little because I was a star pupil. I won one award after another for general scholarship as well as for art and public speaking. Whenever the school had important visitors my teacher always called on me to recite in front of the class.

A significant event that marked me indelibly occurred when I was   10 twelve. That year my school held a music recital and I was one of the students chosen to play the piano. I managed to get up the steps to the stage without any problem, but as I walked across the stage, I fell. Out of the audience, a voice said loudly and clearly, "Ayah! A *baikah* shouldn't be allowed to perform in public." I got up before anyone could get on stage to help me and, with tears streaming uncontrollably down my face, I rushed to the piano and began to play. Beethoven's "Für Elise" had never been played so fiendishly fast before or since, but I managed to finish the whole piece. That I managed to do so made me feel really strong. I never again feared ridicule.

In later years I was reminded of this experience from time to time. During my fourth year as an assistant professor at the University of California at Berkeley, I won a distinguished teaching award. Some weeks later I ran into a former professor who congratulated me enthusiastically. But I said to him, "You know what? I became a distinguished teacher by *limping* across the stage of Dwinelle 155!" (Dwinelle 155 is a large, cold, classroom that most colleagues of mine hate to teach in.) I was rude not because I lacked graciousness but because this man, who had told me that my dissertation was the finest piece of work he had read in fifteen years, had nevertheless advised me to eschew a teaching career.

"Why?" I asked.

"Your leg . . ." he responded.

"What about my leg?" I said, puzzled.

"Well, how would you feel standing in front of a large lecture class?"   15

"If it makes any difference, I want you to know I've won a number of speech contests in my life, and I am not the least bit self-conscious about speaking in front of large audiences. . . . Look, why don't you write me a letter of recommendation to tell people how brilliant I am, and let *me* worry about my leg!"

This incident is worth recounting only because it illustrates a dilemma that handicapped persons face frequently: those who care about us sometimes get so protective that they unwittingly limit our growth. This former professor of mine had been one of my greatest supporters for two decades. Time after time, he had written glowing letters of recommendation on my behalf. He had spoken as he did because he thought he had my best interests at heart; he thought that if I got a desk job rather than one that required me to be a visible, public person, I would be spared the misery of being stared at.

Americans, for the most part, do not believe as Asians do that physically handicapped persons are morally flawed. But they are equally inept at interacting with those of us who are not able-bodied. Cultural differences in the perception and treatment of handicapped people are most clearly expressed by adults. Children, regardless of where they are, tend to be openly curious about people who do not look "normal." Adults in Asia have no hesitation in asking visibly handicapped people what is wrong with them, often expressing their sympathy with looks of pity, whereas adults in the United States try desperately to be polite by pretending not to notice.

One interesting response I often elicited from people in Asia but have never encountered in America is the attempt to link my physical condition to the state of my soul. Many a time while living and traveling in Asia people would ask me what religion I belonged to. I would tell them that my mother is a devout Buddhist, that my father was baptized a Catholic but has never practiced Catholicism, and that I am an agnostic. Upon hearing this, people would try strenuously to convert me to their religion so that whichever God they believed in could bless me. If I would only attend this church or that temple regularly, they urged, I would surely get cured. Catholics and Buddhists alike have pressed religious medallions into my palm, telling me if I would wear these, the relevant deity or saint would make me well. Once while visiting the tomb of Muhammad Ali Jinnah[2] in Karachi, Pakistan, an old Muslim, after finishing his evening prayers, spotted me, gestured toward my legs, raised his arms heavenward, and began a new round of prayers, apparently on my behalf.

---

[2]*Muhammad Ali Jinnah:* Leading Indian politician (1876–1948) who opposed Hindu ideology and the methods of Gandhi for separate Muslim statehood; served as Pakistan's first governor general.

In the United States adults who try to act "civilized" towards handi- 20
capped people by pretending they don't notice anything unusual sometimes
end up ignoring handicapped people completely. In the first few months I
lived in this country, I was struck by the fact that whenever children asked me
what was the matter with my leg, their adult companions would hurriedly
shush them up, furtively look at me, mumble apologies, and rush their children away. After a few months of such encounters, I decided it was my responsibility to educate these people. So I would say to the flustered adults,
"It's okay, let the kid ask." Turning to the child, I would say, "When I was a
little girl, no bigger than you are, I became sick with something called polio.
The muscles of my leg shrank up and I couldn't walk very well. You're much
luckier than I am because now you can get a vaccine to make sure you never
get my disease. So don't cry when your mommy takes you to get a polio vaccine, okay?" Some adults and their little companions I talked to this way were
glad to be rescued from embarrassment; others thought I was strange.

Americans have another way of covering up their uneasiness: they become jovially patronizing. Sometimes when people spot my crutch, they ask
if I've had a skiing accident. When I answer that unfortunately it is something less glamorous than that, they say, "I bet you *could* ski if you put your
mind to it!" Alternately, at parties where people dance, men who ask me to
dance with them get almost belligerent when I decline their invitation.
They say, "Of course you can dance if you *want* to!" Some have given me
pep talks about how if I would only develop the right mental attitude, I
would have more fun in life.

Different cultural attitudes toward handicapped persons came out
clearly during my wedding. My father-in-law, as solid a representative of
middle America as could be found, had no qualms about objecting to the
marriage on racial grounds, but he could bring himself to comment on my
handicap only indirectly. He wondered why his son, who had dated numerous high school and college beauty queens, couldn't marry one of them instead of me. My mother-in-law, a devout Christian, did not share her husband's prejudices, but she worried aloud about whether I could have
children. Some Chinese friends of my parents, on the other hand, said that I
was lucky to have found such a noble man, one who would marry me despite my handicap. I, for my part, appeared in church in a white lace wedding dress I had designed and made myself — a miniskirt!

How Asian Americans treat me with respect to my handicap tells me a
great deal about their degree of acculturation. Recent immigrants behave
just like Asians in Asia; those who have been here longer or who grew up in
the United States behave more like their white counterparts. I have not encountered any distinctly Asian American pattern of response. What makes
the experience of Asian American handicapped people unique is the duality
of responses we elicit.

Regardless of racial or cultural background, most handicapped
people have to learn to find a balance between the desire to attain

physical independence and the need to take care of ourselves by not overtaxing our bodies. In my case, I've had to learn to accept the fact that leading an active life has its price. Between the ages of eight and eighteen, I walked without using crutches or braces but the effort caused my right leg to become badly misaligned. Soon after I came to the United States, I had a series of operations to straighten out the bones of my right leg; afterwards though my leg looked straighter and presumably better, I could no longer walk on my own. Initially my doctors fitted me with a brace, but I found wearing one cumbersome and soon gave it up. I could move around much more easily — and more important, faster — by using one crutch. One orthopedist after another warned me that using a single crutch was a bad practice. They were right. Over the years my spine developed a double-S curve and for the last twenty years I have suffered from severe, chronic back pains, which neither conventional physical therapy nor a lighter work load can eliminate.

The only thing that helps my backaches is a good massage, but the soothing effect lasts no more than a day or two. Massages are expensive, especially when one needs them three times a week. So I found a job that pays better, but at which I have to work longer hours, consequently increasing the physical strain on my body — a sort of vicious circle. When I was in my thirties, my doctors told me that if I kept leading the strenuous life I did, I would be in a wheelchair by the time I was forty. They were right on target: I bought myself a wheelchair when I was forty-one. But being the incorrigible character that I am, I use it only when I am *not* in a hurry!

It is a good thing, however, that I am too busy to think much about my handicap or my backaches because pain can physically debilitate as well as cause depression. And there are days when my spirits get rather low. What has helped me is realizing that being handicapped is akin to growing old at an accelerated rate. The contradiction I experience is that often my mind races along as though I'm only twenty while my body feels about sixty. But fifteen or twenty years hence, unlike my peers who will have to cope with aging for the first time, I shall be full of cheer because I will have already fought, and I hope won, that battle long ago.

Beyond learning how to be physically independent and, for some of us, living with chronic pain or other kinds of discomfort, the most difficult thing a handicapped person has to deal with, especially during puberty and early adulthood, is relating to potential sexual partners. Because American culture places so much emphasis on physical attractiveness, a person with a shriveled limb, or a tilt to the head, or the inability to speak clearly, experiences great uncertainty — indeed trauma — when interacting with someone to whom he or she is attracted. My problem was that I was not only physically handicapped, small, and short, but worse, I also wore glasses and was smarter than all the boys I knew! Alas, an insurmountable combination. Yet somehow I have managed to have intimate relationships, all of them

25

with extraordinary men. Not surprisingly, there have also been countless men who broke my heart — men who enjoyed my company "as a friend," but who never found the courage to date or make love with me, although I am sure my experience in this regard is no different from that of many able-bodied persons.

The day came when my backaches got in the way of having an active sex life. Surprisingly that development was liberating because I stopped worrying about being attractive to men. No matter how headstrong I had been, I, like most women of my generation, had had the desire to be alluring to men ingrained into me. And that longing had always worked like a brake on my behavior. When what men think of me ceased to be compelling, I gained greater freedom to be myself.

I've often wondered if I would have been a different person had I not been physically handicapped. I really don't know, though there is no question that being handicapped has marked me. But at the same time I usually do not *feel* handicapped — and consequently, I do not *act* handicapped. People are therefore less likely to treat me as a handicapped person. There is no doubt, however, that the lives of my parents, sister, husband, other family members, and some close friends have been affected by my physical condition. They have had to learn not to hide me away at home, not to feel embarrassed by how I look or react to people who say silly things to me, and not to resent me for the extra demands my condition makes on them. Perhaps the hardest thing for those who live with handicapped people is to know when and how to offer help. There are no guidelines applicable to all situations. My advice is, when in doubt, ask, but ask in a way that does not smack of pity or embarrassment. Most important, please don't talk to us as though we are children.

So, has being physically handicapped been a handicap? It all depends   30 on one's attitude. Some years ago, I told a friend that I had once said to an affirmative action compliance officer (somewhat sardonically since I do not believe in the head count approach to affirmative action) that the institution which employs me is triply lucky because it can count me as nonwhite, female, and handicapped. He responded, "Why don't you tell them to count you four times? . . . Remember, you're short, besides!"

Engaging the Text

1. How many ways has Chan been a success? How do you think she would define success? What role did her handicap play in her achievements?

2. Chan says that many adults in the United States pretend not to notice visibly handicapped people. Is this a fair assessment of your own behavior? Have family members or others ever instructed you in "how to act" around physically challenged people? Has Chan's narrative changed in any way your attitude about people who face physical challenges?

EXPLORING CONNECTIONS

3. Compare and contrast the stereotypes Chan faces with those described in Studs Terkel's "Stephen Cruz" (p. 326), Curtis Chang's "Streets of Gold: The Myth of the Model Minority" (p. 366), and Judith Ortiz Cofer's "The Story of My Body" (p. 436). What impact, if any, do such stereotypes have on Chan, Cruz, Ortiz Cofer, and the young people described by Chang?

4. Curtis Chang (p. 366) argues that the myth of the model minority has masked the difficulties faced by Asian Americans. Do you think there is a myth of the model handicapped person in American culture? If so, give a nutshell summary of this myth.

EXTENDING THE CRITICAL CONTEXT

5. Do some research in *TV Guide* or your local video rental store to find one or more TV programs or films that include a physically challenged character. How are such characters portrayed? For example, is the "disability" invariably the focal point for that character, or is it just one part of a complex person?

6. Chan mentions that Asians generally have a stronger belief in connections between body, mind, and soul than Americans do. In small groups, discuss your own beliefs about one part of this issue: the power of the mind to heal the body. Report to the class the range of beliefs within your group. Also try to determine whether these beliefs are influenced primarily by parents, by religion, by education, by personal experience, or by other factors.

4

True Women and Real Men

Myths of Gender

"Bree Scott-Hartland as Delphinia Blue," 1992, from *Living Proof: Courage in the Face of AIDS,* by Carolyn Jones, published by Abbeville Press, 1994.

Common sense tells us that there are obvious differences between females and males: after all, biology, not culture, determines whether you're
able to bear children. But culture and cultural myths do shape the roles
men and women play in our public and private relationships: we may be
born female and male, but we are made women and men. Sociologists distinguish between sex and gender — between one's biological identity and
the conventional patterns of behavior we learn to associate with each sex.
While biological sex remains relatively stable, the definition of "appropriate"
gender behavior varies dramatically from one cultural group or historical
period to the next. The variations show up markedly in the way we dress.
For example, in Thailand, men who act and dress like women are not only
socially accepted but encouraged to participate in popular, male-only
beauty pageants; in contemporary Anglo-American culture, on the other
hand, cross-dressers are usually seen as deviant or ridiculous. Male clothing
in late-seventeenth- and early-eighteenth-century England would also have
failed our current "masculinity" tests: in that period, elaborate laces, bro-
cades, wigs, and even makeup signaled wealth, status, and sexual attractiveness for men and women alike.

History shows us how completely our gender derives from cultural
myths about what is proper for men and women to think, enjoy, and do.
And history is replete with examples of how the apparent "naturalness" of
gender has been used to regulate political, economic, and personal relations
between the sexes.

Many nineteenth-century scientists argued that it was "unnatural" for
women to attend college; rigorous intellectual activity, they asserted, would
draw vital energy away from a woman's reproductive organs and make her
sterile. According to this line of reasoning, women who sought higher education threatened the natural order by jeopardizing their ability to bear children and perpetuate the species. Arguments based on nature were likewise
used to justify women's exclusion from political life. In his classic 1832 treatise on American democracy, for instance, James Fenimore Cooper remarked that women's domestic role and "necessary" subordination to men
made them unsuitable for participation in public affairs. Thus, he argued,
denying women the right to vote was perfectly consistent with the principles of American democracy:

> In those countries where the suffrage is said to be universal, exceptions
> exist, that arise from the necessity of things. . . . The interests of women
> being thought to be so identified with those of their male relatives as to
> become, in a great degree, inseparable, females are, almost generally,
> excluded from the possession of political rights. There can be no doubt
> that society is greatly the gainer, by thus excluding one half its members,
> and the half that is best adapted to give a tone to its domestic happiness,
> from the strife of parties, and the fierce struggles of political controver-
> sies. . . . These exceptions, however, do not very materially affect the
> principle of political equality. (*The American Democrat*)

Resistance to gender equality has been remarkably persistent in the United States. It took over seventy years of hard political work by both black and white women's organizations to win the right to vote. But while feminists gained the vote for women in 1920 and the legal right to equal educational and employment opportunities in the 1970s, attitudes change even more slowly than laws. Contemporary antifeminist campaigns voice some of the same anxieties as their nineteenth-century counterparts over the "loss" of femininity and domesticity.

Women continue to suffer economic inequities based on cultural assumptions about gender. What's defined as "women's work" — nurturing, feeding, caring for family and home — is devalued and pays low wages or none at all. When women enter jobs traditionally held by men, they often encounter discrimination, harassment, or "glass ceilings" that limit their advancement. But men, too, pay a high price for their culturally imposed roles. Psychological research shows higher rates of depression among people of both sexes who adhere closely to traditional roles than among those who do not. Moreover, studies of men's mental and physical health suggest that social pressure to "be a man" (that is, to be emotionally controlled, powerful, and successful) can contribute to isolation, anxiety, stress, and illness, and may be partially responsible for men's shorter life spans. As sociologist Margaret Andersen observes, "traditional gender roles limit the psychological and social possibilities for human beings."

Even our assumption that there are "naturally" only two genders is a cultural invention that fails to accommodate the diversity of human experience. Some cultures have three or more gender categories. One of the best-known third genders is the American Indian *berdache,* a role that is found in as many as seventy North and South American tribes. The berdache is a biological male who takes the social role of a woman, does women's work (or in some cases both women's and men's work), and often enjoys high status in the society; the berdache has sex with men who are not themselves berdaches and in some cultures may also marry a man. Euro-American culture, by contrast, offers no socially acceptable alternative gender roles. As a result, gay men, lesbians, bisexuals, transsexuals, cross-dressers, and other gender rebels confront pervasive and often legally sanctioned discrimination similar to that once experienced by women. Just as many Americans in the past considered it "unnatural" and socially destructive for women to vote or go to college, many now consider it "unnatural" and socially destructive for gays and lesbians to marry, bear or adopt children, serve in the military, lead scout groups, or teach school.

This chapter focuses on cultural myths of gender and the influence they wield over human development and personal identity. The first three selections examine how dominant American culture defines female and male gender roles — and how those roles may define us. In "How the Americans Understand the Equality of the Sexes," Alexis de Tocqueville describes the status of American women in the early years of the Republic. Jamaica Kincaid's "Girl," a story framed as a mother's advice to her daughter, presents a more contemporary take on what it means to be raised a woman. Holly Devor's "Becoming Members of Society" examines gender as a socially constructed category and discusses the psychological processes that underlie gender role acquisition.

Next, a series of personal narratives presents strong rereadings of traditional gender roles, introducing us to three individuals who struggle with conventional notions of femininity and masculinity. An oral history, "Nora Quealey," provides an example of a woman torn between the roles she's been socially conditioned to play and the realities of life on a blue-collar job. Judith Ortiz Cofer's personal reflection, "The Story of My Body," traces the shifting meanings of gender and identity for a woman of color who moves among different social and cultural contexts. "Me Macho, You Jane," Dagoberto Gilb's playful riff on masculinity, describes the dilemma of a man who disdains the macho pose of a young coworker but has trouble suppressing his own "macho spasms."

A cluster of essays focusing on popular culture examines the politics of gender in advertising, sports, rap music, and the movies. Jackson Katz, in "Advertising and the Construction of Violent White Masculinity," interprets the popularity of violent masculine images in contemporary media as a sign of men's anxiety about losing power. Mariah Burton Nelson's "Boys Will Be Boys and Girls Will Not" critiques the common assumption that men are naturally better athletes than women and spells out some of the ways that women are kept "in their place" in the sports world. In another media essay, "Sexism and Misogyny: Who Takes the Rap?" bell hooks probes the association between black masculinity and violence and suggests that the misogyny of rap lyrics actually reflects the sexist aggression that is rampant in the dominant culture.

Are we imprisoned by traditional gender roles, or has "liberation" itself become a prison? Christina Hoff Sommers, in "The Gender Wardens," warns that feminist attempts to eradicate traditional roles threaten our freedom of choice. Carmen Vázquez's "Appearances" deals with a different kind of threat to personal freedom: examining the connection between homophobic violence and "gender betrayal," Vázquez documents the penalties — from verbal harassment to murder — paid by both gay and straight people who dare to cross conventional gender boundaries. The chapter ends with two positive redefinitions of gendered identity. "The Two," Gloria Naylor's short story about a lesbian couple, punctures gay stereotypes and invites us to reconsider common assumptions about "natural" roles. In her essay "Where I Come From Is Like This," Paula Gunn Allen counters dominant American myths of gender with an eloquent description of the powerful roles played by women in American Indian cultures.

Sources

Margaret L. Andersen, *Thinking About Women: Sociological Perspectives on Gender,* 3rd ed. New York: Macmillan, 1993.

James Fenimore Cooper, *The American Democrat.* N.p.: Minerva Press, 1969.

Marilyn French, *Beyond Power: On Women, Men, and Morals.* New York: Ballantine Books, 1985.

Paula Giddings, *When and Where I Enter: The Impact of Black Women on Race and Sex in America.* New York: Bantam Books, 1984.

Ruth Hubbard, *The Politics of Women's Biology.* New Brunswick, NJ: Rutgers University Press, 1990.

Judith Lorber, *Paradoxes of Gender.* New Haven and London: Yale University Press, 1994.

James D. Weinrich and Walter L. Williams, "Strange Customs, Familiar Lives: Homosexualities in Other Cultures." *Homosexuality: Research Implications for Public Policy.* Ed. John C. Gonsiorek and James D. Weinrich. Newbury Park, CA: Sage, 1991.

BEFORE READING

- When you think of the following occupations, what's the first image that comes to mind? Do you picture a woman or a man? Quickly read the list, jotting an "f" for "female" or an "m" for "male" next to each occupation.

flight attendant	police officer	construction worker
corporate executive	truck driver	interior designer
lawyer	cook	fashion model
nurse	hair stylist	architect
engineer	doctor	chef
professional athlete	florist	computer programmer
secretary	professor	pilot
judge	farmer	bank teller
supermarket cashier	soldier	teacher
plumber	reporter	daycare worker

  Compare results with classmates: How much consistency do you find in the gender associated with each job? Do you detect any patterns in the types of work associated with women and with men?

- Collect and bring to class images of girls and boys, women and men taken from popular magazines and newspapers. Working in groups, make a collage of either male or female gender images; then compare and discuss your results. What do these media images tell you about what it means to be a woman or a man in this culture?

- Do a brief freewrite focusing on the performer in the frontispiece to this chapter (p. 409). How would you describe this person's gender? In what ways does this image challenge traditional ideas about maleness and femaleness?

How the Americans Understand the Equality of the Sexes

ALEXIS DE TOCQUEVILLE

In 1831, Alexis de Tocqueville (1805–1859), a French aristocrat, left Europe to study the American penal system. The young democracy that he observed in the United States left a deep impression on Tocqueville, and in 1835 he published his reflections on this new way of life in Democracy in America *— a work that has since become the point of departure for many studies of American culture. In the following passage from* Democracy in America, *Tocqueville compares the social condition of American women to that of their European counterparts. Tocqueville's concept of equality and assumptions about women can seem foreign to modern readers, so it would be a good idea to take your time as you read this short passage.*

I have shown how democracy destroys or modifies the different inequalities which originate in society; but is that all? or does it not ultimately affect that great inequality of man and woman which has seemed, up to the present day, to be eternally based in human nature? I believe that the social changes which bring nearer to the same level the father and son, the master and servant, and, in general, superiors and inferiors, will raise woman, and make her more and more the equal of man. But here, more than ever, I feel the necessity of making myself clearly understood; for there is no subject on which the coarse and lawless fancies of our age have taken a freer range.

There are people in Europe who, confounding together the different characteristics of the sexes, would make man and woman into beings not only equal, but alike. They would give to both the same functions, impose on both the same duties, and grant to both the same rights; they would mix them in all things, — their occupations, their pleasures, their business. It may readily be conceived, that, by thus attempting to make one sex equal to the other, both are degraded; and from so preposterous a medley of the works of nature, nothing could ever result but weak men and disorderly women.

It is not thus that the Americans understand that species of democratic equality which may be established between the sexes. They admit that, as nature has appointed such wide differences between the physical and moral constitution of man and woman, her manifest design was to give a distinct employment to their various faculties; and they hold that improvement does not consist in making beings so dissimilar do pretty nearly the same things, but in causing each of them to fulfil their respective tasks in the best possible manner. The Americans have applied to the sexes the great principle of political economy which governs the manufactures of our age, by carefully dividing the duties of man from those of woman, in order that the great work of society may be the better carried on.

In no country has such constant care been taken as in America to trace two clearly distinct lines of action for the two sexes, and to make them keep pace one with the other, but in two pathways which are always different. American women never manage the outward concerns of the family, or conduct a business, or take a part in political life; nor are they, on the other hand, ever compelled to perform the rough labor of the fields, or to make any of those laborious exertions which demand the exertion of physical strength. No families are so poor as to form an exception to this rule. If, on the one hand, an American woman cannot escape from the quiet circle of domestic employments, she is never forced, on the other, to go beyond it. Hence it is, that the women of America, who often exhibit a masculine strength of understanding and a manly energy, generally preserve great delicacy of personal appearance, and always retain the manners of women, although they sometimes show that they have the hearts and minds of men.

Nor have the Americans ever supposed that one consequence of democratic principles is the subversion of marital power, or the confusion of the natural authorities in families. They hold that every association must have a head in order to accomplish its object, and that the natural head of the conjugal association is man. They do not therefore deny him the right of directing his partner; and they maintain that, in the smaller association of husband and wife, as well as in the great social community, the object of democracy is to regulate and legalize the powers which are necessary, and not to subvert all power. 5

This opinion is not peculiar to one sex, and contested by the other: I never observed that the women of America consider conjugal authority as a fortunate usurpation of their rights, nor that they thought themselves degraded by submitting to it. It appeared to me, on the contrary, that they attach a sort of pride to the voluntary surrender of their own will, and make it their boast to bend themselves to the yoke, — not to shake it off. Such, at least, is the feeling expressed by the most virtuous of their sex; the others are silent; and, in the United States, it is not the practice for a guilty wife to clamor for the rights of women, whilst she is trampling on her own holiest duties.[1]

It has often been remarked, that in Europe a certain degree of contempt lurks even in the flattery which men lavish upon women: although a European frequently affects to be the slave of woman, it may be seen that

---

[1]Allusion to Mary Wollstonecraft (1759–1797), English radical, political theorist, and author of *Vindication of the Rights of Woman,* who argued that women should enjoy complete political, economic, and sexual freedom; Wollstonecraft scandalized the "polite" society of her day by living according to her feminist principles.

he never sincerely thinks her his equal. In the United States, men seldom compliment women, but they daily show how much they esteem them. They constantly display an entire confidence in the understanding of a wife, and a profound respect for her freedom; they have decided that her mind is just as fitted as that of a man to discover the plain truth, and her heart as firm to embrace it; and they have never sought to place her virtue, any more than his, under the shelter of prejudice, ignorance, and fear.

It would seem that, in Europe, where man so easily submits to the despotic sway of women, they are nevertheless deprived of some of the greatest attributes of the human species, and considered as seductive but imperfect beings; and (what may well provoke astonishment) women ultimately look upon themselves in the same light, and almost consider it as a privilege that they are entitled to show themselves futile, feeble, and timid. The women of America claim no such privileges.

Again, it may be said that in our morals we have reserved strange immunities to man; so that there is, as it were, one virtue for his use, and another for the guidance of his partner; and that, according to the opinion of the public, the very same act may be punished alternately as a crime, or only as a fault. The Americans know not this iniquitous division of duties and rights; amongst them, the seducer is as much dishonored as his victim.

It is true that the Americans rarely lavish upon women those eager attentions which are commonly paid them in Europe; but their conduct to women always implies that they suppose them to be virtuous and refined; and such is the respect entertained for the moral freedom of the sex, that in the presence of a woman the most guarded language is used, lest her ear should be offended by an expression. In America, a young unmarried woman may, alone and without fear, undertake a long journey. 10

The legislators of the United States, who have mitigated almost all the penalties of criminal law, still make rape a capital offence, and no crime is visited with more inexorable severity by public opinion. This may be accounted for; as the Americans can conceive nothing more precious than a woman's honor, and nothing which ought so much to be respected as her independence, they hold that no punishment is too severe for the man who deprives her of them against her will. In France, where the same offence is visited with far milder penalties, it is frequently difficult to get a verdict from a jury against the prisoner. Is this a consequence of contempt of decency, or contempt of women? I cannot but believe that it is a contempt of both.

Thus, the Americans do not think that man and woman have either the duty or the right to perform the same offices, but they show an equal regard for both their respective parts; and though their lot is different, they consider both of them as beings of equal value. They do not give to the courage of woman the same form or the same direction as to that of man; but they never doubt her courage: and if they hold that man and his partner ought not always to exercise their intellect and understanding in the same manner, they at least believe the understanding of the one to be as sound as that of the other, and her intellect to be as clear. Thus, then, whilst they have allowed the social inferiority of woman to subsist, they have done all they could to raise her morally and intellectually to the level of man; and in this respect they appear to me to have excellently understood the true principle of democratic improvement.

As for myself, I do not hesitate to avow, that, although the women of the United States are confined within the narrow circle of domestic life, and their situation is, in some respects, one of extreme dependence, I have nowhere seen woman occupying a loftier position; and if I were asked, now that I am drawing to the close of this work, in which I have spoken of so many important things done by the Americans, to what the singular prosperity and growing strength of that people ought mainly to be attributed, I should reply, To the superiority of their women.

ENGAGING THE TEXT

1. What roles does Tocqueville assume are natural and appropriate for women? For men? Which of his assumptions, if any, seem contemporary? Which ones seem antiquated, and why?

2. How do American and European attitudes toward women differ, according to Tocqueville? In what ways, according to Tocqueville, is American democracy enabling women to become "more and more the equal of man" (para. 1)?

3. By the time Tocqueville wrote this selection, the first feminist manifesto, Wollstonecraft's *Vindication of the Rights of Woman* (1792), had been read and discussed in Europe for over forty years. Which parts of Tocqueville's essay seem to be intended as a response to feminist arguments for women's equality?

4. Tocqueville finds some forms of equality between women and men more desirable than others. Which forms does he approve, which does he disapprove, and why?

EXPLORING CONNECTIONS

5. Read or review the essays by Paula Gunn Allen (p. 520) and Colin Calloway (p. 688) for information on the various roles assigned to women and men in traditional tribal cultures. How are these roles similar to or different from the ones described by Tocqueville? Do they tend to support or challenge his observation that "the great inequality of man and woman" appears to be "eternally based in human nature" (para. 1)?

6. Both Tocqueville and Thomas Jefferson (p. 532) attempt to justify or rationalize a particular form of inequality. What strategies does each writer use to build his case for the subjection of women or for the enslavement of blacks? Which of their arguments appear least effective to you as a modern reader, and why?

7. Work in groups to list the specific tasks involved in maintaining a household in the 1830s (keep in mind that electricity, indoor plumbing, ready-made clothing, and prepared foods were not available). How credible is Tocqueville's claim that no American woman is "ever compelled . . . to make any of those laborious exertions which demand the exertion of physical strength" (para. 4)? How do you explain his failure to acknowledge the hard physical labor routinely performed by many women during this time?

Girl

JAMAICA KINCAID

Although she now lives in New England, Jamaica Kincaid (b. 1949) retains strong ties, including citizenship, to her birthplace — the island of Antigua in the West Indies. After immigrating to the United States to attend college, she ended up educating herself instead, eventually becoming a staff writer for The New Yorker, *the author of several critically acclaimed books, and an instructor at Harvard University. About the influence of parents on children she says, "The magic is they carry so much you don't know about. They know you in a way you don't know yourself." Some of that magic is exercised in the story "Girl," which was first published in Kincaid's award-winning collection* At the Bottom of the River *(1983). Her latest novel, titled* Autobiography of My Mother, *was published in 1996.*

Wash the white clothes on Monday and put them on the stone heap; wash the color clothes on Tuesday and put them on the clothesline to dry; don't walk barehead in the hot sun; cook pumpkin fritters[1] in very hot sweet oil; soak your little cloths right after you take them off; when buying cotton to make yourself a nice blouse, be sure that it doesn't have gum[2] on it, because that way it won't hold up well after a wash; soak salt fish overnight before you cook it; is it true that you sing benna[3] in Sunday school?; always eat your food in such a way that it won't turn someone

---

[1]*fritters:* Small fried cakes of batter, often containing vegetables, fruit, or other fillings.
[2]*gum:* Plant residue on cotton.
[3]*sing benna:* Sing popular music (not appropriate for Sunday school).

else's stomach; on Sundays try to walk like a lady and not like the slut you are so bent on becoming; don't sing benna in Sunday school; you mustn't speak to wharf-rat boys, not even to give directions; don't eat fruits on the street — flies will follow you; *but I don't sing benna on Sundays at all and never in Sunday school;* this is how to sew on a button; this is how to make a buttonhole for the button you have just sewed on; this is how to hem a dress when you see the hem coming down and so to prevent yourself from looking like the slut I know you are so bent on becoming; this is how you iron your father's khaki shirt so that it doesn't have a crease; this is how you iron your father's khaki pants so that they don't have a crease; this is how you grow okra — far from the house, because okra[4] tree harbors red ants; when you are growing dasheen,[5] make sure it gets plenty of water or else it makes your throat itch when you are eating it; this is how you sweep a corner; this is how you sweep a whole house; this is how you sweep a yard; this is how you smile to someone you don't like too much; this is how you smile to someone you don't like at all; this is how you smile to some-one you like completely; this is how you set a table for tea; this is how you set a table for dinner; this is how you set a table for dinner with an im-portant guest; this is how you set a table for lunch; this is how you set a table for breakfast; this is how to behave in the presence of men who don't know you very well, and this way they won't recognize immediately the slut I have warned you against becoming; be sure to wash every day, even if it is with your own spit; don't squat down to play marbles — you are not a boy, you know; don't pick people's flowers — you might catch something; don't throw stones at blackbirds, because it might not be a blackbird at all; this is how to make a bread pudding; this is how to make doukona;[6] this is how to make pepper pot;[7] this is how to make a good medicine for a cold; this is how to make a good medicine to throw away a child before it even becomes a child; this is how to catch a fish; this is how to throw back a fish you don't like, and that way something bad won't fall on you; this is how to bully a man; this is how a man bullies you; this is how to love a man, and if this doesn't work there are other ways, and if they don't work don't feel too bad about giving up; this is how to spit up in the air if you feel like it, and this is how to move quick so that it doesn't fall on you; this is how to make ends meet; always squeeze bread to make sure it's fresh; *but what if the baker won't let me feel the bread?;* you mean to say that after all you are really going to be the kind of woman who the baker won't let near the bread?

---

[4]*okra:* A shrub whose pods are used in soups, stews, and gumbo.
[5]*dasheen:* The taro plant, cultivated, like the potato, for its edible tuber.
[6]*doukona:* Plaintain pudding; the plaintain fruit is similar to the banana.
[7]*pepper pot:* A spicy West Indian stew.

ENGAGING THE TEXT

1. What are your best guesses as to the time and place of the story? Who is telling the story? What does this dialogue tell you about the relationship between the characters, their values and attitudes? What else can you surmise about these people (for instance, ages, occupation, social status)? On what evidence in the story do you base these conclusions?

2. Why does the story juxtapose advice on cooking and sewing, for example, with the repeated warning not to act like a slut?

3. Explain the meaning of the last line of the story: "you mean to say that after all you are really going to be the kind of woman who the baker won't let near the bread?"

4. What does the story tell us about male-female relationships? According to the speaker, what roles are women and men expected to play? What kinds of power, if any, does the speaker suggest that women may have?

EXPLORING CONNECTIONS

5. To what extent does Patricia Hill Collins's "Black Women and Motherhood" (p. 131) help explain the mother's attitude and advice in this story?

6. What does it mean to be a successful mother in "Girl"? How does this compare to being a good mother or parent in "Growing Pains" (p. 47), "Envy" (p. 118), "An Indian Story" (p. 109), or "Looking for Work" (p. 42)? Of all the parents in these narratives, which do you consider most successful, which least, and why?

EXTENDING THE CRITICAL CONTEXT

7. Write an imitation of the story. If you are a woman, record some of the advice or lessons your mother or another woman gave you; if you are a man, put down advice received from your father or from another male. Read what you have written aloud in class, alternating between male and female speakers, and discuss the results: How does parental guidance vary according to gender?

8. Write a page or two recording what the daughter might be thinking as she listens to her mother's advice; then compare notes with classmates.

Becoming Members of Society: Learning the Social Meanings of Gender

HOLLY DEVOR

Gender is the most transparent of all social categories: we acquire gender roles so early in life and so thoroughly that it's hard to see them as the result of lessons taught and learned. Maleness and femaleness seem "natural," not the product of socialization. In this wide-ranging scholarly essay, Holly Devor suggests that many of our notions of what it means to be female or male are socially constructed. She also touches on the various ways that different cultures define gender. Devor (b. 1951) is a professor of sociology at the University of Victoria in British Columbia and an affiliated scholar at the University of Southern California's Center for Feminist Research. Her award-winning scholarship focuses on female sexuality, transsexuality, and gender. This selection is taken from her book Gender Blending: Confronting the Limits of Duality *(1989).*

The Gendered Self

The task of learning to be properly gendered members of society only begins with the establishment of gender identity. Gender identities act as cognitive filtering devices guiding people to attend to and learn gender role behaviors appropriate to their statuses. Learning to behave in accordance with one's gender identity is a lifelong process. As we move through our lives, society demands different gender performances from us and rewards, tolerates, or punishes us differently for conformity to, or digression from, social norms. As children, and later adults, learn the rules of membership in society, they come to see themselves in terms they have learned from the people around them.

Children begin to settle into a gender identity between the age of eighteen months and two years.[1] By the age of two, children usually understand that they are members of a gender grouping and can correctly identify other members of their gender.[2] By age three they have a fairly firm and consistent concept of gender. Generally, it is not until children are five to seven

[1]Much research has been devoted to determining when gender identity becomes solidified in the sense that a child knows itself to be unequivocally either male or female. John Money and his colleagues have proposed eighteen months of age because it is difficult or impossible to change a child's gender identity once it has been established around the age of eighteen months. Money and Ehrhardt, p. 243. [Author's note]

[2]Mary Driver Leinbach and Beverly I. Fagot, "Acquisition of Gender Labels: A Test for Toddlers," *Sex Roles* 15 (1986), pp. 655–66. [Author's note]

years old that they become convinced that they are permanent members of their gender grouping.[3]

Researchers test the establishment, depth, and tenacity of gender identity through the use of language and the concepts mediated by language. The language systems used in populations studied by most researchers in this field conceptualize gender as binary and permanent. All persons are either male or female. All males are first boys and then men; all females are first girls and then women. People are believed to be unable to change genders without sex change surgery, and those who do change sex are considered to be both disturbed and exceedingly rare.

This is by no means the only way that gender is conceived in all cultures. Many aboriginal cultures have more than two gender categories and accept the idea that, under certain circumstances, gender may be changed without changes being made to biological sex characteristics. Many North and South American native peoples had a legitimate social category for persons who wished to live according to the gender role of another sex. Such people were sometimes revered, sometimes ignored, and occasionally scorned. Each culture had its own word to describe such persons, most commonly translated into English as "berdache." Similar institutions and linguistic concepts have also been recorded in early Siberian, Madagascan, and Polynesian societies, as well as in medieval Europe.[4]

Very young children learn their culture's social definitions of gender   5
and gender identity at the same time that they learn what gender behaviors are appropriate for them. But they only gradually come to understand the meaning of gender in the same way as the adults of their society do. Very young children may learn the words which describe their gender and be able to apply them to themselves appropriately, but their comprehension of their meaning is often different from that used by adults. Five-year-olds, for example, may be able to accurately recognize their own gender and the genders of the people around them, but they will often make such ascriptions on the basis of role information, such as hair style, rather than physical attributes, such as genitals, even when physical cues are clearly known to them. One result of this level of understanding of gender is that children in this age group often believe that people may change their gender with a change in clothing, hair style, or activity.[5]

[3]Maccoby, pp. 225–29; Kohlberg and Ullian, p. 211. [Author's note]

[4]See Susan Baker, "Biological Influences on Human Sex and Gender," in *Women: Sex and Sexuality,* ed. Catherine R. Stimpson and Ethel S. Person (Chicago: University of Chicago Press, 1980), p. 186; Evelyn Blackwood, "Sexuality and Gender in Certain Native American Tribes: The Case of Cross-Gender Females," *Signs* 10 (1984), pp. 27–42; Vern L. Bullough, "Transvestites in the Middle Ages," *American Journal of Sociology* 79 (1974), 1381–89; J. Cl. DuBois, "Transsexualisme et Anthropologie Culturelle," *Gynecologie Practique* 6 (1969), pp. 431–40; Donald C. Forgey, "The Institution of Berdache among the North American Plains Indians," *Journal of Sex Research* 11 (Feb. 1975), pp. 1–15; Walter L. Williams, *The Spirit and the Flesh: Sexual Diversity in American Indian Culture* (Boston: Beacon, 1986). [Author's note]

[5]Maccoby, p. 255. [Author's note]

The characteristics most salient to young minds are the more culturally specific qualities which grow out of gender role prescriptions. In one study, young school age children, who were given dolls and asked to identify their gender, overwhelmingly identified the gender of the dolls on the basis of attributes such as hair length or clothing style, in spite of the fact that the dolls were anatomically correct. Only 17 percent of the children identified the dolls on the basis of their primary or secondary sex characteristics.[6] Children, five to seven years old, understand gender as a function of role rather than as a function of anatomy. Their understanding is that gender (role) is supposed to be stable but that it is possible to alter it at will. This demonstrates that although the standard social definition of gender is based on genitalia, this is not the way that young children first learn to distinguish gender. The process of learning to think about gender in an adult fashion is one prerequisite to becoming a full member of society. Thus, as children grow older, they learn to think of themselves and others in terms more like those used by adults.

Children's developing concepts of themselves as individuals are necessarily bound up in their need to understand the expectations of the society of which they are a part. As they develop concepts of themselves as individuals, they do so while observing themselves as reflected in the eyes of others. Children start to understand themselves as individuals separate from others during the years that they first acquire gender identities and gender roles. As they do so, they begin to understand that others see them and respond to them as particular people. In this way they develop concepts of themselves as individuals, as an "I" (a proactive subject) simultaneously with self-images of themselves as individuals, as a "me" (a member of society, a subjective object). Children learn that they are both as they see themselves and as others see them.[7]

To some extent, children initially acquire the values of the society around them almost indiscriminately. To the degree that children absorb the generalized standards of society into their personal concept of what is correct behavior, they can be said to hold within themselves the attitude of the "generalized other."[8] This "generalized other" functions as a sort of monitoring or measuring device with which individuals may judge their own actions against those of their generalized conceptions of how members of society are expected to act. In this way members of society have available to them a guide, or an internalized observer, to turn the more private "I" into the object of public scrutiny, the "me." In this way, people can monitor their own behavioral impulses and censor actions which might earn them social disapproval or scorn. The tension created by the constant

[6]Ibid., p. 227. [Author's note]

[7]George Herbert Mead, "Self," in *The Social Psychology of George Herbert Mead,* ed. Anselm Strauss (Chicago: Phoenix Books, 1962, 1934), pp. 212–60. [Author's note]

[8]G. H. Mead. [Author's note]

interplay of the personal "I" and the social "me" is the creature known as the "self."

But not all others are of equal significance in our lives, and therefore not all others are of equal impact on the development of the self. Any person is available to become part of one's "generalized other," but certain individuals, by virtue of the sheer volume of time spent in interaction with someone, or by virtue of the nature of particular interactions, become more significant in the shaping of people's values. These "significant others" become prominent in the formation of one's self-image and one's ideals and goals. As such they carry disproportionate weight in one's personal "generalized other."[9] Thus, children's individualistic impulses are shaped into a socially acceptable form both by particular individuals and by a more generalized pressure to conformity exerted by innumerable faceless members of society. Gender identity is one of the most central portions of that developing sense of self. . . .

Gender Role Behaviors and Attitudes

The clusters of social definitions used to identify persons by gender are   10
collectively known as femininity and masculinity. Masculine characteristics are used to identify persons as males, while feminine ones are used as signifiers for femaleness. People use femininity or masculinity to claim and communicate their membership in their assigned, or chosen, sex or gender. Others recognize our sex or gender more on the basis of these characteristics than on the basis of sex characteristics, which are usually largely covered by clothing in daily life.

These two clusters of attributes are most commonly seen as mirror images of one another with masculinity usually characterized by dominance and aggression, and femininity by passivity and submission. A more even-handed description of the social qualities subsumed by femininity and masculinity might be to label masculinity as generally concerned with egoistic dominance and femininity as striving for cooperation or communion.[10] Characterizing femininity and masculinity in such a way does not portray the two clusters of characteristics as being in a hierarchical relationship to one another but rather as being two different approaches to the same question, that question being centrally concerned with the goals, means, and use of power. Such an alternative conception of gender roles captures the hierarchical and competitive masculine thirst for power, which can, but need

---

[9]Hans Gerth and C. Wright Mills, *Character and Social Structure: The Psychology of Social Institutions* (New York: Harcourt, Brace and World, 1953), p. 96. [Author's note]

[10]Egoistic dominance is a striving for superior rewards for oneself or a competitive striving to reduce the rewards for one's competitors even if such action will not increase one's own rewards. Persons who are motivated by desires for egoistic dominance not only wish the best for themselves but also wish to diminish the advantages of others whom they may perceive as competing with them. See Maccoby, p. 217. [Author's note]

not, lead to aggression, and the feminine quest for harmony and communal well-being, which can, but need not, result in passivity and dependence.

Many activities and modes of expression are recognized by most members of society as feminine. Any of these can be, and often are, displayed by persons of either gender. In some cases, cross gender behaviors are ignored by observers, and therefore do not compromise the integrity of a person's gender display. In other cases, they are labeled as inappropriate gender role behaviors. Although these behaviors are closely linked to sexual status in the minds and experiences of most people, research shows that dominant persons of either gender tend to use influence tactics and verbal styles usually associated with men and masculinity, while subordinate persons, of either gender, tend to use those considered to be the province of women.[11] Thus it seems likely that many aspects of masculinity and femininity are the result, rather than the cause, of status inequalities.

Popular conceptions of femininity and masculinity instead revolve around hierarchical appraisals of the "natural" roles of males and females. Members of both genders are believed to share many of the same human characteristics, although in different relative proportions; both males and females are popularly thought to be able to do many of the same things, but most activities are divided into suitable and unsuitable categories for each gender class. Persons who perform the activities considered appropriate for another gender will be expected to perform them poorly; if they succeed adequately, or even well, at their endeavors, they may be rewarded with ridicule or scorn for blurring the gender dividing line.

The patriarchal gender schema[12] currently in use in mainstream North American society reserves highly valued attributes for males and actively supports the high evaluation of any characteristics which might inadvertently become associated with maleness. The ideology which the schema grows out of postulates that the cultural superiority of males is a natural outgrowth of the innate predisposition of males toward aggression and dominance, which is assumed to flow inevitably from evolutionary and biological sources. Female attributes are likewise postulated to find their source in innate predispositions acquired in the evolution of the species. Feminine characteristics are thought to be intrinsic to the female facility for childbirth and breastfeeding. Hence, it is popularly believed that the social position of females is biologically mandated to be intertwined with the care of children and a "natural" dependency on men for the maintenance of mother-child

---

[11]Judith Howard, Philip Blumstein, and Pepper Schwartz, "Sex, Power, and Influence Tactics in Intimate Relationships," *Journal of Personality and Social Psychology* 51 (1986), pp. 102–09; Peter Kollock, Philip Blumstein, and Pepper Schwartz, "Sex and Power in Interaction: Conversational Privileges and Duties," *American Sociological Review* 50 (1985), pp. 34–46. [Author's note]

[12]*schema:* A mental framework, scheme, or pattern that helps us make sense of experience.

units. Thus the goals of femininity and, by implication, of all biological females are presumed to revolve around heterosexuality and maternity.[13]

Femininity, according to this traditional formulation, "would result in   15
warm and continued relationships with men, a sense of maternity, interest in caring for children, and the capacity to work productively and continuously in female occupations."[14] This recipe translates into a vast number of proscriptions and prescriptions. Warm and continued relations with men and an interest in maternity require that females be heterosexually oriented. A heterosexual orientation requires women to dress, move, speak, and act in ways that men will find attractive. As patriarchy has reserved active expressions of power as a masculine attribute, femininity must be expressed through modes of dress, movement, speech, and action which communicate weakness, dependency, ineffectualness, availability for sexual or emotional service, and sensitivity to the needs of others.

Some, but not all, of these modes of interrelation also serve the demands of maternity and many female job ghettos. In many cases, though, femininity is not particularly useful in maternity or employment. Both mothers and workers often need to be strong, independent, and effectual in order to do their jobs well. Thus femininity, as a role, is best suited to satisfying a masculine vision of heterosexual attractiveness.

Body postures and demeanors which communicate subordinate status and vulnerability to trespass through a message of "no threat" make people appear to be feminine. They demonstrate subordination through a minimizing of spatial use: people appear feminine when they keep their arms closer to their bodies, their legs closer together, and their torsos and heads less vertical then do masculine-looking individuals. People also look feminine when they point their toes inward and use their hands in small or childlike gestures. Other people also tend to stand closer to people they see as feminine, often invading their personal space, while people who make frequent appeasement gestures, such as smiling, also give the appearance of femininity. Perhaps as an outgrowth of a subordinate status and the need to avoid conflict with more socially powerful people, women tend to excel over men at the ability to correctly interpret, and effectively display, nonverbal communication cues.[15]

---

[13]Chodorow, p. 134. [Author's note]

[14]Jon K. Meyer and John E. Hoopes, "The Gender Dysphoria Syndromes: A Position Statement on So-Called 'Transsexualism'," *Plastic and Reconstructive Surgery* 54 (Oct. 1974), pp. 444–51. [Author's note]

[15]Erving Goffman, *Gender Advertisements* (New York: Harper Colophon Books, 1976); Judith A. Hall, *Non-Verbal Sex Differences: Communication Accuracy and Expressive Style* (Baltimore: Johns Hopkins University Press, 1984); Nancy M. Henley, *Body Politics: Power, Sex and Non-Verbal Communication* (Englewood Cliffs, New Jersey: Prentice Hall, 1979); Marianne Wex, *"Let's Take Back Our Space": "Female" and "Male" Body Language as a Result of Patriarchal Structures* (Berlin: Frauenliteraturverlag Hermine Fees, 1979). [Author's note]

Speech characterized by inflections, intonations, and phrases that convey nonaggression and subordinate status also make a speaker appear more feminine. Subordinate speakers who use more polite expressions and ask more questions in conversation seem more feminine. Speech characterized by sounds of higher frequencies are often interpreted by listeners as feminine, childlike, and ineffectual.[16] Feminine styles of dress likewise display subordinate status through greater restriction of the free movement of the body, greater exposure of the bare skin, and an emphasis on sexual characteristics. The more gender distinct the dress, the more this is the case.

Masculinity, like femininity, can be demonstrated through a wide variety of cues. Pleck has argued that it is commonly expressed in North American society through the attainment of some level of proficiency at some, or all, of the following four main attitudes of masculinity. Persons who display success and high status in their social group, who exhibit "a manly air of toughness, confidence, and self-reliance" and "the aura of aggression, violence, and daring," and who conscientiously avoid anything associated with femininity are seen as exuding masculinity.[17] These requirements reflect the patriarchal ideology that masculinity results from an excess of testosterone, the assumption being that androgens supply a natural impetus toward aggression, which in turn impels males toward achievement and success. This vision of masculinity also reflects the ideological stance that ideal maleness (masculinity) must remain untainted by female (feminine) pollutants.

Masculinity, then, requires of its actors that they organize themselves   20
and their society in a hierarchical manner so as to be able to explicitly quantify the achievement of success. The achievement of high status in one's social group requires competitive and aggressive behavior from those who wish to obtain it. Competition which is motivated by a goal of individual achievement, or egoistic dominance, also requires of its participants a degree of emotional insensitivity to feelings of hurt and loss in defeated others, and a measure of emotional insularity to protect oneself from becoming vulnerable to manipulation by others. Such values lead those who subscribe to them to view feminine persons as "born losers" and to strive to eliminate any similarities to feminine people from their own personalities. In patriarchally organized societies, masculine values become the ideological structure of the society as a whole. Masculinity thus becomes "innately" valuable and femininity serves a contrapuntal function to delineate and magnify the hierarchical dominance of masculinity.

[16]Karen L. Adams, "Sexism and the English Language: The Linguistic Implications of Being a Woman," in *Women: A Feminist Perspective,* 3rd edition, ed. Jo Freeman (Palo Alto, Calif.: Mayfield, 1984), pp. 478–91; Hall, pp. 37, 130–37. [Author's note]

[17]Elizabeth Hafkin Pleck, *Domestic Tyranny: The Making of Social Policy Against Family Violence from Colonial Times to the Present* (Cambridge: Oxford University Press, 1989), p. 139. [Author's note]

Body postures, speech patterns, and styles of dress which demonstrate and support the assumption of dominance and authority convey an impression of masculinity. Typical masculine body postures tend to be expansive and aggressive. People who hold their arms and hands in positions away from their bodies, and who stand, sit, or lie with their legs apart — thus maximizing the amount of space that they physically occupy — appear most physically masculine. Persons who communicate an air of authority or a readiness for aggression by standing erect and moving forcefully also tend to appear more masculine. Movements that are abrupt and stiff, communicating force and threat rather than flexibility and cooperation, make an actor look masculine. Masculinity can also be conveyed by stern or serious facial expressions that suggest minimal receptivity to the influence of others, a characteristic which is an important element in the attainment and maintenance of egoistic dominance.[18]

Speech and dress which likewise demonstrate or claim superior status are also seen as characteristically masculine behavior patterns. Masculine speech patterns display a tendency toward expansiveness similar to that found in masculine body postures. People who attempt to control the direction of conversations seem more masculine.[19] Those who tend to speak more loudly, use less polite and more assertive forms, and tend to interrupt the conversations of others more often also communicate masculinity to others. Styles of dress which emphasize the size of upper body musculature, allow freedom of movement, and encourage an illusion of physical power and a look of easy physicality all suggest masculinity. Such appearances of strength and readiness to action serve to create or enhance an aura of aggressiveness and intimidation central to an appearance of masculinity. Expansive postures and gestures combine with these qualities to insinuate that a position of secure dominance is a masculine one.

Gender role characteristics reflect the ideological contentions underlying the dominant gender schema in North American society. That schema leads us to believe that female and male behaviors are the result of socially directed hormonal instructions which specify that females will want to have children and will therefore find themselves relatively helpless and dependent on males for support and protection. The schema claims that males are innately aggressive and competitive and therefore will dominate over females. The social hegemony[20] of this ideology ensures that we are all raised to practice gender roles which will confirm this vision of the nature of the sexes. Fortunately, our training to gender roles is neither complete nor uniform. As a result, it is possible to point to multitudinous exceptions to, and variations on, these themes. Biological evidence is equivocal about

[18]Goffman, *Gender Advertisements;* Hall; Henley; Wex. [Author's note]
[19]Adams; Hall, pp. 37, 130–37. [Author's note]
[20]*hegemony:* System of preponderant influence, authority, or dominance.

the source of gender roles,[21] psychological androgyny[22] is a widely accepted concept.[23] It seems most likely that gender roles are the result of systematic power imbalances based on gender discrimination.[24]

[21]See Chapter One. [Author's note]
[22]*androgyny:* The state of having both male and female characteristics.
[23]See Chapter Two. [Author's note]
[24]Howard, Blumstein, and Schwartz; Kollock, Blumstein, and Schwartz. [Author's note]

ENGAGING THE TEXT

1. Devor charges that most languages present gender as "binary and permanent" (para. 3). Has this been your own view? How does Devor challenge this idea — that is, what's the alternative to gender being binary and permanent — and how persuasive do you find her evidence?

2. How, according to Devor, do children "acquire" gender roles? What are the functions of the "generalized other" and the "significant other" in this process?

3. Explain the distinction Devor makes between the "I" and the "me" (paras. 7 and 8). Write a journal entry describing some of the differences between your own "I" and "me."

4. Using examples from Devor and from other reading or observation, list some "activities and modes of expression" (para. 12) that society considers characteristically female and characteristically male. Which are acceptable cross-gender behaviors, and which are not? Search for a "rule" that defines what types of cross-gender behaviors are tolerated.

5. Do some aspects of the traditional gender roles described by Devor seem to be changing? If so, which ones, and how?

EXPLORING CONNECTIONS

6. Review Bebe Moore Campbell's "Envy" (p. 118) or Maxine Hong Kingston's "Silence" (p. 251). What evidence of gender role socialization do you find in the story? To what extent do Moore's or Kingston's childhood experiences complicate Devor's presentation of gender role acquisition?

7. To what extent do Tocqueville's views of women and men (p. 414) reflect the "patriarchal gender schema" as Devor defines it?

8. Drawing on Devor's discussion of gender role formation, analyze the difference between the "I" and the "me" of the girl in Jamaica Kincaid's story (p. 418).

EXTENDING THE CRITICAL CONTEXT

9. As a class, identify at least half a dozen men living today who are widely admired in American culture. To what extent do they embody the "four main attitudes of masculinity" outlined by Devor (para. 19)?

10.   Write an essay or journal entry analyzing your own gender role socialization. To what extent have you been pressured to conform to conventional
roles? To what extent have you resisted them? What roles have "generalized others" and "significant others" played in shaping your identity?

Nora Quealey

JEAN REITH SCHROEDEL

*This interview reveals the thoughts of a woman who has encountered
sexism in a traditionally male occupation — assembly line work on trucks.
Quealey is proud, strong, insightful — and she thinks she would prefer
being a housewife. Jean Reith Schroedel (b. 1951) began collecting oral histories of blue-collar working women when she was an undergraduate at the
University of Washington; she published these interviews in* Alone in a
Crowd *(1985). She has worked as a machinist and a union organizer, and,
fittingly, she supported her work on the book by driving a bus. She now
holds a Ph.D. from the Massachusetts Institute of Technology and is an associate professor in the Center for Politics and Economics at the Claremont
Graduate School in California.*

I was a housewife until five years ago. The best part was being home
when my three kids came in from school. Their papers and their junk that
they made from kindergarten on up — they were my total, whole life. And
then one day I realized when they were grown up and gone, graduated and
married, I was going to be left with nothing. I think there's a lot of women
that way, housewives, that never knew there were other things and people
outside of the neighborhood. I mean the block got together once a week for
coffee and maybe went bowling, but that was it. My whole life was being
there when the kids came home from school.

I never disliked anything. It was just like everything else in a marriage,
there never was enough money to do things that you wanted — never to
take a week's vacation away from the kids. If we did anything, it was just to
take the car on Saturday or Sunday for a little, short drive. But there was
never enough money. The extra money was the reason I decided to go out
and get a job. The kids were getting older, needed more, wanted more, and
there was just not enough.

See, I don't have a high school diploma, so when I went to Boeing and
put an application in, they told me not to come back until I had a diploma

or a G.E.D.[1] On the truck line they didn't mind that I hadn't finished school. I put an application in and got hired on the spot.

My dad works over at Bangor[2] in the ammunition depot, so I asked him what it would be like working with all men. The only thing he told me was if I was gonna work with a lot of men, that I would have to *listen* to swear words and some of the obscene things, but still *act* like a lady, or I'd never fit in. You can still be treated like a lady and act like a lady and work like a man. So I just tried to fit in. It's worked, too. The guys come up and they'll tell me jokes and tease me and a lot of them told me that I'm just like one of the guys. Yet they like to have me around because I wear make-up and I do curl my hair, and I try to wear not really frilly blouses, see-through stuff, but nice blouses.

We had one episode where a gal wore a tank top and when she bent over the guys could see her boobs or whatever you call it, all the way down. Myself and a couple other women went and tried to complain about it. We wanted personnel to ask her to please wear a bra, or at least no tank tops. We were getting a lot of comebacks from the guys like, "When are you gonna dress like so-and-so," or "When are *you* gonna go without a bra," and "We wanna see what *you've* got." And I don't feel any need to show off; you know, I know what I've got. There were only a few women there, so that one gal made a very bad impression. But personnel said there was nothing they could do about it. 5

But in general the guys were really good, I started out in cab building hanging radio brackets and putting heaters in. It was all hand work, and at first I really struggled with the power screwdrivers and big reamers, but the guy training me was super neato. I would think, "Oh, dear, can I ever do this, can I really prove myself or come up to their expectations?" But the guys never gave me the feeling that I was taking the job from a man or food from his family's mouth. If I needed help, I didn't even have to ask, if they saw me struggling, they'd come right over to help.

I've worked in a lot of different places since I went to work there. I was in cab build for I don't know how long, maybe six months, eight months. Then they took me over to sleeper boxes, where I stayed for about two-and-one-half years. I put in upholstery, lined the head liners and the floor mats. After that I went on the line and did air conditioning. When the truck came to me, it had hoses already on it, and I'd have to hook up a little air-condition-pump-type thing and a suction that draws all the dust and dirt from the lines. Then you close that off, put Freon in, and tie down the line. Then I'd tie together a bunch of color-coded electrical wires with tie straps and electrical tape to hook the firewall to the engine. Sometimes I also worked on the sleeper boxes by crawling underneath and tightening down big bolts and washers. Next they sent me over to the radiator shop. I was the first

---

[1]*G.E.D.*: A high school equivalency certificate.
[2]*Bangor*: Site of a Trident nuclear submarine base in the state of Washington.

woman ever to do radiators. That I liked. A driver would bring in the radiators, and you'd put it on a hoist, pick it up and put it on a sling, and work on one side putting your fittings on and wiring and putting in plugs. Then they bounced me back to sleeper boxes for a while and finally ended up putting me in the motor department, where I am now. The motors are brought in on a dolly. The guy behind me hangs the transmission and I hang the pipe with the shift levers and a few other little things and that's about it. Except that we have to work terribly fast.

I was moved into the motor department after the big layoff. At that time we were doing ten motors a day. Now we're up to fourteen without any additional help. When we were down, the supervisor came to me and said we had to help fill in and give extra help to the other guys, which is fine. But the minute production went up, I still had to do my own job plus putting on parts for three different guys. These last two weeks have been really tough. I've been way behind. They've got two guys that are supposed to fill in when you get behind, but I'm stubborn enough that I won't go over and ask for help. The supervisor should be able to see that I'm working super-duper hard while some other guys are taking forty-five minutes in the can and having a sandwich and two cups of coffee. Sometimes I push myself so hard that I'm actually in a trance. And I have to stop every once in a while and ask, "What did I do?" I don't even remember putting parts on, I just go from one to the other, just block everything out — just go, go, go, go. And that is bad, for myself, my own sanity, my own health. I don't take breaks. I don't go to the bathroom. There's so much pressure on me, physical and mental stress. It's hard to handle because then I go home and do a lot of crying and that's bad for my kids because I do a lot of snapping and growling at them. When I'm down, depressed, aching, and sore, to come home and do that to the kids is not fair at all. The last couple of days the attitude I've had is, I don't care whether I get the job done or not. If they can't see I'm going under, then I don't care. And I'll take five or ten minutes to just go to the bathroom, sit on the floor, and take a couple of deep breaths, just anything to get away.

The company doesn't care about us at all. Let me give you an example. When we were having all this hot weather, I asked them please if we couldn't get some fans in here. Extension cords even, because some guys had their own fans. I wasn't just asking for myself, but those guys over working by the oven. They've got a thermometer there and it gets to a hundred and fifteen degrees by that oven! They've got their mouths open, can hardly breathe, and they're barely moving. So I said to the supervisor, "Why can't we have a fan to at least circulate the air?" "Oh yeah, we'll look at it," was as far as it went. We're human. We have no right to be treated like animals. I mean you go out to a dairy farm and you've got air conditioning and music for those cows. I'm a person, and I don't like feeling weak and sick to my stomach and not feel like eating. Then to have the supervisor expect me to put out production as if I was mechanical — a thing, just a robot. I'm human.

You know, I don't even know what my job title is. I'm not sure if it's   10
trainee or not. But I do know I'll never make journeyman. I'll never make
anything. I tried for inspection — took all the classes they offered at the
plant, went to South Seattle Community College on my own time, studied blueprinting, and worked in all the different areas like they said I had
to. I broke ground for the other girls, but they won't let me move up. And
it all comes down to one thing, because I associated with a black man. I've
had people in personnel tell me to stop riding to work with the man, even
if it meant taking the bus to and from work. I said no one will make my
decisions as to who I ride with and who my friends are. Because you walk
into a building with a person, have lunch with him, let him buy you a cup
of coffee, people condemn you. They're crazy, because when I have a
friend, I don't turn my back on them just because of what people think.
What I do outside the plant after quitting time is my own business. If they
don't like it, that's their problem. But in that plant I've conducted myself
as a lady and have nothing to be ashamed of. I plant my feet firmly and I
stand by it.

Early on, I hurt my neck, back, and shoulder while working on
sleeper boxes. When I went into the motor department I damaged them
more by working with power tools above my head and reaching all day
long. I was out for two weeks and then had a ten-week restriction. Personnel said I had to go back to my old job, and if I couldn't handle it I
would have to go home. They wouldn't put me anywhere else, which is
ridiculous, with all the small parts areas that people can sit down and
work in while they are restricted. My doctor said if I went back to doing
what I was doing when I got hurt, I had a fifty-fifty chance of completely
paralyzing myself from the waist down. But like a fool I went back. Some
of the guys helped me with the bending and stooping over. Then the supervisor borrowed a ladder with three steps and on rollers from the paint
department. He wanted me to stand on the top step while working on
motors which are on dollies on a moving chain. I'd be using two-press-
wrenches to tighten fittings down while my right knee was on the transmission and the left leg standing up straight. All this from the top step of
a ladder on rollers. One slip and it would be all over. I backed off and said
it wouldn't work. By this time I'd gotten the shop steward there, but he
didn't do anything. In fact, the next day he left on three weeks' vacation
without doing anything to help me. I called the union hall and was told
they'd send a business rep down the next day. I never saw or heard from
the man.

Anyhow, I'm still doing the same job as when I got hurt. I can feel the
tension in my back and shoulder coming up. I can feel the spasms start and
muscles tightening up. Things just keep gettin' worse and they don't care.
People could be rotated and moved rather than being cramped in the same
position, like in the sleeper boxes, where you never stand up straight and
stretch your neck out. It's eight, ten, twelve hours a day all hunched over. In

the next two years I've got to quit. I don't know what I'll do. If I end up paralyzed from the neck down, the company doesn't give a damn, the union doesn't give a damn, who's gonna take care of me? Who's gonna take care of my girls? I'm gonna be put in some moldy, old, stinkin' nursing home. I'm thirty-seven years old. I could live another thirty, forty years. And who's gonna really care about me?

I mean my husband left me. He was very jealous of my working with a lot of men and used to follow me to work. When I joined the bowling team, I tried to get him to come and meet the guys I worked with. He came but felt left out because there was always an inside joke or something that he couldn't understand. He resented that and the fact that I made more money than he did. And my not being home bothered him. But he never said, "I want you to quit," or "We'll make it on what I get." If he had said that I probably would have quit. Instead we just muddled on. With me working, the whole family had to pitch in and help. When I come home at night my daughter has dinner waiting, and I do a couple loads of wash and everybody folds their own clothes. My husband pitched in for a while. Then he just stopped coming home. He found another lady that didn't work, had four kids, and was on welfare.

It really hurt and I get very confused still. I don't have the confidence and self-assurance I used to have. I think, "Why did I do that," or "Maybe I shouldn't have done it," and I have to force myself to say, "Hey, I felt and said what I wanted to and there's no turning back." It came out of me and I can't be apologizing for everything that I do. And, oh, I don't know, I guess I'm in a spell right now where I'm tired of being dirty. I want my fingernails long and clean. I want to not go up to the bathroom and find a big smudge of grease across my forehead. I want to sit down and be pampered and pretty all day. Maybe that wouldn't satisfy me, but I just can't imagine myself at fifty or sixty or seventy years old trying to climb on these trucks. I've been there for five years. I'm thirty-seven and I want to be out of there before I'm forty. And maybe I will. I've met this nice guy and he's talking of getting married. At the most, I would have to work for one more year and then I could stay at home, go back to being a housewife.

ENGAGING THE TEXT

1. What are Nora Quealey's attitudes toward domesticity? Toward work? Toward money and success? Is she a traditional woman or a feminist?

2. Quealey's life is in some ways tragic. What are the greatest blows she has suffered? Do you think she could have avoided any of them? How — and at what price?

3. What motivates Quealey to persevere in the face of the difficulties she encounters? List as many possible motivations as you can, and review the text to find evidence of them.

EXPLORING CONNECTIONS

4. How might Holly Devor (p. 421) explain the conflicts that Nora Quealey experiences in relation to her work, her male coworkers, and her sense of herself as a woman?

5. Write an imaginary conversation among Nora Quealey, Anndee Hochman (p. 47), and Cora Tucker (p. 390) in which they discuss their attitudes toward work and family.

6. Like Nora, the female executive in the cartoon on page 434 has entered a predominantly male workplace. In what ways does her situation seem to parallel Nora's? In what ways does it differ?

EXTENDING THE CRITICAL CONTEXT

7. When male workers ask "When are *you* gonna go without a bra?" or say "We wanna see what *you've* got," does their speech constitute sexual harassment? How do you think a female employee should respond to such comments? Do you think different standards should apply in different work settings, for example, industrial versus clerical versus professional? Find guidelines defining sexual harassment in your library or Student Affairs office and discuss these in class.

8. Play Ann Landers. Imagine that Quealey has written you a long letter — namely, the text you've just read. Write a confidential response giving advice, encouragement, or an analysis of her situation or feelings, as you see fit. Then write a separate paragraph stating the rationale for your response.

The Story of My Body
JUDITH ORTIZ COFER

Accepting the idea that gender roles are socially constructed might not be too difficult, but it may come as a shock to realize that even the way we see our bodies is filtered through the lens of social values and beliefs. In this personal essay, Judith Ortiz Cofer reflects on the different roles her own body has assumed in different contexts and cultures — the ways that different societies have "read" the meanings of her physical appearance. The story of her body becomes, to some extent, the story of her life, and woven into the tale are intriguing comments on gender and on cross-cultural perception. A native of Puerto Rico, Ortiz Cofer (b. 1952) is a professor of English and creative writing at the University of Georgia. Her publications include The Line of the Sun *(1989), a novel;* Silent Dancing *(1990), a collection of po-*

etry and prose; and The Latin Deli *(1993), in which "The Story of My Body" first appeared.*

> Migration is the story of my body.
> — VICTOR HERNÁNDEZ CRUZ

Skin

I was born a white girl in Puerto Rico but became a brown girl when I came to live in the United States. My Puerto Rican relatives called me tall; at the American school, some of my rougher classmates called me Skinny Bones, and the Shrimp because I was the smallest member of my classes all through grammar school until high school, when the midget Gladys was given the honorary post of front row center for class pictures and score-keeper, bench warmer, in P.E. I reached my full stature of five feet in sixth grade.

I started out life as a pretty baby and learned to be a pretty girl from a pretty mother. Then at ten years of age I suffered one of the worst cases of chicken pox I have ever heard of. My entire body, including the inside of my ears and in between my toes, was covered with pustules which in a fit of panic at my appearance I scratched off my face, leaving permanent scars. A cruel school nurse told me I would always have them — tiny cuts that looked as if a mad cat had plunged its claws deep into my skin. I grew my hair long and hid behind it for the first years of my adolescence. This was when I learned to be invisible.

Color

In the animal world it indicates danger: the most colorful creatures are often the most poisonous. Color is also a way to attract and seduce a mate. In the human world color triggers many more complex and often deadly re-actions. As a Puerto Rican girl born of "white" parents, I spent the first years of my life hearing people refer to me as *blanca,* white. My mother in-sisted that I protect myself from the intense island sun because I was more prone to sunburn than some of my darker, *trigueño*[1] playmates. People were always commenting within my hearing about how my black hair con-trasted so nicely with my "pale" skin. I did not think of the color of my skin consciously except when I heard the adults talking about complexion. It seems to me that the subject is much more common in the conversation of mixed-race peoples than in mainstream United States society, where it is a touchy and sometimes even embarrassing topic to discuss, except in a politi-cal context. In Puerto Rico I heard many conversations about skin color. A

---

[1]*trigueño:* Brown-skinned.

pregnant woman could say, "I hope my baby doesn't turn out *prieto*" (slang for "dark" or "black") "like my husband's grandmother, although she was a good-looking *negra*[2] in her time." I am a combination of both, being olive-skinned — lighter than my mother yet darker than my fair-skinned father. In America, I am a person of color, obviously a Latina. On the Island I have been called everything from a *paloma blanca,*[3] after the song (by a black suitor), to *la gringa.*[4]

My first experience of color prejudice occurred in a supermarket in Paterson, New Jersey. It was Christmastime, and I was eight or nine years old. There was a display of toys in the store where I went two or three times a day to buy things for my mother, who never made lists but sent for milk, cigarettes, a can of this or that, as she remembered from hour to hour. I enjoyed being trusted with money and walking half a city block to the new, modern grocery store. It was owned by three good-looking Italian brothers. I liked the younger one with the crew-cut blond hair. The two older ones watched me and the other Puerto Rican kids as if they thought we were going to steal something. The oldest one would sometimes even try to hurry me with my purchases, although part of my pleasure in these expeditions came from looking at everything in the well-stocked aisles. I was also teaching myself to read English by sounding out the labels in packages: L&M cigarettes, Borden's homogenized milk, Red Devil potted ham, Nestle's chocolate mix, Quaker oats, Bustelo coffee, Wonder bread, Colgate toothpaste, Ivory soap, and Goya (makers of products used in Puerto Rican dishes) everything — these are some of the brand names that taught me nouns. Several times this man had come up to me, wearing his blood-stained butcher's apron, and towering over me had asked in a harsh voice whether there was something he could help me find. On the way out I would glance at the younger brother who ran one of the registers and he would often smile and wink at me.

It was the mean brother who first referred to me as "colored." It was a few days before Christmas, and my parents had already told my brother and me that since we were in Los Estados[5] now, we would get our presents on December 25 instead of Los Reyes, Three Kings Day, when gifts are exchanged in Puerto Rico. We were to give them a wish list that they would take to Santa Claus, who apparently lived in the Macy's store downtown — at least that's where we had caught a glimpse of him when we went shopping. Since my parents were timid about entering the fancy store, we did not approach the huge man in the red suit. I was not interested in sitting on a stranger's lap anyway. But I did covet Susie, the talking schoolteacher doll that was displayed in the center aisle of the Italian brothers' supermarket.

5

[2]*negra:* Black.
[3]*paloma blanca:* White dove.
[4]*la gringa:* A white, non-Latina woman.
[5]*Los Estados:* "The States" — that is, the United States.

She talked when you pulled a string on her back. Susie had a limited repertoire of three sentences: I think she could say: "Hello, I'm Susie Schoolteacher," "Two plus two is four," and one other thing I cannot remember.
The day the older brother chased me away, I was reaching to touch Susie's
blond curls. I had been told many times, as most children have, not to touch
anything in the store that I was not buying. But I had been looking at Susie
for weeks. In my mind, she was my doll. After all, I had put her on my
Christmas wish list. The moment is frozen in my mind as if there were a
photograph of it on file. It was not a turning point, a disaster, or an earth-
shaking revelation. It was simply the first time I considered — if naively —
the meaning of skin color in human relations.

I reached to touch Susie's hair. It seems to me that I had to get on tiptoe, since the toys were stacked on a table and she sat like a princess on top
of the fancy box she came in. Then I heard the booming "Hey, kid, what do
you think you're doing!" spoken very loudly from the meat counter. I felt
caught, although I knew I was not doing anything criminal. I remember not
looking at the man, but standing there, feeling humiliated because I knew
everyone in the store must have heard him yell at me. I felt him approach,
and when I knew he was behind me, I turned around to face the bloody
butcher's apron. His large chest was at my eye level. He blocked my way. I
started to run out of the place, but even as I reached the door I heard him
shout after me: "Don't come in here unless you gonna buy something. You
PR kids put your dirty hands on stuff. You always look dirty. But maybe
dirty brown is your natural color." I heard him laugh and someone else too
in the back. Outside in the sunlight I looked at my hands. My nails needed a
little cleaning as they always did, since I liked to paint with watercolors, but
I took a bath every night. I thought the man was dirtier than I was in his
stained apron. He was also always sweaty — it showed in big yellow circles
under his shirt-sleeves. I sat on the front steps of the apartment building
where we lived and looked closely at my hands, which showed the only skin
I could see, since it was bitter cold and I was wearing my quilted play coat,
dungarees, and a knitted navy cap of my father's. I was not pink like my
friend Charlene and her sister Kathy, who had blue eyes and light brown
hair. My skin is the color of the coffee my grandmother made, which was
half milk, *leche con café* rather than *café con leche*.[6] My mother is the opposite mix. She has a lot of café in her color. I could not understand how my
skin looked like dirt to the supermarket man.

I went in and washed my hands thoroughly with soap and hot water,
and borrowing my mother's nail file, I cleaned the crusted watercolors from
underneath my nails. I was pleased with the results. My skin was the same
color as before, but I knew I was clean. Clean enough to run my fingers
through Susie's fine gold hair when she came home to me.

---

[6]*leche con café . . . café con leche:* Milk with coffee (light brown) . . . coffee with milk
(dark brown).

Size

My mother is barely four feet eleven inches in height, which is average for women in her family. When I grew to five feet by age twelve, she was amazed and began to use the word tall to describe me, as in "Since you are tall, this dress will look good on you." As with the color of my skin, I didn't consciously think about my height or size until other people made an issue of it. It is around the preadolescent years that in America the games children play for fun become fierce competitions where everyone is out to "prove" they are better than others. It was in the playground and sports fields that my size-related problems began. No matter how familiar the story is, every child who is the last chosen for a team knows the torment of waiting to be called up. At the Paterson, New Jersey, public schools that I attended, the volleyball or softball game was the metaphor for the battlefield of life to the inner city kids — the black kids versus the Puerto Rican kids, the whites versus the blacks versus the Puerto Rican kids; and I was 4F,[7] skinny, short, bespectacled, and apparently impervious to the blood thirst that drove many of my classmates to play ball as if their lives depended on it. Perhaps they did. I would rather be reading a book than sweating, grunting, and running the risk of pain and injury. I simply did not see the point in competitive sports. My main form of exercise then was walking to the library, many city blocks away from my barrio.

Still, I wanted to be wanted. I wanted to be chosen for the team. Physical education was compulsory, a class where you were actually given a grade. On my mainly all A report card, the C for compassion I always received from the P.E. teachers shamed me the same as a bad grade in a real class. Invariably, my father would say: "How can you make a low grade for *playing games?*" He did not understand. Even if I had managed to make a hit (it never happened) or get the ball over that ridiculously high net, I already had a reputation as a "shrimp," a hopeless nonathlete. It was an area where the girls who didn't like me for one reason or another — mainly because I did better than they on academic subjects — could lord it over me; the playing field was the place where even the smallest girl could make me feel powerless and inferior. I instinctively understood the politics even then; how the *not* choosing me until the teacher forced one of the team captains to call my name was a coup of sorts — there, you little show-off, tomorrow you can beat us in spelling and geography, but this afternoon you are the loser. Or perhaps those were only my own bitter thoughts as I sat or stood in the sidelines while the big girls were grabbed like fish and I, the little brown tadpole, was ignored until Teacher looked over in my general direction and shouted, "Call Ortiz," or, worse, "Somebody's *got* to take her."

No wonder I read Wonder Woman comics and had Legion of Super Heroes daydreams. Although I wanted to think of myself as "intellectual," my

10

---

[7] *4F:* Draft-board classification meaning "unfit for military service;" hence, not physically fit.

body was demanding that I notice it. I saw the little swelling around my once-flat nipples, the fine hairs growing in secret places; but my knees were still bigger than my thighs, and I always wore long- or half-sleeve blouses to hide my bony upper arms. I wanted flesh on my bones — a thick layer of it. I saw a new product advertised on TV. Wate-On. They showed skinny men and women before and after taking the stuff, and it was a transformation like the ninety-seven-pound-weakling-turned-into-Charles-Atlas ads that I saw on the back covers of my comic books. The Wate-On was very expensive. I tried to explain my need for it in Spanish to my mother, but it didn't translate very well, even to my ears — and she said with a tone of finality, eat more of my good food and you'll get fat — anybody can get fat. Right. Except me. I was going to have to join a circus someday as Skinny Bones, the woman without flesh.

Wonder Woman was stacked. She had a cleavage framed by the spread wings of a golden eagle and a muscular body that has become fashionable with women only recently. But since I wanted a body that would serve me in P.E., hers was my ideal. The breasts were an indulgence I allowed myself. Perhaps the daydreams of bigger girls were more glamorous, since our ambitions are filtered through our needs, but I wanted first a powerful body. I daydreamed of leaping up above the gray landscape of the city to where the sky was clear and blue, and in anger and self-pity, I fantasized about scooping my enemies up by their hair from the playing fields and dumping them on a barren asteroid. I would put the P.E. teachers each on their own rock in space too, where they would be the loneliest people in the universe, since I knew they had no "inner resources," no imagination, and in outer space, there would be no air for them to fill their deflated volleyballs with. In my mind all P.E. teachers have blended into one large spiky-haired woman with a whistle on a string around her neck and a volleyball under one arm. My Wonder Woman fantasies of revenge were a source of comfort to me in my early career as a shrimp.

I was saved from more years of P.E. torment by the fact that in my sophomore year of high school I transferred to a school where the midget, Gladys, was the focal point of interest for the people who must rank according to size. Because her height was considered a handicap, there was an unspoken rule about mentioning size around Gladys, but of course, there was no need to say anything. Gladys knew her place: front row center in class photographs. I gladly moved to the left or to the right of her, as far as I could without leaving the picture completely.

Looks

Many photographs were taken of me as a baby by my mother to send to my father, who was stationed overseas during the first two years of my life. With the army in Panama when I was born, he later traveled often on tours of duty with the navy. I was a healthy, pretty baby. Recently, I read that people are drawn to big-eyed round-faced creatures, like puppies, kittens, and certain other mammals and marsupials, koalas, for example, and, of course, infants. I was all eyes, since my head and body, even as I grew older, remained thin and small-boned. As a young child I got a lot of attention from my relatives and many other people we met in our barrio. My mother's beauty may have had something to do with how much attention we got from strangers in stores and on the street. I can imagine it. In the pictures I have seen of us together, she is a stunning young woman by Latino standards: long, curly black hair, and round curves in a compact frame. From her I learned how to move, smile, and talk like an attractive woman. I remember going into a bodega[8] for our groceries and being given candy by the proprietor as a reward for being *bonita,* pretty.

I can see in the photographs, and I also remember, that I was dressed in the pretty clothes, the stiff, frilly dresses, with layers of crinolines underneath, the glossy patent leather shoes, and, on special occasions, the skull-hugging little hats and the white gloves that were popular in the late fifties and early sixties. My mother was proud of my looks, although I was a bit too thin. She could dress me up like a doll and take me by the hand to visit relatives, or go to the Spanish mass at the Catholic church and show me off. How was I to know that she and the others who called me "pretty" were representatives of an aesthetic that would not apply when I went out into the mainstream world of school?

In my Paterson, New Jersey, public schools there were still quite a few   15
white children, although the demographics of the city were changing rapidly. The original waves of Italian and Irish immigrants, silk-mill workers, and laborers in the cloth industries had been "assimilated." Their children were now the middle-class parents of my peers. Many of them moved their children to the Catholic schools that proliferated enough to have leagues of basketball teams. The names I recall hearing still ring in my ears: Don Bosco High versus St. Mary's High, St. Joseph's versus St. John's. Later I too would be transferred to the safer environment of a Catholic school. But I started school at Public School Number 11. I came there from Puerto Rico, thinking myself a pretty girl, and found that the hierarchy for popularity was as follows: pretty white girl, pretty Jewish girl, pretty Puerto Rican girl, pretty black girl. Drop the last two categories; teachers were too busy to have more than one favorite per class, and it was simply understood that if there was a big part in the school play, or any competition where the main qualification was "presentability" (such as escorting a school visitor to or from the principal's office), the classroom's public address speaker would be requesting the pretty and/or nice-looking white boy or girl. By the time I was in the sixth grade, I was sometimes called by the principal to represent my class because I dressed neatly (I knew this from a progress report sent to my mother, which I translated for her) and because all the "presentable" white girls had moved to the Catholic schools (I later surmised this part).

---

[8]*bodega:* Market.

But I was still not one of the popular girls with the boys. I remember one incident where I stepped out into the playground in my baggy gym shorts and one Puerto Rican boy said to the other: "What do you think?" The other one answered: "Her face is OK, but look at the toothpick legs." The next best thing to a compliment I got was when my favorite male teacher, while handing out the class pictures, commented that with my long neck and delicate features I resembled the movie star Audrey Hepburn. But the Puerto Rican boys had learned to respond to a fuller figure: long necks and a perfect little nose were not what they looked for in a girl. That is when I decided I was a "brain." I did not settle into the role easily. I was nearly devastated by what the chicken pox episode had done to my self-image. But I looked into the mirror less often after I was told that I would always have scars on my face, and I hid behind my long black hair and my books.

After the problems at the public school got to the point where even nonconfrontational little me got beaten up several times, my parents enrolled me at St. Joseph's High School. I was then a minority of one among the Italian and Irish kids. But I found several good friends there — other girls who took their studies seriously. We did our homework together and talked about the Jackies. The Jackies were two popular girls, one blonde and the other red-haired, who had women's bodies. Their curves showed even in the blue jumper uniforms with straps that we all wore. The blonde Jackie would often let one of the straps fall off her shoulder, and although she, like all of us, wore a white blouse underneath, all the boys stared at her arm. My friends and I talked about this and practiced letting our straps fall off our shoulders. But it wasn't the same without breasts or hips.

My final two and a half years of high school were spent in Augusta, Georgia, where my parents moved our family in search of a more peaceful environment. Then we became part of a little community of our army-connected relatives and friends. School was yet another matter. I was enrolled in a huge school of nearly two thousand students that had just that year been forced to integrate. There were two black girls and there was me. I did extremely well academically. As to my social life, it was, for the most part, uneventful — yet it is in my memory blighted by one incident. In my junior year, I became wildly infatuated with a pretty white boy. I'll call him Ted. Oh, he was pretty: yellow hair that fell over his forehead, a smile to die for — and he was a great dancer. I watched him at Teen Town, the youth center at the base where all the military brats gathered on Saturday nights. My father had retired from the navy, and we had all our base privileges — one other reason we moved to Augusta. Ted looked like an angel to me. I worked on him for a year before he asked me out. This meant maneuvering to be within the periphery of his vision at every possible occasion. I took the long way to my classes in school just to pass by his locker, I went to football games, which I detested, and I danced (I too was a good dancer) in front of him at Teen Town — this took some fancy footwork, since it involved subtly moving my partner toward the right spot on the dance floor. When Ted finally approached me, "A Million to One" was playing on the jukebox, and when he took me into his arms, the odds suddenly turned in my favor. He asked me to go to a school dance the following Saturday. I said yes, breathlessly. I said yes, but there were obstacles to surmount at home. My father did not allow me to date casually. I was allowed to go to major events like a prom or a concert with a boy who had been properly screened. There was such a boy in my life, a neighbor who wanted to be a Baptist missionary and was practicing his anthropological skills on my family. If I was desperate to go somewhere and needed a date, I'd resort to Gary. This is the type of religious nut that Gary was: when the school bus did not show up one day, he put his hands over his face and prayed to Christ to get us a way to get to school. Within ten minutes a mother in a station wagon, on her way to town, stopped to ask why we weren't in school. Gary informed her that the Lord had sent her just in time to find us a way to get there in time for roll call. He assumed that I was impressed. Gary was even good-looking in a bland sort of way, but he kissed me with his lips tightly pressed together. I think Gary probably ended up marrying a native woman from wherever he may have gone to preach the Gospel according to Paul. She probably believes that all white men pray to God for transportation and kiss with their mouths closed. But it was Ted's mouth, his whole beautiful self, that concerned me in those days. I knew my father would say no to our date, but I planned to run away from home if necessary. I told my mother how important this date was. I cajoled and pleaded with her from Sunday to Wednesday. She listened to my arguments and must have heard the note of desperation in my voice. She said very gently to me: "You better be ready for disappointment." I did not ask what she meant. I did not want her fears for me to taint my happiness. I asked her to tell my father about my date. Thursday at breakfast my father looked at me across the table with his eyebrows together. My mother looked at him with her mouth set in a straight line. I looked down at my bowl of cereal. Nobody said anything. Friday I tried on every dress in my closet. Ted would be picking me up at six on Saturday: dinner and then the sock hop at school. Friday night I was in my room doing my nails or something else in preparation for Saturday (I know I groomed myself nonstop all week) when the telephone rang. I ran to get it. It was Ted. His voice sounded funny when he said my name, so funny that I felt compelled to ask: "Is something wrong?" Ted blurted it all out without a preamble. His father had asked who he was going out with. Ted had told him my name. "Ortiz? That's Spanish, isn't it?" the father had asked. Ted had told him yes, then shown him my picture in the yearbook. Ted's father had shaken his head. No. Ted would not be taking me out. Ted's father had known Puerto Ricans in the army. He had lived in New York City while studying architecture and had seen how the spics lived. Like rats. Ted repeated his father's words to me as if I should understand *his* predicament when I heard why he was breaking our date. I don't remember what I said before hanging up. I do recall the darkness of my room that sleepless night and the heaviness of my blanket in which I wrapped myself like a shroud. And I remember my parents' respect for my pain and their gentleness toward me that weekend. My mother did not say "I warned you," and I was grateful for her understanding silence.

In college, I suddenly became an "exotic" woman to the men who had survived the popularity wars in high school, who were not practicing to be worldly: they had to act liberal in their politics, in their lifestyles, and in the women they went out with. I dated heavily for a while, then married young. I had discovered that I needed stability more than social life. I had brains for sure and some talent in writing. These facts were a constant in my life. My skin color, my size, and my appearance were variables — things that were judged according to my current self-image, the aesthetic values of the time, the places I was in, and the people I met. My studies, later my writing, the respect of people who saw me as an individual person they cared about, these were the criteria for my sense of self-worth that I would concentrate on in my adult life.

Engaging the Text

1. Ortiz Cofer writes a good deal about how people perceived her and about how their perceptions changed according to time and place. Trace the stages Ortiz Cofer lived through, citing examples from the text, and discuss in each instance how her self-image was affected by people around her. What main point(s) do you think Ortiz Cofer may be trying to make with the narrative?

2. Which of the difficulties Ortiz Cofer faces are related specifically to gender (or made more serious by gender)? Do boys face comparable problems?

3. In your opinion, did Ortiz Cofer make the right decisions throughout her story? Is there anything she or her parents could have done to avoid or resist the various mistreatments she describes?

4. What role do media images play in Ortiz Cofer's story?

5. Does everyone have a similar story to Ortiz Cofer's, or not? Other people may be overweight, wear braces, mature very early or very late, have big noses or unusual voices, and so on. What, if anything, sets Ortiz Cofer's experience apart from the usual "traumas" of childhood?

Exploring Connections

6. Review Holly Devor's "Becoming Members of Society" (p. 421). How do Ortiz Cofer's experiences support and/or complicate Devor's explanation of gender role socialization?

7. Compare and contrast the young Ortiz Cofer with the young Maxine Hong Kingston in "Silence" (p. 251). What similarities do you see in their circumstances, their personalities, and their strategies for dealing with a less-than-friendly environment? Are there important differences between the two?

8. How do Ortiz Cofer's experiences in school confirm or complicate the arguments about women's education made by Myra and David Sadker (p. 228), Blythe Clinchy et al. (p. 256), and Lynne Cheney (p. 263)?

EXTENDING THE CRITICAL CONTEXT

9. In her self-analysis, Ortiz Cofer discusses the "variables" in her physical appearance — the socially determined values that influence her perception of her body. She also reflects on personal "facts" or "constants" — more durable features, like her writing and her need for stability — that contribute to her identity. Write a series of journal entries that tell the story of your own body. What "variables" have influenced your perception of your appearance? What "facts" about yourself have become "constants"?

Me Macho, You Jane
DAGOBERTO GILB

Would you consider a guy who writes short stories and has a degree in philosophy to be macho? How about a tight-lipped union carpenter with an attitude? Dagoberto Gilb is both, and has an understandably complex relationship to the idea of machismo. In this lively personal essay, Gilb explores the tension he feels between his desire to reject macho stereotypes and his inability (or perhaps unwillingness) to escape some of the habits and attitudes embodied in them. Gilb (b. 1950) has received a Guggenheim Fellowship and numerous other awards for his fiction, which includes a collection of short stories, The Magic of Blood *(1993), and a novel,* The Last Known Residence of Mickey Acuña *(1994). This selection first appeared in the anthology* Muy Macho: Latino Men Confront Their Manhood *(1996), edited by Ray González.*

I've been accused of suffering from involuntary macho spasms most of my life. Usually not to my face. Very few got the *cojones*[1] for that! Okay, maybe a couple of people have mentioned it. Tell you the truth, I don't know what it is they're talking about. To me it's a lot like any astrological sign. Which is Leo. I remember this party a long, long time ago. "A Leo, of course he's a *Leo,* what else would he be?" My sign had pissed these people

---

[1]*cojones:* Balls.

off. I was pissed off back. What're you gonna do about it? I snorted, my chin up, the muscles in my hands twitching to knot up, feeling light and quick. I don't remember what I'd done or said, if that was it. Was I too wasted? I didn't belong at that party. Too pseudo-hippie for me (real hippies were too stoned to make accusations). Another one I've often heard is that it's Mexican blood. A hot, spicy *colorado*.[2] Now you see what I'm getting at? That it's usually a complaint about some behavior, or perceived potential for, these people don't approve of. Sort of like when I'm saying I like cockfights. Not as much as certain friends of mine, but I do. I hear the moaning already. People on low-fat, boneless-chicken-is-okay diets. Somehow roosters fighting is a lot worse than football or boxing. But I've sat in stands with all kinds of people, men and women, at all kinds of sporting events, and to me it's the same screaming noises in all of them.

I was raised by my mom. My father lived in the same house as me, maybe my first year or two. My first stepfather lived there when I was thirteen. I was not too fond of this first stepfather. He did not teach me to like manhood. Did my mom teach me to be macho? She had a mean temper, that's true. And I know I got my temper from her. She was a wild, beautiful woman, though. So I'm telling you the truth, I'm not really sure what being macho is. Except sometimes when I see how some wuss behaves.

Is it risk-taking? Danger? Women who take physical risks, look for danger, aren't they being "macho"? Or the threat of violence. Shooting guns. Killing animals. Or men talking about women. Especially a naked woman, real or imagined.

I've come to this office because I need a machine she has offered me the use of, for free. Time and place, from a long time ago to now, from L.A. to El Paso and between or a few miles east or north, I will not specify for reasons of security. Though I barely know her, I sense this woman is interested in me. Twitch, twitch. Okay, score that remark as macho evidence for the prosecution. I know I'm right, though (go ahead, score that one too). I'm not interested in her, though, haven't been. In fact I've avoided her a few times because I don't want the trouble. I'd rather we be friends (score that one for the other side?). She's into the local power movement, is playing that sport. I imagine how someday she'll run for a public office. A Chicana superstar. I'm thinking this as she's talking to me, all these papers strewn everywhere, paper clips and staplers, dirty telephones with long cords all tangled up, posters and bulletin boards, take-out boxes, coffee cups, beer bottles, ashtrays. I'm listening to her quietly, sitting across from her, not really following a story she's telling me about political capital, those who have what and where and how much and the arguments each have about accumulating more and positioning for it, the difficulties she has, as a

---

[2]*colorado:* Red chile.

woman, an attractive woman, elbowing her way in. She is really a nice-looking woman, too. At certain angles, she's unquestionably sexy. She's got a husky laugh because she's large-boned, maybe on the heavy side. She's tough, as fearless and aggressive about her opinions as her desires. Her appetite for fun is as big and loud as she is. Big breasts too. Which all adds up to say that she's not the type I've usually known in a biblical respect. Which is what I'm considering as I'm paying the most superficial attention to what she's saying. Why not? is what I'm thinking. Maybe we ought to get drunk, laugh, take off our clothes in the dark. For the sake of acting bad, to play, not be romantic. Suddenly she says something that startles me into the flow of her monologue:

". . . doesn't like a woman, a tough bitch like me, on stage getting atten-   5
tion. He's so macho. Like you." Who she's talking about is this *político* I don't know personally but can't not know of because he's always news. I ask for an explanation. "You know what I mean," she says. No, I don't. I don't at all. I've never run for any political position. I've never been or even wanted to be anybody's boss. "Yours isn't bad like his," she explains, laughing. Flirting. I don't know *her* well, so how come she decides she knows *me*, knows my "good" or "bad" machismo? In the past I've been nothing less than a gentleman in all respects, and even now, haven't I been sitting here quietly, practically without moving, waiting, listening politely to her about this *pedo* I could care less about so I can use a machine? I have said or done absolutely zero that would give her any knowledge of who I am or how I behave. *Ni una cosa*, nothing.

I worked this four-story in Newport Beach, California, a building so close to Pacific Ocean saltwater that it pushed against a parking structure sheerwall like an aquarium, above which was a view of uncountable masts of million-dollar yachts and catamarans lining the curving bay's piers. All the other carpenters were Anglo. I'd become the Chicano from Texas. From no less than mythical El Paso: the Rio Grande, adobes, Rosa's Cantina, Tony Lama cowboy boots, Juárez whorehouses. I wasn't just me, in other words. I was an embodiment. I was especially as wild as the west Texas wind because I was living in a motel room and I didn't want to continue to work for the company once this job ended. I was even planning to leave sooner than that. Once I'd earned enough, I was outta there, thanks, *hasta la próxima*, and "later"s. The boys knew this about me because I was still there, the only one who'd come out of the union hall still around. The superintendent called men from the hall when some walls had to be formed up in a hurry for a large cement pour; then, a week later, almost two, they were down the road. But he liked my work, and leaving me on was like a long-term employment offer. He kept company men busy all over L.A. and Orange counties. These were guys who talked about which company jobs they'd been at, how many years. It seemed like a good outfit, too, but, complimented as I was, I was there for the money to be made on this job site alone.

I told guys I lived in Texas because I didn't want to live on California free-ways and in stucco tract houses. That I had plans to go my own way. I men-tioned side jobs I got in El Paso and implied that eventually they would lead to something, or, if not, I just didn't care. No, I did not mention my writing. It wasn't like I had to hide it, since it was not a topic that ever popped up. I didn't and wouldn't want it to, anyway, and wouldn't have blinked if it did. With over ten years in the trade at the time, I was a carpenter both to myself and to everyone I worked with, nothing more, nothing less. It's how I wanted it, too. What I inwardly prized about construction (most of the time) was you were judged not by your talk, but what you did, on time, right. What I liked about construction was that, at the end of the day, when you were joint and bone sore, when your feet throbbed, when you required cold beer to numb the pain, you knew you were tired from really working. You rubbed the yellowed calluses, hard as fingernails on your index finger and thumb of your hammer hand, picked at feathery splinters in your palms that seemed to grow hormon-ally like body hair, wiped away dribbling tie-wire cuts you discovered where you didn't feel them happen. What I liked was that at the end of the day you felt like a man, and at the end of the week you got your check, and at the end of a job you knew you'd *earned* your money.

Now I'm ready to tell you about The Asshole. The caps are important in my opinion, descriptive of his transcendent dimension. He's a kid. Looks seventeen, though may be nineteen. Probably twenty-one since he could buy beer. He is pudgy, a soft though unblubbery fat cushioning his belly and wrapping his arms, where there ought at least to be a little muscle tone (we're talking about men in the building trades, you know?). He's a third- or fourth-period apprentice carpenter, meaning he was in his second year of four. He rides what sounds like an uncorked Yamaha. He's got on a black helmet, with black-tint visor, and a black leather jacket. He thinks he is all things bad, and in the morning he struts into work with the attitude. He's a biker. He's a champion football player. He's a sex machine. He's a "lots of lines" doper — meth and coke, but he's done 'em all and can anytime — and he gulps white lightning. He's a musician and an asskicker and killer, if he has to be. His dog is a Doberman, and he's saving for a Harley. He car-ries a buck knife, owns a Luger, wants a magnum.

He does not have a toolbox in the lockup, just hard hat and bags — hammer, tape, tri-square, pencil (often no pencil) — and so one of the first specifically irritating things about him is that he asks to borrow tools the company doesn't supply, but that any carpenter is supposed to carry. A cres-cent wrench, a cat's paw, a flat bar, a level, a chisel, screwdrivers, handsaws. At first the loan was made, like it would be to anyone who asked. When he didn't give a tool back for days, once he was asked, usually it hadn't been lost yet. Usually, though a few times already. Tools getting lost on a job is nothing new, and it's part of the expense. But nobody liked guys who bor-rowed his shit, and nobody liked anyone who lost it. That was just one par-ticular reason the carpenters on the job shook their heads about him.

Mine was different, though. I already couldn't stand him after the first   10
breaktime I sat down, new on the crew, and he opened his mouth. It wasn't
just the boot-high bullshit. It was the whiny, lazy, slow, dumb, loutish
American audacity of it. The seeming privilege of it. I didn't like him because he was a punk, and what made my dislike unique was that I was up-
front about it. I said so to anyone and most of all to him. Right in his face.
"Go away. Go. Away. I do not want you to work anywhere near me. Good-
bye." Guys would find this hysterical. The first few times he'd smile like I
was kidding, even though it was clear to anyone with a two-digit IQ I was
not, and he would bob between staying and leaving. The superintendent
told him to help here, he whimpered. "I don't care. You do not work here.
You work over there, you find anything else to do somewhere else. Away
from me. Leave." If he wavered, I was unhesitant. "Now!" I'd yell to make
my meaning less complex.

I had tried to work with him a few times. He was one of those who'd
stand there forever if you didn't suggest he do *something*, watching me do
everything, all along, like this was his job description. Okay, I was a journeyman, he was an apprentice, so I'd only shake my head: I'd suggest he lift up
the end of this four-by-six — but too heavy for him because it was too wet,
or cement-logged, or he'd been out too late, or he didn't work out last week.
Measure that — he'd stare at the tape, and stare, then give a few numbers,
remeasure, and it'd be wrong. I'd even gotten real simple and asked him to
get nails, or plywood — that was what laborers did! Or he'd be gone so long
I could've forged or glued my own. If he didn't forget, if he came back. He
was enthusiastic only when the lunch wagon blew its horn, though he even
had bad taste in food. Old wrinkled hot dogs on stale yet wet buns, pack-
aged burritos, Twinkies. He savored these like a gourmet. Quitting time was
the only part of the day he was quick. No, I could not understand why he
was on the payroll at all. I told him so. And I told him he should learn to
take a shower, with soap, and to use deodorant, and to brush his teeth, and
to wash his stinking underwear and socks and probably the rest of his
clothes once in a while too, told him he should hang baking soda from his
neck. I was dead serious, too.

The more insulting I got, the more he began to admire me. Yes, you
read that correctly. I'd never heard of such a thing either, and certainly had
never experienced anything so twisted like it. Would this be unwanted, obsessive macho-bonding? I was wild, hooting Texas. I was outlaw Mexican El
Paso. To extinguish the chance of having to sit with him at break or lunch,
I'd often go over with the laborers, all *mexicanos,* who usually sat a distance
away from the English-speaking carpenters. Once or twice I caught him
peering at me with the metaphorical equivalent of his mouth wide open,
tongue limp on his lower lip (I'd move so my back was to him). I was so exotic! Oh, how could *he* become exotic like *me?!* I was a Doberman with
Great Dane size, or a custom Harley. He did finally come to understand
that I was serious about not wanting him near me, not even within my sight.

But he came around anyway, like I was an irresistible force, and I'd have to sling more contempt. You wouldn't believe the words I used to send him off! And he'd say and do nothing. He'd disappear, maybe a day or two, maybe come back hours later to talk to another guy, until he thought, I guess, I'd forgotten or forgiven, and then I'd hurl more paeans of loathing. Did the power of them, their threat and fearsomeness and bravado, sting his wimpy psyche until he was testosterone-numb with envy and fascination for me?

It was like some warped Beauty and the Beast tale. Disgusting. Pathetic. Bizarre. I was not seeking any happy ending. Did I hate the dude? No. I only wanted him to go away, to not be anywhere near me. About his existence I felt an active indifference. That once I was gone, I wouldn't care what his future held, good or bad, and wouldn't care to know. I'd be grateful to never be around the weirdo asshole again, grateful I wouldn't have to.

When the last day came, I'd already said good-bye to the crew, was about to step off the dust and dirt and paraphernalia of the job site, my hard hat on backward, my tool bags looped over one shoulder, the other sagging from the weight of my toolbox, when he struts up. And I can tell he's wanting to act like a man. Like one out of a World War II movie or something.

"You're a real good carpenter," he says with a respect verging on I-don't-want-to-know. And then he puts out his too plump, too soft hand for a handshake.   15

Graduate seminar, Tucson, Arizona, fall 1992. The subject was books of fiction. I sat at the head of the table — six tables shoved together to make one in a nondescript room in the halls of the English department. The color of the room was manila, as in folders. It was a one-semester appointment in the creative writing program. I'd assigned a few writers I valued — John Fanté, Langston Hughes, Juan Rulfo, Naguib Mahfouz, Cormac McCarthy. An initial list also included Paul Bowles, and I was considering Hubert Selby, Jr. Note the shortage of female names. And I was taking over an established, and pre-enrolled, seminar from a professor whose course title was "Women Writers and the World of Their Invention." I hadn't been told this small detail when I accepted the employment. When she sent me her course description, I knew very quickly I was the wrong construction worker for the duty. I had to think and act fast to order books I knew, and I did consider retitling the course "Men and Their Books." With Selby as a possible (my sincere hesitation with him was that a movie had been made; I was interested in the linkage of style and story, and movies cheat close reading), all I'd have to do was add Bukowski and the tanks would be gassed. So I didn't. I wasn't there yet, and they didn't know me, and I was afraid nobody'd laugh. I did have three other books on the list. Ones by Pat Little Dog (Pat Ellis Taylor), J. California Cooper, and Leslie Marmon Silko. Who are women. Since people didn't recognize but one of them, they thought they were men names and men books.

When I arrived there was much less laughter than I could've imagined. Upset students, nervous faculty. A sexual harassment charge draped everyone like a trenchcoat, and, I was to learn, hiring me, a male and a man like I was, was met with such disapproval, it was as though all I wore was a trenchcoat. I was asked to add more books by women, and so I added two, an anthology of stories about and by bad girls, and a novel by Jean Rhys. I'd already decided to pass on Selby, and I dropped Bowles. It wasn't like doing this troubled me in the slightest. I wanted to joke and say how I really, really liked women. How I'd teach any they wanted me to, and I'd read them too! But I left my sense of humor out of it. My physical presence did not seem to inspire too much confidence, either. After my first meeting with those in charge, eyes stumbling around like the words were, after I said I had absolutely no discomfort adding and subtracting books for this course, that I even sincerely agreed with the student complaints (they enrolled for a course for and about women, and this large and loud guy shows up), after that, standing in the busy hall with my first-day escort, I just couldn't hold back one *bromita,* one small crack. "Where's the men's room? They do allow them here still, don't they?" I thought it was a little funny. My escort pointed, unsure, without smiling.

I sat at the head of the tables, a couple of months into it. One woman in the class was the most bitter, unhappy student with the state of Arizona (she was from the east), unhappy with the department's MFA program (evidence my visiting, substitute presence), unhappy specifically with several professors (her unconventional thesis not being received enthusiastically). Since there was much grumbling going on with many students, I didn't know if this was simply a common by-product of all writing programs, or even all graduate schools, or not. I'd read none of her creative work, but she was bright, and most of all she was hardworking, a trait that went a long way with me.

The book assigned to discuss that week was by Rick DeMarinis, a writer whose work I admire as much as I like him. An extremely rare combination. Though DeMarinis is highly regarded among fiction writers, I teased the students, warning them that he lived in El Paso and was my friend. The book, *The Burning Women of Far Cry,* is a comic, coming-of-age novel set in Montana. The women are smart and sexually wild and they drink. The men scam and pine for women and drink.

Usually the student was quiet and needed prodding to speak. This   20 evening she opened the seminar. She picked up DeMarinis's novel by a corner and held it in the air. Picked up the novel like it wasn't a book, with a thumb and finger, at the farthest corner. Like it was soiled. Smelled. Like her fingers would be smeared by it. Holding the very least possible. She turned her eyes away like it didn't deserve their contact. Picked up the novel, eyes averted, held her arm out toward the center of the tables, dropped it, and said, "I can't believe we're expected to read a book like this in a graduate-level seminar." Her tone was contemptuous, defiant, fearlessly in the right.

Her complaint? The portrayal of women. Especially the excessive depiction of them possessing glorious breasts.

To be honest, I hadn't especially noticed the breasts in the novel. And I'd still say that they do not dominate any character description, are not part of even a motif. What interested me in the story was the broken family, the stepfathers, the jobs. What consumed me was the commanding, simple beauty of DeMarinis's prose. Yet the student seemed to have a good, quality argument. I could see how tasteless, how male-fetished the subject might be. So if talking about women's breasts is an inappropriate fixation, how much should be attributed to the writer's character, how much to the character? Is it breasts in general? I'd have to confess that I like women's breasts. I mostly keep this to myself, but is it wrong to admit it openly? When I hear guys talk about them (about tits, to put it bluntly) with other guys, I think so. Is it generalizing? I don't like all women's breasts, or only breasts, not even mainly, just as I don't like all women. Or is it size? Criticize the consistent description of size? When we criticize, do we criticize the writer for willful obsession, or for what is written unaware? Which are his character's flaws, which are his, and how ought they be controlled or not? All of these, and many angles I'm sure I haven't thought of, great topics for discussion in a graduate creative writing seminar.

I say that now. Because when the book plopped on the table, as the room went silent, so did I. I lost sentence consciousness. There was, indeed, only one word left in me, yet inchoate, spiritually forming, physically germinating: *kill*.

As there are differences between men and women, there are differences between men and men. They are bulk and muscle, and they begin to be sensed at an early age. Eventually one boy consciously recognizes another's, and we get in fights to test boundaries. As young men we act more or less on these, bulking and muscling, or not, to a level of satisfaction and resignation. We learn who we are going to be physically smaller than. We accept the larger and smaller distinctions between us. When we are in a dispute with another man, we silently scale one another. At the construction sites where I've so far spent most of my adult work hours, which is where lots of *those* guys go after high school, arguments are too often not subtle. When there's verbal screaming, a real nonverbal howl kicks. Whereas, in a world of ideas, at universities, words are king. Arguments are supposed to be bulky and muscular, not the person advancing them. Even *ad hominem* attacks are too physical in nature. It is the very condition that I love about a university environment. It is a paradise where brutishness is the bottom, where civility and manners are high tools of learning.

No *guy* would have dared done what that student did. Unless he thought he could kick my ass. When male students look me in the eye, and I look back, we've opened a discussion. We have either mutually decided to accept the rules of the idea world, or we have scaled. And we *have* scaled. Because we always scale each other, no matter what. There is no other possibility. He would never have done this without being afraid of me or being ready. But this didn't even occur to the student. She felt right, plain and simple, and self-righteous outrage and behavior never lead to anyone smacking her in the fucking face, which parallel activity on a construction site would lead to almost assuredly. Men don't hit women. The rudeness of dropping the book, my friend's book, a book I assigned for a course with only good intentions, that insult to me, *at* me — a male student would have known the wordless realm he tossed it into.

So what did I do? Nothing. We had none of the potential conversations I spoke of above. I think I tried to maintain some professional decorum. I don't remember if I achieved any. I have no memory of what anyone else said to this day. Stunted conversations, or that was my attention? I do remember how I told myself I was being paid. This was a mental game I learned from miserable construction jobs. I dismissed the class very early. I remember my rage and disgust, seeing around a hot desert light glaring in my eyes as the sun was setting. I remember it as my last class, even though I sat at the head of those tables a few more times.

Several years earlier, I'd taken up coaching because I couldn't stand it anymore. Coaches were either overpraising baby-sitters or Nazis. I picked up a team of seven- and eight-year-olds, which included my youngest boy, but I was too late to get an eleven to twelve group. Meaning my oldest son, Tony, had to find a team, and quick. Which turned out to be one coached by a man I knew because I'd coached his son several times. I will tell you this honestly: His son was not so good an athlete. To put it even more bluntly, he sucked. He was a kind boy with a good and gentle heart who didn't like sports. Not really. He may not have been able to say so in words, but his body wrote clear sentences. It was his dad who wanted sports for him.

There were a few reasons I didn't like this coach very much. A lot had to do with him being an overbearing Christian. A new Christian. One of those who didn't understand that someone else could have a belief that was as well-considered as his. If he wasn't loud, which he was sometimes, his sanctimonious moralism was always screaming. He'd been a foster parent, and now his job, an admirable one, too, was a houseparent for a larger group of boys at a home. He thought they should behave like they were sixty-year-old men, grateful for any conversation. Line up politely and be quiet. Listen to him. Listen when he's talking! It was like school, day and night, and the main lesson was that lessons were to be learned. No time for art or music or any parallel waste of time. Almost all the boys were Chicanos. They spoke Spanish, and their English was strongly accented, often broken. He didn't like that. Not at all. He'd shake his head. What *is it* you're trying to say? he'd snap, intolerant, like stupidity was an accent or a mispronounced word. He didn't think there was anything valuable enough about Mexican culture that wasn't already better in the USA.

His son was to be their example. In all things. I'd coached lots of these boys, just as I had his son. I liked his son, and I liked the boys. And the boys, including his, liked me and our teams because we had fun when we played and we still mostly won and if we lost, no big deal. All of which was why he didn't like me. He didn't say so. It was a sense I had, is all. An instinct. I was inferior, he was sure of it. Something about me. And so, I swore he didn't think these boys ought to like me. I swore he took up coaching because he didn't want someone like me, and my influence, ever again around his boys and his lessons. He didn't want to let it be said that I was a better coach than him.

These were my oldest son's peak years for basketball, and he had   30 quickly become the star of the team, unquestionably the best player. I loved that it was true. I was proud of my Toño. I loved it for him, and I loved him for it, and I loved it because I didn't like the coach. This was true — underneath, I felt I was a better dad and coach and man because my son played basketball better than his. I was proud in larger ways too. Because of how he thought, because my son was a Chicano.

They were winning this game quickly. When Tony got the ball, he scored. It wasn't like he was hogging it, wasn't like he was trying to hot dog. That was never his style. When he got the ball, he tried to get it to others, but they wouldn't shoot it, or missed, or would send it back to him. He shot it and usually made it. The other kids didn't mind. They liked the winning part a lot.

And they were winning easy, and big, when the coach shouted. Games before, he'd been yapping at his son for not taking charge, for not shooting, not rebounding, for standing around doing nothing. He was mad at that deeper level too, as disappointed as I was proud. Then I heard him go after Tony again. It was about not putting it up so much, for having the ball too much. The coach was wrong. In principle, as an idea, he was right, but not in this circumstance. It definitely wouldn't have been true if it were his son, is what I'd say. His logic and principles and understanding would have altered then. There was a kid like Tony on everybody's team, and most boys were closer to his son. But really it wasn't about either boy. No, I'd say. It was about me. It was about me and him. That's what I'd say.

It was when the coach barked at Tony again, told him he had to sit down, even, that I leaped out of my chair across the court. Something uncontrollable gripped me. Even stronger than anger. Pride. Respect. Fairness. Not that I was working around those concepts clearly. "Motherfucker, you leave him alone!"

My hot voice echoed off the hardwood floors and high ceiling of the gym, bounced louder and more rude off east and west walls — a proverbial echo, unobstructed, magnified by cool, whispering autumn air. I couldn't believe it'd come out of me, either, since moments before I'd been sitting there, watching little kids playing ball in a game I sincerely didn't think slightly important. Tony didn't either. He didn't even care that he was being yelled at.

The coach glared at me, appalled. Worse yet, I caught something else too. An I-told-you-so smirk. Now he had confirmed that I was from the crass, violent, low-class, vulgar, gang-ridden, unfit-to-lead culture he so clearly was not from. I'd justified him and his self-righteous fundamentalism. But I was shamed equally about being an American, the ugliest kind. *Abuelitas*,[3] sitting gracious and gently near me, dressed with Sunday shawls over their shoulders, watching their sweet *nietecitos*[4] playing, being nothing but young and sweet, leaned forward, stunned, disgusted, like I'd hocked one onto the foot of the Virgen de Guadalupe. Two little girls on the other side of them got off their seats to step out onto the court to look at the face of a goon. Their innocent mouths were open, and even their eyes wanted to keep their distance. If I could've left I would have. It was that I was in a corner and the door was at the other end, and I couldn't.

Spasms. Twitches. Juice. Blood. Alignment of moon and stars and sun and planets. Hormones. Sex or violence. Meat. Or manners. Nobility, or a lack of. What you're embarrassed about, what you're proud of.

Here's a list: I like women. I like women better than men. I think some people deserve to get their ass kicked. I don't go to bullfights. Well, I've been to a couple, but only because they're in Juárez and it's something to do. My current drink is tequila and grapefruit juice, or vodka and tonic with two squeezes of lemon. I don't drink beer very often, and I love baseball and basketball and I really don't care for football much. You don't like that, screw you. I love my family. I love walking the streets, or up a mountain, or a desert trail, alone. I eat beef. And serrano chiles.

[3]*Abuelitas:* grandmothers
[4]*nietecitos:* little grandchildren

Calvin and Hobbes   by Bill Watterson

Calvin and Hobbes © Watterson. Dist. by Universal Press Syndicate. Reprinted with permission. All rights reserved.

ENGAGING THE TEXT

1. In groups, list the characteristics, behaviors, and attitudes that you associate with "macho" men. Compare your list with those of other groups: Is there any consensus among the definitions? What differences do you find?
2. Although Gilb claims that he's "not really sure what being macho is" (para. 2), he mentions a number of possible characteristics and tells a series of stories that seem to illustrate his own sense of masculinity. Based on the evidence in the essay, work with several classmates to piece together a definition of machismo as Gilb understands it.
3. Look closely at Gilb's account of The Asshole — the young apprentice carpenter. How does the younger man's understanding of masculinity seem to differ from Gilb's? Why does he admire Gilb, and why does Gilb detest him?
4. Debate whether Gilb's behavior was justified or appropriate in his response to The Asshole, to the students in the graduate seminar, and to his son's basketball coach.
5. Gilb appears to both celebrate and mock macho stereotypes. Assuming that he's not just confused, what do you think he's trying to accomplish in this essay?

EXPLORING CONNECTIONS

6. How well does Gilb fit or fail to fit the model of traditional masculinity described by Holly Devor (p. 421)?
7. In the cartoon on page 456, Calvin equates being male with wielding a hammer — that is, with building, destroying, and making as much noise as possible. Do you think Gilb would endorse this definition? To what extent does he embody it?
8. Read Gloria Anzaldúa's discussion of "machismo" in "La conciencia de la mestiza" (p. 665). How does her understanding of machismo compare to Gilb's? How does each of these definitions relate to those generated by the class in response to question 1?

EXTENDING THE CRITICAL CONTEXT

9. Write an imaginary conversation in which Gilb, the Chicana activist, The Asshole, and the angry graduate student discuss what men are and what they should be.
10. Rewrite one of the stories Gilb tells from the perspective of one of the other people involved — for example, the Chicana activist, The Asshole, one of the students in Gilb's seminar, the basketball coach, or Gilb's son.

Advertising and the Construction of Violent White Masculinity

JACKSON KATZ

Advertising offers us a glimpse of our cultural subconscious: designed to sell products by selling us desirable visions of ourselves, ads reflect our dreams and insecurities. According to Jackson Katz, recent advertising presents a disturbing image of American masculinity — an image that equates manhood with bulging muscles, aggression, and violence. Katz (b. 1960) cofounded the Mentors in Violence Prevention Program at Northeastern University's Center for the Study of Sport in Society; this program represented the first nationwide effort to enlist high school, collegiate, and professional athletes in combatting male violence against women. Katz also founded Real Men, an antisexist men's organization based in Boston, and lectures widely on images of violent masculinity in sports and media. Currently he directs worldwide implementation of the United States Marine Corps' gender violence prevention program. This essay appears in Gender, Race and Class in Media *(1995) edited by Gail Dines and Jean M. Humez.*

Violence is one of the most pervasive and serious problems we face in the United States. Increasingly, academics, community activists and politicians have been paying attention to the role of the mass media in producing, reproducing and legitimating this violence.[1]

Unfortunately, however, much of the mainstream debate about the effects of media violence on violence in the "real" world fails to include an analysis of gender. Although, according to the Federal Bureau of Investigation, approximately 90% of violent crime is committed by males, magazine headline writers talk about "youth" violence and "kids'" love affair with guns. It is unusual even to hear mention of "masculinity" or "manhood" in these discussions, much less a thorough deconstruction of the gender order and the way that cultural definitions of masculinity and femininity might be implicated. Under these conditions, a class-conscious discussion of masculine gender construction is even less likely.

[1]*Violence* refers to immediate or chronic situations that result in injury to the psychological, social or physical well-being of individuals or groups. For the purpose of this chapter, I will use the American Psychological Association's (APA) more specific definition of interpersonal violence. Although acknowledging the multidimensional nature of violence, the APA Commission on Violence and Youth defines interpersonal violence as "behavior by persons against persons that threatens, attempts, or completes intentional infliction of physical or psychological harm" (APA, 1993, p. 1). [Author's note]

There is a glaring absence of a thorough body of research into the power of cultural images of masculinity. But this is not surprising. It is in fact consistent with the lack of attention paid to other dominant groups. Discussions about racial representation in media, for example, tend to focus on African Americans, Asians or Hispanics, and not on Anglo Whites.[2] Writing about the representation of Whiteness as an ethnic category in mainstream film, Richard Dyer (cited in Hanke) argues that "white power secures its dominance by seeming not to be anything in particular"; "Whiteness" is constructed as the norm against which nondominant groups are defined as "other." Robert Hanke, in an article about hegemonic masculinity in transition, argues that masculinity, like Whiteness, "does not appear to be a cultural/historical category at all, thus rendering invisible the privileged position from which (white) men in general are able to articulate their interests to the exclusion of the interests of women, men and women of color, and children" (186).

There has been some discussion, since the mid-1970s, of the ways in which cultural definitions of White manhood have been shaped by stereotypical representations in advertising. One area of research has looked at the creation of modern masculine archetypes such as the Marlboro Man. But there has been little attention, in scholarship or antiviolence activism, paid to the relationship between the construction of violent masculinity in what Sut Jhally refers to as the "commodity image-system" of advertising and the pandemic of violence committed by boys and men in the homes and streets of the United States.

This chapter is an attempt to sketch out some of the ways in which   5
hegemonic constructions of masculinity in mainstream magazine advertising normalize male violence. Theorists and researchers in profeminist sociology and men's studies in recent years have developed the concept of *masculinities*, as opposed to *masculinity*, to more adequately describe the complexities of male social position, identity and experience. At any given time, the class structure and gender order produce numerous masculinities stratified by socioeconomic class, racial and ethnic difference and sexual orientation. The central delineation is between the hegemonic, or dominant, masculinity (generally, White and middle-class) and the subordinated masculinities.

But although there are significant differences between the various masculinities, in patriarchal culture, violent behavior is typically gendered male. This doesn't mean that all men are violent but that violent behavior is considered masculine (as opposed to feminine) behavior. This masculine

---

[2]Although hegemonic constructions of masculinity affect men of all races, there are important variables due to racial differences. Because it is not practical to do justice to these variables in a chapter of this length, and because the vast majority of images of men in mainstream magazine advertisements are of White men, for the purpose of this chapter, I will focus on the constructions of various White masculinities. [Author's note]

gendering of violence in part explains why the movie *Thelma and Louise* touched such a chord: Women had appropriated, however briefly, the male prerogative for, and identification with, violence.

One need not look very closely to see how pervasive is the cultural imagery linking various masculinities to the potential for violence. One key source of constructions of dominant masculinity is the movie industry, which has introduced into the culture a seemingly endless stream of violent male icons. Tens of millions of people, disproportionately male and young, flock to theaters and rent videocassettes of the "action-adventure" (a Hollywood euphemism for *violent*) films of Arnold Schwarzenegger, Sylvester Stallone, Bruce Willis, et al.

These cultural heroes rose to prominence in an era, the mid-to-late 1970s into the 1980s, in which working-class White males had to contend with increasing economic instability and dislocation, the perception of gains by people of color at the expense of the White working class, and a women's movement that overtly challenged male hegemony. In the face of these pressures, then, it is not surprising that White men (especially but not exclusively working-class) would latch onto big, muscular, violent men as cinematic heroes. For many males who were experiencing unsettling changes, one area of masculine power remained attainable: physical size and strength and the ability to use violence successfully.

Harry Brod and other theorists have argued that macro changes in postindustrial capitalism have created deep tensions in the various masculinities. For example, according to Brod,

> Persisting images of masculinity hold that "real men" are physically strong, aggressive, and in control of their work. Yet the structural dichotomy between manual and mental labor under capitalism means that no one's work fulfills all these conditions.
>
> Manual laborers work for others at the low end of the class spectrum, while management sits at a desk. Consequently, while the insecurities generated by these contradictions are personally dissatisfying to men, these insecurities also impel them to cling all the more tightly to sources of masculine identity validation offered by the system. (14)

One way that the system allows working-class men (of various races)   10 the opportunity for what Brod refers to as "masculine identity validation" is through the use of their body as an instrument of power, dominance and control. For working-class males, who have less access to more abstract forms of masculinity-validating power (economic power, workplace authority), the physical body and its potential for violence provide a concrete means of achieving and asserting "manhood."

At any given time, individual as well as groups of men are engaged in an ongoing process of creating and maintaining their own masculine identities. Advertising, in a commodity-driven consumer culture, is an omnipresent and rich source of gender ideology. Contemporary ads are filled with images of "dangerous"-looking men. Men's magazines and mainstream newsweeklies are rife with ads featuring violent male icons, such as uniformed football players, big-fisted boxers and leather-clad bikers. Sports magazines aimed at men, and televised sporting events, carry millions of dollars worth of military ads. In the past decade, there have been hundreds of ads for products designed to help men develop muscular physiques, such as weight training machines and nutritional supplements.

Historically, use of gender in advertising has stressed difference, implicitly and even explicitly reaffirming the "natural" dissimilarity of males and females. In late 20th century U.S. culture, advertising that targets young White males (with the exception of fashion advertising, which often features more of an androgynous male look) has the difficult task of stressing gender difference in an era characterized by a loosening of rigid gender distinctions. Stressing gender difference in this context means defining masculinity in opposition to femininity. This requires constantly reasserting what is masculine and what is feminine. One of the ways this is accomplished, in the image system, is to equate masculinity with violence (and femininity with passivity).

The need to differentiate from the feminine by asserting masculinity in the form of power and aggression might at least partially account for the high degree of male violence in contemporary advertising, as well as in video games, children's toys, cartoons, Hollywood film and the sports culture.

By helping to differentiate masculinity from femininity, images of masculine aggression and violence — including violence against women — afford young males across class a degree of self-respect and security (however illusory) within the more socially valued masculine role.

Violent White Masculinity in Advertising

The appeal of violent behavior for men, including its rewards, is coded 15 into mainstream advertising in numerous ways: from violent male icons (such as particularly aggressive athletes or superheroes) overtly threatening consumers to buy products, to ads that exploit men's feelings of not being big, strong or violent enough by promising to provide them with products that will enhance those qualities. These codes are present in television and radio commercials as well, but this chapter focuses on mainstream American magazine ads (*Newsweek, People, Sports Illustrated,* etc.), from the early 1990s.

Several recurring themes in magazine advertising targeting men help support the equation of White masculinity and violence. Among them are violence as genetically programmed male behavior, the use of military and sports symbolism to enhance the masculine appeal and identification of products, the association of muscularity with ideal masculinity, and the equation of heroic masculinity with violent masculinity. Let us now consider, briefly, each of these themes.

Violence as Genetically Programmed Male Behavior

One way that advertisers demonstrate the "masculinity" of a product or service is through the use of violent male icons or types from popular history. This helps to associate the product with manly needs and pursuits that presumably have existed from time immemorial. It also furthers the ideological premise, disguised as common sense, that men have always been aggressive and brutal, and that their dominance over women is biologically based. "Historical" proof for this is shown in a multitude of ways.

An ad for the Chicago Mercantile Exchange, an elite financial institution, depicts a medieval battlefield where muscle-bound toy figurines, accompanied by paradoxically muscular skeleton men, prepare to engage in a sword fight. They might wear formal suits and sit behind desks, the ad implies, but the men in high finance (and those whose money they manage) are actually rugged warriors. Beneath the veneer of wealth and class privilege, *all* men are really brutes. The text reads: "How the Masters of the Universe Overcame the Attack of the Deutschmarks."

An ad for Trojan condoms features a giant-sized Roman centurion, in full uniform, muscles rippling, holding a package of condoms as he towers over the buildings of a modern city. Condom manufacturers know that the purchase and use of condoms by men can be stressful, partially because penis size, in popular Western folklore, is supposedly linked to virility. On way to assuage the anxieties of male consumers is to link the product with a recognizably violent (read: masculine) male archetype. It is no coincidence that the two leading brands of condoms in the United States are named for ancient warriors and kings (Trojan and Ramses).

Sometimes products with no immediately apparent connection to gender or violence nonetheless make the leap. An ad for Dell computers, for example, shows a painting of a group of White cowboys on horseback shooting at mounted Indians who are chasing them. The copy reads "Being Able to Run Faster Could Come in Real Handy." The cowboys are foregrounded and the viewers are positioned to identify with them against the Indian "other." The cowboys' violence is depicted as defensive, a construction that was historically used to justify genocide. The ad explains that "you never know when somebody (read: Indians, Japanese business competitors) is going to come around the corner and surprise you." It thus masculinizes the White middle-class world of the computer business by using the violent historical metaphor of cowboys versus Indians.

An even more sinister use of historical representations involves portraying violence that would not be acceptable if shown in contemporary settings. Norwegian Cruise Line, for example, in an ad that ran in major newsweekly magazines, depicted a colorful painting of a scene on a ship's deck, set sometime in the pirate era, where men, swords drawn, appear simultaneously to be fighting each other while a couple of them are carrying off women. The headline informs us that Norwegian is the "first cruise line whose entertainment doesn't revolve around the bar."

It is highly doubtful that the cruise line could have set what is clearly a rape or gang rape scenario on a modern ship. It would no doubt have prompted feminist protests about the company's glorification of the rape of women. Controversy is avoided by depicting the scene as historical.[3] But Norwegian Cruise Line, which calls itself "The Pleasure Ships," in this ad reinforces the idea that rape is a desirable male pastime. Whether intentional or not, the underlying message is that real men (pirates, swashbucklers) have always enjoyed it.

The Use of Military and Sports Symbolism to Enhance the Masculine Identification and Appeal of Products

Advertisers who want to demonstrate the unquestioned manliness of their products can do so by using one of the two key subsets in the symbolic image system of violent masculinity: the military and sports. Uniformed soldiers and players, as well as their weapons and gear, appear frequently in ads of all sorts. Many of the Camel Smooth Character cartoon ads, for example, display submarines surfacing or fighter jets streaking by as Joe Camel stands confidently in the foreground. One ad features Joe Camel himself wearing an air force bomber pilot's jacket. The message to the young boys and adolescent males targeted by the campaign is obvious: Violence (as signified by the military vehicles) is cool and suave. The sexy blond woman gazing provocatively at the James Bond-like camel provides female ratification of Joe's masculinity.

Ads for the military itself also show the linkage between masculinity and force. The U.S. military spends more than $100 million annually on advertising. Not surprisingly, armed services advertisements appear disproportionately on televised sporting events and in sports and so-called men's magazines. Military ads are characterized by exciting outdoor action scenes with accompanying text replete with references to "leadership," "respect," and "pride." Although these ads sometimes promote the educational and financial benefits of military service, what they're really selling to young working-class males is a vision of masculinity — adventurous, aggressive and violent — that provides men of all classes with a standard of "real manhood" against which to judge themselves.

Boxers and football players appear in ads regularly, promoting products   25
from underwear to deodorants. Sometimes the players are positioned simply to sanction the masculinity of a product. For example, an ad for Bugle

---

[3]Some feminist groups did protest the ad, such as the Cambridge, Massachusetts-based group Challenging Media Images of Women. But the protests never reached a wide audience and had no discernible effect. [Author's note]

Boy clothing depicts a clean-cut young White man, dressed in Bugle Boy jeans and posed in a crouching position, kneeling on a football. Standing behind him, inexplicably, is a large, uniformed football player flexing his muscles. The only copy says, in bold letters, "Bugle Boy Men." It seems reasonable to infer that the goal of this ad was to shore up the masculine image of a product whose name (Bugle Boy) subverts its macho image. The uniformed football player, a signifier of violent masculinity, achieves this task by visually transmitting the message: Real men wear Bugle Boy.

Advertisers know that using high-profile violent male athletes can help to sell products, such as yogurt and light beer, that have historically been gendered female. Because violence establishes masculinity, if these guys (athletes) use traditionally "female" products, they don't lose their masculinity. Rather, the masculinity of the product — and hence the size of the potential market — increases. Miller Brewing Company proved the efficacy of this approach in their long-running television ad campaign for Lite beer. The Miller Lite campaign, which first appeared in the early 1970s, helped bring Miller to the top of the burgeoning light beer market and is often referred to as the most successful TV ad campaign in history.

The Association of Muscularity with Ideal Masculinity

Men across socioeconomic class and race might feel insecure in their masculinity, relatively powerless or vulnerable in the economic sphere and uncertain about how to respond to the challenges of women in many areas of social relations. But, in general, males continue to have an advantage over females in the area of physical size and strength. Because one function of the image system is to legitimate and reinforce existing power relations, representations that equate masculinity with the qualities of size, strength and violence thus become more prevalent.

The anthropologist Alan Klein[4] has looked at how the rise in popularity of bodybuilding is linked to male insecurity. "Muscles," he argues, "are about more than just the functional ability of men to defend home and hearth or perform heavy labor. Muscles are markers that separate men from each other and, most important perhaps, from women. And while he may not realize it, every man — every accountant, science nerd, clergyman, or cop — is engaged in a dialogue with muscles" (16).

Advertising is one area of the popular culture that helps feed this "dialogue." Sports and other magazines with a large male readership are filled with ads offering men products and services to enhance their muscles. Often these ads explicitly equate muscles with violent power, as in an ad for a Marcy weight machine that tells men to "Arm Yourself" under a black and white photograph of a toned, muscular White man, biceps and forearms

[4]The article cited here was excerpted from Klein's book *Little Big Men: Bodybuilding Subculture and Gender Construction* (Albany: State University of New York Press, 1993). [Author's note]

straining, in the middle of a weight lifting workout. The military, too, offers to help men enhance their bodily prowess. An ad for the Army National Guard shows three slender young men, Black and White, working out, over copy that reads "Get a Part-Time Job in Our Body Shop."

The discourse around muscles as signifiers of masculine power involves   30
not only working-class men but also middle- and upper-class males. This is apparent in the male sports subculture, where size and strength are valued by men across class and racial boundaries. But muscularity as masculinity is also a theme in advertisements aimed at upper-income males. Many advertisers use images of physically rugged or muscular male bodies to masculinize products and services geared to elite male consumers. An ad for the business insurance firm Brewer and Lord uses a powerful male body as a metaphor for the more abstract form of (financial) power. The ad shows the torso of a muscular man curling a barbell, accompanied by a headline that reads "the benefits of muscle defined." The text states that "the slow building of strength and definition is no small feat. In fact, that training has shaped the authority that others see in you, as well."

Saab, targeting an upscale, educated market, bills itself as "the most intelligent car ever built." But in one ad, they call their APC Turbo "the muscle car with a social conscience" — which signals to wealthy men that by driving a Saab they can appropriate the working-class tough guy image associated with the concept of a "muscle car" while making clear their more privileged class position.

The Equation of Heroic Masculinity with Violent Masculinity

The cultural power of Hollywood film in the construction of violent masculinity is not limited to the movies themselves. In fact, many more people see the advertising for a given film than see the film itself.

Advertising budgets for major Hollywood releases typically run in the millions of dollars. Larger-than-life billboards enhance the heroic stature of the icons. Movie ads appear frequently on prime time TV and daily in newspapers and magazines. Not surprisingly, these ads highlight the movies' most violent and sexually titillating scenes.

Violence on-screen, like that in real life, is perpetrated overwhelmingly by males. Males constitute the majority of the audience for violent films, as well as violent sports such as football and hockey. It is important to note, then, that what is being sold is not just "violence," but rather a glamorized form of violent masculinity.

Guns are an important signifier of virility and power and hence are an   35
important part of the way violent masculinity is constructed and then sold to audiences. In fact, the presence of guns in magazine and newspaper ads is crucial in communicating the extent of a movie's violent content. Because so many films contain explicit violence, images of gun-toting macho males (police detectives, old west gunslingers, futuristic killing machines) pervade the visual landscape.

Conclusion

Recent research in sociology, media and cultural studies strongly suggests that we need to develop a much more sophisticated approach to understanding cultural constructions of masculinity. Feminists, who have been at the forefront in studying the social construction of gender, have, historically, focused on images and representations of women. Clearly we need a similarly intensive examination of the representation of men — particularly in light of the crisis of men's violence in our society.

This chapter focuses attention on constructions of violent White masculinity in mainstream magazine advertising. But we need also to examine critically a number of other areas where violent masculinities are produced and legitimated: comic books, toys, the sports culture, comedy, interactive video, music video, pornography. This will help us to understand more fully the links between the construction of gender and the prevalence of violence, which might then lead to effective antiviolence interventions.

References

American Psychological Association. (1993). *Violence and youth: Psychology's response*. Washington, DC: Author.

Brod, H. (Ed.). (1987). *The making of masculinities: The new men's studies*. Boston: Allen & Unwin.

Federal Bureau of Investigation. (1992). *Uniform crime reports*. Washington, DC: Author.

Hanke, R. (1992). Redesigning men: Hegemonic masculinity in transition. In S. Craig (Ed.), *Men, masculinity and the media* (pp. 185–198). Newbury Park, CA: Sage.

Jhally, S. (1990, July). Image-based culture: Advertising and popular culture. *The World and I*, pp. 508–519.

Klein, A. (1993, January). Little big men. *Northeastern University Magazine*, p. 14–19.

ENGAGING THE TEXT

1. What does Katz mean when he says that "violent behavior is typically gendered male" (para. 6) in American culture? What evidence do you see to support or challenge this assertion?

2. What role does Katz suggest that the media play in "producing, reproducing, and legitimating . . . violence" (para. 1)? Why does he believe that the issue of gender is typically ignored in discussions of media and violence?

3. How do images of male aggression, strength, and power appeal differently to working-class men and professional men, according to Katz? How does he explain the increasing popularity of such images — for example, in action-adventure movies — since the 1970s?

4. Katz describes and interprets several specific ads (for example, the rampaging pirates in the ad for Norwegian Cruise Lines in para. 21). Sketch out an

alternate interpretation for one or more of these ads based on the details Katz provides. To what extent are the images and texts of the ads ambiguous?

EXPLORING CONNECTIONS

5. Play the role of Holly Devor (p. 421) and write a journal entry explaining how the advertising images described by Katz contribute to the "social hegemony" of the "patriarchal gender schema."

6. While Katz implies that our popular images of masculinity are overwhelmingly sexist and damaging, Judith Ortiz Cofer's (p. 436) account of her Wonder Woman fantasies suggests that images from popular media can influence us in complex and sometimes unexpected ways. Do you see superheroes, comic book characters, and action figures as sexist or liberating for children? Can they be both?

7. Compare the explanations offered by Katz and by Dagoberto Gilb (p. 446) of the connection between masculinity and muscularity. What do muscles signify to men, according to each writer? What role do muscles play in defining a man's identity?

EXTENDING THE CRITICAL CONTEXT

8. Katz maintains that "fashion advertising . . . often features more of an androgynous male look" (para. 12). Skim several magazines aimed at different audiences (for example, *Ebony, GQ, Rolling Stone, Sports Illustrated*) looking for ads that depict conventionally masculine images and others that present more androgynous images of men. What products are associated with each type of image? How are the images in the ads designed to appeal to the audience for each magazine?

9. Using Katz's analysis of "masculine" imagery as a model, survey several magazines designed primarily for women (for example, *Cosmopolitan, Essence, Vogue*) and develop a list of recurrent images that are associated with "femininity" in advertising. Compare your observations with those of classmates.

10. Working in pairs or groups, create an ad designed to appeal to women; the product may be real or imaginary but should be something anyone can use, such as a car, a soft drink, or a bar of soap. Then design another ad for the same product, this time aimed at men. Present the pair of ads to the class and discuss their effectiveness. What changes did you make in the "male" version of the ad, and why?

11. Although Katz concentrates on advertising, he suggests that the images of masculinity he describes also dominate other media like movies, video games, and television cartoons for children. As a class project, survey some of these media and test his claim. Pool your observations: Do they tend to support, challenge, or qualify Katz's argument?

Boys Will Be Boys and Girls Will Not
MARIAH BURTON NELSON

In her years as a serious athlete, first in high school swimming, later in college and professional basketball, Mariah Burton Nelson experienced the exhilaration, power, and confidence that come with developing physical skill and strength. But she also experienced firsthand many of the problems confronted by women in sports, including sexual abuse by one of her coaches. Nelson's book, The Stronger Women Get, the More Men Love Football: Sexism and the American Culture of Sports *(1994), is at once a celebration of female athletic achievement and an indictment of the barriers women still face in the male-dominated world of sports. In the passage reprinted here, she critically examines the common assumption that men make better athletes than women. Nelson (b. 1956) has worked as a columnist for the* Washington Post *and has written for the* New York Times, USA Today, Ms., *and other publications. Her first book is entitled* Are We Winning Yet? How Women Are Changing Sports and Sports Are Changing Women *(1991).*

> My aunts washed the dishes while the uncles
> squirted each other on the lawn with
> garden hoses. Why are we in here,
> I said, and they are out there?
> that's the way it is,
> said aunt Hetty, the shriveled-up one.
> — PAULETTE JILES, "Paper Matches"

Two scientists recently made this forecast: The fastest woman may eventually outrun the fastest man. Their prediction appeared only as a letter to the editor in *Nature* magazine,[1] yet it generated a stampede of interest from the media. *Time,* the *Chicago Tribune, USA Today,* the *New York Times,* the *Washington Post,* and *Sports Illustrated* printed stories. All quoted experts who ridiculed the conjecture as "ludicrous," "sheer ignorance," "a good laugh," "absurd," "asinine," "completely fallacious," and/or "laughable."

In one Associated Press report, the word ridiculous was used five times. *Science News* ran the headline "Women on the verge of an athletic showdown." *Runner's World* entitled its article "Battle of the Sexes." Unlike

---

[1]Brian Whipp and Susan Ward, letter to the editor, *Nature,* (January 2, 1992). [Author's note]

questionable projections that are dismissed without fanfare, this one seems to have struck a nerve.

The researchers, Brian Whipp and Susan Ward of the University of California, Los Angeles, calculated runners' average speeds during record-breaking races over the past seventy years, then compared the rates of increase. Noting that women's average speeds are increasing at a faster rate than are men's, they projected that in the future, the best women may catch up to and even surpass the best men at various distances. For example: By 1998, the best woman and man would, if they continue to improve at current rates, complete the 26.2-mile marathon in two hours, two minutes. In subsequent years, the woman would sprint ahead.

Indisputably, neither women nor men will continue to improve at their current rates forever. Otherwise, humans would one day run the marathon in a matter of minutes. But the very idea that women might someday beat men elicited passionate responses. *Runner's World* writers Amby Burfoot and Marty Post, as if verbally to stop women in their tracks, pointed out that in the past five years, women have made few improvements in world-record times. This is a sure sign, they said, that women "have already stopped" improving.[2]

When I appear on radio and television shows to discuss women's sports or my first book, *Are We Winning Yet? How Women Are Changing Sports and Sports Are Changing Women,* I encounter a similar fury. Female callers are not the problem; they brag about their triceps or gripe about male egos or ask for advice about discrimination. Some male callers tell stories about female martial artists or mountain climbers who taught them, in a way they could understand, about female strength. But at least half of the male callers act as if my views were heretical. Angry and antagonistic, they belittle me, my ideas, my book, and female athletes in general.   5

What seems to make them angriest is my observation that men are not better athletes than women are. In no sport are all men better than all women, I point out, and in many sports, women routinely defeat men. Although single-sex competitions are often appropriate, and men do have physical advantages in some sports, women should see themselves as men's peers, I suggest, rather than exclusively competing against women.

These men don't want to hear any of that. In voices I can only describe as high-pitched and hysterical, they say, "Yeah, but you're never going to see a woman play pro football!"

It is a taunt and, I think, a genuine fear. I'm not talking about football. I've never met a woman who aspires to play pro football. I'm talking about auto racing, horse racing, dog sled racing, equestrian events, rifle shooting,

---

[2]Amby Burfoot and Marty Post, "Battle of the Sexes," *Runner's World* (April 1992), p. 40. [Author's note]

and marathon swimming, where women and men compete together at the elite levels. I'm talking about tennis, golf, racquetball, bowling, skiing, and other recreational sports, where a wife and husband or a female and male pair of friends are likely to find themselves evenly matched. In sports, as in the rest of life, women do compete with men on a daily basis, and often win.

So it intrigues me that in response to my discussion of women's athletic excellence, men change the subject to football. They try to assert football as the sine qua non of athleticism. Because "women could never play football," they imply, men are physically, naturally, biologically superior.

Most men can't play pro football themselves — but they can take vicar-   10
ious comfort in the display of male physical competence and aggression.

They take comfort in professional baseball ("Women could never play pro baseball") and in professional basketball ("Women could never play pro basketball") and in boxing ("Women could never box") and in footraces ("Women could never win the marathon").

Here are a few more quotes from men on radio shows, on airplanes, at restaurants:

"Women can't dunk."

"OK, women can play golf, but they can't drive the ball as far as men can."

"OK, female jockeys win, but there's a horse involved."   15

"Women win at marathon swimming? Who cares? You call that a major sport? I'd like to see a 320-pound female linebacker. That's a laugh."

Most men are not 320-pound linebackers. But, identified with these hulks, average men take great pleasure in the linebackers' exploits (a revealing term). Football, baseball, basketball, boxing, and hockey are important to men in part *because* they seem to be all-male pursuits, because they seem to be activities that *only men can do.* When women demonstrate excellence in sports like running, tennis, and golf, men take great pains to describe that excellence as less important, less worthy, less of an achievement than male excellence.

Psychiatrist Arnold R. Beisser explains the phenomenon this way: "It is small wonder that the American male has a strong affinity for sports. He has learned that this is one area where there is no doubt about sexual differences and where his biology is not obsolete. Athletics help assure his difference from women in a world where his functions have come to resemble theirs."[3]

Sports are about distinction. Who is better? One inch, one point, or one-hundredth of a second can differentiate winner from loser. One pound, one meal, one more set of two-hundred-meter sprints in practice can deter-

[3]Stephanie Twin, *Out of the Bleachers: Writings on Women and Sport* (Old Westbury, New York: The Feminist Press, 1979), p. xxxvi. [Author's note]

mine, or seem to determine, whether a person finishes first or last. Athletes may train for the sheer joy of moving their bodies through space, but eventually they grow curious to see how fast they can move, or how well they can perform, compared to others. They want to compare, to contrast, to differentiate. To know where they stand. To win.

It is in this comparative, competitive arena that we are repeatedly told   20
that women and men are different. And men are better.[4] Women may no longer be weak, granted, but they are still weak*er*. Weaker than men. Still the weaker sex.

Still, as de Beauvoir said, the second sex.[5]

Actually, in many ways, men are the weaker sex. Men die on average seven years earlier than women. Women have a better sense of smell, taste, hearing, and sight (colorblindness affects one woman for every sixteen men). Women are more susceptible to migraines, arthritis, and depression, but men commit suicide more and have higher rates of heart attack and stroke. "Women are sick, but men are dead," Edward Dolnick wrote in his *In Health* magazine article on the subject.[6]

Yet men keep pointing to one physical advantage — upper-body strength — to maintain their illusion of supremacy. Sports that depend on such strength — that, indeed, were designed to showcase that strength — bolster the myth.

Those who claim male sports superiority are not thinking of male gymnasts, who lack the flexibility to use some of the apparatus women use. Or male swimmers, who can't keep up with women over long distances. Or male equestrians, who gallop side by side with — or in the dust of — their female peers.

They are not considering how much women and men have in common: 25
the human experience of sport. These same people would never think of comparing Sugar Ray Leonard to Muhammad Ali. One weighed sixty pounds more than the other. Clearly, they deserved to box in different classes. Yet the top female tennis player is often compared to the top male tennis player ("Yeah but, she could never beat *him*"), who usually outweighs her by sixty pounds.

Those who claim male superiority are not remembering jockstraps. Because men's genitals dangle precariously outside the pelvis, they are vulnerable to speeding baseballs and to angry fists or feet. In addition, "bikes with dropped handlebars bring the rider's legs close to the stomach, and the testicles can get squashed or twisted against the saddle," notes sportswriter

[4]Susan Birrell, "The Woman Athlete: Fact or Fiction?" Paper presented at the National Girls and Women in Sport Symposium, Slippery Rock State University, Slippery Rock, Pennsylvania (February 6–9, 1992). [Author's note]

[5]*Simone de Beauvoir* (1908–1986) published her groundbreaking analysis of patriarchy, *The Second Sex,* in 1949.

[6]Ed Dolnick, "Super Women." *In Health* (July/August 1991), p. 42. [Author's note]

Adrianne Blue in *Faster, Higher, Further.* "This can lead to gangrene and amputation." Such cases have been noted in medical journals.

Blue also suggests that men's bigger bodies make more "dangerous missiles" that are more likely than women's bodies to cause injury when they collide. For this reason a case could be made, she says, for banning men from contact sports.[7]

If women and men were to compete together in noncontact sports, a man would currently win at the elite levels of most existing events: running (as long as the race is under 100 miles); swimming (under about 22 miles); throwing shot, discus, or javelin. On average, men can carry and use more oxygen. They tend to be heavier — an advantage in football — and taller: handy in basketball and volleyball. Men have more lean muscle mass, convenient in sports requiring explosive power — which happens to include most of the sports men have invented.

Less muscle-bound, women generally have better flexibility, useful in gymnastics, diving, and skating. Our lower center of gravity can help in hockey, golf, tennis, baseball, and even basketball. We sweat better (less dripping, therefore better evaporation), which is critical since, like car engines, human bodies need to remain cool and well lubricated to function efficiently.

Physiologist Diane Wakat, associate professor of health education at   30
the University of Virginia, tested athletes under various conditions of heat, humidity, exercise, and nutritional intake, and concluded that women are better able to adjust to the environmental changes. "In every case, females were better able to handle the stress," says Wakat.

The longer the race, the better women do. Women's superior insulation (fat) is, believe it or not, prized by some because it offers buoyancy, heat retention, and efficient use of fuel over long distances, whether by land or by sea.

Ann Trason, a California microbiology teacher, became in 1989 the first woman to win a coed national championship — the twenty-four-hour run — by completing 143 miles. The best male finisher completed four fewer miles. Of Ward and Whipp's prediction that women will one day hold the overall world record in the relatively short (26.2-mile) marathon, Trason says: "I'd be there and be really happy to see it, but it seems unlikely. I do think women will get closer."

Helen Klein's world-record distance in a twenty-four-hour race — 109.5 miles — exceeds the best distance for an American man in her age group (65–69). She says of the possibility that a woman will one day set the overall marathon record, "I would not say no. There is hope. If I were younger, I might try it myself."

---

[7]Adrianne Blue, *Faster, Higher, Further: Women's Triumphs and Disasters at the Olympics* (London: Virago Press, 1988), pp. 154–55. [Author's note]

In marathon and long-distance cold-water swims, "women usually outswim the men," says Bob Duenkel, curator of the International Swimming Hall of Fame. Penny Dean still holds the English Channel record she set in 1978. Diana Nyad is the only athlete to complete the swim from Bimini to Florida. Lynne Cox holds the records for swimming the Bering Strait and the Strait of Magellan. The first person to swim all five Great Lakes, and the first ever to cross Lake Superior (in 1988), was Vicki Keith.

Susan Butcher has been the overall winner of the 1,100-mile Iditarod dog sled race four times. A woman named Seana Hogan recently cycled the four hundred miles from San Francisco to Los Angeles in nineteen hours, forty-nine minutes, breaking the previous men's record by almost an hour. 35

But women's successes are rarely attributable to gender. In ultra-distance running, swimming, and cycling, as well as in equestrian events, horse racing, auto racing, and dog sled racing, success is determined primarily by physical and mental preparation, competitive spirit, self-discipline, or other nongender-related factors. Because upper-body strength is not paramount in these sports, women and men become free to compete together as individuals, even at the highest levels of competition.

Men's strength advantage is actually marginal, meaning that there is more variation among individual men than between the average man and the average woman. It only becomes relevant when comparing trained, competitive athletes. On any recreational doubles tennis team, the female player might be stronger.

Age is also important. Men's strength advantage occurs primarily during the reproductive years. Before puberty, girls, who tend to mature faster, have a height and strength advantage which, if not nullified by institutional and cultural discrimination, would actually render the best of them superior to the best boys. In old age, there is little physical difference between female and male strength.

But we've so long been told that men are better athletes. I even catch myself thinking this way, despite daily evidence to the contrary. For instance, in my masters swimming program, the fastest athletes — including college competitors — swim in Lane 1, while the slowest — including fit, fast, white-haired folks in their seventies — swim in Lane 6. There are women and men in all the lanes.

I swim in Lane 3. In Lane 2 is Ken. Because he's about my age and 40 height, I identify with him. We have the same stroke length, so we look at each other sometimes, his breathing to the left, my breathing to the right, as we windmill through the water. But eventually he pulls ahead. He's faster. At first, I attributed his greater speed to the fact that he is male. His shoulders are broader; his muscles are more prominent than mine.

But then I looked over at Lane 4. There swims Bruce. Also about my height and my age, Bruce is slower than I am. He's got those same broad shoulders and big muscles, but there he is anyway, poking along in Lane 4. I'm faster because I've trained longer, or I have better technique, or I'm in better shape, or I'm more competitive, or some combination of those factors — the same reasons Ken is faster than both Bruce and me, and the same reasons Susie, Karen, Diane, Denise, Lynn, and Martha are faster than Ken. It has nothing to do with gender.

Does it make any sense to ask whether women — even marathoners — will catch up to men? Most women don't think so.

"Let's just run as fast as we can and not compare ourselves to men," proposes Henley Gibble, executive director of the Road Runners Club of America. "It seems like a silly thing to do anyway. In the open distances, we're already winning."

"It's only relevant for me in terms of, Have women been given the same opportunities to explore what their own potential is?" says sports psychologist and University of Virginia professor Linda Bunker. "The bottom line — Will women ever be as good as men? — is not necessarily of interest."

Men are arrogant to think we want to catch up to them, says Susan Birrell, a trailblazing sports sociologist from the University of Iowa. "As if we don't have any ambition at all. As if all we want to do is catch up to men. Remember that quote: 'Women who want to be equal to men lack ambition.'"

In addition to being the overall winner of the twenty-four-hour race, Ann Trason has five times won the women's division and in 1992 and 1993 finished third overall in the Western States 100-Mile Endurance Run. I ask her: "The whole concept of women catching up to men is off the mark for you, because you're already beating men, right?"

"I guess you could look at it that way," she replies. "That's sort of nice."

"Is it nice?" I ask. "Does it matter?"

"Yeah, it is important to me," she says. "It shows what women can do. It's not like I go out there intentionally to outrun men, but I'm proud of that achievement."

Male competitors have told Trason they'd "rather die" than "let" her pass them. But for Trason, competitions are not "athletic showdowns" or "battles of the sexes." In fact, the races nearly transcend gender, which appeals to her. "The nice thing about ultras [one-hundred-mile or twenty-four-hour races] is, you're just competing against whoever's out there. The sex barrier comes down. It's not gone altogether, but it's a lot less than if you were doing a 10K."

Because "being masculine" has included access to diverse sporting opportunities and "being feminine" has not, it's shortsighted to postulate that current gaps between male and female athletic potential will not close, at least partially, in the future — or that, as Post and Burfoot asserted, women "have already stopped improving." Men prevented women from running marathons until 1967. The Olympics did not offer a women's marathon until 1984, and still doesn't offer a women's swimming event longer than eight hundred meters (the men swim fifteen hundred meters). For every college woman who gets a chance to play college sports, 2.24 men do. For every woman who receives a college scholarship, 2.26 men do. The more women run, the greater the likelihood that some of them will run fast. Increased numbers of female runners — along with female-focused training, coaching, scholarships, equipment, and even clothing — account for the historical improvements in women's times, and greater numbers in the future are likely to improve times further.

If marathon swimming were our national sport, as it is in Egypt — if there were a nationally televised Super Bowl of marathon swimming, and spectators packed college swim meets like sardines — we might think differently about women's and men's athletic capabilities. If men competed against women on the balance beam, or in synchronized swimming, or in rhythmic gymnastics, we might rephrase the question about who might catch up to whom.

Maybe, in a world where gender differences were no more relevant than hand sizes, we could innocently wonder if the best women will catch up to the best men in running while also pondering the possibility that the best men will catch up to the best women in gymnastic floor exercise. Neither would have emotional import.

But in this society, the question of women catching up to men has enormous emotional significance. Scientific inquiry is always influenced by the value system of the scientists: What questions are asked? Since most women runners express no desire to "catch up" to men, and indeed seem to want to avoid the comparison, more appropriate questions might be, Do women feel behind? If so, why? In what ways?

We might ask how many women will ultimately have opportunities to   55
play sports. By what date will the percent of college women athletes — currently about one-third — reflect the percent of college women students — one-half? When will women "catch up" in terms of social support?

We might also ask why was the outcry about the letter to the editor of *Nature* far greater than the outcry about the National Collegiate Athletic Association's comprehensive study that described vast gender inequities in college sports.

One reason male-female athletic comparisons are tempting to make, and hard to argue with, is that they seem natural.[8] What could be more natural than human bodies? Sports seem to offer measurable, inarguable proof of human physical potential. Especially when no machines or animals are involved, sports seem to represent a raw, quintessentially fair contest between individuals or teams. *Ready? Set? Go. May the best man win.*

In fact, few professional athletes have "natural" bodies; otherwise we'd bump into pro football-sized men in the supermarkets. The linebacker has been shaped by many behavioral (nutrition, weight lifting) and often

---

[8]Paul Willis, "Women in Sport in Ideology," in Jennifer Hargreaves, ed., *Sport, Culture, and Ideology* (London: Routledge and Kegan Paul, 1982), p. 130. [Author's note]

chemical (steroids, growth hormones) factors. Women who play or do not play sports have also been shaped by various factors, including restricted access to training opportunities, restrictive shoes and clothing, ridicule by peers, and cultural pressure to limit food intake for the sake of creating a thin, rather than strong, body. There's nothing natural about any of that.

But because sports seem natural, and because in the sports media we so often see men who are bigger and stronger than the biggest, strongest women, these men make a convincing subliminal case: not only are men better athletes, men are superior physical specimens. And because the men engaged in sporting events are so often enacting some form of mock combat, we receive the message: Men are inherently, naturally aggressive and, as a gender, dominant.

By framing women as "catching up" — or "naturally" incapable of   60
catching up — writers and researchers obscure the value of women's achievements in and of themselves, regardless of men's achievements. We say that women have an "extra" layer of fat, but not that men have "extra" testosterone. What if we used women's behavior as the standard? In sports, we would compare violent crimes committed by male athletes to violent crimes committed by female athletes. Or sexual abuses committed by male coaches compared to sexual abuses by female coaches. Instead, it's women's physical "inferiority" that captures the public attention.

In Carol Tavris's book, *The Mismeasure of Woman: Why Women Are Not the Better Sex, the Inferior Sex, or the Opposite Sex,* she notes that most gender differences are invented or exaggerated, and women are erroneously compared to a male "norm" for the purpose of maintaining male privilege. "Those who are dominant have an interest in maintaining their differences from others, attributing those differences to 'the harsh dictates of nature' and obscuring the unequal arrangements that benefit them," she writes.[9]

Tavris recently told the audience of a Washington, D.C., radio station, "We see differences as deficiencies and conclude men are better. It's not true that men are better or women are better."

Immediately a male caller protested. "What do you mean, neither men or women are better? It depends what you're talking about: bench-pressing 240 pounds or having labor pains."

Funny: Tavris had not been talking about sports at all. Yet suddenly, irrationally, the caller used a testosterone-aided strength sport (notice he didn't choose gymnastics) to assert not only difference but superiority. Since men do not have labor pains — a rather negative way to refer to women's unique capacity for giving birth — it makes no sense to say women have

[9]Carol Tavris, *The Mismeasure of Woman: Why Women Are Not the Better Sex, the Inferior Sex, or the Opposite Sex* (New York: Simon & Schuster, 1992), p. 24. [Author's note]

labor pains "better" than men do. Yet this man angrily contrasted women's particular reproductive capacity — something men can't do at all — with a sport that men can do "better."

A female caller, obviously unimpressed (and comically unfamiliar with   65 weight lifting), responded, "I hope we get this discussion beyond bench pressing. Maybe someday women will be able to press benches. So what?"

So what? Who cares if men are stronger, heavier, taller? Who benefits when this comparison is repeatedly made, and women come out on the shorter, lighter, weaker end of the stick? Might it be *because* only women can "have labor pains" that men cling so tightly to their strength advantages? Why are some men so vociferously asserting these differences *now?* And what is sport's role in creating and sustaining gender differences?

As every first-grader knows, there are physical differences between women and men, but these differences would be largely irrelevant except in matters of sex, reproduction, urination, and toupee purchases if it weren't for our culture's insistence on categorizing people first and foremost as "male" or "female." It is from these cultural categories — not from biological realities — that most "masculine" and "feminine" behaviors emerge. Cynthia Fuchs Epstein, author of *Deceptive Distinctions*, writes, "The overwhelming evidence created by the past decade of research on gender supports the theory that gender differentiation — as distinct of course from sexual differentiation — is best explained as a social construction rooted in hierarchy."

Here's where the hierarchy part comes in: we don't just say, boys shouldn't play with dolls and girls shouldn't play with pistols. Through our economic structure and through the media, we say that taking care of children — "women's work" — is less important than war — "men's work." We don't just say that football is for boys and cheerleading is for girls. We say that playing football is more valuable than cheerleading or field hockey or volleyball or Double Dutch jump rope or anything girls do — more important, more interesting, more newsworthy: better.

Thus boys have an incentive to cling religiously to "boy behaviors," and they do. Boys are more likely than girls to insist on sex-typed activities and toys,[10] and with good reason — it cements their place in the dominant class. Boys also have an incentive to keep girls out of their tree forts and clubhouses and sports associations and military elite: like "undesirables" moving into a pricey neighborhood, females lower the property value. Women's participation challenges the entire concept of relevant differences between women and men. "To allow women into sport would be an ultimate threat to one of the last strongholds of male security and supremacy," write Mary

---

[10]The Wellesley Center for Research on Women, *How Schools Shortchange Girls.* Report commissioned for the American Association of University Women Educational Foundation (1992), p. 10. [Author's note]

A. Boutilier and Lucinda SanGiovanni in *The Sporting Woman*. To put it another way, if women can play sports then "men aren't really men."[11]

Of course, it's too late to keep women out of sports. But they can be kept out of the public eye and kept out of key, visible, highly paid positions like a football or men's basketball coach. Their accomplishments can be ignored or trivialized or sexualized. They can be barred from "masculine" activities — a term having nothing, really, to do with who men are, and everything to do with what men want to claim as their own.   70

Consider the case of skateboarding. You may have noticed: few girls careen around city streets or suburban malls on skateboards, leaping high over curbs. It's primarily a teenage boys' sport. But in contrast to other male-dominated sports, skateboarders tend not to compete with each other and tend not to establish hierarchies based on ability. Skateboarders value what are often considered feminine qualities: balance, grace, cooperation, and artistic style. One male skateboarder told Greeley, Colorado, researcher Becky Beal, "If you're the worst one on the baseball team, others give you shit and that makes you feel bad. In skating if you are bad, no one makes you feel bad about that." Skaters considered "cool" are those who are supportive, and who do not try to dominate by competing with others.[12]

Yet Beal found during her two-and-a-half-year study of a forty-one-member skateboarding community (37 boys, 4 girls) that teenage boys construe skateboarding as a "naturally" male activity. Despite its cooperative, nonhierarchical, grace-oriented value system, boys insisted that few girls skate because boys and girls are intrinsically different sorts of people suited for different domains. Girls were seen by the boys as lacking the "innate abilities" to skateboard. When Beal pointed out that women succeed at plenty of sports that require balance and coordination such as gymnastics and figure skating, the boys were unshaken in their belief that girls lack what skateboarding requires.

The boys seemed unaware that their own behavior might be making the environment unattractive to young women. Girls who did skate were slighted by the boys as "trying to skate around" or "just trying to balance on the board." Female skaters were labeled "skate Betties" and presumed to be primarily interested in dating the boys. The male skaters did not want to date girls who were engaging in this "masculine" activity. "You don't want your girlfriend to skate," but it's OK for other girls, one boy explained.[13]

---

[11]Mary A. Boutilier and Lucinda SanGiovanni, *The Sporting Woman* (Champaign, Illinois: Human Kinetics Publishers, 1983), p. 102. [Author's note]

[12]Becky Beal, "Skateboarding: Alternative Masculinity and Its Effects on Gender Relations." Paper presented at the North American Society for the Sociology of Sport Conference (Toledo, Ohio: November 4–7, 1992). [Author's note]

[13]Beal, 1992, pp. 5–11. [Author's note]

The four female skaters in the group reported that "skating is seen as un-feminine" and that their male friends were patronizing and overprotective. The boys "feel threatened," one girl said.[14]

In sports, women do various activities men have claimed as masculine.   75
They shove, sweat, strain, flex, groan, take large strides across open spaces, prioritize their own pleasure, and even, occasionally, receive applause for their accomplishments, regardless of their physical beauty. They violate the fundamental principle of gender inequality as expressed by Holly Devor in her book, *Gender Blending*: "Boys will be boys and girls will not."[15]

In sports, girls "will be boys," too. When this happens — when girls trample on "male" territory, men use myriad institutional, cultural, social, and personal means to reinforce the myth of gender difference. These include restricting women's access to sports, ignoring women's participation in sports, controlling women's sports involvement, trivializing women's interest in sports, and sexually harassing women who play sports.

Restricting women's access is becoming increasingly difficult since the law is on women's side, but college administrators plan to go down fighting. In 1993, both Brown and Colgate universities appealed legal decisions that granted their female students expanded sports opportunities. Both schools admitted offering inequitable sports programs, yet resisted, at considerable legal cost, the students' insistence on improved programs. Colgate won; the Second U.S. Circuit Court of Appeals ruled that the Title IX[16] lawsuit was moot because none of the five students who sued would be attending Colgate the following season. Younger students have sued Colgate again. Brown lost the first stage of its appeal; the result is pending as this book goes to press.

Newspapers, magazines, radio, and television ignore women's participation every day. The coverage granted to female athletes — less than 5 percent of total sports coverage — gives the erroneous impression that very few women compete in sports.

Controlling women's sports participation is easy now that more than half of all coaches and administrators of women's sports are men. These men decide what sports will be offered for women, what those women will be taught, what dress and behavior codes will be established, and how the young women will be coached. National and international sports organizations are also overwhelmingly controlled by men. So men can decide, as the Barcelona Taekwondo Federation did in 1992 without consulting its female

[14]Ibid., p. 11. [Author's note]

[15]Holly Devor, *Gender Blending: Confronting the Limits of Duality* (Bloomington: Indiana University Press, 1989).

[16]In 1972 the U.S. Congress passed a gender equity law commonly referred to as Title IX; it states that "no person in the U.S. shall, on the basis of sex . . . be subjected to discrimination under any educational program or activity."

athletes, that women must wear breast protection and groin cups, must undergo pregnancy tests, and must not compete if pregnant.

They can decide, as they often have when female performance matches   80
men's, that women should compete separately. In the case of bowling, this means separating tournaments (and offering men more money) on the pretext that men require different lane conditions. (All pro bowlers use the same size and weight balls, but men's lanes are conditioned with what's known as "longer" oil.) In the case of archery, it means offering slightly different distances for women and men (men shoot at 30, 50, 70, and 90 meters; women at 30, 50, 60, and 70 meters) so that total scores cannot be compared. Segregation begins with children. The National Marbles Tournament, held annually in Wildwood, New Jersey, offers separate competitions for girls and boys.

Rifle-shooting used to be coed. But in the three-position small-bore event, Margaret Murdoch tied teammate Lanny Bassham for first place in the 1976 Olympics. The gold was given to Bassham (a man) based on a tie-breaking rule, though at the awards ceremony, he graciously invited Murdoch up onto the winner's platform with him. Immediately afterward, the international shooting federation segregated most events in the sport. There are now four events for women and seven for men — apparently a more "natural" order of things.

In a variation on the women-shouldn't-go-in-the locker-room rationale, bass fishermen exclude female participants on the grounds that women shouldn't watch men urinate over the side of the boat. When the Army Corps of Engineers recently refused to allow the men use of a lake for a scheduled tournament unless they integrated, the bass men reluctantly admitted one woman. Reporter Julie Vader wrote, "A whole generation of men may now have to learn two of life's most crushing lessons: one, sometimes a woman can catch a lot of fish, and two, she really isn't interested in looking at him with his zipper down."[17]

Go only as far as your nearest college and you'll see that while men's teams tend to have nicknames such as the Panthers, women tend to have nicknames such as the Pantherettes or the Pink Panthers. So men are the norm, women a cutesie deviation from the norm, often absurdly so: consider Lady Rams, Lady Redmen, and my favorite, Lady Gamecocks. To attend a women's sporting event is to have a bizarre zoological experience: fans see Tigerettes, Beaverettes, Eaglettes, Leopardettes, Bulldogettes, Thorobrettes, Yellow Jackettes, Rambelles, Rammettes, Lady Eagles, Lady Centaurs, Teddy Bears, and Wildkittens. More than half of all women's college teams have demeaning or sexist nicknames.[18]

Why can't a panther just be a panther? Because panthers will be panthers, and girl panthers will not.

---

[17]J. E. Vader, "Sex Play." *M Magazine* (February 1992), pp. 41–47. [Author's note]

[18]D. Stanley Eitzen and Maxine Baca Zinn, "The De-Athleticization of Women: The Naming and Gender Marking of Collegiate Sports Teams." *Sociology of Sport Journal* 6 (1989), pp. 362–70. [Author's note]

Sexual harassment is a new term for an old strategy: humiliating women in order to undermine their power. I was sitting in the stands at a women's college basketball game in 1992 when I overheard a vivid illustration of how men employ sexual remarks when threatened by female strength. It was a big game, between the two teams ranked best in the country: the University of Maryland and the University of Virginia. More than 14,500 fans packed Maryland's Cole Field House, screaming when Maryland scored and groaning when they missed. Cheerleaders cheered and band members played, offering the support and enthusiasm most people associate with men's games. For that evening at least, watching women play basketball had become cool. 85

Suddenly a group of male students sitting behind me began loudly harassing the Virginia players with sexual epithets. "You've got too much testosterone," they shouted at one muscular woman. They taunted Virginia's 6'5" Burge twins with, "Amazons!" And when Virginia players stepped to the free-throw line, they tried to rattle them with, "You're bleeding, bitch!"

Male fans are known to be rowdy. But these taunts were telling. All seemed designed to belittle the women *as women* — to punish them for stepping beyond the bounds of traditional femininity, for daring to act like men. The "too much testosterone" accusation implied that muscles and athletic skill are strictly male domain; that the athlete was somehow defective, freakish, or artificially bulked up, not authentically female. The amazon label ridiculed the women for being too tall and too strong; too masculine. With, "You're bleeding, bitch," the men continued their misogynistic tirade, perhaps hoping to remind the women of their inescapable femaleness, to shame and humiliate them about their bodies, and thus to distract them from shooting free throws. (It didn't work.)

Few if any of the male spectators could have won a one-on-one contest with either of the towering Burge twins, or, for that matter, with their 5'6" point guard. These women were more skilled than most if not all of the male fans. This is the reality young men face: female power — physical, political, social — is multiplying daily. By demeaning "amazons," by extolling the sexist traditions inherent in manly sports, and by scrambling to differentiate women from men in a significant, limiting way, men seem to be struggling to nullify the immediate evidence of female strength.

ENGAGING THE TEXT

1. How does Nelson explain the hostility she encounters from many men when she observes that men are not "naturally" better athletes than women? Can you think of other explanations for this antagonism?

2. What differences does Nelson acknowledge between the abilities of male and female athletes? Why do men tend to interpret such differences as evidence of male superiority, according to her analysis?

3. Nelson cites many kinds of evidence to support her argument, including physiological facts, academic studies, sports history, and observations drawn from personal experience. Working in groups, examine the evidence she offers for each of the following claims:

   • that women are not "weaker" than men;
   • that women have been given fewer opportunities to develop their athletic potential;
   • that women's athletic achievements have been minimized or overlooked;
   • that female athletes encounter systematic discrimination.

   Which of these points do you think Nelson has supported most persuasively? Which is least persuasive, and why?

4. Nelson charges that the myth of male superiority is maintained by "restricting women's access to sports, ignoring women's participation in sports, controlling women's sports involvement, trivializing women's interest in sports, and sexually harassing women who play sports" (para. 76). Have you observed or experienced any of these forms of discrimination? Compare notes with classmates and with any women you know who have been actively involved in sports.

EXPLORING CONNECTIONS

5. Compare Nelson's discussion of the sexism directed at female athletes to Myra and David Sadker's account of the sexism experienced by female college students (p. 228). According to these essays, what common obstacles do women face in sports and in higher education? What opportunities exist for women in each of these settings?

6. Judith Ortiz Cofer (p. 436) describes playground sports and mandatory P.E. classes in school as "fierce competitions where everyone is out to 'prove' they are better than others." To what extent, if at all, can Nelson's critique of sexism in sports explain Ortiz Cofer's miserable experiences with athletics? Work in groups to propose ways it might be possible to structure athletic activities so that they would benefit all girls, including nonathletes like Ortiz Cofer.

7. Write or role-play an imaginary talk show in which the guests — Nelson, Holly Devor (p. 421), Nora Quealey (p. 430), Dagoberto Gilb (p. 446), and Jackson Katz (p. 458) — discuss the topic of women, men, and muscles.

EXTENDING THE CRITICAL CONTEXT

8. Based on your own experiences or on interviews with several female athletes, write an essay discussing the personal rewards and costs of being a woman in the world of sports. What can women gain from serious involvement in a sport? What obstacles or difficulties do they confront?

9. Review the coverage of men's and women's sports and the images of female and male athletes in a general interest sports magazine or in your

community's newspaper. What evidence do you find to support or refute Nelson's assertion that the accomplishments of women athletes tend to be "ignored or trivialized or sexualized" (para. 70) by the media?

10. As Nelson points out, Title IX outlaws unequal opportunities and funding for women's athletics, yet many colleges have failed to comply with the law. Has this been an issue on your campus? Sources of information might include campus or community newspaper files, women's athletics coaches and varsity women athletes.

Sexism and Misogyny: Who Takes the Rap?

BELL HOOKS

This essay links Jane Campion's Academy Award–winning film The Piano to "gangsta rap" by such artists as Snoop Doggy Dogg. While this may appear to be an unlikely combination, bell hooks argues that these seemingly different artistic expressions arise from a single sexist ideology. Without absolving rappers, she "contextualizes" their sexism, viewing it from a broader perspective. This perspective might just transform the way you see rap music, not to mention The Piano. *bell hooks is the pen name of Gloria Watkins (b. 1952), who teaches English at City College of New York. She has published twelve books, including collections of essays, interviews, poems, and most recently, a memoir,* Bone Black *(1996). The essay reprinted here appeared in* Z Magazine *in February 1994.*

For the past several months white mainstream media has been calling me to hear my views on gangsta rap. Whether major television networks, or small independent radio shows, they seek me out for the black and feminist "take" on the issue. After I have my say, I am never called back, never invited to do the television shows or the radio spots. I suspect they call, confident that when we talk they will hear the hard-core "feminist" trash of gangsta rap. When they encounter instead the hard-core feminist critique of white-supremacist capitalist patriarchy, they lose interest.

To white-dominated mass media, the controversy over gangsta rap makes great spectacle. Besides the exploitation of these issues to attract audiences, a central motivation for highlighting gangsta rap continues to be the sensationalist drama of demonizing black youth culture in general and the contributions of young black men in particular. It is a contemporary remake of *Birth of a Nation*[1] only this time we are encouraged to believe it is not just vulnerable white womanhood that risks destruction by black hands but everyone. When I counter this demonization of black males by insisting that gangsta rap does not appear in a cultural vacuum, but, rather, is expressive of the cultural crossing, mixings, and engagement of black youth culture with the values, attitudes, and concerns of the white majority, some folks stop listening.

The sexist, misogynist,[2] patriarchal[3] ways of thinking and behaving that are glorified in gangsta rap are a reflection of the prevailing values in our society, values created and sustained by white-supremacist capitalist patriarchy. As the crudest and most brutal expression of sexism, misogynistic attitudes tend to be portrayed by the dominant culture as an expression of male deviance. In reality they are part of a sexist continuum, necessary for the maintenance of patriarchal social order. While patriarchy and sexism continue to be the political and cultural norm in our society, feminist movement has created a climate where crude expressions of male domination are called into question, especially if they are made by men in power. It is useful to think of misogyny as a field that must be labored in and maintained both to sustain patriarchy but also to serve as an ideological antifeminist backlash. And what better group to labor on this "plantation" than young black men.

To see gangsta rap as a reflection of dominant values in our culture rather than as an aberrant "pathological" standpoint does not mean that a rigorous feminist critique of the sexism and misogyny expressed in this music is not needed. Without a doubt black males, young and old, must be held politically accountable for their sexism. Yet this critique must always be contextualized or we risk making it appear that the behaviors this thinking supports and condones — rape, male violence against women, etc. — is a black male thing. And this is what is happening. Young black males are forced to take the "heat" for encouraging, via their music, the hatred of and violence against women that is a central core of patriarchy.

Witness the recent piece by Brent Staples in the *New York Times* titled   5
"The Politics of Gangster Rap: A Music Celebrating Murder and Misogyny." Defining the turf, Staples writes: "For those who haven't caught up, gangster rap is that wildly successful music in which all women are 'bitches' and 'whores' and young men kill each other for sport." No mention of white-supremacist capitalist patriarchy in this piece, not a word about the cultural context that would need to exist for young males to be socialized to think differently about gender. Staples assumes that black males are writing

---

[1]*Birth of a Nation:* 1915 silent movie by D. W. Griffith that has been acclaimed as one of America's greatest films and condemned as a piece of racist propaganda.

[2]*misogynist:* Women-hating.

[3]*patriarchal:* Describing a system in which authority and power belong primarily to males.

their lyrics off in the "jungle," away from the impact of mainstream social-ization and desire. At no point in his piece does he ask why huge audiences, especially young white male consumers, are so turned on by this music, by the misogyny and sexism, by the brutality. Where is the anger and rage at females expressed in this music coming from, the glorification of all acts of violence? These are the difficult questions that Staples feels no need to answer.

One cannot answer them honestly without placing accountability on larger structures of domination and the individuals (often white, usually male but not always) who are hierarchically placed to maintain and perpetu-ate the values that uphold these exploitative and oppressive systems. That means taking a critical look at the politics of hedonistic[4] consumerism, the values of the men and women who produce gangsta rap. It would mean considering the seduction of young black males who find that they can make more money producing lyrics that promote violence, sexism, and misogyny than with any other content. How many disenfranchised black males would not surrender to expressing virulent forms of sexism, if they knew the re-wards would be unprecedented material power and fame?

More than anything gangsta rap celebrates the world of the "material," the dog-eat-dog world where you do what you gotta do to make it. In this worldview, killing is necessary for survival. Significantly, the logic here is a crude expression of the logic of white-supremacist capitalist patriarchy. In his new book *Sexy Dressing Etc.* privileged white male law professor Dun-can Kennedy gives what he calls "a set of general characterizations of U.S. culture" explaining that "It is individual (cowboys), material (gangsters), and philistine."[5] Using this general description of mainstream culture would lead us to place "gangsta rap" not on the margins of what this nation is about, but at the center. Rather than being viewed as a subversion or dis-ruption of the norm we would need to see it as an embodiment of the norm.

That viewpoint was graphically highlighted in the film *Menace II Soci-ety*, which dramatized not only young black males killing for sport, but also mass audiences voyeuristically watching and, in many cases, "enjoying" the kill. Significantly, at one point in the movie we see that the young black males have learned their "gangsta" values from watching television and movies — shows where white male gangsters are center stage. This scene undermines any notion of "essentialist" blackness that would have viewers believe the gangsterism these young black males embraced emerged from some unique black cultural experience.

When I interviewed rap artist Ice Cube for *Spin* magazine last year, he talked about the importance of respecting black women and communica-tion across gender. He spoke against male violence against women, even as he lapsed into a justification for anti-woman rap lyrics by insisting on the

[4]*hedonistic:* Based on the principle that pleasure is the chief good in life.
[5]*philistine:* Unappreciative of artistic values.

madonna/whore split where some females "carry" themselves in a manner that determines how they will be treated. When this interview was published, it was cut to nothing. It was a mass-media set-up. Folks (mostly white and male) had thought if the hard-core feminist talked with the hardened black man, sparks would fly; there would be a knock-down, drag-out spectacle. When Brother Cube and I talked to each other with respect about the political, spiritual, and emotional self-determination of black people, it did not make good copy. Clearly folks at the magazine did not get the darky show[6] they were looking for.

After this conversation, and talking with rappers and folks who listen to   10
rap, it became clear that while black male sexism is a serious problem in our communities and in black music, some of the more misogynist lyrics were there to stir up controversy and appeal to audiences. Nowhere is this more evident than in Snoop Doggy Dogg's record *Doggystyle*. A black male music and cultural critic called me to ask if I had checked this image out, to share that for one of the first times in his music buying life he felt he was seeing an image so offensive in its sexism and misogyny that he did not want to take that image home. That image (complete with doghouse, beware-the-dog sign, with a naked black female head in a doghouse, naked butt sticking out) was reproduced, "uncritically," in the November 29, 1993, issue of *Time* magazine. The positive music review of this album, written by Christopher John Farley and titled "Gangsta Rap, Doggystyle," makes no mention of sexism and misogyny, makes no reference to the cover. I wonder if a naked white female body had been inside the doghouse, presumably waiting to be fucked from behind, if *Time* would have produced an image of the cover along with their review. When I see the pornographic cartoon that graces the cover of *Doggystyle,* I do not think simply about the sexism and misogyny of young black men, I think about the sexist and misogynist politics of the powerful white adult men and women (and folks of color) who helped produce and market this album.

In her book *Misogynies* Joan Smith shares her sense that while most folks are willing to acknowledge unfair treatment of women, discrimination on the basis of gender, they are usually reluctant to admit that hatred of women is encouraged because it helps maintain the structure of male dominance. Smith suggests: "Misogyny wears many guises, reveals itself in different forms which are dictated by class, wealth, education, race, religion, and other factors, but its chief characteristic is its pervasiveness." This point reverberated in my mind when I saw Jane Campion's widely acclaimed film *The Piano,* which I saw in the midst of mass-media focus on sexism and misogyny in "gangsta rap." I had been told by many friends in the art world that this was "an incredible film, a truly compelling love story, etc." Their responses were echoed by numerous positive reviews. No one speaking

---

[6]*darky show:* Demeaning term for a show featuring blacks, such as a minstrel show.

about this film mentions misogyny and sexism or white-supremacist capitalist patriarchy.

The nineteenth-century world of the white invasion of New Zealand is utterly romanticized in this film (complete with docile happy darkies — Maori natives — who appear to have not a care in the world). And when the film suggests they care about white colonizers digging up the graves of their dead ancestors, it is the sympathetic poor white male who comes to the rescue. Just as the conquest of natives and lands is glamorized in this film, so is the conquest of femininity, personified by white womanhood, by the pale speechless corpselike Scotswoman, Ada, who journeys into this dark wilderness because her father has arranged for her to marry the white colonizer Stewart. Although mute, Ada expresses her artistic ability, the intensity of her vision and feelings, through piano playing. This passion attracts Baines, the illiterate white settler who wears the facial tattoos of the Maori — an act of appropriation that makes him (like the traditional figure of Tarzan) appear both dangerous and romantic. He is Norman Mailer's "white negro," seducing Ada by promising to return the piano that Stewart has exchanged with him for land. The film leads us to believe that Ada's passionate piano playing has been a substitution for repressed eroticism. When she learns to let herself go sexually, she ceases to need the piano. We watch the passionate climax of Baines's seduction as she willingly seeks him sexually. And we watch her husband Stewart in the role of voyeur, standing with dog outside the cabin where they fuck, voyeuristically consuming their pleasure. Rather than being turned off by her love for Baines, it appears to excite Stewart's passion; he longs to possess her all the more. Unable to win her back from Baines, he expresses his rage, rooted in misogyny and sexism, by physically attacking her and chopping off her finger with an ax. This act of male violence takes place with Ada's daughter, Flora, as a witness. Though traumatized by the violence she witnesses, she is still able to follow the white male patriarch's orders and take the bloody finger to Baines, along with the message that each time he sees Ada she will suffer physical mutilation.

Violence against land, natives, and women in this film, unlike that of gangsta rap, is portrayed uncritically, as though it is "natural," the inevitable climax of conflicting passions. The outcome of this violence is positive. Ultimately, the film suggests Stewart's rage was only an expression of irrational sexual jealousy, that he comes to his senses and is able to see "reason." In keeping with male exchange of women, he gives Ada and Flora to Baines. They leave the wilderness. On the voyage home Ada demands that her piano be thrown overboard because it is "soiled," tainted with horrible memories. Surrendering it she lets go of her longing to display passion through artistic expression. A nuclear family now, Baines, Ada, and Flora resettle and live happily-ever-after. Suddenly, patriarchal order is restored. Ada becomes a modest wife, wearing a veil over her mouth so that no one will see her lips struggling to speak words. Flora has no memory of trauma and is a happy child turning somersaults. Baines is in charge, even making Ada a new finger.

The Piano seduces and excites audiences with its uncritical portrayal of sexism and misogyny. Reviewers and audiences alike seem to assume that Campion's gender, as well as her breaking of traditional boundaries that inhibit the advancement of women in film, indicate that her work expresses a feminist standpoint. And, indeed, she does employ feminist "tropes,"[7] even as her work betrays feminist visions of female actualization, celebrates and eroticizes male domination. In Smith's discussion of misogyny she emphasizes that woman-hating is not solely the province of men: "We are all exposed to the prevailing ideology of our culture, and some women learn early on that they can prosper by aping the misogyny of men; these are the women who win provisional favor by denigrating other women, by playing on male prejudices, and by acting the 'man's woman.'" Since this is not a documentary film that needs to remain faithful to the ethos of its historical setting, why is it that Campion does not resolve Ada's conflicts by providing us with an imaginary landscape where a woman can express passionate artistic commitment and find fulfillment in a passionate relationship? This would be no more farfetched than her cinematic portrayal of Ada's miraculous transformation from muteness into speech. Ultimately, Campion's *The Piano* advances the sexist assumption that heterosexual women will give up artistic practice to find "true love." That "positive" surrender is encouraged by the "romantic" portrayal of sexism and misogyny.

While I do not think that young black male rappers have been rushing   15 in droves to see *The Piano*, there is a bond between those folks involved with high culture who celebrate and condone the sexist ideas and values upheld in this film and those who celebrate and condone "gangsta rap." Certainly Kennedy's description of the United States as a "cowboy, gangster, philistine" culture would also accurately describe the culture evoked in *The Piano*. Popular movies that are seen by young black males, for example *Indecent Proposal, Mad Dog and Glory, True Romance,* and *One False Move,* all eroticize male domination expressed via the exchange of women, as well as the subjugation of other men, through brutal violence.

Contrary to a racist white imagination which assumes that most young black males, especially those who are poor, live in a self-created cultural vacuum, uninfluenced by mainstream, cultural values, it is the application of those values, largely learned through passive uncritical consumption of mass media, that is revealed in "gangsta rap." Brent Staples is willing to challenge the notion that "urban primitivism is romantic" when it suggests that black males become "real men" by displaying the will to do violence, yet he remains resolutely silent about that world of privileged white culture that has historically romanticized primitivism and eroticized male violence. Contemporary films like *Reservoir Dogs* and *Bad Lieutenant* celebrate urban primitivism and many less well done films *(Trespass, Rising Sun)* create and/or

---

[7]*trope:* Originally a figure of speech such as metaphor or irony; here, "feminist 'tropes'" refers to language or visual images which suggest women's power or independence.

exploit the cultural demand for depictions of hard-core blacks who are willing to kill for sport.

To take "gangsta rap" to task for its sexism and misogyny while critically accepting and perpetuating those expressions of that ideology which reflect bourgeois[8] standards (no rawness, no vulgarity) is not to call for a transformation of the culture of patriarchy. Ironically, many black male ministers, themselves sexist and misogynist, are leading the attacks against gangsta rap. Like the mainstream world that supports white-supremacist capitalist patriarchy, they are most concerned with calling attention to the vulgar obscene portrayals of women to advance the cause of censorship. For them, rethinking and challenging sexism, both in the dominant culture and in black life, is not the issue.

Mainstream white culture is not concerned about black male sexism and misogyny, particularly when it mainly is unleashed against black women and children. It is concerned when young white consumers utilize black vernacular popular culture to disrupt bourgeois values, whether it be the young white boy who expresses his rage at his mother by aping black male vernacular speech (a true story) or the masses of young white males (and middle-class men of color) seeking to throw off the constraints of bourgeois bondage who actively assert in their domestic households via acts of aggression their rejection of the call to be "civilized." These are the audiences who feel such a desperate need for gangsta rap. It is much easier to attack gangsta rap than to confront the culture that produces that need.

Gangsta rap is part of the antifeminist backlash that is the rage right now. When young black males labor in the plantations of misogyny and sexism to produce gangsta rap, their right to speak this violence and be materially rewarded is extended to them by white-supremacist capitalist patriarchy. Far from being an expression of their "manhood," it is an expression of their own subjugation and humiliation by more powerful, less-visible forces of patriarchal gangsterism. They give voice to the brutal raw anger and rage against women that it is taboo for "civilized" adult men to speak. No wonder then that they have the task of tutoring the young, teaching them to eroticize and enjoy the brutal expressions of that rage (teaching them language and acts) before they learn to cloak it in middle-class decorum or Robert Bly[9] style reclaimings of lost manhood. The tragedy for young black males is that they are so easily duped by a vision of manhood that can only lead to their destruction.

Feminist critiques of the sexism and misogyny in gangsta rap, and in all aspects of popular culture, must continue to be bold and fierce. Black females must not be duped into supporting shit that hurts us under the

[8]*bourgeois:* Middle-class, with the connotations here of blandness, materialism, and mediocrity.

[9]*Robert Bly:* Contemporary poet and writer best known as a central figure in the contemporary "men's movement."

guise of standing beside our men. If black men are betraying us through acts of male violence, we save ourselves and the race by resisting. Yet, our feminist critiques of black male sexism fail as meaningful political intervention if they seek to demonize black males and do not recognize that our revolutionary work is to transform white-supremacist capitalist patriarchy in the multiple areas of our lives where it is made manifest, whether in gangsta rap, the black church, or the Clinton administration.

ENGAGING THE TEXT

1. Having read the full essay, return to the first paragraph and explain what hooks thinks the media expected her to say about gangsta rap and why they didn't want to hear what she *did* have to say.

2. Examine hooks's claim that brutal sexism is not "male deviance" (para. 3) but rather "part of a sexist continuum, necessary for the maintenance of patriarchal social order." How does this hypothesis account for the attitudes of the young black men who produce gangsta rap?

3. Why does hooks discuss *The Piano* in the same essay with gangsta rap? Summarize in your own words the argument that links them, and discuss whether or not you find the argument persuasive.

EXPLORING CONNECTIONS

4. According to hooks and to Jackson Katz (p. 458), how do popular media like advertising, movies, and rap music reflect or shape cultural values? To what extent do the two writers agree about the nature and extent of media influence?

5. Read Christina Hoff Sommers's essay, "The Gender Wardens" (p. 491). Debate whether or not hooks's critique of *The Piano* can be interpreted as an attempt to censor artistic expression and to dictate "sexually correct" content in the movies.

EXTENDING THE CRITICAL CONTEXT

6. Watch *The Piano* and test hooks's claims. To what extent do you agree with hooks that the film "excites audiences with its uncritical portrayal of sexism and misogyny" (para. 14)? If you had seen the film before, did reading "Sexism and Misogyny" radically change your understanding of it or your reaction to it?

7. Carefully watch and listen to some current rap videos. How prevalent are sexism and misogyny? Do you find anything in these performances to support or contradict hooks's analysis?

8. hooks claims that the sexism in rap music reflects "mainstream, cultural values ... learned through passive uncritical consumption of mass media" (para. 16). What evidence do you see that mainstream media do or do not promote sexism, misogyny, and violence against women?

The Gender Wardens
CHRISTINA HOFF SOMMERS

In her controversial book, Who Stole Feminism? *(1994), Christina Hoff Sommers argues that the women's movement has been hijacked by "gender feminists," who, in her words, "believe that all our institutions, from the state to the family to the grade schools, perpetuate male dominance. Believing that women are virtually under siege, gender feminists naturally seek recruits to wage their side of the gender war." In the excerpt that follows, Sommers condemns "gender wardens" who try to impose feminist views on others and champions women — from religious conservatives to lipstick lesbians — whom she sees as resistance fighters in the "gender war." Sommers is an associate professor of philosophy at Clark University in Worcester, Massachusetts. She has edited two textbooks on ethics and published articles in the* Wall Street Journal, *the* New Republic, *the* New England Journal of Medicine, *and other periodicals.*

> *Censorship is the strongest drive in human nature; sex is a weak second.*
> — PHIL KERBY, *Los Angeles Times*
> editorial writer, on a postcard to
> Nat Hentoff[1]

QUESTION: How many feminists does it take to screw in a light bulb?
FEMINIST ANSWER: That's not funny.

It is sometimes said that feminists don't have a sense of humor. Yet, there are some situations, not funny to most women, that gender feminists seem to find very amusing.

About a thousand feminists were present at Manhattan's 92nd Street Y on Mother's Day 1992 to hear a debate between Susan Faludi[2] and *Playboy* columnist Asa Baber. Baber opened his talk by observing that on Mother's Day, the phone lines throughout the United States are jammed because everyone is trying to call home to talk to their mothers. On Father's Day, the lines are free. "We have to ask why there is so much less interest in fathers," said Baber.[3]

The assembled women, most of them fans of Ms. Faludi, found this uproarious. "It brought down the house," said Baber. "At first, I didn't get it. I

---

[1]Nat Hentoff, *Free Speech for Me — But Not for Thee* (New York: HarperCollins, 1992), p. 1. [Author's note]

[2]*Susan Faludi:* Faludi documents the rise of conservative resistance to feminism in *Backlash: The Undeclared War Against American Women* (1991).

[3]Jay Overocker, "Ozzie and Harriet in Hell," *Heterodoxy* 1, no. 6 (November 1992): 9. [Author's note]

thought my fly was open." But then he caught on and said, "If you think that is funny, you are going to think this is a laugh riot: I think the fact that our fathers are so much out of the loop is a major tragedy in our culture."

Baber had taken another misstep, but this time he didn't tickle anyone's funny bone. An outraged audience hissed and booed him. Later, when he was asked whether this was because his hecklers believed that men were useless, irrelevant, and potentially dangerous, Baber answered, "You got it."[4] To them he appeared to be just another patriarch exacting homage.

The jeering, hooting atmosphere in which Baber found himself was familiar to me. I had encountered it in the "safe spaces" where gender feminists gather to tell one another put-down stories describing how a sister had routed some male who didn't have a clue at how offensive he was (recall the "Shut up, you fucker" with which one partisan had squelched an unsuspecting male student critic in a feminist classroom). I'd heard it in the appreciative laughter of the audience when feminist academics reported to them on how they had played on the liberal guilt of the faculty to get their projects approved. Baber was in the camp of the enemy, and anything he had to say was regarded as offensive or, if he were lucky, laughable.

The derision of the women who were hooting at Baber was safely directed at "men." One must wonder what Baber's audience would make of the millions of women who still observe the amenities of Father's Day. So intent are gender feminists on condemning the "patriarchy" that they rarely let on how they feel about women who "go along." Nevertheless, it is not hard to see that in jeering at Baber, they were also jeering at most American women.

That is the corrosive paradox of gender feminism's misandrist stance: no group of women can wage war on men without at the same time denigrating the women who respect those men. It is just not possible to incriminate men without implying that large numbers of women are fools or worse. Other groups have had their official enemies — workers against capitalists, whites against blacks, Hindus against Muslims — and for a while such enmities may be stable. But when women set themselves against men, they simultaneously set themselves against other women in a group antagonism that is untenable from the outset. In the end, the gender feminist is always forced to show her disappointment and annoyance with the women who are to be found in the camp of the enemy. Misandry moves on to misogyny.

Betty Friedan once told Simone de Beauvoir[5] that she believed women should have the choice to stay home to raise their children if that is what they wish to do. Beauvoir answered: "No, we don't believe that any woman should have this choice. No woman should be authorized to stay at home to raise her children. Society should be totally different. Women should not

[4]Ibid. [Author's note]

[5]*Friedan . . . Beauvoir:* influential feminist writers and activists. Friedan (b. 1921) is best known for *The Feminine Mystique* (1963) and Beauvoir (1908–1986) for *The Second Sex* (1949).

have that choice, precisely because if there is such a choice, too many women will make that one."[6]

De Beauvoir thought this drastic policy was needed to prevent women from leading blighted conventional lives. Though she does not spell it out, she must have been aware that her "totally different" society would require a legion of Big Sisters endowed by the state with the power to prohibit any woman who wants to marry and stay home with children from carrying out her plans. She betrays the patronizing attitude typical of many gender feminists toward "uninitiated" women.

An illiberal authoritarianism is implicit in the doctrine that women are socialized to want the things the gender feminist believes they *should not want*. For those who believe that what women want and hope for is "constrained" or "coerced" by their upbringing in the patriarchy are led to dismiss the values and aspirations of most women. The next step may not be inevitable, but it is almost irresistible: to regard women as badly brought-up children whose harmful desires and immature choices must be discounted.

Gender feminists, such as Sandra Lee Bartky, argue for a "feminist reconstruction of self and society [that] must go far beyond anything now contemplated in the theory or politics of the mainstream women's movement."[7] Bartky, who writes on "the phenomenology of feminist consciousness," is concerned with what a proper feminist consciousness should be like. In her book *Femininity and Domination,* she says, "A thorough overhaul of desire is clearly on the feminist agenda: the fantasy that we are overwhelmed by Rhett Butler should be traded in for one in which we seize state power and reeducate him."[8] Bartky, however, does not advocate any authoritarian measures to protect women from incorrect values and preferences shaped by "the masters of patriarchal society." She points out that at present we do not know how to "decolonize the imagination."[9] She cautions that "overhauling" desires and "trading in" popular fantasies may have to wait for the day when feminist theorists develop an "adequate theory of sexuality." In her apocalyptic feminist vision, women as well as men may one day be radically reconstructed. We will have learned to *prefer* the "right" way to live.

10

6"Sex, Society, and the Female Dilemma" (a dialogue between Friedan and Beauvoir), *Saturday Review,* June 14, 1975, p. 18. As an equity feminist I find much to admire in de Beauvoir's works, but her bland tolerance for authoritarianism is not part of it. She was perhaps unduly influenced by Jean-Paul Sartre, joining him in his Maoist phase in the seventies. This may help to explain, although it would not excuse, her readiness to use state power to force people to live "correct" lives. [Author's note]

7Sandra Lee Bartky, *Femininity and Domination: Studies in the Phenomenology of Oppression* (New York: Routledge, 1990), p. 5. [Author's note]

8Ibid., p. 51. [Author's note]

9Ibid., pp. 56, 61. Ms. Bartky is also aware that her ideas about the radical reconstruction of self and society are not now popular. It does not worry her: "For it reveals the extent to which the established order of domination has taken root within our very identities." *Femininity and Domination,* p. 5. [Author's note]

Although they may disagree politically about what measures to take with women who make the wrong choices, Beauvoir and her latter-day descendants share a common posture: they condescend to, patronize, and pity the benighted females who, because they have been "socialized" in the sex/gender system, cannot help wanting the wrong things in life. Their disdain for the hapless victims of patriarchy is rarely acknowledged. When feminists talk of a new society and of how people must be changed, they invariably have in mind men who exploit and abuse women. But it is not difficult to see that they regard most women as men's dupes.

Consider how Naomi Wolf (in the *Beauty Myth*) regards the eight million American women members of Weight Watchers — as cultists in need of deprogramming. Most gender feminists may not be ready to advocate coercion of women of low feminist consciousness, but they are very much in favor of a massive and concerted effort to give the desires, aspirations, and values of American women a thorough makeover. As the feminist philosopher Alison Jaggar puts it, "If individual desires and interests are socially constituted . . . , the ultimate authority of individual judgment comes into question. Perhaps people may be mistaken about truth, morality, or even their own interests; perhaps they may be systematically self-deceived."[10] Note that Jaggar explicitly impugns the traditional liberal principle that the many individual judgments and preferences are the ultimate authority. I find that a chilling doctrine: when the people are systematically self-deceived, the ultimate authority is presumed to be vested in a vanguard that unmasks their self-deception. As Ms. Jaggar says, "Certain historical circumstances allow specific groups of women to transcend at least partially the perceptions and theoretical constructs of male dominance."[11] It is these women of high feminist consciousness who "inspire and guide women in a struggle for social change."

Respect for people's preferences is generally thought to be fundamental for democracy. But ideologues find ways of denying this principle. The gender feminist who claims to represent the true interests of women is convinced that she profoundly understands their situation and so is in an exceptional position to know their true interests. In practice, this means she is prepared to dismiss popular preferences in an illiberal way. To justify this, feminist philosopher Marilyn Friedman argues that popular preferences are often "inauthentic" and that even liberals are aware of this:

> Liberal feminists can easily join with other feminists in recognizing that political democracy by itself is insufficient to ensure that preferences are formed without coercion, constraint, undue restriction of options, and so forth. Social, cultural, and economic conditions are as

---

[10]Alison Jaggar, *Feminist Politics and Human Nature* (Totowa, N.J.: Rowman and Littlefield, 1983), p. 44. [Author's note]

[11]Ibid., p. 150. [Author's note]

important as political conditions, if not more so, in ensuring that preferences are, in some important sense, authentic.[12]

Friedman is quite wrong in her assumptions: anyone, liberal or conser-   15
vative, who believes in democracy will sense danger in them. Who will "ensure" that preferences are "authentic"? What additions to political democracy does Friedman have in mind? A constitutional amendment to provide
reeducation camps for men and women of false consciousness? Is she prepared to go the authoritarian route indicated by de Beauvoir?

The feminist who thinks that democracy is insufficient believes that
seemingly free and enlightened American women have values and desires
that, unbeknownst to them, are being manipulated by a system intent on
keeping women subjugated to men. Romance, a major cause of defection
from the gynocentric enclave, is ever a sticking point with gender feminists.
Gloria Steinem, writing on the subject, engages in this kind of debunking
"critique": "Romance itself serves a larger political purpose by offering at
least a temporary reward for gender roles and threatening rebels with loneliness and rejection. . . . It privatizes our hopes and distracts us from making
societal changes. The Roman 'bread and circuses' way of keeping the
masses happy . . . might now be updated."[13] Jaggar, too, sees in romance a
distraction from sexual politics: "The ideology of romantic love has now become so pervasive that most women in contemporary capitalism probably
believe that they marry for love rather than for economic support."[14]

For her authoritarian disdain, de Beauvoir deserves our liberal censure.
But the less authoritarian feminists also deserve it. No intelligent and liberal
person — no one who has read and appreciated the limpid political prose of
George Orwell or who has learned from the savage history of twentieth-
century totalitarianism — can accept the idea of a social agenda to "overhaul" the desires of large numbers of people to make them more "authentic."

In her defense, the gender feminist replies that effective teachers or
political leaders must always try to help others overcome benightedness.
When women are caught in a system designed to perpetuate male domination, they must be enlightened. There is nothing intrinsically illiberal about
seeking to make them conscious of their subjugation. It is the very essence
of a liberal education to open minds and enlighten consciousness. If that entails "reeducating" them and overhauling their desires, so be it.

This argument could easily be made in an earlier era when classically
liberal principles were being applied to men but not to women. In the nineteenth century, the proposition that all men are created equal was taken to

[12]Marilyn Friedman, "Does Sommers Like Women? More on Liberalism, Gender Hierarchy, and Scarlett O'Hara," *Journal of Social Philosophy* 21, no. 2 (Fall–Winter 1990): 83.
[Author's note]
    [13]Gloria Steinem, *Revolution from Within: A Book of Self-Esteem* (Boston: Little, Brown,
1992), p. 260. [Author's note]
    [14]Jaggar, *Feminist Politics and Human Nature,* p. 219. [Author's note]

mean "all males." Women did not have the rights that men had, and, what is more, they were being taught that their subordinate status was fitting and natural. Feminist philosophers like John Stuart Mill and Harriet Taylor rightly feared that such teaching was helping to perpetuate inequities. Under the circumstances, political democracy applied only minimally to women. Because they did not vote, their preferences were not in play, and the question of how authentic their preferences were was of importance inasmuch as it affected their ability to agitate for the rights that were being withheld from them.

But women are no longer disenfranchised, and their preferences are   20
being taken into account. Nor are they now taught that they are subordinate or that a subordinate role for them is fitting and proper. Have any women in history been better informed, more aware of their rights and options? Since women today can no longer be regarded as the victims of an undemocratic indoctrination, we must regard their preferences as "authentic." Any other attitude toward American women is unacceptably patronizing and profoundly illiberal.

Gender feminists are especially disapproving of the lives of traditionally religious women such as evangelical Christian women, Catholic women, or Orthodox Jewish women, whom they see as being conditioned for highly restricted roles. Surely, they say, it is evident that such women are subjugated, and the choices they make inauthentic. As Gloria Steinem explains it, the appeal of religious fundamentalism for women is that "the promise *is* safety in return for obedience, respectability in return for self-respect and freedom — a sad bargain."[15]

That is a harsh judgment to make about millions of American women. Ms. Steinem is of course free to disagree with conventionally religious women on any number of issues, but she is not morally free to cast aspersions on their autonomy and self-respect. The New Feminism is supposed to be about sisterhood. Why are its most prominent practitioners so condescending?

Steinem herself knows a thing or two about how to recruit adherents to a cause by promises of "safety" and "self-respect." The feminist orthodoxy she portrays promises safety in a sisterhood that will offer unhappy or insecure women a venue where they can build self-esteem and attain an authenticity enjoyed by no other group of women.[16]

---

[15]Steinem, *Revolution from Within,* p. 309. [Author's note]

[16]The theme of "safety" is central for gender feminism. Indeed, a favorite phrase for any place where feminists gather is "safe space." In this misogynist world, the "feminist classroom," for example, is advertised as a safe space where women can speak freely without fear of being humiliated by derisive or brutal males. On the other hand, as I tried to show in chapter 6, the feminist classroom can be very *un*safe for those who are not true believers in gender feminism. [Author's note]

The traditionally religious women of today, be they Protestant Christians, Orthodox Jews, or observant Catholics — emphatically do not think of themselves as subjugated, lacking in self-respect, or unfree. Indeed, they very properly resent being described that way. For they are perfectly aware that they have all the rights that men have. If they choose to lead the lives they do, that is their affair.

Of course there are feminists who disapprove of the way these women   25 live, and some may even think of them as pitiable. These feminists are perfectly at liberty to try to persuade them to change their way of life. For their part, traditional women might try to persuade the feminists of the merits of the religious way of life. Mostly, however, gender feminists are content to dismiss and even jeer at the religious women without engaging or confronting them in a respectful dialogue, and it is not surprising that the latter have grown increasingly impatient with their feminist critics.

Several years ago, Liz Harris wrote an extraordinary and much-talked-about article for the *New Yorker* on the ultraorthodox Hasidic women of Brooklyn, New York.[17] She had expected to find oppressed women — "self-effacing drudges" worn down by a family system that exalted men and denigrated women. Instead, she was impressed by their strong marriages, their large, thriving families, and their "remarkably energetic, mutually supportive community of women, an almost Amazonian society." "Most of the [Hasidic] women sped around like intergalactic missiles, and the greater majority of those I was to encounter seemed . . . to be as occupied with worthy projects as Eleanor Roosevelt, as hospitable as Welcome Wagoneers."[18]

My relatives on my husband's side are Jewish, and most are Orthodox. Ms. Harris's description fits them to a T. At family gatherings, I sometimes tell my sister-in-law, my nieces, and their friends about the feminist theorists who pity them and would liberate them from their "gendered families." They are more amused than offended. It might surprise Gloria Steinem to hear they have a rather shrewd understanding of her kind of feminism. They simply want no part of it. They believe they have made an autonomous choice: they also believe their way of life offers them such basic advantages as community, grace, dignity, and spirituality. They see the patriarchal aspects of their tradition as generally benign. Some of them find aspects of Judaism insensitive to important concerns of women, but they are even more put off by the gender feminist's rejection of traditional religion.

But of course it is not only religious women who reject the gender feminist perspective. A clear majority of secular American women enjoy many aspects of "la différence." Many want things that gender feminists are trying

[17]Later expanded and published in book form: Liz Harris, *Holy Days: The World of a Hasidic Family* (New York: Macmillan, 1985), p. 128. [Author's note]
[18]Ibid., p. 129. [Author's note]

to free them from, be it conventional marriages and families, or fashions and makeup that sometimes render them "sex objects." Such feminists are uncomfortably aware that they are not reaching these women; but instead of asking themselves where they may be going wrong, they fall back on the question-begging-theory of false consciousness to explain the mass indifference of the women they want to save.

For the gender feminists do want to save women — from themselves. False consciousness is said to be endemic in the patriarchy. And every feminist has her theory. Feminists who specialize in the theory of feminist consciousness talk about mechanisms by which "patriarchy invades the intimate recesses of personality where it may maim and cripple the spirit forever."[19] However, a growing number of women are questioning whether gender feminism, with its insistence that personal relationships be construed in terms of political power, has taken much of the joy out of male/female intimacy, maiming and crippling the spirit of some of its devotees forever.

A few years ago, an op-ed piece I wrote for the *Chronicle of Higher Education* aroused a storm of protest because it defended the "many women [who] continue to swoon at the sight of Rhett Butler carrying Scarlett O'Hara up the stairs to a fate undreamt of in feminist philosophy."[20] The Society for Women in Philosophy (SWIP), an organization within the American Philosophical Association, arranged for a public debate between Marilyn Friedman, a philosopher from the University of Washington, and me. Ms. Friedman informed the overflow audience that she was stunned by my flippant reaction to Rhett's rape of Scarlett — for rape she considered it to be. "The name of Richard Speck, to take one example, can remind us that real rape is not the pleasurable fantasy intimated in *Gone with the Wind.* To put the point graphically: would 'many women' still swoon over Butler's rape of O'Hara if they knew that he urinated on her?"[21] Lest readers wonder how they could have missed that lurid scene in *Gone with the Wind,* I hasten to say that Ms. Friedman made up this detail presumably to bolster her point. In my rejoinder, I told the audience about a recent poll taken by Harriet Taylor, the feminist author of *Scarlett's Women: "Gone with the Wind" and Its Female Fans.*[22] Ms. Taylor did not pretend that her survey was scientific, but what she found has the ring of truth. She asked GWTW fans what they thought had happened when Scarlett was carried up the stairs. The overwhelming majority of the four hundred respondents indi-

30

---

[19]Bartky, *Femininity and Domination,* p. 58. [Author's note]

[20]Christina Sommers, "Feminist Philosophers Are Oddly Unsympathetic to the Women They Claim to Represent," *Chronicle of Higher Education,* October 11, 1989, p. B3. [Author's note]

[21]Marilyn Friedman, " 'They Lived Happily Ever After': Sommers on Women and Marriage," *Journal of Social Philosophy,* 21, nos. 2 and 3 (Fall–Winter 1990): 58. [Author's note]

[22]Helen Taylor, *Scarlett's Women: "Gone with the Wind" and Its Female Fans* (New Brunswick, N.J.: Rutgers University Press, 1989). [Author's note]

cated that they did not think Rhett raped Scarlett, though there was some "mutually pleasurable rough sex."[23] Almost all reported that they found the scene "erotically exciting." As one respondent put it:

> Scarlett's story is that of a woman who has had lousy sex from two incompetent husbands (a "boy" and an "old man," as Rhett reminds her) [who] knew nothing about women. At last she finds out what *good* sex feels like, even if (or probably because) her first experience takes place in mutual inebriation and a spirit of vengeful anger.[24]

The idea of "mutually pleasurable rough sex" is not high on the gender feminist list of entertainments. All the same, if the New Feminist philosophers were honest about taking women seriously, they would be paying attention to what, in most women's minds, is a fundamental distinction: Scarlett was ravished, not raped. The next morning finds her relishing the memory. Ms. Friedman's insistence that Scarlett was raped was just another example of how gender feminists, estranged from the women they claim to represent, tend to view male/female relations as violent or humiliating to women.

Friedman, like Bartky, takes comfort in the idea that women's desires and aspirations will change in time. Younger women, she says, are already less inclined to be taken in by the Rhett Butler mystique, and his fascination should continue to diminish. That is, unless people like me give younger women the idea that there is nothing wrong with taking pleasure in Scarlett's enraptured submission.

"How sad it would be," she writes, "if Sommers's writings acted as an obstacle to change, bolstering those who interpret the sexual domination of women as pleasurable, and intimidating those who speak out against such domination."[25]

Ms. Friedman considers Sandra Bartky to be one of her mentors and Bartky is, indeed, of the opinion that active measures should be taken to prevent the spread of "harmful" writings. In 1990 I was commissioned by the *Atlantic* to do a piece on campus feminism. When Sandra Bartky somehow learned of this, she wrote to the editors, pleading with them not to publish it. She told them that I was a disreputable philosopher and "a right-wing ideologue." The *Chronicle of Higher Education* found out about the flap, and called Ms. Bartky to ask her why she had written the letter. At first she denied having asked them to suppress my piece, claiming that she had only requested that my article be accompanied by another giving a different point of view. But when the *Chronicle* reporter pointed out that he had a copy of the letter and that it contained no such request, she defiantly admitted having tried to stop the piece: "I wouldn't want a nut case who thinks

---

[23]Ibid., p. 130. [Author's note]
[24]Ibid., p. 133. [Author's note]
[25]Friedman, "Does Sommers Like Women?" p. 87. [Author's note]

there wasn't a Holocaust to write about the Holocaust. Editors exercise discretion. By not asking someone to write a piece, that's not censorship, that's
discretion."[26]

Inadvertently, Bartky got her way. By the time the whole matter was   35
sorted out, the *Atlantic* had gone on to other issues. Editor Michael Curtis
told the *Chronicle* that he was embarrassed that the piece had not been
published. The *Chronicle* reporter asked what he thought of Bartky's letter.
"It seemed to confirm some of the darker aspects of Ms. Sommers's article,
which pointed out the extraordinary lengths some of the women were prepared to go to shape all discussion in which they had an interest," he
replied.[27]

Rhett Butler continues to pique the gender feminists. Naomi Wolf, at
least in her earlier incarnation, was fond of explaining to the public how
women cooperate in their own degradation. When asked why women enjoyed the "rape scene" in *Gone with the Wind,* Ms. Wolf answered that they
had been "trained" to accept that kind of treatment and so grew to like it:
"It's not surprising that, after decades of being exposed to a culture that
consistently eroticizes violence against women, women, too, would often in-
ternalize their own training."[28]

I can't help being amused by how upset the New Feminists get over
the vicarious pleasure women take in Scarlett's transports. All that incorrect
swooning! How are we ever going to get women to see how wrong it is?
Nevertheless, the gender feminists seem to believe that thirty years from
now, with the academy transformed and the feminist consciousness of the
population raised, there will be a new Zeitgeist. Women who interpret sexual domination as pleasurable will then be few and far between, and Scarlett, alas, will be out of style.

Is this scenario out of the question? I think it is. Sexuality has always
been part of our natures, and there is no one right way. Men like Rhett Butler will continue to fascinate many women. Nor will the doctrine that this
demeans them have much of an effect. How many women who like Rhett
Butler-types are in search of support groups to help them change? Such
women are not grateful to the gender feminists for going to war against
male lust. They may even be offended at the suggestion that they themselves are being degraded and humiliated; for that treats their enjoyment as
pathological.

Defending women who enjoy the idea of ravishment is not the same as
holding a brief for any specific kind of fantasy or sexual preference. Fantasies of female domination are also popular. Women are clearly capable of
treating men as "sex objects" with an enthusiasm equal to, and in some

---

[26]*Chronicle of Higher Education,* January 15, 1992, p. A7. [Author's note]

[27]Ibid. [Author's note]

[28]"Men, Sex, and Rape," ABC News Forum, May 5, 1992, Transcript no. ABC-34, p. 9.
[Author's note]

cases exceeding, that of men for treating women as such. Male strip-shows seem to be as popular as Tupperware parties.

The dissident feminist Camille Paglia uses the term *pagan gazers* for   40 those who publicly watch males or females as sex objects. She has no quarrel with the male gazers, but she positively applauds the female ones. "Women are getting much more honest about looking at men, and about leering. Finally we're getting somewhere."[29]

If Paglia is right, sexual liberation may not be going in the direction of eliminating the Other as a sex object; it may instead be going in the direction of encouraging women to objectify the male as Other, too. Such a development would certainly be a far cry from the gender feminist utopia described by University of Massachusetts philosopher Ann Ferguson:

> With the elimination of sex roles, and the disappearance, in an overpopulated world, of any biological need for sex to be associated with procreation, there would be no reason why such a society could not transcend sexual gender. It would no longer matter what biological sex individuals had. Love relationships, and the sexual relationships developing out of them, would be based on the individual meshing together of androgynous human beings.[30]

Ferguson's utopia conjures up visions of a world of gender-neutral characters like Pat on "Saturday Night Live." Although Pat-like people can be very nice (doubtless, never rough), their sexually correct meshings do not invite heated speculation. To put the matter bluntly: the androgynous society has always been a boring feminist fairy tale with no roots in psychological or social reality.

A group of gay women who call themselves "lipstick lesbians" are rebelling against the androgynous ideal that feminists like Ann Ferguson . . . celebrate. According to Lindsy van Gelder, a writer for *Allure* magazine, the lipstick lesbians are tired of Birkenstock and L. L. Bean courtier, "womyn's" music festivals, potluck dinners, and all the "rigid dos and don'ts of feminist ideology."[31] She reports on several lesbian go-go bars in different parts of the country where lipstick lesbians congregate and treat each other in ways that are very much frowned upon in most gender feminist circles.

I believe that the Bartkys, the Friedmans, and the Fergusons are doomed to disappointment but that in any case no feminist should ever have an agenda of managing women's desires and fantasies. For suppose we could succeed in "trading in the fantasy of being overwhelmed by Rhett Butler for one in which we seize state power and reeducate him." Suppose, indeed, that

---

[29]*Boston Globe*, July 30, 1991, p. 54. [Author's note]

[30]Ann Ferguson, *Sexual Democracy: Women, Oppression, and Revolution* (Boulder, Colo.: Westview Press, 1991), p. 207. [Author's note]

[31]Lindsy van Gelder, "Lipstick Liberation," *Los Angeles Times Magazine*, March 15, 1992, p. 30. [Author's note]

we succeeded in getting most people to feel and to behave in ways that are sexually correct by gender feminist lights. Once the methods and institutions for overhauling desires are in place, what would prevent their deployment by new groups who have different conceptions of what is sexually correct and incorrect? Having seized state power, some zealous faction would find ready to hand the apparatus needed for reeducating people to *its* idea of what is "authentic," not only sexually but politically and culturally.

ENGAGING THE TEXT

1. Who are the "gender wardens," according to Sommers? What are their goals and methods? What evidence of their influence does Sommers provide?

2. How do the views of "gender feminists" differ from those of traditionally religious women? How does Sommers's analysis of these differences contribute to her critique of feminism?

3. Sommers asserts that "women are no longer disenfranchised, . . . [n]or are they now taught that they are subordinate or that a subordinate role for them is fitting and proper" (para. 20). Do you agree? What evidence do you see that women today are or are not taught to play a subordinate role?

4. Throughout the essay Sommers evokes the idea of "gender wardens" who have the power to dictate "sexually correct" personal behavior and attitudes; however, she argues that those who endorse such repressive measures "are doomed to disappointment" (para. 44). If she does not believe that the "gender wardens" are likely to succeed, what is her purpose in raising the issue?

5. Sommers defends women who enjoy sexual domination in part by arguing that women are likewise "capable of treating men as 'sex objects'" (para. 39). Do you agree with her assumption that these two situations are equivalent? Why or why not? Is it liberating for women to objectify men?

EXPLORING CONNECTIONS

6. Like Tocqueville, Sommers warns that some feminists may be trying to eliminate all differences between men and women. What "differences" did

Tocqueville wish to preserve? Have any of his fears been realized? How different are Sommers's concerns from Tocqueville's?

7. Sommers argues that contemporary women's choices must be considered "authentic" because they are no longer constrained by law as they were in the past. How might Holly Devor (p. 421), Jackson Katz (p. 458), Mariah Burton Nelson (p. 468), bell hooks (p. 483), or Myra and David Sadker (p. 228) respond to this argument? Besides legal constraints, what forces, if any, shape our values and desires?

8. Do you think that Sommers would see the situation in the cartoon on page 502 as an example of a "gender warden" in action? Do you agree that it's inappropriate to tell a woman that she's sexy? Why or why not? Is it inappropriate to tell a man that he's sexy?

EXTENDING THE CRITICAL CONTEXT

9. What evidence, if any, have you seen in your school, in your community, or in the media that "gender wardens" are enforcing conformity to feminist attitudes and behavior?

10. Sommers reports a heated debate that she has had with feminist scholars about whether Scarlett O'Hara, the heroine of *Gone with the Wind*, was ravished (that is, had "mutually pleasurable rough sex") or was raped by Rhett Butler. Find and read the passage in the novel that describes her ravishment or rape. Which interpretation seems more plausible to you, and why?

Appearances

CARMEN VÁZQUEZ

Have you ever gone for a walk in the evening, ridden a city bus, or gone out dancing? Did these activities make you fear for your life? In this essay, Vázquez writes about what can happen in such everyday situations when the pedestrian, commuter, or dancer is perceived as gay or lesbian. She also discusses some possible causes of homophobia, and she pleads for change. Vázquez (b. 1949) was born in Bayamon, Puerto Rico, and grew up in Harlem, New York. She has been active in the lesbian/gay movement for many years and currently serves as Director of Public Policy for the Lesbian and Gay Community Services Center in New York City; she also codirects Promote the Vote, a registration project sponsored by community centers across the nation. She has published essays and book reviews in a number of publications. "Appearances" comes from an anthology entitled Homophobia: How We All Pay the Price *(1992).*

North of Market Street and east of Twin Peaks, where you can see the white fog mushroom above San Francisco's hills, is a place called the Castro. Gay men, lesbians, and bisexuals stroll leisurely up and down the bustling streets. They jaywalk with abandon. Night and day they fill the cafés and bars, and on weekends they line up for a double feature of vintage classics at their ornate and beloved Castro theater.

The 24 bus line brings people into and out of the Castro. People from all walks of life ride the electric-powered coaches. They come from the opulence of San Francisco's Marina and the squalor of Bayview projects. The very gay Castro is in the middle of its route. Every day, boys in pairs or gangs from either end of the city board the bus for a ride through the Castro and a bit of fun. Sometimes their fun is fulfilled with passionately obscene derision: "Fucking cocksucking faggots." "Dyke cunts." "Diseased butt fuckers." Sometimes, their fun is brutal.

Brian boarded the 24 Divisadero and handed his transfer to the driver one late June night. Epithets were fired at him the moment he turned for a seat. He slid his slight frame into an empty seat next to an old woman with silver blue hair who clutched her handbag and stared straight ahead. Brian stuffed his hands into the pockets of his worn brown bomber jacket and stared with her. He heard the flip of a skateboard in the back. The taunting shouts grew louder. "Faggot!" From the corner of his eye, he saw a beer bottle hurtling past the window and crash on the street. A man in his forties, wearing a Giants baseball cap and warmup jacket, yelled at the driver to stop the bus and get the hoodlums off. The bus driver ignored him and pulled out.

Brian dug his hands deeper into his pockets and clenched his jaw. It was just five stops to the top of the hill. When he got up to move toward the exit, the skateboard slammed into his gut and one kick followed another until every boy had got his kick in. Despite the plea of the passengers, the driver never called the police.

Brian spent a week in a hospital bed, afraid that he would never walk again. A lawsuit filed by Brian against the city states, "As claimant lay crumpled and bleeding on the floor of the bus, the bus driver tried to force claimant off the bus so that the driver could get off work and go home. Claimant was severely beaten by a gang of young men on the #24 Divisadero Bus who perceived that he was gay."

On the south side of Market Street, night brings a chill wind and rough trade. On a brisk November night, men with sculptured torsos and thighs wrapped in leather walked with precision. The clamor of steel on the heels of their boots echoed in the darkness. Young men and women walked by the men in leather, who smiled in silence. They admired the studded bracelets on Mickey's wrists, the shine of his flowing hair, and the rise of his laughter. They were, each of them, eager to be among the safety of like company where they could dance with abandon to the pulse of hard rock, the hypnotism of disco, or the measured steps of country soul. They looked

5

forward to a few drinks, flirting with strangers, finding Mr. or Ms. Right or, maybe, someone to spend the night with.

At the end of the street, a lone black street lamp shone through the mist. The men in leather walked under the light and disappeared into the next street. As they reached the corner, Mickey and his friends could hear the raucous sounds of the Garden spill onto the street. They shimmied and rocked down the block and through the doors.

The Garden was packed with men and women in sweat-stained shirts. Blue smoke stung the eyes. The sour and sweet smell of beer hung in the air. Strobe lights pulsed over the dancers. Mickey pulled off his wash-faded black denim jacket and wrapped it around his waist. An iridescent blue tank top hung easy on his shoulders. Impatient with the wait for a drink, Mickey steered his girlfriend onto the crowded dance floor.

Reeling to the music and immersed in the pleasure of his rhythms, Mickey never saw the ice pick plunge into his neck. It was just a bump with a drunk yelling, "Lame-assed faggot." "Faggot. Faggot. Faggot. Punk faggot." Mickey thought it was a punch to the neck. He ran after the roaring drunk man for seven steps, then lurched and fell on the dance floor, blood gushing everywhere. His girlfriend screamed. The dance floor spun black.

Mickey was rushed to San Francisco General Hospital, where thirty-six   10 stitches were used by trauma staff to close the wound on his neck. Doctors said the pick used in the attack against him was millimeters away from his spinal cord. His assailant, charged with attempted murder, pleaded innocent.

Mickey and Brian were unfortunate stand-ins for any gay man. Mickey was thin and wiry, a great dancer clad in black denim, earrings dangling from his ear. Brian was slight of build, wore a leather jacket, and boarded a bus in the Castro. Dress like a homo, dance like a homo, must be a homo. The homophobic fury directed at lesbians, gay men, and bisexuals in America most often finds its target. Ironclad evidence of sexual orientation, however, is not necessary for someone to qualify as a potential victim of deadly fury. Appearances will do.

The incidents described above are based on actual events reported to the San Francisco Police and Community United Against Violence (CUAV), an agency serving victims of antilesbian and antigay violence where I worked for four years. The names of the victims have been changed. Both men assaulted were straight.

Incidents of antilesbian and antigay violence are not uncommon or limited to San Francisco. A *San Francisco Examiner* survey estimates that over one million hate-motivated physical assaults take place each year against lesbians, gays, and bisexuals. The National Gay and Lesbian Task Force conducted a survey in 1984 that found that 94 percent of all lesbians and gay men surveyed reported being physically assaulted, threatened, or harassed in an antigay incident at one time or another. The great majority of these incidents go unreported.

To my knowledge, no agency other than CUAV keeps track of incidents of antigay violence involving heterosexuals as victims. An average of 3 percent of the over three hundred victims seen by CUAV each year identify as heterosexuals. This may or may not be an accurate gauge of the actual prevalence of antigay violence directed at heterosexuals. Most law enforcement agencies, including those in San Francisco, have no way of documenting this form of assault other than under a generic "harassment" code. The actual incidence of violence directed at heterosexuals that is motivated by homophobia is probably much higher than CUAV's six to nine victims a year. Despite the official paucity of data, however, it is a fact that incidents of antigay and antilesbian violence in which straight men and women are victimized do occur. Shelters for battered women are filled with stories of lesbian baiting of staff and of women whose husbands and boyfriends repeatedly called them "dykes" or "whores" as they beat them.[1] I have personally experienced verbal abuse while in the company of a straight friend, who was assumed to be my lover.

Why does it happen? I have no definitive answers to that question. Understanding homophobic violence is no less complex than understanding racial violence. The institutional and ideological reinforcements of homophobia are myriad and deeply woven into our culture. I offer one perspective that I hope will contribute to a better understanding of how homophobia works and why it threatens all that we value as humane. 15

At the simplest level, looking or behaving like the stereotypical gay man or lesbian is reason enough to provoke a homophobic assault. Beneath the veneer of the effeminate gay male or the butch dyke, however, is a more basic trigger for homophobic violence. I call it *gender betrayal.*

The clearest expression I have heard of this sense of gender betrayal comes from Doug Barr, who was acquitted of murder in an incident of gay bashing in San Francisco that resulted in the death of John O'Connell, a gay man. Barr is currently serving a prison sentence for related assaults on the same night that O'Connell was killed. He was interviewed for a special report on homophobia produced by ABC's *20/20* (10 April 1986). When asked what he and his friends thought of gay men, he said, "We hate homosexuals. They degrade our manhood. We was brought up in a high school where guys are football players, mean and macho. Homosexuals are sissies who wear dresses. I'd rather be seen as a football player."

Doug Barr's perspective is one shared by many young men. I have made about three hundred presentations to high school students in San Francisco, to boards of directors and staff of nonprofit organizations, and at conferences and workshops on the topic of homophobia or "being lesbian or gay." Over and over again, I have asked, "Why do gay men and lesbians bother you?" The most popular response to the question is, "Because they

[1]See Suzanne Pharr, *Homophobia: A Weapon of Sexism* (Inverness, Calif.: Chardon, 1988). [Author's note]

act like girls," or, "Because they think they're men." I have even been told, quite explicitly, "I don't care what they do in bed, but they shouldn't act like that."

They shouldn't act like that. Women who are not identified by their relationship to a man, who value their female friendships, who like and are knowledgeable about sports, or work as blue-collar laborers and wear what they wish are very likely to be "lesbian baited" at some point in their lives. Men who are not pursuing sexual conquests of women at every available opportunity, who disdain sports, who choose to stay at home and be a house-husband, who are employed as hairdressers, designers, or housecleaners, or who dress in any way remotely resembling traditional female attire (an earring will do) are very likely to experience the taunts and sometimes the brutality of "fag bashing."

The straitjacket of gender roles suffocates many lesbians, gay men, and   20
bisexuals, forcing them into closets without an exit and threatening our very existence when we tear the closet open. It also, however, threatens all heterosexuals unwilling to be bound by their assigned gender identity. Why, then, does it persist?

Suzanne Pharr's examination of homophobia as a phenomenon based in sexism and misogyny offers a succinct and logical explanation for the virulence of homophobia in Western civilization:

> It is not by chance that when children approach puberty and increased sexual awareness they begin to taunt each other by calling these names: "queer," "faggot," "pervert." It is at puberty that the full force of society's pressure to conform to heterosexuality and prepare for marriage is brought to bear. Children know what we have taught them, and we have given clear messages that those who deviate from standard expectations are to be made to get back in line. . . .
>
> To be named as lesbian threatens all women, not just lesbians, with great loss. And any woman who steps out of role risks being called a lesbian. To understand how this is a threat to all women, one must understand that any woman can be called a lesbian and there is no real way she can defend herself: there is no real way to credential one's sexuality. (*The Children's Hour,* a Lillian Hellman play, makes this point when a student asserts two teachers are lesbians and they have no way to disprove it.) She may be married or divorced, have children, dress in the most feminine manner, have sex with men, be celibate — but there are lesbians who do all these things. *Lesbians look like all women and all women look like lesbians.*[2]

I would add that gay men look like all men and all men look like gay men. There is no guaranteed method for identifying sexual orientation. Those small or outrageous deviations we sometimes take from the idealized mystique of "real men" and "real women" place all of us — lesbians, gay men,

---

[2]Ibid., 17–19. [Author's note]

bisexuals, and heterosexuals alike — at risk of violence, derision, isolation, and hatred.

It is a frightening reality. Dorothy Ehrlich, executive director of the Northern California American Civil Liberties Union (ACLU), was the victim of a verbal assault in the Castro several years ago. Dorothy lives with her husband, Gary, and her two children, Jill and Paul, in one of those worn and comfortable Victorian homes that grace so many San Francisco neighborhoods. Their home is several blocks from the Castro, but Dorothy recalls the many times she and Gary could hear, from the safety of their bedroom, shouts of "faggot" and men running in the streets.

When Jill was an infant, Gary and Dorothy had occasion to experience for themselves how frightening even the threat of homophobic violence can be. One foggy, chilly night they decided to go for a walk in the Castro. Dorothy is a small woman whom some might call petite; she wore her hair short at the time and delights in the comfort of jeans and oversized wool jackets. Gary is very tall and lean, a bespectacled and bearded cross between a professor and a basketball player who wears jean jackets and tweed jackets with the exact same slouch. On this night they were crossing Castro Street, huddled close together with Jill in Dorothy's arms. As they reached the corner, their backs to the street, they heard a truck rev its engine and roar up Castro, the dreaded "faggot" spewing from young men they could not see in the fog. They looked around them for the intended victims, but there was no one else on the corner with them. They were the target that night: Dorothy and Gary and Jill. They were walking on "gay turf," and it was reason enough to make them a target. "It was so frightening," Dorothy said. "So frightening and unreal."

But it is real. The *20/20* report on homophobia ends with the story of Tom and Jan Matarrase, who are married, have a child, and lived in Brooklyn, New York, at the time of their encounter with homophobic violence. On camera, Tom and Jan are walking down a street in Brooklyn lined with brown townhouses and black wrought-iron gates. It is snowing, and, with hands entwined, they walk slowly down the street where they were assaulted. Tom is wearing a khaki trenchcoat, slacks, and loafers. Snowflakes melt into the tight dark curls on his head. Jan is almost his height, her short bobbed hair moving softly as she walks. She is wearing a black leather jacket, a red scarf, and burnt orange cords. The broadness of her hips and softness of her face belie the tomboy flavor of her carriage and clothes, and it is hard to believe that she was mistaken for a gay man. But she was.

They were walking home, holding hands and engrossed with each   25
other. On the other side of the street, Jan saw a group of boys moving toward them. As the gang approached, Jan heard a distinct taunt meant for her and Tom: "Aw, look at the cute gay couple." Tom and Jan quickened their step, but it was too late. Before they could say anything, Tom was being punched in the face and slammed against a car. Jan ran toward Tom and the car, screaming desperately that Tom was her husband. Fists pum-

meled her face as well. Outnumbered and in fear for their lives, Tom yelled at Jan to please open her jacket and show their assailants that she was a woman. The beating subsided only when Jan was able to show her breasts.

For the 20/20 interview, Jan and Tom sat in the warmth of their living room, their infant son in Jan's lap. The interviewer asked them how they felt when people said they looked like a gay couple. "We used to laugh," they said. "But now we realize how heavy the implications are. Now we know what the gay community goes through. We had no idea how widespread it was. It's on every level."

Sadly, it *is* on every level. Enforced heterosexism and the pressure to conform to aggressive masculine and passive feminine roles place fag bashers and lesbian baiters in the same psychic prison with their victims, gay or straight. Until all children are free to realize their full potential, until all women and men are free from the stigma, threats, alienation, or violence that come from stepping outside their roles, we are all at risk.

The economic and ideological underpinnings of enforced heterosexism and sexism or any other form of systematic oppression are formidable foes and far too complex for the scope of this essay. It is important to remember, however, that bigots are natural allies and that poverty or the fear of it has the power to seduce us all into conformity. In Castro graffiti, *faggot* appears right next to *nigger* and *kike*. Race betrayal or any threat to the sanctimony of light-skinned privilege engenders no less a rage than gender betrayal, most especially when we have a great stake in the elusive privilege of proper gender roles or the right skin color. *Queer lover* and *fag hag* are cut from the same mold that gave us *nigger lover*, a mold forged by fears of change and a loss of privilege.

Unfortunately, our sacrifices to conformity rarely guarantee the privilege or protection we were promised. Lesbians, gay men, and bisexuals who have tried to pass know that. Heterosexuals who have been perceived to be gay know that. Those of us with a vision of tomorrow that goes beyond tolerance to a genuine celebration of humanity's diversity have innumerable fronts to fight on. Homophobia is one of them.

But how will this front be won? With a lot of help, and not easily. Challenges to homophobia and the rigidity of gender roles must go beyond the visible lesbian and gay movement. Lesbians, gay men, and bisexuals alone cannot defuse the power of stigmatization and the license it gives to frighten, wound, or kill. Literally millions of us are needed on this front, straight and gay alike. We invite any heterosexual unwilling to live with the damage that "real men" or "real women" messages wreck on them, on their children, and on lesbians, gay men, and bisexuals to join us. We ask that you not let queer jokes go unchallenged at work, at home, in the media, or anywhere. We ask that you foster in your children a genuine respect for themselves and their right to be who and what they wish to be, regardless of their gender. We ask that you embrace your daughter's desire to swing a bat or be a carpenter, that you nurture your son's efforts to express affection and

30

sentiment. We ask that you teach your children how painful and destructive words like *faggot* or *bulldyke* are. We ask that you invite your lesbian, gay, and bisexual friends and relatives into the routine of your lives without demanding silence or discretion from them. We invite you to study our history, read the literature written by our people, patronize our businesses, come into our homes and neighborhoods. We ask that you give us your vote when we need it to protect our privacy or to elect open lesbians, gay men, and bisexuals to office. We ask that you stand with us in public demonstrations to demand our right to live as free people, without fear. We ask that you respect our dignity by acting to end the poison of homophobia.

Until individuals are free to choose their roles and be bound only by the limits of their own imagination, *faggot, dyke,* and *pervert* will continue to be playground words and adult weapons that hurt and limit far many more people than their intended victims. Whether we like it or not, the romance of virile men and dainty women, of Mother, Father, Dick, Jane, Sally, and Spot is doomed to extinction and dangerous in a world that can no longer meet the expectations conjured by history. There is much to be won and so little to lose in the realization of a world where the dignity of each person is worthy of celebration and protection. The struggle to end homophobia can and must be won, for all our sakes. Personhood is imminent.

ENGAGING THE TEXT

1. Do you think violent events like the ones described above are fairly common or quite rare? How aware of this problem are people in your community? How much attention have you seen paid to gay-bashing in the newspapers, on TV, in books or films, or in everyday conversation?

2. Vázquez waits a while to disclose that "Brian" and "Mickey" were actually straight men, but she *does* disclose this fact. Why does she wait? Why does she disclose it? Does the issue of antigay violence change in any way when we recognize that its victims are sometimes heterosexual?

3. Vázquez cites "gender betrayal" as a possible cause of antigay violence. Explain gender betrayal in your own words; discuss how it works and how well it explains the violence described in the narratives Vázquez recounts.

4. According to Vázquez, Suzanne Pharr links homophobia to misogyny, the hatred of women: the "lesbian" label, she says, can be used to threaten all women. Review and discuss this argument; then discuss how well it can be applied to men, as Vázquez suggests it might be.

5. Besides the threat of physical violence, how does homophobia place us *all* "at risk," according to Vázquez?

EXPLORING CONNECTIONS

6. To what extent does Vázquez's concept of "gender betrayal" (para. 16) explain the attitudes and behavior encountered by Anndee Hochman (p. 47), Nora Quealey (p. 430), Lorraine and Theresa in "The Two" (p. 512), or Kathleen Boatwright (p. 780)?

7. Imagine that you are Vázquez and that you have just read the preceding essay by Christina Hoff Sommers (p. 491). In the role of Vázquez, write a letter to Sommers proposing an alternative definition of "gender wardens" and explaining how and why you see the issue differently than she does.

8. Look at the cartoon on page 510, Alison Bechdel's "Public Display of Affection" (part of her "Dykes to Watch Out For" series). Discuss the cartoon in light of Vázquez's essay. Write an imaginary dialogue between Vázquez and Bechdel on the subject of gay and lesbian harassment.

EXTENDING THE CRITICAL CONTEXT

9. Vázquez writes that "the institutional and ideological reinforcements of homophobia are myriad and deeply woven into our culture" (para. 15). Over a period of days, keep track of all references to gays, lesbians, or homosexuality in casual conversations, news reports, TV programs, and other media. To what extent do you agree with Vázquez that homophobia is deeply ingrained in our culture?

10. San Francisco, the city in which the incidents described took place, is known as one of the most tolerant in the United States. Research your own community's history of assaults on gay and lesbian people. You might begin by talking to gay and lesbian organizations; police or public health departments may also have pertinent information. Report to the class or write a formal paper presenting your findings.

11. Near the end of her essay, Vázquez lists a variety of ways that individuals can combat homophobia (para. 30). Write a journal entry assessing how easy or how difficult it would be for you to follow each of her suggestions, and why.

The Two

GLORIA NAYLOR

This story from Gloria Naylor's The Women of Brewster Place *(1982) paints a fictional portrait of a black lesbian couple as their neighbors begin to discover their secret. As they emerge in the story, Lorraine and Theresa prompt us to reconsider stereotypes of homosexual people. Gloria Naylor (b. 1950) holds a master's degree in Afro-American Studies from Yale University.* The Women of Brewster Place *brought her national recognition and critical acclaim when it won the American Book Award for First Fiction. Naylor has also published a work of nonfiction,* Centennial *(1986), and three other novels:* Linden Hills *(1985),* Mama Day *(1988), and* Bailey's Cafe *(1992).*

At first they seemed like such nice girls. No one could remember exactly when they had moved into Brewster. It was earlier in the year before Ben[1] was killed — of course, it had to be before Ben's death. But no one remembered if it was in the winter or spring of that year that the two had

---

[1]*Ben:* The resident caretaker for the apartments in Brewster Place.

come. People often came and went on Brewster Place like a restless night's dream, moving in and out in the dark to avoid eviction notices or neighborhood bulletins about the dilapidated condition of their furnishings. So it wasn't until the two were clocked leaving in the mornings and returning in the evenings at regular intervals that it was quietly absorbed that they now claimed Brewster as home. And Brewster waited, cautiously prepared to claim them, because you never knew about young women, and obviously single at that. But when no wild music or drunken friends careened out of the corner building on weekends, and especially, when no slightly eager husbands were encouraged to linger around that first-floor apartment and run errands for them, a suspended sigh of relief floated around the two when they dumped their garbage, did their shopping, and headed for the morning bus.

The women of Brewster had readily accepted the lighter, skinny one. There wasn't much threat in her timid mincing walk and the slightly protruding teeth she seemed so eager to show everyone in her bell-like good mornings and evenings. Breaths were held a little longer in the direction of the short dark one — too pretty, and too much behind. And she insisted on wearing those thin Qiana dresses that the summer breeze molded against the maddening rhythm of the twenty pounds of rounded flesh that she swung steadily down the street. Through slitted eyes, the women watched their men watching her pass, knowing the bastards were praying for a wind. But since she seemed oblivious to whether these supplications went answered, their sighs settled around her shoulders too. Nice girls.

And so no one even cared to remember exactly when they had moved into Brewster Place, until the rumor started. It had first spread through the block like a sour odor that's only faintly perceptible and easily ignored until it starts growing in strength from the dozen mouths it had been lying in, among clammy gums and scum-coated teeth. And then it was everywhere — lining the mouth and whitening the lips of everyone as they wrinkled up their noses at its pervading smell, unable to pinpoint the source or time of its initial arrival. Sophie could — she had been there.

It wasn't that the rumor had actually begun with Sophie. A rumor needs no true parent. It only needs a willing carrier, and it found one in Sophie. She had been there — on one of those August evenings when the sun's absence is a mockery because the heat leaves the air so heavy it presses the naked skin down on your body, to the point that a sheet becomes unbearable and sleep impossible. So most of Brewster was outside that night when the two had come in together, probably from one of those air-conditioned movies downtown, and had greeted the ones who were loitering around their building. And they had started up the steps when the skinny one tripped over a child's ball and the darker one had grabbed her by the arm and around the waist to break her fall. "Careful, don't wanna lose you now." And the two of them had laughed into each other's eyes and went into the building.

The smell had begun there. It outlined the image of the stumbling   5
woman and the one who had broken her fall. Sophie and a few other
women sniffed at the spot and then, perplexed, silently looked at each
other. Where had they seen that before? They had often laughed and
touched each other — held each other in joy or its dark twin — but where
had they seen *that* before? It came to them as the scent drifted down the
steps and entered their nostrils on the way to their inner mouths. They had
seen that — done that — with their men. That shared moment of invisible
communion reserved for two and hidden from the rest of the world behind
laughter or tears or a touch. In the days before babies, miscarriages, and
other broken dreams, after stolen caresses in barn stalls and cotton houses,
after intimate walks from church and secret kisses with boys who were now
long forgotten or permanently fixed in their lives — that was where. They
could almost feel the odor moving about in their mouths, and they slowly
knitted themselves together and let it out into the air like a yellow mist that
began to cling to the bricks on Brewster.

So it got around that the two in 312 were *that* way. And they had
seemed like such nice girls. Their regular exits and entrances to the block
were viewed with a jaundiced eye. The quiet that rested around their door
on the weekends hinted of all sorts of secret rituals, and their friendly indifference to the men on the street was an insult to the women as a brazen
flaunting of unnatural ways.

Since Sophie's apartment windows faced theirs from across the air shaft,
she became the official watchman for the block, and her opinions were deferred to whenever the two came up in conversation. Sophie took her position
seriously and was constantly alert for any telltale signs that might creep out
around their drawn shades, across from which she kept a religious vigil. An
entire week of drawn shades was evidence enough to send her flying around
with reports that as soon as it got dark they pulled their shades down and put
on the lights. Heads nodded in knowing unison — a definite sign. If doubt
was voiced with a "But I pull my shades down at night too," a whispered
"yeah, but you're not *that* way" was argument enough to win them over.

Sophie watched the lighter one dumping their garbage, and she went
outside and opened the lid. Her eyes darted over the crushed tin cans, veg-
etable peelings, and empty chocolate chip cookie boxes. What do they do
with all them chocolate chip cookies? It was surely a sign, but it would take
some time to figure that one out. She saw Ben go into their apartment, and
she waited and blocked his path as he came out, carrying his toolbox.

"What ya see?" She grabbed his arm and whispered wetly in his face.

Ben stared at her squinted eyes and drooping lips and shook his head   10
slowly. "Uh, uh, uh, it was terrible."

"Yeah?" She moved in a little closer.

"Worst busted faucet I seen in my whole life." He shook her hand off
his arm and left her standing in the middle of the block.

"You old sop bucket," she muttered, as she went back up on her stoop. A broken faucet, huh? Why did they need to use so much water?

Sophie had plenty to report that day. Ben had said it was terrible in there. No, she didn't know exactly what he had seen, but you can imagine — and they did. Confronted with the difference that had been thrust into their predictable world, they reached into their imaginations and, using an ancient pattern, weaved themselves a reason for its existence. Out of necessity they stitched all of their secret fears and lingering childhood nightmares into this existence, because even though it was deceptive enough to try and look as they looked, talk as they talked, and do as they did, it had to have some hidden stain to invalidate it — it was impossible for them both to be right. So they leaned back, supported by the sheer weight of their numbers and comforted by the woven barrier that kept them protected from the yellow mist that enshrouded the two as they came and went on Brewster Place.

Lorraine was the first to notice the change in the people on Brewster 15 Place. She was a shy but naturally friendly woman who got up early, and had read the morning paper and done fifty sit-ups before it was time to leave for work. She came out of her apartment eager to start her day by greeting any of her neighbors who were outside. But she noticed that some of the people who had spoken to her before made a point of having something else to do with their eyes when she passed, although she could almost feel them staring at her back as she moved on. The ones who still spoke only did so after an uncomfortable pause, in which they seemed to be peering through her before they begrudged her a good morning or evening. She wondered if it was all in her mind and she thought about mentioning it to Theresa, but she didn't want to be accused of being too sensitive again. And how would Tee even notice anything like that anyway? She had a lousy attitude and hardly ever spoke to people. She stayed in that bed until the last moment and rushed out of the house fogged-up and grumpy, and she was used to being stared at — by men at least — because of her body.

Lorraine thought about these things as she came up the block from work, carrying a large paper bag. The group of women on her stoop parted silently and let her pass.

"Good evening," she said, as she climbed the steps.

Sophie was standing on the top step and tried to peek into the bag. "You been shopping, huh? What ya buy?" It was almost an accusation.

"Groceries." Lorraine shielded the top of the bag from view and squeezed past her with a confused frown. She saw Sophie throw a knowing glance to the others at the bottom of the stoop. What was wrong with this old woman? Was she crazy or something?

Lorraine went into her apartment. Theresa was sitting by the window, 20 reading a copy of *Mademoiselle*. She glanced up from her magazine. "Did you get my chocolate chip cookies?"

"Why good evening to you, too, Tee. And how was my day? Just wonderful." She sat the bag down on the couch. "The little Baxter boy brought in a puppy for show-and-tell, and the damn thing pissed all over the floor and then proceeded to chew the heel off my shoe, but, yes, I managed to hobble to the store and bring you your chocolate chip cookies."

Oh, Jesus, Theresa thought, she's got a bug up her ass tonight.

"Well, you should speak to Mrs. Baxter. She ought to train her kid better than that." She didn't wait for Lorraine to stop laughing before she tried to stretch her good mood. "Here, I'll put those things away. Want me to make dinner so you can rest? I only worked half a day, and the most tragic thing that went down was a broken fingernail and that got caught in my typewriter."

Lorraine followed Theresa into the kitchen. "No, I'm not really tired, and fair's fair, you cooked last night. I didn't mean to tick off like that; it's just that . . . well, Tee, have you noticed that people aren't as nice as they used to be?"

Theresa stiffened. Oh, God, here she goes again. "What people, Lorraine? Nice in what way?"   25

"Well, the people in this building and on the street. No one hardly speaks anymore. I mean, I'll come in and say good evening — and just silence. It wasn't like that when we first moved in. I don't know, it just makes you wonder; that's all. What are they thinking?"

"I personally don't give a shit what they're thinking. And their good evenings don't put any bread on my table."

"Yeah, but you didn't see the way that woman looked at me out there. They must feel something or know something. They probably — "

"They, they, they!" Theresa exploded. "You know, I'm not starting up with this again, Lorraine. Who in the hell are they? And where in the hell are we? Living in some dump of a building in this God-forsaken part of town around a bunch of ignorant niggers with the cotton still under their fingernails because of you and your theys. They knew something in Linden Hills, so I gave up an apartment for you that I'd been in for the last four years. And then they knew in Park Heights, and you made me so miserable there we had to leave. Now these mysterious theys are on Brewster Place. Well, look out that window, kid. There's a big wall down that block, and this is the end of the line for me. I'm not moving anymore, so if that's what you're working yourself up to — save it!"

When Theresa became angry she was like a lump of smoldering coal,   30
and her fierce bursts of temper always unsettled Lorraine.

"You see, that's why I didn't want to mention it." Lorraine began to pull at her fingers nervously. "You're always flying up and jumping to conclusions — no one said anything about moving. And I didn't know your life has been so miserable since you met me. I'm sorry about that," she finished tearfully.

Theresa looked at Lorraine, standing in the kitchen door like a wilted leaf, and she wanted to throw something at her. Why didn't she ever fight back? The very softness that had first attracted her to Lorraine was now a frequent cause for irritation. Smoked honey. That's what Lorraine had reminded her of, sitting in her office clutching that application. Dry autumn days in Georgia woods, thick bloated smoke under a beehive, and the first glimpse of amber honey just faintly darkened about the edges by the burning twigs. She had flowed just that heavily into Theresa's mind and had stuck there with a persistent sweetness.

But Theresa hadn't known then that this softness filled Lorraine up to the very middle and that she would bend at the slightest pressure, would be constantly seeking to surround herself with the comfort of everyone's goodwill, and would shrivel up at the least touch of disapproval. It was becoming a drain to be continually called upon for this nurturing and support that she just didn't understand. She had supplied it at first out of love for Lorraine, hoping that she would harden eventually, even as honey does when exposed to the cold. Theresa was growing tired of being clung to — of being the one who was leaned on. She didn't want a child — she wanted someone who could stand toe to toe with her and be willing to slug it out at times. If they practiced that way with each other, then they could turn back to back and beat the hell out of the world for trying to invade their territory. But she had found no such sparring partner in Lorraine, and the strain of fighting alone was beginning to show on her.

"Well, if it was that miserable, I would have been gone a long time ago," she said, watching her words refresh Lorraine like a gentle shower.

"I guess you think I'm some sort of a sick paranoid, but I can't afford to   35
have people calling my job or writing letters to my principal. You know I've already lost a position like that in Detroit. And teaching is my whole life, Tee."

"I know," she sighed, not really knowing at all. There was no danger of that ever happening on Brewster Place. Lorraine taught too far from this neighborhood for anyone here to recognize her in that school. No, it wasn't her job she feared losing this time, but their approval. She wanted to stand out there and chat and trade makeup secrets and cake recipes. She wanted to be secretary of their block association and be asked to mind their kids while they ran to the store. And none of that was going to happen if they couldn't even bring themselves to accept her good evenings.

Theresa silently finished unpacking the groceries. "Why did you buy cottage cheese? Who eats that stuff?"

"Well, I thought we should go on a diet."

"If *we* go on a diet, then you'll disappear. You've got nothing to lose but your hair."

"Oh, I don't know. I thought that we might want to try and reduce our   40
hips or something." Lorraine shrugged playfully.

"No, thank you. We are very happy with our hips the way they are," Theresa said, as she shoved the cottage cheese to the back of the refrigerator. "And even when I lose weight, it never comes off there. My chest and arms just get smaller, and I start looking like a bottle of salad dressing."

The two women laughed, and Theresa sat down to watch Lorraine fix dinner. "You know, this behind has always been my downfall. When I was coming up in Georgia with my grandmother, the boys used to promise me penny candy if I would let them pat my behind. And I used to love those jawbreakers — you know, the kind that lasted all day and kept changing colors in your mouth. So I was glad to oblige them, because in one afternoon I could collect a whole week's worth of jawbreakers."

"Really. That's funny to you? Having some boy feeling all over you."

Theresa sucked her teeth. "We were only kids, Lorraine. You know, you remind me of my grandmother. That was one straight-laced old lady. She had a fit when my brother told her what I was doing. She called me into the smokehouse and told me in this real scary whisper that I could get pregnant from letting little boys pat my butt and that I'd end up like my cousin Willa. But Willa and I had been thick as fleas, and she had already given me a step-by-step summary of how she'd gotten into her predicament. But I sneaked around to her house that night just to double-check her story, since that old lady had seemed so earnest. 'Willa, are you sure?' I whispered through her bedroom window. 'I'm tellin' ya, Tee,' she said. 'Just keep both feet on the ground and you home free.' Much later I learned that advice wasn't too biologically sound, but it worked in Georgia because those country boys didn't have much imagination."

Theresa's laughter bounced off of Lorraine's silent, rigid back and died 45 in her throat. She angrily tore open a pack of the chocolate chip cookies. "Yeah," she said, staring at Lorraine's back and biting down hard into the cookie, "it wasn't until I came up north to college that I found out there's a whole lot of things that a dude with a little imagination can do to you even with both feet on the ground. You see, Willa forgot to tell me not to bend over or squat or — "

"Must you!" Lorraine turned around from the stove with her teeth clenched tightly together.

"Must I what, Lorraine? Must I talk about things that are as much a part of life as eating or breathing or growing old? Why are you always so uptight about sex or men?"

"I'm not uptight about anything. I just think it's disgusting when you go on and on about — "

"There's nothing disgusting about it, Lorraine. You've never been with a man, but I've been with quite a few — some better than others. There were a couple who I still hope to this day will die a slow, painful death, but then there were some who were good to me — in and out of bed."

"If they were so great, then why are you with me?" Lorraine's lips were 50 trembling.

"Because — " Theresa looked steadily into her eyes and then down at the cookie she was twirling on the table. "Because," she continued slowly, "you can take a chocolate chip cookie and put holes in it and attach it to your ears and call it an earring, or hang it around your neck on a silver chain and pretend it's a necklace — but it's still a cookie. See — you can toss it in the air and call it a Frisbee or even a flying saucer, if the mood hits you, and it's still just a cookie. Send it spinning on a table — like this — until it's a wonderful blur of amber and brown light that you can imagine to be topaz or rusted gold or old crystal, but the law of gravity has got to come into play, sometime, and it's got to come to rest — sometime. Then all the spinning and pretending and hoopla is over with. And you know what you got?"

"A chocolate chip cookie," Lorraine said.

"Uh-huh." Theresa put the cookie in her mouth and winked. "A lesbian." She got up from the table. "Call me when dinner's ready, I'm going back to read." She stopped at the kitchen door. "Now, why are you putting gravy on that chicken, Lorraine? You know it's fattening."

ENGAGING THE TEXT

1. What type of community does Naylor describe in her opening two paragraphs, and how, specifically, does she create this atmosphere? Why is this important to the theme of the story?

2. Why does Naylor shift the story's point of view from that of the community to that of Lorraine and Theresa? How does this change of perspective affect the reader?

3. Why does Naylor make a point of details like drawn shades, chocolate chip cookies, and the broken faucet?

4. How important is sexuality in Lorraine and Theresa's relationship? What do they share besides lovemaking?

5. This story is now more than 15 years old. Does its treatment of its main theme hold up well over time? Might a neighborhood today react in the same way to the presence of a homosexual couple? Do you think the story would be as well received today as it was in 1982? Explain.

EXPLORING CONNECTIONS

6. Like "The Two," Jamaica Kincaid's "Girl" (p. 418) and Bebe Moore Campbell's "Envy" (p. 118) depict woman-centered environments. How much power do women have in each of these narratives? How do they use their power, and for what ends?

7. Write an imaginary conversation in which Theresa, Anndee Hochman (p. 47), and Kathleen Boatwright (p. 780) advise Lorraine on the risks and rewards of coming out of the closet.

EXTENDING THE CRITICAL CONTEXT

8. Find one or more psychology texts or articles authored before 1960 that cover homosexuality. How is it defined, described, and classified? How often is lesbianism specifically included in the discussion?

9. Investigate the policies and practices regarding homosexual teachers at various schools in your locale. Are there restrictions, explicit or implicit, against homosexual teachers? Are there restrictions on their behavior or appearance? Report to the class on your findings. Your sources might include interviews with teachers as well as school documents, newspaper stories, or legal cases.

Where I Come From Is Like This

PAULA GUNN ALLEN

Paula Gunn Allen was born in 1939 in Cubero, New Mexico, a Spanish-Mexican land grant village; where she comes from is life as a Laguna Pueblo–Sioux–Lebanese woman. In this essay she discusses some of the ways traditional images of women in American Indian cultures differ from images in mainstream American culture. Allen is a professor of English and American Indian literature at the University of California, Los Angeles. In addition to her scholarship, Allen is widely recognized for her books of poetry and for her novel The Woman Who Owned the Shadows *(1983). Her recent works,* Grandmothers of the Light *(1991) and* Women in American Indian Mythology *(1994), have focused on the female spiritual traditions of Native America. This piece appeared in Allen's collection of essays* The Sacred Hoop: Recovering the Feminine in American Indian Traditions *(1986).*

I

Modern American Indian women, like their non-Indian sisters, are deeply engaged in the struggle to redefine themselves. In their struggle they must reconcile traditional tribal definitions of women with industrial and postindustrial non-Indian definitions. Yet while these definitions seem to be more or less mutually exclusive, Indian women must somehow harmonize and integrate both in their own lives.

An American Indian woman is primarily defined by her tribal identity. In her eyes, her destiny is necessarily that of her people, and her sense of herself as a woman is first and foremost prescribed by her tribe. The definitions of woman's roles are as diverse as tribal cultures in the Americas. In some she is devalued, in others she wields considerable power. In some she is a familial/clan adjunct, in some she is as close to autonomous as her economic circumstances and psychological traits permit. But in no tribal definitions is she perceived in the same way as are women in western industrial and postindustrial cultures.

In the west, few images of women form part of the cultural mythos, and these are largely sexually charged. Among Christians, the madonna is the female prototype, and she is portrayed as essentially passive: her contribution is simply that of birthing. Little else is attributed to her and she certainly possesses few of the characteristics that are attributed to mythic figures among Indian tribes. This image is countered (rather than balanced) by the witch-goddess/whore characteristics designed to reinforce cultural beliefs about women, as well as western adversarial and dualistic perceptions of reality.

The tribes see women variously, but they do not question the power of femininity. Sometimes they see women as fearful, sometimes peaceful, sometimes omnipotent and omniscient, but they never portray women as mindless, helpless, simple, or oppressed. And while the women in a given tribe, clan, or band may be all these things, the individual woman is provided with a variety of images of women from the interconnected supernatural, natural, and social worlds she lives in.

As a half-breed American Indian woman, I cast about in my mind for   5
negative images of Indian women, and I find none that are directed to Indian women alone. The negative images I do have are of Indians in general and in fact are more often of males than of females. All these images come to me from non-Indian sources, and they are always balanced by a positive image. My ideas of womanhood, passed on largely by my mother and grandmothers, Laguna Pueblo women, are about practicality, strength, reasonableness, intelligence, wit, and competence. I also remember vividly the women who came to my father's store, the women who held me and sang to me, the women at Feast Day, at Grab Days,[1] the women in the kitchen of my Cubero home, the women I grew up with; none of them appeared weak or helpless, none of them presented herself tentatively. I remember a certain reserve on those lovely brown faces; I remember the direct gaze of eyes framed by bright-colored shawls draped over their heads and cascading down their backs. I remember the clean cotton dresses and carefully pressed hand-embroidered aprons they always wore; I remember laughter and good food, especially the sweet bread and the oven bread they gave us. Nowhere in my mind is there a foolish woman, a dumb woman, a vain woman, or a plastic woman, though the Indian women I have known have shown a wide range of personal style and demeanor.

My memory includes the Navajo woman who was badly beaten by her Sioux husband; but I also remember that my grandmother abandoned her Sioux husband long ago. I recall the stories about the Laguna woman beaten regularly by her husband in the presence of her children so that the

---

[1]*Grab Days:* Laguna ritual in which women throw food and small items (like pieces of cloth) to those attending.

children would not believe in the strength and power of femininity. And I remember the women who drank, who got into fights with other women and with the men, and who often won those battles. I have memories of tired women, partying women, stubborn women, sullen women, amicable women, selfish women, shy women, and aggressive women. Most of all I remember the women who laugh and scold and sit uncomplaining in the long sun on feast days and who cook wonderful food on wood stoves, in beehive mud ovens, and over open fires outdoors.

Among the images of women that come to me from various tribes as well as my own are White Buffalo Woman, who came to the Lakota long ago and brought them the religion of the Sacred Pipe which they still practice; Tinotzin the goddess who came to Juan Diego to remind him that she still walked the hills of her people and sent him with her message, her demand and her proof to the Catholic bishop in the city nearby. And from Laguna I take the images of Yellow Woman, Coyote Woman, Grandmother Spider (Spider Old Woman), who brought the light, who gave us weaving and medicine, who gave us life. Among the Keres she is known as Thought Woman who created us all and who keeps us in creation even now. I remember Iyatiku, Earth Woman, Corn Woman, who guides and counsels the people to peace and who welcomes us home when we cast off this coil of flesh as huskers cast off the leaves that wrap the corn. I remember Iyatiku's sister, Sun Woman, who held metals and cattle, pigs and sheep, highways and engines and so many things in her bundle, who went away to the east saying that one day she would return.

II

Since the coming of the Anglo-Europeans beginning in the fifteenth century, the fragile web of identity that long held tribal people secure has gradually been weakened and torn. But the oral tradition has prevented the complete destruction of the web, the ultimate disruption of tribal ways. The oral tradition is vital; it heals itself and the tribal web by adapting to the flow of the present while never relinquishing its connection to the past. Its adaptability has always been required, as many generations have experienced. Certainly the modern American Indian woman bears slight resemblance to her forebears — at least on superficial examination — but she is still a tribal woman in her deepest being. Her tribal sense of relationship to all that is continues to flourish. And though she is at times beset by her knowledge of the enormous gap between the life she lives and the life she was raised to live, and while she adapts her mind and being to the circumstances of her present life, she does so in tribal ways, mending the tears in the web of being from which she takes her existence as she goes.

My mother told me stories all the time, though I often did not recognize them as that. My mother told me stories about cooking and childbearing; she told me stories about menstruation and pregnancy; she told me stories about gods and heroes, about fairies and elves, about goddesses and spirits; she told me stories about the land and the sky, about cats and dogs, about snakes and spiders; she told me stories about climbing trees and exploring the mesas; she told me stories about going to dances and getting married; she told me stories about dressing and undressing, about sleeping and waking; she told me stories about herself, about her mother, about her grandmother. She told me stories about grieving and laughing, about thinking and doing; she told me stories about school and about people; about darning and mending; she told me stories about turquoise and about gold; she told me European stories and Laguna stories; she told me Catholic stories and Presbyterian stories; she told me city stories and country stories; she told me political stories and religious stories. She told me stories about living and stories about dying. And in all of those stories she told me who I was, who I was supposed to be, whom I came from, and who would follow me. In this way she taught me the meaning of the words she said, that all life is a circle and everything has a place within it. That's what she said and what she showed me in the things she did and the way she lives.

Of course, through my formal, white, Christian education, I discovered   10
that other people had stories of their own — about women, about Indians, about fact, about reality — and I was amazed by a number of startling suppositions that others made about tribal customs and beliefs. According to the un-Indian, non-Indian view, for instance, Indians barred menstruating women from ceremonies and indeed segregated them from the rest of the people, consigning them to some space specially designed for them. This showed that Indians considered menstruating women unclean and not fit to enjoy the company of decent (nonmenstruating) people, that is, men. I was surprised and confused to hear this because my mother had taught me that white people had strange attitudes toward menstruation: they thought something was bad about it, that it meant you were sick, cursed, sinful, and weak and that you had to be very careful during that time. She taught me that menstruation was a normal occurrence, that I could go swimming or hiking or whatever else I wanted to do during my period. She actively scorned women who took to their beds, who were incapacitated by cramps, who "got the blues."

As I struggled to reconcile these very contradictory interpretations of American Indians' traditional beliefs concerning menstruation, I realized that the menstrual taboos were about power, not about sin or filth. My conclusion was later borne out by some tribes' own explanations, which, as you may well imagine, came as quite a relief to me.

The truth of the matter as many Indians see it is that women who are at the peak of their fecundity are believed to possess power that throws male power totally out of kilter. They emit such force that, in their presence, any male-owned or -dominated ritual or sacred object cannot do its usual task. For instance, the Lakota say that a menstruating woman anywhere near a yuwipi man, who is a special sort of psychic, spirit-empowered healer, for a day or so before he is to do his ceremony will effectively disempower him. Conversely, among many if not most tribes, important ceremonies cannot be held without the presence of women. Sometimes the ritual woman who empowers the ceremony must be unmarried and virginal so that the power she channels is unalloyed, unweakened by sexual arousal and penetration by a male. Other ceremonies require tumescent women, others the presence of mature women who have borne children, and still others depend for empowerment on postmenopausal women. Women may be segregated from the company of the whole band or village on certain occasions, but on certain occasions men are also segregated. In short, each ritual depends on a certain balance of power, and the positions of women within the phases of womanhood are used by tribal people to empower certain rites. This does not derive from a male-dominant view; it is not a ritual observance imposed on women by men. It derives from a tribal view of reality that distinguishes tribal people from feudal and industrial people.

Among the tribes, the occult power of women, inextricably bound to our hormonal life, is thought to be very great; many hold that we possess innately the blood-given power to kill — with a glance, with a step, or with a judicious mixing of menstrual blood into somebody's soup. Medicine women among the Pomo of California cannot practice until they are sufficiently mature; when they are immature, their power is diffuse and is likely to interfere with their practice until time and experience have it under control. So women of the tribes are not especially inclined to see themselves as poor helpless victims of male domination. Even in those tribes where something akin to male domination was present, women are perceived as powerful, socially, physically, and metaphysically. In times past, as in times present, women carried enormous burdens with aplomb. We were far indeed from the "weaker sex," the designation that white aristocratic sisters unhappily earned for us all.

I remember my mother moving furniture all over the house when she wanted it changed. She didn't wait for my father to come home and help — she just went ahead and moved the piano, a huge upright from the old days, the couch, the refrigerator. Nobody had told her she was too weak to do such things. In imitation of her, I would delight in loading trucks at my father's store with cases of pop or fifty-pound sacks of flour. Even when I was quite small I could do it, and it gave me a belief in my own physical strength that advancing middle age can't quite erase. My mother used to tell me about the Acoma Pueblo women she had seen as a child carrying huge ollas (water pots) on their heads as they wound their way up the tortuous stairwell carved into the face of the "Sky City" mesa, a feat I tried to imitate with books and tin buckets. ("Sky City" is the term used by the Chamber of Commerce for the mother village of Acoma, which is situated atop a high sandstone table mountain.) I was never very successful, but even the attempt reminded me that I was supposed to be strong and balanced to be a proper girl.

Of course, my mother's Laguna people are Keres Indian, reputed to be   15
the last extreme mother-right people on earth. So it is no wonder that I got

notably nonwhite notions about the natural strength and prowess of women. Indeed, it is only when I am trying to get non-Indian approval, recognition, or acknowledgement that my "weak sister" emotional and intellectual ploys get the better of my tribal woman's good sense. At such times I forget that I just moved the piano or just wrote a competent paper or just completed a financial transaction satisfactorily or have supported myself and my children for most of my adult life.

Nor is my contradictory behavior atypical. Most Indian women I know are in the same bicultural bind: we vacillate between being dependent and strong, self-reliant and powerless, strongly motivated and hopelessly insecure. We resolve the dilemma in various ways: some of us party all the time; some of us drink to excess; some of us travel and move around a lot; some of us land good jobs and then quit them; some of us engage in violent exchanges; some of us blow our brains out. We act in these destructive ways because we suffer from the societal conflicts caused by having to identify with two hopelessly opposed cultural definitions of women. Through this destructive dissonance we are unhappy prey to the self-disparagement common to, indeed demanded of, Indians living in the United States today. Our situation is caused by the exigencies of a history of invasion, conquest, and colonization whose searing marks are probably ineradicable. A popular bumper sticker on many Indian cars proclaims: "If You're Indian You're In," to which I always find myself adding under my breath, "Trouble."

III

No Indian can grow to any age without being informed that her people were "savages" who interfered with the march of progress pursued by respectable, loving, civilized white people. We are the villains of the scenario when we are mentioned at all. We are absent from much of white history except when we are calmly, rationally, succinctly, and systematically dehumanized. On the few occasions we are noticed in any way other than as howling, bloodthirsty beings, we are acclaimed for our noble quaintness. In this definition, we are exotic curios. Our ancient arts and customs are used to draw tourist money to state coffers, into the pocketbooks and bank accounts of scholars, and into support of the American-in-Disneyland promoters' dream.

As a Roman Catholic child I was treated to bloody tales of how the savage Indians martyred the hapless priests and missionaries who went among them in an attempt to lead them to the one true path. By the time I was through high school I had the idea that Indians were people who had benefitted mightily from the advanced knowledge and superior morality of the Anglo-Europeans. At least I had, perforce, that idea to lay beside the other one that derived from my daily experience of Indian life, an idea less dehumanizing and more accurate because it came from my mother and the other Indian people who raised me. That idea was that Indians are a people who don't tell lies, who care for their children and their old people. You never see an Indian orphan, they said. You always know when you're old that someone will take care of you — one of your children will. Then they'd list the old folks who were being taken care of by this child or that. No child is ever considered illegitimate among the Indians, they said. If a girl gets pregnant, the baby is still part of the family, and the mother is too. That's what they said, and they showed me real people who lived according to those principles.

Of course the ravages of colonization have taken their toll; there are orphans in Indian country now, and abandoned, brutalized old folks; there are even illegitimate children, though the very concept still strikes me as absurd. There are battered children and neglected children, and there are battered wives and women who have been raped by Indian men. Proximity to the "civilizing" effects of white Christians has not improved the moral quality of life in Indian country, though each group, Indian and white, explains the situation differently. Nor is there much yet in the oral tradition that can enable us to adapt to these inhuman changes. But a force is growing in that direction, and it is helping Indian women reclaim their lives. Their power, their sense of direction and of self will soon be visible. It is the force of the women who speak and work and write, and it is formidable.

Through all the centuries of war and death and cultural and psychic destruction have endured the women who raise the children and tend the fires, who pass along the tales and the traditions, who weep and bury the dead, who are the dead, and who never forget. There are always the women, who make pots and weave baskets, who fashion clothes and cheer their children on at powwow, who make fry bread and piki bread, and corn soup and chili stew, who dance and sing and remember and hold within their hearts the dream of their ancient peoples — that one day the woman who thinks will speak to us again, and everywhere there will be peace. Meanwhile we tell the stories and write the books and trade tales of anger and woe and stories of fun and scandal and laugh over all manner of things that happen every day. We watch and we wait. 20

My great-grandmother told my mother: never forget you are Indian. And my mother told me the same thing. This, then, is how I have gone about remembering, so that my children will remember too.

ENGAGING THE TEXT

1. Outline how Allen's views of women differ from traditional Anglo-American views. Do you see any difference between Allen's perspective and "feminism" as you understand the term?

2. What does Allen mean by "bicultural bind" (para. 16)? How has it affected her, and how does she deal with it?

3. How does Allen represent relationships between American Indian women and men?

4. Why is remembering so important to Allen? What roles does it play in helping her live in a world dominated by an alien culture? How does it help her define herself as a woman?

5. Allen's essay includes much personal recollection. Try to "translate" some of this information into more abstract statements of theme or message. (For instance, you might write, "Women's roles in American Indian cultures are maintained through example, through oral tradition, and through ceremonial tribal practices.") What is gained, what lost in such "translations"?

6. Review how Allen uses the image of the web to explain tribal identity. In what ways is this an appropriate and effective metaphor?

EXPLORING CONNECTIONS

7. Review Holly Devor's discussion of gender role socialization (p. 421), and compare the influence of "generalized others" and "significant others" in the experiences of Allen and Judith Ortiz Cofer (p. 436). What tension does each woman feel between her "I" and her "me"? How does she resolve it?

8. Read or reread Roger Jack's "An Indian Story" (p. 109). What similarities do you find in Jack's and Allen's ideas about family and tribal identity?

9. According to Allen and to Patricia Hill Collins (p. 131), in what ways do many American Indian and African American women resist Anglo-European roles?

EXTENDING THE CRITICAL CONTEXT

10. Are you struggling to reconcile different definitions of what you should be? Write an essay or journal entry exploring this issue. (For example, are family, friends, and school pushing you in different directions?)

5

Created Equal
The Myth of the Melting Pot

The myth of the melting pot predates the drafting of the U.S. Constitution. In 1782, a year before the Peace of Paris formally ended the Revolutionary War, Hector St. Jean de Crèvecoeur envisioned the young American republic as a crucible that would forge its disparate immigrant population into a vigorous new society with a grand future:

> What, then, is the American, this new man? He is neither an European, or the descendant of an European. . . . He is an American, who leaving behind him all his ancient prejudices and manners, receives new ones from the new mode of life he has embraced, the new government he obeys, and the new rank he holds. . . . Here individuals of all nations are melted into a new race of men, whose labours and posterity will one day cause great changes in the world.

Crèvecoeur's metaphor has remained a powerful ideal for many generations of American scholars, politicians, artists, and ordinary citizens. Ralph Waldo Emerson, writing in his journal in 1845, celebrated the national vitality produced by the mingling of immigrant cultures: "In this continent — asylum of all nations, — the energy of . . . all the European tribes, — of the Africans, and of the Polynesians — will construct a new race, a new religion, a new state, a new literature." An English Jewish writer named Israel Zangwill, himself an immigrant, popularized the myth in his 1908 drama, *The Melting Pot*. In the play, the hero rhapsodizes, "Yes East and West, and North and South, the palm and the pine, the pole and the equator, the crescent and the cross — how the great Alchemist melts and fuses them with his purging flame! Here shall they all unite to build the Republic of Man and the Kingdom of God." The myth was perhaps most vividly dramatized, though, in a pageant staged by Henry Ford in the early 1920s. Decked out in the costumes of their native lands, Ford's immigrant workers sang traditional songs from their homelands as they danced their way into an enormous replica of a cast-iron pot. They then emerged from the other side wearing identical "American" business suits, waving miniature American flags, and singing "The Star-Spangled Banner."

The drama of becoming an American has deep roots: immigrants take on a new identity — and a new set of cultural myths — because they want to become members of the community, equal members with all the rights, responsibilities, and opportunities of their fellow citizens. The force of the melting pot myth lies in this implied promise that all Americans are indeed "created equal." However, the myth's promises of openness, harmony, unity, and equality were deceptive from the beginning. Crèvecoeur's exclusive concern with the mingling of *European* peoples (he lists the "English, Scotch, Irish, French, Dutch, Germans, and Swedes") utterly ignored the presence of some three-quarters of a million Africans and African Americans who then lived in this country, as well as the tribal peoples who had lived on the land for thousands of years before European contact. Crèvecoeur's vision of a country embracing "all nations" clearly applied only to northern European nations.

Benjamin Franklin, in a 1751 essay, was more blunt: since Africa, Asia, and most of America were inhabited by dark-skinned people, he argued, the American colonies should consciously try to increase the white population and keep out the rest. "Why increase the Sons of Africa, by Planting them in America, where we have so fair an opportunity, by excluding Blacks and Tawneys, of increasing the lovely White . . . ?" If later writers like Emerson and Zangwill saw a more inclusive cultural mix as a source of hope and renewal for the United States, others throughout this country's history have, even more than Franklin, feared that mix as a threat.

The fear of difference underlies another, equally powerful American myth — the myth of racial supremacy. This is the negative counterpart of the melting pot ideal: instead of the equal and harmonious blending of cultures, it proposes a racial and ethnic hierarchy based on the "natural superiority" of Anglo-Americans. Under the sway of this myth, differences become signs of inferiority, and "inferiors" are treated as childlike or even subhuman. This myth has given rise to some of the most shameful passages in our national life: slavery, segregation, and lynching; the near extermination of tribal peoples and cultures; the denial of citizenship and constitutional rights to African Americans, American Indians, Chinese and Japanese immigrants; the brutal exploitation of Mexican and Asian laborers. The catalog of injustices is long and painful. The melting pot ideal itself has often masked the myth of racial and ethnic superiority. "Inferiors" are expected to "melt" into conformity with Anglo-American behavior and values. Henry Ford's pageant conveys the message that ethnic identity is best left behind — exchanged for something "better," more uniform, less threatening.

This chapter explores the interaction between these two related cultural myths: the myth of unity and the myth of difference and hierarchy. It examines how the categories of race and ethnicity are defined and how they operate to divide us. These issues become crucial as the population of the United States grows increasingly diverse. The selections here challenge you to reconsider the fate of the melting pot myth as we enter the era of multi-ethnic, multicultural America. Can we learn to accept and honor our differences?

The first section of the chapter focuses on the problem of racism and racial conflict in American history. It opens with a selection by Thomas Jefferson that presents an unambiguous expression of the myth of racial superiority. Pondering the future of freed slaves, Jefferson concludes that because blacks "are inferior to whites in the endowments both of body and mind," they should be prevented from intermarrying and "staining the blood" of the superior race. The next passage, by Ronald Takaki, offers a thumbnail sketch of ethnic relations in American history — from the first encounter of the English and the Powhatan Indians to the crisis of identity we suffer as a nation in the "post–Rodney King era." The poems that follow, by Wendy Rose and Janice Mirikitani, affirm the vitality of America's minority cultures despite a history of exploitation and racist violence.

Next, a cluster of readings explores the origins of prejudice and the nature of discrimination. Vincent N. Parrillo outlines the most common sociological and psychological theories explaining the causes of prejudiced behavior. The account of C. P. Ellis's transformation from Ku Klux Klan member to union activist examines racism from the inside and raises questions about how, on a larger scale, we can combat the myth of racial superiority. Fred L. Pincus provides a framework for understanding the sometimes subtle ways that discrimination may be perpetuated by institutions and "neutral" social structures as well as by prejudiced individuals. In a personal essay, Leslie Marmon Silko argues passionately that U.S. immigration policy discriminates against people of color. And legal scholar Patricia J. Williams questions the role played by seemingly harmless forms of entertainment — such as jokes and television talk shows — in fostering stereotypes and prejudice.

The remainder of the chapter presents a range of opinion about how to heal our divisions and overcome our long history of conflict. Shelby Steele's "I'm Black, You're White, Who's Innocent?" proposes that African Americans take the initiative by ceasing to blame whites for the injustices of the past and by refusing to play the victim. Jane Lazarre takes the opposite approach in "Color Blind: The Whiteness of Whiteness," calling on white people to acknowledge and resist their "blindness to the dailiness of racism." The last four selections examine the emerging myth of the "new melting pot" of multicultural America. The growing multiracial population of the United States prompts Ellis Cose to ask, "Can a New Race Surmount Old Prejudices?" Ironically, the thing that Jefferson so feared — racial mixing — may offer a solution to the problems created by the myth of superiority that he embraced. Lynell George's essay, "Gray Boys, Funky Aztecs, and Honorary Homegirls," suggests that, even apart from genetic mixing, a new wave of cultural borrowing and blending is already under way. Gloria Anzaldúa's visionary essay calls for a new way of looking at the world: a *mestiza,* or mixed, consciousness that liberates us from outworn and dangerous myths of difference. The chapter ends with Aurora Levins Morales's "Child of the Americas," a poem that affirms both the value of cultural identity and the enduring power of the melting pot myth.

Sources

John Hope Franklin, *Race and History: Selected Essays,* 1938–1988. Baton Rouge: Louisiana State University Press, 1989, pp. 321–31.

Milton M. Gordon, *Assimilation in American Life: The Role of Race, Religion, and National Origins.* New York: Oxford University Press, 1964.

Itabari Njeri, "Beyond the Melting Pot." *Los Angeles Times,* January 13, 1991, pp. E1, E8–9.

Leonard Pitt, *We Americans,* vol. 2, 3rd ed. Dubuque: Kendall/Hunt, 1987.

Ronald Takaki, "Reflections on Racial Patterns in America." In *From Different Shores: Perspectives on Race and Ethnicity in America,* Ronald Takaki, ed. New York: Oxford University Press, 1987, pp. 26–37.

BEFORE READING

- Survey images in the popular media (newspapers, magazines, TV shows, movies, and pop music) for evidence of the myth of the melting pot. Do you find any figures in popular culture who seem to endorse the idea of a "new melting pot" in the United States? How closely do these images reflect your understanding of your own and other ethnic and racial groups? Explore these questions in a journal entry, then discuss in class.

- Alternatively, you might investigate the metaphors that are being used to describe racial and ethnic group relations or interactions between members of different groups on your campus and in your community.

  Consult local news sources and campus publications, and keep your ears open for conversations that touch on these issues. Do some freewriting about what you discover and compare notes with classmates.

- Take a close look at the frontispiece photo for this chapter (p. 528) and then freewrite for five to ten minutes about what you think the wall means to the people on each side. Compare responses in small groups: How much consistency do you find in your interpretations of what the wall represents?

From *Notes on the State of Virginia*

THOMAS JEFFERSON

As third president of the United States (1801–1809), Thomas Jefferson (1743–1826) promoted westward expansion in the form of the Louisiana Purchase and the Lewis and Clark Expedition. In addition to his political career he was a scientist, architect, city planner (Washington, D.C.), and founder of the University of Virginia. This passage from his Notes on the State of Virginia *(1785) reveals a very different and, for many readers, shocking side of Jefferson's character — that of a slave owner and defender of white supremacy. Here he proposes that the new state of Virginia gradually phase out slavery rather than abolish it outright. He also recommends that all newly emancipated slaves be sent out of the state to form separate colonies, in part to prevent racial conflict and in part to prevent intermarriage with whites. Jefferson was not the first and was far from the last politician to advocate solving the nation's racial problems by removing African Americans from its boundaries. In 1862, the Great Emancipator himself, Abraham Lincoln, called a delegation of black leaders to the White House to enlist their support in establishing a colony for African Americans in Central America. Congress had appropriated money for this project, but it was abandoned after the governments of Honduras, Nicaragua, and Costa Rica protested the plan.*

Many of the laws which were in force during the monarchy being relative merely to that form of government, or inculcating principles inconsistent with republicanism, the first assembly which met after the establishment of the commonwealth appointed a committee to revise the whole code, to reduce it into proper form and volume, and report it to the assembly. This work has been executed by three gentlemen,[1] and reported. . . . The following are the most remarkable alterations proposed:

To change the rules of descent, so as that the lands of any person dying intestate shall be divisible equally among all his children, or other representatives, in equal degree.

To make slaves distributable among the next of kin, as other movables. . . .

To emancipate all slaves born after the passing [of] the act. The bill reported by the revisers does not itself contain this proposition; but an amendment containing it was prepared, to be offered to the legislature whenever the bill should be taken up, and farther directing, that they should continue with their parents to a certain age, then to be brought up, at the public expense, to tillage, arts, or sciences, according to their geniuses, till the females should be eighteen, and the males twenty-one years of age, when they should be colonized to such place as the circumstances of the time should render most proper, sending them out with arms, implements of household and of the handicraft arts, seeds, pairs of the useful domestic animals, &c., to declare them a free and independent people, and extend to them our alliance and protection, till they have acquired strength; and to send vessels at the same time to other parts of the world for an equal number of white inhabitants; to induce them to migrate hither, proper encouragements were to be proposed. It will probably be asked, Why not retain and incorporate the blacks into the State, and thus save the expense of supplying by importation of white settlers, the vacancies they will leave?

[1]*executed by three gentlemen:* Jefferson was one of the three men who wrote this set of proposed revisions to the legal code of Virginia.

Deep-rooted prejudices entertained by the whites; ten thousand recollections, by the blacks, of the injuries they have sustained; new provocations; the real distinctions which nature has made; and many other circumstances, will divide us into parties, and produce convulsions, which will probably never end but in the extermination of the one or the other race. To these objections, which are political, may be added others, which are physical and moral. The first difference which strikes us is that of color. Whether the black of the negro resides in the reticular membrane between the skin and scarf-skin, or in the scarf-skin itself; whether it proceeds from the color of the blood, the color of the bile, or from that of some other secretion, the difference is fixed in nature, and is as real as if its seat and cause were better known to us. And is this difference of no importance? Is it not the foundation of a greater or less share of beauty in the two races? Are not the fine mixtures of red and white, the expressions of every passion by greater or less suffusions of color in the one, preferable to that eternal monotony, which reigns in the countenances, that immovable veil of black which covers the emotions of the other race? Add to these, flowing hair, a more elegant symmetry of form, their own judgment in favor of the whites, declared by their preference of them, as uniformly as is the preference of the Oranootan[2] for the black woman over those of his own species. The circumstance of superior beauty, is thought worthy of attention in the propagation of our horses, dogs, and other domestic animals; why not in that of man? Besides those of color, figure, and hair, there are other physical distinctions proving a difference of race. They have less hair on the face and body. They secrete less by the kidneys, and more by the glands of the skin, which gives them a very strong and disagreeable odor. This greater degree of transpiration, renders them more tolerant of heat, and less so of cold than the whites. Perhaps, too, a difference of structure in the pulminary apparatus, which a late ingenious experimentalist has discovered to be the principal regulator of animal heat, may have disabled them from extricating, in the act of inspiration, so much of that fluid from the outer air, or obliged them in expiration, to part with more of it. They seem to require less sleep. A black after hard labor through the day, will be induced by the slightest amusements to sit up till midnight, or later, though knowing he must be out with the first dawn of the morning. They are at least as brave, and more adventuresome. But this may perhaps proceed from a want of forethought, which prevents their seeing a danger till it be present. When present, they do not go through it with more coolness or steadiness than the whites. They are more ardent after their female; but love seems with them to be more an eager desire, than a tender delicate mixture of sentiment and sensation. Their griefs are transient. Those numberless afflictions, which render it doubtful whether heaven has given life to us in mercy or in wrath, are less felt, and sooner forgotten with them. In general, their existence appears to partici-

[2]*Oranootan:* Orangutan.

pate more of sensation than reflection. To this must be ascribed their dispo-sition to sleep when abstracted from their diversions, and unemployed in labor. An animal whose body is at rest, and who does not reflect, must be disposed to sleep of course. Comparing them by their faculties of memory, reason, and imagination, it appears to me that in memory they are equal to the whites; in reason much inferior, as I think one could scarcely be found capable of tracing and comprehending the investigations of Euclid; and that in imagination they are dull, tasteless, and anomalous. It would be unfair to follow them to Africa for this investigation. We will consider them here, on the same stage with the whites, and where the facts are not apochryphal on which a judgment is to be formed. It will be right to make great allowances for the difference of condition, of education, of conversation, of the sphere in which they move. Many millions of them have been brought to, and born in America. Most of them, indeed, have been confined to tillage, to their own homes, and their own society; yet many have been so situated, that they might have availed themselves of the conversation of their masters; many have been brought up to the handicraft arts, and from that circum-stance have always been associated with the whites. Some have been liber-ally educated, and all have lived in countries where the arts and sciences are cultivated to a considerable degree, and all have had before their eyes samples of the best works from abroad. The Indians, with no advantages of this kind, will often carve figures on their pipes not destitute of design and merit. They will crayon out an animal, a plant, or a country, so as to prove the existence of a germ in their minds which only wants cultivation. They astonish you with strokes of the most sublime oratory; such as prove their reason and sentiment strong, their imagination glowing and elevated. But never yet could I find that a black had uttered a thought above the level of plain narration; never saw even an elementary trait of painting or sculpture. In music they are more generally gifted than the whites with accurate ears for tune and time, and they have been found capable of imagining a small catch.[3] Whether they will be equal to the composition of a more extensive run of melody, or of complicated harmony, is yet to be proved. Misery is often the parent of the most affecting touches in poetry. Among the blacks is misery enough, God knows, but no poetry. Love is the peculiar œstrum of the poet. Their love is ardent, but it kindles the senses only, not the imagi-nation. Religion, indeed, has produced a Phyllis Whately [*sic*][4]; but it could not produce a poet. The compositions published under her name are below

[3]The instrument proper to them is the Banjar, which they brought hither from Africa, and which is the original of the guitar, its chords being precisely the four lower chords of the guitar. [Author's note]

[4]*Phyllis Whately:* Phillis Wheatley (175?–1784) was born in Africa but transported to the United States and sold as a slave when she was a young child. Her *Poems on Various Subjects, Religious and Moral* (1773) was the first book of poetry to be published by an African Ameri-can.

the dignity of criticism. The heroes of the Dunciad[5] are to her, as Hercules to the author of that poem. Ignatius Sancho[6] has approached nearer to merit in composition; yet his letters do more honor to the heart than the head. They breathe the purest effusions of friendship and general philanthropy, and show how great a degree of the latter may be compounded with strong religious zeal. He is often happy in the turn of his compliments, and his style is easy and familiar, except when he affects a Shandean[7] fabrication of words. But his imagination is wild and extravagant, escapes incessantly from every restraint of reason and taste, and, in the course of its vagaries, leaves a tract of thought as incoherent and eccentric, as is the course of a meteor through the sky. His subjects should often have led him to a process of sober reasoning; yet we find him always substituting sentiment for demonstration. Upon the whole, though we admit him to the first place among those of his own color who have presented themselves to the public judgment, yet when we compare him with the writers of the race among whom he lived and particularly with the epistolary class in which he has taken his own stand, we are compelled to enrol him at the bottom of the column. This criticism supposes the letters published under his name to be genuine, and to have received amendment from no other hand; points which would not be of easy investigation. The improvement of the blacks in body and mind, in the first instance of their mixture with the whites, has been observed by every one, and proves that their inferiority is not the effect merely of their condition of life. . . .

The opinion that they are inferior in the faculties of reason and imagi-   5
nation, must be hazarded with great diffidence. To justify a general conclusion, requires many observations, even where the subject may be submitted to the anatomical knife, to optical glasses, to analysis by fire or by solvents. How much more then where it is a faculty, not a substance, we are examining; where it eludes the research of all the senses; where the conditions of its existence are various and variously combined; where the effects of those which are present or absent bid defiance to calculation; let me add too, as a circumstance of great tenderness, where our conclusion would degrade a whole race of men from the rank in the scale of beings which their Creater may perhaps have given them. To our reproach it must be said, that though for a century and a half we have had under our eyes the races of black and of red men, they have never yet been viewed by us as subjects of natural

[5]*the heroes of the Dunciad:* In the mock epic poem *The Dunciad* (1728), English satirist Alexander Pope (1688–1744) lampoons his literary rivals as fools and dunces.

[6]*Ignatius Sancho:* Born on a slave ship, Ignatius Sancho (1729–1780) became a servant in the homes of several English aristocrats, where he educated himself and became acquainted with some of the leading writers and artists of the period. He later became a grocer in London and devoted himself to writing. His letters were collected and published in 1782.

[7]*Shandean:* In the style of Laurence Sterne's comic novel, *The Life and Opinions of Tristram Shandy* (1758–1766). Sancho admired Sterne's writing and corresponded regularly with him.

history. I advance it, therefore, as a suspicion only, that the blacks, whether originally a distinct race, or made distinct by time and circumstances, are inferior to the whites in the endowments both of body and mind. It is not against experience to suppose that different species of the same genus, or varieties of the same species, may possess different qualifications. Will not a lover of natural history then, one who views the gradations in all the races of animals with the eye of philosophy, excuse an effort to keep those in the department of man as distinct as nature has formed them? This unfortunate difference of color, and perhaps of faculty, is a powerful obstacle to the emancipation of these people. Many of their advocates, while they wish to vindicate the liberty of human nature, are anxious also to preserve its dignity and beauty. Some of these, embarrassed by the question, "What further is to be done with them?" join themselves in opposition with those who are actuated by sordid avarice only. Among the Romans emancipation required but one effort. The slave, when made free, might mix with, without staining the blood of his master. But with us a second is necessary, unknown to history. When freed, he is to be removed beyond the reach of mixture.

ENGAGING THE TEXT

1. Jefferson proposes colonizing — that is, sending away — all newly emancipated slaves and declaring them "a free and independent people" (para. 4). In what ways would their freedom and independence continue to be limited according to this proposal?

2. Jefferson predicts that racial conflict in the United States "will probably never end but in the extermination of the one or the other race" (para. 4). Which of the divisive issues he mentions, if any, are still sources of conflict today? Given the history of race relations from Jefferson's time to our own, do you think his pessimism was justified? Why or why not?

3. Jefferson presents what seems on the surface to be a systematic and logical catalog of the differences he sees between blacks and whites; he then attempts to demonstrate the "natural" superiority of whites based on these differences. Working in pairs or small groups, look carefully at his observations and the conclusions he draws from them. What flaws do you find in his analysis?

EXPLORING CONNECTIONS

4. Compare this passage by Jefferson to the most famous document he wrote, the Declaration of Independence (p. 684). How do their purposes differ? What ideas and principles, if any, do the two texts have in common, and where do they conflict?

5. Working in groups, write scripts for an imaginary meeting between Jefferson and Malcolm X (p. 219) and present them to the class. After each group has acted out its scenario, compare the different versions of the

meeting. What does each script assume about the motives and character of the two men?

EXTENDING THE CRITICAL CONTEXT

6. Write a journal entry or essay comparing the image of Jefferson you received in American history classes and the image you get from reading this passage. How do you account for the differences?
7. Write a letter to Jefferson responding to this selection and explaining your point of view. What would you tell him about how and why attitudes have changed between his time and ours?
8. Influenced by the heroic image of Jefferson as a champion of freedom and democracy, civic leaders have named libraries, schools, and other public institutions after him for the last two hundred years. Debate whether or not it is appropriate to honor Jefferson in this way given the opinions expressed in this passage.

A Different Mirror

RONALD TAKAKI

The myth of the melting pot was cultivated by generations of historians who portrayed the American story as the saga of a single people. During the past decade, however, scholars have begun to recognize that the distinct, and sometimes conflicting, experiences woven into the tapestry of American history cannot be told as a single narrative with a unified point of view. Ronald Takaki is one of America's foremost new historians. In this excerpt from A Different Mirror: A History of Multicultural America *(1993), Takaki challenges us to look at our history as a chorus of voices or a vast national anthology of stories. The grandson of Japanese immigrant plantation workers in Hawaii, Takaki (b. 1939) is a leading figure in the study of American race relations. His books include* From a Different Shore *(1989) and* Iron Cages: Race and Culture in Nineteenth-Century America *(1990). He currently teaches Asian American and ethnic studies at the University of California, Berkeley.*

I had flown from San Francisco to Norfolk and was riding in a taxi to my hotel to attend a conference on multiculturalism. Hundreds of educators from across the country were meeting to discuss the need for greater cultural diversity in the curriculum. My driver and I chatted about the weather and the tourists. The sky was cloudy, and Virginia Beach was twenty minutes away. The rearview mirror reflected a white man in his forties. "How long have you been in this country?" he asked. "All my life," I replied, wincing. "I was born in the United States." With a strong southern drawl, he remarked, "I was wondering because your English is excellent!" Then, as I had many times before, I explained: "My grandfather came here from Japan in the 1880s. My family has been here, in America, for over a hundred years." He glanced at me in the mirror. Somehow I did not look "American" to him; my eyes and complexion looked foreign.

Suddenly, we both became uncomfortably conscious of a racial divide separating us. An awkward silence turned my gaze from the mirror to the passing landscape, the shore where the English and the Powhatan Indians first encountered each other. Our highway was on land that Sir Walter Raleigh[1] had renamed "Virginia" in honor of Elizabeth I, the Virgin Queen. In the English cultural appropriation of America, the indigenous peoples themselves would become outsiders in their native land. Here, at the eastern edge of the continent, I mused, was the site of the beginning of multicultural America. Jamestown, the English settlement founded in 1607, was nearby: the first twenty Africans were brought here a year before the Pilgrims arrived at Plymouth Rock. Several hundred miles offshore was Bermuda, the "Bermoothes" where William Shakespeare's Prospero had landed and met the native Caliban in *The Tempest*. Earlier, another voyager had made an Atlantic crossing and unexpectedly bumped into some islands to the south. Thinking he had reached Asia, Christopher Columbus mistakenly identified one of the islands as "Cipango" (Japan). In the wake of the admiral, many peoples would come to America from different shores, not only from Europe but also Africa and Asia. One of them would be my grandfather. My mental wandering across terrain and time ended abruptly as we arrived at my destination. I said good-bye to my driver and went into the hotel, carrying a vivid reminder of why I was attending this conference.

Questions like the one my taxi driver asked me are always jarring, but I can understand why he could not see me as American. He had a narrow but widely shared sense of the past — a history that has viewed American as European in ancestry. "Race," Toni Morrison[2] explained, has functioned as a "metaphor" necessary to the "construction of Americanness": in the creation of our national identity, "American" has been defined as "white."[3]

But America has been racially diverse since our very beginning on the Virginia shore, and this reality is increasingly becoming visible and

[1]*Sir Walter Raleigh:* English explorer, statesman, courtier, historian, and poet (1554–1618).

[2]*Toni Morrison:* Nobel Prize–winning African American novelist (b. 1931).

[3]Toni Morrison, *Playing in the Dark: Whiteness in the Literary Imagination* (Cambridge: Harvard University Press, 1992), p. 47. [Author's note]

ubiquitous. Currently, one-third of the American people do not trace their origins to Europe; in California, minorities are fast becoming a majority. They already predominate in major cities across the country — New York, Chicago, Atlanta, Detroit, Philadelphia, San Francisco, and Los Angeles.

This emerging demographic diversity has raised fundamental questions   5
about America's identity and culture. In 1990, *Time* published a cover story on "America's Changing Colors." "Someday soon," the magazine announced, "white Americans will become a minority group." How soon? By 2056, most Americans will trace their descent to "Africa, Asia, the Hispanic world, the Pacific Islands, Arabia — almost anywhere but white Europe." This dramatic change in our nation's ethnic composition is altering the way we think about ourselves. "The deeper significance of America's becoming a majority non-white society is what it means to the national psyche, to individuals' sense of themselves and their nation — their idea of what it is to be American."[4]

Indeed, more than ever before, as we approach the time when whites become a minority, many of us are perplexed about our national identity and our future as one people. This uncertainty has provoked Allan Bloom to reaffirm the preeminence of Western civilization. Author of *The Closing of the American Mind,* he has emerged as a leader of an intellectual backlash against cultural diversity. In his view, students entering the university are "uncivilized," and the university has the responsibility to "civilize" them. Bloom claims he knows what their "hungers" are and "what they can di-gest." Eating is one of his favorite metaphors. Noting the "large black pres-ence" in major universities, he laments the "one failure" in race relations — black students have proven to be "indigestible." They do not "melt as have *all* other groups." The problem, he contends, is that "blacks have become blacks": they have become "ethnic." This separatism has been reinforced by an academic permissiveness that has befouled the curriculum with "Black Studies" along with "Learn Another Culture." The only solution, Bloom in-sists, is "the good old Great Books approach."[5]

Similarly, E. D. Hirsch[6] worries that America is becoming a "tower of Babel," and that this multiplicity of cultures is threatening to rend our social fabric. He, too, longs for a more cohesive culture and a more homogeneous America: "If we *had* to make a choice between the *one* and the *many,* most Americans would choose the principle of unity, since we cannot function as a nation without it." The way to correct this fragmentization, Hirsch argues, is to acculturate "disadvantaged children." What do they need to know? "Only by accumulating shared symbols, and the shared information that

[4]William A. Henry III, "Beyond the Melting Pot," in "America's Changing Colors," *Time,* vol. 135, no. 15 (April 9, 1990), pp. 28–31. [Author's note]

[5]Allan Bloom, *The Closing of the American Mind: How Higher Education Has Failed Democracy and Impoverished the Souls of Today's Students* (New York, 1987), pp. 19, 91–93, 340–41, 344. [Author's note]

[6]*E. D. Hirsch:* American literary and social critic (b. 1928).

symbols represent," Hirsch answers, "can we learn to communicate effectively with one another in our national community." Though he concedes the value of multicultural education, he quickly dismisses it by insisting that it "should not be allowed to supplant or interfere with our schools' responsibility to ensure our children's mastery of American literate culture." In *Cultural Literacy: What Every American Needs to Know,* Hirsch offers a long list of terms that excludes much of the history of minority groups.[7]

While Bloom and Hirsch are reacting defensively to what they regard as a vexatious balkanization of America, many other educators are responding to our diversity as an opportunity to open American minds. In 1990, the Task Force on Minorities for New York emphasized the importance of a culturally diverse education. "Essentially," the *New York Times* commented, "the issue is how to deal with both dimensions of the nation's motto: 'E pluribus unum' — 'Out of many, one.' " Universities from New Hampshire to Berkeley have established American cultural diversity graduation requirements. "Every student needs to know," explained University of Wisconsin's chancellor Donna Shalala,[8] "much more about the origins and history of the particular cultures which, as Americans, we will encounter during our lives." Even the University of Minnesota, located in a state that is 98 percent white, requires its students to take ethnic studies courses. Asked why multiculturalism is so important, Dean Fred Lukermann answered: As a national university, Minnesota has to offer a national curriculum — one that includes all of the peoples of America. He added that after graduation many students move to cities like Chicago and Los Angeles and thus need to know about racial diversity. Moreover, many educators stress, multiculturalism has an intellectual purpose. By allowing us to see events from the viewpoints of different groups, a multicultural curriculum enables us to reach toward a more comprehensive understanding of American history.[9]

What is fueling this debate over our national identity and the content of our curriculum is America's intensifying racial crisis. The alarming signs and symptoms seem to be everywhere — the killing of Vincent Chin[10] in Detroit, the black boycott of a Korean grocery store in Flatbush,[11] the hysteria in Boston over the Carol Stuart murder,[12] the battle between white

[7]E. D. Hirsch, Jr., *Cultural Literacy: What Every American Needs to Know* (Boston, 1987), pp. xiii, xvii, 2, 18, 96. See also "The List," pp. 152–215. [Author's note]

[8]*Donna Shalala:* Appointed Secretary of Housing, Economy, and Welfare in 1993 (b. 1941).

[9]Edward Fiske, "Lessons," *New York Times,* February 7, 1990; "University of Wisconsin–Madison: The Madison Plan," February 9, 1988; interview with Dean Fred Lukermann, University of Minnesota, 1987. [Author's note]

[10]*Vincent Chin:* Chinese American killed by whites angered by competition from the Japanese auto industry during the 1980s.

[11]*Flatbush:* A predominantly African American area of New York.

[12]*Carol Stuart murder:* In this 1989 case, Stuart (a white woman) was murdered by her husband, who then convinced Boston police and the media that she had been killed by a Black assailant.

sportsmen and Indians over tribal fishing rights in Wisconsin, the Jewish-black clashes in Brooklyn's Crown Heights, the black-Hispanic competition for jobs and educational resources in Dallas, which *Newsweek* described as "a conflict of the have-nots," and the Willie Horton campaign commercials,[13] which widened the divide between the suburbs and the inner cities.[14]

This reality of racial tension rudely woke America like a fire bell in the   10
night on April 29, 1992. Immediately after four Los Angeles police officers were found not guilty of brutality against Rodney King,[15] rage exploded in Los Angeles. Race relations reached a new nadir. During the nightmarish rampage, scores of people were killed, over two thousand injured, twelve thousand arrested, and almost a billion dollars' worth of property destroyed. The live televised images mesmerized America. The rioting and the murderous melee on the streets resembled the fighting in Beirut and the West Bank. The thousands of fires burning out of control and the dark smoke filling the skies brought back images of the burning oil fields of Kuwait during Desert Storm. Entire sections of Los Angeles looked like a bombed city. "Is this America?" many shocked viewers asked. "Please, can we get along here," pleaded Rodney King, calling for calm. "We all can get along. I mean, we're all stuck here for a while. Let's try to work it out."[16]

But how should "we" be defined? Who are the people "stuck here" in America? One of the lessons of the Los Angeles explosion is the recognition of the fact that we are a multiracial society and that race can no longer be defined in the binary terms of white and black. "We" will have to include Hispanics and Asians. While blacks currently constitute 13 percent of the Los Angeles population, Hispanics represent 40 percent. The 1990 census revealed that South Central Los Angeles, which was predominantly black in 1965 when the Watts rebellion occurred, is now 45 percent Hispanic. A majority of the first 5,438 people arrested were Hispanic, while 37 percent were black. Of the fifty-eight people who died in the riot, more than a third were Hispanic, and about 40 percent of the businesses destroyed were Hispanic-owned. Most of the other shops and stores were Korean-owned. The dreams of many Korean immigrants went up in smoke during the riot: two thousand Korean-owned businesses were damaged or demolished, totaling about $400 million in losses. There is evidence indicating they were targeted. "After all," explained a black gang member, "we didn't burn our community, just *their* stores."[17]

[13]*Willie Horton campaign commercials:* Commercials supporting former President George Bush's 1988 election, widely criticized for playing on racist fears.

[14]"A Conflict of the Have-Nots," *Newsweek*, December 12, 1988, pp. 28–29. [Author's note]

[15]*Rodney King*: African American motorist severely beaten by four white Los Angeles police officers whose subsequent acquittal sparked the 1992 L.A. uprising.

[16]Rodney King's statement to the press, *New York Times*, May 2, 1992, p. 6. [Author's note]

[17]Tim Rutten, "A New Kind of Riot," *New York Review of Books*, June 11, 1992, pp. 52–53; Maria Newman, "Riots Bring Attention to Growing Hispanic Presence in South-Central Area," *New York Times*, May 11, 1992, p. A10; Mike Davis, "In L.A. Burning All Illusions," *The Nation*, June 1, 1992, pp. 744–745; Jack Viets and Peter Fimrite, "S.F. Mayor Visits Riot-Torn Area to Buoy Businesses," *San Francisco Chronicle*, May 6, 1992, p. A6. [Author's note]

"I don't feel like I'm in America anymore," said Denisse Bustamente as she watched the police protecting the firefighters. "I feel like I am far away." Indeed, Americans have been witnessing ethnic strife erupting around the world — the rise of neo-Nazism and the murder of Turks in Germany, the ugly "ethnic cleansing" in Bosnia, the terrible and bloody clashes between Muslims and Hindus in India. Is the situation here different, we have been nervously wondering, or do ethnic conflicts elsewhere represent a prologue for America? What is the nature of malevolence? Is there a deep, perhaps primordial, need for group identity rooted in hatred for the other? Is ethnic pluralism possible for America? But answers have been limited. Television reports have been little more than thirty-second sound bites. Newspaper articles have been mostly superficial descriptions of racial antagonisms and the current urban malaise. What is lacking is historical context; consequently, we are left feeling bewildered.[18]

How did we get to this point, Americans everywhere are anxiously asking. What does our diversity mean, and where is it leading us? *How* do we work it out in the post–Rodney King era?

Certainly one crucial way is for our society's various ethnic groups to develop a greater understanding of each other. For example, how can African Americans and Korean Americans work it out unless they learn about each other's cultures, histories, and also economic situations? This need to share knowledge about our ethnic diversity has acquired new importance and has given new urgency to the pursuit for a more accurate history.

More than ever before, there is a growing realization that the established scholarship has tended to define America too narrowly. For example, in his prize-winning study *The Uprooted,* Harvard historian Oscar Handlin presented — to use the book's subtitle — "the Epic Story of the Great Migrations That Made the American People." But Handlin's "epic story" excluded the "uprooted" from Africa, Asia, and Latin America — the other "Great Migrations" that also helped to make "the American People." Similarly, in *The Age of Jackson,* Arthur M. Schlesinger, Jr., left out blacks and Indians. There is not even a mention of two marker events — the Nat Turner[19] insurrection and Indian removal,[20] which Andrew Jackson[21] himself would have been surprised to find omitted from a history of his era.[22]

15

Still, Schlesinger and Handlin offered us a refreshing revisionism, paving the way for the study of common people rather than princes and presidents. They inspired the next generation of historians to examine groups such as the artisan laborers of Philadelphia and the Irish immigrants

[18]Rick DelVecchio, Suzanne Espinosa, and Carl Nolte, "Bradley Ready to Lift Curfew," *San Francisco Chronicle,* May 4, 1992, p. A1. [Author's note]

[19]*Nat Turner:* African American slave and leader of a slave revolt (1800–1831).

[20]*Indian removal:* Nineteenth-century U.S. government policy that forced American Indian peoples onto reservations from their native lands.

[21]*Andrew Jackson:* Seventh president of the United States (1767–1845).

[22]Oscar Handlin, *The Uprooted: The Epic Story of the Great Migrations That Made the American People* (New York, 1951); Arthur M. Schlesinger, Jr., *The Age of Jackson* (Boston, 1945). [Author's note]

of Boston. "Once I thought to write a history of the immigrants in America," Handlin confided in his introduction to *The Uprooted*. "I discovered that the immigrants *were* American history." This door, once opened, led to the flowering of a more inclusive scholarship as we began to recognize that ethnic history was American history. Suddenly, there was a proliferation of seminal works such as Irving Howe's *World of Our Fathers: The Journey of the East European Jews to America*, Dee Brown's *Bury My Heart at Wounded Knee: An Indian History of the American West*, Albert Camarillo's *Chicanos in a Changing Society*, Lawrence Levine's *Black Culture and Black Consciousness*, Yuji Ichioka's *The Issei: The World of the First Generation Japanese Immigrants*, and Kerby Miller's *Emigrants and Exiles: Ireland and the Irish Exodus to North America*.[23]

But even this new scholarship, while it has given us a more expanded understanding of the mosaic called America, does not address our needs in the post–Rodney King era. These books and others like them fragment American society, studying each group separately, in isolation from the other groups and the whole. While scrutinizing our specific pieces, we have to step back in order to see the rich and complex portrait they compose. What is needed is a fresh angle, a study of the American past from a comparative perspective.

While all of America's many groups cannot be covered in one book, the English immigrants and their descendants require attention, for they possessed inordinate power to define American culture and make public policy. What men like John Winthrop,[24] Thomas Jefferson, and Andrew Jackson thought as well as did mattered greatly to all of us and was consequential for everyone. A broad range of groups has been selected: African Americans, Asian Americans, Chicanos, Irish, Jews, and Indians. While together they help to explain general patterns in our society, each has contributed to the making of the United States.

African Americans have been the central minority throughout our country's history. They were initially brought here on a slave ship in 1619. Actually, these first twenty Africans might not have been slaves; rather, like most of the white laborers, they were probably indentured servants.[25] The transformation of Africans into slaves is the story of the "hidden" origins of

[23]Handlin, *The Uprooted*, p. 3; Irving Howe, *World of Our Fathers: The Journey of the East European Jews to America and the Life They Found and Made* (New York, 1983); Dee Brown, *Bury My Heart at Wounded Knee: An Indian History of the American West* (New York, 1970); Albert Camarillo, *Chicanos in a Changing Society: From Mexican Pueblos to American Barrios in Santa Barbara and Southern California, 1848–1930* (Cambridge, Mass., 1979); Lawrence W. Levine, *Black Culture and Black Consciousness: Afro-American Folk Thought from Slavery to Freedom* (New York, 1977); Yuji Ichioka, *The Issei: The World of the First Generation Japanese Immigrants* (New York, 1988); Kerby A. Miller, *Emigrants and Exiles: Ireland and the Irish Exodus to North America* (New York, 1985). [Author's note]

[24]*John Winthrop:* First governor of the Massachusetts Bay Colony (1588–1649).

[25]*indentured servants:* Servants who had sold their labor and were bound to a household for a specified period of time.

slavery. How and when was it decided to institute a system of bonded black labor? What happened, while freighted with racial significance, was actually conditioned by class conflicts within white society. Once established, the "peculiar institution" would have consequences for centuries to come. During the nineteenth century, the political storm over slavery almost destroyed the nation. Since the Civil War and emancipation, race has continued to be largely defined in relation to African Americans — segregation, civil rights, the underclass, and affirmative action. Constituting the largest minority group in our society, they have been at the cutting edge of the Civil Rights Movement. Indeed, their struggle has been a constant reminder of America's moral vision as a country committed to the principle of liberty. Martin Luther King clearly understood this truth when he wrote from a jail cell: "We will reach the goal of freedom in Birmingham and all over the nation, because the goal of America is freedom. Abused and scorned though we may be, our destiny is tied up with America's destiny."[26]

Asian Americans have been here for over one hundred and fifty years, before many European immigrant groups. But as "strangers" coming from a "different shore," they have been stereotyped as "heathen," exotic, and unassimilable. Seeking "Gold Mountain," the Chinese arrived first, and what happened to them influenced the reception of the Japanese, Koreans, Filipinos, and Asian Indians as well as the Southeast Asian refugees like the Vietnamese and the Hmong. The 1882 Chinese Exclusion Act was the first law that prohibited the entry of immigrants on the basis of nationality. The Chinese condemned this restriction as racist and tyrannical. "They call us 'Chink,'" complained a Chinese immigrant, cursing the "white demons." "They think we no good! America cuts us off. No more come now, too bad!" This precedent later provided a basis for the restriction of European immigrant groups such as Italians, Russians, Poles, and Greeks. The Japanese painfully discovered that their accomplishments in America did not lead to acceptance, for during World War II, unlike Italian Americans and German Americans, they were placed in internment camps. Two-thirds of them were citizens by birth. "How could I as a six-month-old child born in this country," asked Congressman Robert Matsui years later, "be declared by my own Government to be an enemy alien?" Today, Asian Americans represent the fastest-growing ethnic group. They have also become the focus of much mass media attention as "the Model Minority" not only for blacks and Chicanos, but also for whites on welfare and even middle-class whites experiencing economic difficulties.[27]

20

[26]Abraham Lincoln, "The Gettysburg Address," in *The Annals of America*, vol. 9, *1863–1865: The Crisis of the Union* (Chicago, 1968), pp. 462–63; Martin Luther King, *Why We Can't Wait* (New York, 1964), pp. 92–93. [Author's note]

[27]Interview with old laundryman, in "Interviews with Two Chinese," circa 1924, Box 326, folder 325, Survey of Race Relations, Stanford University, Hoover Institution Archives; Congressman Robert Matsui, speech in the House of Representatives on the 442 bill for redress and reparations, September 17, 1987, *Congressional Record* (Washington, D.C.: GPO, 1987), p. 7584. [Author's note]

Chicanos represent the largest group among the Hispanic population, which is projected to outnumber African Americans. They have been in the United States for a long time, initially incorporated by the war against Mexico. The treaty had moved the border between the two countries, and the people of "occupied" Mexico suddenly found themselves "foreigners" in their "native land." As historian Albert Camarillo pointed out, the Chicano past is an integral part of America's westward expansion, also known as "manifest destiny."[28] But while the early Chicanos were a colonized people, most of them today have immigrant roots. Many began the trek to El Norte[29] in the early twentieth century. "As I had heard a lot about the United States," Jesus Garza recalled, "it was my dream to come here." "We came to know families from Chihuahua, Sonora, Jalisco, and Durango," stated Ernesto Galarza. "Like ourselves, our Mexican neighbors had come this far moving step by step, working and waiting, as if they were feeling their way up a ladder." Nevertheless, the Chicano experience has been unique, for most of them have lived close to their homeland — a proximity that has helped reinforce their language, identity, and culture. This migration to El Norte has continued to the present. Los Angeles has more people of Mexican origin than any other city in the world, except Mexico City. A mostly mestizo[30] people of Indian as well as African and Spanish ancestries, Chicanos currently represent the largest minority group in the Southwest, where they have been visibly transforming culture and society.[31]

The Irish came here in greater numbers than most immigrant groups. Their history has been tied to America's past from the very beginning. Ireland represented the earliest English frontier: the conquest of Ireland occurred before the colonization of America, and the Irish were the first group that the English called "savages." In this context, the Irish past foreshadowed the Indian future. During the nineteenth century, the Irish, like the Chinese, were victims of British colonialism. While the Chinese fled from the ravages of the Opium Wars, the Irish were pushed from their homeland by "English tyranny." Here they became construction workers and factory operatives as well as the "maids" of America. Representing a Catholic group seeking to settle in a fiercely Protestant society, the Irish immigrants were targets of American nativist hostility. They were also what historian Lawrence J. McCaffrey called "the pioneers of the American urban ghetto," "previewing" experiences that would later be shared by the

---

[28]*manifest destiny:* Popular nineteenth-century belief that the United States was "destined" to rule the land west of the Mississippi.

[29]*El Norte:* The North (the United States and Canada).

[30]*mestizo:* Mixed race.

[31]Camarillo, *Chicanos in a Changing Society,* p. 2; Juan Nepomuceno Seguín, in David J. Weber (ed.), *Foreigners in Their Native Land: Historical Roots of the Mexican Americans* (Albuquerque, N. Mex., 1973), p. vi; Jesus Garza, in Manuel Gamio, *The Mexican Immigrant: His Life Story* (Chicago, 1931), p. 15; Ernesto Galarza, *Barrio Boy: The Story of a Boy's Acculturation* (Notre Dame, Ind., 1986), p. 200. [Author's note]

Italians, Poles, and other groups from southern and eastern Europe. Furthermore, they offer contrast to the immigrants from Asia. The Irish came about the same time as the Chinese, but they had a distinct advantage: the Naturalization Law of 1790 had reserved citizenship for "whites" only. Their compatible complexion allowed them to assimilate by blending into American society. In making their journey successfully into the mainstream, however, these immigrants from Erin pursued an Irish "ethnic" strategy: they promoted "Irish" solidarity in order to gain political power and also to dominate the skilled blue-collar occupations, often at the expense of the Chinese and blacks.[32]

Fleeing pogroms[33] and religious persecution in Russia, the Jews were driven from what John Cuddihy[34] described as the "Middle Ages into the Anglo-American world of the *goyim*[35] 'beyond the pale.' " To them, America represented the Promised Land. This vision led Jews to struggle not only for themselves but also for other oppressed groups, especially blacks. After the 1917 East St. Louis race riot, the Yiddish *Forward* of New York compared this anti-black violence to a 1903 pogrom in Russia: "Kishinev and St. Louis — the same soil, the same people." Jews cheered when Jackie Robinson broke into the Brooklyn Dodgers in 1947. "He was adopted as the surrogate hero by many of us growing up at the time," recalled Jack Greenberg of the NAACP Legal Defense Fund. "He was the way we saw ourselves triumphing against the forces of bigotry and ignorance." Jews stood shoulder to shoulder with blacks in the Civil Rights Movement: two-thirds of the white volunteers who went south during the 1964 Freedom Summer were Jewish. Today Jews are considered a highly successful "ethnic" group. How did they make such great socioeconomic strides? This question is often reframed by neoconservative intellectuals like Irving Kristol and Nathan Glazer to read: if Jewish immigrants were able to lift themselves from poverty into the mainstream through self-help and education without welfare and affirmative action, why can't blacks? But what this thinking overlooks is the unique history of Jewish immigrants, especially the initial advantages of many of them as literate and skilled. Moreover, it minimizes the virulence of racial prejudice rooted in American slavery.[36]

Indians represent a critical contrast, for theirs was not an immigrant experience. The Wampanoags were on the shore as the first English

---

[32]Lawrence J. McCaffrey, *The Irish Diaspora in America* (Washington, D.C., 1984), pp. 6, 62. [Author's note]

[33]*pogroms:* Organized attacks in which Jews were terrorized and killed and their property stolen or destroyed.

[34]*John Cuddihy:* American sociologist.

[35]*goyim:* Gentiles.

[36]John Murray Cuddihy, *The Ordeal of Civility: Freud, Marx, Levi Strauss, and the Jewish Struggle with Modernity* (Boston, 1987), p. 165; Jonathan Kaufman, *Broken Alliance: The Turbulent Times between Blacks and Jews in America* (New York, 1989), pp. 28, 82, 83–84, 91, 93, 106. [Author's note]

strangers arrived in what would be called "New England." The encounters between Indians and whites not only shaped the course of race relations, but also influenced the very culture and identity of the general society. The architect of Indian removal, President Andrew Jackson told Congress: "Our conduct toward these people is deeply interesting to the national character." Frederick Jackson Turner[37] understood the meaning of this observation when he identified the frontier as our transforming crucible. At first, the European newcomers had to wear Indian moccasins and shout the war cry. "Little by little," as they subdued the wilderness, the pioneers became "a new product" that was "American." But Indians have had a different view of this entire process. "The white man," Luther Standing Bear of the Sioux explained, "does not understand the Indian for the reason that he does not understand America." Continuing to be "troubled with primitive fears," he has "in his consciousness the perils of this frontier continent. . . . The man from Europe is still a foreigner and an alien. And he still hates the man who questioned his path across the continent." Indians questioned what Jackson and Turner trumpeted as "progress." For them, the frontier had a different "significance": their history was how the West was lost. But their story has also been one of resistance. As Vine Deloria[38] declared, "Custer died for your sins."[39]

By looking at these groups from a multicultural perspective, we can   25
comparatively analyze their experiences in order to develop an understanding of their differences and similarities. Race, we will see, has been a social construction that has historically set apart racial minorities from European immigrant groups. Contrary to the notions of scholars like Nathan Glazer and Thomas Sowell,[40] race in America has not been the same as ethnicity. A broad comparative focus also allows us to see how the varied experiences of different racial and ethnic groups occurred within shared contexts.

During the nineteenth century, for example, the Market Revolution employed Irish immigrant laborers in New England factories as it expanded cotton fields worked by enslaved blacks across Indian lands toward Mexico. Like blacks, the Irish newcomers were stereotyped as "savages," ruled by passions rather than "civilized" virtues such as self-control and hard work.

[37]*Frederick Jackson Turner:* American historian (1861–1932).

[38]*Vine Deloria:* American Indian historian, writer, and activist (b. 1933); author of the influential *Custer Died for Your Sins* (1969).

[39]Andrew Jackson, First Annual Message to Congress, December 8, 1929, in James D. Richardson (ed.), *A Compilation of the Messages and Papers of the Presidents, 1789–1897* (Washington, D.C., 1897), vol. 2, p. 457; Frederick Jackson Turner, "The Significance of the Frontier in American History," in *The Early Writings of Frederick Jackson Turner* (Madison, Wis., 1938), pp. 185ff.; Luther Standing Bear, "What the Indian Means to America," in Wayne Moquin (ed.), *Great Documents in American Indian History* (New York, 1973), p. 307; Vine Deloria, Jr., *Custer Died for Your Sins: An Indian Manifesto* (New York, 1969). [Author's note]

[40]*Nathan Glazer and Thomas Sowell:* Conservative U.S. sociologists (b. 1923 and 1930, respectively).

The Irish saw themselves as the "slaves" of British oppressors, and during a visit to Ireland in the 1840s, Frederick Douglass found that the "wailing notes" of the Irish ballads reminded him of the "wild notes" of slave songs. The United States annexation of California, while incorporating Mexicans, led to trade with Asia and the migration of "strangers" from Pacific shores. In 1870, Chinese immigrant laborers were transported to Massachusetts as scabs to break an Irish immigrant strike; in response, the Irish recognized the need for interethnic working-class solidarity and tried to organize a Chinese lodge of the Knights of St. Crispin. After the Civil War, Mississippi planters recruited Chinese immigrants to discipline the newly freed blacks. During the debate over an immigration exclusion bill in 1882, a senator asked: If Indians could be located on reservations, why not the Chinese?[41]

Other instances of our connectedness abound. In 1903, Mexican and Japanese farm laborers went on strike together in California: their union officers had names like Yamaguchi and Lizarras, and strike meetings were conducted in Japanese and Spanish. The Mexican strikers declared that they were standing in solidarity with their "Japanese brothers" because the two groups had toiled together in the fields and were now fighting together for a fair wage. Speaking in impassioned Yiddish during the 1909 "uprising of twenty thousand" strikers in New York, the charismatic Clara Lemlich compared the abuse of Jewish female garment workers to the experience of blacks: "[The bosses] yell at the girls and 'call them down' even worse than I imagine the Negro slaves were in the South." During the 1920s, elite universities like Harvard worried about the increasing number of Jewish students, and new admissions criteria were instituted to curb their enrollment. Jewish students were scorned for their studiousness and criticized for their "clannishness." Recently, Asian-American students have been the targets of similar complaints: they have been called "nerds" and told there are "too many" of them on campus.[42]

Indians were already here, while blacks were forcibly transported to America, and Mexicans were initially enclosed by America's expanding border. The other groups came here as immigrants: for them, America represented liminality — a new world where they could pursue extravagant urges and do things they had thought beyond their capabilities. Like the land itself, they found themselves "betwixt and between all fixed points of

---

[41]Nathan Glazer, *Affirmative Discrimination: Ethnic Inequality and Public Policy* (New York, 1978); Thomas Sowell, *Ethnic America: A History* (New York, 1981); David R. Roediger, *The Wages of Whiteness: Race and the Making of the American Working Class* (London, 1991), pp. 134–36; Dan Caldwell, "The Negroization of the Chinese Stereotype in California," *Southern California Quarterly*, vol. 33 (June 1971), pp. 123–31. [Author's note]

[42]Tomas Almaguer, "Racial Domination and Class Conflict in Capitalist Agriculture: The Oxnard Sugar Beet Workers' Strike of 1903," *Labor History*, vol. 25, no. 3 (Summer 1984), p. 347; Howard M. Sachar, *A History of the Jews in America* (New York, 1992), p. 183. [Author's note]

classification." No longer fastened as fiercely to their old countries, they felt a stirring to become new people in a society still being defined and formed.[43]

These immigrants made bold and dangerous crossings, pushed by political events and economic hardships in their homelands and pulled by America's demand for labor as well as by their own dreams for a better life. "By all means let me go to America," a young man in Japan begged his parents. He had calculated that in one year as a laborer here he could save almost a thousand yen — an amount equal to the income of a governor in Japan. "My dear Father," wrote an immigrant Irish girl living in New York, "Any man or woman without a family are fools that would not venture and come to this plentyful Country where no man or woman ever hungered." In the shtetls[44] of Russia, the cry "To America!" roared like "wild-fire." "America was in everybody's mouth," a Jewish immigrant recalled. "Businessmen talked [about] it over their accounts; the market women made up their quarrels that they might discuss it from stall to stall; people who had relatives in the famous land went around reading their letters." Similarly, for Mexican immigrants crossing the border in the early twentieth century, El Norte became the stuff of overblown hopes. "If only you could see how nice the United States is," they said, "that is why the Mexicans are crazy about it."[45]

The signs of America's ethnic diversity can be discerned across the continent — Ellis Island, Angel Island,[46] Chinatown, Harlem, South Boston, the Lower East Side, places with Spanish names like Los Angeles and San Antonio or Indian names like Massachusetts and Iowa. Much of what is familiar in America's cultural landscape actually has ethnic origins. The Bing cherry was developed by an early Chinese immigrant named Ah Bing. American Indians were cultivating corn, tomatoes, and tobacco long before the arrival of Columbus. The term *okay* was derived from the Choctaw word *oke*, meaning "it is so." There is evidence indicating that the name *Yankee* came from Indian terms for the English — from *eankke* in Cherokee and *Yankwis* in Delaware. Jazz and blues as well as rock and roll have African American origins. The "Forty-Niners" of the Gold Rush learned mining techniques from the Mexicans; American cowboys acquired herding skills from Mexican *vaqueros* and adopted their range terms — such as *lar-*

30

---

[43]For the concept of liminality, see Victor Turner, *Dramas, Fields, and Metaphors: Symbolic Action in Human Society* (Ithaca, N.Y., 1974), pp. 232, 237; and Arnold Van Gennep, *The Rites of Passage* (Chicago, 1960). What I try to do is to apply liminality to the land called America. [Author's note]

[44]*shtetls:* Villages.

[45]Kazuo Ito, *Issei: A History of Japanese Immigrants in North America* (Seattle, 1973), p. 33; Arnold Schrier, *Ireland and the American Emigration, 1850–1900* (New York, 1970), p. 24; Abraham Cahan, *The Rise of David Levinsky* (New York, 1960; originally published in 1917), pp. 59–61; Mary Antin, quoted in Howe, *World of Our Fathers,* p. 27; Lawrence A. Cardoso, *Mexican Emigration to the United States, 1897–1931* (Tucson, Ariz., 1981), p. 80. [Author's note]

[46]*Ellis Island, Angel Island:* Ports of entry for immigrants on the East and West Coasts.

iat from *la reata, lasso* from *lazo,* and *stampede* from *estampida.* Songs like "God Bless America," "Easter Parade," and "White Christmas" were written by a Russian-Jewish immigrant named Israel Baline, more popularly known as Irving Berlin.[47]

Furthermore, many diverse ethnic groups have contributed to the building of the American economy, forming what Walt Whitman[48] saluted as "a vast, surging, hopeful army of workers." They worked in the South's cotton fields, New England's textile mills, Hawaii's canefields, New York's garment factories, California's orchards, Washington's salmon canneries, and Arizona's copper mines. They built the railroad, the great symbol of America's industrial triumph. Laying railroad ties, black laborers sang:

> Down the railroad, um-huh
> Well, raise the iron, um-huh
> Raise the iron, um-huh.

Irish railroad workers shouted as they stretched an iron ribbon across the continent:

> Then drill, my Paddies, drill —
> Drill, my heroes, drill,
> Drill all day, no sugar in your tay
> Workin' on the U.P. railway.

Japanese laborers in the Northwest chorused as their bodies fought the fickle weather:

> A railroad worker —
> That's me!
> I am great.
> Yes, I am a railroad worker.
> Complaining:
> "It is too hot!"
> "It is too cold!"
> "It rains too often!"
> "It snows too much!"
> They all ran off.
> I alone remained.
> I am a railroad worker!

Chicano workers in the Southwest joined in as they swore at the punishing work:

[47]Ronald Takaki, *Strangers from a Different Shore: A History of Asian Americans* (Boston, 1989), pp. 88–89; Jack Weatherford, *Native Roots: How the Indians Enriched America* (New York, 1991), pp. 210, 212; Carey McWilliams, *North from Mexico: The Spanish-Speaking People of the United States* (New York, 1968), p. 154; Stephan Thernstrom (ed.), *Harvard Encyclopedia of American Ethnic Groups* (Cambridge, Mass., 1980), p. 22; Sachar, *A History of the Jews in America,* p. 367. [Author's note]

[48]*Walt Whitman:* American poet (1819–1892).

Some unloaded rails
Others unloaded ties,
And others of my companions
Threw out thousands of curses.[49]

Moreover, our diversity was tied to America's most serious crisis: the Civil War was fought over a racial issue — slavery. In his "First Inaugural Address," presented on March 4, 1861, President Abraham Lincoln declared: "One section of our country believes slavery is *right* and ought to be extended, while the other believes it is *wrong* and ought not to be extended." Southern secession, he argued, would be anarchy. Lincoln sternly warned the South that he had a solemn oath to defend and preserve the Union. Americans were one people, he explained, bound together by "the mystic chords of memory, stretching from every battlefield and patriot grave to every living heart and hearthstone all over this broad land." The struggle and sacrifices of the War for Independence had enabled Americans to create a new nation out of thirteen separate colonies. But Lincoln's appeal for unity fell on deaf ears in the South. And the war came. Two and a half years later, at Gettysburg, President Lincoln declared that "brave men" had fought and "consecrated" the ground of this battlefield in order to preserve the Union. Among the brave were black men. Shortly after this bloody battle, Lincoln acknowledged the military contribution of blacks. "There will be some black men," he wrote in a letter to an old friend, James C. Conkling, "who can remember that with silent tongue, and clenched teeth, and steady eye, and well-poised bayonet, they have helped mankind on to this great consummation. . . ." Indeed, 186,000 blacks served in the Union Army, and one-third of them were listed as missing or dead. Black men in blue, Frederick Douglass[50] pointed out, were "on the battlefield mingling their blood with that of white men in one common effort to save the country." Now the mystic chords of memory stretched across the new battlefields of the Civil War, and black soldiers were buried in "patriot graves." They, too, had given their lives to ensure that the "government of the people, by the people, for the people shall not perish from the earth."[51]

---

[49]Walt Whitman, *Leaves of Grass* (New York, 1958), p. 284; Mathilde Bunton, "Negro Work Songs" (1940), 1 typescript in Box 91 ("Music"), Illinois Writers Project, U.S.W.P.A., in James R. Grossman, *Land of Hope: Chicago, Black Southerners, and the Great Migration* (Chicago, 1989), p. 192; Carl Wittke, *The Irish in America* (Baton Rouge, La., 1956), p. 39; Ito, *Issei*, p. 343; Manuel Gamio, *Mexican Immigration to the United States* (Chicago, 1930), pp. 84–85. [Author's note]

[50]*Frederick Douglass:* Former slave, abolitionist, orator, and writer (1817?–1895).

[51]Abraham Lincoln, "First Inaugural Address," in *The Annals of America*, vol. 9, *1863–1865: The Crisis of the Union* (Chicago, 1968), p. 255; Lincoln, "The Gettysburg Address," pp. 462–63; Abraham Lincoln, letter to James C. Conkling, August 26, 1863, in *Annals of America*, p. 439; Frederick Douglass, in Herbert Aptheker (ed.), *A Documentary History of the Negro People in the United States* (New York, 1951), vol. 1, p. 496. [Author's note]

Like these black soldiers, the people in our study have been actors in history, not merely victims of discrimination and exploitation. They are entitled to be viewed as subjects — as men and women with minds, wills, and voices.

In the telling and retelling
    of their stories,
They create communities
    of memory.

They also re-vision history. "It is very natural that the history written by the victim," said a Mexican in 1874, "does not altogether chime with the story of the victor." Sometimes they are hesitant to speak, thinking they are only "little people." "I don't know why anybody wants to hear my history," an Irish maid said apologetically in 1900. "Nothing ever happened to me worth the tellin'."[52]

But their stories are worthy. Through their stories, the people who have lived America's history can help all of us, including my taxi driver, understand that Americans originated from many shores, and that all of us are entitled to dignity. "I hope this survey do a lot of good for Chinese people," an immigrant told an interviewer from Stanford University in the 1920s. "Make American people realize that Chinese people are humans. I think very few American people really know anything about Chinese." But the remembering is also for the sake of the children. "This story is dedicated to the descendents of Lazar and Goldie Glauberman," Jewish immigrant Minnie Miller wrote in her autobiography. "My history is bound up in their history and the generations that follow should know where they came from to know better who they are." Similarly, Tomo Shoji, an elderly Nisei[53] woman, urged Asian Americans to learn more about their roots: "We got such good, fantastic stories to tell. All our stories are different." Seeking to know how they fit into America, many young people have become listeners; they are eager to learn about the hardships and humiliations experienced by their parents and grandparents. They want to hear their stories, unwilling to remain ignorant or ashamed of their identity and past.[54]

The telling of stories liberates. By writing about the people on Mango   35 Street, Sandra Cisneros[55] explained, "the ghost does not ache so much." The place no longer holds her with "both arms. She sets me free." Indeed,

---

[52]Weber (ed.), *Foreigners in Their Native Land*, p. vi; Hamilton Holt (ed.), *The Life Stories of Undistinguished Americans as Told by Themselves* (New York, 1906), p. 143. [Author's note]

[53]*Nisei:* Second-generation Japanese Americans.

[54]"Social Document of Pany Lowe, interviewed by C. H. Burnett, Seattle, July 5, 1924," p. 6, Survey of Race Relations, Stanford University, Hoover Institution Archives; Minnie Miller, "Autobiography," private manuscript, copy from Richard Balkin; Tomo Shoji, presentation, Ohana Cultural Center, Oakland, California, March 4, 1988. [Author's note]

[55]*Sandra Cisneros:* Contemporary Mexican American writer (b. 1954).

stories may not be as innocent or simple as they seem to be. Native American novelist Leslie Marmon Silko cautioned:

> I will tell you something about stories . . .
> They aren't just entertainment.
>   Don't be fooled.

Indeed, the accounts given by the people in this study vibrantly re-create moments, capturing the complexities of human emotions and thoughts. They also provide the authenticity of experience. After she escaped from slavery, Harriet Jacobs wrote in her autobiography: "[My purpose] is not to tell you what I have heard but what I have seen — and what I have suffered." In their sharing of memory, the people in this study offer us an opportunity to see ourselves reflected in a mirror called history.[56]

In his recent study of Spain and the New World, *The Buried Mirror*, Carlos Fuentes[57] points out that mirrors have been found in the tombs of ancient Mexico, placed there to guide the dead through the underworld. He also tells us about the legend of Quetzalcoatl, the Plumed Serpent: when this god was given a mirror by the Toltec deity Tezcatlipoca, he saw a man's face in the mirror and realized his own humanity. For us, the "mirror" of history can guide the living and also help us recognize who we have been and hence are. In *A Distant Mirror*, Barbara W. Tuchman[58] finds "phenomenal parallels" between the "calamitous 14th century" of European society and our own era. We can, she observes, have "greater fellow-feeling for a distraught age" as we painfully recognize the "similar disarray," "collapsing assumptions," and "unusual discomfort."[59]

But what is needed in our own perplexing times is not so much a "distant" mirror, as one that is "different." While the study of the past can provide collective self-knowledge, it often reflects the scholar's particular perspective or view of the world. What happens when historians leave out many of America's peoples? What happens, to borrow the words of Adrienne Rich,[60] "when someone with the authority of a teacher" describes our society, and "you are not in it"? Such an experience can be disorienting — "a moment of psychic disequilibrium, as if you looked into a mirror and saw nothing."[61]

---

[56]Sandra Cisneros, *The House on Mango Street* (New York, 1991), pp. 109–110; Leslie Marmon Silko, *Ceremony* (New York, 1978), p. 2; Harriet A. Jacobs, *Incidents in the Life of a Slave Girl, written by herself* (Cambridge, Mass., 1987; originally published in 1857), p. xiii. [Author's note]

[57]*Carlos Fuentes:* Mexican writer (b. 1928).

[58]*Barbara W. Tuchman:* English historian (1912–1989).

[59]Carlos Fuentes, *The Buried Mirror: Reflections on Spain and the New World* (Boston, 1992), pp. 10, 11, 109; Barbara W. Tuchman, *A Distant Mirror: The Calamitous 14th Century* (New York, 1978), pp. xiii, xiv. [Author's note]

[60]*Adrienne Rich:* Jewish American feminist, scholar, writer, and poet (b. 1929).

[61]Adrienne Rich, *Blood, Bread, and Poetry: Selected Prose, 1979–1985* (New York, 1986), p. 199. [Author's note]

Through their narratives about their lives and circumstances, the people of America's diverse groups are able to see themselves and each other in our common past. They celebrate what Ishmael Reed[62] has described as a society "unique" in the world because "the world is here" — a place "where the cultures of the world crisscross." Much of America's past, they point out, has been riddled with racism. At the same time, these people offer hope, affirming the struggle for equality as a central theme in our country's history. At its conception, our nation was dedicated to the proposition of equality. What has given concreteness to this powerful national principle has been our coming together in the creation of a new society. "Stuck here" together, workers of different backgrounds have attempted to get along with each other.

> People harvesting
> Work together unaware
> Of racial problems,

wrote a Japanese immigrant describing a lesson learned by Mexican and Asian farm laborers in California.[63]

Finally, how do we see our prospects for "working out" America's racial crisis? Do we see it as through a glass darkly? Do the televised images of racial hatred and violence that riveted us in 1992 during the days of rage in Los Angeles frame a future of divisive race relations — what Arthur Schlesinger, Jr.,[64] has fearfully denounced as the "disuniting of America"? Or will Americans of diverse races and ethnicities be able to connect themselves to a larger narrative? Whatever happens, we can be certain that much of our society's future will be influenced by which "mirror" we choose to see ourselves. America does not belong to one race or one group, the people in this study remind us, and Americans have been constantly redefining their national identity from the moment of first contact on the Virginia shore. By sharing their stories, they invite us to see ourselves in a different mirror.[65]

[62]*Ishmael Reed:* African American novelist (b. 1938).

[63]Ishmael Reed, "America: The Multinational Society," in Rick Simonson and Scott Walker (eds.), *Multi-cultural Literacy* (St. Paul, 1988), p. 160; Ito, *Issei,* p. 497. [Author's note]

[64]*Arthur Schlesinger, Jr.:* American historian (b. 1917).

[65]Arthur M. Schlesinger, Jr., *The Disuniting of America: Reflections on a Multicultural Society* (Knoxville, Tenn., 1991); Carlos Bulosan, *America Is in the Heart: A Personal History* (Seattle, 1981), pp. 188–189. [Author's note]

ENGAGING THE TEXT

1. What, according to Takaki, are some illustrations that racial tension has become increasingly apparent in American society? Can you think of any others? Do you agree with Takaki that America faces an "intensifying racial crisis" (para. 9)?

2. Takaki suggests that American identity is changing rapidly. Working in small groups, brainstorm a list of qualities that are currently associated with American identity. Then create a similar list for American identity in the year 2010. Overall, which portrait strikes you as more attractive? Why?

3. List the criticisms Takaki levels against traditional historical treatments of the American story. Then think back to the way you were taught American history. To what extent do you agree with Takaki's critique?

4. What kinds of connections does Takaki highlight between the racial and ethnic groups he discusses? What differences does he note?

5. Overall, what does Takaki think of the melting pot myth? How would you describe his vision of American society?

EXPLORING CONNECTIONS

6. Read Paula Gunn Allen (p. 520) and Malcolm X (p. 219) as examples of the historical revision that Takaki is arguing for in this selection. To what extent do these selections fulfill Takaki's assertion that multicultural approaches will give us a "more comprehensive understanding of American history"? What do these revisions of American history add to your understanding of America?

7. Takaki is clearly interested in using a multicultural approach to history as a way of helping to heal racial divisions. How do you think he might address a potentially divisive historical issue like the bigotry expressed by Thomas Jefferson in the previous selection (p. 532)?

8. Role-play a debate between Takaki and Lynne Cheney (p. 263) about whether or not students should have a multicultural education, and if so, what form it should take.

9. The woman in the cartoon below is criticized for fragmenting "good old American history" by highlighting the experiences of particular groups.

Where I'm Coming From © Barbara Brandon. Reprinted with permission of Universal Press Syndicate. All rights reserved.

Could this charge be made of Takaki? Do you think his approach advocates the "balkanization" of America? Why or why not?

EXTENDING THE CRITICAL CONTEXT

10. Research textbooks currently used in American history courses on your campus. Do they represent the experiences of different groups, or do they take a melting pot approach?

11. Research one of the historical events, figures, or ideas mentioned by Takaki. Consult several sources (standard encyclopedias, historical abstracts, indexes of ethnic history, and so forth). Synthesize the information you gather in a brief report, and, in your conclusion, comment on the differences of content, emphasis, or bias you noted in the information presented by each source.

12. After interviewing family members, write your own personal history (or histories) describing your family's experience dealing with the diversity of American culture. You might focus on a family member's immigration experience or on a time when your family had to deal with new cultural attitudes, values, or customs. Share these stories in small groups of students and report back to the class on the similarities and differences you discovered.

Three Thousand Dollar Death Song
WENDY ROSE

Many Native American writers have noted and decried the tendency to treat their heritage as something dead and gone, something to be studied like the fossil record of extinct animals. This poem is a proud song of protest against such dehumanization. Wendy Rose (b. 1948) is a Hopi-Miwok poet, visual artist, editor, and anthropologist. She currently serves as coordinator of American Indian studies at Fresno City College. Twice nominated for the Pulitzer Prize in poetry, Rose is the author of eight volumes of poetry, including Going to War with All My Relations: New and Selected Poems *(1993) and* Bone Dance: New and Selected Poems 1965–1993 *(1995). This poem is from the most acclaimed collection of her poetry,* Lost Copper *(1980), which was nominated for an American Book Award.*

> Nineteen American Indian Skeletons from Nevada
> . . . valued at $3000 . . .
> — MUSEUM INVOICE, 1975

Is it in cold hard cash? the kind
that dusts the insides of men's pockets
lying silver-polished surface along the cloth.
Or in bills? papering the wallets of they
who thread the night with dark words. Or   5
checks? paper promises weighing the same
as words spoken once on the other side
of the grown grass and damned rivers
of history. However it goes, it goes
Through my body it goes   10
assessing each nerve, running its edges
along my arteries, planning ahead
for whose hands will rip me
into pieces of dusty red paper,
whose hands will smooth or smatter me   15
into traces of rubble. Invoiced now,
it's official how our bones are valued
that stretch out pointing to sunrise
or are flexed into one last foetal bend,[1]
that are removed and tossed about,   20
catalogued, numbered with black ink
on newly-white foreheads.
As we were formed to the white soldier's voice,
so we explode under white students' hands.
Death is a long trail of days   25
in our fleshless prison.

From this distant point we watch our bones
auctioned with our careful beadwork,
our quilled medicine bundles, even the bridles
of our shot-down horses. You: who have   30
priced us, you who have removed us: at what cost?
What price the pits where our bones share
a single bit of memory, how one century
turns our dead into specimens, our history
into dust, our survivors into clowns.   35
Our memory might be catching, you know;
picture the mortars,[2] the arrowheads, the labrets[3]
shaking off their labels like bears
suddenly awake to find the seasons have ended
while they slept. Watch them touch each other,   40

---

[1]*foetal bend:* Throughout history, many cultures have buried their dead in a curled position resembling that of a fetus.
[2]*mortars:* Bowl-shaped vessels.
[3]*labrets:* Ornaments of wood or bone worn in holes pierced through the lip.

measure reality, march out the museum door!
Watch as they lift their faces
and smell about for us; watch our bones rise
to meet them and mount the horses once again!
The cost, then, will be paid   45
for our sweetgrass-smelling having-been
in clam shell beads and steatite,[4]
dentalia[5] and woodpecker scalp, turquoise
and copper, blood and oil, coal
and uranium, children, a universe   50
of stolen things.

[4]*steatite:* A soft, easily carved stone; soapstone.
[5]*dentalia:* A type of mollusk shell resembling a tooth.

ENGAGING THE TEXT

1. What do the Indian skeletons mentioned in the epigraph represent?
2. What is the "distant point" Rose mentions in the second stanza?
3. What item seems unusual or out of place in the catalog of "stolen things" that ends the poem? Why does Rose include it in the list? In what way were all these things stolen from the Indians?
4. How do time, place, and point of view shift in the poem? How do these shifts contribute to the poem's meaning?
5. A cynical reader might dismiss lines 36–51 as an empty threat: after all, the bones of slain warriors will not literally rise again and remount their horses. What symbolic or rhetorical purposes might these lines serve?

EXPLORING CONNECTIONS

6. Working in pairs, write an imaginary dialogue between Ronald Takaki (p. 538) and Wendy Rose on the topic of the scholarly study of minority group cultures. How might Rose respond to the idea of multicultural history?
7. Watch a recent film that depicts American Indians (for example, *Squanto, The Last of the Mohicans, Pocahontas*) and draft a letter to the editor from Rose or Paula Gunn Allen (p. 520) responding to it. To extend the assignment, work in small groups to draft a brief statement of principles regarding the portrayal of native peoples in film.

EXTENDING THE CRITICAL CONTEXT

8. Play the role of museum director. Write a letter to the *Reno Times* explaining and defending your museum's purchase of the skeletons. Make up any circumstances you think plausible. Then evaluate the effectiveness of your defense.

9. Investigate a museum in your area with an American Indian collection. What is displayed for public view, and how? What further materials are reserved for research or special exhibits? Has there been any controversy over rightful ownership of skeletons or artifacts? Report your findings to the class.

We, the Dangerous

JANICE MIRIKITANI

Janice Mirikitani is a third-generation Japanese American who was born in 1942, when the United States and Japan were at war. In this poem she presents a sobering catalog of the injustice, oppression, and violence that the United States has inflicted on Asian and Asian American people. Yet this poem also celebrates the persistence, pride, and courage that have enabled them to endure. Mirikitani is an editor, teacher, choreographer, and community activist as well as a poet. Currently she serves as president of the Glide Foundation and Executive Director of Programs at Glide Church/ Urban Center in San Francisco. Her most recent collection of poetry is We, the Dangerous: New and Selected Poems *(1995). The title poem was first published in 1978.*

I swore
it would not devour me
I swore
it would not humble me
I swore   5
it would not break me.

    And they commanded we dwell in the desert
    Our children be spawn of barbed wire and barracks

We, closer to the earth,
squat, short thighed,   10
knowing the dust better.

    And they would have us make the garden
    Rake the grass to soothe their feet

We, akin to the jungle,
plotting with the snake,   15
tails shedding in civilized America.

And they would have us skin their fish
deft hands like blades/sliding back flesh/bloodless

We, who awake in the river
Ocean's child   20
Whale eater.

    And they would have us strange scented women,
    Round shouldered/strong and yellow/like the moon
    to pull the thread to the cloth
    to loosen their backs massaged in myth   25

We, who fill the secret bed,
the sweat shops
the laundries.

    And they would dress us in napalm,
    Skin shred to clothe the earth,   30
    Bodies filling pock marked fields.
    Dead fish bloating our harbors.

We, the dangerous,
Dwelling in the ocean.
Akin to the jungle.   35
Close to the earth.

    Hiroshima
    Vietnam
    Tule Lake[1]

And yet we were not devoured.   40
And yet we were not humbled
And yet we are not broken.

---

[1]*Tule Lake:* The largest of the camps where American citizens of Japanese ancestry, immigrants, and their children were imprisoned in the United States during World War II.

ENGAGING THE TEXT

1. List the images associated with Asian people in the poem. What values and characteristics do these images suggest, and why are they "dangerous"?
2. Who are "they," and what values and characteristics does Mirikitani associate with them?
3. Discuss the significance of the shift from "I" to "we" between stanzas one and two.

4. What does the poem suggest about the social and economic status of Asians in the United States?

5. Explain the structure of the poem. Be sure to comment on the similarity of the first and last stanzas, on the way the two distinct types of stanzas in the rest of the poem play off each other, and on the poem's use of repetition.

EXPLORING CONNECTIONS

6. Compare the roles of the speakers in Wendy Rose's "Three Thousand Dollar Death Song" (p. 557) and "We, the Dangerous." What are their relationships — historical, political, economic, cultural, emotional — to the people they are talking about? How do they portray the people who are the focus of these poems?

7. At the end of "A Different Mirror" (p. 538), Ronald Takaki says, "We can be certain that much of our society's future will be influenced by which 'mirror' we choose to see ourselves. America does not belong to one race or one group." How would you describe the America that is reflected in the "mirrors" held up by Wendy Rose (p. 557) and Mirikitani? Are these poems healing or divisive?

EXTENDING THE CRITICAL CONTEXT

8. Choose a marginalized group in American culture besides Asian Americans — for example, some other ethnic group, lesbians or gays, hearing-impaired people, the aged. Write at least two stanzas in imitation of Mirikitani's poem, keeping your structure identical to Mirikitani's but changing the actual words and ideas. For example, if you wrote from the point of view of a neglected parent, the lines "And they would dress us in napalm / Skin shred to clothe the earth" might become "And they would lock us in nursing homes / Bodies drugged to ease their consciences." Share your effort with classmates.

9. After reading Wendy Rose (p. 557) and Mirikitani, write a poem based on one or more historical incidents involving some marginalized group.

Causes of Prejudice
VINCENT N. PARRILLO

What motivates the creation of racial categories? In the following selection, Vincent Parrillo reviews several theories that seek to explain the motives for prejudiced behavior — from socialization theory to economic competition. As Parrillo indicates, prejudice cannot be linked to any single cause: a whole network of forces and frustrations underlies the reasons for this complex behavior. Parrillo (b. 1938) is chairperson of the Department of Sociology at William Paterson College in New Jersey. His books include Rethinking Today's Minorities *(1991) and* Diversity in America *(1996). He has also written and produced two award-winning documentaries for PBS television. This excerpt originally appeared in* Strangers to These Shores *(1994).*

There appears to be no single cause of prejudice but, rather, many causes that are frequently interrelated. Because fear and suspicion of out-groups[1] are so widespread, scholars and scientists once believed that prejudice was a natural or biological human attribute. Today, because of increased knowledge about the growth of prejudices in children and about the varying patterns of interaction throughout world history, behavioral scientists realize that prejudices are socially determined. A great many theories exist concerning exactly how we become prejudiced.

Socialization

In the socialization process individuals acquire the values, attitudes, beliefs, and perceptions of their culture or subculture, including religion, nationality, and social class. Generally, the child conforms to the parents' expectations in acquiring an understanding of the world and its people. Being young and therefore impressionable and knowing of no alternative conceptions of the world, the child usually accepts these concepts without questioning. We thus learn the prejudices of our parents and others, and they subtly become a part of our values and beliefs. Even if they are based on false stereotypes, prejudices shape our perceptions of various peoples and influence our attitudes and actions toward particular groups. For example, if we develop negative attitudes about Jews because we are taught that they are shrewd, acquisitive, and clannish — all-too-familiar stereotypes — as adults we may refrain from business or social relationships with them. We may not even realize the reason for such avoidance, so subtle has been the prejudice instilled within us.

People may learn certain prejudices because of their pervasiveness. The cultural screen that we develop and through which we view the world around us is not always accurate, but it does reflect shared values and attitudes, which are reinforced by others. Prejudice, like cultural values, is taught and learned through the socialization process. The prevailing prejudicial attitudes and actions often are deeply embedded in custom or law (for

---

[1]*outgroups:* Social groups defined as "outsiders" from a given group's point of view. See "ingroup," note 6.

example, Jim Crow laws), and the new generation may accept them as proper, maintaining them in their adult lives.

Although socialization explains how prejudicial attitudes may be transmitted from one generation to the next, it does not explain their origin or why they intensify or diminish over the years. These aspects of prejudice must be explained in another way.

Herbert Blumer suggests that prejudice always involves the notion of   5
group position in society.[2] Prejudiced people believe that one group is inferior to another, and they place each group in a hierarchical position in society. This perception of group position is an outgrowth of the individual's experiences and understanding of them. The group stereotypes are socially approved images held by members of one group about another.[3]

Self-Justification

Through self-justification, we denigrate a person or group to justify our maltreatment of them. In this situation, self-justification leads to prejudice and discrimination against another's group.

Some philosophers argue that we are not so much rational creatures as we are rationalizing creatures. We require reassurance that the things we do and the lives we live are proper, that good reasons for our actions exist. If we are able to convince ourselves that another group is inferior, immoral, or dangerous, then we can feel justified in discriminating against them, enslaving them, or even killing them.

History is filled with examples of people who thought their maltreatment of others was just and necessary: As defenders of the "truth faith," the Crusaders killed "Christ-killers" (Jews) and "infidels" (Moslems). Participants in the Spanish Inquisition imprisoned, tortured, and executed "heretics," "the disciples of the Devil." The Puritans burned witches, whose refusal to confess "proved" they were evil. Indians were "heathen savages," blacks were "an inferior species," and thus both could be mistreated, enslaved, or killed. The civilians in the Vietnamese village of My Lai were "probably" aiding the Vietcong, so the soldiers felt justified in slaughtering the old men, women, and children they found there.

Some sociologists believe that self-justification works the other way around.[4] That is, instead of self-justification serving as a basis for subjugation of a people, the subjugation occurs first and the self-justification follows, resulting in prejudice and continued discrimination. The evolvement of racism as a concept after the establishment of the African slave trade would seem to support this idea. Philip Mason offers an insight into this view:

[2]Herbert Blumer, "Race Prejudice as a Sense of Group Position," *Pacific Sociological Review* 1 (1958), 3–7. [Author's note]

[3]William M. Newman, *American Pluralism,* Harper & Row, New York, 1973, p. 197. [Author's note]

[4]See Marvin B. Scott and Stanford M. Lyman, "Accounts," *American Sociological Review* 33 (February 1988), 40–62. [Author's note]

A specialized society is likely to defeat a simpler society and provide a lower tier still of enslaved and conquered peoples. The rulers and organizers sought security for themselves and their children; to perpetuate the power, the esteem, and the comfort they had achieved, it was necessary not only that the artisans and labourers should work contentedly but that the rulers should sleep without bad dreams. No one can say with certainty how the myths originated, but it is surely relevant that when one of the founders of Western thought set himself to frame an ideal state that would embody social justice, he — like the earliest city dwellers — not only devised a society stratified in tiers but believed it would be necessary to persuade the traders and workpeople that, by divine decree, they were made from brass and iron, while the warriors were made of silver and the rulers of gold.[5]

Another example of self-justification serving as a cause of prejudice is 10 the dominant group's assumption of an attitude of superiority over other groups. In this respect establishing a prestige hierarchy — ranking the status of various ethnic groups — results in differential association. To enhance or maintain one's own self-esteem, one may avoid social contact with groups deemed inferior and associate only with those identified as being of high status. Through such behavior self-justification may come to intensify the social distance between groups. *Social distance* refers to the degree to which ingroup[6] members do not engage in social or primary relationships with members of various outgroups.

Personality

In 1950 T. W. Adorno and his colleagues reported a correlation between individuals' early childhood experiences of harsh parental discipline and their development of authoritarian personalities as adults.[7] If parents assume an excessively domineering posture in their relations with a child, exercising stern measures and threatening the withdrawal of love if the child does not respond with weakness and submission, then the child tends to be very insecure, nurturing much latent hostility against the parents. When such children become adults, they may demonstrate displaced aggression, directing their hostility against a powerless group as compensation for feelings of insecurity and fear. Highly prejudiced individuals tend to come from families that emphasize obedience.

[5]Philip Mason, *Patterns of Dominance,* Oxford University Press, New York, 1970, p. 7. Also, Philip Mason, *Race Relations,* Oxford University Press, New York, 1970, pp. 17–29. [Author's note]
[6]*ingroup:* A social group whose members are united by a shared identity and a sense of their separateness from the "outgroups" surrounding them.
[7]T. W. Adorno, Else Frankel-Brunswik, Daniel J. Levinson, and R. Nevitt Sanford, *The Authoritarian Personality,* Harper & Row, New York, 1950. [Author's note]

The authors identified authoritarianism by the use of a measuring instrument called an F scale (the F standing for potential fascism). Other tests included the A-S (anti-Semitism) and E (ethnocentrism) scales, the latter measuring attitudes toward various minorities. One of their major findings was that people who scored high on authoritarianism also consistently showed a high degree of prejudice against all minority groups. These highly prejudiced persons were characterized by rigidity of viewpoint, dislike for ambiguity, strict obedience to leaders, and intolerance of weakness in themselves or others.

No sooner did *The Authoritarian Personality* appear than controversy began. H. H. Hyman and P. B. Sheatsley challenged the methodology and analysis.[8] Solomon Asch questioned the assumptions that the F scale responses represented a belief system and that structural variables, such as ideologies, stratification, mobility, and other social factors, do not play a role in shaping personality.[9] E. A. Shils argued that the authors were interested only in measuring authoritarianism of the political right while ignoring such tendencies in those at the other end of the political spectrum.[10] Other investigators sought alternative explanations for the authoritarian personality. D. Stewart and T. Hoult extended the framework beyond family childhood experiences to include other social factors.[11] H. C. Kelman and Janet Barclay demonstrated that substantial evidence exists showing that lower intelligence and less education also correlate with high authoritarianism scores on the F scale.[12]

Despite the critical attacks, the underlying conceptions of *The Authoritarian Personality* were important, and research on personality as a factor in prejudice has continued. Subsequent investigators have refined and modified the original study. Correcting scores for response bias, they have conducted cross-cultural studies. Respondents in Germany and Near East countries, where a more authoritarian social structure exists, scored higher on authoritarianism. In Japan, Germany, and the United States, authoritarianism and social distance were moderately related. Other studies frequently have shown that an inverse relationship exists between social class and F scale scores.[13]

[8]H. H. Hyman and P. B. Sheatsley, "The Authoritarian Personality: A Methodological Critique," in *Studies in the Scope and Method of "The Authoritarian Personality,"* ed. R. Christie and M. Jahoda, Free Press, Glencoe, IL, 1954. [Author's note]

[9]Solomon E. Asch, *Social Psychology,* Prentice-Hall, Englewood Cliffs, NJ, 1952, p. 545. [Author's note]

[10]E. A. Shils, "Authoritarianism: Right and Left," in *Studies in the Scope and Method of "The Authoritarian Personality."* [Author's note]

[11]D. Stewart and T. Hoult, "A Social-Psychological Theory of 'The Authoritarian Personality.'" *American Journal of Sociology* 65 (1959), 274. [Author's note]

[12]H. C. Kelman and Janet Barclay, "The F Scale as a Measure of Breadth of Perspective," *Journal of Abnormal and Social Psychology* 67 (1963), 608–15. [Author's note]

[13]For an excellent summary of authoritarian studies and literature, see John P. Kirscht and Ronald C. Dillehay, *Dimensions of Authoritarianism: A Review of Research and Theory,* University of Kentucky Press, Lexington, 1967. [Author's note]

Although the authoritarian-personality studies have been helpful in the   15
understanding of some aspects of prejudice, they have not provided a causal
explanation. Most of the findings in this area show a correlation, but the
findings do not prove, for example, that harsh discipline of children causes
them to become prejudiced adults. Perhaps the strict parents were themselves prejudiced, and the child learned those attitudes from them. Or, as
George Simpson and J. Milton Yinger say:

> One must be careful not to assume too quickly that a certain tendency —
> rigidity of mind, for example — that is correlated with prejudice neces-
> sarily causes that prejudice. . . . The sequence may be the other way
> around. . . . It is more likely that both are related to more basic factors.[14]

For some people prejudice may indeed be rooted in subconscious
childhood tensions, but we simply do not know whether these tensions directly cause a high degree of prejudice in the adult or whether other powerful social forces are the determinants. Whatever the explanation, authoritarianism is a significant phenomenon worthy of continued investigation.
Recent research, however, has stressed social and situation factors, rather
than personality, as important causes of prejudice and discrimination.[15]

Yet another dimension to the personality component is that people with
low self-esteem are more prejudiced than those who feel good about themselves. Some researchers have argued that individuals with low self-esteem
deprecate others to enhance their feelings about themselves.[16] A recent
study suggests "low self-esteem individuals seem to have a generally negative view of themselves, their ingroup, outgroups, and perhaps the world,"
and thus their tendency to be more prejudiced is not due to rating the outgroup negatively in comparison to their ingroup.[17]

Frustration

Frustration is the result of relative deprivation in which expectations
remain unsatisfied. Relative deprivation refers to a lack of resources, or rewards, in one's standard of living in comparison with others in the society. A
number of investigators have suggested that frustrations tend to increase

---

[14]George E. Simpson and J. Milton Yinger, *Racial and Cultural Minorities: An Analysis of
Prejudice and Discrimination,* Harper & Row, New York, 1953, p. 91. [Author's note]

[15]Ibid., pp. 62–79. [Author's note]

[16]H. J. Ehrlich, *The Social Psychology of Prejudice,* Wiley, New York, 1974: G. Sherwood,
"Self-Serving Biases in Person Perception," *Psychological Bulletin* 90 (1981), 445–59; T. A.
Wills, "Downward Comparison Principles in Social Psychology," *Psychological Bulletin* 90
(1981), 245–71. [Author's note]

[17]Jennifer Crocker and Ian Schwartz, "Prejudice and Ingroup Favoritism in a Minimal Intergroup Situation: Effects of Self-Esteem," *Personality and Social Psychology Bulletin* Vol.
11, No. 4 (December 1985), 379–86. [Author's note]

aggression toward others.[18] Frustrated people may easily strike out against the perceived cause of their frustration. However, this reaction is not always possible because the true source of the frustration is often too nebulous to be identified or too powerful to act against. In such instances the result may be a displaced or free-floating aggression; in this situation the frustrated individual or group usually redirects the aggressiveness against a more visible, vulnerable, and socially sanctioned target, one unable to strike back. Minorities meet these criteria and are thus frequently the recipients of displaced aggression by the dominant group.

Placing blame on others for something that is not their fault is known as scapegoating. The term comes from the ancient Hebrew custom of using a goat during the Day of Atonement as a symbol of the sins of the people. In an annual ceremony a priest placed his hands on the head of a goat and listed the people's sins in a symbolic transference of guilt; he then chased the goat out of the community, thereby freeing the people of sin.[19] Since those times the powerful group has usually punished the scapegoat group rather than allowing it to escape.

There have been many instances throughout world history of minority   20
groups serving as scapegoats, including the Christians in ancient Rome, the French Huguenots, the Jews, the Chinese, the Irish, the Japanese, and the Quakers. Gordon Allport suggests that certain characteristics are necessary for a group to become a suitable scapegoat.[20] The group must be (1) highly visible in physical appearance or observable customs and actions; (2) not strong enough to strike back; (3) situated within easy access of the dominant group or, ideally, concentrated in one area, (4) a past target of hostility for whom latent hostility still exists; and (5) the symbol of an unpopular concept.

Some groups fit this typology better than others, but minority racial and ethnic groups have continually been a favorite choice. Irish, Italians, Catholics, Jews, Quakers, Mormons, Chinese, Japanese, blacks, Puerto Ricans, Chicanos, and Koreans have all been, at one time or another, the scapegoat in the United States. Especially in times of economic hardship,

[18]John Dollard, Leonard W. Doob, Neal E. Miller, O. H. Mowrer, and Robert P. Sears, *Frustration and Aggression,* Yale University Press, New Haven, CT, 1939; A. F. Henry and J. F. Short, Jr., *Suicide and Homicide,* Free Press, New York, 1954; Neal Miller and Richard Bugelski, "Minor Studies in Aggression: The Influence of Frustration Imposed by the Ingroup on Attitudes Expressed Toward Outgroups," *Journal of Psychology* 25 (1948), 437–42; Stuart Palmer, *The Psychology of Murder,* T. Y. Crowell, New York, 1960; Brenden C. Rule and Elizabeth Percival, "The Effects of Frustration and Attack on Physical Aggression," *Journal of Experimental Research on Personality* 5 (1971), 111–88. [Author's note]

[19]Leviticus 16:5–22. [Author's note]

[20]Gordon W. Allport, "The ABC's of Scapegoating," 5th rev. ed., Anti-Defamation League pamphlet, New York. [Author's note]

there seems to be a tendency to blame some group for the general conditions, often leading to aggressive action against the group as an expression of frustration. For example, a study by Carl Hovland and Robert Sears found that between 1882 and 1930, a definite correlation existed between a decline in the price of cotton and an increase in the number of lynchings of blacks.[21]

In several controlled experiments sociologists have attempted to measure the validity of the scapegoat theory. Neal Miller and Richard Bugelski tested a group of young men aged eighteen to twenty working in a government camp about their feelings toward various minority groups.[22] They were reexamined about these feelings after experiencing frustration by being obliged to take a long, difficult test and denied an opportunity to see a film at a local theater. This group showed some evidence of increased prejudicial feelings, whereas a control group, which did not experience any frustration, showed no change in prejudicial attitudes.

Donald Weatherley conducted an experiment with a group of college students to measure the relationship between frustration and aggression against a specific disliked group.[23] After identifying students who were or were not highly anti-Semitic and subjecting them to a strong frustrating experience, he asked the students to write stories about pictures shown to them. Some of the students were shown pictures of people who had been given Jewish names; other students were presented with pictures of unnamed people. When the pictures were unidentified, no difference appeared between the stories of the anti-Semitic students and those of other students. However, when the pictures were identified, the anti-Semitic students wrote stories reflecting much more aggression against the Jews in the pictures than did the other students.

For over twenty years Leonard Berkowitz and his associates have studied and experimented with aggressive behavior. Their conclusions are that, confronted with equally frustrating situations, highly prejudiced individuals are more likely to seek scapegoats than are nonprejudiced individuals. Another intervening variable is that certain kinds of frustrations — personal (marital failure, injury, or mental illness) rather than shared (dangers of flood or hurricane) — make people more likely to seek scapegoats.[24]

[21]Carl I. Hovland and Robert R. Sears, "Minor Studies of Aggression: Correlation of Lynchings with Economic Indices," *Journal of Psychology* 9 (Winter 1940), 301–10. [Author's note]

[22]Miller and Bugelski, "Minor Studies of Aggression," pp. 437–42. [Author's note]

[23]Donald Weatherley, "Anti-Semitism and the Expression of Fantasy Aggression," *Journal of Abnormal and Social Psychology* 62 (1961), 454–57. [Author's note]

[24]See Leonard Berkowitz, "Whatever Happened to the Frustration-Aggression Hypothesis?" *American Behavioral Scientist* 21 (1978), 691–708; L. Berkowitz, *Aggression: A Social Psychological Analysis,* McGraw-Hill, New York, 1962. [Author's note]

Some experiments have shown that aggression does not increase if the 25
frustration is understandable.[25] Other experimenters have found that
people become aggressive *only* if the aggression directly relieves that frustration.[26] Still other studies have shown that anger is a more likely result if
the person frustrating us could have acted otherwise.[27] Clearly, the results
are mixed, depending on the variables within a given social situation.

Talcott Parsons suggests that the family and the occupational system
are both likely to produce anxieties and insecurities that create frustration.[28]
According to this view, the growing-up process (gaining parental affection
and approval, identifying with and imitating sexual role models, and competing with others in adulthood) may involve severe emotional strain. The
result is an adult personality with a large reservoir of repressed aggression
that becomes free-floating — susceptible to redirection against convenient
scapegoats. Similarly, the occupational system is a source of frustration: Its
emphasis on competitiveness and individual achievement, its function of
conferring status, its requirement that people inhibit their natural impulses
at work, and its relationship to the state of the economy are but a few of the
factors that generate emotional anxieties. Parsons pessimistically concludes
that minorities fulfill a functional "need" as targets for displaced aggression
and will therefore remain targets.[29]

Frustration-aggression theory, although helpful, is not completely satisfactory. It ignores the role of culture and the reality of actual social conflict,
while failing to show a causal relationship. Most of the responses measured
in these studies were of people already biased. Why did one group rather
than another become the object of the aggression? Moreover, frustration
does not necessarily precede aggression, and aggression does not necessarily flow from frustration.

Competition

People tend to be more hostile toward others when they feel their security is threatened; thus many social scientists conclude that economic com-

[25]D. Zillman, *Hostility and Aggression,* Lawrence Erlbaum, Hillsdale, NJ, 1979; R. A.
Baron, *Human Aggression,* Plenum Press, New York, 1977; N. Pastore, "The Role of Arbitrari-
ness in the Frustration-Aggression Hypothesis," *Journal of Abnormal and Social Psychology* 47
(1952), 728–31. [Author's note]

[26]A. H. Buss, "Instrumentality of Aggression, Feedback, and Frustration as Determinants
of Physical Aggression," *Journal of Personality and Social Psychology* 3 (1966), 153–62. [Au-
thor's note]

[27]J. R. Averill, "Studies on Anger and Aggression: Implications for Theories of Emotion,"
American Psychologist 38 (1983), 1145–1160. [Author's note]

[28]Talcott Parsons, "Certain Primary Sources and Patterns of Aggression in the Social
Structure of the Western World," *Essays in Sociological Theory,* Free Press, New York, 1964,
pp. 298–322. [Author's note]

[29]For an excellent review of Parsonian theory in this area, see Stanford M. Lyman, *The
Black American in Sociological Thought: A Failure of Perspective,* Putnam, New York, 1972,
pp. 145–69. [Author's note]

petition and conflict breed prejudice. Certainly a great amount of evidence shows that negative stereotyping, prejudice, and discrimination increase strongly whenever competition for a limited number of jobs increases.

An excellent illustration concerns the Chinese sojourners in the nineteenth century. Prior to the 1870s the transcontinental railroad was being built, and the Chinese filled many of the jobs made available by this project in the sparsely populated West. Although they were expelled from the gold mines and schools and had no redress of grievances in the courts, they managed to convey to some whites an image of a clean, hard-working, law-abiding people. The completion of the railroad, the flood of former Civil War soldiers into the job market, and the economic depression of 1873 worsened their situation. The Chinese were even more frequently the victims of open discrimination and hostility. Their positive stereotype among some whites became more commonly a negative one: They were now "conniving," "crafty," "criminal," "the yellow menace." Only after they retreated into Chinatowns and entered specialty occupations not in competition with whites did the intense hostility abate.

One of the early pioneers in the scientific study of prejudice, John Dollard, demonstrated how prejudice against the Germans, which had been virtually nonexistent, came about in a small American industrial town when times got bad.   30

> Local whites largely drawn from the surrounding farms manifested considerable direct aggression toward the newcomers. Scornful and derogatory opinions were expressed about the Germans, and the native whites had a satisfying sense of superiority toward them. . . . The chief element in the permission to be aggressive against the Germans was rivalry for jobs and status in the local woodenware plants. The native whites felt definitely crowded for their jobs by the entering German groups and in case of bad times had a chance to blame the Germans who by their presence provided more competitors for the scarcer jobs. There seemed to be no traditional pattern of prejudice against Germans unless the skeletal suspicion of all out-groupers (always present) be invoked in this place.[30]

Both experimental studies and historical analyses have added credence to the economic-competition theory. Muzafer Sherif directed several experiments showing how intergroup competition at a boys' camp leads to conflict and escalating hostility.[31] Donald Young has shown that, throughout

---

[30]John Dollard, "Hostility and Fear in Social Life," *Social Forces* 17 (1938), 15–26. [Author's note]

[31]Muzafer Sherif, O. J. Harvey, B. Jack White, William Hood, and Carolyn Sherif, *Intergroup Conflict and Cooperation: The Robbers Cave Experiment,* University of Oklahoma Institute of Intergroup Relations, Norman, OK, 1961. See also M. Sherif, "Experiments in Group Conflict," *Scientific American* 195 (1956), 54–58. [Author's note]

American history, in times with high unemployment and thus intense job competition, strong nativist movements against minorities have existed.[32] This pattern has held true regionally — with the Asians on the West Coast, the Italians in Louisiana, and the French Canadians in New England — and nationally, with the antiforeign movements always peaking during periods of depression. So it was with the Native American Party in the 1830s, the Know-Nothing Party in the 1850s, the American Protective Association in the 1890s, and the Ku Klux Klan after World War I. Since the passage of civil rights laws on employment in the twentieth century, researchers have consistently detected the strongest antiblack prejudice among whites who are closest to blacks on the socioeconomic ladder.[33] It seems that any group applying the pressure of job competition most directly on another group becomes its prejudicial target.

Once again, a theory offers some excellent insights into prejudice — there is a correlation between economic conditions and hostility toward minorities — but it also has some serious shortcomings. Not all groups who have been objects of hostility have been economic competitors (for example, Quakers and Mormons). Moreover, why is there greater hostility against some groups than against others? Why do the negative feelings in some communities run against groups whose numbers are so small that they cannot possibly be an economic threat? It would appear that other values besides economic ones cause people to be antagonistic to a group perceived as an actual or potential threat.

Social Norms

Some sociologists have suggested that a relationship exists between prejudice and a person's tendency to conform to societal expectations.[34] Social norms — the norms of one's culture — provide the generally shared rules of what is and is not proper behavior; by learning and automatically accepting the prevailing prejudices, the individual is simply conforming to those norms. This theory says that there is a direct relationship between degree of conformity and degree of prejudice. If this is true, then people's prejudices would decrease or increase significantly when

[32]Donald Young, *Research Memorandum on Minority Peoples in the Depression,* Social Science Research Council, New York, 1937, pp. 133–41. [Author's note]

[33]Andrew Greeley and Paul Sheatsley, "The Acceptance of Desegregation Continues to Advance," *Scientific American* 210 (1971), 13–19; T. F. Pettigrew, "Three Issues in Ethnicity: Boundaries, Deprivations, and Perceptions," in M. Yinger and S. J. Cutler (eds.), *Major Social Issues: A Multidisciplinary View,* Free Press, New York, 1978; R. D. Vanneman and T. F. Pettigrew, "Race and Relative Deprivation in the United States," *Race* 13 (1972), 461–86. [Author's note]

[34]See Harry H. L. Kitano, "Passive Discrimination in the Normal Person," *Journal of Social Psychology* 70 (1966), 23–31. [Author's note]

they move into areas where the prejudicial norm is either lesser or greater. Evidence supports this view. Thomas Pettigrew found that Southerners in the 1950s became less prejudiced against blacks when they interacted with them in the army, where the social norms were less prejudicial.[35] In another study Jeanne Watson found that people moving into an anti-Semitic neighborhood in New York City became more anti-Semitic.[36]

In 1937 John Dollard published his major study, *Caste and Class in a Southern Town,* providing an in-depth look into the emotional adjustment of whites and blacks to rigid social norms.[37] In his study of the processes, functions, and maintenance of accommodation, Dollard shows how the "carrot-and-stick" method is employed. Intimidation, or sometimes even severe reprisals for going against social norms, ensures compliance. However, such actions usually are unnecessary. The advantages whites and blacks gain in psychological, economic, or behavioral terms serve to perpetuate the caste order. These gains in personal security and stability set in motion a vicious circle. They encourage a way of life that reinforces the rationale of the social system in this community.

The problem with the social-norms theory is that although it explains prevailing attitudes, it explains neither their origins nor the reasons for the development of new prejudices when other groups move into an area. In addition the theory does not explain why prejudicial attitudes against a particular group continue to rise and fall in cyclical fashion over the years.

Although many social scientists have attempted to identify the causes of prejudice, no single factor has proven to be an adequate explanation. Prejudice is a complex phenomenon, and it is most likely to be the product of more than one causal agent. Sociologists now tend either to emphasize multiple-causation explanations or else to stress social forces at work in specific and similar situations, such as economic conditions, stratification, or hostility toward an outgroup.

35

[35]Thomas Pettigrew, "Regional Differences in Anti-Negro Prejudice," *Journal of Abnormal and Social Psychology* 59 (1959), 28–36. [Author's note]

[36]Jeanne Watson, "Some Social and Psychological Situations Related to Change in Attitude," *Human Relations* 3 (1950), 15–56. [Author's note]

[37]John Dollard, *Caste and Class in a Southern Town,* 3d ed., Doubleday Anchor Books, Garden City, NY, 1957. [Author's note]

ENGAGING THE TEXT

1. What, according to Parrillo, is the "socialization process"? In what different ways can socialization instill prejudice?

2. How can prejudice arise from self-justification? Offer some examples of how a group can assume an attitude of superiority in order to justify ill-treatment of others.

3. How, according to Parrillo, might personal factors like authoritarian attitudes, low self-esteem, or frustration promote the growth of prejudice?

4. What is the relationship between economic competition and prejudice? Do you think prejudice would continue to exist if everyone had a good job with a comfortable income?

EXPLORING CONNECTIONS

5. Review Ronald Takaki's "A Different Mirror" (p. 538), Wendy Rose's "Three Thousand Dollar Death Song" (p. 557), and Janice Mirikitani's "We, the Dangerous" (p. 560). What evidence can you find in these selections to support Parrillo's theory of economic competition?

6. Review Carmen Vázquez's "Appearances" (p. 503) to determine how useful Parrillo's theories are in analyzing prejudice against gays and lesbians. To what extent can theories like the socialization process, self-justification, authoritarianism, frustration, and economic competition help us understand antigay attitudes?

7. Look at the "Prejudice Workshop" cartoon that appears above. Do you agree with the cartoonist's suggestion that the young blond man is preju-

diced? If so, which of the theories that Parrillo presents best accounts for his attitude? If not, why not?

EXTENDING THE CRITICAL CONTEXT

8. List the various groups (racial, economic, cultural, social, familial, and so forth) that you belong to and arrange them in a status hierarchy. Which groups were you born into? Which groups did you join voluntarily? Which have had the greatest impact on your socialization? Which groups isolate you the most from contact with outsiders?

9. Working in small groups, research recent news stories for examples of incidents involving racism or prejudice. Which of the theories described by Parrillo seem most useful for analyzing the motives underlying these events?

C. P. Ellis

STUDS TERKEL

The following oral history brings us uncomfortably close to unambiguous, deadly prejudice: C. P. Ellis is a former Ku Klux Klan member who claims to have overcome his racist (and sexist) attitudes; he speaks here as a union leader who feels an alliance to other workers, including blacks and women. Studs Terkel (b. 1912) is probably the best-known practitioner of oral history in the United States. He has compiled several books by interviewing dozens of widely varying people — ordinary people for the most part — about important subjects like work, social class, race, and the Great Depression. The edited versions of these interviews are often surprisingly powerful crystallizations of American social history: Terkel's subjects give voice to the frustrations and hopes of whole generations of Americans. Terkel won a Pulitzer Prize in 1985 for "The Good War": An Oral History of World War II. *His most recent work is* Coming of Age: The Story of Our Century by Those Who've Lived It *(1995). "C. P. Ellis" first appeared in* American Dreams: Lost and Found *(1980).*

We're in his office in Durham, North Carolina. He is the business manager of the International Union of Operating Engineers. On the wall is a plaque: "Certificate of Service, in recognition to C. P. Ellis, for your faithful service to the city in having served as a member of the Durham Human Relations Council. February 1977."

At one time, he had been president (exalted cyclops) of the Durham chapter of the Ku Klux Klan. . . .
He is fifty-two years old.

My father worked in a textile mill in Durham. He died at forty-eight years old. It was probably from cotton dust. Back then, we never heard of brown lung. I was about seventeen years old and had a mother and sister depending on somebody to make a livin'. It was just barely enough insurance to cover his burial. I had to quit school and go to work. I was about eighth grade when I quit.

My father worked hard but never had enough money to buy decent   5
clothes. When I went to school, I never seemed to have adequate clothes to wear. I always left school late afternoon with a sense of inferiority. The other kids had nice clothes, and I just had what Daddy could buy. I still got some of those inferiority feelin's now that I have to overcome once in a while.

I loved my father. He would go with me to ball games. We'd go fishin' together. I was really ashamed of the way he'd dress. He would take this money and give it to me instead of putting it on himself. I always had the feeling about somebody looking at him and makin' fun of him and makin' fun of me. I think it had to do somethin' with my life.

My father and I were very close, but we didn't talk about too many intimate things. He did have a drinking problem. During the week, he would work every day, but weekends he was ready to get plastered. I can understand when a guy looks at his paycheck and looks at his bills, and he's worked hard all the week, and his bills are larger than his paycheck. He'd done the best he could the entire week, and there seemed to be no hope. It's an illness thing. Finally you just say: "The heck with it. I'll just get drunk and forget it."

My father was out of work during the depression, and I remember going with him to the finance company uptown, and he was turned down. That's something that's always stuck.

My father never seemed to be happy. It was a constant struggle with him just like it was for me. It's very seldom I'd see him laugh. He was just tryin' to figure out what he could do from one day to the next.

After several years pumping gas at a service station, I got married. We   10
had to have children. Four. One child was born blind and retarded, which was a real additional expense to us. He's never spoken a word. He doesn't know me when I go to see him. But I see him, I hug his neck. I talk to him, tell him I love him. I don't know whether he knows me or not, but I know he's well taken care of. All my life, I had work, never a day without work, worked all the overtime I could get and still could not survive financially. I began to say there's somethin' wrong with this country. I worked my butt off and just never seemed to break even.

I had some real great ideas about this great nation. (Laughs.) They say to abide by the law, go to church, do right and live for the Lord, and everything'll work out. But it didn't work out. It just kept gettin' worse and worse.

I was workin' a bread route. The highest I made one week was seventy-five dollars. The rent on our house was about twelve dollars a week. I will never forget: outside of this house was a 265-gallon oil drum, and I never did get enough money to fill up that oil drum. What I would do every night, I would run up to the store and buy five gallons of oil and climb up the ladder and pour it in that 265-gallon drum. I could hear that five gallons when it hits the bottom of that oil drum, splatters, and it sounds like it's nothin' in there. But it would keep the house warm for the night. Next day you'd have to do the same thing.

I left the bread route with fifty dollars in my pocket. I went to the bank and borrowed four thousand dollars to buy the service station. I worked seven days a week, open and close, and finally had a heart attack. Just about two months before the last payments of that loan. My wife had done the best she could to keep it runnin'. Tryin' to come out of that hole, I just couldn't do it.

I really began to get bitter. I didn't know who to blame. I tried to find somebody. I began to blame it on black people. I had to hate somebody. Hatin' America is hard to do because you can't see it to hate it. You gotta have somethin' to look at to hate. (Laughs.) The natural person for me to hate would be black people, because my father before me was a member of the Klan. As far as he was concerned, it was the savior of the white people. It was the only organization in the world that would take care of the white people. So I began to admire the Klan.

I got active in the Klan while I was at the service station. Every Monday night, a group of men would come by and buy a Coca-Cola, go back to the car, take a few drinks, and come back and stand around talkin'. I couldn't help but wonder: Why are these dudes comin' out every Monday? They said they were with the Klan and have meetings close-by. Would I be interested? Boy, that was an opportunity I really looked forward to! To be part of somethin'. I joined the Klan, went from member to chaplain, from chaplain to vice-president, from vice-president to president. The title is exalted cyclops.

The first night I went with the fellas, they knocked on the door and gave the signal. They sent some robed Klansmen to talk to me and give me some instructions. I was led into a large meeting room, and this was the time of my life! It was thrilling. Here's a guy who's worked all his life and struggled all his life to be something, and here's the moment to be something. I will never forget it. Four robed Klansmen led me into the hall. The lights were dim, and the only thing you could see was an illuminated cross. I knelt before the cross. I had to make certain vows and promises. We promised to uphold the purity of the white race, fight communism, and protect white womanhood.

After I had taken my oath, there was loud applause goin' throughout the building, musta been at least four hundred people. For this one little ol' person. It was a thrilling moment for C. P. Ellis.

It disturbs me when people who do not really know what it's all about are so very critical of individual Klansmen. The majority of 'em are low-income whites, people who really don't have a part in something. They have been shut out as well as the blacks. Some are not very well educated either. Just like myself. We had a lot of support from doctors and lawyers and police officers.

Maybe they've had bitter experiences in this life and they had to hate somebody. So the natural person to hate would be the black person. He's beginnin' to come up, he's beginnin' to learn to read and start votin' and run for political office. Here are white people who are supposed to be superior to them, and we're shut out.

I can understand why people join extreme right-wing or left-wing   20
groups. They're in the same boat I was. Shut out. Deep down inside, we want to be part of this great society. Nobody listens, so we join these groups.

At one time, I was state organizer of the National Rights party. I organized a youth group for the Klan. I felt we were getting old and our generation's gonna die. So I contacted certain kids in schools. They were havin' racial problems. On the first night, we had a hundred high school students. When they came in the door, we had "Dixie" playin'. These kids were just thrilled to death. I begin to hold weekly meetin's with 'em, teachin' the principles of the Klan. At that time, I believed Martin Luther King had Communist connections. I began to teach that Andy Young[1] was affiliated with the Communist party.

I had a call one night from one of our kids. He was about twelve. He said: "I just been robbed downtown by two niggers." I'd had a couple of drinks and that really teed me off. I go downtown and couldn't find the kid. I got worried. I saw two young black people. I had the .32 revolver with me. I said: "Nigger, you seen a little young white boy up here? I just got a call from him and was told that some niggers robbed him of fifteen cents." I pulled my pistol out and put it right at his head. I said: "I've always wanted to kill a nigger and I think I'll make you the first one." I nearly scared the kid to death, and he struck off.

This was the time when the civil rights movement was really beginnin' to peak. The blacks were beginnin' to demonstrate and picket downtown stores. I never will forget some black lady I hated with a purple passion. Ann Atwater. Every time I'd go downtown, she'd be leadin' a boycott. How

---

[1]*Andy Young:* Andrew Jackson Young, Jr. (b. 1932), prominent black leader and politician. Young was a friend and adviser of Martin Luther King, Jr., and served as President Jimmy Carter's ambassador to the United Nations. In the 1980s, he was twice elected mayor of Atlanta.

I hated — pardon the expression, I don't use it much now — how I just hated the black nigger. (Laughs.) Big, fat, heavy woman. She'd pull about eight demonstrations, and first thing you know they had two, three blacks at the checkout counter. Her and I have had some pretty close confrontations.

I felt very big, yeah. (Laughs.) We're more or less a secret organization. We didn't want anybody to know who we were, and I began to do some thinkin'. What am I hidin' for? I've never been convicted of anything in my life. I don't have any court record. What am I, C. P. Ellis, as a citizen and a member of the United Klansmen of America? Why can't I go the city council meeting and say: "This is the way we feel about the matter? We don't want you to purchase mobile units to set in our schoolyards. We don't want niggers in our schools."

We began to come out in the open. We would go to the meetings, and   25 the blacks would be there and we'd be there. It was a confrontation every time. I didn't hold back anything. We began to make some inroads with the city councilmen and county commissioners. They began to call us friend. Call us at night on the telephone: "C. P., glad you came to that meeting last night." They didn't want integration either, but they did it secretively, in order to get elected. They couldn't stand up openly and say it, but they were glad somebody was sayin' it. We visited some of the city leaders in their home and talk to 'em privately. It wasn't long before councilmen would call me up: "The blacks are comin' up tonight and makin' outrageous demands. How about some of you people showin' up and have a little balance?" I'd get on the telephone. "The niggers is comin' to the council meeting tonight. Persons in the city's called me and asked us to be there."

We'd load up our cars and we'd fill up half the council chambers, and the blacks the other half. During these times, I carried weapons to the meetings, outside my belt. We'd go there armed. We would wind up just hollerin' and fussin' at each other. What happened? As a result of our fightin' one another, the city council still had their way. They didn't want to give up control to the blacks nor the Klan. They were usin' us.

I began to realize this later down the road. One day I was walkin' downtown and a certain city council member saw me comin'. I expected him to shake my hand because he was talkin' to me at night on the telephone. I had been in his home and visited with him. He crossed the street. Oh shit, I began to think, somethin's wrong here. Most of 'em are merchants or maybe an attorney, an insurance agent, people like that. As long as they kept low-income whites and low-income blacks fightin', they're gonna maintain control.

I began to get that feeling after I was ignored in public. I thought: Bullshit, you're not gonna use me any more. That's when I began to do some real serious thinkin'.

The same thing is happening in this country today. People are being used by those in control, those who have all the wealth. I'm not espousing communism. We got the greatest system of government in the world. But those who have it simply don't want those who don't have it to have any part of it. Black and white. When it comes to money, the green, the other colors make no difference. (Laughs.)

I spent a lot of sleepless nights. I still didn't like blacks. I didn't want to   30
associate with 'em. Blacks, Jews, or Catholics. My father said: "don't have anything to do with 'em." I didn't until I met a black person and talked with him, eyeball to eyeball, and met a Jewish person and talked to him, eyeball to eyeball. I found out they're people just like me. They cried, they cussed, they prayed, they had desires. Just like myself. Thank God, I got to the point where I can look past labels. But at that time, my mind was closed.

I remember one Monday night Klan meeting. I said something was wrong. Our city fathers were using us. And I didn't like to be used. The reactions of the others was not too pleasant: "Let's just keep fightin' them niggers."

I'd go home at night and I'd have to wrestle with myself. I'd look at a black person walkin' down the street, and the guy'd have ragged shoes or his clothes would be worn. That began to do somethin' to me inside. I went through this for about six months. I felt I just had to get out of the Klan. But I wouldn't get out.

Then something happened. The state AFL–CIO[2] received a grant from the Department of HEW,[3] a $78,000 grant: how to solve racial problems in the school system. I got a telephone call from the president of the state AFL–CIO. "We'd like to get some people together from all walks of life." I said: "All walks of life? Who you talkin' about?" He said: "Blacks, whites, liberals, conservatives, Klansmen, NAACP[4] people."

I said: "No way am I comin' with all those niggers. I'm not gonna be associated with those type of people." A White Citizens Council guy said: "Let's go up there and see what's goin' on. It's tax money bein' spent." I walk in the door, and there was a large number of blacks and white liberals. I knew most of 'em by face 'cause I seen 'em demonstratin' around town. Ann Atwater was there. (Laughs.) I just forced myself to go in and sit down.

The meeting was moderated by a great big black guy who was bushy-   35
headed. (Laughs.) That turned me off. He acted very nice. He said: "I want you all to feel free to say anything you want to say." Some of the blacks stand up and say it's white racism. I took all I could take. I asked for the floor and cut loose. I said: "No, sir, it's black racism. If we didn't have niggers in the schools, we wouldn't have the problems we got today."

---

[2]*AFL–CIO:* American Federation of Labor and Congress of Industrial Organizations — a huge federation of independent labor unions in the United States, Canada, Mexico, Panama, and elsewhere.

[3]*HEW:* Health, Education, and Welfare — at the time, a department of the federal government.

[4]*NAACP:* National Association for the Advancement of Colored People.

I will never forget. Howard Clements, a black guy, stood up. He said: "I'm certainly glad C. P. Ellis come because he's the most honest man here tonight." I said: "What's that nigger tryin' to do?" (Laughs.) At the end of that meeting, some blacks tried to come up shake my hand, but I wouldn't do it. I walked off.

Second night, same group was there. I felt a little more easy because I got some things off my chest. The third night, after they elected all the committees, they want to elect a chairman. Howard Clements stood up and said: "I suggest we elect two co-chairpersons." Joe Beckton, executive director of the Human Relations Commission, just as black as he can be, he nominated me. There was a reaction from some blacks. Nooo. And, of all things, they nominated Ann Atwater, that big old fat black gal that I had just hated with a purple passion, as co-chairman. I thought to myself: Hey, ain't no way I can work with that gal. Finally, I agreed to accept it, 'cause at this point, I was tired of fightin', either for survival or against black people or against Jews or against Catholics.

A Klansman and a militant black woman, co-chairmen of the school committee. It was impossible. How could I work with her? But after about two or three days, it was in our hands. We had to make it a success. This give me another sense of belongin', a sense of pride. This helped this inferiority feelin' I had. A man who has stood up publicly and said he despised black people, all of a sudden he was willin' to work with 'em. Here's a chance for a low-income white man to be somethin'. In spite of all my hatred for blacks and Jews and liberals, I accepted the job. Her and I began to reluctantly work together. (Laughs.) She had as many problems workin' with me as I had workin' with her.

One night, I called her: "Ann, you and I should have a lot of differences and we got 'em now. But there's somethin' laid out here before us, and if it's gonna be a success, you and I are gonna have to make it one. Can we lay aside some of these feelin's?" She said: "I'm willing if you are." I said: "Let's do it."

My old friends would call me at night: "C. P., what the hell is wrong   40
with you? You're sellin' out the white race." This begin to make me have guilt feelin's. Am I doin' right? Am I doin' wrong? Here I am all of a sudden makin' an about-face and tryin' to deal with my feelin's, my heart. My mind was beginnin' to open up. I was beginnin' to see what was right and what was wrong. I don't want the kids to fight forever.

We were gonna go ten nights. By this time, I had went to work at Duke University, in maintenance. Makin' very little money. Terry Sanford give me this ten days off with pay. He was president of Duke at the time. He knew I was a Klansman and realized the importance of blacks and whites getting along.

I said: "If we're gonna make this thing a success, I've got to get to my kind of people." The low-income whites. We walked the streets of Durham, and we knocked on doors and invited people. Ann was goin' into the black community. They just wasn't respondin' to us when we made these house calls. Some of 'em were cussin' us out. "You're sellin' us out, Ellis, get out of my door. I don't want to talk to you." Ann was gettin' the same response from blacks. "What are you doin' messin' with that Klansman?"

One day, Ann and I went back to the school and we sat down. We began to talk and just reflect. Ann said: "My daughter came home cryin' every day. She said her teacher was makin' fun of me in front of the other kids." I said: "Boy, the same thing happened to my kid. White liberal teacher was makin' fun of Tim Ellis's father, the Klansman. In front of other peoples. He came home cryin'." At this point — (he pauses, swallows hard, stifles a sob) — I begin to see, here we are, two people from the far ends of the fence, havin' identical problems, except hers bein' black and me bein' white. From that moment on, I tell ya, that gal and I worked together good. I begin to love the girl, really. (He weeps.)

The amazing thing about it, her and I, up to that point, had cussed each other, bawled each other, we hated each other. Up to that point, we didn't know each other. We didn't know we had things in common.

We worked at it, with the people who came to these meetings. They   45
talked about racism, sex education, about teachers not bein' qualified. After seven, eight nights of real intense discussion, these people, who'd never talked to each other before, all of a sudden came up with resolutions. It was really somethin', you had to be there to get the tone and feelin' of it.

At that point, I didn't like integration, but the law says you do this and I've got to do what the law says, okay? We said: "Let's take these resolutions to the school board." The most disheartening thing I've ever faced was the school system refused to implement any one of these resolutions. These were recommendations from the people who pay taxes and pay their salaries. (Laughs.)

I thought they were good answers. Some of 'em I didn't agree with, but I been in this thing from the beginning, and whatever comes of it, I'm gonna support it. Okay, since the school board refused, I decided I'd just run for the school board.

I spent eighty-five dollars on the campaign. The guy runnin' against me spent several thousand. I really had nobody on my side. The Klan turned against me. The low-income whites turned against me. The liberals didn't particularly like me. The blacks were suspicious of me. The blacks wanted to support me, but they couldn't muster up enough to support a Klansman on the school board. (Laughs.) But I made up my mind that what I was doin' was right, and I was gonna do it regardless what anybody said.

It bothered me when people would call and worry my wife. She's always supported me in anything I wanted to do. She was changing, and my boys were too. I got some of my youth corps kids involved. They still followed me.

I was invited to the Democratic women's social hour as a candidate.   50
Didn't have but one suit to my name. Had it six, seven, eight years. I had it cleaned, put on the best shirt I had and a tie. Here were all this high-class

wealthy candidates shakin' hands. I walked up to the mayor and stuck out my hand. He give me that handshake with that rag type of hand. He said: "C. P., I'm glad to see you." But I could tell by his handshake he was lyin' to me. This was botherin' me. I know I'm a low-income person. I know I'm not wealthy. I know they were sayin': "What's this little ol' dude runnin' for school board?" Yet they had to smile and make like they're glad to see me. I begin to spot some black people in that room. I automatically went to 'em and that was a firm handshake. They said: "I'm glad to see you, C. P." I knew they meant it — you can tell about a handshake.

Every place I appeared, I said I will listen to the voice of the people. I will not make a major decision until I first contacted all the organizations in the city. I got 4,640 votes. The guy beat me by two thousand. Not bad for eighty-five bucks and no constituency.

The whole world was openin' up, and I was learnin' new truths that I had never learned before. I was beginnin' to look at a black person, shake hands with him, and see him as a human bein'. I hadn't got rid of all this stuff, I've still got a little bit of it. But somethin' was happenin' to me.

It was almost like bein' born again. It was a new life. I didn't have these sleepless nights I used to have when I was active in the Klan and slippin' around at night. I could sleep at night and feel good about it. I'd rather live now than at any other time in history. It's a challenge.

Back at Duke, doin' maintenance, I'd pick up my tools, fix the commode, unstop the drains. But this got in my blood. Things weren't right in this country, and what we done in Durham needs to be told. I was so miserable at Duke, I could hardly stand it. I'd go to work every morning just hatin' to go.

My whole life had changed. I got an eighth-grade education, and I wanted to complete high school. Went to high school in the afternoons on a program called PEP — Past Employment Progress. I was about the only white in class, and the oldest. I begin to read about biology. I'd take my books home at night, 'cause I was determined to get through. Sure enough, I graduated. I got the diploma at home.

I come to work one mornin' and some guy says: "We need a union." At this time I wasn't pro-union. My daddy was anti-labor, too. We're not gettin' paid much, we're havin' to work seven days in a row. We're all starvin' to death. The next day, I meet the international representative of the Operating Engineers. He give me authorization cards. "Get these cards out and we'll have an election." There was eighty-eight for the union and seventeen no's. I was elected chief steward for the union.

Shortly after, a union man come down from Charlotte and says we need a full-time rep. We've got only two hundred people at the two plants here. It's just barely enough money comin' in to pay your salary. You'll have to get out and organize more people. I didn't know nothin' about organizin' unions, but I knew how to organize people, stir people up. (Laughs.) That's how I got to be business agent for the union.

When I began to organize, I began to see far deeper. I began to see people again bein' used. Blacks against whites. I say this without any hesitancy: management is vicious. There's two things they want to keep: all the money and all the say-so. They don't want these poor workin' folks to have none of that. I begin to see management fightin' me with everything they had. Hire anti-union law firms, badmouth unions. The people were makin' a dollar ninety-five an hour, barely able to get through weekends. I worked as a business rep for five years and was seein' all this.

Last year, I ran for business manager of the union. He's elected by the workers. The guy that ran against me was black, and our membership is seventy-five percent black. I thought: Claiborne, there's no way you can beat that black guy. People know your background. Even though you've made tremendous strides, those black people are not gonna vote for you. You know how much I beat him? Four to one. (Laughs).

The company used my past against me. They put out letters with a pic-   60
ture of a robe and a cap: would you vote for a Klansman? They wouldn't deal with the issues. I immediately called for a mass meeting. I met with the ladies at an electric component plant. I said: "Okay, this is Claiborne Ellis. This is where I come from. I want you to know right now, you black ladies here, I was at one time a member of the Klan. I want you to know, because they'll tell you about it."

I invited some of my old black friends. I said: "Brother Joe, Brother Howard, be honest now and tell these people how you feel about me." They done it. (Laughs.) Howard Clements kidded me a little bit. He said: "I don't know what I'm doin' here, supportin' an ex-Klansman." (Laughs.) He said: "I know what C. P. Ellis come from. I knew him when he was. I knew him as he grew, and growed with him. I'm tellin' you now: follow, follow this Klansman." (He pauses, swallows hard.) "Any questions?" "No," the black ladies said. "Let's get on with the meeting, we need Ellis." (He laughs and weeps.) Boy, black people sayin' that about me. I won one thirty-four to forty-one. Four to one.

It makes you feel good to go into a plant and butt heads with professional union busters. You see black people and white people join hands to defeat the racist issues they use against people. They're tryin' the same things with the Klan. It's still happenin' today. Can you imagine a guy who's got an adult high school diploma runnin' into professional college graduates who are union busters? I gotta compete with 'em. I work seven days a week, nights and on Saturday and Sunday. The salary's not that great, and if I didn't care, I'd quit. But I care and I can't quit. I got a taste of it. (Laughs.)

I tell people there's a tremendous possibility in this country to stop wars, the battles, the struggles, the fights between people. People say: "That's an impossible dream. You sound like Martin Luther King." An ex-Klansman who sounds like Martin Luther King. (Laughs.) I don't think it's an impossible dream. It's happened in my life. It's happened in other people's lives in America.

I don't know what's ahead of me. I have no desire to be a big union official. I want to be right out here in the field with the workers. I want to walk through their factory and shake hands with that man whose hands are dirty. I'm gonna do all that one little ol' man can do. I'm fifty-two years old, and I ain't got many years left, but I want to make the best of 'em.

When the news came over the radio that Martin Luther King was assas-   65
sinated, I got on the telephone and begin to call other Klansmen. We just had a real party at the service station. Really rejoicin' 'cause that son of a bitch was dead. Our troubles are over with. They say the older you get, the harder it is for you to change. That's not necessarily true. Since I changed, I've set down and listened to tapes of Martin Luther King. I listen to it and tears come to my eyes 'cause I know what he's sayin' now. I know what's happenin'.

POSTSCRIPT:
The phone rings. A conversation.
"This was a black guy who's director of Operation Breakthrough in Durham. I had called his office. I'm interested in employin' some young black person who's interested in learnin' the labor movement. I want somebody who's never had an opportunity, just like myself. Just so he can read and write, that's all."

ENGAGING THE TEXT

1. How does Ellis battle the racism he finds in himself? What gives him the motivation and strength to change? What specific changes does he undergo, and how successful is he in abandoning racist attitudes?
2. Would Ellis say that economic class is more important than race in determining job placement and occupational mobility? Find specific passages that reveal Ellis's beliefs about the connections between economic class, race, and success in American society. What do you believe?
3. How well does Ellis seem to understand himself, his feelings, his motives? Give evidence for your assertions.
4. What is Terkel's role in this selection? Is he unconsciously helping to rationalize or justify the actions of the Ku Klux Klan?

EXPLORING CONNECTIONS

5. Does Ellis's story offer a credible way of overcoming misunderstanding and hatred between races? Do you think such a "solution" would be workable on a large scale? Why or why not?
6. To what extent does Ellis's experience illustrate the theories of prejudice described by Vincent N. Parrillo (p. 563)? Does any one of these theories best account for Ellis's racism and his eventual transformation?

7. Review the account of Malcolm X's self-education (p. 219). How does the dramatic self-transformation he experiences compare with C. P. Ellis's rebirth? What relationships can you find between the circumstances that led to their initial attitudes, the conditions or events that fostered their transformations, and the effects that these transformations had on their characters?

8. Look ahead to Fred L. Pincus's discussion of individual, institutional, and structural discrimination in the selection below. Which of these types of discrimination does Ellis practice or participate in before his change of heart? Which types of discrimination is he subjected to himself?

EXTENDING THE CRITICAL CONTEXT

9. Interview a friend, family member, or fellow student in another class to create your own oral history on the subject of racial attitudes. Ask your subject to describe a time when he or she was forced to re-evaluate his or her thoughts or feelings about someone from a different racial or ethnic group. Try to include as many relevant details as possible in your retelling of the story. Share and edit these oral histories in small groups, and then assemble them into a class anthology.

From Individual to Structural Discrimination
FRED L. PINCUS

For many Americans, words like "racism" and "discrimination" imply overt bigotry. But in the short essay that follows, Fred L. Pincus argues that discrimination can be far more subtle — and may even occur when there is no conscious intention to discriminate. Pincus (b. 1942) is an associate professor of sociology at the University of Maryland Baltimore County; he has taught and written about race relations for thirty years. This piece first appeared in Race and Ethnic Conflict *(1994), a collection of essays edited by Pincus and Howard J. Ehrlich.*

People often think of racial discrimination in terms of the actions of individual prejudiced white people against individual people of color. However, . . . prejudice (an attitude) does not necessarily lead to discrimination (an overt behavior), and discrimination is not always caused by prejudice.

Group discrimination can exist at many different levels. An individual teacher who mistreats a Hispanic student is different from a school system that refuses to admit Hispanics. An individual personnel officer who decides not to hire a qualified black applicant is different from an entire state police department that refuses to hire black officers.

In their influential book *Black Power,* which was published more than a quarter of a century ago, Stokely Carmichael and Charles Hamilton differentiated "individual racism" from "institutional racism." The former involved the behavior of white individuals toward blacks and other minorities, and the latter involved the behavior of the entire white society and its institutions toward people of color.

Since *racism* is a pejorative word often used imprecisely, I shall modify the Carmichael/Hamilton typology and apply it to the concept of discrimination. My discussion here deals with three different types of race/ethnic discrimination: individual, institutional, and structural.

1. *Individual discrimination* refers to the behavior of individual members of one race/ethnic group that is intended to have a differential and/or harmful effect on the members of another race/ethnic group. This category includes a wide range of behavior by majority-group individuals or small groups — from anti-Asian graffiti and name calling, to an employer's refusal to hire blacks or a landlord's refusal to rent to Hispanics, to physical attacks against Native Americans.

According to this definition, actions by individual minority-group members against the majority group can also be characterized as "individual discrimination." Examples might include antiwhite graffiti by blacks, physical attacks against whites by Hispanics, or employment discrimination by Asians against whites. Each of these actions entails intentional antiwhite treatment that has a differential and/or harmful impact.

2. *Institutional discrimination* is quite different in that it refers to the policies of majority institutions, and the behavior of individuals who implement these policies and control these institutions, that are intended to have a differential and/or harmful effect on minority groups. A major goal of institutional discrimination is to keep minority groups in a subordinate position within society. Hence this concept is much broader than that of individual discrimination.

Sometimes, institutional discrimination is embodied in laws and government policy. From the 1890s until the 1950s, for example, most southern states had laws that *legally* discriminated between blacks and whites in all areas of life — from voting, education, and employment to religion, public accommodations, and restaurants. These laws had broad support among the white population and were even given the stamp of approval by the U.S. Supreme Court in 1896.[1] Legal segregation, which has been referred to as

5

---

[1] . . . *1896:* In the landmark case, Plessy v. Ferguson, the Supreme Court upheld southern segregation laws.

the "Jim Crow System," is a clear example of institutional discrimination, and it goes far beyond the level of individual actions.

Blacks are not the only victims of institutional discrimination in the United States. Whites seized the land of Native Americans by brutally defeating them on the battlefield and then confining them to reservations. Treaties with Indian Nations were routinely broken by the government, and entire tribes were forcibly moved from one reservation to another, often with fatal results.

Asians have also been victims. After Japan attacked Pearl Harbor in 1941, all Japanese people on the West Coast were taken from their homes and placed in internment camps for the duration of the war. Both citizens and noncitizens were forced to sell their property at a great loss.

Although most discrimination by federal, state, and local governments is now illegal, examples of institutional discrimination can still be found. One such example is "gerrymandering," the illegal drawing of electoral districts in such a way as to intentionally minimize the electoral power of minority groups. Police and fire departments in many cities across the country have illegally refused to hire and promote *qualified* blacks and Hispanics at the same rate as comparably qualified whites. (This practice has resulted in a series of lawsuits and controversial affirmative action programs. . . .) And even the prestigious Federal Bureau of Investigation illegally discriminated against black and Hispanic agents until 1992, when the FBI entered into a consent decree to end a lawsuit by black agents.

Institutional discrimination can be detected in the private sector as well. Real estate associations often "steer" blacks away from white neighborhoods and show them houses and apartments in predominantly minority neighborhoods. Banks in various cities have "redlined" certain minority areas (that is, they have refused to grant mortgages to people who live in these areas regardless of whether they meet the financial qualifications specified), and they have granted smaller mortgages at higher interest rates. Moreover, large corporations have been convicted of racial discrimination in hiring and promotion, and private social clubs often refuse to admit minority members.

Since the majority group generally controls the major institutions, institutional discrimination is almost always carried out by the majority group against the minority group — not the other way around. For the most part, minority groups lack the power with which to practice institutional discrimination. Nevertheless, the refusal by a black-controlled city government to hire whites would be an example of institutional discrimination.

3. Finally, there is a third type of discrimination that some would say is not really discrimination at all. *Structural discrimination* refers to the policies of majority institutions, and the behavior of the individuals who implement these policies and control these institutions, that are race-neutral in intent but have a differential and/or harmful effect on minority groups. The

key element in structural discrimination is not the intent but the effect of keeping minority groups in a subordinate position.

Although it is sometimes difficult to determine whether a particular   15
phenomenon is an example of institutional or structural discrimination, the differences between the two are important both conceptually and in terms of social policy. Both types have the *effect* of keeping minority groups sub-ordinate, but only institutional discrimination is *intended* to keep minority groups subordinate. Some examples of structural discrimination follow.

It is well known that blacks and Hispanics are underrepresented on the nation's college campuses. Most colleges, however, have what appear to be race-neutral meritocratic entrance requirements: Anyone who meets the re-quirements will be admitted regardless of race, ethnicity, gender, and so on. Requirements usually include high school grades, scores on SAT or ACT tests, teacher recommendations, and the like. And most educators sincerely believe that schools with the most rigorous entrance requirements offer the highest-quality educations.

It is also well known that, for a variety of reasons, blacks and Hispanics on the average tend to get lower high school grades and to score lower on the SAT then do whites. Accordingly, a smaller proportion of blacks and Hispanics than whites are admitted to college, especially to the more presti-gious schools. In this case, we can say that college entrance requirements constitute an example of structural discrimination because they have a neg-ative effect on blacks and Hispanics.

The criteria that educators believe to be important are less accessible to black and Hispanic students than to whites. As a rule, college managers and faculty members do not intend to be racially discriminatory, and many even feel quite badly about the harm done to black and Hispanic students as a re-sult of these requirements. However, most also do not want to change the requirements.

It is possible, of course, that the underrepresentation of blacks and His-panics on college campuses is being caused by institutional discrimination. A few colleges may still refuse to admit any black students. Others may pur-posely inflate entrance requirements as a way of screening out most minor-ity students. Individual discrimination may also be taking place, as when a recruiting officer chooses to avoid black high schools when looking for po-tential students.

Another example of structural discrimination can be found in the con-   20
text of job qualifications. Many employers require new employees to have earned a bachelor's degree even though there may be no direct connection between a college education and the skills required for the job in question. The employer, of course, may *believe* that college-educated people will be better workers. Since a smaller percentage of blacks and Hispanics get bachelor's degrees than do whites, blacks will be underrepresented among those who qualify for the job. This is a case of structural discrimination

because blacks and Hispanics are negatively affected by the educational requirement for the job, even though there may be no intent to subordinate
them.

On the other hand, an employer who used the bachelor's degree requirement intentionally to screen out blacks and Hispanics would be committing a form of institutional discrimination. And an individual personnel
manager who refused to hire a qualified black applicant would be guilty of
individual discrimination.

Consider yet another example: Insurance rates for homes, businesses,
and cars are generally higher in black communities than in white communities, in part because of the higher rates of street crime in lower-income
black communities. Insurance companies argue that it is good business to
charge higher rates in areas where they will have to pay out more in claims,
and they insist that they charge high rates in high-crime white areas as well.
Yet in spite of the apparently race-neutral determination of insurance rates,
the average black ends up paying more than the average white. So this, too,
is an example of structural discrimination.

The "good business" argument can also be seen in the banking practice of
granting loans and mortgages. The lower an individual's income, the less
likely that individual is to be able to pay back the loan. Banks, therefore, are
reluctant to give loans to lower-income people; and if they grant any at all, the
loans are likely to be small. Since blacks tend to earn lower incomes than
whites, they find it more difficult to get loans. Consequently, they have a
harder time buying homes and starting businesses. Accordingly, the lending
practices of banks are examples of structural discrimination, even though the
banks themselves may be following standard business procedures.

Although banks and insurance companies routinely use the "good business" argument to justify structural discrimination, they sometimes practice
institutional discrimination as well. Banks often "redline" black communities, and insurance companies have been known to charge higher rates in
black communities than in white ones, even after controlling for crime
rates.

Many social scientists and much of the general public would be reluctant to apply the term *structural discrimination* to the examples listed here,
given the absence in these examples of any intent to harm minority groups
or keep them subordinate. I assert, however, that the negative *effects* constitute discrimination. Thus even policies that are intended to be race-neutral
and are carried out by well-intentioned people can perpetuate racial
inequality.

Like institutional discrimination, structural discrimination is almost always a matter of majority group against minority group, not the other way
around. Again, since most social institutions work to the advantage of the
majority group, few if any institutional policies favor the minority group.
Groups with little power are generally unable to implement policies that are
structurally discriminatory.

25

Although it is sometimes difficult to know whether a given policy that negatively affects minority-group members is a case of individual, institutional, or structural discrimination, an understanding of the conceptual differences among these three categories is important. Since the different types of discrimination have different origins, different policies are required for their elimination. In trying to eliminate individual and institutional discrimination, for example, activists can appeal to the moral and legal principles of equal opportunity and racial fairness. In particular, they might argue that race-neutral meritocratic policies that promote equal opportunity should be the rule in education, employment, housing, and so on.

Where structural discrimination is concerned, however, policies that are race-neutral in intent are not race-neutral in effect. Since policymakers involved with structural discrimination have not tried to harm or subordinate minorities, it makes no sense for activists to appeal to their sense of racial fairness. The policymakers already believe that they are being racially fair. Instead, activists must convince these policymakers to reevaluate some of the fundamental policies upon which their institutions are based.

If banks are practicing institutional discrimination by "redlining" minority areas, for example, activists can demand that the banks treat each person in that area as a distinct individual. All individuals, inside or outside the redlined area, who meet the banks' universal credit requirements should receive a mortgage. Race or neighborhood should not be a factor.

Confronting the profit-oriented business practices of banks, which I have included in the category of structural discrimination, is more problematic. Even without redlining, banks grant fewer mortgages to blacks than to whites because of racial differences in income and wealth. Bankers can argue that they are simply being good race-neutral capitalists and may even express sincere regret that more blacks do not qualify for loans and mortgages. To deal with this problem, activists must confront the profit-oriented business practices themselves, not the racial views of the bank officials. Perhaps banks have to forgo some of their profits in order to help poor black communities. Perhaps the federal government must subsidize more loans to low-income blacks and create not-for-profit banks in low-income areas. 30

Alternative arguments are also needed to confront racial inequality in higher education. Colleges that refuse to admit Hispanics who meet their admissions standards are practicing institutional discrimination. If activists can successfully show that qualified Hispanics are not being admitted, they can try to bring public pressure on the colleges to get them to stop discriminating. If this effort failed, the activists could probably sue the colleges in a court of law.

Combatting structurally discriminatory admissions standards in higher education requires a different approach. Educators can justify admissions standards by saying that certain grade-point averages and SAT scores are essential to the mission of academic excellence in their institutions, even though a relatively small percentage of Hispanics are able to qualify.

SIGNE
PHILADELPHIA DAILY NEWS
Philadelphia
USA

Activists must call on educators to modify their standards, not their racial views. (Certainly Hispanics do not benefit from the standards currently in place.) Indeed, colleges should devote more resources to remedial and support programs for Hispanics who do not meet the entrance requirements. Also needed are new pedagogical techniques, including a more multicultural curriculum, that would be more suited to Hispanic students. And perhaps colleges could shoulder some of the responsibility for improving the quality of high schools attended by Hispanic students.

All three types of discrimination coexist as major problems in American society. And all three must be confronted if racial equality is to be achieved. Individual and institutional discrimination are the most visible. Yet even if they were completely eliminated, the prospect of racial equality would be jeopardized by continuing structural discrimination.

ENGAGING THE TEXT

1. What distinction does Pincus make between prejudice and discrimination, and why is the difference important to his argument?
2. Pincus notes that individual discrimination can be directed against members of the majority group as well as against members of minorities, but that institutional discrimination against the majority is far less likely to occur. Why?
3. Are grades and test scores fair, race-neutral criteria for college admission, or do they constitute structural discrimination as Pincus claims? What factors, besides individual intelligence, might affect a student's ability to achieve high grades and to do well on standardized tests?

4. Pincus points out that some employers require college degrees on the theory that college graduates are better workers than those without college experience, even when the job itself doesn't demand college-level skills. Is this fair or unfair, and why?

5. Differences in loan approvals and insurance rates for predominantly African American neighborhoods are often explained as a matter of "good business." What's wrong with the "good business" argument, according to Pincus? What do you find persuasive or unpersuasive about his analysis?

6. What remedies does Pincus suggest for structural discrimination? Do they seem workable? If so, how would you persuade institutions like banks, insurance companies, and colleges to implement them? If not, what alternatives would you propose?

EXPLORING CONNECTIONS

7. Which forms of discrimination — individual, institutional, or structural — are evident in the following situations?
   - the "hidden curriculum" observed by Jean Anyon (p. 186)
   - the obstacles encountered by women in college as identified by Myra and David Sadker (p. 228)
   - the treatment of female athletes described by Mariah Burton Nelson (p. 468)
   - the workplace barriers encountered by Stephen Cruz (p. 326)
   - the responses of Kathleen Boatwright's family, friends, and acquaintances when she comes out as a lesbian (p. 780)

8. Pincus suggests that individual and institutional discrimination can be combatted by appealing to "the moral and legal principles of equal opportunity and racial fairness" (para. 27). How do the experiences of C. P. Ellis (p. 575) and Cora Tucker (p. 390) support or complicate this view?

9. What point does the cartoon on page 592 seem to be making about discrimination in college admissions? What common assumptions about affirmative action is the cartoonist calling into question?

EXTENDING THE CRITICAL CONTEXT

10. Working in groups, list any examples of discrimination that you've observed or experienced. Is there any disagreement about whether or not particular examples represent truly discriminatory behavior or policies? If you find examples of discrimination against both minority and majority group members, do you see differences between the types of discrimination encountered by each group?

11. Research your college's admissions criteria: Do they take race and ethnicity into account in any way? Should they?

Fences Against Freedom

LESLIE MARMON SILKO

Despite the reputation of the United States as a nation of immigrants, this country has experienced waves of fierce anti-immigrant feeling throughout its history, particularly during times of economic hardship and rapid social change. Leslie Marmon Silko sees the current political fervor to "control our borders" as a reaction fueled by bigotry and scapegoating; likewise she deplores the climate of fear and constraint created by twelve-foot steel walls on our border and Border Patrol checkpoints on our highways. Silko was born in Albuquerque, New Mexico, in 1948 and grew up on the Laguna Pueblo reservation nearby. Winner of a prestigious MacArthur Foundation grant, Silko has published collections of poems and stories as well as two highly regarded novels, Ceremony *(1977) and* Almanac of the Dead *(1992). "Fences Against Freedom" appears in her recent book of essays on contemporary Native American life,* Yellow Woman and the Beauty of the Spirit *(1996).*

As a person of mixed ancestry, I have always been very sensitive to the prevailing attitudes toward people of color. I remember a time around 1965 when the term *race* was nearly replaced with the term *ancestry* on government forms and applications. For a short time questions about one's ancestry and religion were even deleted from paperwork. During this time, concerted efforts were made by public officials and media people to use the term *ancestry* instead of *race*. Geneticists had scientific evidence that there is only one race, the human race; there is only one species to which all people belong: *Homo sapiens*. This period of conscientious education of the public to eradicate misinformation about "race" grew out of the civil rights movement of the 1950s and from key decisions from the U.S. Supreme Court. Presidents Kennedy and Johnson spoke explicitly about the blot on the honor of the U.S. made by centuries of prejudice; even the U.S. Congress, with the exception of a few senators and congressmen from southern states, joined them in asserting equality for all human beings.[1]

In 1967 I chose "race" as my topic for a paper in one of my college honors seminars. I had taken two semesters of anthropology in my freshman year, and I already knew that "race" had been a hot topic among the physical anthropologists for decades. I understood that the "one race, human race" theorists like Ashley Montagu had finally assembled incontrovertible biological proofs that had swept away the nineteenth-century theories of distinct

---

[1]*even the U.S. Congress . . . all human beings:* In 1964 Congress passed the Civil Rights Acts, outlawing segregation, discriminatory hiring practices, and restrictions on voting.

"races." But I wanted to see exactly how this shift had come about, because I knew that many people still were under the influence of nineteenth-century notions concerning race.

I went to the University of New Mexico library and checked out all the books I could find on the topic of "race." As a person of mixed ancestry, I could not afford to take my anthropology professor or Ashley Montagu's word for it. Segregationists implied that liberals had seized power on campuses and that to mollify blacks and other "racial" minorities these liberals had concocted false data to prove human equality. My parents and the people of the Laguna Pueblo community who raised me taught me that we are all one family — all the offspring of Mother Earth — and no one is better or worse according to skin color or origin. My whole life I had believed this, but now I had to test what I had been taught as a child because I had also been taught that the truth matters more than anything, even more than personal comfort, more than one's own vanity. It was possible that my parents and the people at home, along with people like Ashley Montagu, had deluded themselves just as the segregationists had alleged. I was determined to know the truth even if the truth was unpleasant.

I don't remember all the books I read, but I do remember that Carleton Coon was the name of the leading physical anthropologist whose books and articles argued the "racial superiority" of some "races" over others. I wondered then if Mr. Coon's vehemence about the superiority of the white race had anything to do with his name, which I knew was a common slur used against African Americans. Had the other children teased him about his name in the school yard? Was that why Coon had endured censure by his peers to persist in his "race" research in physical anthropology long after the Nuremberg[2] trials?

I once read an article whose author stated that racism is the only form 5 of mental illness that is communicable. Clever but not entirely true. Racism in the U.S. is learned by us beginning at birth.

As a person of mixed ancestry growing up in the United States in the late 1950s, I knew all of the cruel epithets that might be hurled at others; the knowledge was a sort of solace that I was not alone in my feelings of unease, of not quite belonging to the group that clearly mattered most in the United States.

Human beings need to feel as if they "belong"; I learned from my father to feel comfortable and happy alone in the mesas and hills around Laguna. It was not so easy for me to learn where we Marmons belonged, but gradually I understood that we of mixed ancestry belonged on the outer edge of the circle between the world of the Pueblo and the outside world. The Laguna people were open and accepted children of mixed ancestry because appearance was secondary to behavior. For the generation of my

---

[2]*Nuremberg:* In 1945–1946, following World War II, key Nazi officials were tried for war crimes in Nuremberg, Germany.

great-grandmother and earlier generations, anyone who had not been born in the community was a stranger, regardless of skin color. Strangers were not judged by their appearances — which could deceive — but by their behavior. The old-time people took their time to become acquainted with a person before they made a judgment. The old-time people were very secure in themselves and their identity; and thus they were able to appreciate differences and to even marvel at personal idiosyncrasies so long as no one and nothing was being harmed.

The cosmology of the Pueblo people is all-inclusive; long before the arrival of the Spaniards in the Americas, the Pueblo and other indigenous communities knew that the Mother Creator had many children in faraway places. The ancient stories include all people of the earth, so when the Spaniards marched into Laguna in 1540, the inclination still was to include rather than to exclude the strangers, even though the people had heard frightening stories and rumors about the white men. My great-grandmother and the people of her generation were always very curious and took delight in learning odd facts and strange but true stories. The old-time people believed that we must keep learning as much as we can all of our lives. So the people set out to learn if there was anything at all *good* in these strangers; because they had never met any humans who were completely evil. Sure enough, it was true with these strangers too; some of them had evil hearts, but many were good human beings.

Similarly, when my great-grandfather, a white man, married into the Anaya family, he was adopted into the community by his wife's family and clans. There always had been political factions among these families and clans, and by his marriage, my great-grandfather became a part of the political intrigues at Laguna. Some accounts by anthropologists attempt to portray my great-grandfather and his brother as instigators or meddlers, but the anthropologists have overestimated their importance and their tenuous position in the Pueblo. Naturally, the factions into which the Marmon brothers had married incorporated these new "sons" into their ongoing intrigues and machinations. But the anthropologists who would portray the Marmon brothers as dictators fool themselves about the power of white men in a pueblo. The minute the Marmon brothers crossed over the line, they would have been killed.

Indeed, people at Laguna remember my great-grandfather as a gentle, 10
quiet man, while my beloved Grandma A'mooh is remembered as a stern, formidable woman who ran the show. She was also a Presbyterian. Her family, the Anayas, had kept cattle and sheep for a long time, and I imagine that way back in the past, an ancestor of hers had been curious about the odd animals the strangers brought and decided to give them a try.

I was fortunate to be reared by my great-grandmother and others of her generation. They always took an interest in us children and they were always delighted to answer our questions and to tell us stories about the old days. Although there were very few children of mixed ancestry in those days, the old folks did not seem to notice. But I could sense a difference from younger people, the generation that had gone to the First World War. On rare occasions, I could sense an anger that my appearance stirred in them, although I sensed that the anger was not aimed at me personally. My appearance reminded them of the outside world, where racism was thriving.

I learned about racism firsthand from the Marmon family. My great-grandfather endured the epithet Squaw Man. Once when he and two of his young sons (my Grandpa Hank and his brother Frank) walked through the lobby of Albuquerque's only hotel to reach the café inside, the hotel manager stopped my great-grandfather. He told my great-grandfather that he was welcome to walk through the lobby, but when he had Indians with him, he should use the back door. My great-grandfather informed him that the "Indians" were his sons, and then he left and never went into the hotel again.

There were branches of the Marmon family that, although Laguna, still felt they were better than the rest of us Marmons and the rest of the Lagunas as well. Grandpa Hank's sister, Aunt Esther, was beautiful and vain and light skinned; she boarded at the Sherman Institute in Riverside, California, where my grandfather and other Indian students were taught trades. But Aunt Esther did not get along with the other Indian girls; she refused to speak to them or to have anything to do with them. So she was allowed to attend a Riverside girls school with white girls. My grandfather, who had a broad nose and face and "looked Indian," told the counselor at Sherman that he wanted to become an automobile designer. He was told by the school guidance counselor that Indians weren't able to design automobiles; they taught him to be a store clerk.

I learned about racism firsthand when I started school. We were punished if we spoke the Laguna language once we crossed onto the school grounds. Every fall, all of us were lined up and herded like cattle to the girls' and boys' bathrooms, where our heads were drenched with smelly insecticide regardless of whether we had lice or not. We were vaccinated in both arms without regard to our individual immunization records.

But what I remember most clearly is the white tourists who used to   15
come to the school yard to take our pictures. They would give us kids each a nickel, so naturally when we saw tourists get out of their cars with cameras, we all wanted to get in the picture. Then one day when I was older, in the third grade, white tourists came with cameras. All of my playmates started to bunch together to fit in the picture, and I was right there with them maneuvering myself into the group when I saw the tourist look at me with a particular expression. I knew instantly he did not want me to be in the picture; I stayed close to my playmates, hoping that I had misread the man's face. But the tourist motioned for me to move away to one side, out of his picture. I remember my playmates looked puzzled, but I knew why the man did not want me in his picture: I looked different from my playmates. I was part white and he didn't want me to spoil his snapshots of "Indians." After that incident, the arrival of tourists with cameras at our school filled me with anxiety. I would stand back and watch the expressions on the tourists' faces before trying to join my playmates in the picture. Most times the tourists

were kindly and did not seem to notice my difference, and they would motion for me to join my classmates; but now and then there were tourists who looked relieved that I did not try to join in the group picture.

Racism is a constant factor in the United States; it is always in the picture even if it only forms the background. Now as the condition of the U.S. economy continues to deteriorate and the people grow restive with the U.S. Congress and the president, the tactics of party politicians sink deeper in corruption. Racism is now a trump card, to be played again and again shamelessly by both major political parties. The U.S. government applications that had used the term *ancestry* disappeared; the fiction of "the races" has been reestablished. Soon after Nixon's election the changes began, and racism became a key component once more in the U.S. political arena. The Republican Party found the issue of race to be extremely powerful, so the Democrats, desperate for power, have also begun to pander racism to the U.S. electorate.

Fortunately, the people of the United States are far better human beings than the greedy elected officials who allegedly represent them in Congress and the White House. The elected officials of both parties currently are trying to whip up hysteria over immigration policy in the most blatantly racist manner. Politicians and media people talk about the "illegal aliens" to dehumanize and demonize undocumented immigrants, who are for the most part people of color. The Cold War with the Communist world is over, and now the military defense contractors need to create a new bogeyman to justify U.S. defense spending. The U.S.–Mexico border is fast becoming a militarized zone. The army and marine units from all over the U.S. come to southern Arizona to participate in "training exercises" along the border.

When I was growing up, U.S. politicians called Russia an "Iron Curtain" country, which implied terrible shame. As I got older I learned that there wasn't really a curtain made of iron around the Soviet Union; I was later disappointed to learn that the wall in Berlin was made of concrete, not iron. Now the U.S. government is building a steel wall twelve feet high that eventually will span the entire length of the Mexican border. The steel wall already spans four-mile sections of the border at Mexicali and Naco; and at Nogales, sixty miles south of Tucson, the steel wall is under construction.

Immigration and Naturalization Services, or the Border Patrol, has greatly expanded its manpower and checkpoint stations. Now when you drive down Interstate 10 toward El Paso, you will find a check station. When you drive north from Las Cruces up I-25 about ten miles north of Truth or Consequences, all interstate highway traffic is diverted off the highway into an INS checkpoint. I was detained at that checkpoint in December 1991 on my way from Tucson to Albuquerque for a book signing of my novel *Almanac of the Dead.* My companion and I were detained despite the fact that we showed the Border Patrol our Arizona driver's licenses. Two men from California, both Chicanos, were being detained at the same time, despite the fact that they too presented an ID and spoke English with-

out the thick Texas accents of the Border Patrolmen. While we were detained, we watched as other vehicles were waved through the checkpoint.
The occupants of those vehicles were white. It was quite clear that my appearance — my skin color — was the reason for the detention.

The Border Patrol exercises a power that no highway patrol or county   20
sheriff possesses: the Border Patrol can detain anyone they wish for no reason
at all. A policeman or sheriff needs to have some shred of probable cause, but
not the Border Patrol. In fact, they stop people with Indio-Hispanic characteristics, and they target cars in which white people travel with brown people.
Recent reports of illegal immigration by people of Asian ancestry mean that
the Border Patrol now routinely detain anyone who looks Asian. Once you
have been stopped at a Border Patrol checkpoint, you are under the control of
the Border Patrol agent; the refusal to obey any order by the Border Patrol
agent means you have broken the law and may be arrested for failure to obey
a federal officer. Once the car is stopped, they ask you to step out of the car;
then they ask you to open the trunk. If you ask them why or request a search
warrant, they inform you that it will take them three or four hours to obtain a
search warrant. They make it very clear that if you "force" them to get a search
warrant, they will strip-search your body as well as your car and luggage. On
this particular day I was due in Albuquerque, and I did not have the four
hours to spare. So I opened my car trunk, but not without using my right to
free speech to tell them what I thought of them and their police state procedures. "You are not wanted here," I shouted at them, and they seemed astonished. "Only a few years ago we used to be able to move freely within our own
country," I said. "This is our home. Take all this back where you came from.
You are not wanted here."

Scarcely a year later, my friend and I were driving south from Albuquerque, returning to Tucson after a paperback book promotion. There are
no Border Patrol detention areas on the southbound lanes of I-25, so I
settled back and went to sleep while Gus drove. I awakened when I felt the
car slowing to a stop. It was nearly midnight on New Mexico State Road 26,
a dark lonely stretch of two-lane highway between Hatch and Deming.
When I sat up, I saw the headlights and emergency flashers of six vehicles —
Border Patrol cars and a Border Patrol van blocked both lanes of the road.
Gus stopped the car and rolled down his window to ask what was wrong.
But the Border Patrolman and his companion did not reply; instead the first
officer ordered us to "step out of the car." Gus asked why we had to get out
of the car. His question seemed to set them off — two more Border Patrolmen immediately approached the car and one of them asked, "Are you
looking for trouble?" as if he would relish the opportunity.

I will never forget that night beside the highway. There was an awful
feeling of menace and of violence straining to break loose. It was clear that
they would be happy to drag us out of the car if we did not comply. So we
both got out of the car and they motioned for us to stand on the shoulder of
the road. The night was very dark, and no other traffic had come down the

road since they had stopped us. I thought how easy it would be for the Border Patrolmen to shoot us and leave our bodies and car beside the road. There were two other Border Patrolmen by the van. The man who had asked if we were looking for trouble told his partner to "get the dog," and from the back of the white van another Border Patrolman brought a small female German shepherd on a leash. The dog did not heel well enough to suit him, and I saw the dog's handler jerk the leash. They opened the doors of our car and pulled the dog's head into the car, but I saw immediately from the expression in her eyes that the dog hated them, and she would not serve them. When she showed no interest in the inside of the car, they brought her around back to the trunk, near where we were standing. They half-dragged her up into the trunk, but still she did not indicate stowed-away humans or illegal drugs.

Their mood got uglier; they seemed outraged that the dog could not find any contraband, and they dragged her over to us and commanded her to sniff our legs and feet. To my relief, the strange anger the INS agents had focused at us now had shifted to the dog. I no longer felt so strongly that we would be murdered. We exchanged looks — the dog and I. She was afraid of what they might do, just as I was. The handler jerked the leash violently as she sniffed us, as if to make her perform better, but the dog refused to accuse us. The dog had an innate dignity, an integrity that did not permit her to serve those men. I can't forget the expression in her eyes; it was as if she was embarrassed to be associated with them. I had a small amount of medicinal marijuana in my purse that night, but the dog refused to expose me. I am not partial to dogs, but I can't forget the small German shepherd. She saved us from the strange murderous mood of the Border Patrolmen that night.

In February of 1993, I was invited by the Women's Studies Department at UCLA to be a distinguished visiting lecturer. After I had described my run-ins with the Border Patrol, a professor of history at UCLA related her story. It seems she had been traveling by train from Los Angeles to Albuquerque twice each month to work with an informant. She had noticed that the Border Patrol officers were there each week to meet the Amtrak trains to scrutinize the passengers, but since she is six feet tall and of Irish and German ancestry, she was not particularly concerned. Then one day when she stepped off the train in Albuquerque, two Border Patrolmen accosted her. They wanted to know what she was doing, why she was traveling between Los Angeles and Albuquerque. This is the sort of police state that has developed in the southwest United States. No person, no citizen is free to travel without the scrutiny of the Border Patrol. Because Reverend Fife and the sanctuary movement bring political refugees into the U.S. from Central America, the Border Patrol is suspicious of and detains white people who appear to be clergy, those who wear ethnic clothing or jewelry, and women who wear very long hair or very short hair (they could be nuns). Men with beards and men with long hair are also likely to be detained because INS agents suspect "those sorts" of white people may help political refugees.

In Phoenix the INS agents raid public high schools and drag dark-   25
skinned students away to their vans. In 1992, in El Paso, Texas, a high
school football coach driving a vanload of his players in full uniform was
pulled over on the freeway and INS agents put a cocked revolver to the
coach's head through the van window. That incident was one of many similar abuses by the INS in the El Paso area that finally resulted in a restrain-
ing order against the Border Patrol issued by a federal judge in El Paso.

At about the same time, a Border Patrol agent in Nogales shot an un-
armed undocumented immigrant in the back one night and attempted to
hide the body; a few weeks earlier the same Border Patrol agent had shot
and wounded another undocumented immigrant. His fellow agent, perhaps
realizing Agent Elmer had gone around the bend, refused to help in the
cover-up, so Agent Elmer threatened him. Agent Elmer was arrested and
tried for murder, but his southern Arizona jury empathized with his fear of
brown-skinned people; they believed Agent Elmer's story that he feared for
his life even though the victim was shot in the back trying to flee. Agent
Elmer was also cleared of the charges of wounding in the other case. For
years, undocumented immigrant women have reported sexual assaults by
Border Patrol agents. But it wasn't until Agent Elmer was tried for murder
that another Nogales INS agent was convicted of the rape of a woman he
had taken into custody for detainment. In the city of South Tucson, where
80 percent of the respondents were Chicano or Mexicano, a research project by the University of Wisconsin recently revealed that one out of every
five persons living there had been stopped by INS agents in the past year.

I no longer feel the same about driving from Tucson to Albuquerque
via the southern route. For miles before I approach the INS check stations,
I can feel the anxiety pressing hard against my chest. But I feel anger too, a
deep, abiding anger at the U.S. government, and I know that I am not alone
in my hatred of these racist immigration policies, which are broadcast every
day, teaching racism, demonizing all people of color, labeling indigenous
people from Mexico as "aliens" — creatures not quite human.

The so-called civil wars in El Salvador and Guatemala are actually wars
against the indigenous tribal people conducted by the white and mestizo ruling classes. These are genocidal wars conducted to secure Indian land once
and for all. The Mexican government is buying Black Hawk helicopters in
preparation for the eradication of the Zapatistas[3] after the August elections.

I blame the U.S. government — congressmen and senators and President Clinton. I blame Clinton most of all for playing the covert racism card
marked "Immigration Policy." The elected officials, blinded by greed and
ambition, show great disrespect to the electorate they represent. The people,
the ordinary people in the street, evidence only a fraction of the racist behavior that is exhibited on a daily basis by the elected leaders of the United
States and their sluttish handmaidens, the big television networks.

---

[3]*Zapatistas:* Indigenous people who rebelled against the Mexican government in 1994,
demanding a variety of social and political reforms.

If we truly had a representative democracy in the United States, I do   30
not think we would see such a shameful level of racism in this country. But
so long as huge amounts of money are necessary in order to run for office,
we will not have a representative democracy. The form of government we
have in the United States right now is not representative democracy but
"big capitalism"; big capitalism can't survive for long in the United States
unless the people are divided among themselves into warring factions. Big
capitalism wants the people of the United States to blame "foreigners" for
lost jobs and declining living standards so the people won't place the blame
where it really belongs: with our corrupt U.S. Congress and president.

As I prepare to drive to New Mexico this week, I feel a prickle of anxiety down my spine. Only a few years ago, I used to travel the highways between Arizona and New Mexico with a wonderful sensation of absolute
freedom as I cruised down the open road and across the vast desert plateaus
in southern Arizona and southern New Mexico. We citizens of the United
States grew up believing this freedom of the open road to be our inalienable
right. The freedom of the open road meant we could travel freely from state
to state without special papers or threat of detainment; this was a "right" citizens of Communist and totalitarian governments did not possess. That
wide open highway was what told us we were U.S. citizens. Indeed, some
say, this freedom to travel is an integral part of the American identity.

To deny this right to me, to some of us who because of skin color or
other physical characteristics appear to fit fictional profiles of "undesirables," is to begin the inexorable slide into further government-mandated
"race policies" that can only end in madness and genocide. The slaughters
in Rwanda and Bosnia did not occur spontaneously — with neighbor
butchering neighbor out of the blue; no, politicians and government officials called down these maelstroms of blood on their people by unleashing
the terrible irrational force that racism is.

Take a drive down Interstate 8 or Interstate 10, along the U.S.–Mexico
border. Notice the Border Patrol checkpoints all vehicles must pass
through. When the Border Patrol agent asks you where you are coming
from and where you are going, don't kid around and answer in Spanish —
you could be there all afternoon. Look south into Mexico and enjoy the
view while you are still able, before you find yourself behind the twelve-foot
steel curtain the U.S. government is building.

Engaging the Text

1. Silko asserts that "racism in the U.S. is learned by us beginning at birth"
   (para. 5). Summarize the "lessons" about race that she learns from each of
   the following:
   - college reading
   - family stories

- the traditions and attitudes of the Laguna people
- elementary school
- tourists
- American politicians
- encounters with the Border Patrol

How do these lessons shape her attitude toward U.S. immigration policy?

2. In Silko's two experiences with the Border Patrol, do you think the officers' behavior is justifiable or not? Are her reactions reasonable or unreasonable? Should the Border Patrol have the power to stop a car and interrogate the driver on the basis of that person's appearance?

3. Silko contends that American politicians demonstrate more openly racist attitudes and behavior than "ordinary people in the street" (para. 29). Do your experiences and observations tend to support or contradict this assertion?

4. What kinds of evidence does Silko offer to support her claim that U.S. immigration policy is racist? Do you find some portions of her argument more persuasive than others? If so, which ones, and why?

EXPLORING CONNECTIONS

5. Silko cites a number of incidents — from history, the news, her own experiences and those of family members and friends — as evidence of racism. Review Fred L. Pincus's discussion of individual, institutional, and structural discrimination (p. 586) and try to determine which of these terms, if any, you would use to describe each incident.

6. To what extent does Donald L. Barlett and James B. Steele's essay, "Have-Mores and Have-Lesses" (p. 356), support Silko's analysis of the role played by "big capitalism" in fueling anti-immigrant feeling?

7. Libertarian David Boaz (p. 732) proposes that all freedoms should be based on the concepts of property rights and self-ownership; how would he respond to Silko's argument for "freedom of the open road"? Do illegal immigrants threaten the "property rights" of American citizens? Do Border Patrol checkpoints infringe on the "self-ownership" of Americans traveling within their own country?

EXTENDING THE CRITICAL CONTEXT

8. Write an essay or journal entry modeled on Silko's, in which you recount experiences or stories that have taught you about race relations in general and about the significance of your own racial or ethnic identity.

9. As a class project, read recent articles or editorials on immigration in a variety of publications. What evidence do you find, if any, to support Silko's contention that politicians and media "dehumanize and demonize" illegal immigrants? What differences do you notice in the ways the issue of immigration is addressed in different sources?

10. Watch the classic film *El Norte* on videotape. Does the film support, complicate, or challenge Silko's view of U.S. immigration policy?

Town Hall Television

PATRICIA J. WILLIAMS

Body piercing. Acquaintance rape. Children who want to divorce their parents. Women who marry convicted killers. Television talk shows seem to address every human quirk and tragedy. On occasion, when they deal with serious issues like domestic violence, AIDS, or drug addiction, we may find them sources of useful information; when they sink to tabloid topics like sex with space aliens, we tend to dismiss them as mindless entertainment. But as Patricia J. Williams suggests in this essay, talk shows may be something worse than harmless fluff: they may do great damage by trivializing serious social differences and by perpetuating dangerous stereotypes. Williams (b. 1951) is a professor at Columbia University School of Law. She has published two critically acclaimed collections of essays, The Alchemy of Race and Rights *(1992) and* The Rooster's Egg *(1995); her writing typically blends personal experience with reflections on legal theory, social issues, and popular culture. This essay is taken from her second book.*

Perhaps 6 April 1989 will go down in history as the first "designer drug raid." As heavily armed and flak-jacketed SWAT commandoes stormed the alleged "rock house" near 51st and Main Street in Southcentral L.A., Nancy Reagan and Los Angeles Police Chief Darryl Gates sat across the street nibbling fruit salad in a luxury motor home emblazoned "THE ESTABLISHMENT." According to the *Times,* the former first lady "could be seen freshening her makeup" while the SWATs roughly frisked and cuffed the fourteen "narcoterrorists" captured inside the small stucco bungalow. As hundreds of incredulous neighbors ("Hey, Nancy Reagan. She's over here in the ghetto!") gathered behind the police barriers, the great Nay-sayer, accompanied by Chief Gates and a small army of nervous Secret Service agents, toured the enemy fortress with its occupants still bound on the floor in flabbergasted submission. After frowning at the tawdry wallpaper and drug-bust debris, Nancy, who looked fetching in her LAPD windbreaker, managed to delve instantly into the dark hearts at her feet and declare: "These people in here are beyond the point of teaching and rehabilitating."

— MIKE DAVIS, *CITY OF QUARTZ*

If the pen is mightier than the sword and a picture is worth a thousand words, then a little simple multiplication is all it takes to figure out the enormous propagandistic power that television has to create truth and shape opinion. Within the world of TV land, into which American life has been reduced as well as reproduced, the phenomenon of the talk show has emerged as a genre located somewhere on the spectrum between coffee klatch and town meeting, or perhaps between the psychiatrist's couch and the crowd scene at a bad accident.

Talk-show sets usually resemble the interiors of homes, if not my home; they employ as backdrops what appear to be living rooms or home libraries or other womblike spaces. There are usually some nice comfortable arm-chairs or a sofa or a round (not square) kitcheny table. Coffee mugs are often strewn about, maybe an artsy bunch of jonquils in a nice vase. Yet these womb-rooms are always sawed in half somehow; they offer 180 de-grees of pure schmoozey ambiance and then, at the 181st degree exactly, they open up to an amphitheater of perfect strangers, all of whom always look like my sunny neighbors when I lived in Wisconsin, and none of whom ever look like my lock-jawed neighbors in New York (with the possible ex-ception of the audiences on the old *Morton Downey Show*).

To be a good talk-show host requires a personality that has been similarly sawed in half. "How does it feel," they ask their guests with the soft seduction of a mother cat licking her young; "to know you are feared and loathed by mil-lions of our viewers all over America?" they finish, with the poisonous flick of an impatient rattlesnake. Talk-show hosts act like good parents with an unruly set of teenagers-who-also-happen-to-be-serial-killers: Life's a living hell these days . . . All his friends seem to be going through this phase . . . What's a society to do? Phil as Father-Knows-Best; Oprah as not Mom, because that's too close to Mammy, so Ur-Girlfriend instead.

All of this creates, I think, a very powerful illusion of intimate open-ness . . . yet . . . objectivity — *sincere* objectivity. It creates an illusion of care mixed with an illusion of rigorous inquiry — a species, I guess, of Tough Love. It creates an imagined world in which there is no permission for anyone's feelings ever to be hurt, even when they ought to be; in which good intentions and great attitude rule the day.

This results in a forum that is very persuasive by virtue of its form alone: an atmosphere of overdetermined consensus, much like the scene of that bad accident, in which everyone rushes forth with a blaze of inconsistent opinions and viewpoints, but everyone goes away agreeing or believing they agree that they saw the same thing. A Rorschach test[1] of response in which a catharsis of agreement emerges — such as, sleeping with your girlfriend's boyfriend is right! or it's wrong! — even though the reasons underlying the consensus of rightness or wrongness are extremely varied or vastly contradictory.

Talk shows are sometimes touted as new-age town halls or mini-court-rooms. I suppose this comparison reveals a certain longing for community that has arisen as the common turf of political and judicial space has

5

---

[1]*Rorschach test:* Psychological test in which subjects are shown abstract ink blots and asked to explain what they see in the pattern; predictably, different people perceive very differ-ent meanings in the same blot.

become less and less accessible to all citizens as an arena for debate and resolution. But talk-show politics is hardly that summoned up by the image of the soapbox orator holding forth on the Boston Common or the village green: increasingly plugged into the bottom line of market ratings, the shows' ethics have less and less to do with the democratic constraints of fairness, due process, public accountability, or equality of access. If, again, the general expectation is that talk shows function as a way of airing all points of view or resolving disputes in the manner of a public trial, then we must take stock of the fact that the "talk" is managed with more reference to the rules of football than to any principles of justice; we must begin to wonder if the energy for public debate is not being siphoned off into a market for public spectacle. We must begin to unravel the political function of this jumble of stage-direction-qua-civics. Mangled metaphors of level playing fields tussling with invocations of zero-sum games in which the winner takes all. Bashing the stuffing out of each other but at the end, being good sports and shaking hands and agreeing to disagree and nothing is so important we can't go off and have lunch together. "Can you forgive your father for molesting you?" asks Sally Jesse Raphael. "*No,*" sobs the truly bad sport.

Talk shows as town meetings leave one with the impression of having had a full airing of all viewpoints, no matter how weird, and of having reached a nobler plane, a higher level of illumination, of having wrestled with something till we've exhausted it. And maybe that's true for programs that deal with women who drink their own blood or the joys of body piercing. But I am very concerned that when it comes to some of our most pressing social issues such as anti-Semitism and racism, TV talk shows perform an actual disservice, by (1) creating a sense both of false consensus and false division, and (2) condoning and perpetuating racism, anti-Semitism, and gender stereotypes, even as they supposedly challenge them.

Let me give an example of a Phil Donahue show I saw some time ago. It was a program that purported to be deeply concerned about the rise of anti-Semitism on campuses in general, and the proliferation of Jewish American Princess jokes in particular. "How would *you* feel . . . ?" Phil kept asking by way of challenge to the studio audience.

The program opened with an extraordinarily long volley of Jewish American Princess jokes, not merely recited, but written in large block letters across the screen — for the hearing impaired presumably, although there was no other part of the program so emphatically emblazoned. The jokes played on mean-spirited, vulgar stereotypes; they were just plain offensive, even though they were positioned as merely "models" of the subject to be discussed. Although styled as a repudiation, they reenacted the whole problem — over and over and over again. The audience tittered and giggled its way through this opening volley. It was significant, I think, this tittering — after each joke, the cameras focused as intently as a dentist's drill upon the stunned-rabbit faces of the audience, people caught in a not-quite-sure-how-to-respond mode that implicated them as they struggled to be good sports while being broadcast live to millions of people. It was a marvelously assimilative moment; they were like children trying to decide how to be seen at their best. Smile? Frown? Which is the posture of belonging? So they tittered. Nervously.

I think there is a real risk of destructive impact in jokes that make fun of the supposed characteristics of historically oppressed or shunned people. Of course all humor depends on context, but, if it is possible to speak generally, I think that such jokes too frequently are the enactment of a kind of marking process, in which communities are described, kinship delimited, the enemy imagined. An anecdote will illustrate what I mean by marking, how I think the bright innocence of social divisiveness works:

Some months ago I was riding on a train. In between napping and reading the newspaper, I languidly listened to the conversation of a very well-dressed, well-educated family seated across the aisle from me. Here was a family with traditional values *and* Ralph Lauren looks[2] — mother, father, bright little girl, and a big bearded friend of the family who looked like that seafaring guy on the clam chowder label. It was a fascinatingly upper-class conversation, about investments, photography, and Japanese wood-joinery. It was also soothingly pleasant conversation, full of affection, humor, and great politeness. I enjoyed listening to them, and allowed myself the pleasure of my secret participation in their companionability. Then they started telling redneck jokes.

There was no shift in their voices to warn me of it; they spoke in the same soft, smiling voices as before, with those deliciously crisp *t*'s and delicately rounded *r*'s.

The little girl, who was probably around seven or eight years old, asked, "What's a redneck?" No longer napping, I leaned closer, intrigued by what this moment of sharp but innocent intervention promised in terms of drawing these otherwise thoughtful adults up short in glorious contrition and a renewed sense of social awareness.

"Drinks beer, drives a pickup, low-class, talks bad," came the unselfconscious reply. Then the three adults told more jokes to illustrate. Being very bright, the little girl dumped innocence by the wayside and promptly responded by telling a bunch of blond jokes and then one involving "black" — but I couldn't hear if she was talking about hair or skin.

The father told another joke — what's got ten teeth and something I couldn't hear? The answer was the front row of a Willie Nelson concert.

They were so pleasant and happy. Their conversation was random, wandering. They showed each other pictures of their kids, they played word games, they shared hot dogs. And yet they were transporting a virus.

This process of marking. No wonder it is so hard to get out of our race and class binds. It occurred to me, as I watched this family in all its remarkable

10

15

---

[2] *Ralph Lauren looks:* Ralph Lauren (b. 1939) designs conservative clothing and housewares that are intended to suggest wealth and tastefulness.

typicality, that that little girl will have to leave the warmth of the embracing, completely relaxed circle of those happy people before she can ever appreciate the humanity of someone who drives a pickup, who can't afford a dentist. "Rednecks" were lovingly situated, by that long afternoon of gentle joking, in the terrible vise of the comic, defined by the butt of a joke.

How *givingly* social divisions are transmitted was brought home to me in an essay written by one of my former students. She described her father as a loving family man, who worked six and a half days a week to provide for his wife and children. He always took Sunday afternoons off; that was sacred time, reserved for a "family drive." Yet the family's favorite pastime, as they meandered in Norman Rockwell[3] contentment, was, according to this student, "trying to pick the homosexuals out of the crowd." ("Bill Clinton would have *homosexuals* in his administration!" railed Pat Robertson[4] in his speech to the 1992 Republican National Convention, during which convention homophobic violence reportedly rose by 8 percent in the city of Houston.[5])

Hate learned in a context of love is a complicated phenomenon. Love learned in a context of hate endangers all our family.

But back to our show. The rest of the *Phil Donahue Show* on Jewish   20 American Princesses was a panoply of squirmy ways of dealing with being marked. Phil's guests included not only a Real Live Jewish Princess, but a Black American Princess, an Italian-American Princess, and a WASP[6] Princess as well. While they were all willing to be called *princesses* of X, Y, or Z flavor, they all denied that they were the *bad* kind of princess. They negotiated this good princess/evil princess dichotomy by at least four different maneuvers.

First of all, there was the "role model" response — yeah, well, I'm proud to be pushy, and I've made it into a positive attribute, look at how creative I am with the lemons life has handed me. Doesn't bother me a bit (even though an unfortunate cost of this survival mechanism would seem to be a rather defensive, cynical edge).

Second, there was the "But I really am a princess!" response — the attempt to remove the sarcasm from it and be taken as literal, real. The Real WASP Princess proclaimed herself as the inheritor of society's privilege and all the other ethnic princesses as mere wannabe imitations of herself; the black princess claimed to have been the real princess of a considerably smaller if warmer realm, in having been the apple of her protective family's eye; and the Italian-American princess claimed that her real name *was* Princess, at least that's what Daddy always said.

Third, there was the move to concede that while some women may be like that awful thing at the butt of all those jokes, "all Jewish women are not

[3]*Norman Rockwell:* See page 21.
[4]*Pat Robertson:* Televangelist and conservative Republican presidential candidate.
[5]*Houston:* Site of the 1992 Republican National Convention.
[6]*WASP:* White Anglo-Saxon Protestant.

JAPs." There was, in other words, a concession of the category as validly descriptive, and then the attempt to exceptionalize oneself from it. This is, I think, a powerfully defeatist move because it concedes the category as given, it allows the stereotype legitimacy. The response to racist labeling is thus locked into the logic of merely defining oneself in or out of the label, rather than focused on challenging the prejudice and judgmentalism of the marking process at all. I think this resort to a "them-us" dichotomy or an "I'm different" strategy is perhaps the most prevalent individual response to bigotry, as well as the most destructive.

Fourth, there is the opposite move — and perhaps the most prevalent institutional response to bigotry — the tendency to generalize rather than to exceptionalize, to make shrill self-absorption a general feature of all women, who are arrayed so as to possess a panoply of generally negative qualities. Women of *all* ethnicities are bitchy, stupid, fluffy, greedy, sacrificial, ran the logic of a narrative that played sexism against anti-Semitism, that played general stereotype against its sub-components. Thus "equal opportunity bimboism" is proffered as an odd model of the way in which tolerating intolerance emerges as the new norm for tolerance itself.

Perhaps the best example of the new tolerance of the same old intolerance is the intriguing fact that Howard Stern's sidekick, Robin Quivers, is a black woman who sounds exactly like the quintessential, self-abasing, totally concessionary but not dumb stereotype of a white woman. A *blond* white woman stereotype at that. A shrewdly submissive "bimbo" in blackface. "Oh, *How*ard," she sighs. This weird component is so manifest that Garry Trudeau parodies it in his *Doonesbury* cartoon, in which a movie is supposedly being made of Stern's book *Private Parts*. Boopsie, Trudeau's blonde update of Betty Boop,[7] is sought to play the part of Robin Quivers. "But Quivers is black," says Boopsie. "Don't worry, it's radio," comes the reply. It is a cartoon that echoes the pre-*really*-weird weirdness of Michael Jackson's Unbearable Lightness of Being[8] — specifically, when he attempted to cast a little white boy to play himself as a child in a Japanese-produced video of his life.

Trudeau's cartoon is a complex commentary on the strange post–civil rights era configuration of what integration seems to have become: to the extent that it exists, it does not merge black and white people as much as it hybridizes troublesome stereotypes of women and minorities. Barbie now has cornrows and six little gold earrings. Ken has two-tone hair, one earring, and for a brief moment in doll-making history sported a necklace with a cock ring hanging from it. (Mattell executives claimed they had no *idea* . . .) If black women are still having trouble breaking into the world of high

25

---

[7]*Betty Boop:* Curvaceous cartoon airhead first popularized in the 1920s.

[8]*Michael Jackson's Unbearable Lightness of Being:* Word play linking the African American pop star's habit of bleaching his skin with the title of a 1984 novel by Czech writer Milan Kundera, *The Unbearable Lightness of Being*.

fashion modeling, the same cannot be said of RuPaul, whose glittering, towering, snap-queen transvestism has made him the toast of the MTV crowd. Mammy dolls have gone Hispanic. The most racially and philosophically conservative justice on the Supreme Court in at least fifty years is a black man. The Victorian image of the "fallen woman gotten with child" has merged with that of the black Jezebel and produced the always-rollicking "welfare queen."

It's an interesting development beyond the time-honored use of black-face makeup to mock black people: just use a black *person*. It's a move that was captured in the casting of the movie version of *The Bonfire of the Vanities;*[9] the role of a judge who spews racist claptrap to black defendants was recast from that of white man in the novel to black man in the movie. Let the black judge deliver the racist rebuke because then it's not racist, seems to be the logic of the day. So confined are black bodies by the rigors of puppeted rebuke and suffocating buffoonery that there is a certain sociopathic logic in Michael Jackson's repeated surgical attempts to escape the stereotype of the societally scourged "black male" body.

The powerful weight of stereotypes about blacks as not seriously human was painfully visible in the (how shall I put this gently) incomprehensibly miscalculated spoof undertaken by the actor Ted Danson of his then-girlfriend Whoopi Goldberg, in which Danson donned blackface, ate watermelon, joked about their sex life and her genitalia, and used the word "nigger" repeatedly. Supposedly mystified by the storm of public reaction, Danson made much of the claim that Whoopi had approved of the material, even helped write it, and that therefore it couldn't be racist.

Only weeks after that fiasco, Goldberg's recipe for "Jewish American Princess Fried Chicken" was published in a book entitled *Cooking in Litchfield Hills.* The recipe "instructs you to 'Send a chauffeur to your favorite butcher shop for the chicken,' 'Watch your nails' when you shake the chicken in a brown paper bag, and 'Have Cook prepare rest of meal while you touch up your makeup.'" Again there was a big debate about whether it was funny or whether it was anti-Semitic (as though these are necessarily oppositional). Again the handwringing about subject position, although I'm sure that's not what people imagined they were doing. "'This is in worse taste (than the Friars Club debacle) because she could get away with that because she is black,' said one Litchfield resident." Let's sidestep for just a moment the complicating detail that Goldberg didn't "get away with" much of anything precisely because she employed the body of Danson as the time-honored comedic vehicle of racial minstrelsy — a white man in blackface mouthing too-familiar-to-be-ironic stereotypes, albeit supposedly written by a black woman to parody herself. Rather, I would like to examine the retort by Goldberg's publicist: "Maybe (the critics) are not aware that Whoopi is Jewish, so she is certainly not anti-Semitic." It's a familiar litany: I

[9]*The Bonfire of the Vanities:* Satiric novel by Tom Wolfe (1987).

heard a Jewish person tell this joke so it's not anti-Semitic. And of course, a Jewish person wrote this joke for me, so I couldn't possibly be anti-Semitic just because I'm trying to lighten things up with a little Holocaust humor. In fact, goes the next line of the argument, *you're* intolerant for claiming intolerance. And a bad sport besides. (It is by a reversed but mirror-image logic, perhaps, that two Oakhurst, California, high school youths who dressed up in the white robes and hoods of the Ku Klux Klan and reenacted a lynching of another student for a Halloween party — and who were rewarded with a prize in the costume competition — sought to justify the event by saying that *no* blacks were at the party so it was okay.)

What does this humor mask? At what point does blackface minstrelsy converge with white-hooded threats? Look at *this* and fear for your life; look at *that* and laugh, just laugh and laugh. "My boot came from the area of lower California and connected with the suspect's scrotum around lower Missouri," wrote the Los Angeles police sergeant Stacey Koon of the arrest of a Latino suspect that occurred before his beating of Rodney King. "My boot stopped around Ohio, but the suspect's testicles continued into upper Maine. The suspect was literally lifted off the ground. The suspect tried to speak, but it appeared he had something in his throat, probably his balls." Where are the borders of this cartooned life and that imprisoned one? Is it all just one long joke without end, amen? And when will someone let up on the laugh-track button and just let me breathe?

The *Washington Post* ran an article after the Whoopi and Ted incident that asked all the wrong questions: Was it funny, why not? Was it offensive and why? Yet I wonder if it is not possible to cross well into the realm of the offensive *and* be "funny." I wonder how line-crossing from not-funny seems to redeem any degree of threat or insult. The *Post* article ends with a quote from Tim Conaway, *Hustler* magazine's humor editor, whose last word is "If you're hurt by a cartoon in a magazine . . . I think you ought to look at the real root of that pain." But in bigotry's insistent blindness, humor is precisely the device by which discussion of the roots of pain is most consistently deflected.

ENGAGING THE TEXT

1. What are the attractions of talk show television, according to Williams? What are its dangers or drawbacks? How accurate do you think her assessment is?

2. What does Williams mean when she says that humor based on stereotypes represents a "marking process" (para. 10)? Why does she feel that marking poses "a real risk of destructive impact"? Do you agree that humor can be harmful?

3. Williams lists four strategies used by Phil Donahue's guests to cope with being stereotyped as "princesses." What problems or dangers does she see in each response? How convincing do you find her analysis?

4. What's the significance for Williams of the incident on the train in which she overhears the family telling "redneck" jokes (paras. 11–16)? How does her initial impression of the family intensify her shock at the jokes they tell? Do you think that she overreacts to the situation? Why or why not?

5. Williams cites several incidents in which people attempt to excuse offensive humor because the joke-teller is a member of the targeted group or because no member of the targeted group is present to be offended. In what circumstances, if any, do you think that humor based on stereotypes is acceptable?

6. At the end of the essay, Williams wonders whether a joke can be both offensive *and* funny. Can it? What is Williams's point in raising this issue?

EXPLORING CONNECTIONS

7. Which of the causes of prejudice outlined by Vincent Parrillo (p. 563) are evident in the experiences Williams describes? Imagining yourself as Parrillo, write an analysis of the role that joking and humor can play in perpetuating prejudice.

8. While Williams deplores the stereotyping of women on television talk shows, Elizabeth Dodson Gray (p. 71) argues that talk shows have helped women by raising public awareness about domestic violence. Which view do you find more convincing, and why? Can both be true?

EXTENDING THE CRITICAL CONTEXT

9. Watch several talk shows: What images do they present of particular groups? Do they directly or indirectly reinforce stereotypes as Williams claims?

10. If you have seen a television show or movie recently that relies on humor you consider offensive, compare notes with classmates about shows that have offended them. Do you find any consistency in your perceptions of offensiveness?

I'm Black, You're White, Who's Innocent?

SHELBY STEELE

This essay comes from one of the most controversial American books of the past decade — The Content of Our Character: A New Vision of Race in America. Shelby Steele (b. 1946) believes that black Americans have failed to seize opportunities that would lead to social equality; he is also an outspoken critic of affirmative action, arguing that instead of promoting equal-

ity it locks its recipients into second-class status. Angry critics accuse him of underestimating the power of racism, of blaming victims for their predicament, of being a traitor to his race. In this selection, Steele offers his observations on why black and white Americans have not been able to sustain the kind of dialogue that would make mutual understanding possible. His essays have garnered a number of awards, including a National Book Critics Circle Award. Steele's writings have appeared in Harper's, The American Scholar, The New Republic, *and many other journals and magazines. He is a research fellow at the Hoover Institute, Stanford University, and is writing a book on U.S. race relations and social policy.*

It is a warm, windless California evening, and the dying light that covers the redbrick patio is tinted pale orange by the day's smog. Eight of us, not close friends, sit in lawn chairs sipping chardonnay. A black engineer and I (we had never met before) integrate the group. A psychologist is also among us, and her presence encourages a surprising openness. But not until well after the lovely twilight dinner has been served, when the sky has turned to deep black and the drinks have long since changed to scotch, does the subject of race spring awkwardly upon us. Out of nowhere the engineer announces, with a coloring of accusation in his voice, that it bothers him to send his daughter to a school where she is one of only three black children. "I didn't realize my ambition to get ahead would pull me into a world where my daughter would lose touch with her blackness," he says.

Over the course of the evening we have talked about money, past and present addictions, child abuse, even politics. Intimacies have been revealed, fears named. But this subject, race, sinks us into one of those shaming silences where eye contact terrorizes. Our host looks for something in the bottom of his glass. Two women stare into the black sky as if to locate the Big Dipper and point it out to us. Finally, the psychologist seems to gather herself for a challenge, but it is too late. "Oh, I'm sure she'll be just fine," says our hostess, rising from her chair. When she excuses herself to get the coffee, the psychologist and two sky gazers offer to help.

With four of us now gone, I am surprised to see the engineer still silently holding his ground. There is a willfulness in his eyes, an inner pride. He knows he has said something awkward, but he is determined not to give a damn. His unwavering eyes intimidate even me. At last the host's head snaps erect. He has an idea. "The hell with coffee," he says. "How about some of the smoothest brandy you've ever tasted?" An idea made exciting by the escape it offers. Gratefully, we follow him back into the house, quickly drink his brandy, and say our good-byes.

An autopsy of this party might read: death induced by an abrupt and lethal injection of the American race issue. An accurate if superficial assessment. Since it has been my fate to live a rather integrated life, I have often witnessed sudden deaths like this. The threat of them, if not the reality, is a part of the texture of integration. In the late 1960s, when I was just out of college, I took a delinquent's delight in playing the engineer's role, and actually developed a small reputation for playing it well. Those were the days of flagellatory white guilt: it was such great fun to pinion some professor or housewife or, best of all, a large group of remorseful whites, with the knowledge of both their racism and their denial of it. The adolescent impulse to sneer at convention, to startle the middle-aged with doubt, could be indulged under the guise of racial indignation. And how could I lose? My victims — earnest liberals for the most part — could no more crawl out from under my accusations than Joseph K. in Kafka's *Trial*[1] could escape the amorphous charges brought against him. At this odd moment in history the world was aligned to facilitate my immaturity.

About a year of this was enough: the guilt that follows most cheap   5
thrills caught up to me, and I put myself in check. But the impulse to do it faded more slowly. It was one of those petty talents that is tied to vanity, and when there were ebbs in my self-esteem the impulse to use it would come alive again. In integrated situations I can still feel the faint itch. But then there are many youthful impulses that still itch and now, just inside the door of midlife, this one is least precious to me.

In the literature classes I teach I often see how the presence of whites all but seduces some black students into provocation. When we come to a novel by a black writer, say Toni Morrison, the white students can easily discuss the human motivations of the black characters. But, inevitably, a black student, as if by reflex, will begin to set in relief the various racial problems that are the background of these characters' lives. This student's tone will carry a reprimand: the class is afraid to confront the reality of racism. Classes cannot be allowed to die like dinner parties, however. My latest strategy is to thank that student for his or her moral vigilance and then appoint the young man or woman as the class's official racism monitor. But even if I get a laugh — I usually do, but sometimes the student is particularly indignant, and it gets uncomfortable — the strategy never quite works. Our racial division is suddenly drawn in neon. Overcaution spreads like spilled paint. And, in fact, the black student who started it all does become a kind of monitor. The very presence of this student imposes a new accountability on the class.

I think those who provoke this sort of awkwardness are operating out of a black identity that obliges them to badger white people about race almost on principle. Content hardly matters. (For example, it made little sense for the engineer to expect white people to anguish terribly much over his decision to send his daughter to school with *white* children.) Race indeed re-

---

[1]*Kafka's* Trial: Austrian writer Franz Kafka (1883–1924) is famous for his dreamlike and ominous stories. In his novel *The Trial*, the character known only as Joseph K. battles an intricate legal and police system that never specifies his alleged crime.

mains a source of white shame; the goal of these provocations is to put whites, no matter how indirectly, in touch with this collective guilt. In other words, these provocations I speak of are *power* moves, little shows of power that try to freeze the "enemy" in self-consciousness. They gratify and inflate the provocateur. They are the underdog's bite. And whites, far more secure in their power, respond with self-contained and tolerant silence that is itself a show of power. What greater power than that of nonresponse, the power to let a small enemy sizzle in his own juices, to even feel a little sad at his frustration just as one is also complimented by it. Black anger always, in a way, flatters white power. In America, to know that one is not black is to feel an extra grace, a little boost of impunity.

I think the real trouble between the races in America is that the races are not just races but competing power groups — a fact that is easily minimized, perhaps because it is so obvious. What is not so obvious is that this is true quite apart from the issue of class. Even the well-situated middle-class (or wealthy) black is never completely immune to that peculiar contest of power that his skin color subjects him to. Race is a separate reality in American society, an entity that carries its own potential for power, a mark of fate that class can soften considerably but not eradicate.

The distinction of race has always been used in American life to sanction each race's pursuit of power in relation to the other. The allure of race as a human delineation is the very shallowness of the delineation it makes. Onto this shallowness — mere skin and hair — men can project a false depth, a system of dismal attributions, a series of malevolent or ignoble stereotypes that skin and hair lack the substance to contradict. These dark projections then rationalize the pursuit of power. Your difference from me makes you bad, and your badness justifies, even demands, my pursuit of power over you — the oldest formula for aggression known to man. Whenever much importance is given to race, power is the primary motive.

But the human animal almost never pursues power without first con- 10 vincing himself that he is *entitled* to it. And this feeling of entitlement has its own precondition: to be entitled one must first believe in one's innocence, at least in the area where one wishes to be entitled. By innocence I mean a feeling of essential goodness in relation to others and, therefore, superiority to others. Our innocence always inflates us and deflates those we seek power over. Once inflated we are entitled; we are in fact licensed to go after the power our innocence tells us we deserve. In this sense, *innocence is power.* Of course, innocence need not be genuine or real in any objective sense, as the Nazis demonstrated not long ago. Its only test is whether or not we can convince ourselves of it.

I think the racial struggle in America has always been primarily a struggle for innocence. White racism from the beginning has been a claim of white innocence and therefore of white entitlement to subjugate blacks. And in the sixties, as went innocence so went power. Blacks used the innocence that grew out of their long subjugation to seize more power, while whites lost some of their innocence and so lost a degree of power over blacks. Both races instinctively understand that to lose innocence is to lose power (in relation to each other). To be innocent someone else must be guilty, a natural law that leads the races to forge their innocence on each other's backs. The inferiority of the black always makes the white man superior; the evil might of whites makes blacks good. This pattern means that both races have a hidden investment in racism and racial disharmony despite their good intentions to the contrary. Power defines their relations, and power requires innocence, which, in turn, requires racism and racial division.

I believe it was his hidden investment that the engineer was protecting when he made his remark — the white "evil" he saw in a white school "depriving" his daughter of her black heritage confirmed his innocence. Only the logic of power explained his emphasis — he bent reality to show that he was once again a victim of the white world and, as a victim, innocent. His determined eyes insisted on this. And the whites, in their silence, no doubt protected their innocence by seeing him as an ungracious troublemaker, his bad behavior underscoring their goodness. What none of us saw was the underlying game of power and innocence we were trapped in, or how much we needed a racial impasse to play that game.

When I was a boy of about twelve, a white friend of mine told me one day that his uncle, who would be arriving the next day for a visit, was a racist. Excited by the prospect of seeing such a man, I spent the following afternoon hanging around the alley behind my friend's house, watching from a distance as this uncle worked on the engine of his Buick. Yes, here was evil and I was compelled to look upon it. And I saw evil in the sharp angle of his elbow as he pumped his wrench to tighten nuts. I saw it in the blade-sharp crease of his chinos, in the pack of Lucky Strikes that threatened to slip from his shirt pocket as he bent, and in the way his concentration seemed to shut out the human world. He worked neatly and efficiently, wiping his hands constantly, and I decided that evil worked like this.

I felt a compulsion to have this man look upon me so that I could see evil — so that I could see the face of it. But when he noticed me standing beside his toolbox, he said only, "If you're looking for Bobby, I think he went up to the school to play baseball." He smiled nicely and went back to work. I was stunned for a moment, but then I realized that evil could be sly as well, could smile when it wanted to trick you.

Need, especially hidden need, puts a strong pressure on perception, 15 and my need to have this man embody white evil was stronger than any contravening evidence. As a black person you always hear about racists but rarely meet any who will let you know them as such. And I needed to incarnate this odious category of humanity, those people who hated Martin Luther King, Jr., and thought blacks should "go slow" or not at all. So, in my mental dictionary, behind the term "white racist," I inserted this man's likeness. I would think of him and say to myself, "There is no reason for him to hate black people. Only evil explains unmotivated hatred." And this thought soothed me; I felt innocent. If I hated white people, which I did not, at least I had a reason. His evil commanded me to assert in the world the goodness he made me confident of in myself.

In looking at this man I was *seeing for innocence* — a form of seeing that has more to do with one's hidden need for innocence (and power) than with the person or group one is looking at. It is quite possible, for example, that the man I saw that day was not a racist. He did absolutely nothing in my presence to indicate that he was. I invested an entire afternoon in seeing not the man but in seeing my innocence through the man. *Seeing for innocence* is, in this way, the essence of racism — the use of others as a means to our own goodness and superiority.

The loss of innocence has always to do with guilt, Kierkegaard[2] tells us, and it has never been easy for whites to avoid guilt where blacks are concerned. For whites, *seeing for innocence* means seeing themselves and blacks in ways that minimize white guilt. Often this amounts to a kind of white revisionism,[3] as when President Reagan declared himself "color-blind" in matters of race. The President, like many of us, may have aspired to racial color blindness, but few would grant that he ever reached this sublimely guiltless state. His statement clearly revised reality, moved it forward into some heretofore unknown America where all racial determinism would have vanished. I do not think that Ronald Reagan was a racist, as that term is commonly used, but neither do I think that he was capable of seeing color without making attributions, some of which may have been negative — nor am I, or anyone else I've ever met.

So why make such a statement? I think Reagan's claim of color blindness with regard to race was really a claim of racial innocence and guiltlessness — the preconditions for entitlement and power. This was the claim that grounded Reagan's campaign against special entitlement programs — affirmative action, racial quotas, and so on — that black power had won in the sixties. Color blindness was a strategic assumption of innocence that licensed Reagan's use of government power against black power. . . .

Black Americans have had to find a way to handle white society's presumption of racial innocence whenever they have sought to enter the American mainstream. Louis Armstrong's[4] exaggerated smile honored the presumed innocence of white society — *I will not bring you your racial guilt if you will let me play my music.* Ralph Ellison[5] calls this "masking"; I call it bargaining. But whatever it's called, it points to the power of white society

---

[2]*Kierkegaard:* Danish philosopher and religious thinker Søren Kierkegaard (1813– 1855).

[3]*revisionism:* The reinterpretation or revising of reality to suit one's current purposes.

[4]*Louis Armstrong:* American jazz trumpet virtuoso and singer (1900–1971).

[5]*Ralph Ellison:* American novelist (b. 1914), best known for *Invisible Man,* the account of a nameless black youth coming of age in a hostile society.

to enforce its innocence. I believe this power is greatly diminished today. Society has reformed and transformed — Miles Davis[6] never smiles. Nevertheless, this power has not faded altogether and blacks must still contend with it.

Historically, blacks have handled white society's presumption of inno-   20
cence in two ways: they have bargained with it, granting white society its innocence in exchange for entry into the mainstream, or they have challenged it, holding that innocence hostage until their demand for entry (or other concessions) was met. A bargainer says, *I already believe you are innocent (good, fair-minded) and have faith that you will prove it.* A challenger says, *If you are innocent, then prove it.* Bargainers *give* in hope of receiving; challengers *withhold* until they receive. Of course, there is risk in both approaches, but in each case the black is negotiating his own self-interest against the presumed racial innocence of the larger society.

Clearly, the most visible black bargainer on the American scene today is Bill Cosby. His television show has been a perfect formula for black bargaining in the eighties. The remarkable Huxtable family — with its doctor/lawyer parent combination, its drug-free, college-bound children, and its wise yet youthful grandparents — is a blackface version of the American dream. Cosby is a subscriber to the American identity, and his subscription confirms his belief in its fair-mindedness. His vast audience knows this, knows that Cosby will never assault their innocence with racial guilt. Racial controversy is all but banished from the show. The Huxtable family never discusses affirmative action.

The bargain Cosby offers his white viewers — *I will confirm your racial innocence if you accept me* — is a good deal for all concerned. Not only does it allow whites to enjoy Cosby's humor with no loss of innocence, but it actually enhances their innocence by implying that race is not the serious problem for blacks that it once was. If anything, the success of this handsome, affluent black family points to the fair-mindedness of whites who, out of their essential goodness, changed society so that black families like the Huxtables could succeed. Whites can watch *The Cosby Show* and feel complimented on a job well done.

The power that black bargainers wield is the power of absolution. On Thursday nights, Cosby, like a priest, absolves his white viewers, forgives and forgets the sins of the past. And for this he is rewarded with an almost sacrosanct[7] status. Cosby benefits from what might be called the gratitude factor. His continued number-one rating may have something to do with the (white) public's gratitude at being offered a commodity so rare in our time; he tells his white viewers each week that they are okay, and that this black man is not going to challenge them.

---

[6]*Miles Davis:* Jazz musician and trumpeter (1926–1991).
[7]*sacrosanct:* Sacred.

When a black bargains, he may invoke the gratitude factor and find himself cherished beyond the measure of his achievement; when he challenges, he may draw the dark projections of whites and become a source of irritation to them. If he moves back and forth between these two options, as I think many blacks do today, he will likely baffle whites. It is difficult for whites either to accept or reject such blacks. It seems to me that Jesse Jackson is such a figure — many whites see Jackson as a challenger by instinct and a bargainer by political ambition. They are uneasy with him, more than a little suspicious. His powerful speech at the 1984 Democratic Convention was a masterpiece of bargaining. In it he offered a King-like[8] vision of what America could be, a vision that presupposed Americans had the fair-mindedness to achieve full equality — an offer in hope of a return. A few days after this speech, looking for rest and privacy at a lodge in Big Sur,[9] he and his wife were greeted with standing ovations three times a day when they entered the dining room for meals. So much about Jackson is deeply American — this underdog striving, his irrepressible faith in himself, the daring of his ambition, and even his stubbornness. These qualities point to his underlying faith that Americans can respond to him despite race, and this faith is a compliment to Americans, an offer of innocence.

But Jackson does not always stick to the terms of his bargain as Cosby does on TV. When he hugs Arafat,[10] smokes cigars with Castro,[11] refuses to repudiate Farrakhan,[12] threatens a boycott of major league baseball or, more recently, talks of "corporate barracudas," "pension-fund socialism," and "economic violence," he looks like a challenger in bargainer's clothing, and his positions on the issues look like familiar protests dressed in white-paper formality. At these times he appears to be revoking the innocence so much else about him seems to offer. The old activist seems to come out of hiding once again to take white innocence hostage until whites prove they deserve to have it. In his candidacy there is a suggestion of protest, a fierce insistence on his *right* to run, that sends whites a message that he may secretly see them as a good bit less than innocent. His dilemma is to appear the bargainer while his campaign itself seems to be a challenge.

There are, of course, other problems that hamper Jackson's bid for the Democratic presidential nomination. He has held no elective office, he is thought too flamboyant and opportunistic by many, there are rather loud whispers of "character" problems. As an individual, he may not be the best test of a black man's chances for winning so high an office. Still, I believe it

25

---

[8]*King-like:* Like that of Martin Luther King, Jr.

[9]*Big Sur:* Section of the California coast known for its natural beauty.

[10]*Arafat:* Yasir Arafat (b. 1929), leader of the Palestine Liberation Organization, or PLO.

[11]*Castro:* Fidel Castro (b. 1926), president of Cuba.

[12]*Farrakhan:* Louis Farrakhan (b. 1933), Nation of Islam leader, often accused of making anti-Semitic remarks. Many African American politicians carefully distance themselves from Farrakhan.

is the aura of challenge surrounding him that hurts him most. Whether it is right or wrong, fair or unfair, I think no black candidate will have a serious chance at his party's nomination, much less the presidency, until he can convince white Americans that he can be trusted to preserve their sense of racial innocence. Such a candidate will have to use his power of absolution; he will have to flatly forgive and forget. He will have to bargain with white innocence out of genuine belief that it really exists. There can be no faking it. He will have to offer a vision that is passionately raceless, a vision that strongly condemns any form of racial politics. This will require the most courageous kind of leadership, leadership that asks all the people to meet a new standard.

Now the other side of America's racial impasse: how do blacks lay claim to their racial innocence?

The most obvious and unarguable source of black innocence is the victimization that blacks endured for centuries at the hands of a race that insisted on black inferiority as a means to its own innocence and power. Like all victims, what blacks lost in power they gained in innocence — innocence that, in turn, entitled them to pursue power. This was the innocence that fueled the civil rights movement of the sixties and that gave blacks their first real power in American life — victimization metamorphosed into power via innocence. But this formula carries a drawback that I believe is virtually as devastating to blacks today as victimization once was. It is a formula that binds the victim to his victimization by linking his power to his status as a victim. And this, I'm convinced, is the tragedy of black power in America today. It is primarily a victim's power, grounded too deeply in the entitlement derived from past injustice and in the innocence that Western/Christian tradition has always associated with poverty.

Whatever gains this power brings in the short run through political action, it undermines in the long run. Social victims may be collectively entitled, but they are all too often individually demoralized. Since the social victim has been oppressed by society, he comes to feel that his individual life will be improved more by changes in society than by his own initiative. Without realizing it, he makes society rather than himself the agent of change. The power he finds in his victimization may lead him to collective action against society, but it also encourages passivity within the sphere of his personal life.

Not long ago, I saw a television documentary that examined life in Detroit's inner city on the twentieth anniversary of the riots there in which forty-three people were killed. A comparison of the inner city then and now showed a decline in the quality of life. Residents feel less safe, drug trafficking is far worse, crimes by blacks against blacks are more frequent, housing remains substandard, and the teenage pregnancy rate has skyrocketed. Twenty years of decline and demoralization, even as opportunities for blacks to better themselves have increased. This paradox is not peculiar to

30

Detroit. By many measures, the majority of blacks — those not yet in the middle class — are further behind whites today than before the victories of the civil rights movement. But there is a reluctance among blacks to examine this paradox, I think, because it suggests that racial victimization is not our real problem. If conditions have worsened for most of us as racism has receded, then much of the problem must be of our own making. To admit this fully would cause us to lose the innocence we derive from our victimization. And we would jeopardize the entitlement we've always had to challenge society. We are in the odd and self-defeating position in which taking responsibility for bettering ourselves feels like a surrender to white power.

So we have a hidden investment in victimization and poverty. These distressing conditions have been the source of our own real power, and there is an unconscious sort of gravitation toward them, a complaining celebration of them. One sees evidence of this in the near happiness with which certain black leaders recount the horror of Howard Beach,[13] Bensonhurst,[14] and other recent instances of racial tension. As one is saddened by these tragic events, one is also repelled at the way some black leaders — agitated to near hysteria by the scent of victim power inherent in them — leap forward to exploit them as evidence of black innocence and white guilt. It is as though they sense the decline of black victimization as a loss of standing and dive into the middle of these incidents as if they were reservoirs of pure black innocence swollen with potential power.

Seeing for innocence pressures blacks to focus on racism and to neglect the individual initiative that would deliver them from poverty — the only thing that finally delivers *anyone* from poverty. With our eyes on innocence we see racism everywhere and miss opportunity even as we stumble over it. About 70 percent of black students at my university drop out before graduation — a flight from opportunity that racism cannot explain. It is an injustice that whites can see for innocence with more impunity than blacks can. The price whites pay is a certain blindness to themselves. Moreover, for whites seeing for innocence continues to engender the bad faith of a long-disgruntled minority. But the price blacks pay is an ever-escalating poverty that threatens to make the worst off a permanent underclass. Not fair, but real.

Challenging works best for the collective, while bargaining is more the individual's suit. From this point on, the race's advancement will come from the efforts of its individuals. True, some challenging will be necessary for a long time to come. But bargaining is now — today — a way for the black individual to *join* the larger society, to make a place for himself or herself.

---

[13]*Howard Beach:* Scene in Queens, New York, of a December 1986 racial confrontation in which several young African American men were severely beaten and one died.

[14]*Bensonhurst:* Location in Brooklyn, New York, where the racially motivated murder of sixteen-year-old Yusuf Hawkins took place in August 1989.

"Innocence is ignorance," Kierkegaard says, and if this is so, the claim of innocence amounts to an insistence on ignorance, a refusal to know. In their assertions of innocence both races carve out very functional areas of ignorance for themselves — territories of blindness that license a misguided pursuit of power. Whites gain superiority by not knowing blacks; blacks gain entitlement by not seeing their own responsibility for bettering themselves. The power each race seeks in relation to the other is grounded in a double-edged ignorance of the self as well as of the other.

The original sin that brought us to an impasse at the dinner party I 35 mentioned occurred centuries ago, when it was first decided to exploit racial difference as a means to power. It was a determinism that flowed karmically from this sin that dropped over us like a net that night. What bothered me most was our helplessness. Even the engineer did not know how to go forward. His challenge hadn't worked, and he'd lost the option to bargain. The marriage of race and power depersonalized us, changed us from eight people to six whites and two blacks. The easiest thing was to let silence blanket our situation, our impasse. . . .

What both black and white Americans fear are the sacrifices and risks that true racial harmony demands. This fear is the measure of our racial chasm. And though fear always seeks a thousand justifications, none is ever good enough, and the problems we run from only remain to haunt us. It would be right to suggest courage as an antidote to fear, but the glory of the word might only intimidate us into more fear. I prefer the word effort — relentless effort, moral effort. What I like most about this word are its connotations of everydayness, earnestness, and practical sacrifice. No matter how badly it might have gone for us that warm summer night, we should have talked. We should have made the effort.

ENGAGING THE TEXT

1. What does Steele mean by "innocence" and by "seeing for innocence"? How does he apply these terms to racial conflict and struggles for power in the United States? How do blacks and whites claim innocence through racial conflict? What does Steele mean when he says that "innocence is power?"

2. According to Steele, what strategies have African Americans employed to handle "white society's presumption of racial innocence" (para. 19)? How does he account for public reactions to figures like Bill Cosby and Jesse Jackson in terms of these strategies? Are there other possible explanations of their appeal?

3. Steele believes that "bargaining is now — today — a way for the Black individual to *join* the larger society" (para. 33). Do you agree? Is bargaining an available and acceptable alternative for all African Americans?

4. Steele writes that when the issue of race comes up in classes, "overcaution spreads like spilled paint" (para. 6). If you have observed this phenomenon

in class or in other circumstances, write a journal entry describing one such incident and analyzing the behavior of the people involved.

EXPLORING CONNECTIONS

5. How might Ken Hamblin (p. 376), Vincent N. Parrillo (p. 563), Fred L. Pincus (p. 586), and Jane Lazarre (below) evaluate Steele's assertion that racism grows out of the desire to claim "innocence"? Imagine that they are all participating in a panel discussion and role-play the conversation that would ensue.

6. Compare Steele's notions of bargaining and challenging with Ronald Takaki's idea of sharing stories (p. 538) as strategies for improving race relations. Which seems like the more fruitful or more realistic model for interethnic communication, and why?

7. Write an imaginary dialogue between C. P. Ellis (p. 575), Malcolm X (p. 219), and Steele on American racism. What might they each say about the causes of racist thinking and behavior? About the chances for curbing racism? How would they respond to each other's ideas and strategies for change?

EXTENDING THE CRITICAL CONTEXT

8. Find out the graduation rate for African American students at your school. Then interview a faculty member or administrator to get her or his perceptions of why your school does or does not graduate black students in proportionate numbers. If several students do this assignment, you can begin to analyze prevailing attitudes on campus.

9. At the end of this essay, Steele says, "No matter how badly it might have gone for us . . . we should have talked. We should have made the effort." Working in groups, role-play the conversation that might have occurred that night. How might you initiate such conversations on your campus? Is talk the only or best solution to the kinds of tensions Steele describes?

Color Blind: The Whiteness of Whiteness
Jane Lazarre

Race is often thought of as an African American, Latino, or Asian issue, but it's less often perceived as a white issue, particularly by white people themselves. Jane Lazarre asks us to think again. As a white woman married for nearly thirty years to an African American man and as the mother of two sons who identify themselves as black rather than biracial, Lazarre has contended with white blindness to racism for most of her adult life. In this passage from her memoir, Beyond the Whiteness of Whiteness *(1996), she recounts her struggle to acknowledge the racial barriers that continue to separate her in crucial ways from the people she loves most. Lazarre teaches writing and literature at the New School for Social Research in New York. She is the author of three novels; a collection of essays,* On Loving Men *(1980); and an earlier memoir,* The Mother Knot *(1976).*

> *And there was something so foul in that, something in the crime of in-nocence so revolting it paralyzed him. He had not known because he had not taken the trouble to know. He was satisfied with what he did know. Knowing more was inconvenient and frightening. Like a bucket of water with no bottom. If you know how to tread, bottomlessness need not concern you.* — Toni Morrison, Tar Baby

In the Prologue of Ralph Ellison's *Invisible Man,* a preacher speaks to his congregation: "Brothers and Sisters, my text this morning is the 'Black-ness of Blackness.'"

Some years ago, Gary Lemons, a colleague of mine, gave that term — The Blackness of Blackness — to the title of a course in which he explored with students the often hidden cultural, personal, moral meanings of Black-ness in literature by African Americans.[1]

Intrigued and educated by his conceptualization, I began searching for an understanding of the Blackness of Blackness, even if from the perspec-tive of an outsider/stranger. I have kept a mental record that moves among different layers of consciousness. I read and study literature, its themes and practice, some history, and I listen to a lot of music. Intense focus tends to break down resistances to new consciousness, and I try to attend as carefully as possible to the details of my family's experiences. Years ago, I dreamed repeatedly of wandering in Africa, a blinding sun keeping me away from home. And so I remained for years in a sparse but beautiful room where I had to return again and again, each time I missed my plane back to New York City. For some time, as I became increasingly involved with my chil-dren's African heritage, I interpreted this dream as a turn on the word son, for sun: a representation of the dangerous loss of self and creative transcen-dence of self that is the ambivalent heart of motherhood. Looking back on that state of creative wandering that is the first stage of any deep change in me, I came to understand that any appreciation of the Blackness of Black-ness would have to be accompanied by a willingness to explore whiteness. It was love that kept me from this realization so long. I did not want to be dif-

---

[1]*Gary Lemons,* "The Blackness of Blackness: Representations of Sexuality in African American Literature," Eugene Lang College Course, n.d. [Author's note]

ferent from Douglas[2] and especially my children. Being Jewish was something we might share, but whiteness was the sign of their greatest troubles and I was afraid of getting lost without them. When I thought back on my recurring dream, I saw that the blindness was always in the form of a white light.

Not for a moment do I diminish the difficulty of the task. As I begin to write about whiteness, remembering blindness as well as seeing, afraid of offending, of sentimental guilt, of being just plain wrong, I call up for myself the words I use to en/courage — give courage to — students embarking on the project of autobiographical writing, a project whose dangers they always underestimate:

> "And of course I am afraid, because the transformation of silence into language and action is an act of self-revelation, and that always seems fraught with danger." Audre Lorde, *Sister/Outsider*[3]
>
> "[W]e cannot wait for the undamaged to make our connections for us; we can't wait to speak until we are wholly clear and righteous. There is no purity in our lifetimes, no end to this process." Adrienne Rich, "Split at the Root."[4]

But where can I find the stories, silenced and distorted by years of de-   5
nial and blindness, as the most important stories often are — my students have asked me.

Start with recent memories and work backward, I tell them. Memory leads to consciousness, recollection to the possibility of meaning which always includes a perception of relation between oneself and the world. This is the central principle of an autobiographical attitude we shall try to practice and name.

It is 1992, and Khary is eighteen, a freshman in college. Although he attends a largely white institution, there are enough Black students (98 in the freshmen class) for him to choose a Black social world. Because he concentrates in African and African American Studies, he is often spared the difficulties of being the only Black person in an all-white class, a condition he experienced throughout his high school years in the progressive private school we sent him to, where covert, pervasive racism nevertheless penetrated and often ruined his days. He is clearly happier than he has been in years. He loves his friends, Black Americans, Caribbean, and African students, several of them with one white parent like himself, who nevertheless define themselves, as he does, as Black.

---

[2]*Douglas:* Lazarre's husband.

[3]Audre Lorde, "The Transformation of Silence," in *Sister, Outsider* (Trumansberg, NY: The Crossing Press, 1984), 42. [Author's note]

[4]Adrienne Rich, "Split at the Root," in *Blood, Bread and Poetry, Selected Prose, 1979–1985* (New York: W. W. Norton, 1986), 123. [Author's note]

I am slowly introduced to their perspective on identity. Black Americans have been so-called mixed since the days of slavery, and many still are. Frederick Douglass, who escaped to freedom on September 3, the day of Khary's birth, had a white father, as did many other slaves. Like Douglass, my son tells me, he does not qualify his Blackness. Political and personal life are neatly separated only in academic abstractions. As a feminist, a teacher of feminist studies, as a woman, I know this: the straight, unblurred line between collective and personal stories is an illusion of privilege.

"The world gets inside your head," one Latina student said last semester, defending Jane Eyre's internalized self-doubt, her sometimes overly righteous conviction, to a classmate who criticized that early feminist heroine for her lapses and weaknesses in the face of dominating, erotic love.

"I am Black," Khary explains to me repeatedly during that first year   10
away from home when he has to find and take his place in his own world. "I have a Jewish mother, but I am not 'biracial.' That term is meaningless to me. I reject the identity of the tragic mulatto." He goes on to explain his beliefs and feelings in detail, and when I say, "I understand," he tells me carefully, gently, "I don't think you do, Mom. You can't understand this completely because you're white."

At first, I am slightly stunned, by his vehemence and by the idea. Perhaps even more than most mothers, I have identified with my children. Like other writers of my generation, I have used the experience of motherhood to try to comprehend the essential human conflict between devotion to others and obligations to the self, the lifelong tension between the need for clear boundaries and boundless intimacy. A motherless daughter since early childhood, I have experienced difficulty but also real reparation in mothering children myself. Now, standing in a darkened hallway facing my son, I feel exiled from my not-yet-grown child.

Fierce possessiveness lies at the heart of motherhood right alongside the more reasonable need to see one's children become themselves, and now this emotion rises up and chokes me, obliterating vocabulary. I can not find words to express my feelings, or my feelings are too threatening to find easy language. They are mine fields lining opposite sides of the road of my motherhood of this beloved son. What is this whiteness that threatens to separate me from my own child? Why haven't I seen it lurking, hunkering down, encircling me in some irresistible fog? I want to say the thing that will be most helpful to him, offer some carefully designed, unspontaneous permission for him to discover his own road, even if that means leaving me behind. On the other hand, I want to cry out, don't leave me, as he cried to me when I walked out of day-care centers, away from baby-sitters, out of his first classroom in public school. And always, this double truth, as unresolvable as in any other passion, the paradox: she is me/not me; he is mine/not mine.

A close friend, a Black man who grew up in North Carolina with Douglas, has taken a special interest in Khary, and tells him one day: Your mother isn't really white. She's a Black person in disguise.

Warmed by the love and friendship I know the remark signifies and tempted to relax into its welcome, I also know its message is false. I am white, and I remember long years of childhood and early womanhood when I was as blind to the realities of race as any white American.

I was raised by American Communists who, apart from any of the controversial politics of that period or this one, instilled in their children values of human commonality and internationalist identification. Some of their methods and beliefs can seem ludicrously misguided (one of their favorite words for self-criticism) to the contemporary eye. There was a time, for instance, when the Communist Party was trying to eradicate racism from its ranks, when you could be brought up on charges (before a party tribunal) for ordering a "black and white" soda. "We are all the same, there are no differences between people," was the weird non sequitur in response to any childish notification of color differences among strangers or friends.

We were taught to sing, "You can get good milk from a brown-skinned   15
cow, the color of the skin doesn't matter anyhow." But attributing brown skin to a Negro was considered insulting, a revelation of racial prejudice in itself. The obsessive denial that race mattered was obviously a white creation. I recall very vaguely one or two times when a Black comrade corrected our earnest white parents, suggesting that noticing Blackness was not by definition an offense. Perhaps someone may have tried to explain that invisibility from false tolerance could be just as insulting as invisibility from outright contempt. "Of course she sees I'm Black," I recall a tall, heavy-set man saying to my father who had criticized me for identifying the man's color — which I did, in part, because I was obsessed with color differences in everything, drawing and painting as a means of relief from a lonely and troubled childhood. In part, these memories are vague because, as time passed, I came to accept the idea that any color noticing was a failure of virtue, a departure from good values and an unmasking of prejudice. The moral commandment obliterated real memory, drove the shape of actual experience into a polluted mist of unidentifiable shame.

The memories are also vague, I think, because the experiences were so rare. Black people hardly ever entered the interiors of the intimate collective life of the Communist families I knew. Nearly as much as any other white American community, our life was white. The Blacks we saw most often, apart from the occasional famous artist/comrade who graced a party or meeting with his or her presence, were the women who worked for some of the families as housekeepers and caregivers.

My parents hired a series of women to substitute for my mother, who was a "career woman," a feminist in the terms of her day who worked under her "maiden" name and supported her family, allowing my father to continue his largely unpaid work as a party official. When I was seven and my sister four years old, our mother died after a long illness, and although our substantially lowered income brought us from a life of upper-middle-class privilege into the always money-conscious limitations of my father's working-class life, we nevertheless continued to be dependent on a paid housekeeper rather than the relatives a poorer family might have found to fill the gap.

Before my mother's illness, when my sister was just born, a young woman named Lavinia worked for us. She was harsh and punitive, and I recall very clearly her verbal threats — to lock me in the closet or throw me out the window — and several times being actually pushed or slapped. She was fired when I recounted these stories to my parents, and for many years I remembered the experience only as a source of anger at my parents' casual methods of choosing caretakers for us. When I was a young mother, sitting in the park with babies and toddlers day after day, and noticed the harshness of some Black women toward their young, white charges — which white mothers always notice and comment on righteously, congratulating themselves on staying home with their children — I remembered Lavinia and wondered about her life. I tried to imagine the racial animosities, class and cultural differences regarding standards of children's behavior which might have motivated her threats and slaps. I try to picture her now, but I have lost the memory of her features. I do recall telling her once that she was pretty; I see her hair pulled back behind her ears into a dark net, a slender body always in a white and grey uniform, a long brown arm reaching out to strike me when I tried to poke and scratch my baby sister through the bars of her crib.

After Lavinia, Rose came to work for us. She nursed my mother through her last months of life and, in effect, raised my sister and me for the next ten years. My father called her *Razela,* a Jewish endearment of her name, and like all the other Communists, insisted she was a "member of the family." Politely, softly, she would correct him. "I love you girls, and I love your father, but I work for him."

We ate her cooking, watched her iron our clothes, marveled at the hot   20 comb she used to straighten her hair late at night when she occasionally slept at our house. We got to know her family and visited her small, neat Harlem apartment where the food smelled and tasted exotically different from the food she made for us. But we did not understand, nor were we taught, the simplest facts of her history or heritage. That she had been born in Georgia was all we knew, and had a son in his early twenties who was in the army, stationed in Germany. She had a "boyfriend" — a short, husky musician named Russel who visited our house and was extremely friendly to us. She took care of an aging mother who died while we were still children, but I have no memory of the nature, duration, or quality of Rose's grief.

I know that I did not really know her, and I know that I loved her in a typically childish way: I needed her. Her attentions and protection were essential to me. Her attitudes toward disciplinary clarity, even when harsh — attitudes I know now to be typically southern Black — were a welcome contrast to the immigrant Jewish ambivalence and ambiguity in all things that otherwise characterized our upbringing. If she said something, she meant it, for good or ill. This was new and comforting to me, and years later I would instantly recognize and be drawn to the same quality in Douglas.

She sang us "Summertime" and "Stormy Weather" and, when I had children, I sang those songs to them, hearing her slightly off-key melodies in my head.

Like the sound of my father's voice whispering Yiddish endearments — *ketsaleh, madeleh* — her language remains in my mind as signals of warmth and love — the phrase *Lord have mercy;* the word *ain't;* even *I'm gonna beat your behind.* The first time Douglas called me *Sugar* the echo that rang in me was the sound of her voice.

The hypocrisies twisted into our attitudes toward race were the result of arrogance. Like their largely man-made views on "the woman question" which can now seem so hopelessly naive (it was important for mothers and eventually daughters to "work for a living" but there was no concept of shared housework or child care being an aspect of "women's liberation"; girls were expected to be "smart," but were ruthlessly judged on their looks and physical graces); similarly, their views on race were formed by whites who never, it seems, asked Blacks for their analyses or points of view.

Still, we were explicitly, even rigidly taught an ideology of fairness against the pervasive American tolerance of inequality and white supremacy, and therefore I have no doubt that even in the most racially divided and racist society, children can be taught not to hate. Sheer bigotry was never accorded the respectability of objective truth or even valid argument. I was made ready to learn. When I married Douglas, my father was surprised and pleased and soon, after getting to know him, began to brag incessantly about the strong and reliable "Negro chap" his often "crazy" daughter had married.   25

Shortly before his death (when Adam was barely two years old) my father began having a recurring dream. He was traveling across country with his beloved grandson who in the dream was nineteen or twenty, and they would be unable to find a room in a motel. My father would know that it was because of his grandson's race, and in a variety of ways in a number of different dreams he would begin to battle the racists and haters on his grandson's behalf. Always spiritually charged by the challenges of battle — a fighter by nature or by virtue of his difficult life as a Russian Jew, then as an American Communist — he fashioned his fantasies of victorious conflict from what he understood would be the most predictable burden of his grandson's life. He believed standing up for racial justice in his grandson's behalf would be sufficient, never imagining the hidden narratives of superiority and domination Blacks would identify in white behavior over the next twenty years. He lived in a more naive time for white Americans. I like to think he would have helped my children, coming of age in this difficult, racially polarized time, to hang on to a faith in a nonracial society, a dream to help shape reality, even as reality must demystify our dreams.

I face my younger son in the hallway on the first vacation of his first year away from home, and I watch his face, its bone structure sharpening into beautiful planes as he matures. For years he has towered over me and looks down on me now, his eyes filled with contradictory emotions of his own. He must assert himself, stand by who he is, yet without hurting me.

In that moment we stand there, searching for some new words in which to speak, in a long moment of silence that turns into a silent embrace, I feel my whiteness as a sun-blinded desert of distance from my sons.

When I decided to marry Douglas I had no thoughts of children or their problems, and if I considered their racial identity at all it was with a combination of denial of its importance and a naive faith in imminent, radical social change. It was the sixties and I was twenty-two years old. I had found a man who possessed a temperament which provided a kind of security and reliability utterly lacking in my own childhood, values I shared, and an understated but intense sensuality I desired. The fact that he was Black and I Jewish seemed irrelevant at a time when race relations were at the center of a radical revision of America. It was the time of the civil rights and Black Power movements in which we both had been and continued to be active in different ways.

We met on a picket line, the 1966 strike of public assistance workers against the New York City Welfare Department. It was a multiracial, multiethnic strike, and like the public school teachers whose labor movement battles I had been raised to support, we believed we walked the snowy streets that winter, carrying watery hot chocolate and printed placards, for the benefit not only of ourselves but of our clients whose lives more often than not were made terribly difficult by the punitive, bureaucratic system that purported to serve them. Many of us were recent college graduates who had come of age sitting-in at lunch counters in the South, picketing Woolworth's in the North. The inner divisions which would disturb, enrage, sadden, and educate us in the antiwar, civil rights, and women's movements were not yet upon us. We knew which side we were on and believed we would pretty quickly overcome. 30

During the early days of those explosive social movements, after I quit my job at the Department of Welfare, I began teaching in a New York City high school where my students were only three or four years younger than me. The daughter of a working-class, immigrant father, I was motivated by the salary and benefits, as well as by my love of literature. But also, the destruction of the American Communist Party had left me with a visceral resistance to many forms of organized political action and in teaching I sensed the opportunity for social activism congenial with my temperament, history, and needs.

From that time I remember three small incidents that suggest the complexity of racial experience now so conscious in my life. I still believed that claiming a blindness to color could actually make you blind, that if people only treated each other as equals, centuries of history could be dismissed, even erased. I knew very little about American history, if knowing includes, as I now understand it does, the impact of African American history on the economic, political, artistic, and spiritual development of the United States. *Race Matters,* Cornel West[5] assures us in the title of his collection of essays. *Black Matters,* Toni Morrison[6] instructs in one of hers. But I was assuring myself I was blind to color and failing to see where the true blindness lay.

Each morning in the fall of 1966, I walk ten blocks downtown from my apartment to Brandeis High School on 84th Street to meet my Academic English class with whom I have developed a warm and easy relationship. There are two girls in the class who are especially engaged and interested. They sit in the front row, answer questions quickly and thoughtfully, look at me with such lively response that I often find myself staring intensely into their eyes while I teach. Outside of school, we are becoming friends. They have been to my apartment for dinner, met Douglas, who I am engaged to marry. They have joined in his teasing of my "tired black skirt" which I wear proudly, schooled in the bohemian values of Greenwich Village and the High School of Music and Art. The more worn and used-looking it becomes, the happier I am. But though its slightly ratty, nubbed wool is a symbol of political pride for me, I am a raggedy mystery to the foxy girls of late 1960s Harlem. Perhaps our good-humored teasing about small cultural differences, and our closeness in age, helped me with no prior experience to teach them and my other pupils about formal English grammar, which had always intrigued me, and about reading novels and poetry, which were as crucial as food to me and which I was determined, some day, to write myself.

During one lesson, referring to my particular class, a large number of whom have not done their homework that day, I refer to them as "you people." "You people have to do this work if you want to learn to write better," I say, or something like that. Their faces turn to stone. Eyes move instantly away from mine. Mild, muffled curses are heard. The two girls I count as friends close their books and when I ask why, as the period has not ended, they pretend innocence. "The bell's gonna ring any minute," one of them says with cold formality.

I am dumbfounded and confused, blind to my whiteness which now 35 shines from me like an unwelcome strobe light overheating the room. It has never been gone, of course, not to my students, but only softened, toned down to an unintrusive shine while real friendship and affection grew. I was not wrong in sensing the development of trust; it was the fragility of the connection that I had underestimated. Despite my Jewish heritage which had made me familiar with the details of outsidedness, my olive skin and dark hair which caused me to be mistaken for a "Puerto Rican" almost daily, picket lines and rock-hard faith in our ability to overcome notwithstanding, there was an understanding of the nature of American society evident to my students that was still heavily veiled for me.

[5]*Cornel West:* African American philosopher and religious scholar (b. 1953).
[6]*Toni Morrison:* Nobel Prize-winning African American novelist (b. 1931).

After class, I described my experience to Douglas who explained in one sentence: "When you said 'you people' they thought you meant Black people, and they assumed you meant it derisively, as in *you people never learn*."

But I didn't mean it that way at all," I explained. "I meant you people — in this class."

"It doesn't matter what you meant," I remember him telling me. I was convinced by his interpretation but deaf to his deeper warning. *It doesn't matter what you meant* when you are moving against a tide of history and social reality far more important than one white person's mistake. A white American either accepts the weight of this history or relinquishes the respect and possibility of authentic connection to Black Americans.

This memory might seem quaint now in an age of supposed ultraconsciousness about race. Or it might be buried altogether, if it were not for the fact that I encounter exactly the same sorts of mistakes in my white friends, students, colleagues, even at times in myself, all the time. The mistake is followed quickly by a denial of its importance, as if language itself, individual words and sounds, did not have a history thick with hidden meanings not to be casually undone.

I am hearing a story about common, everyday racism from one of my 40 sons. It is a prototypical story of young Black maleness in an American city, 1990s. Khary's friend has rung the bell one night and is waiting for him to come downstairs. The friend, also Black and nineteen years old, drives the family car, a Toyota. We live on a racially mixed street in a racially mixed neighborhood, yet when Khary comes downstairs, he finds three cops surrounding his friend who is spread-eagle on the front of the car, being searched. Suspecting he had stolen the car, the cops approached him while he was standing against it, and when he objected, turned him around roughly and began their search. I am outraged and shout: "But this is unbelievable!" "Unbelievable?" my son says angrily. "Unbelievable, Mom? It happens to me all the time. If I'm not searched I'm still stopped and questioned, whenever I'm driving a decent-looking car." "It was just a word, a manner of speaking," I insist weakly. Because I already see that neither Douglas nor any other Black person would ever respond with that particular word. It is a small failure on my part, easily forgotten; but it signifies the vast space of white blindness to the dailiness of racism. My son feels that anxiety every time he steps out onto the street. I forget, am privileged to remain innocent.

My ignorance in this case can stand for the broader and deeper ignorance of many white Americans. The shock on their faces when they hear of Douglas's experience on a major highway: he is driving with his son and they are stopped by highway patrol, told to put their hands on the dashboard, cops' hands already on their guns. He has been speeding, they say, although he has not; they search his car, obviously looking for drugs, and only later, when he identifies himself as a government official in New York do they acknowledge that he was doing fifty-eight in a fifty-five mile per hour zone. Providence, Rhode Island, 1993.

The recurring story of young Black women students in white colleges across the country who are subjected to racial and sexual epithets hurled by white male students, so that a system of protection by Black male students has to be initiated to make them feel safe — a story of which most white Americans remain ruthlessly unaware.

Statistics about poverty and especially crime, about the crisis in urban education throughout the country — these realities of modern life are "known" and just as easily "forgotten," the forgetting aided and encouraged by media depictions of "inner city" (Black) children and teenagers as violent, usually orphaned or parented by drug addicts, a generation typically described as having no moral convictions, no sense of connection to society. With this illusion giving us cruel comfort, we can avoid concern, let alone action on behalf of these children.

Several years ago a well-known progressive private school in New York City distributed a questionnaire among its parent body asking for responses to common racial issues that arose year after year. Large percentages of parents, answering anonymously, responded that yes, they encouraged mixed race friendships among the students; yes, they supported extensive scholarships directed to Latinos and African Americans in order to integrate the school; but no, by a large majority, something near 90 percent, they would not be comfortable with interracial dating. When these figures are made public, the parent body in large numbers proclaim their astonishment. None of them can imagine who among them would feel in this way. They claim innocence of their own prejudices and, even after being presented with statistics, deny the obvious reality which would break down their illusions about themselves. The words of my student echo in my ear: *Slavery was always back then. Racism was always out there.* "It is the innocence," wrote James Baldwin in *The Fire Next Time,* "which constitutes the crime."

Last semester, in a class on African American autobiography and auto- 45
biographical writing in which we were discussing, among other themes, the whiteness of whiteness, several white students made the complaint that they were exhausted with talking about race, race, race. This, after half of one semester. The only Black woman student in the class in an overwhelmingly white college countered: "It is exhausting *being* a Black person in this school." I believe it was not the study of race or an introduction to Blackness, but the requirement to think about whiteness that tired them so. The autobiographical project, as the Black student suggested, is far more exhausting than the safer, more distant study of other people's lives.

I have heard numerous white colleagues and friends insist as well that they do not experience whiteness at all, because they are Jewish, or working class, or simply an outsider by personal temperament, as if awareness of skin color privilege might threaten the validity of equally real constraints. I am not a white person, I have heard white people say. I am a writer — a teacher — a woman — a shy and insecure man.

In 1967, a person who defined myself as straightforward and direct about all things, I returned to my class and boldly explained my intended meaning, apologizing for my insensitivity. I was back on track with the class, if I remember correctly, but I am aware that time and desire can replace the grimmer facts of history with pleasing illusions. It would be years, when I had birthed and raised Black children myself, been a disguised witness to white racism and that special form of American unconsciousness that tries to pass for tolerance, before I would really understand the more ominous truth packed at the bottom of Douglas's words: *It doesn't matter what you meant.*

ENGAGING THE TEXT

1. How and why does Lazarre's understanding of color blindness change during the course of her life? Why is this change of perspective so difficult for her to achieve?
2. In the epigraph, Toni Morrison refers to "the crime of innocence." In what ways can innocence be criminal, according to Lazarre? Do you agree?
3. Why does Lazarre's husband tell her that it doesn't matter what she meant when she addressed her students as "you people"? Debate whether good intentions can or should make a difference when someone inadvertently makes a racially insensitive remark.
4. Lazarre constructs an argument by weaving together a series of stories about herself, her family, her students, even her dreams. Outline the argument she makes and think about what other approaches she could have taken to her subject. Why do you think she chose storytelling as a strategy?
5. What does Lazarre feel that other white people can learn from her experience? Do you think she conveys this lesson effectively? Why or why not?

EXPLORING CONNECTIONS

6. Like Lazarre, Shelby Steele (p. 612) identifies innocence as a central problem in race relations; however, the two writers offer different solutions to that problem. Which approach seems better or more workable to you, and why?
7. What does Jules Feiffer's cartoon (p. 635) suggest about the ways that black and white Americans see the world? Would Lazarre agree?
8. Lazarre speaks of the need to recover stories that have been "silenced and distorted by years of denial and blindness" (para. 5). Storytelling also serves an important function for Paula Gunn Allen (p. 520) and Ronald Takaki (p. 538). Compare the purpose and value of stories for these three writers.

EXTENDING THE CRITICAL CONTEXT

9. Write a journal entry describing what has happened when you have unintentionally insulted or offended someone. How did you react to the incident at the time? Has your understanding of the situation changed since then? If so, how?

FEIFFER®

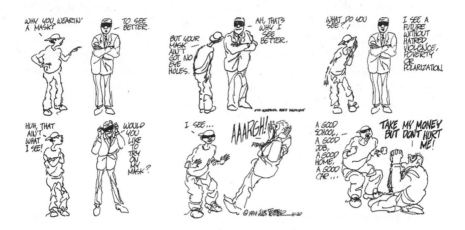

10. Congress eventually issued a public apology and agreed to pay reparations to Japanese Americans who were imprisoned in concentration camps during World War II. What kinds of reparation might be offered to African Americans to compensate them for the suffering of their ancestors under slavery or to American Indians for the systematic theft of their lands and cultures? Would reparations help to address the sources of racial tension identified by Lazarre? Why or why not?

Can a New Race Surmount Old Prejudices?

Ellis Cose

Geneticists have concluded that there is no legitimate biological rationale for dividing people into "racial" groups according to such physical details as skin color, hair texture, or shape of eyes. It would make as much biological sense, they argue, to define "races" according to genetically transmitted characteristics like resistance to malaria or the ability to digest milk (in which case West Africans, Arabs, and northern Europeans could belong to the same "racial" group). Ellis Cose examines some of the absurdities and inconsistencies of our racial classification system in this selection from his most recent book, Color Blind: Seeing Beyond Race in a Race-Obsessed World *(1997). The problems of racial definition are compounded, he observes, by the increasingly multiethnic population of the United States. But a growing uncertainty about old racial categories may also undermine old divisions and hatreds: Can a multiracial nation solve the persistent problem of racism? Cose (b. 1951) has been a journalist for more than two decades and has worked for such major newspapers and magazines as the* Chicago Sun-Times, USA Today, *the* Detroit Free Press, *and* Newsweek. *His half-dozen books address a wide range of topics, including immigration, male privilege, and black anger.*

Americans are accustomed to infinite shades of ebony, but the South African journalist Mzimkulu Malunga found the notion hilarious. So he named one celebrity after another — Tina Turner, Vanessa Williams, Mariah Carey — tickled at the thought that anyone might consider them all black. The impromptu racial-identity game soon had the small group in Soweto in stitches. It seemed an appropriately absurd end to an evening spent, for the most part, in more serious conversation in a country whose governing principle once had been: "Tell me your race, and I'll tell you your place." As his guests finished a dinner of beer, beans, beef, and a grits-like delicacy called pap, Malunga, business editor of *The Sowetan,* finally shrugged as if to say: Race is a strange and flexible concept, with an endless capacity to confound.

That evening took me back to an encounter, some years earlier, on a bus several miles outside Caracas, Venezuela. Upon learning I was from the United States, the dark-skinned woman beside me had peppered me with questions. Did I find Venezuelans to be prejudiced? Was there racism in the United States? Were Canadians less biased than their neighbors to the south? Finally, she focused on her son, seated directly in front of us. He was the color of caramel and about seven years old. His father, she told me, was "white," and the son, despite his dusky appearance and faintly African features, had decided that he was white, too. At first the idea struck me as ridiculous, but, by and by, I found myself thinking, "Why the hell not?" By any logical calculus, he was probably more "white" than "black" (not that, in most of Latin America, he would be considered either). And from the perspective of a child who was old enough to know that whiteness means status but too young to realize how whiteness is defined, wanting to be white was just as natural as wanting to be a quarterback instead of a cheerleader. I wondered, however, if the boy had been American, whether he would have thought he had the option to choose his color. For most of us, race is simply accepted as a given and on faith, no more subject to questioning than the reality of our existence.

Even before the civil rights movement erupted and Jim Crow[1] died, racial definitions in the United States were somewhat different from those in South Africa (and Latin America), and specific policies varied as well. But these countries shared the conceit that the concept of race was reasonably precise and that it told us something important. In fact, those assumptions never really made sense.

Earlier in this century, for instance, Italians, Jews, and Rumanians were widely considered to be of different (and inferior) racial stock compared to the English, Germans, and Swedes. Just a few decades later, those groups were fully accepted into the community of whites. In an essay entitled, "How Did Jews Become White Folks?" Karen Brodkin Sacks asked, "Did Jews and the other Euroethnics become white because they became middle class? That is, did money whiten? Or did being incorporated in an expanded version of whiteness open up the economic doors to middle-class status?" The answer, she concluded, is both. The question, nonetheless, illustrates the absurdity of the premise that racial classifications are fixed.

The supposition, at long last, is under serious challenge — from intel-   5
lectuals who doubt that the concept of race has much meaning; from immigrants who have a different and more elastic view of racial classifications; and, perhaps most interestingly, from those who refuse to consider themselves members of any currently accepted racial category but refer to themselves as multiracial and demand the recognition of a new melded race.

Success in that endeavor, some advocates believe, would be a huge step in the direction of a color-blind society, for by embracing those who are multiracial, the United States would be recognizing, if only implicitly, that the ugly racial lines etched in the nation's soul will, sooner or later, disappear. Alternatively, goes the argument, the nation's failure to recognize formally the existence of multiracial Americans would be a tragedy, not only for mixed-race people but for American society, and would perhaps be a fatal blow to the dream of racial harmony and egalitarianism.

In 1992, in Bethesda, Maryland, several hundred multiracialists came together for the "first national gathering of the multiracial community," as described by Bijan Gilanshah, in the December 1993 issue of the journal *Law and Inequality*. The "Loving Conference" was named in honor of the Supreme Court's decision in the case of *Loving v. Virginia*, which outlawed antimiscegenation statutes in 1967. But the meeting was not simply a celebration of the right to reproduce across racial lines; it would mark — or so its organizers hoped — the public launching of a new and potent political movement.

[1]*Jim Crow:* Laws enacted in the post–Civil War South that mandated racial segregation.

At stake, in Gilanshah's eyes, was nothing less than the prevention of "cultural genocide." Instead of leaving mixed-race people in a vulnerable and nebulous state of official nowhereness, the government, he thought, was obliged to give them full recognition "as a distinct, powerful social unit with idiosyncratic cultural, social and legal interests." Much the same point was made by Charles Byrd, who organized a rally at the Washington Mall in July 1996 to allow mixed-raced Americans, like himself, an opportunity to collectively and "proudly affirm a self-determined identity" while attempting to persuade the federal government to sanction the multiracial category.

Multiracial people with a heritage that is, to some degree, black have a special interest in how mixed-race people are to be defined. "In physical as well as cultural terms every Negro is a little bit colored and a little bit white," observed Martin Luther King, Jr. in *Where Do We Go From Here: Chaos or Community?* Yet it is only the "colored" part that has generally been acknowledged. Unlike Americans of other races, blacks have largely been defined by the so-called one-drop rule: the presumption that even a small percentage of black ancestry effectively cancels out any other racial stock. It is a rule that some biracial people believe compels them either to deny a big part of who they are or to explain constantly to a rigid, "monoracial" world why they reject a patently illogical designation. Why, they ask, should they renounce the ancestry of a nonblack parent or grandparent? What's the point, they ask, in forcing people into narrow boxes that cannot possibly accommodate America's growing racial diversity? — particularly when the black box is fundamentally different from the others, carries the full baggage of slavery, and defies all common sense. As Lawrence Hirschfeld, author of *Race in the Making,* observed: "The absurdity of the biological reading of the one-drop rule is obvious. . . . How reasonable is it to say that a white woman can give birth to a Black baby, but a Black woman can't give birth to a white baby?"

Lise Funderburg, author of *Black, White, Other,* which profiles several children of black-white interracial unions, extracted the following comment from one of the persons she interviewed: "A lot of Blacks get upset if they ask you exactly what you are and you come back and say, 'Biracial.' One response is, 'What? Are you too good to identify with Blacks?' I say, 'It's not that I'm too good at all, but I'm composed of two different races and I choose to value each of those.' It's not as though I'm going to write off my mother's race for the convenience of pleasing somebody else's view of what I should or should not be doing." The one-drop rule, however, demands that biracial children do just that. As novelist Gish Jen noted in an essay in the *New York Times Magazine,* "a mulatto is not a kind of white person, but a kind of black person." Yet there is nothing in biology — indeed, nothing in science at all — that says "black" should trump "white" when it comes to assigning racial categories.

The argument against such an illogical racial-classification scheme ultimately takes you down one of two roads: rejection of the idea of race alto-

10

gether or acceptance of the possibility of an endless proliferation of new races. In recent years, the debate has focused on the census for the year 2000 — specifically on an edict known as "Statistical Policy Directive Number 15." That directive, conjured up by the Office of Management and Budget (OMB) in the late 1970s, sets out the minimum categories that governmental agencies can use when collecting racial and ethnic data. It provides for four racial clusters (white, black, Asian and Pacific Islander, and American Indian and Alaskan Native) and one distinct ethnic group (Hispanic). If someone doesn't quite fit, they are squeezed into the pigeonhole that "most closely reflects the individual's recognition in his community." If that doesn't work, they can always be lumped into "other."

These particular groups are not arbitrary. They reflect OMB's best attempt to capture the American consensus on race. They also reflect the needs of an array of governmental agencies that enforce civil rights laws, run American Indian programs, fight poverty, and calculate health and other statistics — agencies, in short, that need to know something about America's racial makeup to do their jobs. The problem is that America's racial composition is quite different now from the way it was in the 1970s. It is less "monoracial," less black and white, more intermarried, and a hell of a lot more confusing.

At the time of the 1970 census, America had few shades of gray. Whites (at 87.5 percent) and blacks (at 11.1 percent) accounted for more than 98 percent of the total U.S. population. Other racial minorities added up to just over 1 percent. Hispanics, who could be of any race, stood at 4.5 percent. Twenty years later, the nation was spinning from a demographic whirlwind. Newcomers were pouring in from Mexico, the Philippines, Korea, Cuba, India, mainland China, and other non-European countries, while Europeans — no longer favored by U.S. immigration laws — had dwindled to a trickle. America, in short, was no longer nearly so black and white. By 1990, whites and blacks stood at roughly 80 percent and 12 percent, respectively, and Hispanics at 9 percent.

Meanwhile, interracial families were forming apace. In 1960, according to the U.S. census, fewer than half of 1 percent of married couples were interracial. By 1990, the number had risen to about 3 percent — the majority comprised of mixtures other than black and white.

After reanalyzing U.S. Bureau of the Census's survey data for 1985 and 1990, scholars Douglas Besharov and Timothy Sullivan concluded that even black-white marriages were growing faster than had previously been thought. In 1990, they estimated, nearly 10 percent of black grooms married white brides. Although the sample of the Current Population Survey was too small to allow a good estimate for marriages between black brides and white grooms, Besharov and Sullivan conjectured that their number was also rising rapidly. The children of such unions, they declared (in the July–August 1996 issue of *The New Democrat*), "may be the best hope for the future of American race relations."

15

To multiracialists, America's approximately 3 million multiracial children are a forceful argument for the recognition of a new race and a new racial reality — and perhaps, as Besharov and Sullivan suggested, even a way out of America's racial quagmire.

Susan Graham, a white woman married to a black man in Roswell, Georgia, tried to explain the rationale for the new racial category at congressional hearings in 1993. Accompanied by her young son, she related the frustrations of trying to find a comfortable racial niche for biracial children. When she had asked a census official how to identify her two biracial children, the official insulted her. "In cases like these, we always know who the mother is and not always the father," the official said, in explaining why the child should take the mother's race. Her experience, Graham pointed out, was far from unique. A multiracial teenager in North Carolina, she said, had been humiliated by a teacher blurting out in class: "You're so light. Are you sure your mother knows who your father is?" Graham expressed gratitude for a new state policy that had allowed her to identify her five-year-old daughter as "multiracial" when she had enrolled the child in kindergarten. Thanks to Georgia's legislators, her child "was not made to choose between her parents." She urged Congress to protect other children from having to make that painful decision.

"I'm not a scholar, attorney, or lawmaker," Graham continued. "I'm just a mother, a mother who cares about children; and whether I like it or not, I realize that self-esteem is directly tied to accurate racial identity. More and more parents all over our country are instilling new pride in our multiracial children. Can we say we have succeeded if our children leave home only to be denied an equal place in our society?" In closing, she invoked the ever-handy memory of Martin Luther King, Jr.: "I believe Doctor King was speaking thirty years ago for multiracial children too. With your help, their time has finally come."

Carlos Fernández, president of the Association of Multiethnic Americans, was equally impassioned. Governmental administrators' refusal to recognize multiracial children, he suggested, could put them in violation of the U.S. Constitution: "When government compels the multiracial, multiethnic family to signify a factually false identity for their child, it invades their fundamental right of privacy." Fernández made clear, however, that he was primarily concerned not with constitutional issues but with the well-being of multiracial youngsters. The status quo, he intimated, amounted to a form of child abuse. It denied multiracial offspring their "distinctive identity," damaged their self-esteem, and forced them to "favor one parent over the other." Meanwhile, it did nothing to protect them from — or even document — the special form of bigotry aimed at people of mixed race.

Julie C. Lythcott-Haimes made a similar argument in the *Harvard Civil Rights–Civil Liberties Law Review*. "The Multiracial person can hardly advocate the superiority or inferiority of one race without touching   20 off a potentially damaging identity struggle within herself," wrote Lythcott-Haimes. And even if a person's psyche could put up with such turmoil, Lythcott-Haimes saw no reason why anyone should have to. The one-drop rule is not only absurd, she contended, it is blatantly racist, grounded in the central premise "that 'Black blood' is a contaminant while 'White blood' is pure."

Clearly, the multiracialists have flagged a nettlesome problem. Forcing multiracial children into prefabricated "monoracial" boxes is illogical. It is preposterous — not to mention cruel — to ask any child of mixed race to choose one race (and symbolically one parent) arbitrarily over the other. As Gish Jen, a Chinese American married to a man of Irish descent, acknowledged, there is pain in seeing her child stripped of what he considers to be an essential part of his identity. Yet many Americans insist on seeing multiracial children through monochromatic eyes. Some spiteful schoolmates gave her son a taste of what his future might hold when they taunted him for being "Chinese" — even as he futilely insisted that he was not. Though Jen and her husband originally had hoped their son would "grow up embracing his whole complex ethnic heritage," they have had to accept a harsher reality and recognize that their son "is considered a kind of Asian person."

It's unclear whether the federal government's official adoption of a multiracial category would lead to broader public acceptance of multiracialism and eventually make things easier for children such as Jen's son or for families such as Graham's. It is even less clear what effect a multiracial box would have on statistical analyses of America's racial stock. "Multiracial," after all, is not a particularly precise description. It simply means that a person theoretically fits into more than one category. It's a fancy way, in short, of saying "other." Consequently, a multiracial designation conceivably could end up being less accurate (in the sense of grouping people together who are deemed to be phenotypically similar) than the groupings we have now, depending on how it is defined and who decides who belongs to it.

Even if a multiracial designation is taken (as many proponents would like) to apply only to those with two parents of recognizably different racial stocks, it's unclear how useful the descriptor would be. Unless the census spelled out specifically what racial heritages were subsumed by the designation, it would put the offspring of a white person and an American Indian in the same pigeonhole as the child of a black person and a Chinese American or of a black person and a white person. Although the offspring of all the couples would certainly be multiracial, not many Americans would consider them to be of the same race. Many would still consider the black Asian and black-white children to be black (or perhaps mixed) and the white-American Indian child to be white. The children, in any number of circumstances, would be treated differently, as would be the unions of their parents.

A *New York Times* poll in 1991 found that 66 percent of whites were opposed to a relative marrying a black person, whereas 45 percent were opposed to a relative marrying a Hispanic or Asian person. (The survey did not attempt to ascertain whether responses would differ depending on whether the prospective Hispanic spouse was black, white, or something else.) Clearly, in the eyes of many of those respondents, all multiracial families are not created equal. And if part of the purpose of such classifications is to permit researchers to determine how various groups are treated, aggregating groups whose only common denominator is that their parents are racially different would not do much to advance that purpose. One is thus faced with the option of creating at least two multiracial categories — one perhaps labeled "multiracial-dark" and the other called "multiracial-light." But it's unlikely that anyone would see those categories as an improvement over the current system — least of all those who think that the multiracial category is a form of defense against America's obsession with rigid racial categories.

And what about those people who don't care for the multiracial desig- 25 nation? What about the children of black-and-white unions, for instance, who insist on calling themselves black? Providing them with a multiracial box is no guarantee that they will climb into it. And what about the children of "multiracial" parents? If the designation applies only to the first generation, will these children (like many light-skinned "blacks") become monoracial by the second generation? Or will their children, twenty years from now, be fighting for yet another redefinition of race? — for, perhaps, a new box labeled "old multiracial" as opposed to "new multiracial" or even "part multiracial" (which, of course, raises the question of how much multiracial one has to be to be considered truly multiracial).

And what about Latin Americans? Obviously, many Latinos find the current categories lacking. In the 1990 census, 43 percent of Latinos apparently thought of themselves as neither black, white, American Indian, nor Asian. They were "other." In fact, of all American residents who put themselves in the "other" category and indicated an ethnicity, the overwhelming majority (86 percent, according to the census bureau) were Hispanic.

A preliminary test of the multiracial option by the Bureau of Labor Statistics provided only a hazy idea of who might check it. When the option was offered to half of the 60,000 households polled in the May 1995 *Current Population Survey,* it got the biggest response from people in the white, Hispanic, and American Indian–Eskimo–Aleut categories. When Hispanic was offered as a racial (and not just an ethnic) option, the number of Hispanics claiming to be multiracial dropped considerably. Some of the whites who chose to describe themselves as multiracial apparently did so on the basis of belonging to various European ethnic groups. "Multiracial" respondents who did belong to more than one racial group were most likely to be from the American Indian–Eskimo–Aleut cluster. Different ways of asking the question elicited different responses, but it seems likely, on the basis of the results of the 1995 survey (which were essentially replicated in another governmental survey in 1996), that a significant portion of those who choose to be listed as multiracial will not be the children of "mixed"-race unions but either people from traditionally mestizo groups or whites with ancestors whom they consider to be exotic.

Assuming that the technical and definitional issues can be resolved, what will certifying a multirace accomplish? And at what cost? For all the heartfelt concern expressed by the parents of mixed-race children, it's unclear that the U.S. Bureau of the Census's recognition of that category would help. Could a new census category really protect children from crude, callous remarks? Or build self-esteem in those who lack it? Or serve as an effective shield against prejudice? And what influence would it have on the enforcement of laws dealing with housing discrimination and employment discrimination? Or on those private concerns that sell ads, conduct public-opinion research, and do other business based largely on current racial categories? As writer Lawrence Wright asked in the *New Yorker:* "Suppose a court orders a city to hire additional black police officers to make up for past discrimination. Will mixed-race officers count? Will they count wholly or partly?" And as has already been suggested, a new racial category would not even unfailingly provide a reliable anchor for racial identity, since the label is infinitely elastic.

Indeed, many critics would argue — some for scientific and others for sociopolitical reasons — that the creation of more racial pigeonholes is precisely what America doesn't need. The bigger problem, in short, may not be that the current groupings are insufficient, but that they foster a belief that there is something logical, necessary, scientific, or wise about dividing people into groups called races.

Certainly, when it comes to racial "science," not much has changed since 1942, the year anthropologist Ashley Montagu published the first edition of *Man's Most Dangerous Myth: The Fallacy of Race.* "In earlier days we believed in magic, possession, and exorcism, in good and evil supernatural powers, and until recently we believed in witchcraft. Today many of us believe in 'race.' 'Race' is the witchcraft of our time. The means by which we exorcise demons. It is the contemporary myth. Man's most dangerous myth," wrote Montagu.

Montagu acknowledged that racial groups were real. He rejected the notion, however, that the categories amounted to anything important. Racial groups were merely people with geographic origins in common who, to certain European taxonomists, looked somewhat alike. "No one ever asks whether there are mental and temperamental differences between white, black, or brown horses — such a question would seem rather silly," he pointed out, suggesting that the question was no less silly when applied to humans. Having rejected the idea that race represents different evolutionary paths taken en route to becoming Homo sapiens or is linked to fundamentally different capabilities or traits or indicates the existence of any

30

"hard and fast genetic boundaries," Montagu concluded that it is little more than an excuse for prejudice.

Americans are no closer than we were half a century ago to coming up with a sound scientific rationale for the myriad ways we regard race. Certainly, as Montagu admitted, different races exist — if only because we have decided that they do. We can theoretically create races at will. If Americans agreed, for instance, that people with red hair constitute a separate race, these people would be one. And if we proceeded to treat all people with red hair differently from everyone else, they would soon take on all the attributes we associate with "real" races. If, for instance, they were allowed only to do menial labor, refused an education, compelled to intermarry, forced to live in predominantly redhead communities, and told that their only real gifts were drinking and song, they would eventually develop a culture that embodied the new redhead stereotype. But all we would have proved is that human beings have the power to define (and thereby create) races — not that the classification has any value or makes any sense.

Race, in and of itself, is a harmless concept. It is the attributes and meaning we ascribe to race that make it potentially pernicious. And, unfortunately, race began as a value-loaded conceit. As paleontologist Stephen Jay Gould noted, eighteenth-century German naturalist Johann Friedrich Blumenbach created the modern system of racial classification as a "hierarchy of worth, oddly based upon perceived beauty, and fanning out in two directions from a Caucasian ideal." Blumenbach's racial pyramid had Africans and Asians on the bottom, Malays and American Indians in the middle, and whites at the top. That history and the uses to which race was subsequently put go a long way toward explaining why the movement to create a new multirace makes some people uncomfortable. . . .

Indeed, it's impossible to understand much of the resentment of the prospect of a mixed-race governmental category without taking into account America's legacy of colorism. The multiracial category, after all, is not new. The rise of the mulatto class during colonial times was an acknowledgment that the offspring of black-white unions were not necessarily either black or white. But as blacks edged toward freedom, the in-between status of mulattoes posed a growing threat to those who were determined to keep the races (and racial privileges) separate. Though it is not often remembered that way, the landmark 1896 case of *Plessy v. Ferguson,* which gave the Supreme Court imprimatur to the practice of separate (and supposedly equal) public accommodations, was, in part, a case about racial classifications — and whether the privileges of white skin were to be accorded those who were only partially black. As a test of Louisiana's Separate Car Act, Homer Adolph Plessy provoked a prearranged confrontation by sitting in the first-class "white" section of a train on the East Louisiana Railway. Plessy's blood was, by his own reckoning, one-eighth "African." And as the Court noted in its decision, "the mixture of colored blood was not discernible in him."

Plessy argued, among other things, that the reputation of belonging to the white race was a property right and that by denying him a seat in the white section, the statute deprived the white part of him the use of his property.

Still, the Court saw no reason to grant Plessy's demand for "every right, 35 privilege, and immunity secured to citizens . . . of the white race," though Justice Henry B. Brown, writing for the majority, did concede that Louisiana might need to determine whether or not Plessy was white. But Plessy had the last laugh by apparently making the determination on his own. In later years, historian Charles O'Neill reported, Plessy registered to vote as a white man. . . .

As historian Gary Okihiro pointed out in *Margins and Mainstreams,* racial classifications are not inherently stable, even among groups now considered to be racially unambiguous. In Louisiana, for instance, Chinese were classified as whites in 1860 but as Chinese in 1870. Ten years later, children of Chinese men and non-Chinese women were classified as Chinese, but twenty years after that, such children were reclassified as either blacks or whites. Virginia Easley Demarce, a historian with the Bureau of Indian Affairs, noted in a letter to the *Washington Post* that census takers used a form of multiracial classification during parts of the nineteenth century: "In 1870 in Washington Territory and Oregon Territory, for example, white males who had married American Indian women were enumerated on the standard population schedules, while their children were listed as 'half-breeds not otherwise counted' on separate pages. . . . In these two territories, enumerators also often identified native Hawaiians as 'SI' for 'Sandwich Islander.'" Demarce went on to observe that those whose heritage was mixed black and white were, at various times, also separately tallied. "The same family may, in four successive censuses, appear as 'free persons of color' in 1830, white in 1840, mulatto in 1850, and white again in 1860."

Tomorrow's multiracial people could just as easily become the next decade's something else. A name, in the end, is just a name. The problem is that we want those names to mean so much — even if the only result is a perpetuation of an ever-more-refined kind of racial madness.

On the one hand, it makes perfect sense for children of parents of identifiably different races to insist that all their heritages are "honored" in what they are called. Yet, the assumption runs aground of an inescapable reality: that the very function of groups within racial classification is to erase identity, to render us less individuals (whatever our constituent parts) than undifferentiated members of groups within a previously heterogeneous mass. By what logic, for instance, can one take countless African tribes — and the offspring of individuals comprised of any combination of those tribes — and make them all into one race called black? The reasoning is certainly no less specious than that which allows us to ignore the fact that a "black" American may also be Irish or Greek.

In the past, Americans (which is not to exclude much of the rest of the world) have made much more of racial labels than we should. We have seen race as a convenient way of sorting out who is entitled to which rewards, who is capable of what accomplishments, and who is fit to associate with whom. In light of that history, asking whether we should have a new racial category is a trivial question. The infinitely more important question is whether it is possible to divorce any system of racial classification from the practice of racial discrimination, whether a nation splintered along racial lines — a nation that feels compelled to rank people on the basis of race (aesthetically; professionally; socially; and, most insistently, intellectually) — is capable of changing that propensity any time soon.

Selected Bibliography

Books and Monographs

Adamo, Sam. "Race and Povo." In *Modern Brazil,* edited by Michael L. Conniff and Frank D. McCann. Lincoln: University of Nebraska Press, 1989.

Bach, Robert. *Changing Relations.* New York: Ford Foundation, 1993.

Baldwin, James. *The Fire Next Time.* New York: Dial Press, 1963.

Bergmann, Barbara. *In Defense of Affirmative Action.* New York: Basic Books, 1996.

Biddle, Jeff E., and Daniel S. Hamermesh. *Beauty, Productivity and Discrimination: Lawyers' Looks and Lucre.* Cambridge, Mass.: National Bureau of Economic Research, 1995.

Bradlee, Ben. *A Good Life.* New York: Simon & Schuster, 1995.

Brodkin, Karen. "How Did Jews Become White Folks?" In *Race,* edited by Steven Gregory and Roger Sanjek. New Brunswick, NJ: Rutgers University Press, 1994.

Cose, Ellis. *The Press.* New York: William Morrow, 1989.

———. *The Rage of a Privileged Class.* New York: HarperCollins, 1993.

Davidson, Chandler, and Bernard Grofman, eds. *Quiet Revolution in the South.* Princeton, NJ: Princeton University Press, 1994.

Davis, F. James. *Who Is Black?* University Park: Pennsylvania State University Press, 1991.

DeMott, Benjamin. *The Trouble with Friendship.* New York: Atlantic Monthly Press, 1995.

Der, Henry. "The Asian American Factor: Victim or Shortsighted Beneficiary of Race-Conscious Remedies." In *Common Ground,* edited by Gena A. Lew. Los Angeles: Asian Pacific American Public Policy Institute, 1995.

D'Souza, Dinesh. *The End of Racism.* New York: Free Press, 1995.

Du Bois, W. E. B. "The Conservation of Races." *The Oxford W. E. B. Du Bois Reader.* Ed. Eric J. Sundquist. New York: Oxford University Press, 1996.

Duster, Troy, et al. *The Diversity Project: Final Report.* Berkeley: University of California Press, 1991.

Eastland, Terry. *Ending Affirmative Action.* New York: Basic Books, 1996.

Ebling, F. J. G. *Racial Variation in Man.* New York: John Wiley & Sons, 1975.

Ellis, Trey. "How Does It Feel to Be a Problem?" In *Speak My Name,* edited by Don Belton. Boston: Beacon Press, 1995.

Feagin, Joe R., and Melvin P. Sikes. *Living with Racism*. Boston: Beacon Press, 1994.

Franks, Gary. *Searching for the Promised Land*. New York: HarperCollins, 1996.

Friedman, Nathalie, Theresa Rogers, and Elinor Barber. *The Dilemmas of Diversity*. New York: Columbia University Press, 1992.

Funderburg, Lise. *Black, White, Other*. New York: William Morrow, 1994.

Galton, Francis. *Hereditary Genius*. 1869, 1892. Reprint, London: Macmillan, 1925.

Getler, Michael, et al. *Challenge and Change: A Report by the Task Force on the Newsroom*. Washington, D.C.: Washington Post, 1993.

Gill, Lucia, Michael Reilly, and Anne Wheelock. *Looking for America*. Vol. 1. Boston: National Coalition of Advocates for Students, 1994.

Haizlip, Shirlee. *The Sweeter the Juice*. New York: Simon & Schuster, 1994.

Harris, Marvin. *Patterns of Race in the Americas*. New York: Walker, 1964.

Herrnstein, Richard J., and Charles Murray. *The Bell Curve*. New York: Free Press, 1994.

Hirschfeld, Lawrence A. *Race in the Making*. Cambridge: MIT Press, 1996.

King, Martin Luther, Jr. *A Testament of Hope*, edited by James M. Washington. New York: HarperCollins, 1986.

Kotter, John P. *The General Managers*. New York: Free Press, 1982.

Leonard, David, et al. *The Implementation of the Karabel Report on Freshman Admissions at Berkeley: 1990–1993*. Berkeley: University of California Press, 1993.

Lipstadt, Deborah. *Denying the Holocaust*. New York: Free Press, 1993.

Lynch, Frederick R. *Invisible Victims: White Males and the Crisis of Affirmative Action*. New York: Greenwood Press, 1989.

Mandela, Nelson. *Long Walk to Freedom*. Boston: Little Brown, 1994.

Mensh, Elaine, and Henry Mensh. *The IQ Mythology*. Carbondale: Southern Illinois University Press, 1991.

Montagu, Ashley. *Man's Most Dangerous Myth: The Fallacy of Race*. 1952. Reprint, New York: Oxford University Press, 1974.

Montalvo, Frank F. "Phenotyping, Acculturation, and Biracial Assimilation of Mexican Americans." In *Empowering Hispanic Families: A Critical Issue for the '90s,* edited by Marta Sotomayor. Milwaukee: Family Service America, 1991.

Okihiro, Gary. *Margins and Mainstreams*. Seattle: University of Washington Press, 1994.

Oliver, Melvin L. and Tom Shapiro. *Black Wealth, White Wealth*. New York: Routledge, 1995.

Page, Lisa. "High Yellow White Trash." In *Skin Deep*, edited by Marita Golden and Susan Richards Shreve. New York: Doubleday, 1995.

Pompa, Delia, and Michael Reilly. *Looking for America*. Vol. 2. Boston: National Coalition of Advocates for Students, 1995.

Ramphele, Mamphela. *Towards an Equity Environment*. Rondebosch, South Africa: Institute for Democracy in South Africa, 1995.

Review of Federal Measurements of Race and Ethnicity: Hearings Before the Subcommittee on Census, Statistics and Postal Personnel. Washington, D.C.: U.S. Government Printing Office, 1994.

Ross, Thomas. *Just Stories*. Boston: Beacon Press, 1996.

Russell, Kathy, Midge Wilson, and Ronald Hall Sacks. *The Color Complex.* San Diego: Harcourt Brace Jovanovich, 1992.

Rutstein, Nathan. *Healing Racism in America.* Springfield, Mass.: Whitcomb Publishing, 1993.

Scales-Trent, Judy. *Notes of a Black White Woman.* University Park: Pennsylvania State University Press, 1995.

Schofield, Janet Ward. *Black and White in School.* New York: Praeger, 1982.

———. "Black-White Contact in Desegregated Schools." In *Contact and Conflict in Intergroup Encounters,* edited by M. Hewstone and R. Brown. Oxford, England: Basil Blackwell, 1986.

———. "Causes and Consequences of the Colorblind Perspective." In *Prejudice, Discrimination, and Racism,* edited by John F. Dovidio and Samuel L. Gaertner. Orlando, Fla.: Academic Press, 1986.

———. "Review of Research on School Desegregation's Impact on Elementary and Secondary School Students." In *Handbook of Research on Multicultural Education,* edited by J. A. Banks and C. A. McGee. New York: Macmillan, 1995.

Sowell, Thomas. *Affirmative Action Reconsidered.* Washington, D.C.: American Enterprise Institute for Public Policy Research, 1975.

Sykes, Charles J. *A Nation of Victims.* New York: St. Martin's Press, 1992.

Taylor, Jared. *Paved with Good Intentions.* New York: Carroll & Graf, 1992.

Thomas, Piri. *Down These Mean Streets.* New York: Alfred A. Knopf, 1967.

Tien, Chang-Lin. "Affirming Affirmative Action." In *Common Ground,* edited by Gena A. Lew. Los Angeles: Asian Pacific American Public Policy Institute, 1995.

Whimbey, Arthur. *Analytical Reading and Reasoning.* Cary, NC: Innovative Sciences, 1989.

———, Eugene Williams, and Myra J. Linden. *Keys to Quick Writing Skills.* Birmingham, Ala.: EBSCO Curriculum Materials, 1994.

Wilson, William Julius. *The Declining Significance of Race.* Chicago: University of Chicago Press, 1978.

———. *When Work Disappears.* New York: Alfred A. Knopf, 1996.

Wright, Richard. *Uncle Tom's Children.* New York: Harper & Bros., 1940.

Zack, Naomi. *Race and Mixed Race.* Philadelphia: Temple University Press, 1993.

Zenón Cruz, Isabelo. *Narciso descubre su trasero.* 2 vols. Humacao, Puerto Rico: Editorial Furidi, 1975.

Journals and Magazines

Alstyne, William Van. "Rites of Passage: Race, the Supreme Court, and the Constitution." *University of Chicago Law Review* 46 (1979): 775–810.

Andrews, Lori B., and Dorothy Nelkin. "The Bell Curve: A Statement." *Science,* January 5, 1996, 13–14.

Berkowitz, Ari. "Our Genes, Ourselves?" *BioScience* 46 (1996): 42–51.

Besharov, Douglas J., and Timothy S. Sullivan. "One Flesh." *The New Democrat,* July–August 1996, 19–21.

Biddle, Jeff E., and Daniel S. Hamermesh. "Beauty and the Labor Market." *American Economic Review* 84 (1994): 1174–94.

Bok, Derek. "Admitting Success." *New Republic,* February 4, 1985, 14–16.

Carmichael, J. W., et al. "Minorities in the Biological Sciences — The Xavier Success Story and Some Implications." *BioScience* 43 (1993): 564–69.

Cleghorn, Reese. "Taboos and Race in the Newsroom." *American Journalism Review,* November 1995, 4–5.

Dunkel, Tom, et al., "Affirmative Reaction." *Working Woman,* October 1995, 39–48.

English, Rodney K. "What Are Lily-White and Read All Over?" *Folio,* August 15, 1993, 36–38.

Faundez, Julio. "Promoting Affirmative Action." *Indicator SA* 11, no. 4 (Spring 1994): 57–60.

Gilanshah, Bijan. "Multiracial Minorities: Erasing the Color Line." *Law and Inequality* 12 (1993): 183–204.

Gissler, Sig. "Newspapers' Quest for Racial Candor." *Media Studies Journal,* Summer 1994, 123–32.

Gladwell, Malcolm. "Black Like Them." *New Yorker,* April 29 and May 6, 1996, 74–81.

Gould, Stephen Jay. "The Geometer of Race." *Discover,* November 1994, 65–69.

Howard, Jeff, and Ray Hammond. "Rumors of Inferiority." *New Republic,* September 9, 1985, 17–21.

Jen, Gish. "An Ethnic Trump." *New York Times Magazine,* July 7, 1996, 50.

Johnson, James H., Jr., and Walter C. Farrell, Jr. "Race Still Matters." *Chronicle of Higher Education,* July 7, 1995, A48.

Kahlenberg, Richard. "Class, Not Race: Toward a New Affirmative Action." *Current,* September 1995, 3–8.

Kasinitz, Philip, and Jan Rosenberg. "Missing the Connection: Social Isolation and Employment on the Brooklyn Waterfront." *Social Problems* 43 (1996): 501–19.

King, Martin Luther, Jr. "Playboy Interview: Martin Luther King — Candid Conversation." *Playboy,* January 1965, 65–78.

Komaromy, Miriam, Kevin Grumbach, and Michael Drake. "The Role of Black and Hispanic Physicians in Providing Health Care for Underserved Populations." *New England Journal of Medicine* 334 (1996): 1305–14.

Konrad, Alison, and Frank Linnehan. "Formalized Hiring Structures: Coordinating Equal Employment Opportunity or Concealing Organizational Practices?" *Academy of Management Journal* 38 (1995): 785–818.

LaBrecque, Ron. "Racial Resentment Hits Home." *Spectrum,* Summer 1993, 47–50.

Lawrence, Charles R., III. "The Epidemiology of Color-Blindness: Learning to Think and Talk about Race, Again." *Boston College Third World Law Journal* 15 (1995): 1–18.

Leana, Carrie R. "Why Downsizing Won't Work." *Chicago Tribune Magazine,* April 14, 1996, 15–18.

Lemann, Nicholas. "Taking Affirmative Action Apart." *New York Times Magazine,* June 11, 1995, 36–62.

Lodge, Tom. "The South African General Elections, April 1994: Results, Analysis and Implications." *African Affairs* 94 (1995): 471–500.

Lythcott-Haimes, Julie C. "Where Do Mixed Babies Belong?" *Harvard Civil Rights–Civil Liberties Law Review* 29 (1994): 531–58.

Mbatha, Madoda. "Sharing Wealth." *Indicator SA* 11, No. 3 (Winter 1994): 43–46.

McGrath, Mike, and Andrew Whiteford. "Disparate Circumstances." *Indicator SA* 11, No. 3 (Winter 1994): 47–50.

McKinley, Colleen. "Custody Disputes Following the Dissolution of Interracial Marriages: Best Interests of the Child or Judicial Racism?" *Journal of Family Law* 19 (1980): 97–136.

Moller, Valerie. "Post-Election Euphoria." *Indicator SA* 12, No. 12 (Summer 1994): 27–32.

———. "Waiting for Utopia." *Indicator SA* 13, No. 1 (Summer 1995): 47–54.

Murray, Charles. "Affirmative Racism." *New Republic*, December 31, 1984, 18–23.

———, and Richard Herrnstein. "Race, Genes and I.Q. — An Apologia: The Case for Conservative Multiculturalism." *New Republic*, October 31, 1994, 27–38.

"The Negro in America." *Newsweek*, July 29, 1963, 15–36.

Norment, Lynn. "Am I Black, White or In Between? Is There a Plot to Create a 'Colored' Buffer Race in America?" *Ebony*, August 1995, 108–10.

Ogbu, John. "Cultural Problems in Minority Education: Their Interpretations and Consequences — Part One: Theoretical Background." *Urban Review* 27 (1995): 189–205.

———. "Racial Stratification and Education in the United States: Why Inequality Persists." *Teachers College Record* 96 (1994): 264–98.

Pildes, Richard H. "The Politics of Race." *Harvard Law Review* 108 (1995): 1359–92.

Piper, Adrian. "Passing for White, Passing for Black." *Transition: An International Review* 58 (1992): 6–32.

Pogrebin, Robin. "The Best Lawyers in New York." *New York*, March 20, 1995, 32–46.

Pollitt, Katha. "Subject to Debate: Affirmative Action." *The Nation* 260 (March 1995): 336.

Routté-Gómez, Eneid. "So, Are We Racist?" *San Juan*, December 1995–January 1996, 54–58.

Rudenstine, Neil. "The Uses of Diversity." *Harvard Magazine*, April 1996, 49–62.

Samelson, Franz. "From 'Race Psychology' to 'Studies in Prejudice': Some Observations on the Thematic Reversal in Social Psychology." *Journal of the History of the Behavioral Sciences* 14 (1978): 265–78.

Schofield, Janet Ward. "The Impact of Positively Structured Contact on Intergroup Behavior: Does It Last Under Adverse Conditions?" *Social Psychology Quarterly* 42 (1979): 280–84.

Shalit, Ruth. "Race in the Newsroom: The Washington Post in Black and White." *New Republic*, October 2, 1995, 20–37.

Shaya, Stephen B., Howard R. Petty, and Leslie Isler Petty. "A Case Study of Supplemental Instruction in Biology Focused on At-Risk Students." *BioScience* 43 (1993): 709–11.

Shepard, Alicia C. "Too Much Too Soon?" *American Journalism Review*, December 1995, 34–38.

Steele, Claude. "Race and the Schooling of Black Americans." *Atlantic Monthly*, April 1992, 68–78.

———, and Joshua Aronson. "Stereotype Threat and the Intellectual Test Performance of African Americans." *Journal of Personality and Social Psychology* 69 (1995): 797–811.

Wanniski, Jude. "Journalists Who Accept the Findings of The Bell Curve Are 'Benevolent Racists,'" *Forbes Media Critic*, Spring 1995, 85–91.

Webb, Veronica. "Where Have All the Black Models Gone?" *Essence*, September 1996, 108.

Weber, Bruce. "Inside the Meritocracy Machine." *New York Times Magazine*, April 28, 1996, 44–59.

Whimbey, Arthur. "Mastering Reading Through Reasoning." *Journal of Reading* 29 (1986): 466–72.

Wills, Christopher. "The Skin We're In." *Discover*, November 1994, 77–81.

Wilson, William Julius. "Class Consciousness." *New York Times Book Review*, July 14, 1996, 11.

Wright, Lawrence. "One Drop of Blood." *New Yorker*, July 25, 1994, 46–55.

ENGAGING THE TEXT

1. What evidence does Cose provide that race is a social rather than a biological concept? If the idea of race is arbitrary, why does it remain so powerful?

2. What is the "one-drop rule" (para. 9)? Why is the idea both absurd and dangerous, according to Cose?

3. List the arguments cited by Cose for adding a multiracial designation to the next census form; then list the arguments against it. Which position do you find more compelling, and why?

4. The Office of Management and Budget has now decided that people will be allowed to check all the racial categories on the census form that apply to them rather than requiring them to choose just one. What benefits and drawbacks do you see in this plan?

EXPLORING CONNECTIONS

5. Look at Norman Rockwell's depiction of "A Family Tree" on p. 22. Would you consider the little boy at the top of the tree multiracial? Why or why not?

6. Write a letter from Cose to Thomas Jefferson (p. 532) responding to his comments about racial mixing.

7. Cose's title asks, "Can a new race surmount old prejudices?" How might Jane Lazarre (p. 623), as the mother of multiracial children, and Leslie Marmon Silko (p. 594), as a multiracial person herself, answer this question?

8. Read the essay by Lynell George (p. 652). In what ways does her vision of cultural mixing correspond to that offered by Cose? In what ways does it differ?

9. Brainstorm several possible interpretations for the cartoon above. Which interpretation do you prefer, and why? Do you think that the cartoonist would support Cose's vision of a "new race" emerging in the United States?

EXTENDING THE CRITICAL CONTEXT

10. Poll five to ten people of different racial and ethnic backgrounds about whether or not they would favor eliminating all references to race on official forms and documents. Pool your results with those of classmates. How would you interpret the responses offered by people from different groups?

Gray Boys, Funky Aztecs, and Honorary Homegirls

LYNELL GEORGE

A quarter of a century after the civil rights movement some Americans, like Shelby Steele (p. 612), worry about the future of race relations in the United States while others, like the students Lynell George describes in this essay, feel ready to leave old definitions of race behind. According to

George, teens in cities like Los Angeles are living on the edge of a new way of looking at race and ethnicity: they're part of a new melting pot that's merging their varied backgrounds into a new, composite culture. Although George expresses reservations about this cultural ideal, she clearly sees hope that a new generation of Americans has already begun learning how to bridge racial divides. George (b. 1962) was born and raised in Los Angeles where she works as a staff writer for the Los Angeles Times, *the source of this essay. In addition to her work in journalism, she has published* No Crystal Stair: African Americans in the City of Angels *(1992).*

Let's call him "Perry."

If you grew up in Los Angeles (back when it was still hip to dub the mix "melting pot") and sat through a homeroom roll call sandwiching you somewhere between a Martinez, Masjedi, Matsuda, and Meizel, you knew one — but more than likely two. This Culver City "Perry," a classmate of mine, had Farrah Fawcett–feathered blond hair, moist blue-gray eyes, and a *Tiger Beat* dimple in his chin. Tall and gregarious, at first glimpse he seemed destined for the surfers' corner in the cafeteria — that tight tangle of dreamy adolescents who, in wet suits under their hooded Bajas, made their way down to Zuma Beach on slate-gray February mornings. Blaring Led Zeppelin, Boston, or Aerosmith, they trailed westward, away from the sun.

In broad-lapel Qianna shirts and denim flares, Perry, who looked less like Peter Frampton than Barry Gibb, embraced the electronic trickery of Parliament-Funkadelic, the East Coast soul of the Isley Brothers, or some Ohio Players midnight jam swelling from the boombox. He certainly never surfed. He shadowed the intricate steps of the Soul Train dancers, sat with the black basketball players in the back of the bus and attempted to chat up their little sisters in a sonorous baritone carefully fashioned after (who else but) Barry White.

"Oh, man, he's like K.C., you know, in the Sunshine Band," those who knew him would tease. But new faces would take a second look, then bristle and inevitably inquire: "Hasn't anybody told him he ain't black?"

"Chill out," Perry's best partner, the tallest, most imposing BMOC   5 would always defend. "He's OK. He's gray. . . ."

After a while, most everyone forgot what Perry wasn't — even forgot that he was "gray": the hard-won badge worn by those white kids who seemed much more comfortable hovering in the space between.

It often worked other ways, too. White kids, honorary homeboys and homegirls who dressed like *cholos* and talked the grand talk about *mi vida loca.* Blue-blood black kids who surfed and played mean, tireless sets of country club tennis. Japanese kids who saved their lunch money to buy forum floor seats for Earth, Wind and Fire spectaculars and were slipping everyone hallway high-fives during passing period long before it became proball decorum.

Over the years, L.A.'s mix has only evolved into a much more complex jumble as immigration patterns shift and swell, as blurred neighborhood boundaries subdivide or change hands. However, Los Angeles (as shown by the chaos last spring[1]) is still a segregated city, despite such "border towns" as Culver City, Echo Park, or Carson and the disparate bodies that inhabit them, blending and sharing their cultural trappings and identifiers. These contiguous neighborhoods inspire intercultural dialogue. And those living at the fringes have (not without incident) found it necessary to learn something about adaptation. Dealing not in dualities but in pluralities, survival in this city requires a cultural dexterity heretofore unimagined.

L.A. has metamorphosed into a crazy incubator, and the children who live on these streets and submit to their rhythm rise up as exquisite hothouse flowers. They beget their own language, style, codes — a shorthand mode of communication and identification. It's more than learning a handy salutation in Tagalog, being conversant in street slang or sporting hip-hop-inspired styles. This sort of cultural exchange requires active participation and demands that one press past the superficial toward a more meaningful discourse and understanding.

By no means a full-blown movement, these young people, a small coterie, exhibit large-scale possibilities. Unaware and without fanfare, they are compelling examples of how effortless and yet edifying reaching out can be.

Their free-form amalgamation billows up in street style (like the "Gangsta"/*cholo*-style baggy chinos and Pendletons that hit the mainstream fashion pages a few months back) as well as in street music. Latino rapper Kid Frost shook it up with his icy, tough-as-nails Public Enemy delivery, then sharpened the edges with staccato snatches in Spanish. For raw power, post-punk badboys the Red Hot Chili Peppers don't have a thing on their counterparts, the Badbrains.

Recently, the Funky Aztecs have taken the baton. Their new recording, "Chicano Blues," offers samples from soul crooner Bill Withers while vamping on traditional twelve-bar delta blues. When not dipping into reggae dub-style or funk, Merciless, Indio, and Loco pay homage to the rich California melange with the raucous single, "Salsa *con* Soul Food."

For Merciless, who's nineteen, the mixing was almost inevitable. His family moved to an all-black neighborhood in Vallejo when he was nine, and before he shaved his head a year ago, "I had real curly hair," he says. "Just, I guess, by the way I dress, a lot of people mix me up with either being black or mixed with black." And the rhythms of hip-hop were a break from the street. "My Chicano partners they were all into their little gangs, you know, their little Notre XIV. Everyone was talking about gangster stuff: 'I'ma kill

10

---

[1]*the chaos last spring:* The L.A. uprising of 1992 following the acquittal of four police officers in the Rodney King beating case.

you,' 'I gotta gun,' 'this bitch is my "ho."' But I wasn't into that, I was more like expressing myself politically. It was mainly my black friends who were into rapping and deejaying and stuff like that.

"It's a trip because my own race trips off me. I even got chased out of my own barrio. But the brothers are real cool with me. It's not that I side on them or whatever because my race always puts me down. It's not like that, but if you're cool to me, I don't care what color you are — I'm going to give you that love right back."

Lives and attitudes like that wreak havoc with stubborn stereotypes and   15
archaic notions about what it is to be African-American, Latino, Asian-American, or Anglo in a quickly transfiguring metropolitan center. In a recent Village Voice Literary Supplement, L.A. expatriate Paul Beatty eloquently shared a vision of home: "Growing up in Los Angeles," writes Beatty, "I couldn't help noticing that language was closely tied to skin color" but not exclusively. "Black folks was either 'fittin' or 'fixin' to go to Taco Bell. . . . The four Asian kids I knew talked black. . . . When I started writing, I realized that me and my friends had difficulty processing the language. We felt like foreigners because no one understood us. We were a gang of verbal mulattoes. Black kids with black brains but white mouths — inbred with some cognitively dissonant Mexicans who didn't speak Spanish and looked crazy at anyone who thought they did."

Some argue that this sort of mixing dilutes culture and creates innumerable lost souls; but many of those who live it see this sharing as realistically inclusive and ultimately enriching — so long as one holds on to integral bits and pieces of one's own. Those more optimistic hear rumblings in and of this New Age patois as harbingers; these young people are well-equipped bellwethers of the new cultural hybrids of Los Angeles.

The mixing starts earlier and earlier, as Jai Lee Wong of the L.A. County Human Relations Commission points out: "My child is four and a half and is fluent in Spanish because his baby-sitter teaches it to him." He tends, she explains, to identify people by the language they speak, not by their racial or ethnic designations. "If they speak English, they are English or American. If they speak Korean, they're Korean," Wong says. "And even though his father is Chinese and speaks only English, my son thinks he's American. For him it's not based on race or ethnicity. He hears me and his father sitting around identifying people by race and it confuses him. Then one day he started talking about that 'green kid over there.' Turns out that he was talking about a white kid wearing a green shirt." Race is a concept not beyond but perhaps already behind him, Wong realizes; a clumsy piece of baggage that already weighs him down.

The new world view? "It's a people thing," Merciless says. "It's not a black or brown or white or red or orange thing. It's a people thing. We all just need to grow up."

On a recent postcard-bright Saturday afternoon, performance artist Danny Tisdale, assuming his flashy alter ego, Tracey Goodman, sets up a folding table with a matte-black cassette deck and a small P.A. system. Microphone in hand, he begins "hawking" a few specialty products for people of color: skin bleach, rainbow-hued hair extensions, and the "new" Contours Sculpting System ("used for refining the nose, lips and buttocks") to inquisitive Santa Barbara Paseo Nuevo mall denizens. Eyes concealed behind inky black shades, Tisdale/Goodman shouts out carnival-barker style: "Transitions, Incorporated!" just above Frank Sinatra's live, over-the-top rendition of "New York, New York." He promises "the ticket to success" as he displays photos of Michael Jackson, the smiling and yet-unaltered preteen juxtaposed with the blanched and angular post-"Thriller" visage.

Taking the proceedings as the real thing, an African-American woman   20
in a pin-striped suit and patent-leather sling-back heels breaks free from the circle, approaching the display at a quick clip. Interrupting the pitch, she requests a card, asks if surgery is at all involved. For a moment, most everyone gathered around the table incorrectly assumes she's a clever plant, a perfect foil. But as the woman becomes more insistent, arms flailing, voice ascending several octaves, Tisdale's manner appears less certain. He's fresh out of snappy retorts; smiles vanish slowly from the surrounding faces. "But will this really work for me?" She wants to know. "Will it truly help?" She's tried so many others.

The piece makes some people angry and renders others silent and bewildered. On a basic level it forces participants to confront, on the spot, the scope and texture of that uncomfortable quandary: What should one give up to achieve success in contemporary American society? The varied responses of those critiquing from the sidelines mirror the real-life incertitude of people enmeshed in this cultural gamble. A prime place in the mainstream isn't won without a price, or without compromise.

What happens when what was carried over from the Old Country becomes cumbersome, archaic, better to be swept under the rug lest anyone see? It is that loss of organic culture that sits at the heart of many debates about cultural accommodation. Most frequently, we see the conflict in terms of whitewash assimilation versus the "who stole the soul"–style wholesale cultural appropriation. Shelby Steele and Clarence Thomas[2] are trotted around (depending on the camp) as products or "victims" of the former. And rappers the Beastie Boys, Vanilla Ice, or Young Black Teenagers (an all-white rap crew) are seen as the latter: opportunists who pilfer the million-dollar beats and mimic the belligerent stance of this black urban art form without having the cultural understanding or sensitivity to carry it off effectively.

But even the most seemingly clear-cut examples of cultural compromise — like the mainstream-bound black woman tugging at Danny Tis-

---

[2]*Shelby Steele and Clarence Thomas:* African American author (see p. 612) and Supreme Court justice who have been criticized by some as cultural sell-outs.

dale's coat — are shaded or haunted by a wide array of weighty ramifications based on that choice, the consequences of turning one's back on one's culture, ". . . Blacks who imitate whites continue to regard whiteness with suspicion, fear, and even hatred," says professor and culture critic bell hooks in her latest book, *Black Looks,* revealing just one nuance in the many hues of assimilation — this one with a conditional cultural safety net woven in. And hooks suggests that what appears to be, at face, an embrace, is something much more complex, even duplicitous: an ingenious, sophisticated tool fashioned especially for urban survival.

L.A., after all, is not at all the Shangri-La it often presents itself as being, especially when it comes to ethnic/cultural relations. Hate crimes, crosscultural gang violence, ethnic "nationalists" such as skinheads, randomly hurled racial epithets along city byways are all a part of the city's fiber, woven in among flashes of accord and affinity. Xenophobia fueled by ignorance, rigid class stratification and skewed and outmoded media representations have all played a part in stoking interracial tensions in this city as well as across the nation.

That has helped make assimilation, for people of color, a weighty cultural gamble, a risky compromise in the journey toward success within the American status quo. Nowadays, asking one to assume bits and pieces of another's culture at the expense of one's own is viewed as an exercise out of the question, especially when attacks from without are so pointed and regaining what was lost in the past has been so painful. 25

But alternative forms of assimilation — for example, that of slipping in and out of multiple cultural identities — don't demand that people reject their own identifiers. They stress inclusion. In light of L.A.'s rapidly metamorphosing demographics, this drift is likely to become not the exception but the rule.

The mere fact of L.A.'s diversity makes the contentious concept of assimilation far less cut-and-dried than it was in the past, when widespread use of the term *melting pot* suggested that a soul branded with "minority" status in the United States had to "melt down" his or her cultural trappings — language, dress, religious ritual or even body type — to aspire to the American ideal.

Here, where Central and South America meet the Pacific Rim and West Indies, the definitions of what it means to be black, white, brown, or yellow blur, and fitting in requires an entirely different set of tools and techniques. Paule Cruz Takash, a UC San Diego anthropologist and ethnic studies professor, notes that "assimilation is not a one-way street," with everyone striving to adopt Anglo culture. As the phrase "Ellis Island West" spices news reports about the growing lines winding around the city's Immigration and Naturalization Service office, the question of assimilation becomes broader, takes on new definitions.

Ironically enough, in the past two decades, the media and other information arteries, traditional tools for stratifying cultures with the uncomplicated, and erroneous, shorthand of stereotypes, have been invaluable tools for breaking down stereotypes and reworking prevailing theories about cultural identity. New mixes take shape at monster movie-plexes, super-bookstores, and the alternative glitz of underground clubs (and the easy access to them). The ears and eyes take it all in — and the brain then reassembles it, gives it new form.

And an increasing number of L.A. newcomers embody and advance the recombinant culture. Nahom Tassew, a seventeen-year-old Ethiopian who's a junior at Belmont High, came to the United States knowing "just what I saw on movies and TV" about African-Americans. "I thought if I came here, I'd have to become a thief," he says, "or that was what people would think I was." After two and a half years, he has a new attitude ("I saw that [African-Americans at Belmont] were people . . . that there were good people and bad people, that every race has good people") as well as friends from Mexico, Guatemala, El Salvador, Japan, and China. And he's studying Spanish. "I need some Spanish words," he says. Just what will emerge from these admixtures is difficult to say. Tassew, at least, will acquire an early-age sophistication, learning classroom English along with the street Spanish of his neighborhood, finding astonishing cultural parallels (from salutation rituals to food) with his Chinese friends. In that environment, he and others have found, there is no room for xenophobia.

Principals and their support staffs at high schools around the city have been looking closely at their campuses' rapidly altering idiosyncratic mixes and the way students like Tassew work within them. At Carson's Banning High, principal Augustine Herrera has watched the numbers shift dramatically over the past six years. Upon his arrival, the school was 57 percent Latino. That ratio has changed drastically: Banning's population is now 72 percent Latino, 20 percent African-American, and 8 percent Asian/Pacific Islander. "For the most part they get along but I don't want to sugarcoat it." Herrera says: "We have the same problems that the city faces. We have kids who don't get along. What goes on in the city goes on on campus . . . a mindless name-calling that sometimes degenerates into a fight."

Race riots on L.A. high school campuses last fall were physical manifestations of city frictions at the boiling point. Students battling over abstracts or what, at face, seems frivolous — like the kind of music played at a Friday night dance.

"For many, it is the first time they have to mix," Herrera says, and conflicts and more positive exchanges are inevitable. "One feeder junior high is predominantly Latino, one is predominantly black — they must interact. At first there is a sense of distrust, so being in this environment is a good experience for them."

Assistant principal Bea Lamothe has noticed that the hip-hop-inspired cross colors, usually associated with black students, have caught on with the

Samoans and Latinos this year, and she's carefully observed what is a quieter form of cultural exchange and communication as well. "There are a few African-Americans who live on the Eastside in Wilmington who wear white T-shirts and khakis and speak Spanish." Students are often unaware that they are mixing codes or modes, she says. They're living their lives, just trying to fit in.

At this age, these adolescents — native-born or immigrant — are not   35
looking for, or relying on, words to describe or define their lives. They prefer action over theory. For many of them, it's working. And like the music that fuels them and serves as an anthem: It's all in the mix.

The students have unfurled a cloth banner and hung it high above the stage of Belmont High School's cavernous auditorium. In electric, wild-style lettering it proclaims: La Raza Unida (The United Race). As the SRO crowd mills around her, principal Martha Bin stands on the sidelines, blond hair folded into an elegant updo, her walkie-talkie poised in a freshly manicured hand. This year, voting to pass on the usual Columbus Day assembly, the student body, Bin explains, chose instead to pay homage to the campus's Latin cultural mix — spanning several countries and continents.

In what looks like an elaborate show-and-tell, students bring bits and pieces of their culture to Belmont's stage. Since the auditorium won't accommodate the 4,000-plus student body at one seating, there are two assemblies — one morning, another in the afternoon. The second performance begins with several girls in frothy turquoise dresses, their partners in dark, pressed suits, displaying *rancheras*. Later come the *cumbias*, a mambo and an elaborate dance performed with lit candles that originated in Peru. Capping the show is a trio in below-the-knee, extra-large baggy shorts, who rap and joke in English, Spanish, and French.

"We are a school of immigrants," says Bin, sitting down for a moment in a quiet classroom next to the auditorium, her walkie-talkie close by. "Many of the black kids are Hispanic. We have Chinese-Cubans. We have Koreans who speak Portuguese." Belmont, one of the largest high schools in the nation, with 4,500 students on campus, buses out another 3,000 to accommodate the crush of the Temple/Beaudry/Echo Park district youth population from which it draws. Bin says 78 percent of the student body is Latino; the rest is a mix that includes citizens of Romania, Colombia, Armenia, Ethiopia, and Biafra. "You sit them together," Bin says, "they just have to get along — *conjunto* — together."

William Han, an eighteen-year-old Belmont senior, thinks he knows why. "Students who attend Belmont," he says, "are first-generation American students, whereas at other schools they are second or third. We are immigrants. This is our first experience." Han knows the struggle to adjust. It was just four years ago that he and his Korean parents moved here from their home in Brazil. A bright and talkative "American" teen, he wears an oversized jersey with "William" embroidered in green, green-gray pressed slacks, and black sneakers. His black hair is close-cropped and sticks up like the bristles of a stiff brush. Like many of the kids around him, he's something of a citizen of the world — he speaks Portuguese, Spanish, English, and Korean. "Things at Belmont are honest," he says. In the common fight to cope with a new culture, "people accept you for who you are."

Because of the intricate cultural mix surrounding the school, there are   40
concerns and needs that are unique to Belmont. "Our ESL students tend to be Spanish speaking, but a lot of Asians speak Spanish before English on our campus because they hear it in their neighborhood," says assistant principal Rosa Morley, herself an embodiment of ethnic and cultural blending. (She has Chinese parents but grew up in Cuba. Fluent in Spanish, she feels most connected to Cuban culture.)

"The kids feel that the whole world is like this," Bin says, and that can be a problem later on. "They have some difficulty when they move out of this environment and are no longer the majority."

"We don't tell them this isn't the real world," Morley says. "They will find out sooner or later. We are sheltering them in a sense but cannot control what life will bring for them."

By college, one doesn't see as many "Culver City Perrys." The university, for those who make it, is often the startling baptism, a reawakening or first-awakening of self. Students moving out of ethnically/racially diverse environments and into the austere university setting come face to face with cultural stratification. It is, for many, the first time that they are called upon to choose sides or feel a need to become politically active.

The Institute for the Study of Social Change, based at UC Berkeley, reported on diversity at the university level a year ago in a study called the Diversity Project. The study's goal was to address "a vital and constantly unfolding development emerging in American social life," focusing primarily on demographic changes in the country and how they affect interpersonal communication on college campuses. There would be no solution to the problems of diversity, the report stressed, as long as we think in polar terms. The extremes of "assimilation to a single dominant culture where differences merge and disappear vs. a situation where isolated and self-segregated groups [retreat] into . . . enclaves" don't work, researchers concluded. The report was based on sixty-nine focus-group interviews with 291 UC Berkeley students.

The report advises a "third and more viable" option: "the simultaneous   45
possibility of strong ethnic and racial identities (including ethnically homogeneous affiliations and friendships) *alongside* a public participation of multiracial and multiethnic contacts that enriches the public and social sphere of life."

In testimonials in the Diversity Project, students spoke frankly about the problems of bridging two worlds and the inexorable pressure to fit in.

An Asian-American male was traumatized when presented with a completely alien environment: "I was totally unaccustomed to being in [a] social situation where only Asians were there. So I was completely lost. . . . I got so frustrated, I rejected . . . my Asian-American identity and had a lot of Hispanic friends."

In this period of self-searching, what will help these students realize this "third experience" — recognizing diversity while maintaining their own distinctive cultural identity — is to develop the cultural equivalent of achieving bilingual or multilingual proficiency, to be sensitive enough to adapt to one's surroundings without losing sight of self.

This concept of cultural pluralism — where each group makes an influential and duly recognized contribution to American society — may seem naive or merely whimsical, but in light of the tremendous cultural shift, it is tenable. "Racial and ethnic identities are always formed in dialogue with one another," says George Lipsitz, professor of ethnic studies at UC San Diego and author of "Time Passages," a collection of essays on diversity and contemporary pop culture. "So to be Chicano in L.A. means to have a long engagement with black culture. What kind of Anglo you are depends on what group of color you're in dialogue with."

Lipsitz has noted that this mixing once was a more class-based phenomenon, but that drift has altered dramatically in recent years. "When I see desegregated groups of graffiti writers, one of the things that strikes me is that they're also mixed by class," he says. "Style leaders are working-class kids who present themselves as poorer than they are but they have a suburban following. One writer told me: 'Y'know, I go down to the Belmont Tunnel, I go out to the motor yard in Santa Monica, I meet a guy who lives in Beverly Hills, I meet someone who went to Europe last summer.' It's the way they expand what's open to them."

Lipsitz doesn't see this mixing as a grievous threat or as diluting cul-   50
ture, as some nationalists do. People find allies wherever they find them, he believes. "For example, there is a group of graffiti writers who call themselves 'ALZA' — which stands for African, Latino, Zulu, and Anglo. ALZA, Lipsitz says, is Chicano slang for *rise up*. They found each other. Nobody set this up. Nobody put an ad in the paper. They look for spaces that are what we call 'multicultural.' I don't think that they ever think to look at it in those ways. But there's a sense of interest and excitement and delight in difference that makes them look for more complexity."

But painting this phenomena as some sort of "we are the world" harmonious culture fest would be erroneous. Like those in the Diversity Project, Lipsitz has witnessed some of the more painful outcomes of "fitting nowhere," what isolation and alienation can do to a young person's spirit and soul. "I've talked to many students who are either from racially mixed backgrounds or who have what they consider to be an odd history — maybe they were the only black student in a white high school or something like that," he explains. "Then at the university it seems that there is an inside that they are not part of, and there is no obvious subgroup that they can join.

"They don't feel comfortable maybe with African-American culture. Or there are Chicanos who come in but they don't speak Spanish well enough for MEChA [a college-level Latino political organization]; or there are Asian-Americans who are Korean or Vietnamese, and the campus is dominated by Japanese- or Chinese-Americans." It is their love of difference, danger, and heterogeneity that brings them together. When a singer like George Clinton comes along — who's too black for the whites, too white for the blacks — "in a way he's talking to people whose lives are like that."

Susan Straight titled her first short-story collection after one of her favorite herky-jerky, George Clinton–sired Parliament-Funkadelic jams, "Aqua Boogie." Maybe it was something about the rhythm. But probably it was the music's quicksilver spirit — arrogantly individual and all over the map. When Straight's "Aquaboogie" hit the stores, book reviews, and small journals almost two years ago, she inspired quite a few double takes. In her stark, sober portrait, her blond hair framed a steely face out of which light eyes stared boldly into the camera. A novel in short stories, *Aquaboogie* finds its center in a depressed Southern California locale called Rio Seco and its characters among the working-class blacks who live and die there.

The writing — eloquent, sensitive, and honest — wouldn't have riled so many except for the fact that Susan Straight is white, one of the few white artists giving voice to what's considered to be a black experience. "If I was a lousy writer and I was trying to write about a neighborhood like the one I'm writing about and had all these details wrong . . . then I don't think I deserve to be published," Straight says. "I know my little corner of the world and that's what I write about. And I think I do a good job. I don't fit into a box," she adds with that same tough, unblinking stare, "and see this is a big problem for people. It's like everywhere I go, which box do I fit into? I don't. Sorry."

Straight, who balances a UC Riverside lecturing position with writing, 55 leading various local writing workshops and household duties, was born in Riverside. She still makes her home there with her husband (her high school sweetheart, who is black) and two daughters in a sunny, rambling California Craftsman on a wide, tree-lined street. For Straight, fitting in was more of an issue once she left her Riverside friends and environs.

"I went to USC straight from high school. I got a scholarship — my Dad was unemployed at the time. I loved going to USC — once I found some friends," she recalls with a laugh. "When I first got there it was like I talked funny, I came from a bad neighborhood, I had a T-shirt that said 'Itsy-Bit' on the back in that Gothic writing. USC was a really scary place for me coming from Riverside, where everything was country."

She ended up hanging out with athletes — mostly black football players from places like Pomona and Inglewood. "Those were my friends," she says. The problem didn't end at USC's boundaries. It shadowed her cross-country, shot up at the University of Massachusetts, Amherst, where she was constantly embroiled in fiction workshop debates, then later took shape and form in the publishing world when she sent stories to *The New Yorker* and *The Atlantic*. "Of course everybody thought I was black, which I didn't know, but I understand," says Straight. "They just didn't want to read about that kind of stuff. They had problems with the dialect, they had problems with the subject. It was a little bit 'harsh.' One person wrote back: 'Your world view is very bleak. . . .' I thought, 'Man, I'm sorry. Fix the world, and then my view won't be so bleak.' "

What Straight was attempting to do with her body of work made some blacks angry, some whites a shade of uncomfortable that some found difficult to articulate — people like her first agent, who took it upon herself to chastise her client soundly. "She said: 'I didn't know you were white.' And then she said: 'I think you're deceiving people.' She sent all my stories back and wrote me a big, old long letter about '. . . the American public isn't ready for something like me. . . .' She really thought that I should be writing about something different," she says with a shrug, palms upturned. "So what am I supposed to do? Go back and get born again? Have different parents? Grow up in a different place? Marry a different man? Then I'll be writing about different things, right? That's a big order." Confronting her "bleak world view," Straight started writing mostly out of a sense of frustration and a need to take some sort of definitive action.

"Look at me," she says. "I weigh ninety-nine pounds. I mean what can I do? I can't bring my friends back from the dead. I can't stop people from doing what they're doing. Drugs have been a big problem. I've so many friends who have no brains left, and that's not from rock, that's from angel dust. I thought: 'Well I can go home and just write these little stories.' " Her "little" stories deal with enormous and grave issues — death, drug addiction, poverty, abandonment — but they also speak to nurturing aspects, the strength of black family structure, about love, about relationships between fathers and sons, mothers and daughters, community resilience. Not *the* black experience, Straight stresses, but a "particular" black experience.

What rests at the core of understanding, Straight believes, is reaching out and treating others with respect. "People have always said that black people know white people much better than white people know black people, because it's a matter of survival. And that's what I grew up hearing," says Straight. "Now being black is in vogue as far as the movies and stuff. Maybe it should be a matter of survival for white people to know how black people live now." As UC San Diego's Lipsitz notes, "You look around to see who has something to teach you," a new Golden Rule that can be looked upon as an informal paradigm for Twenty-first–Century survival. Kids on the borders of several cultures are "trying to be honest in a dishonest world," he says. "I think if something good were to happen, it would come from them. I think that they're trying to live a life that's not a lie."

Those who might be viewed by some as having "odd histories" because they've spent their lives juggling codes or responding to the various influences within them are breaking down walls and erecting sturdy bridges through the mere act of living their lives. Granted, this vision appears mere chimera, almost utopian. But it is, for them, proving to be an integral component of psychic survival. In this period of uneasy transition, complicated by overwhelmingly rapid change, young people ride the periphery, and their lives do impressive battle with notions of a now-archaic "norm." But their quiet revolution is fueled by much more than simply the adolescent ache to belong. It is a more honest, eyes-wide-open way to reach out and greet a world as confounding as they are.

ENGAGING THE TEXT

1. What, according to George, does it mean to be "gray"? How does someone become a "gray boy," a "funky Aztec," or an "honorary homegirl"?

2. Review several examples of the kind of "recombinant culture" that George describes. Can you think of examples of this new cultural style you have observed in your neighborhood, on campus, or in the media?

3. Working in small groups discuss whether it is possible to adopt multiple cultural styles, as George suggests, without losing your own cultural identity.

4. How does George explain the increase in racially motivated conflict within the new urban melting pot? Can you offer any additional explanations for the increase of racial tension within the new "recombinant culture"?

5. What, according to George, is the impact of college on the complex cultural identities of many entering students?

EXPLORING CONNECTIONS

6. Review the theories of prejudice outlined by Vincent N. Parrillo (p. 563) and Fred L. Pincus (p. 586). How might they respond to George's assertion that the "concept of race" is already "behind" some young Americans — already a "clumsy piece of baggage" from the past that weighs them down?

7. Write a dialogue between Shelby Steele (p. 612) and George on the future of race relations in the United States.

EXTENDING THE CRITICAL CONTEXT

8. Collect as many media images (from films, TV shows, ads, music videos and lyrics, and so forth) as you can that reflect the "recombinant culture" George discusses. Are these images evidence of a genuine cultural shift oc-

curring in the United States or is all this talk of a "new melting pot" just a marketing ploy, a matter of fashion? What evidence do you find, if any, that America's "racial categories" are actually changing?

9. Write a journal entry describing your personal experience of moving from the culture(s) of your neighborhood to the culture of college. To what extent does your experience confirm George's claims that students in college often must deal with "cultural stratification" for the first time in their lives and that they are often forced to "choose sides"? Share your experiences in small groups and discuss whether you feel college works to polarize the racial, cultural, and economic differences between students.

10. Recently there has been growing controversy about whether it is possible or appropriate to speak with authority about the experience of a group whose sexual, racial, economic, and cultural background differs from one's own. In this selection, George presents the case of Susan Straight, a white writer who has published a collection of stories featuring the experiences of African American characters. Do you agree that Straight represents a "quiet revolution" in American society? Would it be equally possible for a white professor to teach African American studies? For a man to write with authority about the experiences of women?

La conciencia de la mestiza[1]
Towards a New Consciousness

GLORIA ANZALDÚA

When Gloria Anzaldúa speaks of a "new consciousness," she's talking about creating a new self, about experiencing the world in a different way. She envisions a cultural evolution bringing new understandings of race, gender, class, and nationality. And in writing of the mestiza *consciousness and the multiple cultures from which it arises, she uses a new language — a hybrid of English, Castilian Spanish, a North Mexican dialect, Tex-Mex, and the Indian language Nahuatl. Anzaldúa is editor of* Haciendo Caras: Making Face/Making Soul *(1990) and coeditor of* This Bridge Called My Back: Writings by Radical Women of Color *(1983). In the last four years she has also published two bilingual children's books. This selection is from her book* Borderlands = La Frontera: The New Mestiza *(1987). Although we've provided translations, we suggest that you not consult these in your first read-*

---

[1]*la conciencia de la mestiza: Mestiza* consciousness; consciousness of the *mestiza* (a woman of mixed racial heritage).

ing. Concentrate instead on Anzaldúa's main points and on her innovative blend of argument and poetry, of myth and manifesto.

> *Por la mujer de mi raza*
> *hablará el espíritu.*[2]

José Vasconcelos, Mexican philosopher, envisaged *una raza mestiza, una mezcla de razas afines, una raza de color — la primera raza síntesis del globo.*[3] He called it a cosmic race, *la raza cosmica,* a fifth race embracing the four major races of the world.[4] Opposite to the theory of the pure Aryan,[5] and to the policy of racial purity that white America practices, his theory is one of inclusivity. At the confluence of two or more genetic streams, with chromosomes constantly "crossing over," this mixture of races, rather than resulting in an inferior being, provides hybrid progeny, a mutable, more malleable species with a rich gene pool. From this racial, ideological, cultural, and biological cross-pollinization, an "alien" consciousness is presently in the making — a new *mestiza* consciousness, *una conciencia de mujer.*[6] It is a consciousness of the Borderlands.

Una lucha de fronteras / A Struggle of Borders

> Because I, a *mestiza,*
> continually walk out of one culture
> and into another,
> because I am in all cultures at the same time,
> *alma entre dos mundos, tres, cuatro,*
> *me zumba la cabeza con lo contradictorio.*
> *Estoy norteada por todas las voces que me hablan*
> *simultáneamente.*[7]

The ambivalence from the clash of voices results in mental and emotional states of perplexity. Internal strife results in insecurity and indecisiveness. The mestiza's dual or multiple personality is plagued by psychic restlessness.

[2]This is my own "take off" on José Vasconcelos's idea. José Vasconcelos, *La Raza Cósmica: Misión de la Raza Ibero-Americana* (México: Aguilar S.A. de Ediciones, 1961). [Author's note]   *Por la mujer de mi raza . . . :* The Spirit shall speak through the women of my race.

[3]*una raza mestiza . . . :* A multiracial race, a mixture of kindred races, a race of color, the first synthetic race of the world.

[4]Vasconcelos. [Author's note]

[5]*the theory of the pure Aryan:* The myth espoused by Adolf Hitler and others of the racial superiority of white northern Europeans.

[6]*una conciencia de mujer:* A female consciousness.

[7]*alma entre dos mundos . . . :* A soul caught between two, three, four worlds. My head aches with contradictions. I'm led north by all the voices that speak to me simultaneously.

In a constant state of mental nepantilism, an Aztec word meaning torn between ways, *la mestiza* is a product of the transfer of the cultural and spiritual values of one group to another. Being tricultural, monolingual, bilingual, or multilingual, speaking a patois,[8] and in a state of perpetual transition, the *mestiza* faces the dilemma of the mixed breed: which collectivity does the daughter of a darkskinned mother listen to?

El choque de un alma atrapado entre el mundo del espíritu y el mundo de la técnica a veces la deja entullada.[9] Cradled in one culture, sandwiched between two cultures, straddling all three cultures and their value systems, *la mestiza* undergoes a struggle of flesh, a struggle of borders, an inner war. Like all people, we perceive the version of reality that our culture communicates. Like others having or living in more than one culture, we get multiple, often opposing messages. The coming together of two self-consistent but habitually incompatible frames of reference[10] causes *un choque,* a cultural collision.

Within us and within *la cultura chicana,*[11] commonly held beliefs of the   5
white culture attack commonly held beliefs of the Mexican culture, and both attack commonly held beliefs of the indigenous culture. Subconsciously, we see an attack on ourselves and our beliefs as a threat and we attempt to block with a counterstance.

But it is not enough to stand on the opposite river bank, shouting questions, challenging patriarchal, white conventions. A counterstance locks one into a duel of oppressor and oppressed; locked in mortal combat, like the cop and the criminal, both are reduced to a common denominator of violence. The counterstance refutes the dominant culture's views and beliefs, and, for this, it is proudly defiant. All reaction is limited by, and dependent on, what it is reacting against. Because the counterstance stems from a problem with authority — outer as well as inner — it's a step towards liberation from cultural domination. But it is not a way of life. At some point, on our way to a new consciousness, we will have to leave the opposite bank, the split between the two mortal combatants somehow healed so that we are on both shores at once and, at once, see through serpent and eagle eyes.[12] Or

---

[8]*patois:* Nonstandard dialect.

[9]*El choque de una alma atrapado . . . . :* The struggle of a soul trapped between the world of the spirit and the world of technology sometimes leaves it paralyzed.

[10]Arthur Koestler termed this "bisociation." Albert Rothenberg, *The Creative Process in Art, Science, and Other Fields* (Chicago, IL: University of Chicago Press, 1979), 12. [Author's note]

[11]*la cultura chicana:* Chicana culture. Elsewhere in *Borderlands,* Anzaldúa writes, "La cultura chicana identifies with the mother (Indian) rather than with the father (Spanish). Our faith is rooted in indigenous attributes, images, symbols, magic, and myth" (Chapter 3).

[12]*see through serpent and eagle eyes:* "The eagle symbolizes the spirit (as the sun, the father); the serpent symbolizes the soul (as the earth, the mother). Together, they symbolize the struggle between the spiritual/celestial/male and the underworld/earth/feminine" (*Borderlands,* Chapter 1).

perhaps we will decide to disengage from the dominant culture, write it off altogether as a lost cause, and cross the border into a wholly new and separate territory. Or we might go another route. The possibilities are numerous once we decide to act and not react.

A Tolerance for Ambiguity

These numerous possibilities leave *la mestiza* floundering in uncharted seas. In perceiving conflicting information and points of view, she is subjected to a swamping of her psychological borders. She has discovered that she can't hold concepts or ideas in rigid boundaries. The borders and walls that are supposed to keep the undesirable ideas out are entrenched habits and patterns of behavior; these habits and patterns are the enemy within. Rigidity means death. Only by remaining flexible is she able to stretch the psyche[13] horizontally and vertically. *La mestiza* constantly has to shift out of habitual formations; from convergent thinking, analytical reasoning that tends to use rationality to move toward a single goal (a Western mode), to divergent thinking,[14] characterized by movement away from set patterns and goals and toward a more whole perspective, one that includes rather than excludes.

The new *mestiza* copes by developing a tolerance for contradictions, a tolerance for ambiguity. She learns to be an Indian in Mexican culture, to be Mexican from an Anglo point of view. She learns to juggle cultures. She has a plural personality, she operates in a pluralistic mode — nothing is thrust out, the good the bad and the ugly, nothing rejected, nothing abandoned. Not only does she sustain contradictions, she turns the ambivalence into something else.

She can be jarred out of ambivalence by an intense, and often painful, emotional event which inverts or resolves the ambivalence. I'm not sure exactly how. The work takes place underground — subconsciously. It is work that the soul performs. That focal point or fulcrum, that juncture where the *mestiza* stands, is where phenomena tend to collide. It is where the possibility of uniting all that is separate occurs. This assembly is not one where severed or separated pieces merely come together. Nor is it a balancing of opposing powers. In attempting to work out a synthesis, the self has added a third element which is greater than the sum of its severed parts. That third element is a new consciousness — a *mestiza* consciousness — and though it is a source of intense pain, its energy comes from continual creative motion that keeps breaking down the unitary aspect of each new paradigm.

---

[13]*the psyche:* The soul or self.

[14]In part, I derive my definitions for "convergent" and "divergent" thinking from Rothenberg, 12–13. [Author's note]

En unas pocas centurias,[15] the future will belong to the *mestiza.* Be-   10
cause the future depends on the breaking down of the paradigms, it
depends on the straddling of two or more cultures. By creating a new mythos — that is, a change in the way we perceive reality, the way we see ourselves, and the ways we behave — *la mestiza* creates a new consciousness.

The work of *mestiza* consciousness is to break down the subject-object
duality that keeps her a prisoner and to show in the flesh and through the
images in her work how duality is transcended. The answer to the problem
between the white race and the colored, between males and females, lies in
healing the split that originates in the very foundation of our lives, our culture, our languages, our thoughts. A massive uprooting of dualistic thinking
in the individual and collective consciousness is the beginning of a long
struggle, but one that could, in our best hopes, bring us to the end of rape,
of violence, of war. . . .

El camino de la mestiza
The Mestiza Way

Caught between the sudden contraction, the breath sucked in and the
endless space, the brown woman stands still, looks at the sky. She decides to go down, digging her way along the roots of trees. Sifting
through the bones, she shakes them to see if there is any marrow in
them. Then, touching the dirt to her forehead, to her tongue, she takes
a few bones, leaves the rest in their burial place.

She goes through her backpack, keeps her journal and address
book, throws away the muni-bart metromaps.[16] The coins are heavy
and they go next, then the greenbacks flutter through the air. She
keeps her knife, can opener, and eyebrow pencil. She puts bones,
pieces of bark, *hierbas,*[17] eagle feather, snakeskin, tape recorder, the
rattle and drum in her pack and she sets out to become the complete
tolteca.[18]

Her first step is to take inventory. *Despojando, desgranando, quitando
paja.*[19] Just what did she inherit from her ancestors? This weight on her
back — which is the baggage from the Indian mother, which the baggage
from the Spanish father, which the baggage from the Anglo?

[15]*En unas pocas centurias:* In a few centuries.

[16]*muni-bart metromaps:* Maps of bus and rail transportation in the San Francisco Bay
area.

[17]*hierbas:* Herbs.

[18]Gina Valdés, *Puentes y Fronteras: Coplas Chicanas* (Los Angeles: Castle Lithograph,
1982), 2. [Author's note] *tolteca:* The Toltec empire predates the Aztec in ancient Mexico. Anzaldúa associates the Toltecs with more woman-centered culture and religion than those of the
warlike, patriarchal Aztecs.

[19]*Despojando, desgranando, quitando paja:* Stripping, removing the grain or the straw.

Pero es difícil[20] differentiating between *lo heredado, lo adquirido, lo impuesto.*[21] She puts history through a sieve, winnows out the lies, looks at the forces that we as a race, as women, have been a part of. *Luego bota lo que no vale, los desmientos, los desencuentros, el embrutecimiento. Aguarda el juicio, hondo y enraízado, de la gente antigua.*[22] This step is a conscious rupture with all oppressive traditions of all cultures and religions. She communicates that rupture, documents the struggle. She reinterprets history and, using new symbols, she shapes new myths. She adopts new perspectives toward the darkskinned, women, and queers. She strengthens her tolerance (and intolerance) for ambiguity. She is willing to share, to make herself vulnerable to foreign ways of seeing and thinking. She surrenders all notions of safety, of the familiar. Deconstruct, construct. She becomes a *nahual*,[23] able to transform herself into a tree, a coyote, into another person. She learns to transform the small "I" into the total Self. *Se hace moldeadora de su alma. Según la concepción que tiene de sí misma, así será.*[24]

Que no se nos olvide los hombres[25]

> *"Tú no sirves pa' nada*[26] —
> you're good for nothing.
> *Eres pura vieja."*[27]

"You're nothing but a woman" means you are defective. Its opposite is to be *un macho*. The modern meaning of the word "machismo," as well as the concept, is actually an Anglo invention. For men like my father, being "macho" meant being strong enough to protect and support my mother and us, yet being able to show love. Today's macho has doubts about his ability to feed and protect his family. His "machismo" is an adaptation to oppression and poverty and low self-esteem. It is the result of hierarchical male dominance. The Anglo, feeling inadequate and inferior and powerless, displaces or transfers these feelings to the Chicano by shaming him. In the Gringo[28] world, the Chicano suffers from excessive humility and self-effacement, shame of self and self-deprecation. Around Latinos he suffers from a sense of language inadequacy and its accompanying discomfort; with Native Americans he suffers from a racial amnesia which ignores our common blood, and

---

[20]*Pero es difícil:* But it is difficult.

[21]*le heredado, lo adquirido, lo impuesto:* The inherited, the acquired, the imposed.

[22]*Luego bota lo que no vale . . . :* Then she discards whatever is useless, falsehoods and brutality. She waits for the deep, probing common sense of the ancient people.

[23]*nahual:* Sorceress.

[24]*Se hace moldeadora, . . . :* She is able to mold her soul. Whatever image she has of herself, so she will be.

[25]*Que no se nos olvide los hombres:* Let us not forget men.

[26]*Tú no sirves pa' nada:* You're good for nothing.

[27]*Eres pura vieja:* You're nothing but a woman.

[28]*Gringo:* Anglo.

from guilt because the Spanish part of him took their land and oppressed them. He has an excessive compensatory hubris[29] when around Mexicans from the other side. It overlays a deep sense of racial shame.

The loss of a sense of dignity and respect in the macho breeds a false 15
machismo which leads him to put down women and even to brutalize them. Coexisting with his sexist behavior is a love for the mother which takes precedence over that of all others. Devoted son, macho pig. To wash down the shame of his acts, of his very being, and to handle the brute in the mirror, he takes to the bottle, the snort, the needle, and the fist.

Though we "understand" the root causes of male hatred and fear, and the subsequent wounding of women, we do not excuse, we do not condone, and we will no longer put up with it. From the men of our race, we demand the admission/acknowledgment/disclosure/testimony that they wound us, violate us, are afraid of us and of our power. We need them to say they will begin to eliminate their hurtful put-down ways. But more than the words, we demand acts. We say to them: We will develop equal power with you and those who have shamed us.

It is imperative that *mestizas* support each other in changing the sexist elements in the Mexican-Indian culture. As long as woman is put down, the Indian and the Black in all of us is put down. The struggle of the *mestiza* is above all a feminist one. As long as *los hombres* think they have to *chingar mujeres*[30] and each other to be men, as long as men are taught that they are superior and therefore culturally favored over *la mujer*,[31] as long as to be a *vieja*[32] is a thing of derision, there can be no real healing of our psyches. We're halfway there — we have such love of the Mother, the good mother. The first step is to unlearn the *puta/virgen*[33] dichotomy and to see *Coatlapopeuh-Coatlicue* in the Mother, *Guadalupe*.[34]

Tenderness, a sign of vulnerability, is so feared that it is showered on women with verbal abuse and blows. Men, even more than women, are fettered to gender roles. Women at least have had the guts to break out of bondage. Only gay men have had the courage to expose themselves to the woman inside them and to challenge the current masculinity. I've encountered a few scattered and isolated gentle straight men, the beginnings of a new breed, but they are confused, and entangled with sexist behaviors that

[29]*hubris:* Exaggerated pride or self-confidence.

[30]*chingar mujeres:* Fuck women.

[31]*la mujer:* The woman.

[32]*vieja:* Old woman.

[33]*puta/virgen:* Whore/virgin.

[34]*Coatlapopeuh-Coatlicue in the Mother, Guadalupe:* A reference to the dual identity (Indian/pagan and Spanish/Christian) of the Virgin of Guadalupe. Anzaldúa argues that "after the conquest, the Spaniards and their Church . . . desexed Guadalupe, taking Coatlapopeuh, the serpent/sexuality, out of her" (*Borderlands*, Chapter 3).

they have not been able to eradicate. We need a new masculinity and the new man needs a movement.

Lumping the males who deviate from the general norm with man, the oppressor, is a gross injustice. *Asombra pensar que nos hemos quedado en ese pozo oscuro donde el mundo encierra a las lesbianas. Asombra pensar que hemos, como femenistas y lesbianas, cerrado nuestros corazónes a los hombres, a nuestros hermanos los jotos, desheredados y marginales como nosotros.*[35] Being the supreme crossers of cultures, homosexuals have strong bonds with the queer white, Black, Asian, Native American, Latino, and with the queer in Italy, Australia, and the rest of the planet. We come from all colors, all classes, all races, all time periods. Our role is to link people with each other — the Blacks with Jews with Indians with Asians with whites with extraterrestrials. It is to transfer ideas and information from one culture to another. Colored homosexuals have more knowledge of other cultures; have always been at the forefront (although sometimes in the closet) of all liberation struggles in this country; have suffered more injustices and have survived them despite all odds. Chicanos need to acknowledge the political and artistic contributions of their queer. People, listen to what your *jotería*[36] is saying.

The mestizo and the queer exist at this time and point on the evolutionary continuum for a purpose. We are a blending that proves that all blood is intricately woven together, and that we are spawned out of similar souls.　　20

Somos una gente[37]

> *Hay tantísimas fronteras*
> *que dividen a la gente,*
> *pero por cada frontera*
> *existe también un puente.*[38]
> — GINA VALDÉS[39]

Divided Loyalties

Many women and men of color do not want to have any dealings with white people. It takes too much time and energy to explain to the downwardly mobile, white middle-class women that it's okay for us to want to

---

[35]*Asombra pensar que nos hemos quedado . . .* : It's astonishing to think that we have stayed in that dark well where the world locks up lesbians. It's astonishing to think that as feminist lesbians, we have closed our hearts to men, to our gay brothers, as disinherited and alienated as we are.

[36]*jotería:* Gayness.

[37]*Somas una gente:* We are one people.

[38]*Hay tantísimas fronteras . . .* : There are so many borders / dividing people / but through each border there / passes a bridge.

[39]Richard Wilhelm, *The I Ching or Book of Changes,* trans. Cary F. Baynes (Princeton, NJ: Princeton University Press, 1950), 98. [Author's note]

own "possessions," never having had any nice furniture on our dirt floors or "luxuries" like washing machines. Many feel that whites should help their own people rid themselves of race hatred and fear first. I, for one, choose to use some of my energy to serve as mediator. I think we need to allow whites to be our allies. Through our literature, art, *corridos*,[40] and folktales we must share our history with them so when they set up committees to help Big Mountain Navajos[41] or the Chicano farmworkers or *los Nicaragüenses*[42] they won't turn people away because of their racial fears and ignorances. They will come to see that they are not helping us but following our lead.

Individually, but also as a racial entity, we need to voice our needs. We need to say to white society: we need you to accept the fact that Chicanos are different, to acknowledge your rejection and negation of us. We need you to own the fact that you looked upon us as less than human, that you stole our lands, our personhood, our self-respect. We need you to make public restitution: to say that, to compensate for your own sense of defectiveness, you strive for power over us, you erase our history and our experience because it makes you feel guilty — you'd rather forget your brutish acts. To say you've split yourself from minority groups, that you disown us, that your dual consciousness splits off parts of yourself, transferring the "negative" parts onto us. (Where there is persecution of minorities, there is shadow projection. Where there is violence and war, there is repression of shadow.) To say that you are afraid of us, that to put distance between us, you wear the mask of contempt. Admit that Mexico is your double, that she exists in the shadow of this country, that we are irrevocably tied to her. Gringo, accept the doppelganger[43] in your psyche. By taking back your collective shadow the intracultural split will heal. And finally, tell us what you need from us.

By Your True Faces We Will Know You

I am visible — see this Indian face — yet I am invisible. I both blind them with my beak nose and am their blind spot. But I exist, we exist. They'd like to think I have melted in the pot. But I haven't, we haven't.

The dominant white culture is killing us slowly with its ignorance. By taking away our self-determination, it has made us weak and empty. As a people we have resisted and we have taken expedient positions, but we have never been allowed to develop unemcumbered — we have never been allowed to be fully ourselves. The whites in power want us people of color to barricade ourselves behind our separate tribal walls so they can pick us off one at a time with

---

[40]*corridos:* Ballads or narrative folk songs of Mexico.
[41]*Big Mountain Navajos:* Big Mountain is an area in New Mexico at the center of a Navaho and Hopi dispute over land rights and treaty conditions.
[42]*los Nicaragüenses:* The Nicaraguans.
[43]*doppelganger:* A double.

their hidden weapons; so they can whitewash and distort history. Ignorance splits people, creates prejudices. A misinformed people is a subjugated people.

Before the Chicano and the undocumented worker and the Mexican from the other side can come together, before the Chicano can have unity with Native Americans and other groups, we need to know the history of their struggle and they need to know ours. Our mothers, our sisters and brothers, the guys who hang out on street corners, the children in the playgrounds, each of us must know our Indian lineage, our afro-*mestisaje*,[44] our history of resistance.

To the immigrant *mexicano* and the recent arrivals we must teach our history. The 80 million *mexicanos* and the Latinos from Central and South America must know of our struggles. Each one of us must know basic facts about Nicaragua, Chile, and the rest of Latin America. The Latinoist movement (Chicanos, Puerto Ricans, Cubans, and other Spanish-speaking people working together to combat racial discrimination in the market place) is good but it is not enough. Other than a common culture we will have nothing to hold us together. We need to meet on a broader communal ground.

The struggle is inner: Chicano, *indio*,[45] American Indian, *mojado*,[46] *mexicano*, immigrant Latino, Anglo in power, working class Anglo, Black, Asian — our psyches resemble the bordertowns and are populated by the same people. The struggle has always been inner, and is played out in the outer terrains. Awareness of our situation must come before inner changes, which in turn come before changes in society. Nothing happens in the "real" world unless it first happens in the images in our heads.

[44]*afro-mestisaje:* Mixed-blood Latino people of African descent.
[45]*indio:* Indian (of Mexico/Central America).
[46]*mojado:* Wetback.

ENGAGING THE TEXT

1. What does Anzaldúa mean by "*mestiza* consciousness"? Why does she think such a new consciousness is necessary? What risks and rewards does she associate with a *mestiza* consciousness?

2. The concept of the *mestiza*, like the myth of the melting pot, involves the coming together of two or more cultures. How does the idea of *mestiza* consciousness differ from the melting pot metaphor?

3. How does Anzaldúa define the concept of *machismo* in this essay? How does it connect to the idea of *mestiza* consciousness? Why, according to Anzaldúa, are homosexuals important to this new way of thinking?

4. In paragraph 7, Anzaldúa distinguishes between a western mode of thinking, which she considers narrow and inadequate, and a more comprehensive "divergent" mode of thought. Do you think a person trained in traditional western thought can or should learn to think differently?

5. Discuss the effects of Anzaldúa's frequent use of Spanish, her mix of prose and poetry, her references to Mexican/Indian deities and folktales, her movement between vivid image and broad generalization, and other distinctive elements of her essay.

EXPLORING CONNECTIONS

6. Compare the idea of "recombinant culture" described by Lynell George (p. 652) with Anzaldúa's concept of *"mestiza* consciousness." Would Anzaldúa be likely to agree that the kind of cultural mixing experienced by the teens in George's essay actually involves a "new consciousness"?
7. Review the essays by Leslie Marmon Silko (p. 594) and Paula Gunn Allen (p. 520) and discuss the cultural, racial, and sexual borderlands that they inhabit as women of Native American and European descent. To what extent would you say that either writer displays the kind of *"mestiza* consciousness" Anzaldúa describes?
8. Anzaldúa and Ellis Cose (p. 635) both suggest the possibility that "the future will belong to the *mestiza* (para. 10). What advantages does each of them see in such a future, and what obstacles must be overcome in order to achieve it?

EXTENDING THE CRITICAL CONTEXT

9. What advice do you think Anzaldúa would give to an American whose experience and family background are essentially monocultural?
10. Anzaldúa suggests that one option for the *mestiza* is "to disengage from the dominant culture, write it off altogether as a lost cause, and cross the border into a wholly new and separate territory" (para. 6). What would it mean to disengage from the dominant culture? Do you think this is possible?

Child of the Americas

AURORA LEVINS MORALES

This poem concentrates on the positive aspects of a multicultural heritage, as Morales celebrates her uniqueness, her diversity, and her wholeness. It's an up-to-date and sophisticated reinterpretation of the melting pot myth and a possible illustration of Gloria Anzaldúa's "mestiza consciousness" finding voice in poetry. As this autobiographical poem states, Aurora Levins Morales (b. 1954) was the child of a Puerto Rican mother and a Jewish father. She moved to the United States when she was thirteen and now writes, performs, and teaches in the San Francisco Bay Area. "Child of the Americas" is from the collection Getting Home Alive *(1986), which she coauthored with her mother, Rosario Morales. Her mother has written that the book "began in long, budget-breaking telephone calls stretched across the width of this country . . . the phone line strung between us like a 3,000-mile umbilical cord from navel to navel, mine to hers, hers to mine, each of us mother and daughter by turns, feeding each other the substance of our dreams."*

I am a child of the Americas,
a light-skinned mestiza of the Caribbean,
a child of many diaspora,[1] born into this continent at a crossroads.

I am a U.S. Puerto Rican Jew,
a product of the ghettos of New York I have never known.   5
An immigrant and the daughter and granddaughter of immigrants.
I speak English with passion: it's the tongue of my consciousness,
a flashing knife blade of crystal, my tool, my craft.

I am Caribeña,[2] island grown. Spanish is in my flesh,
ripples from my tongue, lodges in my hips: 10
the language of garlic and mangoes,
the singing in my poetry, the flying gestures of my hands.
I am of Latinoamerica, rooted in the history of my continent:
I speak from that body.

I am not african. Africa is in me, but I cannot return.   15
I am not taína.[3] Taíno is in me, but there is no way back.
I am not european. Europe lives in me, but I have no home there.

I am new. History made me. My first language was spanglish.[4]
I was born at the crossroads
and I am whole.   20

---

[1]*diaspora:* Scattered colonies. The word originally referred to Jews scattered outside Palestine after the Babylonian exile; it is now used often to refer to African and other peoples scattered around the world.
[2]*Caribeña:* Caribbean woman.
[3]*taína:* Describing the Taino, an aboriginal people of the Greater Antilles and Bahamas.
[4]*spanglish:* Spanish and English combined.

ENGAGING THE TEXT

1. Does this poem do more to challenge or to promote the myth of the melting pot? Explain.
2. Why does the poet list elements of her background that she scarcely knows ("the ghettos of New York" and Taíno)? How can they be part of her?

3. How do you interpret the last stanza? Rephrase its messages in more complete, more explicit statements.

EXPLORING CONNECTIONS

4. To what extent does this poem display a *"mestiza* consciousness" as described by Gloria Anzaldúa (p. 665)? Do you see any important differences between these authors? Explain.

5. Many of the writers and characters in this book — including Gloria Anzaldúa (p. 665), Richard Rodriguez (p. 202), and Maxine Hong Kingston (p. 251) — express a sense of internal fragmentation or cultural conflict. How does the speaker of this poem avoid the feeling of cultural schizophrenia?

EXTENDING THE CRITICAL CONTEXT

6. Write your own version of "Child of the Americas," following Morales's structure but substituting ideas and images from your own heritage. Read it to the class.

6

Liberty and Justice for All

The Myth of Freedom

America's belief in itself as "the land of the free" pervades our mythology: early in our schooling, we are taught that the Pilgrims came to America for religious freedom, that the colonists fought the Revolutionary War for freedom from England, and that the Union defeated the Confederacy to free the slaves. However, a deeper reading of history shows that the motives underlying each of these landmark events were far more complex. Indeed, America's relation to the ideal of freedom has never been uncomplicated.

It's hard to appreciate what America must have meant to religious dissenters like the Puritans in sixteenth-century Europe. Persecuted by what they saw as a corrupt and authoritarian church, the Pilgrims viewed America through the biblical stories of exile, enslavement, and liberation they had read in the Old Testament: they came to see themselves as the new "children of Israel," "the chosen people" destined to venture into the wilderness of a "New Eden." Just as Christ had come to redeem creation from sin, they saw themselves as his agents, freeing humanity from the sordidness and decadence of the "Old World." But the Pilgrims sought a very narrow kind of emancipation: they came to America in pursuit of religious — not personal — liberty; they sought freedom of worship, not the kind of individual liberty that has become the hallmark of American independence. Indeed, in the rigidity of their religious doctrines, the authoritarianism of their social structure, their distrust of difference, and their contempt for worldly pleasures, they seem an unlikely source of inspiration for the American creed of "Life, Liberty, and the pursuit of Happiness."

Some historians trace the American concept of freedom not to the Puritan settlements of New England but to the American Indian cultures the Puritans and other European settlers displaced. Beginning with Christopher Columbus, European explorers were amazed by the personal freedom enjoyed by the Native Americans they encountered: they could scarcely comprehend a life apparently unrestrained by rigid social distinctions, gender roles, financial obligations, religious doctrines, or state regulations. In a 1503 letter to Lorenzo de Medici, Amerigo Vespucci described these remarkable people who seemed to live in harmony with nature:

> The inhabitants of the New World do not have goods of their own, but all things are held in common. They live together without king, without government, and each is his own master. . . . There is a great abundance of gold, and by them it is in no respect esteemed or valued. . . . Surely if the terrestrial paradise be in any part of the earth, I esteem that it is not far distant from these parts.

Europeans raised in cultures dominated by the authority of monarchy, aristocracy, and the church were particularly impressed by the relative freedom of native children. American Indian families often encouraged their sons and daughters to develop a strong sense of independence and personal liberty. Iroquois children, for example, were taught to resist overbearing authority and were rarely punished severely; they were also taught that all tribal members — male, female, adult, and child — were equal and that possessions were to be shared by the entire community. Such attitudes contrasted sharply with those imported to the New World by the Pilgrims, who believed that a child's natural stubbornness and pride had to be broken down through education, discipline, and corporal punishment.

The examples of freedom and equality provided by societies like the Iroquois and the Huron sparked the European imagination and, as some scholars suggest, placed liberty at the top of the Western world's political agenda for the next four hundred years. To political philosophers like Jean-Jacques Rousseau, the "noble savage" was living proof that human beings were born free "in a state of nature" and that tyranny and slavery were the result of social corruption: if tyranny and injustice were not natural or god-given features of human life, then it would be possible — even necessary — for subjects to rebel against royal domination and reclaim their natural "inalienable" human rights. To political activists like Thomas Paine, the freedom and equality enjoyed within many American Indian cultures demonstrated that society could be organized without aristocracy, monarchy, and ecclesiastical authority. The first great advocate of both American independence and the abolition of slavery, Paine based many of his revolutionary ideas on his intimate knowledge of Iroquois customs and values.

The example of America's original inhabitants may have inspired the settlers to take up arms and fight for their own "natural" rights, but, as historian Howard Zinn has pointed out, the Revolutionary War had devastating consequences for Native Americans:

> What did the Revolution mean to the Native Americans, the Indians? They had been ignored by the fine words of the Declaration, had not been considered equal, certainly not in choosing those who would govern the American territories in which they lived, nor in being able to pursue happiness as they had pursued it for centuries before the white Europeans arrived. Now, with the British out of the way, the Americans could begin the inexorable process of pushing the Indians off their lands, killing them if they resisted. In short . . . the white Americans were against British imperial control in the East, and for their own imperialism in the West.

It is one of history's most profound ironies that America's war for independence, the first war ever fought in the name of individual liberty, hastened the destruction of the very societies that had inspired the modern myth of freedom.

America's ambivalence toward the principle of freedom also found expression in the nation's newly drafted Constitution. The American Revolution's idealization of freedom had made slavery appear hypocritical to some patriots; as Abigail Adams wrote during the war, "I wish most sincerely there was not a slave in the province; it always appeared a most iniquitous scheme to me to fight ourselves for what we are daily robbing and plundering from those who have as good a right to freedom as we have." Such feelings prevailed in Vermont, where slavery was outlawed a year after the colonies declared their independence. However, economic and political considerations took precedence over human rights as the Constitutional Convention debated the slavery issue in 1787.

Outright abolition was never discussed at the convention — it would have been politically unacceptable to the many delegates who owned slaves. The question that did arise was whether the United States should continue to allow the importation of Africans for slave labor. Several representatives argued that it was "inconsistent with the principles of the revolution and dishonorable to the American character to have such a feature in the Constitution." But delegates from the South contended that more slaves not only were essential for developing southern agriculture but also would provide economic benefits for the northern states. Thus, a document that sought to "secure the blessings of liberty to ourselves and our posterity" also legitimized the sale and ownership of one human being by another.

The ideal of freedom was compromised again when liberties explicitly protected by the Constitution were denied in practice. The First Amendment guarantee of free speech, for example, was not actively enforced until well into the twentieth century. Dissenters — abolitionists, political activists, labor organizers, feminists, and birth control advocates, among others — were frequently arrested, harassed, fined, denied permits, or otherwise prevented from speaking publicly. The problem was so widespread that, in 1915, a government-sponsored investigative committee reported that

> on numerous occasions in every part of the country, the police of cities and towns have either arbitrarily or under the cloak of a traffic ordinance, interfered with, or prohibited public speaking, both in the open and in halls, by persons connected with organizations of which the police or those from whom they receive their orders, did not approve. In many instances such interference has been carried out with a degree of brutality which would be incredible if it were not vouched for by reliable witnesses.

But while the United States has often failed to uphold the rights of all citizens, the ideals of liberty and self-determination set out in the Declaration and Constitution have inspired many to fight for — and sometimes win — their "inalienable rights." Popular movements throughout the nation's history have organized, marched, struck, sued, and practiced civil disobedience when established political channels failed them. A determined, seventy-five-year campaign by American feminists won women the vote in 1920, and systematic protests and court challenges by the labor movement in the 1930s gave us many of our current protections of free speech. Denied equal protection under the law, equal access to economic opportunity, equal education, and even an equal chance to vote, African Americans sought redress in the courts and on the streets of America for decades, eventually winning substantive legal reforms during the civil rights movement of the 1960s.

In spite of these victories, the struggle for freedom is far from over in America. On college campuses across the nation, students and faculty are debating the need to regulate hate speech and other forms of racially or sexually offensive behavior. Conservatives and libertarians claim that speech codes violate their constitutional rights, while women and new-majority Americans see codes as their only protection against dehumanization and domination. Over the past few years, particularly vulnerable minority groups like gays and lesbians have experienced a backlash of prejudice and seen hard-won protections threatened by initiatives seeking to limit gay rights. Today, perhaps more than ever, America seems ambivalent about the myth of freedom. At times we seem to be foundering amid competing and often contradictory claims of individual rights. It's become nearly impossible to pick up a newspaper without encountering a story about victims' rights, children's rights, the rights of the unborn, animal rights, the right to privacy, the right to pray, freedom of speech, or freedom of the press. The clash of freedoms in contemporary America has even led some social critics to suggest that our devotion to liberty is transforming us into a selfish and dangerously fragmented society. According to "communitarians" like sociologist Amatai Etzioni, America has entered a period of "pervasive moral erosion": our inordinate respect for individual autonomy has led to a breakdown of our shared values and beliefs — "the social glue that helps hold the moral order together." And the communitarians aren't alone. Over the past decade, voices from both ends of the political spectrum — from conservative fundamentalists to radical new-age ecologists — have questioned whether America's experiment with freedom has gone too far and whether the principle of freedom itself may end in the destruction of our nation — or our planet.

This chapter invites you to examine the influence and limitations of the myth of freedom in contemporary American life. The chapter opens with two selections that offer a historical perspective on the American ideal of liberty: The Declaration of Independence is the first and perhaps the best-known proclamation of America's commitment to individual rights; Colin G. Calloway's "New Peoples and New Societies" offers a counterpoint to the Declaration by documenting the history of freedom on American soil before the first colonists arrived. The next three readings present personal meditations on what it means to be free. In "Easy in the Harness," attorney and activist Gerry Spence challenges us to consider how difficult it is to live a free life and invites us to assess our own commitment to the ideal of liberty. Jimmy Santiago Baca offers a different perspective on the meaning of freedom in "Past Present," a personal meditation on the years he spent in prison. June Jordan's "Freedom Time" asks us to consider the troubling possibility that most Americans in the 1990s are losing sight of what freedom really means.

The next section of the chapter is devoted to exploring some of the difficulties that arise in a society that recognizes conflicting freedoms and rights. In one of the several media selections in this chapter, Bill McKibben takes a hard look at the way TV's celebration of freedom has undermined America's sense of community. McKibben's community-based argument for restricting personal liberty is counterpointed by the radical definition of freedom as "self-ownership" offered by David Boaz in "What Rights Do We Have?" Another media essay, Patricia J. Williams's "Hate Radio," asks us if our tolerance of inflammatory talk show hosts like Howard Stern and Rush Limbaugh isn't undermining the spirit of civility that makes life in a free society possible. Next, Stephanie Brail carries the theme of free speech further in her analysis of sexual harassment in the "new wild wild west" of the Internet. Our examination of personal rights concludes with Nancy Mairs's "Freeing Choices," which offers a disabled person's brutally frank analysis of the social implications of in-utero genetic screening and doctor-assisted suicide.

The chapter closes with two selections that bear witness to the enduring power of freedom as an ideal in American life. "The Bridge Builder" offers the story of Kathleen Boatwright, a devout Christian and a lesbian who discovers the meaning of freedom through her relationships with church, God, and community. The chapter and the book close with Langston Hughes's impassioned appeal to make America a land that lives up to its finest myths:

> The land that never has been yet —
> And yet must be — the land where *every* man is free.

Sources

Lerone Bennett, Jr., *Before the Mayflower: A History of Black America.* Rev. 5th ed. New York: Viking Penguin, 1984.

David Kairys, "Freedom of Speech." In *The Politics of Law: A Progressive Critique*, David Kairys, ed. New York: Pantheon Books, 1982.

Ralph Ketchem, ed., *The Anti-Federalist Papers and the Constitutional Convention Debates.* New York: Mentor Books, 1986.

Krishan Kumar, *Utopia and Anti-Utopia in Modern Times.* Oxford: Basil Blackwell, 1987.

Jack Weatherford, *Indian Givers: How the Indians of the Americas Transformed the World.* New York: Ballantine Books, 1988.

Howard Zinn, *A People's History of the United States.* New York: Harper and Row, 1980.

BEFORE READING

- Brainstorm a list of all the freedoms that are important to you, then rank them in the order of their importance. In small groups, compare

684   LIBERTY AND JUSTICE FOR ALL

your list with those of your classmates and discuss patterns or discrepancies that arise.

- Write about a time when freedom or a conflict of freedoms became an issue in your school or workplace. Describe the conflict and the effect it had on you. How was it resolved, and how did you feel about the resolution?

- What does the picture at the beginning of this chapter suggest to you about freedom? In what ways does the woman in this picture appear to be free — or not free? Write a journal entry about a time when you felt the way she appears to feel. Describe the situation you were in. How free did you feel to express yourself or to take action in this situation? What, if anything, constrained you?

Declaration of Independence

THOMAS JEFFERSON

Drafted by Thomas Jefferson when he was only thirty-three years old, the Declaration of Independence was meant to announce and defend the colonies' decision to throw off British rule. But since its adoption by the Second Continental Congress on July 4, 1776, it has come to mean much more: its vision of responsive government and its insistence upon the fundamental equality of the governed have inspired democratic reforms for the past two hundred years — from the Bill of Rights to the civil rights movement. Conceived as a revolutionary manifesto, the Declaration has become the preamble to the most durable of all American myths, the myth of individual liberty. As third president of the United States (1801–1809), Thomas Jefferson (1743–1826) promoted westward expansion in the form of the Louisiana Purchase and the Lewis and Clark Expedition. In addition to his political career he was a scientist, architect, city planner (Washington, D.C.), and founder of the University of Virginia; his writings fill fifty-two volumes. For additional information on Thomas Jefferson, see page 532.

THE UNANIMOUS DECLARATION of the thirteen united
STATES OF AMERICA.

When in the Course of human events, it becomes necessary for one people to dissolve the political bands which have connected them with another, and to assume among the powers of the earth, the separate and equal station to which the Laws of Nature and of Nature's God entitle them, a decent respect to the opinions of mankind requires that they should declare the causes which impel them to the separation. —— We hold these truths to be self-evident, that all men are created equal, that they are endowed by their Creator with certain unalienable Rights, that among these are Life, Liberty and the pursuit of Happiness. — That to secure these rights, Governments are instituted among Men, deriving their just powers from the consent of the governed. — That whenever any Form of Government becomes destructive of these ends, it is the Right of the People to alter or to abolish it, and to institute new Government, laying its foundation on such principles and organizing its powers in such form, as to them shall seem most likely to effect their Safety and Happiness. Prudence, indeed, will dictate that Governments long established should not be changed for light and transient causes; and accordingly all experience hath shewn, that mankind are more disposed to suffer, while evils are sufferable, than to right themselves by abolishing the forms to which they are accustomed. But when a long train of abuses and usurpations, pursuing invariably the same Object[1] evinces a design to reduce them under absolute Despotism, it is their right, it is their duty, to throw off such Government, and to provide new Guards for their future security. — Such has been the patient sufferance of these Colonies; and such is now the necessity which constrains them to alter their former Systems of Government. The history of the present King of Great Britain is a history of repeated injuries and usurpations, all having in direct object the establishment of an absolute Tyranny over these States. To prove this, let Facts be submitted to a candid world. —— He has refused his Assent to Laws, the most wholesome and necessary for the public good. —— He has forbidden his Governors to pass Laws of immediate and pressing importance, unless suspended in their operation till his Assent should be obtained; and when so suspended, he has utterly neglected to attend to them. —— He has refused to pass other Laws for the accommodation of large districts of people, unless those people would relinquish the right of Representation in the Legislature, a right inestimable to them and formidable to tyrants only. —— He has called together legislative bodies at places unusual, uncomfortable, and distant from the depository of their public Records, for the sole purpose of fatiguing them into compliance with his measures. —— He has dissolved Representative Houses repeatedly, for opposing with manly firmness his invasions on the rights of the people. —— He has refused for a long time, after such dissolutions, to cause others to be elected; whereby the Legislative powers, incapable of Annihilation, have returned to the People at large for their exercise; the State remaining in the mean time exposed to all the dangers of invasion from without, and convulsions within. —— He has endeavoured to prevent the population of these

[1]*Object:* Goal, purpose.

States; for that purpose obstructing the Laws for Naturalization of Foreigners; refusing to pass others to encourage their migrations hither, and raising the conditions of new Appropriations of Lands. —— He has obstructed the Administration of Justice, by refusing his Assent to Laws for establishing Judiciary powers. —— He has made Judges dependent on his Will alone, for the tenure of their offices, and the amount and payment of their salaries. —— He has erected a multitude of New Offices, and sent hither swarms of Officers to harass our people, and eat out their substance. —— He has kept among us, in times of peace, Standing Armies without the Consent of our legislatures. —— He has affected to render the Military independent of and superior to the Civil power. —— He has combined with others to subject us to a jurisdiction foreign to our constitution, and unacknowledged by our laws; giving his Assent to their Acts of pretended Legislation: — For Quartering large bodies of armed troops among us: — For protecting them, by a mock Trial, from punishment for any Murders which they should commit on the Inhabitants of these States: — For cutting off our Trade with all parts of the world: — For imposing Taxes on us without our Consent: — For depriving us in many cases, of the benefits of Trial by Jury: — For transporting us beyond Seas to be tried for pretended offences: — For abolishing the free System of English Laws in a neighbouring Province, establishing therein an Arbitrary government, and enlarging its Boundaries so as to render it at once an example and fit instrument for introducing the same absolute rule into these Colonies: — For taking away our Charters, abolishing our most valuable Laws, and altering fundamentally the Forms of our Governments: — For suspending our own Legislatures, and declaring themselves invested with power to legislate for us in all cases whatsoever. — He had abdicated Government here, by declaring us out of his Protection and waging War against us: — He has plundered our seas, ravaged our Coasts, burnt our towns, and destroyed the lives of our people. — He is at this time transporting large Armies of foreign Mercenaries to compleat the works of death, desolation and tyranny, already begun with circumstances of Cruelty & Perfidy scarcely paralleled in the most barbarous ages, and totally unworthy the Head of a civilized nation. — He has constrained our fellow Citizens taken Captive on the high Seas to bear Arms against their Country, to become the executioners of their friends and Brethren, or to fall themselves by their Hands. — He has excited domestic insurrections amongst us, and has endeavoured to bring on the inhabitants of our frontiers, the merciless Indian Savages, whose known rule of warfare, is an undistinguished destruction of all ages, sexes and conditions. In every stage of these Oppressions We have Petitioned for Redress in the most humble terms: Our repeated Petitions have been answered only by repeated injury. A Prince, whose character is thus marked by every act which may define a Tyrant, is unfit to be the ruler of a free people. Nor have We been wanting in attentions to our British brethren. We have warned them from time to time of attempts by their legislature to extend an unwarrantable jurisdiction over us. We have reminded them of the circumstances of our emigration and settlement here. We have appealed to their native justice and magnanimity, and we have conjured them by the ties of our common kindred to disavow these usurpations, which would inevitably interrupt our connections and correspondence. They too have been deaf to the voice of justice and of consanguinity. We must, therefore, acquiesce in the necessity, which denounces our Separation, and hold them, as we hold the rest of mankind, Enemies in War, in Peace Friends.

We, THEREFORE, the Representatives of the UNITED STATES OF AMERICA, in General Congress Assembled, appealing to the Supreme Judge of the world for the rectitude of our intentions, do, in the Name and by Authority of the good People of these Colonies, solemnly publish and declare, That these United Colonies are, and of Right ought to be FREE AND INDEPENDENT STATES; that they are Absolved from all Allegiance to the British Crown, and that all political connection between them and the State of Great Britain, is and ought to be totally dissolved; and that as Free and Independent States, they have full Power to levy War, conclude Peace, contract Alliances, establish Commerce, and to do all other Acts and Things which Independent States may of right do. —— And for the support of this Declaration, with a firm reliance on the protection of divine Providence, we mutually pledge to each other our Lives, our Fortunes and our sacred Honor.

ENGAGING THE TEXT

1. Paraphrase the opening of the Declaration, up to the phrase "former Systems of Government." Are the truths named here "self-evident"?

2. Outline the Declaration in three to five lines. What structure of argument is revealed here?

3. What attitudes toward women and Native Americans does the Declaration reveal?

4. How would you characterize the voice of this document? Read some of it aloud. What is its tone, and how, specifically, is that tone created?

5. Summarize the charges made against the king. Which address matters of individual freedoms? Economic freedoms? Colonial autonomy?

EXPLORING CONNECTIONS

6. Write a dialogue on human rights between the Thomas Jefferson who authored the Declaration and the Jefferson who penned the section on race in *Notes on the State of Virginia* (p. 532). To what extent should we let Jefferson's views on race affect our appreciation of him as a champion of freedom and civil rights?

7. Reread two or more of the following selections: Malcolm X's "Learning to Read" (p. 219), Ronald Takaki's "A Different Mirror" (p. 538), Wendy

Rose's "Three Thousand Dollar Death Song" (p. 557), Janice Mirikitani's "We, the Dangerous: (p. 560), Gregory Mantsios's "Rewards and Opportunities" (p. 331), Fred L. Pincus's "From Individual to Structural Discrimination" (p. 586), and Donald Barlett and James Steele's "Have-Mores and Have-Lesses" (p. 356). Drawing on these readings, write a response to the vision of freedom offered by Jefferson.

EXTENDING THE CRITICAL CONTEXT

8. Working in small groups, go to the library and compare the Declaration with the Constitution in terms of their tone, their approach to individual rights, and the notion of freedom they convey.

New Peoples and New Societies
COLIN G. CALLOWAY

Americans tend to think of freedom as an American invention. Maybe it's because generations of schoolbooks have taught that the Puritans who arrived on the Mayflower *came in search of religious freedom after having been persecuted for their beliefs in Europe. But, as Colin G. Calloway reminds us in this selection, freedom predated the Pilgrims in America: long before the first Europeans arrived in the so-called New World, Native American peoples like the Iroquois and Mohawk had developed societies dedicated to the principle of individual liberty. It was the living models of freedom they found among Native Americans that encouraged revolutionaries like Benjamin Franklin and Thomas Jefferson to believe that people are, in fact, born with certain "unalienable Rights." Calloway is the Chair of Native American Studies at Dartmouth University and the author of many scholarly articles and books on Native American history, including the source of this selection,* New Worlds for All: Indians, Europeans, and the Remaking of Early America *(1997).*

Not only did Indians and Europeans create new societies in the new world that emerged after contact, but existing societies experienced significant changes and responded to new influences. Those were greatest for Indian societies, of course, but Indian ways left subtle imprints in the societies of the Europeans who sought to displace them.

In 1987, two centuries after the adoption of the Constitution of the United States, the U.S. Senate passed a resolution that acknowledged "the historical debt which this Republic of the United States of America owes to the Iroquois Confederacy and other Indian Nations for their demonstration of enlightened, democratic principles of government and their example of a free association of independent Indian nations." Shortly after, several Iroquoian scholars signed an open letter to the *New York Times,* criticizing the Senate resolution for its misuse of history, but the notion that the Iroquois provided the model for the U.S. Constitution has remained popular — it is an article of faith in some circles. Those who believe that the founders used the Iroquois system point to evidence such as the speech of the Onondaga orator Canasatego to the commissioners of Virginia, Maryland, and Pennsylvania at the Treaty of Lancaster in 1744. On the final day of the conference (ironically, July 4), Canasatego urged the colonists to seek strength in unity: "Our wise Forefathers established Union and Amity between the *Five Nations;* this has made us formidable; this has given us great Weight and Authority with our neighboring Nations," he said. "We are a powerful Confederacy; and, by your observing the same Methods our wise Forefathers have taken, you will acquire fresh Strength and Power; therefore whatever befalls you, never fall out one with another." The message was not lost on Benjamin Franklin, who later wrote that "it would be a very strange Thing, if six Nations of ignorant Savages should be capable of forming a Scheme for such a Union, and be able to execute it in such a Manner, as that it has subsisted [for] Ages, and appears indissoluble; and yet a like Union should be impracticable for ten or a Dozen Colonies, to whom it is more necessary, and must be more advantageous." Some writers insist that the Iroquois system and Indian ideas of liberty provided Franklin and other leaders the rationale for the American Revolution.

As had the Iroquois, the founding fathers created a system of government where power was distributed not concentrated, where new tribes or states could join, where authority was derived from the people, where individual freedoms, group autonomy, and freedom of speech were protected, but where member groups united on matters of common concern. Like the Iroquois League of Peace, the United States became a haven for refugee people. Evidence that the founders copied the Iroquois model in drawing up the Constitution, however, is largely circumstantial and inferential. The fact that they knew about the league and the remarkable Iroquois system does not mean that they sought to emulate it. There was much in the Iroquois matrilineal, clan-based system that the founders chose not to use: they rejected the idea of government by consensus, excluded women from participation, separated church and state, and protected individual rather than communal property rights. If the founders looked to the Indians to help build the new nation, it was the Indians' lands, not their systems of government, they were interested in.

The debate over the Iroquois and the Constitution is part of a larger question concerning Indian influences on American liberty. Even as

Europeans sought to displace and destroy Indian societies, some found much to admire. Indian ways seemed to infiltrate their own societies, and, at the very least, they were exposed to Indian ideas and social values. To say that American democracy emerged as a synthesis of European and Indian political traditions may be an overstatement, but to deny it may be placing too much weight on the written record: ideas and customs tend to seep subtly from one group to another rather than being formally acknowledged. Such indirect influences are difficult to establish with certainty, but they would be in keeping with the flow of Indian ways into Euro-American societies.

Many have attributed to American Indians an impact on European social thought. From Roger Williams and the baron de Lahontan in the seventeenth century, to Thomas Jefferson and Benjamin Franklin in the eighteenth, and on to the present, numerous writers have found much to admire in Indian societies. French missionary Marc Lescarbot compared the social ills of European society with the merits he found in Micmac communities: "If only through considerations of humanity, and because these people of whom we shall treat are men like ourselves, we have reason to be roused with the desire of understanding their modes of life." Montaigne, Rousseau, and others used Indian society — that is, their understanding of it — as a yardstick by which to judge European civilization. Canadian historian Alfred Bailey suggested that by alerting Frenchmen to the inequities in their own society, contact with the Indians was "a remote precursor of the French Revolution." Historian William Brandon argues that Indian notions of liberty filtered into European social thought via reports from the New World. Seneca John Mohawk and Onondaga Oren Lyons claim democracy as an "export item, perhaps Native America's greatest contribution to the world," which toppled European monarchies and resulted in the formation of the United States. Wendat (Huron) scholar Georges Sioui sees a degenerate Europe finding the sources of its own regeneration in Native America. "A dehumanized European civilization," he writes, "began to rediscover the reality of human nature and, with the help of its Amerindian teachers, lead the rest of the world along the path of world socialization."

Certainly, some American colonists and European philosophers were impressed by the freedom, egalitarianism, and communal ethics they saw in Indian society. Indians lived in functioning democracies, enjoyed "natural" rights and freedom, and were not burdened by "unnatural" monarchy and government oppression. Roger Williams noted that Indian chiefs in New England led by "gentle persuasion" and would do nothing "unto which the people are averse." Daniel Gookin agreed that Indian sachems won and retained support by "acting obligingly and lovingly unto their people, lest they should desert them." William Penn said that Indian chiefs "move by the Breath of their People." Trader James Adair, who lived among the Indians of the Southeast before the Revolution, said the Indians' "whole constitution breathes nothing but liberty." Trader John Long said the Iroquois

5

"laugh when you talk to them of Kings; for they cannot reconcile the idea of submission with the dignity of man." Cadwallader Colden said that each Iroquois nation was "an Absolute Republick by itself, governed in all Publick affairs of War and Peace by the Sachems or Old Men, whose Authority and Power is gained by and consists wholly in the opinions of the rest of the Nation in their Wisdom and Integrity. They never execute their Resolutions by Compulsion or Force Upon any of their People." A French officer, writing in the closing years of the French regime, commented that Frenchmen who lived among Indians found greater freedom than they had ever been accustomed to: "'Liberty,' they say, 'is no where more perfectly enjoyed, than where no subordination is known, but what is recommended by natural reason, the veneration of old age, or the respect of personal merit.'" A Mohawk said more simply: "We have no forcing rules or laws amongst us."

Indian communities were living proof that human beings could construct and maintain societies based on liberty, examples of political systems where those who governed derived their authority from the people. Some colonists went to live in these societies, and some writers advocated injecting healthy doses of Indian-style freedom and equality into their own ailing societies. John Lawson maintained that Indians were "the freest People in the World," and he urged settlers to emulate their ways.

Some Europeans saw in Indian societies practices that put "civilization" to shame. Father Claude Chauchetière was impressed by the sharing, hospitality, and patience in dealing with children he witnessed in Indian communities. "In fine," he said, "all our fathers and the French who have lived with the savages consider that life flows on more gently among them than with us." Crèvecoeur maintained that Indians had "in their social bond something singularly captivating, and far superior to anything to be boasted of among us." In marked contrast to Europe, where wealth and poverty existed side by side, Recollect missionary Gabriel Sagard reported that the Hurons "make hospitality reciprocal and are so helpful to one another that they provide for the needs of all, so that there are no poor beggars in any of their towns and villages." William Wood, in *New England's Prospect*, reported that the Indians were "reddy to communicate the best of their wealth to the mutual good of one another." Roger Williams pointed out that, in contrast to European society, Indians had "no beggars amongst them, nor fatherlesse children unprovided for." Revolutionary writer Thomas Paine said that Indian societies lacked "any of those species of human misery which poverty and want present to our eyes in all the towns and streets of Europe."

Sharing in Indian societies was not an ideal; it was an obligation. People acquired honor and established reciprocal relations by giving things away, not by accumulating them. Observing how an item given to an Indian "may pas twenty hands before it sticks," William Penn said, "Wealth circulateth like the blood, all parts partake." Refusal to share was regarded as antisocial, even hostile behavior: in 1712, Cree Indians around Hudson Bay killed seven Frenchmen who would not share food and ammunition with a band of Indians who were on the verge of starvation. Indians thought Europeans were selfish and uncaring; many Europeans felt that Indians who gave things away and failed to "get ahead" were "shiftless" and "improvident."

Many Indian societies also accorded women and children a measure of   10
respect unusual in Europe. In societies where women produced food as well as prepared it, their economic role seems to have translated into higher status than that of their European or colonial counterparts. Iroquoian women in particular exerted an influence undreamed of by Europeans. "All real authority is vested in them," wrote Joseph François Lafitau in the seventeenth century. "The land, the fields, and their harvest all belong to them. They are the souls of the Councils and the arbiters of peace and of war. . . . The children are their domain, and it is through their blood that the order of succession is transmitted." While women gave and sustained life, raising crops and rearing children in the villages, men took life, fighting and hunting away from the villages.

Gender relations often changed after contact with Europeans. Women's participation in public affairs sometimes declined, since Europeans insisted on dealing with men, and the new demands generated by the fur trade and the increased absences of men on hunting and war expeditions placed additional economic burdens on women. Europeans interpreted egalitarian gender relations as a lack of social and family hierarchy, and they sought to subordinate women in their program of restructuring Indian societies along European lines: men, not clan mothers, must dominate society.

European travelers frequently noted that Indian people were indulgent parents, eschewing corporal punishment in child-rearing. Cabeza de Vaca said, "These people love their offspring more than any in the world and treat them very mildly." What attracted de Vaca in the sixteenth century, however, alarmed Puritans in the seventeenth century. They feared the effects of the New World and its Indian inhabitants, and they worried that in building a new "civilization" in America, they might become like the Indians they sought to displace. The Puritan minister Cotton Mather lamented that "tho' the first English planters of this country had usually a government and a discipline in their families that had a sufficient severity in it, yet, as if the climate had taught us to Indianize, the relaxation of it is now such that it seems wholly laid aside, and a foolish indulgence to children is become an epidemical miscarriage of the country, and like to be attended with many evil consequences." Increase Mather also lamented the decline of family government and the indulgence of parents and masters toward children and servants: "Christians in this Land, have become too like unto the Indians," he said. Subordination of children, as of women, was part of the invaders' agenda for Indian society. Nevertheless, travelers noted, backcountry settlers often seemed to follow Indian examples in their indulgent treatment of children.

Colonists who borrowed from Indian societies and shook off the restraints of eastern elites created what scholars of French-Canadian history call "new social types." Denys Delâge notes that one can only imagine the impact of egalitarian and freedom-loving Indian societies on coureurs de bois, who generally were the sons of indentured servants and other members of the underclasses. Some Europeans found liberty and equality more threatening than attractive and endeavored to keep them out of the societies they were building. Delâge points to the colonists' dilemma: "It was the very existence of these relatively egalitarian societies, so different in their structure and social relationships from those of Europe, that exercised the greatest influence on the newcomers and, at the same time, repelled them most."

The egalitarian nature of Indian societies was antagonistic to the class societies of Europe. Individual freedom threatened to undermine patterns of hierarchy, discipline, and self-restraint. To contemporaries, the freedom of Indian society was largely inherent in what they saw as a wilderness environment, where land was plentiful and colonial authority was weak. In the seventeenth century, William Hubbard worried that the settlers scattered along New England's frontier "were contented to live without, yea, desirous to shake off all *yoake of Government,* both *sacred* and *Civil,* and so *Transforming* themselves as much as well they could into the manners of the Indians they lived amongst." In the 1750s, Louis Antoine de Bougainville complained that Montcalm's soldiers became "corrupted . . . by the example of the Indians and Canadians, breathing an air permeated with independence."

The patterns of communal sharing, leadership dependent upon the   15
good will of one's followers, individual liberty, and egalitarian relations that typified many Indian societies contrasted starkly with the vision of society articulated by John Winthrop in a sermon to fellow Puritans aboard the *Arbella:* "God Almighty . . . hath so disposed of the Condition of mankind, as in all times some must be rich[,] some poor, some high and eminent in power and dignity; others mean and in subjection." The collision and occasional fusion of different concepts of society is part of the American historical experience, but how far European colonists, or American founding fathers, went in adopting Indian ways as they modified Winthrop's vision is difficult to say. Awareness and even admiration of Indian political systems and social ethics did not mean that Europeans would adopt them as permanent features of the new societies they were creating. Immigrants tended to cling to many of their own ways and to adopt new ways of life when and for as long as it suited them to do so. Gary Nash reviews the process by which admired values came to be suppressed:

> Idealistic Europeans saw the "wilderness" of North America as a place where tired, corrupt, materialistic, self-seeking Europeans might begin a new life centered around the frayed but vital values of

reciprocity, spirituality and community. . . . Yet as time passed and Europeans became more numerous, it became evident that the people in North America who best upheld these values were the people who were being driven from the land. . . . Indians seemed to embody these Christian virtues almost without effort while colonizing Europeans, attempting to build a society with similar characteristics, were being pulled in the opposite direction by the natural abundance around them — toward individualism, disputatiousness, aggrandizement of wealth, and the exploitation of other humans.

In the end, European imperial ambitions, settlement patterns, laws, and institutions prevailed at the expense of idealistic notions that a truly new world could be created that incorporated the best of Indian and European societies. Ultimately, the invaders of North America succeeded in their goal of building new societies that were more like their old ones in Europe than the Native societies they encountered in America.

Nevertheless, those societies developed where Native American roots ran deep. How much of what was new in them derived from the human environment and how much from the physical is difficult to ascertain, but the early settlers themselves often regarded Indians and "wilderness" as inseparable. European colonists, like the Indians whose world they invaded, were compelled to combine old and new ways, to experiment and innovate as well as adhere to traditions for guidance. Although many social experiments did not endure, by the end of the colonial era, Europeans, Indians, and Africans had all created new societies. Each one, in James Merrell's words, was "similar to, yet very different from, its parent culture." The New England town meeting is a far cry from Winthrop's vision of an ordered and orderly society and displays more attributes of Algonkian government by consensus than of Puritan government by the divinely ordained.

ENGAGING THE TEXT

1. In what ways did American Indians influence early American institutions and beliefs, according to Calloway? Which aspects of tribal society did colonists emulate? Which did they reject, and why?

2. Summarize in a page or less the social, political, and cultural differences that distinguished American Indians from the Europeans who first colonized North America. What was the result of such political and cultural differences?

3. How does Calloway characterize the attitudes of early colonists toward their Native American neighbors? Why did they feel this way?

4. Toward the conclusion of this selection Calloway says that "In the end, European imperial ambitions, settlement patterns, laws, and institutions prevailed at the expense of idealistic notions that a truly new world could be created that incorporated the best of Indian and European societies" (para. 15). What evidence, if any, do you see in contemporary American

culture that the values and ideals of early American Indian society have, in fact, survived?

EXPLORING CONNECTIONS

5. Review the Declaration of Independence (p. 684) and identify the sections that seem inspired by the kinds of values and beliefs that Calloway ascribes to Native American societies at the time of colonization. Which sections seem to reflect values, beliefs, or attitudes that might be more closely identified with the Old World of Europe? How do you think the Native American leaders of the Five Nations would have responded to the Declaration?

6. To what extent are Paula Gunn Allen's description of gender roles in contemporary American Indian cultures (p. 520) and/or Roger Jack's depiction of modern Native American family values (p. 109) consistent with Calloway's depiction of earlier American Indian cultures?

EXTENDING THE CRITICAL CONTEXT

7. Working in small groups, discuss recent depictions of Native American culture in the mass media. How common in these depictions are the values and beliefs that Calloway describes? What values and beliefs currently dominate media depictions of Native American society?

8. Divide into small research groups, with each group focusing on a specific Native American tribe, and use your library resources to learn as much as you can about each tribe's social structure and political organization before contact with Europeans. What were the tribe's attitudes toward power and authority? How were decisions made and enforced? What roles were played by men, women, children, and the elderly? Summarize your findings in a collective research paper and compare your efforts in class.

Easy in the Harness: The Tyranny of Freedom
GERRY SPENCE

As one of America's most outspoken and successful trial lawyers, Gerry Spence has more than a passing acquaintance with issues of freedom. In 1979 Spence came to national attention when he took on and defeated one of the largest nuclear power companies in the United States; representing Karen Silkwood, a power-plant employee exposed to lethal doses of radiation, Spence won fame as a champion of individual rights and as a relentless critic of corporate excess. In this selection, Spence wonders if Americans understand the meaning of freedom and claims that genuine freedom is, in fact, too painful for most of us to bear. The author of several books on justice and injustice in American society, Spence (b. 1929) is the host of The Gerry Spence Show *on CNBC and continues to practice law in Jackson Hole, Wyoming. His most recent publication is the autobiographical* The Making of a Country Lawyer *(1996). "Easy in the Harness" originally appeared in* From Freedom to Slavery: The Rebirth of Tyranny in America *(1994).*

"What is freedom?" an enlightened teacher asked her class.

"It's when you can leave home and go wherever you want, and do whatever you want, and your parents can't tell you what to do," a child replied.

"But what if you get hungry? Are you now free to starve?"

"I would go home," the child says.

We are not free. Nor have we ever been. Perfect freedom demands a   5
perfect vision of reality, one too painful for the healthy to endure. It requires that we be alive, alert, and exquisitely aware of our raw being. Faced with the pain of freedom, man begs for his shackles. Afraid of death, he seeks the stultifying boundaries of religion. Afraid of loneliness, he imprisons himself in relationships. Afraid of want, he accepts the bondage of employment. Afraid of rejection, he conforms to the commands of society. If our knowledge of freedom were perfect we would not choose it. Pure freedom is pure terror.

Freedom is like a blank, white canvas when no commitments, no relationships, no plans, no values, no moral restraints have been painted on the free soul. A state of perfect freedom is a state of nothingness. When we care for another, when we make room for another's wants and needs, we have lost an equal portion of our freedom, but in the bargain we are freed of loneliness. When we take on marriage and a family, we are bound by our vows, the law, and our moral commitments to spouse and child, but our bargain frees us of detachment and meaninglessness. When we live in the country we can drive our trucks across the prairies, but when we join a community we cannot drive our cars across our neighbors' lawns. We can abide by no moral values without being limited by them. We can belong to no clubs without agreeing to their rules, or to a neighborhood without recognizing the rights of our neighbors. When we become residents of a village, a state, or a nation, we must obey its laws. In short, when we join into any relationship our dues are always paid in freedom.

Robert Frost[1] understood freedom and expressed its essence in a typical Frostian metaphor: "Freedom is when you are easy in the harness." Easy in the harness. I used to sit behind a team of good horses, Star and Spiffy,

[1]*Robert Frost:* American poet (1874–1963).

and together we mowed the meadow hay. Their flanks foamed with sweat and after struggling for weeks at their tugs, sores developed on their necks from their rubbing collars. I remember a deep, sad look in the eyes of the horses. I liked to touch to horses, to feel their softer-than-velvet noses against my cheek. I liked their smell. I loved old Star and Spiffy.

I suppose that team of horses was mostly "easy in the harness." Willingly they would trudge up and down the field all day, their heads down, their tugs tight, their flanks digging like the pistons of engines, and at the end of the day when I lifted the wet harnesses from their backs they would run for the corral and lie down in the deep dust and roll, and roll again. Then they would get up and shake the dust from their backs and wait for me to open the corral gate to the pasture.

One spring when I returned to the ranch I found Star and Spiffy gone. Nobody wanted to talk about it. "They're just gone," the old rancher said.

"But where?" I asked.   10

"Gone," was all he would say, and the way he said it with such finality made it clear that was to be the end of it. Later I learned that each fall a horse buyer visited the neighboring ranches to buy the ranchers' worn-out nags. They brought a few cents a pound for dog meat. Some claimed the meat was shipped to Europe where horse meat was allegedly a delicacy, especially with the French, but I never confirmed it.

As I look back on it the horses were as easy in their harnesses as we. And their deaths were perhaps better than our own. I could see in my mind's eye the old team being shipped off, the eyes of the old horses as sad as ever. But it was only another ride to them. They were not being trucked to their execution. Their bellies were not gripped with fear. There was no sadness, no regrets. And as the truck rumbled down the highway toward the slaughterhouse, the fall air must have blown through their manes and made their old tired eyes water, and they must have felt joy.

Every day we spend our freedom like careless children with too many pennies. In exchange for acceptance by our friends we give up the right to say what we think. Being socially proper is more important than possessing a fresh, uncompromised soul. Being acceptable to our neighbors is often more important than being acceptable to ourselves. For nearly two hundred years slavery thrived in America over the silent protestations of decent citizens enslaved themselves by the tyranny of convention. The price of freedom is often rejection, even banishment.

I knew an old rancher who lived on the Wind River in Wyoming. People didn't have much good to say about old Jack. His chief crime was that he told the truth as he saw it and laughed at things we were all afraid to laugh at. Every once in a while I'd stop by to see him. He was usually in his garden. That day he was hoeing his corn, a special hybrid variety he had developed for our short growing season, and he was also locally famous for his high-altitude peas and potatoes.

"Well, what has God wrought today?" I asked, knowing full well my   15
question would engender a strong response.

"You talkin' 'bout *me*," he replied. "I'm my own god."

"Jack, aren't you afraid of going to hell for saying such irreligious
things?"

"There ain't no hell 'cept on earth." He went on hoeing. His shirt was
wet with good fresh summer sweat.

"Suppose God heard you say that," I said prodding him a little. "What if
he condemned you to burn in hell for an eternity for such heresy?" I'd been
introduced to such horrors as a child in Sunday school.

"No just god would condemn ya fer usin' the power of reason he give   20
ya," he said, "and the idea of hell is plumb unreasonable." He stopped,
leaned on his hoe handle, and squinted at me. "Besides, who would want ta
worship a god that would send yer ass to hell forever fer such a triflin' trans-
gression as not believin' somethin' that is unreasonable? That would be no
just god, and if he ain't just I don't want nothin' ta do with him."

The old boy was already well past eighty and he knew that by all odds
his days were numbered. "How you been feeling, Jack?" I asked, trying to
change the subject.

"Feel just perty perfect," he said. Then he went back to hoeing. "But I
may not make it another winter."

The following spring I stopped by. He was on his hands and knees
planting his garden.

"Well, Jack, I see you make it through another winter."

"Yep," he said. "See ya done the same."   25

"God willing," I said.

"God didn't have nothin' to do with it," he said.

"How come you're so tough on God?" I asked.

"On accounta those kinda ideas hurt a lotta innocent folks," he said. He
never looked up from his planting while he talked. He dropped the brown
bean seeds about an inch apart in the shallow furrow. "Christ taught that
love is the supreme law. But they got it all mixed up. I got a lotta neighbors
that love God and hate each other. I say if yer gonna love, ya oughta love
something ya can see, say, yer neighbor fer instance."

He had radical ideas for his time, for instance his views on birth con-   30
trol, about which he spoke often and freely. "This here earth is overrun with
people. The multitudes is starving everywhere. Now when I can't feed no
more cows on this little ranch I sure don't raise no more calves. There ain't
no starvin' calves here," he said. He covered the seed with his old crooked
fingers and tamped the fresh, moist soil over them with the heels of his
hands. "So how come my cows has got better rights than people? What kind
of a god would want ya to raise up kids ta starve?"

When he got to the end of the row he stood up, stretched his old stiff
back, and looked at me for the first time. "Why them churchgoin' neighbors
a mine claim to love the fetus in the womb. But as soon as the kid is born,

they say it's all right if it's left ta starve. I never could figure out why little kids who never done nothin' ta nobody should be punished by bein' sentenced ta starve ta death fer no worse crime than being born in the first place." When he looked at me I never saw a kinder set of eyes. I never knew a more honest man. I never knew a man who was more free than old Jack. But I think Jack was lonely sometimes. And, to the wonder and secret disappointment of some of his neighbors who were put off by his harsh and unedited comments on religion, and who thought for sure he'd never make it another winter, he lived through a dozen more after that.

Sometimes when I think of old Jack I realize how unfree I am, how afraid, how timid and intimidated and how the bargains I make sometimes leave me feeling cheated, how I sometimes trade honest convictions for silence to gain acceptance by those around me. Yet, in the end, I doubt that my neighbors love me any more than Jack's loved him. They respected him, that much I know, and maybe Jack valued their respect more than their love. Yet respect and love are sometimes hard to separate.

Jack's neighbors all came to his funeral, and some who had been his most severe critics had tears in their eyes. I doubt that Jack would have been surprised. I think he knew.

They buried old Jack out behind his garden where he wanted, close to the creek. As they lowered the pine box into the ground I could hear his creaky old voice arguing away. "Why, Spence," he said, "we kick our dogs if they shit in the house, but we shit all over this beautiful planet like a herd a hogs sufferin' from terminal diarrhea. Baby owls are smarter'n that. Ya never seen a baby owl that ever fouled its nest. These human bein's ain't too smart a species."

And I thought, Well, Jack, your old bones won't pollute this little plot   35
behind your garden, that's for sure. Next spring you'll turn into fresh buds on the cottonwood trees, and maybe you won't think that's too bad a place to be. Maybe that's eternity after all. Earth to earth.

"Beats hell outta hell," I could hear hold Jack reply. And then I turned away before the neighbors could catch up with me to tell me all about how old Jack was. One thing I knew: old Jack was free. Always had been.

The notion of "being American" is heavily laden with ideas of freedom. Being American and being free are often thought synonymous. As Americans we envision Washington's battered patriots marching to the beat of the boy drummer. We see Washington crossing the Delaware. We think of the Constitution and the Bill of Rights, and remember the Civil War, Lincoln and the Gettysburg Address, the freeing of the slaves, the great world wars "to keep America free." We see the billowing smoke of the ships sinking at Pearl Harbor and our American heroes raising the flag at Iwo Jima. And we remember the marches of Martin Luther King, Jr. We believe we are free in the same way we believe in God. Freedom is an article of faith, not a fact, not a condition. True, the freedom we enjoy in America, when set against the freedom of peoples in other lands, is emblazoned like a single candle lighting the gloom.

Law and order and rules, although antithetical to freedom, provide us with safeguards by which we are free to live with reasonable safety among those who are stronger. But the strong impose themselves upon us nevertheless. Although our younger, stronger neighbor is not free to force us out of our homes, the bank can do so if we fail to pay it its tribute of green flesh. Although we argue we are free to labor where we please for whomever we please, unless we show up in the morning, unless like old Star and Spiffy, we take our places in our stanchions and consent to the harness, we will be free to join the depressed and desperate masses of the unemployed who become harnessed to yet another master — fear.

If we are American, we believe in an American religion called "free enterprise," the principal tenet of which holds that it is not only moral but divine to reserve for the corporate oligarchy substantially all the wealth — leaving to the people the blessed right to obtain whatever, if any, dribbles down. The religion called "free enterprise" holds that in exchange for corporate America's right to squash and squeeze from all below it, the next in power possess the right to squash and squeeze those below them, and so on down the line until there is nothing left but the empty dredges of humanity. Some of these we discard on the streets, where they are free to die of hunger, disease, and shame. Those who rebel are at last housed — in prisons. . . .

Today we are more concerned with extracting freedom from our enemies than in preserving our own. We wish into prison those who terrorize us in the streets and who break into our cars and homes. We wish the executioner's hand against those who kill our innocent without just cause. At last we wish to eliminate all those from our society who threaten us and frighten us and injure and kill us, and we seem willing to diminish or release our constitutional rights, indeed, our freedom, to be safer. In truth, we long for a more successful domestication of the human species.   40

I recall a certain white heifer at the ranch, a full-blown renegade. When she was disturbed in the slightest she would run bellowing and bawling and wildly kicking at everything and anything, including the air. To get her from one pasture to another took half a dozen good men on good horses half a day. I would have sent her to the butcher but for the fact that I had paid a pretty price for her one crazy afternoon at a fancy purebred sale that had been held in the lobby of the Hilton Hotel in Denver.

When her calf came, the calf was just like her. The little renegade wasn't more than a few days old when it kicked the old dog and broke his jaw. But for the fact that the calf in all other respects was quite a beautiful specimen and would bring a good price, I would have rid the ranch of her as well. But the calf's calf was even worse. Finally I realized I was breeding back to the wildebeest, and that unless I abandoned that bloodline, I would end up with an utterly unmanageable herd of cattle that would eventually do me in.

Domestication has been the specialty of man from the beginning. He domesticated the wolf into the dog, the wildcat into the lap pussy, the wild horse into the plow horse, the wildebeest into the Hereford and the Holstein. He has also been busily domesticating himself. As in the domestication of animals he has been selecting the most compliant members of his species and eliminating the least.

Today, America imprisons more people than any nation in the world. Those who occupy our prisons have been our noncomplying social deviants, whom we have removed from the reproductive cycle. In recent times we have become more willing to impose the death penalty against our own for a broader assortment of crimes. Facing proof that the death penalty has no deterring effect on crime whatsoever, we nevertheless encourage its imposition out of our true purpose, not to punish, not to prevent future crimes, but to further domesticate the species by eliminating those who are less compliant than we.

Something about servitude stills. Something about domestication stifles.   45
The wolf, now the poodle, no longer howls. The wild boar lies on its side in the hog pen and grunts. The wildebeest stands in her stall placidly chewing her cud while she's milked dry. Domestication of man and beast muffles the cry of freedom and suffocates the spirit of liberty.

As we continue to domesticate the species, we tend toward the creation of a mass of mankind that is as easily herded as a flock of dead-eyed sheep. This amorphous glob faithfully mumbles the liturgy demanded by the corporate oligarchy, which holds that it is moral to take first and most from the weakest and the poorest. The dogma also holds that it is laudable to create classes of people based on wealth, not virtue, that is to say, it makes no difference how miserly, how greedy, how uncaring and spiteful the individual may be, if he has wealth he is of a different and better class than the virtuous without wealth. This religion to which the people are bound delivers to the corporate oligarchy the prerogative to ply its enormous powers against the people in order to become yet more powerful. And so it has been throughout human history as man struggles for his freedom, fights and dies for it, but having once achieved it, squanders it or casts it aside as too naked, too frightening, too painful to long possess.

I think of the wars that have been fought, allegedly for freedom. More often the blood and suffering and death were sacrificed so that massively powerful moneyed interests might remain free to use us up in our harnesses. I think of the endless list of the dead who were said to have given their lives so that we might be free. But after the wars nothing much changed. As usual we arose every morning, slipped into our harnesses, plodded to our work, and believed we were free. Then we died.

We all wear our harnesses, and if we are easy in them, if we feel free, is not the illusion of freedom as satisfactory as freedom itself? Should we fret over our servitudes, petty or grand, when the fictions of freedom we embrace often serve as satisfactorily? Is not a shackled slave who cannot see or feel his chains as free as if he had no chains at all? Should we free the happy slave and cast him into the chaos and horrors of pure freedom? Indeed, have we not at last achieved the prediction of *Brave New World*,[2] in which Aldous Huxley observed that the "really efficient totalitarian state would be one in which the all-powerful executive of political bosses and their army of managers control a population of slaves who do not have to be coerced, because they love their servitude"? Huxley argued that, "To make them love it [their bondage] is the task assigned, in present-day totalitarian states. . . ." Ought we not consider the possibility that the *1984*[3] of George Orwell has come and gone and that his once chilling oracle is the culture of our time, one in which we do, in fact, love our bondage, one where, in fact, we happily accept the clichés, the images, the fables, and the fictions of freedom in the place of freedom itself?

Freedom, "that sweet bondage," as Shelley[4] called it, is a marvelous thing in small doses. Not to be afraid of our government is blessed. Not to be lied to, not to be cheated, not to be exploited and poisoned and hurt for corporate greed, not to be used up like old rags; to be heard, to be respected, to grow and to discover our uniqueness — these are the freedoms we most cherish, freedoms we, by reason of our occupancy of this earth, are entitled to enjoy.

Yet most of our freedoms lie within. As the poem goes, "Stone walls do   50 not a prison make, nor iron bars a cage." Most freedoms cannot be given, except as we give them to ourselves.

I think of old Jack who cherished his freedom above all. He is, at last, free, totally free, since freedom, by common definition, is a condition in which the individual may do what he wants, and since the dead have no wants they are, are they not, totally free? Or perhaps as the Greeks argued, "Only Zeus is free."

And I also think of old Star and Spiffy, and of their freedom. Were I as successful, as free. Were I able to mow the meadows of my life and live by my own work as well. Were I able to remove the harness from within — such is freedom. And when finally the legs have given out, when the bones are old and brittle and crooked, and at last the shoulders too crippled to pull the load, I should hope that on the way to wherever it is that old horses and old men go I feel the wind through my hair, and that my eyes do not water from tears, but from having felt the joy of the trip, the trip to the last and only freedom.

---

[2]*Brave New World:* A 1932 novel by Aldous Huxley (1894–1963) portraying a future technocratic society in which life is completely controlled from cradle to grave.

[3]*1984:* A 1949 novel by George Orwell (1903–1950) portraying life in an imagined totalitarian state.

[4]*Shelley:* Percy Bysshe Shelley (1792–1822), English Romantic poet also known for his radical politics, atheism, and advocacy of sexual freedom.

ENGAGING THE TEXT

1. What, according to Spence, is perfect freedom, and why is it so hard to bear?

2. Explain the point of the story Spence tells about Star and Spiffy. How does he feel about these horses and their fate? What does their story say about freedom?

3. Spence says that each American wears a "harness" within. What forces and institutions, according to Spence, impose this invisible harness? What other social forces or institutions would you add to this list? To what extent do you agree with Spence that "we long for a more successful domestication of the human species" (para. 40)?

4. What's particularly free about "old Jack"? Do you think it's inevitable that a genuinely free human being must also be offensive? Why?

EXPLORING CONNECTIONS

5. Review two or more selections involving the following individuals or characters:

Richard Rodriguez (p. 202)	Sylvia in "The Lesson" (p. 348)
the narrator in *"Para Teresa"* (p. 216)	Sucheng Chan (p. 401)
	Nora Quealcy (p. 430)
Malcolm X (p. 219)	Judith Ortiz Cofer (p. 436)
Gary Soto (p. 42)	Paula Gunn Allen (p. 520)
Anndee Hochman (p. 47)	C. P. Ellis (p. 575)
Stephen Cruz (p. 326)	Leslie Marmon Silko (p. 594)

   Which of these individuals or characters seem the most free to you in Spence's sense of the word? Which seem most "domesticated"? Which challenge or complicate Spence's definition of what it means to be free?

6. Spence suggests that being free means being an outsider. How might Malcolm X (p. 219), Carmen Vázquez (p. 503) and/or Paula Gunn Allen (p. 520) respond to this idea?

7. How might Spence interpret "Minimum Security Freedom," the cartoon that follows this selection on page 704?

EXTENDING THE CRITICAL CONTEXT

8. Make an inventory of the "deals," "bargains," or "trades" that you make with your friends, family, employer, school, and society every day. How do these implied agreements limit your freedom? What do you get in return for honoring them? Which of these "deals" impinge most on your freedom?

9. Write a profile of a person you've known who, as Jack does for Spence, symbolizes freedom for you. In this portrait, try to clarify how this person expresses her freeness and how her freedom has affected others.

10. Spence suggests that America is more concerned with the "illusion" of freedom than with its reality. Working in groups, survey a number of music videos and print ads for contemporary images of freedom. How is freedom portrayed in American culture? What costs or consequences are typically associated with it?

Past Present

JIMMY SANTIAGO BACA

Lately, the myth of freedom has fallen on hard times in America. During the 1940s Franklin D. Roosevelt could electrify a nation huddled around living room radios by urging Americans to defend their freedoms against aggressors east and west. But as we approach the century's end, the idea of freedom seems increasingly abstract and old-fashioned; even politicians on the stump seem to avoid its use: today's candidates might talk about productivity or jobs or rights, but they rarely if ever evoke the idea that lies at the heart of American ideology. Of course, not all Americans need to be reminded of what freedom really means — certainly not those who have lived under a totalitarian regime or who have ever spent time behind bars. Jimmy Santiago Baca shares this gut-level understanding of what it means to be free. Born in New Mexico in 1952, Baca lived in an orphanage until he escaped to the streets at the age of eleven. By the time he was twenty he was doing time in prison for possession and sale of drugs. During the six years he spent in jail, Baca taught himself how to read and began to write and publish poetry in nationally recognized magazines. Since his release he has authored three award-winning collections of verse, several screenplays, and a novel. This selection originally appeared in Writing in the Dark: Reflections of a Poet of the Barrio *(1992).*

When I finished my last prison term twelve years ago, I never dreamed I would go back. But not long ago I found myself looking up at the famous San Quentin tower as I followed an escort guard through the main gates. I should have been overjoyed since this time I was a free man, the writer of a film which required a month of location-shooting there. But being there had a disquieting effect on me. I was confused. I knew that I would be able to leave every night after filming, but the enclosing walls, the barbed wire, and the guards in the towers shouldering their carbines made old feelings erupt in me. While my mind told me I was free, my spirit snarled as if I were a prisoner again, and I couldn't shake the feeling. Emotionally, I could not convince myself that I was not going to be subjected once more to horrible indignities, that I would not have to live through it all again. Each morning when the guards checked my shoulder bag and clanked shut the iron door behind me, the old convict in me rose up full of hatred and rage for the guards, the walls, the terrible indecency of the place. I was still the same man who had entered there freely, a man full of love for his family and his life. But another self from the past reawakened, an imprisoned self, seething with the desire for vengeance on all things not imprisoned.

As I followed the guard, passing with the crew and the actors from one compound to another, a hollow feeling of disbelief possessed me and I was struck dumb. The grounds were impeccably planted and groomed, serene as a cemetery. Streamlined circles of flowers and swatches of smooth lawn rolled to trimmed green margins of pruned shrubbery, perfectly laid out against the limestone and red brick cellblocks. But I knew that when you penetrated beyond this pretty landscaping, past the offices, also with their bouquets of flowers, past the cellblock's thick walls, there thrived America's worst nightmare. There the green, concealing surface lifted from the bubbling swamp, a monster about to rise from its dark depths. There writhed scaly demons, their claws and fangs primed for secret and unspeakable brutalities.

Even within those walls, the free man that I am eventually found himself able to forgive the sufferings of the past. But the convict in me was inflamed by everything I saw. It was all so familiar, so full of bitter memory: the milk-paned windows and linoleum tiles of the offices, the flyers thumbtacked to cork boards on the walls; the vast lower yard, and the great upper yard with its corrugated shed pocked with light-pierced, jagged bullet holes; the looming limestone cellblocks. The thought of the thousands of human beings whose souls were murdered here in the last hundred years made my blood run cold. The faintly humming body energy of six thousand imprisoned human beings bored a smoking hole in my brain. And through that hole, as if through a prison-door peephole, I saw all the free people going about their lives on the other side, while my place was again with the convicts. Anyone opening that door from the other side must die, or be taken hostage and forced to understand our hatred, made to experience the insane brutality that is the convict's daily lot, and that makes him, in turn, brutal and insane.

Since I was acting in the film, I had to dress out daily in banaroos, prison-issue blue denims. I was made up to look younger than I am, as I might have looked in 1973. After this outer transformation, I seemed more and more to become the person I had left behind twelve years ago, until finally that former self began to consume the poet and husband and father who had taken his place. I didn't know what was happening to me.

Dragged back into dangerous backwaters, I encountered my old ·5 demons. The crew seemed to sense this and gave me a wide berth. The familiar despair and rage of the prisoners was like a current sucking me down into the sadness of their wasted lives. The guards who paced the cellblocks now were no different from the guards who had leered and spit at me, beaten and insulted me. Even though I knew that now I wouldn't have to take their shit and that now I could speak up for the cons who had to hold their tongues, part of me was still caught in this time warp of displacement.

When we went to the recreational building, where I was to choose some of the convicts to act as extras, I was surprised by how young they were. I realized I was now the old man among them. In my prison days, the convicts had always seemed to be grizzled older guys, but now, for the most part, they were young kids in their twenties. After I selected the group of extras, I explained to them that the movie was about three kids from East L.A., one of whom goes to prison. As I spoke, my convict stance and manners came back to me, and the old slang rolled off my tongue as if I had never left. Memories of my own imprisonment assailed me, dissolving the barrier between us.

Although technically I was free, that first week I used my freedom in a strange way, venting hatred on anyone who looked at me, the cons included, because they, too, in the prison world, are joined in their own hierarchy of brutality.

One day a documentary crew came to where we were filming in the weight pit and asked to interview me. Prisoners of every race were present. I looked around me and was filled with contempt for every living soul there. After repeatedly refusing to speak, while microphones were shoved in my face, I suddenly decided to answer their questions.

How did I feel about returning to a prison to help film and act in this movie I had written? Was I proud and pleased? I sat on a bench-press seat curling about thirty pounds as I spoke.

I said I hated being back and that no movie could begin to show the in- 10 justices practiced here. I said that fame was nothing weighed against the suffering and brutality of prison life. I told them that these cons should tear the fucking walls down and allow no one to dehumanize them in this way. What were my feelings about being here?

I said that I hated everyone and just wanted to be left alone, and fuck them all. Just leave me alone!

I got up and walked away. There was a terrible tearing wound in my heart that I thought no one could see. But Gina, the associate producer, came up to me weeping, pleading for me to come back to myself, to be again the man she knew. She hugged me. One of the actors also approached and talked to me quietly. In spite of their attempts to confront me, I felt helplessly encaged by powers I couldn't vanquish or control. I was ensnared in a net of memories. When the few convicts who had been hanging with me started to put some distance between us, I felt as if no one could see me or hear me. I was disoriented, as if I had smashed full force into some invisible barrier.

After a couple of days, I came out of it, dazed and bewildered, shocked and weak as if after major surgery. People I previously couldn't bring myself to speak to, I spoke with now. I felt that sense of wonder one feels after a narrow escape from death.

As I continued to live my double life, I became a keen observer of both worlds. On the streets people could cry freely, but in prison tears led to challenges and deep, embittered stares. In prison no one shakes hands, that common gesture of friendship and trust. The talk never varies from the subjects of freedom and imprisonment, the stories and the laughs are about con jobs and scams. Outside everything is always changing, there are surprises, and you talk about that. But in prison the only news is old news. It is a dead land, filled with threat, where there is no appeal from the death sentence meted out for infractions of the convict code. Imagine being hunted through the jungles of Nam day after day for twenty years, and that will tell you a little of what prison is about.

The days went by. When we finished filming, late in the evenings, I 15 would go back to my trailer, change into my street clothes, and walk alone across the lower yard. The dead exercise pit, where many of the men spend a lot of time buffing themselves out, looked forlorn. It was very late as I crossed the lower yard to a waiting van, but the lights around the lower yard, huge, looming, twenty-eyed klieg lights, made it seem like daytime. Everything about prison life distorts reality, starting with the basic assumption that imprisonment can alter criminal behavior, when the truth is that it entrenches it more firmly. Confinement perverts and destroys every skill a man needs to live productively in society.

As I walked on, my mind full of these thoughts, buses from all over California pulled up in the eerie yellow light, disgorging new inmates who were lined up to get their prison clothes before being marched off to the cellblocks. A van was waiting to take me back to my corporate-paid condo, where there was fresh food waiting for me, where I could relax and phone my wife, turn on some soft music and write a little, read a little, in the silence; walk to the window and smell the cool night air and look across the bay to the Golden Gate Bridge and beyond to San Francisco, a city as angelic at night as any heavenly sanctum conjured up in medieval tapestries.

But all of these anticipated pleasures only intensified my anguish for those I was leaving behind, for those imprisoned who have — nothing. The cells in San Quentin's Carson block are so small that a man cannot bend or stretch without bruising himself against some obstacle. And two men share each cell. The cellblocks stink of mildew and drying feces. The noise is a dull, constant, numbing beating against the brain. Had I really inhabited such a cell for seven years? It didn't happen, it couldn't have happened. How did I survive? Who was that kid that lived through this horror? It was me. Since that time I had grown, changed; but I was still afraid to touch that reality with my mind, that unspeakable pain.

On those lonely night walks into freedom, the tremendous grief and iron rage of the convict revived in me. The empty yard, with its watchful glare, mercilessly mirrored the cold, soul-eaten barrenness of those confined within. In the world outside, convicts have mothers and wives and children, but here, in this world, they have nothing but the speed of their fists. They have only this one weapon of protest against the oppression of brain-dead keepers who represent a society whose judicial standards are so disparate for rich and poor.

When a man leaves prison, he cannot look into the mirror for fear of seeing what he has become. In the truest sense, he no longer knows himself. Treated like a child by the guards, forced to relinquish every vestige of dignity, searched at whim, cursed, beaten, stripped, deprived of all privacy, he has lived for years in fear; and this takes a terrible toll. The saddest and most unforgivable thing of all is that most first-time felons could be rehabilitated, if anyone cared or tried. But society opts for the quickest and least expensive alternative — stark confinement, with no attempt at help — that in the future will come to haunt it.

Each day that we filmed at San Quentin, where I was surrounded by   20
men whose sensibilities were being progressively eroded by prison society, the urge grew in me to foment a revolt: tear down the walls, herd the guards into the bay, burn down everything until nothing was left but a smoldering heap of blackened bricks and molten iron. And I was filled with a yearning to escape, to go home and live the new life I had fought so hard to make. The two worlds I inhabited then were so far apart I could find no bridge between them, no balance in myself. My disorientation was radical.

My days were spent in this prison, among men who had been stripped of everything, who had no future; and of an evening I might find myself in the affluence of Mill Valley, attending a ballet with my visiting wife and two sons, my wife's cousin's daughter dancing on stage in a mist of soft lights. . . .

As the weeks passed, I realized I had gone through changes that left me incapable of recognizing my own life. What was most shocking to me was not that I had survived prison, but that the prisons still stood, that the cruelty of that life was still going on; that in San Quentin six thousand men endured it daily, and that the system was growing stronger day by day. I realized that America is two countries: a country of the poor and deprived, and a country of those who had a chance to make something of their lives. Two societies, two ways of living, going on side by side every hour of every day. And in every aspect of life, from opportunities to manners and morals, the two societies stand in absolute opposition. Most Americans remain ignorant of this, of the fact that they live in a country that holds hostage behind bars another populous country of their fellow citizens.

I do not advocate the liberation of murderers, rapists, and sociopaths. But what of the vast majority of convicts, imprisoned for petty crimes that have more to do with wrong judgment than serious criminal intent or character defect? They are not yet confirmed in criminality, but the system makes them criminals. Society must protect itself against those who are truly dangerous. But they comprise only a small proportion of our prison population.

One day, late in the afternoon after we had shot a riot scene, the cell-block was in disarray: burning mattresses, men screaming, hundreds of cons shaking the bars with such force that the whole concrete and iron cellblock groaned and creaked with their rage. The cons were not acting. The scene had triggered an outrage waiting to be expressed. Finally, all that was left were a few wisps of black smoke, the tiers dripped water, and hundreds of pounds of soaked, charred newspapers were heaped on the concrete. Clothing and bed sheets, shredded to rags, dangled from the concertina wire surrounding the catwalks.

Quiet fell, the kind of dead quiet that comes after hundreds of men have been venting their wrath for hours, cursing and flailing and threatening. The smoldering trash on the cellblock floor testified to a fury that now withdrew, expressing itself only in their eyes. One of the convicts walked over to me through the silence. He told me that another convict wanted to speak with me, and led me to a cell that was in total darkness, where he spoke my name. A voice from the top bunk replied. I heard the man jump from the bunk to the floor and come to the bars. He was a tall, young Chicano with a crew cut, whose eyes were white orbs. He lived in the absolute darkness of the blind, in this small cell no bigger than a phone booth. In a soft voice he told me he had a story to tell, and asked my advice. He wanted his story to go out into the world, in print or on film.

Never has a man evoked from me such sympathy and tenderness as this blind warrior. It was plain to me that he had suffered terribly in this manmade hell, and that, somehow, his spirit had survived. I knew that his courage and his heart were mountains compared to the sand grains of my heart and courage. From behind the bars, this tall, lean brown kid with blind eyes told me how, after the guards had fired random warning shots into a group of convicts, he found himself blinded for life. I looked at him and saw the beautiful face of a young Spanish aristocrat who might be standing on a white balcony overlooking a garden of roses and lilies at dawn. I could also see in him the warrior. How softly he spoke and how he listened, so attentive to the currents of sound.

Blind Chicano brother of mine, these words are for you, and my work must henceforth be a frail attempt to translate your heart for the world, your courage and *carnalismo*.[1] While the world blindly grabs at and gorges on cheap titillations, you go on in your darkness, in your dark cell, year after year, groping in your imagination for illumination that will help you make sense of your life and your terrible fate. I couldn't understand you. I could only look at you humbly, young Chicano warrior. You spoke to me, spoke to me with the words and in the spirit in which I have written my poems. Looking at you, I reaffirmed my vow to never give up struggling for my people's right to live with dignity. From you I take the power to go on fighting until my last breath for our right to live in freedom, secure from the brutality in which you are imprisoned. From your blind eyes, I reimagined my vision and my quest to find words that can cut through steel. You asked me to tell your story. I promised I would.

---

[1]*carnalismo:* Chicano slang meaning, roughly, "brotherhood."

Today, as I was writing these words, a sociologist consulting on the movie led me to a viewing screen to see the eclipse: July 11th, 1991, 11:00 A.M. I looked through the shade glass and saw the sun and moon meet. I thought of you, my blind brother, and how our eyes met, yours and mine, dark moons and white suns that touched for a moment in our own eclipse, exchanging light and lives before we parted: I to tell my people's stories as truly as I can, you to live on in your vision-illuminated darkness. And I thought how the Mayans, at the time of eclipse, would rekindle with their torches at the altar flame, bringing the temples to new light; how their great cities and pyramids came out of darkness and they journeyed to the sun in their hearts, prepared to live for another age with new hope and love, forgiveness and courage. The darkness again gave way to the light, and I thought of you in your darkness, and of myself, living in what light I can make or find; and of our meeting each in our own eclipse and lighting the altar flame in each other's hearts, before passing on in our journeys to give light to our people's future.

Copies of my books that I had ordered from New York arrived in San Quentin on the last day of filming. I signed them and handed them out to the convicts who had helped us. As they accepted these books of my poems, I saw respect in their eyes. To me, I was still one of them; for them, I was someone who had made it into a free and successful life. This sojourn in prison had confused me, reawakening the old consuming dragons of hatred and fear. But I had faced them, finally, and perhaps I will be a better poet for it. Time will tell.

The next morning, I woke up early and packed my bags. Then I went   30 back to San Quentin for the last time. The production company vans and trailers, the mountains of gear, the crew and the actors, were gone. I made my way across the sad and vacant yard to make my last farewells. This final visit was a purposeful one: I would probably never set foot in a prison again. I was struck with pity for those who had to stay, and with simple compassion, too, for myself: for the pain I had endured in this month, and for that eighteen-year-old kid I once was, who had been confined behind walls like these and had survived, but who would never entirely be free of the demons he met behind bars. This last pilgrimage was for him, who is the better part of me and the foundation for the man I am today, still working in the dark to create for my people our own unique light.

Engaging the Text

1. How does returning to prison affect Baca? Why does it have this impact on him?

2. What does the experience of prison do to inmates, according to Baca?

3. What does Baca's encounter with the inmate he calls the "blind warrior" mean to him? Overall, what does he learn during his return to San Quentin?

EXPLORING CONNECTIONS

4. Write a brief dialogue between Baca and Gerry Spence (p. 695) on the price of freedom. How free is Baca as a successful poet and filmmaker, from Spence's point of view? How might Baca react to Spence's notion that most Americans live their lives "easy in the harness"?

5. Reread Malcolm X's description of his experience in jail in "Learning to Read" (p. 219), and compare his view of prison with that presented by Baca. How might you account for the differences you find between their perspectives on prison life?

EXTENDING THE CRITICAL CONTEXT

6. Write a journal entry about a particular moment in your own life when you felt unfree. If you're comfortable doing so, share these in small groups and discuss how your own experiences compare with that of Baca.

7. Do some informal research to find out about the men, women, and young people who are currently doing time in American prisons or other correctional institutions. What can you discover about the average age, ethnicity, economic status, and crimes committed by inmates? How large is the current prison population? How large is it likely to become over the next ten to twenty years? How effective is the prison system in "reforming" inmates? To what extent does your research support or challenge Baca's claim that America is becoming "a country that holds hostage behind bars another populous country of their fellow citizens" (para. 22)?

8. Review one or more recent movies set in prison (some good possibilities are *The Shawshank Redemption, Dead Man Walking,* or *Murder in the First*). To what extent does the portrait of prison life offered in the movie you view coincide with Baca's? Which seems more credible?

Freedom Time

JUNE JORDAN

Does freedom come in colors? In the following essay, poet and activist June Jordan suggests that "white" conceptions of freedom may be very different from her own. She also warns that freedoms hard-won during the civil rights movement may be threatened in an America that's growing more divisive and bad-tempered by the day. A professor of African American studies at the University of California, Berkeley, Jordan (b. 1936) has authored several collections of poetry and political essays, including Living Room *(1985),* Naming Our Destiny *(1989),* Civil Wars *(1981),* On Call

(1985), Technical Difficulties *(1992), and* Haruko Love Poems: New and Selected Love Poems *(1994). This essay was first published in* The Progressive.

A million years ago, Janis Joplin was singing, "Freedom's just another word for nothing left to lose." I found that puzzling, back then. Or, "white."

To my mind, freedom was an obvious good. It meant looking at an apartment and, if you liked it, being able to put down a deposit and sign a lease. It meant looking for a job and, if you found something for which you qualified — on the basis of education and/or experience — being able to take that position. Freedom had to do with getting into college if your grades were good enough. Freedom meant you could register to vote and live to talk about it.

A lot of other Americans felt the same way, thirty years ago. And black and white, we sang militant songs and we tested public transportation and restaurants and universities and corporate hiring policies and nice, clean neighborhoods for freedom. And we rallied and we marched and we risked everything for freedom because we believed that freedom would deliver us into pride and happiness and middle-class incomes and middle-class safety.

Thirty years later and freedom is no longer a word that most folks remember to use, jokingly or otherwise. And the declining popularity of the word is matched by our declining commitment to protect, and to deepen, and to extend, the meanings of freedom in the United States.

Today we know that "black and white" does not adequately describe 5 anything real. Individual, economic, racial, ethnic, and sexual realities defy such long-ago simplicity. "Black" has become Nigerian or Afro-Caribbean or Senegalese or African-American or Zulu. "White" has become Serbo-Croatian or Bosnian Muslim or Irish Republican or Italian-American or Greek or Norwegian. And, even as collective identities inside America have multiplied, our political presence here has intensified as well: women, Latino, Asian, Native, gay, lesbian, senior citizen, and so-called legal and illegal aliens. (As for the very popular concept of "aliens," you would think that, by now, anybody other than Native Americans or Chicanos/Mexicans would be pretty embarrassed to mouth such an obnoxious pejorative.)

But rather than recognize galvanizing intersections among us, too often we yield to divisive media notions such as women's rights, for example, threatening the rights of black folks or Chicanos. There is a dismal competition among Americans who should know better and who should join together for their own good. There is an acquiescence in the worst knavery of the mass media, as those top TV shows and those major weekly magazines inflame our egocentric and paranoid inclinations. In consequence, we are muddling through a terrifying period of atomization and bitterness and misdirected anger.

What the new emerging majority of these United States holds in common, at its core, is a need for freedom to exist equally and a need to become the most knowledgeable, happy, productive, interconnected, and healthy men and women that we can. Ours is a need for freedom that does not omit any racial, gender, ethnic, sexual, or physical identity from its protection. But unless we will, each of us, reach around all of these identities and embrace them even as we cherish our own, no one's freedom will be assumed.

In Margaret Atwood's novel *The Handmaid's Tale,* the reader comes upon this remarkable one-liner: "Nothing changes instantaneously: In a gradually heating bathtub, you'd be burned to death before you knew it." I think we're jammed inside that bathtub and the water's getting hot.

About five weeks ago, I was walking my dog, Amigo, along the rather quiet streets of North Berkeley when a young white man yelled something in my direction and asked me to stop. I stopped. He bolted in front of me and, excitedly, inquired whether I had seen "anything or anyone unusual." I said no, and waited to hear him out.

It seems that twice on that one day, somebody had "delivered" an anti-   10
Semitic bound book of neo-Nazi filth to the lawn in front of his house. He, Eric, was the father of a newborn baby and his Jewish wife, he told me, was completely freaked out by these scary events.

"How about you?" I asked him. Eric shrugged, and kept repeating that he "didn't understand it" and "couldn't believe" that none of his neighbors had seen anything. We talked a little while and I gave Eric my name and telephone number, as well as the numbers of some active people who might rally, fast, against this hatefulness.

In subsequent weeks, Eric invited me (and Amigo) into his house to meet his wife and to see their new baby boy, but I never had the time. Or, I never made the time to visit them.

Shortly after the first delivery of neo-Nazi literature to my neighborhood, I got on a plane bound for Madison, Wisconsin. *The Progressive*[1] was putting on a benefit show and the editors arranged for me to join the celebration. Madison, Wisconsin, is a lot like North Berkeley except Madison gets cold, and stays cold, during the winter. Similar to my northern California habitat, there are abundant public indications of environmental concern and civility: sheltered bus stops, wheelchair-accessible street crossings, bike lanes, public tennis courts, fabulous public libraries, a wonderful public university, and bookstores and backpackers all over the place.

I stayed with Dr. Elizabeth Ann Karlin during my visit to Madison. The morning after my arrival, Dr. Karlin and I sat at the dining table looking at newspapers, drinking coffee, and pushing bagels away from the butter and the cream cheese. At some point, Dr. Karlin stopped talking, and I glanced

---

[1]*The Progressive:* A leftist newsmagazine.

at her face: it was flushed, and she fell silent. Now her dogs were wild with barking and ferocious agitation.

I got up and went to the windows. Outside, two white men were marching back and forth carrying placards that said, ABORTION, A BABY CAN LIVE WITHOUT IT, and LIBERTY AND JUSTICE FOR SOME.

Breakfast was over.

I located my press pass, my ballpoint pen, yellow pad, and I tied my sneaker shoelaces and went outside to interview these members of "Operation Rescue" and "Missionaries to the Pre-born." Why were they there?

"We're picketing Elizabeth Karlin's house because she kills babies in her Women's Medical Health Center."

I talked with Kermit Simpson and David Terpstra for more than two hours. It was eerie. It was familiar. They spoke about the futility of the courts, the brutality of the police, and their determination, regardless, to rescue "innocent babies" from "murder." It was familiar because their complaints and their moral certitude echoed the regular complaints and the moral certainty of the civil rights movement.

But these groups were white. These groups were right-wing religious fundamentalists. And the only freedom they were concerned about was the freedom of the "unborn."

In fact, throughout our lengthy conversation, neither one of these men ever referred to any woman or anything female: "the baby" had to be saved from murder. That was the formulation. No woman's mind or body or feelings or predicament, at any moment, entered their consideration. What mattered was "the baby."

As I listened to David Terpstra, a good-looking white man in his twenties, it occurred to me that he was the kind of person who might have shot and killed Dr. Gunn.[2] Certainly he would see no reason not to kill a doctor who "kills babies." David told me there are twenty-two warrants out for his arrest, and he keeps moving.

He has no wife and no children and nothing special besides his mission to save "the baby."

Inside Dr. Karlin's house, the day was ruined. Even if the sun had returned to the sky (which it refused to do), there was terror and dread palpable, now, in every room.

And where were the good people of Madison who love their civil liberties and who hold Dr. Karlin in highest esteem as a warrior of our times and who used to understand that individual freedom depends upon a mass demand for its blessings and opportunities?

And what could I do for my friend, the doctor, before I got back on a plane, and left the scene of her clear and present danger?

[2]*Dr. Gunn:* A gynecologist killed outside his Florida clinic by an antiabortionist in 1993.

The next weekend was a memorial reading for Tede Matthews, a gay white American who had managed the Modern Times bookstore in San Francisco, and who had died of AIDS in July. Tede Matthews had also distinguished himself as an activist for human rights in Central America. And he had helped many, many writers and poets to acquire a community of support. He was/he is much beloved. And he died of AIDS.

In the overflow audience of several hundred people who came to honor Tede Matthews's life and to establish a Tede Matthews fund for civil rights for gay men and lesbians in Central America and in the United States, there were many gay men and lesbians.

And I heard in my brain the helter-skelter of selective scripture that the Operation Rescue guys hurled into that Wisconsin silence. And I reflected on the tragedy of Tede Matthews's death, and the death of thousands upon thousands of young men whom we have loved and lost. And I wanted to rise from my seat in a towering, prophetic rage and denounce any scripture/any construct of divinity that does not cherish all of the living people on earth and does not grieve for the cruelties of daily life that afflict every one of us if basic freedom is denied.

But this was a memorial service. And Tede Matthews is no longer alive.   30

On my return to U.C. Berkeley, one of my students alerted me to a forthcoming issue of *Mother Jones*[3] that would trash women's studies in general and our department in particular. This student, Pamela Wilson, had been quoted out of context and she explained things to me. And she was mad.

The *Mother Jones* article proved to be a juicyfruit of irresponsible, sleazy journalism: a hatchet job with malice toward every facet of the subject under scrutiny and entitled, "Off Course."

Since its appearance, several other national publications have chimed in, applauding the "exposure" of "fraud" perpetrated upon students beguiled into taking courses that let them study themselves and sometimes sit in a circle of chairs.

The head of Women's Studies, Professor Evelyn Glenn, called a special departmental meeting. The faculty decided to respond to the attack, in writing, and on national public radio.

One student, Catherine Cook, has received hate mail from loquacious   35
bigots who believe that women's studies, along with ethnic studies, make it clear that public education is wasting taxpayer money. Furthermore, these "nonacademic" studies "debase" the minds of young Americans who, instead, should "get a job," and so forth.

As a matter of fact, this latest assault on freedom of inquiry and the pivotal role of public education within that categorical mandate, this most recent effort to roll things back to "the basics" of white men studies taught by white men

[3]*Mother Jones:* A magazine focusing on American culture.

with the assistance of books written by and about white men has upset our students. The young woman who received hate mail because she thought she had a right to pursue her (women's) studies had trouble breathing, and her hands shook, as she brought those items of hatred into our faculty meeting. Students in my class, Coming Into the World Female, seemed puzzled, at first, and then stunned, and now furious with brilliant energies as they prepare for a press conference, a mock women's studies class, and a demonstration that will take place just outside the entrance to the office building of *Mother Jones*.

The students voted to create those public reactions. They have spent hours and hours in solemn, wearisome research and composition. They believe that the truth of their intentions — and the truth of the necessity for women's studies and ethnic studies and African American studies — will become apparent to most of America if only they, the students, do all of this homework into the facts, and if only they give the design and the wording of their flyers maximal painstaking and meticulous execution.

They believe that there is a mainstream majority America that will try to be fair, and that will respect their courage, and admire the intelligence of their defense. They believe that there is a mainstream majority America that will overwhelm the enemies of public and democratic education. They believe that most of us, out here, will despise and resist every assault on freedom in the United States.

And I hope they're right. With all my heart, I hope so. But the water's boiling. And not a whole lot of people seem to notice, or care, so far.

Freedom is not "another word for nothing left to lose." And we are letting it go; we are losing it. Freedom requires our steady and passionate devotion. Are we up to that?   40

ENGAGING THE TEXT

1. Why does Jordan criticize the Janis Joplin song lyrics she uses to introduce this essay? Why do you think the idea expressed in this song strikes her as particularly "white"? Do you agree?

2. What did freedom mean to Jordan during the years of the civil rights movement? How did she view the purpose of freedom in those days? How has her view of freedom changed?

3. In the second half of the essay Jordan offers a series of examples meant to illustrate the weakening of freedom in contemporary America. In what ways is freedom challenged in the incidents involving Eric, Elizabeth Karlin, Tede Matthews, and the attack on her women's studies course? Can you think of any other incidents you have heard about recently that illustrate this danger?

4. Jordan shows some ambivalence about the two abortion protesters she talks to outside Elizabeth Karlin's home. What is her attitude toward these young men and their right to protest? Is her attitude consistent with her ideas about freedom in America?

Exploring Connections

5. Compare the visions of freedom presented by Jordan and Gerry Spence (p. 695). What concerns do they share about the current health of freedom in the United States? How compatible are their views of freedom? What aspects of Spence's idea of freedom might strike Jordan as particularly "white"? What aspects of Jordan's idea of freedom might strike Spence as just another bit of "harness"? Which view do you find more honest or attractive?

6. Read or review Carmen Vázquez's "Appearances" (p. 503), Ronald Takaki's "A Different Mirror" (p. 538), Leslie Marmon Silko's "Fences Against Freedom" (p. 594), Jimmy Santiago Baca's "Past Present" (705), and Patricia J. Williams's "Hate Radio" (p. 746), and write an essay exploring Jordan's claim that "we are muddling through a terrifying period of atomization and bitterness and misdirected anger" (para. 6). What evidence, if any, do you see that America is becoming an increasingly angry and alienated nation?

Extending the Critical Context

7. Jordan claims that the media pose a threat to American freedom because they portray America as a country torn apart by "dismal competition" between a number of different factions. Working in groups, survey TV news programs over a few evenings. In general, how are relations between various American social, religious, economic, and ethnic groups portrayed? To what extent do your observations confirm or challenge Jordan's assertion?

8. Jordan suggests that we are in danger of losing the freedoms that were won during the 1960s and '70s. Make a list of freedoms that were gained or expanded during these years. Do you agree with Jordan that they are endangered by the media? Can you think of other forces that are placing these freedoms in jeopardy?

TV, Freedom, and the Loss of Community
BILL McKIBBEN

To Bill McKibben, freedom is far from being an unqualified social good. From his perspective as an ecological advocate and lay minister, freedom is a double-edged sword that threatens to destroy our sense of community connection as it enhances our individual autonomy. A former staff writer for The New Yorker, McKibben (b. 1960) *is the author of* The End of Nature *(1989), an important work on global warming. This selection comes from his second collection of essays,* The Age of Missing Information *(1992). His most recent book,* Hope, Human and Wild: True Stories of Living Lightly on the Earth, *appeared in 1995. McKibben lives in the Adirondack Mountains where he is an avid hiker, a Sunday school teacher, and the treasurer of the local volunteer fire department.*

The light lasted a long time; as it was finally fading, I saw a pickup head down the part of the road visible from the ridge. I knew, by the size of the truck and the time of the day, who it was and what he'd been doing — he'd been working on an addition for a summer house down at the lake, working late, since it was the month with no bugs, no cold, and not much dark. Not many cars drive down the road — most of them I can identify. And my sense of the community is relatively shallow. A neighbor of mine used to man a nearby fire tower for the state. From the top he could look out and see the lake where he was born and grew up, and the long unnamed ridge where he learned to hunt whitetail deer. He could see the houses of four of his eight children, and his house, or at least the valley where it sat. His mother's house, too, and the old pastures where she ran a dairy, and the church where her funeral would take place the next year, a service led by his daughter who was a sometime lay preacher there. His whole world spread out before him. He'd been to New York City exactly once, to help someone move, and somehow he'd gotten his piled-high pickup onto the bus ramp at the Port Authority bus station, and all in all it wasn't quite worth it even for a hundred dollars a day. Why leave when you're as tied in as that — when you can see a puff of smoke and know by the location and the hour if it's so-and-so burning trash or a forest fire starting up. Why leave when you live in a place you can understand and that understands you. I was putting storm windows on the church last fall with a neighbor, an older man who'd lived here all his life. He suggested we crawl up into the belfry, where I'd never been. The boards up there were covered with carved initials, most of them dating from the 1920s or earlier — some were a hundred years old. My neighbor hadn't been up there for four or five decades, but he knew whom most of the initials belonged to and whether or not they'd ended up with the female initials carved next to them. "This is my brother's," he said. "And this is mine," he added, pointing to a "DA" carved before the Depression. He pulled a knife out of his pocket and added a fresh set, complete with the initials of his wife of fifty years.

"For most of human history," writes psychologist Paul Wachtel in his book *The Poverty of Affluence,* "people lived in tightly knit communities in which each individual had a specified place and in which there was a strong sense of shared fate. The sense of belonging, of being part of something larger than oneself, was an important source of comfort. In the face of the dangers and the terrifying mysteries that the lonely individual encountered, this sense of connectedness — along with one's religious faith, which often could hardly be separated from one's membership in the community — was for most people the main way of achieving some sense of security and the courage to go on."

"For most of human history." I have used this phrase before in this book, to try to make it clear just how different our moment is, just how much information we may be missing. In this case, the information is about "community." Many of us are used to living without strong community ties — we have friends, of course, and perhaps we're involved in the community, but we're essentially autonomous. (A 1990 survey found 72 percent of Americans didn't know their next-door neighbors.) We do our own work. We're able to pick up and move and start again. And this feels natural. It is, after all, how most modern Americans grew up. On occasion, though, we get small reminders of what a tighter community must have felt like. Camp, maybe, or senior year in high school. I can remember spring vacations when I was a teenager — the youth group from our suburban church would pile in a bus and head south for some week-long work project in a poor community. Twenty-four hours on a chartered Greyhound began to bring us together; after a week of working and eating and hanging out we had changed into a group. I can recall, too, the empty feeling when we got back to the church parking lot and our parents picked us up and we went back to the semi-isolation of suburbia — much of the fellow feeling just evaporated. I do not mean that a group of adolescents working together for a week somehow equaled a community — I do mean that there was something exhilarating about it. This twining together of lives, this intense though not always friendly communion. It seemed nearly natural. As if we were built to live that way.

"Community" is a vexed concept, of course — the ties that bind can bind too tight. Clearly, all over the world, people have felt as if they were liberating themselves when they moved to places where they could be anonymous, to the cities and suburbs that in the last seventy-five years have come to dominate the Western world. All of us have learned to luxuriate in privacy. But even just watching TV you can tell there's still a pull in the other direction, too. Fairfax Cable, on its Welcome Channel, promises you that "in our busy, fast-paced, congested world, cable TV is helping to revitalize the concept of community involvement" — in other words, they let each town in their service area operate a channel. Most of the time there is just a slow "crawl" of bulletin-board announcements, and it is from these that you can sense the desire and need for community, or at least for like-minded supportive people to whom you can turn in times of crisis. Thus there are innumerable announcements about hotlines and support groups — the child abuse hotline, the support group for mothers of AIDS patients, and so on. But in ordinary times how much community is there? The crawl of messages sheds some light on our aloneness, too. The town of Falls Church offers a service to all its elderly residents: a computer will call you at home once a day. If you don't answer, help is automatically summoned. Surely very few societies have ever needed such a thing — surely

very few people lived such unaffiliated lives that their death could go un-
noticed for a day.

Other functions nearly as central to the working of a community are   5
automated too, and sold. For just ninety-five cents a minute, the 900 phone
lines allow you to hear "real people" trading "confessions." That is, you can
pay someone to let you gossip, or to gossip to you; eliminating communities
doesn't eliminate their mild vices — it just makes them duller and costlier.
New York's Channel 13, perhaps the most cerebral television channel in
America, recently installed a 900 line so that people could call up after
MacNeil/Lehrer or *Frontline* and chat with five other viewers for up to an
hour — again only ninety-five cents a minute. Singles bars, once the classic
symptom of modern loneliness, now involve too much contact, according to
TV producer Rick Rosner; instead, you can stay at home and watch Rosner's
new boy-meets-girl show, *Personals,* or maybe *Studs,* or *Love Connection,*
"where old-fashioned romance meets modern technology." On May 3, a
man appeared on *Love Connection* to say that the hips of the woman he had
dated the night before — a lady sitting there in full view of the nation —
were too large.

It's true that you can go altogether too warm and trembly at the idea of
community solidarity. (The actor Alec Baldwin, for instance, told *Hollywood Insider* how "refreshing" he had found the three days he spent in
prison while researching his role in a film called *Miami Blues.* "A lot of the
guys in the joint lift weights and stuff," he said. "I don't like to do that, and
the other option was a lot of them box. It was the best workout I ever had.
There's no cruising girls at the juice bar and all that other health-club
crap.") The idea that, say, small towns hum with peace and good cheer is
nonsense — both *Good Morning America* and *Larry King Live* featured
one tough mother from Crystal Falls, Michigan, who had gone undercover
for the local cops and busted twenty-three of her friends and neighbors for
selling drugs. She was not some church lady baking pies — she was mean.
(On *Larry King Live,* a man phoned in to explain that *he* would teach his
kids "responsible drug use." "What are you going to do, one nostril at a
time?" she asked). She left for the big city because her small-town neighbors were threatening to kill her kids.

Still, TV clearly understands that at least the *idea* of community ties attracts us. What is *Cheers* but an enclosed neighborhood where people depend on one another when the chips are down? "Where everybody knows
your name. And they're always glad you came." No one moves away, no one
can break up the kind of love that constantly makes jokes to keep from acknowledging that it is a kind of love. "You want to go where everybody
knows your name." That's right — we do. That's why we loved *M°A°S°H,*
another great TV community. But on TV, of course, while *you* know everybody's name, they've never heard of yours.

There were two Cosby episodes on this day, and both exploited this
yearning. On the rerun, his former basketball coach returned to tell stories

of Cliff as a youth; in the evening, it was his great-great-aunt, an ancient but vivacious lady who had taught the children of ex-slaves to read in a one-room schoolhouse. "Many of the kids had to walk twelve miles. And when they went home they had to work their farms till sundown." She told stories of the good old days, of courting, of chaperones — of community. The program ended in church, with Mavis Staples[1] singing a booming gospel number: "People, we all have to come together, 'cuz we need the strength and the power." It's a tribute to ties, to history — a meaningless tribute, of course, because it's all in the past tense and the present Cosbys need no one to help them lead their lives of muffled, appliance-swaddled affluence. The great-great-aunt represents a different, more primitive species, one that TV helped us "evolve" away from. But the sticky sentiment obviously plucks some strings in our hearts.

For every Hallmark card it mails to the idea of community, though, TV sends ten telegrams with the opposite meaning. Thinking of living in the same place your whole life, or even for a good long stretch of time? "No one said moving was easy. But Moving Means Moving Ahead," Allied Van Lines declares. When you reach your new home, of course, the TV will provide continuity — the same shows at the same times. And TV, of course, can provide you with people to be interested in, to gossip about — people you can take with you when you move. Not just TV actors but real-life people, like the Trumps.[2] An interesting episode of *Donahue* focused on gossips — he interviewed a woman who ceaselessly peeked out windows to find out what her neighbors were doing. The crowd was hostile — "Get a life," one lady shouted. But all day long the same demographic group that watches *Donahue* was watching, say, *Nine Broadcast Plaza,* where an "audiologist" and a "body language analyst" analyzed the videotape of an interview that Diane Sawyer had conducted the day before with Marla Maples, the other woman in the Trump divorce. On the tape, Marla grew flustered and inarticulate when asked, "Was it the best sex you ever had?" The audiologist, despite "two independent scientific instruments," could only classify her response as "inaudible," but the body language analyst thought she may have had better sex with someone else. Did she love Trump? Yes, the audiologist declared — definitely. "I don't think she knows what love is — she's too young," said the body language expert, who added that Maples was "lying through her teeth" when she said she didn't take cash from Donald. (*Nine Broadcast Plaza* also devoted time to a claim from Jessica Hahn that her encounter with Jim Bakker[3] involved "the *worst* sex I ever had.") That night on ABC, Sam Donaldson grilled Mr. Trump himself — he refused to talk about Marla or Ivana, but did say that his yacht was "the greatest yacht in the world," and that while he bought it for $24 million, he could *easily* sell it

---

[1]*Mavis Staples:* Gospel singer (b. 1940).
[2]*the Trumps:* Multimillionaire Donald Trump and his (now former) wife, Ivana.
[3]*Jim Bakker:* Televangelist involved in sexual and financial scandals in 1987.

for $115 million. Who needs eccentric uncles or town characters when you've got the Trumps?

TV's real comment on community, though, is slyer and more potent   10
than the ones I've described so far. Day after day on sitcom after talk show
after cartoon after drama, TV actively participates in the savaging of an old
order it once helped set in stone. TV history, as I've said, goes back forty
years. At its dawn are the shows like *Ozzie and Harriet,* synonyms for the
way things were. Every day we can watch Ozzie and Harriet and Beaver and
the 1950s. They represent a certain sort of community. It is no longer a
physical community, really — it's faceless suburbia. But there is still some
sense of shared values, albeit white and patriarchal and square and repressive values, values largely worthy of being overthrown. And TV joined gleefully in this overthrow. Every day, over and over, we relive the vanquishing
of that order in the name of self-expression and human liberation and fun.
The greatest story of the TV age is the transition from the fifties to the sixties — the demolition of the last ordered American "way of life." And TV
tells us this story incessantly.

It begins by repeating the old shows, and therefore the old verities. On
Father Knows Best, Bud is trying out for the football team. To win the notice of the coach, he decides to date his daughter, a sweet and innocent girl.
He makes the team — but of course he doesn't feel right, so he talks to his
dad. "You got what you wanted, but you feel you didn't get it fairly," Pop
says gravely. "Now your conscience is bothering you, and you'll figure some
way to straighten it out." Which he does, quitting the team and genuinely
falling in love with her. That plot seems so exceptionally familiar and yet so
distant — the football team as the pinnacle of boyish desire, the formal
courtship of the girl complete with long talks with her father. And especially
the act of going to one's own parents to talk about such matters. It is resolutely unhip, almost as unhip as the *Leave It to Beaver* episode that begins
with Eddie Haskell's[4] attempts to cheat on a history exam (a history exam
with questions on Clemenceau[5] and Lloyd George[6]) and ends as, reformed,
he dutifully recites the first six countries to ratify the League of Nations[7]
charter.

But TV doesn't simply offer us these shows as relics — consciously and
unconsciously it pokes fun at them. Consider this promo for Nick at Nite's
nonstop week of *Donna Reed Show* reruns: "This is Donna Reed, super-
competent mother of two and wife of one," says the announcer, who is

---

[4]*Eddie Haskell:* Wally Cleaver's best friend on the 1950s *Leave It to Beaver* TV show.

[5]*Clemenceau:* Georges Clemenceau (1841–1929), French statesman and premier of
France from 1906 to 1909 and 1917 to 1920.

[6]*Lloyd George:* Lloyd David George (1863–1945), English statesman and prime minister
from 1916 to 1922.

[7]*The League of Nations:* Predecessor of the United Nations, established in 1920.

imitating Robin Leach.[8] "She lives in this spectacular American dream house, which she cleans for her husband, the handsome Dr. Stone. Dinnertime at Chez Stone features meat, usually accompanied by potatoes, and takes place in this spotless dream kitchen!" Over pictures of people in gas masks and belching factories, the announcer says mockingly, "Out to save a world that's made a mess of things, she comes — mighty Hoover vacuum in hand. It's Donna Reed, sent from TV land to lead us politely into the new millennium."

Even when the ridicule is less explicit, it's fascinating to see the old order break down in front of your eyes each night. Over two hours on a single channel I watched a progression that began with Lucy trying desperately to get the handsome new teacher to ask her out on a date. Then came *That Girl!*, where Marlo Thomas was living alone in the city and faring well but still desperate for her parents to like her cooking. *Rhoda* was next — she went to the house of her husband's ex-wife to pick up the kids and they got roaring drunk. And finally, on *Phyllis,* most of the humor came from a cackling granny who loved to watch golf on TV because the golfers keep bending over and displaying their rear ends. In case you weren't getting the point, the shows were interspersed with ads like this one, for a videotape library of old TV shows: "The fifties — life seemed simpler then. Drive-ins, chrome-covered cars, and every Monday night there was *Lucy.*"

This account of our liberation from the repressive mores of society is not an entirely new story (as the Zeffirelli version of *Romeo and Juliet* on Showtime made clear), but never has it been told so ceaselessly. Steve Vai had a tune in heavy rotation this week on MTV — it showed a young boy with a prim old lady for a teacher. He jumps up on the desk to play his guitar for show-and-tell, and the kids, liberated by the beat, tear the room apart; the teacher goes screaming out into the hall. The children watching this video have likely never known this sort of school, where learning is by rote and repression is the rule. And yet this mythical liberation survives, celebrated over and over again, as it will as long as the people who lived through that revolution are writing TV shows. (And perhaps as long as the people who grew up watching those shows are writing them, and so on forever.)

Any revolution this constant and thorough breeds counterrevolt, or at   15
least uneasiness. Sometimes it is explicit, as with the conservatives who haunt the religious channels preaching "traditional family values." Usually, though, the uneasiness creeps in around the edges. On pay-per-view, *Field of Dreams* concerned a fellow, Ray Kinsella, who was a big wheel in the antiwar movement. He retains a fair amount of contempt for the stolid farmers around him, and his wife certainly stands up against book-burning bigots. But there's also a lot in the movie about his dad, who just wanted to play catch with him. Ray rejected all that family stuff in a huff and went off

---

[8]*Robin Leach:* Host of popular 1980s TV show *Lifestyles of the Rich and Famous.*

to college to protest — and now, more or less, he has to build a big stadium in the cornfield in order to get his daddy back. He'd gone a little bit too far back then.

Other, lesser movies made the same kind of point. HBO ran a fascinating film, *Irreconcilable Differences,* about a little girl who was suing her parents for divorce. They had been the classic sixties couple — they met as *semihippies* on a *road trip* across America. He'd written his thesis about *sexual overtones* in *early films.* She decided to dump her *Navy fiancé.* They drank *tequila* and listened to *James Taylor* and *cried* at films. And then they got rich writing movies on their own and fulfilled themselves in all sorts of predictable ways — divorces, bimbos, personal masseuses, big houses, fast cars. They were "doing their thing," "following their bliss." Which is why their daughter ends up explaining to the judge that she wants to go live with the Mexican housekeeper in her tiny bungalow, where the children sleep three to a bed. "I don't expect my mom to be a person who vacuums all day and bakes cookies for me when I get home from school, and I don't expect my dad to be some kind of real understanding person who wants to take me fishing all the time. But my mom and dad are just too mixed up for anyone to be around. I'm just a kid, and I don't know what I'm doing sometimes. But I think you should know better when you grow up." Their reconciliation comes in a cheap chain restaurant — utter normality as salvation.

This kind of reaction, though, has not really slowed the trend away from Ozzie and Harriet. One critic described Fox's *Married . . . With Children* as "antimatter to the Huxtables. . . . Sex (both the desire for and aversion to), the body at its grossest, stupidity, and familial contempt are the stuff of this sitcom." And yet, as CBS programmer Howard Stringer pointed out ruefully, more children were watching the program than any show on CBS. Therefore, he said, he was sending a signal to producers of comedy shows that they had an "open throttle" to change the network's image as "stuffy, stodgy, and old." He pointed with pride to an upcoming CBS pilot show that, in the words of the *Times,* "contains a provocative line of dialogue from a six-year-old girl." On *Leave It to Beaver,* Wally talks to his girlfriend on the phone in the living room in front of his parents and thinks nothing of it. By the *Brady Bunch,* the girls are giggling secretly over the princess phone. When you get to *One Day at a Time,* the children listen in as the mother talks to *her* boyfriend, who's trying to persuade her to come to a South Pacific island. "He's probably down there starving for your body, lusting for your lips," the daughter says. And *One Day at a Time* is already in reruns.

Ozzie and Harriet represented all sorts of things that needed to be overthrown, or at least badly shaken up — a world where women did what housework remained, where children never talked back, where appearance and conformity counted above all, where black people never showed their faces, where sex was dirty or absent, where God lived in some church, where America was the only country that counted. The problem is only that the rebellion against this world never ended, never helped create a new and better order to take its place. The American Revolution tossed out the tyrants and set up something fresh; the French Revolution tossed out tyrants and then looked for more tyrants.

The main idea that emerges from the breakup of this Donna Reed order is "freedom," or, more accurately, not being told what to do. You can listen to, say, sociologist Robert Bellah when he says "personal freedom, autonomy, and independence are the highest values for Americans," or you can listen to the crowd on one of the morning talk shows responding to the plight of a man whose XXXtasy hard-core pornography television service has been shut down by an Alabama sheriff. "It's just total censorship," someone in the studio audience said. "It all comes down to the same thing — our rights." "Everyone out there has to make their own decisions." The same kind of sentiments attended the 2 Live Crew controversy, which came to a head while I was working on this book. The Crew, you will recall, was the rap group that specialized in lyrics like "Suck my dick, bitch, and make it puke," and which finally found one cooperative Florida district attorney who rose to the bait and charged them with obscenity. As Sara Rimer reported in the *Times,* Luther Campbell, the group's leader, said he was worried that the six jurors, who included three women over age sixty and only one black, might be "too old, too white, and too middle-class" to "understand" his music. His worry was misplaced; after they quickly acquitted him, one juror said, "I thought it would've been cute if we could of come out with the verdict like we were doing a rap song," and another said the content of the lyrics had not affected her: "Those were their songs. They were doing their poetry in song."

The jurors made the right decision — "You take away one freedom and   20
pretty soon they're all gone," said one, and he was telling the truth. So were the people on *Nine Broadcast Plaza* — an Alabama sheriff shouldn't care what folks watch on their TVs. Tolerance is an unqualified good — a world where people of all races and all sexual orientations and both genders and all political persuasions can express themselves openly is so manifestly superior to the bigoted and repressed world we're leaving behind that they hardly bear comparison. And it's probably even useful to have occasional phenomena like 2 Live Crew to make us stand up once again and reassert our principles.

But tolerance by itself can be a cover for moral laziness. In a world with real and pressing problems, tolerance is merely a precondition for politics — it is not itself a meaningful politics. We try to pretend that "liberation" is enough because it's so much easier to eternally rebel: "Kicking against social repression and moral vapidity — that's an activity rock 'n' roll has managed to do better than virtually any other art or entertainment form," *Rolling Stone* boasted in a year-end editorial in 1990 that called for forming a "bulwark against those who would gladly muzzle that spirit . . . of insolent liberty." Good, fine, we all agree — "I thought it would've been cute if we could of come out with the verdict like we were doing a rap song." But is that all there is? Don't popular music and art and politics have a good deal more to do than "kick against social repression and moral vapidity"? Isn't it time to focus harder on substantive problems, such as, how do we build a society that doesn't destroy the planet by its greed, and doesn't *ignore* the weak and poor? (Not repress them, just ignore them.) I don't mean a lot of sappy records and TV shows with syrupy messages about saving dolphins — I mean popular art that fulfills the old functions of popular art, that reminds us of our connections with one another and with the places we live. An art that reminds us that our own lives shouldn't merely be free — that they should be of value to others, connected to others, and that if our lives are like that they will become finer. That's what a culture is. It's true that we don't need all the old "traditional" values — but as a society we desperately need *values*.

We need them because a culture primarily obsessed with "tolerance" as an end instead of a means is, finally, a selfish culture, a have-it-your-way world. A place where nothing interferes with desire, the definition of a perfect consumer society. Listen to Jerry Della Femina, the adman, on *Good Morning America*. He's excoriating Disney for not letting movie theaters show commercials with its films: "Disney is blackmailing the movie theaters. . . . It should be up to the audience. If you hate the commercial, boo and hiss. If you like the commercial, buy the product. That's the American way." Or listen to Marion Barry, who in 1990 was still the mayor of Washington but had already been indicted on any number of drug and malfeasance charges. The city Democratic committee was voting that night on a motion urging him not to run for re-election. "It amounts to a type of censorship," he told one network. "Our country was founded on the principle that all men have a right to life, liberty, and the pursuit of happiness. And I intend to pursue my happiness as I see fit." By the late news, he's Daniel Webster[9] — "I'd rather die losing and stand on principle." The principle is that no one should tell him what to do, never mind that his city was a grotesque shambles. That night, a woman stood up at the Democratic meeting to defend Barry: "We're not Hitler, and we can't say who should run and who should not run." This is tolerance replacing sense.

Though it's rarely mentioned on TV, the gay community in the wake of the AIDS crisis provides an alternative example. Randy Shilts's eloquent history of the crisis, *And the Band Played On*, begins in San Francisco, where gay people had carved out an enclave of freedom and tolerance in a hostile world. And then, out of nowhere, not as a punishment but as a fact, came a strange disease. It was a proud community, and a community tolerant, even indulgent, of all desires. The emerging understanding of the disease — that it was sexually transmitted, that safety lay in limiting both partners and practices — conflicted sharply with that tolerant ethos. Some

---

[9]*Daniel Webster:* American statesman and orator (1782–1852).

people said that closing the bathhouses or educating people about what not to stick where would force people back into the closet, interfere with their freedom, return them to the repressed past. But AIDS was a fact. Gradually — a little too gradually, probably — the gay community came as a group to embrace other values, to form a community that in its organized compassion, active caring, and political toughness is a model for every other community in America. A mature community. This does not mean that AIDS was a good thing. Far, far better it had never come, and life had gone on as before, and none of those tens of thousands had died. But AIDS was and is a fact, a shocking enough fact to force people into changing, into realizing that along with tolerance and liberation they now need commitment and selflessness.

By accepting the idea that we should never limit desire or choose from the options our material and spiritual liberations give us, we ignore similarly pressing facts about our larger community. In a different world perhaps we'd never need to limit our intake of goods, to slow down our consumption of resources, to stop and share with others. But we live in this world — a world approaching ecological disaster, riven by proverty. A world of limits, demanding choices. TV gives us infinite information about choice — it celebrates choice as a great blessing, which it is, and over the course of a single day it lays out a nearly infinite smorgasbord of options. As much as it loves choice, though, it doesn't actually believe in choosing. It urges us to choose *everything* — this and this and this as well. And it does nothing to help us create the communities that might make wise choices possible on a scale large enough to make a difference.

In this case, the mountain is useful mostly as a vantage point. It can   25
offer scant advice about how humans should organize their lives together, but it does provide an aerial view; from up here on the ridge I can recognize each home by its kitchen lights, and see how they stand in relation to one another. And now the all-night light has switched on at the volunteer fire department, whose noon siren was about the only mechanical sound I heard all day.

No need, as I said, to romanticize small towns — they can be home to vicious feud and rankling gossip and small-minded prejudice and all the other things that made leaving them appear so liberating. But there are a few things to be said for them, and the volunteer fire department is one. A house fire is no joke — when you take the state qualifying course, they show you film after film of houses exploding with folks inside, just as in *Backdraft*. On this day, in fact, the Washington TV stations were covering a tragedy in a tiny Pennsylvania village, Hustontown. The firemen had been called to clean out a well for an old lady. It smelled funny, but they thought there was just a dead animal down there. The first man down suddenly lost consciousness — two more jumped down to get him. All three died from some gas that had collected there. The fiancée of one of the men sobbed hysterically on the porch of a nearby house — she'd begged him not to go, but "he told me it was his duty as a volunteer firefighter." His duty, that is, to friends, neighbors, community.

It may be more sensible, by some utilitarian calculation, to entrust your safety to trained professionals and to insurance companies — more reliable, perhaps, and in places of a certain size clearly necessary. But it comes at a cost in information. Abstracted from others, you begin to believe in your own independence, forgetting that at some level you depend on everyone else and they depend on you, even if it's only to pay taxes. (Pretty soon you don't want to pay taxes anymore.) "We place a high value on being left alone, on not being interfered with," says Bellah, the sociologist who has interviewed hundreds of Americans. "The most important thing is to be able to take care of yourself. . . . It's illegitimate to depend on another human being." And this belief is so lonely — it's something human beings have never had to contend with before.

Public television was airing a Bill Moyers interview with a businessman named James Autry. A former brand manager for Colgate, he was trained at Benton & Bowles advertising agency and now worked as the publisher of *Better Homes & Gardens.* He is also a poet. He took Moyers back to the Mississippi town where he'd grown up — where his father, Reverend Autry, had spent his life preaching at the local church in the piney woods. The son had left the South in part to escape its ugly, intolerant side — he didn't want all that went with being a white Southerner. But he'd started coming back in recent years — he sat in the graveyard next to his daddy's church and read a poem. "She was a McKinstry, and his mother was a Smith / And the listeners nod at what that combination will produce / Those generations to come of honesty or thievery / Of heathens or Christians / Of slovenly men or worthy. / Course his mother was a Sprayberry. . . ." And he said, this man who publishes *Better Homes & Gardens,* which convinces millions that a better home is a home with better furniture, "I've thought about my own sons. What are they connected to? Some house on Fifty-sixth Street in Des Moines? What will they remember?" And this is a hard and terrible question for all of us who grew up liberated.

ENGAGING THE TEXT

1. What, according to McKibben, does a community offer its members? Write a brief journal entry about a time you felt you belonged to a community as McKibben defines it — whether a town, neighborhood, school, work situation, club, or other organization. What made this group of people a community? What did belonging to this community offer you?

2. What evidence does McKibben offer to support the claim that America's sense of community is in decline? Do you agree with him? What examples can you think of that demonstrate the health or decay of America's sense of community?

3. McKibben portrays TV as playing a complex — almost a contradictory — role in relation to America's eroding sense of community. Using examples he provides, explain his analysis of the way that TV simultaneously exploits the myth of freedom and appeals to our need for social connection.

4. Toward the end of the essay, McKibben offers gay San Francisco as a model of a mature community. What qualities make this gay community such a positive example for McKibben? What other model communities can you think of?

EXPLORING CONNECTIONS

5. Compare and contrast the concepts of freedom presented by Gerry Spence (p. 695), June Jordan (p. 712), and McKibben. How does each of these authors view freedom? What virtues and hazards does each associate with being free?

6. Discuss one or more of the following communities in light of McKibben's argument. For example, what do these communities offer their members? What does each demand or expect in return? To what extent do these examples challenge or confirm McKibben's account of the value of community life?

   - the school featured in Deborah Meier and Paul Schwarz's "The Hard Part Is Making It Happen" (p. 289)
   - the Native American tribes in Paula Gunn Allen's "Where I Come From Is Like This" (p. 520)
   - the network of mothers in Patricia Hill Collins's "Black Women and Motherhood" (p. 131)
   - the town C. P. Ellis grew up in (p. 575)
   - the new "melting pot" of Los Angeles in Lynell George's "Gray Boys, Funky Aztecs, and Honorary Homegirls" (p. 653)

7. Using the analyses of television provided by McKibben, Elizabeth Dodson Gray (p. 71), and Patricia J. Williams (p. 604) as a point of departure, write an essay on the impact of TV on American values and attitudes.

8. Compare McKibben's analysis of why America's sense of community is weakening with that suggested by the Ted Rall cartoon that follows this selection on page 731. Which do you think is a greater threat to our sense of community — the broadcast programming that McKibben criticizes or the kind of "narrowcasting" that Rall spoofs in his cartoon? Why?

EXTENDING THE CRITICAL CONTEXT

9. Watch an hour or so of MTV videos and analyze the messages that they convey about community and liberation. How well do your observations mesh with McKibben's claims about TV?

10. What community or communities do you participate in on your college campus? Would you consider your college as a whole to be a community? Your dorm? Your composition class? If not, why not? If so, what common

values, beliefs, goals, or mutual responsibilities hold each of these communities together? What other organizations do you belong to that offer you a sense of community on campus?

11. McKibben suggests that the media occasionally go through periods of "counterrevolution" when so-called traditional values and beliefs are glamorized at the expense of more rebellious messages (para. 15). As a class, discuss the current state of the media in relation to the themes of community and liberation. Are TV shows and films currently highlighting what might be considered traditional values? Has there ever been a period when the media emphasized liberation at the expense of traditional values?

What Rights Do We Have?

DAVID BOAZ

Freedom is the favorite topic of David Boaz. Executive Vice President of the Cato Institute and a central figure in the Libertarian party, Boaz gained national recognition in 1988 when he wrote an article for the New York Times calling for the decriminalization of all illegal drugs. This radical solution to the country's drug problems shocked many Americans, but it was completely consistent with Boaz's faith in the power of freedom. In this selection from Libertarianism: A Primer *(1997), Boaz argues that our preoccupation with guaranteeing individual "rights" is actually eroding our essential liberty. "Self-ownership," not rights, is the foundation of American freedoms, according to Boaz. Since joining the Cato Institute, Boaz has written editorials and articles for the* New York Times, *the* Wall Street Journal, *and the* Washington Post. *He has also edited the* Libertarian Reader *(1997) and* Assessing the Reagan Years *(1988).*

Critics on both left and right have complained that America in the 1990s is awash in talk about rights. No political debate proceeds for very long without one side, or both, resting its argument on rights — property rights, welfare rights, women's rights, nonsmokers' rights, the right to life, abortion rights, gay rights, gun rights, you name it.

A journalist asked me recently what I thought of a proposal by self-proclaimed communitarians to "suspend for a while the minting of new rights." Communitarians in late twentieth-century America are people who believe that "the community" should in some way take precedence over the individual, so naturally they would respond to rights-talk overload by saying, "Let's just stop doing it." How many ways, I mused, does that get it wrong? Communitarians seem to see rights as little boxes; when you have too many, the room won't hold them all. In the libertarian view, we have an infinite number of rights contained in one natural right. That one fundamental human right is the right to live your life as you choose so long as you don't infringe on the equal rights of others.

That one right has infinite implications. As James Wilson, a signer of the Constitution, said in response to a proposal that a Bill of Rights be added to the Constitution: "Enumerate all the rights of man! I am sure, sirs, that no gentleman in the late Convention would have attempted such a thing." After all, a person has a right to wear a hat, or not; to marry, or not; to grow beans, or apples; or to open a haberdashery. Indeed, to cite a specific example, a person has a right to sell an orange to a willing buyer even though the orange is only 2⅜ inches in diameter (although under current federal law, that is illegal).

It is impossible to enumerate in advance all the rights we have; we usually go to the trouble of identifying them only when someone proposes to limit one or another. Treating rights as tangible claims that must be limited in number gets the whole concept wrong.

But the complaint about "the proliferation of rights" is not all wrong. 5 There is indeed a problem in modern America with the proliferation of phony "rights." When rights become merely legal claims attached to interests and preferences, the stage is set for political and social conflict. Interests and preferences may conflict, but *rights* cannot. There is no conflict of genuine human rights in a free society. There are, however, many conflicts among the holders of so-called welfare rights, which require someone else to provide us with things we want, whether that is education, health care, social security, welfare, farm subsidies, or unobstructed views across someone else's land. This is a fundamental problem of interest-group democracy and the interventionist stage. In a liberal society, people *assume* risks and obligations through contract; an interventionist state *imposes* obligations on people through the political process, obligations that conflict with their natural rights.

So what rights *do* we have, and how can we tell a real right from a phony one? Let's start by returning to one of the basic documents in the history of human rights, the Declaration of Independence. In the second paragraph of the Declaration, Thomas Jefferson laid out a statement of rights and their meaning that has rarely been equaled for grace and brevity. . . . Jefferson's task in writing the Declaration was to express the common sentiments of the American colonists, and he was chosen for the job not because he had new ideas but because of his "peculiar felicity of expression." Introducing the American cause to the world, Jefferson explained:

> We hold these truths to be self-evident, that all men are created equal, that they are endowed by their Creator with certain unalienable Rights, that among these are life, liberty, and the pursuit of happiness. That to secure these rights, governments are instituted among men, deriving their just powers from the consent of the governed. That whenever any form of government becomes destructive of these ends, it is the right of the people to alter or abolish it.

Let's try to draw out the implications of America's founding document.

Basic Rights

Any theory of rights has to begin somewhere. Most libertarian philosophers would begin the argument earlier than Jefferson did. Humans, unlike animals, come into the world without an instinctive knowledge of what their needs are and how to fulfill them. As Aristotle said, man is a reasoning and deliberating animal; humans use the power of reason to understand their own needs, the world around them, and how to use the world to satisfy their needs. So they need a social system that allows them to use their reason, to act in the world, and to cooperate with others to achieve purposes that no one individual could accomplish.

Every person is a unique individual. Humans are social animals — we like interacting with others, and we profit from it — but we think and act individually. Each individual owns himself or herself. What other possibilities besides self-ownership are there?

Someone — a king or a master race — could own others.   Plato and Aristotle did argue that there were different kinds of humans, some more competent than others and thus endowed with the right and responsibility to rule, just as adults guide children. Some forms of socialism and collectivism are — explicitly or implicitly — based on the notion that many people are not competent to make decisions about their own lives, so that the more talented should make decisions for them. But that would mean there were no universal human rights, only rights that some have and others do not, denying the essential humanity of those who are deemed to be owned.

Everyone owns everyone, a full-fledged communist system.   In such a   10
system, before anyone could take an action, he would need to get permission from everyone else. But how could each other person grant permission without consulting everyone else? You'd have an infinite regress, making any action at all logically impossible. In practice, since such mutual ownership is impossible, this system would break down into the previous one: someone, or some group, would own everyone else. That is what happened in the communist states: the party became a dictatorial ruling elite.

Thus, either communism or aristocratic rule would divide the world into factions or classes. The only possibility that is humane, logical, and suited to the nature of human beings is *self-ownership*. Obviously, this discussion has only scratched the surface of the question of self-ownership; in any event, I rather like Jefferson's simple declaration: Natural rights are self-evident.

Conquerors and oppressors told people for millennia that men were *not* created equal, that some were destined to rule and others to be ruled. By the eighteenth century, people had thrown off such ancient superstition; Jefferson denounced it with his usual felicity of expression: "The mass of mankind has not been born with saddles on their backs, nor a favored few booted and spurred ready to ride them legitimately by the grace of God." As we enter the twenty-first century, the idea of equality is almost universally accepted. Of course, people are not equally tall, equally beautiful, equally smart, equally kind, equally graceful, or equally successful. But they have equal rights, so they should be equally free. As the Stoic lawyer Cicero wrote, "While it is undesirable to equalize wealth, and everyone cannot have the same talents, legal rights at least should be equal among citizens of the same commonwealth."

In our own time we've seen much confusion on this point. People have advocated public policies both mild and repressive to bring about equality of outcomes. Advocates of material equality apparently don't feel the need to defend it as a principle; ironically, they seem to take it as self-evident. In defending equality, they typically confuse three concepts:

- A right to equality before the law, which is the kind of equality Jefferson had in mind.

- A right to equality of results or outcomes, meaning that everyone has the same amount of — of what? Usually egalitarians mean the same amount of money, but why is money the only test? Why not equality of beauty, or of hair, or of work? The fact is, equality of outcomes requires a political decision about measurement and allocation, a decision no society can make without some group forcing its view on others. True equality of results is logically impossible in a diverse world, and the attempt to achieve it leads to nightmarish results. Producing equal outcomes would require treating people unequally.

- A right to equality of opportunity, meaning an equal chance to succeed in life. People who use "equality" this way usually mean equal rights, but an attempt to create true equality of opportunity could be as dictatorial as equality of results. Children raised in different households will never be equally prepared for the adult world, yet any alternative to family freedom would mean a nanny state of the worst order. Full equality of opportunity might indeed lead to the solution posed in Kurt Vonnegut's short story "Harrison Bergeron," in which the beautiful are scarred, the graceful are shackled, and the smart have their brain patterns continuously disrupted.

The kind of equality suitable for a free society is *equal rights*. As the Declaration stated clearly, rights are not a gift from government. They are natural and unchanging, inherent in the nature of mankind and possessed by people by virtue of their humanity, specifically their ability to take responsibility for their actions. Whether rights come from God or from nature is not essential in this context. Remember, the first paragraph of the Declaration referred to "the laws of nature and of nature's God." What is important is that rights are imprescriptible, that is, not granted by any other human. In particular, they are not granted by government; people form governments in order to protect the rights they already possess.

Self-Ownership

Because every person owns himself, his body and his mind, he has the   15
right to life. To unjustifiably take another person's life — to murder him —
is the greatest possible violation of his rights.

Unfortunately, the term "right to life" is used in two confusing ways in our time. We might do better to stick to "right to self-ownership." Some people, mostly on the political right, use "right to life" to defend the rights of fetuses (or unborn children) against abortion. Obviously, that is not the sense in which Jefferson used the term.

Other people, mostly on the political left, would argue that the "right to life" means that everyone has a fundamental right to the necessities of life: food, clothing, shelter, medical care, maybe even an eight-hour day and two weeks of vacation. But if the right to life means this, then it means that one person has a right to force other people to give him things, violating their equal rights. The philosopher Judith Jarvis Thomson writes, "If I am sick unto death, and the only thing that will save my life is the touch of Henry Fonda's cool hand on my fevered brow, then all the same, I have no right to be given the touch of Henry Fonda's cool hand on my fevered brow." And if not the right to Henry Fonda's touch, then why would she have the right to a room in Henry Fonda's house, or a portion of his money with which to buy food? That would mean forcing him to serve her, taking the product of his labor without his consent. No, the right to life means that each person has the right to take action in the furtherance of his life and flourishing, not to force others to serve his needs.

Ethical universalism, the most common framework for moral theory, holds that a valid ethical theory must be applicable for all men and women, at whatever time and place we find them. The natural rights to life, liberty, and property can be enjoyed by people under any normal circumstances. But so-called rights to housing, education, medical care, cable television, or the "periodic holidays with pay" generously proclaimed in the United Nations' Universal Declaration of Human Rights, cannot be enjoyed everywhere. Some societies are too poor to provide everyone with leisure or housing or even food. And remember that there is no collective entity known as "education" or "medical care"; there are only specific, particular goods, such as a seat for a year in the Hudson Street School or an operation performed by kindly Dr. Johnson on Tuesday. Some person or group of people would have to provide each particular unit of "housing" or "education," and providing it to one person necessarily means denying it to other people. Therefore, it is logically impossible to make such desirable things "universal human rights."

The right to self-ownership leads immediately to the right to liberty; indeed, we may say that "right to life" and "right to liberty" are just two ways of expressing the same point. If people own themselves, and have both the right and the obligation to take the actions necessary for their survival and flourishing, then they must enjoy freedom of thought and action. Freedom of thought is an obvious implication of self-ownership; in a sense, though, it's difficult to deny freedom of thought. Who can regulate the content of someone else's mind? Freedom of speech is also logically implied by self-ownership. Many governments have tried to outlaw or restrict freedom of speech, but speech is inherently fleeting, so control is difficult. Freedom of the press — including, in modern times, broadcasting, cable, electronic mail, and other new forms of communications — is the aspect of intellectual freedom that oppressive governments usually target. And when we defend freedom of the press, we are necessarily talking about property rights, because ideas are expressed *through property* — printing presses, auditoriums, sound trucks, billboards, radio equipment, broadcast frequencies, computer networks, and so on.

Property Rights

In fact, the ownership of property is a necessary implication of self-ownership because all human action involves property. How else could happiness be pursued? If nothing else, we need a place to stand. We need the right to use land and other property to produce new goods and services. We shall see that all rights can be understood as property rights. But this is a contentious point, not always easily understood. Many people wonder why we couldn't voluntarily share our goods and property.   20

Property is a *necessity*. "Property" doesn't mean simply land, or any other physical good. Property is anything that people can use, control, or dispose of. A property right means the freedom to use, control, or dispose of an object or entity. Is this a bad, exploitative necessity? Not at all.

If our world were not characterized by scarcity, we wouldn't need property rights. That is, if we had infinite amounts of everything people wanted, we would need no theory of how to allocate such things. But of course scarcity is a basic characteristic of our world. Note that scarcity doesn't imply poverty or a lack of basic subsistence. Scarcity simply means that human wants are essentially unlimited, so we never have enough productive resources to supply all of them. Even an ascetic who had transcended the desire for material goods beyond bare subsistence would face the most basic scarcity of all: the scarcity of one's own body and life and time. Whatever time he devoted to prayer would not be available for manual labor, for reading the sacred texts, or for performing good works. No matter how rich our society gets — nor how indifferent to material goods we become — we will always have to make choices, which means that we need a system for deciding who gets to use productive resources.

We can never abolish property rights, as socialist visionaries promise to do. As long as things exist, someone will have the power to use them. In a civilized society, we don't want that power to be exercised simply by the strongest or most violent person; we want a theory of justice in property titles. When socialist governments "abolish" property, what they promise is that the entire community will own all property. But since — visionary theory or no — only one person can eat a particular apple, or sleep in a particular bed, or stand on a particular spot, someone will have to decide who. That someone — the party official, or the bureaucrat, or the czar — is the real possessor of the property right.

Libertarians believe that the right to self-ownership means that individuals must have the right to acquire and exchange property in order to fulfill their needs and desires. To feed ourselves, or provide shelter for our families, or open a business, we must make use of property. And for people to be willing to save and invest, we need to be confident that our property rights are legally secure, that someone else can't come and confiscate the wealth we've created, whether that means the crop we've planted, the house we've built, the car we've bought, or the complex corporation we've created through a network of contracts with many other people.

Original Acquisition of Property.   How do men and women come to   25 acquire property in the first place? Perhaps if a spaceship full of men and women landed on Mars, there would seem to be no need for conflict over land. Just pick a spot and start building or planting. A cartoonist once depicted one caveman saying to another, "Let's cut the earth into little squares and sell them." Put like that, it sounds absurd. Why do that? And who would buy the little squares? And with what? But as population increases, it becomes necessary to decide what land — or water or frequency spectrum — belongs to whom. John Locke[1] described one way to acquire property: Whoever first "mixed his labor with" a piece of land acquired title to it. By mixing his own labor with a piece of previously unowned land, he made it his own. He then had the right to build a house on it, put a fence around it, sell it, or otherwise dispose of it.

For each entity there is in fact a bundle of property rights, which can be disaggregated. There can be as many property rights attached to one entity as there are aspects of that entity. For instance, you might purchase or lease the right to drill for oil on a piece of land, but not the right to farm or build on it. You might own the land but not the water under it. You might donate your house to a charity but retain the right to live there for your lifetime. As Roy Childs wrote in *Liberty Against Power,* "Before there was a technology available to broadcast through the airwaves, certain kinds of things . . . could not have been property, because they could not have been specified by any technological means." But once we understand the physics of broadcasting, we can create property rights in the frequency spectrum. Childs went on, "As a society gets more complicated . . . and technology advances, the kinds of ownership that are possible to people become more and more complex."

The homesteading principle — initially acquiring a property title by being the first to use or transform the property — may operate differently with different kinds of property. For instance, in a state of nature, when most land is unowned (as if men landed on a new planet), we might say that simply camping on a piece of land and remaining there is sufficient to acquire the property right. Surely laying out the foundation for a house

[1]*John Locke:* English philosopher (1632–1704).

and then beginning to build it would establish a property right. Rights to water — whether in lakes, rivers, or underground pools — have traditionally been acquired in ways different from land acquisition. When people began to use the frequency spectrum to broadcast in the 1920s, they generally adopted a homestead principle: start broadcasting on a particular frequency, and you acquire a right to continue using that frequency. (The role of government in all these cases is simply to *protect*, largely through the courts, the rights that individuals acquire on their own.) The important thing, as I'll discuss later, is that we have some way of establishing property rights and then that we allow people to transfer them to others by mutual consent.

Property Rights Are Human Rights.   What exactly does it mean to own property? We might cite Jan Narveson's definition: "'x is A's property' means 'A has the right to determine the disposition of x.'" Note that a property right is not a right *of* property, or a right *belonging to* a piece of property, as opponents of property rights often suggest. Rather, a property right is a human right *to* property, the right of an individual to use and dispose of property that he has justly acquired. Property rights are human rights.

Indeed, as argued above, all human rights can be seen as property rights, stemming from the one fundamental right of self-ownership, our ownership of our own bodies. As Murray Rothbard put it in *Power and Market,*

> In the profoundest sense there *are* no rights but property rights. . . . There are several senses in which this is true. In the first place, each individual, as a natural fact, is the owner of *himself*, the ruler of his own person. The "human" rights of the person that are defended in the purely free-market society are, in effect, each man's *property right* in his own being, and from *this* property right stems his right to the material goods that he has produced.
>
> In the second place, alleged "human rights" can be boiled down to property rights . . . for example, the "human right" of free speech. Freedom of speech is supposed to mean the right of everyone to say whatever he likes. But the neglected question is: Where? Where does a man have this right? He certainly does not have it on property on which he is trespassing. In short, he has this right only either on his *own* property or on the property of someone who has agreed, as a gift or in a rental contract, to allow him on the premises. In fact, then, there is no such thing as a separate "right to free speech"; there is only a man's *property* right: the right to do as he wills with his own or to make voluntary agreements with other property owners [including those whose property may consist only of their own labor].

When we understand free speech this way, we see what's wrong with Justice Oliver Wendell Holmes's famous statement that free speech rights cannot be absolute because there is no right to falsely shout "Fire!" in a crowded theater. Who would be shouting "Fire"? Possibly the owner, or one of his agents, in which case the owner has defrauded his customers: he sold them tickets to a play or movie and then disrupted the show, not to mention endangered their lives. If not the owner, then one of the customers, who is violating the terms of his contract; his ticket entitles him to enjoy the show, not to disrupt it. The falsely-shouting-fire-in-a-crowded-theater argument is no reason to limit the right of free speech; it's an illustration of the way that property rights solve problems and of the need to protect and enforce them.

The same analysis applies to the much-debated right to privacy. In the   30
1965 case *Griswold v. Connecticut,* the Supreme Court struck down a Connecticut law prohibiting the use of contraceptives. Justice William O. Douglas found a right to privacy for married couples in "penumbras, formed by emanations" from various parts of the Constitution. Conservatives such as Judge Robert Bork have ridiculed such vague, rootless reasoning for thirty years. The penumbras kept on emanating to take in an unmarried couple's right to contraception and a woman's right to terminate a pregnancy, but suddenly in 1986 they were found not to emanate far enough to cover consensual homosexual acts in a private bedroom. A theory of privacy rooted in property rights wouldn't have needed penumbras and emanations — which, penumbras being imperfect shadows, are necessarily pretty vague — to find that a person has a right to purchase contraceptives from willing sellers or to engage in sexual relations with consenting partners in one's own home. "A man's home is his castle" provides a stronger foundation for privacy than "penumbras, formed by emanations."

Those who reject the libertarian principle of property rights need to do more than criticize. They need to offer an alternative system that would as effectively define who may use each particular resource and in what ways, ensure that land and other property is adequately cared for, provide a framework for economic development, and avoid the war of all against all that can ensue when control over valuable goods is not clearly defined. . . .

Freedom of Conscience

It's . . . easy for most people to see the implications of libertarianism for freedom of conscience, free speech, and personal freedom. The modern ideas of libertarianism began in the struggle for religious toleration. What can be more inherent, more personal, to an individual than the thoughts in his mind? As religious dissidents developed their defense of toleration, the ideas of natural rights and a sphere of privacy emerged. Freedom of speech and freedom of the press are other aspects of the liberty of conscience. No one has the right to prevent another person from expressing his thoughts and trying to persuade others of his opinions. That argument today must extend to radio and television, cable, the Internet, and other forms of electronic communications. People who don't want to read books by communists (or libertarians!), or watch gory movies, or download pornographic pictures, don't have to; but they have no right to prevent others from making their own choices.

The ways that governments interfere with freedom of speech are legion. American governments have constantly tried to ban or regulate allegedly indecent, obscene, or pornographic literature and movies, despite the clear wording of the First Amendment: "Congress shall make no law . . . abridging the freedom of speech or of the press." As a headline in *Wired* magazine put it, "What part of 'no law' don't you understand?"

Libertarians see dozens of violations of free speech in American law. Information about abortion has been banned, most recently in the 1996 law regulating communication over the Internet. The federal government has often used its monopoly post office to prevent the delivery of morally or politically offensive material. Radio and television broadcasters must get federal licenses and then comply with various federal regulations on the content of broadcasts. The Bureau of Alcohol, Tobacco, and Firearms forbids the producers of wine and other alcoholic beverages from noting on their labels that medical studies indicate that moderate consumption of alcohol reduces the risk of heart disease and increases longevity — even though the latest dietary guidelines from the Department of Health and Human Services note the benefits of moderate alcohol use. In the 1990s, more than a dozen states have passed laws making it illegal to publicly disparage the quality of perishable items — that is, fruits and vegetables — without having "sound scientific inquiry, facts, or data" to back you up.

Landlords can't advertise that an apartment is "within walking distance to synagogue" — an effective marketing point for Orthodox Jews, who aren't supposed to drive on the Sabbath — because it allegedly implies an intent to discriminate. Colleges try to ban politically incorrect speech; the University of Connecticut ordered students not to engage in "inappropriately directed laughter, inconsiderate jokes, and conspicuous exclusion [of another student] from conversation." (To be precise here, I believe that private colleges have the right to set rules for how their faculty and students will interact, including speech codes — which is not to say that such codes would be wise. But state colleges are bound by the First Amendment.)

And of course every new technology brings with it new demands for censorship from those who don't understand it, or who understand all too well that new forms of communication may shake up established orders. The 1996 telecommunications reform act, which admirably deregulated much of the industry, nevertheless included a Communications Decency Act that would prevent adults from seeing material that might be inappropriate for children. A 1996 law in France requires that at least 40 percent of the music broadcast by radio stations be French. It also requires that every second French song come from an artist who has never had a hit. "We're forcing listeners to listen to music they don't want to hear," says a radio programmer.

Most important, people who want to spend money to support the political candidates of their choice are limited to contributions of $1,000 — sort of like telling the *New York Times* that it can write an editorial endorsing Bill Clinton but it can only print 1,000 copies of the paper. That's how the political establishment, while proclaiming its devotion to free speech, hobbles the kind of speech that might actually threaten its power.

There's a utilitarian argument for freedom of expression, of course: out of the clash of different opinions, truth will emerge. As John Milton[2] put it, "Who ever knew Truth put to the worse in the free and open encounter?" But for most libertarians, the *primary* reason to defend free expression is individual rights.

The right of self-ownership certainly implies the right to decide for ourselves what food, drink, or drugs we will put into our own bodies; with whom we will make love (assuming our chosen partner agrees); and what kind of medical treatment we want (assuming a doctor agrees to provide it). These decisions are surely as personal and intimate as the choice of what to believe. We may make mistakes (at least in the eyes of others), but our ownership of our own lives means that others must confine their interference to advice and moral suasion, not coercion. And in a free society, such advice should come from private parties, not from government, which is at least potentially coercive (and in our own society is indeed quite coercive). The role of government is to protect our rights, not to poke its nose into our personal lives. Yet a few state governments as recently as 1980 banned alcohol in restaurants, and some twenty states today outlaw homosexual relations. The federal government currently prohibits the use of certain lifesaving and pain-relieving drugs that are available in Europe. It threatens us with prison if we choose to use such drugs as marijuana or cocaine. Even when it doesn't ban something, the government intrudes into our personal choices. It hectors us about smoking, nags us to eat a proper diet — all our daily foods organized into a neat pyramid chart — and advises us on how to have safe and happy sex. Libertarians don't mind advice, but we don't think the government should forcibly take our tax money and then use it to advise everyone in society on how to live. . . .

What Rights Aren't

As the complaints about a proliferation of rights indicate, political debate in modern America is indeed driven by claims of rights. To some extent this reflects the overwhelming triumph of (classical) rights-based liberalism in the United States. Locke, Jefferson, Madison, and the abolitionists laid down as a fundamental rule of both law and public opinion that the function of government is to protect rights. Thus, any rights claim effectively trumps any other consideration in public policy.

Unfortunately, academic and popular understanding of natural rights has declined over the years. Too many Americans now believe that any de-

40

---

[2]*John Milton:* English poet and defender of a free press (1608–74).

sirable thing is a right. They fail to distinguish between a right and a value. Some claim a right to a job, others a right to be protected from the existence of pornography somewhere in town. Some claim a right not to be bothered by cigarette smoke in restaurants, others a right not to be fired if they are smokers. Gay activists claim a right not to be discriminated against; their opponents — echoing Mencken's jibe that Puritanism is "the haunting fear that someone, somewhere may be happy" — claim a right to know that no one is engaging in homosexual relationships. Thousands of lobbyists roam the halls of Congress claiming for their clients a right to welfare, housing, education, Social Security, farm subsidies, protection from imports, and so on.

As courts and legislatures recognize more and more such "rights," rights claims become ever more audacious. A woman in Boston claims "my constitutional right to work out with [the heaviest] weights I can lift," even if the heaviest weights at her gym are in the men's weight room, which is off limits to women. A man in Annapolis, Maryland, demands that the city council require pizza and other food-delivery companies to deliver to his neighborhood, which the companies say is too dangerous, and the council is receptive to his request. He says, "I want the same rights any other Annapolitan has." But no Annapolitan has the right to force anyone else to do business with him, especially when the company feels it would be putting its employees in danger. A deaf man is suing the YMCA, which won't certify him for lifeguard duty because, according to the YMCA, a lifeguard needs to be able to hear cries of distress. An unmarried couple in California claim a right to rent an apartment from a woman who says their relationship offends her religious beliefs.

How do we sort out all these rights claims? There are two basic approaches. First, we can decide on the basis of political power. Anyone who can persuade a majority of Congress, or a state legislature, or the Supreme Court, will have a "right" to whatever he desires. In that case, we will have a plethora of conflicting rights claims, and the demands on the public treasury will be limitless, but we'll have no theory to deal with them; when conflicts occur, the courts and legislatures will sort them out on an ad hoc basis. Whoever seems most sympathetic, or has the most political power, wins.

The other approach is to go back to first principles, to assess each rights claim in the light of each individual's right to life, liberty, and property. Fundamental rights *cannot* conflict. Any claim of conflicting rights must represent a misinterpretation of fundamental rights. That's one of the premises, and the virtues, of rights theory: because rights are universal, they can be enjoyed by every person at the same time in any society. Adherence to first principles may require us, in any given instance, to reject a rights claim by a sympathetic petitioner or to acknowledge someone else's right to engage in actions that most of us find offensive. What does it mean to have a right, after all, if it doesn't include the right to do wrong?

To acknowledge people's ability to take responsibility for their actions, 45
the very essence of a rights-bearing entity, is to accept each person's right to

be "irresponsible" in his exercise of those rights, subject to the minimal condition that he not violate the rights of others. David Hume[3] recognized that justice frequently required us to make decisions that seem unfortunate in a given context: "However single acts of justice may be contrary, either to public or private interest, 'tis certain, that the whole plan or scheme is highly conducive, or indeed absolutely requisite, both to the support of society, and the well-being of every individual." Thus, he says, we may sometimes have to "restore a great fortune to a miser or a seditious bigot," but "every individual person must find himself a gainer" from the peace, order, and prosperity that a system of property rights establishes in society.

[3]*David Hume:* Scottish philosopher and historian (1711–1776).

Engaging the Text

1. What's wrong with the concept of individual rights, according to Boaz? What evidence, if any, do you see that Americans have become overly concerned with the issue of rights?

2. Explain the distinction Boaz makes between a "liberal" and an "interventionist" state. Are there any rights (for example, the right to education, safe working conditions, clean water, a minimum wage, or medical treatment) that should be guaranteed by the government? Why or why not?

3. Why, according to Boaz, do all rights, like the right of free speech, boil down to property rights? Can you think of any fundamental rights (like the right to vote, to assemble, or to protest) that might challenge this definition? To what extent do you agree with his belief that "fundamental rights" never conflict?

4. Toward the end of the selection, Boaz asks what it means "to have a right, after all, if it doesn't include the right to do wrong?" (para. 44). What exactly does Boaz mean by this? Do you agree that all real rights should entail the "right to do wrong"?

Exploring Connections

5. Compare Boaz's understanding of rights with that expressed in the Declaration of Independence (p. 684). How would Boaz probably interpret the Declaration's assertion that all people are endowed with "certain unalienable Rights," including the right to "Life, Liberty, and the pursuit of Happiness"?

6. How might the Native Americans mentioned in Colin G. Calloway's "New Peoples and New Societies" (p. 688) respond to Boaz's claim that all human rights derive from the "homesteading principle" (para. 27) and the right to own property? Which rights might the Native Americans described by Calloway have recognized as "fundamental" rights? Which would they have been likely to label "phony"?

7. Compare Boaz's view of the individual and society to that of Bill McKibben in "TV, Freedom, and the Loss of Community" (p. 718). To what extent do their views of individual rights appear to differ? How would you expect each of them to envision the ideal society? Which of these visions would be more attractive to you, and why?

EXTENDING THE CRITICAL CONTEXT

8. Review a week's worth of newspapers to determine just how "awash" America seems to be in talk about rights. Does your research confirm or challenge the impression that America is overly focused on issues of individual rights?

9. Boaz claims that all human rights derive from the primary right to own property and implies that all conflicts between rights can be resolved by applying this principle. How might the principle of property rights be applied to resolve conflict in the following situations:

   - An elementary school teacher sues his school district after he is fired when it is discovered that he operates a child pornography Web site from his home.
   - A Christian landlord is sued when he refuses to rent to a rap musician because he believes that rap music is influenced by the devil.
   - Several African American cadets at a private military academy refuse to obey orders until their classmates remove Confederate and Nazi flags from their dormitory doors.
   - A group of gay and lesbian Irish Americans sue the organizers of a St. Patrick's Day parade when they are banned from participating.
   - A women's group at a state university calls for disciplinary action against a fraternity that publishes a songbook that includes lyrics advocating violence against women.
   - A fast food chain is sued by a national civil rights organization after an independent study shows that the chain consistently refuses or slows service to Mexican Americans.
   - A Rastafarian Jamaican American is jailed because she insists on smoking marijuana as part of her religious observance.
   - A coalition of American Indian tribes files suit asking for compensation for the loss of Indian lands.

   Does the principle of property rights lead to a clear and just resolution of these cases? Can you think of any other basic principles that might provide a more adequate foundation for all other human rights?

Hate Radio

Patricia J. Williams

> *America's fascination with in-your-face free speech has no better em-*
> *bodiment than talk radio: millions tune in daily to hear commentators like*
> *Howard Stern and Rush Limbaugh hold forth on everything from phone sex*
> *to the state of the union. But not every American is charmed by the new*
> *candor on the airwaves. In the following essay, Patricia J. Williams asks if*
> *the hatred vented on talk radio isn't preparing America for a renaissance of*
> *intolerance and bigotry. For more information on Patricia J. Williams, see*
> *page 604. This essay originally appeared in* Ms. *(March/April 1994).*

Three years ago I stood at my sink, washing the dishes and listening to
the radio. I was tuned to rock and roll so I could avoid thinking about the
big news from the day before — George Bush had just nominated Clarence
Thomas to replace Thurgood Marshall on the Supreme Court. I was
squeezing a dot of lemon Joy into each of the wineglasses when I realized
that two smoothly radio-cultured voices, a man's and a woman's, had replaced the music.

"I think it's a stroke of genius on the president's part," said the female
voice.

"Yeah," said the male voice. "Then those blacks, those African Americans, those Negroes — hey 'Negro' is good enough for Thurgood Marshall —
whatever, they can't make up their minds [what] they want to be called. I'm
gonna call them Blafricans. Black Africans. Yeah, I like it. Blafricans. Then
they can get all upset because now the president appointed a Blafrican."

"Yeah, well, that's the way those liberals think. It's just crazy."

"And then after they turn down his nomination the president can say   5
he tried to please 'em, and then he can appoint someone with some
intelligence."

Back then, this conversation seemed so horrendously unusual, so singularly hateful, that I picked up a pencil and wrote it down. I was certain that
a firestorm of protest was going to engulf the station and purge those foul
radio mouths with the good clean soap of social outrage.

I am so naive. When I finally turned on the radio and rolled my dial to
where everyone else had been tuned while I was busy watching Cosby reruns, it took me a while to understand that there's a firestorm all right, but
not of protest. In the two and a half years since Thomas has assumed his
post on the Supreme Court, the underlying assumptions of the conversation
I heard as uniquely outrageous have become commonplace, popularly ex-

pressed, and louder in volume. I hear the style of that snide polemicism everywhere, among acquaintances, on the street, on television in toned-down versions. It is a crude demagoguery that makes me heartsick. I feel more and more surrounded by that point of view, the assumptions of being without intelligence, the coded epithets, the "Blafrican"-like stand-ins for "nigger," the mocking angry glee, the endless tirades filled with nonspecific, nonempirically based slurs against "these people" or "those minorities" or "feminazis" or "liberals" or "scumbags" or "pansies" or "jerks" or "sleaze-balls" or "loonies" or "animals" or "foreigners."

At the same time I am not so naive as to suppose that this is something new. In clearheaded moments I realize I am not listening to the radio anymore, I am listening to a large segment of white America think aloud in ever louder resurgent thoughts that have generations of historical precedent. It's as though the radio has split open like an egg, Morton Downey, Jr.'s[1] clones and Joe McCarthy's[2] ghost spilling out, broken yolks, a great collective of sometimes clever, sometimes small, but uniformly threatened brains — they have all come gushing out. Just as they were about to pass into oblivion, Jack Benny and his humble black sidekick Rochester get resurrected in the ungainly bodies of Howard Stern and his faithful black henchwoman, Robin Quivers. The culture of Amos and Andy[3] has been revived and re-assembled in Bob Grant's radio minstrelsy and radio newcomer Daryl Gates's[4] sanctimonious imprecations on behalf of decent white people. And in striking imitation of Jesse Helms's[5] nearly forgotten days as a radio host, the far Right has found its undisputed king in the personage of Rush Limbaugh — a polished demagogue with a weekly radio audience of at least twenty million, a television show that vies for ratings with the likes of Jay Leno, a newsletter with a circulation of 380,000, and two best-selling books whose combined sales are closing in on six million copies.

From Churchill to Hitler to the old Soviet Union, it's clear that radio and television have the power to change the course of history, to proselytize, and to coalesce not merely the good and the noble, but the very worst in human nature as well. Likewise, when Orson Welles[6] made his famous radio broadcast "witnessing" the landing of a spaceship full of hostile Martians, the United States ought to have learned a lesson about the power of

[1]*Morton Downey, Jr.:* 1980s talk show host famed for baiting guests and discussing incendiary topics.

[2]*Joe McCarthy:* Joseph R. McCarthy (1908–1957), U.S. senator and chairman of the infamous Senate subcommittee that investigated so-called un-American activities during the anti-communist hysteria of the 1950s.

[3]*Amos and Andy:* Popular 1950s TV series often seen as promoting racist stereotypes of African Americans.

[4]*Daryl Gates:* Former Los Angeles Police Department chief and host of his own conservative radio show.

[5]*Jesse Helms:* Conservative U.S. senator (b. 1921).

[6]*Orson Welles:* American actor and movie director (1915–1985).

radio to appeal to mass instincts and incite mass hysteria. Radio remains a peculiarly powerful medium even today, its visual emptiness in a world of six trillion flashing images allowing one of the few remaining playgrounds for the aural subconscious. Perhaps its power is attributable to our need for an oral tradition after all, some conveying of stories, feelings, myths of ancestors, epics of alienation, and the need to rejoin ancestral roots, even ignorant bigoted roots. Perhaps the visual quiescence of radio is related to the popularity of E-mail or electronic networking. Only the voice is made manifest, unmasking worlds that cannot — or dare not? — be seen. Just yet. Nostalgia crystallizing into a dangerous future. The preconscious voice erupting into the expressed, the prime time.

What comes out of the modern radio mouth could be the *Iliad*,[7] the   10
Rubaiyat,[8] the griot's[9] song of our times. If indeed radio is a vessel for the American "Song of Songs," then what does it mean that a manic, adolescent Howard Stern is so popular among radio listeners, that Rush Limbaugh's wittily smooth sadism has gone the way of prime-time television, and that both vie for the number one slot on all the best-selling book lists? What to make of the stories being told by our modern radio evangelists and their tragic unloved chorus of callers? Is it really just a collapsing economy that spawns this drama of grown people sitting around scaring themselves to death with fantasies of black feminist Mexican able-bodied gay soldiers earning $100,000 a year on welfare who are so criminally depraved that Hillary Clinton or the Antichrist-of-the-moment had no choice but to invite them onto the government payroll so they can run the country? The panicky exaggeration reminds me of a child's fear. . . . *And then, and then, a huge lion jumped out of the shadows and was about to gobble me up, and I can't ever sleep again for a whole week.*

As I spin the dial on my radio, I can't help thinking that this stuff must be related to that most poignant of fiber-optic phenomena, phone sex. Aural Sex. Radio Racism with a touch of S & M. High-priest hosts with the power and run-amok ego to discipline listeners, to smack with the verbal back of the hand, to smash the button that shuts you up once and for all. "Idiot!" shouts New York City radio demagogue Bob Grant and then the sound of droning telephone emptiness, the voice of dissent dumped out some trapdoor in aural space.

As I listened to a range of such programs what struck me as the most unifying theme was not merely the specific intolerance on such hot topics as race and gender, but a much more general contempt for the world, a verbal stoning of anything different. It is like some unusually violent game of

---

[7]*Iliad:* Ancient Greek epic poem of Trojan war commonly attributed to Homer (9th–8th? century B.C.).

[8]*Rubaiyat:* Persian epic poem written by Omar Khayyám (1048?–1131?).

[9]*griot:* A singer of tales in African oral tradition.

"Simon Says," this mockery and shouting down of callers, this roar of incantations, the insistence on agreement.

But, ah, if you *will* but only agree, what sweet and safe reward, what soft enfolding by a stern and angry radio god. And as an added bonus, the invisible shield of an AM community, a family of fans who are Exactly Like You, to whom you can express, in anonymity, all the filthy stuff you imagine "them" doing to you. The comfort and relief of being able to ejaculate, to those who understand, about the dark imagined excess overtaking, robbing, needing to be held down and taught a good lesson, needing to put it in its place before the ravenous demon enervates all that is true and good and pure in this life.

The audience for this genre of radio flagellation is mostly young, white, and male. Two thirds of Rush Limbaugh's audience is male. According to *Time* magazine, 75 percent of Howard Stern's listeners are white men. Most of the callers have spent their lives walling themselves off from any real experience with blacks, feminists, lesbians, or gays. In this regard, it is probably true, as former Secretary of Education William Bennett says, that Rush Limbaugh "tells his audience that what you believe inside, you can talk about in the marketplace." Unfortunately, what's "inside" is then mistaken for what's outside, treated as empirical and political reality. The *National Review* extols Limbaugh's conservative leadership as no less than that of Ronald Reagan, and the Republican party provides Limbaugh with books to discuss, stories, angles, and public support. "People were afraid of censure by gay activists, feminists, environmentalists — now they are not because Rush takes them on," says Bennett.

U.S. history has been marked by cycles in which brands of this or that 15 hatred come into fashion and go out, are unleashed and then restrained. If racism, homophobia, jingoism, and woman-hating have been features of national life in pretty much all of modern history, it rather begs the question to spend a lot of time wondering if right-wing radio is a symptom or a cause. For at least 400 years, prevailing attitudes in the West have considered African Americans less intelligent. Recent statistics show that 53 percent of people in the United States agree that blacks and Latinos are less intelligent than whites, and a majority believe that blacks are lazy, violent, welfare-dependent, and unpatriotic.

I think that what has made life more or less tolerable for "out" groups have been those moments in history when those "inside" feelings were relatively restrained. In fact, if I could believe that right-wing radio were only about idiosyncratic, singular, rough-hewn individuals thinking those inside thoughts, I'd be much more inclined to agree with Columbia University media expert Everette Dennis, who says that Stern's and Limbaugh's popularity represents the "triumph of the individual" or with *Time* magazine's bottom line that "the fact that either is seriously considered a threat . . . is more worrisome than Stern or Limbaugh will ever be." If what I were hearing had even a tad more to do with real oppressions, with real white *and* black levels of joblessness and homelessness, or with the real problems of real white men, then I wouldn't have bothered to slog my way through hours of Howard Stern's miserable obsessions.

Yet at the heart of my anxiety is the worry that Stern, Limbaugh, Grant, et al. represent the very antithesis of individualism's triumph. As the *National Review* said of Limbaugh's ascent, "It was a feat not only of the loudest voice but also of a keen political brain to round up, as Rush did, the media herd and drive them into the conservative corral." When asked about his political aspirations, Bob Grant gloated to the *Washington Post*, "I think I would make rather a good dictator."

The polemics of right-wing radio are putting nothing less than hate onto the airwaves, into the marketplace, electing it to office, teaching it in schools, and exalting it as freedom. What worries me is the increasing-to-constant commerce of retribution, control, and lashing out, fed not by fact but fantasy. What worries me is the re-emergence, more powerfully than at any time since the institution of Jim Crow,[10] of a socio-centered self that excludes "the likes of," well, me for example, from the civic circle, and that would rob me of my worth and claim and identity as a citizen. As the *Economist* rightly observes, "Mr. Limbaugh takes a mass market — white, mainly male, middle-class, ordinary America — and talks to it as an endangered minority."

I worry about this identity whose external reference is a set of beliefs, ethics, and practices that excludes, restricts, and acts in the world on me, or mine, as the perceived if not real enemy. I am acutely aware of losing *my* mythic individualism to the surface shapes of my mythic group fearsomeness as black, as female, as left wing. "I" merge not fluidly but irretrievably into a category of "them." I become a suspect self, a moving target of loathsome properties, not merely different but dangerous. And that worries me a lot.

What happens in my life with all this translated license, this permission   20
to be uncivil? What happens to the social space that was supposedly at the sweet mountaintop of the civil rights movement's trail? Can I get a seat on the bus without having to be reminded that I *should* be standing? Did the civil rights movement guarantee us nothing more than to use public accommodations while surrounded by raving lunatic bigots? "They didn't beat this idiot [Rodney King] enough," says Howard Stern.

Not long ago I had the misfortune to hail a taxicab in which the driver was listening to Howard Stern undress some woman. After some blocks, I had to get out. I was, frankly, afraid to ask the driver to turn it off — not because I was afraid of "censoring" him, which seems to be the only thing people will talk about anymore, but because the driver was stripping me

---

[10]*Jim Crow:* Laws enacted in the post–Civil War South that mandated racial segregation.

too, as he leered through the rearview mirror. "Something the matter?" he demanded, as I asked him to pull over and let me out well short of my destination. (I'll spare you the full story of what happened from there — trying to get another cab, as the cabbies stopped for all the white businessmen who so much as scratched their heads near the curb; a nice young white man, seeing my plight, giving me his cab, having to thank him, he hero, me saved-but-humiliated, cabdriver pissed and surly. I fight my way to my destination, finally arriving in bad mood, militant black woman, cranky feminazi.)

When Yeltsin blared rock music at his opponents holed up in the parliament building in Moscow, in imitation of the U.S. Marines trying to torture Manuel Noriega in Panama, all I could think of was that it must be like being trapped in a crowded subway car when all the portable stereos are tuned to Bob Grant or Howard Stern. With Howard Stern's voice a tinny, screeching backdrop, with all the faces growing dreamily mean as though some soporifically evil hallucinogen were gushing into their bloodstreams, I'd start begging to surrender.

Surrender to what? Surrender to the laissez-faire resegregation that is the metaphoric significance of the hundreds of "Rush rooms" that have cropped up in restaurants around the country; rooms broadcasting Limbaugh's words, rooms for your listening pleasure, rooms where bigots can capture the purity of a Rush-only lunch counter, rooms where all those unpleasant others just "choose" not to eat? Surrender to the naughty luxury of a room in which a Ku Klux Klan meeting could take place in orderly, First Amendment fashion? Everyone's "free" to come in (and a few of you outsiders do), but mostly the undesirable nonconformists are gently repulsed away. It's a high-tech world of enhanced choice. Whites choose mostly to sit in the Rush room. Feminists, blacks, lesbians, and gays "choose" to sit elsewhere. No need to buy black votes, you must pay them not to vote; no need to insist on white only schools, you just sell the desirability of black-only schools. Just sit back and watch it work, like those invisible shock shields that keep dogs cowering in their own backyards.

How real is the driving perception behind all the Sturm und Drang[11] of this genre of radio-harangue — the perception that white men are an oppressed minority, with no power and no opportunity in the land that they made great? While it is true that power and opportunity are shrinking for all but the very wealthy in this country (and would that Limbaugh would take that issue on), the fact remains that white men are still this country's most privileged citizens and market actors. To give just a small example, according to the *Wall Street Journal*, blacks were the only racial group to suffer a net job loss during the 1990–91 economic downturn at the companies reporting to the Equal Employment Opportunity Commission. Whites,

---

[11]*Sturm und Drang:* "Storm and Passion": a Romantic German literary movement of the eighteenth century; here, something like impassioned posturing.

Latinos, and Asians, meanwhile, gained thousands of jobs. While whites gained 71,144 jobs at these companies, Latinos gained 60,040, Asians gained 55,104, and blacks lost 59,479. If every black were hired in the United States tomorrow, the numbers would not be sufficient to account for white men's expanding balloon of fear that they have been specifically dispossessed by African Americans.

Given deep patterns of social segregation and general ignorance of history, particularly racial history, media remain the principal source of most Americans' knowledge of each other. Media can provoke violence or induce passivity. In San Francisco, for example, a radio show on KMEL called "Street Soldiers" has taken this power as a responsibility with great consequence: "Unquestionably," writes Ken Auletta in *The New Yorker*, "the show has helped avert violence. When a Samoan teenager was slain, apparently by Filipino gang members, in a drive-by shooting, the phones lit up with calls from Samoans wanting to tell [the hosts] they would not rest until they had exacted revenge. Threats filled the air for a couple of weeks. Then the dead Samoan's father called in, and, in a poignant exchange, the father said he couldn't tolerate the thought of more young men senselessly slaughtered. There would be no retaliation, he vowed. And there was none." In contrast, we must wonder at the phenomenon of the very powerful leadership of the Republican party, from Ronald Reagan to Robert Dole to William Bennett, giving advice, counsel, and friendship to Rush Limbaugh's passionate divisiveness.

25

The outright denial of the material crisis at every level of U.S. society, most urgently in black inner-city neighborhoods but facing us all, is a kind of political circus, dissembling as it feeds the frustrations of the moment. We as a nation can no longer afford to deal with such crises by *imagining* an excess of bodies, of babies, of job-stealers, of welfare mothers, of overreaching immigrants, of too-powerful (Jewish, in whispers) liberal Hollywood, of lesbians and gays, of gang members ("gangsters" remain white, and no matter what the atrocity, less vilified than "gang members," who are black), of Arab terrorists, and uppity women. The reality of our social poverty far exceeds these scapegoats. This right-wing backlash resembles, in form if not substance, phenomena like anti-Semitism in Poland: there aren't but a handful of Jews left in that whole country, but the giant balloon of heated anti-Semitism flourishes apace, Jews blamed for the world's evils.

The overwhelming response to right-wing excesses in the United States has been to seek an odd sort of comfort in the fact that the First Amendment is working so well that you can't suppress this sort of thing. Look what's happened in Eastern Europe. Granted. So let's not talk about censorship or the First Amendment for the next ten minutes. But in Western Europe, where fascism is rising at an appalling rate, suppression is hardly the problem. In Eastern and Western Europe as well as the United States, we must begin to think just a little bit about the fiercely coalescing power of media to spark mistrust, to fan it into forest fires of fear and revenge. We must begin to think about the levels of national and social complacence in the face of such resolute ignorance. We must ask ourselves what the expected result is, not of censorship or suppression, but of so much encouragement, so much support, so much investment in the fashionability of hate. What future is it that we are designing with the devotion of such tremendous resources to the disgraceful propaganda of bigotry?

ENGAGING THE TEXT

1. What does Williams mean when she says that she hears the "snide polemicism" of talk radio everywhere in contemporary America? To what extent do you agree that "crude demagoguery" has infected the way Americans think and relate to each other?

2. How does Williams account for talk radio's popularity? Which of her explanations strikes you as the most plausible? Why? What other reasons can you offer?

3. What worries does Williams express about talk shows like Rush Limbaugh's? What, according to her, are such shows doing to America? Do you agree?

4. Williams mentions an incident in which she was forced to leave a cab because its driver was listening to Howard Stern "undress" a woman on the air. Should she have asked the cabdriver to turn the radio off? Should

people in public places be allowed to listen to shows that may be racially or sexually offensive?

5. What is "laissez-faire segregation"? Is segregation acceptable if it is a matter of choice?

6. Although Williams criticizes talk radio, she offers little sense of what should be done to curb "the disgraceful propaganda of bigotry" it produces. What, if anything, should be done to address the excesses of shows like Howard Stern's and Rush Limbaugh's?

EXPLORING CONNECTIONS

7. Drawing on June Jordan's "Freedom Time" (p. 712), Bill McKibben's "TV, Freedom, and the Loss of Community" (p. 718), and Williams's "Hate Radio," write a paper exploring the dangers that the mass media may pose in a democracy.

8. Review Gerry Spence's discussion of the risks entailed by real freedom in "Easy in the Harness" (p. 695), paying special attention to his observations on "old Jack" (para. 14). How might Spence interpret the "hate" Williams condemns on talk radio? How different are the opinions and the confrontational style of "old Jack" from those of talk radio stars like Howard Stern and Rush Limbaugh?

9. Write a brief dialogue between Williams and David Boaz (p. 732) on the right of radio station owners to broadcast any content they see fit. Ultimately, whose position do you find more sympathetic, and why?

10. Imagine what TV show the characters are about to watch in the Callahan cartoon (p. 752) and write a sample of the language they are likely to hear. Who would be offended by it? Who would enjoy it? Why? Compare notes with your classmates and discuss.

EXTENDING THE CRITICAL CONTEXT

11. Working in small groups, listen to an hour or more of "hate radio" hosted by any of the commentators Williams mentions. How many unsupported assertions are made during the show? How many derogatory labels or slurs are used? Overall, would you agree that such shows are providing America with "the disgraceful propaganda of bigotry"?

The Price of Admission:
Harassment and Free Speech
in the Wild, Wild West

STEPHANIE BRAIL

Since the first European expeditions settled on the East Coast, Americans have associated the idea of freedom with life on the frontier. It was on the edges of western expansion that Americans seemed to be most liberated from the dogmas and traditions associated with the Old World of Europe. Today, America's frontiers are electronic, not geographic. If you want to experience real freedom in contemporary America, you have to get on the electronic superhighway and travel on the Internet. But as Stephanie Brail points out in the following article, while the "new wild west" offers freedom of expression, it may also be just as inhospitable to women as any sagebrush outpost of the 1800s. An "Internet resident" since 1988, Brail discovered the price of freedom when she became the focus of the first case of sexual harassment on the Net to attract national attention. Brail created the Spiderwoman mailing list for women Web designers and is also cofounder of Digital Amazon, an Internet company dedicated to promoting the interests of women online. You can visit her acclaimed Web site, Amazon City, the first "electronic city" for women, at http://www.amazoncity.com. This essay was authologized in Wired Women: Gender and New Realities in Cyberspace *(1996), Lynn Cherny and Elizabeth R. Weire, editors.*

Online harassment has become a media headliner in the last few years. I should know: I was the target of one of the more sensationalized cases of "sexual harassment" on the Internet. When I wrote about my and others' experiences with online harassment, I found myself inundated by requests for interviews with other reporters writing the same story. I've been quoted in *USA Today,* interviewed by *Glamour,* pursued by the local ABC news affiliate and pounced on by editors at *Mademoiselle,* who wanted, I assume, a juicy tale of cyberspace stalking to sell more issues of their magazine.

Online harassment is a tough issue. Finding the fine line between censorship and safety and creating a better environment for women in cyberspace, are complex tasks. As I've wrestled with these issues, one of the sharpest areas of concern for me has become the effect harassment has on our most precious online commodity: Free speech.

Wanna Fuck?

Just what is online harassment? If someone sends you a request for sex in email, is that harassment? What if someone calls you a name online? A woman is called a "curmudgeon" and complains that the poster is harassing and slandering her. Is he? Many might define online harassment as unwanted, threatening or offensive email, "instant messages" ("sends" or "chats" on some systems) or other personal communication that persists in spite of requests that it stop. But this is a poor definition, because what is unwanted, threatening, or offensive to one person may not be to another. Sometimes it seems as if the definition boils down to a personal one of "I know it when I see it."

There is a huge gap between legal definitions of harassment and what we describe as online harassment in common parlance. The legal aspects will come later; for now, let's look at the nonlegal definition.

Much of what is termed "online harassment" is "wanna fuck" email. A   5
"wanna fuck" is simply an email request for a date or sex. An email asking for a date is not in and of itself harassment, but what bothers many women on the Internet and on online services is the frequency and persistence of these kinds of messages. America Online's (AOL) chat rooms, for example, are notorious for having a barlike atmosphere . . . should you enter a chat room using a woman's login name, you're likely to find yourself the target of a wanna fuck "instant message" from some man you've never even heard of. Though AOL has strict rules of conduct, called their Terms of Service, which explicitly ban harassment, as well as obscenity, chain letters, and other "offensive" types of online communication, the staff at AOL is hard-pressed to be at all places at once, so the Terms of Service do not guarantee a "safe environment," however hard AOL tries.

I would guess that wanna fuck email generates the bulk of online harassment complaints, and that repeated, targeted harassment of the kind I experienced is actually quite rare. So I'm not sure if online harassment has become a media hot-button because it is a matter of concern or because it creates another sensational headline, or both. So much hype and angst has been whipped up over this issue, it's hard to look at it objectively anymore. Many users get really riled up about having a safe environment online, but equal numbers, many of them women, are so sick of this subject they don't ever want to see another article about it as long as they live.

Enter the Online Harassment Poster Queen

That I had a harrowing online experience in 1993 was one thing. That it brought me my fifteen minutes of fame was more disappointing, to say the least. When I first spoke out about online harassment, I meant it as a call to arms, a message to women that it was time to take hold of the keyboard and carve out some female space in the online world. I was apparently riding a wave of media interest, set in motion by some genuine activism on the part of many dedicated women activists and computer mavens, but the bigger force was, of course, the American lust for a new victim.

My experience of harassment coincided with an article I was writing on sexism online for *On the Issues,* a small feminist quarterly out of New York. When my editor found out I was being harassed, she thought it would be great to add that personal touch to my story, which turned into an article about online harassment called "Take Back the Net."

When I began writing the article I noticed that what seemed like every other reporter and freelance writer in the business was working on the same story I was. Next thing I knew, I was being interviewed about my experience instead of writing about it. That was 1993, when the Internet was still just a blip on the national media scene. If the number of interviews I did is any indication, harassment took up an inordinate amount of ink that year. Two years later I was still getting calls from reporters.

I believe these stories of online harassment are told and retold partially 10
because of the "car wreck fascination" factor, but more importantly because we all keenly feel our vulnerability in the new medium of computer-mediated communication. Women, especially, need to discuss and understand the implications of online harassment because it affects our ability to use the medium and, thereby, to take part in something that will only become more important to our freedom. How many women would have voted had polling places been in dark alleys?

The Online Car Wreck

Here's my story. It has become, even in my mind, more of a sound bite than something real. The gory details have been swept away in the interest of something quotable; the actual event a faint memory while the intellectualizations I created around it abound.

What happened is less interesting than why it happened. I was harassed not because I was an innocent bystander, or another female using the Internet, but because I had a mouth. I dared to speak out in the common space of the Internet, Usenet.

Usenet is a collection of online discussion conferences or forums available to almost all Internet users. My boyfriend and I had been reading the Usenet newsgroup *alt.zines* to discuss underground, homemade publications, because we were in the process of creating our own zine.

I don't remember exactly how the flame war/argument started, but a young woman had posted to the group a request to talk about Riot Grrls zines. Riot Grrls is a political and social movement of young punk postfeminists, inspired by girl bands like Bikini Kill and the Breeders, and a hallmark of the movement is the numerous fanzines created to support these bands. At the mention of Riot Grrls, some of the men on the group started posting vehemently in protest. They didn't want to talk about those stupid girl bands; the girls couldn't play anyway. Someone suggested that the young woman start her own newsgroup called "alt.grrl.dumbcunts."

In spite of having been online for years, I had never really participated   15 in Usenet before and had no idea how much anti-female sentiment was running, seemingly unchecked, on many Usenet forums. When I saw the treatment this woman was getting in response to her request to discuss Riot Grrls, I was not only appalled, but also incredibly angry.

The woman who wrote the original note fought back, posting angry, curt responses to the one or two men who were leading the charge against the "stupid" Riot Grrls. My blood pressure increasing, my heart pounding and my body aching for justice, I joined the fray. I'm a natural writer — wordy, passionate — and, in a world where you are your words, I am loud. I bellow, I scream, I prognosticate. I was writing what I thought at the time were noble words, defending the honor of all women.

That was my first flame war. Probably my best. What an ego-driven experience! I had fans of both sexes emailing me letters of encouragement. Most of my detractors responded with a lot of sexist drivel, and several people, who identified themselves as Internet old-timers, tried to explain (to my deaf ears) that I obviously must be a newbie or I wouldn't be getting so upset. (Looking back, they were right; being online for a while makes you increasingly blasé about online slights.) To a certain extent, the whole thing embarrasses me now, but at the time, I didn't think I was doing anything wrong. I felt I had to speak up, largely because a few men were telling us women to sit down, shut up and go away.

It's hard to explain the kind of high you can get while participating in a flame war; in some ways it's like being on a roller coaster — your stomach may be churning, but it is a delicious kind of sickening feeling, steeped with adrenaline. I had never participated so much online. I came home from work dying to see what the responses were to my posts. Then the harassment started.

I was not the first target. One of the women sticking up for Riot Grrls, perhaps the one who originally started the topic, received obscene email from a guy named "Mike." The email was anonymous — sent with no real name and with a fake return email address. She posted the letter to the group to show how the flame war had degraded. Others received similar emails. Then my boyfriend, who had been one of the guys sticking up for women, received a few nasty ones, asking him why he supported Riot Grrls — "fuck 'em, their daddies did," one anonymous email said. Another one said: "Heh heh — I'd love to see a porno with a father doing his Riot Grrl daughter — she has a bad haircut and is wearing boots with a pink mini. He says, this will give you something to rant about! As he sodomizes her little riot ass."

"What should I do with this?" my boyfriend asked.   20

"Just ignore it," I responded. "What a jerk."

Easier said than done. My boyfriend posted one of the notes back to the group anyway, with a sarcastic message of disapproval. Even though

"Mike" had no idea my boyfriend and I knew each other, soon after that I became the target.

When I received email with the word "cunt" splashed across the screen, I became sick to my stomach. The harassment was a shock; in spite of the mess on the newsgroup, I hadn't expected it. But I was shaking, less from fear than from anger. I tried to email a response to the guy, but the message automatically bounced back to my mailbox, compounding the insult. So, as everyone else had done, I posted the note back to the group, coupled with some very nasty comments.

In response, I found more email messages in my box the next day, and the next day, and the next. Reams of pornographic text detailing gang rapes. Strange, poorly formatted messages full of long ramblings about how the poster was a writer and how he found all this so interesting. There were details about a girlfriend, Valerie, who purportedly worked at some great book publisher in New York. He was harassing me because he was going to write a story about it, he told me.

Each message was from a different fake email address, with a different   25
name on it. I had no way of telling which messages were from friends and which were from my foe. It made me sick to read much of the stuff he sent me, but I went through most of it, trying to find a clue as to who this person was.

At this same time, a man on the group sympathetic to our side, Ron, was receiving several emails a day from the same person, although his were less frequent and much tamer. Ron had taken up my cause like the proverbial knight in shining armor. I didn't know him but was relieved to have an ally. We were now battling detractors on the newsgroup, who were sick of the flame wars and totally unsympathetic when we posed public notes telling Mike to stop. Some even told us that by complaining about Mike we were censoring him!

Mike wreaked havoc with my email inbox for several weeks. He wrote a story about the incident, which he posted to the group, but in his warped version of events, I was supposedly turned on by the whole thing. He also faked some posts to another Usenet group, to make it look as if I had posted something he had written. It was only when I got a strange message from someone from *alt.sex.bondage* that I found out Mike had been emailing people there and putting my name and return address on the messages.

Ron and I tried to get help from the system administrators at the university from which the posts originated, but to no avail. The sysadmins told us the only way they could catch him was "in the act." We considered calling the police and the FBI, and only after we made the threat "in public" on the newsgroup did Mike's email slow down to a trickle, though I continued to receive occasional pornographic email from him. Months later I received an email from him at one of my other email addresses. I have no idea how he found the address, but the message he chose to send was chilling: "I know you're in Los Angeles," he wrote. "Maybe I can come for a date and fix your 'plumbing.'"

By this time I was incredibly paranoid. I made sure the doors to our bungalow were always locked; I practiced self-defense. When a male friend called us and left a prank message, I thought Mike had found our number, and I panicked.

But finally, Mike goofed. He sent a message to my boyfriend that left   30
some tracks. My months of dealing with the inner workings of Internet mail paid off, and I was able to track him down. I forwarded the message to his real email box without comment, and I haven't heard from him since.

Although the experience was horrific, it was a tempering kind of fire. It forced me to learn UNIX, the computer language much of the Internet is based on. In response to similar types of harassment, other women created their own spaces to be free of attacks of this kind. In response to the events on *alt.zines,* one young woman began a private female-only mailing list called Riot Grrls, which is still going strong. The support and advice I received on that mailing list during that time were invaluable in keeping me sane and active on the net.

The whole incident has taken its toll, though. I don't trust that this is the last I'll ever hear from Mike, or anyone else, for that matter. I'm careful what kind of information I give out online now — never my home phone number and certainly not my home address. I certainly know how easy it is to make an enemy on the Internet, and I stopped participating in *alt.zines* long ago. I'll probably never post there again. And that's the true fallout: I've censored myself out of fear.

The Big C-word: Censorship

I've censored myself. My choice, right? I'm not so sure. Do I or do I not have the right to speak my mind in public without being harassed, stalked, and threatened because of what I say?

The Internet is the Wild Wild West — as far from the civilized, or at least patrolled, corridors of the commercial online services such as Prodigy as the West was from the streets of Boston. And just as it's easy to romanticize the Wild West, forgetting the abuses that took place during that savage time, it's easy to romanticize these pioneer days of the Internet as well. I myself have loved this time of openness on the net, when relative freedom and a lack of government control made it one of the coolest places to be. It saddens me that some people abuse the freedoms many have taken for granted on the Internet, and that these freedoms are now threatened thanks to such immaturity.

It seems that a truly free space for public discourse is too threatening to   35
the American public and we've only begun to see the start of what's likely to be a long and drawn-out fight to keep alive the delicious anarchy that's been such a fertile ground. Without free speech, the Internet will be as lifeless as, well, corporate broadcasting.

At the same time, I believe that online harassment is, to some extent, already killing free speech on the Internet, in particular the free speech of women, although women aren't the only targets of these vigilante censors.

Shut Up or Put Up

Unfortunately, because of rightful fear of government control, many people see this harassment issue as one that shouldn't be mentioned. And many don't believe it should matter anyway. Just fight back, they tell you. This is easy advice for a loud-mouthed, college-aged know-it-all who has all the time in the world, but does it apply to real, working women, who don't have the time and luxury to "fight back" against online jerks? And should we have to, as the price of admission? Men don't usually have to jump through a hoop of sexual innuendo and anti-feminist backlash simply to participate. They use their energy for posting, while we often use ours wondering if we'll be punished for opening our mouths. And with all our training to be "nice," are most women even prepared to do such battle?

This is not to say that supportive people aren't out there to help. When I was being harassed, new Internet friends from all over the world offered me technical assistance.[1] Many gave freely of their time and knowledge, and some offered to help me construct mail filters to keep out the offensive messages. Some offered to track the harasser down. Many friends offered to email bomb the perpetrator in return, but I declined.

For years a laissez-faire attitude has governed behavior on the Internet. Users didn't turn to lawsuits to solve their problems; they dealt with them using the technical tools available. Any talk of regulation scares users. When I first started talking about online harassment, people criticized me for trying to bring the regulators down on our heads. They should have been yelling at the jerks who abuse the system. For speaking out against online harassment I was likened to an Andrea Dworkin[2] disciple, or worse, Phyllis Schlafly,[3] out to wipe the Internet clean of smut.

Pornography Is Not Harassment

Despite those who believe that certain types of sexual content are harm-   40 ful to women, there is a difference between pornography available online and harassment. If someone wants to post nude pictures to a newsgroup, I

---

[1]Thanks to such help, I now know exactly how "Mike" faked his email messages to me, through a loophole in the UNIX mail system that anyone could exploit. (Mike's not a hacker, but a hack.) Remember: There is no guarantee on the Internet that you are talking to whom you think you are. [Author's note]

[2]*Andrea Dworkin:* Feminist theorist best known for "radical" theories like her belief that all acts of intercourse amount to rape.

[3]*Phyllis Schlafly:* Conservative activist and former president of the Eagle Forum who gained fame by championing antifeminist positions on social issues.

don't have to see them. Not only would I have to decide to go to the news-group myself to see the pictures, I would have to download them *and* decode them *and* have the proper configuration on my computer to see them. If I accidentally went to one of these newsgroups, all I would see on my screen is a bunch of garbled text: the encoded version of the smut. (And maybe some lewd words, but that's about it.)

Unwanted erotica and pornography do become more of an issue with the World Wide Web, where the availability of embedded graphics makes it harder to avoid the online equivalent of *Hustler*. A friend looking for do-mestic violence resources on the net checked out an address and within two "clicks" was looking at pornography. A page linked to another page linked to another page, and she'd gone from an informational Web site to a porno-graphic one. It can be disconcerting.

Fortunately, new software is making it easy to avoid explicit material on the Internet and World Wide Web. All you have to do is screen it out. But when someone starts sending detailed descriptions of gang rape to my email box as a veiled threat or starts to post pornographic stories with me as a main character, the issue has gone far beyond pornography. I am concerned that harassment and pornography have somehow become confused in the minds of our lawmakers: The harassment issue has been co-opted to create an ex-cuse for banning so-called indecent material. The two are not the same at all.

So What About the Law?

From my discussions with many women online, I have found that most forms of online harassment are mere annoyances, desperate men looking for sex in the electronic ether and hitting on anything vaguely female. To give them the benefit of the doubt, many do stop when asked; many don't mean to hurt people. Many (and I've heard from some of them) are really not trying to scare anyone and are simply trying to make new friends. They may be kind of awkward and clueless, but they're mostly harmless.

Women are often annoyed and put out by this behavior, but as many of the strong women online will tell you, they can handle it. The problem is when the date requests (or "wanna fucks") continue after you've said no twice, or when you're sent repeated email messages calling you a "bitch" for stating something on *alt.feminism*. The question then becomes, how does this atmosphere affect the culture, and does it discourage women from being online in the first place? Is this behavior against the law? And can women speak in this atmosphere?

When I was harassed, I thought a lot about going to the police, but I 45 didn't relish being the start of a high-profile online harassment case, and at the time I thought it would be incredibly difficult to prosecute.

According to Mike Godwin, staff counsel for the Electronic Frontier Foundation, the legal definition of harassment does not apply to most on-line harassment cases, since harassment is something that technically occurs in a school or work environment. However, civil and criminal laws that deal with issues of online harassment do exist. For example, on the civil side, you might sue for "intentional infliction of emotional distress." It is also against the law to misappropriate someone's name or license, that is, to send mail under another person's name. And Godwin points out that laws of defamation and libel also apply to the online world. In addition, federal laws exist that outlaw threats "through a means of interstate commerce."

Unfortunately, these legal remedies are often either unknown or misunderstood. And, while the good news is that someone can't threaten you in email legally, not every wanna fuck email is legally a "threat" (which is probably for the better in the long run, what with lawsuits running rampant in this country). As Godwin says: "It's not whether you feel threatened, it's whether an objective person looking at it would say it was a threat."

It's also perfectly legal to insult someone in public or by email. While sometimes I believe the laissez-faire attitude regarding net behavior goes overboard, those who call for banning words that hurt are way off base. When I see women call for strict email conduct rules (as I've seen on the women's online service, Women's Wire), or when women call it sexist and harassment when their Web pages are linked to the "Babes of the Web" site, I'm concerned that their fear is constricting free speech as much as real and perceived harassment might be.

Dealing with the Current Atmosphere

Because not everyone is going to file a lawsuit, and not everything is prosecutable, women have come up with many different ways to battle the bombardment online. Many women I've talked to have resorted to using male or gender-neutral names to avoid getting hit on online.

One young woman I spoke with, a college senior majoring in English, decided to put "MRS!" next to her name on all her electronic correspondence because of the constant requests for dates. Her comments on sexism online included: 50

> I think (the Internet) is the last bastion of real ugly sexism because it's unmoderated and faceless. I've received more 'wanna fucks' . . . and 'shut up bitch' mail than I care to count. I've posted to *alt.feminism* and had men posting me back screamingly hateful email calling me everything from a lesbian to a whore. One man told me that as a woman "you have so little to complain about in real life that you stay on the net all day whining about how bad things are."

I've talked with system administrators who've dealt with harassment on the Internet Relay Chat (IRC) simply by shutting down the service altogether. The IRC is a CB-like collection of live chat "channels," much like the notorious chat rooms on America Online. Like those on America Online, many IRC channels are harmless, fun places to hang out, but many others are places where certain men apparently like to "camp out," waiting for an unsuspecting female to log on. It is unfortunate that shutting down the system has been one of the only ways to deal with annoying people online.

While it can be said that "wanna fuck" email is "only words" and "not real," I can't help but wonder how many women are discouraged from speaking up online for fear of being targeted for some sort of sexual advance or another. I wonder how many women have stopped posting their words because they were sick of constantly being attacked for their opinions. I'll be the first person to stand up for good old-fashioned disagreement and even flaming, but I have a problem with women being silenced through sexist attacks and vague physical threats. It is the threat of the physical behind the virtual that makes online harassment a very scary thing.

Sandy's Story

Sandy,[4] a polite and friendly forty-year-old woman with a soft Southern accent, loves cats and frequented the newsgroup *rec.pets.cats*.

In 1993 a gang of people from several newsgroups, *alt.tasteless,* *alt.syntax.tactical* and *alt.bigfoot,* "invaded" the *rec.pets.cats* newsgroup. By the time the invasion had ended, Sandy had received death threats, hate mail and harassing phone calls, was having her email monitored at work and had almost lost her job.

The incident began when one of the invaders who joined her newsgroup posted a message asking if he could get help destroying his girlfriend's cat. He said the cat was bothering him, but he didn't want the girlfriend to find out if he killed it. When he began discussing poison and drowning as options, Sandy spoke up.   55

First she sent email urging him not to kill the cat, but if he insisted, to have it "put to sleep" humanely. When the email didn't help, Sandy became concerned, then terrified for the cat. She had nightmares. Eventually she wrote a letter to the police that was subsequently distributed on the Internet.

The flame war exploded. The request for help in killing the cat was actually a fake. The poster and his friends had purposefully chosen a quiet little newsgroup to start a flame war of mythic proportions. Their stated goal was to inflame the members of the group with their posts. And it worked. But when Sandy contacted the police, the invaders became ugly and turned their attention to her.

Soon Sandy found herself on the member list of a *Net.Invaderz* FAQ (Frequently Asked Questions document) that was being passed around Usenet and even several computer conventions. Rather than being a victim, Sandy was singled out as one of the victimizers. "Those of us that opposed the group coming in and invading us (were added to the list)," she

[4]Sandy is a fictitious name. The woman described prefers to remain anonymous. [Author's note]

said. "It was spammed all over the network as a true document with our names on it."

Sandy was disturbed but tried to ignore the problems as much as possible until she found herself under investigation by her own company. An irate "U.S. taxpayer" had written her employer complaining that he didn't want the Internet used for actions such as those described in the *Net.Invaderz* document. "I'm a twenty-two year employee with this company, with a good reputation which is now in the pooper because of this," she said.

Sandy hasn't prosecuted but the incident exhausted her and made her 60
fearful. She no longer participates in or even reads *rec.pets.cats;* concerned friends email her posts of interest privately. She cannot afford her own home computer, so she can only access the Internet through work, where her supervisor now watches her every move.

Because she acted (in this case alerting the authorities to what she believed to be cruelty to animals), Sandy became the target of a vicious attack launched by a group of people she had never even met.

In part, the wars going on in cyberspace are cultural wars. Who is to decide what is polite and acceptable? Some time ago, I talked with one of the founders of *alt.syntax.tactical,* who calls himself Antebi. His response to those who suggest his tactics are uncivilized? "Learn to use killfiles," he says. "Grow up, welcome to reality."

After talking with him, I understood his group to be somewhat like an Internet fraternity, a bunch of young men who like to do virtual "panty raids" on unsuspecting newsgroups. They per se aren't the problem (I do not think *alt.syntax.tactical* was responsible for the death threats to Sandy), but that kind of mischievous mentality, coupled with a lot of free time, means that certain people can abuse their power in the virtual world.

But should the virtual world be one where war is the only metaphor? An invading army swept through Sandy's village, and when she reached out to protect someone else, they turned their sights on her. She was attacked, accused, harassed and threatened — with no possible recourse. The army captain merely says she should have armed herself. But perhaps there are other ways to live than by the rule of the strongest? Isn't that what civilization is supposed to be about?

Tools, Not Rules

A popular phrase you'll hear on the venerable California-based online 65
service, the WELL, is "Tools, Not Rules." In other words, don't regulate the Internet, train people how to use it and let them decide for themselves what they want to read and see.

I'm all for it, since I believe that overregulation would stifle the Internet. Women can and should learn more about their online environment so they can exert more control over their corner of cyberspace. The move of many women to create mailing lists and online services is a positive one.

Rather than playing the victim, we can take charge and fight back with the same tools being used against us.

But the Tools, Not Rules philosophy has its limits. On the WELL, a small cybercommunity of 12,000, where such issues of free speech and community are cherished and routinely thrashed about, user Preston Stern wrote:

> Like any other good thing, though, embraced wholly with no conditional moderation [Tools, Not Rules] can easily be turned over and create effects opposite to those intended.... We can insure that everyone has equal access to the tools, but we cannot guarantee that everyone will have equal proficiency. This means that some people, by virtue of having more expertise, more time and/or more experience with the tools, are able to become more powerful, to bend the public discourse and agenda toward their own ends.

Stern wasn't writing this in response to a topic about online harassment, but the concern is the same. Tools can empower, but they can also be a barrier. Women, especially, have a greater problem using Internet "tools" — the typical barriers being lack of time and knowledge and the male domination of all things technical in our society.

Whose Responsibility?

Harassment isn't just a women's issue. In this kind of free-for-all climate, the only people who will have free speech are those who have the gall to stand up to threats or frequent requests for sex, and those who have been lucky enough not to step on the wrong person's toes yet. And while women bear the brunt of this climate, men can also be affected. The man who spoke up in my case, Ron, was harassed and at one point challenged to meet his attacker "face-to-face" — for what, we can only imagine.

Is this the atmosphere that encourages enlightened discourse and free speech? Sandy compares the current atmosphere online to the dark science fiction movie *Blade Runner:*

> It's like another world, it's like another planet. It's like a totally unregulated dirty nasty little underworld. It's got some really nice, great, shining pockets of humanity and education and conversation, and then it's got this horrible seamy gutter-ridden filth . . . they're spreading like a cancer. As far as how to eradicate that without cutting out the good, I don't know what's going to happen to it. I really sincerely do not think censorship and government regulation is the way to go, I just wish people were a little nicer to each other.

So what can be done? Most women will continue to receive wanna fucks, and many will not even prosecute when they do receive a legitimate threat.

I don't think a legal remedy is the real answer anyway. Like Sandy, most women I know online are opposed to censorship. I would rather put up with the harassment than have Uncle Sam reading all my email. But I don't think that living with harassment should be necessary to enjoy the Internet, nor do I think the current "everything goes" environment is healthy. I think we can take steps to make the online world a little more safe. Part of what I would consider to be healthy would be an environment where community responsibility, not rampant individualism, was more the emphasis.

Unfortunately, whenever you so much as mention that you want something done about harassment, you are accused of being pro-censorship. Certainly, the strict rules you can find on online services such as Prodigy and America Online are double-edged swords. Perhaps these services are a little "safer," but is that truly free speech? Maybe the price of freedom is tolerance. Tolerance of jerks who want to put up a "Rate the Babes Home Page," tolerance of a few unwanted emails, tolerance of women online. But sometimes it feels as if the price of freedom also means I must be willing to risk my personal safety for free speech.

In real life, harassment isn't confused with free speech. If I get death threats through regular mail and I report that to the police, am I "censoring" the person who sent the threat? Threats are not free speech. Extortion is not free speech. Defamation is not free speech. Shouldn't the question be: Do we really have free speech on the Internet in its present form? Isn't the tyranny of vigilante bullies, however rare and arbitrary, the same as tyranny by an officially sanctioned body like a government or corporation? When people tell me the Internet is just words I can't help but remember checking the locks on my house, looking for a young man who might have decided that words weren't enough.

Easy answers are hard to come by, and extreme positions on either side will do more harm than good. An Internet police state, for example, would undoubtedly not have the freedom of women as its first concern.   75

Although I would hope that our vigilante friends would take responsibility for their actions and realize that each abuse bodes ill for their and our future enjoyment of the Internet, the burden of action lies with ourselves. Women must take action. The more of us that speak up, the more of us that exist online, the harder it will be to silence us. Perhaps there are places that we won't want to go to — if a place offends us, perhaps we should just stay away — but instead of withdrawing totally from the online world, with all its riches and opportunities, we can form our own networks, online support groups, and places to speak. We can support each other in existing online forums. Women cannot be left behind, and we cannot afford to be intimidated.

ENGAGING THE TEXT

1. What are some of the complex, contrasting feelings Brail expresses about the "flame war" she became involved in? Why didn't she simply withdraw from her usergroup? Should she have? Why or why not?

2. Do you agree with Brail's claim that an antifemale culture dominates life online? Would you agree that "wanna fucks" constitute a serious form of

sexual harassment? In what ways do such "electronic" propositions resemble or differ from the kind of sexual harassment that occurs on a college campus or in a workplace?

3. What is Brail's attitude toward free speech, pornography, and censorship on the Internet? What options do women currently have for dealing with harassment and pornography, according to Brail? What solutions does she offer? Do you think her response to this problem is appropriate? Why or why not?

EXPLORING CONNECTIONS

4. Compare Brail's account of harassment on the Internet with Patricia J. Williams's analysis of bigotry and sexism on the airwaves in "Hate Radio" (p. 746). To what extent are the situations of the Internet and broadcast radio equivalent? To what extent should they submit to the same level of public scrutiny and control? Why?

5. How might Bill McKibben (p. 718) and David Boaz (p. 732) respond to the problem of sexual harassment on the Internet? What solutions might these writers offer? Which would you find more attractive, and why?

6. Reread Christina Hoff Sommers's "The Gender Wardens" (p. 491). Do you think that Brail is just another "gender warden," trying to dictate "sexually correct" behavior and attitudes to Internet users?

EXTENDING THE CRITICAL CONTEXT

7. Working in small groups, cruise a number of Web sites for an hour or so to survey the kinds of information currently available on the Net. Keep track of your findings and compare them with those of the rest of the class. Based on this informal research, do you agree with Brail that the Net has become the "new wild, wild west"?

8. Investigate the issue of freedom of speech on the Internet at your college. Has your campus instituted any rules or restrictions concerning the types of information that may be communicated using college facilities? If so, what topics or types of speech are restricted, and why? How effective and fair are these rules?

Freeing Choices

NANCY MAIRS

Over the past fifty years the range of choices available to most Americans has been expanding at an astronomical rate. Advances in modern technology are extending the reach of individual decision making far beyond the realms dreamt of by the men who penned the Declaration of Independence. Thinkers like Thomas Jefferson guaranteed us the right to "Life, Liberty, and the pursuit of Happiness," but how could they foresee a time when prospective parents could genetically screen children in utero to "guarantee" a healthy birth, or a time when modern medicine would make it possible to choose painless self-termination over a more "natural" death? Nancy Mairs is in a unique position to contemplate the implications of such new freedoms. Diagnosed with multiple sclerosis at the age of twenty-nine, Mairs has spent most of her adult life grappling with her "disability" and the reactions it inspires in the people around her. The author of five books of personal essays and a volume of poetry, Mairs lives with her husband George in Tucson, Arizona. This selection originally appeared in Waist-high in the World: A Life Among the Non-disabled *(1997).*

A September Sunday morning, still and hot. George and I munch our ritual scones with strawberry jam as we leaf through the *New York Times* and half listen to Weekend Edition on NPR. An interview comes on that I begin to heed more closely: a discussion of the increasingly common practice of using amniocentesis to determine the sex of a fetus, followed by abortion if the parents don't want the sort they've begun. What they generally want, as parents have done from time immemorial, is a boy.

The person being interviewed plainly shared my distaste for sexual selectivity. But the way she articulates it brings me up short. "Sex," she tells her interlocuter emphatically, "is not a birth defect."

"That sort of statement strikes a chill straight through my heart," I say to George, who has begun to listen more closely, too. He looks puzzled for a moment and then responds: "Oh. Yes. I can see how it might. I never thought of it that way."

Not very many people would. The implicit argument appears self-evident: the use of abortion to fulfill the desire for a male (or female) child is impermissible, but the same use to prevent an imperfect one is not merely legitimate but, many would argue, socially responsible. As a defective myself, however, I have some doubts.

Although mine was not a birth defect, some evidence suggests a genetic   5
predisposition toward MS, and one day — perhaps even quite soon — this
may be detectable. What then? What if, I find myself wondering, such a test
had been devised more than half a century ago? Suppose a genetic counselor had said to my mother, "Your baby will be born healthy, and she will
probably remain so throughout childhood. But as some point, perhaps in
her twenties, she is likely to develop a chronic incurable degenerative disease of the central nervous system. She may go blind. She may not be able
to speak. Her bladder and bowels may cease to function normally. She may
become incapable of walking or even of moving at all. She could experience
tingling, numbness, or intractable pain. In the end, she might have to be
fed, bathed, dressed and undressed, turned over in bed, as helpless as an infant." What would Mother have done then? What should she have done?

I don't know. Morally, I feel a lot more confident asking questions
than answering them. What I do know, from my own circumstances, is that
I am glad Mother never faced the option to "spare" me my fate, as she
might have felt obliged to do. I simply cannot say — have never been able
to say, even at my most depressed, when I have easily enough wished myself dead — that I wish I had never been born. Nor do I believe that MS
has poisoned my existence. Plenty of people find my life unappealing, I
know. To be truthful, it doesn't altogether appeal to me. But a good scone
with a cup of hot coffee does much to set things right.

I know I am lucky. There are conditions crueler than MS, including
many birth defects, and some of these are already detectable by amniocentesis and ultrasound. Suppose — and I'm being far less speculative here
than I was in imagining my own mother — that a woman learns that her
fetus has spina bifida.[1] The degree of disability may be impossible to predict, but the risks, she is told, include intellectual impairment, bladder and
bowel dysfunction, repeated infections, and the inability to walk. Bright,
healthy, and active herself, the woman strains to imagine what quality a life
thus impaired might possess. Such a child can adapt to her circumstances,
of course, and grow into an energetic and resourceful woman like my friend
Martha, now in her sixties, married, the moderator of her own radio show.

Even if persuaded of this potentiality, the mother still must decide
whether she is emotionally and financially equipped for such an undertaking, with access to medical care and educational programs, reliable assistance from the child's father, a supportive community, a flexible attitude toward surprises and obstacles, and an indefatigable sense of humor. You
can't decide that you're in the middle of a great book, and anyway you're
sick unto death of the four-hour catheterization schedule, and the kid's
bladder can damned well wait a couple of hours till you're more in the
mood. Caring for children, even undamaged ones, never ceases, and in our
society mothers are customarily expected to provide or arrange it. Much as I

---

[1]*spina bifida:* A sometimes fatal birth defect that involves the splitting of the spinal cord.

admire the mothers of variously disabled children I have known — and much as I believe their extraordinary qualities to derive, at least in part, from the rigors of their lives — I could not blame a woman who chose not to test her mettle in this way.

If I make her appear to be choosing in a social vacuum, I do so because, in a society where the rearing of even a healthy child is not viewed as a community undertaking, where much-touted "family values" are always ascribed to the nuclear and not the human family, the parents of a disabled child will find themselves pretty much on their own. If they are lucky enough to have health insurance, the insurer, whose goal is to maximize shareholders' profits rather than the well-being of patients, is not about to spring for a $7,000 power wheelchair that would enable a child with muscular dystrophy to mingle independently with his classmates on an almost equal "footing," though it might provide $425 for a manual wheelchair to be pushed by an attendant (which it would not pay for). A school system, underfunded by screaming taxpayers, is not likely to procure a Kurtzweil machine that would permit its blind students to "read" their own textbooks. Unless they are wealthy, Mom and Dad do the pushing, the reading, and whatever other extra duties are required, on top of their jobs and their care for any other children in the family.

"Eric and I plan to have only a couple of children," my daughter tells   10
me, contemplating the start of a family. "Why should we expend our resources on a damaged one?" A plausible point, as I have come to expect from this most clearheaded of young women. And in fact, as she knows, her father and I took great care to avoid conceiving another child after her younger brother was born in distress because of Rh incompatibility. After a couple of blood exchanges, he recovered, but we were told that another baby would likely be damaged, perhaps gravely, by the antibodies in my blood. I was no more eager to raise a deformed or retarded child than Anne is. I might have chosen an abortion if contraception had failed.

But then I think of my godson, the product of contraceptive failure, who shares with his sister a possibly unique genetic condition that has caused severe visual impairment in them both. Many seeing people have a dread of blindness so overwhelming that they might well consider abortion if such a defect could be detected (as it could not in this case). But these are otherwise ideal children — healthy, smart, funny, confident, affectionate — and I think they're going to become terrific adults. The problem is that if you eliminate one flaw, you throw out the whole complicated creature, and my world would be a poorer place without Michael and Megan.

Obviously, I don't have an unambiguous answer to this dilemma. I don't think one exists. I do feel certain, in view of the human propensity for exploiting whatever techniques we can devise with virtually no regard for consequences, that more and more people will choose, either for their own reasons or in response to the social pressure not to produce "unnecessary" burdens, to terminate pregnancies so as to avoid birth defects (and to select for sex as well). This development won't eradicate people with disabilities, of course: birth trauma, accidental injury, and disease will continue to create them from those who started out as even the healthiest fetuses. What it will do is to make their social position even more marginal by emphasizing that no one with the power to choose would ever have permitted them to exist. Their own choice to survive will seem suspect. *We're doing everything we can to exterminate your kind,* the social message will read, *and we'd get rid of you too if only we knew how.* No one will ever say this. No one will have to.

This mute message — that one is an accident that ought not to have happened — is communicated again, in the issues surrounding the other end of life, by the current movement to legally protect the "right to die." This phrase always strikes me as a little odd, since the right to do a thing presupposes the option not to do it. Although one's conception and birth are chancy at best (will a sperm reach the egg, and if so, which one? will the egg implant? will the fetus reach viability?), one's death is absolutely not; and legislation in such matters seems wildly inappropriate. Human beings have never been able to leave one another's bodies alone, however, but seem compelled to regulate even their most private moments, and so I suppose it is inevitable that some of them are going to set out to protect one's legal right to do what one can't help doing anyway.

The phrase "right to die" is shorthand, of course, and seems considerably less reductive when spelled out: what is generally being called for by right-to-die advocates is the protection of one's freedom to choose the time and circumstances of one's own death and to receive assistance from willing accomplices if necessary. I am as adamantly pro-choice in this matter as I am with regard to abortion; but as with abortion, the question of "choice" here is vastly more complex than politicians, legislators, and religious fundamentalists make it. Their (self-)delegated task is to reduce the rich ambiguities of life to a set of binaries — us/them, law/transgression, right/wrong. The labels vary but the underlying aim is constant — so that we can all stretch out on the couch every Saturday afternoon in front of some quintessentially binary sports contest rather than on a moral rack. Just as your team wins or loses, you either vote for a candidate or you don't, who upon election either does or does not enact certain promised laws, which you either break or obey, and in the end, depending on the choices made, both you and your representative go to Heaven or to Hell.

For absolutists, the "right to die" issue is as indisputable as abortion: killing oneself, or helping another to die, is murder; although the first act is humanly unpunishable, the second ought to be penalized to the full extent of the law, which, in most states, requires that the perpetrator receive assistance in dying by electrocution, suffocation, or lethal injection. Oh well, "a foolish consistency is the hobgoblin of little minds," and all that. Absolutists come in more than one stripe, however (though such a pluralistic view

15

would be repudiated by absolutists themselves), and some of those who crusade to pass legislation permitting assisted suicide seem just as scarily single-minded as their opponents: Jack Kevorkian,[2] "Dr. Death," the principal figure among them.

My own relationship to suicide renders this an unusually vexed topic for me. I have suffered from clinical depression for several decades now, and although not all depressives become suicidal during an episode, I do. I have tried to kill myself more than once, and the last time I so nearly succeeded, taking an overdose of antidepressant medication, that I am unlikely to fail another time. Thus, I must monitor myself ceaselessly for symptoms that signal a downward spiral in order to seek timely treatment. I have spent a good deal of my life struggling to deny myself the death to which activists would like to guarantee me the right.

To complicate matters, I am as vulnerable as the next person to the ordinary situational depression that surges in response to painful life events. The triggers vary from person to person — a broken friendship, a miscarriage, divorce, the departure of children, even a failed exam or the death of a pet — but almost all of us have endured at least brief periods of sleeplessness, loss of appetite, panic attacks, distractability, or ill-defined malaise following some personal catastrophe. Although my own situation gladdens more than it pains me, it does contain some grimmish elements, especially the threat of my husband's death. And because I am a suicidal depressive, I respond to this threat by wanting to kill myself.

A couple of years ago, George began to experience severe bowel problems, and because his melanoma had last recurred in his small bowel, these strongly suggested a relapse. Although I have always known that this may happen at some point, knowledge is no proof against terror, and I went instantly into a tailspin that very nearly carried me over the precipice of panic into the eternal abyss. I procured twice the amount of the medication that had nearly killed me the last time, and I began to plan: "Some afternoon while George is still teaching, so as to have plenty of time," I wrote in my journal. "Drink a beer to relax. Spread out an underpad to avoid soiling the bed. Lie down on it. That way I can't chicken out — once down, I can't get up again. Put on the white-noise machine. Go to sleep forever." Fortunately, I've been in the depression business long enough now to remain a little skeptical about my urges. "It would be stupid to die for no reason," I noted, "so I suppose I should wait until the tumor has been located." That shred of rationality held me back long enough to learn that this time George had not cancer but an antibiotic-induced colitis, and we have both lived to tell the tale.

My intimacy with self-destructive urges leads me to question the term "rational" suicide, which right-to-die proponents use supposedly to

[2]*Jack Kevorkian:* A Michigan physician who has championed and stood trial for doctor-assisted suicide for terminally ill patients.

distinguish the death they have in mind from the one I have approached so closely. Suicide appears imperative only when one loses sight of all other alternatives (and there is always at least one other). Since hopelessness is a distinctive symptom of depression, which is an emotional disorder, actions carried out in a despairing state seem to me intrinsically irrational. This last time I clung to some shreds of reason, which saved me.

I also remembered my son-in-law's words during a family discussion of   20
the precarious future, his voice flat and slightly muffled as it can get with strong feeling: "I think it would be very inconsiderate of you to kill yourself." If there's anything that chagrins me, it's acting stupid or inconsiderate. Better I should stay alive.

Seriously, consideration for others is one of the motives often expressed by people who argue for the license to end their own lives: the desire, sometimes quite desperate, not to be a "burden" on others. Perhaps as a legacy of the rugged individualism that fueled colonial settlement, our society has developed a peculiar structure, in which we create small units that, after a certain amount of time, break and expel even smaller fragments who will form their own similarly friable units: children can't wait to escape their parents, who sometimes can't wait to be escaped, and have families of their "own." The parent who becomes more than a peripheral part of the new constellation, especially one who because of incapacity requires a child's assistance, is considered an intrusion.

Shucking the previous generation in this way doesn't appear to have a practical basis. I mean, we hardly live under the conditions that forced the Eskimos to float their aged and ill off on ice floes in order to conserve scarce resources. The hardships entailed in keeping three or even four generations under one roof are, I think, psychological rather than material. And, as our staggering divorce rate makes clear, we are not, as a society, tolerant of the kind of psychological hardship I have in mind, caused by the tensions that inevitably arise between people living in intimacy. Our notion of satisfactory relationships is incurably romantic in the least wholesome sense of the phrase. We are so bombarded in the media by various and garbled messages about intimate interactions — from the pictorial rapture of a perfume advertisement to the pop-psych-speak of experts on television talk shows to horrific newspaper accounts of domestic abuse — that instead of accepting ordinary conflict as one of the fixed, though less agreeable features, of the human condition, we label it "bad," "sick," and damp it down as best we can, sticking the latest Arnold Schwarzenegger movie into the VCR, pouring a drink or popping a Prozac, heading out for a day at the mall, filing for divorce, whatever it takes to disengage from the maddening other. Or we explode, savaging or even killing the source of irritation.

No wonder the presence of another can seem a burden. No wonder some people would rather die than play such a role.

Many years ago, when I first became active in securing low-income housing for my community, I asked a friend from Israel, whose descriptions of various social programs there had impressed me, about housing for the elderly. He looked a little puzzled, and thinking he didn't understand the term, though his English was excellent, I explained the concept.

"Yes, I understand," he said. "We don't have any."   25

"What do you do with your old people, then?"

"They live with their families."

This notion was hardly foreign to me, since my grandmother had lived with us from the time I was nine; but the idea that an entire society could accept such an arrangement seemed strange indeed. Even though my own experience proved the contrary, I assumed that each generation naturally desired to be quit of the other, except perhaps at holidays, as soon as possible.

The horror of functioning as one of Job's afflictions[3] can be so overwhelming that it obscures the needs and desires of others. That day years back when, panic-stricken at George's impending death, I told my neurologist that I didn't want my children to take care of me because "that's not who I want to be in their lives," Dr. Johnson merely nodded, and we went on to discuss home help, Meals on Wheels, assisted-living arrangements in retirement communities, and other alternatives to the nursing home that evokes dread in just about all of us. I had then, and still have, no idea whether Anne (and now her husband) would consider taking me into their lives, and how burdensome they would find me if they did, but that's just the point: *I have no idea.* Anne was sitting right there, but I blurted what I thought she'd be relieved to hear — that she'd never be saddled with me — without taking the time to ask. At that moment, in the presence of a woman we scarcely knew, both of us distraught over George's illness, we could hardly have delved into the matter. But I could have said, should have said, something open-ended: "I don't know about living with my children. We haven't yet talked about it." Instead, I played Boss Mom, as I have done all too often, decreeing that only what I wanted could be done.

What I wanted — and what I think all of us want who demand the right   30
to die on our own terms — was to maintain a sense of control. Even more than the dread of becoming a burden, helplessness triggers in us a manic terror that things are slipping from our grasp, and I was feeling more impotent than I had ever felt before. A few months earlier, a severe fall had signaled the dreaded end of my walking days. Since then, I had watched George's flesh melt mysteriously away, and now the bony remains huddled like jetsam on a hospital bed, tubes in his arms, his nose, his penis, and nothing I could do would bring him back. These circumstances struck me as intolerable, and I wanted the right to refuse them permanently and irreversibly.

---

[3]*one of Job's afflictions:* In the Bible, God tests the faith of Job by inflicting many hardships on him, including disease; hence, any great burden or unwarranted suffering.

I still do. I want to be the one in charge of my life, including its end, and I want to be able to enlist someone to help me terminate it if I choose "rational" suicide. I have a friend, a doctor whom I admire deeply, who has told me about assisting a patient, irreversibly ill and on a ventilator, to die: listening carefully to the man's clear and repeated requests, calling together his family for their last goodbyes, administering a shot of morphine to ease his passage, turning off the ventilator, remaining with him until he had gone. I would hope to find someone as brave and compassionate if I were to make a similar appeal.

But I would not seek out Dr. Kevorkian or any other crusader for euthanasia, because people who act on principle are likely to sacrifice the individual for the agenda, which is frequently shaped by their own, often deeply buried, presuppositions about what constitutes an acceptable life. Doctors despise disease, or else they wouldn't become doctors, and I have heard of those who couldn't bring themselves to tell a patient she or he had multiple sclerosis because the diagnosis seemed too horrible to bear. Isn't a doctor suffering from this kind of anxiety all too likely to tell me: "You have MS? Of course you want to die! Here, let me write you a prescription so you can peacefully end it all."

In other words, the social construction of disability which makes me uneasy about urging abortion to prevent defective children disturbs me here, too. Behind the view of death as a "right" to be seized and defended lurks the hidden assumption that some lives are not worth living and that damaged creatures may be put out of their misery. True, all kinds of safeguards would be put into place to ensure that only the person doing the dying could make the ultimate decision; but no amount of regulation can eliminate the subtle pressure to end a life perceived by others to be insufferable. If, ideally, I ought never to have [been] born, and if my dependent existence creates a burden on those who must care for me, then don't I have not merely the right but the obligation to die? How can I honorably choose otherwise?

My purpose in raising questions about abortion and euthanasia is not to condemn these procedures, which I believe ought to be freely available, in strict privacy, to any fully informed person who elects them. In fact, I would educate doctors more, and regulate them less, so that they and their patients could explore options, reach decisions, and take action without intrusion. My concern is that these issues be confronted in such a way as to create a social climate in which people with disabilities perceive life to be an honorable choice. And that means sending the social message that disabled people are valued and valuable, precious even, by investing, financially and emotionally, in institutions and practices that help them out.

Everybody, well or ill, disabled or not, imagines a boundary of suffering 35 and loss beyond which, she or he is certain, life will no longer be worth living. I know that I do. I also know that my line, far from being scored in stone, has inched across the sands of my life: at various times, I could not possibly do without long walks on the beach or rambles through the woods; use a cane, a brace, a wheelchair; stop teaching; give up driving; let someone else put on and take off my underwear. One at a time, with the encouragement of others, I have taken each of these (highly figurative) steps. Now I believe my limit to lie at George's death, but I am prepared to let it move if it will. When I reach the wall, I think I'll know. Meanwhile, I go on being, now more than ever, the woman I once thought I could never bear to be.

I cannot excuse or condemn those women with MS, less crippled than I, who sought out Dr. Kevorkian's services. They had their lines. They may have lacked adequate support: familial, medical, psychological, spiritual. I can, however, defend the human right to choose actions that the nondisabled find unfathomable and perhaps even indecent. If a woman, upon learning that her fetus has spina bifida, may choose abortion, then she ought also to feel free to decide, without apology, to bear and rear the child, certain that she will have the same access to medical care and educational programs that a nondisabled child enjoys. If, after consulting with family, spiritual counselors, and medical personnel, a diabetic with gangrenous legs may ask for an easeful death, he should also be fully supported in his decision to live on as an amputee, confident that he can continue to work, shop, attend church, take his wife out for dinner and a movie, just as he has always done. Only in a society that respects, and enables, these choices are atrocities against the disabled truly unthinkable.

"But provisions for these people cost *money*," fiscal conservatives squeal, "and why should *I* pay for someone else's misfortune?" Because that's what human beings do: take care of one another. "But we can't *afford* it." In my experience, this argument is most commonly made by those who mean they can't afford both high taxes or charitable donations and membership in the country club or a winter home in Florida, but never mind. The perception of scarcity is highly subjective, and if you believe yourself on the doorsill of the poorhouse, nothing I say can comfort your fears (though, as Thomas Friedman once pointed out in an editorial in the *New York Times*, a short trip to Africa might have a salutory effect).

Let me point out, instead, being something of a fiscal conservative myself, that we're not talking huge amounts here, nothing like the billions squandered on Star Wars[4] and the B-2 stealth bomber, which plenty of people believed we could afford. If the money is spent wisely, it will constitute not a drain but an investment. Thousands of people with disabilities are already productive citizens; with adequate funds for medical care and research into preventable and treatable conditions, education, structural modifications, and adaptive equipment, we can create thousands more. They will support themselves! They will pay taxes! They will make charitable donations! Their

---

[4]*Star Wars:* An extremely expensive satellite-based nuclear defense system planned during the early 1980s.

potential contributions to culture are impossible to gauge. (Alexander Pope and Toulouse-Lautrec were hunchbacks, after all; Milton went blind; Beethoven, deaf, and so on, and so on. We can ill afford to kill off our geniuses, and every live birth holds such promise.) They will weave into the social fabric important strands of tenacity, patience, and ingenuity. We will all be glad they were born, I think. We will be glad they chose to live on.

ENGAGING THE TEXT

1. What are some of the reasons Mairs offers for the termination of a pregnancy when the fetus shows indications of genetic "abnormalities"? What reasons does she offer for continuing such a pregnancy? Do you think that genetic screening should be a regular part of maternity medical care? Why or why not?

2. Why does Mairs criticize the "binary" or "right/wrong" approach to issues like abortion or the right to die? What do such approaches fail to consider, according to Mairs?

3. How does Mairs redefine the right to "rational suicide"? What personal experiences does she discuss in her attempt to explain why "the right to die" is important to her? What other arguments can you think of that are commonly forwarded to support or condemn doctor-assisted suicide?

4. What, according to Mairs, are the "hidden assumptions" involved in genetic screening and rational suicide? How effective do you think such assumptions are in shaping attitudes toward the handicapped? What is Mairs's proposal for combating such assumptions? Do you agree with her conclusion? Why or why not?

EXPLORING CONNECTIONS

5. Drawing on June Jordan's "Freedom Time" (p. 712), Bill McKibben's "TV, Freedom, and the Loss of Community" (p. 718), Patricia J. Williams's "Hate Radio" (p. 746), and Mairs's "Freeing Choices," write an essay on the erosion of community in contemporary American society.

6. How might you expect David Boaz (p. 732) to respond to the issue of the right to die? How might he respond to Mairs's suggestion that society should bear the costs if a mother chooses to have a child even if the child tests positive in utero for a serious problem like spina bifida?

7. What does the Bolling cartoon that follows this selection on page 779 suggest about social attitudes toward the right to die?

EXTENDING THE CRITICAL CONTEXT

8. Survey people on campus to find out how they would rank the top four or five rights they enjoy as Americans. Then ask them where they would rank the right to doctor-assisted suicide and why. Share your findings in class and discuss how they compare with Mairs's view of the issue.

9. Working in small groups, brainstorm a list of all the ways that the government intervenes in issues or decisions that affect your body. These might

include laws or regulations specifying how old you have to be to enjoy certain "privileges," the sexual acts you can engage in, the foods and drugs you can consume, and so on. Which of these regulations seem reasonable? Which seem to be unjustified restrictions of personal freedom? Why?

10. Write a journal entry in which you explore your own personal "boundary of suffering or loss" — the point at which you would feel that you were no longer living an acceptable life and would seriously consider rational suicide. Compare your responses in small groups and discuss why you made the choice that you did.

The Bridge Builder:
Kathleen Boatwright

ERIC MARCUS

*As the title of this personal history implies, freedom isn't always a mat-
ter of standing alone against the crowd: sometimes real freedom emerges
from the relationships we build with new friends and communities. "The
Bridge Builder" tells the story of Kathleen Boatwright, a devout Christian
fundamentalist and mother of four who discovers freedom — and happiness — as she begins to explore her life as a lesbian. This selection originally
appeared in* Making History: The Struggle for Gay and Lesbian Equal
Rights 1945–1990 *(1992), a collection of oral histories edited by Eric Marcus. A former associate producer for* CBS This Morning *and* Good Morning
America, *Marcus (b. 1958) is the author of* The Male Couple's Guide *(1988)
and* Is It a Choice? Answers to 33 of the Most Frequently Asked Questions
about Gays and Lesbians *(1993). His most recent publication,* Breaking the
Surface, *which he coauthored with Olympic diving champion Greg Louga-
nis, appeared in 1995.*

*Invariably wearing a sensible Sears dress or skirt and jacket, Kathleen
Boatwright doesn't look the part of a social activist, as she describes herself.
But as vice president of the Western Region of Integrity, the gay and lesbian
Episcopal ministry, Kathleen uses her conventional appearance, her status
as a mother of four, her Christian roots, her knowledge of the scriptures,
and her disarming personal warmth to wage a gentle battle for reform in the
church she loves — and to change the hearts and minds of individuals
within the church. According to Kathleen, "I see myself uniquely gifted to
show people what we do to each other in ignorance."*

*Kathleen Boatwright's very difficult and painful journey from funda-
mentalist Christian, director of the children's choir at her local church, and
pillar of her community to Episcopal lesbian activist began one day in August 1984, when Jean, a veterinary student at Oregon State University,
walked through the door of Kathleen's church in Corvallis, Oregon.*

The first time I met Jean, she was having a nice conversation with my
fifteen-year-old daughter at our church. I was very impressed by the mature
way in which she spoke to my daughter. Then, during the service, I sat in
the front row and watched Jean sing. I was so enamored by her presence
that she stuck in my mind. But then she left town and was gone until January the following year.

Come January, I was sitting in church and I looked across the room, and there was Jean, carrying her guitar, walking down the aisle with such determination. I had this incredible lump in my throat, and I said to myself, *Jean's back.* After the service, and despite my difficulty talking to new people, I just had to ask Jean where she had been. I had to talk to her.

I found out that she was back in Corvallis for five months to finish her degree. She didn't have a place to live. So I said to her, "Don't worry, my parents have always wanted to take in a college student. You're redheaded like Dad. They'll love it!" I went and dragged my mother away from where she was talking and I said, "You remember Jean, she's looking for a place to stay. Why don't you and Dad take her in and board her?"

From early on my parents encouraged the friendship because they saw how much Jean meant to me. Meeting her brought me to life in a way they hadn't seen before. They knew that I used to cry for hours on end when I was a child because no girls liked me at school. My mother would come in and rub my leg or pat my hand. I was extremely intelligent and bright, but I had low self-esteem because I wasn't able to find friendship. So my parents encouraged Jean to invite me to lunch or to take me for a drive or go horse-back riding. They felt that her friendship was really wonderful for me. They were glad I was happy. For a while.

My husband didn't pay much attention — at first. He was a state po-liceman and had always been nonparticipatory, both as a parent and a spouse.

After four months of being friends, of having this wonderful platonic relationship, Jean had to go away for a month for her externship. While she was away she met a fundamentalist couple. Well, Jean sent me a postcard and said, "Something's going on. I'm playing with fire. I can't handle it. I've got to talk to you." My heart wrenched. What was going on?

When we were finally able to meet and talk, Jean explained to me how she and this fundamentalist woman started sharing in an intimate way. My response was to put my arm through hers and say, "Don't worry. We'll get it fixed." Jean couldn't be homosexual because it was wrong. Besides, if she was homosexual, then she would be leaving my life. And I think on a deeper level, I didn't want Jean exploring these things with anyone but me.

After her externship, Jean wanted to be more sensual with me. Her at-titude was, "Now I'm going to show *you.*" She said, "I'll give you a back rub some night." So one night — after Bible study, no less — she was over at my house and said, "Why don't you lay down on the blanket on the floor and take off your blouse and bra and I'll rub your back?" And I was like, "Okaaay!" My husband was working all night, and this just seemed like a great setup. So this nice little Christian lady rubbed my back, and I said to myself, *Gee, this is it!*

All the little pieces, all the little feelings came together. Even com-ments my mother made to me over the years began to make sense. She'd say things like, "don't cut your hair too short." "You can't wear tailored clothes." It was then that I also realized that the neighbors I had grown up with were a lesbian couple, even though I had never thought about that before. I recalled the feeling of walking through the Waldenbooks bookstore, looking at *The Joy of Lesbian Sex* and longing for that kind of intimacy. It all came upon me at that moment, and I felt a real willingness to release myself to this person in a way I had never done before. Then the phone rang. It was my son from Bible college. I thought, *Oh, God, saved by the bell! I don't know where this would have gone.*

By the end of the month, Jean was graduating, taking her national boards, and trying to figure out what to do about her feelings toward me and what to do about the fundamentalist woman. It was Pentecostal hysteria.

Now don't forget, at this time I still had a husband and four kids. I had a nineteen-year-old son at a conservative Bible college. I had a sixteen-year-old daughter in the evangelical Christian high school, of which I was a board member. Two children were in parochial day school. My father was the worship leader at church. And I was still very bound to my parents for emotional support. I was the favorite child. And my grandparents lived in town.

Well, shit, I was in way over my head. I was really painted into a corner because there wasn't a single place I could turn for even questioning. So I started looking to some Christian sources. Some of the advice was so incredible, like, "If you feel homosexual tendencies, you can't have the person you have those feelings for over to your house in the evening." "You can never let a member of the same sex sit on your bed while you're chatting." "Meet only in a public place." I thought this advice was ridiculous, but I also thought it was my only option because my spiritual nature was more important than my physical nature. Intellectually and emotionally, I was so hungry and so turned on that I didn't know what to do with my feelings.

At this point, people pull the trigger, turn to the bottle, take drugs, leave town. But I didn't do any of those things because I was madly in love. If I had pulled the trigger, I wouldn't have been able to express the part of me I had discovered. I had found someone, someone who shared the same sort of values I had.

Everything reached a crisis point. I acknowledged to myself and to Jean that I was a lesbian and that I loved her. By this time we had already been sexually active. My husband began to get suspicious that something was going on, and he and I went into counseling. Jean was leaving for a job in Colorado and told me that I couldn't go with her because she was a responsible woman and didn't want to destroy my family. And I still hadn't yet found the spiritual guidance that I needed.

I had to get away and do some soul-searching. I needed to figure out if there was any Christian support somewhere that said I could reconcile my love for Jean and my love for my faith. I didn't feel I could build a life of love if I rejected my faith. So I packed my bags and told my parents that I was leaving to go to stay with my great-aunt in Los Angeles for ten days. I told my husband, "I am going to get away and I'm going to think about a bunch of issues, and then I'm coming back."

For the first time in my entire life, at the age of thirty-six, I was by myself with my own agenda. I had left my husband, my children, my parents, my support structures; got in a car; and started driving to West Hollywood, where I knew there was a lesbian mayor and a gay community. So surely, I thought, there had to be a spiritual gay community.

In West Hollywood I found Evangelicals Together. It's not a church, just a storefront ministry to the gay community for people coming out of an evangelical Christian background. It's led by a former American Baptist minister who talked my language. He said to me, "In order to deal with your dilemma, you have to take a step back from your relationship with Jean. Lay her aside and ask yourself, *Who did God create me to be?*"

Through our sharing, and by looking from a different perspective at the   20
gospel and what Jesus had to say, I could embrace the theology that said, "God knew me before I was born. He accepted me as I was made to be, uniquely and wholly." Ultimately, in an obedience to God, you answer that call to be all that He has created you to be. I felt firmly and wholly that what I had experienced with Jean was no demonic possession, was not Satan tempting me with sins of lust, but an intimacy and a love that was beautiful and was God given. So now I had to figure out how to deal with it.

When you're my age, you're either going to go back to the way it's always been — go for the security you've always known — or take a chance. I felt that for the love I felt for Jean I was willing to risk all. Of course, having Jean there, I was hedging my bet a bit. I was jumping off a cliff, but I was holding somebody's hand.

Jean flew down a few days later to join me in Los Angeles. She agreed to commit to me and I to her. The first Sunday after we affirmed our relationship, we worshiped at All Saints' Episcopal Church in Pasadena because I was told that the Episcopals had the framework of faith I loved, as well as an ability to use reason in light of tradition and scripture.

It was God answering the cry of my heart to send me to that worshiping place. Jean and I had never been to an Episcopal church before. We went into this beautiful place with the largest Episcopal congregation west of the Mississippi River. We sat in the fourth row. It was just this incredible Gothic wonderful place. It was All Saints' Day at All Saints' Church. They played the Mozart Requiem with a full choir and a chamber ensemble, and a female celebrant sang the liturgy. We held hands and wept and wept. We could go forward because in the Anglican tradition, the Eucharist is open for everyone. God extends himself. There are no outcasts in the Episcopal church.

When I got back to town, I met with my husband at a counselor's office. I said, "Yes, you're right. I am gay and I'm going to ask for a divorce.

I'm going to take this stand. I want to meet with my older children and my parents to talk about the decisions I've made." I felt at least I had a right to make my own decisions. I went to pick up my two youngest girls at my father's house. I went to open the door and I heard a flurry of activity, and the children saw me. "Oh, Mommy's home! Mommy's home!" And my dad stepped out on the front porch and pushed the children away and slammed the door. He took me forcibly by the arm and led me down the stairs and said, "You're never seeing your children again without a court order! Just go shack up with your girlfriend!" And he forced me down to the street.

It took going to court to see my two youngest children. They hadn't   25
seen me for two weeks. They asked, "Mommy, Mommy, what's wrong?" I leaned over and whispered in their ears, "Mommy loves you." My husband wanted to know, "What are you telling the children?" I had only a minute with them, then went downstairs, and my husband told me that he wanted me to come back, that he would be my brother, not my husband.

I tell you, my whole world came down upon my ears. I wasn't allowed to see my children. I was denied access to my residence. The church had an open prayer meeting disclosing my relationship with Jean. They tried to get Jean fired from her job. And when that didn't work, they called Jean's parents, who then tried to have her committed or have me arrested. My family physically disinherited me and emotionally cut me off. My older daughter, upon the advice of her counselor-pastor, shook my hand and said, "Thank you for being my biological mother. I never want to have anything to do with you again." After that, whenever she saw me in town, she hid from me. I saw her lay flat on the asphalt in the grocery store parking lot so I wouldn't see her. People I'd known all my life avoided me like I had the plague. I was surprised that Jean didn't just say, "Hey, lady, I'm out of here!"

Fortunately, I wasn't entirely without support. I went to Parents and Friends of Lesbians and Gays and I met some wonderful loving, Christian, supportive parents and gay children who said, "You're not sick. You're not weird. Everybody's hysterical." They offered any kind of assistance possible. Through their emotional support, I felt like it was possible to survive the crush.

Living in a small rural county in Oregon, I didn't know anything about women's rights, let alone gay rights. So it's not surprising that I bought into the lie that children of lesbians or gays are better off living with the custodial heterosexual parent. I believed my husband could provide a sense of normality that I could not. So I signed away my custodial rights and became a secondary parent. After being the primary-care parent for twenty devoted years, the judge only let me see the children two days a week.

By then I'd had enough. So I packed one suitcase and a few things in grocery sacks and left my family and children behind. Jean and I just rode quietly out of town in the sunset to her job in Denver, Colorado.

As you drive into Denver, you go over this big hill about fifteen miles   30
from town. We stopped at a phone booth and called the local Parents FLAG president to ask if there was a supportive Episcopal parish in town.

She said, "Yes, go to this place, look up this person." It was getting to be evening. It was clear, and we were going over the mountain. It was a whole new adventure. It was real closure to my past and a real opening toward my future. Still, the guiding force in my life was, "The church has the answers."

Jean and I called the church and found out when services were and asked if they had an Integrity chapter. Integrity is the Episcopal ministry to the gay and lesbian community. There was one, so two nights later we walked into our first Integrity meeting. There were twelve attractive men in their thirties and the rector. They were shocked to see two women because it's unusual for women to be in Integrity. The only thing dirtier than being a lesbian in a Christian community is being a Christian in the lesbian community because it brings in so many other issues besides sexual orientation, like women's issues and patriarchy and all that stuff.

Denver Integrity was an affirming congregation. We were out as a couple. We were healed of so many things through the unconditional love and acceptance of this parish of eighty people. The rector there encouraged me to become involved. Out of his own pocket he sent me to the first regional convention I went to, in 1987 in San Francisco. Now, I'm vice president of the Western Region for Integrity, and I'm on the national board of directors, I'm one of only maybe 125 women in Integrity's membership of about 1,500.

Integrity gives me a forum for the things I want to say, both as a lesbian woman and as a committed Christian. And because of my background and experience, I can speak to the church I love on a variety of issues that others cannot. I can say, "I call you into accountability. You are bastardizing children raised in nontraditional households. You're not affirming the people that love and guide them. You say you welcome us, but on the other hand you don't affirm us. You don't give us rites of passage and ritual and celebration like you do for heterosexual families."

The church needs to change. What we're asking for are equal *rites*. We're asking the church to bless same-sex unions. I'm asking for canonical changes that affirm my wholeness as a child of Christ who is at the same time in a loving committed relationship with a woman. We're also challenging the church to make statements asking the government to legitimize our relationships and give us the same sorts of tax breaks, pension benefits, et cetera. But most importantly, we need the church to get off the dime and start affirming gay and lesbian children's lives. I never want a girl to go through what I went through. I want to spare everybody right up front.

To get my point across when I go out and talk to groups as a representative of Integrity, I personalize the issue. I personalize my political activism by speaking to people as a person, as Kathleen Boatwright. People don't need to hear dogma or doctrine or facts or theology. They need to meet people.

Here's a great example. For the first time, the women of Integrity got seated at Triennial, which is this gigantic group of very traditional women

35

who have a convention every three years. It used to be that while the men were making the decisions, the women held their own convention. With women's issues having changed so dramatically in the Episcopal church, that's no longer true. Now that women are allowed to serve in the House of Deputies and can be ordained into the priesthood, we've become full team members in the canonical process.

Triennial was made for me. Everybody wears their Sears Roebuck dress. Everybody is a mom. Everybody lived like I had lived for twenty years. I know how to network and how to deal with those women. But I also have a new truth to tell them that will have an impact on their lives in very special ways. Gays and lesbians are 10 percent of the population. Everybody is personally affected by that issue, including these women at Triennial.

During the convention, I attended a seminar given by conservative Episcopals who said gays and lesbians have confused gender identity. Later, we had an open meeting in which we talked about human sexuality. But no one talked about sexuality. Instead, we only talked about information on biological reproduction. After about forty minutes of hearing these women drone on, I stood up in my Sears Roebuck dress and said, "OK ladies, put on your seat belts because you're going to take a trip into reality. You won't want to hear it, but I need to say it because you need to know what people's lives are really like."

I talked to them about my journey. I talked to them about the misnomers, about "confused gender identity." I was wearing this circle skirt and I said, "As you can see from my appearance," and I curtsied, "I do not have a 'confused gender identity.'" Everybody who had been really stiff started laughing — and they started listening. The key is that I take risks. I risk being vulnerable. I risk sharing the secrets of my heart. We already know what the straight people feel in their hearts. But no one talks about how the lesbian or gay person feels in his or her heart.

For the next hour and a half, people talked about where they really live. They talked about their pregnant teenagers or the suicide attempts in their families. All those gut-level issues. But you have to have someone lead you to that. That's me — because I'm safe. I've also learned that instead of having all the answers, that God calls me to listen to people's pain, and not to judge it.

This one woman told me that she had been driving by her daughter's house for eight years and that her husband had never let her stop because her daughter was a lesbian. "But," she said, "I'm going to go home and I'm going to see her. My daughter's name is also Kathleen." Then she started to cry. She had never even told the women from her church about what had happened to her daughter. It's like the living dead for many Christian families. They just have a child who is lost prematurely in so many senses of the word.

Inevitably, everywhere I go I hear about parents who have made ultimatums. This one mother said, "I've never told anybody, but I said to my son, 'I wish you were dead.' And by forcing him into the closet, I fulfilled that prophecy. Three years later, he was dead." Then there was a woman

40

who said to me, "Kathleen, I'm questioning my sexuality at seventy. Could you send me some information?"

I think in my heart that I represent the hidden majority of lesbian women because many, many are married or have been married, have children, and have too much to risk — like I've risked and lost — to come out. And those women who are out, who are much more political and aggressive, have seen enough successes happen, enough bridges built by my approach, that they're beginning to respect the fact that I can go through doors they never can.

The first time I spoke publicly to the leadership of the women of the church, I spoke along with another lesbian. She was politically correct and a strong feminist. *Feminist* was always a dirty word for me, so I've had to overcome a lot of my own bias. I said to her, "Please don't speak about politics. Don't brow beat these people. Stand up and say that you're a doctor, that you've never been in a committed relationship, that you're a feminist. Because I want to stand up and say, 'I've been a Blue Bird leader.' What that will say is that we represent the gamut of human experience, just like the heterosexual community. It's just our ability to develop intimate relationships with the same sex that makes us different."

People don't have to identify with my ideology. They identify with my person, and then the questions come from them. We don't have to tell them. They start asking us. People say to me, "What do you call your partner?" "You don't have any medical insurance?" To me that's the best sort of teaching process: answering questions rather than giving information.

My husband remarried; he married the baby-sitter. At Easter of 1987, I got a call informing me that he had removed my ten-year-old daughter from his house, accusing her of using "inappropriate touch" with his new stepsons. He wanted to unload the difficult child. Then he used that child as a weapon to try and deny me visitation for the younger one. The end result was that I had one child and he had one child. I filed suit against him without any hope or prayer of winning back custody of my other child.

I went to a lesbian minister to ask her about finding a lawyer to handle my case, and she said to me, "The best attorney in this town is Hal Harding, but he's your husband's attorney. Maybe that will prove to be a blessing." So I had to find another attorney.

As part of the custody proceedings, Jean and I eventually met with my husband's attorney. He took depositions and asked Jean and me really heartfelt questions. Then he advised his client — my ex-husband — to go ahead and have a psychological evaluation. The court had not ordered it and, in fact, would not order it because there was no precedent in that county. But my former husband agreed to go to the psychologist of his choice. That psychologist, a woman, took the time and energy to interview every person involved and recommended to the court that Jean and I become custodial parents. We now have custody of both children, sole custody. It was indeed a blessing.

We just added Jean's ninety-one-year-old grandmother to our family. So we are all-American lesbians living here in Greenacres, Washington. We are Miss and Mrs. America living together. The thing that we need in our life now that our faith doesn't give us is a community of supportive women. We have yet to find that place.

Not long ago, I went to the National Organization for Women lesbian   50
rights agenda meeting and gave a workshop on spirituality for women, from the Christian perspective. And I took a deep breath in my Betty Crocker suit — if I ever write a book it's going to be *The Radicalization of Betty Crocker* — and thought, *I wonder what the Assemblies of God girls would say now? From their perspective, I'm walking into the total pit of hell, and I'm bringing the very gift that they should be giving.* Who would have believed it?

ENGAGING THE TEXT

1. What family, religious, and cultural bonds restrained Boatwright from acknowledging her sexuality? What were her options? How do you think she should have reacted when she realized that she was attracted to Jean? Why?

2. In what different ways does Boatwright's emerging lesbian identity change her and her life? What price does she pay?

3. How do Boatwright's attitudes toward the church develop during her story? How does her self-image change?

4. How do you interpret the title of this oral history? In what different senses is Boatwright a "bridge builder"?

5. From the information available about her past, write a brief character sketch of Boatwright, tracing the development of her personality from childhood through the occasion of this oral history.

EXPLORING CONNECTIONS

6. Compare what freedom and oppression mean to Gerry Spence (p. 695), Jimmy Santiago Baca (p. 705), and Boatwright. What forms does oppression take in these selections? How does the experience of oppression shape each writer's understanding of what it means to be free?

7. Write a dialogue between Boatwright and Christina Hoff Sommers (p. 491) on the question of whether women continue to be disenfranchised or taught to play subordinate roles in American society.

EXTENDING THE CRITICAL CONTEXT

8. Several of the selections in this chapter refer to the "risk" associated with real freedom. Write a personal essay about the risks you feel are necessary in order to live a free life — or about a specific risk you once ran in order to be free.

Let America Be America Again
Langston Hughes

Our survey of American culture closes with a reflection on the power that the myth of freedom has to inspire hope, even in the face of despair. Written nine years into the great Depression, "Let America Be America Again" (1938) offers a stinging indictment of the hypocrisy that Langston Hughes perceived everywhere in American life. Yet Hughes transcends his rage and dares to hope for America's future; in so doing he pays homage to ideals that retain their potency even in the 1990s. (James) Langston Hughes (1902–1967) was a major figure in the Harlem Renaissance — a flowering of African American artists, musicians, and writers in New York City in the 1920s. His poems, often examining the experiences of urban African American life, use the rhythms of jazz, spirituals, and the blues. Among the most popular of his works today are The Ways of White Folks *(1934), a collection of short stories, and* Montage of a Dream Deferred *(1951), a selection of his poetry.*

Let America be America again.
Let it be the dream it used to be.
Let it be the pioneer on the plain
Seeking a home where he himself is free.

(America never was America to me.)   5

Let America be the dream the dreamers dreamed —
Let it be that great strong land of love
Where never kings connive nor tyrants scheme
That any man be crushed by one above.

(It never was America to me.)   10

O, let my land be a land where Liberty
Is crowned with no false patriotic wreath,
But opportunity is real, and life is free,
Equality is in the air we breathe.

(There's never been equality for me,   15
Nor freedom in this "homeland of the free.")

Say who are you that mumbles in the dark?
And who are you that draws your veil across the stars?

I am the poor white, fooled and pushed apart,
I am the red man driven from the land.   20
I am the refugee clutching the hope I seek —

But finding only the same old stupid plan
Of dog eat dog, of mighty crush the weak.
I am the Negro, "problem" to you all.
I am the people, humble, hungry, mean —   25
Hungry yet today despite the dream.
Beaten yet today — O, Pioneers!
I am the man who never got ahead.
The poorest worker bartered through the years.
Yet I'm the one who dreamt our basic dream   30
In that Old World while still a serf of kings,
Who dreamt a dream so strong, so brave, so true,
That even yet its mighty daring sings
In every brick and stone, in every furrow turned
That's made America the land it has become.   35
O, I'm the man who sailed those early seas
In search of what I meant to be my home —
For I'm the one who left dark Ireland's shore,
And Poland's plain, and England's grassy lea,
And torn from Black Africa's strand I came   40
To build a "homeland of the free."

The free?
Who said the free? Not me?
Surely not me? The millions on relief today?
The millions who have nothing for our pay   45
For all the dreams we've dreamed
And all the songs we sung
And all the hopes we've held
And all the flags we've hung,
The millions who have nothing for our pay —   50
Except the dream we keep alive today.

O, let America be America again —
The land that never has been yet —
And yet must be — the land where *every* man is free.
The land that's mine — the poor man's, Indian's, Negro's, ME —   55
Who made America,
Whose sweat and blood, whose faith and pain,
Whose hand at the foundry, whose plow in the rain,
Must bring back our mighty dream again.

    O, yes,   60
    I say it plain,
    America never was America to me,
    And yet I swear this oath —
    America will be!

ENGAGING THE TEXT

1. Explain the two senses of the word "America" as Hughes uses it in the title and refrain of the poem.
2. What different types of freedom does Hughes address in this poem?
3. According to Hughes, who must rebuild the dream, and why?
4. Why does Hughes reaffirm the dream of an ideal America in the face of so much evidence to the contrary?
5. Explain the irony of lines 40–41 ("And torn from Black Africa's strand I came / to build a 'homeland of the free.' ")
6. Examine the way Hughes uses line length, repetition, stanza breaks, typography, and indentation to call attention to particular lines of the poem. Why does he emphasize these passages?

EXPLORING CONNECTIONS

7. Review some or all of the poems in *Rereading America:*
    Melvin Dixon's "Aunt Ida Pieces a Quilt" (p. 149)
    Wendy Rose's "Three Thousand Dollar Death Song" (p. 557)
    Janice Mirikitani's "We, the Dangerous" (p. 560)
    Aurora Levins Morales's "Child of the Americas" (p. 675)
    Inés Hernández-Ávila's "Para Teresa" (p. 216)
    Langston Hughes's "Let America Be America Again"
Then write an essay on poetry as a form of social action. What are the characteristics of this type of poetry? How does it differ from the poetry you have read before in school?

EXTENDING THE CRITICAL CONTEXT

8. Working in groups, "stage" a reading of the poem, using multiple speakers. Consider carefully how to divide up the lines for the most effective presentation. After the readings, discuss the choices made by the different groups in the class.
9. Working in pairs or in small groups, write prose descriptions of the two versions of America Hughes evokes. Read these aloud and discuss which description more closely matches your own view of the United States.

Acknowledgments

Horatio Alger, from *Ragged Dick*. Reprinted with the permission of Simon and Schuster from *Ragged Dick and Mark the Match Boy* by Horatio Alger. Copyright © 1962 by Macmillan Publishing Company.

Paula Gunn Allen, "Where I Come From Is Like This" from *The Sacred Hoop* by Paula Gunn Allen. Copyright © 1986, 1992 by Paula Gunn Allen. Reprinted by permission of Beacon Press, Boston.

Jean Anyon, from *Social Class and the Hidden Curriculum of Work*, edited. Reprinted from *Journal of Education*, Boston University School of Education (1980), Vol. 162, no. 1, with permission from The Trustees of Boston University and the author.

Gloria Anzaldúa, "La conciencia de la mestiza/Towards a New Consciousness" from *Borderlands/La Frontera: The New Mestiza*. Copyright © 1987 by Gloria Anzaldúa.

Toni Cade Bambara, "The Lesson" from *Gorilla, My Love* by Toni Cade Bambara. Copyright © 1972 by Toni Cade Bambara. Reprinted with permission of Random House, Inc.

Donald Barlett and James B. Steele, "Have Mores and Have Lesses" from *America: Who Stole the Dream?* Copyright © 1996 by Donald Barlett and James B. Steele. Reprinted with permission of Andrews and McMeel. All rights reserved.

Rose Blue and Corinne J. Naden, from *Colin Powell: Straight to the Top*. Copyright © 1991 by Rose Blue and Corinne J. Naden and reprinted by permission of the Millbrook Press, Inc.

David Boaz, "What Rights Do We Have?" Reprinted with permission of The Free Press, a Division of Simon & Schuster, from *Libertarianism: A Primer* by David Boaz. Copyright © 1997 by David Boaz.

Stephanie Brail, "The Price of Admission: Harassment and Free Speech in the Wild, Wild West" from *Wired Women*, Lynn Cherny and Elizabeth Reba Weise, eds. Copyright © 1996. Published by Seal Press.

Colin G. Calloway, "New Peoples and New Societies" from *New Worlds for All*, pp. 187–194. Copyright © 1997 by Colin G. Calloway. Reprinted by permission of Johns Hopkins University Press.

Bebe Moore Campbell, "Envy." Reprinted by permission of The Putnam Publishing Group from *Sweet Summer: Growing Up With and Without My Dad* by Bebe Moore Campbell. Copyright © 1989 by Bebe Moore Campbell.

Sucheng Chan, "You're Short, Besides!" from *Making Waves*, ed. by Asian Women United. Copyright © 1989 by Asian Women United; copyright © 1994 by Sucheng Chan. Reprinted by permission of the author.

Lynne Cheney, "Politics in the Schoolroom." Reprinted by permission of Simon & Schuster from *Telling the Truth* by Lynne Cheney. Copyright © 1995 by Lynne V. Cheney.

Blythe McVicker Clinchy, Mary Field Belenky, Nancy Goldberger, and Jill Mattuck Tarule, "Connected Education for Women." Reprinted from *Journal of Education*, Boston University School of Education (1985), Vol. 167, no. 3, with permission from The Trustees of Boston University and the authors.

Judith Ortiz Cofer, "The Story of My Body." From *The Latin Deli: Prose & Poetry*. Copyright © 1993 by Judith Ortiz Cofer. Reprinted by permission of the University of Georgia Press.

Patricia Hill Collins, "Black Women and Motherhood." Reprinted from *Black Feminist Thought: Knowledge, Consciousness, and the Politics of Empowerment* by Patricia Hill Collins (1990) by permission of the publisher, Routledge: New York and London.

Stephanie Coontz, "What We Really Miss About the 1950s" from *The Way We Really Are* by Stephanie Coontz. Copyright © 1997 by BasicBooks, a division of HarperCollins Publishers, Inc. Reprinted by permission of BasicBooks, a division of HarperCollins Publishers, Inc.

Ellis Cose, "Can A New Race Surmount Old Prejudices?" from *Color Blind* by Ellis Cose. Copyright © 1996 by Ellis Cose. Reprinted by permission of HarperCollins Publishers, Inc.

Harlon L. Dalton, "Horatio Alger" from *Racial Healing* by Harlon L. Dalton. Copyright © 1995 by Harlon L. Dalton. Used by permission of Doubleday, a division of Bantam Doubleday Dell Publishing Group, Inc.

Holly Devor, "Becoming Members of Society: Learning the Social Meanings of Gender" from *Gender Bending: Confronting the Limits of Duality* by Holly Devor. Copyright © 1989 by Indiana University Press, Bloomington, IN. Reprinted by permission of Indiana University Press and the author.

Melvin Dixon, "Aunt Ida Pieces a Quilt" reprinted with permission of the Estate of Melvin Dixon.

Anne Witte Garland, "Good Noise: Cora Tucker" from *Women Activists: Challenging the Abuse of Power* by Anne Witte Garland, published by The Feminist Press at the City University of New York. Copyright © 1988 by the Center for the Study of Responsive Law. Reprinted by permission. All rights reserved.

John Taylor Gatto, "The Seven Lesson Schoolteacher." From *Dumbing Us Down: The Hidden Curriculum of Compulsory Schooling* by John Taylor Gatto, 1992, New Society Publishers, P.O. Box 189, Gabriola Island, BC V0R 1X0, Canada.

Lynell George, "Gray Boys, Funky Aztecs and Honorary Homegirls" from the January 17, 1993 issue of *The Los Angeles Times Magazine*. Copyright © by Lynell George. Reprinted by permission of the author. Lynell George lives in Los Angeles and is a staff writer for *The Los Angeles Times*.

Dagoberto Gilb, "Me Macho, You Jane." Copyright © 1996 by Dagoberto Gilb. From *Muy Macho: Latino Men Confront Their Manhood* by Ray Gonzales. Used by permission of Doubleday, a division of Bantam Doubleday Dell Publishing Group, Inc.

John R. Gillis, "Myths of Family Past" from *A World of Their Own Making* by John Gillis. Copyright © 1996 by BasicBooks, Inc. Reprinted by permission of BasicBooks, a division of HarperCollins Publishers, Inc.

Elizabeth Dodson Gray, "Television's Transformative Role in Courtroom Justice for Women and Children." Excerpt from *Women Transforming Communications*. Copyright © 1996 by Donna Allen et al. Reprinted by permission of Sage Publications, Inc.

Ken Hamblin, "The Black Avenger." Reprinted with permission of Simon & Schuster from *Pick a Better Country* by Ken Hamblin. Copyright © 1996 by Ken Hamblin.

Inés Hernández-Ávila, "Para Teresa" from *Con Rázon, Corazón* by Inés Hernández-Ávila. Copyright © 1987 by Inés Hernández-Ávila. Reprinted by permission.

Deborah Meier and Paul Schwarz, "The Hard Part Is Making It Happen" from *Democratic Schools,* 1995. "The Hard Part Is Making It Happen" by Deborah Meier and Paul Schwarz, Alexandria, VA: Association for Supervision and Curriculum Development. Copyright © 1981 by ASCD. Used with permission. All rights reserved.

Janice Mirikitani, "We, the Dangerous" from *Awake in the River, Poetry and Prose* by Janice Mirikitani. Copyright © 1978 by Janice Mirikitani. Reprinted by permission of the author.

Aurora Levins Morales, "Child of the Americas" from *Getting Home Alive* by Aurora Levins Morales and Rosario Morales. Copyright © 1986 by Aurora Levins Morales. Reprinted by permission of Firebrand Books, Ithaca, NY.

Charles Murray, "The Coming White Underclass," from *The Wall Street Journal.* October 29, 1993. Reprinted with permission of The Wall Street Journal. Copyright © 1993 Dow Jones & Company, Inc. All rights reserved.

Gloria Naylor, "The Two" from *The Women of Brewster Place* by Gloria Naylor. Copyright © 1980, 1982 by Gloria Naylor. Used by permission of Viking Penguin, a division of Penguin Books USA Inc.

Jill Nelson, "Number One!" Excerpt from *Volunteer Slavery* was reprinted with the permission of Jill Nelson.

Mariah Burton Nelson, "Boys Will Be Boys and Girls Will Not" from *The Stronger Women Get, The More Men Love Football.* Copyright © 1994 by Mariah Burton Nelson, reprinted by permission of Harcourt Brace & Company.

Vincent N. Parrillo, "Causes of Prejudice" from *Strangers to These Shores: Race and Ethnic Relations in the United States, 3/e* by Vincent N. Parrillo. Copyright © 1990. All rights reserved. Reprinted by permission of Allyn & Bacon.

Fred L. Pincus, "From Individual to Structural Discrimination" from *Race and Ethnic Conflict: Contending Views on Prejudice, Discrimination, and Ethnoviolence* by Fred L. Pincus. Copyright © 1994 by WestviewPress. Reprinted by permission of WestviewPress.

Richard Rodriguez, "The Achievement of Desire" from *Hunger of Memory* by Richard Rodriguez. Reprinted by permission of David R. Godine, Publisher, Inc. Copyright © 1982 by Richard Rodriguez.

Mike Rose, "I Just Wanna Be Average." Reprinted with the permission of The Free Press, a Division of Simon & Schuster, from *Lives on the Boundary: The Struggles and Achievements of America's Underprepared* by Mike Rose. Copyright © 1989 by Mike Rose.

Wendy Rose, "Three Thousand Dollar Death Song" from *Lost Copper* by Wendy Rose (Malki Museum Press). Copyright © 1980 by Wendy Rose. Reprinted by permission of the author.

Theodore Roszak, "The Computerized Campus" from *The Cult of Information: The Folklore of Computers and the True Art of Thinking.* Copyright © 1994. Permission granted by the Regents of the University of California Press.

Myra Sadker and David Sadker, "Higher Education: Colder by Degrees." Reprinted with the permission of Scribner, a Division of Simon & Schuster, from *Failing at Fairness* by Myra Sadker and David Sadker. Copyright © 1994 by Myra Sadker and David Sadker.

Jean Reith Schroedel, "Nora Quealey" from *Alone in a Crowd: Women in the Trades Tell Their Stories* by Jean Reith Schroedel. Copyright © 1990 by Temple University Press. Reprinted by permission of Temple University Press.

Leslie Marmon Silko, "Fences Against Freedom." Reprinted with the permission of Simon & Schuster from *Yellow Woman and a Beauty of the Spirit: Essays on Native American Life Today* by Leslie Marmon Silko. Copyright © 1996 by Leslie Marmon Silko.

Christina Hoff Sommers, "The Gender Wardens." Reprinted with the permission of Simon & Schuster from *Who Stole Feminism? How Women Have Betrayed Women* by Christina Hoff Sommers. Copyright © 1994 by Christina Hoff Sommers.

Gary Soto, "Looking for Work" from *Living Up the Street: Narrative Recollections* by Gary Soto, Dell, 1992. Copyright © 1985 by Gary Soto. Used by permission of the author.

Gerry Spence, "Easy in the Harness: The Tyranny of Freedom." Copyright © 1993 by Gerry Spence. From *From Freedom to Slavery* by Gerry Spence. Reprinted with the permission of St. Martin's Press Inc., New York, NY.

Shelby Steele, "I'm Black, You're White, Who's Innocent?" from *The Content of Our Character*. Copyright © 1990 by Shelby Steele. Reprinted with the permission of St. Martin's Press Inc., New York, NY.

Ronald Takaki, "A Different Mirror" from *A Different Mirror* by Ronald Takaki. Copyright © 1993 by Ronald Takaki. By permission of Little, Brown and Company.

Studs Terkel, "C. P. Ellis" and "Stephen Cruz" from *American Dreams: Lost and Found*. Reprinted by permission of Donadio & Ashworth, Inc. Copyright © 1980 by Studs Terkel.

Carmen Vázquez, "Appearances" from *Homophobia: How We All Pay the Price* by Warren J. Blumenfeld. Copyright © 1992 by Warren J. Blumenfeld. Reprinted by permission of Beacon Press, Boston.

Patricia J. Williams, "Hate Radio." Reprinted by permission of *Ms. Magazine*. Copyright © 1994.

Patricia J. Williams, "Town Hall Television." Reprinted by permission of the publisher from *The Rooster's Egg* by Patricia J. Williams, Cambridge, Mass.: Harvard University Press. Copyright © 1995 by the President and Fellows of Harvard College.

Art Acknowledgments

CHAPTER 1: HARMONY AT HOME

"Boy with Mother" (p. 17) photograph by Mary Kate Denny/PhotoEdit.

"A Family Tree" (p. 22) by Norman Rockwell. Photo courtesy of The Norman Rockwell Museum at Stockbridge. Printed by permission of the Norman Rockwell Family Trust. Copyright © 1997 the Norman Rockwell Family Trust.

"Freedom from Want" (p. 23) by Norman Rockwell. Photo courtesy of The Norman Rockwell Museum at Stockbridge. Printed by permission of the Norman Rockwell Family Trust. Copyright © 1997 the Norman Rockwell Family Trust.

"Freedom from Fear" (p. 24) by Norman Rockwell. Photo courtesy of The Norman Rockwell Museum at Stockbridge. Printed by permission of the Norman Rockwell Family Trust. Copyright © 1997 the Norman Rockwell Family Trust.

CHAPTER 5: CREATED EQUAL

CHAPTER 6: LIBERTY AND JUSTICE FOR ALL

Index of Authors and Titles